THE ROMANOVS

Also by W. Bruce Lincoln

NIKOLAI MILIUTIN: *An Enlightened Russian Bureaucrat*
NICHOLAS I: *Emperor and Autocrat of All the Russias*
PETR SEMENOV-TIAN-SHANSKII: *The Life of a Russian Geographer*

W. BRUCE LINCOLN

THE ROMANOVS

Autocrats of All the Russias

THE DIAL PRESS

NEW YORK

For Patti

Published by
THE DIAL PRESS
1 DAG HAMMARSKJOLD PLAZA
NEW YORK, NEW YORK 10017

ACKNOWLEDGMENTS

Excerpts from THE TRAVELS OF OLEARIUS IN SEVENTEENTH-CENTURY RUSSIA translated and edited by Samuel H. Baron: Reprinted by permission of the publishers, Stanford University Press. © 1967 by the Board of Trustees of the Leland Stanford Junior University.

Excerpts from THE LETTERS OF NICHOLAS TO THE EMPRESS MARIE by E.J. Bing: Published by Longman, Green, 1938.

"The Twelve" by Aleksandr Blok: translated by Babette Deutsch and Avrahm Yarmolinksy. First published in *The Slavonic Review*, June 1929. Used by permission of *The Slavonic & East European Review*.

"The Bronze Horseman" by Alexander Pushkin: translated by Oliver Elton. Used by permission of Leonard S. Elton.

Excerpts from THE LITERATURE OF EIGHTEENTH-CENTURY RUSSIA by Harold Segal, editor and translator. Copyright © 1967 by Harold B. Segal. Reprinted by permission of the publisher, E.P. Dutton.

Excerpts from THE LETTERS OF THE TSAR TO THE TSARITA used by permission of Academic International Press.

Manufactured in the United States of America
First printing
Design by Francesca Belanger

Library of Congress Cataloging in Publication Data

Lincoln, W. Bruce.
The Romanovs.

Bibliography: p.
Includes index.
1. Russia—History. 2. Romanov, House of.
I. Title.
DK113.L54   947'.046   80-39902
ISBN 0-385-27187-5

CONTENTS

CONTENTS

Contents

PREFACE

This is the story of the Romanovs, those fifteen men and four women who ruled Russia between 1613 and 1917. In the broadest sense, it is their collective biography, an effort to portray not only their personalities and personal lives but also their aspirations, policies, accomplishments, and failures as rulers of the modern world's largest empire. Yet the drama of the Romanovs extends over a canvas far too vast for any one historian to paint in its entirety, and theirs is a tale that, in all its complexity, would require far more than one volume to recount. Thus, the account I have set forth in the following pages is not a history of Russia, nor is it a history of everything the Romanovs attempted during the 304 years in which they sat upon Russia's throne. *The Romanovs: Autocrats of All the Russias* reflects most of all my own interests, preferences, and prejudices about the Romanovs and their Russia. As such, it is an attempt to set forth their biographies and the drama of their reigns as I have come to perceive them during some two decades of study and reflection about Imperial Russia.

ACKNOWLEDGMENTS

It would require far more space than is available here to acknowledge the generosity and kindness of the many people who have in some way aided my efforts to write this book. During the past two decades I have had the good fortune to have been taught by some of the greatest modern scholars in the field of Russian studies, especially Professors Leopold Haimson (U.S.A.), Marc Raeff (U.S.A.), Petr Zaionchkovskii (U.S.S.R.), and Michael Cherniavsky (U.S.A.). I also have profited greatly from discussions with many scholars in the United States and abroad. In this respect Samuel Baron, Valentina Chernukha, James Cracraft, Daniel Field, Ralph Fisher, Jacob Hoptner, Bruce McCully, Brenda Meehan-Waters, Sidney Monas, Daniel Orlovsky, Alexander Rabinowitch, Benjamin Uroff, and Richard Wortman are at the top of what is, to my good fortune, a very lengthy list. Helen Barrett was the person who first urged me to write this book and offered me far more in the way of encouragement, advice, and suggestions than I had any right to expect, while Joyce Johnson at Dial Press did much to clarify its style and improve its narrative. My wife Patti set aside her own writing for more than a year in order to take command of life's time-consuming daily tasks so that I could devote all of my efforts to completing this book. As a token of my gratitude, I have dedicated this volume to her.

Institutions, too, have aided me in my efforts to study the Romanovs and to write this volume. The International Research and Exchanges Board supported me as an exchange scholar in Moscow and Leningrad, where the Academy of Sciences of the U.S.S.R. proved a generous and helpful host. The Fulbright-Hays Faculty Research Abroad Program supported my research both in the Soviet Union and in Poland, where the Historical Institute of Warsaw University outdid itself in efforts to make my stay pleasant and productive. Finally, a senior research fellowship at Columbia University's Russian Institute, and various grants and logistical support from Northern Illinois University, the American Council of Learned Societies, and the Russian and East European Center at the University of Illinois, helped me to complete this book.

Yet, the best efforts of family, colleagues, friends, and generous research organizations cannot help a scholar in his work unless libraries and archives make their resources available to him. In that respect I have been especially fortunate. Many archivists and librarians at the Lenin Library and the Archive of the October Revolution in Moscow, the Saltykov-Shchedrin Public Library and the Central State Historical Archive in Leningrad, the Warsaw University Library, the British Museum, Butler Library at Columbia University, and the Regenstein Library at the University of Chicago must remain the unsung heroes in the lengthy tale of the research that went into this book. As helpful as the efforts of these many people were, I must acknowledge a further debt of gratitude to Marianna Tax Choldin, Laurence Miller, Frankie Mosborg, and June Pachuta at the University of Illinois Library for the efforts they expended on my behalf and for the dedication and good humor with which they always met my sometimes outrageous requests for assistance. To them, and to many others in the United States, England, Poland, and the Soviet Union, I owe a special debt that formal acknowledgment and thanks such as this cannot begin to repay.

W. Bruce Lincoln
Sycamore, Illinois
March 21, 1980

A NOTE ON RUSSIAN NAMES AND DATES

The spelling of names in this volume may appear somewhat unfamiliar to readers who are accustomed to reading books that employ English counterparts for Russian names (Peter, Paul, Mary, Alexandra, Catherine, etc.) rather than such transliterations as Petr, Pavel, Maria, Aleksandra, and Ekaterina. Nevertheless, because this is a book about Russia, not about England or the United States, I have avoided Anglicizing most Russian proper names. Readers should remember that the feminine form of family names in Russian usually ends in the letter "a," while the masculine does not. Thus, Tsar Aleksei Mikhailovich's second wife was born Natalia Naryshkina, but her brother was Ivan Naryshkin. Generally, I have used Russian transliterations for all but the names of most rulers, such familiar place names as Moscow and St. Petersburg, and a handful of people especially well known to Western readers. Therefore, the name of the famous nineteenth-century composer appears as Tchaikovsky, as it has on countless concert and ballet programs during the past century, not as Chaikovskii, as it would if it were transliterated directly from the Russian.

All this being said, I confess to violating these principles on several occasions where there seemed good reason to do so. I have not Anglicized the names of seventeenth-century Tsars in an effort to convey to readers a greater sense of their comparative isolation from Europe, while, in the case of their eighteenth- and nineteenth-century successors, I have used Anglicized forms to symbolize their growing involvement in European affairs. Further, although I have Anglicized the names of reigning Romanovs in the eighteenth and nineteenth centuries, I have used the Russian forms in referring to their spouses. Readers thus will encounter the Empress Elizabeth (1741–61), while the wife of Alexander I (1801–25) will be referred to as the Empress Elisaveta Alekseevna. Finally, where transliterations produced double vowels in the middle of a first name, I have eliminated them, with the result that the wife of Paul I, for example, appears as Maria (not Mariia) Feodorovna, and Peter the Great's half-sister is referred to as Sofia, not Sofiia. In the case of patronymics, however, they have been preserved as in Elisaveta Alekseevna.

As far as dates are concerned, I again admit to a certain amount of caprice in an effort to balance clarity against historical precision. I have dated all Western European events according to the Gregorian calendar, as is the usual practice among historians. Russian dates are more of a problem because Russians employed three different calendars during the centuries covered by this book. Until February 1, 1918, I have given the dates of all Russian events according to the Julian calendar, although that calendar was adopted in Russia only in 1699. Seventeenth-century Russians celebrated the New Year on September 1 and calculated dates from the year 5508 B.C., which they considered to be the year in which the world had been created. Thus, Tsar Mikhail Feodorovich, the first Romanov, came to the throne in 1613 according to the Julian calendar, but in "the year 7121 since the creation of the world" according to the one in use in Russia at the time. Obviously, any effort to date events according to the seventeenth-century Russian calendar would produce only confusion and chaos, and, to my knowledge, no modern historian has ever attempted it.

Yet, dating according to the Julian calendar, in use in Russia between 1699 and 1918, is not without some difficulties as well because Western Europeans used the more modern Gregorian calendar during most of the Romanov period of Russia's history. During the seventeenth century, the Julian (Old Style) calendar was ten days behind the Gregorian (New Style) one. The gap widened by one day in each subsequent century, with the result that, by the early twentieth century, Russia's calendar was thirteen days behind the one used in the West. Only in 1918 was the problem resolved when Lenin's government decreed that February 1 (Old Style) would become February 14, thereby adopting the Western calendar in Russia. The only present-day legacy of this centuries-long divergence of calendars is that citizens of the Soviet Union now celebrate on November 7 the Great October Revolution that brought the Bolsheviks to power on October 25, 1917, according to the Julian calendar then in use.

THE ROMANOVS

PROLOGUE

Hidden from the eyes of Europeans, deep in the then-unknown regions of the inner Asian continent, a people known as the Mongols lived, tended their flocks, and raided their neighbors during the eleventh and twelfth centuries. At that point in their history, they built no great cities or lasting monuments to themselves, for they were a nomadic people whose lives were spent on the backs of their shaggy, sturdy ponies. In raids upon their neighbors, they traveled great distances with a speed that astounded their enemies; so mobile were their forces that they usually struck without warning. Mongol horsemen could fire their short, sharply curved bows with deadly accuracy while riding at a full gallop, and their ability to survive the rigors of long campaigns in distant lands was phenomenal. The European traveler Marco Polo, who lived among the Mongols for nearly two decades toward the end of the thirteenth century, remarked that they could subsist for a month or more from a kind of porridge made from mare's milk and that they would draw blood from their horses' veins to sustain themselves if they could find no other food.

Ranging over the vast region that lies in the neighborhood of Lake Baikal and the Gobi Desert, the Mongols multiplied with remarkable rapidity. Hardened by the rigors of life in some of the most inhospitable terrain in Eurasia, they, like the Indians of the American plains, became some of the finest light cavalry the world has ever seen. Military prowess soon turned them from vassals into masters. At the very beginning of the thirteenth century, they began to challenge the authority of their Chinese overlords, and, in less than fifty years, they became world conquerors. Led by their chieftain Temuchin, who later took the name Genghis Khan, they conquered much of northern China in the brief space of five years, between 1211 and 1216. Then they turned westward, smashed the Moslem states of Central Asia, and reached the passes of the Caucasus that stood as the gateway to the rich and fertile plains of southern Russia.[1]

The Mongol armies first attacked the Russian land in the year 1223 when, like an unforeseen pestilence, they swept into the south Russian plain, eager for more conquests and confident of victory. The Russians hastily concluded an alliance with their former enemies, the steppe nomads known as the Polovtsy, and assembled a large army comprised of the vassals and retainers of those petty princes who ruled in the Russian land. Two of these princes, Mstislav the Brave and Danil Romanovich, were chosen to command the Russo-Polovtsian force, but they were unable to unify their command because of quarrels among the other princes. In June they met the Mongol host on the banks of the Kalka River. For three days, say the chronicles, the battle raged. Abandoned by the Polovtsy, the Russians suffered defeat; many were taken prisoner. According to legend, the Mongols built a great wooden platform upon the backs of their captives, held a great victory feast, and crushed their hapless victims in the process.[2] Then, as swiftly as they had come, the Mongols vanished from the Russian land. In the fall of 1237, they returned, suddenly and without warning. With an even larger army they swept everything before them.

The Russian territory upon which the Mongols fell with such ferocity was not the great and powerful state that the Romanovs would rule a half-millennium later. Russia in the thirteenth century was a collection of independent principalities, wracked by internecine strife, and ruled by a motley collection of petty princes whose position within a broad and complex network of family relationships determined which thrones they occupied. To unite these warring princes against the Mongol's new attack would have demanded a leader who combined heroic qualities with finely honed diplomatic skills. Only Prince Aleksandr Nevskii, one of Russia's earliest national heroes, a man of vast energy, courage, and a great measure of military genius, might have done so. But Prince Aleksandr's first and most immediate duty was to his principality of Novgorod, located in the far northwest corner of the Russian land, far from the scene of the Mongol invasion. At the very time the Mongols fell upon Russia from the south and east, Novgorod faced attacks by powerful armies of Swedes and Teutonic Knights from the north and west. By the time Aleksandr had defeated the Swedes on the banks of the Neva River and had routed the Teutonic Knights, in the spring of 1242, in the famous "battle on the ice" at Lake Peipus in Estonia, it was too late. The Russian land lay firmly beneath the Mongol yoke, and Aleksandr himself was obliged to pay homage and tribute to Russia's new masters.[3]

Such seemingly invincible military machines as Napoleon's Grande Armée and Hitler's Wehrmacht first tasted the bitter dregs of defeat when their commanders launched winter campaigns into the vastness of Russia. By contrast, the Mongols' campaign in the winter of 1237–38, directed by Genghis Khan's grandson Batu and led by the brilliant strategist General Subudey, enjoyed resounding and uninterrupted success. The combat was so brutal that, in the words of an ancient chronicler, "even the earth began to moan."[4] The Russians, weakened by petty quarrels among themselves, were no match for Batu's armies, which won victory after victory. In the month of February 1238 alone, the Mongol invaders seized no less than fourteen major towns and cities in Russia.[5] Their three-year campaign culminated with the looting of Kiev, which in earlier times had been the political and cultural center of the Russian land. In December 1240 the Mongols took the inner defenses of Kiev by storm. The women and children who had retreated to the shelter of the city's many and beautiful churches were immediately put to the sword by the invaders. Then the city was destroyed. "When we were journeying through that land we came across countless skulls and bones of dead men lying about on the ground," wrote the Minorite friar John of Plano Carpini, who traveled through the region six years later. "Kiev," he continued, "had been a very large and thickly populated town, but now it has been reduced almost to nothing, for there are at the present time scarce two hundred houses there and the inhabitants are kept in complete slavery."[6] A century earlier, Kiev had boasted twice as many churches as the handful of houses Friar John found in 1246.

The Mongols often have been depicted as cruel and brutal masters who destroyed Russia's earlier cultural achievements, cut her off from Europe, and plunged her into several centuries of isolation and darkness. Yet the Mongol lords interfered remarkably little in Russian affairs after their initial conquest, and, although they were first pagans and then Moslems, they even patronized the Russian Orthodox Church. Unlike his brother princes in China, Persia, and Central Asia, Batu Khan did not establish his dynasty among the Russians. Instead, he chose to rule his domains, which became known as the Golden Horde, from his capital at Sarai, on the lower reaches of the Volga River.[7]

Although Batu Khan did not attempt to Mongolize his new conquests, he demanded an annual tribute in men and treasure from each of the ruling Russian princes. This involved him and his successors in bitter conflicts and endless negotiations with their reluctant vassals. Tribute sometimes had to be collected by force, and it has been estimated that Russia suffered at least forty-eight Mongol attacks of varying magnitude between 1237 and 1462 as a result. Some of these were at the invitation of individual Russian princes who sought and obtained Mongol aid in their continuing conflicts with neighbors and rivals. More often, however, the purpose of these invasions was to put down revolts against taxation or to extort taxes from a reluctant populace when the Khan's specially appointed *baskaks* failed to do so with the usual means at their disposal.[8]

The Mongols sought to ease their difficulties in collecting tribute by assigning the task to those Russian princes who demonstrated a particular willingness to employ their energies in that direction. In 1327 Prince Ivan I of Moscow, known as "Ivan the Moneybag" because of his talent for filling his private coffers, won responsibility for collecting the annual tribute not only from his native Moscow but also from the neighboring and, originally, far more important principality of Vladimir. The Khan permitted Ivan to bequeath the title of Grand Prince of Moscow and Vladimir to his descendants, clever politicians who maneuvered to increase their power over other Russian princes while they continued to be abjectly submissive to their masters at Sarai. Thus began the process known as the "gathering of the Russian lands," which enabled the once-insignificant princes of Moscow to become Tsars of All the Russias. During the course of three centuries, the mere six hundred square miles of territory Ivan the Moneybag inherited increased almost four thousand-fold to some 2,347,800 square miles in 1613.[9]

If the Russian lands were to be gathered into a single, unified state, some means had to be established for determining which lands in eastern Europe were "Russian" and which were not. The Russian Orthodox Church, owing its first allegiance to Byzantium, not the Khan at Sarai, played an important role in this vital task. Those lands that lay within the realm of the Church's authority came to be defined as "Russian," for the all-Russian concept emerged within the Church before it gained a political dimension. Thus, there was a Metropolitan of All Russia before any secular prince dared take the title. Ivan the Moneybag's clever maneuvering, aided by a considerable measure of good fortune, caused both the religious and secular all-Russian concepts to become centered in Moscow. Ivan's first stroke of good luck came in 1326 when Petr, Metropolitan of All Russia, died while on a visit to Moscow, and his remains, worshipped by Russians as sacred, were enshrined in the Kremlin.[10] Then Ivan convinced Petr's successor to move his permanent residence from Vladimir to Moscow.

These events marked the beginning of a close alliance between the Russian Orthodox Church and the political power of Moscow's princes that would continue for several centuries. Each supported the other in expanding its authority over the Russian land, and the cumulative effect was to make Moscow the most powerful religious and political center in all of Russia. The Grand Princes of Moscow and Vladimir, soon to be known as Grand Princes of All Russia, restored a measure of order and stability in the Russian land, thereby strengthening the Church's control over its vast landed estates and improving its economic position. At the same time, the Metropolitans of All Russia used their ecclesiastical authority to strengthen the power of the Grand Princes. Those who opposed the Grand Princes' political demands were declared enemies of Christ and suffered excommunication. Within the relatively short space of less than two centuries, earthly well-being and eternal salvation for all Russians became the monopoly of Moscow.

Those who refused to recognize that fact suffered the temporal wrath of the Grand Princes and, at the same time, the eternal damnation cast upon them by the Russian Church.[11]

Moscow's growing political and religious power in the fourteenth century meant that it was only a matter of time before the Grand Prince of All Russia would challenge Mongol hegemony over the Russian land. Given the extensive nature of Mongol power, and the political and ideological realities of Russia at the time, such a challenge needed to be overwhelming in its dimensions in order to succeed. Thus, the Grand Prince not only would have to defeat the Khan in battle but he would have to replace him as master of the Russian land. To do so, he would have to command greater resources than those of the Mongols. In his haste to free Russia from its Mongol lords, the Grand Prince proved too anxious and struck before his strength was sufficient to overpower Mongol authority. Although the Grand Prince defeated the Khan's armies in his first great challenge to the Mongols, he could not consolidate his victory, and Russia had to suffer still another century beneath the Mongol yoke.

The first confrontation between Russian and Mongol came when the armies of Grand Prince Dmitrii met those of Khan Mamai in a titanic encounter at Kulikovo Field, on the eastern bank of the Don River, in September 1380. Dmitrii was one of old Russia's great heroes, tall and physically powerful, a man above others in thought and deed. He was a temperate man, religious, deeply patriotic, and every inch a prince. Resolved to free the Russian land from the Mongol scourge, he raised an army of 150,000 men to destroy the suzerainty of Khan Mamai. Confident of his mighty army's invincibility, Mamai took up Dmitrii's challenge. After a day of desperate fighting, the Mongols were driven in rout from the field of battle. Mamai thus led the Mongols to their first major defeat against the Russians, but his successor would win the war because Dmitrii could not follow up his victory.[12]

For his victory, Dmitrii was hailed as Russia's savior and named "Donskoi," in commemoration of the river on whose banks the battle was fought. He had destroyed forever the myth of Mongol invincibility, and that was an important first step in Russia's liberation. But much more was needed to free Russia from her Mongol masters. The Golden

Horde still commanded vast resources, while Dmitrii Donskoi had drained every possible source of wealth and manpower in his domains. As a result, when Mamai's successor, Khan Toktamysh, burned Moscow two years after the battle in retribution for Mamai's defeat, Dmitrii Donskoi could mount no effective resistance. It was clear that the Grand Prince of All Russia would have to become yet more powerful and command still greater resources of wealth and manpower before the Mongol yoke could be lifted.[13]

During the next century, Moscow's rulers sought to increase their power within Russia, while continuing Ivan the Moneybag's policy of servility to their Mongol masters at Sarai. As Dmitrii's able successors brought principality after principality under their control, the size of their domains increased and their wealth and power grew apace. Perhaps Moscow's most important territorial conquests of the century came during the reign of Ivan the Great, who has been described as a "mighty figure" of "unusual statesmanship and vision."[14] In 1478 Ivan annexed the great trading center of Novgorod, whose domains swept across the vast reaches of Russia's far north. Less than a decade later, he seized the principality of Tver, Moscow's greatest rival for control of the Russian lands a century earlier. As a result, when Ivan the Great turned to face the Mongols, he commanded more than four times the territory and manpower, and many more times the wealth, than had Dmitrii Donskoi. Equally important, through the century factional strife within the Golden Horde had brought it to the brink of disintegration.

When the armies of Ivan the Great and Khan Akmad met in their final confrontation on the banks of the Ugra River in 1480, the Muscovites emerged victorious. So dramatically had the balance of power shifted in the course of a century that, in fact, there was no real battle, no clash of giants, as had occurred at Kulikovo. For several months, the two armies faced each other from opposite sides of the river while Akmad awaited reinforcements from his Lithuanian allies. By November, the Lithuanians still had not arrived and Akmad retreated. He was assassinated by agents of a rival Mongol faction before he reached his capital. Russia no longer lay helpless beneath the heel of her Mongol conquerors, and Moscow soon emerged as an independent and powerful state in Eastern Europe.[15] Within a few decades of Ivan's victory, Moscow had defeated Lithuania, her greatest enemy in the West, and had established diplomatic relations with the Holy Roman Empire, the Papacy, the Ottoman Empire, and even the great Mogul Empire in India.

The reign of Ivan the Great also saw the Russian Church free itself from the spiritual domination of Byzantium, which had held sway ever since the Christianization of the Russian lands, traditionally dated as occurring in 988. Russia's most dramatic and important form of religious art, the icon, was originally painted according to Byzantine models, and the design of Russian churches, especially in the south, followed the Byzantine pattern. Even many of the bishops in Russia came directly from Byzantium and knew little or no Russian until the early fifteenth century. Throughout the Kievan and Mongol periods of Russia's history, the Byzantines continued to regard the Russians and their Church as poor and inferior relations.[16]

The Mongol invasion, the increased hazards of travel to Constantinople, especially after the Metropolitanate had been moved to Moscow, and the growing threat of the Mohammedan Turks to Byzantine sovereignty had eroded this subjugation between the thirteenth and fifteenth centuries, but it remained a religious, even political, fact nonetheless. Within the context of Eastern Orthodoxy, it was essential that there be a Christian Emperor and a Christian Empire to establish a temporal framework within which the Church could exist and flourish. For nearly a millennium after the split between Eastern and Western churches, these were supplied by the political institution of the Byzantine Empire and the person of the Byzantine Emperor. The fall of Constantinople to the Turks in 1453, a cataclysmic and apocalyptic event that threatened the spiritual foundations of Eastern Christianity, marked the destruction of both Emperor and Empire. This, in turn, abruptly changed Russia's position within the Orthodox Church as a whole. For, although the Grand Prince of All Russia still was nominally subject to the Mongol Khan, he was the most independent of any Christian Monarch within the domains of the Eastern Church.

That the Grand Prince of All Russia had fallen heir to the Byzantine inheritance was first demonstrated by the marriage in 1472 of Ivan the Great to Sofia Paleologina, niece of the last Byzantine Emperor. But before Ivan could claim this heritage by adding the Byzantine two-headed eagle to his royal crest, and by adopting the high title of Tsar (from the Byzantine, *Caesar*), he had to be freed from his vassalage to the Mongol Khan. Once that was accomplished in 1480, he proceeded to adopt Byzantine Court ritual and all the other attributes of his Byzantine heritage. The Grand Prince of All Russia soon became Tsar and Autocrat of All the Russias, and claimed descent from Prus, the legendary brother of Augustus Caesar. At the same time, Muscovite churchmen proclaimed Moscow to be the Third Rome, thereby placing upon the Tsar's shoulders a new and awesome burden. In their view, the first two Romes (Rome and Constantinople) had fallen to the infidel; Moscow was the third, and there could not be a fourth. Russia thus stood as the last independent vessel of pure Christianity on earth, and it must be preserved inviolate at all costs. The Tsar and Autocrat of All the Russias thus became the last and final hope of all Christians everywhere, in the view of Moscow's theologians, and he must make Russia yet stronger and more powerful to defend the purity of the Holy Faith.[17]

The events of the late fifteenth and early sixteenth centuries thus made the Grand Prince of All Russia into a far more awesome being. As Tsar and Autocrat of All the Russias, he possessed vast lands and great wealth. Russia's clerics proclaimed that his domains held a monopoly on the most precious of all commodities, salvation itself. An added measure of his new status was the fact that large numbers of Mongol nobles, formerly vassals of the Khan at Sarai, began to seek places in his service. Among them were the Godunovs, one of whom would himself become Tsar during the upheavals that began the Time of Troubles at the end of the sixteenth century. So considerable was this migration of Mongol lords into the service of the Tsar, according to the calculations of the Russian historian Kliuchevskii, that by the end of the seventeenth century approximately seventeen percent of the Muscovite nobility was of Mongol or other eastern origin.

Western Europeans also began to enter the service of the Tsar in the fifteenth and sixteenth centuries. While under the Mongol yoke, Russians had used wood rather than stone in their buildings, and the construction of large stone edifices had become something of a lost art. As a reflection of his new grandeur, Ivan the Great dreamed of building in stone once again and on a massive scale. He sought architects and engineers in the West since there were none in Russia. In 1474 he sent a special envoy to Venice, one of the greatest centers of Renaissance art, and obtained the services of such prominent Italian builders as Pietro Solario, Alevisio, and Marco Ruffo, as well as the engineer Aristotle Fieravanti. Together with architects from the city of Pskov, near Russia's western frontier, these men erected the brilliant architectural ensemble that comprised the heart of Moscow's Kremlin: the Cathedrals of the Assumption, the Annunciation, and the Archangel, and a fittingly impressive palace for the Tsar of All the Russias.[18]

The greater glory and power Ivan the Great won for Moscow was increased by his son Vasilii III and, especially, his grandson Ivan the Terrible, who provided a dramatic and stunning personification of the Tsar's new power. The image of this "terrible" Tsar would evoke in later times a panorama of overwhelming and awesome terror, tortures of the most horrible kinds, bloody and brutal executions, violence for the sake of violence alone. Even the very epithet attached to him in Russian—*Groznyi*—transmitted the sense of Ivan's great power, but for his contemporaries it did so in a positive, rather than profoundly negative, sense. For above all, Ivan "the Terrible" inspired awe, just as did Pope Julius II, *il Papa Terribile*, for example. As Ivan himself once wrote, "at all times, a Tsar must be . . . sometimes gentle and sometimes cruel, merciful to the good and cruel toward those who are evil. And if this is not the case, then he is not a Tsar."[19] More than any Russian ruler before or since, Ivan personified the classic tyrant who, by his use of terror, punished evil and protected the good, to defend Russia, God's earthly kingdom. He lived in an age when cruel tortures and barbaric executions were commonplace in the West as well as in the East. Like his European contemporaries—Henry VIII and Elizabeth I in England, Philip II in Spain, Pope Alexander VI and Cesare Borgia in Italy—he sought to curb violence by greater violence.[20]

One historian tells us that, on the day of Ivan the Terrible's birth, "the whole country was filled with the noise of thunder, and with awful flashes of lightning,"[21] an omen, perhaps, of the thunderous shocks that his fifty-year reign would bring to Russia. His father, Vasilii III, died when Ivan was three, and his mother, possibly a victim of poison, followed her husband to the grave before her son reached the age of eight. Rival factions of great nobles (*boiars*) despoiled the Russian land during Ivan's childhood, and he was powerless to stop them. His closest friend, Feodor Vorontsov, was incarcerated in a monastery when Ivan was thirteen, and another friend, Prince Ivan Obolenskii, died of starvation in prison. In 1547, the year of Ivan's coronation, a great fire and riot swept Moscow. His thirtieth year was marked by the death of his beloved first wife, Anastasia Romanova, like his mother, a possible victim of poison.[22]

Ivan the Terrible thus grew up in an atmosphere of brutality, even outright terror, and he would rule in a like manner once he took the reins of government into his hands in 1547. His reign began in triumph but ended in disaster. One by one, the Khanates of Kazan and Astrakhan, Russia's enemies to the southeast, fell before the onslaught of the young prince's conquering armies. In the northwest, he seized a foothold on the Baltic Sea and, in 1558 alone, captured more than twenty enemy fortresses in that region, including the important city of Dorpat. To beautify Moscow and to modernize his armies, Ivan brought Western European artists, craftsmen, army officers, and armaments experts to Moscow. In 1554 he concluded Russia's first commercial treaty with England, and thus established economic ties that would be of critical importance to Russia until well into the nineteenth century.

But there was a dark and foreboding side even to these years of triumph, for Ivan was forced to confront treachery among his *boiars*. When he suffered a grave illness in 1553, and thought himself near death, these men opposed his request that they swear allegiance to his infant son. His suspicions aroused by this apparent act of disloyalty, Ivan blamed the *boiars* for his wife's sudden death a few years later. Although their role in the death of the Tsarina Anastasia Romanova remains in dispute, there was no doubt of their treason when some of them, including Ivan's close friend Prince Andrei Kurbskii, defected to Lithuania soon afterward. In response to these and other challenges to his power, Ivan struck out against the *boiars* with brutal vengeance.

Aided by the *oprichniki,* a new corps of loyal retainers, he unleashed terror throughout his domains. Astride their black steeds and garbed in black from head to toe, these new agents of the Tsar swept the length and breadth of the Russian land, destroying the families, friends, even servants, of those *boiars* whom Ivan suspected of disloyalty.[23]

Some historians have argued that Ivan lost his emotional balance after the death of his first wife and that the reign of terror, which lasted from 1564 until at least 1572, was the act of a madman. But it must be pointed out that the reign of terror was rationally planned and implemented, and thus does not appear to have been a purely capricious act of madness. Indeed, it seems to have had the very calculated purpose of strengthening the power of the Tsar over the Muscovite state, whose territorial consolidation only recently had been completed. Many in Ivan the Terrible's domains still remembered the days when they had owed allegiance to lords other than the one who reigned in Moscow, and the descendants of those princes still lived and continued to maintain territorial bases from which they might conceivably challenge the supremacy of the Tsar. Ivan's *oprichniki* destroyed those princes. At the same time, they made certain that all in Russia understood the deadly consequences that would result from even the faintest hint of disloyalty to Moscow's ruler. As Aleksandr Zimin, a leading Soviet expert, wrote some years ago, "the edifice of the centralized state [in Russia] was erected upon the bones of many thousands . . . who paid a dear price for the triumph of autocracy."[24]

The immediate result of the "terrible" Tsar's efforts to consolidate his power was that vast areas of his domains were laid waste, and the Russian land resembled a country ravaged by the horrors of civil war. Perhaps even more critical for Russia's immediate future, Ivan's violent temper deprived her of the successor who might have brought order out of the chaos he had created. For, in 1581, consumed by a fit of blind rage, Ivan struck his eldest son with an iron-tipped staff and mortally wounded him. When the Tsar died in March 1584, his domains were left in the hands of Feodor Ivanovich, his feebleminded younger son, who produced no heirs and whose death in 1598 heralded the demise of the House of Riurik, whose descendants had ruled Russia for some seven centuries. In her search for a new dynasty, Russia plunged into a period of strife and chaos that would see three Tsars rise and fall in the brief space of twelve years.

The Time of Troubles began when an Assembly of the Land, a *zemskii sobor,* elevated Feodor Ivanovich's chief adviser, Boris Godunov, to the Russian throne. Boris was an able statesman, who sent Russians to study modern technology in the West, promoted foreign trade, and sought to preserve peace at home and abroad. Contemporaries sang his praises and wrote glowingly of his virtues: "His love of justice had no price." "He mercilessly killed those given to all sorts of bribery, so loathsome was it to him." "Against every evil that contravened the good, he was as implacable as he was an unflattering rewarder of virtue."[25] Yet, despite Boris's appealing personal qualities and these promising beginnings, his "contemporaries found that God did not give his blessing to the reign of Tsar Boris," as one Russian historian wrote many years ago.[26] Beginning in the third year of Boris's reign, Russia suffered a three-year famine of appalling severity. Starving by the tens of thousands, Russia's masses devoured bark, grass, dead and rotting animals, even the cadavers of their fellows who had died of hunger or plague. In great numbers, men and women turned to brigandage, pillaging town and country in a desperate bid for survival. Order collapsed throughout Russia, and lawlessness became a way of life, nurturing a series of political and social crises that shook the state to its very roots and raised a new Tsar to the throne.[27]

Soon after Boris's accession, rumors had begun to spread that Ivan the Terrible's last and youngest son, the Tsarevich Dmitrii, who had died under mysterious circumstances in Uglich in 1591, still lived. Such romantic myths have long been a part of Russia's political experience and frequently have been given added substance by the appearance of a pretender, the most recent being "Anastasia," daughter of Nicholas II and Aleksandra. In the case of Ivan the Terrible's youngest son, the pretender was a man by the name of Grigorii Otrepiev, known in history as "the False Dmitrii." Unlike the supposed Grand Duchess Anastasia, however, the False Dmitrii sought to make good his claim by force. In October 1604 he invaded Russia at the head of a small and motley band of Polish aventurers and Cossacks. Under normal conditions, such an enterprise would have been doomed. Yet, within the larger social and political turmoil that surged across Russia in the early seventeenth century, it captured the popular imagination. Thus, when Boris Godunov died suddenly in April 1605, the False Dmitrii hastened to Moscow and was proclaimed Tsar.[28]

The False Dmitrii's accession did not ease the social and political crises that rent the fabric of the Russian state and society in the early seventeenth century. On the contrary, it made them more intense and bitter—culminating in the deposition and murder of the Tsar. Vasilii Shuiskii, a man of ancient and illustrious lineage, succeeded him, but he had no greater success in bringing order and peace. Further pretenders appeared, a vast rebellion led by Ivan Bolotnikov burst forth in the south, the Swedes threatened Novgorod in the north, and the Poles launched an invasion from the west. Powerless to defend Russia or even himself, Shuiskii was deposed in 1610 by an Assembly of the Land and forced to become a monk. For a time, a council of seven great *boiars* pulled the reins of government in as many different directions, as Russia continued to wrestle with what appeared to be unsolvable dynastic, political, social, and military crises that culminated in the fall of Novgorod to the Swedes and the occupation of Moscow by a Polish army in 1611. With a Polish garrison in the heart of the Kremlin, Russia lay prostrate beneath a new conqueror's heel.[29]

Three men—Prince Dmitrii Pozharskii, the Patriarch of Moscow Germogen, and Kuzma Minin, a butcher from the Volga trading center of Nizhnii-Novgorod—led Russia out of these dark days of peril. Together they raised an army, instilled it with patriotic fervor, and took it to victory against the Polish conquerors. Early in November 1612, the army of Minin and Pozharskii stormed the Kremlin, and Moscow was restored to her rightful owners. Headed by Prince Pozharskii, Patriarch Germogen, and several other great *boiars,* the victors set about reestablishing a firm, nationally acceptable government to end the Time of Troubles. For that purpose, an Assembly of the Land was summoned to Moscow. There, early in 1613, some five hundred delegates met to decide Russia's fate. On February 7 they chose as Russia's new Tsar Mikhail Feodorovich Romanov, the son of Filaret, Metropolitan of Rostov. Two weeks later, on February 21, they proclaimed Mikhail Tsar and Autocrat of All the Russias in the Great Kremlin Palace amid the clutter, filth, and debris left behind by Russia's Polish invaders. Mikhail was only sixteen, sickly, unassuming; hardly a man, it seemed, to bring Russia greatness.[30]

Even though the first Romanov appeared unpretentious, he established a dynasty that would guide Russia's destiny from July 1613 until March 1917, and in his wake would come a line of dynamic Russian sovereigns that included Tsar Aleksei, Peter the Great, Catherine the Great, Alexander I, Nicholas I, Alexander II, and eleven others in between. Under their stewardship, Russia would grow into a vast Empire of more than one hundred million subjects, encompassing one-sixth of the earth's surface. At its height in the mid-nineteenth century, the Romanovs' Empire would stretch almost halfway around the globe, from Prussia's eastern frontier to Canada's northwestern boundary and, even, to California. The Romanov men and women who ruled this vast and complex domain will be the subject of this book. Theirs is a tale of glory and pathos, of heroism and cowardice, of victory and defeat. Their story is an intimate part of the drama that surrounds the rise and fall of the modern world's largest Empire.

PART ONE

MUSCOVITE BEGINNINGS

(1613–1689)

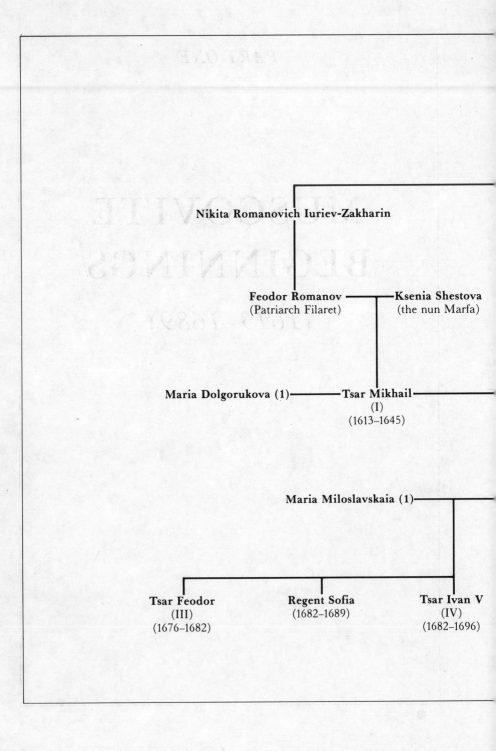

Nikita Romanovich Iuriev-Zakharin

Feodor Romanov ———— Ksenia Shestova
(Patriarch Filaret)   (the nun Marfa)

Maria Dolgorukova (1)———— Tsar Mikhail
                                              (I)
                                        (1613–1645)

Maria Miloslavskaia (1)

Tsar Feodor   Regent Sofia   Tsar Ivan V
(III)   (1682–1689)   (IV)
(1676–1682)   (1682–1696)

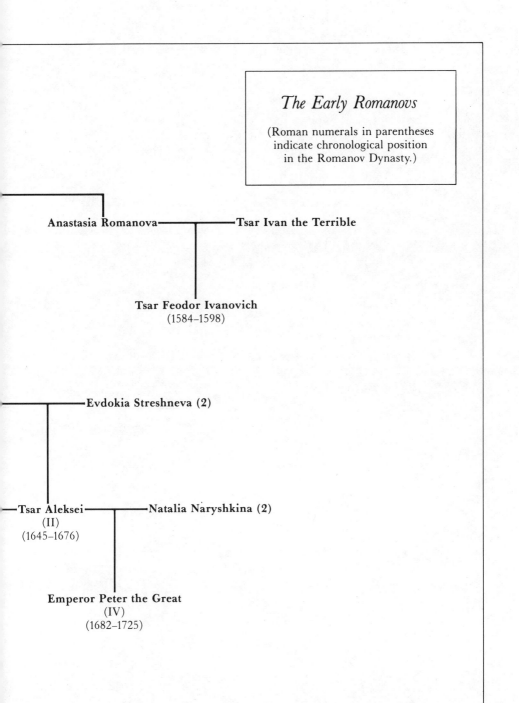

The Early Romanovs

(Roman numerals in parentheses
indicate chronological position
in the Romanov Dynasty.)

Anastasia Romanova — Tsar Ivan the Terrible

Tsar Feodor Ivanovich
(1584–1598)

Evdokia Streshneva (2)

Tsar Aleksei — Natalia Naryshkina (2)
(II)
(1645–1676)

Emperor Peter the Great
(IV)
(1682–1725)

CHAPTER I

Tsars and Tsarinas

On March 2, 1613, a large procession of notables set out from Moscow toward the northeast. They carried supplies for a fortnight's journey and went well armed, for, in the region around Russia's capital, runaway serfs and army deserters still threatened even large bands of travelers. A dangerous journey faced them, and many must have felt a certain longing for the safety of the Kremlin's great brick ramparts that stood silhouetted against the horizon in their rear. Some sixty-five feet high, and almost half that thick, those walls radiated an aura of solidity, of security against invaders, that belied the disturbing fact that they had so recently been manned by Polish invaders. Above the line formed by the ramparts' crenellated rim rose other monuments to those past glories that Russians hoped to recapture and, perhaps, even surpass one day. Glinting dimly in the watery light of the winter sun, which sat low on the horizon even at midday, rose the heavy golden dome of the Uspenskii Cathedral, the repository of Russia's most sacred relics and witness to some of the greatest dramas in her history. Ivan the Terrible had walked there, and so had his grandfather Ivan the Great. The present Cathedral had risen only in the 1470s, but it stood on ground trodden by Dmitrii Donskoi and many other famous Russian princes of earlier times. Slightly to the east of the Cathedral's huge dome, the great Bell Tower of Ivan the Great soared skyward, a brilliant white shaft against the wintry sky. From its peak, a sharp-eyed watchman could see twenty miles in every direction and could follow the windings of the Moskva River to the Virgins' Convent, past Sparrow Hills, and beyond to the summer estate of Moscow's Tsars at Kolo-

menskoe. Somewhat nearer to the departing caravan, its dozen
varicolored domes and spires set off against the Kremlin's dull red
walls, stood the Cathedral of St. Basil the Blessed, which Ivan the Terrible had raised to commemorate the great victory of Russia's armies
over the Mongol defenders of Kazan in the 1550s. Like the Kremlin itself, it too had known the indignity of the Poles' invasion during the
Time of Troubles.

Yet it was not Russia's past, but Russia's future, that must have
been foremost in the minds of the richly adorned travelers as the
Kremlin and its great buildings faded into the distance. If they failed in
their mission, the peace so recently established could be destroyed, and
the Poles, or even the Swedes, again might hold their land in bondage.
The great prominence of those who had agreed to make this arduous
journey testified to the seriousness of its purpose. At their head rode
the great princes of the Russian Church, led by the Archbishop of
Riazan, the Elder of the famous Trinity Monastery, and the archpriests
from Moscow's several great cathedrals. Behind them rode a number
of *boiars,* the greatest temporal lords in the realm, and, in their wake,
came rank upon rank of lesser nobles, great merchants, Cossacks, elite
musketeers known as *streltsy,* and important government officials. Their
destination was the Ipatiev Monastery near Kostroma, some two
hundred twenty-five miles away, where the sixteen-year-old Mikhail
Romanov had taken refuge with his mother, the nun Marfa. Their purpose was to carry word to this young lord, weak and sickly though he
was, that the *zemskii sobor,* the Assembly of the Land, had chosen him to
reign as Tsar and Autocrat of All the Russias. The Archbishop of
Riazan and the great *boiar* Feodor Sheremetiev had been chosen to
speak for all those in the Russian land who craved an end to war and
prayed for the return of peace. According to their instructions, these
two great lords, as representatives of the Russian Church and the great
nobles, were to "bow low before the Sovereign, and to entreat him,
their Sovereign, in every way, that he, their Sovereign Lord, should
show them his favor and not disdain to accept their entreaties that he
become Lord of Vladimir and Moscow, and Tsar and Grand Prince of
All Russia, and [they should beg him] to deign to come to Moscow as
quickly as possible."[1]

Through bitter winds and freezing temperatures, the delegation from the *zemskii sobor* wended its way along snow-covered paths that led through villages burnt out and devastated by the waves of warfare that had swept over Russia during the past fifteen years. On the evening of their journey's eleventh day they reached the outskirts of Kostroma, where little more than three hundred households remained of the many that had flourished only a few decades before. Worn from their journey, the caravan rested; its travelers dined as best they could and prepared to spend the night wherever they could find shelter among the many ruined and abandoned buildings. The next morning they formed a solemn procession that slowly made its way from the ruined city to the Ipatiev Monastery. There, Mikhail received them in the company of his mother. He seemed frightened and appeared reluctant to accept the proffered crown. Several times during the past ten years of his short life, sudden shifts in Russia's political winds had left him exposed to mortal danger, and he was fearful of venturing into those treacherous currents again. He was also concerned for the safety of his mother, who had shared his lonely wanderings, and, even more, for the life of his father, the Metropolitan Filaret of Rostov, who still languished in a Polish castle dungeon. If Mikhail should take up the crown that Russia's great nobles and churchmen offered, the Polish king, who also claimed it, might take his father's life in revenge.

Yet the great temporal and spiritual lords who had come to the monastery on that cold March day were not to be denied. They swore that if their new Tsar and his mother left the monastery, they would guarantee their safety; they also assured Mikhail that the *zemskii sobor* was willing to exchange as many Polish captives as necessary to obtain his father's freedom. Mikhail finally agreed to become Tsar and prepared to return to Moscow. After wandering in the war-torn Russian land for almost a decade, he had little to carry with him. In less than a week, he began his journey to the ancient capital that was now his. He traveled slowly, still fearful of the many brigands and rebellious soldiers who lurked in the forests. On the way to Moscow, he was saddened at the devastation that greeted him at every village he entered.[2] Everywhere, cottages and barns lay in ruins. Peasants' livestock had been killed or driven away, and their grain had been burned or left exposed to rot in the fall rain and winter snow. Many people were without food and went about starving and dressed in rags. To restore order and prosperity to Russia would have taxed the talents of the greatest statesman. Yet Mikhail Romanov was utterly inexperienced in government. The great nineteenth-century historian Nikolai Kostomarov once wrote that "few examples can be found in history when a new sovereign ascended the throne in conditions so extremely sad as those in which Mikhail Feodorovich [Romanov], a minor, was elected."[3]

The sixteen-year-old youth who entered Moscow's Kremlin in triumph on Sunday, May 2, 1613, to become the first of eighteen Romanov autocrats who would reign over Russia during the next three centuries, belonged to a family that had served Russia loyally in high office for many years. Mikhail's great-aunt had been the Tsarina Anastasia, the gentle woman upon whom Ivan the Terrible had lavished so much love before her mysterious death at the age of thirty. Anastasia's elder brother, Nikita Romanovich Iuriev-Zakharin, had risen in his sister's wake to serve Ivan as a general, courtier, and statesman. Nikita had won important victories for his Tsar during the Great Livonian War and had defended Russia's southern frontier against the Tatar cavalry. Unlike Ivan's other favorites, he had refused to serve with the dreaded *oprichniki* and had become known as a humane and honest man during an age notorious for its cruelty and corruption. Peasants and Cossacks immortalized him in legend and sang his praises long after his death.[4] The honesty, decency, and personal warmth of the Tsarina Anastasia and her brother thus created an aura of popular affection for the Romanov family during the turbulent reign of Ivan the Terrible that would stand their descendants in good stead for decades to come. These descendants were the first in Russia to use the name of Romanov, taken from Nikita's patronymic, and almost immediately they won a place for it among the most prominent names of the age. Most important of all, Nikita's eldest son Feodor became the Patriarch of the Russian Orthodox Church and the father of Mikhail Romanov.

Mikhail Romanov's very existence proved that his father had not always intended to devote his life to Holy Orders and the Church. Until he was well into middle age, Feodor had been very much a man of the world, the close friend of the Tsar and the confidant of the

Tsar's chief adviser, Boris Godunov. Even more than his father, Feodor Romanov was closely involved in deciding weighty affairs of state, and his opinions were heard with respect and attention in the Tsar's chamber and the *Boiar* Council. Yet Feodor Romanov had even greater ambitions, which would prove his undoing as a Kremlin politician and courtier and would change the course of his life in a dramatic fashion. As one who stood close to the throne and whose aunt had been Russia's Tsarina, Feodor Romanov dreamed of seizing the crown for himself when Ivan's son died in 1598. His pretensions drew him into a deadly feud with Boris Godunov, who also intended to sit upon Ivan's great ivory throne, and whose political resources outmatched Feodor Romanov's by a considerable margin. In bitter frustration, Feodor once struck at his rival with a dagger and brought upon himself and his family a brutal and terrible revenge. For it was Boris Godunov, not Feodor Romanov, who realized his ambition to become Russia's Tsar, and he would not soon forget the former friend who had tried to bar his path to the throne. Boris Godunov accused the entire Romanov family of treason, sorcery, and witchcraft. These were particularly fearsome crimes in the minds of Muscovites, the latter two even more so than the first. For treason was directed against the temporal power of man, while sorcery and witchcraft invoked the dark and evil powers of the supernatural and threatened not only man's life but his very soul.

To prove his charges against Feodor Romanov and his family, Tsar Boris planted false evidence in their homes and bribed their servants to swear false testimony against them. The Romanovs were found guilty and condemned to exile in the remote Arctic regions of Russia, where bitter winds sliced through the warmest clothing, and a man's breath froze solid upon his beard in an instant. In that land of brutal cold, winters lasted for more than eight months of every year. During the coldest months, the sun barely rose above the horizon. Men and women lived in darkness broken only by the flickering light cast by oil lamps and candles. In an effort to keep warm, an exile's body demanded inordinate amounts of calories, yet food was always scarce. Disease quickly attacked debilitated organisms, and death came more quickly than in warmer regions. During the first year of their exile, a number of the Romanovs succumbed to these hazards as Godunov had intended, but Feodor and his immediate family survived. As the leading member of his family, Feodor himself spent the first part of his exile on the bleak northern reaches of the Dvina River, where Godunov's agents forced him to take the name of Filaret and become a monk. Weeks later, a similar fate befell his wife Ksenia, who was coerced into taking the veil and the name of Marfa.[5] As the churchmen who did Godunov's bidding shaved the crown of his head and dressed him in a monk's cowl, Feodor Romanov was obliged to bid farewell to his dream of sitting upon Russia's throne. Yet he did not abandon his ambition to rule in Moscow's Kremlin; there were other ways to rule the Russian land than from the throne of Moscow's Tsars. Two decades later, Filaret would show how effective these other ways could be.

Once Boris Godunov had forced them to don the cowl and the veil, Feodor and Ksenia Romanov no longer could live as husband and wife, but the Tsar's cruel misuse of the Church's authority was not the first deep sadness to enter their lives. Ksenia Romanova had happily borne her husband five sons, but fate had obliged them to look on in impotent despair while the first four died in their cradles. Born on July 12, 1596, just two years before the Time of Troubles engulfed Russia in its waves of war and terror, Mikhail was their fifth and last son. Desperate not to lose him, Feodor and Ksenia Romanov lavished affection and attention upon Mikhail from the moment of his birth. He played with toys made of beautifully wrought silver and slept in an ornately carved oaken cradle. Although never robust, Mikhail survived the first years of infancy and childhood and even began to flourish under his parents' doting gaze. But this happiness was not to last for very long. Just before his fifth birthday, Mikhail's comfortable and secure world collapsed in ruins when his family was sent into exile. Godunov's agents sent the boy to live with one of his aunts in the remote village of Belozersk, where they were left in want and uncertainty while Russia sank deeper into bitter political conflicts and ruinous economic crises that brought poverty, starvation, and death in their wake.[6]

After they had suffered for some fifteen months in Belozersk, Mikhail and his aunt were allowed to move to one of the smaller Romanov estates located some fifty miles north of Moscow. There they lived simply, but free from the suffering they had known before. A few years later, the death of Boris Godunov enabled Mikhail and his mother and father, to resume a more normal life. Filaret returned to Moscow and soon was raised to high Church office as Metropolitan of Rostov, while Marfa took Mikhail directly to Rostov to await Filaret's arrival. Although forced by the Church to live separately, Filaret and Marfa enjoyed relative peace with their ten-year-old son until a new political crisis burst upon them. Again, the ambitions of other men tore the Romanovs apart and condemned them to further wanderings.

In 1606 Moscow's masses murdered the False Dmitrii, the prince who had ruled Russia since Boris Godunov's death, and the great *boiars* chose Vasilii Shuiskii to sit upon Russia's throne. Soon afterward, a second False Dmitrii, often called the Felon of Tushino, appeared near Russia's western border to march against Moscow at the head of an army of Cossacks and Poles. Brigands and Cossacks who proclaimed themselves his followers attacked Rostov in October 1608. As the most prestigious lord in the city, Filaret urged the townsfolk to resist with all their strength. Days and weeks of brutal fighting followed, as Rostov's citizens fought to save their city and defend their honor. But they were outnumbered by their foes, and weakened by hunger and disease. Rostov finally fell, and its attackers sent Filaret to the Felon of Tushino's camp near Moscow. When the Poles fled from Moscow in the fall of 1612, they took their high-born prisoner with them, and it was another seven years before he was freed. In the meantime, Mikhail Romanov and his mother had fled from Rostov's burning center, to begin four years of wandering through many of Russia's monasteries, convents, and provincial towns. News of Mikhail's election to the throne reached them in Kostroma some days before the great procession of temporal and spiritual lords arrived.[7]

In choosing Mikhail Romanov to be Russia's Tsar, the *zemskii sobor* had rejected several other candidates, and the best estimates are that Mikhail won its approval because, several powerful, often antagonistic, political groups found that they could agree upon him. Mikhail's family ties to the popular Tsarina Anastasia and her famous brother Nikita Romanovich also made him popular with the masses. He appealed to many Russians because he had no close ties to such great *boiar* families as the Godunovs and Shuiskiis, whose feuds had weakened Russia so severely during the Time of Troubles. Russia's great lords thought that Mikhail was too young and inexperienced to threaten their power, and the masses thought that he would not favor the great lords.[8] Both were correct in their judgments. At the time of his election, Mikhail had had little political training and had built no Court alliances. He mounted Russia's throne alone. There were no strong and able men among his immediate family in Moscow, and his dynamic and assertive father still languished as a prisoner in a foreign land. Marfa probably was the major influence in Mikhail's life during his first years on the throne, although she generally confined herself to such personal matters as obtaining Court sinecures for her relatives. Certainly, she did not play that decisive political role that some historians have assigned to her.[9]

One of the first requests Mikhail Romanov received from the *zemskii sobor* after his arrival in Moscow at the beginning of May was that he take up his crown without further delay. He therefore set July 11 as the date for his coronation, and all Moscow was soon caught up in a frenzied effort to make the necessary preparations. There were only two months to prepare a coronation worthy of the new Tsar and the new order that men and women fervently hoped had been born out of fifteen years of bloody struggle and suffering. From the Kremlin's treasury, Court officials brought a throne of "Persian gold," set with many large and rare gems, upon which they planned to seat Russia's first Romanov ruler. There seemed to be a unity of purpose such as no one had seen in the Kremlin since the early years of Ivan the Terrible's reign more than a half-century earlier, as greater and lesser lords joined in a common effort to crown and pay tribute to Mikhail. To lessen tensions still more, the new Tsar decreed that the distinctions between various types of noble rank would not be observed at his coronation. That way, the day could not be marred by those endless disputes over precedence that so often embroiled Muscovite lords in bitter personal and political conflict. Mikhail also bestowed special honors upon Prince Dmitrii Pozharskii and Kuzma Minin, the two national heroes who had driven the Poles from Moscow that fall. By July 10, all was ready and the Muscovites awaited the morrow with ill-contained anticipation. That evening, all of the city's churches celebrated special masses to commemorate the dawn of a new age for Russia.

On Sunday, July 11, 1613, Russia's great nobles and state officials assembled in the Kremlin's Palace of Facets to await their sovereign. At two o'clock in the afternoon, Mikhail entered, his youth and pallor accentuated by the heavy golden robes that hung from his frail shoulders. Prince Pozharskii brought forward the Tsar's symbols of office: the crown of Monomakh, rimmed with sable and surmounted by rubies and emeralds the size of pigeon eggs; the diamond-studded orb; and the golden Muscovite sceptre. These he then carried to the Uspenskii Cathedral, where Russia's Tsars were traditionally crowned. As Pozharskii crossed the square, all thirty-three bells, including the huge Bell of the Assumption, rang out from the Bell Tower of Ivan the Great to announce the beginning of the ceremony. The great *boiar* Vasilii Morozov than led the procession from the Palace to the Cathedral. A number of other nobles, all chosen for their prominence in state affairs, came after him, followed by the Cathedral's archpriest, who sprinkled the way behind him with holy water so that Mikhail would walk only on consecrated pavement. Small and alone, Mikhail came next in the great procession. Quite probably he looked ill at ease and uncertain about the events that lay ahead. It was the day before his seventeenth birthday, and, until that moment, he never had played even a minor part in an important official ceremony.

People of all ranks crowded joyfully into the Kremlin's vast square as the procession made its way toward the great Uspenskii Cathedral that towered in its center. Slowly, Russia's greatest lords, followed by their Tsar, passed through the arched doorway and walked beneath its towering frescoes to enter the holy sanctum of Russia's spiritual heritage. On their right, the great golden iconostasis held Russia's most treasured icons, gathered from all corners of the realm to adorn the great cathedral that Aristotle Fieravanti had built to the greater glory of God and the Grand Prince of Moscow in the 1470s. As Mikhail entered, the sacred and ancient image of Our Lord of the Golden Hair, which unknown artists had created even before the Mongols had swept through the Russian land, gazed down upon him. Nearby hung the awesome and frightening Savior of the Chastening Eye, painted when Ivan the Moneybag had ruled Moscow's far more modest domains. So, too, did the tender and loving countenance of the Blessed Virgin of

Vladimir, who held a special place in the hearts of all Russians, and who had been painted by a student of the greatest of all Russian icon painters, Andrei Rublev. From the Cathedral's great columns, frescoes of Christ's twelve disciples, the Archangels Michael and Gabriel, Russia's patron St. George, and St. Nicholas the Miracle Worker—all were illuminated by the rays of the sun and the flickering of holy candles. Around the young prince about to be crowned Tsar stood the sarcophagi in which the holiest of Russia's Church Fathers slept their eternal sleep. Every square inch of wall or ceiling was adorned with sacred images. All served to remind every mortal who entered the Cathedral that life on earth was but a brief moment of eternity and that it was man's first and greatest duty to serve his Heavenly Sovereign, for whom the Tsar of All the Russias stood as an earthly representative.

Before all those assembled, Metropolitan Efrem asked God's blessing upon the young prince about to be crowned, and Mikhail then spoke about the many trials that Russia had faced since the death of Tsar Feodor Ivanovich fifteen years before. Russians must rebuild their national unity, he said, and they must restore peace and order throughout their land. Efrem placed the crown upon his brow, blessed him and gave him Holy Communion. Mikhail then took up the orb and sceptre to reign as Tsar of All the Russias, and Moscow burst into a frenzy of celebration.[10]

Although his subjects rejoiced, Mikhail Romanov faced immense difficulties on the day of his accession. Filaret, his father, was still a prisoner of the Poles. Armies of brigands and thieves still roamed his country's forests, and much of his domain lay in ruins from the devastation of foreign armies. Trade and commerce had ceased, taxes remained uncollected, and the treasury was nearly empty. Throughout the kingdom there was widespread hunger and disease. Mikhail faced these crises alone, with no political experience and no astute advisers in whom he could place his trust.

While the zemskii sobor that had elected him traditionally had been summoned by Russia's Tsars only for very brief meetings, Mikhail kept it in session, with rare recesses for new elections, for almost a decade. The zemskii sobor, the people's elected representatives, thus took an active part in Russia's reconstruction and even went so far as to suspend for several years the operation of *mestnichestvo,* that complex rank-ordering system of ancestral precedents that had led to such bitter disputes among the Tsar's servitors that affairs of state, even battlefield commands, had been paralyzed during the years before Mikhail's accession.[11]

Before they could begin Russia's domestic reconstruction, the *zemskii sobor* and, especially, Mikhail had to deal with the marauding Swedish and Polish armies who remained in Russia and continued to threaten the survival of her new government. Mikhail had few resources with which to continue an armed struggle, yet he could not leave foreign armies unchallenged, especially when they occupied some of Russia's most important cities. He dealt first with the Swedes' army, still in the important commercial center of Novgorod. The Swedish King's brother, Prince Charles Philip, still claimed the Russian throne. For several years, nothing in the way of a peace could be arranged, but finally, with the help of the English King James I, Mikhail signed the Peace of Stolbovo on February 27, 1617. Sweden's King restored Novgorod to Russia and ordered Prince Charles Philip to abandon his claim to Mikhail's throne. Mikhail paid Sweden an indemnity of twenty thousand rubles and gave up all the lands that the armies of Ivan the Terrible and Boris Godunov had won along the Baltic coast. The cost of peace was exorbitantly high: Russia lost her outlet to the Baltic Sea and could ill afford the indemnity. Yet Mikhail had no choice and was grateful to the British for helping him obtain the terms of the settlement. He turned next to negotiations with Poland and, two years later, agreed to cede a number of important Russian towns and cities to the Poles in return for a fourteen-year armistice and the release of his father.[12] Both treaties were humiliating, but with them Mikhail bought the peace that was so necessary to restore order. He postponed any threat of foreign invasion and won Filaret's freedom. Both would be of great importance in the reconstruction of Russia during the coming decade.

On June 10, 1619, two men faced each other on the eastern bank of the Presna River, a small stream that ran some five miles to the north of Moscow's Kremlin. One was tall and robust, even though he was near seventy. The other was short and slight. He was only twenty-three, but he walked with considerable difficulty. As Filaret and Mikhail approached each other, both men fell to their knees and wept with joy. Within eight days, the Tsar had named his father Patriarch of the Russian Church, the *zemskii sobor* had given its assent, and, after a proper amount of hesitation, Filaret had accepted.[13] Yet the Patriarch Filaret was not content to rule only the Church; faithful to his earlier ambitions, he was determined to rule the Russian state as well. He did so by imposing his powerful will upon his weaker and less assertive son. He insisted upon assuming the exalted title of *velikii gosudar,* which translates roughly as "sovereign majesty" and which only the Tsar had borne until that time. Filaret, not Mikhail, made policy decisions in the Kremlin; under his stern hand, Russia's policies began to take on a more positive, even aggressive, character at home and abroad.[14]

One of Filaret's greatest political concerns upon his return to Russia was the very disturbing fact that his son had reached the age of twenty-three but was unmarried and had no heirs. Even before his return, the question of Mikhail's marriage had become a major issue at the Court, all the more so because Tsars always had married Russian noblewomen. For centuries, political alliances at the Russian Court had been based upon the shifting loyalties among various great clans, and the relationships between men in the Tsar's service had become so intertwined that the unexpected rise of one family through marriage could throw everything into turmoil.

Some four years before Filaret returned from Poland, when Mikhail still was naïve and inexperienced in Court politics, he had announced his decision to wed Maria Khlopova, the daughter of a provincial nobleman who had no friends or allies at Court. Maria was brought to the Kremlin, where Mikhail announced their betrothal with proper ceremony, but vicious political intrigue soon reversed her family's fortunes. The Khlopovs' sudden elevation to high office at Court sparked fierce jealousies among the Saltykovs, who were relatives of Mikhail's mother. Obviously, they stood to lose a great deal of the influence they had gained from Marfa's patronage, and they struggled to defend their position by every foul means at their command. The Saltykovs first arranged to have a strong emetic placed in Maria Khlopova's food as she sat at dinner one evening in the Kremlin. Almost immediately, spasms of violent wretching wracked her body, while the other guests looked on in ill-concealed horror. The first part of their scheme accomplished, the Saltykovs bribed several physicians to tell the Tsar that his bride-to-be suffered from an incurable disease she had knowingly concealed in her effort to become Russia's Tsarina. They then persuaded Mikhail to send the Khlopovs to Siberia as punishment for "deceiving" him about the health of his intended bride. It was Filaret who first learned the truth about what had happened that evening several years later. When he reported this discovery to his son, Mikhail was consumed by a rare moment of rage. He drove the Saltykovs from Court, and confiscated many of the vast estates they had gotten through illegal means. Still, even though he knew Maria Khlopova had been wronged, he could not marry his first betrothed because Marfa, now angered by the revenge he had taken against her family, refused to give her consent. Mikhail's clumsily bestowed favor had cost the Khlopovs dearly.[15]

Probably in an effort to avoid a similar outcome, Filaret first sought a wife for Mikhail among Europe's many lesser princesses. But this search in foreign lands had a broader significance as well; it indicated that Russia, and especially the Orthodox Church, was ready to turn outward after several centuries of self-imposed isolation. Ivan the Terrible's Great Livonian War in the 1560s and 1570s had marked the first serious effort by Moscow's rulers to break with the Church's efforts to isolate Russia from the West. Boris Godunov continued that policy, but, like Ivan, he had been obliged to violate the Church's decrees in order to do so. Now at last both Church and State were prepared to see Russia become a part of the European political community.

But Europe's rulers were not yet willing to ally themselves with Russia's new masters. The King of Denmark would not even make the gesture of receiving Filaret's envoy. When approached about a marriage between Mikhail and his sister-in-law, Sweden's King Gustavus Adolphus refused on the patently hypocritical ground that her required conversion to Orthodoxy would endanger her immortal soul. The only available foreign candidates seemed to be the two unmarried sisters of Dorothea, Princess of Altenburg, who, one chagrined Russian diplomat reported, were "so obese that no one would think of proposing marriage to them."[16] Filaret did not dispute his envoy's conclusions and left the two sisters to commiserate in their spinsterhood.

Since no bride could be found in the West, Filaret prepared to marry Mikhail to a Russian, even though such a union would create new political rivalries at Court and oblige the Romanovs to share some of their power and influence with others. At his mother's urging, Mikhail agreed to marry the Princess Maria Dolgorukova, whose family was related to Marfa's relatives. The wedding was celebrated in September 1624. Yet Mikhail's marriage did not resolve the succession question in Russia because the Princess Maria died in less than a year. Again the search for a suitable bride began, but this time Mikhail conducted it with more of the pomp and circumstance that tradition required. Late in 1625, specially appointed agents assembled some sixty maidens in Moscow. From them Mikhail chose Evdokia Streshneva. Like Maria Khlopova, she was the daughter of a rural squire. Unlike the Khlopovs, the Streshnevs were better connected at Court and more aware of the dangers that lurked in the dark corridors of the Kremlin. They were also fortunate to have Filaret's support and protection. Evdokia was guarded well. No enemies hid emetic potions in her food, and it would have done little good had they tried. The Streshnevs and Filaret already knew that Evdokia was in perfect health well before she set foot in the Kremlin. On February 5, 1626, Mikhail Romanov and Evdokia Streshneva were wed in a magnificent but uneventful ceremony. They would spend the rest of their lives together.[17] Most important to the Muscovite lords and ladies who lived around them, in little more than three years Evdokia gave birth to the first heir to be born since the Romanovs had ascended the throne. Although not secure, the succession had finally been established. By then, it was 1629, a full sixteen years since Mikhail had been crowned as a lonely, frail youth in the vastness of the Uspenskii Cathedral.

Mikhail's marriage resolved only one of the many crises that Russia faced during the three decades in which he sat upon the throne. The first years of his reign had been a desperate attempt to assure Russia's survival as an independent state in a world in which she was surrounded by rapacious and powerful neighbors, and in which her own great lords lusted for personal power and influence at the Court of an apparently weak monarch. Yet, for a young man who had spent his youth in painful wanderings far from the center of political power in Russia, Mikhail did remarkably well in keeping his kingdom from being torn apart from within or consumed by greedy neighbors from without. It was a task that must have stretched his abilities and physical resources to the breaking point, and, once Filaret returned to Moscow in 1619, Mikhail seemed only too willing to relinquish many of his responsibilities. While Filaret ruled for more than a decade, his son enjoyed the family happiness he found in his life with the Tsarina Evdokia.

Mikhail's emancipation from some of the burdens of ruling his tumultuous kingdom came to a sudden end on October 1, 1633, when Filaret died at the age of eighty. Russia was in the midst of a ruinous war with Poland. That summer, the conflict had turned against her, and, by early fall, the Polish King Władysław IV was on the march with more than thirty thousand men to lift the Russian siege of the fortress city of Smolensk. Filaret breathed his last at the very moment when his decisive leadership was needed most, leaving Mikhail, weakened in body and worn in spirit, to finish the war on his own terms. It was then that he proved his true mettle as Russia's Tsar. Russia lost no lands to the Poles in the treaty he signed the next year. He paid a large war indemnity he could ill afford, but he forced the Poles to recognize his claim to Russia's crown.[18]

During the decade after he had signed the peace of 1634 with Poland, Mikhail saw a growing aura of stability spread over his domains. Russia still faced many crises, yet the situation was no longer desperate, and her survival as a nation no longer was at stake in her relations with foreign powers. To add to the sense of stability that Mikhail was beginning to enjoy, his wife bore him six children, three of them sons. Certainly, there seemed to be little danger that Russia would be left without an heir at his death. Equally gratifying, Mikhail found Western rulers moderately receptive to his attempts to find husbands for his daughters, and, for the first time in several centuries it seemed possible that a Russian princess might wed a foreign prince. Denmark's King Christian greeted Mikhail's suggestion that his daughter Irina should marry the Danish Prince Waldemar quite warmly.

Soon after the New Year's celebrations in 1644, Waldemar arrived in Moscow with a large retinue to pursue the matter further.

There was a great deal more at stake in Mikhail's plan to marry Irina to Prince Waldemar than the mere acceptance of a Romanov daughter by a reigning house in Europe. In 1639 Mikhail's two youngest sons had died suddenly, and only Grand Duke Aleksei Mikhailovich remained as his heir. If Aleksei should die, Mikhail realized that his own death would plunge Russia into turmoil. Once again, great *boiars* and princes would tear the Russian land asunder in their struggles for power and wealth, and Russia well might not survive a second Time of Troubles. Mikhail hoped that this problem might be avoided through Irina's marriage to a Western prince who could be proclaimed his heir if the need arose. There was one major obstacle to his plan: Waldemar's refusal to convert to Orthodoxy. Mikhail was so eager for the marriage to take place, however, that he was willing to set the question of conversion aside.

The Patriarch Iosif and a number of great temporal lords were not willing to be so tolerant. When Waldemar arrived in Moscow, the Patriarch and several leading *boiars* insisted on his conversion. A religious debate between Waldemar's chaplain and the Orthodox theologian Ivan Nasedka ensued, and Muscovites followed its course with avid attention throughout the spring and summer of 1644. One of Nasedka's refutations of Waldemar's chaplain and the Lutheran faith sold over a thousand copies in three months, an unheard-of quantity that no other book would match for almost a century. Yet, if Muscovites found the debate engrossing, the question of Waldemar's faith remained unresolved. Mikhail had no stomach for a head-on confrontation with the Church, but he feared that it would heap international ridicule upon Russia if he sent Waldemar back to Denmark unmarried. He held Waldemar a virtual prisoner until the summer of 1645. A year had passed, and still there seemed no way out of the dilemma. Then, on July 13, 1645, the day after his forty-ninth birthday, Mikhail died, and his wife followed him to the grave in less than a month.[19] As in 1613, Russia once again became the domain of a sixteen-year-old youth who had no experience in politics or statecraft. This youth, however, had great talent and energy. Aleksei Mikhailovich would be known in history as the "most gentle" Tsar. One of his first acts was to send Prince Waldemar back to Denmark, unconverted and unwed.[20]

His parents' second child and their first son, Aleksei Mikhailovich was born on March 19, 1629. He was far more robust in body than his father, his mind was more brilliant, and his character more lively and appealing. For the first five years of his life, he lived mainly in his mother's *terem,* those secluded rooms on the upper floors of seventeenth-century aristocratic and royal Russian dwellings that were the exclusive preserve of women and their small children, an inner sanctum into which men rarely ventured and where masculine voices were almost never heard. There, women still lived according to principles and ideals of the *Domostroi* set forth by the monk Silvestr early in the sixteenth century, when secular and spiritual lords saw women as pure and passive creatures, who seldom spoke except to pray or reply to their fathers' or husbands' questions. Such models of Muscovite female virtue were never to be seen in public, nor were they to set eyes upon any of the men who visited their fathers, brothers, or husbands in their own homes. They were to devote their higher thoughts to prayer, their lesser thoughts to children, and their hands to sewing and embroidery. Thus the *Domostroi* decreed, and thus did Russia's women live.

For the women in his mother's *terem,* Aleksei was the object of continuous petting and concern. They cherished him as the prince who one day would inherit the Russian throne and made every effort to protect him from injury. They watched in fear for the symptoms of such childhood diseases as measles, scarlet fever, and diphtheria, which, in those days, struck down infants with frightening quickness. Aleksei was a treasure to be guarded with the utmost care, and his mother, her companions, and servants dedicated their lives to that effort. But tradition dictated that they could not hold him for long. Soon after his fifth birthday, Aleksei Mikhailovich left the world of women and entered that of men, where Boris Morozov, a politically astute nobleman, taught him to read and write and oversaw his schooling in the rituals and liturgy of the Russian Church. Although custom dictated that a Muscovite prince should receive no more than this elementary schooling, Morozov cautiously pushed beyond those limits. He saw that the young prince had an intellectual curiosity that was unusual for the time and milieu in which he lived. One day, he gave him a small collection of German engravings that depicted life in the modern West, and his pupil studied them avidly. In his enthusiasm for the new world about which Morozov's engravings gave only the most tantalizing hints, Aleksei Mikhailovich began to assemble a small personal library. Not only were there religious books in Russian but secular volumes written in Polish, Greek, even Latin. The young prince collected translations of foreign works on such practical subjects as military strategy and tactics, a science no Muscovite Tsar had studied formally before, and began to read them with attention. There were Latin and Greek lexicons, an indication that Aleksei Mikhailovich may have begun to study those languages at that time.[21] Thanks to Morozov's efforts, the second Romanov to rule Russia discovered things in the West that seemed worthwhile, important, and attractive. Aleksei Mikhailovich would draw upon Western technology and experience to an ever-increasing degree when he became Russia's sovereign. He would blaze the trail his youngest son, Peter the Great, would follow with such energy and passion a half-century later.

As Tsar and Autocrat of All the Russias, Aleksei Mikhailovich has been called "the most attractive figure ever to appear upon the throne of the Muscovite Tsars."[22] Contemporaries and historians have remembered him in warm and flattering terms, although few have been so immoderate as Jakob Reutenfels, the brother of one of the Tsar's physicians, who described him as "the kind of sovereign all Christian peoples desire, but few ever obtain."[23] Still, even after proper allowances are made for exaggeration and overstatement, there was much about Aleksei Mikhailovich that was appealing. Dr. Samuel Collins, another of his physicians, wrote that he was "a goodly person, about six feet high, well set, inclined to fat, of a clear complexion, lightish hair, somewhat low forehead, of a stern countenance, severe in his chastisements, but very careful of his subjects' love,"[24] and that probably was an accurate description. As a person, Aleksei Mikhailovich was a humane and kindly man who lived in a cruel and heartless age. Aleksei, too, could be heartless on occasion. In performing his duties as Russia's Tsar, he could be as bad tempered and "terrible" as Ivan the Terrible had been.

Aleksei was deeply religious, "Christ-loving and pious" in the words of the prayer that was said at the end of every Church service.[25] His day began with prayers at four in the morning in his private chapel, followed by matins, a late morning service, and other devotions throughout the afternoon and evening. Often there were services that lasted the entire night, leaving everyone exhausted.[26] As one noted scholar wrote about him some years ago, "his every action necessitated a religious ceremony, and every religious occasion required his personal participation. . . . Through all these vigils moved the figure of the Tsar—praying, giving his hands to bishops to kiss, and in turn kissing their hands, listening to army reports, and praying again."[27] Aleksei Mikhailovich dedicated himself to the ritual of reigning with a passion and intensity that no other Tsar matched at any time in Russia's history.

During the first few years of his reign, Aleksei Mikhailovich left the direction of state affairs to his tutor Morozov, to whom he gave control of the elite *streltsy* guards, those foreign mercenaries in Russia's service, and the State Exchequer.[28] For a while, Morozov virtually ruled the land, while his youthful master went in search of a bride who would bear his sons to assure an orderly succession. Early in 1647 Aleksei's agents brought two hundred of Russia's most beautiful maidens to Moscow. There they were examined and observed by the Tsar's most trusted chamberlains. All of them were beautiful, but which met the ideal? Which lived most faithfully the principles of the *terem* and the *Domostroi*? Which combined beauty with a healthy body and a fertile womb? Aleksei's chamberlains and physicians chose the six whom they judged the most perfect in all respects. These they presented to their young sovereign, and he chose the daughter of Feodor Vsevolizhskii, a beautiful but shy maiden who fell into a dead faint when she heard that she was to become the Tsar's bride. Schemers who opposed the marriage, and Morozov may very well have been among them, immediately spread the vicious rumor that Aleksei's choice had fainted because she suffered from the curse of epilepsy. Like the Khlopovs before them, she and her family were exiled to Siberia, where they were kept in want and misery for several years. In the meantime, at Morozov's urging, Aleksei married Maria Miloslavskaia on January 16, 1648. The wily

Morozov hastened to wed her younger sister Anna, and, before the end of the month, he had become the Tsar's brother-in-law.[29] Morozov soon fell from his pinnacle of power, but those Miloslavskiis he had sponsored proved more durable and fortunate. For the next half-century, they exercised a major influence on Russia's domestic affairs and played a frequently disruptive role in Muscovite Court politics. By the end of the century, the name Miloslavskii had become feared and hated throughout Russia. When Peter the Great seized the throne in 1689, the Miloslavskiis' enemies would exact a vicious and ruinous vengeance upon them. No Miloslavskii ever held a high government position in Russia after 1689.

Almost from the moment of his accession, Aleksei Mikhailovich faced revolts and threats to his crown, and he always was obliged to be on the lookout for new rebel attacks in various corners of his domains. The first great revolt burst forth in the heart of Moscow, at the very gates of the Kremlin, early in the summer of 1648. It came not long after Aleksei's marriage, and less than three months after he had turned nineteen. Its underlying causes were complex, and of long standing, but it was sparked by the unrelenting demands of Morozov and his favorites for more money from the people of Moscow. Perhaps most hated among the new taxes Morozov sought to impose was the new government monopoly upon salt, which raised the tax levied upon that vital commodity by some four hundred percent. The result was catastrophic and predictable. All but the very rich reduced their use of salt, and it was left in government storehouses where dampness and rain turned it to brine. It merely "dribbled away," one contemporary recalled. "A year later," a foreign observer remarked, "it was necessary to calculate how many thousands [of rubles] had been lost on salted fish—used as food in Russia more than meat—that spoiled because it was not properly preserved, owing to the high price of salt."[30] Bitterly, Muscovites carried their complaints to Morozov, but he doggedly refused to take them to the Tsar. The crowd soon took matters into their own hands.[31]

On June 1, 1648, Aleksei Mikhailovich returned to Moscow from a brief pilgrimage to the Trinity Monastery some fifty miles away. As always, his return was celebrated by a great procession as the people of

Moscow welcomed their "most gentle" Tsar back into their midst. "According to local custom," wrote one witness, "the masses went out of the city to greet him with offerings of bread and salt [the gifts traditionally presented to honored visitors]. Along with wishes for long life and good fortune, they also begged him to accept their petition against Pleshcheev [one of Morozov's most corrupt and arrogant deputies]. The *streltsy* drove them away with their whips and made a number of arrests."[32] Desperate to be heard, the crowd tried to present their petition to the young Tsarina Maria some thirty minutes later. Again, the guards drove them away. This time, a few fought back against the *streltsy* whips and cudgels. It was an ominous sign. Frustrated in their peaceful efforts to carry grievances to their Tsar, the Moscow crowd turned violent in the presence of the Romanovs for the first time since they had ascended the throne. It had been more than three decades since a Russian Tsar had seen an angry crowd in Moscow's streets, and it was not a sight that Aleksei Mikhailovich would forget quickly.

During the night after their first efforts to petition Aleksei Mikhailovich about the arrogance and corruption of his officials, the Moscow crowd became more unruly and irate. The next morning, June 2, they assembled in front of the Kremlin Palace and demanded that their Tsar surrender Pleshcheev to them for execution. When Morozov misjudged the depths of their anger and urged Aleksei to refuse, the crowd broke into open rebellion. Lusting for blood, a raging mob killed several of Morozov's assistants and plundered their palatial homes. Then they stormed through the Kremlin to Morozov's palace itself. Adam Olearius, a Holsteiner who had visited Moscow on four occasions between 1634 and 1643 and who kept a close watch upon events in Russia's capital for some years afterward, described the crowd's anger in an account he published just a few years later. "Although they found Morozov's wife at home [Morozov was hiding in the Tsar's apartments]," Olearius wrote, "they caused her no bodily harm, but only said, 'Were you not the sister of the Grand Princess [Aleksei's wife] we would hack you to bits.' They were so furious that they spared not even the holy icons, which they usually venerate highly. They tore from them the pearls and precious stones with which they were embellished and flung them into the square. . . . Some of the mob broke into the cellar to the barrels of mead and vodka, drank their fill, and smashing the barrels they were unable to drink up, they waded knee-deep in liquor. . . . When the fire that had been set in the house reached the cellar, they were burned along with the building."[33]

By their generous treatment of Morozov's royal wife, the Moscow mob made it clear that their anger was directed not against their young Tsar but against his counselors. In their fury they clamored for victims, and, despite his deep repugnance at the deed, Aleksei surrendered several of his advisers to them. Obviously Pleshcheev could not be saved, nor could his immediate superior, Nazarii Chistoi. Bowing to the inevitable, Aleksei Mikhailovich allowed Pleshcheev and Chistoi to be taken by the crowd at different times on different days. Both were brutally murdered before his eyes, a sight he would never forget and one for which he would exact a high price from the Muscovites at a later date. "Pleshcheev was clubbed to death," wrote Olearius. "His head was beaten to such a pulp that his brains spattered over his face. His clothing was torn off, and the naked body dragged through the dirt around the market place, while they cried: 'Thus will all such scoundrels and thieves be treated. God preserve His Tsarist Majesty's health for many years!' The corpse was left lying in the dirt and was trampled on."[34] Only after four days of revolt and murder could Aleksei's agents bring the crowd under control. The final price he was obliged to pay for peace was Morozov's disgrace. He sent him into exile at a monastery that stood in the midst of those remote Arctic wastes that formed the shores of the White Sea. It was the first time, but far from the last, that a Romanov would sacrifice one of his closest and most valued counselors to pacify irate Russians. Aleksei Mikhailovich then followed his father's example and summoned a *zemskii sobor* to assemble in Moscow. At his urging, they began to draft a new code of laws for Russia that would be called the *Ulozhenie* of 1649. This code made a serious effort to satisfy the demands of all Russians except for serfs and slaves, who were forced to bend under an even more oppressive yoke than ever before.[35]

Although Aleksei Mikhailovich had brought order to Moscow, he had not succeeded in pacifying the entire Russian land. In the fall of 1649, famine struck Russia's northwestern province of Pskov, and large numbers of people began to die from hunger and disease. Just a few months later, in February 1650, Aleksei's government sent more than fifty thousand bushels of grain to Sweden as part of an agreement that had been signed some years earlier. Furious that the Swedes should eat while they went hungry, Pskov's starving masses seized the grain as it passed through their territory and drove the Tsar's agents in panic back to Moscow. A month later, Pskov's sister city, the great trading center of Novgorod, joined her in revolt, and threatened to turn the entire northwest region of Russia into a hotbed of rebellion. Aleksei brought these townsmen to heel only after he sent Prince Ivan Khovanskii with several thousand troops to unleash a reign of terror against them. Khovanskii accomplished his task by a brutal wave of executions, tortures, and vicious floggings, after which he sent many of the victims into exile. By the middle of the summer, he had restored order and forced those who had survived the violence to pay large sums of treasure to atone for their political sins.[36]

Conditions in Russia continued to be so bad, and the demands of government agents so exorbitant, that even greater revolts soon followed. In a little more than a decade, the people of Moscow again took to the streets. The famous Moscow Copper Riot of 1662 had its origin in a scheme by which some of Aleksei Mikhailovich's advisers hoped to amass vast sums of treasure for their financially troubled government without taking the always unpopular course of raising taxes. In 1654 they had begun to mint copper coins that were identical is size, shape, and denomination to the existing silver ones, and simply decreed that they were equal in value to their silver counterparts. According to one knowledgeable observer, while silver coinage contained its face value in silver, the Moscow Mint needed less than two rubles' worth of copper to mint one hundred rubles' worth of coins. At the same time, Aleksei Mikhailovich's officials insisted that all foreign trade be carried on in silver or gold, so that, in exchange for such much-desired commodities as sable, marten, and lynx pelts, caviar, leather, and potash, the treasury continued to receive large sums of foreign specie. On the eve of a new war with Sweden, when the government desperately needed to buy large quantities of armaments in the West, the plan truly seemed heaven-sent to Russia's much-harassed treasury officials, and, during the next five years, they blithely minted some twenty million rubles' worth of valueless copper coins to yield an astronomical profit.[37]

Counterfeiters sprang up like the fall mushrooms of which Russians are so inordinately fond. One especially clever criminal minted the staggering sum of six hundred fifty thousand rubles' worth of counterfeit coins (almost thirty-five times the war indemnity Tsar Mikhail had paid the Swedes in 1617) before he was arrested. According to one knowledgeable contemporary estimate, there were more than four hundred counterfeiters in Moscow's prisons in 1661, when there had been none a decade earlier.[38] There was simply no way to tell which coins were real and which were not, because the government had not foreseen the counterfeit threat. Government agents began to insist that all taxes and other monies due the treasury be paid in silver, and the value of copper coins plummeted. Simultaneously, Russia suffered another great famine, which caused food prices to soar. By the beginning of 1662, a Russian needed four copper rubles to buy one silver ruble's worth of goods, and everyone expected the gap to widen still more.[39]

What made this situation particularly explosive in Moscow was that Aleksei Mikhailovich's government insisted upon paying all its debts, including the salaries of soldiers and state officials, in the devalued copper coins. This posed an especially critical problem for Muscovites because they, unlike their country cousins, had no choice but to purchase all of life's necessities at soaring prices. High officials turned a deaf ear to their complaints. As in 1648, angry citizens took matters into their own hands. On the morning of June 25, 1662, Muscovites awakened to an unusual sight. Throughout the center of the city, hand-printed placards proclaimed that Aleksei Mikhailovich's counselors were thieves and speculators. Comparatively few in Moscow were literate, but there were a number of men who willingly read out the message to crowds that grew larger by the minute. The city police began to tear down the placards. The crowds protested vehemently. The police insisted that they were taking down the printed complaints only so that they could take them to the Tsar, but long-held suspicions spilled forth from the bitter Muscovites. "You're taking the placards to the traitors themselves, because the Tsar isn't even in Moscow!" someone bellowed. "These posters should be read by everyone!"[40] Quickly the crowd swelled until it numbered more than five thousand. In a spontaneous rush, the mob decided to take their grievances to Aleksei Mikhailovich himself, who was staying at a Romanov estate at Kolomenskoe, just a few miles outside Moscow.

Even for the modern-day tourist, Kolomenskoe is a breathtaking sight. For seventeenth-century Russians it was awesome indeed. Atop a bluff overlooking the Moskva River stands a unique church built of brick, the focal point of the small village and estate that surrounds it. Quite unlike any other church in all of Moscow, it boasts no drum-shaped towers topped by onion domes. Instead, it flaunts a single, lofty, conical spire that rises so high above the riverbank it seems to pierce the heavens themselves as if to merit its name of the Church of the Ascension. Just below the base of the church's conical roof, the "Tsar's seat" is cut into the brickwork. There, Ivan the Terrible, and the Tsars who came after him, sat to watch their armies parade on the plain far below. Not far from the Church of the Ascension, Aleksei Mikhailovich's royal architects had completed in the early 1650s the Church of the Virgin of Kazan. Nearby stood a small royal lodge he soon would transform into a remarkable palace with some two hundred fifty rooms and more than three thousand mica windows, all ornamented with that superb wood carving for which the Russians are so justly famous. On the morning the Copper Riot broke out, Aleksei Mikhailovich was attending a special Mass to celebrate the birth of his seventh daughter, Feodosia. Long before the Moscow mob came near the church, he could hear them shouting the names of the Miloslavskiis, and calling for his trusted adviser Feodor Rtishchev. Calmly, he told Rtishchev and the Miloslavskiis to take refuge in the Tsarina Maria's *terem,* a sanctum he hoped the mob would not dare to violate, and he sent couriers to Moscow with orders for his senior officers to bring up the elite *streltsy* guards from the Kremlin. Then he turned to face the angry crowd of some five thousand Muscovites.[41]

Aleksei Mikhailovich proved that day at Kolomenskoe that he possessed nerves of steel. He did not summon his bodyguards, not even when some of the crowd clutched at his robes, seized his buttons, and pleaded with him to punish those whom they thought had joined with the counterfeiters to reap vast profits. Aleksei spoke calmly. "Go back to your homes. As soon as the Mass is finished, I shall go to Moscow myself to make an investigation and settle this matter immediately."[42] Apparently satisfied, the crowd fell silent and turned back to the city, only to meet a larger mob coming to protest as they had just done. The mood of the second wave was more savage, and they were far less willing to let themselves be sent home with promises. Together they all surged back to Kolomenskoe to demand that the Tsar give them the "traitors" for immediate punishment. In reply, Aleksei Mikhailovich ordered the *streltsy* into action. Without a moment's hesitation, these elite guards began to hack and stab their way through the crowd. Some seven thousand Muscovites fell before their weapons, drowned in the Moskva River as they tried to flee, or were rounded up for interrogation, torture, and further punishment. Yet Aleksei demanded still more punishment for his subjects' treason, for he was not inclined to be lenient as he had been in 1648. This time, he was more secure, more confident of his ability to face a crisis, and the crowd had tried his autocratic patience once too often. When he returned to the Kremlin, he condemned another fifteen thousand Muscovites to various fates: losing their arms or legs, being branded, being sent into exile, being dispossessed of all their property. The "most gentle" Tsar's retribution rivaled that which Ivan the Terrible had wrought upon such rebellious cities as Novgorod some three-quarters of a century earlier.[43]

The rebellious spirit of the Moscow crowd was quelled, but discontent festered among Russia's masses. To rebuild and modernize Russia and fight costly wars with Sweden and Poland, the Tsar's officials demanded greater and greater amounts of blood and treasure from the oppressed peasants who had reaped no rewards from the Romanovs' government. Aleksei Mikhailovich had decided to build his government's support upon the Russian nobility. In an effort to win their fuller support, he had used the *Ulozhenie* of 1649 to strengthen those bonds of serfdom that held many of Russia's peasants in ever-increasing servitude to their noble lords. Many fled to the southern and southeastern frontiers to join the great Cossack hosts that lived on the lower reaches of the Don, Volga, and Iaik rivers. There, they found freedom in a great and close brotherhood of army deserters, religious dissidents, and fugitive serfs. The nineteenth-century revolutionary Aleksandr Herzen called them the "knights-errant of the Russian common people,"[44] and, indeed, they were. Their vigorous, dangerous life was not for the fainthearted or weak. But it stood as the ideal for oppressed Russian peasants, whose backs were bent ever lower by the demands of their masters.

For more than a century, these Cossacks had been the most explosive social group in the Russian land. It was they who had supported various pretenders during the Time of Troubles, and it was from among them that Ivan Bolotnikov had risen to launch a great uprising against Tsar Vasilii Shuiskii in the early 1600s. Bolotnikov and his host of Cossack and peasant followers had been crushed by Shuiskii's better-trained and better-armed forces, but the great rebel tradition to which he had given birth lived on long after Shuiskii's executioner gouged out his eyes and drowned him at Kargopol.[45] For the next sixty years, Russia's oppressed masses kept the memory of Bolotnikov alive in ballads and folk tales that were recounted around Cossack campfires and in smoke-blackened huts whenever men spoke of oppression and dreamed of freedom. And then, in the manner of Bolotnikov, a new leader rose among them. As the great historian Kostomarov wrote more than a century ago, serf and Cossack alike knew him by his "enormous will and impulsive activity. . . . Now stern and gloomy, now working himself into a fury, now given up to drunken carousing, now ready to suffer any hardship with superhuman endurance. There was something fascinating in his speech; reckless courage was written in his coarse and slightly pock-marked features. The crowd sensed some supernatural strength in him, against which it was useless to struggle. They called him a sorcerer; and in fact there was in his soul some dreadful and mysterious darkness."[46] This new hero, violent, courageous, and dark souled, was Stenka Razin, destined to become the leader of the first great "peasant war" against the Romanovs.

Stenka Razin was born around 1630 into one of the most prominent Don Cossack families. We know nothing about his life until he reached his early twenties when, in keeping with Cossack tradition, he traveled nearly two thousand miles to the famous Solovetskii Monastery on the shores of the White Sea to pray to its founders. Razin soon grew into a Cossack of importance and stature. He undertook a number of diplomatic missions for the Cossack brotherhood and led them with distinction against the Tatars in the Crimea. For reasons that still are not clear, Razin turned against Moscow in 1667, even though Aleksei Mikhailovich's agents had been paying an annual subsidy to the Cossacks for many years. His campaign began as a freebooting expedition near Russia's southeastern frontier. It was directed against the Moscow authorities only to the extent that they opposed his progress toward the Caspian Sea to plunder Turkish and Persian shipping. Somewhat to the north of the Volga city of Tsaritsyn, Razin and his band seized a large flotilla of trading ships and barges belonging to several great Moscow merchants, an enterprise in which Aleksei Mikhailovich had a financial interest. The Cossacks' ambush was brilliantly successful, and within a few hours they had the ships they needed to plunder the Caspian at will. But success had come at a terrible cost; to obtain the ships, Razin had turned himself and his followers into state criminals. In mid-July, Aleksei Mikhailovich branded them "brigands" and enemies of Christ.[47]

Razin remained blissfully unmindful of the Tsar's anger. He easily defeated several *streltsy* detachments sent against him, seized the fortress of Iaitsk for his winter headquarters, and, the next spring, began his "furious inroad into Persia." Throughout 1668 and part of 1669, Razin ravaged Persia's Caspian coastlands, and destroyed all forces the Shah sent against him. He then returned to Russia, accepted the pardon that Aleksei's governor of Astrakhan offered in return for his promise to abandon his piratical ways, and then promptly violated his oath. It was at that point that Razin's movement began to turn from a freebooting expedition into a social protest. Razin's deeds against the Shah's and Tsar's armies had made him into a great popular hero, and he began to unite various groups of dissidents under his banner. With more than seven thousand men under his command, he began his march against Moscow in the spring of 1670, and everything fell before his attack. Russia's nobles trembled before his advance. Aleksei Mikhailovich cursed him as a brigand and a rebel, and the Patriarch denounced him as "the bandit Stenka Razin who had lost his fear of God and forsaken the Holy Orthodox and Apostolic Church." But the masses adored him more than ever, considered him invincible, and hailed him as their savior. As one man, Razin and his rebel army swore "to stand together and to exterminate the treacherous *boiars*, to throw off the yoke of slavery, and to become free men."[48] By mid-1670, Razin's plundering expedition had become a very powerful, and immensely explosive, social rebellion, which threatened to engulf much of southeastern and central Russia in its flames.

During the early summer of 1670, Razin made what many historians consider to be the error that destroyed him. Rather than continue his march against Moscow, which might well have fallen before his attack at that point, he decided to seize Astrakhan, Russia's great gateway to Persia and the East, a city rich in precious silks, rare perfumes, and exotic spices. He fell upon the city "like a wolf falling on the Christian flock,"[49] looted it from one end to the other, and tortured its defenders. Some were thrown from the walls, to lie broken and bleeding upon the rocks below, while others were hung by the ribs on meat hooks to die a slow and agonizing death. Only after Razin held Russia's gateway to the East in his hands did he turn to seize its center. As he marched up the Volga toward Moscow, city after city opened its gates at his call. The residents of Saratov and Samara greeted him in ecstasy and flocked to his standard. His agents ranged far and wide to recruit serfs to his rebellious legions. "Whoever wants to serve God and the Tsar," they proclaimed, were summoned to join Stenka Razin to "drive out the traitors and the bloodsuckers from the peasant villages."[50] It was a siren call of an immensely seductive kind to peasants who hated their lords but remained fiercely loyal to their Tsar. As in all great peasant revolts in Russia before the twentieth century, Razin and his lieutenants cast themselves in the role of fighting *against* the nobles *for* the Tsar. Peasants flocked to his side, cheering their liberator and brandishing their scythes, pitchforks, and axes.

Obviously, Aleksei Mikhailovich did not share Razin's view about the crimes he was committing against the Tsar's agents along the Volga. Now that his armies were freed from Russia's long war with Poland, he prepared to send them against Razin's hordes. As always, the Church rose to support him with the full might of divine sanction.

Like the great and wrathful Jehovah of the Old Testament, the Patriarch Iosif thundered against this "enemy of Christ," who had arisen in the people's midst, in an effort to offset Razin's immensely effective propaganda. "From the vipers' cave comes the brigand and traitor, the enemy of Christ, the Don Cossack Stenka Razin," the Patriarch proclaimed to all true believers throughout the Russian land. "With his accursed accomplices, who share all his sins, he, like the serpent [in the Garden of Eden], has enticed true Christians into his clutches and has dragged them down with him into the depths of perdition." Razin was "a brigand who has betrayed His Sovereign Majesty [Aleksei Mikhailovich] and the whole Moscow state,"[51] Iosif warned, and those who followed him were doomed to earthly punishment and eternal damnation. Yet the Patriarch's warnings often fell upon deaf ears; thousands continued to flock to Razin's side. By September of 1670, he controlled almost a thousand miles of the great Volga riverway between Astrakhan and Simbirsk and had more than twenty thousand insurgents in his motley army. Clearly his was no ordinary peasant revolt and could not be suppressed by sending a few contingents of *streltsy* against it, as Aleksei Mikhailovich had done when he faced rebellious crowds in Nóvgorod, Pskov, and Moscow in earlier years.

During the latter months of 1670, Aleksei Mikhailovich assembled his most seasoned and best-equipped troops under the command of Prince Iurii Dolgorukii, one of his best and most experienced generals. Dolgorukii planned to stop Razin at Kazan, where the Volga began a giant sweep westward toward Moscow. But first it was necessary to delay the rebels until he could march the five hundred miles from Moscow to Kazan. The task of delaying Razin's advance fell to Prince Ivan Miloslavskii, commander of the Simbirsk garrison, who barricaded himself and his troops in the city's citadel and swore to "die before I yield to this brigand."[52] Miloslavskii, his men, and their women, remained true to their oath and their Tsar. Day after day, night after night, they beat back attacks by rebels who outnumbered them by more than four to one. Their heroism was rewarded. From Kazan, Dolgorukii sent a relief column that arrived just in time to rout Razin's ill-disciplined irregulars with their well-placed cannon and musketry fire. Razin and the nucleus of his Cossack force escaped, but thousands of rebels died in battle or were executed by Aleksei Mikhailovich's commanders. Razin had suffered his first defeat. Once his followers saw that he was not invincible, it was the beginning of his end.[53]

During the following weeks, Prince Dolgorukii moved relentlessly to crush the rebellion with a brutality calculated to remind each and every one of the Tsar's subjects of the agonizing fate that awaited all brigands, traitors, and "enemies of Christ." One anonymous English observer remarked that Dolgorukii's field headquarters "had the resemblance of the suburbs of Hell. Round about it were gallows, each of which was loaded with forty or fifty men. In another place, many lay beheaded and covered with blood. Here and there stood some impaled, whereof not a few lived unto the third day and were heard to speak. Within the space of three months, there were by the hands of the executioners put to death eleven thousand men, in a legal way, upon the hearing of witnesses."[54] Still, Dolgorukii demanded more tortures and executions. His captains led their detachments up and down Russia's countryside in search of rebels and their sympathizers. In every rebellious village they entered, they hanged numbers of peasants; disemboweled others; beheaded, impaled, or quartered still more. Some they crucified against trees or buildings. Others they tore apart with butchers' hooks. No village that had succored the rebels escaped Dolgorukii's retribution.

Razin's days of freedom now were closely numbered. In April 1671, a band of Cossacks loyal to Aleksei Mikhailovich seized him, chained him hand and foot, and took him to Moscow. Aleksei spared no cruelty in punishing the man who had posed the greatest threat to the Romanovs' power since the Time of Troubles had ended. For this "enemy of Christ," who was guilty of "evil and loathsome acts against God" as well as treason against his sovereign, Aleksei Mikhailovich ordered brutal beatings with the knout (a particularly vicious type of lash with weighted ends), burnings with hot irons, and a torture in which Razin's head was shaved and cold water dripped upon it, one drop at a time. His arms and legs were torn out of their sockets and then forced back into place. Finally, he was quartered alive and, while a crowd looked on, his torso and innards were thrown to the dogs that roamed Moscow's streets.[55]

The years of Razin's revolt were a sad time for the Tsar for reasons other than those associated with social and political tension. Just as the rebel armies were approaching the peak of their success, he suffered several personal tragedies that added to his emotional burdens. His son Simeon died in July 1669 at the age of four. Just six months later, his eldest son and heir, the Tsarevich Aleksei, died at the age of sixteen. Even more tragic, the Tsarina Maria died in March 1669. She had borne him thirteen children and had shared his life for twenty-one years. Together, they had faced the revolts in Moscow, Novgorod, and Pskov. Together, they had seen Russia defeat the Poles and push back the Swedes. Suddenly, she was gone, and her death served to remind Aleksei of his own mortality as he crossed the threshold of middle age.

Although the Tsar felt the death of his wife deeply, its impact upon his policies was to be liberating. Throughout her years as Russia's Tsarina, Maria Miloslavskaia had opposed modernization and had defended the old ways. Reared according to rigid Muscovite tradition, she had upheld the ideal of the *terem* and had been a model of Old Russian female virtue. Her private apartments were dominated by a "Red Corner," in which holy icons hung, and before which everyone knelt and uttered a prayer as they entered. Maria began her day with prayers and devotions in her private chapel as the *Domostroi* required. She then spent most of her morning in overseeing the work of her many ladies-in-waiting and serving women upon whom she imposed the same strict daily regimen she herself observed. Cosmetics were forbidden, and mirrors were kept in closets or covered with heavy cloths—they could be used only for arranging one's hair, never to make one alluring or sexually enticing in any way. Clothing was loose and flowing, and designed to mask the female form. Thus modestly attired, and with their thoughts supposedly on exalted and holy things, Maria's ladies worked religious objects with golden and silver thread in intricate designs, and decorated them with pearls and semiprecious stones, or they embroidered more modestly ornamented towels, cloths, and clothing.

Once her ladies were all well embarked upon their labors, Maria herself turned to the affairs of her household, and then heard reports about the many charities she supported. Concern for the poor and needy was an important part of the *Domostroi's* precepts, and she tended to such matters assiduously. An appeal to her mercy often served as a court of last resort for those who had exhausted all other avenues of relief. Carefully observing the rules of the *terem*, Maria began each of these new tasks, no matter how small, with a special prayer and a moment devoted to asking God for His blessing upon her work. As it had begun, so her day ended, with more prayers and devotions, with thanks for the blessings of the day that had passed, and with the invocation of divine protection for the night that had fallen.[56] The only change in this daily routine came when Maria moved to one of the Romanovs' suburban estates, such as that at Kolomenskoe, or when she, usually in the company of her husband, made a pilgrimage to some nearby shrine or monastery. Her prayers then were said in different surroundings, but the substance of her life—pious, humble, and placidly uneventful—never altered. A woman who served the ideal of the *Domostroi* was supposed to serve God, her husband, and her sons, never herself.

Although Aleksei Mikhailovich tended to be less bound by tradition, there is no doubt that his first wife's conservatism made an impact upon the regime he established at Court. He continued to import Western technology and military know-how as his father had done, but he curtailed sharply the Court's adaptation of Western cultural forms. Early in his reign, he ordered all Western musical instruments to be burned in an *auto-da-fé* on Red Square. Not long afterward, he drove out his father's Western European acrobats and clowns and brought back good, traditional, Russian fighting bears in their place. Church choirs, hunting, feasts from which forks and all but the most rudimentary eating and drinking utensils were excluded, became an integral part of Kremlin life during Aleksei's reign. How much this policy may have resulted from Maria Miloslavskaia's urgings is suggested by the rapidity with which the "most gentle" Tsar began to restore Western objects and amusements after her death in 1669. Very soon after he had emerged from mourning his first wife's death, Aleksei Mikhailovich established a theatrical troupe in the Kremlin and brought back the Western Court musicians his father had so loved.[57]

The apparently rapid change in his attitude was closely connected with the entrance of Natalia Naryshkina into his life. Born in 1651, she was more than two decades younger than he and a year younger than his eldest daughter Evdokia. An orphan, Natalia was raised by Artamon Matveev, Aleksei Mikhailovich's closest adviser during the late 1660s and early 1670s. Matveev was one of those rare individuals in mid-seventeenth century Russia who was much attracted to the culture of the West. In utter disregard for all of Moscow's social conventions, Matveev had married Eudoxie Hamilton, a Scotswoman. To please her, he had made his home into a rare Western oasis in the midst of Moscow. There, Natalia Naryshkina grew up, surrounded by Western furniture, books, and art. For a woman, this milieu stood light-years apart from the life of the *terem*.

Lively, vivacious, and curious, Natalia Naryshkina was the antithesis of most Muscovite noblewomen. She was fascinated by the trivia of Western technology, by "mechanical birds which sing in the trees" and "automatons which blow on trumpets."[58] When measured against the *Domostroi* ideal, she was naughtily irreverent and even a bit scandalous. Although not very intelligent, she evidently was extremely beautiful in a buxom Slavic way. Laughter came as easily to her as prayer had come to the Tsarina Maria. Already into middle age when he met her, Aleksei Mikhailovich was utterly captivated by the joy this young woman, without family or means, radiated into the world around her. He was anxious to bed her in an effort to recapture his fading youth. Most marvelous of all, his desires could be justified in terms of state interest because he had only two surviving sons, both of whom were sickly and not expected to live very long. It seemed a reasonable hope that the sparkling and robust Natalia Naryshkina would provide more Romanov heirs to guarantee the succession at his death.

On January 22, 1671, twenty-one months after the Tsarina Maria's death, Aleksei Mikhailovich wedded Natalia in a small ceremony at the Kremlin. The young bride wore a gown so laden with pearls and precious stones that she could scarcely walk. Determined not to relinquish the westernized life she had known in Matveev's household, Russia's new Tsarina began to change the daily regimen at the Kremlin in ways that astounded Muscovites. During her first ceremonial procession among the people of Moscow, one shocked observer noted, she "opened the window of her carriage slightly," an action that produced confusion and dismay among those who thought it sinful for them to set eyes upon their Tsarina and equally sinful for her to look upon them. But their view was not Natalia's. For a brief moment, she heeded the protests that poured into the Kremlin, but soon she was driving in what one foreigner called an "open" carriage. Even more shocking to Muscovite convention, on the feast given to commemorate her name day, she greeted all of the great *boiars* in person and served them small meat pastries with her own hands. In acts such as these, the Tsarina Natalia was indeed a worthy mother of Peter the Great, who would tear down so many of those stout walls of medieval convention and prejudice that hemmed in life in Russia.[59]

During the first two decades of his reign, when contemporaries remarked so admiringly about his piety, Aleksei Mikhailovich might have found it difficult to permit the innovations that his young wife insisted upon at the beginning of the 1670s. But his attitudes had begun to change even before his second marriage. If Russia were to compete successfully with Poland and Sweden for influence in Eastern Europe and the Baltic, she must equal her enemies in technology—an obvious reason for Aleksei Mikhailovich to develop closer ties with the West. But as time went on, it also seemed that he found Western ways more and more appealing. He built Western-style gardens at his Izmailovskoe estate in the early 1660s and, at the end of the decade, built even larger and more impressive ones at Kolomenskoe, where he had raised an immense wooden palace for his new wife. Although built in the Russian style, the new palace had a number of features that indicated Aleksei's intent to integrate Western and Muscovite ways. The *Domostroi* had proclaimed it sinful for women to set eyes upon men who were not of their family. At Kolomenskoe, where he often received foreign dignitaries, Aleksei had a secret compartment constructed in his audience chamber from which the Tsarina Natalia could watch the comings and goings not only of Russian, but also of foreign, men. At about the same time, he agreed to permit the grille that screened her theatre box to be removed so that she could see and be seen by all.[60]

During the first year of their marriage, Aleksei Mikhailovich delighted in the laughter and humor of his young bride, but this happiness was but a pale shade of the ecstasy he knew on May 30, 1672, the feast of St. Isaac, when the Tsarina presented him with a healthy, robust son. Named Peter, the infant bawled lustily in his cradle, and contrasted vividly with those five sickly and delicate sons that had been born to the Tsarina Maria. News of Peter's birth raced through the Kremlin and beyond its walls into the streets and alleys of Moscow. When Peter was less than four hours old, Aleksei ordered a thanksgiving Mass at the Kremlin's Uspenskii Cathedral and summoned to it Russia's greatest *boiars,* officials, and army captains.[61] Afterward, Aleksei bestowed honors and promotions upon his courtiers, especially the relatives of his young wife. For three days, cannon boomed out their salutes and the Kremlin bells pealed. After a month, the celebrations culminated in Peter's christening at the famous Chudovo Monastery, where the False Dmitrii had lived during the Time of Troubles.[62] Aleksei placed such hopes in his newborn son that he ordered a medal struck to commemorate his birth. On the reverse was engraved, "the hope for a great future."[63]

It seems quite clear that, at the time of Peter's birth, Aleksei Mikhailovich expected neither of his two elder sons to outlive him. Feodor, the eldest, was sickly and distinguished especially by his excessive piety, while his younger brother, Ivan, apparently a victim of Down's syndrome, was mentally retarded, suffered a speech impediment, and was partly blind.[64] The unsuitability of these two elder sons to rule Russia had been a matter of considerable concern to Aleksei during the first quarter-century of his reign, but Peter's birth appeared to lift that burden from his shoulders. Aleksei, after all, was only forty-three, still brimming with energy, and it seemed to him and those who advised him that many years remained before a successor would be called upon to step forward. Almost certainly by that time, the healthy young Peter would have reached manhood and would be the obvious candidate to succeed his father. Yet, less than four years later, on January 30, 1676, Aleksei Mikhailovich was dead. Feodor Alekseevich, the eldest of his living sons, became Tsar and Autocrat of All the Russias. Because Peter was still too young to wear the crown, Aleksei had bowed to the inevitable and named Feodor his successor as he lay upon his deathbed.

Born in May 1661, Tsar Feodor Alekseevich was Aleksei Mikhailovich's third son and the second to live beyond infancy. No one ever expected him to sit upon the throne, and there were probably few who expected him to survive childhood. Delicate from birth, he suffered an attack of scurvy as a child and never fully recovered. He was gentle, without his father's passion and violent temper, and somewhat bookish. Because of his interest in learning and the changing times in which he lived, he received an education that was far more comprehensive than his father's had been. He was allowed to spend his days with Simeon Polotskii, a West Russian monk who was one of the most learned and erudite men of his age. Feodor became the first Russian prince to speak foreign languages fluently. From Polotskii, he learned Polish and Latin well, and even translated a number of psalms from Latin into Russian.[65] But the boy's body was as weak and diseased as his mind was strong and active. He would not be a stupid Tsar, but a very unassertive one. He came to the throne at a time when a strong and dynamic ruler was needed to keep the warring factions at Court under control. Often confined to his chamber by illness, and only fourteen years old at the time of his accession, there was not even a remote possibility that he could become the sort of Tsar that conditions in Russia required.

Aleksei Mikhailovich's sudden and unexpected death unleashed a deadly struggle in the Kremlin. His marriage to Natalia Naryshkina had condemned the Miloslavskiis to an obscurity that they bitterly resented. Unable to deny his young wife whatever she desired, and eternally grateful to Artamon Matveev for bringing her into his life, Aleksei had parceled out rewards in generous measure. To Matveev, he gave more and more ranks and responsibilities in the government. At the same time, he raised Natalia's Naryshkin relations to lucrative Court posts, often at the expense of the Miloslavskiis. Especially after Natalia gave birth to the Grand Duke Peter, the Naryshkins' fortunes soared, while the Miloslavskiis suffered further slights and indignities. What was at first bitter jealousy between the two families soon became deep dark hatred. The feud had reached dangerous proportions even before Peter's birth, but the Miloslavskiis were powerless to reassert themselves so long as Aleksei Mikhailovich lived and while so astute a politician as Matveev remained in high office to defend the Tsarina and the Naryshkins against their attacks. For those Miloslavskiis who awaited Feodor's accession in order to wreak their revenge upon the Naryshkins, Aleksei's favoritism toward Natalia's son Peter increased their bitterness. It would have been the ultimate indignity for them if the Tsar had denied the crown to his elder son in favor of the vigorous, lusty lad to whom his second wife had given birth.

Because of these long-standing feuds, Aleksei Mikhailovich's death agony was the signal for the Court to burst into open clan warfare, as the Miloslavskiis struggled to regain their position and the Naryshkins tried to deny their ambitions. Matveev's fate was central to the outcome of the struggle. If he could remain in power, then the primacy of the Naryshkins and the Tsarina Natalia was assured. If, on the other hand, the Miloslavskiis and their allies could bring him down, there was little chance that the Naryshkins could survive his fall, for none of them possessed more than a small fraction of his political acumen. Greedy for recognition, and arrogant in their newfound splendor, the Tsarina Natalia's uncle and brothers had turned many in the Kremlin against them, and even those who had not previously allied with the Miloslavskiis were willing to support them in an anti-Naryshkin campaign. Like any great statesman, Matveev, too, had made enemies only too willing to join an attack against him.

To defend himself, Matveev had attempted to construct a small but powerful faction at Court during the last years of Aleksei Mikhailovich's reign, and there is even some evidence to suggest that he and these allies were planning to proclaim the four-year-old Peter as Tsar in the event of Aleksei's death. But Matveev had overlooked the Khitrovos, an obscure *boiar* family who would eventually bring him to ruin. This family had gained a strong influence over the mind of the sickly young Feodor. Anna Khitrovo had been one of his nannies, and Ivan Khitrovo, who had been his closest friend since earliest childhood, had been appointed one of his two chamberlains.

To turn the gentle Feodor against Matveev at first seemed no easy task. But the Khitrovos soon found the weapon they needed in Feodor's poor health. In an effort to keep the young prince from growing any weaker, Matveev had sought the advice of several foreign physicians and had insisted that Feodor take the medicines and tonics they prepared. The medicines did no good, and Ivan Khitrovo used that fact to destroy his enemy. Again and again, he whispered to Feodor that the medicines Matveev brought from the palace pharmacy were being used to poison him and that such treason must be punished. In vain did Matveev protest to his accusers that, before Feodor took these medicines, they were tasted by his physician and two chamberlains, including Ivan Khitrovo himself. As one final precaution against poison, Matveev also had insisted upon taking the medicines himself in the presence of Feodor and his chamberlains before the Tsar took his daily dosage. Despite all of Matveev's assurances, Feodor could not deny that he had indeed grown weaker since he had begun to take the prescriptions prepared by the Kremlin's foreign doctors. Convinced that Ivan Khitrovo would not lie, Feodor drove Matveev into exile; his vast estates were confiscated, and he was left to live on the beggarly allowance of a common state criminal.[66]

Feodor's coronation reflected the triumph of the Khitrovo-Miloslavskii faction at Court. Khitrovo and his father, Bogdan, both played conspicuous parts in the ceremony, and, although many courtiers were invested with higher ranks and showered with costly gifts, not one Naryshkin stood among them. By the end of the year, the Miloslavskiis and the Khitrovos appeared to reign supreme in the Kremlin. Yet, as so often happens between allies joined by political intrigue, their very success undermined their alliance. Bogdan Khitrovo feared the Miloslavskiis, and they, in turn, distrusted him and his son Ivan. Likewise, the Miloslavskiis were especially wary of Anna Khitrovo, long recognized as a genius at *terem* politics, and vicious in dealing with her political opponents. Feeling themselves outnumbered by the numerous Miloslavskiis, the Khitrovos tried to strengthen their position by pushing forward three men whom they made a part of Feodor's inner circle. The eldest, and the one who had already become a close associate of the Tsar by the time of his coronation, was Aleksei Likhachev, a man of middle age, to whom Feodor had given the honor of carrying the bowl of golden coins that were traditionally scattered among the masses during the coronation procession. The other two were much younger. Ivan Iazykov would become immensely powerful in Feodor's councils during the last two years of his reign. Prince Vasilii Golitsyn's greatest opportunities would come later when, as the lover of Feodor's eldest sister

Sofia, he would become the most powerful man in Russia during the regency she established at the time of Feodor's death.[67]

All three of these men, however, were able and responsible statesmen. Their policies were governed by their loyalty to Feodor and their love for Russia. Iazykov and Golitsyn, in particular, soon replaced the Khitrovos and the Miloslavskiis in Feodor's confidence and sought to implement a number of reforms in Russia. The most important of these was the abolition of the much-criticized institution known as *mestnichestvo,* the system of defining a *boiar*'s rank and position according to ancestral precedents. Under *mestnichestvo,* talent and experience counted for little, while the offices a *boiar*'s ancestors had held were all important. No *boiar* could be asked to accept any appointment that would oblige him to serve under another nobleman if that nobleman's ancestors had served in positions subordinate to those held by the ancestors of the *boiar* in question. As a result, the Tsar often could appoint his most talented officers and officials to the highest posts only during those moments of national crisis when the *zemskii sobor* agreed to suspend *mestnichestvo* for a period of time. Golitsyn's ability to convince Feodor to call for *mestnichestvo*'s abolition in January 1682, and his ability to convince the *Boiar* Council to agree to the Tsar's decision, was an important factor in enabling Russia to enter the modern age.[68] Without the abolition of *mestnichestvo* few of the reforms of Peter the Great would have been possible.

Yet the abolition of *mestnichestvo* was but an infrequent instance where Feodor's ever-weakening health improved momentarily and permitted him to take an active part in state affairs for a brief time. Feodor spent most of his days in his Kremlin chambers or in prayer in his private chapel. Constantly reminded of his mortality by his disease-ridden body, he became increasingly preoccupied with thoughts of life after death.[69] Meanwhile, even though the Naryshkins had been driven from Court, the bitter feuds of Kremlin politics continued to swirl around him. This was especially true of the events surrounding his marriage in 1680.

The question of Feodor's marriage had even more urgent political significance than the marriages of Tsars Mikhail and Aleksei. Because it seemed likely that Feodor would not live for very long, it was necessary to consider the question of his successor. There were, in fact, only two possible candidates for the throne, and each represented a major political faction in Moscow. The Tsarina Natalia's son Peter stood as the hope of the Naryshkins. He was an active child, large for his age, and promised to grow into an energetic prince. For the Miloslavskii's there was Feodor's younger brother, Ivan Alekseevich, half-witted, sickly, and almost blind, a fragile reed indeed. There was only one way the Miloslavskiis could hope to preserve their power—by arranging for Feodor to marry a daughter of one of their political allies, who might produce a son before Feodor died.

But there were others in Feodor's inner circle who also sought to strengthen their position by arranging his marriage. Soon Aleksei Likhachev and Ivan Iazykov entered the fray. They had the advantage over the Miloslavskiis because their duties kept them close to the Tsar, and they could observe his reactions to even the most inconsequential events. As a result, it was they who were present when Feodor caught sight of a young maiden in a church procession during the late spring of 1680. The Tsar betrayed his feelings only for a second, but it was obvious to his attentive companions that he was smitten by the young woman's beauty. Iazykov therefore made discreet inquiries and learned that she was Agafia Grushetskaia.[70] Like the wives of his grandfather and father, the woman whom Feodor soon would marry was from an obscure noble family. Unlike Russia's earlier Tsarinas, however, she was part Polish, and her rise would foster Polish influence at Court.

Although he evidently was much infatuated with Agafia Grushetskaia and determined to wed her, Feodor, again like his father and grandfather, went through the charade of ordering his chamberlains to search throughout Russia for eligible maidens and to bring those judged the most beautiful to Moscow. But once the twenty young women had been assembled at the Kremlin, he gave the golden ring and symbolic pearl-embroidered handkerchief to Agafia as he had planned to do all along. Realizing that Feodor's choice could only strengthen the position of Iazykov and Likhachev, and weaken his own and that of his family, Ivan Miloslavskii launched a vicious campaign to ruin the girl's reputation and blacken her character in Feodor's eyes, but he grossly understimated Feodor's strength of character. Infuriated by Miloslavskii's efforts to drive his fiancée from the Kremlin, Feodor forbade him to appear again at Court. Miloslavskii's disgrace marked the final triumph of Likhachev, Iazykov, and Prince Golitsyn in the Tsar's inner councils, for their efforts to help him wed Agafia Grushetskaia established them forever in his favor. They would hold their privileged positions until Feodor's death some two years later.[71]

Triumphant over those who had opposed his decision, Feodor wed Agafia Grushetskaia in mid-July, but he did so without the pomp and splendor usually associated with royal weddings. Most probably because of his poor health, there was no great procession across the Kremlin Square to the Uspenskii Cathedral and no great banquet in the Palace of Facets to celebrate the royal nuptials. For several days, Feodor and his inner circle simply remained in seclusion, and no one knew precisely what was taking place. There was one group of wedding customs, however, that must have been scrupulously observed. Given the anxiety with which they awaited the birth of an heir, Feodor's courtiers and their ladies must have hastened to scatter a liberal measure of the traditional kernels of wheat between the sheets of the royal bed, to pile sheaves of rye beneath it, and to make certain that the icons of the Blessed Virgin and the Nativity hung above it in their proper places in an effort to ensure that their royal master's union would prove fertile.[72]

Although fate had condemned him to ill health, the Tsar's consummation of his marriage proved fertile indeed. On July 11, 1681, just one week before their first anniversary, the Tsarina Agafia gave birth to a son whom his delighted parents named Ilia. But only three days after her son was born, Agafia died from complications resulting from his difficult birth. In less than a week, her child followed her to the grave.

The woman whom the Miloslavskiis had sought to keep from Russia's throne was dead, but they had little cause to rejoice. Iazykov, Likhachev, and Prince Golitsyn retained their influence at Court, and the Miloslavskiis fell even further from favor during the next six months. Nothing could have made more clear the Miloslavskiis' plummeting fortunes than the moment when, on February 12, 1682, with no advance announcement or ceremony, the Patriarch Ioakim emerged from Feodor's apartments to announce that the Tsar had just wed Marfa Apraksina, one of Iazykov's relatives. One of the new young Tsarina's godparents was Matveev, the man the Miloslavskiis had driven into exile half a decade earlier. A full month before his marriage, Feodor had heeded the pleas of his bride-to-be to restore all of Matveev's estates to him, and free him from confinement in Pustozersk in the far north. To please his intended, the Tsar had ordered Matveev to travel to the village of Lukh, just three hundred miles northwest of Moscow, and to await new instructions from him there.[73] The instructions never came. On April 27, 1682, Feodor finally succumbed to the poor health that had made each of his days on earth a torment.

For the Miloslavskiis, his death was more than a reprieve; it offered them an unexpected opportunity to regain all the power they had lost since that day in 1671 when Aleksei Mikhailovich had married Natalia Naryshkina and first created a rival to their family's power. Now, both the sickly Ivan and ten-year-old Peter became pawns in the deadly rivalry between the Miloslavskii and Naryshkin clans.[74]

At first, it seemed that good sense and a preference for a Tsar who promised soon to grow into a forceful monarch would win the day, especially since there was growing resentment in Moscow toward the high-handed manner in which the Miloslavskiis had exploited their privileged position under Feodor. Soon after Feodor's death, the Patriarch Ioakim, Moscow's leading churchman, and the city's great *boiars* gathered in the Kremlin's Palace of Facets. There in its vaulted audience chamber, a vast room some seventy feet square, overshadowed by its enormous golden central pillar, they considered the crisis that faced them. After a brief debate, they decided to summon an Assembly of the Land, as had been done when the Time of Troubles had ended in 1613. The *zemskii sobor* that convened a few hours later in the square outside the audience chamber was scarcely representative of Russia, but it did represent the various social, economic, and political groups of Moscow. Prodded by the Patriarch and his Naryshkin allies, the Assembly chose Peter, though the choice was by no means unanimous. Perhaps too willing to discount those voices that had called out their preference for Ivan, Patriarch Ioakim blessed Peter as Russia's new Tsar. The Assembly dispersed, the majority confident that the Tsarina

Natalia would become Regent, with Matveev as her chief adviser, until Peter came of age. For many, Matveev's recall from the Arctic monastery of Pustozersk promised a return to the more sensible policies of Tsar Aleksei and an end to the arrogant rapaciousness of the Miloslavskiis.[75] But those supporting Peter had failed to take into account the ambitions of Feodor's elder sister Sofia who, at the moment of Peter's accession, burst the constricting traditional bonds of the Kremlin's *terem* to enter the political turmoil that seethed in the inner halls of the Palace of Facets. For the next seven years, she, and she alone, ruled the Kremlin in a manner reminiscent of Catherine de Medici in sixteenth-century France and her contemporary, Elizabeth Tudor, in England. Within a few weeks, Sofia had murdered Matveev and most of the Naryshkins within the Kremlin's very walls and had restored the Miloslavskiis to a position of unchallenged power in Russia.

Sofia, the fourth daughter of Aleksei Mikhailovich and Maria Miloslavskaia, was born in September 17, 1657, and christened two weeks later by the famous Patriarch Nikon. Her childhood and adolescent years coincided with the lifting of many restrictions upon the lives of aristocratic Russian women in general and Romanov women in particular. In a dramatic break with tradition, Aleksei Mikhailovich allowed men to enter the *terem* and sent the monkish scholars Simeon Polotskii and Silvester Medvedev into its previously sacrosanct halls to teach his daughters in addition to his son Feodor. Most of the royal daughters showed little interest in learning and little inclination toward serious study, but Sofia stood out as a brilliant exception. From Polotskii and Medvedev she learned Polish, French, and Latin. Her thirst for knowledge vied with her passion for intrigue to make her an especially unique personality in seventeenth-century Moscow. She quickly became dissatisfied with the traditional constraints upon a Tsar's daughters. Unless some foreign prince would have them, and none had married a Tsar's sister or daughter for several hundred years, Sofia, her sisters, and aunts, were condemned to lifelong virginity, for tradition dictated that no Russian could possibly be their equal. Theirs was a life made dull by its monotony and vicious by the bitterness that gnawed at hearts denied the warmth of love, the comfort of children, and the satisfaction of lives lived for a worthwhile purpose. "They were born, lived, and died," in the words of one Russian scholar, "without knowing of what occurred around them, and themselves unknown to anyone."[76]

Determined that hers would not be a life wasted in the service of empty and meaningless ideals, Sofia ventured into the arena of Kremlin politics during Feodor's reign. She stepped timidly at first, but quickly trod more boldly. It was a heady emancipation for a woman who had lived within the *terem* for almost two decades, and it made her daring and aggressive. Because the constraints of tradition operated less effectively while the Romanov scepter was held in Feodor's weak grasp, and because he himself tended to favor Western European customs and styles, Sofia probed deeper along the boundaries of tradition to determine how far they could be stretched. She frequently went to her brother's apartments to nurse him in his many illnesses, and there she met those men who advised him and sat in his inner councils. Especially after the eclipse of the Khitrovo family, Feodor's confidants tended to be men who held tradition in less reverence than did many great *boiars,* with the result that they were more willing to accept Sofia into their midst. She was especially drawn to Prince Vasilii Golitsyn, who combined intellectual brilliance with a dashing and chivalrous manner. Sofia at first shared with him a passion for Western learning, a respect for Western technology, and a conviction that Russia needed to follow a path similar to that already taken by Western Europe.[77] Soon, she became consumed by more urgent passions, and these led her to violate the most sacred of the constraints that tradition and the precepts of the *Domostroi* imposed upon royal women in Russia. In an act of supreme self-liberation, Sofia took Golitsyn to her bed and made him her lover.

Less cosmopolitan than he, Sofia was a more astute and realistic politician. Further, unlike a number of her successors, she was obliged to rely primarily upon her intellect to gain victory during the chaotic weeks of political struggle that followed Feodor's death because she had none of the physical charms with which to seduce men to her cause. Indeed, her appearance evidently bordered upon the grotesque. In the memorable words of one of her contemporaries, she had "a shapeless body, monstrously fat, a head as big as a bushel measure, [and] hair growing on her face."[78] But this body housed a brilliant mind. While the Kremlin's leading political figures flailed at each other in ineffectual intrigue during the spring of 1682, Sofia moved decisively, guided by a sure and unerring instinct that enabled her to draw all the reins of power into her hands. Only twenty-five at the time of Feodor's death, she fully understood that her retarded brother could serve as her instrument for gaining great personal power. If Peter had won the throne by a hasty election, she was determined that Ivan could gain it through more forceful means. For the first time since the election of Mikhail Romanov in 1613, a new factor thus appeared in Russian politics. Confronted by Sofia's determination to wrest Ivan the Terrible's ivory throne from Peter, his allies would have to defend it by force. The key to the struggle was the Tsar's bodyguard, the *streltsy*. Whoever could command their support could command the throne. In the intrigues that followed, Sofia's cunning proved more than a match for Peter's supporters, especially since the Tsarina Natalia possessed none of her stepdaughter's political instincts and, during the critical days after her son's election, remained cloistered in her royal apartments awaiting the arrival of Matveev, who did not reach Moscow until the evening of May 12, more than two weeks later.[79]

The *streltsy*, who were to prove such a critical factor in the events of late April and early May 1682, had been established in the mid-sixteenth century as a privileged force to guard the persons of the Tsar and his family and to serve as elite assault troops in time of war. In return for their service, the Tsar provided them with pay, clothing, and food. Even more important, he granted them numerous concessions to engage in trade during peacetime and allowed them exemption from taxation. But their many privileges had corrupted them. By the late seventeenth century, many of the *streltsy* had grown fat upon the rich profits they reaped from their commercial ventures. As a result, during the political crisis of 1682, some twenty thousand *streltsy* were prepared to sell their loyalty to the highest bidder. On the very day of Feodor's death, the Naryshkins sought to woo them by promises of money, further economic concessions, and religious toleration.[80] For the moment, they succeeded. *Streltsy* voices were among those who called out Peter's name at the Assembly of the Land.

During the two weeks that separated Peter's election from Matveev's return to Moscow, Sofia sought to win the *streltsy* to Ivan's cause. Aided by her uncle Ivan Miloslavskii and by the popular *streltsy* officer Ivan Khovanskii, she plied them with gold and vodka until, as one historian has written, "they became a rampaging instrument of violence."[81] To these more tangible inducements, she added a campaign of whispers designed to inflame the *streltsy* against the Naryshkins and Peter. Carefully planted rumors raced up and down Moscow's narrow streets that the Naryshkins had poisoned Feodor, that they were plotting to murder Ivan, that a Naryshkin regency would grant concessions to foreign merchants at the expense of Russians, and that Matveev, whose preference for Western European ways was well known, would introduce Western heresies into Moscow if he returned to power.[82]

Sofia's sly campaign of rumor and slander had little basis in fact, but the political ineptitude of the Tsarina Natalia predisposed the *streltsy* to give it credence. During Feodor's reign, their senior officers had abused their authority, even to the extent of withholding pay and exacting forced labor from their subordinates. In early April, a number of the *streltsy* had petitioned the Tsar for redress, and in the days after his death, their complaints had become more bitter. Unable to consult Matveev, and fearful for her safety, the Tsarina Natalia had panicked and had ordered the arrest and public flogging of sixteen *streltsy* colonels on April 30. The rank and file among the *streltsy* had administered the whippings themselves.[83] The sight of blood and the collapse of discipline caused by the punishment of sixteen senior officers had inflamed their subordinates further. Sofia thus had fertile soil in which to sow the seeds of disaffection. For the next two weeks, she assiduously tended her crop. On May 15, less than three days after Matveev's return, she reaped the harvest.

On the morning of Monday, May 15, Artamon Matveev, once again Russia's chief minister of state, took his seat in the *Boiar* Council. Just before noon, he reported to the Tsarina Natalia and prepared to return home for his midday meal. Despite the fact that Mondays were considered unlucky by Russians, this seemed a normal day, with nothing out of the ordinary to command his attention. Indeed, just two days earlier, representatives of the restless *streltsy* regiments had come to the Kremlin to pay him their respects and seemed to be firmly under the control of the new officers the Tsarina had appointed a few days before his arrival in Moscow.[84] Matveev had no way of knowing that he would not live to see the sun set, or that the *streltsy* would be the instruments of his death.

Earlier that morning, Aleksandr Miloslavskii and Petr Tolstoi, both of them in the service of Sofia's cause, had galloped through the *Streltsy* Quarter of Moscow shouting, "The Naryshkins have strangled the Tsarevich Ivan!"[85] A list of "traitors" prepared by Sofia already in their hands, Miloslavskii and Tolstoi had ordered the *streltsy* to the Kremlin to avenge the murder. Unaware that Ivan was unharmed, the *streltsy* seized their pikes and muskets and marched to the Kremlin to the toll of tocsins and the roll of drums. With banners embroidered with pictures of the Virgin flying at the heads of their columns, and with their regimental cannon bringing up the rear, they swept into the square in front of the Palace of Facets just moments after Matveev had received word of their advance. Faced by regiments of raging *streltsy* within the Kremlin's walls, Matveev urged the Tsarina Natalia to show them that Ivan was unharmed. Although nearly paralyzed by fear, and trembling at every step, she complied. Together with Patriarch Ioakim and a number of the great *boiars,* she took the hand of Peter in her right and that of Ivan in her left and made her way to the head of the Red Staircase that stretched from the audience chamber to the square below. The crowd fell silent. A few of the *streltsy* mounted the staircase for a closer look. Satisfied that Ivan was unhurt, they stood for a moment in a quandary. Bewildered, they then retreated to the ranks their comrades had drawn up on the square. For a moment, it appeared that order could be restored.[86]

But Sofia and her confederates had prepared for just such a moment. A small group of her agents began to shout that "traitors" among the great *boiars* threatened the safety of the throne and that they must be delivered to them for punishment. From Sofia's list they called out the names:

> Artamon Matveev!
> Kyrill Naryshkin!
> Ivan Naryshkin!
> Afanasii Naryshkin!

Lev Naryshkin!
Martemian Naryshkin!
Feodor Naryshkin!
Vasilii Naryshkin!
Petr Naryshkin!
Prince Iurii Dolgorukii!
Prince Mikhail Dolgorukii!
Prince Grigorii Romodanovskii!

To these names they added others to include all of the Naryshkin allies.[87] Yet those who called for the blood of the Naryshkins and their followers were only a small portion of the troops who stood on the square; most of the *streltsy* remained undecided. In an effort to exploit their hesitation, the Patriarch Ioakim stepped forward. Speaking with all the great authority his exalted office commanded, Ioakim told them that they had been deceived, that, as they could see, Ivan was alive and unharmed. He called upon them to disperse. After their great deeds on behalf of Moscow's Tsars in the past, he asked, how could they now threaten those who served the Tsar most faithfully? Again, the *streltsy* wavered.

Sofia's carefully laid plans might well have come to naught after Ioakim's moving plea had not one of her most bitter opponents unwittingly aided her cause. Prince Mikhail Dolgorukii, deputy commander of the *streltsy*, undoubtedly enraged at the inclusion of his name on a list of "traitors," and as reckless as he was brave, could contain his wrath no longer. His judgment clouded by his fury, Prince Mikhail strode to the head of the Red Staircase. In a thunderous voice he ordered the *streltsy* back to their homes, cursed them for their invasion of the Kremlin, and threatened them with the knout.

Dolgorukii's threats reminded the *streltsy* of those arrogant colonels whom they had punished some two weeks before. They surged toward the Red Staircase in anger. From that moment, they became Sofia's willing instruments, and what is known as the *Streltsy* Revolt of 1682 began in gruesome earnest. The first to fall before their onslaught was Prince Mikhail Dolgorukii himself. Before he had finished his abusive remarks, they seized him and hurled him from the top of the staircase onto the erect pikes of the men below. Their appetite for blood only whetted by Dolgorukii's murder, they rampaged through the Palace of Facets in search of more "traitors." Those they found—Matveev, Afanasii Naryshkin, Prince Romodanovskii, and Feodor Saltykov—were also impaled upon the mass of upturned pikes in the square. Other *streltsy* then dragged the torn corpses to the execution block on Red Square where they hacked them to pieces. All were on Sofia's list except for Saltykov, an innocent victim of mistaken identity who died because of his resemblance to Ivan Naryshkin. Recognizing their error, the *streltsy* carried Saltykov's mutilated corpse to his father, humbly begging his pardon for the murder of his son. His chambers filled with his son's murderers, the old man remarked that "it is God's will!" and, according to one account, offered them wine and beer. But once they had departed, he told his widowed daughter-in-law that "soon they shall hang upon pikes from the [city] walls." When a disgruntled servant reported his remark to the *streltsy,* the men who had drunk his wine and begged his pardon returned and murdered him where he stood.[88]

At dusk, the *streltsy* left the Kremlin. During the course of the day, they had driven their pikes through mattresses, chopped down draperies with their halberds, slashed upholstery with their swords, and even desecrated altars in a futile search for other "traitors." Because they had not found the rest of the Naryshkins, especially Natalia's eldest brother Ivan, they sealed the Kremlin gates and vowed to finish their work the next day. At dawn on May 16, they returned, lusting for more blood after a night spent in murder and drinking in Moscow's streets. Still, they failed to find their chief quarry. Frustrated, they departed, posted guards at the gates again, and swore to return in the morning.

On May 17, the *streltsy* assembled for the third time in the Kremlin square. This time they brought not only their weapons but also an ultimatum. Ivan Naryshkin, they proclaimed, must be delivered into their hands at once or they would kill every great *boiar* they could find in the Kremlin. At that point, Sofia, who in fact continued to hold firm command of the *streltsy* through the loyalty of Ivan Khovanskii and Ivan Miloslavskii, turned to the Tsarina Natalia. In a voice that feigned terror, she proclaimed within hearing of a number of *boiars,* "Your brother will not escape the *streltsy.* Don't let us all be murdered on his account!"[89] For Natalia, this was a moment of supreme terror. Raised in the urbane, Europeanized atmosphere of Matveev's home, she was unaccustomed to violence. Yet, during the past two days, she had seen her guardian and a number of her brothers suffer gruesome deaths. She had neither Sofia's intelligence nor her ruthless nature and, in earlier moments of crisis, had turned to Matveev and her brothers for guidance. Now she must decide alone, and without delay. Not only her life and that of her brother but that of her son Peter hung upon her decision. In her darkest hour of tragedy, Natalia chose to sacrifice her brother to spare her son, the ten-year-old lad who would grow up to become Peter the Great.

Ivan Naryshkin answered his sister's summons in the sure and certain knowledge that an agonizing death awaited him. Bravely, he went with her to the Church of the Savior, where he calmly made his confession and received the last rites. Grief-stricken, Natalia fell into his arms to bid him farewell, but even that last solace was cut short. Within a few moments, Prince Iakov Odoevskii, a kindly and timorous old man, interrupted their final leave-taking. His voice quavering with terror, he begged Naryshkin to hurry to his death. "You must go in haste, Ivan, or they will murder us all on your account."[90] Holding the icon of the Blessed Virgin in his hands, Ivan Naryshkin gave himself into the hands of the mob, who dragged him by his feet across the square to the torture chamber. Before he died, he bore their tortures for many hours while they sought in vain to force from his lips a confession that he had murdered Feodor at the bidding of his sister and Matveev.[91] Sofia had triumphed. She now turned to consolidate her power.

Although Sofia had incited the *streltsy* to murder Matveev and the Naryshkins by branding them traitorous enemies of the princes Peter and Ivan, she could not use similar tactics against Peter himself. Yet, if she were to realize her political ambitions, it was necessary to alter in some manner his election as Tsar, which had handed the regency to the Tsarina Natalia. Again, she used the *streltsy* to further her plans. On April 23, less than a week after the revolt, her agents prompted the *streltsy* to petition that Peter and Ivan be appointed joint Tsars; two days later, they petitioned that Ivan be recognized as the senior of the two. Finally, on May 29, they presented yet a third petition, this time

[73]

urging that Sofia replace Natalia as Regent. To deal with these petitions, the *Boiar* Council decided to summon yet another Assembly of
the Land. Finding sufficient precedents in the history of the Byzantine
Empire, from which the Muscovite state had drawn much of its spiritual and temporal heritage, the Assembly approved these unusual arrangements.[92]

For the first time in her history, Russia was to be ruled by two
Tsars. Of more immediate importance, Sofia had realized her ambition
to gain supreme power. Yet Sofia's regency embodied one potential
threat that posed a greater challenge to her power with every year that
passed. No one was prepared to argue that her half-wit brother Ivan
ever could wield the scepter on his own, but her half-brother Peter was
a very different prince indeed. Energetic, insatiably curious, and well
over six feet tall before he reached the age of fifteen, Peter obviously
was capable of ruling Russia, and one day would demand to do so.
Tragically, he shared many of Sofia's deepest convictions about the
need to modernize Russia on the model of Western Europe, but, because of the bitter rivalry between the families he and Sofia represented, and the vast ambitions that consumed them both, they could
not work together in a common cause. The survival of one could be
only at the expense of driving the other from the Kremlin.

Bitter as their rivalry would become in the late 1680s, neither Peter
nor Sofia seriously considered the most obvious and effective means to
resolve their conflict. Assassination had a long and ignominious history
in the Russian land, and it had been used frequently to resolve political
conflicts before the Time of Troubles. Yet both Sofia and Peter shrank
from such an undertaking. Although there were frequent rumors that
she plotted to take her half-brother's life, Sofia never attempted to do
so, although her agents killed many of Peter's relatives during the 1682
streltsy uprising and could easily have included him in that number had
they been ordered to do so. Likewise, when Peter finally drove Sofia
from the Kremlin in 1689, he sent her to a convent, not to the scaffold.
But this tacit rejection of what was, after all, the ultimate weapon of political struggle proved a far greater tactical sacrifice for Sofia than for
Peter. The normal course of events would bring Peter to power, while
Sofia would have to alter the direction of that process if she were to

remain in the Kremlin. As Peter approached his majority, Sofia thus faced the bitter reality that she either must step down as Regent or seize the throne in her own name. Not surprisingly, she chose the latter course. In doing so, she proposed to break with a tradition of male rulers that stretched more than seven centuries back into Russia's history. If she succeeded in her quest, she would become the first woman to reign in Russia since the Princess Olga in the tenth century.

During the mid-1680s, Sofia's desire to seize the crown and rule Russia in her own right was intensified by events within her family circle. In 1682 she had not only forced the great *boiars* and a hastily summoned *zemskii sobor* to recognize Ivan as Russia's co-Tsar but had applied sufficient political pressure to have him proclaimed senior to her half-brother Peter. Realizing that Ivan lacked the wit and the will to rule Russia, Sofia at first had hoped to perpetuate her regency by using him as her docile instrument. If she could arrange for Ivan's marriage, if his dim and childish mind could be made to grasp the process of sexual intercourse, and if he could impregnate his bride with a son, then Sofia might well secure his recognition as Russia's sole heir, since he had the senior claim to the throne. She then could remain Ivan's Regent until his death. If his poor health brought death while his son was a minor, she could continue to rule as Regent, at least until the son reached his majority. All that was needed was for Ivan to take a wife, and for a son to appear in due course and by the proper means.

The easiest part of Sofia's task was to find a wife for Ivan. Fated to suffer the indignity of arranged marriages, and condemned to lifetimes of isolation in the *terem,* there was no shortage of Russian noblewomen who were willing to exchange the prospect of a life with an abusive lord for a life with a gentle and pious idiot, especially when that life could be spent in a *terem* whose opulence was unmatched anywhere in Russia. At the beginning of January 1684, soon after Ivan had passed his seventeenth birthday, Sofia married him to Praskovia Saltykova, a young woman from that family that had risen so high under the patronage of Tsar Mikhail's mother, only to be driven into disgrace by Patriarch Filaret as punishment for their base intrigues. But the remainder of Sofia's scheme proved far more difficult to realize. Not until 1688 did Ivan impregnate his wife, and Praskovia's first child was not born until

March of the following year. After that, the Tsarina gave birth almost every twelvemonth until the year before Ivan's death, although this did little to advance Sofia's designs. Ivan's children would come too late for her political needs, and, in any case, of the five children born to the Tsarina Praskovia between 1689 and 1694, all would be daughters.[93] At the age of thirty-seven, the fourth, Anna, would one day become Russia's second Empress; by that time not only Sofia but the future Peter the Great would be dead.

As Sofia watched her scheme fail, she began to think seriously about seizing the throne herself and, perhaps, sharing it with Prince Golitsyn. Yet, by the time she began to contemplate that drastic course, opinion in Russia had turned solidly against her. She had diverged too far from the model of female virtue set forth in the *Domostroi* for Russians to accept her on the throne. Dynamic, and often seen in public, Sofia shocked to the depths of their hearts and souls those Russians who still thought women should live within the confines of the *terem*. Although she never flaunted her liaison with Golitsyn and, in public, always appeared to be sober and regally proper, Muscovites continued to proclaim her a whore because her style of life diverged so sharply from tradition.[94]

There were also hard political reasons for Sofia's loss of popularity that had nothing to do with her personal behavior. Russia's domestic crises continued during her regency, as did the menace of Tatar incursions along the southern frontier. Russia's domestic economic problems were the result of an extremely complex interplay of forces and events, but they were made much worse by the ineffectual campaigns Sofia and Golitsyn launched against the Tatars. These campaigns, always led by Golitsyn, drained vast quantities of money from Russia's treasury and consumed the lives of tens of thousands of men to little purpose. They cast a pall over all of Sofia's regency and surrounded it with an aura of failure.

By the late .1680s, Sofia had become blinded to Golitsyn's faults and weaknesses. In search of a man whose deeds were as brilliant as his ideas and personality, she convinced herself that her prince had the makings of a great general and that he could match his intellectual brilliance with equally dazzling feats of arms. Toward the end of the decade, Sofia twice sent Golitsyn to the south against the Tatars, and both times he suffered crushing defeats. On his campaign in the summer of 1689, Golitsyn lost nearly a third of the 112,000 men under his command, but won no victories. Sofia proclaimed him a second Moses, a hero who had driven off the Tatar army and had avoided surrender despite great losses. In Golitsyn's refusal to surrender, she saw a great Russian victory "renowned throughout the entire world."[95] When her prince returned to Moscow, she planned not only a great victory celebration but also a coup to drive Peter from the throne. As she had done before, she planned to use the *streltsy* as her instruments. With their help, she had succeeded brilliantly in 1682. Why should she not succeed in a second, even more ambitious, effort? This time, her trust in the *streltsy* proved her undoing. When they failed to heed her exhortations, she had no choice but to flee the Kremlin and leave the field to Peter, the young prince she had so hoped to depose. In September 1689, at the age of seventeen, Peter brought Sofia to ruin.

Sofia had breached the wall of medieval prejudice that isolated highborn Russian women from the world around them. But in the seven short years during which she ruled as Russia's Regent, she could not accustom Russians to accepting a woman as their ruler. The revolution she envisaged would come less than a half-century after her defeat. Ironically, it would be made possible by the even broader revolution that her rival, the young Tsar Peter, launched soon after he drove her from the Kremlin.

CHAPTER II

In the Eye
of the Storm

The first century of Romanov rule brought no order or peace to Russia. Foreign and domestic crises came one after another in dizzying succession, mystifying in their complexity and awesome in their dimensions. War, famine, and plague decimated Russia in a manner not seen in the West since the late Middle Ages. "It seems not excessive to estimate that twice during the seventeenth century—in the early years of the Time of Troubles and of the First Northern War respectively—a third of the population of Great Russia perished," wrote one noted scholar not long ago.[1] During the First Northern War with Poland in the 1650s and 1660s, so many Russians were killed or fled to the frontier to escape conscription by their noble lords that Samuel Collins, an English physician at Aleksei Mikhailovich's Court, estimated that there were ten women for every man in the region around Moscow.[2] The first century under the Romanovs also saw Russia torn asunder by a religious debate that was as soul-shaking and bitter as the Reformation in the West had been a century earlier, and it saw great areas of the land ravaged by the peasant war of Stenka Razin. No aspect of Russian life, no part of the Russian experience remained untouched by these catastrophic crises.

As frightening as they were, there was a greater, even more vital, issue bound up with them. The seventeenth-century Romanovs reigned at a time when Europe was in the midst of an age of geographical and scientific discovery. Her armies, merchant fleets, and missionaries reached outward with an urgency that seemed all but irresistible. Regardless of her own preferences and desires, Russia was drawn ever deeper into the European world, as the Romanovs struggled to defend their lands against direct attacks from Poland and Sweden and to parry the more subtle, but no less threatening, commercial thrusts of England and Holland. From the moment the Romanovs ascended Russia's throne, they had to define their relationship to the technological skill and sophistication of an increasingly secularized West. The ardent, pious, instinctive loyalty of Russians to their Tsar, Church, and traditions had to compete with the rationality, vigorous energy, and technological convenience that the life and culture of the West displayed wherever its agents set foot.[3] The resolution of this issue was perhaps the most critical of any crisis that Russians faced in their history. How they met the Western challenge and defined their relation to it would determine their country's course forever after.

The critical task for the first Romanovs was to determine how far European technology and culture should impinge upon Russian daily life and experience. To put the issue in somewhat different terms, how far should the modern, rationalistic, European experience be permitted to redefine the relationship of Russians to their God, Tsar, and Country? Only in the nineteenth century, when Nicholas I adopted the slogan of "Orthodoxy, Autocracy, and Nationality," did the Romanovs finally resolve this issue, but the controversy would reach its bitterest point two hundred years earlier, when the West seemed to threaten not only Russia's national survival but the access of Russians to salvation. The Romanovs' Court provided the central arena for this great cultural and ideological struggle.

At first, the Romanovs defined Russia's contact with the West in such a way that it excluded all but the most narrow and pragmatic relationship. This was partly the result of an acute sense of inferiority that stemmed from the need to import Western experts and their technology; it was also a result of those precepts according to which Russians had defined themselves as superior to the West in religious and cultural terms for several centuries. This strange duality of inferiority and superiority found expressions on many levels in Russia and at the Romanovs' Court in particular. It was perhaps most dramatically expressed in the Romanovs' repeated invitations to Western diplomats, merchants, and military personnel to visit their domains so that the

Russians could utilize the technological expertise the West had to offer. At the same time, the Romanovs continued to perform an elaborate ritual, which went back several centuries, whenever it was necessary for their hands to be kissed by foreign dignitaries on ceremonial occasions. "Beside the Grand Prince's throne . . . stood a gold basin and ewer, and a hand towel, so that His Tsarist Majesty could wash his hand after the ambassadors had kissed it," wrote Adam Olearius, a Holstein diplomat, in 1634. "This washing is done," he added, "in the presence of a large number of magnates, confirming their hatred of their fellow [non-Orthodox] Christians."[4]

This ritual was practiced by the Romanovs upon those very foreigners who were in the process of modernizing their armies, building their cannon foundries and weapons manufactures, and designing new buildings for the Kremlin and Moscow. From the moment they entered Tsar Mikhail's domains, foreign delegations found themselves under the direct care of the Tsar's special agents (*pristavs*) who accompanied them to Moscow and provided all the necessary food, transportation, and housing along the way. As the foreigners made their way toward Moscow, other special agents went to all the towns and villages in the region and ordered the people to turn out along their route in their holiday finest in order to impress the Tsar's visitors with the numbers and prosperity of his subjects.[5] Once they reached the vicinity of Moscow, the Tsar's agents redoubled their efforts to control and impress the Europeans while at the same time isolating them from the Russian population.

"A quarter league from the city, we came upon four thousand mounted Russians, in costly dress, drawn up in very fine ranks, and we were obliged to pass between them," Olearius wrote. "Two *pristavs* dressed in gold brocade and high sable hats rode up on beautifully groomed white horses. . . . Behind the *pristavs* came the Grand Prince's Master of the Stable, with twenty white horses led by their bridles; he was followed by many people, some mounted and some on foot." Olearius then discussed the exchange of formalities between the two Holstein ambassadors and Mikhail's agents. When the two ambassadors had been mounted on "two large white steeds with embroidered German saddles," the procession began its journey into Moscow itself. Olearius recounted further details:

A throng of other Russians on horseback accompanied us into the city and to the ambassadors' residence. We were put up in the area called Tsargorod (the emperor's city), which is within the white wall. During our entry we were watched from the streets and houses by countless numbers of people. . . . Half an hour after our arrival, by way of welcome we received provisions from the Grand Prince's kitchen and cellar, namely eight sheep, 30 chickens, many wheat and rye loaves, and 22 kinds of drinks—wine, beer, mead, and vodka—each one more delicious than the others. They were brought by 32 Russians who came in single file. We were daily supplied in the same manner with similar, but only half as many, provisions.[6]

Since the embassy of which Olearius was a part included only thirty-four members, Mikhail's supplies were generous indeed. They were all the more impressive because Moscow had only a short time before suffered a major fire. Yet there was another side to Mikhail's generosity that spoke with equal eloquence about his attitude toward the foreigners who had come to his capital. "When the provisions had been handed over," Olearius continued, "the porch of our dwelling was locked and 12 *streltsi* were placed there as a guard so that none of us could go out and no stranger could visit us until we had had our first audience. Each day, the *pristav* came to visit the ambassadors and to see whether anything was needed. One of the Russian interpreters stayed in the house with us to dispatch musketeers to buy various things requested."[7] Sir Dudley Diggs, an English diplomat at the Court of Tsar Mikhail, dubbed his Russian escort "my gentleman Jaylor," and William Prideaux, sent by Oliver Cromwell as a special envoy to Aleksei Mikhailovich, called his lodgings in Moscow "the house where I am for my prison" because he was kept under such strict surveillance.[8]

By mid-century Tsar Aleksei Mikhailovich decreed that foreigners could not wear Russian clothing and thus branded them a race apart. He drove them from Moscow's inner city and required them to live in a ghetto that stood between the Iauza and Kukui rivers a short distance outside the city. Muscovites immediately dubbed the New Foreign Quarter "Cockville" because the name Kukui sounded rather like "khui," an obscene Russian word for the male organ.[9] There, foreigners were isolated from daily contact with the Russians. In the words of Johann de Rodes, a Swedish merchant and diplomat, the New

Foreign Quarter was "surrounded by a fence in which there was only one gate, which was guarded by *streltsy*."[10]

Yet as so often has happened in the history of mankind, the new, the innovative, and, above all, the forbidden, presented a lure to which men and women seem destined to succumb. Thus, "Cockville" proved to be one of the strangest ghettos in history, for it eventually became the model for Russians to emulate, as the traditional life of Orthodox constraint gave way to the more joyous, more exciting, and, especially, freer direction the Foreign Quarter represented. When the young Tsar Peter chose the life of the Foreign Quarter over that of the Kremlin at the end of the seventeenth century, the dilemma of Russia's relationship with the West finally was resolved in the most radical manner possible. Russia would emulate the West in technology, culture, and the manner of her daily life. The revolutionary "artisan Tsar" insisted that his people follow him along this new and unknown path.

In 1613, when Mikhail Romanov entered Moscow as Russia's chosen Tsar, a Court, in the sense of a cultural and political entity such as had flourished under his predecessors, simply did not exist. The first Romanov Tsar entered a Kremlin that had been laid waste by its Polish conquerors and by the struggle of the Russian national army that had liberated it. With devastation all around them, Mikhail and the men who stood close to him searched for something to grasp, something to serve as an anchor in the uncertain world they faced. It seemed essential to return to the old order, tried and true. As one Russian historian wrote not long after another great revolution had swept over his country in 1917 to condemn many to search again for new values, "as a result of the Time of Troubles, the Russian people had 'lost heart and were shattered' in their values and outlooks. The fall of the old social principles, the incursion of masses of foreigners into Russian life, the civil war, and all of the 'perfidies' connected with it—all these had shattered the old world view of Muscovites and had led men to doubt their earlier certainty that Russia was a 'new Israel,' a people chosen by God."[11]

Mikhail and his courtiers turned to the traditional precepts of the *Domostroi* that had served their ancestors so well. Indeed, the *Domostroi* commanded more observance during the seventeenth century than when the monk Silvestr had written it. "Fear the Tsar, and serve him faithfully," he had instructed his readers. "Devote yourself to your Prince and your masters with all your heart. Harbor no evil thoughts against them. For the Apostle Paul has said that 'all power is instituted by God.' "[12] Certainly such a vision of authority fit the needs of the first Romanovs as they turned to the immense task of reestablishing order. For more than a decade, their subjects had switched allegiance among several claimants to the throne, and it was therefore especially important that the Russian people be convinced that there was only one true Tsar, that that Tsar sat in the Kremlin, and that there could be no other.

Above all, Silvestr stressed the need for absolute authority within the family and extended that authority upward in an absolute hierarchy that terminated at the throne of God Almighty. Men ruled with iron hands in the world of the *Domostroi,* and women, servants, and children were to be totally subject to their will. Fathers were exhorted to "punish your children while they are young, and you will enjoy a peaceful old age," and women were instructed to devote their lives to the service of others and, in all things, to be subordinate to the will of their husbands, Tsar, and God. "A good wife, who loves labor and is silent and meek, becomes her husband's crown," Silvestr had proclaimed in an ecstatic panegyric to women.[13] Russians thus were to be constrained by a strict code of morality and daily behavior, and every departure from its narrow precepts was proclaimed a mortal sin. To serve as an example to others, the Romanovs instituted this rigid morality and unbending ritual at their Court.

Yet Mikhail Romanov's effort to glorify tradition, to return to the old values and the old ways, was offset from the very first by the influences of Western Europeans. Numbers of them had been in Moscow since the mid-fifteenth century, when Tsar Ivan the Great had brought Italian architects and engineers to rebuild and beautify the Kremlin. But they had tended to become assimilated among the Russians and therefore presented no cultural threat to the order the Tsars and their churchmen sought to preserve in Russia. During the late sixteenth century, and particularly during the Time of Troubles, however, their numbers increased significantly, and they tended to resist assimilation and to preserve their own customs more enthusiastically.

It was during the Time of Troubles that Europeans first began to serve a major military function at the Muscovite Court. Tsar Vasilii Shuiskii was the first to hire European mercenaries to fight the Poles and Swedes, and it very soon became clear to Russians that they could not stand against their foes without the weapons and expertise these Western troops had at their command. As a result, from the very moment that Mikhail Romanov ascended Russia's throne, European professional soldiers became a part of Moscow's population. Likewise, European merchants, anxious to tap Russia's rich supplies of furs, naval stores, and other raw materials, poured back into Russia in larger numbers than ever, even before a semblance of peace had come.[14] Both groups—the "master technicians" of the military and the merchants from the expanding Western commercial empires—were essential to Russia's development, but they posed a serious threat to that conservative, traditional order that Filaret, his son Mikhail, and his grandson Aleksei Mikhailovich sought to establish as a bulwark to their new regime. Clearly, if Europeans were to be allowed in Russia, and if the Romanovs were to continue to base their regime upon tradition, very strict measures had to be taken to keep foreigners and Russians apart.

If Tsar Mikhail, his advisers, and his churchmen sought to isolate foreigners from contact with Russian life so that they would not corrupt the Russians, what was the life that they offered as the model for Russians to imitate? Historians have often argued that "the Byzantine idea of asceticism" was the ideal that governed Court life in the Russia of Tsars Mikhail and Aleksei Mikhailovich.[15] But even the most rigid religious precepts could not drive all forms of entertainment from the Court that began to develop around Mikhail in the 1620s. Jesters, fools, and dwarfs played a major part in Court amusements, and the Tsar evidently brought a favorite jester by the name of Mosiaga with him when he moved into the Kremlin in the spring of 1613. Clad in their red or yellow garments, and wearing fox-skin caps, usually with pointed ears, Mosiaga and his male and female companions were permitted free rein in expressing whatever sorts of humor struck their fancy at any given moment. Their only obligation was to move the Tsar and his Court to laughter.[16] In the words of one historian, they acted as "a sort of moral safety-valve for the society of the day, which, outwardly grave and reverent, was inwardly bubbling over with artificially repressed animal spirits."[17]

But jesters, fools, and dwarfs could hardly release the full measure of tension that such a rigid moral order produced. Muscovites found widespread relief in drunkenness that was excessive by any standard. "The entire nation is given to drunkenness, from the smallest to the greatest, including priests and parishioners, from the lowest peasants to the highest lords," wrote Iurii Krizhanich, a Croation priest, in the 1670s.[18] A half-century earlier, Olearius had written that "the vice of drunkenness is prevalent among this people in all classes, both secular and ecclesiastical, high and low, men and women, young and old,"[19] and there is evidence that the Tsar himself indulged that vice on occasion.[20]

Krizhanich and Olearius were not referring simply to occasional overindulgence on the part of the Tsars, their courtiers, and their subjects. Certainly Europeans were no paragons of sobriety in the seventeenth century, and alcoholism was a problem in Western societies as well. The drunkenness that so shocked Europeans in Russia was of the utterly degrading and totally uncontrolled variety. It left Russians unable to stand, to move, or to speak. Sometimes it left them blind or paralyzed, and, on occasion, it killed them from alcohol poisoning. Indeed, Olearius wrote that an ambassador sent by the Swedish King Charles IX in 1608 died from the strong vodka his Russian hosts served him during a ceremonial dinner.[21] Numerous Westerners commented upon Russians' filthiness, crudity, and, even, gross bestiality. After a Russian delegation had left Copenhagen in the 1630s, the Danish King Christian IV reportedly remarked that "if these people come to me again, I shall build for them a pigsty because no one can live for at least six months in any building they have occupied due to the stench they leave behind."[22] Olearius spoke of rich and rare delicacies served at Mikhail Romanov's own table in dishes that were "silver, but not especially clean," and he continually returned to the theme of Russians' filth in language and way of life. "They have nothing on their tongues more often than 'son of a whore,' 'son of a bitch,' 'cur,' [and] 'I fuck your mother.' " In amazement, he added, "Not only adults and old people behave thus, but also little children who do not yet know the name of God, or father, or mother, already have on their lips 'fuck you,' and say it as well to their parents as their parents to them."[23] Olearius also spoke of Russians' taste for sodomy, "and not only with young boys but also with men and horses."[24] Truly, Western visitors found the Tsar, his Court, and his subjects an amazing morass of contradictions as they insisted upon remaining passionately and uncritically loyal to the traditional order that spawned this life of pent-up tension and violent release, extreme piety and excessive lust, abysmal ignorance and an exaltation of superstition.

Secular Western influences had broadened in Moscow during the three decades of Mikhail's reign despite these many constraints. Mikhail himself had broken down some of the barriers, probably unwittingly, when he commissioned the Dutch masters Johan and Melchior Lunn to build a great organ in the Kremlin, although such was forbidden by the puritanical precepts of the Church.[25] Further, when Filaret returned from his Polish captivity in 1619, he brought with him a taste for such seemingly innocent secular entertainments as jugglers and theatricals. These and similar amusements remained very much a part of Court life until Filaret's death in 1633, although conservative churchmen preached against them as evil and sinful. This slight tendency toward liberalization was suppressed during the last years of Mikhail's reign as the Tsar began to feel his age and sought to constrain the joys of this world in an effort to win laurels for himself when he passed into the next. Likewise, when the energetic Iosif became Patriarch in 1642, he gave enthusiastic support to Mikhail's increasingly puritanical tendencies. Yet the generally passive Mikhail did little to initiate efforts to root out external signs of Western influences in Russia. His son, the "most gentle" Tsar Aleksei Mikhailovich, not content to follow his father's less dynamic religious policies, became an energetic crusader in a fundamentalist campaign to return Russians to the traditional moral and cultural precepts of Orthodoxy. Together, he and Iosif railed against all foreigners and their culture as instruments of Satan.

Although we cannot doubt Aleksei's piety, it is also true that he urged a religious revival upon Russians for a very concrete political purpose. The Moscow Riot of 1648, followed by the grain riots in Pskov and Novgorod, made him fear for his crown. During the early 1650s, Aleksei Mikhailovich thus sought to spark a xenophobic upsurge in Russia to distract his subjects from famine, plague, and economic crises.[26]

He and the Patriarch Iosif also sought to educate Russians more broadly in those rigid and uncompromising Orthodox beliefs that had served as a bulwark against social and political upheaval in earlier times. They employed the revolutionary and dangerous instruments of literacy and the printing press in their efforts. Led by Ivan Nasedka, whose polemical tract against Lutheranism had been Russia's first bestseller in 1644, the patriarchal printing press, which enjoyed an absolute monopoly over the printed word in Russia, turned out between 1647 and 1652 nearly ten thousand copies of the first Russian primer, as well as nine printings of the psalter and eight of the book of hours.[27] Clearly, the Church intended to intensify Russians' devotion by teaching a larger number of them to read the fundamental writings of the Orthodox faith.

When Iosif died in 1652, Aleksei Mikhailovich appointed as his successor Nikon, Metropolitan of the chaotic and far-flung see of Novgorod, which stretched all across Russia's far north. For six years, Nikon would drive the Church with a passion and energy equaled in Russian history only by Filipp, that wrathful and unforgiving Metropolitan of Moscow whose opposition to Ivan the Terrible's demands had led the Tsar to order his murder a century earlier.

Nikon quickly and obviously intimidated the young Tsar, who called him "the great sun."[28] His huge, raw-boned, six-foot six-inch frame towered over friend and foe alike, and his piercing eyes and intense religiosity were immensely compelling. His intellect also set other men in his shadow. Along with such leading churchmen as Stefan Vonifatiev, he was a part of a group of Grecophiles in seventeenth-century Moscow who sought to purify tradition and find the "true" religion through scholarly inquiry.[29]

Once he became Patriarch in 1652, Nikon built upon the work of his predecessor and moved rapidly to direct Moscow along the path to becoming the new center of the Orthodox East. Nikon insisted that Aleksei Mikhailovich's early victories against Roman Catholic Poland in the First Northern War gave proof that Russia had a special mission within the context of universal culture and that she had been chosen by God for a special purpose.[30] Therefore, if Russia were to stand as the political *and* spiritual hope of the Orthodox East, she must become the source of ritualistic and religious purity. Nikon insisted upon a "purification" of Russian Church books to remove errors in translation and ritual that had appeared over the centuries. Shocked Russian clerics and their flocks found that they had been writing Christ's name incorrectly and that it was spelled Iisus, not Isus. To their dismay, they learned that three fingers must be used to make the sign of the cross and that it besmirched the name of God to use two fingers, as all Russians had done for centuries. In this and many other ways, Nikon sought to purify tradition, but many saw his effort as a terrible attack against it. How, they asked in amazement, could a missal published less than a half-century ago in Venice, that den of Roman Catholic apostasy, serve as the basis for banning prayers and rituals that Russians had venerated for centuries? The fact that Nikon had chosen the 1602 edition because it was considered accurate, definitive, and the closest to the original Greek was not an argument that minds steeped in superstition and unaccustomed to scholarly debate could comprehend.[31] Almost instantly, serious opposition to Nikon's policy of purification exploded throughout Russia. Undaunted, he insisted that men must follow his path regardless of their personal views. The result would be religious and social catastrophe—splitting the Russian Church into two factions that remain bitter enemies to this day.

Yet Nikon had even greater dreams. Above all, he aspired to establish the position of Patriarch as equal to the Tsar himself. Like Filaret, he assumed the title of "Sovereign Majesty." Unlike his politically astute predecessor, he established a Patriarchal Court whose grandeur rivaled the Tsar's own, surrounded his each and every act with an elaborate and royal ritual, and built an opulent new Patriarchal palace within the Kremlin's inner walls. From the moment he became part of Aleksei Mikhailovich's inner circle, Nikon exploited the young Tsar's favor to increase the power of his own office. This became especially blatant in 1652, when Aleksei Mikhailovich offered him the Patriarchate. As good form demanded, Nikon refused the office. When the Tsar came to the Cathedral to beg him on his knees to accept, Nikon exacted an amazing and terrible pledge from him. At Nikon's dogged insistence, Aleksei Mikhailovich swore "before Our Lord and Savior, before our Holy Mother, the angels, and all the saints" that he would obey the Patriarch as his "first pastor and father" in everything he taught "in matters of dogma, discipline, and morality."[32] Such vague terms as "discipline and morality" could have almost any meaning Nikon chose to give them, and it soon became clear that he intended to endow them with a meaning so broad that it included the newly established *Ulozhenie*, the Law Code of 1649 and day-to-day political affairs. Never had a Russian churchman demanded such a pledge from a Tsar. The powerful and assertive Filaret had not even dared ask it from his son.

Yet Aleksei Mikhailovich agreed to Nikon's demand. He went even further, and allowed him to function as Russia's co-ruler during the long months when he was at the Polish front between May 1654 and late 1656. So great did Nikon's power become in Aleksei Mikhailovich's absence that the Patriarch conducted state business on a daily basis and often did not consult with the Tsar before making major policy decisions. But clouds were gathering upon the horizon, and they soon would unleash a terrible storm, a tempest so violent that its fury would sweep Nikon from the Kremlin and into exile in a distant monastery. For Nikon usurped Russia's temporal power in an arrogant and tactless manner that turned Russia's great *boiars* against him. At the same time, Aleksei Mikhailovich's success at the front made the young Tsar into a man at last. Confident of his judgment, he became reluctant to subordinate himself to the Patriarch as he had done so willingly before. Therefore, in July 1658, he revoked Nikon's title of "Sovereign Majesty" and ordered him to cease attacking the Law Code of 1649. In angry protest, and proclaiming that Aleksei Mikhailovich had violated his sacred oath to follow him in all matters of dogma, discipline, and morality, Nikon left Moscow and entered a monastery.[33] In the struggle between Church and State, Nikon was determined that the Church should emerge at least as an equal. At the same time, Aleksei Mikhailovich was determined to rule Russia with all of the absolute authority at his command. For the next decade, both issues—the conflict between Church and State and the matter of Church reforms—seethed throughout the Russian land as they awaited the resolution that came only with the great Church Council of 1667.

Although a number of Russian churchmen opposed Nikon's efforts to purge church texts of inaccuracies and errors, his most famous opponent was the Archpriest Avvakum. Like the Patriarch, Avvakum had grown up among the peasants in the Russian northeast and had been a part of Vonifatiev's and Rtishchev's Moscow circle of friends. Avvakum also opposed Western influence but, unlike Nikon, he hated everything that was not Russian, including those Balkan and Near Eastern influences to which Nikon paid such homage in the 1650s. Avvakum advocated a puritanical morality that was so unyielding it made those conservative constraints Aleksei Mikhailovich and Nikon hoped to impose upon Russian society seem liberal, even licentious, by comparison. He and his followers damned tobacco as "bewitched grass" and cursed hops as "bewitched Lithuanian grapes."[34] Avvakum castigated all secular art, and all religious art that was in any way true to life. Most of all, he saw in Nikon's effort to correct Church texts and liturgy a direct attack upon the fundamental precepts of Russian Orthodoxy. Nikon's reforms made Russians' relationship with God, Christ, and the Church less direct, less warm, and more impersonal. What Nikon regarded as simple, scholarly errors that had been compounded over time, Avvakum and his impassioned followers saw as the spiritual treasures that made Russian Orthodoxy unique among all other forms of Christianity. To alter the manner in which devout men and women made the sign of the cross, wrote the name of Christ, or called upon the name of God in the Lord's Prayer, Avvakum insisted, destroyed the very things that made Russian Orthodoxy the most perfect of all religions.[35]

Violent as it was, Avvakum's xenophobic and obscurantist attack against Nikon's reforms was not merely the view of one angry priest. It represented an angry assault of the noncelibate, nonmonastic, parish clergy against that monkish elite that had ruled the Church for so long, and with so little concern for the concerns of its flock. Although the Patriarch sent the wrathful Archpriest into Siberian exile in the fall of 1653, Avvakum's followers continued vehemently to voice their protest into the mid-1660s, for, like the Church-State conflict, the debate on reform was not resolved until the Church Council of 1667. By the time the Council voted to uphold Nikon's purification of the liturgy's form and content and to reject his pretensions to vie with the Tsar's power,

Avvakum's supporters had turned his protest into a grass-roots movement that rejected both the Church that had altered the liturgy and the State that had given it temporal support.[36]

Because he was exiled to Siberia so early in the conflict, Avvakum's protest might never have been organized into a powerful religious movement had it not been for one of the most remarkable women in Russia's history. The great *boiarina* Feodosia Morozova's passion and energy rivaled that of the Tsarevna Sofia who, as Regent, would persecute her followers. A woman of great wealth and even greater courage and spirit, Morozova owned vast estates and ruled the lives of more than more than eight thousand serfs; her Moscow palace employed more than three hundred servants. She drove about the city in a coach inlaid with pure gold and silver as she went on errands of charity and mercy. Not counting her estates and serfs, her fortune in gold, silver, jewels, and other riches was estimated at almost a quarter-million rubles, which easily made her one of the wealthiest of Aleksei Mikhailovich's subjects. She was the sister-in-law of Boris Morozov, the tutor whom the Tsar had been obliged to exile in 1648, and she was a great favorite of the Tsarina Maria, who became her protectress and sympathizer in religious causes.[37] Yet it was not as a woman of great wealth and high position but as a religious zealot that Morozova made her indelible mark on history. She became the most ardent of Avvakum's disciples, and it was she who gave organization and substance to his protest after he was sent to Siberia.

The true test of Morozova's faith began in 1667, when Aleksei Mikhailovich ordered all Russians to swear allegiance to the new Church texts that Nikon had produced. It was at that time that the Church was officially split by schism, and the Old Belief, as it was known, became a crime. It was then that the convictions of Avvakum and his followers were put to the bitterest of tests. Together, they refused the oath, went to prison, and suffered appalling tortures. Steadfast in their faith, they continued to refuse the oath as they fell, one by one, as martyrs to the Old Belief. Morozova's torment was postponed so long as her protectress, the Tsarina Maria, lived. When she died in 1669, Morozova's fate was sealed, although the blow did not fall until the end of 1671.[38]

During the late night hours of November 14, 1671, the Archimandrite Ioakim (soon to become Russia's Patriarch), an army officer, and a detachment of burly soldiers knocked at Morozova's door. Ioakim proclaimed that the Tsar had ordered her to recant her Old Belief. If she refused, she must suffer as all heretics must suffer. Her spirit hardened by the martyrdom of many friends, Morozova boldly refused. At Ioakim's order, the soldiers placed her in chains and took her away to prison. The scene was later immortalized by the great nineteenth-century painter Vasilii Surikov, who portrayed Morozova, clad in black and ever defiant, being borne away on a sledge with her hand raised in the defiant two-fingered blessing of the Old Belief. Morozova was destined to bear her torture under three Patriarchs, for Iosafat II died in early 1672 and Pitirim died in the spring of 1673. Thus it was the same Ioakim who had arrested her who presided as Patriarch over her final martyrdom in 1675. During the four years of her imprisonment, Morozova bore whippings, brandings, and other tortures with the same triumphant defiance that Surikov captured in his great canvas. Finally, in the summer of 1675, she was condemned to a cruel and lingering death. She and her sister Evdokia, who had shared her beliefs and her sufferings from the very beginning, were ordered into a dungeon that was devoid of all light and air. On pain of death, their guards were ordered to deny them all food and water. The fate of the two sisters was to be martyrdom by starvation. Their deaths were postponed by guards who pitied them and smuggled bits of food to their cell, although such moments of kindness could not save them and probably only increased their suffering. Evdokia died in mid-September, some ten weeks after her torture began, her wasted body unable to move beneath the weight of her chains.

Aleksei Mikhailovich and the Patriarch Ioakim both thought that her sister's death would at last destroy Morozova's will, that she would swear the oath, and that her recanting would bring a flood of others once the Old Believers thought themselves abandoned by the woman who stood as the symbol of their opposition. They could not have been more mistaken. Weak, hardly more than a skeleton, Morozova remained defiant, her will, like the strongest steel, unbent by all the forces that were directed against it. Determined to resist all efforts of her persecutors, she refused the oath and swore to remain faithful to the Old Belief unto death. Six weeks later, on November 1, 1675, she finally met her end by starvation.

A quicker, but even more painful, end awaited her mentor Avvakum, but it did not come until a few years later. In 1682, just two weeks before the death of Tsar Feodor, Avvakum was burned at the stake. As the flames rose around him, he raised high the cross of the Old Belief and perished with a dire warning on his lips. "If you ever abandon this cross, your city will perish," he cried as he neared his final agony. "Its end will be the end of the world."[39]

The split between the official Church and the Old Belief had of course been an unequal struggle from the very beginning, for neither poor peasants and parish priests, nor even the wealth and prestige of Morozova, could stand against the growing might of the state over which the Romanovs ruled. Yet the *Raskol,* as the split was known to all Russians, was a religious and social catastrophe of ruinous dimensions, for it turned large numbers of Russians away from their country and their Tsar. Over the next half-century, thousands upon thousands of Russians faithful to the Old Belief chose death over reconciliation with the Tsar and his agents. Throughout the far north and western Siberia, entire congregations ecstatically followed the example of those seventeen hundred Old Believers who, in 1679, barred themselves in their church, set fire to it, and perished in the flames rather than fall into the hands of Tsar Feodor's troops.[40] A half-century before Peter the Great launched his revolutionary changes upon his frightened subjects, the Russian body politic thus was split into two utterly irreconcilable segments. Until the day they fell from the throne in 1917, the Romanovs would be denied the support of millions of Russians who remained faithful to the Old Belief and rejected as heretical instruments of the Devil, utterly unworthy of allegiance, the state, the rulers, and the laws that came after the Council of 1667.

Aleksei Mikhailovich's victory over Nikon, and the war he declared against the Old Belief, which martyred Avvakum, Morozova, and so many others, also marked a dramatic shift in his attitudes toward the question of Western influences and the relationship of Russia and the Russians to them. Even by the time his conservative and deeply pious

Tsarina Maria died in 1669, opposition to foreign ideas and culture was becoming identified with opposition to the Tsar's authority because xenophobia was so intrinsically a part of the Old Belief. Not long afterward, hatred of the West also became identified with social revolt as Old Believers joined the many thousands who followed Stenka Razin's rebel army up the Volga. By the early 1670s, it had become almost impossible to differentiate between the more controlled opposition to Western influences that the Tsar himself had championed during the first decade of his reign and the passionate, unthinking, rejection of all things foreign that characterized Avvakum and his followers. Quite probably because opposition to the West was becoming identified with the Old Belief, Aleksei Mikhailovich began to support the influx of that Western culture his young wife Natalia and his adviser Matveev pressed upon him. Their urgings, however, were part of a broader movement led not only by Matveev but by Iurii Krizhanich, one of the most complex personalities to appear in Russia in the quarter-century before Peter the Great rose to the throne.

Iurii Krizhanich was born in Croatia in 1617, studied at a Roman Catholic seminary in Vienna, and trained in Rome to become a missionary. He first visited Russia in 1647 as part of a Polish diplomatic delegation. He returned to Moscow twelve years later, this time disguised as a Ukrainian refugee, and became a librarian in the Kremlin. His purpose was to preach his favorite theme of Slav religious unity among the Russians, but we have no record of just when or where he preached or if, in fact, he did. All we know is that in 1661, for reasons that are not clear, he was sent to the western Siberian frontier outpost of Tobolsk, where he remained until the year after Aleksei Mikhailovich's death. In Tobolsk, probably between 1663 and 1666, he wrote his most famous work, *Conversations on Government,* which was best described as "an argument for absolute monarchy based largely on classical and Renaissance authorities," not the least of whom was Machiavelli.[41]

While the Old Believers challenged the Tsar's authority, the Croatian Roman Catholic priest Krizhanich supported it without reservation and insisted that absolute monarchy was one of the most vital underpinnings of Russia's national welfare. But he also insisted that Russians must not allow the superiority of their system of government to blind them to certain other inadequacies and failures they suffered in comparison with the West; nor must they allow themselves to become blind defenders of tradition or slavish advocates of innovation. "Reason tells us that nothing can be good or bad simply because it is new. Everything good and everything bad was at one time new," he wrote.[42] Krizhanich argued that there was much of practical value to be learned from the "German" world. Most Russian homes, he pointed out, were poorly designed, had little ventilation, and no chimneys. Garbage and excrement collected in an appalling manner, and Russians had become notorious for the utter filth they left behind when they traveled in foreign lands. Russian weapons were primitive, and many things were poorly made. Yet Krizhanich saw something even more disturbing among the Russians, which he identified as the key to resolving the dilemmas they faced in the 1660s. "A much greater failure of ours stems from what I shall call xenomania, or hatred of foreigners," he warned. It was this attitude that had cut Russia off from the valuable and positive aspects of Western culture, accounting for that backwardness from which she suffered.[43] Obviously, the gap between East and West needed to be bridged.

After several centuries of condemning everything Western as anathema, it required daring men to reverse Russia's course in the 1660s and 1670s. Perhaps most prominent among these early Westernizers was Artamon Matveev, Aleksei Mikhailovich's closest adviser during the last decade of his reign. Matveev came from origins that were noble but far from illustrious. There is no record of his grandparents' names, what they did, or where they lived in Russia. It was Matveev's father who began to make a name for his family, and his achievements in the service of Mikhail Romanov won him a position as an official Kremlin secretary and several estates in Moscow, Kaluga, and Riazan. We do not know how the elder Matveev earned the Tsar's favor, but he must have proved meritorious indeed because, in 1638, his thirteen-year-old son Artamon was brought into the Kremlin to be educated along with the Grand Duke Aleksei Mikhailovich, heir to the Russian throne. Artamon Matveev proved an apt student and was fascinated by those bits of Western culture to which the Grand Duke's tutor Morozov timidly introduced them. Evidently, Matveev secured the Grand Duke Aleksei's friendship during their student years together. When he became Tsar in 1645, the young monarch bestowed upon Matveev the rank of colonel and named him chief of the Moscow *streltsy*. For the next two decades, Matveev held a number of military and diplomatic commissions, performed ably in them all, and rose to new heights in the Tsar's favor.[44]

While several of Aleksei Mikhailovich's counselors advocated that Russia establish closer connections with the West out of necessity, Matveev became the rare Muscovite who preferred to live in the Western manner. Everything about Matveev's household must have shocked Muscovites. He became friendly with a number of the Europeans who lived in the New Foreign Quarter that was rising outside the city gates, and, in an act of boldness that exceeded all bounds of propriety in Muscovite society, he was known to entertain such men and women in his home. While the Church condemned as utterly sinful all secular art, particularly portraits, Matveev's reception room boasted more than two dozen, including one of a woman. Indeed, it was in the matter of women that Matveev probably most shocked Russian visitors to his home. Mirrors were displayed openly in the halls and rooms of his dwelling, and his Scottish wife Eudoxie blatantly used them for primping and other feminine purposes at a time when the Church decreed that mirrors must be covered except when being used for such essential purposes as pinning up one's hair. Most shocking of all, Matveev's wife joined him in greeting guests as they arrived, and dined with them, although the *Domostroi* forbade such behavior. A *terem* did not exist at the Matveevs, and *terem* rules went unobserved. A visit to the Matveevs thus must have been an amazing, unnerving, and probably deeply disturbing experience for Muscovite lords in the 1660s. There was one, however, who found this new way of life increasingly appealing, and that was no less a figure than the Tsar himself.[45] As Aleksei Mikhailovich broke with the Patriarch Nikon, as his saintly adviser Feodor Rtishchev went into retirement, and as he began to draw away from the religious conservatism of the Tsarina Maria in the year or two before her death, he began to see closer connections with the West as desirable from a standpoint of personal taste as well as political necessity.

Aleksei Mikhailovich's new tastes produced such a dramatic cultural shift in Moscow during the 1660s that one historian has concluded that "there was a kind of restoration atmosphere" about the city during these years.[46] Indeed, this was the most exciting and vibrant cultural period in the entire seventeenth century, for it was then that the great storm of religious and cultural conflict, which had swirled around the Romanovs for more than half a century, began to find some hint of the direction it would follow in the years ahead. No longer would Russia's culture remain frozen by medieval precepts that opposed progress. The Tsar and his Court began to map out a path toward modernization in late seventeenth-century terms. Their first efforts seem timid in retrospect, especially when compared to the cultural and political turmoil Peter the Great brought to Russia a quarter-century later. But, for the time and place in which they occurred, Aleksei Mikhailovich's first steps were very bold, for they crossed the threshold from the medieval world into a modern one.

The few years between about 1663 and 1676 brought to Russia early attempts at worldly art, the beginnings of instrumental music, and the first performances of the secular theatre. Aleksei Mikhailovich urged the diplomatic agent he sent to England to have "masters in the art of presenting comedies" dispatched to Moscow. Restoration England's first Ambassador to Moscow did indeed stage "a handsome Comedie in Prose" in the mid-1660s.[47] Artists no longer devoted their brushes solely to the glorification of God in the highly stylized form the Church had demanded for so long. First foreign, and then Russian, artists began to paint true-to-life portraits of living men and women. In vain did such xenophobes as Avvakum rail against those Russian modernists who painted the image of Emmanuel the Savior "with a puffy face, dark red lips, curly hair, thick arms and muscles, with chubby fingers and legs, and heavy hips so as to make him resemble a German, pot-bellied and fat, the only difference being that a sword was not painted at his hip."[48] Very slowly to be sure, but with a persistence that left no doubt about their growing taste for things secular, Russians began to display this sort of art in their homes. Woodcuts became so popular during the last quarter of the century that they were sold in stalls near the Spasskii Gate in Moscow, and the government even sponsored a *Book of Titled Figures,* featuring lifelike portraits of some sixty-five foreign and Russian rulers.[49] All of these new endeavors reflected Russians' concern with the earthly life, and that was perhaps the most important innovation of all.

Nowhere was this revolutionary shift in Russian attitudes more evident than in the poetry of Simeon Polotskii, tutor to the future Tsar Feodor Alekseevich and the Regent Sofia in the 1660s and 1670s. As Aleksei Mikhailovich's Court poet, Polotskii produced *The Multi-Flowered Garden,* a weighty volume of 1,246 poems totaling some 30,000 lines of verse. Polotskii pursued a number of secular themes and drew heavily upon historical collections of the medieval West for his subjects. Most innovative, even revolutionary, in his work was the manner in which he portrayed women, their lives, and their aspirations. Polotskii wrote for an audience that had been reared upon the precepts of the *Domostroi;* to the traditional image of female virtue and modesty, Polotskii counterposed another, in which women were very legitimately concerned with the earthly life. "His wife has clothes that make me look a slattern," a woman complained in his poem "The Marriage," but she complained not because she was greedy or sinful but because she wanted to hold the love and attention of her husband. Thus, she lauded physical beauty and endeavored to make herself attractive to men in physical terms. As Polotskii explained to her husband, "For she wishes to have you always fondly gazing,/The beauty of her face and temper praising."[50] That was indeed a far cry from the ideal woman of the *Domostroi* world, the woman who was never even to think of physical beauty, and certainly would not think of competing for her husband's attention in society, since she never was permitted to enter it.[51]

Polotskii's new portrayal of women, which his former pupil, the Tsarevna Sofia, would live out to the fullest during the decade after his death in 1679, gained wider currency and further articulation in theatrical works and, especially, in those "English comedies" Aleksei Mikhailovich found so appealing. Not only did the Tsar import secular plays, he built a large theatre at Preobrazhenskoe, another in the Kremlin, and established a theatrical company under the direction of Johann-Gottfried Gregory, formerly a soldier in the armies of Poland and Sweden, but, since 1658, a German pastor in Moscow's New Foreign Quarter. Although Gregory's troupe functioned as a Court theatre only from 1672 until Aleksei Mikhailovich's death four years later, it presented at least eight plays and a ballet, some of which featured large casts and grandiose sets. The play *Judith,* for example, had a cast of more than sixty. By seventeenth-century Russian standards, its dialogue was clearly revolutionary because it dealt with a secular theme and some of its lines dealt very explicitly with amorous passion and sexual attraction. "Don't you see, lovely goddess, how the power of your beauty has already in part overcome me?" one of the characters proclaimed to Judith.[52] We do not know how many Court women attended these plays, but we know that the Tsarina Natalia and some of her stepdaughters did. Certainly, Matveev's Scottish wife was a regular theatregoer. According to a Danish diplomat who knew him, Matveev's passion for the theatre was so intense that he even took part in theatricals himself.[53]

Lives devoted to the pursuit of secular interests and worldly pleasures demanded a different setting than that which had surrounded the Romanov Court throughout most of the seventeenth century. Ever since 1613, the form and design of the Romanovs' residences had been focused around the secular and religious ceremonial that formed such an integral part of their effort to control the turbulent domain they ruled. Chapels occupied a central position in their residences, and the decor of their palaces emphasized religion and the God-given superiority of the Tsar over all men. At mid-century, one new element was added to the ceremonial setting in which the Romanovs lived, and that centered upon Aleksei Mikhailovich's passion for the hunt, which gradually encroached upon the dawn-to-dusk religious ritual that had governed Court life during the 1640s. The hunting lodges the Tsar built during the 1650s were almost completely without the stultifying ceremonial trappings of Muscovite royal life; they were small, rustic, and quite spartan. From them, Aleksei Mikhailovich pursued the falconry he loved so ardently that the Kings of England, Poland, and Denmark, as well as the Ottoman Sultan and the Shah of Persia sent him birds of prey as gifts.[54] Yet hunting lodges symbolized only the beginning of a break in that ceremonial screen with which the Romanovs had surrounded their Court since 1613. Beginning in the 1660s, Aleksei Mikhailovich began to build two country palaces of a very different sort from his earlier hunting lodges.

Izmailovo was the first suburban estate to which Aleksei Mikhailovich brought his growing interest in things Western and technological. He first built a palace of Westernized design, had a large moat dug around it, and laid a drawbridge across it. But Aleksei Mikhailovich's greatest concern at Izmailovo was not the palace, but the vast gardens that surrounded it. They were the first gardens that a Romanov, or any other Russian for that matter, had laid out according to Western designs. Like those eighteenth-century Romanovs who borrowed so heavily from the West, Tsar Aleksei insisted that his adaptation be on a massive scale, with the result that his new gardens were as immense as they were impressive. Also like his successors, and especially his son Peter the Great, Aleksei Mikhailovich demanded that his gardens stand as a monument to the triumph of his power over nature. Lush melons from Central Asia, pears from Hungary, even date palms from the Caucasus flourished in open defiance of Moscow's brutal winter climate, as the Tsar's gardeners used heavy straw matting to protect fragile plants from the bitter winds and devised a variety of ingenious means to warm the air and ground. But rare fruits and flowers were not the only new and curious attractions to be found in Aleksei's vast gardens. There also was Russia's first zoological exhibit, with wild beasts and rare birds of all sorts, and an herb garden in which rare foreign medicinal plants intermixed with the more common Russian ones. There were smaller gardens for courtly relaxation and amusement, including a hanging garden, a French garden, and a labyrinth. Elsewhere there were a number of other monuments to Western technology, including windmills and a glassworks. And there were monuments to Russian ingenuity as well. Thousands of peasants brought in from other Romanov estates saw their grain threshed by an air-driven machine a Russian mechanic had put together.[55] Like so many of the great technological discoveries made in the Romanovs' Russia, the thresher was never put into production or general use; typical of his countrymen, Aleksei Mikhailovich regarded many technological achievements as marvelous curiosities, but never considered that they could have a broader, more "practical" application.

There was much at Izmailovo that conflicted with Muscovite tradition. Yet the most significant departure from the past was the least tangible and the most difficult to document and measure. At Izmailovo, there was a sense of progress, of movement, of invention. It was a place where things were not supposed to remain unchanged, a place where life was expected to be different a decade hence than it was today. Izmailovo stood for an interest in science, in technology, in progress, all three of which were antithetical to the Church-dominated, tradition-centered culture that had characterized the first half-century of Romanov rule in Russia.

If the new Izmailovo stood as a precursor to that adulation of Western technology that Peter the Great would impose upon Russians, Aleksei Mikhailovich's second suburban estate, the rebuilt and greatly expanded Kolomenskoe, stood for the gaiety and frivolity of the West's achievements. At Kolomenskoe, Aleksei Mikhailovich built a vast new palace for his young Tsarina Natalia. He opened it to the light with some three thousand mica windows and filled it with Western furniture and mirrors. The foreign observer Jakob Reutenfels wrote that "thanks to its carved decoration set off by brilliant gilding, it is of such a remarkable sort that it seems as if it had just been taken out of a jewelry chest."[56] There were, of course, icons in their proper places, but on the palace's walls also hung proud portraits of such worldly heroes as Julius Caesar, Alexander the Great, the great Persian King Darius, and a number of others. In an early tribute to Russian craftsmen's talent for putting technology to frivolous but fascinating uses, there were two large mechanical lions of gilded copper and sheepskin that were able to roar, roll their eyes, and move their jaws when a servant squeezed a pair of hidden bellows. Outside the palace, more than five thousand fruit trees and bushes filled some one hundred fifty acres of gardens. From them the Tsarina's servants prepared those exotic fruit wines and brandies that always graced the royal table. In one of his many poems, Simeon Polotskii called Kolomenskoe the eighth wonder of the world.[57] It was hardly that to those worldly Europeans who were watching Louis XIV's magnificent Versailles rise before them, but certainly it was a wonder to Russians who still regarded any sort of reasonably complex technology as nothing short of miraculous. Kolomenskoe stood for a world most of them had never seen and had only just begun to think about.

The decor and design of Kolomenskoe symbolized Aleksei's attempt to add Western elements to Russia's culture in a manner that would modernize, not destroy, it. He seemed to sense that the modern Western ways might easily swallow up their more medieval Russian counterparts if the two were brought into direct confrontation. Unlike his revolutionary son Peter the Great, he sought to integrate the Western experience into a Russian framework rather than permit tradition to be overwhelmed. His effort was made easier because much of the Western influence that reached Moscow in the 1670s came by way of Poland and had become somewhat Slavicized before the Tsar and his contemporaries were obliged to come to grips with it. Indeed, Polish influence at the Russian Court increased markedly during the 1670s and reached a peak during the reign of Aleksei Mikhailovich's elder son, Tsar Feodor, who spoke Polish fluently, favored Polish styles and fashions, and chose a bride who was part Polish. Feodor's interest in things Polish brought Russians their first sustained view of Western life through translations of Polish versions of Western heroic tales. The *Tale of Melusine* and the *Tale of Otto,* both of them widely read French romances dating from the fourteenth and sixteenth centuries, were translated from Polish into Russian in the 1670s. They circulated widely, but only in manuscript copies, probably because Moscow's patriarchal printing press would not publish such works. Both tales told of noble princes who ruled distant lands and of lovely maidens who were rescued from danger by virtuous and heroic knights. In doing so, they opened to Russians a world that seemed as exciting and exotic as the Russian world seemed to Europeans. These romances so captured the imagination of the aristocrats who read them that one of Feodor's sisters even arranged for a shortened version of Otto's tale to be performed in the Kremlin's new theatre.[58]

The view of Western life that Russians drew from these early romances was not, of course, of the contemporary European scene but of a romantic, chivalrous one that had long since passed into oblivion. They therefore presented no direct cultural or social challenge to Feodor's Russia. Nonetheless, they violated the Church's proscription against secular literature, art, and theatre. Especially in the context of greater Polish influence, these translations added another dimension to the attack against the Church's conservatism that Aleksei Mikhailovich first had launched in the 1660s. This attack gained a serious intellectual dimension during the regency of Sofia, when she raised her lover, Prince Vasilii Golitsyn, to a position of great authority in Russia. As Sofia's most cherished cultural and intellectual model, Golitsyn personified Russians' first serious efforts to enter into the mainstream of Western philosophical and political thought, come to grips with its principles, and apply them to Russian conditions without destroying the cultural and social precepts that underlay the society in which they lived. Golitsyn had become convinced that Russia must abandon her medieval mores and take up the modernism of the West. Concerned not to disrupt Russian life, he sought a more balanced, gradual means to achieve the ends that Peter the Great attempted to gain by driving his subjects forward in a relentless and brutal fashion. Golitsyn lauded reason and moderation as the two greatest allies of progress. Peter preferred the raw force of his unfettered autocratic will.

Prince Vasilii Golitsyn was easily the best-educated minister to serve any Romanov in the seventeenth century. Portraits show that he was a striking figure of a man, with wide-set eyes, a high forehead, and a firm jaw. In an age when the Church decreed that beards should be worn long and full (because man was made in God's image and to cut the beard defiled that image), Golitsyn wore a well-shaped moustache and a closely trimmed beard. One famous portrait in Moscow's Historical Museum shows him holding one of his treasured books, with others piled on a table that was obviously of Western design. Golitsyn spoke Greek, Polish, and especially Latin with an ease that amazed European visitors, and he was knowledgeable about Western European politics. Adrien de la Neuville, a contemporary French observer who arrived in Moscow at the beginning of 1689, tells us that Golitsyn discussed the English Revolution of 1688 with him in considerable detail, although it had occurred only a few months before. His library contained what was easily the largest collection of Western European books and manuscripts in all of Russia, and he was known to have read them with care.[59] Even more than Matveev, who preferred Western culture but followed a very Russian political course, Golitsyn wanted to integrate Russia into Europe's political order.

Unlike his predecessors and contemporaries, Golitsyn lived in a grand European manner that shocked Russians and astounded the Europeans who visited him. Although his information was admittedly fragmentary, the great nineteenth-century historian Vasilii Kliuchevskii reconstructed what is still the best portrait we have of Golitsyn's Moscow palace, and it is clear that it was a work of art as out of place in the Moscow of the 1680s as a Baroque silver tea service would have been in Boonesboro, Kentucky, a century later. "In his spacious Moscow home, which foreigners considered one of the most magnificent in Europe, everything was arranged according to the European style," Kliuchevskii wrote. "In the great halls, the wall space between the windows was adorned with large mirrors. Along the walls were hung paintings, portraits of Russian and foreign monarchs, and German geographical maps in gilded frames. On the ceiling was painted the planetary system, and a quantity of clocks and thermometers of artistic design completed the rooms' decoration." Yet Golitsyn's palace showed not only the extent of his westernization but also his acknowledgment of its limitations. He was convinced that before his and Russia's westernization could go beyond simple borrowings of technology and decoration, it was necessary to understand the West in intellectual and political terms. "Golitsyn's palace was a meeting place for educated foreigners who turned up in Moscow," Kliuchevskii added. "His hospitality surpassed that of those other pro-Western Muscovites, and he even received Jesuits, whom no one else could tolerate."[60]

Golitsyn was somewhat more of a dreamer than a man of deeds, and much of what he is said to have planned for Russia has come down to us only in the remarks of his contemporaries, since his personal papers seem not to have survived the turmoil of Sofia's fall in 1689. Still, it seems clear that he hoped to reform and modernize Russia's army, establish regular diplomatic relations with the countries of Western Europe, and grant Russians freedom to worship and think as they pleased. He hoped to educate Russians in the West, foster economic development along the lines already taken by Europe, and free his country's millions of serfs. He discussed his ambitious program with knowledgeable men in Moscow's Foreign Quarter, considered their comments, and pondered volumes of Western political theory.[61] Yet, conditions in Russia were too volatile, and his own position too uncertain, for him to work toward the goals he envisioned. Long before Golitsyn even began to draft his ideas into concrete reform plans, the young Tsar Peter drove Sofia from the Kremlin, and her lover fell with her.

Golitsyn's fall, and Peter's accession in 1689, meant that Russians would embark upon an era of social and cultural transformation that would leave her citizens reeling from shock and bewilderment. For the next half-century, Russians would grope their way, seeking that less tumultuous path that had almost been found but had so quickly been lost sight of. When they finally emerged from the Petrine upheavals and began to walk with surer steps once again, it was along a very different path and through a very different world than any of the seventeenth-century Romanovs had envisioned.

CHAPTER III

The Politics of Muscovy

"The Russian land is ruled by the mercy of God, the grace of the most pure Mother of God, the prayers of all the Saints, with the blessings of our parents and, finally, by us, its sovereign," Ivan the Terrible once wrote.[1] During the hundred years or so before the Romanovs came to power, Russians came to see their country as the land upon which God had bestowed his special grace and favor. Moscow for them became heir to the fallen Roman and Byzantine empires and the last hope for the salvation of mankind, undefiled by the Roman Catholic apostasy in the West and still secure against the infidel Turk in the East. The Tsar's very title, which Ivan the Terrible took at his coronation, came from the Caesar of Byzantium, who had fallen before the Turks' onslaught in 1453.

For men consumed by medieval prejudice, the belief that Moscow was the Third and last Rome was of great import, for it promised one last chance at salvation in a world where heresy and impiety raged unchecked, where men and women had forgotten God and given themselves up to the pursuit of earthly pleasures and eternal sins. The Tsar not only controlled the life and death of his people, but had the even more awesome power of salvation and damnation. He, and he alone, became the arbiter of what was forbidden and what was permitted among the Russian faithful. Ivan the Terrible therefore could admit the first English merchants ever to enter Russia's domains and, at the same time, insist that Russia was superior to all other nations in the grand design of universal history, even though the foreigners represented a state that clearly was superior in terms of military power and technology.

But even Russians' conviction that they were God's chosen people and that Russia was "a new Israel"[2] did not allow them to pass through the Time of Troubles unscathed. As Swedish and Polish armies, and the Scottish and German mercenaries who fought in their ranks, defiled Russia's land, her churches, her women, and her honor, Russians were forced to realize how much foreigners looked down upon them and, even, despised them.

Europeans' disdain and the humiliation of defeats on the battlefield were not the only injuries Russians suffered during the Time of Troubles. The King of Sweden led his armies into Russia's northern lands, regained all of the territories won by Tsar Boris Godunov's armies a decade earlier, and occupied the great commercial center of Novgorod in Russia's northwest. At the same time, Polish armies marched east and occupied all of the West Russian lands between the Polish border and Moscow itself. When Mikhail Romanov became Tsar of All the Russias in 1613, tens of thousands of square miles of lands that had been a part of Ivan the Terrible's domains had been seized by foreign armies. Russia's economy lay in shambles, and the national treasury stood nearly empty. The seventeenth-century Romanovs would be obliged to marshal all of Russia's domestic resources for the great and glorious task of winning back her lost lands.

First of all, Tsar Mikhail had to restore order to those domains that lay within Russia's shrunken borders, for brigands and Cossacks still roamed the fields and forests, seizing food and treasure as they went. From their island strongholds in the lower reaches of Russia's great rivers, the Cossacks ranged far and wide, especially in times of social and political crisis, when their ranks were swollen by army deserters, escaped criminals, and fugitive serfs. Superb horsemen and expert sailors, they were equally at home on the great rivers of the Ukraine and southern Russia or on the vast steppes through which the rivers had cut their way hundreds of centuries earlier. They paid homage to no prince, be he Russian, Turk, or Pole, and took intense pride in being masters of their own destiny.

Yet the refusal of the Cossacks to bow before temporal lords did not prevent them from entering the service of those sovereigns who bestowed the proper gifts upon them, or won their favor in some other manner. During the Time of Troubles, groups of Cossacks therefore had served several masters, and, although a large number of them had supported Mikhail Romanov's election, there were others who favored different candidates. The Cossack General Ivan Zarutskii, whose detachments had supported Tsar Vasilii Shuiskii, the Polish King Sigismund, and the False Dmitrii's wife Marina between 1610 and 1612, openly opposed Mikhail Romanov's government after his election in 1613. Together with Marina and her infant son, Zarutskii retreated to Astrakhan and began to plan a campaign to destroy the new Romanov government, summoning all Cossacks to join him in a march upon Moscow. Should they support him, Zarutskii might well sweep up the Volga to Kazan and then launch a whirlwind cavalry attack westward into the heart of Old Russia to the very walls of the Kremlin.[3] Mikhail faced the real possibility of losing his throne even before the ancient crown of Monomakh had been placed upon his brow.

Mikhail was young and inexperienced, but he had a valuable ally in the *zemskii sobor* that had elected him and that he had kept in session in Moscow to give him advice and support. Recognizing that Zarutskii commanded only a fragment of the Don Cossacks, the Tsar and his Assembly of the Land bestowed lavish gifts of gunpowder, lead, vodka, food, and a special charter of privileges upon the rest. In return, most of the Don Host swore to support Mikhail and urged other branches of the Cossack brotherhood on the Volga, Terek, and Iaik rivers to join them. Gifts similar to those bestowed upon the Don Cossacks won them to Mikhail's cause. By the spring of 1614, Zarutskii stood alone, abandoned by his allies, and surrounded by hostile armies. At the end of June, the Iaik Cossacks seized him, Marina, and her son, and sent them under heavy guard to Moscow with strict orders that they be slain on the spot if any sympathizers attempted to free them. Marina was imprisoned in a convent, where she soon died from grief at seeing her eight-year-old son hanged. At Mikhail's order, Zarutskii was taken to the scaffold, bound hand and foot, and left standing with a sharpened stake driven deep into his bowels. Eventually the pain and loss of blood weakened him so that he collapsed, forcing the fixed upright stake upward into his lungs and heart.[4]

Once Mikhail had restored a modicum of order to the turbulent Russian land, he and the *zemskii sobor* were free to resume the struggle against those Swedish and Polish armies that remained on Russian soil. Because the Poles were occupied with problems at home, they at first contented themselves with minor operations in Russia and left Mikhail to focus his attention upon the Swedes who remained in Novgorod and northern Russia. Mikhail's armies were unable to fight more than a holding action against the Swedes, but they were aided by a doughty population that had grown weary of strife and Swedish oppression. Following the path of passive resistance that has always served them so well, masses of Russian peasants slipped away from the regions under Swedish occupation. Silently, they disappeared into the area's vast forests and made their way south to Romanov territory, leaving the Swedes to govern depopulated provinces from which they could collect neither taxes nor recruits.[5] In the city of Novgorod, all but a handful of Russian citizens swore to oppose the Swedish yoke. "The Novgorodians value their independence so highly, they are so inspired by the idea of having their own Russian tsar, that they are ready to sacrifice their life for it," wrote Swedish General Horn to King Gustavus Adolphus in December 1614. Ominously, he added, "an example of their attitude toward us is that after harvesting they immediately burn all straw in order to deprive the Swedes of fodder for their horses. Hay is unobtainable. In two months our last horses will die. Many men are dying too."[6]

Faced by the sullen hatred of the Russians subject to his control and the frustrating fact that, although they suffered no great defeats, his armies won no resounding victories, Gustavus Adolphus agreed to peace negotiations in October 1615. John Merrick, an ambassador especially appointed by the English King James I "to intercede betwixt [Sweden and Russia] . . . and conclude such a peace between them as may binde uppe all their former dissentions in amity and love,"[7] played a crucial role in mediating between the two enemies. Largely due to Merrick's persistence, the Peace of Stolbovo was signed in February 1617. It was a far better treaty than Mikhail had any reason to expect. Thanks to Merrick's willingness to press Russia's demands upon the Swedes in the hope that Mikhail and his advisers in turn might grant further trading concessions to the English Muscovy Company, the Russians regained Novgorod and its surrounding territories, although they could not avoid surrendering Karelia and Ingria, their foothold on the Baltic, to Sweden.[8]

The armistice of 1615 and the Peace of Stolbovo that followed just a year later saved Mikhail from facing a hopeless two-front war with Sweden and Poland. In the summer of 1616, the Polish *Sejm* (National Assembly) voted the funds for a new campaign against Russia, as King Sigismund III swore to drive Mikhail from the Kremlin, place his son Władysław on the throne, and conclude a permanent union between Russia and the Polish-Lithuanian Commonwealth.[9] Even more than in his struggle with Sweden, Mikhail had to stem the Polish tide or lose his throne. At first, his chances appeared slim, as several key Russian border forts fell to the invaders. As has always been the case in their history, Russians fought more valiantly on their own soil, and, as the Poles drove deeper into Muscovite territory, Russian resistance stiffened. Early in the winter of 1617, Polish attacks against Kaluga, Tver, and Mozhaisk all were driven back by stalwart Russian defenders. By late 1617, Mikhail had gained enough confidence in his armies to refuse Sigismund's offer of peace negotiations, and the war remained stalemated for the next nine months. The next fall, however, the Poles regrouped and attacked in force with a two-pronged thrust that reached the walls of Moscow itself. As he had done in 1612, Prince Pozharskii rallied the Russians in Moscow's defense. For hours, vicious hand-to-hand fighting raged in the city's narrow streets, as the Russians defended five inner city gates against the invaders' assault. Finally, the Poles fell back and broke into retreat. By that time, Sigismund was embroiled in the recently begun Thirty Years' War and needed his armies to fight in the West. Convinced by the defeat at Moscow's gates that a continued war with Russia would be a long one, he again proposed peace negotiations; this time Mikhail agreed. On the day before Christmas 1618, they signed the Armistice of Deulino. Mikhail and Sigismund agreed to halt their conflict for fourteen and a half years, and the Poles released Mikhail's father, Filaret, from his long captivity. Yet Sigismund returned none of Russia's western lands and remained steadfast in his refusal to recognize Mikhail as Russia's Tsar.[10] Although the Romanovs would have to fight further wars with Poland, as they would with Sweden, the achievements of Mikhail's first decade of war and diplomacy were far from inconsequential. He had won back Novgorod and had gained for himself and Russia a desperately needed, albeit uneasy, peace with two of his greatest enemies.

Now that there was peace, some means had to be found to increase state revenues, since the government tottered on the brink of bankruptcy. "The *streltsy* and Cossacks," Mikhail had lamented in 1613, "cannot continue in Our service because of their great impoverishment. We have no funds in Our treasury, no grain in Our storehouses, and thus have nothing with which to pay the men in Our service."[11] In what would become a traditional Romanov response to setbacks in the West, Mikhail and Filaret turned toward the East for solutions. Siberia, with its immensely rich fur trade, would yield up the wealth to finance Russia's much-needed reconstruction after the Time of Troubles. Gold from the sale of tens of thousands of ermine, sable, lynx, otter, and marten pelts began to fill the Kremlin's near-empty coffers.

By 1624 Romanov agents were collecting some forty-five thousand rubles from the fur trade annually, and, by the time of Mikhail's death in 1645, the income had risen by almost two hundred and fifty percent. Since most of this income came from a tithe they imposed upon trappers and fur traders, it is obvious that the quantity of furs taken out of Siberia in the seventeenth century must have been immense. The animal population in western Siberia was depleted so significantly that the center of pelt-gathering activity was driven more than a thousand miles eastward in the brief span of a quarter-century.[12]

Although life in Russia remained far from easy throughout the seventeenth century, the return of many peasants to the northern and central regions was striking evidence that Mikhail's and Filaret's reconstruction policies enjoyed some success. As noted earlier, perhaps as much as one-third of Great Russia's population had been lost to the ravages of war, famine, plague, and flight during the Time of Troubles. By the late 1620s, however, the population levels in the region around Moscow had begun to return to the levels of the 1590s. These would be somewhat reduced when peasants again fled famine and cattle plague in 1630,[13] but the speed with which the peasants had returned in the brief span of years since Mikhail's accession indicated that the Romanovs' policies were bringing some measure of stability to central Russia. It was at about this time that Russian peasants began to show a marked preference for living in communities rather than in isolated homesteads or tiny hamlets, perhaps for the feeling of protection it afforded them.[14]

The fragile foreign and domestic peace that Mikhail and Filaret established in the decade after 1619 was destined to be painfully short-lived. The Deulino armistice was due to expire in 1632, and there was no chance that it could be renewed or converted into a full-fledged peace. Both Mikhail and his Polish adversaries were anxious for war, and, this time, he was better prepared. Soon after Filaret had returned from Poland, he had urged his son to recruit foreign army officers to train Russia's army, and, with the advice of a number of high-ranking European officers, most of them Scottish or English, they had begun a broad effort to modernize the army's organization and equipment. General Mikhail Shein, a great *boiar* who had won fame throughout Russia and Eastern Europe for his valiant defense of Smolensk against the Polish invaders during the last years of the Time of Troubles, played the most active role in these efforts.

Not long before Minin and Pozharskii had freed Moscow in 1612, Shein had been captured by the Poles and, along with Filaret, had remained their captive until the Deulino armistice. Impressed by Shein's military genius, the Poles had been reluctant to free him even then and had done so only after forcing him to swear a sacred oath never to take up arms against them. Shein's oath at first posed no dilemma for him because Russia and Poland remained at peace for the next fourteen years. For most of that time, he directed the Kremlin's Artillery Department and supported Mikhail's newly hired European officers in their efforts to reorganize the Russian army. In doing so, he incurred the hatred of many senior Russian army officers. As Shein well knew, the Russians most of all needed training in the use of firearms, and they needed to be drilled in that precision and discipline that the massed use of clumsy and slow-firing muskets required. But Russians tended to resist such discipline. Adam Olearius remarked in 1633 that even the elite *streltsy* performed musket drill "without the slightest semblance of order, as if each wanted to be the first to finish" and noted with some apprehension that one of their salutes "was executed so carelessly that the secretary to the Swedish Resident, who was standing by us watching the ceremony, had a large hole torn in his jacket."[15] If Europeans found it difficult to drill Russia's infantry, Shein had more success in his efforts to modernize the artillery. Under his direction, the Moscow Cannon Foundry began to use waterpower and to turn out sizable numbers of cannon ranging from very small half pounders to long-range and heavy twenty-six pounders. Thanks to Shein's efforts, when war with Poland broke out, Russia had a modern train of artillery to use against the enemy.[16]

Like Filaret, Shein urged that Russia attack Poland when the armistice ended in order to recapture those West Russian lands the Poles had seized during the Time of Troubles. When war began late in 1632, he won command of Russia's armies. Shein's first great objective was to drive the Poles from Smolensk, to avenge that surrender into which he had been forced after months of heroic defense. This time, his failure would be resounding. At the siege of Smolensk, Shein faced a myriad of problems. Not all of them were of his own making, but he was obliged to bear the blame for them all. When he advanced against the city, it was garrisoned by a skeleton force of between twelve and fifteen hundred Polish troops. Knowing the Poles' weakness, Shein had not brought heavy and slow-moving siege artillery from Moscow but had raced forward in hopes of launching a surprise assault. He should have known better, for he had constructed the nearly impregnable fortifications at Smolensk himself. In a spirited defense, the Poles held the walls of Smolensk against Shein's attack. Unable to sustain further losses, he withdrew to await his siege artillery. By the time it arrived some three months later, it was more than counterbalanced by the Poles' reinforcements.[17]

In April, May, and June 1633, Shein battered Smolensk's walls with his siege guns, but could not take the fortress, for the Poles greeted his men with massed cannon fire whenever they poured through a new breach. Shein finally settled down to a classic and time-consuming siege operation, much to the delight of his many enemies in Moscow, who deluged Mikhail with whispers that the *boiar* general's failure to take Smolensk bordered upon treason. When Poland's new King Władysław IV arrived to raise the siege in the fall of 1633, the whispers in the Kremlin grew louder, especially after Shein's protector and friend of many years, Patriarch Filaret, died at the beginning of October. Because Shein's soldiers were in need of supplies, weapons, and, above all, reinforcements to offset the twenty-five thousand Cossacks and Poles that Władysław had brought from Poland, he warned the Tsar that they would be forced to surrender if more troops did not arrive. "You can tell all of your soldiers that the expected reinforcements are on the way, that they soon can expect help against the enemies against whom they have stood so bravely and resolutely," Mikhail replied.[18] But Filaret's death had thrown Russia's government into a turmoil that bordered on paralysis. The reinforcements never arrived, and Shein's troops continued to be depleted by disease and battle losses. To make matters worse, his foreign advisers began to quarrel among themselves. The Scottish Colonel Leslie accused the English Colonel Sanderson of betraying his plans to the Poles, drew a pistol, and shot him dead in front of Shein's very eyes. Finally, Shein had no choice left. He surrendered his starving, freezing, outnumbered army to the Poles on condition that he and his men be allowed to return to Moscow; Władysław required them to leave their artillery behind. When Shein reached the Kremlin, he was arrested, tried for treason, found guilty, and beheaded.[19] Fortunately for Mikhail, his other commanders did not repeat Shein's failures, and Władysław was not able to follow up his victory at Smolensk with others. Because the Turks were about to launch a campaign against the south of Poland, Władysław agreed to peace. Mikhail had to pay an indemnity of twenty thousand rubles and recognize Władysław's claim to Smolensk and a number of other West Russian lands. On his part, Władysław recognized Mikhail's claim to the Russian throne and hailed him as Russia's legitimate sovereign.

During the Smolensk War, several groups of Cossacks had fought on the side of Russia and of Poland, and their shifting allegiances were an important factor in complicating the Romanovs' foreign policy in the decades between the 1620s and 1660s. The central question was whether Russia or Poland would rule the Ukraine, a land of rich soil and bountiful grain harvests, through which flowed the greatest waterways of Eastern Europe: the Dniestr, South Bug, and Dniepr rivers. The dispute about the Ukraine was made more complex because Poland relied upon the Ukrainian Cossacks to play a major role in the defense of her southern frontier against Turk or Tatar raids, while the Russians had other Cossacks on the Don and the Volga to serve that function. The Poles thus lost no opportunity to turn the Ukrainian Cossacks against Russia. Ukrainian Cossacks played major roles in Sigismund's attack against Moscow in 1617 and in Władysław's victory over Shein at Smolensk. Yet the Cossacks were devout Russian Orthodox Christians, and that fact ultimately inclined them toward the Romanovs, as the equally devout Roman Catholic Poles began to pursue an increasingly anti-Orthodox policy in the seventeenth century. After the Smolensk War ended, the Poles also attempted to increase their political control over the Ukrainian Cossacks, and that policy sparked a rebellion in 1637 that would be crushed only by fifteen thousand crack Polish regulars under the command of General Mikołaj Potocki.[20] Two major consequences of Potocki's victory were that a large number of Ukrainian Cossacks fled to Southern Russia and that an unknown man by the name of Bogdan Khmelnitskii rose to a prominent position among those who remained behind. Both events would be of major significance in the lives and policies of Mikhail Romanov and his son, Tsar Aleksei Mikhailovich.

When the Ukrainian Cossacks rebelled against the Poles, the Don Cossacks, generally loyal to the Romanovs since 1612, had launched an expedition against the Turkish fortress of Azov, which commanded the mouth of the Don River. On June 18, 1637, some forty-four hundred Cossacks stormed the fortress and, despite losses of more than one thousand, overwhelmed the Turks' defenses and drove them from the city. In a raging fury at the loss of so many comrades, the Cossacks killed every Moslem within the walls, freed all the Christian slaves they could find, and seized thousands of rubles' worth of booty.[21] Fearful of Turkish reprisals against his domains, Tsar Mikhail hastened to disavow the Cossacks' action and publicly criticized them for killing an envoy the Turks had sent to their camp before the battle. Even when the Sultan ordered his Crimean Tatar allies to invade southern Russia in retaliation, Mikhail remained unmoved to support the Cossacks' cause.

Mikhail's refusal to send reinforcements and supplies to the Don Cossacks made them doubly overjoyed when hundreds of Ukrainian Cossacks, driven from their homes by Potocki's victorious advance, joined them at Azov.[22] These men and their women provided much-needed reinforcements for the depleted Cossack units within the fortress. More came during the next three years, possibly a major factor in the Cossacks' victory when the Turks returned in force in the spring of 1641. Throughout the summer, more than thirty thousand Turks besieged the fortress using massed artillery to batter the walls and hundreds of sappers to dig beneath them. Inside the walls, somewhat fewer than ten thousand Cossacks, including about eight hundred women, fought with unmatched fury. One out of every three died during the three-month siege, but they killed more than six thousand Turks and wounded thousands of others. At the end of September, the Turks retreated. For the moment, the Cossacks remained in proud possession of the great fortress.[23]

Although flushed by their victory, the Cossacks realized that, even with further recruits from among their Ukrainian brethren, they would eventually be overwhelmed by the Turks. They therefore offered Azov to Mikhail with the request that it be incorporated into Russia's domains. It was a tempting prospect, for it would bring to Mikhail's side a number of native allies in Russia's south and would open to Russian merchants river access to the Sea of Azov and the Black Sea beyond. But to accept the fortress meant certain war with the Ottoman Empire and its Tatar allies in the Crimea. Unwilling to take such a risk on his own initiative, Mikhail summoned a *zemskii sobor*. A majority of its members urged him to accept the Cossacks' offer.[24] Yet Mikhail still feared to do so. His government had not yet fully recovered from the ruinous costs of the Smolensk War, the peace with Poland was so fragile that he feared the Poles might strike across his western frontiers if he committed his forces to a war against the Turks, and, even if the Poles respected the peace, the Ottoman Empire was a formidable adversary. Perhaps equally important, although only in his mid-forties, Mikhail was beginning to feel the approach of death as his many illnesses sapped his strength. Certainly, he did not want to risk leaving a devastating war as his major bequest to his only son, the teen-aged

Aleksei Mikhailovich. Mikhail therefore ordered the Cossacks to abandon Azov, which they did only with reluctance and a sense of betrayal. But when the time came for them to decide between Russia and Poland somewhat more than a decade later, they chose Russia and the Romanovs.

The leading figure in bringing the Ukrainian Cossacks and their lands into the Romanovs' hands was Bodgan Khmelnitskii, Hetman of the Cossacks and a devout Orthodox Christian. Khmelnitskii had been born around 1595 to parents who stood high in the Ukrainian Cossack hierarchy. For the times in which he lived he was immensely well educated, for he had studied at a university and knew Latin and Polish in addition to his native language. When he was in his mid-twenties, Khmelnitskii was captured by the Turks and lived among them for more than two years, while his widowed mother struggled to raise his ransom. He returned to his family estate in 1623, wiser in the ways of intrigue and politics and fluent in Turkish and Tatar. During the next fifteen years, Khmelnitskii rose within the Cossack ranks. When Potocki suppressed the revolt of 1637, he appointed the young Cossack lord to a prominent post. It was Potocki's firm expectation that the urbane, well-educated Khmelnitskii would serve as an effective ally in bringing his people more fully under Polish control. But Khmelnitskii was first of all a Cossack, a Ukrainian, and an Orthodox Christian. In 1648 he and his Cossacks once again rose in open rebellion against their Polish lords, and Potocki once again marched to crush them. This time, Potocki was too confident. Many of his troops succumbed to Khmelnitskii's personal magnetism and deserted to serve his cause. Soon Potocki found himself surrounded and badly outnumbered by the Cossacks and their Tatar allies. After a series of brutal battles in which his son and many of his loyal officers were killed, Potocki was taken prisoner. Haughty and defiant even in defeat, he was brought before Khmelnitskii. Unmindful of his personal safety and enraged that the man he had thought an ally had turned against him, he berated the Cossack lord in front of his men. "Boor! With what wilt thou pay the Tatars [for their aid]?" he asked in derision. Perhaps remembering the fate he once had suffered when he had fought on the side of the Poles, Khmelnitskii calmly replied, "With thee and thy like," and turned Potocki and his senior officers over to his allies to be held for ransom.[25]

Khmelnitskii's victory over Potocki brought more bloodshed to the Ukraine. Peasants and townsmen throughout the region took his success as a signal to rise and massacre their Polish lords. Their actions were further encouraged by the widespread upheavals that flared all over Eastern Europe at the time. Aleksei Mikhailovich faced the salt riots in Moscow and grain riots in Pskov and Novgorod. In the Ukraine, and in adjacent regions of Poland, the Cossacks plundered indiscriminately and perpetrated what one scholar has called "the single greatest massacre of Jews prior to Hitler."[26] Cursing the Jews as "Christ killers," the Cossacks hunted them down and butchered them with heartless abandon. The best estimates are that some two hundred thousand Jews, or about 35 percent of all those in Eastern Europe, were murdereded by the Cossacks and their peasant allies in 1648 and 1649.[27] Obviously, such upheaval could not continue unchecked. To restore some semblance of order, and to prepare for the inevitable war against Poland, Khmelnitskii attempted to "Cossackify" the Ukraine. The masses responded to his call with an enthusiasm that even he had not foreseen. "Everyone turned Cossack," wrote a contemporary.[28] Thus began almost twenty years of bitter fighting between Cossack and Pole, which brought about a formal union between Russia and the Ukraine and launched Russia into the long and bitter First Northern War with Poland. Not until 1667 would Russians and Cossacks be at peace with the Poles.

Ever since his accession in 1645, Tsar Aleksei Mikhailovich had followed closely the progress of Bogdan Khmelnitskii's struggle against the Poles. After some hesitation, he brought the matter to the attention of a specially summoned *zemskii sobor* in 1651 and, at the same time, sought the advice of the Patriarch Iosif about Khmelnitskii's petition that his people be allowed to enter a Russian protectorate. Opinion for and against such a union was about evenly divided in Church and government circles at the time, and the result was that neither *zemskii sobor* nor Patriarch took a clear-cut position on the matter.[29] During the next two years, however, opinion in Moscow shifted dramatically in favor of a break with Poland and a union of Russia and the Ukraine. The new Patriarch Nikon favored closer ties with the Ukraine, and the Poles refused to make amends for the grievances Aleksei Mikhailovich had presented to them two years earlier. As a result, Aleksei Mikhailovich decided to grant Khmelnitskii's request, to take the Ukrainian Cossacks "under the great arm of the Sovereign" in the language of the day, even though it might well mean war with Poland. To Khmelnitskii, he wrote, "our military forces are assembling in accordance with Our Sovereign Tsarist order, and the militia also is assembling."[30]

To give his decision the highest validity, Aleksei Mikhailovich summoned a *zemskii sobor*. Throughout the spring and summer of 1653, delegates were elected from among the townsmen, merchants, nobles, great *boiars,* and regular army officers. They assembled, as the Tsar had ordered, on October 1 within the Italianate walls of the great Palace of Facets in the Kremlin. The Patriarch Nikon, the Metropolitan of Serbia, and Russia's greatest church lords were there. So, too, were all the members of the great *Boiar* Council and all the elected representatives. Of all the assemblies of the seventeenth century, this one was to make the most momentous decision of any since the one that had elected Mikhail Romanov to the Russian throne. First, they discussed how the Poles had violated the treaty of 1634. Then they considered Khmelnitskii's petition. Unanimously, the *zemskii sobor* urged Aleksei Mikhailovich not only to accept the Ukrainian Cossacks' request for a protectorate but also to break diplomatic relations with Poland. On October 9, Aleksei Mikhailovich sent a delegation of great Muscovite notables to tell Khmelnitskii of the decision.[31]

When Aleksei Mikhailovich's delegation reached Khmelnitskii's headquarters at Periaslavl, the Cossack chieftain summoned a general assembly in the town's central square. He spoke to his people of the great trials they had borne since they had broken with Poland six years before. "We now see that we can no longer live without a Tsar," he proclaimed. Already confident of their reply, he posed the fateful question to the masses of Cossacks assembled before him. Would they choose to be ruled by the Tatar Khan of the Crimea, the Turkish Sultan, the King of Poland, or the Tsar of All the Russias? The first two rulers, he hastened to remind his listeners, were Moslems, and hardly sympathetic to Orthodox Christians. The King of Poland not only was a Roman Catholic but he already had subjected them to great tribulations and abuse. The answer came back with resounding conviction from his listeners: "We choose the Eastern [Russian] Tsar, the Orthodox one."[32] The Ukraine and its Cossacks had become a part of Russia. It was an event of the greatest historical significance; in the struggle between Russian and Pole that had dominated the vast steppes of Eastern Europe for more than a century, the balance of power shifted decisively to Russia's side. As the great Professor Vernadsky once wrote, "the foundation was laid for the eventual transformation of the Tsardom of Moscow into the Russian Empire."[33]

In some ways, it would be the most costly territorial acquisition Russia ever made. Boldly, Aleksei Mikhailovich entered into the First Northern War with Poland to defend his annexation. Thirteen years later, half of the Ukraine was his. But, in addition to untold amounts of treasure, the war directly and indirectly would cost the lives of one-third of all the population of Great Russia.[34]

The war began in the spring of 1654 with three Russian armies and one Ukrainian Cossack force advancing against Poland and Lithuania. Aleksei Mikhailovich himself led the main Russian force against Smolensk, the objective that had cost Shein his reputation and his head two decades before. Aleksei Mikhailovich commanded far greater resources than had Shein, and the local peasants gave him their wholehearted support in a manner enjoyed by no previous Russian sovereign. "The peasants are extremely hostile to us," wrote a Polish observer. "Everywhere, they submit to the Tsar's authority and do even greater damage to us than do the forces of Moscow." Ominously, the Polish reports predicted that "this evil will spread further."[35] At first, the Poles and Lithuanians fought desperately for their King and their faith; nowhere was this more evident than at Smolensk itself. Russian casualties in the attack can be estimated as high as seven thousand killed with more than twice that number wounded. "Our soldiers attacked bravely and scaled the tower and the walls," Aleksei wrote in a letter to his sisters describing an assault against one of the thirty-four bastions that rose above the fortifications of the city. "More than two hundred Lithuanians were killed, and our soldiers had some three hundred killed and upwards of a thousand wounded."[36] Smolensk fell in September, and the Tsar's victorious armies took the fortress town

of Vitebsk less than two months later. After that, the towns and fortresses of Belorussia opened their gates to the approaching tsarist armies. Within a few months, thirty-three towns and fortresses had
surrendered to the Russians.[37] No Russian Tsar had led his armies with
such success since Dmitrii Donskoi had defeated the Tatars at Kulikovo
Field some three centuries before.

Despite these victories, the campaign of 1654 had a very dark and
tragic side for Russian and Ukrainian alike. While Aleksei Mikhailovich
enjoyed great success at the front, the plague struck his rear. Moscow
and much of central Russia were decimated by its fury. Estimates are that
something over three-quarters of a million Russians died in the space
of a few months. The virulence of the disease is indicated by the fact
that fatalities usually exceeded fifty percent of those who contracted it;
often the deaths were dramatically more numerous than even that astronomical figure. No one kept records of fatalities among the masses
at that time, but those special instances in which figures were kept indicate appalling losses. Among 362 servants of the great *boiar* Boris
Morozov, 343 died from the plague. Prince Aleksei Trubetskoi lost 270
of his 278 servants, and Prince Odoevskii lost 295 out of 310. Outside
of Moscow, and among social and economic groups who were better
provided for, the survival rate was higher, but the death rate still was
terrifyingly high. In the Voznesensk Convent, 90 nuns died and 38 survived; in Ivanovsk the ratio was about the same. One of the highest
recorded recovery rates was among the translators and interpreters in
the Kremlin's Foreign Office, where thirty died and thirty lived to tell
of their suffering.[38] "The wrath of God is on all people," wrote one
bewildered contemporary, and most Russians must have shared his
view.[39]

But plague was not the only catastrophe to strike Russians and
Ukrainians during the first year of the First Northern War, for Bogdan
Khmelnitskii's military fortunes turned out to be as dismal as Aleksei
Mikhailovich's were brilliant. For reasons that are still not clear, Khmelnitskii delayed taking the field that spring and summer and lost the initiative to General Potocki, his former enemy, who by that time had
been ransomed from the Tatars and returned to Poland. Aided by the
brutal and bloodthirsty Stefan Czarnecki, Potocki invaded the Ukraine

and put every living soul to the sword, including every woman and child he could lay his hands on. The Poles burned more than a thousand churches, razed some fifty villages, and killed about one hundred thousand people in all. At the same time, the Poles' Tatar allies attacked the Ukraine from the south and carried another three hundred thousand men, women, and children away to be sold into slavery. By the time Khmelnitskii finally halted Potocki's advance at the end of 1654, nearly a half-million Ukrainians had been killed in battle, murdered in their villages, or seized and carried off into captivity.[40]

The high point of Aleksei Mikhailovich's fortunes in the war against Poland probably came in mid-1655. During the first half of the year, he had seized more Lithuanian towns, and Khmelnitskii had begun to push back Potocki's forces. Then, in June 1655, the Swedish King Charles X attacked Poland and laid claim to the Polish crown. Khmelnitskii welcomed the added military pressure on the Poles, but the prospect of a Swedish-Polish union, no matter how remote, terrified Aleksei Mikhailovich and his advisers beyond all reason. If Charles seized the Polish crown, it would give the Swedes a stranglehold on the Baltic at a time when Russian statesmen were becoming acutely aware that their country needed warm water outlets to increase their access to Western technology and trade. It gave little consolation to the Russians that, even if Sweden should win a war with Poland, her King would find it extremely difficult to seize the Polish crown because of the pressures that would come from the Habsburgs in Europe. As fearful of the Swedes as he was of the Poles, Aleksei Mikhailovich sent General Prince Ivan Cherkasskii to attack the Swedish domains in the southern and eastern Baltic during the summer of 1657. For a brief time, Russia was at war with both of her traditional northern foes. To Aleksei Mikhailovich's good fortune, neither saw Russia as a major threat to its power; therefore the two did not settle their differences and ally against her. Because Polish statesmen thought Charles by far the more formidable enemy, they agreed to an armistice with Russia so that the Tsar could turn his arms against the Swedes.

Although complex in themselves, the diplomatic shifts of 1656–57 were but a prelude to the convoluted intrigues that dominated Eastern Europe during the next decade. As one might expect, the difficulties centered in the south among the ever-turbulent Cossacks. Not long after Aleksei Mikhailovich's armies turned to attack Sweden, Russia's newly established ties with the Ukraine began to unravel. If the Cossacks had chafed under the constraints of Polish rule, they soon found that ties with Russia also imposed unwelcome restraints upon their freewheeling behavior. Within months of his agreement to place the Ukraine under Aleksei Mikhailovich's protection, Khmelnitskii had begun to act independently; indeed, it was in part due to his diplomatic maneuverings that Sweden had declared war against Poland in 1656. Although he found Russia's declaration of war against Sweden distasteful, he made no effort to break his recent union with Moscow, perhaps because he heeded his own warning that the Cossacks could "no longer live without a Tsar."

Others, however, soon came to see that warning as unfounded and ill-advised. When Khmelnitskii died later in 1657, his son, who succeeded him, returned the Cossacks to the Polish fold, although there were a number who opposed that course as well. By the early 1660s, the Ukraine had split. The region east of the Dniepr River ("Left Bank Ukraine") swore allegiance to Moscow, while "Right Bank Ukraine," under Khmelnitskii's son, remained loyal to the Polish King. "It is impossible to rely upon the Cossacks. One cannot believe anything they say, for they bend with every breeze, just as a reed bends before the wind," wrote a frustrated Aleksei Mikhailovich to one of his advisers in 1660.[41] Yet frustration did not leave him without an alternative course to follow in dealing with the Cossacks; he and his advisers began to introduce serfdom and an aristocracy organized along Muscovite lines into the Ukraine. Such a scheme was designed to split the egalitarian Cossack society and to create a small group of lords loyal to Russia, who then could be called upon to use their power to keep the masses under control. It was a tactic the Romanovs would employ again and again as they brought new lands under their control during the next two centuries. Some of the eighteenth-century Romanovs, especially Catherine the Great, would use it with great finesse, but Aleksei Mikhailovich's first attempt produced a bizarre mixture of control and chaos. The ensuing rivalries and conflicts so ruined the Ukraine that it took more than a century for it to recover. Profiting from its chaos, the Tatars began to carry off peasants and townspeople from the Ukraine in ever-larger numbers. In 1666 alone, they seized approximately one hundred thousand captives, and their incursions continued until the end of the century.[42] Not without reason have Ukrainian historians called the period that followed Khmelnitskii's death the "time of ruin."

Although the Ukraine continued to be ravaged by Tatar raids and torn by internal strife, Aleksei Mikhailovich and Poland's King Jan Kazimir finally reached a peace settlement that ended the First Northern War. Both nations had exhausted themselves in the struggle, and both had suffered serious civil unrest as a result of the war. Because internal conflicts had so drained their resources, neither Poland nor Russia had waged a decisive campaign since 1656. Therefore, Aleksei Mikhailovich's early victories, although more than a decade past, still counted for something in 1667, and the Peace of Andrusovo marked the first Romanov victory against Russia's western enemies. For the first time since Boris Godunov's Baltic campaigns in the 1590s, Russia had fought and won a war that was not purely defensive. Also for the first time since the Romanovs had begun to rule Russia, a western sovereign had ceded to them territory that he had come to regard as a permanent part of his domain. Despite the immense cost of the victory, Aleksei Mikhailovich thus emerged with some valuable prizes. Most notable of all, he now was master of the great cities of Smolensk and Kiev and lord of all the "Left Bank Ukraine."[43] Poland always had been the stronger of the two, but she could enforce that claim no longer. Although Russia and Poland would fight other wars in the coming centuries, the Romanovs never again would have to fear Poland as a serious threat to their sovereignty.

In fighting successfully against the Swedes and the Poles, Aleksei Mikhailovich had marshaled all of Russia's limited resources in the struggle. He was able to do so because he and his father had imposed a harsh regime upon their subjects and had prevented the vast majority from rebelling against it. In order to make this sort of regime effective, the Romanovs emphasized governmental centralization. To that end, they relied heavily upon *voevody*, specially appointed military governors who served as their chief representatives in Russia's cities and provinces. It was the *voevoda* to whom they turned when something needed to be done, and it was the *voevoda* upon whom they heaped ruin and abuse if their orders were not carried out.

In the region where he held sway, the *voevoda* wielded nearly absolute power. He stood high above all other men and walked with the authority of the Tsar himself. Despite the risks of the position, few men could resist the attraction of such power over their fellows, nor did they fail to become corrupted by it and amass vast wealth during their tenure in office. Although the earlier Muscovite practice of *kormlenie** had been abolished before the Romanovs came to power, *voevodas* continued to function very much in the *kormlenie* tradition. Everywhere they went, they expected and received numerous costly gifts from subordinates and private citizens. Provincial delegates who attended the *zemskii sobor* in 1642 complained to Tsar Mikhail that his *voevodas* had "reduced the people of all stations to beggary, and have stripped them to the bone." [44] But the *voevodas'* exploitation of their subjects was a price the Romanovs were more than willing to pay to sustain their power.

Illegality figured in the actions of many Russians who held positions of authority during the 1630s and 1640s. At the root of the problem was the fact that the old law code of 1550 was totally out of date, and no viable code had taken its place. Aleksei Mikhailovich thus set a special commission to draft a modern code of laws that would apply to Russian society of the 1650s. Part of his purpose obviously was to meet some of the most pressing demands of the nobles and townsmen in Russia. At the same time, he wished to constrain the peasantry even further, so that the state could continue to squeeze their slender purses to obtain the wealth needed to support the army and administration.

Both of these purposes were clearly reflected in the law code that Aleksei Mikhailovich and the *zemskii sobor* approved as the *Ulozhenie* of 1649. A number of its articles defended the rights of nobles and townsmen to life and property, while others further established the sanctity of autocratic power. Yet it was not these issues to which the *Ulozhenie* devoted most of its attention. If nobles' estates and crown lands were to

---

*The literal meaning of *kormlenie* is "feeding." In earlier periods of Russia's history, officials had been granted the right to exact tribute from the populations they governed, or, in the Russian phrase, to engage in "feeding" upon them.

have any value, there had to be a guaranteed labor force to farm them. For that reason, the *Ulozhenie* sought to marshal the peasantry to do the bidding of the state and its nobles. Peasants were tied to the land, no longer free to leave the estates upon which they labored. Not yet slaves, still their purpose in life was to fulfil their landlords' will. Obviously, Russia's peasants did not accept this service status passively, and it is probably no accident that Razin's revolt, the greatest Russia ever had seen, came just two decades after the *Ulozhenie* was promulgated. Aleksei Mikhailovich's preoccupation with control of Russia's peasant masses was most dramatically indicated by the brutal punishments he and his advisers decreed for peasants who committed even minor offenses. As in seventeenth-century England, many crimes were punishable by death or loss of limbs. The knout, which could wound, maim, or even kill, was mentioned in 141 different instances in the *Ulozhenie*.[45]

Aleksei Mikhailovich placed rigid constraints upon his people because Russia suffered from an ongoing manpower shortage as well as a scarcity of most other resources. Plague, famine, and war with Poland and Sweden all played a part in claiming the lives of millions of Russians during the seventeenth century and helped to drain hundreds of thousands of rubles from the Romanovs' meager treasury. But it was the Tatars of the Crimea, not the Swedes or the Poles, who proved to be the Romanovs' most debilitating enemy, and the one they were least able to hold in check. One Soviet historian has calculated that, between 1613 and 1650, the Romanovs paid almost a million rubles in tribute to the Tatars.[46] That was an astronomical sum by seventeenth-century standards, especially if we remember that it was *fifty* times the indemnity Mikhail had paid to the Swedes at the Peace of Stolbovo in 1617. But gold alone could not even begin to measure the cost of the tribute the Tatars exacted from the Russians. As a consequence of their lightning raids into Russia's southern provinces to gather captives for sale in the slave markets of Constantinople and other Near Eastern urban centers, they deprived the Romanovs of hundreds of thousands of subjects. Sometimes in groups of a few dozen, sometimes in vast hordes numbering in the tens of thousands, the Tatars swept through Russia's southern regions in search of men, women, and children to be sold into bondage—especially the tall, blond, and buxom young women of the Ukraine who brought high prices from slave traders.

For more than two centuries, Tatar raids became almost an an- √. nual event. As the spring floods receded, and the early summer sun shrank the swollen streams and dried the land, Tatar horsemen would begin to appear in the southern steppe. Like their ancestors, the Mongols, they were superb horsemen and masters of the surprise attack. Without warning, small groups of them would descend upon isolated hamlets while terrified peasants sought in vain to hide themselves. In such cases, the Tatar assault was brief. Slung over their saddles would be the children and young adults of the community, destined for slavery in some Near Eastern household.

The Tatar cavalry did not always attack in small groups against far-flung peasant homesteads. On occasion, large numbers attacked towns with the same result, and they were known to range far beyond the south when their strength permitted them to probe into Russia's interior. In 1521 their raiding parties had reached the walls of Moscow, only to be driven back and kept from returning for a half-century by Ivan the Terrible's aggressive policies. Yet, the moment Ivan's defenses weakened, an army of fifty thousand Tatars attacked Moscow in 1571. Again the Russians drove them off, but, as they retreated southward, they carried more than one hundred thousand captives back to their strongholds in the Crimea. Two decades later, they again reached Moscow; in the intervening years, they had invaded Russia's southern lands on sixteen different occasions.[47]

Throughout much of the seventeenth century, the Romanovs' two great Western foes, Sweden and Poland, were deeply involved in European affairs, with the result that both played major roles in the Thirty Years' War that engulfed so much of Europe in bloody conflict between 1618 and 1648. Their animosity toward Russia clearly took second place during those years. By contrast, the Tatars had long been allied with the Ottoman Empire, the greatest power in the Near and Middle East, and were confident of the protection of the Sultan. Secure from attack by the one neighbor with the power to crush them, the Tatars were free to direct all their military resources against the Romanovs.

The Time of Troubles had left the Russians so weak and exhausted that they simply had no resources to direct against the Tatars during the first years of Mikhail Romanov's reign. Until peace agreements were signed with the Swedes and the Poles, Mikhail had no choice but to allow his southern foes to range at will in the steppes, and they very soon penetrated deep into the interior. In 1614, Russian prisoners of war told their Swedish captors that a large force of twenty thousand Tatars had been within a half-mile of Moscow. By early 1615, the Tatars had seized so many captives that the price of Russian slaves in the markets of the Near East plummeted by almost eighty percent. Partly as a consequence of these falling slave prices, but also because Tsar Mikhail's peace with Sweden and Poland had left his troops free to retaliate against the Tatars, the 1620s were a time of relative calm on Russia's southern frontier, and, in some years, the Tatar raiders did not appear at all. As the demand for slaves resumed in the Near East in the mid-1630s, the Tatars launched large-scale raids again, but the Cossacks' successful attack against Azov at the end of the decade turned their attention away from Russia's southern steppes. Only when the Cossacks complied with Mikhail's order to abandon Azov in 1642 did the Tatars again begin their raids in earnest.[48]

Between the 1640s and the 1670s, Russia's relations with the Tatars formed a part of that large and complex network of international struggles that involved the Ottoman Empire, Hungary, Poland, and the Ukrainian Cossacks, culminating in the Russo-Turkish War of 1677–81. The European struggles during most of the seventeenth and eighteenth centuries have accustomed historians of that period to think of war in terms of small mercenary armies that generally did not involve civilian populations to any significant degree. The experience of Eastern Europe was very different, and far more brutal. Armies of vast numbers marched and attacked over equally vast distances. During the summer of 1677, almost one hundred twenty thousand Turks and Tatars invaded the Romanovs' southern lands, burning, pillaging, and seizing thousands of captives as they went. Certainly the sickly young Tsar Feodor, who had ascended the throne the year before, was unfit to lead an army against them, and it seemed a time when Russia was particularly vulnerable to attack. But Feodor had the good fortune to find two outstanding commanders in Prince Grigorii Romodanovskii and the Cossack chieftain Ivan Samoilovich. Under their generalship, Russia's armies proved very different from those troops the Turks and Tatars had grown accustomed to fighting during the first half of the century. To the Turks' amazement, these Russian troops were formidable. Better trained and better disciplined, they commanded three times more artillery than did the Turks. In late August, they drove the Turks into headlong retreat and killed a great number of their senior officers, including the sons of the Turkish Pasha and the Tatar Khan. Yet this victory did not bring success. As so often was the case with the Romanovs' armies, supply problems finally forced the Russians to withdraw into the interior. By the end of the year, they had lost the advantage won that summer.[49]

The Turks and Tatars returned to southern Russia in 1678 with an army fully as large as the one they had raised the year before. For the entire summer, the armies of Romodanovskii and Samoilovich engaged them in numerous bloody battles, and again the Turks suffered defeat at their hands. This second campaign cost Russia's enemies so dearly that, the next year, they could send only small raiding expeditions into the steppe. Realizing that the Turks and their allies had been weakened seriously, Tsar Feodor and his advisers began a vigorous diplomatic campaign at all of Europe's Courts for an anti-Turk crusade. At Vienna, Paris, London, Warsaw, the Vatican, and any number of lesser German Courts, Russian agents urged Europe's princes that 1679 and 1680 was the time for all of Christendom to strike a mortal blow against the infidel. Yet the dream of a new crusade came to naught. Since Europe would not support Russia in her struggle, Feodor authorized his diplomats to begin peace negotiations with the Turks and the Tatars in the fall of 1680. After eighteen months of negotiations, Russia made peace. Temporarily it seemed that the balance in the south had shifted in her favor.[50]

Shortly after his representatives signed a peace treaty with the Turkish Sultan, Tsar Feodor died. For several years, the Regent Sofia devoted her attention to consolidating her power at home, while the Turks and their Tatar allies were occupied with their great struggle against the armies of the Habsburgs and the Polish King Jan Sobieski. By the spring of 1687, however, Prince Vasilii Golitsyn was seeking glory in battle to raise himself even further in the eyes of Sofia. With the blessings of his august mistress, and in alliance with the Habsburgs, Poland, and Venice, Golitsyn marched south to crush the Tatars with more than one hundred thousand men. Overconfident and inexperienced, he failed in his first attempt, although his campaign kept the Tatars from joining with the Turkish Sultan against the Habsburgs and Poland. Soon, Sofia and her ministers were forced to accept the bitter realization that their allies were unwilling to aid Russia in return. When Golitsyn launched a second campaign against the Tatars in 1689, Russia had to fight alone.[51]

When he began to assemble his armies in midwinter 1689, Prince Golitsyn had no inkling that his brilliant career would collapse in ruins before fall and that his patroness and royal mistress would greet the year's end as a prisoner in the Virgin's Convent to the south of Moscow. Golitsyn planned to have his forces ready by February, so that they could begin their march south before the ice broke and the melting snow began to turn Russia's primitive roads into rivers of mud over which neither man nor beast could pass. In all, he had about 112,000 men under his command, and they were supported by more than four hundred pieces of artillery. With this force, he intended to strike directly against the Tatar stronghold of Perekop, the great fortress that guarded the entrance to the Crimea, in order to end, once and for all, Tatar raids into Russia's southern lands.

But Golitsyn and his men were not prepared to confront the surprise tactics the Tatars employed with such devastating effect once the Russians entered their territory. Well acquainted with the terrain, and using every topographical feature to the very best advantage, Tatar cavalry demoralized the Russians and inflicted heavy damage upon them. On May 15, ten thousand Tatars caught one of Golitsyn's army groups in the open steppe and killed a large number before being driven off by Russian artillery. The next day, they attacked in the midst of a driving rainstorm, inflicting many more casualties. Golitsyn continued his advance, but only after he had abandoned large numbers of horses and heavy equipment.[52]

On May 20 he and his armies came within sight of the high walls of Perekop. Yet, for reasons historians still have not determined, Golitsyn did not press on. To everyone's surprise, he let himself be drawn into negotiations while the Tatar Khan strengthened his defenses and the Russian army consumed precious provisions to no purpose. When the negotiations produced no immediate results, Golitsyn, still for reasons unknown, decided to withdraw without reaching any formal terms with the Tatars. His decision was little short of foolhardy. Only the Khan's lack of troops saved Golitsyn's armies from complete annihilation. As the Russians withdrew, steppe fires set by the Tatars raged along their route and destroyed all forage and supplies. The heat was intense, and there was almost no water to be had. Men and horses fell at an appalling rate. Only when they had recrossed the Dniepr River were Golitsyn and his troops safe.

Tens of thousands of soldiers had died to no purpose in Golitsyn's disastrous campaign, and the triumphal reception Sofia planned for her lover did not conceal the magnitude of his failure or protect him from its consequences. When Golitsyn returned to Moscow in mid-July, Tsar Peter openly upbraided him. For an entire week, the young Tsar postponed signing the decree Sofia had prepared to confer rewards upon her favorite and his officers and adamantly refused to grant Golitsyn an audience to receive his thanks once he did sign it. For Sofia and Golitsyn, it was the beginning of the end.[53]

Although the seventeenth-century Romanovs' foreign policy had ended upon a note of failure, they still could claim considerable accomplishment. They had ascended Russia's throne when the country was in a state of near-collapse and foreign armies occupied much of Russia's western and northern lands. Far weaker than any of her enemies, Russia seemed doomed to defeat and the loss of vast territories. Europeans called her the rude and barbarous kingdom of Muscovy, and their only interest in her was to seize as many of her abundant natural resources as possible. Certainly, the Western merchants and diplomats who sought to wheedle concessions from Tsar Mikhail and his son Aleksei Mikhailovich had little expectation that they ever would be obliged to confront Muscovy on any but the most unequal and advantageous terms.

When Peter drove Sofia and Golitsyn from the Kremlin, the Romanovs had won the advantage in Russia's struggle with Poland, and, within another quarter-century, her growing might would overwhelm Sweden as well. The Tatars and the Turks would continue to be a menace for somewhat longer, but they never were a truly serious threat after Peter's successful campaign against Azov in 1696. Well before the end of their first century on the Russian throne, the Romanovs thus had raised Russia to a position of importance and power in Eastern Europe. Beginning with Peter the Great, the eighteenth-century Romanovs would lead Russia to far greater heights of power and glory throughout the Western world than Tsar Mikhail or Aleksei Mikhailovich could have imagined in their wildest dreams.

PART TWO

THE RISE
OF AN
EMPIRE

(1689–1796)

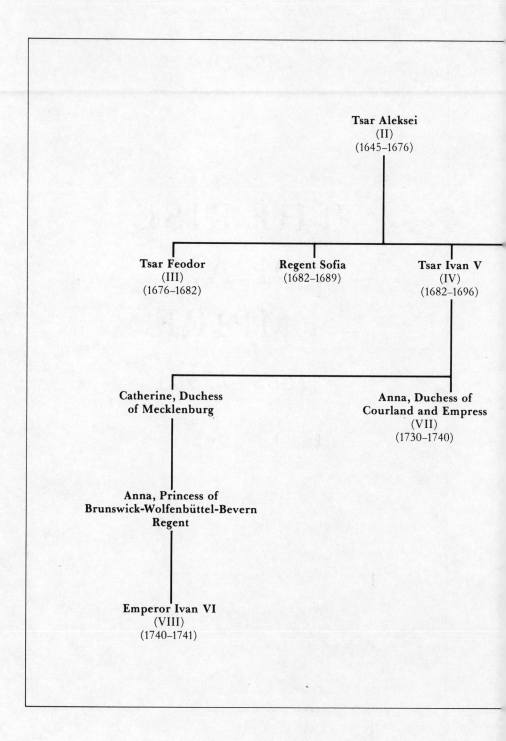

Tsar Aleksei
(II)
(1645–1676)

Tsar Feodor
(III)
(1676–1682)

Regent Sofia
(1682–1689)

Tsar Ivan V
(IV)
(1682–1696)

Catherine, Duchess
of Mecklenburg

Anna, Duchess of
Courland and Empress
(VII)
(1730–1740)

Anna, Princess of
Brunswick-Wolfenbüttel-Bevern
Regent

Emperor Ivan VI
(VIII)
(1740–1741)

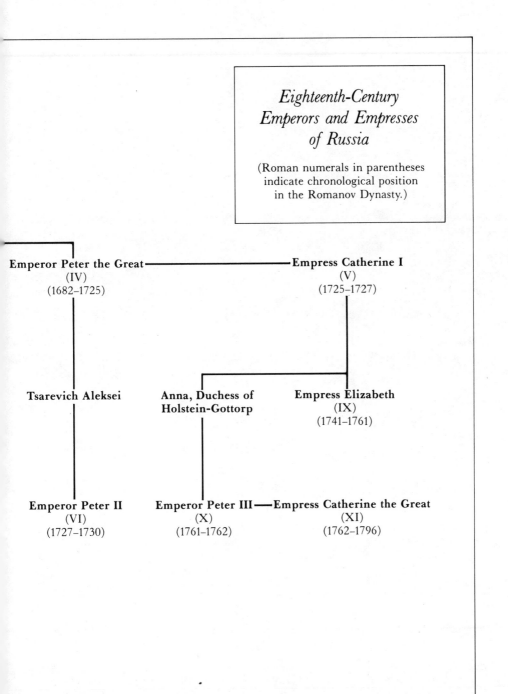

**Eighteenth-Century
Emperors and Empresses
of Russia**

(Roman numerals in parentheses
indicate chronological position
in the Romanov Dynasty.)

Emperor Peter the Great————————————Empress Catherine I
(IV)　　　　　　　　　　　　　　　　　(V)
(1682–1725)　　　　　　　　　　　　(1725–1727)

Tsarevich Aleksei　　　Anna, Duchess of　　　Empress Elizabeth
　　　　　　　　　　Holstein-Gottorp　　　　　(IX)
　　　　　　　　　　　　　　　　　　　　(1741–1761)

Emperor Peter II　　　Emperor Peter III——Empress Catherine the Great
(VI)　　　　　　　　　(X)　　　　　　　　(XI)
(1727–1730)　　　　(1761–1762)　　　　(1762–1796)

CHAPTER IV

Eighteenth-Century
Emperors and Empresses

In 1721, when the Imperial Senate proclaimed him Russia's first Emperor, Peter the Great's Imperial title reflected principally his success in wresting Russia away from her Muscovite past and launching her firmly into the mainstream of European politics. Yet his early years gave no hint that he would deviate from the course of more gradual change and cautious Europeanization charted by his father, Tsar Aleksei Mikhailovich. As an infant Peter was surrounded by that luxury all Muscovite royal heirs enjoyed in the seventeenth century. He was not weaned until he was well beyond the age of two, and more than a dozen women of high birth spent their days and nights anticipating his every whim. The walls of one of his rooms were covered with fine leather stamped with silver designs, his cradle was of Turkish velvet encrusted with gold and silver embroidery, and he slept on sheets of the finest white silk. His nursery overflowed with toys lavished upon him by doting parents, relatives, and future subjects. For his first birthday, six of the finest icon painters in the town of Kostroma presented him with a picture book. He also received two toy drums, miniature cymbals with golden cords and tassels, and a wooden horse that moved on tiny iron wheels, complete with bridle and saddle adorned with silver. A few months later a guard at the Kremlin's famous Armory carved for him a set of wooden horses and cannon from maple and lime wood. Only in the gift he received on his second birthday from his father's chief minister, the Tsarina Natalia's former guardian Matveev, was there a portent of the future course Peter would pursue. Matveev presented him with a toy boat made of silver and inlaid with gems.[1] A quarter-century later Peter would build Russia's first navy; in the south it would defeat the Turks and then in the north it would open Russia's maritime window on the West, the new capital of St. Petersburg.

From the moment he took his first steps, Peter was surrounded by companions who joined him in his games and later would serve him as royal counselors. Among them were Matveev's eight-year-old son Andrei, Peter's future Chancellor Gavriil Golovkin, and Avtonom Golovin. Peter also had a retinue of dwarfs that numbered fourteen by the time he reached the age of ten. With these companions, he played in the Kremlin and at various palaces and estates outside Moscow, including those in the royal villages of Preobrazhenskoe, Kolomenskoe, and Vorobevo, and with them he took part in royal progresses to more distant places such as the famous Trinity Monastery some sixty miles away. Peter always made these journeys in opulence and grandeur, in a manner befitting the Tsar's heir, rather than the youngest of three living princes. "Following the entourage of the Tsar came that of the Tsarina," wrote one foreign ambassador in the fall of 1675. "In front rode a steward with two footmen, and behind them came twelve large horses, white as snow and harnessed in silken reins, drawing the Tsarina's carriage. Then came the small carriage of the youngest prince, all encrusted with gold and drawn by four ponies. Alongside rode four dwarfs, while another rode behind, all astride mounts of similar minute stature."[2] The young prince was then three years old. Four months before Peter's fourth birthday, Tsar Aleksei died and Peter's childhood world of opulence and regal ceremony collapsed in a storm of misfortune and intrigue.

By the end of that year, the Miloslavskii clan held unchallenged sway in the Kremlin. Although they allowed her to remain in her former royal apartments, Peter's mother, the Tsarina Natalia, was a virtual prisoner, powerless to aid those of her family and friends who fell before the Miloslavskiis' wrath.[3]

But the bitter feuds that drove his mother's family and friends into disgrace and exile during the late 1670s at first had little impact upon Peter's daily life. During the first three years of his half-brother Feodor's reign, he continued to live the carefree life of a royal child. The most significant event in his life during these years occurred in 1679, when a group of male attendants, headed by R. M. Streshnev, replaced his nannies and woman servants. At the age of seven, Peter thus moved from the world of women into that of men. Soon afterward, according to the best estimates we have, his education began. We do not know who first taught him to read and write, nor do we know what books he studied. Like so much of what took place within the Kremlin's dark walls during the late 1670s and the 1680s, Peter's early education is shrouded in mystery.[4]

One thing we know for certain is that the *Streltsy* Revolt of 1682, when Sofia seized power as Regent, left a deep and permanent scar upon Peter, who was extremely precocious. He never forgot the terror of seeing his mother's brothers slaughtered. Nor would he forget the arrogance and rudeness of the *streltsy* as they invaded his private apartments and desecrated his personal possessions. These events awakened in him a hatred not only of the *streltsy* but of Moscow itself. As Peter grew older, he turned his back upon all that reminded him of the spiritual and temporal Muscovite precepts upon which the first Romanovs had built their state. In his adolescence, the Foreign Quarter on the outskirts of the city became his haven, and it was there that he sought the models for the Russia he envisioned. Eventually, he built for Russia a western capital, a city in which to emulate the life of the Foreign Quarter.

Peter spent the years of Sofia's regency in the Kremlin and at the Romanovs' country estates on the outskirts of Moscow. Active and impatient, he evidently had a strong distaste for the complex Court and Church ceremonial his father had so adored, though he was obliged to take part as Ivan's co-Tsar. As the historian Bogoslovskii, the leading expert on Peter's early life, has shown, Peter avoided many of the assemblies that so occupied the attention of the Muscovite Court in the 1680s.[5] Yet it is from his rare attendance at these functions that we have some of our best portraits of him in his early years. He was so tall and robust that, in 1683, the German traveler Engelbert Kämpfer estimated his age to be sixteen, even though he was only eleven.[6] Two years later, another foreigner, Van Keller, sketched him in precise and prophetic terms: "Nature develops herself with advantage and good fortune in his whole personality; his stature is great and his mien fine;

he grows visibly, and advances as much in intelligence and understanding as he gains the affection and love of all. He has such a strong preference for military pursuits that when he comes of age we may expect from him brave actions and heroic deeds."[7]

Peter's love of things military was the dominant characteristic of his adolescent years. While earlier Muscovite princes had been schooled in the learning of the Church and, in some cases, had received a limited secular education, Peter devoted a minimum of attention to such pursuits. For him, deeds, not words, gave the measure of men, and he valued learning only for its immediate or potential practical applications. His boyhood games all centered upon weapons and war. At the end of 1683 he formed his first "play regiment," the Preobrazhenskii, which took its name from the village of Preobrazhenskoe where he and his mother often spent part of their summers. Soon its numbers increased to the point where it could no longer be quartered in the village, and Peter formed a second regiment, the Semenovskii, again taking its name from a nearby village.[8] These two regiments would eventually become the core of a new elite military force in Russia, the Imperial Guards. Throughout the eighteenth century, they would play a major role in deciding the succession. Until the revolution of 1917, they would serve as the Emperor's own regiments.

Even though he took no part in the actual business of governing Russia ·during the 1680s, Peter had at his command the resources of the Kremlin's Armory. He drew upon them frequently for the matériel he required for the activities of his "play regiments" in the fields outside Moscow. Beginning in January 1683 he began to order a variety of weapons from the Armory, including not only sabers, pistols, and muskets but even cannon, of which he received sixteen during the month of July 1683 alone.[9] Peter also recruited soldiers, and officers to train them. It was his efforts to find such instructors that first took him into Moscow's Foreign Quarter. There he found his first advisers: the artillery expert Simon Zommer, who first acquainted Peter with the use of mortars, and Franz Timmerman, a Dutchman, who taught him arithmetic, geometry, and the rudiments of ballistics. Peter soon added to their number more prominent men, especially Patrick Gordon, a Catholic Royalist from Aberdeenshire who had fled Scotland at the age of sixteen, and Franz Lefort, who had rejected the stern Calvinist morality of his native Geneva and become a soldier of fortune.

There were of course many more Russians who entered Peter's service as well. By 1689 his "play soldiers" numbered about one thousand. They were a diverse lot, for over the years the young Tsar showed himself not to be overly particular about his companions' social origins. His first recruits were Sergei Bukhvastov and Ekim Voronin, who were sent to him by the Armory in 1683. So impressed was he by Bukhvastov's abilities that he dubbed him the "first Russian soldier" and later ordered the famed sculptor Rastrelli the Elder to cast a life-size statue of him.[10] Peter soon added others. Chief among them was Aleksandr Menshikov, his lifelong comrade, who rose to become Generalissimus of Russia's armies and a Prince of the Holy Roman Empire. According to various accounts, Menshikov was the son of a corporal or a groom and reputedly sold pies in the streets of Moscow before he entered Peter's service in 1686. Pavel Iaguzhinskii, who later rose to become Procurator-General of the Senate, was said to have herded swine in Lithuania in his youth, and Petr Shafirov, Peter's future Vice-Chancellor, had been a clerk in a small shop. Aleksei Kurbatov, who rose to become Vice-Governor of Arkhangelsk Province, began his life as a house serf. At the other end of the social spectrum were Prince Iakov Dolgorukii, who became a Senator, and Boris Sheremetiev, a future Field Marshal, both of whom came from some of Moscow's oldest families.

Although his "play soldiers" were Peter's chief passion during the 1680s, he developed another interest toward the end of the decade. According to Peter's own account, published some three decades later as the introduction to Russia's first Naval Regulations, in the late spring of 1688 he and Franz Timmerman discovered an ancient and rotting craft in a storehouse on one of the Romanov estates near the village of Izmailovo. It may have been the remains of a yacht sent as a gift by Elizabeth I of England to Ivan the, Terrible. Timmerman termed it an "English boat" and explained that, unlike those flat-bottomed vessels that plied Russia's inland waterways and could sail only with the wind, this craft could sail against the wind as well. Peter ordered it to be repaired, even though there were no Russian shipwrights capable of the task. In the Foreign Quarter, Timmerman found Karsten Brant, a Dutch shipbuilder Aleksei Mikhailovich had brought to Russia in the 1660s, and Brant made the craft seaworthy. Peter spent the remainder of that summer and most of the next one sailing first on the Iauza River and then at Lake Periaslavl, where he also commissioned Brant to construct a number of other small vessels.[11] In later years, Peter would remember this as the beginning of Russia's navy.

Peter's passion for ships and soldiers, and the hours and days he was beginning to devote to drinking, lovemaking, and riotous living in Moscow's Foreign Quarter, led his mother in January 1689 to arrange his marriage at the age of sixteen to Evdokia Lopukhina. From the first, they were a sadly mismatched pair. Evdokia was nineteen at the time and is said to have been pretty, quiet, and shy, scrupulously reared in the best traditions of an old Moscow noble family. Peter's opposite in every sense, she could in no way share his life and interests. Within three months, he had impregnated and abandoned her.

During the late summer of 1689, Peter began to assert his independence. Suddenly the issues posed in 1682 required settlement in a life-or-death struggle. Most obviously, he was full grown, and his half-sister Sofia's regency was no longer necessary. During the previous year, ambitious men with sound political judgment had begun to gravitate to his entourage. First, there were his uncles Lev and Martemian Naryshkin, who had old scores to settle with Sofia and evidently had concluded that they could better achieve their aims through Peter than through his mother. Much more important was the astute politician Prince Boris Golitsyn, a cousin of Vasilii Golitsyn, Sofia's lover and chief minister. Finally, there was General Patrick Gordon, whose role in the events leading up to the confrontation of 1689 remains murky, but who was a clever and ambitious political opportunist. Gordon's diary begins to make frequent mention of the young Tsar in 1688, when Peter drafted some soldiers from his regiment for service with his "play soldiers." As a foreign adviser in the pay of the Russian government, Gordon still was officially in Sofia's service, and, although he did not make his final break with her until the last possible moment, it is quite probable that he encouraged Peter to assert himself against her.[12]

What may have further strengthened Peter's resolution to depose

Sofia was the disastrous outcome of Prince Vasilii Golitsyn's campaign against the Crimean Tatars in the south. The young Tsar snubbed Golitsyn on his return to Moscow and made his growing rejection of Sofia's regency even clearer on July 8, when he abruptly ordered her not to take part in an important religious procession, virtually an open declaration of war.[13] By late summer the situation had grown so tense that, at the beginning of August, Sofia ordered a *streltsy* regiment to escort her on a pilgrimage to the Donskoi Monastery, evidently because she feared that Peter's troops might attack her on the way. A group of *streltsy* loyal to Peter mistook this as preparation for an attack against him at Preobrazhenskoe and rode to warn him that troops commanded by his enemy Feodor Shaklovityi were on the march. Rudely awakened by these well-intentioned emissaries just before midnight on August 7, Peter fled to the Trinity Monastery, where his mother and pregnant wife joined him a few hours later. There he marshaled his forces: two regiments of "play soldiers" that were, in fact, well-armed, well-trained troops, a number of *streltsy* loyal to him, and, most important, the Patriarch Ioakim, who abandoned Moscow in order to stand at the young Tsar's side. Peter now had a formidable military force and the power of the Church behind him. Perhaps equally important, his flight to the Trinity Monastery brought him popular approval as well, for, in the minds of the masses, the Tsar would flee to such a holy place only if his life were truly in danger.

With this support behind him, Peter continued to apply pressure on Sofia in the Kremlin. First, he ordered all eighteen colonels of the *streltsy* regiments to report to him at the Monastery. Sofia managed to dissuade them, but Peter's second summons, which threatened them with death if they refused, could not be disobeyed. On September 4, General Gordon and his elite cadre of foreign officers joined Peter. Three days later, Vasilii Golitsyn made his way to the Monastery. Since his cousin Boris was one of Peter's closest advisers, Golitsyn evidently hoped to avoid punishment; he was spared torture and execution, but Peter deprived him of all his estates and noble rank and sent him into exile in Pustozersk.

By mid-September Sofia stood utterly alone, for even her brother Ivan agreed to support Peter. In return, Peter allowed Ivan to retain his title of co-Tsar until his death in 1696. Powerless, Sofia had no choice but to accept her fate. Peter decreed that she be incarcerated in the Virgins' Convent on the southern outskirts of Moscow. In the context of Muscovite tradition, Peter dealt gently with his first formidable political foe. He would be far more brutal with those who opposed him in future years.[14]

Sofia's fall did not mean that Peter immediately took the reins of Russia's government into his own hands, however. For the next six years, he left the day-to-day conduct of state affairs in the hands of those men who had clustered around him or his mother during the years of Sofia's ascendancy: his uncle Lev Naryshkin; Prince Petr Prozorovskii and Tikhon Streshnev, two of his former tutors; and Petr Lopukin, an uncle of his now-estranged wife. The only man of real talent among Peter's early counselors continued to be Prince Boris Golitsyn, whom a contemporary described as "a man with great intellect and a keen sense of humor, but one who lacked diligence because, most of all, he loved amusement and was especially devoted to drinking."[15] Unlike most Muscovite aristocrats, Boris Golitsyn was especially close to Moscow's foreign community. Both General Gordon and Franz Lefort were among his frequent companions, and he had been instrumental in bringing Peter into their circle during the last years of Sofia's regency.[16] Although considerably older than Peter, Gordon and Lefort became two of his closest comrades. To show his admiration, Peter violated the most sacred canons of Muscovite custom and entertained them in the Kremlin itself. They became his most frequent advisers on military affairs, were generals in his army, and admirals in his nonexistent navy. In their company, Peter came to know life in the Foreign Quarter not as a curiosity but as a model for daily existence.

By now Peter was in the prime of his manhood, a powerful young giant whose 230 pounds of hardened muscle were distributed over a frame some six feet eight inches in height.[17] Unaware of his physical strength, and evidently with a high tolerance for discomfort himself, Peter frequently inflicted physical pain upon others in giving rein to his rough sense of humor. He had a savage temper that expressed itself in sudden outbursts of fury. He could not tolerate stupidity or incompetence and frequently used his massive fists to drive his commands deeply into the minds of those who failed to carry out his will. Yet, if he was quick to anger, he was equally quick to forgive. He was devoted to his friends, and many of them took advantage of that fact. "Aleksasha" Menshikov stole vast sums from Russia's treasury during Peter's reign and often bore the bruises of Peter's cudgel for his sins, yet he remained firmly in the Tsar's favor throughout his life.

To his life in Moscow's Foreign Quarter, Peter brought his hatred for ritual and formality. Often gathering at Lefort's spacious dwelling, he and his friends held riotous feasts and dances in which all inhibitions were left outside. Peter loved to dance, had a gargantuan appetite, and a taste for lusty foreign women. In the passionate embraces of the belles of the Foreign Quarter, he sought to forget the boredom of his marriage bed, and it was there he found his first mistress. Anna Mons, the daughter of a German wine merchant, was seventeen when Peter first took her to his bed. According to Gordon's son Alexander, she was "an exceedingly beautiful young woman, endowed with all the talents to please, except prudence and good sense."[18] While Peter was in Moscow, Anna was his daily companion and even began to fulfill some of the ceremonial functions of the Tsarina. When Peter stood as sponsor at the christening of the Danish envoy's son, it was Anna, not Evdokia, who stood with him. Yet, although she was beautiful and, from all reports, deeply sensual, Anna also was peevish, even ill tempered, especially when money and power were at stake. She gave herself to Peter with real passion, but she bestowed her favors upon others as well.[19] Peter eventually left her for a young Lithuanian peasant girl named Marfa Skavronska, who was known not only for her beauty but for her good temper. First Peter's mistress and then his wife, Marfa rose from camp follower to Empress in the space of three decades.

Peter's most notorious pasttime was drinking; his bouts with Menshikov, Gordon, Lefort, and a number of others in the Foreign Quarter took on a truly orgiastic character. Drunken orgies, of course, are not rarities in history, but in Peter's time Russians consumed vast quantities of spirits even by seventeenth-century European standards. To the amazement of his contemporaries, Peter endowed his orgies with a curious ceremonial structure. Around 1690 he created The Vastly Extravagant, Supremely Absurd, Omni-Intoxicated Synod, which continued to assemble until his death. It was indeed vastly extravagant and its members were frequently intoxicated, but it was absurd only in its outer manifestations. Indeed, everything about the Synod was a gross parody on the rituals and hierarchy of the Church. Under the headship of a Prince-Pope, the Synod included, in the historian Vasilii Kliuchevskii's memorable description, "a conclave of twelve cardinals, all inveterate drunkards and gluttons, with a large staff having the titles of bishops, archimandrites, and other clerical ranks, and all bearing sobriquets which are too dirty and disgusting to print."[20] Peter endowed this complex hierarchy with all the elaborate ritual he otherwise shunned, as if to proclaim that ceremony was fit only for drunken orgies, not for serious affairs of state. Throughout his reign, he devoted considerable attention to the grotesque parodies for which the Synod became notorious. The most memorable among its celebrations were the mock weddings of Court jesters in 1694 and 1702; the real wedding in 1715 of Nikita Zotov, the Synod's Prince-Pope and Peter's former tutor; and the marriage of Zotov's successor, Petr Buturlin, to Zotov's aged widow in 1720.[21]

It was not Peter's public debauchery but his public blasphemy that began to stir fears in the breasts of Russians. These fears became more concrete after his return from Western Europe in 1698 when he decreed that his courtiers must shave their beards and don Western fashions in place of the long robes that Muscovite noblemen customarily wore. The Russian popular imagination, which had given birth to so many pretender legends in the past, once again began to produce explanations for the Tsar's strange conduct and his love for things foreign. Was Peter, in fact, an impostor and not their true Tsar? Soon tales began to fly thick and fast, spread by word of mouth across all of Russia. Peter was the bastard offspring of some foreign wench, substituted for a daughter that the Tsarina Natalia had borne, to satisfy Tsar Aleksei's longing for a son. Peter had been fathered by one of the *streltsy*, or even Lefort. Still others whispered fearfully that "when our Tsar was abroad, they chained him into a cask and threw him into the sea. This is not our Sovereign, but a foreigner."[22]

It was feared by some that Peter might be something even worse than a foreign impostor; that he was, in fact, none other than the Antichrist come to preside over the end of the world. As early as June 1700, the scribe Grishka Talitskii confessed that he held such a view and had sought to spread it among Russia's common folk. Talitskii was executed, but the legend of Peter as the Antichrist flourished so widely that one of his leading Church propagandists, Stefan Iavorskii, was obliged to write *Signs of the Antichrist's Coming* in a futile effort to refute the myth. So strongly did the tales about Peter grip the popular imagination that in October 1702 he was obliged to establish the Preobrazhenskii Office, and to assign the task of dealing with them to one of its departments, the so-called Secret Office. Under the direction of Prince Feodor Romodanovskii, one of Peter's earliest and most loyal supporters, the Secret Office became Russia's first institutionalized secret police, and the dread phrase "Word and Deed," with which it identified such cases of popular treason, became synonymous with the agonies of its torture chambers.[23]

In the minds of the masses, it was Peter's journey to the West that accounted for the many and momentous changes he imposed upon Russia during the first quarter of the eighteenth century. This journey began in March 1697 and lasted for some eighteen months during which the Tsar briefly visited a number of Baltic ports and German cities, spent four months in Holland, made a lengthy visit to England, and a briefer journey to Vienna. Peter at first traveled *incognito* as Peter Mikhailov, a noncommissioned officer in the Preobrazhenskii Guards; accompanying him was the Grand Embassy, a suite of some two hundred fifty men headed by Lefort and Feodor Golovin, the Governor-General of Siberia. The official purpose of the Grand Embassy was to negotiate a Grand Alliance of all Christian states of Europe against the Turks. Its real purpose was to hire Western naval and military experts for service in Russia and to provide Peter with an opportunity to view the West at first hand. Peter aspired to become a royal jack-of-all-trades, for, as he once remarked, "a monarch would feel ashamed to lag behind his subjects in any craft."[24] In the West, he studied a number of artisan trades and took pride and delight in mastering the rudiments of everything from shipbuilding to dentistry.

In Germany Peter first encountered the elegant Court society of Europe, upon whom he made a poor impression. Even by seventeenth-century standards, he and his companions were revoltingly unclean. In a society where elegant manners had become the rule, he knew not even the rudimentary rules of decent behavior. In Courland, Baron Blumberg dubbed Peter and his entourage "baptised bears,"[25] and most others shared that view. As one historian summarized the impression Peter made upon Europeans, "the strangeness of his appearance and behavior, his fits of uncontrollable temper, his revolting untidiness, his ignorance of the elementary rules of decent conduct, and his aversion to the use of knives and forks made him a most embarrassing guest at court functions."[26] Certainly, Sir John Evelyn, in whose manor Peter stayed while in England, must have felt an even stronger aversion when he presented his government with a bill for the large sum of £350 to repair the damage Peter and his companions had done to his dwelling. According to Evelyn's complaint, the walls were scarred, the windows smashed, the floorboards torn up and smeared with vomit and filth, while the lovely formal gardens were utterly destroyed.[27] Only Sophia Charlotte, the Electress of Brandenburg, found redeeming qualities beneath Peter's seemingly primitive exterior. "That he has not been taught to eat in a tidy manner," she wrote, "is obvious. But I was much taken with his natural and easy manner." She and her mother found "the Northern Barbarian's" ignorance of whalebone corsetry, which led him to remark that "German women have damnably hard bones," charming and concluded that "this is a sovereign who, at one and the same time, is very good and very evil, whose character precisely reflects that of his country. If he had received a better education, he would be a superb man, because he has much merit and unlimited native intelligence."[28]

Peter's purpose in going to the West was not, of course, to shine in high society. He far preferred the shipyards of Zaandam or the excitement of the mock naval battles Vice-Admiral Giles Scheij and King William III arranged for him. The young Tsar arrived in Holland consumed by curiosity and impatient to comprehend that new world about which he had heard so much in Moscow's Foreign Quarter. Nicholas Witsen, the Amsterdam Burgomeister who shared his passion for ships, often aided him in these first efforts. Witsen arranged for him to visit Dutch factories, museums, and hospitals and even granted his fondest wish, which was to spend several weeks working as a common carpenter in the shipyards of the Dutch East India Company. During his spare moments in Amsterdam, Peter became fascinated with the science of anatomy, a passion that later led him to establish in St. Petersburg Russia's first anatomical museum. The core of the museum's exhibit was the collection of the eminent Dutch anatomist Professor Ruysch, which Peter purchased some years after his visit to Amsterdam. Throughout the latter part of his reign, he built upon Ruysch's collection and decreed that the bodies of all grossly malformed fetuses that were miscarried or stillborn must be preserved and sent to his museum so that the foreign scientists he maintained in his capital might begin to study the causes of extreme birth defects.[29]

Despite his enthusiasm for Holland's many technological and scientific wonders, her shipwrights ultimately disappointed Peter, for he could discern in their work no fundamental principles upon which to base nautical design and construction. Dutch craftsmen seemed to build ships according to the rule of thumb, while he sought a more scientific approach. He therefore resolved to visit England, his enthusiasm heightened by the gift of a yacht, carrying twenty brass cannon and named the "Royal Transport," that King William III bestowed upon him at the end of 1697.[30] In early 1698, Peter and some of his entourage therefore went to England. After a brief stay in London, they went to Deptford, one of the most important centers for English shipbuilding. John Perry, one of the Englishmen Peter recruited into his service, left us an account of the young Tsar's activities in the Deptford shipyards. English shipwrights, Perry wrote in his memoirs, "shew'd him their Draughts, and the Method of laying down by Proportion any Ship or Vessel, of what Body soever required, with the Rules for moulding and building a ship . . . which made him repent that he had spent so much time in Holland." Perry added, "His Majesty often says that if he had not come to England he had certainly been a Bungler as long as he had lived."[31]

Peter devoted much of the six weeks he spent in Deptford to the study of English naval design, considered to be the most advanced in the world. Yet he also found time to visit the Greenwich Observatory, the Woolwich Arsenal, the Tower of London, and the Royal Mint. In the late seventeenth century, Russian coinage still was primitive, comprised mainly of lesser coins struck from lengths of silver wire. Peter soon would reform it upon the English model. In addition to technological matters, Peter also probed the nature of England's Church-State relations in frequent conversations with Gilbert Burnet, Bishop of Salisbury. He was especially impressed by the manner in which the Anglican Church was subordinated to King and Parliament and may have seen in that relationship a possible solution to the conflicts he faced with the Patriarch and Church in Moscow.[32]

Although Peter was fascinated by England, he had been away from Russia for more than a year, and the political situation in Moscow was becoming dangerous because of disaffection among the *streltsy*. He therefore left England at the end of April 1698, planning to return to Moscow by way of Amsterdam, Vienna, and Venice. In Amsterdam, he received word from Andrei Vinius, Prince Feodor Romodanovskii, and General Gordon, his chief ministers and military advisers in Moscow, that four *streltsy* regiments garrisoned in Azov, the southern port he had so recently seized from the Turks, had revolted rather than obey his orders to march to the frontier of Lithuania.[33] General Gordon concluded that "it was hardly worth while to take the matter seriously, or anticipate great danger,"[34] and he evidently had convinced Prince Romodanovskii to share his view. Peter was furious and wrote to Romodanovskii that his failure to question the ringleaders under torture was inexcusable.[35] Nevertheless, he concluded that the revolt had been put down and continued with his plans to visit Vienna and Venice.

The situation was far more explosive than Gordon had first realized. On June 8, 1698, he wrote in his diary that "a report was spread that four Strelitz [*streltsy*] regiments at Toropets were disposed to insurrection." Three days later, he learned more details: "Two captains returned from Toropets and reported that the Strelitzes, after repeated secret consultations, had resolved not to march to the stations appointed for them, but to go straight to Moscow." Romodanovskii and Vinius decided to send Gordon with artillery and some two thousand infantry drawn from Peter's new Guards regiments to crush them. Gordon met the rebels near the Voskresenskoe Monastery and performed his task efficiently, though not without a considerable measure of charity for the enemy.[36]

[*150*]

Peter heard of the revolt only after it had been crushed. Although Romodanovskii had written to him on June 11, the letter, with its ominous postscript that the rebels were only sixty miles from Moscow, did not reach Vienna until July 15.[37] Peter reacted to Romodanovskii's report with barely contained fury. Not knowing that Gordon had the situation well in hand, he abandoned his plans to visit Venice and made straight for Moscow. He traveled from Vienna to Krakow with amazing speed, sometimes covering as many as eighty-five miles in a single day. At Krakow, word finally reached him that the *streltsy* no longer threatened Moscow; Peter traveled the remaining distance more slowly, still intent upon dealing ruthlessly with the men whose political volatility threatened his government.[38]

Late on the night of August 25, 1698, Peter slipped into the Kremlin unnoticed. Within a week, he ordered his courtiers to shave their beards in violation of the Church's dictates, insisted that they exchange their flowing kaftans for Western fashions, and forced his uncomprehending, tradition-bound wife Evdokia into a convent where she was separated from Aleksei, the son she had borne eight years earlier. Because she stood for the old ways he was determined to abandon, Peter wanted neither his wife, nor the son upon whom she doted and in whom she sought to instill the religious and cultural precepts of Old Russia, to become the focus of political dissension once he had embarked upon his plans to transform Russia into a European power.

His wife disposed of, his courtiers clean shaven and garbed in coats and trousers, Peter turned to deal with the *streltsy*. Brutal in his vengeance, he unleashed a bloodbath such as Muscovites had not seen since the days of Ivan the Terrible. He was determined to provide his subjects with a vivid example of the consequences political dissenters could expect to suffer. Hundreds of *streltsy* were sent to Prince Romodanovskii's torture chambers at Preobrazhenskoe, where Peter himself often did the questioning. Within the space of a few days, he hanged, beheaded, or broke upon the wheel a total of 799 men. Johann Korb's diary describes the scene of one of Peter's more barbaric executions:

> All the Boyars and Magnates that were present at the Council by which the fate of the rebel *streltsy* was decreed, this day were summoned to a new tribunal. A criminal was set before each, and each

had to carry out with the axe the sentence which had been passed. Prince Romodanovskii . . . laid four *streltsy* low with the same weapon—His Majesty urging him to it. The more cruel Alexsasha [Menshikov] went boasting of twenty heads that he had chopped off. . . . The Czar himself, sitting in his saddle, looked on with dry eyes at the whole tragedy . . . being only irate that several of the Boyars had performed this unaccustomed function with trembling hands.[39]

For those of the *streltsy* who escaped execution and survived Romoda-novskii's torture chambers, Peter had further punishments in store. In June 1699 he disbanded all regiments of the Moscow *streltsy*, confiscated their property, dispersed them to distant parts of Russia, and forbade them to serve as soldiers again. In doing so, he eliminated the one dissident group in Russia that possessed the military force to challenge his power. At the same time, he condemned the former *streltsy* to lives of insignificance and obscurity, since military service soon became perhaps the major vehicle for upward social mobility in Peter's Russia.

Peter spent the decade after his return from Western Europe in frenzied activity that touched every aspect of Old Russia's economic, social, and political life. Between 1699 and 1709, he abandoned Moscow as his capital and built a new one, St. Petersburg, near the point where the Neva River flowed into the Gulf of Finland. Yet, before the first cornerstone of Peter's new capital could be laid, the land on which it was to stand had to be won by the force of Russian arms. For upon it stood the small Swedish fort of Nienschanz, an ever-present reminder that the Swedish King Charles XII claimed the eastern-most reaches of the Baltic as his own. Peter's refusal to recognize that claim led to his ignominious defeat at Narva, where he had lost much of his army, many of his generals, and most of his artillery to Charles's surprise attack in November 1700. Charles then had scornfully turned his back upon Russia to deal with the Poles and the Saxons, whom he deemed more worthy opponents. In the meantime, Peter had reorganized and rebuilt his army with furious energy, and he was ready by the fall of 1702 to try the Swedes again. This time, he faced lesser captains than the great Charles himself, and, for the first time in more than a century, Russia tasted the sweet nectar of victory against the Swedes. In

October 1702 Peter's armies under Field Marshal Boris Sheremetiev seized the Swedish fortress of Noteburg, which they renamed Schlüsselberg, and gained a foothold on the Neva River. The next step was to conquer the Neva's mouth. On April 23, 1703, less than three years after his defeat at Narva, Peter sent Field Marshal Sheremetiev with sixteen thousand infantry against Nienschanz. Sheremetiev's advance guard easily seized the fort's outer works but, because he had no artillery, he began to construct siege entrenchments before he attacked the fort itself. A few days later, Peter himself brought up sixteen siege mortars and forty-eight pieces of heavy artillery. After one day's bombardment, the Swedes surrendered on May 1. With few casualties, and a minimal amount of cannon fire, Peter had gained the foothold on the Baltic for which Russia had struggled since the time of Ivan the Terrible.

Noteburg and Nienschanz were Peter's first victories against the Swedes, but they were by no means his last or his greatest, for the relatively small modern force he threw against Charles's army in 1702 and 1703 represented but a beginning in a vast undertaking to reorganize, rearm, and retrain the entire Russian army according to the latest European models. So successful was Peter's effort that he would crush Sweden's regulars at Poltava in a defeat that marked the end of Charles XII's great battles in Russia. After 1709 the war would shift to Charles's Finnish lands and to Sweden itself as Peter built Russia's first Baltic fleet and learned to use it effectively against a nation that had been until recently a major seapower. These achievements were in themselves impressive, but the extent of Peter's modernizing effort becomes truly awesome if we remember that he rebuilt his army and built his navy at a time when he faced serious political and social unrest at home. For, during the same decade that he won the land on which to build St. Petersburg and defeated Charles XII's army at Poltava, Peter crushed major revolts in Astrakhan and among the Don Cossacks in the Ukraine and the Bashkirs along the Volga.

At the same time as he waged war against Sweden and his rebellious subjects, Peter began to reorganize Russia's central and provincial administration along European lines, and he sought to develop a system of taxation that would more effectively tap the wealth of his domains.

To make Russia less dependent upon manufactured goods from Europe, he began a large-scale program of subsidizing the development of new industries throughout Russia. How extensive these efforts were can be seen if we look ahead to the end of Peter's reign in 1725. By that time, the number of Russia's industries had increased tenfold, a new tax system based on a head tax upon all lower-class males had been implemented, and a new system of central administration—the so-called administrative colleges—had been put into practice. Perhaps most significant of all, Peter had forced Russia's nobles to shoulder the onerous burden of lifetime service and made their social and economic position dependent upon their success in the service of their country.[40]

During the same decade as he won his first victories against Sweden, Peter's personal life became more settled, even happy, for it was at that time that he found the woman with whom he would share the rest of his life. Marfa Skavronska was a Lithuanian peasant girl whose early life, from the sparse information we have, was filled with sadness and tragedy. Orphaned at an early age, she spent her childhood and adolescence in the home of Ernst Gluck, a Lutheran pastor in Marienburg, where she performed menial household chores that, according to some accounts, even included tending the pastor's swine. By the age of seventeen, she had become a beautiful young woman, whose masses of curls and voluptuous figure drew admiring glances wherever she went. To her physical charms, she added a ready smile, flashing dark eyes, and an easy manner. Her first love was Johann Raabe, a Swedish dragoon garrisoned at Marienburg, who was called away to defend the town on the day of their marriage. She never saw him again. The days after the fall of Marienburg in 1702 found Marfa, by then presumably a widow, in the Russian baggage train, "dressed in nothing but a shirt."[41] One of the foreigners in Russia's service, an officer by the name of Bauer, soon discovered her, rescued her, and made her his mistress. But she was not long destined for Bauer's bed. Soon she became the mistress of Field Marshal Sheremetiev himself, and from his hands passed into those of Peter's favorite, "Aleksasha" Menshikov.[42]

Toward the end of 1703, at Menshikov's table, where her task was to fill the guests' wine goblets, Peter first saw Marfa. Within a few months, Tsar and serving wench had formed a relationship that would endure until his death in 1725. Soon she converted to Orthodoxy and took the name of Catherine. She traveled with Peter, even on his campaigns, and became his closest friend. During their years together, Catherine bore Peter four sons and six daughters, although all but three daughters died in childhood, most probably weakened and left vulnerable to disease by the syphilis Peter had contracted during his youthful carousals in Moscow's Foreign Quarter. Yet Catherine became far more than a fecund bedmate for the Tsar. Well aware that her physical charms would one day fade and that, in any case, her body alone could not command the Tsar's loyalty during their long separations, she enveloped him in a warmth and comradeship he had never known and had always craved. With Catherine, Peter found rare moments of peace. He soon began to call her "little mother" and found time to send her a steady stream of endearing notes from all corners of Russia. Although illiterate, Catherine treasured them as evidence of his affection, had them read and reread by her companion Anisia Tolstaia, and dictated the replies for which Peter waited impatiently during the weeks and months they sometimes were apart. "It has been three weeks since I have heard from you," he wrote from the marshes of St. Petersburg in March 1708. "For the love of God, come to me with all speed or, if that is not possible, write, for it makes me so sad not to hear from you or see you." So strong was Catherine's hold upon the Tsar's heart that he married her privately in 1707; on February 9, 1712, he did so publicly. Their children, Anna and Elizaveta, were the bridal attendants.[43]

On June 27, 1709, Peter sent one of his many notes to Catherine, which began: "Hello to you, little mother! I announce that the All-merciful God has this day granted us an indescribable victory over the enemy. In a word, the entire enemy force is smashed. You will hear all about it from us. Come here and give us your congratulations in person."[44] These simple phrases told Catherine that her Tsar had realized the dream he had carried in his heart for nearly a decade. At long last, Peter had avenged Russia's humiliating defeat at Narva and had demolished the armies of Charles XII in a great battle at the gates of Poltava. At Narva even the forces of Nature had turned against the Russians and had provided Charles with a raging blizzard to mask his advance. In 1709 Nature allied herself with Peter. As would happen with the armies of Napoleon in 1812 and those of Hitler in 1941, the Russian winter decimated the ranks of Sweden's armies long before they faced Peter's guns.

The year 1709 had opened with savage frosts and bitter winds that caught the Swedes in the open and caused thousands to suffer frostbite, amputated limbs, and death. They suffered as well the ravages of hunger. Contrary to his expectations, Charles XII found the population of the Ukraine hostile, and, as a result, when he laid siege at the beginning of May to Poltava, a small commercial center on the west bank of the Vorskla River, the magnificent army of forty thousand with which he had marched from Saxony the previous autumn had but a shade of its former might. Two months later, Peter's armies attacked. For several hours bitter fighting raged across the plain in front of the city. Always in the thick of the fray, Peter lost his hat to a musket ball, had his saddle struck by another, and felt yet a third glance off the crucifix he wore around his neck. By noon, the battle was over. The Russians had lost thirteen hundred men. They had killed more than three thousand Swedes and taken some two thousand more captive, including Field Marshal Rehnskjold, four Major Generals, and five Colonels. A day later, the Swedish General Lewenhaupt surrendered with another twelve thousand men at Perevolochna. When Charles, wounded and exhausted, finally escaped across the Bug River, he had fewer than a thousand men with him. Overjoyed at his victory, Peter, who had assigned himself the lowly rank of bombardier in 1689, now promoted himself to the rank of Lieutenant General to celebrate his apparent mastery of military science.[45]

As Peter wrote to General-Admiral Feodor Apraksin, the victory at Poltava "laid the final stone in the foundation of St. Petersburg,"[46] thus ensuring the safety of his newly opened "window on the West." Russia's war with Sweden had not ended, however, and there were still battles with other enemies to be fought. In 1711 Peter suffered a humiliating defeat on the Pruth River at the hands of the Turks and lost the southern ports he had struggled so valiantly to wrest from the Ottoman Empire at the beginning of his reign. It was not until 1721 that he achieved final victory over the Swedes. His successful campaign against Persia came two years later.

By the 1720s, Peter had lost many of the comrades with whom he had stood shoulder to shoulder in the darker moments of his reign. Field Marshal Sheremetiev, that imposing and magnificently clad figure who had so dazzled the captive Marfa Skavronska after the fall of Marienburg, had become a querulous old man before he died in 1718. Prince Boris Golitsyn had become an arthritic cripple well before the end of the Great Northern War, and Prince Feodor Romodanovskii, for so many years master of the torture chambers at Preobrazhenskoe and one of Peter's most devoted drinking companions, died in 1717 at the age of seventy-seven. The passing of these comrades served to remind Peter of his own mortality, an awareness probably strengthened by the signs of advancing venereal disease, which caused him to lose the use of his left hand on occasion and made it necessary for him to take a variety of cures in Western Europe.[47] Although he tried to accept other minor infirmities with some humor, there was an element of pathos in his efforts. "Hello, darling little Kate, my dearest friend," he wrote to Catherine in May 1716 after she had sent him a pair of spectacles. "My thanks for your gift. I have sent you something from here in return. Truly our presents for each other are fitting on both sides. You have sent me something to counter the ravages of age, and I am sending you something for the adornment of your youth."[48]

Peter's growing awareness of his mortality forced him to face the question of his successor. One by one, he had seen three of the treasured sons Catherine had borne him sicken and die. By 1717, only the sickly two-year-old Petr Petrovich remained. Beyond that, there still were a number of other Romanov candidates: Evdokia's son Aleksei, three daughters, a variety of nieces, and Petr Alekseevich, the son who had been born in 1715 to Aleksei and his wife, Princess Charlotte of Wolfenbüttel. Among those who stood in line to inherit his throne, Peter favored Petr Petrovich, whose birth came on the eve of his own recovery from a serious illness. "God has given me a recruit. God has given me a little seaman," he had proclaimed when he heard the news.[49] Together he and Catherine placed their hopes upon this boy, the first son born to them since 1706. In doing so, they ignored the obvious fact that he was somewhat backward.

Peter's joy at Petr Petrovich's birth apparently caused him to take a firmer stand in dealing with his eldest son Aleksei, that disappointing fruit of those few weeks he had spent with Evdokia in 1689. Born on February 19, 1690, Aleksei had spent the first eight years of his life in the company of his mother and her circle of traditionalists who stood united against the violent path of rapid westernization Peter had mapped out for Russia. Aleksei had been steeped in the teachings and rituals of the Church from infancy. Like the grandfather whose name he bore, he had a deep love for religious reading and contemplation.

When Peter sent Evdokia to a convent in 1698, he placed Aleksei's education in the hands of Western tutors and sought to introduce him to the life of war and ships that he so loved himself. Yet, in doing so, Peter crushed his son's spirit, for he was an awkward, even brutal, teacher. Aleksei lacked his father's indomitable will, strength, and boundless energy, and he could not perform the physical tasks his father imposed upon him. He lived in constant terror of Peter's displeasure, and this soon overwhelmed whatever love or admiration he may have had for him. He sought solace in the company of men who offered sympathy, those who also had reason to hate his father. As Aleksei grew to manhood, he became a drunkard and a man of brutal temper. Like Peter, he soon rejected the company of his well-born wife Charlotte and sought solace in the arms of a peasant girl, whom he made his mistress. Aleksei's peasant mistress, Afrosinia, was, like her lover, weak. At best a stupid and simple wench, she could not be for him the emotional buttress in times of crisis that Peter found in Catherine. Nor could she moderate his violent temper with common sense.[50]

Just before the birth of Petr Petrovich in late October 1715, Peter resolved to force Aleksei to mend his ways. He sent him a stern document entitled "A Declaration to My Son," which left no doubt about his intentions. It was a brief but dramatic statement, the final cry of frustration from a father whose son had failed him so utterly that there was no common ground left between them. After referring to his pride in Russia's new military strength, Peter continued:

> When I survey in my mind the line of succession, a grief almost equal to my joy [at Russia's military might] consumes me, for I see you, my heir, to be unfit for directing the affairs of state. . . . Moreover, you want to hear nothing of military matters, by means

of which we have come out of the darkness into the light, and because of which the world, which previously scorned us, now does us honor. . . . Thinking about all this, I turn again to my original point about you, for I am a man and one day shall die. To whom have I to bequeath . . . what I have sown? To him who can be likened to the idle servant in the Scriptures who buried his single coin in the ground! Then I also recall what an evil and obstinate temper you possess! How often have I cursed you for that, and not only cursed, but even beaten you. . . . Taking all this into account, I have concluded that nothing can make you mend your ways. For the good of all, I have contrived to write this last testament to you, but to wait yet a little longer to see if you will honestly mend your ways. If you do not, then you can be certain that I shall deprive you of your inheritance, that I shall cut you off like a gangrenous limb. . . . As God is my witness, I shall do so. For, if I have not spared my own life in the service of our motherland, then why should I spare yours which is unnecessary to her? [51]

Aleksei's reply to his father's ultimatum came three days later. "Most Gracious Sovereign Father," he wrote. "I have nothing more to report except that, if you desire to deprive me of my right to the Russian crown, let your will be done. . . . I see myself as incapable and unfit for such a task, for I am of poor memory (without which it is possible to do nothing), and, with all my intellectual and physical powers weakened by various illnesses, I have become unfit to govern the [Russian] people, for such is a task that requires a far less decayed sort of man than I." He signed himself "Your most humble slave and son, Aleksei." [52]

It is difficult to gauge accurately Aleksei's thoughts and motivations at this point, for he had become accustomed to concealing his true intentions from his father beneath a veil of craven submissiveness. Certainly he was in no way as mild and humble as his replies to his father's demands made him appear. He was willful and spiteful, and he loved wealth and the luxury money could buy. He enjoyed forcing others to bend to his will but had no understanding of the obligations of power. Certainly he had no notion of service to Russia. He did not want to govern, as his father had done, but he did want to sit upon the throne.

In the context of that Muscovite upbringing in which Aleksei had been immersed since infancy, a Tsar did not renounce his throne. Yet a

Tsar could retire from public life when his personal safety was threatened or when his hold upon the throne was insecure. Ivan the Terrible had done so in 1564, and Sofia had employed a similar tactic in 1682 when she had gone to the Trinity Monastery to bring Khovanskii and his *streltsy* to heel in the days immediately after their revolt. Aleksei seemed prepared to follow a similar course in 1715; the fact that Peter was gravely ill in the weeks before and after he sent his "Declaration" to his eldest son adds further circumstantial evidence to such an explanation for Aleksei's actions. Quite probably, he simply wanted to retire from view until he could ascend the throne on his own terms. Although they must have frightened him momentarily, his father's next warnings in January 1716, which told him to "change your ways and honestly act like an heir to the throne or become a monk,"[53] posed no great threat to his peace of mind once his closest adviser, Aleksandr Kikin, assured him that "to put on the monk's cowl does not mean that it is nailed to your head; it can be taken off again." Aleksei therefore wrote to his father on January 20, 1716, that "I desire the monk's state and beg your gracious leave to become such."[54]

For Peter, Aleksei's willingness to withdraw from state affairs and his refusal to "act like an heir to the throne" posed a dilemma to which he could find no ready solution. It seems quite clear that he would have preferred to see the throne go to the infant Petr Petrovich, but his childhood had shown him the perils that lay in store for Russia with the accession of a minor. At the age of forty-four, he could not reasonably plan to live until his newborn son reached adulthood. His own father had died at the age of forty-seven, his grandfather had lived only two years longer. Rather than permit Aleksei to take monastic vows, he asked him to consider again the alternative of "acting like an heir to the throne." Relieved that his father had not forced the issue, Aleksei returned to the joys of drunkenness and the arms of his serf mistress. In his delight, he overlooked the ominous last line Peter had penned in January 1716: "'If you do not do this [that is, either mend your ways or become a monk], I shall treat you like a criminal."[55] The Tsar had come near to the end of his patience; he could not be pushed much further.

Peter did not intend this reprieve to continue indefinitely. He had given Aleksei six months to consider his final course, and, at the end of August, he demanded an answer. "Upon receipt of this letter," he wrote in his characteristically brusque manner, "make your choice immediately. It must be one or the other."[56] Forced to action by his father's demands, Aleksei chose a third course that drove Peter well beyond the limits of his patience. At the end of September 1716, Aleksei fled to Vienna and begged the Holy Roman Emperor, Charles VI, for asylum. "I have come to beg the Emperor . . . to save my life. They want to murder me," he pleaded with the Imperial Vice-Chancellor Count Schönborn. "Do not turn me over to my father, for he is surrounded by evil counselors and is himself a cruel man who does not value human life and thinks that, like God, he has the power over life and death."[57] Fearing that Russia was on the brink of a serious political upheaval since the Austrian resident in St. Petersburg had recently reported that "everything here is ripe for rebellion,"[58] Charles VI could not simply send his troublesome brother-in-law back to St. Petersburg. At the same time, it would be awkward indeed to give him asylum, for that would be tantamount to a public proclamation that Peter was guilty of plotting his son's murder. Charles chose to keep Aleksei in hiding and waited for Peter to make the next move.

It was not long before Peter learned of his son's whereabouts, but he shrank from the embarrassment of raising the matter with the Emperor. In July 1717, his patience finally exhausted, he sent Count Petr Tolstoi and Captain Aleksandr Rumiantsov to Vienna to seek a private audience with the Emperor and to inform him that, if Aleksei were not sent back, he would take whatever further steps were necessary to obtain his return. Through a combination of charm and bribery, Tolstoi obtained an interview with Aleksei. He had with him a letter from the Tsar in which he promised that his son would "suffer no punishment" and that he would bestow upon him his "best love if you obey my will and return."[59] At the same time, Tolstoi contrived that Aleksei be given the impression that Charles VI was about to withdraw his protection and that Afrosinia, the serf mistress he now hoped to wed, would be taken from him. Confused, terrified, and desperate at the prospect of being parted from Afrosinia, Aleksei agreed to return to Russia. Tolstoi even promised that he could wed his mistress. Everyone breathed a sigh of relief except for those Russians who had supported Aleksei secretly against his father. "He'll get a coffin, not a wedding," Prince Vasilii Dolgorukii remarked bitterly.[60]

Peter chose to confront his wayward son not in St. Petersburg but in the Kremlin, that symbol of Muscovite tradition that Aleksei and his supporters held so dear. He was brought in as an officer under arrest, stripped of his sword. Begging his father for mercy on his knees, he was forced by Peter to publicly renounce the throne in favor of the three-year-old Petr Petrovich and to name all who had aided and encouraged him. Without a moment's hesitation, Aleksei condemned them all: Aleksandr Kikin, Prince Vasilii Dolgorukii, General Aide-de-Camp Semën Naryshkin, his tutor Nikifor Viazemskii, his chamberlain Ivan Afanasiev, and a number of others. Fearing a conspiracy, Peter had many of them questioned under torture. Some were executed; others suffered exile and disgrace. All lived to rue the day they had placed their confidence in a weak-willed drunkard. Aleksei himself did not escape, although it was not the testimony of these men but that of Afrosinia that doomed him. Peter himself questioned her, and, whether through fear, contempt, indifference, or plain stupidity, she readily condemned him. Above all, her testimony made it clear that Aleksei had wished his father's death, had plotted rebellion, and hated everything his father stood for.

Confronted by his mistress's testimony, Aleksei confessed. To Peter it was now clear that his eldest son was guilty not only of opposing his will but of high treason. A court composed of Russia's highest dignitaries examined him under torture, found him guilty, and sentenced him to death. The signatures affixed to his sentence read like an honor roll of the families who would render the Romanovs the most faithful service for the next two centuries: Prince Menshikov, Count Apraksin, Count Golovkin, Prince Iakov Dolgorukii, Count Musin-Pushkin, Prince Dmitrii Golitsyn, Petr Tolstoi, General Ivan Buturlin, General Grigorii Chernyshev, Prince Matvei Gagarin, and 116 others.[61] But Aleksei cheated his father's executioner. Probably as a result of the torture he had suffered, he died on June 26, 1718, two days after his death sentence had been signed but before it could be carried out.

Aleksei's death did not resolve Peter's difficulties in finding a successor. Indeed, that would become one of the insoluble problems of his reign, and his inability to find a solution would, in large measure, account for the unfortunate legacy of instability and crisis he left at his death. Less than a year after Aleksei's death, Petr Petrovich followed him to the grave, leaving Peter with no sons to follow in his steps. Indeed, the only surviving male Romanov, aside from Peter himself, was his grandson Petr Alekseevich, the product of that ill-fated union between Aleksei and the Princess Charlotte of Wolfenbüttel. Evidently convinced that his successor could not be a male Romanov, Peter proclaimed in 1722 that the Emperor could choose whomever he thought best qualified to succeed him.[62] It may well have been that he had Catherine in mind when he took such an unprecedented step; his formal coronation of her as Empress in May 1724 lends weight to that supposition. Certainly the decree he published prior to her coronation stressed her virtues as a consort and her talent for statecraft: "Our most beloved Spouse, the Sovereign Empress Catherine," it read, "has been of great help to us . . . in many military campaigns. She has set aside feminine weaknesses, and willingly has assisted us as much as possible. Especially in the Pruth campaign against the Turks, in our most desperate hour, she acted like a man, not a woman. This is known to our entire army and, through it, undoubtedly to the entire nation."[63] Given the popular prejudice against having a woman on the throne, Peter's emphasis upon Catherine's ability to "act like a man" in state affairs and her willingness to "set aside feminine weaknesses" was especially significant. Yet he never formally proclaimed her his heir, and during his last years on the throne there were some who feared that he might even name a foreigner to succeed him. Despite his efforts to prepare for the future, death caught Peter by surprise in early 1725. He died without naming a successor, thereby plunging Russia into a half-century of succession crises that at times, would leave the ship of state dangerously adrift.

Although his failure to produce a healthy male heir continued to plague Peter during the last decade of his reign, there were other aspects of his life in which he found considerable satisfaction. In 1721 the Treaty of Nystadt with Sweden gave Russia mastery over the eastern Baltic and formal title to the land upon which the new city of St.

Petersburg stood eighteen years after its first stone had been laid. Peter was exultant. "All students usually complete their course of study in seven years, but for our schooling, the course had to be thrice-repeated," he wrote to Prince Dolgorukii in Paris. "Thank God that it all ended so well that it could not have been better." [64]

Peter's triumph over the Swedes marked more than a military victory and the corresponding acquisition of new territory. It marked the emergence of Russia as a major power. Peter's regular army of 130,000 men, supplemented by 100,000 Cossacks, was easily the largest in Europe. Further, it was an army equipped with modern weapons and trained in up-to-date tactics, a far cry from the feudal levies Vasilii Golitsyn had led into the Crimea in 1689. Perhaps particularly satisfying to Peter, Russia's defeat of Sweden was a naval victory won with a navy that, at the outset of the war, had been nonexistent. Although Peter's Black Sea fleet never became a reality, his Baltic fleet had become a formidable force in the space of a single decade. It was a measure of the Tsar's vast energy and indomitable will that, while there was not a single Russian warship on the Baltic in 1710, the fleet numbered 48 ships of the line, 750 lesser vessels, and 28,000 sailors by 1725. [65]

The fleet, the army, and the fact of St. Petersburg's existence were great achievements, but Peter realized them only at a stupendous cost. Tens of thousands died in the construction of Russia's new capital, and tens of thousands more died of wounds or disease in his many campaigns. Yet it was the achievement that the Imperial Senate and the Holy Synod lauded in October 1721, when they conferred upon Peter the title of Emperor and the epithet "the Great." There was much truth in the ringing praises the Bishop of Pskov, Feofan Prokopovich, delivered on that occasion. From the Trinity Cathedral, in the city that owed its very existence to Peter, Prokopovich proclaimed: "We take it upon ourselves in the name of the All-Russian state and your subjects of all ranks, to most humbly implore Your Majesty to favor us with a small measure of your fatherly concern by taking upon yourself, as a small mark of our acknowledgment of the blessings you have brought to our entire nation, the title of Father of Our Country, Peter the Great, Emperor of All Russia. Vivat, Vivat, Vivat Peter the Great, Father of Our Country, Emperor of All Russia!" [66]

During his lifetime, and throughout the two hundred fifty-odd years since his death on the morning of January 28, 1725, scholars and publicists have tried to evaluate Peter the Great's accomplishments, to weigh them in the balance of history against their cost and against his failures. Certainly, it is clear that many of the changes he implemented had their roots in the policies of his father, even in the policies of the Regent Sofia and Vasilii Golitsyn. But, while some of his predecessors may have caught glimpses of the path Russia would be obliged to follow to modernization, they had been cautious and timid in approaching it. Lacking Peter's daring, and fearful of the political and social costs involved in Russia's transformation, they sought to integrate Western innovations into the fabric of the Russian state and society. Impatient, and unafraid to chart new courses, Peter declared war upon the life and culture of Old Russia as well as upon the Swedes and the Turks. He seized upon time-honored customs and tore them out by the very roots, leaving Russia's cultural landscape disordered in his wake. Yet, in his passion to clear away the old ways, Peter failed to give Russians new values to replace the ones he had destroyed. If he failed to designate a successor, so too did he fail to bequeath a clear view of the course he had charted. As Russians later in the eighteenth century would say, "Peter created the body of Russia, but Catherine [the Great] gave it a soul."[67] The soul would be created only after a half-century of political, social, and intellectual chaos during which Russians sought first to perceive, and then to come to grips with, the legacy of the man known as the "Tsar-Transformer."

During the four centuries that separated the accession of Ivan the Moneybag and the death of Peter the Great, Russia's rulers had been blessed with an unbroken line of heirs, except for that brief span of the decade that bridged the sixteenth and seventeenth centuries. As a result, the problem Russians faced at Peter's death, and the means for resolving it, were relatively unfamiliar to them. This was especially so because Peter had left no hint about how he thought a successor might be chosen. Only one thing was clear: he did not intend to have his nine-year-old grandson Petr Alekseevich succeed him, even though he was the only living male Romanov. Those who had opposed the Emperor's policies and hoped to return to the comparative calm of Muscovite ways after his death saw in Petr Alekseevich a means for achieving those ambitions. But there were others—those who had risen by supporting Peter's reforms—who stood to suffer exile, disgrace, perhaps even death, if his grandson, rather than the Empress Catherine, ascended the throne. Inevitably, the elite regiments of Imperial Guards, which had evolved from Peter's "play regiments," assumed a leading role in the matter. For the next four decades, with the notable exceptions of the accessions of Peter II in 1727 and Peter III in 1761, the Imperial Guards would be the arbiters of the succession. Within the space of thirty-seven years, they would place four autocrats upon the Russian throne.

The first to reap the benefits of the Guards' support was the Empress Catherine, who had arrayed on her side many of the men who had wielded vast influence under her husband. Most important among them were: Pavel Iaguzhinskii, Russia's Procurator-General, who like Catherine had begun life as a Lithuanian peasant; Petr Tolstoi, a Senator regarded by many as the murderer of Peter's eldest son; Feodor Apraksin, General-Admiral of the Russian fleet; General Ivan Buturlin; Feofan Prokopovich, who had risen from humble origins to become Bishop of Pskov; and, most important, Menshikov, Catherine's former lover and Peter's closest confidant. Even before Peter had breathed his last, they had begun to lay their plans. Fearful that a majority of Russia's senior statesmen might refuse to support their arguments on Catherine's behalf, they turned to the Guards for assistance. In that respect, their task was relatively simple. Catherine's easy ways and good humor had won for her the loyalty of Russia's soldiers when she had accompanied Peter on his campaigns. Menshikov, Tolstoi, and Apraksin hastened to fortify those sentiments by distributing sixteen months of back pay to the Guards and St. Petersburg's garrison in Catherine's name.

Confident that they held the power to assert Catherine's claim, Menshikov, Iaguzhinskii, Apraksin, Buturlin, and Tolstoi went to a meeting of Russia's leading statesmen and senior officials on the night after Peter's death. There they were confronted by Prince Dmitrii Golitsyn, Prince Grigorii Dolgorukii, Prince Nikita Repnin, and Apraksin's younger brother Petr. Already these elder statesmen were beginning to sense that it would be impossible to assert Petr Alekseevich's claim directly. Prince Golitsyn therefore attempted a compromise: their candidate would be proclaimed as Emperor, while Catherine, guided by the Senate, would serve as Regent. Knowing that they held the power to enforce their claim, Catherine's supporters, with Tolstoi as their spokesman, rejected Golitsyn's compromise as useless, even dangerous, because "this proposal would lead to civil strife, which we want to avoid at all costs." "Under present conditions," Tolstoi continued, "the Russian Empire has need of a steadfast sovereign, firm in the affairs of state, who would be able to defend that importance and glory won through the continued labors of our [deceased] Emperor, and who, at the same time, would be distinguished by a concern for making our people happy and loyal to the government. All these necessary qualities," he concluded, "are possessed by the Empress. She has learned the art of governing from her husband, who confided to her the most vital state secrets. She has, without doubt, displayed her heroic courage, her magnanimity, and her love for the people upon whom she has bestowed endless blessings both in general and individually, for she has never done evil to anyone."[68]

A number of Guards officers had drifted into one end of the council chamber as Tolstoi spoke, and they greeted his words with acclamations of support. If those elder statesmen who supported the candidacy of Petr Alekseevich had any doubts in their minds about which group held the power to assert its will, these were quickly dispelled by the roll of drums in the square below where the Preobrazhenskii and Semenovskii Guards were drawn up in full parade array. "Who dared bring these troops here without my orders? Am I not the Field Marshal?" Prince Repnin asked. "I ordered them to come here in accordance with the wishes of the Empress to whom every Russian, including you, owes allegiance," Buturlin replied.[69] Those of Russia's elder statesmen who doubted the legitimacy of a Lithuanian peasant wench who had borne five royal bastards before her marriage to a Tsar who had never properly divorced his first wife kept their reservations to themselves. Catherine was proclaimed Empress Catherine I before Peter had been dead a full day. What some historians have labeled as the "Era of Palace Revolutions" had begun.

Catherine did not take lightly the awesome responsibilities of her exalted office. One of her first concerns was to lighten the tax burdens of Russia's oppressed peasantry. Since Russia was now at peace, she was determined to reduce the state's ruinous military expenditures, which during the last years of Peter's reign had consumed some 65 percent of the state's annual revenue. She ordered the Senate to report to her every Friday, so that she could be well versed in Russia's internal policy.[70] These admirable efforts showed that Catherine did not intend to reign as a mere figurehead. But she was unable to rule effectively. The chief ministers she had inherited from Peter were a rough and ready crew, men of explosive temperament and vast personal ambition; only an extraordinary monarch such as Peter could harness them to positive ends and Catherine was not such a ruler. The entire concept of a female sovereign was totally alien to the experience of such men, and long years spent in Peter's inner circle had accustomed them to viewing Catherine as a woman, not a monarch. Menshikov at one time had shared her bed, and would do so again. Unlike her brilliant successor, the Empress Catherine the Great, she could not impose upon her lovers that personal discipline that separated the boudoir from the council chamber. Nor could she keep her avaricious and ambitious advisers in check. Aware of her failure, she allowed their personalities and ambitions to clash directly, perhaps hoping that the rapaciousness of one would counterbalance the greed of another, that the limitless ambitions of Menshikov could be checked by the conflicting aspirations of his associates. On February 8, 1726, she therefore established the Supreme Privy Council, which replaced the Senate as Russia's supreme administrative body.[71]

Besides the volatile Procurator-General of the Senate, Pavel Iaguzhinskii, the Supreme Privy Council included the six most powerful personalities to emerge in the upper reaches of Russia's government during Catherine's reign. In addition to Menshikov, she appointed General-Admiral Count Feodor Apraksin, Chancellor Count Gavriil Golovkin, Senator Count Petr Tolstoi, Senator Prince Dmitrii Golitsyn, and Vice-Chancellor Baron Andrei Ostermann, most probably hoping to achieve a balance in membership that would prevent any one member from gaining absolute control of state affairs. They were a diverse assembly, reflecting the varied sources from which Peter had drawn his advisers and assistants. With the exception of the forty-year-old Ostermann, all were well beyond middle age. Golovkin, a relative of the Naryshkins, came from exalted origins and had been one of Peter's most trusted advisers on foreign policy, but he was now sixty-six and had lost much of his youthful dynamism. Like Golovkin, Apraksin also was in his mid-sixties, and less assertive than in former days. He, too, had been one of Peter's earliest allies, and perhaps his closest adviser on naval affairs. Petr Tolstoi, now over eighty, had been a supporter of Sofia, but quickly had switched his loyalty to Peter before the coup of 1689. A master at Court politics and intrigue, he had convinced Peter's wayward son Aleksei to return to Russia and death, and had championed Catherine's candidacy at the time of Peter's death. Regarded by traditionalists as a traitor to the cause of Sofia, Aleksei, and Petr Alekseevich, he could only expect disgrace if they regained power. Ostermann, also the only foreigner among Catherine's appointees, had built his entire career upon his Emperor's favor and confidence. The son of a Westphalian Lutheran pastor, he had entered Peter's service in 1703 at the age of seventeen. A consummate diplomat, he rivaled Golovkin in his influence in foreign affairs. All these men owed their success to Peter and had broken their ties with Russia's traditionalists. Only Prince Golitsyn, just over sixty, held status in the old-line camp. Of Peter's former advisers, he was perhaps the best read in Western European political theory, and his reading and experience had convinced him that the Emperor had marched too quickly along the path to modernization. Nevertheless, Peter had kept him in high positions, probably because of his brilliant mind and broad education.

Catherine may have expected the Supreme Privy Council to hold the rapacity of "Aleksasha" Menshikov in check but, if that was her plan, it succeeded only to a very limited extent. The fault was her own. Menshikov continued to assail her with requests for honors and favors, and she granted many of them. From her hands he received the lordship of the vast region of Baturino in the Ukraine and, finally, the title of Generalissimus. If the Supreme Privy Council could not control Menshikov, it also could boast few accomplishments in directing Russia's internal affairs. The provinces became more impoverished, and the tax payments of the peasantry fell further into arrears. Only in foreign affairs did the Supreme Privy Council succeed in preserving a certain continuity in Russia's relations with the states of Western Europe.

As an Empress, Catherine thus enjoyed little success, and her failure to carry on the work of her husband must have made her last years bitter. The great void left in her life by the death of Peter and of her youngest daughter Natalia later in 1725 increased her bitterness. Natalia was the eighth of her ten children to die before they reached adulthood. Catherine sought refuge in the wild festivities and revels she had so enjoyed during Peter's lifetime, perhaps in a futile effort to make his presence seem nearer. Foreign observers in particular relished tales of her vast debauches and numerous lovers, but many of them can be discounted as rumors created by men whose minds inevitably focused upon such themes when a woman sat upon the throne. Still, there is no doubt that Catherine's health was destroyed by excessive drinking and the irregular hours she kept as she restlessly sought to bring her life back into focus. In her time of personal trial, she turned increasingly to "Aleksasha" Menshikov, the man to whom she had been close for nearly a quarter-century and whose great height and rough manners so reminded her of Peter.

As Catherine's condition deteriorated, Russians became preoccupied with the succession. Petr Alekseevich was still the only living male Romanov. Anna and Elizaveta, the two living daughters of Peter and Catherine, also could lay claim to the throne, and Catherine had always been sensitive to her childrens' interests. Yet all the candidates had serious disabilities. Petr Alekseevich was only ten years old when Catherine's health began to decline, and many Russians feared a regency, while others thought his accession would mark the undoing of what Peter the Great had begun. Catherine's eldest daughter, Anna, had married the Duke of Holstein-Gottorp soon after her father's death; Russians feared that he might attempt to seize the throne himself should his wife be named Catherine's heir. Elizaveta was yet unmarried but, like Anna, bore the stigma of illegitimacy. The two girls had been born well before Peter and Catherine were married publicly; many Russians could remember that both had been Catherine's bridal attendants. There also was the fear that Elizaveta might wed a foreign prince; Peter's efforts to arrange a marriage for her with a member of the Bourbon dynasty were well known.

It was Andrei Ostermann who first proposed a solution to the dilemma. Elizaveta had grown into a beautiful woman by the age of sixteen, and the precocious Petr Alekseevich was by no means indifferent to his young aunt's seductive charms. Ostermann proposed to marry them to each other, thereby uniting the divergent political interests each represented. Yet his plan had serious flaws, the most critical being that the marriage of two such close relatives was forbidden by the Church. Before a final decision could be made, Menshikov, possibly aided by the Austrian Ambassador Count Rabutin, conceived a plan of his own, the implications of which were utterly dazzling from his point of view. Catherine was persuaded to agree to a marriage between Petr Alekseevich and Menshikov's daughter Maria.[72]

Like Ostermann's proposal for marrying the young Grand Duke Petr to his aunt, Menshikov's plan seemed to promise the reconciliation of rival factions. Yet it really indicated that Menshikov was seeking to build new bridges to the camp of his former enemies in order to ensure his continued aggrandizement after Catherine's death. As a result, his former close associates, Count Tolstoi and General Buturlin, secretly opposed the marriage and tried to force him from office. At the same time, they prepared to defend the claims of Catherine's daughters. But their attack was premature, and their allies carelessly chosen. Some unguarded words from one of their ambitious confederates, General Anton de Vière, led to discovery, and they were disgraced and sent into exile.[73] Menshikov's power still was too strong to be opposed, yet in shifting his loyalty to the cause of Petr Alekseevich, he had set in motion the events that would lead to his own destruction.

Menshikov's patroness, the Empress Catherine I, died on May 6, 1727, at the age of forty-three, her sturdy peasant constitution undermined by the birth of ten children, more than two decades of rough and ready life with Peter, the venereal disease with which he had infected her, and her excessive drinking during the years after his death. Of her two surviving daughters, Anna no longer could contend for the throne because Russians feared the ambitions of her foreign husband. Elizaveta too, had little political support at that point, since her two chief advocates, Buturlin and Count Tolstoi, were exiled. Without difficulty or dispute, Peter the Great's eleven-year-old grandson, Petr Alekseevich, succeeded Catherine and was proclaimed Emperor and Autocrat of All the Russias immediately after her death. The Supreme Privy Council, now composed of nine members, including the Duke of Holstein-Gottorp and the princesses Elizaveta and Anna, was to serve as regent during Peter II's minority, but Menshikov seemed more in control than ever. He moved the young Emperor into his own palace where he could keep a watchful eye upon those who came into his presence. In May 1727 few in Russia would have disputed General Christopher von Manstein's remark that Menshikov "was exercising a perfect despotism."[74]

Yet even apparently perfect despotisms have their flaws, and a tempest was brewing that would sweep Menshikov into Siberia's bleak and endless wastes. Having abandoned his allies among the men who had risen under Peter the Great, he courted new ones among Russia's old aristocracy by dispensing favors as he had done during Catherine's reign. Yet he was no longer dealing with men who, like himself, had sprung from humble origins and craved honors to gloss over their obscure beginnings. The great lords among whom he now sought to make his way were men whose nobility had its origins in the time of Ivan the Terrible or even before, and they would never regard him as anything more than an upstart. Menshikov courted the Golitsyn princes and, even more, the princes Dolgorukii, men descended from the founder of Moscow himself.[75] These men accepted favors from his hands not to glorify their social position but to strengthen their political power. Once their position was strong enough, they would drive him from the scene as ruthlessly as he had dealt with their brothers, fathers, uncles, and grandfathers in the past.

Although he was only eleven at the time of his accession, Peter II had a mind of his own and proved far from a pliant tool for his prospective father-in-law's ambitions. A slender lad who had inherited the weak constitution that so often plagued male Romanovs, he was frequently ill. His chief passions were hunting, strong drink, and his blond, blue-eyed, and very buxom aunt Elizaveta.[76] Like his father and grandfather, he abhorred formal study but, again like them, he formed a deep personal attachment for his tutor. This was the same Baron Ostermann who had been one of Catherine's chief advisers on foreign affairs. Peter's closest friend was Prince Ivan Dolgorukii, a jovial and robust youth of nineteen, with whom he established a relationship not unlike that which the youthful Peter the Great had enjoyed with Franz Lefort in the 1690s. All of Peter II's entourage nourished secret, but burning, hatreds against Menshikov; Menshikov's greatest political blunder was that he had appointed them to their positions in the first place. Even Baron Ostermann would use his position as Peter's friend and tutor to undermine the power of his former ally.

Peter II also despised Menshikov, and his feelings for Menshikov's daughter Maria were only slightly warmer. Even at the age of eleven, he was acutely conscious of his position as Autocrat, and bitterly resented the high-handed manner in which Menshikov ordered him about. At one point, Peter reacted violently and shouted, "I will make you know that I am Emperor, and that I will be obeyed."[77] Yet his prospective father-in-law kept such a tight rein upon him that it seemed impossible for the boy to break free.

During the summer of 1727, however, Peter had his first taste of freedom despite Menshikov's best efforts, for Menshikov fell grievously ill. Wracked by a raging fever and coughing great quantities of blood, even he thought death was at hand. To everyone's amazement, he recovered.[78] But the consequence of his illness was just as lethal as if he had never risen from his deathbed. For, during the days in which Menshikov had lain ill, the fortnight between August 26 and September 7, 1727, the young Emperor proclaimed "I shall not marry before the age of twenty-five," despite the fact that Menshikov expected him to wed his daughter within a year. Peter refused to attend a celebration at Menshikov's suburban palace at Oranienbaum and removed all of his personal belongings from Menshikov's palace in St. Petersburg. When the Supreme Privy Council worried that he was challenging Menshikov too openly, Peter replied bluntly, "I will show you who is Emperor: Menshikov or me." The following day, he showed them indeed. On the morning of September 8, he sent Lieutenant General Semën Saltykov to Oranienbaum with a warrant for Menshikov's arrest. Later that day, he decreed that "no orders or letters from Prince

Menshikov relating to any matter whatsoever . . . are to be obeyed under pain of Our wrath." He then deprived Menshikov of all his titles and ranks, confined him to Oranienbaum and, the following spring, sent him, his wife, and daughter to Siberia.[79]

"We have suffered from a tyranny which, thanks be to God, has now gone up in smoke," wrote Feofan Prokopovich, Menshikov's former close ally.[80] The general reaction to Menshikov's fall was perhaps best summed up by Egor Pashkov, an official in the army's administrative center, who wrote to a friend in Moscow: "The vain and empty glory of the arrogant Goliath, whom God has smashed with his mighty right hand, has perished. Everyone is ecstatic about it, and I . . . now live without fear. Everything here goes extremely well, and the terror we all knew under Prince Menshikov is gone."[81]

Although Peter II had driven Menshikov from office, he had neither the maturity nor the experience to govern Russia himself. He still remained a willful, unlettered youth whose passion for the hunt consumed his days. The tasks of ruling Russia thus fell to others, and this unleashed a bitter power struggle within the Supreme Privy Council and at Court. The chief antagonists were Baron Ostermann, who, as Peter's tutor and friend, enjoyed his confidence; the Golitsyn brothers, Prince Dmitrii and Prince Mikhail; and the powerful Dolgorukii clan, led by Peter's inseparable companion Prince Ivan, along with Ivan's father Prince Aleksei and his uncle Prince Vasilii Lukich. Their rivalry would nearly paralyze Russia's policy-making process as everyone waited to see who would emerge as Menshikov's successor. "Everything in Russia is in a terrible state of chaos," a foreign ambassador reported. "The Tsar does not deal with state affairs and does not intend to start doing so. No one is being paid, and God only knows what will happen to the state's finances. Everyone steals as much as he can. All the members of the Supreme Privy Council are 'unwell' and do not attend its meetings. Other government agencies also have ceased to function. Complaints are endless. Everyone does whatever happens to come to mind."[82]

At least until late 1728, it was unclear who held the authority to conduct the day-to-day business of government in Russia. First Prince Dmitrii Golitsyn, then Baron Ostermann, then the Dolgorukiis, then

Count Aleksandr Buturlin, and then again the Dolgorukiis, seemed about to rise to the top of the churning political caldron. The Spanish Ambassador, the Duke de Liria, thought for a brief moment in late 1727 that the rise of Buturlin might establish some sort of political truce between the warring Golitsyn and Dolgorukii clans, but that proved an idle hope. Buturlin's personality charmed not only the young Emperor but also Peter's sensual aunt Elizaveta. She and Buturlin quickly became lovers, and Peter jealously reassigned the dashing officer to the Army of the Ukraine.[83] With Buturlin gone, it seemed that the Dolgorukiis would emerge triumphant. Yet no one had any real certainty about it. As the Duke de Liria wrote to his superiors in Madrid in early 1728, "I will not guarantee that a week from now everything will not again be completely turned upside down, because there is no Court in all of Europe that is so volatile as this one."[84]

Despite the near-paralysis of policy that characterized his reign, the one thing that seemed certain was that Peter II would move Russia's capital back to Moscow. St. Petersburg represented the antithesis of everything his father had stood for, and, once free of Menshikov's control, he began to share openly the preference of his friend Prince Ivan Dolgorukii for Russia's ancient capital. When he prepared to visit Moscow for his coronation at the beginning of 1728, many assumed that he would remain there. The Duke de Liria reported that "the Tsar cannot endure either the sea or ships, but he passionately loves to follow the hounds. Here in St. Petersburg, there are few places to hunt, while around Moscow there are vast tracts of land for it. That is why people say and, it seems to me, they have sufficient reason for doing so, that once he [Peter II] goes to Moscow he will not return here." The Duke was certain enough of his opinion to sign a year's lease for a residence in Moscow and to purchase eighty horses to move his entire suite to Russia's old capital.[85]

De Liria proved correct. After arriving in Moscow at the beginning of February 1728, Peter lived alternately in the Kremlin and in the palace his grandfather had given to Franz Lefort. During the summer of 1729, he began to transfer a number of Russia's central government agencies to Moscow. Yet his abandonment of St. Petersburg was more than symbolic; Peter II also turned his back upon some of his grandfather's most dramatic achievements. After Menshikov's fall, he refused to appoint a new head for the College of War, the army's central administrative agency, despite pleas from the Supreme Privy Council. So little, in fact, did Peter II concern himself with the state of Russia's army that, when the College of War was moved to Moscow in 1729, he ordered its Vice-President, General Count Burkhard Münnich, to remain in St. Petersburg.[86] He similarly ignored the navy. When one of his advisers suggested that he might wish to sail aboard one of Russia's ships, he reportedly remarked that "I do not intend to sail the seas as did my grandfather."[87] By the end of his reign, Russia had not even a dozen seaworthy ships-of-the-line left from the fleet in which Peter the Great had taken so much pride.

Although Peter II's lack of interest in military matters promised to diminish Russia's status among the nations of Europe, the immediate effect of his neglect was to lessen popular discontent in Russia. No longer obliged to endure Peter the Great's hated annual troop levies, Russians found state authority less onerous. There were few popular protests and little seditious activity during Peter II's brief reign. In April 1728 he abolished the Preobrazhenskii Office, feared and hated by Russians for so long, and, for a brief span of two years, Russians no longer needed to fear the torture chambers Prince Romodanovskii had made so notorious.

The Tsar's passivity reduced the economic and political pressures upon his subjects, but Russia's governmental paralysis also meant that the state could neither respond to the needs of its inhabitants nor meet challenges to its authority and prestige abroad. Whether Peter II as an adult would have paid more serious attention to Russia's needs and problems than he did as an adolescent is impossible to determine, but as he grew older he appeared to become even less interested in affairs of state and left everything to his feuding advisers. At the beginning of September 1729, he left Moscow in the company of several Dolgorukiis and six hundred twenty hounds. He spent the next two months at a nearby Dolgorukii estate and seemed quite unconcerned that state affairs languished in the meantime. "There is no Tsar here, nor any ministers either. Consequently, we can accomplish nothing," complained the Duke de Liria from Moscow in mid-September.[88]

Surprising news accompanied Peter's return to Moscow in November. During the weeks the Emperor had been a guest on his estate, Prince Aleksei Dolgorukii had taken advantage of every opportunity to throw his daughter Ekaterina into the young ruler's path. Peter had become infatuated and agreed to marry her. Soon after he returned to Moscow, the couple formally announced their betrothal. Peter was fourteen at the time, Princess Ekaterina Dolgorukaia three years older. General von Manstein described her as a woman who "without being absolutely a beauty, had a very pretty face. She was above the middle stature, and very well shaped. She had something of a languishing expression in her large blue eyes, and wanted for neither wit nor education."[89] Peter planned to wed her soon after the beginning of the new year. Field Marshal Vasilii Dolgorukii opposed the marriage, fearing that, by arranging such a union, his cousin might follow Menshikov down the road to unpopularity and disgrace, but the rest of the clan was ecstatic. Once their relative became Russia's Tsarina, their triumph over the Golitsyns would be assured. In vain, the Field Marshal counseled the young princess to remember that "if someone asks you to use your influence on their behalf, serve not the interests of your family, but those of merit and virtue."[90]

Events soon proved the wisdom of Field Marshal Dolgorukii's good sense and caution. Just a month after his formal betrothal to Ekaterina Dolgorukaia, Peter fell ill. At first, his doctors did not consider his illness serious, but it soon became clear that he was suffering not from a simple chill but from the dread smallpox. A few days later, at one o'clock in the morning of January 19, 1730, the very day he was to have been married, Peter II died. Immediately after his death, Prince Aleksei Dolgorukii tried to convince the Court and the Supreme Privy Council that the young Emperor had named the Princess Ekaterina to be his successor. But Dolgorukii's claim was too absurd to be creditable, and his words fell upon deaf and sullen ears. For the third time in five years, Russia's ruling class was obliged to debate the succession question. For the second time since the death of Peter the Great, the Imperial Guards would play a central role.

The situation that confronted Russian statesmen in the hours after the young Emperor's death was more complex than the one they had faced after the death of Peter the Great, for Peter II was the last of the male Romanovs. There was now no question but that the crown must pass to a woman. The difficulty was to determine which one. To resolve this dilemma, the Supreme Privy Council met at ten that morning. There were present four Dolgorukiis, two Golitsyns, and Russia's aged Chancellor Gavriil Golovkin. Ever the diplomat, and concerned most of all with his political survival, Vice-Chancellor Baron Andrei Ostermann remained absent, pleading illness, as he sometimes did to avoid being involved in difficult political decisions. "It was by means of these sicknesses, which occurred at proper times, that this minister kept his ground so long," remarked one observer.[91] Especially in Ostermann's absence, Prince Dmitrii Golitsyn emerged as the dominant voice in the Council. Well educated, articulate, and taking advantage of the fact that the Dolgorukiis were divided among themselves and hated by everyone else, Golitsyn was able to impose his views upon the others.[92]

Aside from the Princess Ekaterina Dolgorukaia, whose candidacy not even all of the Dolgorukiis took seriously, there were five women whose birth and position brought them to the Council's attention. Although incarcerated in a convent since 1698, Peter the Great's first wife, the Tsarina Evdokia, had continued to consider herself Russia's Tsarina and had been allowed to return to Court by Peter II. She now demanded that she be considered her grandson's successor. Her personal plight evoked sympathy among Russian statesmen, but they were not inclined to give serious consideration to the claim of a narrowminded woman, who had been out of touch with the world for more than a quarter-century. At the urging of Prince Dmitrii Golitsyn, who argued that her illegitimacy was an insurmountable barrier, the Council also rejected the claim of the Grand Duchess Elizaveta. Thus, the choice almost immediately was narrowed to the three living daughters of Ivan V, Peter the Great's co-Tsar in the 1680s and 1690s. Ekaterina, the eldest, was married to the Duke of Mecklenburg, whom one historian has rightly called "one of the most worthless German princelets and a source of infinite trouble."[93] She thus was rejected, as was her youngest sister Praskovia. The Council settled upon Anna Ivanovna, the second daughter of Ivan V, and long-time widow of the Duke of Courland.

Anna Ivanovna seemed an attractive candidate to the members of the Supreme Privy Council for a number of reasons. Her husband's death had left her in near-destitute circumstances, and she had turned to her homeland for aid. Forced by necessity into the role of supplicant, she had corresponded with a number of the men who now sat on the Council to beg for funds, and her apparent docility had impressed them. In 1726 she had hoped to free herself from penury by wedding Maurice de Saxe, the illegitimate son of Augustus II of Poland and a future Marshal of France, who sought to eclipse his bastardy by becoming Duke of Courland. Her hopes had conflicted with Russian policy and Menshikov's aspirations to become Duke of Courland himself. Catherine I therefore had refused her permission for this marriage. Anna had raised no objections to Catherine's refusal, especially since, by that time, she had realized that de Saxe's suit was motivated only by his lust for Courland and not for her. Yet her apparent submissiveness had again impressed Russian statesmen.[94] Thus, in 1730, Anna appeared to them an ideal choice, a docile and easily influenced woman, whose undoubted gratitude at being rescued from obscurity in Mitau would make her a pliant tool in the hands of those who made her Russia's Empress.

The Supreme Privy Council, however, was not inclined to leave the expression of Anna's gratitude to chance. At Prince Golitsyn's suggestion, they secretly agreed among themselves to impose a number of conditions upon her that would circumscribe her power as an autocrat and assure their continued control of Russia's government. That very evening, Prince Vasilii Lukich Dolgorukii hastened in greatest secrecy to Mitau with a document pledging Anna to consult the Council in all matters. According to the agreement Dolgorukii carried, only with its consent could she marry, appoint an heir, declare war or make peace, levy new taxes, promote men to high ranks in the army and civil service, deprive nobles of life, property, or honor, or spend state revenues.[95] Anna signed the conditions immediately. On February 2, General Mikhail Leont'ev returned to the Supreme Privy Council with her agreement to rule as they decreed. For the moment, the traditionally unlimited power of Russia's Autocrat had been reduced to impotence, leaving the government in the hands of a small clique of oligarchs.

Yet there were a number of political forces at work in addition to the great lords in the Supreme Privy Council. Many greater and lesser nobles had come to Moscow to celebrate Peter II's wedding, and they were by no means satisfied to be excluded from the Council's deliberations. Even before Golitsyn and his associates had finished drafting the "Conditions," word of their plans filtered out to others in Moscow and created both consternation and an awareness of new political opportunities. Former Procurator-General of the Senate Pavel Iaguzhinskii, now a bitter enemy of the Supreme Privy Council, sent a messenger racing to Mitau to tell Anna that the conditions carried by Prince Dolgorukii were the work of a tiny oligarchy and were not ascribed to by the majority of the nobility or the Imperial Guards. At the same time, various other groupings of nobles hastily drafted twelve different petitions to the Empress. All sought to curb the pretensions of the Golitsyn-Dolgorukii oligarchy that dominated the Council, but none was especially concerned with limiting the power of the Autocrat.

Indeed, the vast majority of the 1,218 men who signed the petitions saw themselves as the Autocrat's creations. For centuries, Russia's noblemen had been dependent upon the Autocrat's favors for those privileges that set them apart from other classes. They saw little reason to change that relationship, and they therefore opposed the efforts of the Council to limit Anna's power. At the same time, they urged her to reduce their obligations and to grant them more privileges: to shorten the term of military service required of them by the state, to allow them to enter the army as officers rather than as privates, and to repeal Peter the Great's decree by which he had sought to introduce primogeniture in 1714.[96] These petitions clearly showed Anna that most of the nobility then in Moscow would support a restoration of her autocratic power. At the same time, they indicated the price she must pay for the support of the nobility and the Imperial Guards if she wished to rule as an Autocrat. She was more than willing to pay that price.

On Sunday, February 15, 1730, Anna entered Moscow with all the pomp befitting an Autocrat. She rode in a carriage drawn by nine horses, all richly adorned with gold. Before her marched the Preobrazhenskii Guards, chosen from among the most handsome men in the Empire, all over six feet tall, and led by Russia's three Field Marshals. Behind her came still more Preobrazhenskiis, followed by the Semenovskiis in full parade array. A salute of 156 cannon accompanied her progress to the gates of the Kremlin, where she was met by Russia's leading churchmen. At the entrance to the Cathedral of the Assumption stood Russia's Senators and the heads of the twelve administrative colleges Peter the Great had established. As she entered the Cathedral, a salute of one hundred more cannon boomed out, and all the troops who had lined her route through Moscow fired their muskets three times into the air.[97] If Anna had surrendered any of her autocratic powers, she did not act it. Significantly, the members of the Supreme Privy Council had been assigned no ceremonial role in her welcome to the Kremlin; they had been obliged to ride in her entourage.

Once word of their plans to limit Anna's powers had begun to circulate in Moscow, the Supreme Privy Council had realized that it would be difficult to enforce the agreement she had signed, especially since it could not be proclaimed publicly. Their plan had been to have Anna incorporate the "Conditions" into her coronation speech, thus making it appear that she had limited her power voluntarily. That way, it would seem that she had chosen them to govern Russia and would obscure the fact that they had seized power for themselves. To prevent any of those who opposed their plan from staging a countercoup, they had their new Empress closely guarded. Their spies were everywhere, and she was forbidden to speak with anyone except in the presence of witnesses. Yet they had not reckoned upon the cleverness of their opponents, especially Baron Ostermann.

Ostermann had conveniently suffered a crippling attack of gout in his right hand at the very moment when the rest of the Council had signed Prince Golitsyn's conditions. Fearing that, as the only foreigner in their midst, he would be the first to fall if they remained in power, Ostermann planned to bring about their ruin. Once Anna reached Moscow, he proceeded to put his plans into operation and found willing allies among those 180 senior statesmen and army officers (the so-called *Generalitet*) whom the Council had excluded from their deliberations. Ostermann arranged for Anna's ladies-in-waiting to be appointed from among the wives of these men, and thus passed secret messages to the Empress through their hands. So great was the need for secrecy that, on one occasion, messages were hidden behind the face of a clock sent as a gift from the Moscow clergy by Ostermann's ally, the Archbishop of Novgorod Feofan Prokopovich. Another time, messages were secreted in the swaddling clothes of the Empress's godchild.[98]

Their preparations complete, Ostermann, Prince Aleksei Cherkasskii, the Princes Ivan and Nikita Trubetskoi, General Grigorii Chernyshev, and 160 others of the *Generalitet* chose to act on February 25. Supported by the Guards, they demanded an audience with Anna in the Council chamber at four o'clock that afternoon. They begged her to restore the autocracy in the manner of "your glorious and worthy predecessors, and to destroy those conditions sent to your Imperial Highness by the Supreme Privy Council and signed by your own hand." Prepared for this petition by the secret messages she had received, Anna innocently asked, "Do you mean that the conditions that were brought to me in Mitau did not reflect the desires of all my subjects?" When told that they did not, she replied, "Then that means that you, Prince Vasilii Lukich [Dolgorukii], have deceived me."[99] In response to the *Generalitet* petition that she rule as an Autocrat, Anna demanded public agreement from those Supreme Privy Councillors who had sought to limit her power. "My constant intention is to rule my subjects peacefully and justly. But, because I have signed their conditions, I now must know if the members of the Supreme Privy Council agree that I should accept that which is now offered to me by my subjects." Silently, the Golitsyns and the Dolgorukiis bowed their heads in assent. Anna sent her secretary, Anisim Maslov, to fetch the document she had signed, and when he returned with it, she tore it into bits.[100] "It was fortunate that the ministers of the Supreme Council did not propose anything at that point, for if they had opposed the decision of the nobility, those nobles and Guards officers would have thrown them through the window," reported the French Ambassador Magnan.[101] The next evening, the Moscow sky was illuminated by an aurora borealis that, according to one account, "overspreading the whole horizon, made it appear as if all were drenched in blood."[102] Some took it as an omen. In some ways, they would not be mistaken.

By the end of February 1730, Anna had become Russia's Empress, with a public mandate from her senior officials, high-ranking officers, and the Imperial Guards to rule as an Autocrat. Her power was unlimited and undivided, and she exercised it in a manner that many would regret. Not only the Golitsyns and Dolgorukiis but also a number of those who had supported her in 1730 would fall victim to her capriciousness during the next decade. Aware that she owed her throne in large measure to the Guards, she established a new regiment, the Izmailovskii Guards. She named her former lover, Count Karl Gustavus Löwenwolde, to command it and recruited its officers from the nobility of Russia's Baltic provinces, whose loyalty she trusted. Within a year, she revived Russia's secret police. Renamed the Office of Secret Investigations and headed by General Andrei Ushakov, one of Peter the Great's most energetic officers, its torture chambers became as feared as they had been under Prince Romodanovskii. With these twin supports for her power, Anna then proceeded to enjoy her emancipation from the draughty thirteenth-century castle of the Teutonic Order that she had inhabited in the backwater of Mitau for the past two decades.

Because much of the information we have about the Russian Court during Anna's reign comes from the reports, letters, and memoirs of European diplomats, historians have portrayed Anna in uniformly black shades. We must remember, however, that although her tastes often were crude, they were no more so than those of her predecessors. Even her most notorious escapades did not equal those of Peter the Great in his more barbaric and drunken moments. The problem that we have in making judgments about Anna's Court is that the expectations of Europeans had grown even more rapidly between 1700 and 1730 than had the changes in Russian Court behavior. Before Peter the Great had transformed Russia into a Great Power, Europeans had expected Russians to be crude and barbaric precisely because they considered them Asiatics and, therefore, inferior. By the 1730s, they had raised their expectations for Russians and the Russian Court in particular, because Peter had forced them to treat Russia as a European power. They therefore began to judge Russia according to the measure of other European states rather than Asiatic ones. Further, Europeans tended to be less tolerant of Anna's excesses because she was a woman. They found it droll, even deliciously shocking, when the gigantic and roisterous Peter behaved in a grotesque and absurd manner. They found similar acts when committed by a woman deeply offensive. Even the great nineteenth-century historian Vasilii Kliuchevskii shared such a view and dubbed Anna's reign as "one of the darkest pages in our history, and the darkest stain was the Empress [Anna] herself."[103]

Like Peter the Great, Anna was fond of crude practical jokes that degraded those she forced to serve as the butts of her humor. She made three of the Empire's leading nobles—Prince Mikhail Golitsyn, Prince Nikita Volkonskii, and Aleksei Apraksin—into Court jesters and decreed that these great lords were to greet her return from church every Sunday by squatting in corners and cackling like hens. Sometimes, she ordered them and other jesters to mount each other's shoulders and to entertain her with bloody jousting tournaments. In 1740 she ordered Prince Golitsyn to marry a hideous Kalmyk serving woman and then forced the couple to spend their wedding night in a palace built entirely of ice.[104]

Such behavior on the part of their Empress made other courtiers fearful that they too might suffer such degradations. Anna may have played upon this fear as a form of control to ensure her safety on the throne and, if so, her frequent farces, although crude, served a sophisticated political purpose. Yet she devoted far too much attention to such matters. Most of all, she occupied herself with the trivia of daily life. She wrote many letters to her officials, but most were devoted to petty affairs unworthy of the attention of a state minister or a provincial governor, let alone an Empress. Thus, for example, she wrote to Semën Saltykov, Governor-General of Moscow: "Let me know if my chamberlain [Prince] Iusupov is still married. Here [in St. Petersburg] it is rumored that he is divorced. . . . I am writing to you about this in absolute secrecy so that he will not know about my inquiry." "When you receive this memorandum," she wrote to Saltykov again in January 1734, "look for a bride for Davydov. Send her here escorted by a soldier, but do not send any of her relatives, not even her mother."[105]

In addition to her courtiers' personal lives, Anna was passionately concerned with what they wore at Court. She insisted that only bright clothing be worn in her presence because, as Count Ernst Münnich wrote, "she could not abide dark colors."[106] She herself loved to don sky blue or bright green robes with "a red kerchief tied round her head in the style usually worn by tradeswomen."[107] An accomplished marks-woman, she was also much preoccupied with hunting and went about it in what eighteenth-century Europeans considered a bloody and utterly unladylike manner. Russia's only newspaper, the *St. Petersburg Gazette,* which appeared twice weekly during her reign, published ac-counts of her many kills, and, just so there would be no shortage of game for her guns, it was proclaimed a serious crime for anyone else to hunt game within a hundred-*versty** radius of the capital. Anna even kept loaded fowling pieces near the windows of her palaces so that she could shoot at birds that might fly past.

Anna had had numerous lovers which was natural enough for a senuous and robust young woman who had been widowed at the age of eighteen. Here again her taste left much to be desired. Before her ac-cession, she had made no protest when, in the words of one observer, one of her lovers, General Count Petr Bestuzhev, turned her palace in Mitau into "a dishonorable whorehouse," and at one point in her liai-son with Bestuzhev, she also had an affair with Mademoiselle Ogińska, the daughter of an important official in Lithuania. Her passion for the young woman was so obvious that Madame Rondeau, the English Am-bassador's wife, remarked that the two "were continually together and they very often even lay in the same bed." After Anna became Russia's Empress, one of her first acts was to send Ogińska a miniature of her-self framed in diamonds.[108]

Perhaps Anna's most scandalous liaison, and the one that Russians resented most bitterly, was with Count Biron, an adventurer whose wife and children Anna insisted upon having in her presence during the day, while she kept the Count in her bed at night. Ernst Johann Bühren was born in 1690, some four years before his Imperial mis-tress. His father and grandfather had been grooms in the service of the Dukes of Courland. A passionate Francophile, he changed his name to Biron and, according to some accounts, adopted the arms of the extinct French noble family that had borne the name before him. One contem-porary described him as "haughty, and ambitious beyond all bounds,

---

*A *versta* (pl. *versty*) was a Russian measure of distance equivalent to approximately two-thirds of a mile.

abrupt, even brutal, avaricious, an implacable enemy, and cruel in his revenge."[109] Count Ernst Münnich, whose father was Anna's leading general, remarked that "there was not a single language which he could speak properly."[110] Yet, whatever his shortcomings, Biron was energetic and not easily discouraged. Like many European adventurers, he looked upon Russia as a land of opportunity where fortunes could be made and high rank won through bravery or intrigue. He chose the latter course. In 1714 he had sought a position in St. Petersburg at the Court of Charlotte of Wolfenbüttel, but evidently was so arrogant that he was refused. Ordered to leave St. Petersburg at once, he returned to Mitau and obtained a sinecure at Court, where he soon came to Anna's attention.

Contemporaries agree that Biron was handsome, dashing, and, like Anna herself, an ardent huntsman. Horses were his chief passion, and he was at his best in dealing with them. Indeed, the Austrian Ambassador Count Ostein reportedly once remarked that "when the Count Biron talks of horses, or to horses, he speaks like a man, but when he speaks of men, or to men, he speaks as a horse might do."[111] At some point in the mid-1720s, probably soon after the failure of her plans to marry Maurice de Saxe, Anna had installed Biron as her lover, a position he held, although sometimes obliged to share with others, until her death in 1740. By 1730 his influence over her had become sufficiently notorious for the members of the Supreme Privy Council to insist that she not bring him to Russia. As soon as Anna regained her autocratic power, however, her first act was to install Biron in her palace. She doted upon him, granted him countless favors, and reacted to his every mood. As Count Münnich once remarked, "one could tell the mood of her lover on any particular day by the Empress's face. . . . When the former was happy, joy shone in her eyes. If something had displeased her lover, it was immediately reflected in the Empress's obvious unhappiness."[112] Although Biron held no formal position in Russia's government, his power was unrivaled to such an extent that Russians have long dubbed Anna's reign as the *Bironovshchina* (the era of Bironism). Foreign ambassadors who saw him as the key to the Empress sought to buy his favors. "Her Majesty thinks . . . to heap up riches and honor on Count Biron," reported England's Ambassador

Claude Rondeau on January 4, 1731. Somewhat later he wrote, "I believe the best way to secure Count Biron would be to follow Count Wratislau's advice, for in this country one may do almost anything with money."[113] While his Imperial mistress lovingly looked on, Biron amassed a vast fortune and a list of titles that raised him high above his humble beginnings. He was named a Count in 1730. In 1737 Anna's support assured his election as Duke of Courland.

Like other eighteenth-century Russian monarchs, with the exception of Peter II, Anna came to the throne proclaiming her intention to reign in the spirit of Peter the Great. She symbolized her intention to do so by moving Russia's Court and government back to St. Petersburg at the end of 1731. But in other areas of Russian policy, Anna violated some of Peter's most cherished principles. Most important of all, she broke with his insistence that the nobility must serve Russia throughout their entire adult lives and that they must enter Russia's service in the bottom ranks and work their way up. Mindful that it was the nobility who had installed her as Autocrat in Russia, Anna paid her debt to them willingly. In 1730 they had demanded release from compulsory lifetime service, more control over their serfs, and the opportunity to enter the service at officer rank. The Empress began to meet their demands in less than a year. As we shall see, Anna's concessions to Russia's nobility would mark the beginning of their evolution from a servile class to one that enjoyed extensive special treatment but bore no obligations to the government that had granted them their privileged status.

For a number of years, Anna had been tortured by kidney stones and, when she reached middle age, she also began to suffer from gout. Although painful, these maladies alarmed no one in her entourage until early October 1740. On October 7, the British Ambassador Edward Finch warned his government that "no ill consequences apprehended from the Czarinna's gout till Sunday morning, when, by strong vomitings attended with vast quantities of putrid blood, it appeared that . . . Her Czarish Majesty was in great danger." Her illness was diagnosed as "an ulcer in the kidneys" but, in an effort to disguise the seriousness of her condition, her physicians reported that she was suffering only from the onset of menopause, "the great critical turn of her sex," as Ambassador Finch termed it. On October 8, 1740, however,

Finch was obliged to report that the Empress had died the day before from "a mortification in her kidneys."[114]

Evidently sterile and, in any case, unmarried, Anna left no direct heirs to whom she could bequeath the crown. But unlike her immediate predecessors, she had made some serious effort to arrange the succession before her death, although her arrangements would prove immensely unpopular with her Russian subjects. On August 24, 1740, her niece, Anna Leopoldovna, Princess of Brunswick-Wolfenbüttel-Bevern, had given birth to a son in St. Petersburg. Just six days before she died, the Empress had proclaimed the infant Ivan her successor and ordered the Imperial Guards to swear allegiance to him in a ceremony that, according to Ambassador Finch, was "transacted with more tranquility than a regiment of guards would have passed in Hyde-park."[115] The critical question at the Empress's deathbed thus was not who would succeed her but who would serve as Regent for the two-month-old Ivan VI. The morning after her death it was learned that, according to the will she had signed in the presence of Baron Ostermann a day or two before, Biron was named to the post. Given the hatred Biron had inspired in the hearts of all Russians, no one was certain how long he could remain in power. The answer to that question came with amazing speed.

Shortly after two o'clock on the morning of November 9, a small coach drew up at a side door of the Winter Palace where the infant Emperor Ivan VI and his parents were sleeping. Two men quickly entered, hurried up a small stairway, and slipped into Anna Leopoldovna's apartments. In an anteroom they awakened her favorite lady-in-waiting Julie Mengden. When the startled young woman had gathered her wits and rubbed the sleep from her eyes, she realized that the two men standing before her were none other than Field Marshal Count Münnich, thought by all to be one of Biron's strongest supporters, and his aide-de-camp Colonel Manstein. They demanded to speak with her mistress. When Anna Leopoldovna appeared some minutes later, Münnich hastily explained that all was ready for the coup d'état he had discussed with her in secret a day or two before. All that was needed to set it in motion was her approval. Anna Leopoldovna nodded in agreement. Manstein ordered the officers who were on guard at the palace to gather in the Princess's apartments, where they kissed her hand and swore allegiance to her as Russia's new Regent. With them and eighty of their men at their backs, Münnich and Manstein marched to the palace where Biron and his wife were sleeping. After they had convinced Biron's guards to join them, Münnich sent Manstein with twenty men into the palace. Silently he and his men slipped into the Regent's bedchamber. Manstein stepped forward, threw back the curtains, and placed Biron under arrest. In fear and rage, Biron lashed out with his fists. Manstein's men retaliated with the butts of their muskets, stuffed a handkerchief into his mouth, bound his hands, and carried Russia's formerly all-powerful Regent, stark naked and still struggling, to the palace guardroom. Refusing even to allow him time to dress, they wrapped Biron in a cloak and escorted him to the Winter Palace where Anna Leopoldovna waited. At the same time, Münnich's agents were arresting Biron's brother and Aleksei Bestuzhev, his chief ally in the Foreign Office. By noon on November 9, Anna Leopoldovna had proclaimed herself Regent, the Guards had sworn their allegiance, and Biron and his family had been sent to the fortress of Schlüsselberg as prisoners. The coup had been remarkedly easy. As Manstein later confessed, he was "unable to conceive how it was possible for the attempt to succeed, for . . . the affair ought, naturally speaking, to have miscarried."[116] England's Ambassador Finch concluded, "This great change has been conducted with a tranquility, which nothing can equal but the general joy it has produced."[117] He could not have been more mistaken. Anna Leopoldovna's regency lasted just over a year.

During the reign of the Empress Anna, Russians had resented the great role she had assigned to foreigners in their country's government. Baron Ostermann had directed Russia's foreign policy; Field Marshal Count Burkhard Münnich had commanded her armies; Count Karl Gustavus Löwenwolde had been Master of the Horse, Commander of the Izmailovskii Guards, and, at various times, lover of the Empress; his brother had been Marshal of the Imperial Court, and above them all had stood Count Biron. Yet, if Russians had been sensitive about the Empress Anna's appointments of foreigners to high state office, they faced an even more galling situation under the Regent Anna Leopoldovna whose first official act was to declare her husband, Prince Anton-Ulrich, Generalissimus of Russia's armies, a post Münnich coveted. Then, in an attempt to satisfy Münnich, she appointed him "first minister" and then sought to pacify Baron Ostermann, who thought that post should be his, by naming him Grand Admiral in addition to leaving him in control of foreign affairs. To be sure, Anna Leopoldovna named the Russians Prince Aleksei Cherkasskii as Chancellor and Count Mikhail Golovkin as Vice-Chancellor, but her grants of appointments, awards, and favors in the days after her victory over Biron left no doubt where her sentiments lay. To Münnich she gave Biron's palace; to the Prince of Hesse-Homburg she gave command of the Izmailovskii Guards; to Count Löwenwolde she granted eighty thousand rubles to pay his debts; to Münnich's brother she gave twenty thousand more; to Manstein went command of the Astrakhan Regiment, the core of the Petersburg garrison; to Baron Mengden, cousin of her favorite lady-in-waiting, she gave the presidency of the College of Commerce; and to Münnich's wife she gave "precedency immediately after the princesses of the blood" at all Court ceremonies. What she gave to Russians—ten thousand rubles to Field Marshal Nikita Trubetskoi; the Orders of St. Aleksandr Nevskii to Vasilii Streshnev and Prince Iusupov; the Orders of St. Andrei the First Called to Prince Aleksandr Kurakin, General Count Andrei Ushakov, Count Mikhail Golovkin, and Count Aleksandr Golovkin—paled by comparison.[118] Under Anna Leopoldovna, Russia was to be ruled by a clique of Germans who had known nothing but poverty in their petty princedoms and duchies and now sought to make their fortunes by dipping greedy hands into Russia's treasury.

When her infant son became Russia's Emperor and she, at the age of twenty-two, its Regent, Anna Leopoldovna enjoyed the prospect of wealth and power that stretched far beyond her wildest dreams. Yet neither she nor her husband had any notion of how to realize such visions. Instead, domestic quarrels and petty Court intrigues came to dominate their lives. Married to a weak and docile prince, Anna Leopoldovna always had lived a life that violated the bounds of good taste and common sense, and her new power and position served mainly to stimulate her more bizarre appetites. Pregnant when she became Regent, she began a passionate affair with her lady-in-waiting Julie Mengden, with whom she evidently spent days on end locked in her private apartments "without any other dress than a petticoat" allowing only a few favorites to enter.[119] Her obsession with her lady-in-waiting was so intense that, as Ambassador Finch wrote to his chief, Lord Harrington, "I should give your lordship but a faint idea of it by adding that the passion of a lover for a new mistress is but a jest to it."[120] As soon as her daughter Catherine was born, Anna Leopoldovna became consumed by an equal passion for the Saxon Ambassador Count Maurice Lynar, whom she had first taken as a lover when she was a girl of sixteen. She often used Mengden's apartments for meetings with him, while her lady-in-waiting stood guard to bar her husband Prince Anton-Ulrich from interrupting them. During the last weeks of her regency in the fall of 1741, for reasons that are not clear, Anna Leopoldovna became obsessed with the idea of marrying Lynar to Julie Mengden. That, and not her crumbling political alliances, occupied her attention.[121]

The grotesque comedy of Germans attempting to rule Russia while devoting themselves mainly to intrigues and scandalous love affairs suddenly came to an end in late November 1741. For a number of months during the summer and fall, the Grand Duchess Elizaveta, daughter of Peter the Great and Catherine I, had been the focus of a plot conceived by men who hoped to overthrow Ivan VI and his mother. Chief among them were the French Ambassador Marquis de la Chétardie, who hoped to turn Russian policy from its German orientation to one more acceptable to his master King Louis XV, and Elizaveta's personal physician, Armand Lestocq, a Frenchman who supported the conspiracy from motives of personal gain. We do not know how much Elizaveta encouraged these men in their plots, but certainly they could not have continued to lay their plans had she forbidden them to do so. Throughout the fall of 1741, she seems to have let them continue their work, neither giving nor withholding her formal consent.

Precisely how long this state of affairs would have continued is not clear, but the conspirators suddenly were forced to act in late November. As Manstein remarked, Lestocq, "the most giddy man alive and the least capable of keeping a secret, had often said in coffee houses, before a great number of people, that there would soon be great changes in St. Petersburg."[122] Lestocq's remarks soon reached Baron Ostermann's ears, and he warned Anna Leopoldovna that something was afoot. Although Elizaveta was able to allay the Regent's fears in an interview they had on November 23, she realized that she soon must move against her or suffer unpleasant consequences. According to several accounts, Lestocq himself dramatized the choice she must make when he visited her on the morning of November 24. Bursting in upon her while she was still dressing, he gave her a card. On one side was a drawing of her crowned as Russia's Empress; the reverse showed her wearing a nun's veil and surrounded by gallows and instruments of torture. "Take your choice, my Lady," Lestocq reportedly said. "Become Empress or be incarcerated in a convent and watch your loyal supporters be killed."[123] Whether or not Lestocq made such a dramatic plea, other factors probably moved the Grand Duchess to action. That very day, some of the Guards regiments upon whose support her coup would depend had been ordered to the Finnish frontier. Further, she had just learned that Anna Leopoldovna planned to declare herself Empress on December 18.

Just after midnight on the morning of November 25, the Grand Duchess Elizaveta knelt before an icon of the Virgin in her private chamber, begged for divine guidance, and promised to abolish capital punishment in Russia if she were successful in seizing power. She then donned a guardsman's cuirass and, holding a silver cross in her hands, went to meet the men who had assembled in her outer rooms. Most prominent among them were her lover Aleksei Razumovskii; the three Shuvalov brothers, Petr, Aleksandr, and Ivan; her chamberlain Mikhail Vorontsov; Vasilii Saltykov; and Lestocq. Together they hastened to sleighs waiting outside and sped through St. Petersburg's deserted streets, Elizaveta and Lestocq in the first sleigh, with Vorontsov and the Shuvalovs on its running boards. Behind them came Razumovskii and Saltykov, accompanied by three Preobrazhenskii grenadiers. Their destination was the Preobrazhenskii Guards barracks less than a mile away.

Within minutes they were at their destination. The next few moments were a blur of activity. A guard started to beat the alarm, Lestocq leaped from the sleigh, slashed the drum head, and some thirty grenadiers, who had been told of the plot beforehand, burst from the barracks shouting their support for their "little mother." A true daughter of Peter and Catherine, Elizaveta rose from her sleigh. "You know whose daughter I am! They want to force me into marriage or put me into a nunnery! Will you follow me?" The Guards greeted her with roars of enthusiasm. "We're ready, little Mother! We'll slay them all!" "If that is what you intend to do, I shan't go with you," she replied. She then raised her silver cross. "I shall swear to die for you and you shall vow to give your lives for me. But let no blood be shed unjustly!" "We agree," they replied.[124]

Three hundred sixty strong, the Preobrazhenskii grenadiers followed her down the Nevskii Prospekt toward the Winter Palace. Four groups of twenty-five each went to arrest Münnich, Ostermann, Löwenwolde, and Golovkin, Anna Leopoldovna's chief advisers. As the rest neared the Winter Palace, Elizaveta left her sleigh to go forward on foot so that the sound of the horses' hooves would not alert the Palace Guard. She found it difficult to move in the deep snow. Gallantly, the grenadiers lifted her onto their shoulders and carried her the rest of the way. The Palace Guard joined them. Once in the Palace, Elizaveta roused Anna Leopoldovna and told her that she, Elizaveta, was now Russia's Empress. A few hours later, the Empire's leading officials, senior statesmen, and all the regiments of the Guards and the Petersburg garrison assembled at the Palace and swore allegiance to her as Elizabeth I, Russia's new Empress. Anna Leopoldovna, Prince Anton-Ulrich, and their infant daughter Catherine were sent back to Germany. The new Empress bore the fifteen-month-old Ivan VI no malice, and her first inclination was to send him to Germany as well. Yet, the fact of his having held the crown made him too great a threat to her political power. Knowing that he could at any time become the focus for dissident elements who might want to overthrow her, she sent him to the fortress of Schlüsselberg. There he would remain for the next quarter-century until he was killed by his jailers on orders from the Empress Catherine II.

Elizabeth became Russia's third Empress just twenty-three days before her thirty-second birthday. Unlike her mother, she was blond and blue-eyed. She had little formal education, but spoke French and German fluently, and danced superbly, for her father had intended for her to wed a French prince. Contemporaries agree that during her youth she was strikingly beautiful and utterly charming, two qualities that made her irresistible to men. "Her physical charms are marvelous to behold, her beauty indescribable," wrote the Duke de Liria in 1728.[125] Others echoed his sentiments. Unrestrained by any moral scruples, the young princess had found enjoyment in the company of handsome Guards officers. When she was nineteen, the Duke de Liria remarked that "she shamelessly does things that would make even the most uninhibited individual blush."[126] England's Ambassador Finch wrote that "she had not one bit of nun's flesh about her and is extremely well beloved and very popular."[127] These qualities endeared her to the Guards and were instrumental in their readiness to join her cause. She rewarded them generously for their support and named the company of grenadiers who had followed her to the Winter Palace "Her Majesty's Own Company"; she proclaimed herself their captain.[128] Elizabeth's "Own Company" of Guards would replace the Empress Anna's freaks, dwarfs, and buffoons at Court. Russia's new Empress might not have been well educated in the formal sense, but certainly her accession heralded an era of better taste and greater civility in St. Petersburg.

Having been obliged to live in relative penury during the reigns of Peter II and Anna,[129] Elizabeth spent lavish sums upon clothing and entertainment when she became Empress. She could not bear to wear a gown more than once, and, although she reputedly lost four thousand dresses in a fire in 1744, she left some fifteen thousand gowns and two trunks filled with stockings when she died less than two decades later.[130] She loved the theatre, the opera, and rich banquets. Most of all she adored the masquerade balls she held every Tuesday during the winter season, and she especially loved to attend them in the masculine attire in which she cut such a striking figure. Beginning in 1744, she decreed that men should attend these balls dressed as women, while women must don masculine garb. According to the

Grand Duchess Catherine, later to become the Empress Catherine the Great, only Elizabeth enjoyed these gatherings, which put the entire Court in an ill humor because they all felt foolish and unattractive in the attire of the opposite sex. "Only the Empress appeared to really good advantage in men's clothing," Catherine wrote. "Because she was very tall and somewhat powerfully built, male attire suited her marvelously. She had the most beautifully proportioned leg I have ever seen on any man, and her foot was similarly well-turned. She danced to perfection, and everything she did had a particular grace about it whether she was dressed as a man or a woman. One always wished to stare at her, and could only tear one's eyes away with regret, because no other object in the room could hold such fascination."[131]

Elizabeth's love of entertainment obviously contained an element of frivolity, but there was a vein of hard discipline that ran beneath her seemingly gay and gregarious exterior. To be sure, she could not equal her successor Catherine the Great in that respect, and she has suffered at historians' hands as a result. In comparison with her predecessors, however, she had considerable personal integrity and a strong sense of duty, tempered by common sense, that made her the first Autocrat since Peter the Great to understand what it meant to rule Russia. Although she had lovers, and loved them all warmly, she never allowed any of them to rule her or Russia, not even Aleksei Razumovskii, whom she made a Count and may have secretly married.[132] Nor did she seek to employ Russia's power and resources abroad to satisfy the pretensions of her lovers as the Empress Anna had done.

Having risen to the throne of a country weary of seeing foreigners close to the person of its ruler, Elizabeth did much to restore Russian national pride. Her lovers were Russian to a man, and, although foreigners were the chief architects of her coup d'état in November 1741, most of her advisers and counselors were also Russian. Not since Peter the Great did any ruler leave such a positive imprint upon Russia. In architecture, in theatre, even in literature, Elizabeth presided over an "Elizabethan Age" that laid the foundations for Catherine's so-called "Golden Age of the Nobility." Elizabeth was the first of Russia's rulers since 1725 to understand the course her father had charted and to begin to unravel the complexities of Peter's vision.

Having lived through insecurity and turmoil during the reigns of Peter II and Anna, and knowing that she would not marry publicly or have children, Elizabeth appointed a successor within a year of her accession. Determined to pass the crown to the descendants of her father and mother, she brought Peter, Duke of Holstein, the only son of her elder sister Anna, to Russia in 1742 and proclaimed him her heir. Peter was fourteen at the time, tall, frail, and unhealthy. Elizabeth lavished affection upon him, nursed him through the smallpox in 1744, and tried in every way to mold him into a worthy successor. She succeeded only in spoiling him, and he tried her patience sorely. According to Catherine the Great, who married Peter in 1745, Elizabeth soon reached a point where she could barely stand to have her nephew in her presence. "She could not spend even a quarter of an hour with him without becoming disgusted, angry, or sad," Catherine wrote. "I later found among her papers two notes written in her own hand. . . . In one was the remark 'my damned nephew has vexed me beyond the point of endurance.' In the other, she wrote, 'my nephew is a monster; he can go to Hell.' "[133]

Peter would grow up to be boastful, cruel, selfish, and capricious. Yet Elizabeth could never bring herself to disinherit him. Instead, she hastened to find him a wife in the hope that he would produce a more dynamic heir. There too she was disappointed. The best opinions are that Peter was impotent or, at least, sterile. Certainly, his many childhood and adolescent illnesses, including measles and smallpox, could have caused sterility, and his deep feelings of inferiority toward his wife Catherine could well have made him impotent in his relations with her. His several mistresses never became pregnant as a result of his attentions, although they bore children to other men. The son whom the Grand Duchess Catherine bore in 1754 thus was most probably the fruit of her liaison with the young nobleman Sergei Saltykov.[134] Realizing that Catherine's bastard offspring Paul was the best she could hope for, Elizabeth bore him away in triumph and doted upon him for the last seven years of her life, perhaps hoping to live long enough to name him heir in place of her troublesome nephew.

Peter was not Elizabeth's only source of difficulty during the two decades of her rule. Although Russia was still regarded as backward, many European statesmen were anxious to draw her large army and vast resources into the military conflicts that raged on the continent during the three decades between 1733 (the outbreak of the War of the Polish Succession) and 1763 (the end of the Seven Years' War). St. Petersburg thus seethed with diplomatic intrigue, as well as with the still-bitter feuds among Russian aristocrats. As a result, Elizabeth was forced to live through two decades of plots and counterplots, which demanded that she stem some of her natural openness and be wary of those around her. Some of these plots would threaten her closest advisers, some would threaten her policies, and some would threaten her life.

The first of these intrigues came to light in July 1742, less than eight months after she had ascended the throne. Elizabeth was in Moscow for her coronation when she learned that Aleksandr Turchaninov, one of her servants; Petr Ivashkin, an ensign in the Preobrazhenskii Guards; and Ivan Snovidov, a sergeant in the Izmailovskii Guards, were plotting to seize her and her heir Peter, murder them, and place the deposed Ivan VI back on the throne. Elizabeth's inquisitors were unable to learn who stood behind these men, but it was doubtful that they had acted on their own.[135] The Empress sent the three to Siberia, increased General Ushakov's secret police force, and took her Court back to St. Petersburg where she felt more secure. Yet she did not have long to wait for further threats to her person and position. In July 1743 another plot was discovered; this time, the conspirators were not low-ranking soldiers and servants but some of the most prominent figures at her Court. Among them were General Stepan Lopukin, his wife Natalia, and their son Ivan, as well as the Countess Anna Bestuzheva and Count Mikhail Golovkin. All of them had risen to high positions under Anna Leopoldovna and had reason to regret Elizabeth's accession. Together with the Austrian Ambassador, the Marquis de Botta, they were accused of conspiring to restore Ivan VI to the throne. Just how much serious plotting was involved is not clear, for there may have been other issues at stake as well. Certainly Dr. Lestocq, who was intent upon undermining Russia's alliance with Austria and hoped to bring down Vice-Chancellor Aleksei Bestuzhev by attacking his sister-in-law Anna, employed at least one *agent provocateur* to encourage Ivan Lopukin in treasonous public statements. In any case, Elizabeth's counselors took the conspiracy seriously and recommended that the three Lopukins and Countess Bestuzheva be broken on the wheel. Elizabeth commuted their death sentences to public flogging and having their tongues cut out, after which their estates were confiscated and they were sent to Siberia.[136]

Scarcely had she recovered from the shock of the so-called "Botta Conspiracy" than Elizabeth was confronted by another. This time, it was revealed that her long-time ally, the Marquis de la Chétardie, and several of her other close associates were plotting with Prussia and France to bring about the fall of Vice-Chancellor Bestuzhev and thus reverse his policy of alliance with Austria. This plot was especially painful to Elizabeth because she had always regarded la Chétardie as a close personal friend. Yet its discovery had the very positive consequence of elevating Bestuzhev to the post of Chancellor, thus enabling him to follow a consistent foreign policy. For a decade, Bestuzhev's system of alliances would restore to Russia's foreign policy a large measure of that continuity it had enjoyed under the wily Baron Ostermann during the late 1720s and 1730s. The plot's discovery also had the positive effect of removing some of the most inveterate schemers from Elizabeth's Court and establishing a more tranquil atmosphere among her courtiers.[137] La Chétardie would be the last foreigner to gain such a dominant voice in Russian affairs; matters of state would be left mainly in the hands of Russians for the rest of the Romanov era. Russia thus attained a level of maturity she had not known since before the Time of Troubles. No longer were foreigners deemed superior in their ability to fight battles and conduct state affairs. Russians and Russia's rulers now considered themselves equal to the task of governing the world's largest Empire. The inferiority complex Peter had imposed upon his subjects had at last dropped away.

Unfortunately, the relative calm that settled upon Elizabeth's Court in the wake of the la Chétardie affair did not extend to the Empire as a whole. The Empress's immediate predecessors and their foreign advisers had been too occupied with Court intrigue and Russia's new role in European affairs to pay sufficient attention to domestic affairs. Not even Peter the Great had fully understood how important rural calm and an effective system of local administration were to the well-being of his Empire, and his immediate successors had comprehended these needs even less clearly. As a result, the peasantry was impoverished and the countryside was in a state of chaos. Perhaps most critical from the point of view of state security, there was no effective means of political control. It fell to Elizabeth to pay the price for this neglect. Her reign would see increasingly violent and widespread outbreaks of peasant discontent, as well as other forms of protest among Russia's enserfed millions.

As in Muscovite times, Russian peasants often protested against increased demands from the government and their masters by simply running away. During the fifteen years after the death of Catherine I, it has been estimated that over a half-million peasants fled from their masters' estates to havens on Russia's frontiers and beyond; the number rose significantly during Elizabeth's reign.[138] Such mass flights narrowed the state's tax base and reduced state revenues. At the same time, however, those serfs who chose open revolt rather than flight also increased in numbers. According to the best available estimates, the number of serious serf revolts increased by more than three hundred percent during Elizabeth's reign.[139] This presented a truly terrifying prospect to Elizabeth and her advisers since these were not mere bands of serfs armed with scythes and pitchforks; sometimes they numbered in the thousands and were armed with muskets and even cannon.[140]

Elizabeth had neither the resolution nor the knowledge to contend with this serious domestic crisis. Moreover, the twin burdens of her gay social life and the demands of ruling Russia had taxed her health. In the years after her accession, her statuesque figure turned rapidly to fat, and by the end of her first decade on the throne she had become seriously overweight.[141] She suffered from colic and constipation, aggravated by the strain of her daily existence. Her life became one of behavioral extremes. For a time she would throw herself into gay festivities; then she would enter a period of penance, visiting monasteries far away from her capital. Both her festivities and her pilgrimages were exhausting and debilitating. By the mid-1750s, she began to suffer from shortness of breath and dropsy. Her legs began to swell, and at times she coughed blood.[142] In June 1756 she suffered a stroke, and her physicians and courtiers feared she would die. To their amazement she recovered by early September and began to pay serious attention to determining what part Russia should play in the Seven Years' War.

The war was one in which Elizabeth could participate wholeheartedly. She had nurtured a deep hatred for Frederick the Great of Prussia for nearly two decades, and the bitter defeats her armies inflicted upon him gave her great satisfaction. She was delighted with General Stefan Apraksin's victory over the Prussians at Gross-Jägersdorf in August 1757 and even more so with that of General Count Petr Saltykov at Kunersdorf almost two years later.

Yet Elizabeth would not live to see the war's end. She began to suffer from more frequent seizures, perhaps caused by epilepsy, which left her unable to speak for several days at a time. In September 1759 she collapsed outside the church at Tsarskoe Selo, and it was several hours before her physicians could revive her. She became increasingly depressed and melancholy, and there were rumors that she wanted to spend her last days as a nun.[143] By the summer of 1761, her legs had become so swollen that she could not walk. During the early winter she improved, and her doctors declared her out of danger. But on December 12 she again began to vomit blood. She recovered, but the attacks returned on December 22, complicated by what seemed to have been a severe stroke. She asked her confessor to read the *Otkhodnaia*, the Orthodox Church's solemn prayer for the dying. The next day, she could not comprehend the news of Russia's great victory at Kolberg nor the significance of the keys to the city that General Count Petr Rumiantsev, commander of Russia's armies in Pomerania, had sent to her. Clearly, she was dying.

On Christmas Day, 1761, at four o'clock in the afternoon, Prince Nikita Trubetskoi, Field Marshal and Procurator-General of the Senate, opened the doors of her bedchamber and walked into the anteroom crowded with dignitaries and courtiers. With tears streaming down his cheeks, the old man announced the accession of Peter III. The Empress Elizabeth, under whom "Russia had regained her consciousness," as the great historian Solovev once wrote, was dead.[144]

According to one witness, when Prince Trubetskoi made his an-

nouncement, "the entire Court was filled with moans and weeping."[145]
Peter was not popular with his subjects, and few looked forward to life
under his rule. The memoirs of Princess Ekaterina Dashkova, later to
become Director of the Russian Academy of Sciences, give a dramatic
account of that afternoon:

> The Guards regiments (including the Semenovskii and Iz-
> mailovskii, which passed under my window) looked gloomy and
> dejected. The men all spoke at once but in a low voice, and the con-
> fused stifled murmur which arose from the ranks sounded so men-
> acing and alarming, so desperate even, that I could not help
> wishing myself a hundred miles away so as not to hear it. . . . That
> day, which our Church celebrates as one of its greatest festivals and
> which is as a rule the occasion for popular rejoicing, [thus] wore an
> almost sinister aspect, with grief painted on every face.[146]

At seven o'clock in the evening, all of Russia's Senators, high officials, and Guards officers gathered to take the oath of allegiance to
their new Emperor. Peter insisted that they all wear bright clothing
and, after the ceremony, gave a festive banquet for nearly a hundred
guests.[147] He was delighted to be Emperor and equally delighted to insult the memory of the woman who had given him the throne. During
the weeks that Elizabeth's body lay in state, he behaved rudely at every
opportunity. On those rare occasions that he came to the chamber of
mourning, he joked with the ladies in attendance, ridiculed the clergy,
and scolded the Duty Officers. According to the Princess Dashkova,
when he attended memorial masses, "he made faces, acted the buffoon,
and imitated poor old ladies."[148] In every way, he acted with unpar-
donable boorishness, which did little to win him friends among Elizabeth's loyal courtiers.

Peter III was almost thirty-four when he became Russia's Emperor. His mother, who died a few days after his birth, was Peter the
Great's daughter Anna, and his father, Karl-Friedrich, was the Duke of
Holstein-Gottorp. Born on February 10, 1728, Peter had spent his
childhood in the Baltic backwater of Kiel. The Duke of Holstein-Gottorp had a passion for drilling troops and a weakness for alcohol.
These devotions consumed most of his waking hours, and he ignored
his son. Peter thus grew up in the care of Holstein's household guards

officers. Their only interest was the army; they taught him the manual of arms and parade drill. They put sergeant's stripes on his sleeve and let him drill the Holstein household troops. Knowing nothing else, Peter became passionately enamored of drill field trivia. In every way, his childhood and early adolescence were undistinguished by any serious effort at education or training in the arts of governing.[149]

Peter's life had changed dramatically when his aunt Elizabeth brought him to St. Petersburg and proclaimed him her heir. Elizabeth had attempted to educate her nephew, but since she herself was poorly educated (she was convinced, for example, that the early death of Peter's mother was caused by her passion for reading), she chose for him pedantic and untalented tutors. Peter's education thus proceeded without system or direction. His tutors showed him pictures, medals, and portraits and from them sought to teach him history. To teach him physics, they told him stories about "physical phenomena"; they introduced him to mathematics by playing number games.[150] He was devoted to his regiments of toy soldiers and loved to saw away on his violin, although his efforts produced more noise than music.[151] According to his wife Catherine, even when he was in his late teens, Peter played with dolls and often covered their bed with them at night. So intense was his passion for parade drill that he spent long hours instructing Catherine in the manual of arms and made her stand guard at their door.[152] He had a voice like a drill sergeant, "loud, foul-mouthed, and unpleasant," according to one contemporary,[153] and on one occasion, referred in public to the distinguished General Buturlin as "a son of a bitch."[154] He often was so drunk that he could not remember what he said or did and liked his courtiers to behave in a similar fashion.[155] "To be general and drill sergeant on parade in the morning, to have an excellent dinner with a good bottle of burgundy, to spend the evening with his buffoons and a few women, and to do whatever he was ordered by the King of Prussia—this was Peter III's idea of bliss," was the way the sister of his mistress characterized him.[156] Above all, he was a fanatical Holstein patriot. As a Grand Duke, he looked forward to the day when he would ascend the throne and be able to turn Russia's vast military resources to the service of his Duchy in its perpetual conflicts with Denmark.

Yet Peter III's character and personality have been condemned to some extent unjustly, by the unflattering portraits left by his wife and her friend Princess Dashkova, both of whom had good reason to dislike him. While it is true, for example, that his education was superficial, it was no worse than that of any of the Emperors and Empresses who had preceded him. Unlike his Aunt Elizabeth, he had a love and respect for books, owned a sizable library, and took considerable pride in it, although he evidently was not well versed in its contents. He knew German and French well and spoke Russian passably, which marked a considerable improvement over the linguistic deficiencies of Peter the Great, Catherine I, and the Empress Anna.[157] Beyond that, as we shall see further on, some of his domestic policies were remarkably liberal. He freed the nobility from obligatory service to the state, allowed many of the men and women whom the Empresses Anna and Elizabeth had sent into exile to return to St. Petersburg, and made no effort to persecute those Elizabethan courtiers who had treated him shabbily, even cruelly, before he became Emperor.

In his foreign policy, however, there is no way to escape the conclusion that Peter III was extremely unwise, even foolhardy. At the time of Elizabeth's death, Russia was on the verge of defeating Prussia's armies but, rather than finish the destruction of Frederick the Great, Peter immediately made peace with his idol. Yet even this did not turn Russian opinion against him so much as did his impatience to make war on Denmark to recover the territory of Schleswig for his native Duchy of Holstein. Everyone realized that such a war could bring no benefit to Russia. Even Frederick counseled him against it. But Peter was determined to continue and on May 21, 1762, told General Count Petr Rumiantsev that he should consider Russia at war with Denmark.[158] Before hostilities began, however, Peter III was deposed and his wife Catherine elevated to the throne in his place.

If Peter's foreign policy did little to win him supporters at Court, the manner in which he treated the army, and the Guards regiments in particular, increased his unpopularity. One of his first acts as Emperor was to abolish "Her Majesty's Own Company," which Elizabeth had created from those Preobrazhenskii grenadiers who led her coup in 1741. He replaced this "guard within the Guard" with his beloved Holsteiners and frequently spoke about their superiority to Russians. He referred to Russia's Guards as "janissaries" and ordered them, and all army units, to don Prussian-style uniforms and march according to Prussian military regulations.[159] At the same time, Peter made himself thoroughly unpopular with senior officials and statesmen by insisting that all who held honorary rank in the army don proper uniforms and take part in parades, no matter how old, fat, or infirm they might be. Andrei Bolotov, one of eighteenth-century Russia's greatest memoirists, has left us an account of the indignities some elder statesmen suffered at such military reviews. Bolotov had just returned to St. Petersburg from the Russian army in Pomerania and saw a detachment of Guards on parade. They wore the new Prussian uniforms and marched wonderfully. Yet the perfection of their performance was marred by the awkwardness of their leader. "Nothing," Bolotov wrote, "astonished me more than the short, fat, old man in a uniform covered with gold braid, with a star on his chest and a blue ribbon over his coat, who marched in front of the first platoon carrying a spontoon [who turned out to be] Prince Nikita Iurievich Trubetskoi."[160] Prince Trubetskoi was sixty-three years old. During the last years of Elizabeth's reign, his legs had pained him so badly that he could not go to Court or the Senate for weeks on end. Although the Empress had given him the title of Field Marshal in 1756 as recognition for his work as Procurator-General of the Senate, he had not seen active service in more than two decades. Forced to engage in acts that held them up to ridicule, senior statesmen such as Trubetskoi soon came to hate their Emperor, and when Catherine seized his throne, not one of them lifted a hand to defend him. As Catherine herself later remarked, "Peter III was his own worst enemy."[161]

While Peter angered the Guards, his senior statesmen, and Russia's leading clerics, his wife, the Grand Duchess Catherine, spared no effort to win them to her cause. An immensely ambitious and talented woman, Catherine had a flair for political intrigue. She had been born in Stettin, in Pomerania, on April 21, 1729. Her father was Prince Christian August of Anhalt-Zerbst, and her mother was Johanna of Holstein-Gottorp. Like many of Germany's petty princelets, they were part of that inbred society of Central European royalty from which eighteenth- and nineteenth-century Romanovs so often chose their mates. Christened Sophie Auguste Friedrike, this princess who was to become Catherine the Great was called "Fike" by her family. As a child, she was adored by her father, ignored by her mother, and cared for by two French *émigrée* nurses. Her early education was left in the hands of Herr Wagner, a narrow-minded Lutheran pastor. By her own account, she was headstrong, somewhat devious, and convinced that she was nei-ther pretty nor talented in the feminine arts of drawing or music.[162]

When Sophie Auguste Friedrike was fourteen, the pattern of her life took an unexpected and momentous turn. On New Year's Day, 1744, she received an invitation from Russia's Empress Elizabeth to come to St. Petersburg. She had been chosen to wed the Grand Duke Peter Feodorovich, heir to the Russian throne. As Russian custom required, she was rebaptized into the Orthodox faith and took the name Ekaterina Alekseevna. Her wedding took place on August 21, 1745, in the Cathedral of the Virgin of Kazan in St. Petersburg. After a magnificent wedding feast in the Winter Palace, followed by a ball at which only polonaises were danced, she and the Grand Duke Peter were taken to their bedchamber and put to bed. That night, their mar-riage was not consummated. Nor would it ever be, according to the best estimates. What physical love Catherine enjoyed she found in the arms of lovers, of which she had at least a dozen during her life. These in-cluded Sergei Saltykov (1752–54), Count Stanislaw Poniatowski (1755–58), Grigorii Orlov (1761–72), Aleksandr Vasilchikov (1772–74), Grigorii Potemkin (1774–76), Count Petr Zavadovskii (1776–77), Simon Zorich (1777–78), Ivan Rimskii-Korsakov (1778–80), Aleksandr Lanskoi (1780–84), Aleksandr Ermolov (1785–86), Count Aleksandr Dmitriev-Mamonov (1786–89), and Platon Zubov (1789–96).[163] Although she and her first six lovers were approximate contemporaries, Catherine began to choose younger men as she aged. She was sixteen years older than Zorich, twenty-five years older than Rimskii-Korsakov and Ermolov, thirty years older than Lanskoi and Dmitriev-Mamonov, and thirty-eight years older than Zubov. Catherine called these men her "pupils," although only three—Orlov, Potemkin, and Zubov—ever exercised great influence in Russia's affairs. Of these three, Potemkin had great talents as a statesman, Orlov less, and Zubov none at all. Aged twenty-two when he became the lover of Russia's sixty-year-old Empress, Zubov was both ignorant and arrogant. Of all her lovers, he was the only one who seems to have turned her head to such an extent that his physical attractions interfered with Catherine's political judgment.

Unhappy in her marriage to the Grand Duke Peter and, for almost a decade, denied any chance at romance by the watchful spies of the Empress Elizabeth, Catherine sought solace in books. During her first years in Russia, her reading was haphazard and undirected. She began with novels and then turned "accidentally [to] the letters of Madame Sévigné [which] fell into my hands and gave me great pleasure." She later read the works of Voltaire, which she "never again got loose from," and the writings of Plato and Tacitus.[164] She claimed to have read all of Pierre Bayle's *Dictionnaire historique et critique,* and, as her own later writings would show, she was well acquainted with the work of Montesquieu, Diderot, and the other eighteenth-century French *Encyclopédistes.* She knew something of Shakespeare's plays and later in her life became impressed with the German writings of Thümmel and Nicolais. While her husband claimed that Frederick the Great was his "master," Catherine found hers in Voltaire, who "is my teacher, or better said, his works have formed my mind and spirit."[165] Nothing could have characterized better the vast chasm that separated husband and wife than their choice of mentors.

Yet the world of books and ideas was not enough to satisfy Catherine's passionate, ambitious nature. During the mid-1750s, she found distraction in the arms of her first lover, Sergei Saltykov, and in the birth of her son, the Grand Duke Paul. But her thoughts soon turned in other directions. Saltykov had been ardent and attentive, but he was above all a courtier and concerned with his career at a Court where a lasting relationship with a Grand Duchess could be of little value once he had performed the function that enabled her to produce an heir. Intellectually, he was a poor match for Catherine, and, although both were ambitious, their ambitions led them in very different directions. Catherine's second lover would be far more her equal.

Count Stanisław Poniatowski, a tall, dashing Polish aristocrat related to the powerful Czartoryski family, was three years younger than

Catherine. His looks enabled him to play precisely that role a young woman steeped in French romances craved in a lover, while his education made him the ideal confidant. In the summer of 1755, when Catherine was twenty-six, Poniatowski arrived in St. Petersburg as a member of the suite of Sir Charles Hanbury-Williams, England's new Ambassador to Russia. Saltykov had been posted as Russia's minister to Hamburg a few months before; Catherine's son Paul had been taken from her by the Empress, and she was lonely and at loose ends. Poniatowski soon brought Catherine to his bed. He also brought her into those intrigues in which Hanbury-Williams was engaged with Russia's Chancellor Bestuzhev, and thus into Russian politics. Catherine's intelligence and circumspect behavior won her allies among important men. These included Field Marshal Count Kyril Razumovskii, Field Marshal Alexandre Villebois, Baron Nikolai Korf (soon to become Peter III's Director of Police), and Count Nikita Panin, tutor to her son Paul—all of whom would rally to her when she seized the throne at the end of June 1762.[166]

During the six months of Peter III's reign, Catherine's position deteriorated along with that of the clergy, Russia's senior statesmen, and the Imperial Guards. Peter reportedly began to contemplate divorcing her so that he could marry Elizaveta Vorontsova, the woman who had been his mistress for the past seven years, whom one observer described as "fat and stupid looking, with flabby jowls."[167] During these months, Catherine strengthened her ties with all three major dissident groups in St. Petersburg. She was dutiful and reverent in her observance of Church ritual, and she remained calm and dignified, even in the face of the gross insults Peter heaped upon her in public. This won her sympathy from clergy and courtiers alike. Moreover, the devotion of the Guards to her cause was certain, not only because they were thoroughly disenchanted with their Emperor but because Grigorii Orlov, one of their most popular commanders, had by that time become her lover. Orlov was then twenty-eight. Four years earlier, at the battle of Zorndorf, he had been wounded three times, yet continued to lead his men. His soldiers idolized him; his brother officers respected his valor and judgment. With his four brothers, themselves all popular Guards officers, he was the ideal champion for Catherine's cause.

Thus a plot began to form. In addition to the five Orlov brothers, it involved Nikita Panin, his niece Princess Dashkova, Kyril Razumovskii, the Guards officers Vasilii Bibikov and Petr Passek, and several others. All were prepared to support Catherine's cause, although some originally hoped she would rule as Regent for her son Paul. They tilled fertile soil. By mid-June the Guards, and the army in general, had become totally disaffected and bitter about receiving orders to march against Denmark. "It was evident," wrote the historian Bilbassov eight decades ago, "that just one spark would ignite an explosion."[168] That spark proved to be the arrest of Captain Passek on the afternoon of June 27, 1762. Fearful that Passek's inquisitors might force him to reveal the conspiracy, Catherine's supporters decided to act.[169] Catherine was at Peterhof, a summer palace Peter the Great had built on the Gulf of Finland, some twenty-eight *versty* from St. Petersburg, while Peter III was vacationing with his mistress at Oranienbaum, another summer palace some fifteen *versty* farther away. Just after midnight on the morning of June 28, Aleksei Orlov and Vasilii Bibikov slipped out of St. Petersburg and galloped to warn Catherine, prepared to risk everything on the success of their efforts during the next twenty-four hours. They must succeed or face disgrace, exile, perhaps even death. When the long, low silhouette of Peterhof Palace came into view at six o'clock that morning, they knew that they were about to face the most critical battle of their lives.

While Orlov and Bibikov were making their journey, Catherine lay asleep in Monplaisir, a small cottage nestled in the gardens at Peterhof. In her dressing room, her maids had laid out the ceremonial dress she was to wear later that day at a formal dinner celebrating Peter III's name day. Although she knew that a plot was in the making, she had no inkling that the time for action was at hand until Orlov entered her room and awakened her. In low and urgent tones he said, "Passek has been arrested." Catherine needed to hear no more. Quickly she donned a plain black dress, left the cottage, and entered a small carriage Orlov had waiting. Together, they hastened toward the capital. They were met on the way by Orlov's brother, Catherine's lover Grigorii. On the outskirts of the city, they came first to the barracks of the Izmailovskii Regiment. Quickly and enthusiastically, the soldiers swore allegiance to Catherine as Empress and trouped behind her carriage to the Semenovskii Guards barracks where the performance was repeated. By the time she reached the Church of Our Lady of Kazan at nine o'clock in the morning, Catherine's entourage, which had numbered a mere two persons when she left Monplaisir, had become a triumphal procession. Not only the Semenovskiis and Izmailovskiis but the Preobrazhenskiis and the Horse Guards marched in her train. Outside the Church, a number of Russia's senior statesmen assembled to greet her. As she entered, the city's leading churchmen proclaimed her "Empress and Autocrat Catherine the Second." From the Church she went to the Winter Palace, where Russia's leading courtiers, officials, and army officers added their oaths of allegiance to those she had already received.[170]

While Catherine was gathering the military and political forces of St. Petersburg around her on the morning of June 28, Peter III lay asleep at Oranienbaum. He awakened late with a terrible hangover from the wine he had drunk the night before. As usual, his first act was to review the battalion of Holstein troops stationed at the palace. Somewhat after noon he set out with a large retinue, including his mistress, her father, two field marshals, five generals, and a number of courtiers, to attend his name day dinner with his wife. When the caravan from Oranienbaum drew up at Catherine's Peterhof cottage at two o'clock that afternoon, they were surprised to learn that she had left early that morning. Another hour passed before Peter and his advisers began to suspect what had happened. The Emperor then sent Colonel Neelov to Kronstadt, the naval fortress at the mouth of the Neva River, to take command of its garrison, load the men on ships, and sail them to St. Petersburg. At the same time, Peter sent Ivan Kostomarov, adjutant of the Ingermanland Regiment, to St. Petersburg with orders to bring the Astrakhan Regiment along with his own to Peterhof. Half an hour later, Peter countermanded his order to Neelov and sent his aide-de-camp Prince Ivan Bariatinskii to Kronstadt with instructions to prepare the fortress for his arrival. That single change in orders proved to be a critical blunder; indeed, it may have cost Peter his throne. Knowing nothing of the coup d'état in St. Petersburg, the Kronstadt commander, General Gustav Nummers, first told Bariatinskii that the fortress was always ready to receive the Emperor. The Prince set sail again for Peterhof, not knowing that at that very moment orders were arriving in Kronstadt from Admiral Ivan Talyzin, now loyal to Catherine, that no one should be allowed in or out of the fortress.[171] If Peter had not countermanded Colonel Neelov's orders, the fortress would have been in his hands before Talyzin's messenger arrived, and he would have been able to sail up the Neva and attack St. Petersburg, which was defenseless against such an assault.

When Prince Bariatinskii reached Peterhof at ten o'clock that evening, he found the Emperor distraught and alarmed. Throughout the late afternoon and early evening, he had been sending members of his suite to St. Petersburg to learn what was afoot, but almost none had returned. However, he had managed to learn that Catherine had proclaimed herself Empress and that she had all of the Guards, St. Petersburg's senior officials, and leading churchmen on her side. The only troops over which Peter still held control were his battalion of Holsteiners. At his orders they had taken up defensive positions, fortified by artillery, in Peterhof's park, but feared to tell their Emperor that they had no cannon balls to fire. But even in terms of sheer paucity of numbers, it was not an impressive defense. At one point, Peter therefore contemplated flight. To his chagrin, he was told that there were no horses available since his suite had come from Oranienbaum in carriages. Things looked black indeed until Bariatinskii arrived with word that the commandant of Kronstadt was still loyal. Immediately, Peter seized upon that as a means for salvaging his crown. They all would sail to Kronstadt and use the fortress, with its three-thousand-man garrison, as their base of operations. However, when they reached Kronstadt somewhat after midnight, sentries refused them permission to land. In response to Peter's angry orders, they replied that he was no longer Emperor and that their loyalty was to the Empress Catherine II. Peter was at his wit's end. Field Marshal Münnich urged him to sail directly to the Baltic port of Reval, board a Russian frigate, and sail to Prussia where there were still some eighty thousand Russian troops. Instead, Peter chose to sail back to his palace at Oranienbaum. In doing so, he lost his last opportunity to save his crown.[172]

Meanwhile, Catherine was preparing to launch a final assault against Peter. On the evening of June 28, she donned a uniform lent her by one of the Semenovskii officers. Astride a white stallion, and holding a saber aloft, she led her regiments along the road she had taken early that morning. During the past twelve hours, she had encountered success at every turn. The soldiers had cheered their "little mother" whenever she appeared, and their officers had sworn allegiance to her as Russia's Autocrat. Russia's high churchmen stood at her side, and the government was functioning under her authority. Yet her claim to the throne would not be complete until Peter had been forced to abdicate; in the eyes of all Europe, he still ruled Russia. Catherine had the necessary military force to impose her will upon her husband. What she did not have was information about his exact whereabouts. Knowing Peter's character, however, she assumed he would take refuge in the miniature fortifications he had constructed several years earlier at Oranienbaum.[173]

Because many of her troops were infantry, Catherine was obliged to move slowly. The hour of one o'clock in the morning of June 29 found them at the "Krasnyi Kabachok," a small tavern located some nine *versty* outside St. Petersburg on the Peterhof-Oranienbaum road. There they stopped until morning to rest men and horses. Catherine set up her headquarters in the tavern's small second-floor parlor, while the soldiers made camp and cooked their rations outside. At six o'clock in the morning of June 29 Vice-Chancellor Prince Aleksandr Golitsyn arrived with a letter from Peter. Golitsyn immediately swore allegiance to Catherine and also told her that Aleksei Orlov, whose hussars had reached Peterhof earlier that night, had learned of Peter's whereabouts and had occupied all the entrances to the gardens that surrounded the palace at Oranienbaum. Peter and his Holstein troops were now sealed within its gates. The problem was to dislodge them without a bloody attack that might cost the lives of many good troops. Catherine issued no orders about her husband, but moved on toward Peterhof, probably hoping that Peter might take some action. Again, good fortune favored her. At Peterhof, she met General Mikhail Izmailov bearing another letter from the deposed Emperor. Peter now offered to renounce the throne and asked only that he, his mistress, and his favorite general Andrei Gudovich be allowed to return to Holstein.

Catherine sent General Izmailov and Grigorii Orlov to Oranienbaum with a formal announcement of abdication, which she insisted Peter must copy in his own hand and sign. Orlov was to deal with the abdication. Izmailov had a different task: he was to lure Peter to Peterhof in order to avert bloodshed at Oranienbaum. Both officers succeeded in their commissions with remarkable ease. Peter signed the notice of abdication immediately, and Orlov galloped back to Peterhof with the precious document in his hands. Soon afterward, Izmailov convinced the fallen Emperor that his best course of action was to travel to Peterhof with his mistress and General Gudovich and throw himself upon his wife's mercy. When Izmailov reached Peterhof, all three of his companions were placed under arrest, and Peter was obliged to surrender his sword and decorations. Catherine ordered that he be taken under a guard headed by Aleksei Orlov to Ropsha, a country estate some thirty-six *versty* from St. Petersburg.[174] As his idol Frederick the Great later wrote, Peter III had "allowed himself to be overthrown like a child being sent off to bed."[175]

Peter's continued existence presented a serious political dilemma to Catherine for, as long as he was alive, he was a potential threat to the security of her throne. She had sent him to Ropsha only temporarily, while preparations were made to incarcerate him in the far more secure fortress of Schlüsselberg, where Ivan VI still languished more than two decades after he had been overthrown. But Catherine was not obliged to live with the burden of an imprisoned husband for long. A week after her coup, a frightened courier arrived from Ropsha bearing a sealed packet from Aleksei Orlov. Inside Catherine found a crumpled sheet of paper, stained and smeared, in Orlov's handwriting. Although only partially coherent, for Orlov obviously had been drunk when he wrote it, the note contained vitally important news. Aside from repeated and semicoherent statements about his fear of the Empress's wrath and his readiness to face death at her command, Orlov's message read: "Little Mother, our most merciful Sovereign Mistress! How can I explain, how can I even begin to write about what has happened? You won't believe your faithful slave, but, just as if I were standing before God himself, I speak the truth. . . . Little Mother—he [Peter III] is no longer in this world. . . . He got into an argument with Prince Feodor [Bariatinskii] during dinner. We couldn't separate them and he no longer lives. We really don't remember exactly what happened."[176]

Although she has often been accused of plotting her husband's murder, there is no direct evidence that Catherine did so, and the remorse, even fear, in Orlov's drunken note seems genuine enough. Still, there is no doubt that Peter's death removed a great burden from Catherine's shoulders, and she was grateful to be rid of it. She never punished the men involved. In fact, they figured prominently in the list who received rewards even before her coronation.[177] During the three weeks after Peter's death, she bestowed upon them the following favors:

> *To Aleksei Orlov:*
> Promotion to the rank of Major General "for outstanding service to his motherland," a gift of 50,000 rubles, and an estate with eight hundred male serfs.*
>
> *To Grigorii Orlov:*
> Appointment to the post of Lord High Chamberlain, a gift of 50,000 rubles, and an estate with eight hundred male serfs.
>
> *To Grigorii Potemkin:*
> Promotion from the rank of sergeant-major to that of lieutenant in the Horse Guards, and an estate with four hundred male serfs.
>
> *To Feodor Bariatinskii:*
> A gift of 20,000 rubles.

Peter's death had to be explained to his former subjects, and Catherine hastened to do so. On July 7, 1762, she decreed: "On the seventh day after We ascended Our All-Russian throne, We received news that the former Emperor Peter the Third had suffered an acute attack of colic during one of his frequent bouts with hemorrhoids. For the sake of not shunning Our Christian duty and the Sacred Commandments by which We are obliged to protect the life of someone close to Us, We gave orders that everything necessary to restore him to health be done

---

* Eighteenth-century Russian censuses recorded only males among the peasant population. Hence, the actual population of the estates Catherine granted to these and other courtiers during her reign was slightly more than twice the number mentioned in the documents, since there were slightly more females than males in Russia's population.

immediately. But, to Our extreme grief and deep sorrow, yesterday evening We received further news that he, according to the will of Almighty God, had departed from this earth."[178] Eight days after Orlov had awakened Catherine in the early morning hours at Monplaisir, what is sometimes called the Revolution of 1762 was over. A petty German princess, whose only accomplishment when she had arrived in Russia eighteen years earlier had been a fluent command of French, had become Empress and Autocrat of All the Russias. Not one drop of Romanov blood flowed in her veins, and it is more than likely that none flowed in the veins of her son. Nevertheless, she would be remembered as one of the greatest "Romanov" autocrats.

Catherine was well aware that her claim to the throne was devoid of any legal basis, and she also knew that a number of Russia's statesmen had supported her in the expectation that she would act as Regent for her son Paul. Once she had seized power, however, she was determined to remove all threats to her authority. Peter III's death had eliminated one such threat. There remained two others: her son Paul and the deposed Emperor Ivan VI, the "nameless convict," as Catherine called him, still languishing in a cell in Schlüsselberg fortress. Since Paul was only eight years old, she had a decade in which to consolidate her power so that she could refuse to hand over the crown when he reached his majority. Ivan VI was a more difficult problem. He was twenty-two, his claim to the throne already established by the fact that he once had been proclaimed Emperor, and Catherine realized that he could easily become the focus of any foreign or domestic attempts to unseat her. Indeed, less than three months after her accession, the French King had instructed Baron de Breteuil, his Ambassador to St. Petersburg, to obtain all possible information about Ivan, to learn who his supporters were and, if possible, to "establish communications with him."[179]

There were some who suggested to Catherine that she marry Ivan VI, and she evidently did interview him soon after she became Empress. But long years of imprisonment had reduced him to a state of mental and physical dereliction. Having just escaped from one husband whose mental state and personality left much to be desired, Catherine was not inclined to take another whose condition was even worse. She gave orders to return the "nameless convict" to Schlüsselberg and to put him to death should any attempt be made to free him. Conveniently for her, Lieutenant Vasilii Mirovich, a Ukrainian separatist, made just such an attempt in June 1764. Apparently delighted at the opportunity to be freed from their burdensome task of guarding Ivan, his jailers promptly killed him.[180] The last rival claimant to Catherine's throne was eliminated; by the time her son Paul reached his majority, she simply let it be known that he would succeed her after her death.

Peter III had been blatantly offensive in his disdain for Russia and Russians. Remembering the ease with which she had won supporters, Catherine would not make the same mistake. German by birth, she vowed to become more Russian than any monarch since Peter the Great. Unrelated to Peter by blood, she promised to become heir to his aspirations and dreams. As a Grand Duchess, she had been conspicuous in observing Church rituals; she continued to be so as Empress. At the same time, she surrounded herself with Russians and appointed Russians to command the Empire's armies. Finally, Catherine began to plan an elaborate coronation. A consummate politician, she saw vast potential for winning her subjects' hearts and loyalty in Russia's intricate coronation ritual. If she could not claim the throne by Divine Right, she would invest her crown with the aura of Divine Sanction in her coronation.

Two days after Peter had signed his abdication manifesto, Catherine appointed Prince Nikita Trubetskoi to plan her coronation and allocated 50,000 rubles for the ceremony. She ordered a magnificent fireworks display costing thousands of rubles, and sent 600,000 rubles in silver coins to Moscow to be thrown among the throngs who would line the route of her triumphal procession. She moved not only her Court but most of Russia's government offices to Moscow for the ceremony. She would exploit Russians' love for their ancient capital and make amends for the many slights the city had suffered during the previous half-century. Her progress to Moscow was slow and regal, taking her thirteen days to travel the six hundred *versty* from St. Petersburg. When she made her triumphal entry into the city on September 13, 1762, Moscow was like a city reborn. Dull rows of long, low fences were concealed by thousands of evergreen trees cut especially for that purpose, the walls of many houses were covered with ornate rugs, and balconies were draped with brightly colored banners. Shouting, joyous throngs lined her route. "The chime of bells, the roar of the people's greetings, and the thunder of cannon greeted Catherine and accompanied her to the Kremlin," wrote one historian.[181] It was more than the blatant, gaudy opulence that had marked the ceremonial entries of the Empresses Anna and Elizabeth. It was magnificence, done with taste and elegance.

Catherine's coronation took place on Sunday, September 22. Early in the morning the Guards regiments assembled in parade dress on the square that lies in the midst of the Kremlin's three great cathedrals. At ten o'clock, a fanfare of trumpets and kettle drums signaled that the procession was about to begin. Garbed in the Imperial mantle of Russia's sovereigns, Catherine entered the Kremlin's great audience chamber, where she was met by all of Russia's Senators in full ceremonial regalia. Her confessor proceeding her to sprinkle holy water in her path, Catherine and her Senators stepped onto that very balcony from which Matveev and the Naryshkins had been thrown to their deaths upon *streltsy* pikes nearly a century before. Catherine moved to the head of the Red Staircase. As she began her descent, the bells in the Tower of Ivan the Great rang out and cannon roared in salute. Before she entered the Cathedral of the Assumption, the Archbishop of Novgorod raised a cross before her. Reverently, Catherine kissed the cross and entered into that holy sanctum where Russia's rulers had been crowned for centuries. Every inch the Autocrat, Catherine seated herself upon the Imperial throne. Two of her maids-of-honor helped her don her Imperial robes and placed over them the blue watered silk ribbon representing the Order of St. Andrei the First Called. Field Marshals Count Razumovskii and Prince Aleksandr Golitsyn came forward bearing her Imperial crown on a golden pillow. Solemnly, Catherine raised it and placed it upon her head. Then began the magnificent liturgy, while the Empress remained on the throne, with the Imperial scepter in her right hand, the orb in her left. At the end of the service, she emerged into the Kremlin square, resplendent in her Imperial garments and crown, still bearing the orb and scepter. Slowly she crossed first to the Cathedral of the Archangel and then to the Cathedral of the Annunciation. In each, she knelt to kiss the holy relics of Russia's early saints. She then returned to the Kremlin Palace where, enthroned under a rich canopy, she bestowed marks of favor upon her courtiers.[182]

Catherine had given careful thought to these. Most important, she wished to reward those who had supported her coup d'état. At the same time, she needed to ensure the further political support of Russia's senior statesmen and army commanders. She granted the title of Count to all five Orlov brothers and presented sabers inset with diamonds to Field Marshal Aleksandr Buturlin, Field Marshal Count Petr Saltykov, Field Marshal Alexandre Villebois, General Petr Panin, and General Prince Mikhail Volkinskii, five of Russia's most senior and popular commanders. To Field Marshal Prince Golitsyn, Prince Iakov Shakhovskoi, and General Count Zakhar Chernyshev, she gave the coveted Order of St. Andrei the First Called, Russia's highest decoration, and twelve others received the Order of St. Aleksandr Nevskii. She named Grigorii Orlov, who would remain her lover for another decade, her general aide-de-camp, and Princess Ekaterina Dashkova and Anna Matiushkina became senior ladies-in-waiting. Beyond that, Catherine bestowed fifteen promotions upon other members of the *Generalitet* and more upon men of lower rank. Nor did she forget the rank and file who had marched in her train during the revolt. The entire St. Petersburg garrison received six months' extra pay.[183] By the evening of September 22, it was clear to all in the Kremlin that loyal service to Catherine brought prompt and handsome rewards.

As Frederick the Great once remarked to Count Kaunitz, "the Empress of Russia is very proud, very ambitious, and very vain."[184] A better characterization of her might have added that she also possessed immense political talent and a flair for publicity. Catherine regarded Russia as a great Empire and was determined to be considered a great Empress. Therefore, she saw herself not only as a Russian monarch but as a world figure. As such, she intended to do more than build for herself a secure political position within Russia. More than any of her predecessors since Peter the Great, she was concerned about Russia's image in Europe. When Catherine ascended the throne, Russia's military prestige in Europe had reached new heights because of her recent victories over the armies of Frederick the Great during the Seven Years' War, but she wanted Russia to be respected for more than raw military might.

"Russia's ruler is an Autocrat," Catherine wrote, "because only by placing all power in the hands of one person can so vast an Empire be governed effectively." But she did not equate autocracy with tyranny. "The intention and purpose of autocratic government," she insisted, "is the glory of its citizens, the state, and the ruler . . . The object of autocracy . . . is not to deprive men of their natural liberty, but to direct their actions in such a manner as to achieve the greatest good for all."[185]

To achieve the recognition she desired for herself and Russia, Catherine embarked upon one of the most energetic and remarkable public-relations campaigns in the history of the eighteenth century. She had been Empress for scarcely more than a week when she launched the dramatic opening of her effort to pose as an apostle and patron of the Enlightenment. In 1751 the renowned French *philosophe* Denis Diderot had begun to publish his world-famous *Encyclopédie* with the help of the mathematician Jean D'Alembert. It was a monumental undertaking, a compendium of the Western world's historical and scientific knowledge that ultimately would fill seventeen large volumes and boast contributions from such leading thinkers of the day as Voltaire, Montesquieu, and Rousseau. From the beginning, Diderot's work epitomized the rational, skeptical, and scientific spirit of the mid-eighteenth century and embodied a pronounced criticism of Europe's *ancien régime* institutions and society. As a result, the Parisian authorities had suspended its publication, and, at the time of Catherine's accession, Diderot was looking for a place to resume his work. With a dramatic flourish, Catherine invited both Diderot and D'Alembert to St. Petersburg, where Diderot could continue with his *Encyclopédie* and D'Alembert could see to the education of her son Paul. Both refused, but Catherine continued to press them to accept her patronage. In response to D'Alembert's first refusal, she urged, "[I invite you to] come here with all your friends. I promise all of you every possible comfort and pleasure which I have the power to grant and, perhaps, you will find here more freedom and tranquility than you have now."[186]

D'Alembert continued to refuse, pleading the demands of his work in the West. Although Diderot also resisted her invitations, she continued to seek ways to serve as his patron. When he found himself in dire financial straits in 1765, she purchased his library for 15,000 livres, left it in his hands, and appointed him as its librarian at an annual salary of 1,000 livres.

Such acts of Imperial munificence served Catherine's cause well. All over Europe, leading thinkers and writers responded to her overtures with praise and enthusiasm. Madame Marie Geoffrin, who reigned over one of Paris's leading political and literary salons; Frau Johanna Bielcke, who presided over a similar one in Hamburg; Baron Melchior von Grimm, whose literary newsletter reached subscribers all over Europe, and a number of others were flattered by her personal notes and sang her praises across the length and breadth of the continent. Most vocal of all her panegyrists was the great Voltaire himself. Far sooner than other Europeans, Voltaire had perceived the rewards that lay in store for men and women who turned their pens to Russia's praise. Through the efforts of the French Ambassador to St. Petersburg, Voltaire had been elected an honorary member of Russia's Academy of Sciences in 1745 and, with the patronage of the great Elizabethan courtier Ivan Shuvalov, he had obtained the necessary documents to begin work on his *Histoire de l'Empire de Russie sous Pierre le Grand.* Despite Frederick the Great's caustic remark that it was incomprehensible why anyone would want to write "the history of wolves and Siberian bears" and that he "would not read the history of these barbarians," Voltaire knew such a work could bring him considerable profit. "After all," he remarked to D'Alembert, "these bears were very well-mannered in Berlin," a cutting reference to one of Frederick's most embarrassing military defeats.[187] Voltaire called Catherine the Semiramis of the North after the Assyrian queen noted for her beauty and wisdom, and he heaped fulsome praise upon her every act. "Who could have even imagined fifty years ago that the time would come when the Scythians [i.e. barbaric Russians] would so nobly reward virtue, knowledge, and philosophy in Paris?" he wrote when Catherine purchased Diderot's library.[188]

Some of Voltaire's greatest praises were reserved for Catherine's efforts to draft a new code of laws for Russia, one that would embody the most advanced legal theories of the Enlightenment. By the mid-1760s, Russia was in dire need of a code of laws that would reflect the many changes that had occurred since Peter the Great had ascended the throne. Peter himself had been the first to recognize the need for such a new code as early as 1700, but his efforts to have one written had come to naught, as had the efforts of a number of his successors, especially the Empress Elizabeth. Now Catherine vowed to succeed where so many others had failed. Although she was almost completely ignorant of Russian law, she attempted to formulate basic principles to guide the Legislative Commission she planned to summon in 1767.

Catherine wrote to Voltaire in 1765 that, although her heraldic device was a bee flitting from flower to flower gathering honey for its hive, her storehouse of political knowledge resembled an anthill.[189] She spent the next two years attempting to impose order upon the anthill of political notions she had amassed during some two decades of un-directed reading. The result was the *Nakaz* (the Instructions), which she completed at the beginning of 1767 and presented to Russia's Legislative Commission to guide them in their work. The *Nakaz* was mainly a compilation of ideas Catherine took from the writings of those *philosophes* whose favor she had courted from the moment of her accession. Of its 655 articles, she copied almost 300 from Montesquieu and more than one hundred from the Marquis di Beccaria, whose ideas about law, crime, and punishment she found appealing in an abstract sense. Many of the remaining articles came from Diderot's *Encyclopédie* and from the writings of a number of contemporary German publicists and jurists.[190] Very little of the text was written in Catherine's own words, a fact she frankly acknowledged when she wrote to Frederick the Great that "you will see that, like the crow in the fable, I have arrayed myself in a peacock's feathers. In this document, only the arrangement of the material, and a line here and a word there, belongs to me."[191]

The Legislative Commission summoned by Catherine to Moscow was comprised of 428 deputies chosen from Russia's military and civil services, the nobility, townsmen, peasants living on state lands, and various non-Russian ethnic groups. It could hardly have been expected to draft an enlightened code of laws for Russia for a number of reasons, not the least of which was the inexperience of the deputies and their general lack of education in those Western theories and precepts the Empress expected them to implement during the course of their deliberations. As Britain's Ambassador to St. Petersburg, Henry Shirley, wrote to Lord Viscount Weymouth in February 1768, after the Commission had been meeting for more than half a year:

> To give your Lordship a right idea of this choice collection of men, and their operations, permit me to suppose a certain number of the most ignorant of our petty merchants and shopkeepers in Great Britain and Ireland gathered as the several deputies of those nations in America, who either are subjects, or under the protection of His Majesty, and a few gentlemen unacquainted with the general principles, which constitute the basis of good government; this would perhaps be too favourable a copy of the original, now in the possession of what Russia prides herself so much upon.[192]

Beyond their inexperience and ignorance, the Legislative Commission deputies represented such very diverse interest groups that, even had they been better prepared, it would have been difficult for them to accomplish much. Each carried a statement of the expectations and demands of his "constituents," and these were so contradictory it was immediately obvious that they shared no common ground.

Although these statements have yet to be studied thoroughly by scholars, even a cursory examination reveals a number of quite surprising things about Russian society in the 1760s. First of all, Russia had become a sharply divided caste society in which various social groups were so separate in their aspirations and demands that they could not even hope to join in working for a common goal. None of the deputies thought in terms of Russia's welfare, but only of their narrower caste interests. Equally important, it was shockingly obvious from the information presented by the deputies that almost none of those vast changes that had occurred in Russia since the accession of Peter the Great had penetrated into the towns, villages, and countryside of the Empire. Outside the cities, Russians had no access to doctors, medicine, or teachers. The machinery of local administration and justice either was nonexistent or functioned as it had in the sixteenth and seventeenth centuries; Russians still lived in a premodern world.[193] As Ambassador Shirley wrote:

> Was even the Empress one of those great geniuses created to enlighten the world; how could Russia hope to be governed for the future by just, equal, and solid laws, if she considers, that were even these laws to be brought to a certain degree of perfection, the extreme want of respected and disinterested magistrates would still prevent her feeling the good effects of these laws. One cannot help pitying the Russians, who think themselves so wise, so powerful, when they are at such an immense distance from the happy situation of some nations in Europe.[194]

Catherine had written the *Nakaz* when she was almost totally ignorant of the reality of Russian life, and the ideas and hopes she had incorporated into it obviously bore little relation to the conditions that actually existed in her Empire. This did not lessen her disappointment when the Legislative Commission failed. As she later remarked to the *philosophe* Melchior Grimm in one of her characteristic flashes of candor, the *Nakaz* was "pure prattle in which one can find neither any understanding of [Russian] conditions, nor any discretion, nor foresight."[195] She was far closer to the truth than Voltaire was when, from his home in Fermy, he pronounced the *Nakaz* "the most beautiful monument of the century."[196]

From the failure of the Legislative Commission, Catherine drew two important conclusions. First, it was painfully clear that widespread administrative reforms were needed if the Autocrat's will and the Autocrat's benevolence were to be felt in Russia's counties, towns, and villages. Second, the Empress realized that her hopes for an educated Russian society had been wildly optimistic and that she could not be an enlightened sovereign without first becoming an *enlightening* monarch. Even the nobility required basic education in Western thought, and that must be her first task before such grandiose aspirations as an enlightened code of laws could become a reality. At the end of her *Nakaz*, she had written that "labor and diligence will overcome any obstacle."[197] After the Legislative Commission's failure, she turned to apply those virtues to the task of educating Russia's nobles. Eventually, she would succeed, but the result would be far different from what she had expected. When the younger generation of Russia's nobles began to assimilate the ideals of the Enlightenment, they would turn to criticize the social and political order Catherine had created.

The great nineteenth-century historian Vasilii Kliuchevskii once observed that the *Nakaz* was "not an historical stage in our [Russian] legislative process . . . but a feature in the biography of the document's composer."[198] That is true in part. But it is also true that in her unique organization of the *philosophes'* ideas, and in her additions and excisions to the *Nakaz,* Catherine made a fundamental statement about her political views and the character of Russian autocracy as she perceived it. As we mentioned earlier, Catherine believed that autocracy was the only system of government proper for her Empire and that "any other form of government not only would be harmful for Russia but, in the end, would lead to her ruin."[199] Such a statement clearly contradicted the views of the *philosophes* whom she had sought to marshal in support of Russia's cause. Yet, through the clever use of "a line here and a word there," Catherine succeeded in reconciling for public consumption her defense of autocracy with their ideas. She did so by blurring the distinction between the very different principles of division of power and division of function as they were institutionalized in the government of Russia. Thus, she proposed separate legislative, judicial, and executive agencies, but, instead of permitting them to limit the power of the monarch, she placed the Autocrat on a pedestal above them all, implying that autocracy was capable of limiting itself in the service of the common good.

All noble aspirations aside, the sad truth was that Catherine was not even in a position to perceive the common good, let alone serve it. Because the Russian ruler's power was absolute, whoever sat upon the throne could raise men to great heights or cast them into the lowest depths. Russia's history throughout the eighteenth century provided ample evidence of that fact. No longer hindered by the restraints tradition had placed upon the power of seventeenth-century Tsars to elevate servitors to high positions, Peter the Great had raised lowborn men and foreigners to dizzying heights and, at the same time, had reduced a number of men with long and distinguished aristocratic lineage to misery and poverty. His example had been followed far more capriciously by his successors, as men's careers soared upward and plummeted into disgrace and exile with every change of ruler in St. Petersburg. As a result, eighteenth-century Russian autocrats were surrounded by men and women who told them only what they wanted to hear. They were insulated from unpleasant reality by an impenetrable screen of sycophants who sought to curry favor and advance their positions and those of their families. Thus, the realities of Russian conditions were hidden from Catherine so thoroughly that she knew little of what her subjects really needed to improve their lives. That fact would become painfully clear in the fall of 1773, just after the first decade of her reign had passed when out of the southeastern corner of Russia burst the most violent social revolution the country had ever known—called by Soviet historians the Peasant War of Emelian Pugachev.

During the eighteenth and nineteenth centuries, Russia, like the United States, was mistress of a vast frontier that stretched some two thousand miles from the Arctic Ocean to the Caspian Sea and gradually moved eastward from the city of Kazan on the Volga River across some four thousand miles of unsettled territory toward the Pacific. Particularly along the lower reaches of Russia's great rivers—the Don, the Volga, and the Iaik—communities of freebooting Cossacks had settled; throughout the eighteenth century, their numbers had been augmented by peasants fleeing the more settled regions of the Empire to escape the heavy burdens of serfdom. To bring these outlying areas in the southeast more firmly under control, Catherine's government sought to establish Russian military authority and, along with it, serfdom and other aspects of the Imperial society and administration. Yet, in the 1760s and early 1770s, the Russian military and administrative presence was still feeble and widely scattered. Orenburg province, the region in which Pugachev first raised his standard of rebellion, encompassed an area larger in size than the British Isles, with a population of about seven hundred thousand, nearly all of it dissident national minorities and Cossacks, who were hostile to Russian authority.[200] The task of representing Imperial authority in this vast and hostile area fell to some seven thousand troops spread out over two dozen forts that were as primitive as those on the eighteenth-century American frontier, and often even more so.[201] As in the case of America's frontier experience, these forts were adequate to protect their garrisons against natives armed with primitive weapons. Against any substantial force with firearms, they were totally undefendable. By the late summer of 1773, Pugachev commanded just such a force.

Before he rose to notoriety, Pugachev had enjoyed a checkered career typical of a number of eighteenth-century Russian borderers. He was born a Cossack on the lower reaches of the Don River around 1742, fought in the Seven Years' War and a number of other campaigns, deserted from the army, wandered in Poland and southern Russia for some years, got into difficulty with the authorities, was sentenced to hard labor in Siberia and escaped, all before he was thirty.[202] His escape at the end of May 1773 led him into Russia's turbulent and isolated frontier region of the Iaik River on the western fringes of Siberia. There he found shelter among those Iaik Cossacks who were at the moment in an angry and rebellious mood because of the Imperial administration's increasing incursions into those lands where they held sway. In his flight from Russian justice, Pugachev thus found himself in the midst of burgeoning social and political upheaval.[203] Proclaiming himself "Amperor" Peter III and claiming that he had miraculously escaped the murderous clutches of Catherine's agents at Ropsha, he began his march with fewer than eighty followers. His army grew like an avalanche. By the beginning of 1774, almost thirty thousand rebels with nearly one hundred cannon marched beneath his banners. On a hitherto unknown scale, they pillaged manor houses, murdered provincial noble families, overran government outposts, and finally laid siege to the provincial capital of Orenburg.[204]

During the fall and winter of 1773, when Pugachev was enjoying his first successes, Catherine's Court was particularly brilliant and festive. At the beginning of October, all of Petersburg's high society was agog over the elaborate festivities she had arranged for the wedding of her son, the Grand Duke Paul, to the Princess of Hesse-Darmstadt. A few weeks later, the great *encyclopédist* Diderot at last favored his Imperial patroness with a visit, and, at the same time, the famous German publicist Melchior Grimm visited the Court. Catherine was in her glory. For at least a moment, her Court almost equaled Europe's salons in terms of the brilliant figures assembled, and far exceeded them in the opulence of its setting. She played her role of Europe's northern Semiramis to the hilt. Before all, she posed as the champion of reason and proclaimed the benefits her enlightened rule had brought to Russia.

Right in the midst of Catherine's carefully staged cultural and intellectual charade dropped the tainted fruit of Pugachev's rebellion, and it produced a stench that no amount of verbal perfumery could mask. Before many weeks had passed, all foreigners in St. Petersburg knew that the lives of Catherine's subjects were, in fact, so wretched that they flocked in droves to the rebel standards of a burly and bearded Cossack who claimed to be her murdered husband. At first, Catherine tried to suppress all news about Pugachev and his rebel host. But by December the rebellion had become so immense that it could not be concealed. Soon it spread through an area greater than all of France, and by some estimates, nearly fifty thousand rebels were involved.[205] Fear among Russia's serf owners reached hysterical dimensions, heightened by tales of Pugachev's brutality that began to filter into those areas not yet touched by the revolt.

"Depending upon the circumstance, the time, and the man . . . it is necessary to have the teeth of a wolf and the tail of a fox," Catherine had written to her newly appointed Governor-General of the Ukraine, another traditionally turbulent area of her Empire, not long after she became Empress.[206] She now sought to show the fox's tail to Western Europe by writing to her correspondents that Pugachev was a mere "highwayman," dubbing him "le Marquis Pugacheff."[207] At the same time, Catherine turned her wolf's teeth upon Pugachev himself, sending general after general against him. First General Vasilii Kar was ordered to "make a search for the miscreant and try to catch both him and his scurrilous band."[208] In mid-October, Kar raced toward Orenburg confident of victory, only to have his ragtag army of garrison troops and armed settlers smashed the following month. Following Kar's failure, Catherine sent out General Aleksandr Bibikov, giving him full military and civil powers over the southeastern region so that he could draw upon all resources to crush his foe.[209] Bibikov was neither as rash as Kar nor as ready to underestimate that "pig Pugachev's villainous bunch."[210] He therefore waited in Kazan for reinforcements of regular troops to arrive, inflicting in the meantime some minor defeats on Pugachev's forces. By the end of March, his reinforcements had seized Pugachev's stronghold at Tatishchev Station and relieved Orenburg. At Kargala and Sakmarvsk, they reduced his forces to less than five hundred effectives, but Pugachev himself escaped. A few days later, Bibikov died of fever.[211]

With Bibikov dead, Pugachev retreated to the north, gathered new forces, and seized a number of ironworks and lesser forts. Then, to everyone's astonishment and terror, he turned and stormed Kazan, the largest Russian city in the southwest, in mid-July. Yet on the heels of Pugachev's greatest victory came the beginnings of his final defeat. That same month, Russia ended her war with the Ottoman Empire, and Catherine thus had more regular troops and some of her greatest generals, including Petr Panin and Aleksandr Suvorov, to throw against the rebels. Faced by better troops led by talented commanders, Pugachev's rebel hordes suffered defeat after defeat. Finally, the Iaik Cossacks, the men who had first joined his cause a year earlier, betrayed Pugachev in return for pardons. On September 14, 1774, they delivered him bound hand and foot into the hands of Captain Savva Mavrin at the town of Iaitsk, not far from where the revolt had begun. Pugachev, alias "Amperor" Peter III, was delivered to Moscow in November in an iron cage.[212]

On Saturday morning, January 10, 1775, Pugachev was brought to a specially constructed platform on the bank of the Moscow River within sight of the Kremlin. His sentence was read to him as he crossed himself and prepared for what promised to be a painful death. His arms and legs were to be cut off and then he was to be beheaded. But the executioner, having never performed such a task before, either became confused or had been bribed by Pugachev's sympathizers to end his agony. As one witness described the scene: "Instead of first quartering him by cutting off his arms and legs as the sentence decreed, the executioner suddenly beheaded him. . . . One of the officials turned on the executioner and bellowed: 'You dumb son of a bitch! How did you manage to screw this up? Cut off his arms and legs and be quick about it!' "[213] Pugachev thus was spared the suffering the enlightened

Catherine had intended for him. After the execution, his head was exhibited on a spike, and parts of his dismembered corpse were taken to various quarters of Moscow where they were burned and the ashes scattered. Russians may have become Europeanized, but the death inflicted upon Pugachev had a great deal in common with the execution of the False Dmitrii more than a century and a half earlier. Myths would circulate that someone else had died in Pugachev's place, but the greatest peasant war in Russia history was ended.[214]

Catherine was well aware that the oppressive nature of serfdom was the main reason so many had flocked to Pugachev's standard. Indeed, soon after his execution, she wrote, "If we do not consent to diminish cruelty and to moderate a situation which is intolerable to the human race, then sooner or later they [the masses] will take this step themselves."[215] But, if she recognized the problem, Catherine was in no position to provide the solution. To improve conditions for the masses would mean an assault upon the privileged position of the nobility, which she was by no means prepared to undertake. Indeed, she chose to strengthen the control of her government over the lower classes by making an even firmer alliance with the nobility and placing the control of Russia's provincial affairs more fully in their hands.

Although Catherine had tried to conceal the extent of Pugachev's revolt from Europe, it was widely reported and commented upon in the Western press; an account of it even appeared in Williamsburg's *Virginia Gazette*.[216] In a moment of depression, Catherine wrote that the rebellion had set Russia back some two centuries in the eyes of Europe, but it is doubtful that she believed that statement.[217] In fact, the rebellion did little to disrupt that polite mutual admiration society she had established with the *philosophes* of France and Germany, and almost a decade more would pass before those circles began to criticize her openly. Her Court became even more elegant, even more magnificent, and, in the years after the revolt, she embellished her capital with more beautiful buildings. Much of this new exuberance was sparked by Grigorii Potemkin, a moody, passionate, one-eyed giant, known as the "Cyclops," who became her lover in 1774.

Grigorii Potemkin was the first man in Catherine's life to share fully her political, intellectual, and cultural interests. Born in the village of Chizhovo in the western province of Smolensk in 1739, he grew up in a turbulent household ruled by a morose father who suffered an almost pathological jealousy of his young and intelligent wife. Because his family was too poor to hire one of the foreign tutors who were coming into vogue among Russia's nobility, Grigorii was first taught by the village priest and by a cousin who was a high-ranking civil servant. Even as an adolescent, he had a brilliant mind and a ready wit. He was torn between becoming a priest and entering the army, a conflict that continued to plague him throughout his life. In 1756 he entered the *gymnasium* at the newly founded University of Moscow, but was expelled for "laziness and missing classes" four years later. He then joined the elite Horse Guards as a corporal and very soon became friendly with the Orlovs and their circle. Catherine's coup d'état found Potemkin, then a sergeant major, among those who escorted Peter III from Oranienbaum to Peterhof, and he was one of those charged with guarding the deposed Emperor at Ropsha. Less than three weeks after Peter's death, he was promoted to the rank of lieutenant and given an estate with four hundred male serfs, the first of many marks of favor he would receive from Catherine's hands.[218]

Although Catherine was much taken by the dashing and brilliant young Potemkin at the beginning of her reign, they did not become lovers for more than a decade. For one thing, it was difficult for her to break her ties with Grigorii Orlov. She could not forget that, during the dark days of Peter III's reign, when her husband's insults had made her an awkward guest even at her own Court, Orlov had wooed her and loved her. Nor could she forget their shared experience in the Revolution of 1762 and the fact that Orlov and his four brothers wielded great political power because of their popularity among the Guards. Until her hold upon the throne was truly secure, she could not displace Orlov, although she may well have wished to do so by the mid-1760s.

As Catherine turned from problems of political survival to the business of ruling Russia, Orlov's shortcomings became patently obvious. He was a dashing officer, a clever politician, and an exciting lover, although fidelity evidently was not one of his virtues. But his mind was primitive, his conduct sometimes boorish, and he had little talent for diplomacy or statecraft. During the Russo-Turkish War of 1768–74, the Moscow plague of 1771, and Pugachev's revolt, Catherine began to feel even more acutely the loneliness that came with absolute power as crisis after crisis burst upon her. More than ever she needed a lover who could do more than satisfy her physical needs. At the beginning of 1774, she found him in Potemkin, whose professional progress she had carefully charted for the past decade.

During the first decade of Catherine's reign, Potemkin's career had flourished, partly because of her patronage but also because he had shown himself to be one of those rare men who are talented both in war and statecraft. He had been one of the government representatives on Catherine's abortive Legislative Commission, had acquitted himself admirably there, and had proved an effective administrator in a number of other government offices. Yet he was not satisfied to hang his star only upon his talent as a civil official. As was often the case with eighteenth-century Russian officials, he had kept his army commission; when the Russo-Turkish War began in 1768, he demanded the chance to prove himself on the battlefield. Catherine granted his wish.

Potemkin distinguished himself in some of the war's bloodiest battles. At Khotin he was cited for "conspicuous bravery and talent in military affairs" and promoted to the rank of major general. At Fokshan, his cavalry routed a force of some ten thousand Turks, and in early 1770 he fought with distinction in the battles of Braila, Larga, Kargul, and Izmail. In September, Count Petr Rumiantsev, Commander-in-Chief of Russia's armies in the Balkans, wrote of Potemkin's prowess to Catherine: "Not knowing what it is to be urged into action, he [Potemkin], of his own free will, sought every opportunity to join in the fray." To this, Field Marshal Prince Aleksandr Golitsyn added, "Russia's cavalry has never fought with such order and bravery as it does under the command of Major General Potemkin." The next year, he won more victories and was promoted to lieutenant general. From the reports she received from the front, Catherine came to see Potemkin not only as a brilliant man but as a hero of great stature. "Dear Lieutenant General and Chevalier!" she wrote to him in late 1773. "Because I am very anxious to retain the services of zealous, brave, intelligent, and skilful men, I beg you not to put yourself into unnecessary danger."[219] When he received her letter, Potemkin knew that his moment had come. He took leave of his command and galloped to St. Petersburg.

During the first decade of Catherine's reign, Potemkin had proved a worthy servant of his Empress and one upon whom she might rely for counsel. Yet she had waited to summon him to her side until the end of the Russo-Turkish War was in sight. When she dismissed Grigorii Orlov in 1772, she had installed as his successor not Potemkin, but the young Guards Officer Aleksandr Vasilchikov, as the result of what she later called a "choice at random," resulting from her desire to let Potemkin cover himself with glory on the battlefield.[220] In any case, Vasilchikov remained as her lover for some eighteen months until Potemkin returned from the siege of Silestria in January 1774.

Potemkin hastened to St. Petersburg fully expecting to be installed in those apartments that connected with Catherine's own by a special staircase. To his amazement, he found that Vasilchikov still held his post as favorite. Unlike Vasilchikov, Potemkin was far from being a biddable courtier. He had an audience with Catherine, briefly appeared satisfied with the result, then became morose and withdrawn. Soon he retired to the Aleksandr Nevskii Monastery, donned a monk's habit, and began to grow a beard. Knowing that the contemplative monastic life held a certain attraction for him (indeed, one of the achievements that had first brought Potemkin to Catherine's attention was his knowledge of the Scriptures and his fluency in Greek),[221] the Empress feared she might lose him. She sent her *Eprouveuse*, Countess Bruce, whose task it was to test the prowess of the Empress's prospective lovers, to promise him the highest favors if he returned to Court.[222] Catherine dispatched Vasilchikov to Moscow, laden with the usual presents she bestowed upon a departing lover, and prepared to install Potemkin in his place. Honors and appointments were heaped upon her new lover. At the beginning of March, she named Potemkin her personal general aide-de-camp, Deputy Commander of the Preobrazhenskii Guards (of which she herself was the Commander), and decorated him with the Order of St. Aleksandr Nevskii. Later that year, she promoted him to the rank of full general, named him Vice-President of the War College, made him a Count of the Russian Empire, and a Knight of the Order of St. Andrei. She gave him a saber set with diamonds, and her portrait, also set in diamonds, to wear over his heart. In 1775 he received the Order of St. George; in 1776 she appointed him to several high military commands, made him a Prince, and in June gave him the Anichkov Palace.[223]

Catherine and Potemkin shared a taste for Western ideas and culture, a love of Russia, and a passion for work. She adored him madly, probably more than any man she had met before and more than any she would know afterward. For a woman who always had been disciplined and calculating and whose greatest passion was the love of power, she permitted her heart unusual freedom with him. Potemkin returned her love with equal passion. When they were apart, if only for a few hours, they exchanged tender notes. Theirs was a mutually shared, total passion and, although Catherine herself was at a loss to understand it fully, she let herself be swept up in it. As she wrote to Melchoir Grimm, Vasilchikov had been "immediately replaced, I myself know not exactly how, by one of the greatest, strangest, and most amusing eccentrics of this iron age."[224]

Yet, while they shared many interests and aspirations, Catherine and Potemkin were very different. Although she was Russian by conviction, Catherine would always remain a precise, orderly, diligent German to the very depths of her being. She had long since established a rigid daily routine, rising at six in the morning and working for twelve or fifteen hours. While she rarely scaled emotional peaks, she seldom fell into emotional abysses. By contrast, Potemkin had a mercurial Slavic temperament. He was exuberant or morose, feverishly energetic or totally lethargic. One day he could write, "You have enclosed me in your heart. I wish to stand there higher than all others"; the next day he could refuse Catherine admittance to his chambers.[225] "I came to see you to tell you how much I love you, but found your door locked," read one plaintive note from Russia's usually vain and proud Empress.[226]

Catherine might swallow her pride and vanity when caught up in the first throes of love, but her submission would not last long or be often repeated. Potemkin understood his Empress well enough to realize that. Yet he also knew that his own nature could not change. Like his Imperial mistress, he loved power above all else. When it became clear that the conflicts of their passion might destroy his political relationship with his mistress, he resolved to replace himself as Catherine's lover with a creature he could control and to retire gracefully from her bed while their intellectual and political relationship still flourished. To this arrangement, Catherine evidently agreed, also realizing that their stormy passion might one day destroy Potemkin's ability to function as her chief adviser—it was far easier to find a new lover than an able and talented statesman. Catherine replaced Potemkin as her personal general aide-de-camp in 1776 with Count Petr Zavadovskii, a man of Potemkin's own choosing, while Potemkin continued to be her close personal friend and political counselor. This arrangement would last through seven changes in lovers until Potemkin's death in 1791.

None of Potemkin's successors possessed his intellectual brilliance or his talent for statecraft, and that was as he intended it should be. For the next fifteen years, he continued to serve Catherine as her leading statesman. He took a major part in foreign policy discussions and also spoke with authority on domestic and military affairs. Together, he and Catherine would plan Russia's annexation of the Crimea in 1783 and the opening of the Black Sea to Russian trade. Together they would dream of Catherine's "Greek Project," which evoked the image of a reborn Byzantine Empire ruled by her second grandson, the Grand Duke Konstantin, and which led to the outbreak of the second Russo-Turkish War in 1787. After its annexation, Catherine left the Crimea and the other provinces of the southern region known as New Russia in Potemkin's charge. He proved an energetic and capable administrator.

Catherine came to view the results of Potemkin's labors in the south herself during the spring of 1787. She was so confident of his success in developing the Crimea and the northern littoral of the Black Sea that she invited the Austrian Emperor Joseph II and several foreign ambassadors to accompany her. Her progress from St. Petersburg to the Crimea was Potemkin's greatest triumph, a combination of brilliant showmanship and prodigious attention to details. Catherine began her journey on January 18, 1787, from the summer palace at Tsarskoe Selo, some twenty-five *versty* from St. Petersburg. There were

14 great sledges and 184 smaller ones to carry the Empress and her entourage, with 560 horses waiting at each post station to replace those that had grown weary of their burdens. Catherine's sledge had a drawing room, a study, a library, and a bedroom. She shared it with her current "pupil," Count Aleksandr Dmitriev-Mamonov, and her favorite lady-in-waiting, Mademoiselle Protasova, who was Countess Bruce's successor to the unique office of *l'Eprouveuse*.[227] Because night fell in midafternoon during the winter in that part of Russia, Potemkin had arranged for their way to be lighted by gigantic bonfires. After each day's journey, they stopped for the night at a palace or mansion, often belonging to a high local official, which Potemkin had specially refurbished for the occasion. Beginning at Smolensk, there were impressive receptions and entertainments for Catherine and her guests. In this manner, the entire company passed the next three weeks until on February 9 they reached Kiev, center of the first Russian state and cradle of Russian Christianity. There they remained for almost three months until May 1, 1787, when the ice had cleared from the Dniepr River, making it possible for them to continue their journey by water.

They traveled in seven galleys "of elegant form and of a majestic size, skilfully painted, and manned with crews, numerous, active, and uniformly dressed. The splendid apartments constructed on the decks glittered with gold and silk," according to Count Louis Philippe de Ségur, the French Ambassador. "Each of us found in ours a room and cabinet as sumptuous as it was elegant, a convenient sofa, an excellent bed of chinese taffeta, and a mahogany secretary." Everyone was impressed by the elegance and comfort in which they traveled. But Potemkin's display was just beginning. De Ségur remarked that "all the stations were so measured as to avoid even the slightest fatigue, and care had been taken that the fleet should anchor only before towns or villages in picturesque situations. Large flocks gave animation to the meadows; groups of peasants enlivened the banks; and numerous boats full of youths and girls, who were singing the rustic airs of their country, incessantly surrounded us. Nothing was forgotten."[228] The culmination of the journey was Sevastopol, the new naval base Potemkin had built for Russia's new Black Sea fleet. From the Inkerman Heights outside the new town, Catherine first saw her new fleet. Forty men-of-war flying the Russian flag lay at anchor and greeted her with broadsides from their cannon.[229] Wrote de Ségur, "It appeared to us quite incomprehensible how Prince Potemkin, at eight hundred leagues from the capital, and in a country so recently conquered, could find the means to form, in two years, such an establishment, build a town, raise a fleet, make forts, and gather together so many inhabitants; it was indeed a prodigious display of activity."[230]

So incomprehensible was Potemkin's achievement to some, especially to the Saxon Ambassador Helbig, that they sought to explain it by declaring it a gigantic hoax, claiming that Potemkin had built sham villages filled with structures that were only facades. In fact, Potemkin's accomplishments in the south were immensely impressive, and they embodied substance, not sham. A mere listing of known historical facts proves the extent of his labors. Between 1783 and 1787, Potemkin founded most of Russia's major southern cities: Kherson, Nikolaev, Ekaterinoslav, and Sevastopol. Although they were still under construction in 1787 (de Ségur noted, for example, that "no quays had been constructed nor any commercial storehouses" in Kherson), a great deal of building had been completed. According to de Ségur's account, Kherson had two thousand houses and a nearly completed fortress.[231] Certainly, these were no sham cities. Indeed, later in 1787, Count Kyril Razumovskii wrote that, in Kherson, there were "increasing numbers of stone buildings, a fortress enclosing a citadel and the best buildings, an admiralty office . . . [and] an extensive suburb in which reside merchants and petty tradesmen on one side and barracks housing ten thousand troops on the other."[232] Most of all, Potemkin's newly established southern ports and shipyards produced the Black Sea Fleet with which Russia would win two naval victories against the Turks in July 1788.

The grandeur and festivity of Potemkin's southern spectacle, unfortunately, were far from indicative of the conditions that Catherine faced during her last decade on the throne. The years between 1787 and 1796 saw Russia fight a victorious though ruinous and bloody war with the Turks, an inconclusive war with Sweden, and a desperate campaign against Tadeusz Kościuszko's Polish patriots. Beginning in 1789, Catherine had to face the political threat of the French Revolution, along with the realization that it was a logical outgrowth of the ideas she had toyed with early in her reign. Likewise, she had to face criticism of her policies from that younger generation of Russians who held those ideas more deeply than did she. Among them, Aleksandr Radishchev, one of a select group of protégés she had sent to study in the West, published a moving indictment of serfdom and autocracy in 1790 under the title *A Journey from St. Petersburg to Moscow*. As we shall see, Catherine was horrified by Radishchev's book. But an even greater shock soon followed. On October 12, 1791, a courier from the south arrived at the Winter Palace with the news that Potemkin had died a week before on the road between Jassy and Nikolaev.

For Catherine, the shock of Potemkin's death was overwhelming. Her private secretary Aleksandr Khrapovitskii's brief diary notes are perhaps a more dramatic expression of her grief and loss than some of the more romantic and florid accounts that have been written:

> Tears and despair. At 8 PM she was bled. At 10 PM she was put to bed. Entry for October 12, 1791.
>
> She awoke in grief and tears. Entry for October 13, 1791.
>
> The weeping continues. She said to me: "How can I replace Potemkin? No one can do so. Who would have thought that [Count Ivan] Chernyshev and other old men would have outlived him? He was a true aristocrat, a wise man. He never tried to sell me to others. No one could buy him." Entry for October 16, 1791.[233]

No monarch's servant could have asked for a better epitaph from his sovereign than that which Catherine penned to Melchoir Grimm a few days later. "To an excellent heart, he added a rare understanding, and an extraordinary broadness of mind; his views were always broad and magnanimous; he was very humane, full of knowledge, singularly amiable, and his ideas were always unique. . . . No one in the world could be led by others less than he. . . . In a word, he was a statesman."[234]

Perhaps in an effort to keep alive Potemkin's heritage and perhaps to create the illusion that the world of the 1760s and 1770s, in which she had cut such a brilliant figure, still existed in the 1790s, Catherine continued to dream those grandiose dreams she had shared for so many years with Potemkin. But she now lacked the means and the will that had been hers in earlier times. "Now I am an old woman," she told her secretary Khrapovitskii in a rare flash of candor.[235] As a result, those dreams that once had been underlain by an element of reality now became pure flights of fantasy. To lend them an air of reality, she tried to recapture her precious relationship with Potemkin in the arms and confidences of Platon Zubov, the youth who had become her lover in 1789, two years before Potemkin's death.

According to contemporaries, Zubov was not tall, but broad shouldered and strong, with especially striking eyes and a talent for playing the violin.[236] When he became Catherine's twelfth official lover, he was twenty-two and she had just turned sixty. She had ruled Russia for twenty-seven years, and the burden had taken a heavy toll. Her face had grown lined and sagging, and the figure in which she once had taken such pride lay buried beneath a deep layer of fat. "Toward the close of her life, Catherine had so increased in size, as to be an object almost of deformity [and] her legs . . . were always swollen and often ulcerated," wrote the Frenchman Charles Masson, in an observation that was shared by the young Polish courtier Prince Adam Czartoryski.[237] Thus, for Russia's vain and proud Empress, the burden of physical ugliness was added to those of the political and economic crises she faced. She became infatuated with her young and handsome "pupil," nearly four decades younger than she, immediately made him a general, ordered books from abroad to improve his mind, and lavished gifts and attentions upon him. She gave him vast estates and tens of thousands of serfs. For the first time in her life, her infatuation with a lover began to impair her political judgment.[238]

Totally lacking the talent and knowledge to play a statesman's role, the petty and greedy Zubov strode about Court "with a large hat and feather on his head," surrounded by lackeys and sycophants.[239] At first he flattered his mistress immensely, but even with her he was at times so arrogant that her courtiers were appalled. According to some accounts, he even attempted to seduce the sixteen-year-old Grand Duchess Elisaveta Alekseevna, wife of the future Alexander I. Wrote the young Prince Czartoryski, aghast at such behavior: "This arrogant and chimerical conceit brought him great ridicule, and one is amazed that he dared to conceive of this idea under the very eyes of Catherine."[240] Catherine, however, was utterly blind to Zubov's faults. She made him a Knight of Saint Andrei and Governor-General of New Russia (Potemkin's former post) when he was twenty-six, a Prince at the age of twenty-eight, and, although he had never even been to sea, Commander of the Black Sea fleet in the same year.[241] It was Zubov who, in a vain effort to emulate Potemkin, conceived of a grandiose "Oriental Project," which would involve Russia's invasion of the Caucasus and Persia, establish a link with India, and isolate Constantinople from the East, while another Russian army under General Suvorov would drive across the Balkans and seize Constantinople. It was a pretentious and preposterous scheme made downright ridiculous by the fact that Zubov convinced Catherine to appoint his twenty-four-year-old brother Valerii as Commander-in-Chief.[242] The one certainty was that the venture would cost vast amounts of money and tens of thousands of troops, neither of which Russia could afford to commit to such a chimerical quest for Oriental glory.

Fortunately, Russia was spared these absurd burdens by Catherine's death. On November 4, 1796, she attended one of her smaller evening assemblies and seemed in good spirits, although she had been somewhat ill the day before. She left early, however, saying that she had a slight touch of colic. The next day she seemed well enough, gave some audiences to her counselors, and spoke briefly with Zubov. At one point, she excused herself and went to her water closet. She did not return. Her valet finally became concerned and went in search of his mistress, only to find her lying unconscious on the floor. Catherine had suffered a massive stroke and died some thirty hours later, on November 6, without regaining consciousness.[243]

That same day, her son, now aged forty-two, was proclaimed Emperor Paul I after having waited more than a quarter-century for the throne that was rightly his. Paul would become the first nineteenth-century Russian Emperor. One of his major goals would be to restore the authority of the Autocrat, which Catherine had weakened by granting so much power over local affairs to the nobility. Never again in the history of Imperial Russia would the nobility know such a time of privilege. Not without good reason would they remember Catherine as their "little mother" and her reign as their Golden Age.

CHAPTER V

An Imperial City in the Making

There, by the billows desolate,
He stood, with mighty thoughts elate,
And gazed: but in the distance only
A sorry skiff on the broad spate
Of Neva drifted seaward, lonely.
The moss-grown miry banks with rare
Hovels were dotted here and there
Where wretched Finns for shelter crowded;
The murmuring woodlands had no share
Of sunshine, all in mist beshrouded.
And thus he mused: From here, indeed
We shall strike terror in the Swede;
And here a city by our labour
Founded, shall gall our haughty neighbour;
Here cut—so Nature gives command—
Your window through on Europe; stand
Firm-footed by the sea, unchanging!
Ay, ships of every flag shall come
By waters they have never swum,
And we shall revel, freely ranging.
A century—and that city young,
Gem of the Northern world, amazing,
From gloomy wood and swamp upsprung,
Had risen, in pride and splendour blazing.[1]

T hus, did Aleksandr Pushkin, Russia's greatest romantic poet, describe the first century of St. Petersburg's history. Its construction was a feat worthy of a romantic poet's pen, for in it there was heroism, tragedy, and, above all, glory. Men died by the thousands to build it, but their achievement stood as a monument to man's triumph over nature. Parks and gardens flourished where bogs once had held sway. Muddy streams and rivulets were transformed into majestic canals. In place of mud huts inhabited by primitive fishermen there arose magnificent palaces in which elegant lords and ladies dined and danced the polonaise and minuet until dawn. In less than a century, St. Petersburg grew from a small Swedish fort into Russia's first Imperial city and one of Europe's most beautiful capitals. Originally given the Dutch name of Sankt Pieter Burkh, it bore the name of its founder's patron saint and became a worthy monument to Russia's first great Emperor, Peter the Great. It was his "window on the West," an expression of what he wanted Russia to become in the eyes of Europe. St. Petersburg was, and always would be, Peter's city.

The construction of St. Petersburg began after Peter's victory at Nienschanz in 1703 when the Tsar built a fortress to defend the land he had won from the Swedes. For its location, he chose Hare Island, on the Neva River, where his cannon could block the passage of enemy ships. On May 16, his closest lieutenant, "Aleksasha" Menshikov, laid the first stone of the fortifications that would become the famous Fortress of Saints Peter and Paul.

To finish the fortress quickly, Peter assigned more than twenty thousand men to the backbreaking job of raising its dirt and wood walls. A difficult task under ideal conditions, the work at the Peter-Paul Fortress was made more grueling by shortages of everything except manpower. As the German diplomat Friedrich Weber described it, "There were neither sufficient provisions for subsisting such a number of men, nor care taken to furnish them with the necessary tools as pickaxes, spades, shovels, wheel-barrows, plants, and the like. They even had not so much as houses or huts. . . . The earth [for fortifications], which is very scarce thereabouts, was for the greater part carried by the laborers in the skirts of their clothes, and in bags made of rags and old mats, the use of wheel-barrows being then unknown to them."[2] By fall, the fortress was completed, although its earthen and wood walls later would be replaced by ones of brick and stone faced with granite.[3]

Erecting a fortress, however, is not the same thing as building a city, and it would be a number of years before the city of Peter's dreams began to emerge. When he began in 1703, there were no per-

manent buildings. The climate was wretched, even hostile—hot and
steamy in the summer, because of the surrounding marshes, but bitter
cold, with bone-chilling winds in the winter. Diseases of all sorts thrived
in the delta's many swamps, and the city always would be plagued by a
shortage of drinking water. Even at the beginning of the twentieth century, Karl Baedeker's famous guidebook on Russia warned travelers
that, in St. Petersburg, *"unboiled water should on no account be drunk."*[4]
Perhaps most disquieting of all, the area on which Peter planned to
build his city was only four to six feet above sea level. Even strong west-
erly winds could raise tides over the river's banks to flood the entire
region. As early as August 1703, General Prince Nikita Repnin complained of the flooding at the fortress he and his men were building.
"Your Majesty, we have terrible weather coming in from the sea and it
floods into the bivouacs of my troops." Repnin added an ominous
warning: "The natives around here say that at this time of year this
place is always flooded."[5] His information was all too accurate. St. Petersburg would be plagued by periodic inundations until well into the
second quarter of the nineteenth century, when Nicholas I ordered
locks built to control the spring flood waters that flowed down from the
melting ice in Lake Ladoga.

Peter never explained why he chose such an inhospitable location
for his city. It may well be that he already had conceived a dream of
reproducing Amsterdam, the city he had so loved when he had visited
the West a half-decade earlier, and the many streams in the Neva delta
seemed suited to that purpose. By 1704 he had begun to call it his capital,[6] and to the men in whose hands he left the arduous task of overseeing its construction he sent a steady stream of instructions,
comments, and orders. Wherever he was in Russia, and whatever crises
faced him, he always found time to attend to St. Petersburg's beginnings. Before his impatient eyes, it soon began to rise on the Neva's
marshy delta despite floods, disease, and the harsh climate. At first, the
buildings were mere log huts, and Peter himself lived in a small cottage, which had wood and clay walls painted to resemble masonry,
whenever it was possible for him to spend time in what he called his
"paradise."[7] But larger and more permanent buildings also began to be
built beginning with the Admiralty, whose site was chosen by Peter for

further protection against enemy ships. St. Petersburg still stood upon occupied Swedish territory, and there was the very real danger that Charles XII might turn away from his campaigns in Eastern Europe to wrest it from Peter's hands. As Sweden's young King had remarked when he learned that St. Petersburg was being founded, "Let the Tsar tire himself with founding new towns; we will keep for ourselves the honour of taking them later."[8] Thus it was not until his great victory over the Swedes at Poltava that Peter began to feel secure about the strength of Russia's claim to the land upon which the city stood. As he wrote to General-Admiral Feodor Apraksin, his triumph over the Swedes had "laid the final stone in the foundation of St. Petersburg."[9] Only after 1709, therefore, did the building of St. Petersburg as a capital city begin in earnest. When Russia's armies captured Vyborg, the last Swedish fortress in the eastern Baltic, in 1710, the security of St. Petersburg was assured.[10]

How much the victory at Poltava increased Peter's sense of security about his hold on the Neva delta can be judged by the speed with which St. Petersburg began to rise after 1709. Not only did the number of buildings increase but the character of the city began to emerge along the lines he had envisioned. Originally, Peter proposed to develop Vasilevskii Island as the center of his new city and planned to locate government buildings there, while the palaces of his nobles were to be arrayed alongside the Admiralty on the Neva's south bank. Thus, he had the Summer Palace, his first real residence, built on the south bank in 1710; under his continued prodding, large stone houses began to rise along the embankment between the Summer Palace and the Admiralty. The following year, he ordered work to begin on the Winter Palace and in 1712 commanded that a large stone cathedral be built in the center of the Peter-Paul Fortress. To compel stonemasons to move to St. Petersburg, he decreed in 1714 that no stone buildings could be built anywhere in Russia except in his new capital. To stimulate trade, he offered large cash bounties and exemption from customs duties to the first ships to arrive in St. Petersburg from the West; and to populate his city and make it into a functioning capital, he moved Russia's government offices from Moscow in the years between 1709 and 1712.[11]

The half-decade after Peter's victory at Poltava thus saw a number of impressive stone structures appear along the banks of the Neva. But the overall impression still was one of chaos and impermanence. "I was surprised to find instead of a regular city, as I expected, a heap of villages linked together like some plantation in the West Indies," was Friedrich Weber's first impression when he arrived in 1714. He described many of Petersburg's buildings as being "all of wood, beam upon beam, rough without, and smoothed within by the help of a hatchet," and remarked that "many poor and small ones [were so flimsy that], in two hours time, [they] may be taken to pieces and put up again in another place."[12] Peter had been so impatient to see his city grow that he had uprooted his nobles and many others and brought them to his capital long before there was sufficient housing for them. Buildings thus had been thrown up in immense haste, and the result had been rough and unattractive. St. Petersburg in 1714 resembled a boom town, with a few large and impressive stone structures scattered among its many shoddy buildings. Still, it was not an unusual situation for a new city, especially one that was to be a national capital, and not so very different from Washington, D. C., during its early days. What was different was that wolves still were to be found in St. Petersburg's unlit streets, and robberies and murders were nightly occurrences.

Yet, even as Weber and others like him were noting Petersburg's disordered appearance, Peter was taking steps to give his capital an air of permanence and majesty. By that time, he had thoroughly assimilated the many impressions of Western architecture that had flooded upon him during his visits to Prussia, Holland, England, Austria, and Poland more than a decade earlier. Most of all, the appearance of Amsterdam, with its rows of elegant buildings fronting on its three major canals—the Prinzengracht, the Heerengracht, and the Kiesergracht—had captured his fancy, and he proceeded to impose his now definite ideas upon the architects he brought to his new capital.

The architect who played the greatest role in translating Peter's dream into substance was Domenico Tressini. Tressini was an Italian, born in Lugano in 1670, in a climate very different from St. Petersburg's, and among architectural styles that diverged widely from those Peter favored. Before he had come to Russia in 1705, however, Tres-

sini had worked in Copenhagen and thus had experience in constructing stone buildings upon marshy subsoil. Regarded in the West as a
mediocre architect, Tressini was more diligent than creative. He did
not seek to impose his architectural preferences upon his master. Instead, he was more than willing to accept Peter's tastes and translate
them into concrete designs. Perhaps most important, Tressini incorporated Peter's infatuation with Amsterdam's buildings into a series of
model designs according to which housing for the nobility, "prosperous
citizens," and the lower classes was to be built. Each of the three models
differed in terms of size, height, and ornamentation, but they all
blended into a preconceived and harmonious whole that conformed to
the Dutch Baroque style Peter favored. By using such model designs,
Peter sought to avoid the architectural hodgepodge, so common to
most cities, when Petersburg's wooden buildings were replaced by stone
structures and to instill a sense of order and uniformity as the city
began to develop.[13]

In the years immediately after 1714, Tressini's models had a particularly great influence upon the development of Vasilevskii Island,
and it was Tressini who designed the Summer Palace, the Cathedral
and the Petrine Gates at the Peter-Paul Fortress, and the vast structure
that housed Peter's administrative colleges under a single roof, but
gave the impression of being twelve identical, terraced, three-story
Dutch houses. As would frequently happen in the eighteenth and nineteenth centuries, Russia provided an environment in which men who
had not been able to flourish in the West could develop their limited
talents to the fullest, often with impressive results.[14]

What St. Petersburg needed most of all was an overall plan to integrate those separate parts of the city that Weber had characterized as
"a heap of villages." It was in this realm that Peter's own ideas were the
least developed. He wanted the view from the eastern tip of Vasilevskii
Island to become the focal point for visitors arriving by sea. At the
same time, he desired the city's center to be located in the middle of
that island, which was the lowest area in the city and the one most subject to floods. Finally, to increase the grandeur of the panorama from
the island's eastern tip, Peter insisted that most of the city's major resi-
dential palaces be built upon the Neva's south bank, thus separating

them by water from St. Petersburg's administrative and commercial center.

To integrate these diverse requirements was virtually an impossible task. Tressini attempted to do so and failed, and so did the German architect Georg Mattarnovi. When he visited Paris and Versailles in 1716, Peter engaged the French architect Jean Baptiste Leblond, a pupil of Louis XIV's famed architect LeNôtre, appointed him to be St. Petersburg's first chief architect, and assigned him to draft a city plan. Heavily influenced by the fortifications of seventeenth-century French castles and the plan of Versailles itself, Leblond proposed to surround St. Petersburg by a ring of monumental fortifications, which left no room for the city to expand and grow into the commercial center Peter envisioned. Perhaps most critical of all, his fortifications would have cut all of the mainland off from the rest of the city, except for the narrow littoral on which the Admiralty and the Summer and Winter palaces stood.[15] Although he had little training in architecture and city planning, Peter readily perceived the flaws in Leblond's plan and simply allowed it to fall into abeyance while he used the Frenchman's architectural talents elsewhere.

During the last decade of Peter's life, St. Petersburg's development followed lines that seemed predestined by nature and grew away from those low-lying areas on Vasilevskii Island to the more elevated lands behind the Admiralty. The mainland area behind the Admiralty, centering especially on the famous Nevskii Prospekt, became St. Petersburg's center. Indeed, so much more convenient was the mainland than Vasilevskii Island that Mrs. Rondeau, wife of England's Ambassador to St. Petersburg, wrote in 1730: "Here [on the island] the merchants were designed to live; but though the houses and streets are very handsome, they are mostly uninhabited, for the Admiralty [Quarter] is by much the most populous."[16] Yet, the Admiralty Quarter lacked that order and symmetry Tressini's model designs had given to the island. Much of the new area behind the Admiralty continued to be dotted with those flimsy wooden structures that had so offended Weber's eye in 1714.

Shoddy impermanent buildings reflected the immense dislike many of St. Petersburg's residents had for their city. Of course, some of

Peter's favorites shared his enthusiasm, or at least pretended to. Menshikov built St. Petersburg's largest palace, a vast structure constructed of red brick according to the designs of the German architect Gottfried Schädel.[17] A few others followed his example, but the majority of St. Petersburg's inhabitants viewed life in the city as a monstrous inconvenience and a heavy financial burden. Friedrich Weber estimated in 1716 that "a man may live at Moscow for one-third of what it will cost him at Petersburg, where everything is excessive dear"; Weber reported that the nobles, whom Peter ordered to move to his new capital, "complained that, by this change, they lost about two-thirds of their estates, considering they were obliged to build houses at Petersbourg, and pay ready money for what they wanted; whereas in Russia they could live cheaper and subsist on the produce of their land."[18]

The personal discomfort and financial burdens of his subjects posed no deterrent to Peter's insistence that Russians move to his new city, and he uprooted them from all parts of his Empire. First, he conscripted tens of thousands of Russian peasants to work on construction, beginning with a levy of forty thousand men in 1704.[19] But he also insisted that nobles, merchants, artisans, and officials settle there. In August 1710 alone, Peter compelled four thousand seven hundred twenty master artisans to move to St. Petersburg "for permanent residence" with their wives and children and, four years later, decreed that three hundred fifty nobles, three hundred merchants, and another three hundred master artisans must become Petersburgers.[20] By the time of his death, there were between twenty-five and thirty thousand permanent residents plus many more thousands of transient laborers.[21] Most were responsible for building their own dwellings at great expense. They resented being forced to tear up their ancestral roots and, at first, made little effort to meet any but the most punitive of their Emperor's demands in regard to construction and landscaping.[22] For these Russians, St. Petersburg was a curse, a disease-infested swamp, from which they hoped to be freed by Peter's death.

When Peter II ascended the throne in 1727, it seemed that their wish was about to be realized. In 1728 Russia's child-Emperor moved his capital back to Moscow, and St. Petersburg remained little more than a port city. But the accession of the Empress Anna, and the disgrace of those Dolgorukiis and Golitsyns who represented the old Muscovite aristocracy, meant that St. Petersburg's moment had come. Anna made St. Petersburg her capital at the beginning of 1732, and there it remained until 1918. Under Anna, and those Romanov Empresses and Emperors who followed, St. Petersburg more than realized Peter's dream of an Imperial city on the Neva's delta. By 1750 it had almost seventy-five thousand residents.[23] During the next half-century, its population increased threefold to 220,208, and by the mid-nineteenth century it reached a half-million.[24] During the last seven decades of the eighteenth century, St. Petersburg also lost its shabby and disordered appearance, as its wooden structures gave way to stately stone buildings. By the end of the century, the Count de Ségur could describe it as "an astonishing monument of the triumph obtained by a man of genius over nature."[25]

Beginning with the Empress Anna, all the Romanov sovereigns endeavored to place an imprint upon the capital, to leave it more beautiful than they had found it. In her first efforts, Anna spared no expense. As her Court architect, she appointed a young Italian named Bartolomeo Francesco Rastrelli. The son of a well-known sculptor, Rastrelli was born and educated in Paris. In 1716 Peter the Great invited his father to Russia, and Rastrelli, aged sixteen, accompanied him. In St. Petersburg, the young man developed a passion for building. He had no formal training in architecture but plunged boldly ahead at the age of twenty-one to design a palace for Prince Kantemir. His first creation could have been found acceptable only in a country where tastes for Western architectural styles had not yet been formed, and it bore almost none of the marks that distinguished Rastrelli's mature work. It was obvious that he had talent, but he desperately needed formal training. Therefore, a few months after Peter the Great's death in 1725, Rastrelli's father sent him to northern Italy to study under first-rate masters.

Although scholars have never been able to discover with whom he studied, or even how long Rastrelli stayed in the West, the best estimates are that he was away from St. Petersburg for not much more than a year. During that time, he must have put his time to extremely good use for, when he returned to Russia, his work took on a more mature, much more integrated, character. When the Empress Anna announced in 1730 that she planned to move the capital back to St. Petersburg, Rastrelli was commissioned to build for her a wooden Summer Palace in Peter's Summer Gardens. He completed the task in time for her return at the beginning of 1732. Anna and her lover Count Biron were so pleased with the result that they flooded Rastrelli with commissions. During the 1730s, he built in two months a three-tiered opera house, in which Italian opera was first performed in Russia in 1736;[26] a riding school large enough for seventy-five horsemen at one time; two large palaces in Courland for Count Biron, and a number of lesser buildings in St. Petersburg. His major task, however, was the Winter Palace, which he enlarged during the early 1730s. In architectural terms, his creation was less than satisfying, largely because he was obliged to incorporate smaller adjoining palaces into his structure. Thus, it was in the interior of the Palace that Rastrelli did his best work. The Great Hall was particularly magnificent. Completed in time for Anna's birthday celebration in January 1734, it was one hundred eighty feet long, its walls entirely gilded and set off by rows of colonnades.[27] Although she had been critical of the old Winter Palace, the wife of England's ambassador described Rastrelli's creation in glowing terms in a letter to a friend soon after she had attended the Empress's birthday celebrations:

> It was decorated with orange-trees and myrtles, in full bloom: these were ranged in rows that formed a walk on each side of the hall, and only left room for the dancers in the middle. . . . The beauty, fragrance, and warmth of this new-formed grove, when you saw nothing but ice and snow through the windows, looked like enchantment. . . . The walks and trees filled with beaux and belles, in all their birthday finery, instead of the shepherds and nymphs of Arcadia, made me fancy myself in a Fairy-land, and Shakespeare's *Midsummer Night's Dream* was in my head all the evening.[28]

In contrast to the far more moderate tastes of Peter the Great, Anna clearly intended that the palace of the Autocrat of all the Russias would surpass all others in grandeur.

Yet Anna did more than break with Peter's modest style of living in St. Petersburg. She decided to abandon his plan to locate the city's center in the midst of Vasilevskii Island and chose instead to accept its tendency to develop in the Admiralty Quarter and along the Nevskii Prospekt. But the many small and unattractive wooden homes and shops of humble tradesfolk that crowded into that area hardly lent to St. Petersburg that majestic image she thought proper for Russia's capital city. The best solution would have been to raze much of the entire area, but that obviously could not be done. St. Petersburg was still filled with reluctant residents, those thousands of master artisans and nobles whom Peter had transported from all over Russia, and Anna knew that if her government announced any intention to destroy their poorly built homes, discontent would rise to a dangerous, perhaps explosive, level. Uncertain about how to proceed, she let the problem remain for the first half of her reign. It suddenly was resolved in 1736 and 1737, when St. Petersburg suffered two of the greatest fires in its history. To this day, no one is certain how the fires started, although the authorities officially blamed them upon arsonists. What is certain, however, is that nearly all of the one- and two-storied wooden buildings in the Admiralty Quarter were destroyed in a remarkably precise and methodical manner. The way now was clear to build along new and more majestic lines.[29]

Once fire had cleared the Admiralty Quarter of its wooden buildings, Anna issued a series of decrees that excluded tradesmen and artisans from that part of the capital and prohibited any but stone buildings from being constructed to replace those that had burned. At the same time, she decreed that her courtiers could no longer live in the Winter Palace, thus forcing them to build new residences in the Admiralty Quarter. Finally, in June 1737, she established the St. Petersburg Construction Commission to plan the development of her capital. No longer would Petersburg's new center grow in a hit-or-miss fashion, but according to a carefully designed plan.

Although Anna's reign is often regarded as the high point of foreign influence in Russian state affairs, it marked a brief triumph for Russians in architecture. Although she gave major commissions to Rastrelli, Anna appointed only Russians to the St. Petersburg Construction Commission. Chief among them were Mikhail Zemtsov, St. Petersburg's city architect; Ivan Korobov, who had designed the new

Admiralty buildings; and Petr Eropkin, who had some experience in city planning. When they began work after the fire of 1737, the shape of St. Petersburg still was unclear, and they enjoyed remarkable freedom in arranging the city to suit their tastes and plans for the future.[30]

Central to the plan they drew up for St. Petersburg's development were three great avenues radiating outward from the Admiralty. The first of these, and the one that became the most famous, was the Nevskii Prospekt, which stretched for some three miles from the Admiralty to the Aleksandr Nevskii Monastery, which Peter had founded in memory of one of Russia's greatest and most heroic saintly princes. The other two were Gorokhovaia Street and Voznesenskii Prospekt, which stretched outward from the Admiralty to the barracks of the Semenovskii and Izmailovskii Guards. To integrate these broad avenues more fully into the structure of the city, Anna's architects planned a network of semicircular streets and canals.[31] The result was both pleasing and impressive, and, even today, as one walks along the streets and avenues of Leningrad, the effect still is strikingly evident, focusing the visitor's attention upon the Admiralty and the area along the Neva that once was the seat of Russia's Imperial power.

The St. Petersburg Construction Commission did much more than draft a plan for the capital's development and oversee the construction of brick and stone palaces. Petr Eropkin, perhaps its most talented member, sought to use it as a means for establishing serious architectural training within Russia itself. Eropkin translated Palladio's four books on architecture and drafted a lengthy and farseeing essay on "The Responsibilities of the Architectural Department," in which he attempted to define the role of architects in Russian society and advocated centralizing their work in order to achieve uniformity in design. Such a program took far too little account of individual initiative and the need to foster artists' creative spirit. But, as a city planner, Eropkin was most concerned with integrating St. Petersburg's architecture into a broader framework and avoiding the construction of buildings that fit in poorly with their surroundings. He saw architects more as technicians than as artists.[32] Political difficulties made it impossible for Eropkin to realize his plans, however. He became involved with the political circle of Artemii Volynskii, a cabinet minister who was found guilty of high treason in 1740. Along with Volynskii, Eropkin was executed on June 27, the thirty-first anniversary of the Poltava victory that had made it possible for St. Petersburg to become Russia's new capital city. His manuscripts and translations remained unpublished until the twentieth century because he had been branded a traitor.

At a time when Germans reigned supreme at Court, men such as Eropkin, Korobov, and Zemtsov laid the foundations for what the Soviet art historian S. S. Bronshtein has called "an independent national school, and paved the way for the flowering of Russian architecture in the middle of the eighteenth century."[33] Without the work these men accomplished under Anna's patronage, those masters who beautified St. Petersburg during the reigns of the Empresses Elizabeth and Catherine the Great would have found their task far more difficult.

Despite the Empress Anna's architectural achievements, her gauche tastes did not set a very high cultural standard for Russia's Court nobility. During her reign, St. Petersburg was a strange mixture of elegance and barbarity, a city of impressive palaces in which lords and ladies were just learning to behave decently. Court life was at best a parody of European culture rather than a sincere imitation of it. A foreign visitor to the city in the 1730s captured this phenomenon quite accurately in his description of the young Princess Kurakina:

> She rides in a coach and six, with two postilions and four footmen, keeps two dozen maidservants and as many lackeys, dines sumptuously and at odd hours, sleeps until noon, dresses like a singer at the Petersburg opera, speaks only Russian, but mixes in so many French and Italian words with Russian endings that Russians have a more difficult time understanding her than they do a foreigner. In her conversation, she mostly praises French fashions and free living. She laughs at God-fearing women who pine for worldly vanity, because they cannot find suitors and get married. . . . Her sexual escapades show that one may play amorous dramas just as well in Moscow [and St. Petersburg] as one can in Paris and London.[34]

Judging by a book of manners and rules of behavior first published in 1718, and republished in 1740 at Anna's express order, even Princess Kurakina was ahead of many of her peers. Entitled *The Honest Mirror of Youth* this little volume instructed Russia's aspiring courtiers and their ladies in how to sit at table, the proper way to use a knife and fork, how to use a handkerchief, and how to converse in polite society. They were admonished not to spit on the floor, not to blow their noses with their fingers, and not to jab others with their elbows at formal dinners. The author of the volume even found it necessary to instruct his readers that "when speaking about sad things, it is necessary to look sorrowful and to use a sad tone, while, on joyful occasions, it is necessary to appear pleased and to speak with a happy lilt."[35]

It is probably safe to say that many of the nobles who populated Anna's Court still followed the Muscovite traditions Peter the Great had sought to destroy during his reign. Certainly, they still preferred life in Moscow, and it would be at least another decade before that attitude changed. As Edward Finch, Britain's Ambassador to St. Petersburg, reported to his superiors in London in June 1741, "there is not one of them who would not wish St. Petersburg at the bottom of the sea, and all the conquered provinces at the devil, so they could but remove to Moscow, where, by being in the neighborhood of their estates, they could all live in greater splendour and with less expense."[36]

Empress Elizabeth I, daughter of Peter the Great and Catherine I, was a woman of Westernized, elegant tastes, who represented everything that Peter had dreamed Russia would become. Like all the Romanovs, she was crowned in Moscow, but St. Petersburg was her capital and the city upon which she lavished love and attention. Throughout her reign, she would build, rebuild, and elaborate upon the foundations her father and the Empress Anna had laid. When she died two decades later, St. Petersburg would have become a city that much better represented Russia's newfound power and glory. No longer would it appear rough, architecturally undefined, and uncertain of its future development. In the center of the city, swamps had begun to give way to parks, gardens, impressive squares, and wide streets, their waters drained into elegant canals that served to set off the overall plan that Korobov, Eropkin, and Zemtsov had designed. The cost of living continued to be high, since all foodstuffs had to be shipped to St. Petersburg from the interior of Russia or from abroad. But, by 1761, it was a price that many Russian courtiers were more willing to pay in order to enjoy the advantages they perceived in life in the capital.

By the end of Elizabeth's reign, Western cuisine and entertainment had become an integral part of nobles' daily lives, and they had begun to compete with each other in beautifying the interiors of their palaces. Western fashions became critically important in determining a courtier's social success. Women changed their gowns three or four times each day, and it was considered poor taste to appear in the same gown too frequently. Dinners became lengthy and elegant affairs, and culinary innovations became a subject of competition among Petersburg's aristocrats. Count Petr Shuvalov became the talk and envy of St. Petersburg society when he introduced his guests to bananas and pineapples at one of his dinners in the 1750s. Although foreign wines had been popular since the time of Peter the Great, it became a matter of social necessity for a nobleman to offer his guests a long list of them so that each could choose the one most to his taste. So intense did the quest for elegance become that first-rate chefs commanded the astronomical annual wage of five hundred rubles, more than fifty times the income of an average serf family.[37] By 1761 Elizabethan society had come a vast distance from Anna's courtiers, who a scant quarter of a century earlier had required instruction in the proper use of knives and forks.

The architect who provided the physical setting for the Elizabethan transformation in manners and culture was the same Bartolomeo Rastrelli who had served the Empress Anna in the 1730s. At the time of Elizabeth's accession, Rastrelli was just entering into the most creative and productive period of his career, and Elizabeth's own tastes, ill-defined though they were, provided just the proper stimulation for his work. Under her patronage, Rastrelli developed a distinctive style that combined elements of Muscovite church architecture with Baroque lightness and symmetry. The result, in the words of the art historian Tamara Rice, was "a style which, while superficially flamboyant and ornate, was fundamentally so classical and severe that it had the purity and unity essential to all truly great architecture."[38] For Elizabeth, Rastrelli would build churches and great palaces. He would also design breathtaking interiors and plan some of the elaborate and opulent celebrations for which Elizabeth's reign became justly famous. It was Rastrelli who paneled an entire room in Elizabeth's Summer Palace at Tsarskoe Selo with those carved amber panels Peter the Great had received from the King of Prussia in exchange for fifty of his tallest Preobrazhenskii grenadiers.[39]

Rastrelli produced five great architectural monuments that together expressed the spirit and grandeur of Russia's Elizabethan Age. His first creation was a summer palace in St. Petersburg, built on the banks of the Fontanka River between 1741 and 1744. We have only drawings and engravings to tell us how it looked, because it was later torn down to make room for the Mikhailovskii Castle, which Paul I built at the end of the century and which later became the famous Engineer's School where the writer Dostoevskii studied in the 1840s. Nevertheless, we know that it was built on a monumental scale and its design was far more sophisticated than anything Rastrelli had produced during the reign of the Empress Anna; set in the midst of extensive parks and gardens, it far more resembled those summer palaces he would build in the 1740s and early 1750s. Its ballroom was narrower than the one at Versailles, but it was longer and could hold more people, and its parks and gardens were magnificent by any standard. Indeed, Rastrelli's creation would provide dramatic testimony that Russia, which Europeans had only just begun to cease regarding as Oriental and barbaric, was more than capable of equalling those architectural achievements with which Louis XIV had captured the imagination and admiration of eighteenth-century Europeans.[40]

Rastrelli devoted much of his effort during the 1740s and 1750s to the design and construction of suburban palaces. The second monument he produced for Elizabeth was the summer palace at Peterhof, situated on the Gulf of Finland some twenty-eight *versty* from St. Petersburg. Beginning work in 1747, Rastrelli sought to elaborate upon the architectural themes Peter the Great had established more than a quarter of a century earlier, for Peter himself had chosen the palace's location and had lavished considerable care upon its design. Built in 1722 by the French architect Leblond, the first Peterhof Palace was a small two-storied structure in which Peter had established Russia's first major art gallery. The palace itself stood on a small rise overlooking the Finnish gulf, and, beneath it, a large formal park stretched out to the water's edge. In front of the palace Peter had built a grotto of fountains from which jets rose to a height of some fifty feet and, in the lower portions of the park, had erected a small villa in his beloved Dutch style to which he had given the name Monplaisir. In all, Peterhof commanded a beautiful location, and its buildings were well designed and carefully integrated into their natural setting. Rastrelli sought to develop the site's full potential by constructing a dramatic architectural ensemble.

As would often be the case in the work he did for the Empress Elizabeth, Rastrelli preferred to preserve the work of his predecessors and incorporate it into a larger structure. Therefore, he made Leblond's palace the center of a much larger one that extended outward in the form of two low-lying wings, each about two hundred fifty feet in length. For the interior of his new palace, Rastrelli made extensive use of intricate parquet floors set off by vast amounts of gilt and mirrors. His Hall of Mirrors, in which he consciously set out to surpass Versailles, was indeed a masterpiece, and it was one of the few interiors that Catherine the Great, whose tastes were markedly different from Elizabeth's, left intact. When it was completed in 1752, Peterhof was far more than the informal Summer Palace Elizabeth had envisoned when Rastrelli had begun work a half-decade earlier. But it satisfied her love for vast interior space and reflected her taste as much as Rastrelli's. It was a monument of which the daughter of Peter the Great could be justly proud, and, even today, its restored form, rising above the shores of the Finnish Gulf, is a breathtaking sight.[41]

During the late 1740s and early 1750s, Peterhof consumed only part of Rastrelli's energies and talents because he was commissioned by Elizabeth to enlarge another suburban palace. Tsarskoe Selo, meaning the Tsar's Village, was an enchanting spot, situated some twenty-five *versty* from St. Petersburg in the opposite direction from Peterhof. Catherine I had originally acquired it as a gift for Peter the Great, and in 1718 Peter had commissioned the architect Johann Braunstein to build a small country palace there as a private retreat. Peter and Catherine spent some of their happiest moments there during the last years of their lives, and they both were deeply attached to it. When Catherine bequeathed it to Elizabeth, the young Grand Duchess quickly came to share the feelings of her parents. When she became Empress, Elizabeth commissioned Mikhail Zemtsov to enlarge it. After his death in 1743, two other famous Russian architects, Kvasov and Chevakinskii, took on the project. They already had begun building when Rastrelli took over the task in 1748. He worked on the enlargement for the next four years from the plans Kvasov and Chevakinskii had developed, but neither he nor his Imperial mistress was satisfied with the result. In 1752 Elizabeth ordered him to begin again and to rebuild according to his own new designs. By 1756 he had completed what the Russian scholar and scientist Mikhail Lomonosov called "the Russian Versailles."[42]

In his final plans for the Summer Palace at Tsarskoe Selo, Rastrelli chose to preserve only the original palace Braunstein had built as the center of the new structure Elizabeth would name the Catherine Palace, in memory of her mother. Rastrelli gave Braunstein's building an entirely new facade and extended the palace on a straight line so that its total length was 326 meters. It was immense, but well proportioned, with portions of the facade set slightly back from the rest, its monotony broken by columns. From the palace's two extremities, Rastrelli designed wings that curved inward to culminate in superbly fashioned wrought iron gates, thus creating a vast, but magnificent, courtyard. Painted a light turquoise blue, with white columns and gilded sculptures, the Catherine Palace was easily one of the most beautiful in Europe, and its interior even surpassed its external magnificence. As at Peterhof, a Hall of Mirrors was one of its main features, and, at night, when lighted with 695 candles, it was truly splendid.[43] In all, Rastrelli's creation at Tsarskoe Selo bubbled with that gay, lively atmosphere Elizabeth so adored. She had taken a passionate interest in the project, and it fully reflected her tastes and whims. Perhaps at no other palace did she feel so much in her element.

Yet Elizabeth and Rastrelli were not content to build a superb palace with magnificent interiors; they also devoted great care to its setting. Thus, the grounds around the Catherine Palace were expertly landscaped, filled with marble statues done by some of Venice's greatest seventeenth- and eighteenth-century masters, and designed to include grottoes, carefully constructed ruins, and various follies so popular at the time.[44] At the far end of the park's central *allée* stood one of Rastrelli's miniature masterpieces, a small Hermitage, nestled in a natural hollow. Designed for intimate gatherings, although large enough to accommodate a small orchestra, it included every conceivable device to add to its atmosphere of quiet elegance and luxury. Its dining room was especially unique. The table was fixed to the floor, and each of its twelve plate rests, as well as its central section, were designed to function as lifts so that, when Elizabeth rang a bell at the end of a course, all of the plates and serving dishes would disappear from the table, and new ones, holding the next course, would rise to take their place.[45] Beyond the Hermitage, Rastrelli constructed a number of pavilions where Elizabeth's lords and ladies could rest during promenades or hunts and where intimate suppers could be served in the open air. There was also a Toboggan Hill built of wood for winter sledding, which became an eighteenth-century version of a roller coaster in the summer.

So much of Rastrelli's work during the first half of Elizabeth's reign was devoted to gay and lively summer palaces designed more for informal amusement than for formal gatherings that it would be relatively easy to characterize him by those achievements were it not for the last two monuments he built to his mistress during the 1750s. The first of these was the Smolnyi Convent in which he combined elements of Moscow's religious architecture with his own characteristically showy Baroque style, a marriage of genres he had already tested in Kiev's Cathedral of St. Andrew and in the chapels at Tsarskoe Selo and Peterhof. Ornate in the extreme, and decorated by flamboyant high-relief sculptures, Smolnyi Convent still preserved a dignity and purity in design. Originally planned to include a number of buildings, its focal points were its bell tower and cathedral, the four corner domes of which, arranged in the traditional Muscovite style, were elongated to resemble turrets. Such was the effect of Rastrelli's cathedral at Smolnyi that the Catherinian architect Giacomo Quarenghi, who found Baroque distasteful, reportedly used to remove his hat each time he passed and exclaim, "There is a *real* cathedral!"[46]

Rastrelli's final creation, and the one that represented his greatest monument to the Elizabethan Age, was the "fourth" Winter Palace, which he began in 1754 but did not complete before Elizabeth's death. Elizabeth must have seen in it the culmination of her passion for building, for she allocated vast sums for its construction. During the last six years of her reign, she spent some two and a half million rubles on it, and much more was needed to complete it after her death. The final product was a building that covered 42,118 square feet of ground, had 1,054 rooms and almost 2,000 windows. It surpassed anything Russia had ever seen and had few equals anywhere in the world.[47]

In constructing the fourth Winter Palace, Rastrelli had the rare opportunity to redo his own work. The result of his first effort had been less than satisfying, partly because of his inexperience and partly because he had been obliged to work within the constraints imposed by existing buildings and limited funds. This time, Rastrelli had finally found the style of building that suited him best and had funds to build in the manner he loved most: opulently and extravagantly. The palace he constructed was made up of four great facades, each one somewhat different in design, and richly ornamented with high-relief sculptures, white columns, and gilded statues at the roof. Its interior surpassed that of either Peterhof or the Catherine Palace in richness, with one room paneled entirely in malachite.

With Elizabeth's death in 1761 would come the end of Rastrelli's major work. The accession of Catherine the Great the following year brought new architectural tastes to St. Petersburg; in 1764 Rastrelli moved to Mitau to enter the service of one of his early patrons who had just returned from Siberian exile: Count Ernst Biron. It is the height of irony that Rastrelli lies in an unmarked grave somewhere in the city where his palaces and cathedrals still stand.[48]

There were other architects of great talent during Elizabeth's reign whose work is sometimes lost sight of as a result of Rastrelli's preeminence. That some of their designs reflected principles similar to those used by Rastrelli was, in large measure, due to the influence of the Empress who demanded from St. Petersburg's architects designs that combined native Russian elements with her passion for the Baroque. Thus, she patronized the native Russian architect Savva Chevakinskii, a student of Korobov; Grigorii Dmitriev, a protégé of Zemtsov; and a number of others. From their fertile minds emerged a plethora of new structures including the famous Anichkov Palace, the palace of Count Ivan Shuvalov, that of Count Sheremetiev, and a number of other important state buildings and churches.[49] Elizabeth's predecessor had left a plan for St. Petersburg's future development and the beginnings of the monumental architecture that would characterize Russia's capital in the later eighteenth and nineteenth centuries. Elizabeth built extensively upon those foundations. When she died, she bequeathed to her successors a capital that had indeed begun to resemble an Imperial city.

During the thirty-four years Catherine II reigned as Russia's Empress, she would change the city even more by encouraging among the St. Petersburg nobility that passion for building the Empress Elizabeth had first instilled in them. Under the protective mantle of her patronage, St. Petersburg enjoyed the services of dozens of architects, a number of whom were so talented that no one of them would ever gain the preeminent position Rastrelli had enjoyed earlier. In 1792 the German scholar Heinrich Storch described St. Petersburg as an Imperial capital with which few others in Europe could compete:

> The aspect [of the city] is gay and cheerful. Straight, broad and generally long streets, frequently intersecting each other in abrupt and sharp corners—spacious open squares—variety in the architecture of the houses—in short, the numerous canals and the beautiful river Neva, with their substantial and elegant embankations, render the general view brilliant and enchanting. In regard to regularity and capacity for embellishment but few capital cities in Europe can be compared with St. Petersburg. Paris, notwithstanding the multitude of its palaces and the perpetual attention that is paid to the correction of its defective construction, can never become an elegant city, and London can only apply that Epithet to some of its modern annexations. Berlin may vie with any other capital in regard to its beautiful symmetry, but Petersburg has more grand capabilities.[50]

Fully sharing Storch's enthusiasm, the Count de Ségur wrote in the mid-1780s that Petersburg was a city of "elegant fashions, magnificent dresses, sumptuous repasts, splendid fêtes, [and] theatres equal to those which embellish and animate Paris and London."[51]

During Catherine's reign, Russians for the first time also began to pay serious attention to the furnishings of their new and grand palaces and town houses. Throughout the first half of the eighteenth century, Western furnishings had been in chronically short supply in Russia. Especially during the Elizabethan Age, when the Empress's courtiers began to live in the Western manner at home as well as at Court, the demand far exceeded the supply. Russian artisans began to produce some furniture in Western styles in the 1730s, but their efforts were timid and the scarcity continued. Even Elizabeth found it difficult to purchase sufficient furniture for her needs. When she traveled from one palace to another, she was obliged to carry vast amounts of furniture with her, much as medieval European monarchs used to travel with immense baggage trains when they made progresses through their kingdoms. By the 1750s, the shortage of good furniture was so severe that Rastrelli had to produce in his own workshops the furniture for the palaces he built at Peterhof and Tsarskoe Selo.[52] Many aristocrats simply did without, and used the aged, often crude furniture left over from the Muscovite era. The famous eighteenth-century memoirist Andrei Bolotov described a nobleman's country estate that he visited in the 1750s as lacking any sort of Western furniture such as "sofas, canapés, armchairs, tambours, and commodes." Its owner, Bolotov sadly remarked, was obliged to use old Muscovite furnishings that comprised "smooth and clean benches set along the walls, many . . . ancient wooden chairs [that] had to serve in place of armchairs and canapés, and a long oaken table and a variety of nondescript folding objects [that] had to take the place of all [elegant] small tables."[53]

Under Catherine's prodding, Russia's nobles no longer were willing to accept such primitive furnishings. As a result, a number of skilled craftsmen began to produce furniture on a large scale; artisans from Germany, especially, found a ready market for their work. By the end of Catherine's reign, Western furniture had become common enough in noble palaces that aristocrats, in order to compete with each other in elegance, began to demand unique and cleverly constructed pieces that were more works of art than simply furniture. Catherine herself once paid some twenty-five thousand rubles to the German craftsman Roentgen for an intricately constructed desk that included, among other things, disappearing gilt bas-reliefs and a built-in burglar alarm that played "the most charming strains of soft and plaintive music." Lesser though still unique and elegant pieces by this craftsman commanded several thousand rubles. Indeed, long before he produced his unique desk for the Empress, Roentgen had built a solid reputation as a furniture maker because, in his pieces, "all is fitted so exactly together as though it were molded at one cast."[54]

While Elizabeth had been concerned more with building than with broader planning and design, Catherine pursued both on an immense scale. One of her first and greatest projects involved the Neva waterfront, especially the Palace Embankment and that of the Peter-Paul Fortress that faced it. Beginning in 1764, she commissioned the architect Georg Veldten to face the Neva waterfront and the walls of the fortress with granite, a vast task that demanded great artistry to prevent the granite from becoming simply a cold and dark band rimming the water's edge. Since the embankments of the Neva were the main foundation upon which were erected many of St. Petersburg's most impressive palaces and government buildings—including the Senate, the Admiralty, the Winter Palace, and the new Marble Palace—it was necessary that the quays be designed in such a way as to provide the waterfront with continuity and architectural unity. This was of particular importance because the Neva itself was used extensively as a means of urban transportation in the eighteenth century, since at that time St. Petersburg lacked permanent bridges to connect the islands with the mainland. Thus, elegant barges, yachts, and galleys carrying noble passengers along the Neva's embankments were a common sight, and one of the most frequent views residents had of their city was from the waterways that flowed through it. Veldten's granite embankments became one of St. Petersburg's most brilliant architectural features and gave an unrivaled majesty to its riverfront area, especially when a number of the buildings situated along it were heightened to bring them into proper harmony with Veldten's achievement.[55]

Of the main buildings Catherine commissioned to grace Veldten's new embankment, the Marble Palace was perhaps the most impressive. Its designer, the architect Antonio Rinaldi, was born in Italy in 1709. He was invited to Russia in 1751 by Count Kyril Razumovskii, Hetman of the Ukraine and one of Elizabeth's favorite courtiers, to build a vast complex of buildings at Baturino. Rinaldi completed only one palace for Razumovskii before he came to St. Petersburg in 1754. Two years later, he was named architect to the Grand Ducal Court of Peter and Catherine. The Grand Duke Peter, soon to become Emperor Peter III, opposed his Aunt Elizabeth in all things, and architectural taste was no exception. As a result, Rinaldi was able to work with the classical designs he preferred at a time when Russia's Empress insisted that the architects who served her work only within the framework of her beloved Baroque. Rinaldi built Peter a small palace on the grounds of Oranienbaum, which had been owned originally by Aleksandr Menshikov, but had reverted to the Crown after his disgrace and exile. Peter immediately surrounded Rinaldi's creation with miniature fortifications and called it Peterstadt. It was in Rinaldi's palace that he took refuge during the Revolution of 1762 before he surrendered to his wife Catherine.

Before Peter III was deposed, however, Rinaldi began the Chinese Palace at Oranienbaum for Catherine. It was one of Rinaldi's finest early works, and one of the few eighteenth-century Russian structures to incorporate Chinese elements into its interior design. Small, elegant, with clean and uncluttered lines, it was a dramatic departure from the more monumental works of Rastrelli, Chevakinskii, and Dmitriev, whose designs had been so popular during the Elizabethan Age. As such, it earned Catherine's respect, and when she began to plan a palace in St. Petersburg for her lover, Grigorii Orlov, she turned to Rinaldi for its design.[56]

Catherine's gift to Orlov, the Marble Palace, was Rinaldi's greatest achievement, and he devoted almost two decades (1768–85) to building it. The lower portion of its exterior was of gray granite to tie it more closely with Veldten's embankment, but the resulting severity was relieved by the bluish gray marble of its upper stories, its reddish marble columns, and by rich, though muted, ornamentation. A special expedition was sent to the Ural Mountains to obtain the marble, and master stonemasons from all over the Empire were brought to St. Petersburg to work with it. The roof of the palace was made of sheet copper supported by thick iron bars so that, when the rays of the sun played upon it, it looked like pure gold. More than 164 tons of copper went into the roof alone, and the cast window frames each contained a half-ton more. (Both copper roofing and cast window frames were replaced by the Soviet government in the 1930s, when copper was in desperately short supply.)[57] The palace's main facade faced toward the Summer

Gardens of Peter the Great and boasted marvelous wrought iron gates decorated with gold-plated bronze roseates. Rastrelli and his fellow Elizabethan architects had built palaces of brick covered with heavy stucco, which was then painted in the pale blues, greens, yellows, and pinks for which St. Petersburg became so famous. Only Rinaldi's Marble Palace relied upon natural elements—granite and marble set off by copper and bronze—to produce an effect of grandeur and majesty. In that respect, it was, and still remains, unique among those buildings that line the Palace Embankment.

Although Catherine the Great was a petty German princess by birth and had no legitimate claim to the Russian throne, she was determined to leave an imprint upon St. Petersburg that would surpass that left by any of her predecessors. One of her first efforts in that direction was to recruit architects throughout Russia and Europe on a scale unmatched by any Romanov before her. In November 1763, she announced an international competition in which she encouraged Russian and European architects to submit "such proposals as would bestow upon the city of St. Petersburg a state of dignity and grandeur, commensurate with its position as the capital of a large country."[58] The designs submitted to this competition have not survived, nor do we have a complete list of the entrants. What is certain, however, is that architecture flourished to an incredible degree under Catherine's patronage, with the result that, between 1762 and 1787 (the twenty-fifth anniversary of her accession), the number of brick and stone buildings in St. Petersburg nearly tripled. The German scholar Heinrich Storch has left us a vivid account of the result of Catherine's efforts. Writing in 1792, he remarked:

> The brick houses in St. Petersburg are generally built with great taste and a proper regard to convenience, but not with equal solidity. They are entirely of brick, not of brick and timber together, usually consisting of only two stories, seldom less, and still seldomer more. There are indeed houses of extraordinary height, but, as in regard to habitation luxury here is more studied than in any other place that I know, so the same elevation which at Paris, for example, is sufficient for five stories, is here employed only for two. Most of the houses being built on the Italian plan of architecture, have a basement story, rising but little above the level of the pave-

ment, and is fitted up as apartments for the upper servants, or let out as . . . shops for petty wares. This basement story is now generally built of granite, and produces a very noble and substantial effect. The fronts of the houses are in an excellent style and display uncommon taste, only at times overloaded with ornaments, being no less subject to the dominion of fashion than the forms of dress. The taste at present runs upon columns, and as long as that lasts it will be carried to excess like every other reigning mode. These structures being always of brick, covered with stucco, the outside is washed with some particular colour: formerly the favourite colour was pink or yellow; at present it seems to be green and café au lait. The coverings are sometimes of sheet-iron, sometimes of cast iron, occasionally of sheet copper, which, besides their duration and security, present an agreeable view, when, as is now frequently done, they are painted green or red.[59]

It would be impossible to list all the architects whose designs contributed to the beautification of St. Petersburg during Catherine's reign, and a discussion of even their major works would fill a very large volume. Between 1762 and 1796, Vallin de la Mothe designed St. Petersburg's famous Merchants' Arcade (*Gostinnyi Dvor*), the Catholic Church of St. Catherine, the Little Hermitage, and the Palace of Count I. G. Chernyshev; while Georg Veldten built the Lutheran Church of St. Anna, the Boarding School for Tradesmen's Daughters, and (perhaps with the help of Petr Egorov) the marvelous wrought iron grille along the front of the Summer Gardens. Later in Catherine's reign, Giacomo Quarenghi added to these creations by designing the Concert Hall at Tsarskoe Selo, the Hermitage Theatre, the Academy of Sciences, and, perhaps his greatest achievement, the Alexander Palace at Tsarskoe Selo. At about the same time, the Scot, Charles Cameron, produced his famous Gallery at Tsarskoe Selo, the Palace at Pavlovsk, and created a number of truly breathtaking interiors for his Imperial mistress in Rastrelli's Catherine Palace at Tsarskoe Selo. Nor were native architects far behind their Western European colleagues. Egor Sokolov built the beautiful Public Library during Catherine's reign; Feodor Volkov designed the building that housed the Naval Cadet Corps; and Aleksandr Kokorinov collaborated with de la Mothe to produce the Academy of Fine Arts.

Catherine's reign also saw the emergence of three truly great native Russian architects, all sons of poor men and educated entirely in Russia. Ivan Starov produced most of his major work in the capital city. He built the Trinity Church at the Aleksandr Nevskii Monastery, the Taurida Palace, which Catherine commissioned as a gift for Potemkin, and a number of other buildings. Matvei Kazakov, a student of Dmitrii Ukhtomskii, the founder of Russia's first architectural school, designed the Senate building in Moscow and the main building of Moscow University. Vasilii Bazhenov, also educated in Ukhtomskii's school, designed the great Kremlin Palace in Moscow and the facade of the Semenovskii Regimental Church in St. Petersburg. Russian architecture came of age during the reign of Catherine the Great and Russian architects could hold their own with some of the best in Europe.[60]

St. Petersburg's physical emergence as an Imperial city during the eighteenth century involved more than the design and construction of great palaces and public buildings, although all of Peter the Great's successors, beginning with the Empress Anna, devoted themselves to that task. Almost from the moment he had begun to lay out his new capital, Peter the Great had planned a number of extensive parks and gardens to set off his city and its buildings. The first of these was the Summer Garden, the plans for which were drafted in 1707 by Peter's first Russian architect, Ivan Matveev. When Matveev died that year, Tressini took over the task and built Peter's first Summer Palace in 1710 in one corner of the Summer Garden. Peter loved the Summer Garden and devoted considerable effort to planning its development; he sent agents to the West to purchase dozens of marble statues to ornament its arbors and grottoes. He especially loved the works of seventeenth-century Venetian masters, had them mounted upon elegant pedestals marked with the sculptor's name and the name of the work, and had them taken up and put into storage during the winter. This practice led to considerable confusion during the first half of the eighteenth century because illiterate workmen failed to match the statues with their proper bases. Thus, in 1739, the Italian Francesco Algarotti would make a caustic comment about seeing marble busts of "Ceres bearded and Domitian crowned," and Giacomo Cassanova would relate a quarter-century later that he had seen in the same garden a statue of an aged and bearded man labeled as Sappho.[61] Still, the overall effect was impressive; just a decade after Peter had begun his Summer Garden, Friedrich Weber would remark that "considering its situation and the short time since it was raised [the Summer Garden] is perfectly well-contrived and cannot be found fault with. . . . In this Garden is a plantation or nursery of oaks, which thrive according to wish, a thing so much the more remarkable because not only the neighboring country, but all the Northern Russia does not produce that sort of trees, whence it appears how far things may be carried by industry. There are also in this garden a green-house, water-works, and particularly, a grotto, which when finished, will yield to no other whatsoever."[62]

As was the case with St. Petersburg itself, Peter's successors would add to the Summer Garden and seek to leave their mark upon it. The Empresses Anna, Elizabeth, and Catherine the Great held frequent festive gatherings there, and, by the late eighteenth century, it had become the established place for elegant aristocratic promenades on holidays. Elizabeth and Catherine both remained faithful to Peter's original Dutch design. The result was pleasing and restful, a haven of tree-lined walks and marble statuary nestled in groves, in the midst of the growing bustle of St. Petersburg.

> Notwithstanding the uniformity of the Dutch taste in which it is laid out [wrote Heinrich Storch], it is not deficient in interesting objects. Its neat walks, shaded by lime-trees, venerable for their age, afford an agreeable refuge from the oppressive heats . . . and the charming prospect towards the Neva presents a view that perhaps could be vainly sought for in the most splendid capitals of Europe.[63]

Elsewhere, both Elizabeth and Catherine gave free rein to their own tastes. At Elizabeth's urging, Rastrelli designed elegant French gardens for his palaces at Peterhof and Tsarskoe Selo, and Catherine added a large English Park to the latter, which testified to her admiration for Capability Brown's more informal theories about landscaping Nature.[64] Under the watchful eyes of his successors, Peter's orangeries grew greater, and the culture of exotic tropical trees, flowers, and fruits in St. Petersburg's frigid climate became a passion among some of Russia's greatest nobles as well as her rulers. The Empress Elizabeth had twenty-five thousand lime trees sent to St. Petersburg in 1744 (among them were those Storch later described as "venerable for their age"), and all eighteenth-century Russian monarchs sought to grow bananas and palms in the city.[65] The entire area of Elagin Island came to boast impressive parks in which the summer palaces of the Stroganovs and Bezborodkos nestled, and Storch wrote enthusiastically about the gardens Catherine commissioned at the Taurida Palace. "The charming simplicity of its plan, entirely in the English taste, forms its peculiar excellence." He added that "hills and lakes, shrubberies and water-falls render it extremely romantic."[66]

What St. Petersburg lacked during much of the eighteenth century were great works of sculpture to adorn its vast squares, courtyards, and avenues. Indeed, sculpture developed very slowly in Russia despite the efforts of her rulers to encourage it. At the time Peter the Great ascended the throne, Russians traditionally had shown little interest in objects worked in the round, although wood carving in the production of bas-reliefs was finely developed. Russians at first showed strong prejudices against the marble statues and busts that Peter's agents had purchased in Italy, Holland, and England to ornament his Summer Garden. Even Petr Tolstoi, that widely traveled statesman who reflected Peter's desires in so many things, could see in Greek and Roman statues nothing more than graven images forbidden by the Church.[67]

The first great sculptor to work in Russia was Italian—Carlo Rastrelli, father of Bartolomeo Rastrelli, the architect. Invited to St. Petersburg in 1716 by Peter the Great, Rastrelli the Elder remained there until his death in 1744. Much of his most important work was cast in bronze. His bust of Peter the Great, the face taken from a mask cast during the Emperor's lifetime, has given us one of the best images of Peter, and his full-length statue of the Empress Anna, also in bronze, remains a true masterpiece and the finest likeness of the Empress we have. Rastrelli's equestrian statue of Peter, done in the early 1720s and cast just after the artist's death, became the first of many monumental sculptures that would adorn the squares of St. Petersburg in the late eighteenth and nineteenth centuries.[68]

Rastrelli the Elder, however, produced most of his work to grace the interiors of palaces. It was his son Bartolomeo who popularized the use of exterior sculpture by utilizing large statues to adorn the rooftops of his palaces and by employing high-relief work to break up the facades of his immense architectural creations such as the Catherine and Winter Palaces. Some of Russia's first native sculptors followed the path of the elder Rastrelli, particularly the gifted Fedot Shubin (1740–1805), the son of a White Sea fisherman and largely self-taught, who, in the brief span of about sixteen years, produced a series of dramatic portrait busts that included marble likenesses of the Countess Panina, several Chernyshevs and Golitsyns, Russia's great scientist and scholar Mikhail Lomonosov, Catherine's son Paul and her lover Grigorii Potemkin, a work Shubin completed in the year of Potemkin's death.[69] Those who followed the urgings of Rastrelli the Younger included especially Mikhail Kozlovskii, who produced the dramatic gilded figure of Samson for the main cascade at the Peterhof Fountains and a number of other great bronze and marble works, including the figure of General Aleksandr Suvorov done in the form of Mars.[70]

Perhaps the greatest, and certainly the most famous, piece of monumental sculpture to grace St. Petersburg during the entire eighteenth century was done by a Frenchman, Etienne Falconet, who produced the immortal Bronze Horseman, that great equestrian statue of Peter the Great that still adorns the Senate Square. Falconet was born the son of a poor Parisian joiner in 1716. He began to study sculpture in 1734 and, some twenty years later, became a member of the French Academy. His early work was adequate, but certainly not outstanding. Had he remained in France, he might well be remembered only as one of a host of competent sculptors who lived and worked in Paris during the half-century before the French Revolution. But Falconet was more than an artist. He also aspired to be a philosopher and became very much a part of that circle of *philosophes* that surrounded Diderot. Indeed, it was Diderot who recommended Falconet to Prince Golitsyn, Russia's Ambassador to Paris, as the artist to do the great monument Catherine wanted to dedicate to Peter the Great.[71]

Catherine's plan to commission a statue of Peter the Great was part of a carefully conceived effort to surround herself with an aura of political legitimacy by identifying her regime and person closely with the memory of Russia's first great Emperor. Falconet was fifty years old when he began the task, and he had never worked on such a vast scale as Catherine's plans demanded. "My monument will be simple," he wrote to Diderot. "I shall confine myself only to a statue of this hero [uncluttered by lesser figures], whom I shall interpret not merely as a great captain or a victor, although he, of course, was both of these things. Much more important will be the personality of the founder, the law-giver, the benefactor, of his country. That is what I want people to see in my work."[72]

Falconet himself sculpted the horse and Peter's body, but he called upon Marie Callot, one of his pupils and future wife of his son, to work with him in producing the Emperor's head from Rastrelli the Elder's famous plaster mask. Much of the modeling was done by 1773 when Diderot visited St. Petersburg; he wrote Falconet: "I always knew that you are a very able man; but may I die if I thought that you had anything like this in your head. How could I have guessed that this astounding conception could exist in the same understanding by the side of the dainty image of the statue of Pygmalion?"[73] Falconet's monumental Bronze Horseman required an equally dramatic base upon which to mount it. For that purpose, he chose a rough-hewn boulder of granite, some 275 tons in weight, that had been discovered by a peasant in a distant Finnish bog. In one of the greatest engineering feats of the century, the boulder was brought by water to St. Petersburg and Falconet's statue put into place upon it. It bore only the simple inscription "To Peter the First from Catherine the Second. Summer, 1782." From the moment it was unveiled, it became one of Europe's greatest monuments, and one that won its creator worldwide acclaim. There could have been no more fitting monument to Russia's first and greatest Emperor and to the Imperial city he had founded. There Peter sat, astride his great charger, rearing over the Neva upon whose banks he had built his city. As Aleksandr Pushkin later wrote, Falconet's statue was indeed a personification of

> . . . . him
> Who, moveless and aloft and dim,
> Our city by the sea had founded,
> Whose will was Fate. Appalling there
> He sat, begirt with mist and air.
> What thoughts engrave his brow! What hidden
> Power and authority he claims!

What fire in yonder charger flames!
Proud charger, whither are thou ridden,
Where leapest thou? And where, on whom,
Wilt plant thy hoof?—Ah, lord of doom
And potentate, 'twas thus, appearing
Above the void, and in thy hold
A curb of iron, thou sat'st of old
O'er Russia, on her haunches rearing! [74]

By the end of Catherine the Great's reign, St. Petersburg had become in every sense the Imperial city Pushkin's "Bronze Horseman" had dreamed of during his lifetime. But the achievement was as much Catherine's as it was Peter's. One of Europe's most beautiful cities, St. Petersburg was the fitting capital of a great Empire that spanned one-sixth of the globe's surface. The city would grow yet larger and more elegant during the century to come.

CHAPTER VI

From Debauchery to Philosophy

A vast cultural and intellectual gulf separated Russia and Europe at the time of Peter the Great's Grand Embassy in the late 1690s. By that time, Europeans already were well into the age of exploration and scientific discovery. During the previous two centuries, their ships had discovered the New World and circumvented the globe. The men and women they had carried across the Atlantic had put down firm roots in colonial empires. In technology and science, Europeans had made discoveries that would change forever the nature of men's lives. In philosophy, they had moved resolutely from the medieval world into the Age of Reason and now viewed the world as dynamic rather than static. Men and women had come to accept as inevitable, even desirable, the notion that their children would live in a world different from their own. For the European aristocracy, the late seventeenth century was the Age of Louis XIV, the Sun King, whose world revolved around questions of economic and political power and whose achievement was reflected in the brilliance of Versailles and its Court. Elegant fashions, exquisite manners, and luxurious dwellings had become the marks of distinction that men and women craved, and their leisure hours were devoted not to religious contemplation but to the enjoyment of music, literature, and haute cuisine.

By contrast, for Russians the late seventeenth century was not so very different from the fifteenth. Men and women were still far more preoccupied with the fate of their immortal souls than with the nature of their daily lives. The average Russian nobleman was usually illiterate, his vision limited to the world encompassed by his lands. Indeed, he usually preferred not to live in Moscow, and his life, as the historian Marc Raeff once wrote, was "entirely centered on the satisfaction of the simplest, even the grossest, personal pleasures . . . without meaning, without purposeful activity, or energy-absorbing concerns."[1] European ideas, and abstract thought generally, were alien to him, and he had no notion of service to such impersonal entities as the State or Society. He spent his life either on his estate or in the Tsar's service, and if he served the Tsar he did so in a very direct and personal sense. He had no other options. All the careers and activities open to Europeans— in law, medicine, science, letters, exploration, even the Church —were closed to the Russian nobleman simply because they did not exist. In seventeenth-century Russia, the clergy was a closed caste, law was administered by the Tsar's officials as a direct expression of his personal will, science was frowned upon as godless, and secular literature was virtually nonexistent. Men and society remained introspective. Very many Europeans who encountered this world shared the views of the Venetian diplomat who remarked that "it is impossible to tell whether or not the observations made during the journey of the Tsar [Peter to the West], and the invitation of so many people to Russia for the purpose of training its people and developing its industry, will prove sufficient to transform these barbarians into civilized people."[2]

Into this medieval, rigidly traditionalistic world burst Peter the Great. Dynamic, energetic, and unfettered by tradition, he swept aside prejudice, restraints, and lethargy. Relentlessly, he beat, cajoled, dragged, even terrorized the sleeping Russian giant, forced him to flex his unused and flabby muscles, and dragged him into the modern world. Although he drove them at a merciless pace, Peter did not regard his subjects as inferior to Europeans. Rather, he thought they had as much talent, ingenuity, inventiveness, and capacity for greatness as the peoples of the West. But he understood that Russia and her people must become modern if they were to realize that potential. He saw European states reaching out for empires and new worlds to conquer; he also saw that they had begun to reach into Russia in search of vital foods and raw materials such as grain, pitch, tar, and hemp, which the Russian land possessed in such abundant measure.[3] At an early point in his life, he realized that if Russia did not move quickly to become a part of the modern world, the modern world would devour her.

In spite of the hundreds of books that have been written about Peter and the times in which he lived, it is still difficult to say conclusively why he was so very different from his predecessors and so much ahead of the world into which he was born. Why did Peter find the Muscovite world so unattractive? How did a modern man such as he appear in the midst of a medieval world? And why did he develop such a new, even revolutionary, vision of Russia's future? Peter was not given to articulating his views in writing, for he was a man of deeds. Therefore, we have no such clearly reasoned statements of his principles and aspirations as we have in the case of Catherine the Great. Nevertheless, it is clear that much of Peter's early attack on Russian traditionalism was based upon instinct. Living as he did in two worlds during the 1680s and 1690s, he saw intuitively that the old Muscovite values had to be destroyed before the new vision of life he had glimpsed in the Foreign Quarter could become a part of Russia's experience. And, since Muscovite values were so intimately intertwined with those of the Church, Peter chose to focus his first assaults against the pride and prejudice of the Church. As we have seen, the Church dominated men's lives in Russia, and the rigid precepts of Orthodoxy formed a bulwark against modernization. The Church thus stood for the medieval world Peter wanted to destroy and against the modern one he wanted to create.

The gross parodies and debaucheries of The Vastly Extravagant, Supremely Absurd, Omni-Intoxicated Synod marked Peter's first attacks upon the traditionalism and obscurantism of the established Church and also upon the medieval and Byzantine worlds represented by the titles of Prince-Pope and Prince Caesar, which he bestowed upon Nikita Zotov and Prince Feodor Romodanovskii. These two men presided over the Synod's activities during much of Peter's reign, and both were noted for their capacity to consume spirits and their willingness to commit blasphemy. Yet the elaborate rituals of the Synod were not merely designed for Peter's personal entertainment, and that of his Western and westernized companions, for he insisted that they be performed publicly, in full view of his subjects. The Austrian diplomat

Johann Korb was a witness to one of the Synod's lesser celebrations and his diary entry for February 21, 1699, describes it in some detail:

> A sham Patriarch and a complete set of scenic clergy dedicated to Bacchus, with solemn festivities, the palace which was built at the Czar's expense, and which it has pleased him now to have called Lefort's. . . . He that bore the assumed honours of the Patriarch was conspicuous in the vestments proper to a bishop. Bacchus was decked with a mitre and went stark naked, to betoken lasciviousness to the lookers on. Cupid and Venus were the insignia on his crozier, lest there should be any mistake about what flock he was pastor of. The remaining rout of Bacchanalians came after him, some carrying great bowls full of wine, others mead, others again beer and brandy, that last joy of the heated Bacchus. As the wintry cold hindered their binding their brows with laurel, they carried great dishes of dried tobacco leaves, with which, when ignited, they went to the remotest corners of the palace, exhaling those most delectable odours and most pleasant incense to Bacchus from their smutty jaws. Two of those pipes through which some people are pleased to puff smoke—a most empty fancy—being set crosswise, served the scenic bishop to confirm the rites of consecration. Now, who would believe that the sign of the cross—that most precious pledge of our redemption—was held up to mockery?[4]

Yet Peter was not against religion per se. Although he attacked the established Church, he also sought to use it as an instrument in his cause. Thus, when the Patriarch Adrian died in 1700, Peter did not appoint a successor but left the Church in the hands of two clerics, Feofan Prokopovich and Stefan Iavorskii, who shared his vision of a modern and progressive Russia. Peter's elevation of these unusual men to high office once again indicated his determination to break down those barriers the Church and its tradition had thrown up in the way of change and progress.

Stefan Iavorskii had been educated at the Kievan Academy but had converted to Roman Catholicism and continued his studies at Jesuit schools in Lwów, Lublin, Vilna, and Poznan in the 1680s. When he returned to Russia, he abandoned Catholicism to become an Orthodox monk and taught at the Kievan Academy for some years. Just before the end of 1699, he went to Moscow, where Peter met him quite by chance in February 1700, when Iavorskii preached a moving sermon at the funeral of the great *boiar* Aleksei Shein.[5] Peter was immensely impressed by Iavorskii's oratorical gifts and by his broad Western learning that made him so different from the churchmen the Tsar had met before. Iavorskii believed that "the basis of religion is faith alone." He had a good command of Latin and Western theology and appeared more than willing to place his gifts at Peter's disposal; as a result, his rise was meteoric. In March 1700 Peter named him Metropolitan of Riazan and in October, after the death of the Patriarch Adrian, appointed him "Keeper and Administrator of the Patriarchal See." The result was a flood of pompous sermons glorifying Peter's early work. "Iavorskii can serve as an example of the style of scholasticism carried to its greatest extremes," wrote the Russian literary scholar Aleksandr Pypin. Yet Iavorskii was not willing to remain the Tsar's mere instrument. He nurtured vast ambitions to become the head of the Eastern Church and, after a decade had passed, began to criticize Peter's policies and his unorthodox personal life. In later years, he defended the Tsarevich Aleksei against Peter's wrath. His voluminous treatise, *The Stone of Faith*, was a turgid scholastical argument against many of the things Peter had originally thought he stood for. As a result, Peter turned increasingly to Feofan Prokopovich, whom he made Rector of the Kievan Academy and Bishop of Pskov.[6]

Prokopovich's background was remarkably similar to Iavorskii's. More than twenty years younger, he had been born the son of a petty tradesman in Kiev, orphaned as a child, and, like Iavorskii, first educated at the Kievan Academy. Following in Iavorskii's path, he went to Poland to study, became a Uniate monk, and went to Rome, where he studied for three years at the College of St. Athanasius, which had been founded by Pope Gregory XIII at the end of the sixteenth century to train missionaries for work among Orthodox believers. Prokopovich returned to Russia in 1702, reconverted to Orthodoxy, and became a teacher at the Kievan Academy. He was a brilliant man, probably the best-educated Russian of his day. He amassed a large library, was a publicist, poet, and dramatist, in addition to being a theologian, and wrote voluminously in all those fields. Indeed, the most complete scholarly bibliography of his writings contains almost two hundred items. Prokopovich also was a consummate schemer and political intriguer, and his rise coincided directly with an eloquent panegyric about Peter and the Poltava victory that he unabashedly delivered in Peter's presence in 1709.[7]

Far more than Iavorskii's, Prokopovich's ideas coincided with Peter's and promised to serve his purpose in marshaling opinion behind his efforts to modernize Russia. Prokopovich insisted that the clergy ought not to comprise a state within a state, and that, just as soldiers and civil servants had a duty to perform certain tasks for the state, so were churchmen obliged to subjugate themselves to what he called the "supreme state power." Thus, he argued that the Church could not stand above, or even coequal with, the temporal power, as Muscovite theologians had maintained, but that it must serve as a willing instrument of the Autocrat's policies. Such a view could not have coincided better with Peter's own, and he ultimately called upon Prokopovich to draft the famous Ecclesiastical Statute of 1721. This law made Church administration another branch of Russian civil government under the aegis of the Holy Synod, which, in reality, was merely another of Peter's administrative colleges.[8]

Prokopovich established the first gathering in Russia that resembled a Western European literary salon and dubbed its leading members the "Learned Guard." These men devoted their pens to glorifying Peter's reign and to defending his accomplishments against what Prokopovich called the "big beards" of the established Church hierarchy. In addition to Prokopovich, the two leading members of the Learned Guard were Prince Antioch Kantemir and Vasilii Tatishchev. Although Prokopovich was a churchman, Kantemir a poet, satirist, and diplomat, and Tatishchev a state official and historian, they all played an important role as political theorists during and immediately after Peter's reign. They were among the first ideologists of absolute monarchy in Russia, and Tatishchev probably expressed their credo most concisely when he wrote that he owed "everything I have: rank, honor, estates, and, most of all, reason," to the Russian Autocrat.[9] To aid the Autocrat in the task of modernization, they argued, was the sacred obligation of every Russian, high or low, rich or poor.

In the view of the Learned Guard, Russia prospered only under the hand of a strong Autocrat and, when the ruler was weak, all of Russia suffered accordingly.[10] For these reasons, all three regarded Peter the Great as a heroic figure, the creator of modern Russia. In Prokopovich's ringing funeral oration, Peter was Russia's "Samson [who] found in you a weak strength and made it stone-like and adamantine in accordance with his own name of Peter. He found an army dangerous at home, weak in the field, scorned by its enemies, and brought to his fatherland one that was useful, fearful to the enemy, everywhere terrible and renowned." He was Russia's "first Japheth who . . . [built] a fleet new in the world." He was Moses, Solomon, David, and Constantine all rolled into one. He brought to Russia glory, laws, and "sciences, crafts, and skills hithertofore unheard of among us, and, moreover . . . ranks and degrees, civil orders, exemplary models of social intercourse, and the rules of acceptable customs and manners."[11] "In a word," Kantemir added, "he was everything."[12]

Probably even Feofan Prokopovich did not believe the immoderate praise he rendered to Peter's memory in 1725. Certainly Peter had been more concerned with creating a powerful Empire and a new social order to support it than with establishing new values and a culture to express them. His "exemplary models of social intercourse" were but dim shades in the understanding of many Russians, even those at Court. First and foremost, Peter had approached the West from a utilitarian-technological perspective. He wanted Western technology, and he wanted it for the very utilitarian purpose of making Russia into a great nation in European terms. Thus, he wanted Russians to learn how to make muskets, cast cannon, and produce iron and cloth for his armies. He wanted them to learn how to build and sail ships for his navy. And he wanted Russia to have a state administration that would govern her more efficiently and effectively than had been the case in Muscovite times.

Yet in order to introduce Western technology into Russia, he had been obliged to attack those values that were so intimately connected with Muscovite Church-centered culture. The mere fact that it was no longer acceptable in Peter's Russia to look and act like a seventeenth-century Muscovite left a social and cultural vacuum. Further, when he freed Russian noblewomen from the confines of the *terem* and ordered that they appear at social functions, the vacuum increased. Not only Russian women, but Russian men as well, needed new models for social behavior. How should women behave in public? How should men behave toward them? If one ought not to act like a Muscovite, then how should one act? Since Peter accorded privileged status to those Europeans who had come to Russia, it was only natural that Russians should turn to them for answers to these and many other questions and to regard them as models for social behavior. Thus, during the second half of Peter's reign, Russians began to develop a social-utilitarian attitude toward the West, which dictated that, if men and women wished to succeed, they must emulate Western social behavior. In 1718 Peter made it clear that he shared that view when he commissioned the publication of *An Honest Mirror of Youth,* a handbook to instruct Russians in Western manners and values.

A second factor that made it necessary for Russians to draw upon the cultural experience of the West was connected with the construction of St. Petersburg itself. Peter insisted that St. Petersburg be a European city, with palaces and other buildings constructed according to Western designs. To be sure, Tressini, Mattarnovi, Leblond, and Schädel built only a handful of palaces during his reign. But even these obliged Russians to draw more heavily upon the cultural experience of the West and to adopt Western social and cultural values more extensively. In 1718 Peter ordered his leading courtiers to hold informal social gatherings (*assemblées*) and laid down detailed rules of etiquette for guests and hosts.[13] Social relationships were further defined along Western lines when he introduced the Table of Ranks in 1722. As we shall see, the Table of Ranks established a hierarchical order of fourteen ranks (a number of which were Russianized forms of European ranks), which defined an individual's position in Russia's military, civil, or Court services. Since *mestnichestvo,* the Muscovite system of defining social and service relationships according to genealogical precedents, had been abolished in 1682, and nothing had replaced it during the intervening four decades, the standing an individual held in the Table of Ranks quickly began to determine the order of social relationships in Russia.

At least among his closest associates, Peter's informal *assemblées* quickly became popular. All members of St. Petersburg's noble society were expected to appear, to dance the minuet and polonaise, play cards or chess, and engage in polite conversation. In addition to these gatherings, some of Peter's greatest courtiers sometimes gave banquets and other more formal entertainments, and these always were held in European settings. Menshikov's palace was especially elegant, its rooms filled with splendid furniture and its walls hung with rich tapestries and brocades. Further, although Peter himself lived modestly, his wife Catherine's Court had become elegant and westernized by the early 1720s. Pages, lackeys, and other servants proudly strutted in elegant green uniforms faced with red and trimmed with gold lace, and a large orchestra played Western music at dinner.[14] By the early 1720s, Muscovite fashions, which Peter had forbidden his courtiers to wear after he returned from the West in 1698, were worn in St. Petersburg only at masquerade balls.[15]

These cultural innovations meant that, while Europeans continued to remark upon the rudeness of Russians, they also began to comment about the flashes of elegance at social gatherings. "Nowhere in all of Europe do they dance the minuet with more grace than at the Petersburg Court," wrote the French dancing master Landet.[16] The Holstein courtier Bergholtz wrote in the early 1720s that ladies at the Russian Court were not inferior to their French and German counterparts in their worldly manners, elegant fashions, and dramatic coiffures. Although Bergholtz's native Holstein was hardly a center of Europe's high culture and society, he had visited Paris and Berlin and could draw at least superficial comparisons. Of course, Russia's cultural westernization remained a thin veneer that overlay centuries of Muscovite cultural experience. But, if its early shoots seemed fragile, its roots went far deeper by the time of Peter the Great's death than contemporaries and a number of historians realized.[17] With Peter's encouragement, Russians began to translate foreign literature and works on political theory into Russian, and, thanks to Peter's decree of 1708, they were printed in a modern alphabet.

Given the general opinion among contemporaries and historians that Russians had adopted the external forms of Western culture reluctantly, and only to protect themselves from Peter's wrath, one might expect to have seen a massive reversion to Muscovite ways once Peter II moved Russia's capital back to Moscow in 1728. In fact, somewhat the reverse happened. Peter II's courtiers did not hasten to don Muscovite kaftans, return their women to the *terem*, and spend long hours upon their knees in church. Instead, they preserved their newly acquired European pretensions and continued to demand Western luxury goods. Their westernized social life continued in Moscow and, according to the wife of England's ambassador, was similar to that which Peter the Great had established in St. Petersburg. "The Polish minister's lady has an assembly every night, where all the people of fashion meet," she wrote to a friend, and remarked that "one might find agreeable conversation if cards were not known in Russia."[18] Certainly, the balls, the *assemblées* where men and women played cards and conversed together, and Western theatrical performances were far from what Moscow had known during the times of Tsar Aleksei. Indeed, by the end of Peter II's reign, young Russians who carried their infatuation with things Western *ad absurdum* had become sufficiently numerous to impel Prince Kantemir, one of Prokopovich's Learned Guard, to create the first satirical portraits of them in Russian literature. In Kantemir's first satire, Medor, the powdered and painted young fop who lived only for fashion, was a personification of the growing infatuation with the West.[19]

When the Empress Anna ascended the throne early in 1730, the higher nobility began to demand institutions in which their sons could be educated in the manners and culture of Europe. Historians often have characterized this demand as the result of nobles' reluctance to enter the army or civil service at the bottom ranks but, although that was a factor, it hardly could have been the major one. The Cadet Corps Anna established in 1731 had a student body of approximately two hundred fifty during its early years. As such, it could not educate a sufficient number of noble youths to reduce in any significant way the number of aristocrats who were obliged to enter Russia's service at the bottom ranks. It could, however, educate youths from Russia's most prominent families who aspired to become successful courtiers. During the early 1730s, the most popular classes were German, French, dancing, fencing, and music—all subjects that were essential to the successful education of an aspiring courtier anywhere in Europe.[20]

That certain young Russian noblemen pursued these studies

should not lead us to conclude that the veneer of cultural westernization had thickened appreciably in the decade after Peter the Great's death. Even in St. Petersburg, many Russian nobles still were in the rudimentary stages of learning Western ways, as indicated by the Empress Anna's order in 1740 that *An Honest Mirror of Youth* be reprinted. In the provinces, of course, Western culture had scarcely begun to penetrate. Even as late as the 1750s, the noted memoirist Andrei Bolotov described places in Russia where nobles still wore kaftans and lived as they had in the seventeenth century.

It was during the reign of the Empress Elizabeth that cultural westernization became an intrinsic part of Russian aristocratic life. Indeed, the two decades between 1741 and 1761 saw the emergence of an aristocratic culture, patterned after the West, but produced, at least in part, by Russians. Elizabeth's reign witnessed the first performance of a Russian opera by Russians, the founding of Russia's first university at Moscow, the beginnings of a periodical press with essays written by Russians, and serious literary works by three great mid-eighteenth-century Russian writers: Vasilii Trediakovskii, Mikhail Lomonosov, and Aleksandr Sumarokov. During Elizabeth's reign, students from the Cadet Corps began to give dramatic performances at Court, often using works by Russian writers.[21] French replaced German as the language of polite society, thus setting the stage for a surge of cultural Francophilia.

The impressive achievements of the Elizabethan Age in some ways caused a split in the cultural personalities of St. Petersburg's lords and ladies. They aspired to speak French, behave like Versailles courtiers, and wear the very latest in Parisian fashions, but they were surrounded by a world that was still overwhelmingly Russian and grossly medieval. They lived in the capital of Russia, but it resembled the Dutch city of Amsterdam, and was beginning to take on Italian overtones from the work of Elizabeth's chief architect Bartolomeo Rastrelli. They wandered through artificial Roman and Greek ruins in the park at Tsarskoe Selo, sat in Chinese pagodas in the midst of Russian birch groves, and danced among tropical gardens in the dead of the northern winter. As one scholar wrote some years ago, an "unconscious realization of this unreality" may explain Elizabeth's passion for masquerades, especially those that parodied reality by having men dressed as women and women clad in the attire of men. So great was the fascination with unreality among aristocratic Russians in the mid-eighteenth century that there even was a chair of allegory at the Academy of Sciences.[22]

Later in the eighteenth century, the split in the cultural personalities of Russia's westernized aristocrats became even more extreme as they came to enjoy vast privileges, but bore no obligation to serve Tsar and country. Men and women read the works of the *philosophes* but perceived no conflict between the ideas of the Enlightenment and the absolute and arbitrary authority they wielded over their serfs, a dichotomy that found one of its most extreme expressions in Catherine the Great's ardent espousal of the Enlightenment and her equally strong defense of autocracy. Most important, however, this split cultural personality of the nobility expressed a far greater and more dramatic schism in Russia as a whole. By the mid-eighteenth century, noble status had come to be defined in terms of an individual's cultural westernization, with the result that two cultures came to exist side by side in Russia: the Western culture of the nobility and Court and the Russian culture of the peasants. Since peasants, by definition, were not nobles, they also, by definition, could not be westernized. There developed a vast chasm between the two separate worlds of lord and peasant that led Russian lords to consider their serfs to be less than human. In the 1870s, when educated Russians sought to bridge the gap by returning to the people, they would find the chasm had become unbridgeable.

One of the most dramatic distinctions between these two cultures was that Russia's peasant society was communal, while the world of the nobles was individualistic. The emergence of individualism in Russia was a direct consequence of Peter the Great's turn to the West for, until his reign, Muscovite noblemen had been governed by group loyalties and clan ties. Long before Peter's time, Europeans had abandoned the medieval ideal of a static world order in which tradition held unchallenged sway and the notion of progress was virtually nonexistent. The triumph of reason, as expressed in Descartes's axiom, "I think, therefore I am," meant that the individual came to reign supreme in the minds of Europeans. All the achievements of the Age of Explorations, all the discoveries of science in the seventeenth century, all the new patterns of entrepreneurship established by Europe's industrious and venturesome merchants, all the thought of the Age of Reason and afterward—all were the products of the critically thinking individual's triumph over medieval groups that had functioned according to the dictates of tradition. Peter wanted his nobles to function as individuals and to possess all the characteristics of their individualistic European counterparts: energetic behavior, a belief in progress, and unlimited creativity. Thus he established the principle that men would rise as a result of merit, not birth, and he rewarded men for what they did, not for what family they came from. He decreed that men could gain noble status through meritorious service to the state, and he institutionalized that principle in the Table of Ranks in 1722. As Marc Raeff once wrote, "The merit clause of the Table of Ranks provided both the stimulus and the foundation for the development of individualism [in Russia]." [23]

Peter's emphasis upon individualism had a broad and far-reaching impact upon all areas of Russian life. Most significant for our purposes, it stimulated men's creative powers in art, literature, science, and thought. Even by the 1730s, there was evidence of modern individual cultural accomplishment among such Russians as Prokopovich, Kantemir, and Tatishchev. Most important was Mikhail Lomonosov, whom Aleksandr Pypin once called "the greatest name in our eighteenth-century literature," a man who could say truthfully that "I have adorned the Academy of Sciences before the whole world for twenty years." [24] Indeed, Lomonosov was the first Russian Renaissance man, an intellectual colossus who was his country's first great scientist and much more. "Historian, rhetorician, specialist in mechanics, chemist, minerologist, artist, and poet, he probed everything, and fathomed everything," wrote Pushkin. "He founded our first university. In truth, he himself *was* our first university." [25]

Lomonosov was a striking example of the new Petrine man. Like Prokopovich, he was a commoner, but he grew up under very different circumstances. He was born in 1711 in the village of Denisovka, which was located on an island near the mouth of the Dvina River on the shores of the White Sea about fifty miles from the Arctic port of

Arkhangelsk. Far from Moscow, and surrounded by frozen wastes, this region was deemed so desolate and inhospitable that the early Romanovs often sent political enemies into exile there. At first glance, it hardly seemed a place that was likely to produce Russia's greatest eighteenth-century intellectual figure.[26]

In fact, the region was the most unusual in Russia in terms of its contact with the West during the latter half of the sixteenth and seventeenth centuries. Ever since Richard Chancellor had sailed the *Edward Bonaventure* into the White Sea and cast anchor in the mouth of the Dvina late in the summer of 1553, the area around Lomonosov's birthplace had enjoyed continuous and intimate contacts with the West. Ivan the Terrible had received Chancellor as King Edward VI's emissary and had agreed to allow English merchants "free marte with all free liberties" in Russia.[27] As a result, the English had begun a flourishing trade and had established a number of factories on the White Sea coast to produce rope and process other naval stores. English factors lived there year round and brought with them their culture and learning. Thus, during the century before Lomonosov's birth, the Dvina region came to resemble Moscow's Foreign Quarter, but with the very important difference that it was far away from the constricting and rigidly traditionalist influence of the capital. During the last third of the seventeenth century, one of Russia's first printing houses was established there, and books thus began to circulate more frequently and in greater numbers than in other parts of Russia.[28]

These unusual factors produced a population of Russians in the Far North who were, in many ways, prototypical of the new, dynamic men Peter the Great hoped to create. Since the land generally was too poor and the climate too cold for farming, serfdom had not become firmly established. Many of the population were free peasants, and they made their living in a rough and ready manner common to seafarers. Some were fishermen, others were coastal traders, and a number were quite prosperous. Like his neighbors, Lomonosov's father, Vasilii, earned his living from the sea. Among them, he stood out as an innovator, a man who was even more willing than they to take risks for a profit. By the time of his first son's birth, he owned several ships, and he was the first among the northern coastal folk to build a vessel according to European designs. With the *Sea Gull*, he began a prosperous business in transporting government supplies from Arkhangelsk to other settlements along the coast.[29]

Lomonosov grew up in a world of hardy seafaring folk who were energetic and daring. He learned to read as an adolescent and devoted the long nights of the Arctic winter to study. The precision of science and mathematics appealed to him, but he did not know Latin, the language of communication among scholars and scientists in the early eighteenth century. Therefore, in 1730, he went to Moscow's Zaikonospasskii Monastery to enroll in the Slaviano-Graeco-Latin Academy, popularly known as the Spasskii School. Since his father technically was a peasant, and since sons of peasants were prohibited from entering the academy, Lomonosov lied about his origins and claimed to be the son of a nobleman in distant Kholmogory. His ruse succeeded, and he was admitted to the school. The twenty-year-old Lomonosov thus took his place next to children in the beginners' Latin class. For almost five years he studied at the Spasskii School, living on a half-kopek's worth of bread a day, but mastering Latin and entering the world of Homer, Ovid, Livy, Virgil, and Horace.[30]

Because of his brilliant record at the Spasskii School, Lomonosov's teachers chose him in 1735 to become one of the first Russians to study at the Academy of Sciences where, until that time, German scholars had educated German students at Russian expense. A year later, his mentors at the Academy sent him to the University of Marburg, where he studied under the great physicist Christian von Wolff. From Marburg, he went to Freiburg to study mining and metallurgy, and returned to St. Petersburg in 1741, just a few months before Elizabeth seized the throne. He spent the next several years at the Academy of Sciences writing a number of dissertations in physics and being frustrated by the Academy's conservative German establishment in his efforts to begin serious scientific experiments. He lived a wild, undisciplined life, drank heavily, and brawled often. At one point he was arrested and obliged to make a public apology to the entire Academy. He restored himself in the authorities' good graces by composing a series of odes to great Russian courtiers and, in 1747, composed one to Elizabeth herself, "the great daughter of Tsar Peter," as he called her.[31]

In 1745 Lomonosov was named a professor of chemistry and a full member of the Academy. His new position enabled him to gain the necessary support to build the first chemical laboratory in Russia that provided facilities for chemical research and instruction. At the same time, he continued with numerous research projects in physics, all of them directed toward his dream of producing a vast work that would unite physics and chemistry by means of the "corpuscular theory" he had developed from his study of Robert Boyle's writings. Lomonosov's "corpuscular theory," all of which remained unpublished until 1904, anticipated by more than a century those molecular theories that form the basis for modern chemistry. Likewise, he discovered the law of the conservation of matter and energy a full quarter-century before Lavoisier and did brilliant work in electricity, optics, and the theory of heat, much of which was far ahead of his time. It is one of the tragedies of modern science that Lomonosov lived and worked at a time when Russia had no real scientific community and no means for communicating the substance of his discoveries. He thus remained a lone figure working in isolation, and many of his scientific discoveries remained unknown to the world until his papers were studied by specialists in the twentieth century.[32]

Lomonosov once wrote that "poetry is my solace—physics, my profession."[33] Throughout the many difficult times he experienced in his conflicts with the conservative authorities at the Academy, he produced a great deal of poetry, as well as a number of other literary works. He prepared the first effective Russian grammar, wrote one of the first scholarly histories of Russia, and developed his own literary language. He held knowledge and learning sacred above all and dreamed of "a Russian Academy comprised of the sons of Russia."[34] At that time, the vast majority of Russia's scholarly establishment were foreigners, but Lomonosov was convinced that Russia could produce scientists and thinkers equal to any in the world. As he wrote in his "Ode on the Ascension of Elizaveta Petrovna":

> *O men of learning, whom our nation*
> *Expects to come from its own womb,*
> *And wishes to be not inferior*
> *To those it calls from foreign lands,*
> *Oh, may your days on earth be blessed!*
> *Emboldened now be not reluctant*

To show by all your ardent zeal
That Mother Russia can give birth to
Its own philosophers like Plato
And Newtons of brisk intellect.[35]

In 1755 Lomonosov succeeded in convincing the Empress Elizabeth that a university should be established in Russia. He must have taken considerable pride in the fact that one-fifth of its faculty were Russians whereas, when Peter the Great had founded the Academy of Sciences three decades earlier, all of the faculty had to be imported from the West. Moscow University (now named after Lomonosov) soon became and remains to this day Russia's greatest university.[36]

Lomonosov's choice of Moscow as the university's site was an important symbolic statement. While Moscow was the home of Old Russian culture and the center of the traditionalism that Peter the Great had vowed to destroy, Western ideas actually found a better climate in which to develop there than in St. Petersburg. The origins of this seemingly strange phenomenon can be traced back to Tsar Aleksei's westernized advisers Artamon Matveev and Afanasii Ordin-Nashchokin in the 1660s, as well as to Sofia's westernized lover Prince Vasilii Golitsyn in the 1680s. These nobles were not opposed to change, but they thought change should be gradual and integrated into the fabric of Russia's life and experience. They therefore opposed Peter's rapid pace of westernization and its inevitable upheavals. As early as the 1730s, when the Court aristocracy in St. Petersburg had assimilated only the thinnest veneer of Western culture, a narrow circle of aristocrats in Moscow were already discussing sophisticated Western political and philosophical systems in a serious and thoughtful manner.[37] As a result, what intellectual dissent there was in Russia during the eighteenth century tended to originate there.

While in science Lomonosov had no peer, in literature he found a number of rivals whose works vied with his own for popular acclaim. Most prominent was a man whose writings commanded great attention among Elizabeth's courtiers and that widening circle of westernized Russians outside the Court. This was the playwright and poet Aleksandr Sumarokov, the originator of the elegant literary classicism of the Elizabethan Age and founder of a tradition from which such giants as

Dostoevskii and Tolstoi would emerge in the nineteenth century. Unlike Lomonosov, he came from aristocratic roots and was one of the first outstanding products of the elite schools Anna had established during the 1730s. Schooled in the arts of the Western European courtier, he extolled the ideals of patriotism and service to Russia; the conflict of duty and honor with base egotism and the passions became a central theme in most of his plays. As Director of Russian Theatres during the last years of Elizabeth's reign, Sumarokov did much to develop the dramatic arts. Like Lomonosov, he championed the development of a modern Russian language, yet he did not want modern Russian to become a language made up of adopted foreign words, although he was not against foreign incursions used to broaden and enrich his native tongue. What he opposed most vehemently was the Francomania of Russia's courtiers who, by the mid-eighteenth century, had begun to flood their speech with French words when perfectly good ones already existed in Russian. "We overload our language with foreign words," he wrote. "Finally we may forget Russian altogether, which would be a great pity, for no people has yet killed its native tongue, although ours is threatened with final extinction."[38] As one historian later remarked, many Russian nobles "tried eternally to be at home among foreigners and succeeded only in becoming foreigners at home."[39]

Unlike Lomonosov, Sumarokov became a critic of the society and attitudes that had arisen in Russia by the mid-eighteenth century. To spread his views, he founded Russia's first privately owned and edited periodical, *The Industrious Bee,* in 1759, and used its pages to criticize the baseness of the Russian nobility. He urged that educated men dedicate their pens to bettering the moral quality of Russia's political elite in order to improve society and government. The well-ordered state and society, he argued in a brief essay entitled "A Dream—The Happy Society," was one in which statesmen were chosen only for their talent and where renown could not be won "except through merit." Justice should be the province of all subjects, from the highest to the lowest, and the ideal ruler should think only of their well-being, never of his personal interests.[40] Sumarokov insisted that the virtuous nobleman, like the ideal ruler, had a duty to serve the good of society and that it was the moral superiority he gained as a result, not the mere title of nobleman, that distinguished him from the lower classes.[41] As he wrote in his satire "On Nobility":

> I am worthy if I myself can earn honor.
> But if there is no duty I can well perform, it means
> That I am not a nobleman as was my father.[42]

For Sumarokov, it was the moral superiority of the nobleman who served society that justified the continuing enserfment of Russia's masses, and he sharply criticized those who did not conform to his ideal or treated their serfs in a cruel and arbitrary fashion.

Sumarokov reflected an important characteristic of Russian thought in the mid-eighteenth century that often has been overlooked. This was the tendency of Russians to draw their first Western intellectual precepts from Central Europe rather than from France or England, although they followed the French example in questions of fashion and manners. Beginning with the faculty of the Academy of Sciences, the foreign scholars who settled in Russia tended to be Germans. These men maintained close ties with their homeland and sent their Russian protégés to study there. The Russians who studied abroad drew directly upon the ideas of such German jurists and philosophers as Christian von Wolff (Lomonosov's mentor at Marburg) and Friedrich Christian Baumeister and, through them, such great jurists as Samuel Pufendorf and Hugo Grotius.[43]

Of all the ideas of the seventeenth and eighteenth centuries, the concepts of natural law fostered by these men most appealed to Russians and best conformed to their aspirations and self-image. As one scholar has written, "German philosophers and jurists of the *Aufklärung* always conceived of the individual within the context of a community, with rights being conferred on him only in return for the fulfillment of his obligations to his fellow men and to the group."[44] As a result, writings that grew out of the *Aufklärung* were among the earliest nontechnical Western works to be translated into Russian. Pufendorf's work *On the Duties of Man and the Citizen According to Natural Law* was published in Russian as early as 1726, in accordance with Peter the Great's order that it be translated "as soon as possible and with all speed."[45] By 1760 the Russian reader also could read some of the writings of Baumeister and Wolff in Russian translation, and there was much in the writings of Sumarokov, and his predecessors among Prokopovich's "Learned Guard," that came directly from them.

That Lomonosov and Sumarokov found an audience in Russia indicates that a reading public had begun to emerge during the Elizabethan Age. This had not been the case during the Petrine era, or even during the reign of Anna, and the result was that much of the work of such early intellectuals and writers as Tatishchev and Kantemir went unpublished until after their deaths. Kantemir's satires, although written in the 1730s, were first published in French translation by a London printer in 1750, and the first Russian edition appeared only in 1762. Even more amazing, Tatishchev completed his great history of Russia in 1739, but the first volume was not published until 1768, and the last appeared only in 1848! So limited was the demand for books during the reign of Anna that only 140 were published during the entire decade. During the first decade of Catherine the Great's reign, the total increased to just over one thousand.[46] Clearly, the demand for books existed during the last years of the Elizabethan Age, but Elizabeth was too preoccupied by her age-ravaged beauty, her poor health, and the pressures of the Seven Years' War to encourage the publication of translations and original literary works. Catherine the Great would do so almost from the moment of her accession.

When Elizabeth died in 1761, Russia's cultural landscape was far more verdant than it had been at the time of her accession. At least at Court, and among the nobility of Moscow and St. Petersburg, Russia's relationship with the West and its culture had undergone a great transformation. There, Western culture had become an integral part of the lives and outlooks of the aristocracy. By mid-century, educated Russians dressed, entertained, and dined in the Western manner because the old Muscovite ways seemed to lack grace and appeared rather absurd. The Petersburg courtier of 1760 would have found ludicrous the refusal of the Muscovite *boiar* at the turn of the century to shave his flowing beard for fear of losing his place in Paradise. Like their Western counterparts, St. Petersburg's nobility had become more concerned with the problems and pleasures of their present lives and were far less preoccupied with the fate of their eternal souls in the hereafter.

Rationalism, individualism, even a touch of skepticism had taken the place of those Church-centered views Peter the Great had struggled to eradicate. In that sense, the Petrine transformation had succeeded.

The result, however, was by no means without flaw. Once they had set foot upon the path to westernization, Russia's nobles had embraced the West with a passion that was as ardent as it was undiscriminating. By the late 1730s, the *petit-maître* and the *coquette* (the coxcomb and female dandy) had begun to see Western fashions and manners as ends unto themselves, forgetting that their privileged position was predicated upon responsible behavior and service to Russia. By mid-century, such a high premium had come to be placed upon French style and manners at Court that a young man simply could not hope to succeed in the highest social and political circles without such attributes. Because Russia's few elite schools could educate only a handful of noble youths, many of the aristocracy in St. Petersburg and Moscow sought to hire tutors for their children. It was *de rigueur* that they be foreign and very much preferred that they be French. It was fervently hoped that they could instill in their charges the graces necessary to succeed, although they did not always have the ability or background to do so. Nevertheless, any sort of tutor was preferable to none, especially since it became a mark of distinction to have a full-time tutor in a noble household. Later in the century, when cultural westernization began to filter into the provinces, a tutor became one of the highest marks of status. Wrote one observer, "In the provinces, the phrase 'they have a tutor' tells you that a family is very wealthy indeed."[47]

Since the demand for tutors far exceeded the supply, any and every available foreigner was pressed into service, and the flotsam and jetsam of the Parisian streets found in Russia a land of vast opportunity. "I hired eight French lackeys for the students at the Corps of Cadets and, two months later, they had all left to become tutors in eight separate households," complained one frustrated official.[48] The Chevalier de Corberon remarked in the mid-1770s that "a prostitute from the rue Saint-Honoré could, if she were slightly trained in proper manners, gain a position as a governess" at the prestigious Smolnyi Institute, which Catherine the Great had just founded to educate young ladies of high birth. Joseph Ribas, "some sort of Italian," began his career in Russia as a tutor in the Cadet Corps where, according to Corberon, "he introduced gambling, roguery, and sodomy."[49] Ribas later became the Corps's director and an admiral in the Russian navy. One enterprising Frenchman reportedly embroidered a *fleur de lis* on his sleeve, boldly told one noble family that he was a cousin of the French King, and was taken into service immediately by gullible Russians who were proud to have such an "exalted" personage in their employ. There was even a persistent rumor that one shameless Finn spent a number of years in the provinces teaching his native language in the households of nobles who thought he was teaching their children French.[50]

Russians clearly would employ anyone at almost any price to have a tutor. "My *mamzell* [governess] costs me dear, the little minx! One hundred and eighty rubles a month, five pounds of sugar, and a pound of tea!" "Oh, I have to pay even more: two hundred and fifty rubles a month, and all the food she can eat. But she also washes my laces and sews my bonnets, and is teaching our servant how to do it"—such was the gist of one reported conversation between two Russian noble matrons. *Mamzell* and her male counterpart may have had considerable talent as washerwomen, ladies of the night, and teachers of gambling and sodomy, for a number of them had left Paris just one step ahead of the French police. Their knowledge of their native tongue, however, left much to be desired. Around 1750 the Russian authorities made an effort to sift out the incompetents among them by instituting an examination, sometimes with ludicrous results. There is the tale of the prospective tutor who sat for his examination and was asked to explain the moods of verbs. He replied that it was impossible to give a precise answer because he had left Paris quite sometime earlier and that verbs changed their moods very often.[51]

Such superficiality and warped understanding among westernized Russians concerned Catherine the Great from the moment of her accession, and she attempted to add an intellectual dimension to their experience. She thus introduced an intellectual-utilitarian element into Russia's cultural westernization process. Just as European manners and dress had been a prerequisite for success at the Courts of Anna and Elizabeth, so a polite acquaintance with western ideas, especially those of Voltaire, became essential for the successful Catherinian courtier. For the scant number of thinking Russians, this meant adding another dimension to the ideas of the *Aufklärung*. For most of the westernized nobility, however, it simply meant another fashion to be adopted and slavishly followed. As one satirist characterized them in the pages of the short-lived Moscow journal, *The Sunset:*

> *If you don't know the ideas now in style,*
> *You just can't stand among the noble file . . .*
> *You style your locks, and wear the latest mode . . .*
> *Sit proudly in your cariole, all dandified . . .*
> *You trample folk, and put on airs where 'ere you ride;*
> *You strut about, speak only Franco-Russian . . .*
> *But serious thought is not your taste for musing . . .*
>
> *Your serfs, you've ruined, pawned, or sold.*
> *On games of cards you gamble all your gold . . .*
> *To sum it up: your life's the latest mode.*[52]

Instead of creating a society that had firm intellectual roots in the West, Catherine generally succeeded only in making many of her courtiers and their ladies into intellectual *petits-maîtres* and *coquettes*. Perhaps that was to be expected, because Catherine herself was something of an intellectual *coquette*. She read widely in the works of the Enlightenment and eighteenth-century European literature generally, but her reading was undirected and haphazard. She was hardly the philosopher upon the throne that she aspired to become; indeed, she herself fell victim to intellectual infatuations as did her courtiers. Catherine was "a great temperament, not a great intellect," one historian wrote.[53]

Catherine's efforts to become an enlightening monarch took many forms. More than any previous Russian sovereign, she was determined to become a patron of the arts and to make her Court a monument to the cultural and intellectual westernization she aspired to promote among her subjects. Most of all, she wanted her Court to reflect that image of Russia's glory she endeavored to foster at home and abroad. She therefore commissioned sculptors to produce busts of marble and statues of bronze, the greatest being Falconet's great Bronze Horseman. She purchased art on a vast scale, and her agents combed Europe for ancient and contemporary treasures. Cost was of almost no consequence in her effort. In 1768 she bought the famous Dresden gallery of Count Brühl for 180,000 rubles. Four years later, through the efforts of Diderot, she purchased the even more famous Crozat collection in Paris. There were over a thousand paintings—works by Raphael, Van Dyck, Rembrandt, Tenier, Poussin, and many others—and the price was an astounding five hundred thousand francs.[54]

But these collections were just a beginning. Three months after she obtained the Crozat collection, Catherine bought fifty more great paintings from the Duke de Choiseul for another five hundred thousand francs and paid Madame Geoffrin thirty thousand more for two paintings by Van Loo. She bought the Duke of Orleans's entire collection of engraved gems in one avid swoop, commissioned the artists Vernet and Chardin to do landscapes for her palace, and had German artists make copies of Raphael's immortal frescoes in the Vatican. In 1765 she purchased Diderot's library, although she allowed him to retain it until his death. At Voltaire's death, she purchased his library of seven thousand beautifully bound volumes as well, thus acquiring for Russia a wealth of rare literary and historical treasures, all annotated by the Sage of Fermy himself. No one in Europe could match Catherine's resources, so her treasure grew more and more impressive. By 1790 she could write to Melchior Grimm that "[my museum] at the Hermitage consists of pictures, the panels of Raphael, thirty-eight thousand books, four rooms filled with books and prints, ten thousand engraved gems, [and] nearly ten thousand drawings."[55]

Catherine aspired also to be a patron of literature. Again, her thirst for personal renown, which she identified with Russia's greater glory, inspired her. Among other things, she encouraged the work of a number of poets, especially Gavrila Derzhavin, whom the great nineteenth-century literary critic Vissarion Belinskii once called "the hero of our poetry."[56] During the course of a sporadic career, Derzhavin rose from impoverished beginnings to stand among the top one percent of the Russian nobility in terms of wealth.[57] Yet he was not destined to become merely a wealthy landowner, living idly on the income from his estates and serfs. In 1782 he wrote a satirical "Ode to the Wise Princess Felitsa," in which he flattered Catherine's self-image by portraying her as an enlightened ruler, a wise and just sovereign who lived frugally and devoted her life to good government and serious thought:

Not following your murzas' *custom,*
You often go about on foot,
And only have the simplest dishes
Permitted in your dining room.
Not valuing your leisure hours,
You read and write before a lectern,
And grant a true felicity
Unto all mortals by your writings.[58]

Derzhavin's ode raised him to new heights in Catherine's favor. She decided to call him back into Russia's service, made him governor first of the province of Olonets, then of Tambov, and finally appointed him her personal secretary and a Senator. Yet his tongue was too sharp, his personality too abrasive, and his fundamentalist self-righteousness too galling. He could not resist making critical comments about society and people among whom he lived. He was obsessed by the notion of justice, and wrote as his epitaph: "Here lies Derzhavin,/ Who upheld legal justice,/ But crushed by wrong,/ Fell in defense of the laws."[59] Wherever he served, Derzhavin became embroiled in conflicts with his superiors, and often got himself out of trouble only by penning another flattering piece of verse to his August Imperial patroness. Even so, he could not restrain himself from reminding Catherine of her mortality in his poem "To Rulers and Judges":

And you shall fall, in no way different,
As withered leaves shall fall from trees;
And you shall die, in no way different,
As your most humble slave shall die![60]

Derzhavin's moralistic and self-righteous proclamations about Russian society were heavy and unbending. His contemporary, the dramatist Denis Fonvizin, creator of some of Russia's greatest comedies, was a very different kind of social critic. Unlike Derzhavin, Fonvizin came from a prosperous background where family serfs coddled him, entertained him with an endless stream of those folk tales in which Russia's peasant culture is so rich, and he grew up happy and sheltered. Fonvizin received a good education at Moscow University and was an outstanding student. Long before he left Moscow, he showed his great talent for satire and his brilliance in highlighting the frailties of the society in which he lived. When he was eighteen, he wrote "A Letter to My Servants Vanka and Petrushka Shumilov," a comico-philosophical conversation in the style of Voltaire, in which he summarized the purpose of the universe in caustic and satirical tones:

> Priests cheat without ceasing their pastoral hordes,
> While in palaces the servants do the same to their lords,
> And the nobles themselves seek to swindle each other,
> While the greatest among them do the same to the Tsar;
> Thus, each seeks to fill his purse up to the brim,
> And it's just for this purpose so much fraud does set in.
> So fond of money are nobles and merchants,
> Judges and scribes, soldiers brave, even peasants.
> And the priests who have charge of our hearts' and souls' keep
> They allow to extort a quit-rent from their sheep:
> Docile creatures get married, multiply, and decease,
> While the priests keep getting great wealth without cease.
> For money, they will free the elite from their sin,
> While the masses must settle for joy in Heaven.
> But if one can speak out with the truth in this world,
> I would say with all candor that I now do behold:
> That for money, the Lord God Himself to surfeit
> Would deceive without question his priests and their sheep.[61]

Fonvizin soon was to continue in a much more subtle vein. At the age of twenty-one, he wrote the first of his comedies, *The Brigadier*, which focused upon the flaws of the faulty (and false) europeanization of Russia's nobles and their shallow Francophilia. "I was never there, but still I already have a very good idea of what France is like. Isn't it true that mostly Frenchmen live in France?" asks one of his characters. Later, in complimenting her lover upon his French ways, the same character rejoices that "it is your good fortune and mine, dear, that you fell into the hands of a French coachman [who came to St. Petersburg and established a boarding school]."[62]

Fonvizin's greatest comedy was *The Young Ignoramus*, upon which he labored for two decades. Because he believed that a writer must be "the guardian of general welfare, and raise his voice against abuses and prejudices,"[63] Fonvizin returned to the themes of his early "Letter to My Servants" and focused upon one of the major problems Catherine faced throughout her reign: the boorishness and brutishness of Russia's provincial nobility. Unlike Catherine, who thought that education could solve that problem, Fonvizin made it clear that the national backwardness, personified in the young ignoramus Mitrofanushka and the people around him, was an inevitable consequence of their primitively despotic world of serfs crushed by stupid and base masters. Although virtue triumphed in the end, it did not resolve the broader problem of ignorance, sloth, and greed that the system of serfdom engendered in Russia's provinces. For such people, Fonvizin insisted, education provided no solution, because they saw it as useless and were even too lazy and too ignorant to become semi-Frenchified *petits-maîtres* such as he had inveighed against in *The Brigadier.*

Derzhavin, Fonvizin, and a number of other Russian poets and dramatists wrote for a reading audience that grew rapidly during the last three decades of the eighteenth century. The years 1762–96 saw six times as many books published as in the entire six preceding decades. Many of these were translations of Western European works, a part of Catherine's effort to bring Russia more firmly into the intellectual life of the West as she understood it. During her reign, Russians thus became able to read not only translations of major works of the French Enlightenment and the German *Aufklärung* but the writings of John Locke and William Pitt, most of the major Greek and Roman classics, and the works of Swift, Defoe, Fielding, Racine, Molière, Alexander Pope, Scarron, Smollet, and many others.[64] Among these foreign translations, the ones Russians enjoyed most were novels. During the last years of Elizabeth's reign, novels became an integral part of their lives as they searched for broader and more sophisticated models of behavior in the new and westernized world that was emerging around them. Once the westernized Russian had mastered the rudimentary rules of behavior set forth in such books as *An Honest Mirror of Youth,* a whole new series of questions arose. How did European lords and ladies spend their days? How did they spend their evenings? What sorts of conversations took place at dinners, at salons, at balls? Books on manners could tell Russians how to behave in public, but they could not tell them how to behave in private. How did European lords and ladies conduct love affairs? How did they treat their servants? How did they act in the boudoir?

Russians sought the answers in those European novels that presented large slices of life and broad panoramas of Western society. The famous memoirist Andrei Bolotov, in describing his experiences as a young man in the late 1750s, has left us a brilliant account of this process. "In reading the description of incidents which took place in all countries and in all parts of the world," he wrote, "I imperceptibly became much closer acquainted with all types of people and, especially, with the great lords and ladies of urban society. I discovered, and then acquired a fuller understanding of, the various mores and customs of people . . . and learned how people lived in other countries. . . . Worldly life, the life of high society in all its complexities, and the entire world in general, seemed much clearer to me than before, and I thus acquired a much better grasp of many things that I had only known about in a vague and imprecise way."[65]

Such reading elevated upper-class Russians' image of proper behavior. At the same time, it led them to denounce the superficially westernized behavior of some of their fellows as undesirable and, even, barbaric. "I began to see everything from a far more elegant perspective," wrote Bolotov. "All this caused me to become disgusted with crude and vile manners, and the company of boors and louts."[66] A certain sensitivity, even sensibility, thus became a part of some nobles' outlooks. But, as was so often the case with Russians' efforts to confront European cultural forms in the eighteenth century, some went too far and accepted as gospel every form of behavior they read about in Western books. Paris became for them a sort of Mecca to which they paid an emotional, if absurd, tribute. Remarked the fictional Ivan in Fonvizin's *The Brigadier,* "Every person who's been to Paris has the right, speaking about Russians, not to include himself in their number because he has already become more a Frenchman than a Russian."[67]

Such superficial and extreme manifestations of Francophilia were among the blemishes on the face of Russia's cultural westernization that Catherine sought to erase. Like Fonvizin, she chose satire as her weapon, but she sought to wield it in the pages of satirical journals rather than in comedy. She modeled her efforts upon *The Tatler* and *The Spectator,* those English weeklies that Steele and Addison had made so famous, when she founded *Odds and Ends* (*Vsiakaia vsiachina*) in 1769. For a bit more than a year, she used its pages to poke fun at those nobles who dressed and acted like Europeans but had no interest in serious thought or service for Russia's greater glory. Yet Catherine's effort was doomed because those who found *Odds and Ends* amusing were precisely those better educated men and women who could laugh at the absurdities of the *petit-maître* and *coquette*. Her message did not reach the superficial coxcombs against whom the satire was directed.

Aleksandr Pushkin once wrote that "if reigning successfully means to know the frailties of the human spirit and how to use them to advantage, then, in this respect, Catherine deserves to be marveled at by posterity."[68] In her efforts to promote satire as a weapon against the cultural and intellectual superficiality of Russian society in the 1760s and early 1770s, Catherine encouraged Russians to establish other weeklies modeled upon *Odds and Ends*, and between 1769 and 1773 a number appeared in St. Petersburg. Indeed, during those five years, fifteen new journals appeared in Russia, a quantity that equaled the number founded during all the preceding years of the eighteenth century.[69]

Ironically, Catherine proved unable to control the new and awesome force she had unleashed by encouraging Russia's periodical press. At first, she attempted to stimulate a polite controversy between *Odds and Ends* and the other weeklies about the purpose of satire. But that soon led to a much broader debate in which she argued that satire ought to call attention to Russia's shortcomings in an abstract and impersonal way, while others insisted that it should be employed to criticize specific faults and social ills. Just beneath the surface of these polite literary and stylistic disputes lay the far more vital issue of the press's role in unmasking society's flaws in the name of social, cultural, even political progress.[70] As a result, while *Odds and Ends* criticized the superficiality of the westernization process among Russia's nobles, other editors soon began to challenge some of those very principles and institutions Catherine thought vital to Russia's welfare. Most vocal among them was Nikolai Novikov, editor of *The Drone*.

Novikov was the first writer of consequence to question Russia's eighteenth-century social and economic order, and he thus founded that noble tradition from which sprang the first revolutionary challenges to the Russian autocracy in the nineteenth century. Like Derzhavin, his early career had its ups and downs as he moved from one branch of the service to another. In 1767, at the age of twenty-three, he served as a secretary on Catherine's Legislative Commission, where he saw at first hand the failings of the Russian bureaucracy, the flaws of Russian society, and the injustices of the serf system, as the deputies discussed questions of runaways, the economic plight of the serfs, and the ineffectiveness of provincial administration in the Empire.[71] Novikov left the Legislative Commission with a conviction that these failings must be remedied if his country were to prosper. He founded *The Drone* in 1769 and turned his pen against favoritism and corruption in Russia's government. "Madame Odds and Ends," that is, Catherine herself, replied that no one enjoyed "nasty jokes" and "melancholy letters." Yet Novikov persisted in his criticism and found support among a number of other editors and their journals. He began to criticize the venality and ignorance of Russia's judges and the ineffectuality of her courts; instead of laughing, as Catherine did, at the pretensions of Russia's semi-Europeanized provincial nobles, he detailed the manner in which they abused their serfs. Catherine responded as a frustrated Autocrat, not as an enlightened sovereign who sought the advice and counsel of public opinion. Even if she did not force Novikov to close *The Drone,* as historians often have contended, she certainly lost her taste for the debate she had brought into being, and turned to the theatre and satirical comedy, which was easier to control. By mid-1770, the satirical weeklies whose founding she had encouraged just over a year before had all ceased to appear.[72]

Novikov was not prepared to abandon his campaign to repair the flaws in Russia's social and economic order. In 1770 he launched the weekly journal *The Tatler,* which survived for only two issues. Two years later, he founded another satirical journal, *The Artist.* When that was closed in mid-1773, he made a final effort with *The Purse* (dedicated "to my homeland"), which survived a mere three months. His criticism took on ever sharper tones. He railed against corruption and branded Catherine as "the moralizer, reprimanding all critics, and believing that satires only harden morals, while moralizing improves them."[73] Most of all, he focused upon the moral indignity and economic ruin serfdom brought to Russia. "Everywhere dire poverty and slavery met me," he wrote in chronicling a journey into the countryside (a theme the more radical writer Aleksandr Radishchev would develop much further at the end of the century). "I always found that the masters themselves were at fault for this," he continued. "O, humanity! You are unknown in these villages. O, mastery! You lord tyranny over the people subjected to your care. . . . Stupid serfowners! These poor slaves seem to you more like horses and dogs than people."[74] Despite the fervor of his pleas, Novikov's criticisms stirred little positive response among Russia's serfowners, and he soon abandoned his effort in order to devote full attention to the serfs themselves. This was partly because of his disillusionment with the nobility but also the consequence of his growing commitment to the precepts of freemasonry, which emphasized service to society by educating and enlightening the masses. ,

It is difficult to explain why Novikov embraced freemasonry with such fervor at this point in his life because he later destroyed many of the personal papers that related to his masonic activities. From the detailed account of his close friend and fellow freemason Ivan Lopukhin, it seems that freemasonry attracted them both because the officially fostered version of westernization, with its emphasis upon rationalism and the teachings of the Enlightenment, had failed them. Both men had come from the provinces and were more deeply imbued with traditional Russian values than their St. Petersburg counterparts. Because of that universal instinct that impels adolescents to rebel against the precepts of their fathers and also because of current literary and philosophical tastes, they had turned to the teachings of the Enlightenment soon after they went out into the world on their own and for several years were avid readers of Voltaire and a number of other *philosophes*. Yet these works proved too cold, too rationalistic, and too far removed from their previous experiences and values. Unlike the *hommes nouveaux* who filled the Court and St. Petersburg society, and who made their way by adopting first the social, then the intellectual, values that were in vogue, Lopukin and Novikov could not entirely abandon the tradition in which they had been reared. Although they believed that the existing order should be made more humane, that noble lords should not abuse their serfs, and that culture and ideas should be more firmly rooted in national experience, they were not prepared to reject the class and the system in which they had a vested interest.[75] They thus sought an intellectual compromise that would improve the existing social and economic system in Russia without requiring its destruction. They found this compromise in the socially oriented doctrines of freemasonry, which stressed the moral and social perfectability of man. As freemasons, they thus committed themselves to enlightening Russia's peasantry and, indeed, "all those others in Russia who were culturally still very backward in spite of their relatively high social and economic level."[76]

Novikov and his fellow freemasons sought to achieve that end by printing and distributing books that emphasized moral and social enlightenment. Called the Typographical Company, this enterprise marked the first private effort to spread Western ideas among a broad stratum of Russians, and its symbolic importance was of more consequence than the results it achieved. The Typographical Company was the first concrete indication of a major shift in the process of Russia's cultural westernization. Ever since Peter the Great had returned from the West in 1698, Russia's Autocrats had led the way in their country's technological, social, and cultural westernization. In an important sense, the Romanovs thus had assumed a social revolutionary role throughout most of the eighteenth century. The activities of the Typographical Company indicated that this role was now being taken up by others, and when Catherine arrested Novikov and a number of his associates in 1792, it was clear that the autocracy had begun to relinquish its social revolutionary function.

The path taken by the Moscow freemasons remained fundamentally conservative, for it stressed moral and social improvement within the context of Russia's existing serf and autocratic order. As the end of the eighteenth century approached, there were other young men who followed the values and teachings of the Enlightenment to the logical conclusion that the freemasons had rejected. Most important among them was Aleksandr Radishchev, often called the first Russian radical. Like Novikov and Lopukin, Radishchev spent his childhood in Russia's provinces. The son of rich serfowners, he studied at the Corps of Pages in St. Petersburg until 1767, when Catherine chose him to be one of twelve students to be trained as an elite corps of jurists at the University of Leipzig. Radishchev thus lived in Leipzig at a time when it still was an impressive cultural and intellectual center. It was there that J. C. Gottsched, along with Professor Christian Gellert, presided over the development of German literature. The city was the home of the philosopher Leibnitz and the great composer Johann Sebastian Bach. Its university was the alma mater of Goethe, Fichte, and Schelling; G. E. Lessing, one of the great figures of the *Aufklärung,* had his first play produced there.[77]

At Leipzig, Radishchev and his fellow Russian students delved into the works of the Enlightenment and the *Aufklärung* in a seemingly endless orgy of reading and passionate dispute. They read Voltaire and Diderot, Montesquieu and Rousseau, Leibnitz and Baron d'Holbach. They read and argued over the Abbé Mably's *Le Droit public de l'Europe* and Helvetius's *De l'ésprit.* They also read Locke, Fénélon, Helvetius, and the Abbé Raynal. They overruled their guardian, Major von Bokum, whom Catherine had sent along to oversee their work, and voted to study independently rather than follow the prescribed course of study at the university.[78] During his years in Leipzig, Radishchev came to equate autocracy with despotism and saw it as a system of government that violated the most sacred principles of natural law and the social contract. As he would write just two years after his return to Russia, "autocracy is the condition most contrary to the nature of men. We cannot give anyone unlimited power over ourselves." Further, he added, "injustice on the part of the sovereign gives the people, who are his judges, an even greater right over him than the law gives him to punish criminals."[79]

Radishchev returned to Russia in 1771 to find that events had altered his future prospects dramatically. He had expected to come back as one of a chosen elite, to be among that handful of jurists through whom an enlightened Empress would implement a code of enlightened laws. By 1771, however, Catherine had abandoned her idealistic plans and had vastly reduced her hopes for Russian society. At the age of twenty-two, Radishchev became a clerk in the Senate. He left that position to become a junior officer in the Russo-Turkish War, then a civil servant in the College of Commerce, and, finally, chief of the St. Petersburg customs house. Catherine's failure to grant him a position commensurate with the expectations she had nurtured in him as a young man must have made him bitter and probably encouraged him to chronicle the failures of the sociopolitical amalgam his Empress had created. He never became a revolutionary as some have maintained. But he urgently demanded broad and far-reaching reforms and warned that revolution could be the price Catherine and her advisers might pay if they ignored his pleas.

During the 1780s, Radishchev devoted his leisure hours to writing a book that was ostensibly a traveler's account of a journey from St. Petersburg to Moscow. And, indeed, his book did include accurate descriptions of Russia's social, economic, and cultural life at the time. But his purpose was not merely to describe the places and people a traveler might encounter on a journey between Russia's new and old capitals. Cast in a style very similar to Laurence Sterne's *Sentimental Journey,* and reminiscent of Goethe's *Sorrows of the Young Werther* and Defoe's *Tour Through the Whole Island of Great Britain,* his tale was designed to comment upon the cruel indignities of serfdom, the failings of autocracy, the baseness of the nobility, the venality of the bureaucracy, and the low cunning of the clergy and their lack of Christian virtues. Among all the classes and social groups in Russian society, Radishchev saw only the peasantry as noble and virtuous and, while his peasants were highly idealized and sentimentalized, there was much truth in his chronicle of their daily sufferings.[80]

On July 7, 1790, Catherine's private secretary Aleksandr Khrapovitskii wrote in his diary that, after reading Radishchev's newly published book, Catherine "deigned to remark that he was a worse rebel than Pugachev." He added that "this was said with deep feeling and passion."[81] Indeed, the bitter truths in Radishchev's book, which paraded Catherine's failures as an enlightened sovereign before all the world, enraged the Empress. "The intention of this book is obvious on every page," she wrote. "The author, totally infected with the delusions of the French, seeks in every possible way to disparage respect for power and authority, and to goad the masses to indignation against their leaders and government."[82] For publishing a book that was "filled with the most pernicious philosophizing, destructive to civic peace, disparaging of citizens' respect for authority . . . and, finally, replete with insulting and frenzied remarks against the dignity and power of the sovereign," Catherine condemned Radishchev to death and decreed that "all copies of his book, wheresoever they may be found, [are] to be destroyed."[83] Thus did the sovereign, who had once promised Diderot and D'Alembert "more freedom and tranquility than you have [in France],"[84] deal with the man who had been bold enough to take to heart her admonitions to study the thought of the Enlightenment. Catherine soon commuted Radishchev's sentence to exile in Siberia, and then turned to punish Novikov, whom she sentenced to fifteen years' imprisonment in the fortress prison at Schlüsselberg.

Catherine dealt especially harshly with Radishchev and Novikov because she feared the revolution that had broken out in Paris in 1789. A number of Russians, among them some of her most prominent courtiers and statesmen, had been expecting revolution in France for a number of years, but she had not shared their views. When Count Semën Vorontsov wrote in 1787 that "the upheavals in France will be violent,"[85] Catherine remarked that she was not "one of those who thinks that we are on the eve of a great revolution."[86] The storming of the Bastille on July 14, 1789, caught her by surprise. Nevertheless, her reaction was swift and showed that she had no sympathy for the ideals of her cherished *philosophes* when they were carried to their logical conclusion. While some in St. Petersburg "congratulated and embraced one another in the streets, as if they had been relieved from the weight of heavy chains,"[87] Catherine quickly moved to set her house in order and to erect defenses against revolutionary ferment. She prohibited Diderot's *Grande Encyclopédie*, stopped the translation of Voltaire's works that she had commissioned, and confiscated the volumes already in print. "It is necessary to throw all the works of the best writers, and all that which their words have spread throughout Europe, into the flames," she wrote to Melchior von Grimm.[88] She endeavored to exclude all writings of the Enlightenment from Russia and, at the same time, meted out severe punishments to those who even hinted that they shared the *philosophes'* views. Clearly, she had no intention of permitting Russians to take seriously the ideas she herself had once championed. When forced to choose between enlightenment and strict autocracy, she chose the latter without question.

If Catherine failed to become an enlightened sovereign and defender of Western thought, she was far more successful in raising the general cultural level among Russia's nobility. While a handful of those she had introduced to the works of the *philosophes* took them seriously, and thus threatened her established order, the vast majority of educated Russians regarded the Enlightenment in just the manner Catherine had intended. They read and discussed in a vacuum whatever ideas were in vogue and never thought of actually applying them to Russia. They appeared as supremely cultured, well-read Europeans, but remained loyal to the precepts of autocracy and the system of serfdom that supported it.

By the end of Catherine's reign, Russia's cultural westernization had spread outward into the provinces, at least on a superficial level. In St. Petersburg and Moscow, the process had proceeded by leaps and bounds during the 1770s and 1780s to the point where a polite and elegant society, the equal of its counterparts in Paris, Berlin, and London, had arisen among Russia's great nobles. Within the confines of this hermetic little European world, so far removed from the realities of Russian life, men and women spoke French and lived *à la Française.* Their society became a hospitable haven for noble émigrés fleeing France after 1789. A number of these émigrés even entered Russia's service as they stayed in St. Petersburg to enjoy the *ancien régime* society no longer possible in their homeland, but which the Romanovs had created in Russia.[89] "[On the Nevskii Prospekt], I would have thought myself in Paris, on the Terrasse de Feuillans or the Boulevard de Coblentz," wrote the Comte de Puibusque. "I heard French spoken everywhere. The attire of the lords and ladies . . . is precisely the same as in Paris. The civility and brilliance of their conversations, this agreeable chatter of a joyous and contented crowd, made me forget the distance which separates us."[90] The Empresses Elizabeth and Catherine the Great, who together had ruled Russia for more than half of the eighteenth century, undoubtedly would have regarded his remark as a pleasing tribute to their labors.

CHAPTER VII

Imperial Aspirations

W hen Peter the Great drove his half-sister Sofia from the Kremlin in 1689, Russia was of little consequence anywhere in the world. During the seventeenth century, she had barely managed to defeat Poland, had found the Ottoman Empire too formidable a foe, and was overawed by the military might of such European powers as France, England, Holland, and Sweden. Europeans regarded Russians as inferior Asiatics, and thought their state was of little political or military consequence. They considered Russians primitive, sunk in sloth and all sorts of vice, and uncivilized by any decent standard. Without exception, Europeans luxuriated in a comfortable sense of superiority when they visited the Tsar's domains. As one Holsteiner described the Russians in the seventeenth century:

> *Churches, ikons, crosses, bells,*
> *Painted whores and garlic smells,*
> *Vice and vodka everyplace—*
> *This is Moscow's daily face.*
>
> *To loiter in the market air,*
> *To bathe in common, bodies bare,*
> *To sleep by day and gorge by night,*
> *To belch and fart is their delight.*
>
> *Thieving, murdering, fornication*
> *Are so common in this nation,*
> *No one thinks a brow to raise—*
> *Such are Moscow's sordid days.*[1]

Although Russia and her people were looked down upon, the country had become a critical factor in the efforts of European states to expand their economic and political power. As we mentioned earlier, the English and the Dutch attempted to exploit Russia's resources throughout the seventeenth century as they applied new mercantilist theories to their economic and foreign policies. Their purpose was to gain unchallenged access to the raw materials needed to expand their production and feed their growing populations at home. By importing cheap raw materials, while producing and exporting more costly manufactured goods, they expected to increase their national wealth, which, in turn, would augment their power. As early as 1623, one English writer had written that "if the native commodities exported do weight down and exceed in value the foreign commodities imported, it is a rule that never fails that then the kingdom grows rich and prospers." To this, Daniel Defoe added in mid-century, "Tis the longest purse that conquers now, not the longest sword."[2]

Throughout the seventeenth century, the English and the Dutch applied these precepts to Russia. "The wealth of our Netherlands is based upon trade and shipping," wrote one seventeenth-century Dutch legislator. "If we do not engage in them, then not only will we fail to gain the means for waging war, but our entire nation will become impoverished, and disorders may break out. There is . . . a new path, which is just as profitable as the sea trade with [New] Spain. This is the path to Moscow."[3] The English and the Dutch thus concluded that Russia's raw materials, themselves "of no great worth," could be used to employ their countrymen in trade, shipping, and manufacture, thereby increasing their national wealth and assuring the stability of their societies. So avaricious did they become in their efforts to control Russia's resources that the English established Russia's first rope walk in Kholmogory, and the Dutch established mills to produce gunpowder, glass, paper, and lumber before 1689. Most dramatic of all, the Dutch established a foundry in Tula that exported to Holland nearly one thousand first-rate cannon a year in the mid-seventeenth century; they sold the inferior pieces to the Russians.[4] The Romanovs thus suffered the ultimate indignity of a colonized state. Although an efficient armaments industry existed within their borders, their armies were chronically short of good weapons, and they could obtain them only in Sweden or in Holland, the very country whose agents operated the armaments works in Russia.

By the time of Peter's accession, it was clear that, should this state of affairs continue, Russia could only become weaker and even more dependent upon the advanced nations of the West. Throughout Peter's reign, advisers continued to warn him of the danger. Ivan Pososhkov, whose *Book on Poverty and Wealth* was the first partially mercantilist tract to be written by a Russian, argued that his countrymen should control their own industries and reap the profits from them "so that the monies gained thereby will remain in Russia."[5] The Baron Johann von Luberas, a Holsteiner who became Vice-President of the College of Mines and Manufactures, sternly reminded Peter that "when the natives sell their products in a raw state . . . it is the inhabitants of other countries who work up the raw materials and receive the great return on their labors, while the former possessors receive only a meagre sustenance."[6] No one could have stated more clearly the threat Russia faced. Nor could the course of action to defend Russia against it have been more obvious. Peter's foreign policy thus would be directed toward gaining access to the Black Sea and the Baltic, building a commercial fleet to carry Russia's overseas trade, and maintaining a powerful naval force to defend it.

When Peter took over full command of Russia's government, he first turned his attention to the south in his search for outlets to the sea. A number of important factors must have played a part in his decision. The Black Sea probably seemed a more accessible outlet than the Baltic, since Sweden was a stronger power than the Ottoman Empire at that time. Equally important, the Ottoman Empire, and its Tatar vassals, were far more bothersome neighbors than Sweden because of their incessant demands for tribute and captives. Obviously, if Peter were to realize his dreams to make Russia a Great Power, he could not continue to pay tribute to the Tatars. Nor could he allow them to continue selling one out of every thirty-five Russians into slavery.[7] He thus launched his first campaign in the south; he would punish the Tatars and open the Black Sea to Russia's shipping at one stroke. His main objective was Azov, about ten miles upriver from the sea, where there was a garrison of some twenty-six thousand Turks.[8]

Peter began his campaign when the snows were still deep in the fields around Moscow. He assembled almost thirty thousand of Russia's best troops, including his new Guards regiments, which he supplied with two hundred cannon, thirty-three thousand bombs, cannon balls, and grenades, and more than three-quarters of a million pounds of gunpowder. General Patrick Gordon led 9,393 men to Azov in February. The remainder left Moscow at the beginning of May under the command of Generals Avtonom Golovin and Franz Lefort. With them marched "Bombardier Peter Alekseev," private soldier in the Preobrazhenskii Guards Regiment, who set out in a lighthearted mood as if on one of the many maneuvers on which he had led his "play soldiers" during the previous decade.[9] He soon learned through sad experience that this was very different from mock battles in the fields around Moscow. His first bitter discovery was that it required careful planning and considerable effort to move large numbers of troops over long distances. The slow and arduous river journey to Azov was made much worse by what Peter called "stupid pilots and workmen, who call themselves masters, but in reality are as far from being so as heaven is from earth."[10] They reached Azov only at the very end of June.

Once the armies of Golovin and Lefort were united with those of Gordon, the siege of Azov began. At best, it was a pointless exercise, for Peter had no navy to command the Don River. The Russians laid their siege works, and the Turks promptly sailed up the river from the Black Sea to provision their fortress. Throughout the summer and early fall, Peter's generals tried several times to take Azov by storm, but failed. To make matters worse, Gordon almost lost his entire army in mid-July when Jacob Jansen, a Dutch seaman whom Peter had taken into his service and upon whom he had showered favors, defected to the Turks and told them of the Russians' plans. By fall, Peter was obliged to admit failure and return to Moscow. Bad weather and floods hindered his retreat, while his rear guard was butchered by the Turkish cavalry.[11] Peter had learned that to "plow the field of Mars" was a brutal and deadly task. Still, he took his first defeat well, made no excuses, and admitted that he had erred seriously in leaving the decisions to three squabbling commanders and not appointing a commander-in-chief.[12] Most of all, he realized that he must have a navy if he was to vanquish the Turks. He plunged into the task with his characteristic energy and enthusiasm, demanding more from himself than from anyone else.

During the winter of 1695–96, Russians first felt the frenetic pace at which Peter would drive them throughout his reign. At the town of Voronezh, situated on one of the Don's tributaries and surrounded by forests of oak and evergreen, Peter put some thirty thousand men to work felling trees to build ships for his navy. In less than five months, a fleet of thirteen hundred barges, numerous fireships, and thirty seagoing vessels took shape. At the same time, Peter amassed an army that was more than twice the size of that which Lefort, Gordon, and Golovin had commanded the previous year. This time, he gave command to Generalissimus Aleksei Shein. When the Russians began a murderous bombardment of Azov in the late spring of 1696, Peter's new navy prevented the Turks from relieving their besieged forces. As always, the young Tsar was in the thick of the fighting. When his younger sister urged him to take care, he replied that "I am not going anywhere near cannon balls and bullets, but they somehow keep coming near me."[13] In July the Turks surrendered, and Peter claimed his first military victory. It was a heady experience, and it made him hunger for new triumphs. His next thrust to the sea would come in the north against Sweden, the most formidable of the Baltic powers.

In alliance with Denmark and Poland, Peter launched the first campaign of the Great Northern War on August 19, 1700, just a month after he had signed a peace treaty with the Ottoman Empire. The war could not have had a worse beginning. Sweden's eighteen-year-old King Charles XII proved to be a military genius, recklessly courageous and utterly contemptuous of danger. He defeated Denmark in a few weeks and then turned to deal with the Russians, who were besieging his Baltic fortress at Narva. For two months, the Russians sought in vain to take the city. Then, at the end of November, eight thousand Swedes under Charles's personal command burst out of a blinding snowstorm to capture all of Peter's artillery and several of his generals. The Russians fled in headlong retreat.[14]

Diligence and hard work would be Peter's watchwords during the decade after his bitter defeat at Narva. While Charles XII turned his attention to Poland and Saxony, Peter worked at top speed to establish the bases for a powerful modern Empire in Russia. In his desperate need for metal from which to make new cannon, he ordered church bells cut down and collected for casting weapons. From all corners of Russia, he summoned new conscripts and began training them in European tactics. By the spring of 1701, he had a new army, equipped with some two hundred fifty siege guns, field pieces, and mortars.[15] With these new forces, he began to win back what he had lost and more. During the next three years, he seized most of Sweden's territory along the southern shore of the Finnish Gulf and the Baltic, while Charles basked in the false confidence that he could recapture it at will.

Peter was extremely fortunate that his foe made no effort to march against him at that time. Between 1705 and 1707, he was in no position to face any hostile foreign force because he was obliged to devote most of his resources to suppressing serious revolts within his domains. The revolts broke out in 1705 in the southeastern city of Astrakhan and spread quickly along the Volga to the Bashkirs, a people of Turkic origin, who opposed the extension of Imperial power into their homeland, continuing to resist until 1711.[16] Yet these revolts were of lesser consequence compared with the one that broke out among the Don Cossacks in 1707. Kondraty Bulavin was a Cossack chieftain who had fought in the campaigns against Azov. He was acutely aware of the great deeds of Stenka Razin, the rebel Cossack chieftain who had led a vast revolt against the Romanovs in the 1670s. "I am the direct heir of Stenka," he proclaimed to the Cossacks in 1707, "and I shall be your leader." Provoked by the government's persecution of Old Believers and its decision to hunt down runaway serfs among them, the Don Cossacks flocked to Bulavin's standard by the tens of thousands and occupied a large part of southern Russia for almost a year. Only in mid-1708 did Prince Vasilii Dolgorukii bring them to heel. In June, Bulavin shot himself; by the fall, the last of his followers had been dispersed, arrested, or hanged.[17]

It was not until the end of 1707 that Charles XII turned his attention to Peter's lands once again. By that time, Peter and his generals had restored internal peace and had built a much larger and more formidable army. During the decade after Narva, Peter was so desperately in need of funds to finance his growing army that he levied taxes on almost everything imaginable: mills, fisheries, harnesses, hats, boots, beehives, cellars, chimneys, bathhouses, bridges, ferries, ice storehouses, tallow, pitch, tar, horses, hides, and bread, just to name a few additions to the list of commodities already taxed. His taxes, although much resented, brought in the needed money. As a result, when he again faced Charles XII, his armies were four times larger than at Narva; they were better trained, better armed, better led, and more confident.

Anxious for final victory, Charles had left Saxony in late August to launch an attack against Russia. With his usual impatience, he had raced across Poland with an army of thirty-eight thousand combat-hardened, well-equipped veterans. By Christmas, he had reached the Vistula River in Poland. A month more, and he had crossed the Niemen and stormed Grodno, a strategic position from which he could turn north into Russia's newly won Baltic provinces or strike east toward Moscow itself. Charles chose the latter course, but, rather than press the Russians, he took up quarters near Minsk and remained there for more than three months to rest his troops. By early June, the Swedes were on the march again, eager for battle and new victories. Charles breached the Berezina River and entered Russia unopposed. Although his advance soon bogged down in muddy roads, he won further victories against the Russians at Golovchina and soon seized the important town of Mogilev. Everyone thought that he soon would dictate the terms of Russia's surrender in Moscow itself.[18]

Yet Charles's victory at Golovchina had not come easily, and the battle had been in doubt for several hours before the Swedes finally had broken Prince Nikita Repnin's left wing. From that, the Russians took heart. They had cause for greater rejoicing as the summer drew to a close. As they withdrew further into Russia, Peter's armies employed those scorched-earth tactics that later would serve so well against the armies of Napoleon and Hitler. Each foot of ground Charles seized was blackened and desolate. Each loaf of bread his soldiers ate could not be replaced, and each man who died from a Russian bullet or bayonet thrust reduced his effective combat force. At the same time, with all of Russia's material and human resources at his rear, Peter made good his losses and even increased the size of his armies.

Advancing over desolated terrain and running short of supplies and men, Charles placed his hopes for victory on two critical factors: the sixteen thousand troops and vast stores General Count Adam

Löwenhaupt held in Riga, and the men and supplies commanded by the Ukrainian Cossack Hetman Ivan Mazeppa. During 1707 and 1708, Mazeppa had secretly informed Stanisław Leszczynski, the man whom Charles had placed upon the Polish throne in place of Augustus II, that he was prepared to betray Peter in order to free the Ukraine from Russian rule.[19] To take advantage of Mazeppa's offer, Charles turned south from Mogilev to join him. At the same time, he ordered General Löwenhaupt to advance from Riga. Once he had effected a union of these forces and supplies, Charles planned to strike directly at Moscow in the spring of 1709.

At his King's command, Löwenhaupt raced south with his army and a great supply train, only to be intercepted by Peter at the village of Lesnaia in late September. Although outnumbered by the Swedes, the Russians won a brilliant victory. "During the entire day, it was impossible to see who would win the battle. But then, by the grace of God, the giver of victories, the enemy was smashed," Peter wrote exuberantly.[20] He later remarked that "this victory can be regarded as our first. Never before had we won such a triumph over regular troops with a force that was inferior in numbers to our enemy. Truly, it was the cause for all the successes which Russian arms have enjoyed since then."[21] Löwenhaupt's defeat denied Charles the supplies and replacements upon which he had counted so heavily. He now placed all his hopes upon the wily Mazeppa's ability to raise the Ukraine against his Russian lord and open its vast granaries to Sweden's troops. Charles continued his march south, always advancing over charred fields and through burning hamlets, his rear continually harassed by Russian cavalry. Grimly, his starving soldiers began to remark that they had three physicians—Dr. Vodka, Dr. Garlic, and Dr. Death—to succor them in their march.[22]

The sufferings of Charles's troops in the Ukraine during the bitter winter of 1708–9 left them vulnerable to disease and weakened their ability to face Peter's better-fed armies. Now Peter's troops had the impetus and enthusiasm the Swedes had lost. Buoyed by their victories, and further encouraged by news that only a handful of Ukrainians had followed Mazeppa into Charles's camp, Peter and his army anxiously awaited the arrival of spring. Summer brought the total defeat of

Charles's army at the historic battle of Poltava. All of Europe was stunned. The armies of the Muscovites, whom they had looked upon with disdain for so long, had defeated one of the world's greatest captains.[23] A new Great Power had arisen in Europe, one that boasted a larger army than that of any other European state and one that threatened to dominate the Baltic, where the Dutch, Swedes, and English had long held sway. Peter had "become formidable to his neighbors" and had "given the [Habsburg] Emperor and the maritime powers [of Europe] good reason to be envious," remarked Louix XIV's Minister of Foreign Affairs de Torcy.[24] Wrote the great philosopher Leibnitz, who in 1700 had predicted that Charles XII would seize Moscow and conquer all of Russia to the Amur River and the frontiers of China, Europe now "feared the extreme power of the Tsar, calling him the Turk of the North."[25]

Although Russia's victory at Poltava did not end the Great Northern War, it freed Peter from the immediate threat of Charles XII's armies and gave him a respite in which to attend to domestic affairs. During the next two years, he began to build St. Petersburg in earnest and gradually moved Russia's central administrative offices there from Moscow. He appointed Governors to head those new provinces he had established in 1708, and, since their major task was to oversee the collection of taxes and conscripts, he chose them from among his most capable assistants. To resolve one of Russia's most fundamental administrative problems—the fact that the Tsar held both supreme power and supreme executive authority—he established the Governing Senate, authorized it to make administrative decisions in his absence, and thereby freed Russia's daily administration from dependence upon his personal direction. Peter appointed nine senior statesmen to this new body in late February 1711. They were not among his closest confidants but were men of proven administrative ability and long governmental experience.[26]

The Governing Senate had an opportunity to exercise its new powers almost immediately. After his defeat at Poltava, Charles XII had taken refuge in the Ottoman Empire where, in league with the warlike Grand Vizir Baltadji Mahomet, he convinced the Sultan to declare war upon Russia. On November 20, 1710, the Ottoman Divan cast Russia's

Ambassador Petr Tolstoi into the dungeon of the Castle of the Seven Bastions and set out to recapture Azov and those southern territories Peter had wrested from them a decade earlier. Peter had no choice but to take the field once again. On February 25, he declared the Turks enemies of Christ, ordered General-Admiral Feodor Apraksin to strengthen Azov's defenses, and instructed his generals in the Ukraine to prepare for an attack against the Ottoman Empire. On March 2, he gave the Governing Senate its first instructions "to watch over expenditures throughout the entire state and . . . collect as much money as possible, because money is the artery of war."[27] Four days later, he began his ill-fated campaign on the Pruth River.

Peter planned to strike boldly into Ottoman territory to prevent a Turkish attack on the Ukraine or against Azov. It was an aggressive plan, but its success depended upon the willingness of Orthodox Christians to rise up against their Turkish masters in the Danubian principalities of Wallachia and Moldavia. Since the leading Orthodox Christians had been calling for such a campaign for a number of years, Peter had every anticipation of success. Yet he failed to receive the support he expected. As a result, the early days of July found him and his army on the banks of the Pruth River, without supplies and surrounded by a Turko-Tatar army that outnumbered them five to one. The victor of Poltava found himself in very real danger of becoming a Turkish captive.

Even while staring into the jaws of ignominious defeat, Peter was touched by the hand of fortune. His troops had inflicted such terrible losses upon the Turks in their desperate fighting that the Sultan's elite janissaries refused to attack again. Apprehensive about these rebellious troops and fearful that General Ronne's Russian cavalry might attack his rear after their victory at Braïla, the Grand Vizir agreed to a truce that Peter had proposed at Catherine's urging. So desperate was Peter's situation on July 10, 1711, that he was prepared to surrender Azov and all other fortifications in the south, return all of the Baltic provinces except for Ingria and St. Petersburg to the Swedes, and even pay a quarter of a million rubles in bribes to the Grand Vizir and his advisers.[28] But the wily Baron Petr Shafirov, whom Peter sent as his emissary to the Grand Vizir, found it necessary to pay only a fraction of that price. He had only to surrender Azov, destroy Taganrog and the fortresses he had built along the Turkish frontier, grant Charles XII safe conduct to Sweden, and agree not to interfere in Polish affairs.[29] Peter ordered Shafirov to sign the treaty immediately. The next day, he led his army back into Russia, saved from utter humiliation by clever negotiations and the Turks' ignorance of his true plight. Shafirov and Field Marshal Sheremetiev's son were obliged to remain with the Turks as surety that the Russians would fulfill their commitments. It was more than eighteen months before they were permitted to return to Russia.

Although the Great Northern War dragged on for another decade after Peter's defeat on the Pruth, no more major battles were fought on Russian soil. In 1713, Russian armies occupied much of Finland, and, the next summer, Peter's new Baltic fleet won a brilliant victory off Cape Hangö. Soon afterward, Russian troops occupied the Åland Islands, which put them within fifteen miles of Stockholm itself. Anxious to join a winning cause, Friedrich Wilhelm I of Prussia and George I (as Elector of Hanover, not as King of England) declared war upon Sweden. But their support for Peter's cause was brief. Long before Charles XII was shot through the head at Fredrikshald in December 1718, it was obvious that Peter's new Russia had replaced Sweden as the greatest power in the Baltic region. Apprehensive about Russia's growing might during the summer of 1719, George I concluded a separate peace with the Swedes; Prussia and Denmark followed his example before the middle of 1720, leaving Peter to face Sweden alone once again. England's fear of Peter's Imperial aspirations in the Baltic had become so great that George I even sent an English fleet under Admiral Norris in 1720 with orders to cooperate with the Swedish navy in an effort to force Peter to accept England's mediation. Peter's response was to send Brigadier Iurii von Mengden to burn almost fifty Swedish towns and hamlets while Admiral Norris was staging a show of strength before Russia's Baltic port of Reval.[30]

Not easily intimidated, Peter was determined to establish Russia's supremacy on the Baltic to supplant the power the English and the Dutch had exercised for more than a century. "England has permitted the Tsar to win vast conquests, and to consolidate his position on the Baltic," Lord Stanhope remarked grandly to Feodor Veselovskii, Russia's representative in London. "England has allowed His Majesty the Tsar to undertake these conquests because she could not stop him from doing so," was Veselovskii's confident reply.[31] At the beginning of 1721, the French Ambassador to Sweden succeeded in arranging a peace conference at Nystadt. Negotiations dragged on for months while Europe's Great Powers tried to convince Russia's diplomats that some of the lands they had won must be returned to Sweden. "God would punish me if I should give away any of the fruits which my Empire has won by so much blood, pain, and treasure simply to please another," Peter replied. To which Prince Menshikov added, "The Tsar will not cede [to Sweden] one inch of soil in Livonia or Estonia, and [in the direction of Finland] he does not want to look out upon the territory of his neighbor from his own window."[32]

On August 30, 1721, Peter's representatives signed the Treaty of Nystadt by which Sweden recognized Russia's preeminent position in the Baltic. Yet Peter did far more than establish Russia as a major force in European affairs during the last decade of his reign. Between 1715 and 1725, he constructed the domestic supports for the Empire he proclaimed after his victory over Sweden. If Russia were to support the military colossus her newly proclaimed Emperor had created and if the government were to look after the welfare of Russians as he envisioned, a far more sophisticated central administration was needed. Peter assigned Heinrich Fick, a former Holstein official, and the Baron Johann von Luberas to study the problem. Both were authorities on the collegial form of government that functioned in Sweden and a number of other Northern European countries at the time, and Peter had chosen them for that reason. For he fully shared Leibnitz's opinion that "there cannot be good administration without the [administrative] colleges. Their mechanism is like that of watches, whose wheels mutually keep each other in movement."[33] After Fick, Luberas, and several others had studied the Russian situation, Peter established in 1717 nine administrative colleges for foreign affairs, state revenue, justice, state control, the army, the navy, commerce, state expenditures, and mining and industry. Responsible for one major area of administration, each was directed by a board of eleven members including a president, a vice-president, and a foreign adviser.[34] Three more colleges would be added later. They would comprise the fundamental units of Russia's central administration for the rest of the eighteenth century.

Peter then turned to an equally critical area of domestic affairs. Strained almost to the breaking point by the cost of his military ventures, Russia's finances were in catastrophic disarray. The household tax, collected from each peasant household, and the basic source of state revenue in the seventeenth century, could no longer provide the great sums Peter's new state required, especially since peasants had begun to merge their households in order to evade taxation.[35] Peter had tried to offset these difficulties by levying a greater number of indirect taxes, but they were even more difficult to collect. If Russia was to have sufficient revenue to meet the Tsar's demands, a new tax base was needed and the population must be fixed more firmly to the areas in which they lived so that taxes could be collected more readily. In 1718 Peter therefore introduced the head tax (*podushnaia podal*), which was a tax levied upon each male peasant rather than upon households. Before implementing this new tax, Peter ordered a complete census of all Russian peasants and other lower classes subject to the tax, "not excluding the oldest men to the very latest infants."[36] Begun in early 1719, the census was completed four years later. Its most important result was to tie the masses even more firmly to the estates upon which they resided and strengthen further the bonds of serfdom in Russia. The head tax almost tripled Russia's revenue from direct taxes. The price the Empire's peasant masses were forced to pay for Peter's success was the loss of their last vestiges of freedom.

Especially during the last half of his reign, Peter attempted to develop an industrial establishment to produce such essential products as iron, cloth, and weapons in an effort to free Russia from that economic and technological dependence upon Europe that had characterized the first century of Romanov rule. At first, he emphasized those industries directly related to Russia's military needs with the result that, by 1715, his army had about thirteen thousand cannon of Russian manufacture, and, by 1720, Russia's armaments industry was producing about twenty thousand muskets a year. At the same time his efforts to develop an iron industry in the Urals were so successful that, by 1780, Russia would become Europe's leading producer of pig iron. In other areas, however, Russians proved reluctant to embark upon new ventures even though Peter offered them generous grants of serf labor, subsidies, and tax exemptions. Merchants' still-medieval attitudes made them fear the risks involved, and the profit motive that was so much a part of industrial expansion in the West remained foreign to them for decades to come. Peter often resorted to coercion, but with mixed results at best.[37]

That neither his administrative reforms nor his efforts to stimulate Russia's industrial development were as successful as Peter had hoped was partially due to the widespread corruption and inefficiency among those upon whom he was obliged to rely to implement his orders and decrees. Corruption in government was sanctified by centuries of Muscovite tradition and even made necessary by the miserable salaries state officials received. As a result, Peter never even attempted to stamp out bribery, and, like those Romanovs who came before and after, he tended to regard it as a necessary evil. Yet he did try to punish those who embezzled state funds on a massive scale. He established a corps of special agents, known as *fiskali*, whom he charged with uncovering tax evasion and corruption. As a result of his efforts, Prince Gagarin, Governor of Siberia, who was notorious for the blatant manner in which he filled his wallet from the public coffers, died on the gallows, and a number of others suffered a similar fate. Yet corruption was too deeply rooted to be routed out, even by such extraordinary measures. Some of Peter's closest associates ranked among Russia's greatest embezzlers, and Menshikov was the most notorious of them all. Even two of Peter's chief *fiskali*, Aleksei Kurbatov and Aleksei Nesterov, were executed for embezzlement toward the end of his reign.

If Peter could not deal with corruption successfully, he also could not remedy the chronic shortage of officials that plagued his efforts to modernize Russia. He never was able to establish an effective system of education, and, even though the number of officials had increased significantly during the seventeenth century, there were not nearly enough to meet the needs of the more complex state Peter had created.[38] Most significant, perhaps, this shortage of officials made it impossible for Peter to extend his administration effectively beyond St. Petersburg, Moscow, and a few other centers in Russia. He had to rely upon military agents to carry out his decrees on a sporadic basis, and this simple fact limited his theoretically autocratic power and made it difficult for him to impose his will upon increasingly obdurate and often resentful subjects.

Peter nevertheless sought to draft Russia's entire population into the service of their country. The peasants provided the manpower for his army, the money to support it, and the labor for agriculture and industry, while he called upon the nobility to staff his officer corps and administration. Peasant and noble alike were obliged to serve Russia throughout their adult lives. Peter made it possible even for peasants to become ennobled for meritorious service. By doing so, he changed the composition of Russia's noble class dramatically and firmly tied noble status to service in Russia's military or civil offices.

There has been continued and impassioned debate among historians about whether the many changes Peter imposed upon Russia were good or evil, successes or failures, reformist or revolutionary, and the passage of more than two and a half centuries since his death still has not resolved the issue. One thing, however, is certainly clear. Peter was the first of the Romanovs to establish Russia's Imperial aspirations. When he died in 1725, Muscovite Russia had broken out of the Asiatic mold Europeans had cast about her and had achieved full recognition as a European power. During the rest of the century, Russia and the Romanovs would seek to maintain this new and awesome status and integrate it into the ever-changing and increasingly complex fabric of European international politics.

After Peter's dynamic and tempestuous reign, those of his successors over the next four decades seem pallid and unassertive, and the rapidity with which the throne changed hands has made it appear as if state policy was formed and applied in a hit-or-miss fashion. Yet there was a certain continuity in domestic and foreign policy during the "Era of Palace Revolutions," as it has often been called by historians. During these years, the army and bureaucracy Peter had established developed a set of principles that diverged sharply from his insistence that all Russians must serve their country. At the same time, Russia continued to strengthen her Great Power status, largely through the efforts of the statesmen Baron Andrei Ostermann and Aleksei Bestuzhev. Although they were bitter political rivals, their policies were remarkably similar, and they were especially important in determining the contours of Russia's foreign policy between 1725 and 1761.

Baron Ostermann had filled a variety of diplomatic posts under Peter and had been Count Jacob Bruce's deputy at the Nystadt negotiations. Catherine I appointed him Vice-Chancellor, and he soon supplanted Count Golovkin as her chief adviser on foreign affairs. Despite several changes in sovereigns, he continued to direct Russia's foreign policy until Elizabeth seized the throne at the end of 1741. To pursue a consistent policy was no easy task at the Courts of Catherine I, Peter II, and Anna, for these were hotbeds of intrigue in which one false step could bring disgrace and exile as foreign agents plotted to bring men favorable to their countries' interests into positions of power and influence. To survive in this atmosphere, any minister had to be a consummate intriguer, and Ostermann played that part with rare virtuosity. The fundamental elements of his policy were close alliance with Austria, continued enmity toward France, and, for most of the time, a hostile attitude toward England, who had allied herself with France by the Treaty of Herrenhausen in September 1725. Both England and France sought a Russian alliance to counterbalance the combination Austria and Spain had forged at the Treaty of Vienna in 1725, but Ostermann feared France's interests in Poland, Sweden, and the Ottoman Empire, and was equally wary of Britain's designs in the Baltic. Therefore, he sought to counterbalance them by maintaining a close alliance with their enemies.

During his first years as Russia's Vice-Chancellor, Ostermann's most pressing concerns were to limit his country's involvement in North German affairs, to end her conflict with Persia, and to broaden her diplomatic alliance system with the West. He succeeded in all three areas. The death of Catherine I and Peter II's decision to exile Menshikov removed much of the pressure at the Russian Court for involvements in Holstein and Courland and thus enabled Ostermann to withdraw somewhat from that area. By 1735 he had managed to end the Russo-Persian War, even though the price was Russia's temporary abandonment of Peter's policy of expansion in the Caspian region. In broadening the base of Russia's diplomatic alliances with the West, Ostermann was perhaps most successful of all. He defended Russia's alliance with Austria in view of the increasing tensions in his country's relations with the Ottoman Empire and Poland. But the Treaty of Seville, by which Spain agreed in 1729 to recognize England's occupation of Gibraltar, and Austria's ratification of that agreement in 1731 in return for England's support of the Pragmatic Sanction, by which Charles VI had in 1713 proclaimed the indivisibility of Habsburg lands, muted some of the more rigid diplomatic divisions that had characterized European affairs since the mid-1720s. This, and his decision to withdraw Russia from Persia, made it possible for Ostermann to establish better relations with England, while the Empress Anna's willingness to abandon Holstein's claims to Schleswig meant that Russia was able to sign a mutual-assistance treaty with Denmark in 1731.[39] As a result of Ostermann's policies, Russia enjoyed a stable and broadly based diplomatic position when new wars loomed on the horizon.

When the pro-Russian Polish King Augustus II died in 1733, his subjects stood evenly divided in support of his son, Friedrich Augustus, and Stanislaw Leszczynski who, with the support of Sweden, had occupied Poland's throne between 1707 and 1709. Leszczynski's daughter had married France's King Louis XV, and, with the support of Poland's Catholic Primate Teodor Potocki, France engineered Leszczynski's election as King.[40] Ostermann and his supporters viewed Leszczynski's restoration as a dangerous threat because it promised to strengthen France's influence on Russia's western borders. Therefore, they urged the Empress Anna to send her armies under General Count Peter Lacy into Poland in support of Friedrich Augustus's claim to his father's throne. Within a week, Lacy proclaimed him King Augustus III and drove Leszczynski to seek refuge in Danzig. Lacy's army then laid siege to the city. It fell in June 1734. Although Leszczynski managed to escape disguised as a peasant, the French threat in Poland was ended for more than a decade.[41]

While Anna's armies were occupied in Poland, the Turks encouraged their Tatar allies to send raiding parties into Russia's southern frontier settlements. Field Marshal Count Münnich convinced the Empress that Russia must retaliate, and, over Ostermann's objections, she declared war on the Tatars in the summer of 1735 and upon the

Ottoman Empire a few months later.[42] Russia's armies invaded the Crimea, stormed the defenses of Perekop, and sacked the Tatar capital of Bakhchisarai. Yet hopes for a brief and decisive war died quickly as the gross ineptitude of Russia's commissariat negated the victories of her troops and caused the war to drag on until September 1739. In making the peace, Russia regained Azov, but had to agree not to maintain a navy on the Black Sea.[43] Such meager results hardly justified the loss of some one hundred thousand men. Ostermann's inability to overcome the bellicosity of such hotheads as Münnich had proved costly indeed.

Coming on the heels of the Empress Anna's death in October 1740, Elizabeth's palace revolution caused a temporary paralysis of policy in St. Petersburg as the new Empress sought to organize her government and bring under control the freewheeling intrigue that had flourished at Court. Yet a conspiracy had brought her to power, and two of her closest collaborators, Lestocq and la Chétardie, had been agents of France. These men sought to drive Ostermann from power in order to draw Russia away from his anti-French alliance system. Ostermann therefore was arrested during the night of Elizabeth's coup d'état and sent to Siberia soon afterward. Nonetheless, despite their best efforts, France's agents could not destroy the alliance system Ostermann had forged. In his place, Elizabeth appointed Count Aleksei Bestuzhev, whose foreign policy had an equally strong anti-French focus. In addition, he favored a close alliance with Austria and England and opposed the expansionist ambitions of Prussia. Yet he found it difficult to express his convictions openly at first because of the influence Lestocq and la Chétardie exercised over the Empress. Patiently and carefully, Bestuzhev worked against them behind the scenes for over two years.[44]

Bestuzhev's opportunity to destroy la Chétardie came in 1742, when France refused Elizabeth's request to mediate the conflict that had recently broken out between Russia and Sweden. The French Minister Cardinal Amelot had in fact reprimanded la Chétardie sharply for speaking on Elizabeth's behalf. "I cannot reconcile your recommendations with the knowledge of His Majesty's views on this subject that you most assuredly possess," he wrote. "Nor can I reconcile it with your frequent reports on the poor state of the Muscovite army, which lacks even the basic necessities, and which, in your opinion, would certainly suffer defeat in its first encounter with the Swedes."[45] Unable to move his government to support the Russians, la Chétardie tried to win Bestuzhev over to the cause of the Swedes by offering him an annual bribe of some fifteen thousand livres. To his amazement, Bestuzhev refused and told him that he would not consent to ceding "one inch of Russian territory to the Swedes."[46] La Chétardie and Lestocq then decided to arrange for Bestuzhev to suffer Ostermann's fate. Supported by the Grand Duke Peter's Holstein advisers Bergholtz and Brümmer, the Prussian Ambassador, and the Grand Duchess Catherine's mother, the Princess Johanna, they felt confident of success. They did not know that Bestuzhev had deciphered the code la Chétardie had used in corresponding with Amelot. Although he found a wealth of incriminating material in la Chétardie's reports, he had decided to play a waiting game; in June 1744, when the quantity of evidence had become overwhelming, he quietly gave decoded copies of the letters to Elizabeth who, in a rage, drove la Chétardie from Russia within twenty-four hours. Elizabeth's disillusionment with la Chétardie was so bitter that she never again permitted a foreigner to gain a decisive voice in Russian affairs. At the same time, the Prussian influence represented by Brümmer, Bergholtz, and the Princess Johanna also collapsed when Elizabeth expelled them from Russia soon after la Chétardie.

Elizabeth recognized Bestuzhev's victory over the French and Prussian cabal that had intrigued against him by elevating him to the office of Chancellor. He then began to press his own policy, which he defined as mere elaborations upon the "system of Peter the Great" in an effort to appeal to Elizabeth's avowed ambition to rule in the spirit of her father, and modestly expressed his views in muted marginal comments the Empress later could claim as her own. There was little to be gained, Bestuzhev insisted, from an alliance with Prussia, England's enemy at the time. "Experience has shown us that the King of Prussia rarely keeps to his word, that he does not observe his commitments, and that, therefore, one can place little faith in his lavish flattery," he warned Elizabeth. Therefore, he concluded that Russia ought to take a firm stand against Prussia, but that, above all, she should draw closer to England. "The English buy and sell goods worth more than a million rubles here every year, and, because they buy more than they sell, this means that more than a half-million rubles' profit remains in Russia," he wrote, adding that: "Peter the Great was so convinced of the need for continuing friendship with England that, even during his dispute with King George I [as Elector of Hanover] over Mecklenberg, he always sought to preserve friendly relations with England."[47] Only toward the middle of the second decade of Elizabeth's reign did Bestuzhev's quest for this alliance succeed. On September 19, 1755, an Anglo-Russian agreement was signed. Russia agreed to station fifty-five thousand troops on her western frontiers to be available to defend the continental possessions of George II. In return, England agreed to pay Russia an annual subsidy of one hundred thousand pounds sterling, which would be raised to five hundred thousand pounds if the troops actually marched beyond Russia's frontiers.[48]

Rather than cementing Bestuzhev's system, his new alliance with England proved his undoing, for he had become blinded to the great and critical turns that European diplomatic alignments were about to take. In January of 1756, England formed an alliance with Prussia in the treaty of Westminster, and the Treaty of Versailles bound France and Austria together in May of the same year. This new alignment of the West's leading states meant that Bestuzhev's system suddenly became filled with destructive contradictions. If the Austrian alliance were preserved, it meant also alignment with Russia's traditional enemy France. Yet, if his newly drafted Anglo-Russian alliance remained, it meant that Russia also must ally with Prussia, whose King, Bestuzhev still believed, was unalterably opposed to Russia's interests in Constantinople, Sweden, and North Europe. He continued to press his pro-English views, but, in August 1756, the Prussian King Frederick invaded Saxony with the support of England, an act Russia could not leave unchallenged. Russia now was driven into the Austro-French camp to enter the Seven Years' War against Prussia and England. Bestuzhev's system crumbled. In February 1758, he was accused of conspiring to overthrow the Empress, arrested, and sent into exile.[49]

Russia's performance in the Seven Years' War strengthened the reputation her armies had won under Peter the Great. In the summer of 1757, General Stepan Apraksin's armies poured into East Prussia and defeated the Prussians at Gross-Jägersdorf, but glacially slow supply services, poor transportation, and disease forced him to withdraw into Poland for the winter. The next spring, this time under General Count William Fermor, the Russian army again stormed into East Prussia to capture the city of Königsberg. Fermor then turned to besiege the fortress of Cüstrin, but was amazed to learn that Frederick the Great had raced north by forced marches and was about to attack him with his entire army. The two armies met at Zorndorf in one of the bloodiest battles of the eighteenth century, in which the Prussians lost twelve thousand killed and wounded, and the Russians lost almost twice that number. The battle was indecisive, although it was celebrated as a great victory in St. Petersburg.[50] Like Apraksin, Fermor was obliged to shorten his supply lines and withdrew into Poland for the winter.

The campaigns of 1759, 1760, and 1761 followed similar patterns. Fermor was replaced in 1759 by General Count Petr Saltykov who, in 1760, relinquished his command to Field Marshal Count Aleksandr Buturlin. Buturlin, in turn, was saved from disgrace only by Elizabeth's death on Christmas Day, 1761. During the last three years of the war, all three generals won important battles; yet Russia never was able to follow up these victories. It was on the diplomatic front that Frederick really began to lose the war. When George II died in October 1760 and William Pitt resigned a year later, Frederick lost his two major allies in England. By the end of 1761, he stood virtually alone against France, Austria, and Russia, while Russian Cossacks ranged over his eastern lands, wreaking havoc and destruction as they went.

At the last moment, Frederick was snatched from the jaws of certain defeat by Russia's new Emperor Peter III, who could not bear to be at war with the man he often called "the King, my master."[51] When Frederick's emissary, Colonel Baron Goltz, arrived in St. Petersburg, Peter insisted that Frederick should draft the peace treaty himself. Frederick did so gladly, sending him a treaty that returned to Prussia everything Russia's troops had won during the previous five years. Wrote Frederick to his new ally: "Adjust this proposal as you see fit. I shall sign everything, because what benefits you shall also benefit me."

"I was in despair about my situation when I found a true and faithful friend in Europe's greatest monarch," he confided.[52] To be called "Europe's greatest monarch" by his idol sent Peter III into ecstasy. Senselessly, he signed the treaty Frederick had drafted, which cost Russia all of the gains she had won at the cost of great sacrifice and suffering.

Despite Peter's disgraceful treaty with Prussia, the Seven Years' War reminded Europe's rulers and statesmen of Russia's military might, and it raised her prestige to greater heights. As they would do again during the second quarter of the nineteenth century, Europeans overlooked the vast supply problems and the timid generalship that characterized Russia's military ventures, and remembered only the victories. Most of all, they remembered with fear and awe the tread of Russian troops along the streets of Berlin. These armies were the product of that social and political order Peter the Great and his successors had forged; we should examine more closely how this order evolved at home.

At the time of Peter's death in 1725, the nobility included at least three groups hostile to each other's social position and political aspirations. For a time those great Muscovite *boiar* families, whose monopoly on political power and social prominence had been critically weakened by Peter's reforms, attempted to recoup their former grandeur in such a way as to threaten other noble groups in Russia. Likewise, those "new men" who had risen from obscure beginnings to great heights under Peter defended their position against the old *boiars* who bitterly resented their presence close to the throne. Finally, Peter's emphasis upon achievement over birth had enabled tens of thousands of Russians to rise into the noble class. While there had been approximately thirty thousand heads of noble families in Russia in 1689, there were approximately two hundred thousand in 1725, and all of them intended to keep their newly won privileges and prominence.

In the political and social turmoil of the next years, the *boiars* employed their traditional tactics of Court intrigue, while Russia's noble newcomers defended their interests by using as a political instrument those Guards regiments that so often had been their initial vehicle for upward social and political mobility. The "new men" dominated the events that led to the elevation of Catherine I as Empress because they were able to enlist the support of the rank-and-file nobility in the Guards, while the *boiars* began to reassert themselves during the reign of Peter II. The succession crisis of 1730 found the *boiars* and the Petrine nobility more evenly matched. The *boiars* dominated the Supreme Privy Council and convinced Anna to sign the famous "Conditions" as their price for offering her the crown. But the Petrine nobility controlled the Imperial Guards and soon used them to destroy the oligarchical order the *boiars* had established. Indeed, the victory of the Petrine nobility in 1730 marked the end of the *boiars'* efforts to reassert their former preeminence. Gradually, they made common cause with those "new men" whom they had so despised in the years immediately after Peter's death. Between 1730 and 1762, a more unified nobility therefore emerged in Russia, and its formerly fragmented elements began to assert their newfound power against the Autocrat.

During the "Era of Palace Revolutions," Russia's nobles tried most of all to increase their privileges and reduce the onerous demands Peter had imposed upon them as the price of noble status. They also obtained greater control over the enserfed population on their estates. These trends complemented each other and enabled them to become masters of the Russian countryside while the Autocrat remained mistress of the Empire. So many were the concessions they obtained from their eighteenth-century Empresses that historians sometimes refer to the last three-quarters of the century as the "era of gentry monarchy."

Despite their increased privileges and authority, the life of the nobility was not without problems. Most important, their traditional system of inheritance, which made it customary for all noble children to inherit a portion of their father's lands, had the very negative consequence of rapidly fragmenting their estates. Peter had attempted to halt this process by his *maiorat* law of March 23, 1714, in which he decreed that a nobleman could have only one heir, but the rank-and-file nobility remained bitterly opposed and demanded its repeal soon after Anna arrived in Moscow. Anna abolished the *maiorat* at the end of 1730, and permitted the process of fragmentation to begin anew.[53] Especially in the Empire's western provinces, large numbers of nobles became impoverished as a result. Catherine the Great and her son Paul I granted large quantities of Crown lands and serfs to their noble servitors in a futile attempt to offset this process, but the impoverished noble, who owned less than twenty male serfs, soon became commonplace in Russia.[54]

Increased access to education and promotion, and the right to dispose of their estates as they saw fit, were important benefits the nobility obtained from the Empress Anna during the first years of her reign. Their central demand for emancipation from compulsory lifetime service, however, struck directly at the heart of the system Peter the Great had established. This was a concession Anna was reluctant to grant because she feared it would reduce Russia's already inadequate corps of state officials and military officers. Yet there were other factors, in addition to the selfish demands of the nobility, that obliged her to consider at least limiting her nobles' terms of service and freeing some of them altogether.

By the mid-1730s, it had become clear to Anna and her counselors that many estates were on the verge of ruin. Obliged to be away from their homes for years at a time, noblemen had left their lands in the hands of bailiffs, who often had proven incompetent or corrupt. As a result, large sums of tax payments never reached the Imperial treasury. Especially after famine struck large areas of Russia in 1733–34, large bands of peasants turned from farming to brigandage, murdering and stealing in order to stay alive.[55] Unable to extend the authority of Russia's central government into the countryside because officials were in such short supply, Anna decided to make the nobility responsible for tax collection, recruit levies, and law and order. At the end of 1736, she therefore decreed that, once the war with Turkey had ended, "whoever has two or more sons may choose one of them to remain at home to tend to the management of the family estate" and that the others would be obliged to serve for only twenty-five years. "All noble youths between the ages of seven and twenty must devote themselves to their studies, and each must serve for twenty-five years beginning at the age of twenty," she decreed.[56] The nobles had achieved their first breach in the state organization Peter the Great had built upon the conviction that all men must serve Russia as long as they lived.

Peter the Great had instituted his regime of compulsory service because Russia's nobles had not yet developed the Western attitude that service to one's country was a fundamental attribute of noble status. By the end of the Russo-Turkish War, the harness he had buckled upon them still fit the nobles awkwardly, and they chafed at its restraints. They longed to return to their estates, far from the troublesome pressures that life in the army, the bureaucracy, and St. Petersburg heaped upon them. When Anna's decree went into effect, they petitioned for retirement in droves. Wrote General Manstein:

> No sooner was this ordinance published than the number of petitioners was infinite. Half at least of the officers presented petitions for leave to resign, each pretending to have served above twenty years. There were instances of young men who were scarce past thirty, that insisted on their discharge; for having, at the age of ten or twelve years, had their names enrolled in some regiment, they reckoned the time of their service from that date. Several even who had not a farthing in their purses, still preferred cultivating their fields with their own hands, to military service.[57]

Faced with this deluge of petitions, Anna hastened to limit her initial decree. She insisted that the twenty-five-year limit applied only to active service and that some of it had to be in the military forces. Men in Russia's civil service had to serve an additional ten years, an indication, perhaps, that the Russian government suffered an even more acute shortage of men who were literate enough to wield a pen than of men able to wield a sword.[58]

In 1739 Russia's westernization process had not yet made a deep enough impression upon the nobility to oblige them to serve voluntarily, but the roots were there and bore fruit in another quarter-century. Especially as a consequence of serving in St. Petersburg and Moscow, and in such Western lands as Poland and Prussia, Russian noblemen acquired the habit of looking to the West for their patterns of behavior, and lost contact with the more traditional Russian countryside.[59] By the end of Elizabeth's reign, many of them had acquired a taste for the style of life that could be found only in St. Petersburg or Moscow. To leave the service meant to return to an isolated and deadening provincial existence.

Because Russia's nobles had altered their view of service so dramatically during the reign of Elizabeth, her nephew and successor Peter III felt confident enough to take the final step in their emancipation. On January 17, 1762, at ten o'clock in the morning, he and a large suite of dignitaries crossed the frozen Neva River to the building that housed Russia's central administrative colleges. There, in the presence of the Empire's Senators and other high officials, Peter signed a brief decree of only nine paragraphs to free the nobility from all compulsory service.[60] A month and a day later, on February 18, the decree was published and became law. "I cannot describe what great joy this document produced in the hearts of all nobles of our beloved homeland," wrote one contemporary.[61] Yet Russia's nobles rejoiced not because an onerous burden had been lifted from their shoulders but because they regarded Peter III's decree as recognition of their status as true noblemen who served not as slaves but freely and willingly like their Western counterparts.[62]

Destruction of the concept of universal service upon which Peter the Great had built his new state earlier in the century brought no improvement in the lives of the other major social group from whom he had required lifelong service, the serfs. Indeed, the four decades during which the nobility had sought their own emancipation had seen the bonds of serfdom tighten. In law, the Russian nobleman had come to possess all but the power of life and death over his serfs; in practice, he often claimed that as well. Short of purchasing his freedom, which required a great deal of money as well as his master's consent, perhaps the only legal means by which a serf could escape from bondage during the reign of Peter the Great had been by voluntary enlistment in the army. In 1727 Catherine I revoked that right; other restrictive measures followed. In 1736 masters were allowed to punish captured runaways as they saw fit, and, a year later, serfs were forbidden to purchase land except in the name of their masters and with their masters' permission. So low had Russia's serfs sunk in status that, when Elizabeth ascended the throne, she did not even require them to take an oath of allegiance. She no longer considered them subjects; they were chattels of their lords. Finally, in 1760, noble masters received the right to exile serfs to Siberia without government approval.[63] Until that time, only the Autocrat had possessed the power to send men and women into exile.

According to Russian law and tradition, masters owned not the persons of their serfs but the land to which they were bound. Decrees of the Empresses Catherine I, Anna, and Elizabeth blurred that fine distinction so that nobles could sell their serfs in much the same manner as plantation owners in the American South sold their slaves. Noble lords also could dictate whom their serfs married, and some of them began to breed serfs in much the same manner as they bred horses and cattle. At the same time, in order to pay the rising costs of their cultural westernization, nobles increased the obligations their serfs were bound to pay. Most important of all, perhaps, they established a claim upon their bondsmen's resources and incomes that took precedence over that of the government. In matters of tax collection and other feudal duties, the nobles took their share first and the state received what remained.[64]

Peter the Great had imposed unprecedented burdens upon his subjects, and only his monumental presence had made it certain that enough of them would obey his will to enable him to transform Russia into a Great European Power. But his effort left his nation exhausted and his people confused, with no clear sense of direction. Under a succession of weak rulers between 1725 and 1762, Russians had come to terms with a new system of government, a new and foreign culture, and a way of life that was based upon technology more than ever before. Nobles had to function effectively within an entirely new framework of values that were often unclear to them, while peasants had to reconcile themselves to a more rigid and exploitative social and economic order than any they had known before. By 1762 Russians had made considerable progress toward adjusting their lives and values to these new demands. But, in doing so, they had changed the nature of Peter's system significantly. No eighteenth-century Romanov better understood the intricate balance required to keep this domestic order functioning than did Catherine the Great. She also understood the importance of raising Russia's status in Europe.

"Peace is essential to this vast Empire," Catherine wrote a few years before she became Russia's Empress. "Peace will bring us greater esteem than the always ruinous uncertainties of war."[65] As Empress, she failed to shield her subjects from the pain and uncertainties of war, but she began her reign on a note of peace. On June 28, 1762, she canceled the absurd declaration of war against Denmark that Peter III had so foolishly proclaimed a month earlier in a pointless effort to win Schleswig for his native Duchy of Holstein. Well aware that Peter's war had nothing to do with Russia's foreign or domestic interests, Catherine instructed Baron Nikolai Korf, her ambassador in Copenhagen, to tell King Frederick V that the interests of Holstein would no longer be a factor in determining Russia's relations with Denmark. "Not only the Court, but all the people in those Danish provinces through which I traveled, were filled with joy at this unexpected turn of events," Korf later wrote. "They reacted very differently, however, in Berlin and Brandenburg when they learned of Your Majesty's accession. There, the terror was so great that they moved the Royal treasury to Magdeburg under the cover of night." [66]

Korf's report capsulized the broad range of Europeans' reactions to Catherine's accession. While the Danes were delighted to be freed from a war they did not want, Frederick the Great feared that Prussia might suffer severe consequences from the fall of that Emperor who had so foolishly signed a peace with his Prussian enemies while his armies had been marching to victory in the Seven Years' War. Certainly, the activities of Field Marshal Saltykov had given Frederick good cause for alarm. As part of the peace he had concluded with Prussia at the beginning of 1762, Peter III had ordered Saltykov to abandon the offensive positions he had held at the time of Elizabeth's death and to consider his armies under Frederick's command. Saltykov had moved his troops slowly and with reluctance. The moment he heard of Peter's overthrow, he reoccupied his former battle lines and waited orders to attack the Prussians once more. He soon was disappointed, and Frederick immensely relieved. Catherine had no intention of beginning the war again, for she wanted peace abroad in order to consolidate her political position at home. Frederick hastened to congratulate her on her accession and to express his hope that "the agreement and likemindedness, which has [recently] been established between our two nations," would be preserved.[67]

Frederick's relief at Catherine's decision not to reopen hostilities was soon tempered by disappointment. For, if she did not intend to take the field against Elizabeth's sworn enemy, she also was unwilling to join him in battle against Austria. The treaty by which Peter III had agreed to commit Russia's armies against Austria had not yet been signed when he was overthrown, and Catherine made it clear that she had no intention of ratifying that part of her husband's folly either. She therefore concluded a defensive alliance with Frederick, but refused to make any agreements that might force Russia to commit her armies anywhere in the West. Nevertheless, the basis for Russo-Prussian cooperation had been established. In another decade, it would produce its first fruit, as Catherine and Frederick joined in seizing portions of Poland to satisfy their Imperial ambitions.

Cautious and correct in her relations with Frederick the Great, Catherine followed a similar policy with other European powers. The Austrians were anxious to reestablish the ties that had grown so strong under the tutelage of the Empress Elizabeth and her Chancellor Bestuzhev. Less than three weeks after Catherine had seized Russia's crown, the Austrian Empress Maria Theresa penned a personal note to congratulate her new sister sovereign on her accession and to confide that "I most ardently desire to have an opportunity to provide proofs of my [warm] feelings to Your Majesty."[68] Catherine responded with equal warmth. "Nothing could have given me more pleasure than to receive your protestations of friendship," she replied. "I hope soon to give you proof of my friendship, especially because this friendship is confirmed by our common interests."[69] Yet Catherine refrained from making any offensive comitments to other powers until she could determine where Russia's true interests lay.

During the first months of her reign, she found fertile soil for her policy of peace in England as well. England's commercial interests had suffered severely during the Seven Years' War, and the British looked to Catherine to play an active role in reestablishing peace, despite the desires of Prussia to continue the conflict. "There could not be a more natural alliance than one between Britain and Russia," England's ministers told Catherine's Ambassador Count Aleksandr Vorontsov, as they assured him that "all territorial gains made by the Russian Empire, and every increase in its prestige in Europe, could only be agreeable to the King of England and advantageous to Great Britain in general."[70] Despite these assurances, Catherine held back from committing Russia to a full alliance. "Given the undefined nature of European affairs at the moment, we must adopt caution in the matter of concluding new alliances while we first reestablish order in our domestic affairs," she wrote to her Chancellor Mikhail Vorontsov. "We must persuade the English Court that we recognize the value of an alliance, and that we are clearly disposed toward reviving it. But we must indicate confidentially that we must defer putting it into effect for the moment because . . . we have postponed renewing our time-honored alliances with the Court of Vienna."[71]

When Catherine turned to relations with France, she found things difficult in the extreme. Peter III's alliance with Prussia had brought Franco-Russian relations to such a low point that Louis XV had recalled Baron de Breteuil, his Ambassador to St. Petersburg, and had left only a *chargé d'affaires* to represent him in Russia's capital. Once Catherine had seized the throne, the French King ordered Breteuil to return to his post, he left him with no doubt about his intentions. "I shall repeat in the most emphatic manner possible, that *the main purpose of my policy toward Russia is to remove her from European affairs as fully as possible,*" Louis wrote to Breteuil on the eve of his departure for St. Petersburg in September 1762. *"Anything that might help to throw that Empire into chaos, and force it to fall back into obscurity, is in keeping with my interests!* There is no chance that I would agree to any alliance with Russia. It will be sufficient simply to keep our relations on a decorous footing for the moment."[72] Louis XV's attitude coincided with Catherine's own preferences, for Russia had more grounds for potential conflict with France than with any other Western power. In Poland and in the Ottoman Empire, they followed antagonistic policies. In both regions, those conflicts would become heightened during the first decade of Catherine's reign.

Among other things, Catherine proceeded cautiously in her relations with Western powers during the first year of her reign because a bitter struggle had developed about Russia's foreign policy between two rival factions at her Court. Elizabeth's former Chancellor Bestuzhev had returned from exile to head a pro-Austrian faction, while Count Nikita Panin urged a pro-Prussian policy upon his new mistress. Catherine at first sought to learn more about foreign affairs from both groups, but refused to commit herself to either. When forced to take a clear position in mid-1763, she clarified the lines of Russia's foreign policy for the first time since her coup d'état.[73]

The political situation in Poland was the catalyst that finally impelled Catherine to support Count Panin's pro-Prussian policy in spite of Bestuzhev's warnings. By the summer of 1763, it had become evident to everyone that King Augustus III was at death's door and that the Poles soon must elect another King. France and Austria supported Augustus's eldest son Frederick Christian, his successor as Elector of Saxony. Determined to maintain Russian supremacy in Poland, Catherine put forward her former lover, the Polish aristocrat Count Stanisław Poniatowski, who, she cynically remarked, "had less right than any other candidate [to the Polish throne] and therefore should be all the more grateful to Russia."[74] Since Austria and France stood against her, Catherine ordered Prince Vladimir Dolgorukii, her Ambassador to Berlin, to ask Frederick the Great if he would support her choice. Frederick replied that he was "willing to join forces with the Empress in the event that the King of Poland died, if she will promise that she will not permit any prince related to the Austrian ruling house to ascend the throne."[75] Catherine had indeed found a willing ally, for Frederick did not relish the prospect of either a Saxon prince on the Polish throne or a Polish King who owed his crown to the Austrian Empress. Catherine thus lent a sympathetic ear to Count Panin's urgings for a firm alliance with Prussia; in the fall of 1763, she instructed him to negotiate a treaty.[76]

By the time Catherine and Frederick had agreed upon a formal alliance in April 1764, the situation in Poland had changed dramatically. Augustus III had died at the beginning of October 1763, and his son Frederick Christian had followed him to the grave two months later, long before the Polish National Diet had assembled to elect a new King. Augustus's brother, Prince Ksawery, became Regent in Saxony and announced his candidacy for Poland's throne. The refusal of France and Austria to support him destroyed his chance for the crown, especially after Russian troops entered Poland in April 1764 at the request of the pro-Russian Czartoryski party.[77] In August the Polish National Diet assembled outside Warsaw on Wola Field and elected Poniatowski their next King. "In all our history there is no example of an election as quiet and as perfectly unanimous [as this one]," Poniatowski wrote to Madame Geoffrin a few days later. Indeed, it could not have been otherwise; the entire field had been surrounded by Catherine's troops to ensure that her will was carried out.[78] "I congratulate you on the King we have just created," Catherine smugly wrote to Count Panin.[79]

Once they had placed Poniatowski on Poland's throne, Catherine and her new ally Frederick expanded their influence in Polish affairs. At first glance, their ability to do so seems surprising. With more than 280,000 square miles of territory and a population of over eleven million, Poland was one of the largest and most populous states in Europe. Yet she was incredibly weak because her archaic political system enabled her feuding nobles to keep her in a state of perpetual chaos.[80] Catherine and Frederick proceeded to exploit that weakness to advance their Imperial ambitions at Poland's expense. Catherine played the leading role, and she used as her excuse the religious disabilities the so-called "dissidents," members of the Orthodox faith living in Poland, suffered at the hands of the Polish authorities. On the pretext of defending their rights, Catherine kept troops in or near Poland during the first years of Poniatowski's reign and sponsored a number of confederations to support Russia's cause. In the spring of 1767, her representatives formed a "general confederation" at Radom and demanded a meeting of the National Diet to discuss freeing the "dissidents" from their civil and religious disabilities. At the same time, Prince Nikolai Repnin and Otto von Saldern proceeded to undermine Poland's Catholic establishment by threats, bribes, and even arrests. When the Diet assembled to discuss the "dissident" question in early 1768, Prince Repnin told them that he would arrest any deputy who opposed Catherine's will. The Diet therefore approved a treaty in February 1768 that made Russia the guarantor of Poland's constitution and proclaimed political and religious freedom for the "dissidents." It seemed Catherine had won an easy victory, but she soon saw her grave error. She had pushed too far, and thousands of Polish patriots hastened to form the Confederation of Bar. Poland plunged into several years of bloody civil war in which Catherine had to confront not only the guns of Polish patriots but also those of the Turks. Just months after the Confederation of Bar had taken the field against Catherine and her Polish supporters, the Sultan cast her Ambassador, Aleksei Obrezkov, into Constantinople's dungeons. Again, Russia and Turkey were at war.[81]

Louis XV and his Foreign Minister, the Duke de Choiseul, had been forced to acquiesce in Catherine's forced election of Poniatowski as Poland's King because France's armies had been weakened by the Seven Years' War. They found it much easier to oppose Russia's Empress in Constantinople. Throughout the early and mid-1760s, France's Ambassador to the Ottoman Porte, Count Vergennes, found fertile soil for his intrigues (and an outstretched palm for French gold in the person of the Sultan Mustafa III) as he stirred the Turks' smoldering hatred for the Russians into open flame.[82] During the summer of 1768, Mustafa dismissed in disgrace those counselors who opposed war with Russia; by the end of September, he was free to follow his and France's bellicose inclinations.[83] "The Turks and their French allies have seen fit to awaken the sleeping cat," Catherine wrote to Count Ivan Chernyshev in London. "This cat promises to give them a lesson they shan't soon forget."[84]

The Russo-Turkish War of 1768–74 saw Catherine's armies launch assaults against the Ottoman domains in the Balkans and the lands of their Tatar allies in the Crimea. Sometimes successful, these campaigns more often were inconclusive, interspersed by long intervals of suspended hostilities as the belligerents sought peace at the negotiating table. The most astounding Russian victory came in June 1770, when the Russian fleet under Count Aleksei Orlov annihilated its Turkish opponents in the Gulf of Chesme. A novice at naval warface, Orlov was aided by the outstanding British Admirals John Elphinston and Sir Samuel Greig, who served under his command. Theirs was a naval victory that surpassed anything Russia had known since the time of Peter the Great.[85]

Yet Chesme did little to end the war. During the next two years, Russia's international position deteriorated as France supported the Turks and the Confederation of Bar more energetically than ever. Apprehensive about further Russian expansion, England and Austria drew so close to the Turks that Catherine's advisers feared that Maria Theresa might conclude a military alliance with the Sultan. Even Frederick the Great looked for a means to end the conflict before other major European powers became involved and he was forced to honor his alliance with Russia. Still, Catherine insisted that the Crimea must be freed from Ottoman domination before she would consent to peace. By late 1771, it seemed probable that Austria would join the Turks and that Prussia might be drawn into the conflict on the side of Russia.[86]

In 1772, though the Russo-Turkish War ground on, Austria, Russia, and Prussia eased their mutual antagonisms. To prevent Prussia from being drawn into an unwanted war, to gain those territories that separated East Prussia from the rest of his domains, and to satisfy Catherine's Imperial ambitions, Frederick proposed a partition of Poland. When their representatives signed the treaty on July 25, 1772, Catherine received the White Russian lands of Vitebsk, Mogilev, most of Podolsk, and part of Livonia as compensation for renouncing her designs on Wallachia and Moldavia in the Balkans. In doing so, she added almost two million subjects to her Empire. Maria Theresa and Frederick made equally important gains from the Polish territories bordering on their lands. Poland lost almost one-third of her territory and more than one-third of her population.[87]

When they heard of the First Partition of Poland, the Turks stiffened their resistance for they feared that the Great Powers of Eastern Europe might plan a similar fate for them. Now it was Catherine who sought peace. During the summer of 1772, she sent Grigorii Orlov and Aleksei Obrezkov to discuss peace with the Sultan's representatives at Fokshani.[88] The negotiations failed because Catherine insisted that the Crimea be made independent from the Ottoman Empire and that Russia be permitted to maintain a navy on the Black Sea. She refused to compromise on those points. "If the peace treaty does not include independence for the Tatars [in the Crimea], and the right [for Russia] to sail the Black Sea," she wrote, "then all our victories over the Turks will have accomplished nothing. I will be the first to say that such a peace would be as shameful as that made on the Pruth [by Peter the Great in 1711] or in Belgrade [by Anna Ivanovna in 1739]."[89] Catherine's generals thus prepared for a new campaign. "I shall soon begin a new correspondence with Mustafa," she wrote to Voltaire. "But this time it will be with cannon fire, because he was pleased to command his representatives to leave the Fokshani Conference and break the armistice."[90]

In the spring of 1773, Catherine ordered her armies to strike across the Danube into the Balkans. On the night of May 10, General Aleksandr Suvorov stormed across the river, captured the Turks' river fleet of some fifty vessels, and seized sixteen of their cannon. Yet Field Marshal Petr Rumiantsev could not sustain the impetus of Suvorov's advance. His armies bogged down in an abortive effort to capture the Turkish fortress of Silestria, and he withdrew in late June. Catherine was dismayed by Rumiantsev's retreat. To make matters worse, the rebel Emelian Pugachev chose that moment to launch his great revolt and forced her to face the unpleasant reality of a two-front war. Yet Catherine remained firm in her insistence that Turkey permit a Russian fleet in the Black Sea and that the Crimea be independent. Refusing all offers from Austria, Prussia, and even France to mediate her conflict with the Sultan, she remained determined not to throw away the fruits of Russia's earlier victories.

It turned out that the Turks were even more exhausted by the prolonged conflict than were the Russians. When Sultan Mustafa's death in January 1774 broke the strength of the pro-war faction at the Porte, Russian and Turkish representatives met at the village of Kuchuk-Kainarji. Peace was signed on July 10, 1774, and Catherine won her demands. Russia gained the strategic points of Kerch, Enikale, Kinburn, a portion of the North Black Sea coast, and the right to establish a navy on the Black Sea. The Crimean Tatars were declared independent. Turkey recognized Russia's right to protect the Orthodox Christians in Moldavia and Wallachia and agreed to pay war indemnities totaling 4,500,000 rubles. The Treaty of Kuchuk-Kainarji marked Russia's first decisive defeat of the Ottoman Empire, but it also left the Turks burning for revenge. Little more than a decade later, Catherine's armies had to face Turkish guns once again.[91]

Austria's fear of Prussia's expansionist ambitions throughout the eighteenth century was a major factor in Russia's growing role in the affairs of Central and Eastern Europe, as Catherine played one power against the other. Particularly at the urging of Count Nikita Panin, she maintained close relations with Frederick during the first half of her reign at the expense of Russia's long-standing alliance with Austria. Around 1780, however, Catherine began to shift the focus of her alliances.[92] This was partly a consequence of Panin's eclipse in the late 1770s. More importantly, it was connected with the rise of Grigorii Potemkin as Catherine's chief minister and their joint infatuation with a "Greek Project" that aimed to expel the Turks from Europe and reestablish the Byzantine Empire under Catherine's infant grandson Konstantin. The Greek Project was a romantic, somewhat improbable scheme. Without the cooperation of Austria, however, its success was absolutely impossible.

A number of factors interfered with Catherine's efforts to strengthen Russia's ties with Austria. Despite her protestations of friendship, Maria Theresa had detested Catherine and Russia, and that fact kept the two nations apart so long as she lived. Her son Joseph II did not share her prejudices, and his accession in November 1780 opened the way to better relations. In fact, a full year before his mother's death, Joseph began to pave the way for closer ties with Russia by visiting Catherine incognito as Count Falkenstein. Together, they attended the comic opera, held long and weighty conversations, and sought to charm each other at every opportunity.[93] "Monsieur Falkenstein told me things in our conversations that were worthy of being printed, and [shared with me] a number of profound thoughts which, if he should put them into practice, will assuredly do him infinite honor," Catherine wrote to Baron Grimm. "I found him extremely well informed," she confided. "He loves to speak, and speaks very well indeed."[94] The two rulers spoke often of Frederick the Great and of his passion for intrigue. Both sought closer and more formal ties. "I told Her Majesty that We have decided to let her know Our most candid opinions and to seek her advice about all important matters," Joseph wrote. Britain's Ambassador James Harris reported to his superiors in London, "Count Falkenstein has struck [such] a terrible blow against the influence of the Prussian King here [in St. Petersburg] . . . that I would guess that this influence will never be restored."[95]

So disturbed was Frederick by Joseph's apparent success that he sent Prussia's Crown Prince Frederick William to St. Petersburg that fall to repair the damage. "The Crown Prince of Prussia is coming here in September for the purpose of spoiling everything useful that I have managed to accomplish," Joseph complained to his mother a few weeks after his meetings with Catherine.[96] He need not have feared for the results of his efforts: at the end of 1780, Count Cobenzl, Austria's new Ambassador to St. Petersburg, proposed a formal alliance. Several months of negotiations produced a treaty in May 1781. Although directed mainly against the Ottoman Empire, the alliance also pledged to preserve peace in Poland and defend the revised constitution that the Polish National Diet had drafted between 1773 and 1775. Equally important, the treaty marked Catherine's decisive turn to an alliance system that centered upon Austria.[97]

Once she had assured herself of Austria's friendship and support against the Ottoman Empire, Catherine moved to expand Russia's territory along the north shore of the Black Sea. She and Joseph had spoken of partitioning the Ottoman lands but had reached no agreement when, spurred on by Potemkin, she took a bold step. As Governor-General of New Russia since 1776, Potemkin had worked assiduously to create a Russian party among the Crimean Tatars. He had done so partly to counter Ottoman intrigues at the Crimean Court, but also for his own and Russia's aggrandizement, for he wanted to add the Crimea to the vast domain he administered in the south. In 1782 his efforts began to bear fruit when Shagin-Girei, a Tatar prince educated in St. Petersburg, became the Crimean Khan. Shagin-Girei asked Catherine for aid against his political opponents, and she immediately dispatched General Count Aleksandr Samoilov to the Crimea. Throughout the late winter and early spring of 1783, Catherine increased the number of troops under Samoilov's command so that, by the end of March, Russia's occupation of the Crimea had become an accomplished fact. Bowing to the inevitable, Shagin-Girei abdicated in favor of the Romanovs; on April 8, 1783, Catherine annexed the Crimea without firing a shot. A few months later, she extended her influence into the Caucasus when Georgia accepted a Russian protectorate.[98] It was only a matter of time before the Turks would be forced to respond to such bold provocation.

Under Potemkin's energetic direction, Russia's new Black Sea territories flourished. When Catherine visited the south in 1787, cities were rising at Kherson, Nikolaev, Ekaterinoslav, and Sevastopol, and Potemkin had constructed a Black Sea fleet of more than forty men-of-war.[99] The south was becoming one of the most brilliant jewels in the Romanov Imperial crown and one that Catherine vowed to defend at all costs. She was determined to keep the Ottoman Empire weak and preserve the gains the Turks had conceded to Russia at the end of the First Russo-Turkish War. "You are not willing that I should drive from my neighborhood your children the Turks," she told Count Louis Philippe de Ségur on the eve of her departure for the Crimea in 1787. "If you [Frenchmen] had similar neighbors in Piedmont or in Spain, who brought you annually plague and famine, and killed or destroyed every year twenty thousand people, would you find it agreeable that I should take them under my protection? I believe that then you would indeed treat me as a barbarian."[100]

Nonetheless, Catherine hesitated to commit Russia to another war in the south, although she spoke of driving the Turks from Europe and continued to dream of her grandiose Greek Project. Her indecision ended soon after she returned from her tour of the Crimea; as in 1768, the Turks struck the first blow. "So long as the Crimea remains in Russian hands," the Sultan told France's Ambassador Count Vergennes, "Turkey is like a house with no doors which thieves can enter at will."[101] Therefore, in August 1787, he demanded that Catherine nullify her annexation of the Crimea. When she refused, he cast her Ambassador Iakov Bulgakov into the dungeons of the Castle of the Seven Bastions. Before the end of the month, Joseph II reaffirmed his pledge to support Russia if she were attacked by the Ottoman Empire; in February 1788 he joined Catherine in war against the Turks.[102]

The Second Russo-Turkish War followed the pattern of the first. The Russians won brilliant victories at Ochakov, Fokshani, Rymnik, Bender, and Akkerman, while the Austrians occupied Belgrade and won other engagements. Yet the Russians were unable to follow up their victories, and their international position went from bad to worse as Prussia, France, England, Holland, and Spain all used their influence to oppose Catherine's openly announced Greek Project. To make matters worse, King Gustavus III of Sweden declared war on Russia in an attempt to regain some of the territory his country had lost over the past eighty years. Fortunately for Catherine, his offensive was weakened by a domestic revolt and posed no serious threat to Russia's security. Still, it proved a costly annoyance, for Russia lost fifty-three ships and ten thousand men at the naval battle of Svenskund. Finally, both powers agreed to recognize the *status quo ante bellum* and signed the Treaty of Verelä in August 1790.[103]

Once freed of the Swedes, Catherine returned to Russia's conflict with the Ottoman Empire. The death of Joseph II and the threatening situation in Poland complicated her task. When Joseph had died in February 1790, his brother Leopold II, with resources dangerously depleted by the Turkish conflict, had had to face revolts in the Austrian Netherlands, Hungary, Bohemia, and Galicia. At the same time, Prussia's new King, Frederick William II, had made clear his intention to seize the important Polish cities of Gdańsk and Toruń while Russia and Austria were occupied in the south. Leopold therefore had hastened to arrange an armistice with the Turks and sign a Convention with Prussia at Reichenbach in July 1790,[104] leaving Catherine to face the Turks alone at a time when England and Prussia were becoming more bellicose about her Greek Project. She thus was obliged to shelve her grandiose plans for reestablishing a new Byzantine Empire. At the Peace of Jassy, in late December 1791, she settled for the fortress of Ochakov, all the Black Sea coast between the Dniestr and Southern Bug rivers, and Ottoman recognition of her annexation of the Crimea.

With Catherine's armies fighting the Turks and the Swedes, the Poles saw an opportunity to free themselves from Russian domination. With the support of Prussia, they demanded that Catherine withdraw her troops; since she could not fight a three-front war, she agreed. The Poles then summoned their Great Diet to Warsaw at the beginning of October 1788. For the next four years, it met amid feverish excitement and burning patriotic fervor that touched virtually all groups in the country. "Our sons and grandsons will not live to see a better occasion than we now have for setting our house in order, increasing the forces of the Republic [and] assuring our liberties," proclaimed one member. Freed for the moment from Russian interference in their affairs, the Poles proceeded to initiate just the sort of broad reform program that Catherine had opposed ever since she had placed Poniatowski on the throne. Exclaimed Stanislaw Stasic, one of Poland's leading liberal reformers, "This matter will brook no delay. The sickness is violent: it demands violent remedies."[105] It seemed that Poland's great opportunity to modernize her archaic constitution and political system had come at last.

Between 1788 and 1791, men such as Stanisław Małachowski, Ignac Potocki, Prince Adam Czartoryski, and Hugo Kołłątaj directed the passage of major reform programs through the enthusiastic, sometimes tumultuous Great Diet. Their labors produced the famous constitution of May 3, 1791, which abolished the *liberum veto* that had enabled any member of the Diet to wield an absolute veto over any piece of proposed legislation, did away with Poland's elective kingship, and made illegal those armed confederations that had kept Poland in a state of perpetual political turmoil.[106] In England, the great Edmund Burke proclaimed it one of the greatest constitutions any nation had ever received. The Danish minister, Count Bernsdorff, saw it as a joyful event, and, much to everyone's amazement, both Prussia and Austria announced their support.[107] Catherine was livid with rage. "This Polish Diet has just outdone the madness of the National Assembly [in Paris]," she wrote to Melchior Grimm. "They have abolished the *liberum veto*, the palladium of their Polish liberties."[108] She held her peace for the moment and ordered her ambassador to Warsaw to make no formal or public protest. After she settled matters with the Turks, she would deal with Poland. When it came, her blow would be vicious and fatal.

If 1791 had been a brilliant year for the Poles on the international scene, 1792 would be ruinous, as a disruptive and unforeseen factor appeared on the western horizon. For almost three years since the mob had stormed the Bastille on July 14, 1789, revolutionary France had been occupied with domestic affairs as the National Assembly drafted a Republican constitution and inaugurated a vast program of social and political change. In early 1792, however, the revolution changed course dramatically as the Girondists rose to proclaim that revolution in France could never be secure until it had been carried into other nations. Their fears spurred by the Austrian Emperor's declaration at Pillnitz that he would restore order in France if other European sovereigns would join him, the National Assembly declared war against Austria. In reply, Austrian and Prussian armies marched west to eradicate the scourge of revolution from France. With the two major powers of Central Europe thus occupied in the West, Catherine was left free to deal with Poland in the manner she thought most fitting.

In March 1792, Catherine invited Feliks Potocki, Seweryn Rzewuski, and Jan Branicki to St. Petersburg. Potocki was one of Poland's richest lords, proud, arrogant, and scornful of all authority but his own. Rzewuski was the Crown Hetman, the "Cato of Poland," who saw himself as the defender of Poland's ancient liberties. Branicki was an adventurer, like most of his kind guided purely by self-interest. His life was a "succession of treasons" against Poland. As one historian once remarked, in these three men "the worst vices of Poland stand incorporated."[109] With Catherine's support, they formed the Confederation of Targowica, which branded Poland's new constitution an "audacious crime" and a "contagion of democratic ideas" that had imposed the "shackles of slavery" upon Poland. Actually drafted by one of Catherine's officials and signed in St. Petersburg, this illegal confederation became the basis for Catherine's invasion of Poland.[110]

On the night of May 18, 1792, thirty-two thousand combat-hardened regulars under Catherine's most brilliant general, Aleksandr Suvorov, stormed across the Russo-Polish frontier into Lithuania to face less than fifteen thousand green Polish troops. A few days later, another sixty-four thousand Russian veterans under General Kakhovskii invaded the Ukraine, where they were opposed by only seventeen thousand Poles under Prince Jozef Poniatowski and Tadeusz Kościuszko, one of the heroes of the American War of Independence. The Poles fought valiantly and covered themselves with glory at Zieleńce and Dubienka, where Kościuszko momentarily halted the advance of almost twenty thousand Russians with a force of six thousand and almost no artillery.[111] But the weight of Russia's might was too overwhelming, and the resolution of Poland's King Stanisław Augustus too weak. Although he had sworn to lay down his life for Poland's constitution, the King was far too cowardly to put himself in danger. His main thoughts were for his safety and personal comfort, and his major concern, when his advisers urged him to join the army in the field, was whether he would find "a proper cuisine" there.[112] Hurriedly, he sought peace with the Empress whose bed he had shared more than three decades before. He allowed Suvorov's armies to occupy Warsaw and the Confederation of Targowica to take control of Polish affairs. Catherine was in full command of Poland. When she and Frederick William signed the Second Partition of Poland in January 1793, three million Poles became Russian subjects and another million fell under the sway of Prussia. Poland lost the important cities of Gdańsk (called Danzig by the Prussians) and Toruń. The country also lost her richest grain-growing region, the Polish Ukraine.[113]

Although the Poles had acquiesced in the rape of their lands by Austria, Prussia, and Russia in 1772, they proved far less biddable two decades later. On March 12, 1794, a brigade of the Polish army mutinied at Ostrołęke to begin what became known as the Kościuszko Revolt. Quickly, the insurgents seized Kraków. Less than two weeks later, Kościuszko defeated Catherine's armies at Racławice, and, on April 17, the population of Warsaw rose up to massacre half of its Russian garrison. Five days later, the insurgents destroyed the Russian garrison at Vilno. Led by Frederick William himself, a Prussian army failed to retake Warsaw and beat an inglorious retreat across the Prussian frontier. Kościuszko then turned to face Suvorov's Russians. Aided by Generals Zajączek and Sierakowski, Kościuszko at first won a number of brilliant victories. But the sheer weight of numbers again proved too great. On October 9, Kościuszko's army of seven thousand faced fourteen thousand Russians under General Fersen. After a brutal all-day battle, Fersen annihilated the Polish forces and took the gravely wounded Kościuszko prisoner. Suvorov then advanced. On November 3, he stormed the Polish defenses at Praga, directly across the Vistula from Warsaw, and slaughtered soldiers and civilians indiscriminately. Terrified, the inhabitants of the capital surrendered. By the middle of November, the revolt was over. Suvorov sent Kościuszko and a number of other Polish generals to St. Petersburg as prisoners of war.[114]

The massacre of the Russian garrison in Warsaw had driven Catherine into a fury; she vowed brutal revenge. While her troops were still marching on Warsaw, she announced to Prussia and Austria that "the time has come for the three Courts to take measures not only to extinguish the last spark of the fire that has burst forth in the neighboring land [of Poland], but also to prevent it from ever flaming up again from the ashes."[115] Yet the division of Poland's remaining territories proved no easy task, as the Austrians and Prussians fell to squabbling over which power would possess the important southern city of Kraków. Frederick William's retreat from Warsaw soon afterward drove Catherine into a further rage, for she realized that Russia now must bear the brunt of the fighting against Kościuszko's rebels. "Oh God! I dare not say what I think," she wrote to Baron Grimm. "Our public opinion is outraged."[116] But the failure of the Prussians, whom Catherine branded "so odious that one must expect from them everything that is morally evil," left her better able to dictate a settlement of the Polish question.[117] After Suvorov's army occupied Warsaw, Russia and Austria signed the Third Partition Treaty in January 1795, but two more years of negotiations were needed before Prussia was satisfied. Russia gained Lithuania, Courland, and the western portions of Podolia and Volynia, while Austria and Prussia divided the rest between them. To protect their subjects from "the scandalous and often contagious example [of Poland]," Russia, Prussia, and Austria erased her from the map.[118]

Catherine's foreign policy had been successful, even brilliant in some respects. During the thirty-four years of her reign, she added almost a quarter-million square miles to Russia's territory and almost doubled her population.[119] But she purchased these gains at a very dear price. Especially in the case of the Poles, she brought into her Empire an ardently nationalistic people who despised their Russian masters and continued to struggle against them. The nineteenth century would see bitter outbreaks of Polish hatred that always proved costly for the Romanovs. Further, Catherine's foreign policy had been immensely expensive, and she had been obliged to squeeze her subjects very hard to keep her armies in the field. Although her reign was a time of expanding trade and rapid industrial growth, it was also a time of dramatic inflation and fiscal crisis.

To finance her wars, Catherine printed large quantities of paper money, which fueled the fires of inflation and negated the increased revenues her treasury collected.[120] She therefore printed still larger quantities, which, in turn, aggravated the problem further. In all, during the last two decades of her reign she issued nearly 200,000,000 paper rubles that were unsupported by gold or silver.[121] But that was only one of many crises her policies brought to Russia. Her incessant recruit levies took large numbers of peasants from the fields, thereby lowering the productivity of the nobles' estates, and increasing poverty in the Russian countryside. As Edmond Genet, French *chargé d'affaires* in St. Petersburg, reported in January 1790, "The people frown in every province to see the best cultivators being continually torn from the land and lamenting families being robbed of their sole means of support; money has completely vanished from circulation and it is evident that the Government, under the guise of banknotes, is manufacturing a veritable paper currency."[122]

Although she had not one drop of Romanov blood in her veins, Catherine had set out to make herself Russian in every way and to create a powerful state that would give Russians pride in their nationality. To do so, she needed national acquiescence in her continued usurpation of her son Paul's crown, and she needed loyal noble servitors to administer Russia's provinces and to lead her armies. She therefore struck a firmer alliance with the nobility, whose support constituted her only claim to the Russian crown. The first major piece of legislation through which Catherine sought to achieve these aims was the Law on the Administration of the Provinces, which she published on November 7, 1775. To streamline Russia's provincial administration, she reduced the sprawling Petrine provinces to more manageable dimensions and appointed a governor, answerable directly to the Senate and to the Autocrat, to head each one. She also created a number of elective offices to be filled by the nobility at the lower, county level, and assigned these positions status in the Table of Ranks and a salary from the treasury. By doing so, she brought back into the framework of the state service a number of those nobles who had retired to the provinces and reinforced their ascendancy over other classes in Russia by giving them a dominant voice in district affairs.[123]

On April 23, 1785, Catherine broadened the principles of her law on provincial administration in a Charter of the Nobility. Although she reconfirmed the nobles' emancipation from state obligations, she stressed that their status would continue to be associated with loyal service to the Empire. Nobles were exempted from all personal taxation, given the right to travel abroad, and even permitted to enter the military or civil services of friendly foreign powers. They also received the right to meet in county and provincial assemblies, a privilege given to no other social class. There, too, Catherine stressed the importance of duty to the state, for only those who had reached officer rank in the army, or its equivalent in the civil service, could vote in the Provincial and District Assemblies of the Nobility.[124] In this manner, she blunted the emancipation from compulsory service that Peter III had granted to the nobles in early 1762. Throughout her reign, nobles continued to be free not to serve the Autocrat if they so desired. Nevertheless, all the paths to social status, wealth, and success passed through loyal service to the Empress.

More than any other ruler before her, Catherine used the practice of granting estates and serfs to reward those who served her faithfully. Yet, these were not only a mark of Imperial favor during her reign; they also were a matter of economic necessity for many nobles, rich and poor alike. The new Western culture, which had become so much a way of life at Court and in the capital by the time of Catherine's accession, was extremely expensive, as were the grand palaces and town houses the Romanovs encouraged their nobles to build. So great was the expense of the new culture that nobles frequently went deeply into debt to maintain what was considered to be a proper standard of living. "I leave my inheritors in extreme poverty, since my debts, most illustrious Madame, exceed half a million rubles," complained Count Ivan Chernyshev, one of Russia's richest noblemen, to Catherine in 1794. They accumulated, he continued, "during my thirty years of service in the Admiralty, where, particularly in the beginning, I was compelled to entertain many guests, to feed almost everybody, and to get them accustomed not only to high society, but also to affluence."[125] Because such indebtedness was aggravated further by nobles' steadfast opposition to primogeniture, the only way to offset these difficulties was for the monarch to grant additional estates. Catherine bestowed them in profusion upon those who served her. During the three months between her accession and her coronation, she granted estates upon which more than thirty thousand serfs lived to those who had supported her coup d'état; during the next thirty-four years, she gave away well over a million peasants in all. Most of these went to a mere handful of great lords, forty-two of whom received a total of more than four hundred thousand peasants.[126] But she also gave many smaller grants of serfs and lands to lesser men, thereby giving them hope for even greater grants in the future.

While Catherine's reign thus proved to be the Golden Age of the Russian nobility, it was a difficult time for the Empire's peasants. The same high costs of westernization that enabled the Empress to make the nobility more dependent than ever before upon her generosity also increased the burdens borne by their serfs. In an effort to pay for their new palaces, Western fashions, and luxury goods, nobles pressed their serfs to supply more labor services and to provide a larger variety of duties and cash payments. According to recent studies, the real value of serfs' money payments did not increase substantially during Catherine's reign,[127] but certainly their sense of oppression did. Rarely were masters punished for abusing their serfs except in cases of utterly notorious abuse such as that of Daria Saltykova, the noblewoman who tortured scores of her serfs to death in a brutal and sadistic manner.[128] As a result of this near-total lack of governmental restraint, the sale of serfs reached a peak during Catherine's reign. The largest trade flourished in serfs sold as recruit substitutes, but there also was an ongoing trade in field hands, and young and beautiful serf girls brought five hundred rubles or more at the Ivanovo wench market, as compared to about one hundred rubles for field workers. Serfs with special skills or talents commanded even higher prices; Potemkin once paid 40,000 rubles for an entire serf orchestra.[129]

For the mass of Catherine's subjects, her reign thus was a sore and trying time, and the lip service she paid to the ideals of the Enlightenment made her willingness to concede so much to Russia's nobles appear all the more duplistic. Nevertheless, it was in Catherine's hands that Peter the Great's dreams finally found their full realization, and the Imperial aspirations that had been hardly more than dim images when he had overthrown the Regent Sofia in 1689 became a startling and undisputed reality. In the course of a century, Russia had risen from an obscure and backward nation on the eastern fringe of Europe to become one of its most formidable powers. Catherine left behind a triumphant Empire. In the hands of her immediate successors, it soared to even greater heights.

PART THREE

EMPIRE TRIUMPHANT

(1796–1894)

Emperor Peter III————————Empress Catherine the Great
(X)   (XI)
(1761–1762)   (1762–1796)

Wilhelmina of Hesse-Darmstadt————Emperor Paul I————
(Natalia Alekseevna)   (XII)
                                                   (1796–1801)

Emperor Alexander I————Louisa of Baden   Emperor Constantine I
(XIII)   (Elisaveta Alekseevna)   (XIV)
(1801–1825)   (1825)

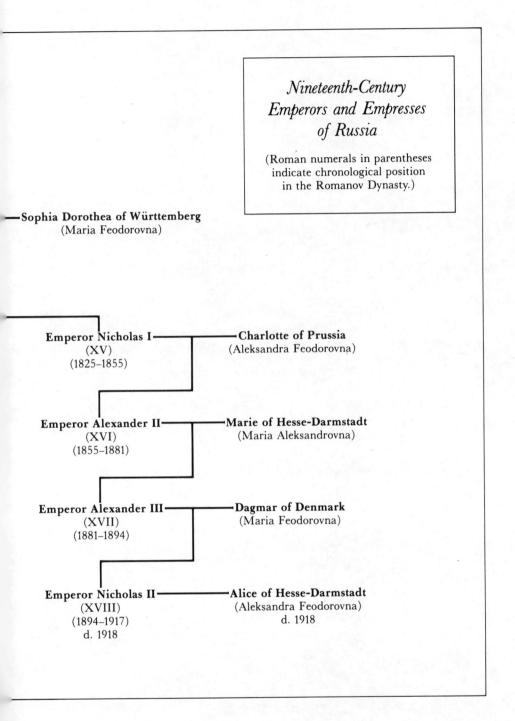

Nineteenth-Century
Emperors and Empresses
of Russia

(Roman numerals in parentheses
indicate chronological position
in the Romanov Dynasty.)

—Sophia Dorothea of Württemberg
(Maria Feodorovna)

Emperor Nicholas I——————Charlotte of Prussia
(XV)   (Aleksandra Feodorovna)
(1825–1855)

Emperor Alexander II——————Marie of Hesse-Darmstadt
(XVI)   (Maria Aleksandrovna)
(1855–1881)

Emperor Alexander III——————Dagmar of Denmark
(XVII)   (Maria Feodorovna)
(1881–1894)

Emperor Nicholas II——————Alice of Hesse-Darmstadt
(XVIII)   (Aleksandra Feodorovna)
(1894–1917)   d. 1918
d. 1918

CHAPTER VIII

The Imperial Dynasty

It is one of the great ironies of Russia's history that Paul I, the monarch who established the Romanovs as an Imperial dynasty, may well not have had a single drop of Romanov blood in his veins. The doubts relating to Paul's parentage began in the spring of 1754, when the Grand Duchess Catherine announced to an amazed Court and an overly delighted Empress Elizabeth that, after a decade of marriage to the Grand Duke Peter, she was pregnant. By that time, it was generally assumed that Peter was impotent or sterile. Certainly, he had never fathered a child or, to the best of anyone's knowledge, even impregnated anyone. At the same time, Catherine's liaison with the handsome young Sergei Saltykov had not been as well concealed as she had thought, and there undoubtedly were those who could testify that she and Saltykov had lain together on a number of occasions. Yet Elizabeth was in no way inclined to punish her; there is even some evidence that Catherine's affair with Saltykov was begun and carried on with Elizabeth's approval.

All of this may explain why Catherine seemed curiously uninvolved with the progress of her pregnancy, while the Empress Elizabeth began to lay elaborate plans for the heir whose birth she had awaited for so long. She placed Catherine in a special palace apartment next to her own and allowed her to be attended only by those women in whom she had absolute confidence. But, if she was at pains to assure Catherine's physical well-being, Elizabeth offered her no warmth or affection, and left her isolated, "without any companionship, and as unhappy as a stone," as Catherine later recalled.[1]

Catherine's account of her son's birth, on September 20, 1754, provides a vivid statement about the extreme psychological injury she suffered at the Empress Elizabeth's hands and may well explain why she never expressed much maternal warmth for her only son. Even at the moment of Paul's birth, Elizabeth reminded her of her lowly position as a human incubator and left no doubt that she considered Catherine insignificant in comparison to the task she was expected to accomplish. Thus, Catherine later wrote:

> Toward noon . . . on September 20th, I gave birth to a son. They had only just wrapped him in swaddling clothes, when the Empress summoned her confessor and gave him the name of Paul, after which she ordered the midwife to pick up the child and follow her. I remained alone on my bed of pain. . . . I had perspired a great deal, and I begged Madame Vladislava [who attended me] to have my linen changed, and to have me put into my own bed. She replied that she dared not do so. She sent for the midwife on several occasions, but the woman never came. I begged for a drink, but received the same answer. Finally, somewhat after three o'clock, the Countess Shuvalova appeared, dressed in her finest. Seeing me lying in the same place where she had left me [three hours earlier], she was irate, saying that they must be trying to kill me. . . . Shuvalova left immediately and, evidently, she summoned the midwife, because, a half-hour later, the midwife appeared and apologized, saying that the Empress had been so occupied with the newborn infant that she would not permit her to leave, even for a moment. The Empress had no thought for me whatsoever.[2]

To be left abandoned upon a bed stained by the struggle of childbirth must have been extremely painful for someone of Catherine's monumental ego. Elizabeth's conduct during the weeks after Paul's birth must have been equally galling. For the services her womb had performed for the Russian state, Catherine received a gift of one hundred thousand rubles, which she had to return a few days later when Elizabeth's private secretary lamented that there was not a kopek left in the Empress's coffers to pay the Grand Duke Peter a similar sum that he had demanded for himself.[3] Catherine was left with a necklace, earrings, and two rings that, she later wrote, were so worthless that "I would have been ashamed to present them to my lady-in-waiting."[4]

Aside from the act of childbirth, Catherine had almost no contact with the Grand Duke Paul during his infancy and early childhood because the Empress took over his care and upbringing. Elizabeth kept Paul in her private chambers and ran to him every time he whimpered. Catherine the mother was left to become Catherine the lonely Grand Duchess once again. She could inquire about her son's welfare only in secret because such questions could be interpreted as criticisms of Elizabeth's care for her child. She did not even see Paul until forty days after his birth, and did not set eyes upon him again until the spring of 1755. Gradually, she put him out of her mind. When he passed his sixth birthday, she was given permission to visit him once each week. By that time, he was no longer a child of her body, but a stranger to whom she had a strange and indefinite connection.[5]

At first, Elizabeth was enthusiastic about rearing the infant prince she had taken into her private chambers. He was the child she had never borne, the heir she had always hoped to rear according to her principles and personal tastes. Hers from the moment of birth, she hoped he might become the adoring child the Grand Duke Peter had never been, the reflection of her own personality. But poor health soon distracted Elizabeth from the duties of motherhood, and, at forty-five, she was too set in her ways to tolerate the disruptions that child rearing inevitably entails. Very quickly she began to leave Paul's daily care to nursemaids and nannies, and he soon fell victim to their conflicting folkish beliefs. At one point, they fed him only dishes made of milk and cheese. When these gave him diarrhea, they fed him huge quantities of meat, which made him vomit. Fearful for his health, they kept him bundled in flannel garments, winter and summer, and continued to overwhelm him with tender but oppressive ministrations. Without proper, balanced nourishment, Paul grew into a sickly and fragile child, unusually susceptible to colds, and quite probably a victim of rickets.[6] His nannies made no effort to form his character, and their bickering made him nervous and easily frightened. Elizabeth was dismayed to see him, as a child of four, cower beneath a table in his nursery when a door slammed too loudly, and she hastened to turn his training and education over to men in an effort to repair the damage inflicted upon his character by too many women.

Thanks to the efforts of Count Nikita Panin, Paul received a first-rate education from the age of six onward. Brilliant, articulate, and talented, Panin was one of the most westernized Russians of his day. His family had served Tsars Mikhail and Aleksei Mikhailovich in minor Court posts, but they had risen to great heights under Peter the Great and thus were deeply committed to his westernized path. Panin himself was blessed with an incisive mind and broad interests, which ranged from history and politics to literature and science, and Elizabeth was quick to enlist him in her service. Just after he turned thirty, she appointed him ambassador to Sweden, one of the most sensitive and demanding posts in Russia's Foreign Service; he represented Russia's interests in the torturous maze of Swedish political intrigues for the next twelve years. When Elizabeth recalled him to St. Petersburg in 1760, he had become an even stronger devoté of Western ideas, culture, technology, and medicine. His wide readings in Western thought and literature had made him an advocate of the modern educational theories of Leibnitz, Fénélon, and John Locke, which meant that he preferred active debate to dry, rote learning. One of his favorite methods for teaching Paul was to assemble a number of knowledgeable and prominent men around the dinner table to discuss the subjects they knew best. Not only leading statesmen were invited to these dinners but men such as the great playwrights Sumarokov and Fonvizin. Panin used their discussions to emphasize the ideas and principles he considered important for a prince to learn.[7]

Panin once wrote that "a good monarch does not, and, indeed, cannot, have any true interest or true glory apart from the prosperity and well-being of those peoples subjected to him by God's grace."[8] This conviction formed the core of his teaching as he continued to play father and mother to a youth who, in effect, had neither. He insisted that Paul study history, foreign languages, science, and, especially, mathematics, in order to develop the habits of clear, logical, and precise thought. At the same time, he encouraged him to become a collector of books and art in order to stimulate his enthusiasm for culture and learning. Yet Panin also wanted his pupil to enjoy life and to develop a healthy body in addition to an active mind. Paul never would be large or strong, but Panin hoped that he could develop coordination, grace, and a sense of proportion. Therefore, the young prince was taught to draw well and dance elegantly. He became an excellent horseman and loved to ride through the fields near St. Petersburg, although he was too short, and his head too round, to gain that commanding presence on horseback that would come so naturally to all four of his tall, imposing sons.[9]

When Paul reached adolescence, Panin began to educate him in the intricacies of domestic and international politics in order to prepare him to rule Russia at Catherine's death. Most of all, Panin emphasized that a virtuous monarch must regulate his government and establish it upon the firm foundation of law. Paul took up these principles willingly and incorporated them into his first political writings. "The state should be regarded as a body," he wrote in 1774. "The ruler is its head, the laws are its soul, morals its heart, and abundance its health, military power its arms and all other parts serving its defense, and religion is the law under which everything is constituted."[10] Panin had trained him to think much more precisely than his mother, and his writings were clearer and more original. Paul's view of what a government should be, and how a monarch should rule, embodied some of the real substance of the Enlightenment, not merely its external forms.

Her son's superior education and obvious talent gave Catherine much pause when he reached adulthood. Clearly, he could lay claim to the Romanov throne, and there were those in Russia who still considered him Peter III's legitimate heir, even though Catherine had ruled for a decade. In March 1768, Paul was greeted by delirious crowds in Moscow, and the gesture was repeated often enough in other cities to make Catherine apprehensive. Not long afterward, some of Russia's greatest writers began to celebrate his virtues in odes and literary discourses, a form of tribute Catherine especially envied. In 1771 Fonvizin called Paul "the hope of our homeland, the single, precious pledge of our peace and tranquillity," and Sumarokov echoed those words a year later. The journalist Nikolai Novikov, whose conflicts with Catherine were growing more bitter by the moment, dedicated his *Historical Dictionary of Russian Writers* to the young prince, and other Russian poets sang his praises.[11] Many of these were the men whom Panin frequently invited to dinners and evening gatherings at Paul's apartments, and that fact alarmed Catherine further, since it appeared that her son might become the focus for political opposition.

The Panins themselves were one of the most powerful and astute clans in the Empire, and they had long been known for their political ambitions. Although there is no evidence that they ever conspired to put Paul upon the throne during Catherine's lifetime, she feared that they might, and she acted accordingly. She decided to remove Paul from Panin's tutelage. The easiest way was to find him a wife and to establish him in an independent household where he could be kept more hidden from public view. Catherine chose as her son's bride the Princess Wilhelmina of Hesse-Darmstadt, who took the name of Natalia Alekseevna when she converted to Russian Orthodoxy as required by Russian tradition and Church law. Paul and the Grand Duchess Natalia were officially betrothed in August 1773. A week later, Catherine relieved Panin of all his tutorial duties with effusive thanks and monumental rewards. To ensure Panin's future loyalty, she bestowed upon him the ranks of Field Marshal and Chancellor, granted him estates with some fifteen thousand serfs, and gave him a town house of his own choosing in St. Petersburg plus wines and provisions for an entire year and one hundred thousand rubles for its furnishings. She also gave him a silver service valued at fifty thousand rubles, a yearly salary of fourteen thousand more, and another twenty-five thousand rubles each year as a pension.[12]

Paul married Natalia Alekseevna on September 29, 1773, just nine days after his nineteenth birthday. He was happy with his bride, and she was on excellent terms with Catherine. So diligent was Natalia Alekseevna in attempting to reconcile mother and son that Catherine reportedly remarked that "I am indebted to the Grand Duchess for returning my son to me."[13] But this newly found family bliss soon was tarnished by discord, for the Grand Duchess's character was very different from what it seemed at first. Energetic and vivacious, she also was far too fond of politics and intrigue. "If she cannot make a revolution, no one can," remarked the Chevalier de Corberon.[14] To make matters more difficult, Natalia Alekseevna did not think much of her new husband, and she shared Corberon's well-publicized opinion that "the Grand Duke not only has a weak character, he has none at all."[15]

She sought pleasure elsewhere, soon finding it in the arms of Count Andrei Razumovskii, a fact of which Paul evidently remained ignorant, because he always considered Razumovskii his best friend.[16] All of this made Catherine's relations with the so-called "young Court" difficult in the extreme. "There is no pleasure, no caution, no prudence, in any of this, and only God alone knows what will come of it, because no one listens, and everyone does just as they wish," she wrote to one of her close friends.[17]

Married or single, Paul was destined to live a life of neglect. Perhaps most galling of all, his marital difficulties coincided with the meteoric rise of Potemkin, and he had to sit by and watch his mother bestow upon her new favorite a number of the offices he himself might reasonably have expected to possess. During the first half of 1774, Catherine named her lover second in command of the Preobrazhenskii Guards, although Paul was entitled to that honor. She also appointed Potemkin Vice-President of the College of War and made him a member of her Council, when she knew that her son would have liked to hold either of those posts. Yet Catherine's callous treatment of Paul did not stem only from her fear that he might seize the throne, nor even from her dislike for him. There was another, more complex, psychological factor involved. Because Paul's very existence as her heir proclaimed the fact of her mortality, anything she might have done to prepare him to rule Russia would have reminded her of her eventual death. She thus continued to deny Paul any position in Russia's administration at a time when he was becoming increasingly anxious to prepare himself for the Imperial duties that one day would be his.[18]

He thus remained isolated from the inner circles of his mother's government, a Grand Duke with no important duties or function. He became bitter, his hatred for his mother festered, and Catherine made no attempt to soothe his injured pride. Indeed, she did just the reverse. When she celebrated her forty-fifth birthday in April 1774, she gave her son an inexpensive watch to commemorate the occasion, while she bestowed upon Potemkin a gift of fifty thousand rubles, the precise amount Paul had requested not many days before to pay the debts run up by his extravagant young wife.[19] The Grand Duchess Natalia had expensive tastes indeed, but she was not destined to continue in her ways for long. After three days of agonizing labor, she died in mid-April 1776, as she struggled to give birth to an infant that could not leave her body. "No human ministrations could save this princess," Catherine wrote to a friend a few days later. "Her unfortunate physical structure would not allow her to give birth to the child she carried."[20]

Paul was not overly dismayed by his wife's sudden death. During her life, Natalia had ruled him in despotic fashion, and he had become apathetic under her influence.[21] Catherine, too, shed no tears at her passing and, by early summer, had begun to seek a new wife for her son. This time, her choice was Princess Sophia Dorothea Augusta Louisa of Württemberg. She broached the subject to Paul soon after Natalia's funeral. "Is she dark or fair, short or tall?" he reportedly asked with eager interest. "She is tall, lovely, charming; in a word, she is a treasure, a real treasure, a treasure who will bring joy with her," Catherine replied.[22] By early July, Paul was on his way to Berlin to discover for himself this new "treasure" and see what joy she might bring to his life.

Princess Sophia Dorothea was born in Stettin on October 25, 1759. She was very different from Paul, and she ultimately would grow into an impressive Russian Empress. She was tall, fair, and somewhat inclined to stoutness, but her carriage was indisputably regal, and she loved the pomp and ceremony associated with Court life. Unlike the Romanovs, she was frugal, a rare virtue in any eighteenth-century European ruling family. She was remarkably well educated, and her family seat of Montbéliard was a well-known center of learning and culture. Joseph II of Austria, Prince Henry of Prussia, the great Abbé Raynal, and many other European intellectual and political figures frequented her parents' dinner table, and the princess avidly kept diaries and wrote letters to preserve her impressions of their comings and goings. Sophia Dorothea loved all the arts and, in Russia, would support them generously.[23] At the age of seventeen, she already was wise in the ways of the world. When her mother lamented that "unfortunate things often happen to Russian sovereigns, and who knows what fate has in store for my daughter?" Sophia replied that "I fear the Empress Catherine greatly. I will get all confused in front of her and undoubtedly will seem stupid. If only she and the Grand Duke will like me!"[24] Obviously she did not fear the Russian Court but only worried about making her way in it quickly and successfully. She made every effort to charm her new courtiers and their ladies in order to ensure her success in St. Petersburg. She has been best characterized as "a mixture cunningly blended of patriarchal simplicity and worldly wisdom, of intellectual and artistic culture, and bourgeois simplicity, of German *Gemütlichkeit* and French refinement."[25]

Paul met his future bride at a state dinner given in honor of his arrival in Berlin by the Prussian Queen. He was as delighted with the young princess as she was with him. "I found my intended to be such as I could only have dreamed of," he wrote to his mother. "She is tall, shapely, intelligent, quick-witted, and not at all shy."[26] Sophia Dorothea's first impressions were no less enthusiastic. "I am more than content," she wrote. "Never, dear friend, could I be more happy. The Grand Duke could not be more kind. I pride myself on the fact that my dear bridegroom loves me a great deal, and this makes me very, very fortunate."[27] By early fall, she had fallen deeply in love with her future husband. "I cannot go to bed, my dear and adored Prince, without telling you once again that I love and adore you madly," she wrote to Paul soon after she reached St. Petersburg that September. Her first letter to him after she took the Russian name Maria Feodorovna spoke only of her love. "By this paper I swear to love and adore you as long as I shall live." Paul's reply was, "I swear to you that, with each day, I love you more and more."[28] They were wed on September 26, 1776. The Grand Duchess Maria Feodorovna would make a nearly perfect Imperial wife, and Paul for many years would be a model husband, deeply in love with the woman he married.

Perhaps because Catherine denied him any role in state affairs, Paul became very conscious of himself as the founder of a dynasty that would end those succession crises that had plagued Russia for so long. He and Maria Feodorovna awaited the birth of their first child with special excitement, and they were delighted when a son, Alexander, was born in December 1777. "I am very happy that the Almighty has seen fit to use me as an instrument for fulfilling the hopes of our beloved homeland," Maria Feodorovna wrote to the Moscow Metropolitan Platon a month later.[29] But the young couple's joy was painfully short lived, for Catherine hastened to inflict upon her son and daughter-in-law the same cruel indignity she had suffered at the hands of the Empress Elizabeth. Just three months after Alexander's birth, Catherine took him away to live in her own apartments, to raise him as an enlightened prince who would one day rule Russia. In April 1779, Maria Feodorovna bore a second son, Konstantin, and, again, Catherine spirited him away to raise him to reign over her latest, but never-to-be-realized dream—a reborn Greek Empire. "Here I am with Alexander on my right and Konstantin on my left," she crowed in a letter to Baron Grimm.[30] She seemed to give no thought to the pain she had inflicted by denying her son and his wife the joys of rearing their first children. Nor was she concerned about the deep humiliation they must have felt when she proclaimed that she had taken Alexander and Konstantin from them because they were incapable of rearing their children properly and responsibly.

Maria Feodorovna bore no children for four years after Konstantin's birth. In the meantime, Paul had little to occupy his time, for Catherine continued to refuse him any role in state affairs. So determined was she to exclude him from her government that she did not even tell him about the manner in which she and Potemkin were shifting Russia's international alliance system. Paul held only the empty title of Grand Admiral, and the small estate of Pavlovsk, which his mother had given him and Maria Feodorovna to celebrate Alexander's birth. Like most of the things Catherine bestowed upon her son during her lifetime, Pavlovsk was a flawed gift, for it was a primeval tract, a region of dense forests and dark swamps, visited only by a few sturdy hunters in search of game. In the spring and fall, the rough, narrow road that led to it from Tsarskoe Selo was impassable. By contrast with the brilliant and flourishing estates Catherine bestowed upon Potemkin at the same time, it was a poor gift indeed.

Yet Maria Feodorovna saw possibilities in Pavlovsk that eluded Catherine's less imaginative gaze, and her efforts would produce one of the most beautiful estates in all of Russia. At first, her dreams were restrained by her limited means, but during 1778 and 1779 she had two modest summer houses built in an effort to relive fond memories of the summer residence she had so loved during her Württemberg childhood.[31] A few years later, she would commission the great architect Charles Cameron to grace the hill that rose above the estate with a small palace that was as elegant as it was beautiful, a rare Russian monument to good taste and moderation, which led the Count de Ségur to exclaim that "everything there was stamped with the seal of the greatest dignity, good form, and refinement."[32]

In the fall of 1781, Paul and Maria Feodorovna left St. Petersburg for a grand tour of Europe that took them to Austria, Italy, France, the Netherlands, Switzerland, and Southern Germany. Although they traveled incognito as the Count and Countess du Nord, Paul and Maria Feodorovna received royal honors wherever they went. They basked in the attention they received, yet even in the midst of his joy, Paul made little effort to conceal his growing frustration at being excluded from Russian affairs, and he proclaimed his bitterness at foreign courts. When asked about his mother's leading advisers, he exclaimed, "when I have power, I shall flog them, ruin them, and kick all of them out."[33]

But Paul's immoderate criticisms of his mother's ministers were not what made the greatest impression upon the Europeans who met him. Most of all, they were impressed by his civility, sharp intellect, never-ending curiosity, and charming ways. These impressions are especially worth noting to balance the portraits drawn by a number of contemporaries and historians, who painted Paul as a hopeless madman. Certainly, those who met him in 1781–82 had no such impression, and he won many plaudits for his good humor and honesty. "I make no pretensions at being brilliant," he wrote from Rome. "A man becomes awkward in spite of himself if he tries to be anything other than what he truly is."[34] "At Versailles, the Grand Duke seemed to know the French Court as if it were his own," wrote one observer. "His conversations and everything he said that I can recall, revealed not only an extremely penetrating and very educated mind, but also a subtle understanding of all the nuances of our customs and all the subtleties of our language."[35] Perhaps the best portrait of Paul and Maria Feodorovna was penned by the Austrian Emperor Joseph II, who knew them well. "Good music, or a good play, especially if it is not too long or too late in the evening, seems to please their Imperial Highnesses," Joseph wrote to his brother Leopold, Duke of Tuscany. "The Grand

Duchess plays the harpsichord extremely well," he added, "and, for the Grand Duke, who loves to explore his surroundings, it is necessary to have both maps of the immediate area and plans of the various buildings in which you live or will show him."[36]

Paul and Maria Feodorovna returned to Russia at the end of 1782 to devote their attention to Pavlovsk, where Cameron was raising his architectural masterpiece. There, Maria Feodorovna gave birth to Aleksandra Pavlovna, the first of six daughters she would bear during the next twelve years. "I love boys far more than girls," Catherine remarked, leaving Aleksandra and the five sisters who followed—Elena, Maria, Ekaterina, Olga, and Anna—to their parents' care.[37] For Paul and Maria Feodorovna, life in 1783 seemed pleasant, happy, and vaguely promising, the horizon unclouded by crises or family cares. Yet the very events that brought them joy in that year also sowed the seeds of bitterness and discord in their lives. To celebrate the birth of their first daughter, Catherine gave them Gatchina, an estate situated some forty-five *versty* from St. Petersburg, which once had been owned by her lover, Grigorii Orlov. There, Paul and his wife would spend much of the next decade, living in retirement and isolated from political affairs.

Gatchina was a large and flourishing estate, with more than six thousand serfs, and Paul viewed it as a miniature version of the Empire he one day would rule, a minikingdom in which to test his ideas about government, economy, and reform. Paul wheedled a battalion of troops from his mother in order to defend his peasants against the brigands who infested the neighborhood, and he soon began to test his ideas about military reform and tactics upon them. Therein lay the makings of a tragedy. Nikita Panin, an enlightened, high-minded man, had taught Paul the principles of government. Sadly, it was Baron Steinwehr, a rigid Prussian, thoroughly schooled in the automatonlike parade-ground techniques of Frederick the Great's drill sergeants, who taught him how to command. The regulations Steinwehr so adored were already obsolete, but Paul viewed them as the epitome of military efficiency. He had an absolute, but totally misplaced, confidence in Steinwehr's very limited abilities. "This man will be for me what [Franz] Lefort was for Peter the Great," he proclaimed enthusiastically.[38] It was at best an unfortunate hope. More properly, it was an absurd dream. Steinwehr implemented his cherished and antiquated Prussian system under Paul's watchful and approving eye, seemingly unaware of the anachronistic product he had created. "The officers of the Grand Duke's entourage are like figures cut out of an old scrapbook," remarked the Duchess of Saxe-Coburg when she saw them a few years later.[39]

There was no real and immediate danger in Paul's passion for dressing his battalion up in outdated Prussian uniforms and marching them according to equally antiquated Prussian regulations. There was, however, another sort of danger, very real indeed. Under Steinwehr's tutelege, he tasted absolute power for the first time, and he did so in a brutal military environment. Physically a small man, and denied power for too long, his first taste left him thirsting for more. He turned Gatchina into a military camp and its grounds into a vast drill field for that handful of soldiers over whom he could exercise absolute authority. There, he evolved the retrograde "Gatchina system." To direct his "system," he chose men of flawed character who had been unable to make their way in Russia's regular military establishment. In addition to Baron Steinwehr, Paul's most trusted deputies were Count Feodor Rostopchin, Aleksei Arakcheev, and Ivan Kutaisov. Together, they established a regime that was notorious for its brutality, its worship of Prussian ideals and regulations, and its passion for the details of parade drill. Paul had fallen victim to the paradomania that had so afflicted Peter III. Under its influence, such trivia as the cut of parade uniforms, the size and shape of buttons, and the length of a parade step became matters of high state policy in the administrations of every Romanov who followed him.

There were mitigating aspects to life at Gatchina, however. By the late 1780s, Paul's private library had grown to number some forty thousand volumes, and he used them in a diligent effort to prepare himself for the Imperial duties he hoped one day to assume. As master of Gatchina's serfs, he proved a benevolent and enlightened lord. Most of his serfs were Lutheran Finns, and he was surprisingly tolerant of their faith. He subsidized the construction of four new churches, only one of them Russian Orthodox. Paul allotted more land for his serfs' use, lent them money in time of need, instructed them in more advanced agricultural techniques, and established a variety of industrial enterprises to occupy them during the winter months. He founded schools where peasant children were taught to read and write, and he built a hospital where peasants, who usually lived and died without seeing a physician, could receive free medical care. Paul introduced the latest ideas about sanitation into his hospital and ordered the quarantine of patients with infectious diseases. He also established a system of itinerant doctors, who visited patients who could not travel to the hospital. Gatchina became a model estate whose example was emulated all too rarely by Russia's noble serfowners.[40]

Although Paul and his wife were not as close as they once had been, there remained a good deal of warmth between them during the years they lived in isolation. Maria Feodorovna moderated the extreme elements in Paul's character that had begun to emerge on the drill field, continued her efforts to beautify Pavlovsk, and dedicated herself to charitable work among its inhabitants. She was devoted to expanding her modest literary salon and ardently planned infrequent theatrical and musical evenings for her family and friends. Except for these rare moments, their life was uneventful. "We usually dine at four or five o'clock," Maria Feodorovna wrote in the fall of 1790. "There are the Grand Duke, myself, Mademoiselle Nelidova, kind Count Pushkin, and Lafermière. After dinner, we pass the time in reading. In the evening, I play chess with our good Pushkin and, when the clock strikes eight, Lafermière, hat in hand, invites me for a stroll."[41] During these years, she kept voluminous diaries that recorded their daily life in great detail. But she was a person who treasured her privacy above all. In keeping with her last wishes, Nicholas I burned all these volumes after her death in 1828. Even most of the letters she wrote have not survived. Maria Feodorovna usually ended whatever she wrote with an admonition to "burn this letter."[42] We therefore know far less about the years she and Paul spent at Gatchina and Pavlovsk than we would wish, and much of our view of their life must rest upon fragmentary documents and a certain amount of conjecture.

One thing we know for certain is that Paul's fascination with his militaristic regime at Gatchina began to drive him and his wife apart during the late 1780s. The crude military manner he found so attractive, and adopted so slavishly after his brief visit to the Finnish front during the Russo-Swedish War, did violence to everything in which Maria Feodorovna believed. It was during these years that Paul began to turn to other women, although he never had his mother's prodigious appetite for lovers. Even in his extramarital affairs, Paul was inclined to monogamy, and there were only two other women in his life. The first of his mistresses was Ekaterina Nelidova, one of Maria Feodorovna's ladies-in-waiting. Maria Feodorovna was crushed by Paul's first infidelity, and her relations with Nelidova were very bitter for several years. Around 1794, however, the two women made their peace and vowed to use their combined influence in an attempt to moderate Paul's increasingly frequent rages. Their alliance endured until 1798, when the nineteen-year-old Anna Lopukina displaced Nelidova as Paul's official mistress.[43]

Neurotically sensitive, Paul saw even the slightest infraction of his orders as a challenge to his authority at Gatchina, and that unfortunate perception remained with him when he became Russia's Emperor late in 1796. Paul thus viewed the French Revolution in even more negative terms than did his mother because he saw in it a direct and immediate threat to his personal power. At Gatchina, he therefore adopted extreme precautions against every real or imaginary revolutionary menace. "The Grand Duke sees the offshoots of revolution everywhere," Feodor Rostopchin reported in May 1974. "He finds Jacobins everywhere, and, the other day, he ordered the arrest of four unfortunate officers of his battalions because their plaits were too short—a true sign of revolutionary spirit!"[44] Catherine began to fear the "sort of hands my Empire will fall into after my death," as she once wrote.[45] Indeed, there is some evidence that she became so apprehensive about Paul's tyrannical behavior at Gatchina that she considered excluding him from the succession and naming her grandson Alexander as her heir. Whatever her thoughts, her sudden death in November 1796 prevented her from disinheriting her son. On November 6, 1796, Paul became Emperor of All the Russias at the age of forty-three.

Paul had never made a secret of his contempt for his mother's advisers, and there were many in St. Petersburg who awaited his first acts as Emperor with trepidation. Yet Paul's conduct at first belied the frightening rumors that Catherine's courtiers had repeated in hushed whispers for so long. Charles Masson, a Frenchman who had become the future Alexander I's personal secretary, was a witness to the beginning of Paul's reign, and has left us a striking account of the new Emperor as a sober, cautious, and sensible monarch, generous toward his enemies:

> The first steps which he took seemed to contradict the reports of his stern and capricious disposition. His conduct towards [Catherine's] favourite [Platon Zubov] likewise had every feature of generosity. He . . . continued him in his offices in flattering terms; saying, when he delivered to him the cane of command, which is borne by the general *aide-de-camp* upon duty: "Continue to execute those functions about the corpse of my mother; I hope you will serve me as faithfully as you have served her." . . . The ministers, and the heads of the different departments, were likewise confirmed in their employ . . . and the most powerful were even promoted. . . . Every hour, every moment, announced some wise change, some just punishment, or some merited favour. The court and city were surprised. People began to imagine that his character had been mistaken, and that his long melancholy pupillage had not entirely depraved it. All the world saw itself happily deceived in its expectations, and the conduct of the grand-duke was forgotten in that of the emperor.[46]

Paul's first acts as Emperor thus promised a policy of peace abroad and moderate reform at home. He pardoned Tadeusz Kościuszko, the Polish patriot who had led a rebellion against Russia in 1794, and rehabilitated Peter III, interring his remains in the cathedral at the Peter-Paul Fortress in their proper place next to Russia's other rulers. His only vengeful act was to order Count Aleksei Orlov to follow Peter III's coffin in the funeral cortege. Now old and infirm, Orlov was obliged to hold an Imperial crown above the coffin of the Emperor he had helped to murder.

On the day of his mother's funeral, Paul announced that his coronation would take place in Moscow on April 5, 1797. At the beginning of January, the Imperial Guards began to move to Russia's ancient capital to prepare for the ceremony, and Paul himself went there in the middle of March to oversee their final efforts. His was to be a coronation filled with Prussian military ceremonial, and it would be difficult to name a Romanov crowning that contrasted more with Catherine the Great's than his. Catherine had used her coronation as a psychological and ceremonial instrument to proclaim her close ties to the nation she ruled. She had glorified Russian tradition, courted the Muscovites, made amends for the slights they had suffered at the hands of her predecessors, and emphasized her love for the Orthodox Church. By contrast, Paul made Moscow and his coronation ceremony into a reflection of the Gatchina system. Moscow became "a city transformed along Prussian lines," wrote one observer. "Everything was according to the German style in order to please the taste of the new Tsar."[47] Despite snow and bitter cold, dress parades were the order of the day as Paul inflicted humiliating punishments for minor infractions of his newly established military regulations upon officers and men unaccustomed to the Gatchina regime. So enamored had he become with things military that, during the coronation ceremony, he strode to the altar to take Holy Communion with a saber still hanging from the sword knot at his hip.[48] Catherine's coronation had been festive, regal, and elegant. Paul's resembled the ceremony of a general taking command of his armies. No festive atmosphere greeted his coronation; the hearts of his subjects began to fill with fear and a dark sense of foreboding.

No sooner had he taken up Russia's crown than Paul read a manifesto that delineated a firm order of succession through the male line of the Romanov family.[49] Together with the Statute on the Imperial Family, which he decreed later that day, Paul's proclamation established the legal basis for the Romanov dynasty. Modeled upon the "House Statutes" of German ruling families, Paul's dynastic laws placed all members of the House of Romanov in an intricate hierarchy that made clear their place in the line of succession and bestowed upon them a unique position within Russia's state and society. As one historian wrote more than a half-century ago, "The entire 'family' was abruptly separated from civil society. The 'Imperial Family,' the 'Reigning House,' from that moment became a unique organization, whose members all occupied a completely exclusive position outside the general framework of public and civil law."[50] On the day of Paul's coronation, all Romanovs, no matter how distantly related to the reigning monarch, became potential heirs to the throne. The Romanovs no longer were a part of Russian society, but stood above it and outside it.

For those who pleased him, Paul's coronation was a time of glorious rewards, and he outdid his mother in showering favors upon his courtiers. He created seven counts, one prince, and two barons, and bestowed Russia's highest decoration, the Order of St. Andrei, upon no less than thirteen men. He appointed three new field marshals, and awarded twenty-one Orders of St. Aleksandr Nevskii. One hundred twenty-five men and women received First and Second Class Crosses of St. Anne. Beyond that, he gave away nearly two hundred thousand serfs to those he considered faithful servitors.[51]

Catherine the Great had bestowed rewards and marks of favor at her coronation with care and forethought in order to assure herself of political support among Russia's leading generals and statesmen. The bonanza of ranks, titles, estates, and serfs that Paul showered with wild abandon served no such positive political purpose. Although his first acts after Catherine's death had calmed the apprehensions of those who had served his mother, their fears soon returned and grew more intense. Paul substituted rigid regularity for the more subtle shades that had characterized his mother's methods of governing, and he attempted to reestablish the service system of Peter the Great. Widespread feelings of persecution were stirred as he drove nobles into exile for minor, sometimes imagined, infractions of his rigid regulations. "The general dissatisfaction began to express itself in conversations within families, then among friends and acquaintances, and finally became the topic of the day. The more it spread, the more energetic became the efforts of the secret police," wrote Nikolai Sablukov, a young officer in the Horse Guards. "The officers of our regiment," he added, "became the objects of special attention, and the slightest slip on the parade ground was punished by arrest."[52] Men soon began to whisper of ridding Russia of Paul's tyranny. As early as the fall of 1797, the Swedish Ambassador to St. Petersburg reported rumors of conspiracies to his superiors in Stockholm.[53]

Despite the early rumors, it seems that the actual plot that overthrew Paul originated during the fall of 1799. Three men were instrumental in setting it in motion. The first was Count Nikita Petrovich Panin, who in October 1799, at the age of twenty-eight, became Russia's Vice-Chancellor and was probably the only one of all the conspirators to be motivated by deep concern for Russia's welfare. He truly feared the growing influence of Count Feodor Rostopchin, who, at the time, was Paul's closest confidant, and Panin was convinced that Paul's increasingly capricious domestic and foreign policies would ruin Russia. Panin's first ally was Joseph Ribas, a man of very different caliber. Probably the son of an Italian porter, Ribas had come to Russia during the reign of Catherine the Great, gotten a post as tutor in the Cadet Corps, and married Anastasia Sokolova, one of the great Potemkin's protégées. Through intrigue and great good fortune, Ribas became an Admiral in the Russian navy, and, after a brief period of disfavor for his shameless thefts from the state exchequer, he had risen to become Paul's Deputy Vice-President of the Admiralty. Ribas has been characterized as "an adventurer with the soul of a bandit," a description probably not far off the mark.[54] Certainly, he was ready for any intrigue that would increase his rank and fortune, and his brief period of disgrace had given him cause to protect himself from Paul's wrath.

Although they had the will, neither Panin nor Ribas had the resources to carry out a plot against their Emperor, and, for that reason, they enlisted Count Petr Pahlen in their cause. To everyone, Pahlen seemed a witty, charming, and honest man, and he had risen high in Catherine's service. "Pahlen was a tall, broad-shouldered man, with a high forehead and a frank, cordial, good-natured expression," recalled the Princess Daria Lieven. "He had a carefree attitude toward life. He was the embodiment of straightforwardness, joviality, and lightheartedness."[55] "It is impossible to know this good old man and not to love him," Maria Feodorovna wrote to a friend in September 1798.[56] Yet there was another and sinister side to Count Pahlen's character that would betray all the trust that Paul and his Empress placed in him. He was immensely ambitious, and his great pretensions had been sorely deflated when Paul had dismissed him as Governor of Riga early in his reign. Although Paul soon restored him to favor and bestowed even higher posts upon him, Pahlen remained fearful and insecure because of his one brush with disgrace. He sought to protect himself, his wealth, and his career by every fair and foul means. "Under that attractive exterior, [there was] an abyss of perfidy and ferocity, an iron will, and a reckless audacity at the service of an ambition as boundless as it was unscrupulous," remarked one commentator.[57] Although by 1799 Pahlen had become Military Governor-General of St. Petersburg, Military Governor of Riga, and Civil Governor of the Baltic provinces, he was more than ready to join the plot against his Emperor in an effort to make certain that he would never again suffer disfavor or disgrace.

The growth of a plot against Paul during 1800 represents a tortuous web of foreign and domestic intrigue, and we still cannot be certain about the reputed involvement of several prominent figures. There is some circumstantial evidence that implicates Charles Whitworth, Britain's Ambassador to St. Petersburg, and Austria's Ambassador Count Cobenzl must have some blame laid at his door as well. These men gathered frequently at the town house of Madame Olga Zherebtsova, whose beautiful body, loose morals, and elegant, intimate suppers made her a prominent figure in St. Petersburg society. Zherebtsova was the sister of Catherine's last lover, Prince Platon Zubov, and, for a time, she also was Whitworth's mistress, although she never allowed him exclusive access to her favors. Devious in her sometimes complex sex life, she was by nature a conniver, loved intrigue, and despised Paul because he had sent her three brothers into exile and sequestered their estates. Certainly the men who visited her residence discussed a variety of underhanded dealings. Yet the content of these early discussions at Zherebtsova's remains shrouded in mystery, largely because Count Pahlen, as chief of Paul's military police, kept the conspirators' work a well-guarded secret. We can only begin to trace the full development of the conspiracy against Paul from documents that date from mid-1800.[58]

Toward the end of 1800, it seemed that the conspiracy to overthrow Paul was about to collapse. Cobenzl was declared *persona non grata* in February 1800, and Whitworth was expelled in June. Five months later, Paul disgraced Panin and sent him to live on one of his estates far from St. Petersburg. A fortnight later, Admiral Ribas died. Of the three original conspirators, only Pahlen remained; unfortunately for Paul, he was the most dangerous, and events soon turned to his advantage. Paul's general amnesty of November 1800 strengthened Pahlen's support by bringing the Zubovs, anxious to regain their influence and eager for revenge, flocking back to St. Petersburg. In February 1801 Paul exiled Count Rostopchin and left Pahlen even more fully in control of state security. Pahlen now held the military command of St. Petersburg and the Baltic provinces. He controlled the Empire's postal service and, with Prince Aleksandr Kurakin, directed Russia's Foreign Office.[59] Unwittingly, the Emperor had delivered himself into the hands of the very man who was the chief conspirator against him. Confident that his plot against Paul could succeed, Pahlen prepared for action.

A number of Russia's leading generals and statesmen enlisted in the ranks of the conspiracy. By February 1801, there were more than fifty men, including all three of the Zubov brothers, five Senators, the Commanders of the Preobrazhenskii and Semenovskii Guards, and two of Paul's general aides-de-camp.[60] As more men learned about the plot, its existence became ·more difficult to conceal, even with all the resources at Pahlen's command. By the beginning of March 1801, Paul himself had begun to hear vague rumors about it, and he grew wary of Pahlen's charming manner. Seeing that he might fall into disfavor at any moment, Pahlen hastened to set Sunday, March 11, as the fateful night.[61]

On that evening, the conspirators dined in small groups at the lodgings of several of their senior officers who shared in the plans to depose their Emperor. At about eleven o'clock, they assembled at the quarters of General Talyzin, where some of them began to lose their nerve. It seemed that the conspiracy might collapse until Pahlen stepped into the breach and urged them on. "Remember, gentlemen, that in order to eat an omelet, one must begin by breaking some eggs," someone remembered him saying at that moment.[62] He ordered more toasts. The young officers did not need to be asked a second time to refill their glasses. That night, more than one of them rediscovered his courage at the bottom of a cognac bottle.

Once certain that his men would stand firm, Pahlen divided them into two groups. He placed Platon Zubov and General Count Leontii Bennigsen at the head of one group and led the other himself. Then the conspirators made their way to the Mikhailovskii Castle, Paul's new castle-fortress, where he lived protected by moats, drawbridges, and battalions of armed guards. Anyone who has spent a winter in St. Petersburg knows the misery that city can hold for the traveler who goes on foot through a cold, rainy November night, and the conspirators found the weather at its worst. Freezing rain, driven by great gusts of bone-chilling arctic wind that swept in from the Gulf of Finland, slashed at their faces and cut through their greatcoats. The streets were dark, alleys even darker, and the cobbles slippery with ice. Cautiously the officers picked their way along streets that would not know the glow of streetlights for several more decades.

Ever the crafty politician who thinks first and foremost of self-preservation, Pahlen made certain that Zubov and Bennigsen reached the Mikhailovskii Castle ahead of him so that he would be in a position to claim that he had rushed to Paul's defense if their assault failed. But Zubov and Bennigsen crossed the moat and the drawbridge with ease because they had with them General Petr Argamakov, the very aide-de-camp whose duty it was to warn Paul of any emergency. Once across the drawbridge, they entered the palace by a side door, climbed a back staircase, and broke into Paul's bedchamber. To their amazement, his bed was empty, its sheets rumpled and tossed aside as evidence that its recent occupant had made a hasty retreat. "He has escaped!" Zubov shouted. Then Bennigsen, his eyes sharper and his wits less dulled by alcohol than the others, saw Paul's feet just showing beneath a screen that shielded the room's huge fireplace. Silently, he motioned to Zubov. The two men drew their swords, tossed the screen aside, told Paul that he was Emperor no longer, and placed him under arrest.[63]

Accounts differ about what happened in the moments after Paul's arrest, and none of the participants seemed willing to admit his full role. We therefore do not know who struck the blow that killed Paul, but it seems clear that one of the conspirators felled him with a heavy gold snuffbox, while another strangled him with a scarf. There is some evidence that Nikolai Zubov, a huge bear of a man, may have killed him with his fists. In any case, some moments before Pahlen and his companions reached the second floor of the Mikhailovskii Castle, Paul lay dead upon the floor of his bedchamber.[64] Pahlen then awakened the Grand Duke Alexander, who knew of the plot but did not expect his father to be murdered. Dismayed when he heard the news, Alexander evidently first thought of refusing a crown stained by his own father's blood. "How shall I have the strength to rule with the constant remembrance that my father has been assassinated?" he reportedly asked his wife. "I cannot. I resign my power to whomever wants it. Let those who have committed the crime be responsible for what can come of it."⁶⁵ "Enough of being a child," Pahlen commanded. "Go and reign. Show yourself to the Guards. The well-being of millions of people depends upon your firmness."⁶⁶ Alexander did as he was told. To the detachment of Semenovskii Guards on duty at the Mikhailovskii Castle, he announced: "My father has died from an apoplectic seizure. During my reign, everything will be as it was during the time of my grandmother."⁶⁷

Paul had held the crown for a mere four years. In the early morning hours of March 12, 1801, he had met the same tragic fate as Peter III in what was to be the last of Russia's palace revolutions—and for much the same reason. Despite his long years of waiting and study, Paul had not learned to wield absolute power, and it had perverted his good intentions. "Paul came to the throne at that period, propitious for autocracy, when the terrors of the French Revolution had cured Europe of the dreams of civil freedom and equality," wrote one of his contemporaries. But he failed to make proper use of his opportunities. "What the Jacobins had done to the republican system, Paul did to the autocratic one," the writer continued. "He treated us not as his subjects, but as his slaves. He executed the innocent and rewarded the worthless. . . . Heroes, accustomed to victories, he taught to parade. . . . Although inwardly disposed to goodness, he secreted gall. Each day, he devised ways to frighten others, yet he himself was the most frightened of all. He wanted to build himself an inaccessible palace—and built himself a tomb instead!"⁶⁸

The tragedy of Paul's murder was eclipsed by the joy of his subjects at being freed from his despotic regime. "After four years, Catherine has arisen from her tomb in the form of a handsome youth. The child of her heart, her beloved grandson, proclaims that he will return us to her era," rejoiced one young official. "I don't know how to describe what happened," he recalled in his memoires. "Everyone felt some sort of moral emancipation. Everyone's outlook became more optimistic, their steps bolder, and their breathing freer."[69] "He will be just like Peter [the Great]: great in justice and great in war," proclaimed Admiral A. S. Shishkov.[70] Europeans in St. Petersburg felt the same way. "What priceless good fortune for Russia and for all of Europe," wrote the Austrian Consul Viazzoli to his superiors in Vienna. "I am convinced that this prince will march with rapid steps along the true path of glory, and that they will bestow upon him the well-deserved title of 'the Great.' " "Terror has taken flight, and joy reigns supreme in this capital," Viazzoli's colleague Locatelli added.[71] In the streets of St. Petersburg, people wept with joy and strangers embraced each other. "Even greengrocers congratulated their customers on the change in the same manner as they offered congratulations on important holidays," wrote another observer.[72] Never had the accession of a Russian sovereign been greeted by such general and heartfelt rejoicing.

Alexander I was twenty-three years and three months old when he became Russia's Emperor. He was tall, blond, and handsome. He walked with a slight limp, which added an air of romance to his presence, and he was easily the most charming Romanov that Russians had yet seen. Alexander was blessed with a rare gift for putting others at ease by his courteous and simple manners. More than any of his native-born predecessors, he was European in culture and outlook. He spoke French better than Russian, and he was steeped in the teachings of the Enlightenment. Yet Alexander was a sphinx, "the enigmatic Tsar," a man wracked by deep inner torment and a gnawing sense of personal inadequacy that would lead him to become a reactionary and a mystic who spent his last years in a tortured quest for salvation. Alexander, the prince who liberated Europe from the tyranny of Napoleon, ultimately became a tyrant himself, as he came to fear the dreams of his youth.

Alexander had spent his childhood at Catherine's Court, where he began his princely education at the age of six under the doting gaze of his grandmother and his chief tutor, General Nikolai Saltykov. Saltykov was a biddable courtier of limited ability, with a knack for making himself pleasing to others. Certainly, some of his manner rubbed off on Alexander, who grew into a lad with winning ways. Catherine was enthralled and loved him with a deep maternal passion. As a child, Alexander returned her love in full measure. His first letters were to his "dearest granny" and left no doubt about his feelings: "Dearest granny Empress thank you for all the letters you wrote me, and I hope you will come back to us very soon we are well, we hope you were well too. I kiss your hands and feet and your little finger. Your little grand-son Alexander."[73]

In time, Catherine was not content to leave Alexander's formal ed-ucation in Saltykov's hands. At her instruction, the ever-diligent Mel-chior von Grimm searched Europe for a tutor and recommended Frédérick-César LaHarpe, an ardent Swiss republican. LaHarpe once described himself as a man who was "filled with republican principles, educated in solitude, completely alien to the real world, [who] lived more with books and the creation of fantasies than with people."[74] It was that world he showed Alexander. "LaHarpe endeavored to in-troduce his pupil to the enchanted realm where the abstract notions of reason, justice, equality, and the common good assumed an appearance of reality and moved majestically amidst the romantic figures of heroes and social reformers drawn from ancient and modern history," the his-torian Michael Florinsky once wrote.[75] He taught Alexander nothing about the reality of Russia because he knew nothing about it. Russians complained that LaHarpe wanted to make his pupil into a Marcus Aurelius when their country desperately needed a Genghis Khan or a Tiberius.

Although he spent most of his childhood at Catherine's Court, Alexander came under the influence of Paul's Gatchina system during his weekly visits to his parents' estate. He began to speak of doing things "in our way, in the Gatchina style," and this unfortunate new passion stayed with him throughout his life. As his close friend Prince Adam Czartoryski later remarked, "The trivia of [this sort of] military service, and the practice of attaching extreme importance to them, per-verted the mind of the Grand Duke Alexander. He developed a liking for them from which he never recovered."[76] Indeed, the Gatchina sys-tem became as much a part of Alexander's character as did the studied charm of General Saltykov and the abstract intellectual world of La-Harpe.

The great Goethe once wrote that "man is unable to free himself from the impressions of his youth"; while that is undoubtedly true, men and women usually succeed in reconciling the contradictory influences of their formative years into a more or less integrated outlook and set of values. In other times and under other circumstances, this process probably would have been a part of Alexander's adolescent experience, but the unique circumstances of his youth prevented it from occurring. Paul openly despised the elaborate civility of Catherine's Court, and she was equally scornful of the rude, militaristic regime he had established at Gatchina. Anxious to please both grandmother and father, Alexander lived two completely different lives as an adolescent. Yet the worlds of Catherine and Paul were so contradictory that neither permitted compromise with the other. Alexander therefore developed two different personalities and never integrated them into what might be called the "real" Alexander. In Catherine's presence, he was Alexander the enlightened prince, the sensitive and charming youth, steeped in the writings of the Enlightenment and early sentimentalism. At Gatchina, he became the parade-ground commander, a part of that raw militarism of jackbooted officers and sharp, brusque commands that his father so adored. The first role reinforced Alexander's image of himself as a prince whose superior sensitivity and intellect could envision a state in which justice, reason, and concern for the common good prevailed. The second role reinforced his awareness of the absolute power of autocracy that could provide the means for implementing his enlightened dreams. Both were fantasy worlds but, for Alexander the Grand Duke, they seemed very real. The tragedy of Alexander the Emperor would be that he attempted to live in both, while their contradictions made it impossible for him to establish either one in Russia. His failure to do so made his adult life a succession of soul-shaking psychological crises, which would drive him to the brink of emotional breakdown toward the end of his life.

These crises were still in the future as the youthful Grand Duke Alexander studied with LaHarpe under Catherine's doting gaze and drilled the Gatchina troops under his father's critical eye. He was tall for his age and had become fascinated with women by the time he reached fourteen. Catherine decided that he must marry, and she chose Princess Louisa of Baden as his future bride. "Even though she will not be fourteen until January [1793], she is majestic and pleasing to the eye," wrote one of Alexander's tutors. "She is tall. There is something especially fetching about her manner and the way she walks. . . . Everything she does shows great modesty. . . . I venture to predict," he concluded, "that in a few years, when she matures, she will become a great beauty."[77]

Princess Louisa came to St. Petersburg in the fall of 1792 to become the Grand Duchess Elisaveta Alekseevna and Alexander's wife. Catherine thought her a model of beauty, charm, and honesty, gave her rich apartments unlike anything she had ever known, and showered her with marks of affection. "Her voice goes straight to your heart," Catherine later wrote to her friend Grimm.[78] At first, Alexander was shy with his future bride, and she mistook his reserve for dislike. "The Grand Duke treated the Princess very bashfully," one of his courtiers confided to his diary, while Louisa lamented that "he did not come near me, and stared in an unfriendly manner."[79] But the young couple soon grew fond of each other, and that feeling soon bloomed into love. "You tell me that I hold the happiness of a certain person in my hands," she wrote to Alexander. "If that is true, then his happiness is assured forever. . . . This person loves me tenderly, and I love him in return, and that will be my happiness. . . . You can be certain that I love you more than I can ever say," she added.[80] Alexander and Elisaveta Alekseevna were betrothed in May 1793, looking like "a pair of angels," in Catherine's fond words.[81] On September 28, 1793, Elisaveta Alekseevna donned a gorgeous gown of silver brocade and, with the diamond-studded Order of St. Andrei flashing upon her breast, became Alexander's wife while a twenty-one-gun salute boomed out over the Neva. "It was a marriage between Psyche and Cupid," Catherine wrote to the Prince de Ligne.[82] Psyche was fourteen years old; Cupid was just a year older.

Alexander and his bride were too young to marry, and soon they were crushed by a world that posed expectations they could not satisfy. Elisaveta was overwhelmed by the grandeur of the Court and frightened by the vicious intrigues Russian lords and ladies waged with such cold calculation. Her own family life had been warm and close, and it had taught her to cherish marriage as a sacred institution. She was appalled by the intense sexual intrigues that flourished all around her in a Court where adultery was an accepted form of entertainment and where the Empress's own lover tried to seduce her before she reached her sixteenth birthday.[83] Elisaveta Alekseevna felt abandoned in an alien world where she could never be herself, even among her servants and ladies-in-waiting. Alexander was her only source of solace. "Without my husband, who alone makes me happy, I should have died a thousand deaths," she wrote to her mother less than six months after her wedding.[84]

But Alexander could not become the psychological bulwark his child bride needed, for he was scarcely more than a child himself, and his marriage was only one of several interests.[85] Yet he too became exhausted by the tensions of the dual life he led at Gatchina and at his grandmother's Court. There were persistent rumors that Catherine meant to disinherit his father and name him heir apparent. Alexander was not yet ready for the burden of ruling Russia, but the rumors forced him to take a serious look at the Empire he one day must rule. He was terrified by what he saw. "Our affairs are in unbelievable disarray, and we are being plundered from all sides," he wrote to his friend Viktor Kochubei a few months before Catherine's death. "It is an absolute impossibility even for a genius, let alone an ordinary person like me, to deal with these problems, and I have always held to the principle that it is better not to take on a task than to do it badly. Thus my plan is that, having at some point renounced this scabrous place, I shall set myself up with my wife on the banks of the Rhine, where I shall live a life of peace and simplicity, devoted to the company of my friends and to the study of nature."[86] Alexander often returned to his dream of a simple, pastoral life, but he never renounced the Russian throne, nor did he ever make serious plans to do so. Whatever their dreams, he and Elisaveta were destined to reign as Emperor and Empress of Russia for a quarter-century.

Alexander's first acts as Emperor showed him to be generous, tolerant, and charitable. On the first day of his reign, he freed an estimated twelve thousand Russians whom his father had sentenced to prison or exile without trial. In less than a month, he decreed that Russians could travel abroad once again, import books and musical scores, and reopen private presses, although he did not free booksellers and publishers from responsibility for what they imported or printed. To bring back the droves of talented statesmen, officers, and nobles who had fled abroad during Paul's reign, he issued an amnesty to all except murderers, restored Catherine's Charter of the Nobility, and abolished Paul's secret police.[87]

So generous and noble hearted did their new Emperor appear that Russians rejoiced when he and Elisaveta Alekseevna went to Moscow for their coronation in September. It was a beautiful time of year, the weather sunny and warm during the day, with the nights tinged by the crispness of the coming fall. It was that fleeting season called *bab'e leto,* the equivalent of Indian summer, a time when summer's somnolence has passed and vigor returns to the men and women of Russia. There is a certain romance in the days and nights of *bab'e leto,* as Muscovites strain to catch those last warm rays of sun before they become blotted out by winter's cold. It was just the right moment for a dashing young prince to be crowned in the great Uspenskii Cathedral and just the time for Muscovites to meet the Empress Elisaveta, now grown into a breathtakingly beautiful woman.

Alexander was far less formal and much less concerned with pomp than his predecessors had been. On some occasions, he even rode through the streets of Russia's ancient capital alone, and the people instantly took him to their hearts. "There were no shouts, no noise, but awed whispers of 'little father,' 'our very own,' and 'our beautiful sun,' " wrote one young official.[88] Alexander was loved by his people for what his modest manner seemed to promise, not for the wealth and prestige he had it in his power to bestow. Unlike his predecessors, he granted few marks of favor at his coronation and heaped no gifts of serfs upon his courtiers. "The vast majority of our peasants in Russia are slaves," he explained. "I have vowed not to increase their numbers, and therefore have made it a rule not to give away peasants as property."[89] Instead, Alexander spoke of laws, justice, and constitutions. Many Russians soon fell into a quandary about what their "little father" meant to do.

Alexander himself was not certain about what he would do, but he was determined to do something impressive, for there were times when his adolescent dreams of a rural idyll on the Rhine faded before the more brilliant vision of himself as an enlightened sovereign who brought to Russians a glorious government based upon well-ordered laws, justice, and the rights of man. He had shared these dreams with a circle of four friends, but three of them, Count Viktor Kochubei, Nikolai Novosiltsev, and Prince Adam Czartoryski, had left Russia to escape the uncertainties of Paul's capricious regime. The only one still in St. Petersburg was Count Pavel Stroganov, a young man who had studied under the famous mathematician-revolutionary Gilbert Romme and had established close ties with Jacobin clubs in Paris during the early days of the French Revolution.[90] Quietly and discreetly, Alexander summoned the rest of his young friends back to Court. Together, they planned an era of enlightenment and progress for Russia. "Alexander reigns," wrote Stroganov to Novosiltsev in London. "Come, my friend, we are going to have a constitution."[91]

Constitution! The word was a ringing cry during the days of the American and French revolutions, and it was one that Alexander and his young friends spoke with passion and reverence. Indeed, most accounts of the beginning of Alexander's reign have fastened upon it, proclaiming him one who wanted to bring to Russia a new and "liberal" order, modeled upon that of the West. To Alexander and his young friends, however, "constitution" meant something very different than it did in the American or Western European experience. They spoke of "a constitution made to conform to the true spirit of the nation," which meant rules and regulations established by an absolute monarch, not rights and freedoms defined by the will of common men.[92] "The welfare of men consists in the security of their property and in the freedom to do with it everything that is not detrimental to others," Stroganov wrote. Such a statement might have been made by Edmund Burke, Thomas Jefferson, or any number of other political figures at the end of the eighteenth century, but Stroganov added a very important qualification: "The means of assuring this [welfare of men] are the regulations of the [state's] administration. The guardian of these regulations is the fundamental law of the state or, in other words, a constitution. A constitution is the law which regulates the manner in which a watch is kept over the making of *administrative laws* . . . which reduces the wrong which can come from the differences in abilities of those who are at the head of the state."[93] Alexander and his advisers thus viewed a constitution as an instrument for protecting men and their property from such abuses of autocratic power as Russians had suffered under Paul. Ideally, a constitution would achieve what the Prussians called *Rechtsstaat,* a system in which the rights and obligations of all subjects were defined and protected by laws and regulations.

As typical children of the Enlightenment, Alexander and his young friends thought that their elite educations and superior sensitivity made them uniquely able to serve the best interests of Russia and her people. Convinced that they must preserve the Emperor's despotic power if they were to impose an enlightened order from above, they reached the strange and contradictory view that only a monarch who wielded unlimited authority could bring a constitution to Russia. In a word, they planned to use despotism in the pursuit of liberty and justice. So sensitive were they to the perils of regularizing power relationships in Russia that they called themselves the "Private Committee" and met in secret. "It is of such importance to keep the public in ignorance of the government's purpose that, before we go any further, we should establish the principle that *secrecy* ought to be one of the fundamental principles [of our work]," Stroganov wrote in the spring of 1801.[94] After eighteen months, their concern for the sanctity of autocratic power and their fear of public opinion led them to conclude their discussions after having accomplished little beyond restructuring Russia's central administration.

Alexander's failure to play the role of enlightened monarch in Russia coincided with a dramatic change in his personal life: he began a love affair that would continue for almost two decades. Maria Czetwertynska, who has been described as a woman possessed of "a courtesan's cunning and a harlot's outlook,"[95] was a beautiful Polish princess who had married Dmitrii Naryshkin, Grand Master of Alexander's hounds. She paraded her Polish origin before a Court that was wary of Poles, and she flaunted her liaison with Alexander in a tasteless and blatant fashion. When the Empress inquired about her health at a ball, Naryshkina remarked, "I think I am pregnant," before a large group of courtiers and their ladies who, as Elisaveta Alekseevna later lamented to her mother, "could not be ignorant of the means by which she had been impregnated."[96] Despite her vicious tongue and petty meanness, Maria Naryshkina and Alexander shared a passion that endured until 1819, when his conversion to mysticism broke the long-standing bond between them. After visiting Paris for a number of months in late 1819 and early 1820, Naryshkina returned to St. Petersburg to find that her Imperial lover, to whom she had returned with such longing and passion, talked of "nothing except the cross and divine love."[97] The man who had shared her bed for so many years wanted to become her father confessor, and that ended their union.

As much as he loved her, Alexander's relationship with Naryshkina could not blunt the sense of failure that overwhelmed him when the "Private Committee" broke up in 1803. Unable to become the emancipator of Russia, he attempted to become the deliverer of Europe. In the fall of 1805, he rode at the head of his armies to free Europe from the scourge of Napoleon Bonaparte, who had just proclaimed himself Emperor of France. We shall return to the complexities of Alexander's wars and foreign policy in a later chapter, but here we should point out that he was no more successful abroad than he had been at home. During his first campaigns, Alexander drained the bitter draught of defeat again and again, as Napoleon scored one triumph after another over his armies and those of Russia's allies. At Austerlitz, in late November 1805, Napoleon inflicted some twenty-six thousand casualties upon a Russian army of about ninety thousand and captured all their artillery. After some talk of peace, the war began anew, but it went no better for Russia. In November 1806, Alexander watched his armies stand aside while Napoleon's flamboyant Marshal Joachim Murat occupied Warsaw. Then, in late January 1807 (February 8, according to the Western calendar), Russia's armies fought the indecisive, but immensely bloody, battle of Preussische-Eylau—only to be crushed by Napoleon at Friedland in June, where Alexander's forces suffered some fifteen thousand casualties in a single day.[98] "Sire," the Grand Duke Konstantin Pavlovich reportedly said to Alexander when this last bitter news arrived, "if you would not make peace with France now, then give each of your soldiers a well-primed pistol and order them to blow out their brains. That will give you the same result as you would achieve by fighting another and final battle."[99] Proclaiming that "an alliance between France and Russia has always been the object of my desires" and that only such an alliance was "capable of assuring the welfare and security of the world," Alexander sued for peace.[100]

In mid-June 1807, Alexander and Napoleon met on a gaily festooned raft that had been anchored near Tilsit at midstream in the Niemen River, which formed the border between Prussia and Russia. Their manner was jovial, their words friendly. It was as if they never had been enemies. The two Emperors met alone, and their conversation went unrecorded. Still, after a thorough study of remarks they made to their closest advisers before and after the meeting, a careful diplomatic historian has reconstructed the course their conversation probably followed. "I loathe the English as much as you, and shall be delighted to support you in anything you may undertake against them," Alexander reportedly said in beginning discussions with his adversary. "In that case," Napoleon supposedly replied, "Everything is taken care of and the peace is made." "Let us deal directly with each other," he is said to have continued. "In an hour, the two of us can accomplish more than our representatives could in several days. Let no one stand between us. I shall be your secretary, Sire, and you shall serve as mine."[101] Each Emperor did his utmost to charm the other and to give away as little as possible. "God has saved us," Alexander wrote to his sister a few days later. "Instead of sacrifices, we are leaving the conflict with a certain luster."[102] Napoleon left Tilsit thinking he had gotten the best of his foe. He might have felt less certain of his ground had he seen the last line in a letter Alexander penned to the Grand Duchess Ekaterina Pavlovna just nine days later. "Bonaparte pretends that I am nothing but a fool," he wrote. *"He who laughs last, laughs best!"*[103]

Before his turn came to laugh, Alexander faced more hardship and failure, for he returned to Russia determined to take up the course of reform he had abandoned in 1803. This time, he relied not upon his inner circle of friends but upon Mikhail Speranskii, a humble priest's son, who was an administrative genius and one of a mere handful of truly farseeing statesmen to serve the Romanovs in the nineteenth century. With Alexander's approval, he studied the government of Napoleonic France and drafted an ambitious plan for modernizing Russian society and the administration that served it. He presented his recommendations to Alexander in 1809. Once again, Alexander was torn between his enlightened dreams and his apprehension about restricting his personal power, and he never put Speranskii's plan into effect. He approved only a few of the plan's lesser reforms, which regularized Russia's civil service and established more rigid qualifications for promotions. Because even these modest measures undercut some of the fradulent schemes Russia's nobles used to advance their careers in their nation's service, Speranskii became perhaps the most unpopular statesman in Russia.

During the years immediately after Alexander signed the peace at Tilsit, there was rising discontent in Russia, but it was far less the result of the Tsar's limited reforms than of his stubborn participation in Napoleon's Continental System. Britain's blockade of Russia's port prevented the nobility from exporting the products their serfs produced and caused them to suffer serious economic losses. Their discontent reached a peak early in 1812, and one of its most vocal centers was the Court the Grand Duchess Ekaterina Pavlovna maintained at her provincial estate in Tver. There she assembled those nobles who criticized her brother and encouraged the historian and belletrist Nikolai Karamzin to write his famous *Memoir on Ancient and Modern Russia,* which urged the Emperor to return to the policies of his grandmother.[104]

That Ekaterina Pavlovna allowed her Court to become a center of opposition must have pained Alexander extremely. She was an energetic, vivacious woman, short and petite, with ringlets of closely cropped, tightly curled chestnut hair framing her cameolike face. She drew men to her with irresistible charm, and they took delight in doing her bidding. She claimed the hearts of many in Russia, but her greatest conquest was her brother himself. She was Alexander's favorite sister, one of the great feminine influences in his life. Indeed, his intense passion, expressed in such phrases as "I am yours, heart and soul, for life," "I think that I love you more with each day that passes," and "to love you more than I do is impossible,"[105] adds yet another element of mystery to his already complex character. Ekaterina Pavlovna's letters to her brother expressed no such yearnings, but she was indeed a scheming woman with a burning interest in politics, who missed no opportunity to influence state policy. Certainly, she was an important leader in the opposition against the commoner Speranskii.

Although he was not to blame for the nobility's economic difficulties, Speranskii became the focus of their hatred just as Russia's relations with France fell into a serious decline. Recognizing the need to establish a united front to face the approaching French menace, Alexander sacrificed his favorite adviser in what must have been one of the most painful decisions of his life. On March 17, 1812, he sent Speranskii into exile in the wastes of Viatka. It was a sad and bitter moment for the Tsar and minister. "When I left him," Speranskii later recalled, "my cheeks were still wet with his tears."[106] On June 13/25, 1812, the fifth anniversary of their meeting at Tilsit, Napoleon invaded Russia with his Grande Armée. Without a declaration of war, he began his fateful march on Moscow.

Throughout his first decade as Russia's Emperor, Alexander had known only failure as he attempted to fulfill those great roles he thought an enlightened Emperor should play. He was unable either to give Russia enlightened laws and a constitution or to free Europe from the scourge of Napoleon, whom he once cursed as an enemy of Christ. At the same time, Napoleon had enjoyed brilliant successes. His *Code Napoléon* created a state in which all citizens were equal before the law and guaranteed its protection. In addition, he gave France an efficient civil administration and showed himself to be one of the world's greatest captains. With a poor education and little training, Napoleon had risen from obscure beginnings to become all those things to which Alexander aspired in his dreams. Napoleon's invasion of Russia would shift the balance completely. For the campaign of 1812 marked the beginning of his ruin, while it heralded the onset of Alexander's greatest hour. Alexander not only would defend his Empire against Napoleon but would lead a victorious crusade back across Europe to sweep the Corsican conqueror into exile on the island of St. Helena more than a thousand miles off the southeast coast of Africa.

Napoleon crossed the Neimen on June 13 with every intention of crushing Russia before the first flakes of snow began to fall. He was supremely confident, for the Grande Armée was the greatest military force ever assembled in the Western world. Not only Frenchmen, but Germans, Poles, Italians, Portuguese, Hollanders, Scots, Irishmen, and Hungarians marched beneath his famed Imperial eagles. Except for England, all of Europe stood against Russia in the summer of 1812; the Grande Armée was a dramatic affirmation of that fact. It was 575,000 strong and had more than 1,100 cannon. How could a mere 195,000 Russians bar its way? Because Europeans thought Alexander weak, they saw nothing but empty rhetoric in his vow that "I shall not lay down my arms so long as a single enemy soldier remains in my domains." Wrote the Prussian Field Marshal Count von Gneisenau, "After his first defeat, [Alexander] will cede all the lands between the Dvina and the Dniepr. After his second—Petersburg and Moscow, and [he then] will be content to keep Kazan and Astrakhan."[107]

The campaign of 1812 was a titanic clash of great armies locked in bloody struggle, of vast ambitions in deadly conflict, of heroic deeds and daring heroes who fought and died in their Emperors' causes. The poet Mikhail Lermontov later painted it as a duel between giants in the style of the ancient gods. There was Alexander, "His helmet cast of gold/ The ancient Russian titan/ Stood waiting for another/ From distant lands." And, against him, stood Napoleon, who "came with martial thunder . . . To raise his insolent fist/ Against his royal foe."[108] Alexander thought of the struggle in much the same way. "It is Napoleon or me. Me or Napoleon. But we cannot reign at the same time [on this planet]," he wrote at the time.[109]

Napoleon began his campaign in Russia by driving everything and everyone before him. In rapid succession, some of Russia's most important western cities fell before his onslaught, and, on August 18, he entered the smoking ruins of Smolensk after a battle that had cost each army some twenty thousand casualties. It was a costly defeat, but part of the grand strategy Alexander and his generals had settled upon that summer. They gave battle when necessary, always retired in good order, and, with every step of their retreat, drew Napoleon deeper into Russia. They did so with a clear purpose. "Your Empire has two powerful defenders in its vastness and its climate," wrote the Governor-General of Moscow to Alexander. "The Emperor of Russia will always be formidable in Moscow, terrible in Kazan, and invincible in Tobolsk [in Western Siberia]."[110] Throughout the summer and fall, Russia's armies continued in their slow retreat, waiting for these two powerful allies to bring their awesome forces into play.

Alexander brought yet another force to bear against Napoleon, and it proved even more powerful. This was the emotional and psychological power of Russians' love for their Mother Russia, who was being ravished by the Western conqueror. At no time did Alexander play upon this theme with more virtuosity than during his visit to Moscow in mid-July. His armies were in retreat from Vitebsk, but he made no attempt to conceal Russia's first defeats and even warned his subjects that more would follow. But, as he spoke simply and movingly of his people's greatness and strength in times of adversity, he promised them final victory. Summoning the nation to rise in arms, he called upon the shades of Kuzma Minin and Prince Pozharskii, and the people of Moscow took him to their hearts in an outpouring of patriotic fervor such as no Romanov had yet seen. "Lead us where you will! Lead us, father. We shall triumph or die!" "Take heart! You see how many of us there are in Moscow alone. Think how many there are in all of Russia! We all are ready to die for you!"[111] Nobles formed their serfs into companies and battalions of militia, while merchants emptied their purses in a fervent orgy of national sacrifice. Based upon his careful study of historical sources, Count Lev Tolstoi captured brilliantly in his epic novel *War and Peace* the intense emotions that seized Moscow's lords and great merchants as he described the assembly that met on July 15 to consider Alexander's plea for troops and treasure:

> The great halls were packed. In the first were the nobility in their uniforms and, in the second, the great merchants with their beards and blue kaftans, bedecked with medals. There was a hum of voices and continual movement in the chamber where the noblemen assembled. The greatest lords sat on high-backed chairs at a great table beneath the Emperor's portrait, but most of the nobles were walking back and forth through the room. . . .
>
> "Yes, and this is not the time for deliberation, but for action," said [one] nobleman. "The war is in Russia. Our enemy advances to destroy Russia, to defile the graves of our fathers, to carry off our wives and children." This nobleman smote his breast. "We all shall

rise up. All of us. Every man shall go. All of us shall follow our Tsar!" . . . Several voices spoke up in approval. "We are Russians and we shall not begrudge our blood to defend the faith, the throne, and our motherland. We must set aside our fantasies if we are to be true sons of our homeland. We shall show Europe how Russia rises in the defense of Russia!" shouted a nobleman. . . . Then the Emperor entered along a wide pathway between two walls of nobles. . . . From the nobles' chamber, the Emperor went to the merchants' hall. . . . A stout liquor merchant sobbed like a child and kept repeating: "My life and my property—take both, Your Majesty!"[112]

The struggle against Napoleon had become Russia's first Great Patriotic War.

Soon after he left Moscow, Alexander appointed the popular Field Marshal Mikhail Kutuzov to command Russia's armies. At one time, Kutuzov had been known for his élan and disregard for danger under fire. Twice he had been gravely wounded during Catherine's Turkish wars; in the first one, a Turkish ball had cost him an eye. In those days, Kutuzov also had been a wencher of Sybaritic proportions and a courtier of some accomplishment. By 1812 he was sixty-seven years old, enormously corpulent, and anything but a dashing figure. His greatest loves seemed to be food, drink, and women, as many and as varied as could be found. "Let the Lord give him a Field Marshal's baton, tranquility, and thirty women," was one Russian general's fond wish for him on the eve of Napoleon's invasion.[113] Yet there was another side to this fat, one-eyed, aging lecher. He spoke little and often seemed to sleep during staff meetings, but he was one of Russia's greatest commanders and bound men to him as only great captains can. Napoleon called him "the old fox of the North," a careful fox who knew his country and his soldiers perfectly and who husbanded his resources when less patient men would have rushed into the fray. In 1812 Kutuzov turned his craft against Napoleon, and, just when the invader thought he had triumphed, he found that he stood perilously close to the brink of destruction. Kutuzov never pushed him over the edge, but left Napoleon to take that step himself.

Kutuzov and Napoleon first clashed on August 26 in a titanic struggle some fifty miles to the west of Moscow near the village of

Borodino. Few battles have been more brutal, and few have seen more men committed to combat at one time. As the first artillery shells began to scream overhead at dawn, 130,000 of Napoleon's soldiers launched their attack against some 120,000 Russians. For fifteen hours the battle raged. The rattle of musketry, the clang of sabers and bayonets, and the thunder of cannon blended with the roars and screams of desperate and dying men. Deadly artillery fire and vicious hand-to-hand struggles reduced several army corps on both sides to the size of battalions. General Count Mikhail Vorontsov led a division of four thousand grenadiers into battle that morning only to emerge from the fray with fewer than three hundred that afternoon. When night fell, fifty-eight thousand Russians and fifty thousand of the Grande Armée lay dead or wounded upon the field. Among them were forty-seven of Napoleon's best generals and some of Kutuzov's most able commanders, including the popular hero General Prince Petr Bagration.

Veteran of so many great and bloody conflicts, Napoleon later wrote that "the most terrible of all my battles was the one [at Borodino] before Moscow. The French showed themselves worthy of victory, and the Russians worthy of being invincible." [114] Both sides claimed victory, but neither had inflicted a fatal blow. For Napoleon, the only satisfaction was that Kutuzov fell back toward Moscow rather than continue the battle the next morning, a small consolation indeed. As he continued his advance toward Moscow, grave doubts gnawed at the French Emperor's resolve. "Peace lies in Moscow," Napoleon proclaimed to his aides. "When the great nobles of Russia see us masters of the capital, they will think twice about fighting on." Yet, even as he spoke these encouraging words, his close aides noted that he had become "very thoughtful and worried." [115]

No one ever has explained why Napoleon was so certain that Alexander would sue for peace once the French occupied Moscow. He had hoped to smash the Russians at its gates, but Kutuzov was too clever to risk his army. He saw no strategic value in Moscow's defense, and he refused to give battle merely to satisfy public opinion. On September 1, Kutuzov summoned all of his commanders to a final conference at Fili, a small village on the western edge of the city. In a blaze of decorations and brilliant uniforms, men who had fought under Russia's banners for decades gathered in a peasant's hut and urged their views upon their commander in chief. After listening to them for an hour, Kutuzov rose. "I see that I shall have to pay the fiddler myself," he muttered. "I shall sacrifice myself for the good of our country. I order a retreat [from Moscow]."[116] And so it happened. While Muscovites looked on in disbelief, Kutuzov led his armies to the southeast, through the city and out of Napoleon's path. Through Moscow's main streets, the Russian soldiers marched with measured tread, their eyes downcast, their hearts bitter at being ordered to abandon the holy city of their ancestors to the invaders. Some of the peasant conscripts, who made up the army's rank and file, were weeping. Rather than face occupation by the French, as many of Moscow's citizens as could find transportation followed in Kutuzov's wake. By the morning of September 2, the only people left were those who had not been able to find horses or carts or carriages or wheelbarrows or who, for some other reason, could not leave the city. Shops along the Arbat, the Tverskaia, and Kuznetskii Bridge were boarded up, their owners having fled with whatever they could carry. Those who remained in Moscow hid in their homes, fearfully awaiting the arrival of the dreaded French conqueror.

If a lookout had been standing in the belfry of the Bell Tower of Ivan the Great at two o'clock on the afternoon of September 2, he would have seen a brilliant suite of general staff officers in the splendid uniforms of the French Empire appear on the crest of the Sparrow Hills to the southwest of Moscow. Several hundred feet below them, and less than a mile away, rose the domes of the Virgins' Convent, where Peter the Great had incarcerated Sofia during the last years of her life. But it was not toward the serene beauty of that cloister that the officers gazed. All of them, including a short, swarthy man whose black hair was receding and whose paunch was beginning to bulge, riveted their eyes upon a point some three miles further to the northeast. There before them rose the ancient ramparts, towering spires, and gilded domes of the Kremlin. It was a sight they had ridden more than two thousand miles to see and one for which many of their comrades had paid with their lives. Napoleon and his officers sat gazing in silence at the sight below, then the silence was shattered as the Old Guard, heroes of so many of Napoleon's greatest battles, rushed forward. From throats long accustomed to cheering France's glories came the cry, "Moscow! Moscow! Long Live the Emperor!"[117] Napoleon had won his prize. Moscow, Russia's ancient capital and the key to Eurasia, lay at his feet.

At first Napoleon made no move to enter the city he had so longed to add to his list of great conquests. From all of these other cities—Cairo, Jaffa, Alexandria, Milan, Venice, Berlin, Lisbon, Madrid, Warsaw, Amsterdam, Rome, and Antwerp—deputations of city fathers had come forth to lay their beloved city and its treasures at the conqueror's feet. Napoleon was determined that Moscow should be no different; he waited on the Sparrow Hills for a deputation of city elders to surrender Russia's ancient capital to him. To his amazement, none arrived. Soon his advance guards sent back a report that seemed too absurd to be believed: Moscow was empty. "All had fled," Napoleon's adjutant, General Armand Caulaincourt recalled. "Moscow was a deserted city, where one came across none but a few wretches of the lowest class. . . . A gloomy silence reigned throughout the deserted city. During the whole of our long progress [through the city streets] we met not a single person."[118] Napoleon bowed to the inevitable and rode on to the Kremlin. No amount of cheering by his own soldiers could mask the fact that no Russians greeted his arrival.

Before Napoleon went to bed that night, a number of adjutants began to report fires breaking out in various corners of Moscow. None of them was large, and few threatened to get out of control, yet it was the beginning of disaster. Unlike St. Petersburg, a city of broad avenues, great squares, and majestic brick and stone buildings, Moscow's medieval heritage had left her with narrow streets lined with closely crowded wooden buildings. A spark from a carelessly tended stove or from any one of a hundred other sources was all that was needed to set tinder-dry shingles ablaze. Once started, the flames spread faster than any fire-fighting equipment known in the early nineteenth century could control. The French soon found themselves in a city consumed by flames. "A demon inspires these people!" exclaimed Napoleon, as he received reports that it was the Russians themselves who were setting the fires. "What savage determination! What a people!"[119] He had entered a city with all its buildings, supplies, and facilities intact. In less than a week, three-quarters of it was in ruins.

To this day, no one is certain if the Moscow fires began because

Napoleon's soldiers were careless or because the city's Governor-General, Count Feodor Rostopchin, ordered them set; there is considerable evidence to support both conclusions. In any case, the Russian reaction to Moscow's burning was fearsome and swift. They had felt grief, even a sense of betrayal, when Kutuzov had abandoned the capital without a fight. But, as news of the city's burning spread, the Russians' grief turned to anger and their anger soon boiled into a seething fury against the invaders who had destroyed the holy city of their ancestors. By the middle of September 1812, Napoleon faced not only Kutuzov's armies but an entire nation welded into a single deadly weapon bent upon his destruction. Alexander spoke for all Russians that fall when he wrote to his sister that "my resolution *to struggle is more unyielding than ever.*"[120]

Throughout the fall of 1812, Napoleon waited in vain for Alexander's peace proposals to arrive in the Kremlin. When none came, he made overtures on his own, but Alexander sent no reply. As days stretched into weeks, Napoleon came to see that he, not Alexander, faced a truly desperate situation, for Russia's armies grew stronger by the day while his own dwindled from desertions and the ravages of disease. He faced the hopeless prospect of wintering in Russia without adequate food, shelter, or supplies, surrounded by people so hostile that they burned their grain rather than sell it for French gold.[121] As winter approached and as the Russian partisans stepped up their attacks in his rear, Napoleon saw that his line of communications, which relied upon a perilously vulnerable corps of couriers who raced from Paris to Moscow in fourteen days, must soon collapse. By early October, he admitted the hopelessness of his situation. At seven o'clock in the morning of October 7, 1812, the Grande Armée abandoned Moscow. "I am on my way to winter quarters," Napoleon wrote to his wife.[122] At the time, he could not admit even to himself that he would spend the winter in Paris, for he thought only of revenge as he left Russia's ancient capital. One of his last orders as he passed through Moscow's gates was to detonate the gunpowder charges that had been placed in the Kremlin.

Napoleon retreated along the road by which he had invaded Russia that summer. Although the first part of the winter of 1812 was unusually mild, his horses had no fodder and his men were without food and proper clothing. They moved slowly, surviving only because the temperatures had not yet fallen below freezing. Then, in mid-November, bitter cold struck and what remained of the Grande Armée collapsed. "The greater part of our artillery has been put out of action because the horses have died and the majority of the gunners have had their feet and hands frozen off," reported Napoleon's Marshal Berthier. "The army is in a state of complete chaos."[123] Napoleon's soldiers limped westward, hoping against hope to escape the Russian partisans and cavalry that dogged their steps. Finally, the great Niemen River came into view, and, on December 2, the last tattered remnants of the once-proud Grande Armée recrossed it into the safety of Prussia. Six months earlier, Napoleon had led 575,000 men eastward into Alexander's domains. Only one in twenty returned. Using Nature's perils as his chief weapons, Kutuzov had inflicted an overwhelming defeat upon his adversary.

Kutuzov's victory brought him little thanks, for Alexander and most of his advisers considered his strategy during Napoleon's retreat grossly incompetent. Kutuzov had dedicated all of his efforts to driving Napoleon from Russia at the least cost to Russia's armies. He had kept steady pressure upon the retreating Grande Armée and always had stood between it and Russian supply centers. But he had spared his troops the agony of pitched battles, knowing that the elements, and Napoleon's overextended supply lines, would complete the task for him. Kutuzov wanted only to liberate Russian soil, but Alexander immediately saw an opportunity to launch a European crusade against the Corsican conqueror he so despised. While Kutuzov continued to insist that there was no reason to spill Russian blood to liberate Prussians and Austrians who might later turn against Russia as they had in the past, Alexander could think of little else. This victory over Napoleon offered him the opportunity he had sought for almost a decade to become Europe's liberator.

When Alexander led his armies across the Niemen on New Year's Day, 1813, he plunged Europe into two years of bloody war. Napoleon fought with desperate fury to protect his crown, and he assembled a vast new army to meet Alexander's attack. Even before the last remnants of the Grande Armée had crossed the Niemen into Prussia, he was in Paris, raising new forces and planning a new campaign. Alexander's advance and the defection of Prussia from the French alliance obliged him to fight a different campaign than he had intended, but he fought it brilliantly with the aid of his enemies' impetuosity and carelessness. In mid-April, Kutuzov's death removed the last voice of caution from the Allied war councils, and Alexander at last could have his way. Freed from the aged Field Marshal's restraints, he and his allies raced ahead to be soundly defeated by Napoleon at Lützen a week later. On May 20, they suffered further losses at the bloody, but indecisive, battle of Bautzen. As in 1805, it appeared that Alexander's dream of liberating Europe was to be short lived.

In June 1813, Napoleon made what most historians consider a fatal error, when he proposed a two-month armistice in an affort to strengthen his forces. During the summer, he increased his army to nearly seven hundred thousand men, but that achievement was offset by the advantage the Russians, Prussians, and British gained from being able to regroup their forces and bring Austria firmly into their camp. Although still outnumbered, the new Allied coalition faced Napoleon in August with an army of more than a half-million, and they had assembled impressive reserves of men and supplies that would prove crucial later in the year.[124] Napoleon showed his old genius by defeating the Allies at Dresden on August 26, but four days later they turned the tables at Kulm, which marked the beginning of the end. In October the Allies inflicted a shattering defeat upon Napoleon at Leipzig. After three days of unrelenting combat, and one hundred twenty thousand casualties, they seized three hundred French cannon, twenty-two French generals, and thirty-seven thousand prisoners of war. Alexander himself led the Cossack attack that turned the initially victorious French advance into a defeat.[125]

During late 1813 and early 1814, Alexander scaled the heights of greatness. Triumphant in all things, he became the hero of the hour and Europe's proclaimed savior. With careful precision, he welded the Allies together to serve the welfare of Europe and instilled in them a sense of common purpose that transcended their narrow national interests. Wrote the Prussian statesman Freiherr vom Stein at the beginning of 1814, "the Emperor Alexander continually acts in a brilliant and fine manner. One cannot help but be amazed by the extent to which this sovereign is devoted to the needs of the moment."[126] It was Alexander who convinced his Allies to fight a winter campaign against Napoleon and it was he who led them across the Rhine into France in early January 1814. Most of all, it was Alexander who negotiated in secret with France's Foreign Minister Talleyrand to learn that the French had lost the will to resist and that the Allies had every chance for victory if they pressed on. When Alexander and his armies reached the outskirts of Paris on March 25, the Russian corps of Generals Count Alexandre Langeron and Aleksandr Rudziewicz stormed Montmartre and the city fell. At *Le Petit Jardinier,* a small inn near the St. Denis gate, the French signed an armistice; on March 31, Alexander entered Paris at the head of his armies.[127] Against all predictions, he had fulfilled the vow he had made when Napoleon had invaded Russia almost two years earlier. The Russians held Paris, and Napoleon's Empire lay in shambles.

Napoleon had come to Moscow as an arrogant conqueror, but Alexander took pride in entering Paris as a prince of peace. The popular adulation he received caused the Countess Choiseul-Gouffier to remark that "one would have said that he was a beloved monarch, re-entering his own capital upon his return from a fortunate and glorious campaign." As in many things, the Countess's account tended to exaggeration, but there is no doubt that Alexander's generosity and kindness won him popular acclaim. "I have only one enemy in all of France," he assured the Parisians. "This is the man who deceived me in a most unworthy manner, who abused my confidence, who betrayed all his oaths to me, and who brought to my country an unlawful and brutal war. Any reconciliation between him and me is impossible. But, I repeat, I have no other enemy in all of France. All the French, with the exception of this one man, have my good will."[128] Alexander turned Paris over to the French National Guard and decreed that the French should choose their own form of government to replace Napoleon's Empire. He even was magnanimous to Napoleon himself, permitting him to retain his title of Emperor and bestowing upon him the island of Elba as a sovereign domain.[129]

When he signed the First Peace of Paris on May 30, 1814, and forced the reluctant Louis XVIII to grant a charter to his French subjects a fortnight later, Alexander saw his most dazzling ambitions realized. For a brief moment before Napoleon escaped from Elba to launch his Hundred Days' Campaign in 1815, Alexander was both the enlightened prince of his grandmother's dreams and the awesome conqueror who epitomized the Gatchina commander grown to international dimensions. But this reconciliation of his character's contradictory facets was of brief duration, for the seeds for a new and destructive crisis already had taken root in his mind. Soon Alexander came to see himself as God's chosen instrument, a prince whose earthly mission was to create a world order of peace and brotherhood based upon the teachings of Christ.

We do not know precisely when Alexander, the princely skeptic, turned to God, but the theme of divine guidance and mercy appeared frequently in his letters once Napoleon began his retreat from Moscow. "God has done everything. It is He who has turned things in our favor so suddenly," Alexander wrote to the Grand Duchess Ekaterina Pavlovna in November 1812.[130] A few weeks later, he joined the Bible Society, which his lifelong friend Prince Aleksandr Golitsyn established at the end of 1812, and arranged for it to receive a government subsidy.[131] Under Golitsyn's guidance, he read the Bible with new attention and devotion, and it left a deep imprint upon him. "My faith is fervent and sincere," he wrote at the beginning of 1813. "It is impossible to describe the good that has come out of my readings of the Scriptures, which I knew only very superficially before. . . . Address your prayers to the Supreme Being, to Our Savior, and to the Holy Spirit, which flows from Them, so that They shall guide me and strengthen me in the only path which can lead to Salvation. And pray that They shall give me the strength needed to carry out my earthly tasks and thus make my people happy. . . . It is to the cause of hastening the true reign of Jesus Christ that I devote all my earthly glory."[132]

Alexander's devotion to "hastening the true reign of Jesus Christ" on earth led him to seek out a strange company of devout Christians, religious fanatics, vulgar charlatans, and shadowy figures of dubious merit. He met the Quakers William Allen and Etienne de Grellet in

Tsar Mikhail Feodorovich

Tsar Aleksei Mikhailovich

Tsar Aleksei Mikhailovich's suburban palace at Kolomenskoe

The Battle of Poltava, 1709

Emperor Peter the Great
(THE SALTYKOV-SHCHEDRIN PUBLIC
LIBRARY, LENINGRAD)

The Admiralty, St. Petersburg, 1716
(THE SALTYKOV-SHCHEDRIN PUBLIC
LIBRARY, LENINGRAD)

The unveiling of Falconet's statue of Peter the Great,
"The Bronze Horseman," 1782

The Regent Sofia Alekseevna

Empress Elizabeth I

Empress Anna Ivanovna
(THE SALTYKOV-SHCHEDRIN PUBLIC LIBRARY,
LENINGRAD)

Empress Catherine I

Empress Catherine the Great

Catherine the Great in 1794

Field Marshal Grigorii Potemkin

The rebel Emelian Pugachev

The Winter Palace, St. Petersburg, 1716

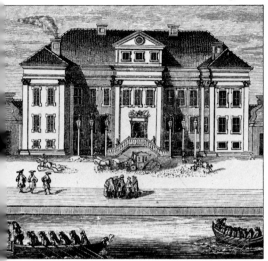

Aleksandr Radishchev

The Moscow Kremlin, early eighteenth century

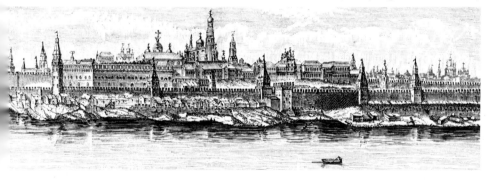

The Winter Palace seen from the Neva River,
late eighteenth century
(THE SALTYKOV-SHCHEDRIN PUBLIC LIBRARY,
LENINGRAD)

1. De Thomon's Bourse*
2. Rastrelli's Winter Palace
3. Voronikhin's Kazan
    Cathedral*
4. Rinaldi's Marble Palace
5. Field of Mars
6. Merchants' Arcade
7. Peter the Great's summer
    gardens
8. Brenna's Mikhailovskii Castle*
9. Rastrelli's Summer Palace
10. Rossi's Mikhailovskii
    Palace*

11. Znamenskaia Square
12. Rossi's General Staff
    Headquarters*
13. Rasputin's apartment*
14. Nevskii Prospekt
15. Haymarket
16. Monferrand's St. Isaac's
    Cathedral*
17. Rossi's Holy Synod*
18. Rossi's Imperial Senate*
19. Falconet's statue of Peter the
    Great ("The Bronze Horseman")

Asterisk (*) denotes buildings constructed after this map was drawn.

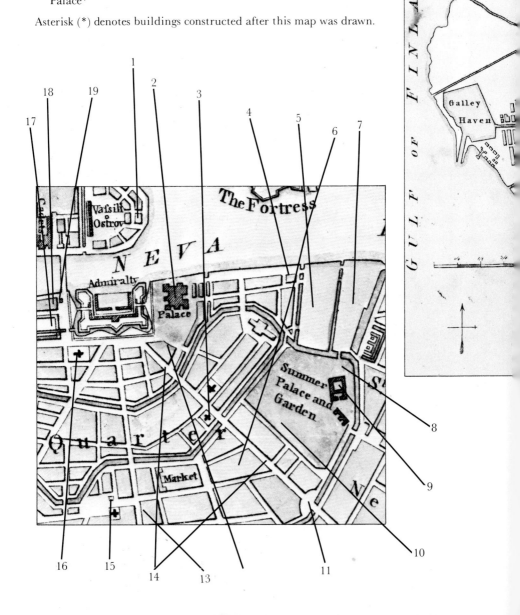

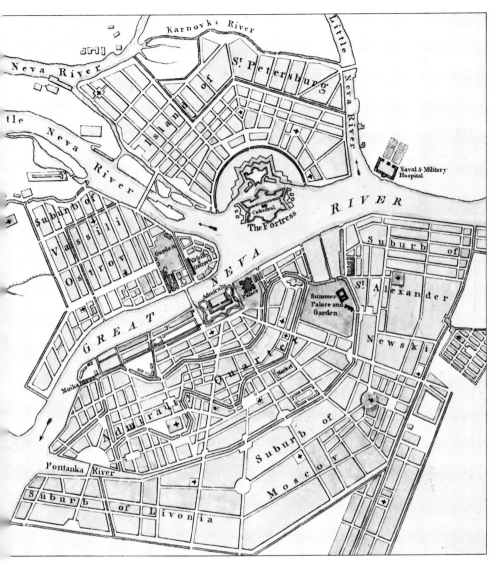

Late-eighteenth-century map of St. Petersburg

Emperor Paul I

Emperor Alexander II

Emperor Nicholas I

Emperor Alexander III

Empress Maria Feodorovna

Emperor Alexander I

Field Marshal Aleksandr Suvorov

The Decembrist Revolt, December 14, 1825

Count Mikhail Speranskii, 1838

Nikolai Karamzin

Count Aleksei Arakcheev

Konstantin Pobedonostsev

The Catherine Palace at Tsarskoe Selo, central courtyard

The Nevskii Prospekt in St. Petersburg

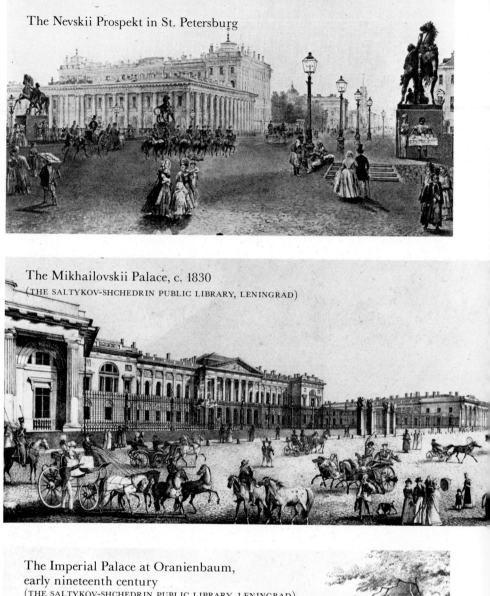

The Mikhailovskii Palace, c. 1830

The Imperial Palace at Oranienbaum,
early nineteenth century

Aleksandr Pushkin

Count Lev Tolstoi

Feodor Dostoevskii

Ivan Turgenev

Bloody Sunday, 1905

The Empress Alexandra
in her mauve boudoir

The children of Nicholas and
Alexandra; the Tsarevitch is
standing below his sisters.

Opposite: Nicholas with Grand Duke
Nikolai Nikolaevich

Tsarevitch Aleksei with three of the royal princesses interned at Tsarskoe Selo
(THE BETTMANN ARCHIVE, INC.)

Vladimir Ilich Lenin, April 1917

London in 1814, conversed with the German mystic Johann Jung-Stilling, became acquainted with the doctrines of Eckhartshausen, and studied the precepts of Böhme and Swedenborg.[133] Alexander's first spiritual mentors were men of strong character, fertile mind, and un-doubted virtue, but none of them struck a truly responsive chord in his mind or heart. That note was sounded by the Livonian Baroness Julia von Krüdener, with whom the confused Tsar had a celebrated mid-night meeting at Heilbronn. An itinerant salon prophetess with a strong personality, Baroness von Krüdener claimed to speak for God Himself and instructed Alexander to surrender his soul to God because he was His chosen instrument. For a moment, she so captured the Tsar's heart and imagination that he arranged a special military review on the Plain of Vertus, where his entire army stood in formation around altars constructed for her benefit.[134] But the Baltic prophetess's influence upon Alexander waned soon after Napoleon's second defeat in 1815, and he became bored with her pretentious ravings as her let-ters became more rambling and absurd. As his infatuation waned, he turned to pursue his dream of a Holy Alliance, which he envisioned as a moral union of European monarchs designed to create a pan-European community based upon Christian principles and to which he would devote his thoughts and policies for the last decade of his life.

Alexander once insisted to Chateaubriand that "there no longer exists an English policy, a French, Russian, Prussian, or Austrian pol-icy; there is now only one common policy, which, for the welfare of all, ought to be adopted in common by all states and all peoples."[135] Such a view was at best a hopeless dream, but Alexander saw his Holy Alliance as the most important instrument for transforming his dream into real-ity. Prominent statesmen such as Britain's Viscount Castlereagh charac-terized Alexander's Holy Alliance as "a piece of sublime mysticism and nonsense"[136] and confessed that, when he and the Duke of Wellington first saw the draft, "it was not without difficulty that we went through the interview with becoming gravity."[137] Other statesmen shared Cas-tlereagh's unflattering opinion.

The principles that underlay Alexander's Holy Alliance were not new to Europe—not long before, Franz Baader had urged a closer identification between politics and religion as the only cure for the evils of the French Revolution, and Chateaubriand himself had argued similarly in his *Génie du Christianisme*.[138] Nor did they stem entirely from the Tsar's growing commitment to pietism. As early as September 1804, he had sent Nikolai Novosiltsev to London to argue for an anti-Napoleonic league in which the Allies would agree to a system of collective security and something resembling a league of nations.[139] He had returned to these ideas again in 1812, when he urged the monarchs of Europe to "live like brothers, aiding each other in their need, and comforting each other in their adversity."[140] When he sought to incorporate similar principles into his Holy Alliance in 1815, however, the mystical terms in which he couched them hardly seemed appropriate to the increased antagonism and suspicion emerging among Napoleon's recent conquerors at the Congress of Vienna.

The Holy Alliance thus embodied Alexander's futile attempt to impose static and outdated principles upon a dynamic and rapidly changing world. The early nineteenth century had seen the first stirrings of nationalistic sentiments in the hearts of many European peoples ruled too long by others. Soon, Alexander's vision of a "common policy" clashed violently with the liberal sentiments he once had cherished. As nationalistic challenges to the stability and order of Europe flared up in Spain, Naples, and Greece during the decade after the Congress of Vienna, Alexander saw his Holy Alliance become identified with the forces of obscurantism and reaction. At the same time, he began to identify liberalism and progress with the dark forces of revolution and upheaval. "We find ourselves in a situation somewhat similar [to what we faced in 1812–14], but I would say that the present evil is still more dangerous than the devastating despotism of Napoleon because the present doctrines are more seductive for the masses than the military yoke under which [Napoleon] held them," Alexander wrote to his friend Prince Golitsyn in February 1821. He thought that he, and all defenders of order, faced a powerful and numerous enemy whose ranks included "revolutionary liberals, radical levelers, and members of the *carbonari* from all corners of the world." He was certain that there was "a general conspiracy of all these societies . . . who have sworn to wreak a most bitter vengeance upon all governments." Even worse, these groups represented "the implementation of doctrines preached

[*406*]

by Voltaire, Mirabeau, Condorcet, and all the pretended philosophers known by the name of *Encyclopédistes*" and were determined to destroy "the Religion of our Savior," a fact proven by "thousands upon thousands of authentic documents."[141] Alexander swore "not to bow before the Satanical power." "The methods we employ must correspond to the magnitude of the danger which threatens us," he wrote to Prince Golitsyn a month later. "Only now do I understand why the Lord God has kept me here until this moment!"[142] The man who had adored the ideas of Voltaire and Rousseau as a youth and had dreamed of establishing a just order based upon the principles of the Enlightenment now damned those precepts as Satan's own and saw himself as God's instrument in a mortal struggle against them.

As God's chosen agent, Alexander served his Divine Master at home and abroad during the last years of his life. His efforts produced complex foreign and domestic intrigues that left Russian state affairs in a shambles at the time of his sudden and unexpected death. Almost immediately, his younger brother and successor had to face a revolutionary threat that came not from the dark "reign of Satan" but from the flower of Russia's nobility grown bitter at Alexander's failure to live up to his promise of an enlightened regime at home.

Alexander's death in the remote southern port town of Taganrog on November 19, 1825, posed the first serious test to the dynastic decrees that Paul I had enacted in 1797. Because he and his Empress had no sons, Alexander's younger brother, Grand Duke Konstantin Pavlovich, was next in line for the throne. Konstantin, however, had divorced his first wife some years before in order to enter a morganatic marriage with the Polish Countess Joanna Grudzinska. Because his new wife could not reign with him in Russia, Konstantin had relinquished his right to the throne in favor of Grand Duke Nikolai Pavlovich in 1823, but he and Alexander had kept his renunciation a closely guarded secret. That unexplained fact presented Nikolai Pavlovich with an immensely awkward dilemma when he learned of Alexander's death. Although he knew that his elder brothers had designated him to rule Russia, his father's dynastic laws of 1797 had established a clearly ordered line of succession within the House of Romanov and had made it illegal for a reigning Emperor to alter it in any manner. Because Konstantin had not renounced the throne publicly, Nikolai swore allegiance to him as Emperor and sent messengers to announce that fact throughout the Empire.[143] For reasons known only to himself, Konstantin refused to accept the Imperial title even for the brief time it would have required for him to abdicate. "My resolve is unshakable," he wrote to his younger brother from Warsaw.[144] After almost two weeks of this ridiculous charade, Nikolai Pavlovich bowed to the inevitable and set December 14, 1825, as the date for his official accession, even though Konstantin still refused to make a formal abdication. That day would go down in history as the "first Russian revolution," more commonly known as the Decembrist revolt.[145]

The men who have been remembered as the Decembrists were young army officers who decided that autocracy must be overthrown in Russia and replaced by a constitutional order. Most of them were scarcely out of their teens, and their reasons for joining in Russia's newly emerged revolutionary movement are not at all clear. Contrary to what most historians have written, the vast majority of them never had been to the West and thus had experienced no direct contact with Western revolutionary societies, but that in no way lessened their ardor.[146] Certainly, adolescent enthusiasm and the tendency of youths to become alienated from the established order cannot be discounted as important factors in their revolutionary development. Of more immediate importance, however, was the ideological and political motivation of their leaders. These men were somewhat older, had marched with Alexander's armies to the West, and had experienced the entire spectrum of political, intellectual, and emotional influences associated with the defeat of Napoleon. When they returned to Russia, they founded secret societies modeled upon the *Tugendbund,* a German patriotic society of the Napoleonic era, which had advocated Prussia's spiritual and national regeneration. The Decembrists' secret societies advocated a mixture of the ideals of Russian freemasonry, the *Aufklärung,* the French Enlightenment, and German Romanticism. Their first aim had been to promote social and political progress within the framework of the autocratic system, but as Alexander became more reactionary in his sympathies, they concluded that revolution was the only way to achieve their goals. During the last year of Alexander's reign, they increased the membership in their secret societies and laid plans for a coup d'état.[147]

December 14, 1825, the day of Nicholas I's accession, was a Monday, an unlucky day according to Russian superstition. The temperature in St. Petersburg was eight degrees below freezing, and an icy wind swept over the city. Nikolai Pavlovich arose well before dawn to receive oaths of allegiance from ranking Guards officers, ministers of state, and senior officials. He knew that a revolt probably would occur among the Imperial Guards that day, but he refused to arrest even the best-known conspirators. "I do not wish the oath [to me] to be preceded by arrests," he had told Minister of War General Aleksandr Tatishchev. "Think of what an ugly impression we should make upon everyone."[148] At first, all was quiet, and for a few hours Nicholas continued to hope that perhaps his advisers' fears about a revolt had been exaggerated.[149] Before the morning was over, however, everyone's worst apprehensions were confirmed. Just before noon, Major General Neidhardt, Chief of Staff of the Guards Corps, galloped to the Winter Palace to report: "Sire! The Moskovskii Regiment is in full revolt. [Brigade Commander General V. N.] Shenshin and [Regimental Commander General Baron P. A.] Frederiks have been grievously wounded and the rebels are marching toward the Senate!"[150]

By early afternoon, some three thousand rebels had gathered on the Senate Square around Falconet's statue of Peter the Great. Nicholas acted swiftly. First, he ordered trusted aides to assemble loyal Guards regiments around the Senate Square and sent others to escort his Empress and children to safety. He then led the Preobrazhenskii Guards to the scene of the revolt to deal with the rebels himself.[151] For some time, neither side moved. The rebels had no plan of action beyond assembling at the Senate Square, and Nicholas was still reluctant to fire upon his subjects on the first day of his reign, especially upon young officers who represented some of Russia's greatest noble families. Yet nightfall would be approaching shortly, and he could not allow so many rebels to escape unpunished under the cover of darkness. He ordered the Horse Guards to attack, but their charge failed "because of the confined space, the icy pavement, and, in particular, because they did not have sharpened sabres," he later recalled.[152] Finally, only one course of action remained. "Sir, there is not a moment to lose! You must give the order [for the artillery] to fire!" pleaded Nicholas's Aide-de-Camp General Prince Ilarion Vasilchikov. In reply, Nicholas posed a fateful question. "Would you have me spill the blood of my subjects on the first day of my reign?" "Yes, Sire," Vasilchikov replied, "to save your Empire."[153] Nicholas ordered the Guards Artillery to load their cannon. After more hesitation, he gave the command: "The guns are to fire in sequence beginning from the right!"[154] Unable to withstand the deadly iron hail that tore into their midst, the rebels broke ranks. Just hours later, Nicholas took up his pen and wrote: "Dear, dear Konstantin. Your will has been done. I am Emperor, but, my God, at what a price! At the price of my subjects' blood!"[155]

Everyone who met Nicholas agreed that he looked every inch a man born to rule an Empire. "He is taller than ordinary men by half a head. . . . His carriage and attitudes are naturally imposing. . . . The Emperor Nicholas is more sincere [than his brother Alexander] but has a habitual expression of severity which sometimes gives the impression of harshness and inflexibility. However, if he is less charming [than his late brother] he is more firm. The Emperor Nicholas . . . desires to be obeyed, where others desire to be loved," wrote the French Marquis de Custine in 1839.[156] In 1844 Queen Victoria rounded out de Custine's portrait by adding that "he is stern and severe—with fixed principles of *duty* which *nothing* on earth will make him change; very *clever* I do *not* think him, and his mind is an uncivilized one; his education has been neglected; politics and military concerns are the only things he takes great interest in; the arts and all softer occupations he is insensible to, but he is sincere, I am certain, *sincere* even in his most despotic acts, from a sense that that *is* the *only* way to govern."[157]

Catherine the Great was more prophetic than she knew when, on June 26, 1796, the day after Nicholas's birth, she wrote to Melchior Grimm that "his brothers will prove to be dwarfs before this colossus."[158] Nicholas grew up under very different circumstances from those of his two elder brothers Alexander and Konstantin. He was only four months old when Catherine died, so his parents, not his grandmother, saw to his education. Paul set the tone for his upbringing by immediately appointing his infant son a colonel in the Imperial Horse Guards.[159] Emphasis upon things military took on a more concrete form as Nicholas grew from infancy into childhood. Just after his second birthday he received his first toy musket. In April 1799, when he was not quite three, he donned the crimson-and-white parade uniform of a Horse Guards colonel for the first time.[160] In November 1800 Paul named General Count Matvei Lamsdorf, a man of no intellectual accomplishment whatever, to be his son's tutor. Symbolic of the continued militaristic German influence that surrounded Nicholas, his father and tutor discussed his early education in German. "I have chosen you as chief tutor for my sons [Nicholas and Mikhail]" Paul told Lamsdorf. "You must do this for Russia."[161]

As a child and a youth, Nicholas was an indifferent student, often bored, and easily distracted from his studies. His teachers, although some of Russia's leading scholars, jurists, and statesmen, were far from inspiring. "I remember how these men tormented us," Nicholas later wrote. "They meant well . . . and were very learned. But they were the most insupportable pedants imaginable. [Professor] Kukolnik lectured to us about Roman, Greek, and God only knows what other kinds of laws, in a mixture of languages of which we understood not even one well. [Professor] Balugianskii talked about some sort of imaginary 'natural' law. In addition, they sent [Professor Heinrich] Storch to us with lectures about political economy that were certain to put you to sleep."[162] Of all his tutors, the only one who remotely stirred Nicholas's interest was Monsieur Puget d'Yverdon, a native of Lausanne, who taught him French and history. Under the tutelage of LaHarpe, the Emperor Alexander had come to idealize the French Revolution. Under Puget's direction, Nicholas reached precisely the opposite view. As a ten-year-old child, he concluded that "King Louis XVI did not do his duty, and for that he was punished. One is not merciful by being weak," he added. "Louis XVI was faced with what was, in fact, a conspiracy disguised under the false name of liberty. He would have spared his people a great deal of misery if he had not spared the conspirators."[163] As Russia's Emperor, Nicholas would rule as he thought Louis XVI ought to have ruled. Most significant of all, perhaps, he suffered no marks of the split personality that had plagued Alexander I so sorely. Nicholas knew where he stood in relation to Russia and where Russia stood in relation to the West.

As a child, Nicholas found relief from the boredom of his lessons in a fascination with the army, an interest he shared with his younger brother Mikhail. Together, they built fortresses out of tables and chairs and sometimes constructed even more realistic fortifications out of earth in the palace gardens. Nicholas always was careful to place cannon "for defense" around any structure he built.[164] Indeed, he seems to have been preoccupied with defense as a child. When still in the care of Jane Lyon, his stern but loving Scots nurse, he used to grow pale when he met army officers for fear that they might take him "prisoner."[165] Perhaps his father's murder had scarred him more deeply than anyone suspected. Certainly, defense became a key factor in his policies as he sought to defend his state against revolution and shield his subjects from ideas he considered harmful. Most of all, Nicholas sought to defend Russia from Europe—from its constitutions, its revolutions, and the breakdown of its *ancien régime* mores. Indeed, the notion of defense sharply differentiated his foreign policy from that of his brother Alexander. While Alexander saw Russia as a part of Europe, Nicholas always considered his Empire as unique and separate from the West.

Firm in his determination to shield his people from sedition and conspiracies "disguised under the false name of liberty," Nicholas dealt severely with the Decembrists. "It is my duty to give this lesson to Russia *and to Europe*," he told the French Ambassador before he announced the Decembrists' sentences.[166] He sent more than a hundred officers to Siberian exile and penal servitude. Most shocking of all to Russian public opinion, Nicholas ordered five Decembrists—Pavel Pestel, Petr Kakhovskii, Kondratii Ryleev, Sergei Muravev-Apostol, and Mikhail Bestuzhev-Riumin—to be hanged. It was the first such execution in Russia since that of Pugachev a half-century earlier, and an executioner had to be imported from Sweden because there was none to be found in Russia.

At three o'clock in the morning of July 13, 1826, the five condemned Decembrists were led out to the square behind the Peter-Paul

Fortress. Their insignia of rank were stripped from their tunics, their swords broken over their heads, and their uniforms taken away. Clad only in loose robes, they were led to the scaffold. The executioner tightened the nooses around their necks and then kicked away the stools upon which they stood. In three cases, the knots slipped and the victims fell to the scaffold floor. Muravev-Apostol, his leg broken in the fall, cried out, "Poor Russia! Here we can't even hang a man properly!"[167] The executioner and his assistants then lifted him and his two companions up to be hanged a second time, thereby confirming the radical intelligentsia in their view that Nicholas was cruel, brutal, and tyrannical.

Yet Nicholas was not a tyrant, nor was he especially cruel or brutal. As Russia's supreme commander he thought that he bore full responsibility to God for all that was done within his command. It was a crushing burden and carried awesome obligations, for he believed he must serve as a model of devotion and piety and conduct himself in a manner that would "serve as a living example to all." Nicholas thought that an autocrat should be "gentle, courteous, and *just*," in the sense of being merciful, yet firm. He should be "benevolent and approachable to all unfortunates" but "must not squander treasure." He should not seek confrontations with foreign powers, but "must always defend the dignity of Russia." Above all, he must remember that he was Russian. "That," Nicholas once remarked, "means everything."[168] To bear the burdens of his office, Nicholas thus was firm, stern, and severe, and that was the image he projected to most Russians. Yet, in his private life, he also was warm and open-hearted. He preferred to live modestly, without ostentatious display, and saw Court ceremonial as a duty, not a pleasure. Nowhere were these parts of his character more evident than in his relationship with his wife, the Empress Aleksandra Feodorovna.

Raisons d'état had figured prominently in eighteenth-century Romanov marriages as Peter the Great and his successors sought to establish family ties with a number of European dynasties. Therefore, none of Peter the Great's successors between 1715 and 1815 had been allowed much choice about whom they wed. For Nicholas, however, it was different, for he chose his own bride and swore that there could be no other. He met Princess Charlotte of Prussia in the fall of 1814 and returned to Berlin a year later to declare his love and win her hand. For a brief time, he wooed his princess with uncharacteristic passion, and, as the tall and slender Russian Grand Duke and the romantic, starry-eyed Prussian princess wandered through the picturesque Potsdam countryside, the rest of the world was forgotten. Nicholas proposed to his princess that autumn, and she came to Russia to become his bride less than a year later.[169] Within a few weeks, she converted to Russian Orthodoxy, took the name of Aleksandra Feodorovna, and married Nicholas on July 1, 1817. "I felt myself very, very happy when our hands joined," she later wrote about her wedding. "With complete confidence and trust, I gave my life into the hands of my Nicholas, and he never once betrayed it."[170]

Nicholas and Aleksandra Feodorovna were private people who found great pleasure in each other's company. She once wrote that "we both were truly happy only when we found ourselves alone in our apartments," and they were taken aback when Alexander I first told them that he intended Nicholas to replace him on the throne one day.[171] "My wife and I remained in a position which I can liken only to that sensation that would strike a man if he were going calmly along a comfortable road sown with flowers and with marvelous scenery on all sides when, suddenly, an abyss yawns wide beneath his feet, and an irresistible force draws him into it, without allowing him to step back or turn aside," Nicholas once wrote in describing their reactions to Alexander's decision.[172] Neither welcomed the duties that Alexander's death thrust upon them, but both were resolved to perform them to the fullest.

Nicholas's devotion to Russia brought him great joy and even greater pain. He often was deeply moved by the greatness of the people he ruled and the vast potential of the Empire he governed. "God, what fine and good people these are! May God keep them so. One is truly proud to belong to them," he once wrote to Aleksandra Feodorovna from the banks of the Volga.[173] Yet the Decembrists' revolt and their testimony during lengthy interrogations by his most trusted adjutants had made it very clear that there were flaws in the Empire he had inherited from his brother.[174] Despite his honest effort to improve conditions in Russia, even his greatest achievement—the codification of the laws Speranskii completed in 1833—failed to establish a society founded upon the principles of law. Arbitrary power, capriciously applied, continued to stain Russian life. Because he defined his autocratic role in very broad terms, failure was especially painful for Nicholas. He believed that he alone must motivate and direct everything in Russia and that generals, admirals, ambassadors, and senior statesmen were mere extensions of his autocratic *persona*. Just as their successes were his, so were their failures. The balance shifted heavily toward failures toward the end of his reign, and Nicholas had to face repeated reminders of his inadequacies from a periodical press and a full-fledged intelligentsia that had not existed in the days of his predecessors.

During the first two decades of his reign, Nicholas's power was undiluted at home, respected abroad, and he was served by advisers he trusted. These were men of integrity and honor, whom he had known since the days of his youth; they had shared his values and dreams as well as the crises of his accession. Even General Count Aleksandr Benkendorf, head of the Imperial Gendarmerie that Nicholas created in 1826, generally was well regarded during the 1830s because he stood for values in which many Russians believed and did not use the awesome powers of his office for evil or petty purposes. These decades also were good years for Nicholas in terms of his personal life. Vigorous and handsome, he was at the peak of his physical and intellectual powers, and age would not begin to leave its mark upon him until well into the 1840s. Even as late as 1844, when he was nearing fifty, Queen Victoria would describe him as "a very *striking* man; still very handsome; his profile is beautiful and his manners most dignified."[175] Death did not begin to separate him from his closest comrades until near the end of these years.

Personal friendships with men such as Benkendorf were important to Nicholas, but even more important were the very close relationships he had with his family. Nicholas knew of his brother Konstantin's capricious behavior in Warsaw. He realized that it had proved costly for Russia, but no word of reproach ever crept into the letters he wrote to Konstantin as Viceroy.[176] Much the same was true of his relations with his younger brother Mikhail who, at best, was a reasonably competent regimental staff officer. Mikhail's barracks-room manners and his strange relationship with his elegant and beautiful wife, the Grand Duchess Elena Pavlovna, caused considerable embarrassment to the entire Romanov family. His behavior on their wedding night, when he galloped off to review a Guards regiment rather than escort his bride to their new apartments, was the talk of St. Petersburg.[177] Many contemporaries considered him utterly boorish, yet Nicholas, who normally insisted upon propriety and good form, remained close to his younger brother and took pains to share with him the glory he won for Russia. He immediately appointed Mikhail to the Imperial State Council when he became Emperor and gave him the honor of leading the first regiment of victorious Russian Guards into Warsaw in September 1831, even though the victory belonged to Field Marshal Ivan Paskevich.

Nicholas's relations with his children were even closer than with his brothers. There were seven in all: three Grand Duchesses and four Grand Dukes. Aleksandr, the eldest, one day became Alexander II, Russia's "Tsar-Emancipator," and Konstantin played important parts in the naval reforms of the 1850s and the Great Reforms of the 1860s. Of Nicholas's three daughters, blond and blue-eyed Maria, the eldest, became Duchess of Leuchtenberg and the pale, black-haired Olga, Queen of Württemberg. The youngest daughter, Aleksandra, a talented musician, married the Prince of Hesse-Cassel. Two more sons were born to Nicholas and Aleksandra Feodorova in the 1830s: Nikolai, who became commander in chief in the Russo-Turkish War of 1877–78, and Mikhail, later Inspector-General of the Russian Artillery.

Always the "father-commander," Nicholas required his children to report each morning on how they had spent the previous day and what progress they had made with their studies. He chose more talented tutors for his children than he had had; among them were the poet Zhukovskii, the statesman Baron Modest Korf, and the reformer and legal expert Mikhail Speranskii. Nicholas examined his children's lesson books himself and was a firm taskmaster who meted out punishments far more frequently than rewards. Duty, love for Russia, and diligence were the virtues he sought to instill, and when he punished his children, it was for that purpose. "It is for the Motherland that you must do your duty," he always began. "It is not I, but the Motherland, who punishes or rewards you. I am here to carry out her orders and her intentions."[178] None of Nicholas's children ever dared even to think, as Alexander I once actually wrote, that "it is better not to take on a task than to do it badly."[179] Nicholas taught his children that, if their duty as Romanovs demanded that they take on a task, they were honor bound to do it well. Yet his severity did not condemn his children to the cold and loveless existence he had suffered as a child, for parental love and warmth tempered the demands he imposed upon them.

Nicholas was very conscious that he and Aleksandra were breathing life into that dynasty his father had created in law, but which his brothers had failed to perpetuate.[180] He thought it his duty to be stern with those who held Russia's future in their hands but he loved his children deeply nevertheless. For many years he followed a rigid daily routine that permitted him to spend at least two hours with them. Each morning he arose early, worked several hours at his desk and came to the Empress's apartments promptly at ten o'clock. There, he spent an hour breakfasting and holding what he called *"la revue de la famille."*[181] Until his sons and daughters were grown and married, he dined with them at precisely four o'clock each afternoon. Such dinners usually lasted less than an hour. Afterward, Nicholas and any guests would retire briefly to Aleksandra's study for coffee and conversation until he excused himself and returned to work. Later in the evening, the family sometimes gathered again to read out loud or for small concerts in which Nicholas played the cornet.[182]

Nicholas's love for the Empress, "Mouffy" as he called her, continued unabated. "God has bestowed upon you such a happy character that it is no merit to love you," he wrote her in 1836, nearly twenty years after their marriage.[183] When the Winter Palace burned the following year, he reportedly told an aide-de-camp to "let everything else burn up, only just save for me the small case of letters in my study which my wife wrote to me when she was my betrothed."[184] Theirs was an attraction of opposites: Nicholas, tall, robust, dynamic, and Aleksandra, slender, frail, often in poor health. Only after more than a quarter-century of marriage, at a time when he was beginning to show

signs of age, did Nicholas take a mistress. He turned to Varvara Nelidova, one of Aleksandra's young ladies-in-waiting, to recapture his lost
youth and to find the physical solace that the Empress's recurring heart
attacks made it impossible for her to provide.

Even after Nelidova made her appearance, much love remained
between Nicholas and Aleksandra. In 1845 Nicholas wept when Court
doctors urged the Empress to visit Palermo for several months. "Leave
me my wife," he begged his physicians, and when he learned that she
indeed must go, he made plans to join her, if only for a brief time.[185] If
physical love was forbidden by the Empress's doctors, a deep comradeship endured between the two, and Nicholas continued to seek refuge
from the cares of state in Aleksandra's company. "Happiness, joy, and
repose—that is what I seek and find in my old Mouffy," he once
wrote.[186] His letters always were filled with those detailed accounts
Aleksandra so loved to read about costumes, furnishings, uniforms,
and military reviews at the Courts he visited. Always he found time to
remember her in small but tender ways when they were apart.

Nicholas's private life with his family was an intimate haven into
which he admitted few, and from which he excluded the pomp, splendor, and opulence of the Imperial Court for a frugal and spartan existence. While Aleksandra Feodorovna's apartments were elegant and
richly decorated, his own were utterly modest. His study was a small
room with a cot and the straw-filled leather pallet upon which he always slept, a desk, a sofa, a few odd chairs and tables, and various
personal mementos, including the gray army greatcoat he had worn
during the Russo-Turkish campaign of 1828.[187] Family, a few friends,
and immense amounts of work comprised Nicholas's daily life in the
Winter Palace during the first two decades of his reign.

As the year 1848 opened, most upper-class Russians expected the
orderly life they had enjoyed since the day Nicholas mounted the
throne to continue. For many of them, these had been times of prosperity and promise. "No dissonances marred the general harmony, for
there was a conservative monarchical sentiment in all strata [of society],
and there seemed to be no possibility of any other" was how one observer summed up his impressions in the 1840s.[188] Gone were the uncertainties of Alexander's time, when talk of constitutions and eman-

cipating the serfs had disturbed the comfortable lives of the nobility. Gone, too, were the devastations Russia had suffered during Napoleon's invasion and the great and ruinous wars with other enemies. Of course, the first two decades of Nicholas's reign had seen Russian soldiers take the field against the Persians, the Turks, and the Polish rebels, and they had continued their annual campaigns against the natives of the Caucasus. But these conflicts were but distant rumblings about which few heard and in which fewer participated. Only periodic announcements of glorious victories brought these struggles into the everyday consciousness of most Russians. It had been more than three decades since an enemy soldier had set foot upon Russian soil, and Russian arms appeared invincible in Europe and in Asia. Not until 1854 would Russian society be mobilized for war as it had been during Alexander I's Napoleonic campaigns.

Despite its promising beginnings, 1848 would be the most difficult year Nicholas had faced since his accession. Russia suffered the ravages of a great famine, when the average harvest was "in general not more than half the amount planted," according to official estimates.[189] At the same time, a cholera epidemic spread into every corner of European Russia and even some parts of Siberia. Cholera was a dread disease in the 1840s, killing a large percentage of its victims. That fateful year also saw a great revolutionary upsurge in Western and Central Europe, which posed a direct threat to the system Nicholas had erected at home and abroad, at a time when he had fewer personal and material resources to meet it than ever before.

Even before 1848, Nicholas had shown signs of age as the strain of ruling Russia began to take a toll upon his powerful constitution. "He has to make an effort to conquer fatigue, to do what seemed easy to him until now. He has become silent. He avoids assemblies. He says that society, balls, and fêtes have become a drudgery, and that he prefers to live like a bourgeois," the Austrian Ambassador reported to Metternich in 1846. "The conviction is gaining more and more ground," he added, "that the Emperor, in spite of his constant work and energy, will not succeed in doing the good he wants to do, nor in destroying the evil he sees."[190] No longer was Nicholas the self-possessed young paladin who had returned to the arms of his Empress on the night of December 14, 1825, after crushing the Decembrists. Nor was he the dynamic conqueror who had strode through the palace halls of Müchengrätz some fifteen years earlier to dictate the political order of Central and Eastern Europe. Like his two brothers before him, Nicholas aged quickly once he neared fifty. As with Alexander and Konstantin, a nagging sense of frustration about what he had not accomplished, tinged with vague feelings of fatalism and defeat, set in. Early in 1847, Nicholas suffered a serious abdominal inflammation and thought he was dying. A few months later, another illness struck, lingered briefly, and strengthened further his awareness of his mortality.[191]

The inevitability of his death must have occupied Nicholas increasingly. Grand Duchess Aleksandra Nikolaevna, his youngest daughter, whom he loved so dearly as the image of her mother, died just before he reached his fiftieth birthday. Even more depressing, the fragile and beautiful "Mouffy" had become worn and gaunt, aged well before her time, a woman "to whom one would give sixty years . . . [when] she only had passed her fortieth."[192] The Empress's health got no better after 1840, and there were several times that she seemed at death's door.[193] Death also began to claim Nicholas's closest advisers. General Count Benkendorf, perhaps his closest companion and a comrade-in-arms for more than two decades, passed away in 1844. Minister of Finance General Count Egor Kankrin died the following year, General Prince Iarion Vasilchikov in 1847, and General Vasilii Levashov in 1848. By 1848 nearly all of Nicholas's closest confidants, men with whom he had shaped the Nicholas "system" of government, were dead. Gone forever were the intimate gatherings at the Winter Palace where he had met in the late afternoons and evenings with energetic counselors to discuss policy issues and resolve crises. In the place of these men now sat weaker, less assertive, less honest bureaucrats. Nicholas, the commander who saw "each one of his days . . . [as] a day of battle,"[194] thus faced the crises of 1848 with weakened reserves.

The contrast between the domestic policies Nicholas adopted after the revolutionary crises of 1830 and those he followed after the revolutions of 1848 could not have been more striking. The decade after 1830 saw the first compilation of Russia's laws since 1649 and a number of attempts to modernize Russia's economy and government, as Nicholas and General Count Pavel Kiselev, his "Chief of Staff for Peasant Affairs," made serious efforts to improve the conditions under which the state peasants lived in Russia. The 1830s and the first part of the 1840s brought no appreciable intensification of censorship and marked the Golden Age of Russian Literature, as the great poet Pushkin, and the writers Lermontov and Gogol, reached the zenith of their careers. Toward the end of these years, Ivan Turgenev and Feodor Dostoevskii published their first works, Nikolai Nekrasov began to write, as did a number of others. In the pages of the "thick journals," the literary criticism of Vissarion Belinskii commanded the attention of Russia's youth and educated society. It was a time that much of educated society would recall with fondness, even longing, during the trying years of the 1860s and 1870s, when Russia had to cope with the traumatic adjustments demanded by the Great Reforms and had to face the rising threat of revolutionary terror.

The worst thing about Nicholas's response to the crises of 1848 was the capricious manner in which he and his senior officials exercised their authority. Such arbitrariness was a fundamental part of Russia's autocracy and of the Nicholas "system" in particular, for all Russians were subject to the unlimited power of the Emperor and his adjutants. Before 1848, however, tradition, regulations, even certain laws, had limited the capricious exercise of absolute power. Afterward, Nicholas allowed despotism a freer rein, even encouraging it by some of the regulations he insisted upon putting into effect. In the realm of censorship, this meant probing into the "inner meanings" of published work and manuscripts. Elsewhere, it took such forms as an 1850 regulation that declared that any senior official could remove subordinates from office for "faults or misdemeanors which cannot be proved" and that no explanation need accompany such dismissals.[195] With a single stroke of his pen, Nicholas thus deprived all Russian civil servants of any protection of the laws.

The crucial question is why Nicholas, who believed that an autocrat should be "gentle, courteous, and *just*" and that the "best theory of law is good morality," should have condoned arbitrary and despotic behavior on such a scale.[196] Obviously, he overreacted to the revolutionary events of 1848. He had reason to see them as a threat to the system he had so laboriously constructed against revolution in Central and Eastern Europe, to be sure, but his fear of revolution within Russia's frontiers bordered upon a paranoia not unlike the Emperor Paul's reaction to the French Revolution of 1789. Nicholas saw every revolutionary pamphlet confiscated by his police as a real threat to Russia's internal security and wrote to his "father-commander" Prince Ivan Paskevich that "only God alone can save us from general ruin!" [197] Yet a few inflammatory pamphlets, almost always printed abroad and smuggled into Russia in small numbers, were the most visible and threatening revolutionary disturbances that Nicholas faced within his domains at any time during 1848, while in 1830 and 1831 he had waged a full-scale war to crush revolution in his Polish lands. In the final analysis, one cannot say decisively why Nicholas saw the events of 1848 as such a threat to his country's internal security. Certainly his growing sense of isolation from the political and economic realities of Russia was an important factor, for his ministers and advisers in 1848 were not bound to him by their common experience in suppressing the Decembrists or by their service with the Russian army in the West at the time of Napoleon's defeat. After those men died, there was not that deep sense of trust, that close personal bond, between their successors and their Emperor that was so vital to the success of Nicholas's "system."

It is one of the ironies of Russia's history that Nicholas, who had attempted to make all Russians virtuous by insulating them from moral and intellectual evils, found his own policies being conditioned by the very system he had created. Anxious to advance their careers and win their sovereign's approval, senior officials and advisers surrounded him with a screen of censorship, which he succeeded in drawing aside only rarely. Too worn by the strain of ruling to continue those inspection tours that had enabled him to motivate his government personally, Nicholas came to see his Empire not as it was but as his senior officials wished him to see it. To reflect well upon themselves and to secure their positions, they painted Russian conditions in terms that were as glowing as they were inaccurate. "Under the sacred, beneficial protection of autocracy, this fortunate land of Russia blossoms," wrote High State Counselor Aleksandr Kamenskii in 1850. "Foreigners gaze upon her prosperity with intense regret. To them it is evident that . . . this awe-inspiring colossus towers above them."[198] Kamenskii's claims were utter nonsense. Weighed down by an antiquated serf-based economic system that produced acute technological backwardness and chronic social unrest, the Russian bloom had become limp, even withered.

Indeed, what Kamenskii had called the "awe-inspiring colossus" would not tower above foreign powers for much longer. Nicholas soon was to face his most trying hour in a military crisis that would destroy his system of government. He did not really expect war with the Ottoman Empire in the autumn of 1853, yet it came, and as a result of his own misjudgments. "The Emperor Nicholas has in himself something of Peter the Great, of Paul I, and of a medieval knight. But, as the years have passed, it is now the qualities of Paul I which rise more to the fore," wrote the French diplomat Marquis de Castelbajac that September. Castelbajac did not mean, of course, that Nicholas was on the verge of madness, as most Russians thought Paul had been. But, like all autocrats, and especially like his father, his judgment had grown impaired by the absolute power he wielded. "This sovereign, born with the best possible qualities, has been spoiled by adulation, by success, and by the religious and political prejudices of the Muscovite nation," Castelbajac added somewhat later.[199] Nicholas had ruled too long. He had come to believe too much in his and Russia's God-given mission, which the disciples of Official Nationality had glorified for some two decades.

Early in October 1853, a young lady-in-waiting by the name of Anna Tiutcheva confided to her diary that "a terrible struggle has burst upon us. Monumental and contradictory forces are on a collision course: the East and the West, the Slavic world and the Latin world. . . . Filled with dread and anguish, one asks, what will be the outcome of this struggle between two worlds? There can be no doubt. We, Russia, are on the side of truth and ideals: Russia fights not for material gain and worldly interest, but for ideas which are eternal."[200] For this tragic confrontation, first between Russia and the Ottoman Empire, and then between Russia and the West, Nicholas summoned his remaining reserves of physical and spiritual strength. Wrote General Castelbajac at the beginning of 1854, "In his painful indecision, his religious scruples on one hand, and his humanitarian scruples on the other; in his wounded pride, in the face of national feeling and the dangers which pursue his Empire; in the violent struggle with these various feelings, the Emperor Nicholas has aged ten years. He is truly sick, physically and morally."[201]

Despite his tired spirit and weakened body, despite the antiquated weapons his soldiers carried, and despite the ever-present logistical obstacles that plagued Russian planners, Nicholas and Russia still were powerful forces to be reckoned with, as the campaigns of 1853 and 1854 made very clear. Russia's major fault in the Crimean War would be miscalculations in the diplomatic arena and in the upper reaches of her military command. There lay the greatest shortcoming of the system Nicholas had created, and it was the one that most directly caused Russia's defeat. Set in patterns of thought that had become fixed over the course of nearly three decades, Nicholas could not alter his views or his evaluations of diplomatic alignments. He expected the animosity of France, but he did not anticipate, nor could he comprehend, the hostility of Britain. As for Austria and Prussia, nearly three decades of joint defense against revolution through a conservative coalition in which Russia always had been the dominant power made it nearly impossible for Nicholas to realize that these were new times, that Central Europe faced other problems, and that Austria and Prussia could not be relied upon as in the 1830s and 1840s. And, since there was no well-established means for replacing aging counselors with younger, more energetic, and clearer-thinking ones less constrained by decisions taken in years past, there was no one among Nicholas's advisers who could tell him otherwise. Count Karl Nesselrode had been Russia's Foreign Minister since 1814. The men with whom he had labored to construct the Concert of Europe and the Nicholas system abroad—Metternich, Castlereagh, Talleyrand, Canning, Wellington, and Frederick William III—had long since left the scene for retirement or the grave. A second, even a third, generation of diplomats had replaced them, and Nesselrode was not a part of their new and modern world. What was true of Nesselrode on the diplomatic front was equally true for Prince Ivan Paskevich and Admiral Aleksandr Menshikov, the two men who advised Nicholas most closely on military matters at the outbreak of the war. They had grown used to thinking in terms of tactics and alignments that had become utterly antiquated by mid-century, and their advice proved ruinous.

During his last year of life, Nicholas saw Russia's armies suffer their first defeats in more than three decades. In September 1854, Admiral Menshikov allowed an Anglo-French expeditionary force to land unopposed at Eupatoria in the Crimea and, a week later, lost the battle of Alma. Russian defeats at Balaklava and Inkerman followed; although they were not losses of major significance, they took a heavy toll upon Nicholas. Throughout his reign, his soldiers had advanced, his soldiers had attacked. They had died for their Faith, their Tsar, and their motherland. With them, behind a wall of a million bayonets, Russia had seemed safe. News that Russian arms were not everywhere victorious thus was bitter for Nicholas to hear. On top of this, toward the end of 1854, many feared that Aleksandra Feodorovna was dying. "The Empress is critically ill," wrote Anna Tiutcheva. "For several days her life was in danger. . . . The slightest upset could cause the illness to return." During these days, most of Nicholas's concern was for his wife. "He neither sleeps nor eats," wrote one observer.[202] The illness of his Empress, the defeats of his armies in the Crimea, the loneliness of standing against the European Allies, the grueling strain of ruling Russia for nearly three decades—all these placed a tremendous psychological and physical burden upon Nicholas during the winter of 1854–55. The strain exacted a far greater toll than anyone expected, for it cost Nicholas his life.

On February 15, 1855, Nicholas finally relieved Admiral Menshikov from command of Russia's land armies in the Crimea and named General Prince Mikhail Gorchakov, a younger and more energetic commander, to replace him. This would be his last major act as Russia's supreme commander. He had caught a slight cold three days before at a wedding, but, as he often had done in the past, he ignored his doctors' advice and went about his daily routine. His cold became worse after he reviewed troops at the Riding School in temperatures that were well below freezing, but no one felt any real alarm, for heavy colds were common in St. Petersburg's damp climate. Even on the evening of Wednesday, February 16, one of the Imperial ladies-in-waiting would recall that "the Empress still was calm in view of the assurances of Doctor Mandt that there was absolutely nothing dangerous about the condition of His Majesty."[203] Mandt repeated his assurance as late as nine o'clock on the evening of February 17.

Very early in the morning of February 18, Doctor Mandt suddenly realized that Nicholas's life was in danger and urged him to summon a priest. Nicholas fixed an imperious and penetrating stare upon his doctor. "Then I am dying?" he asked. Recalling a promise he once had made to his sovereign many years ago, Mandt replied, "Your Majesty, you have only a few hours left."[204] Nicholas accepted the news with Imperial dignity. He took the sacrament and bade farewell to those servants, close friends, and family who were with him. He then turned again to affairs of state. Until his last hour, he continued to rule Russia as he thought an autocrat should. He ordered all the Guards regiments brought to the palace so that they would be on hand to swear allegiance to his son the moment he breathed his last for, even in death, Nicholas could not forget the tragic circumstances of his own accession. His suffering grew worse as the night drew to a close. "If this is the beginning of the end, it is very painful," he told Mandt.[205] To his son, about to become Alexander II, he spoke his last words: "I wanted to take everything difficult, everything serious, upon my shoulders and to leave to you a peaceful, well-ordered, and happy realm. Providence decreed otherwise. Now I go to pray for Russia and for you all. After Russia, I loved you [my family] more than anything else in the world. Serve Russia."[206] "Never have I seen anyone die like this," wrote Mandt. "There was something superhuman in this carrying out of one's duty to the last breath."[207]

News of Nicholas's death stirred intense sentiments in all who heard it. In London, the émigré radical Aleksandr Herzen uncorked his best champagne, summoned his friends, and gave silver coins "for beer and candy" to the street urchins to shout "Hurrah! Hurrah! Impernikel is dead! Impernikel is dead!"[208] In St. Petersburg, the publicist and jurist Konstantin Kavelin called Nicholas's reign "a thirty-year tyranny of madness, brutality, and misfortunes of all sorts, the likes of which history has never seen,"[209] and the censor Aleksandr Nikitenko remarked that "the main shortcoming of the reign of Nikolai Pavlovich consisted in the fact that it was all a mistake."[210] But there also were those who felt a deep emptiness, an intense sense of loss, as if a vast chasm had opened before them. "Only two days have passed since all this occurred, but it seems to me that, after these two days, the world has come tumbling down," wrote Anna Tiutcheva. "Papa said, 'It is as if we had been told that a god had died,' " she added.[211] General Count Kiselev, for nearly two decades Nicholas's "Chief of Staff for Peasant Affairs," perhaps summed up such reactions best when he wrote that "history will give him his due. I shall only say in this initial surge of my soul's grief, that in his valiant heart were reflected all the noble feelings with which the Almighty in his mercy adorns man."[212]

Nicholas I was the last of the Romanovs to hold undivided power. He was, in a very real sense, Russia's last absolute monarch, for the collapse of his system, which became so dramatically and painfully obvious in the year after his death, forced Russia upon a new course. A multitude of problems had arisen in the first half of the nineteenth century, and they demanded solutions that he and his system could not provide. Russia's continuing financial crisis, her economic backwardness and underdeveloped industry, her inefficient bureaucracy, and, underlying all of these problems, the antiquated institution of serfdom, all required serious attention. It became the task of Alexander II to take them up after his father's death. He would usher in the period of Russia's history known as the Era of Great Reforms. Paradoxically, this reform era also would see an upsurge of revolutionary terror, and Alexander II, the Romanov who freed Russia's enserfed millions, would become the first Romanov to be murdered by the masses.

Grand Duke Alexander Nikolaevich, the future Emperor Alexander II, was born four days before Easter on April 17, 1818. He was the first Russian ruler since Peter the Great to be born in Moscow and the first Grand Duke born into the Romanov family in two decades. Feverish excitement gripped Muscovites when they heard the news. Wrote one contemporary in a flurry of enthusiasm, "The Grand Duchess Aleksandra Feodorovna has given birth without mishap. Where? In Moscow, in the Kremlin! When? During Easter week! To whom? A son! A Grand Duke named Alexander! What happy coincidences these are! In the city there is great rejoicing and happiness, and the people stream toward the Kremlin in their coaches and carriages. According to Moscow custom there is a great celebration here."[213] The Dowager Empress Maria Feodorovna gave a great dinner for Moscow's highest officials and clerics, the entire city was illuminated by a gigantic fireworks display, and the poet Vasilii Zhukovskii penned a verse to celebrate the occasion. As soon as he heard the news, Alexander I appointed his infant nephew and namesake chief of the Hussar Lifeguards. Nothing could have pleased his father more and nothing could have symbolized better the environment in which he would grow to manhood.

As with all Romanov Grand Dukes, Alexander Nikolaevich spent the first few years of his life in the company of women. He was cared for by women of high birth, and his grandmother, the Dowager Empress, played an important part in his early life. Only after he had passed his sixth birthday did Alexander make the abrupt transition into the world of men. Captain Karl Merder, an officer who taught at St. Petersburg's new School for Guards Ensigns and Cavalry Cadets, became his tutor and began to teach him about those parades and maneuvers for which he already had developed an intense passion. Merder was a veteran of the Napoleonic Wars who had received a head wound at Austerlitz while leading a handful of hussars in a daring charge to free their commander from the French dragoons. After he recovered, he went on to fight again at Preussische-Eylau and Friedland and then became an instructor at the Cadet Corps until the School for Guards Ensigns and Cavalry Cadets opened some fifteen years later.[214] Merder thus was very different from the typical parade-ground officer, and he tried to direct the young Alexander away from the more extreme forms of paradomania. It was he, and he alone, who kept him from becoming an uncompromising martinet at an early age.

When Nicholas I became Emperor, the nature of Merder's responsibility changed dramatically. No longer was he training a junior Grand Duke, but the heir to the Russian throne. To his credit, he realized that such a task was beyond his ability, and urged Nicholas to appoint others. Chief among the men Nicholas chose was Vasilii Zhukovskii, the poet who had tutored Aleksandra in Russian when she first came to St.

Petersburg, and who had become a close friend of Russia's new Imperial family in the intervening years.

Zhukovskii took up his task with a dramatic flurry of preparations. He devoted the winter and spring of 1827 to planning a grandiose course of study for his pupil. "According to the plan I have prepared for educating the Grand Duke," he wrote from Dresden in January 1827, "everything will fall upon my shoulders alone. All of his lectures will be my responsibility. The work of his other tutors merely will serve to embellish and repeat my own."[215] The responsibility for a future Emperor's education was heady stuff, and Zhukovskii was thoroughly intoxicated by it. "Glory, duty, religion, love of country, in a word, everything that is inherent in the spiritual nature of man, no longer attracts me purely for my own interest, but for the sake of him in whose spirit these exalted thoughts would yield useful benefits for humanity," he wrote before he returned to Russia.[216] Like a number of his predecessors, Zhukovskii was supremely confident that his efforts would produce a prince whose enlightenment and brilliance would astound the world. Also like his predecessors, he was disappointed. Just as Nikita Panin and LaHarpe had learned before him, Zhukovskii found that humanistic learning could not compete in a world that adored military organization and glorified military command. Like the three Emperors who had reigned before him, Alexander II loved the army first and learning second.

Zhukovskii feared that a sovereign who allowed military principles to govern his actions could serve neither justice nor truth, and his fondest wish was for the Grand Duke Alexander to become a sovereign who honored both. "Should he be only a soldier, destined to act only within the narrow horizons of a general?" he wrote to the Empress. "Oh, Sovereign Mistress, forgive my outburst, but a passion for the art of war only will crush his spirit. He will come to see our people only as regiments, and he will look upon our country only as a barracks."[217] Zhukovskii pleaded for the chance to mold Alexander into a humane and humanitarian prince who could cope with the rapidly changing world men and women were beginning to encounter in the 1830s and 1840s.

More clearly than most Russian courtiers and statesmen, Zhukovskii foresaw that Alexander would rule in a world very different from the one into which he had been born. Europe's Industrial Revolution was creating a world in which rulers would be called upon to resolve problems more complex than any that eighteenth-century monarchs had imagined. The rapid advance of technology meant that state policy decisions soon must involve specialized economic and social expertise such as had never even touched the educations of eighteenth-century statesmen. The development of railroads alone raised social, economic, even political issues that called for new technical expertise. Nicholas's solution to these difficulties was to insist that Alexander "must be military in spirit, or he will be lost in this present age."[218] Nevertheless, he permitted Zhukovskii to broaden his son's education by bringing in experts in many of those areas of knowledge and policy making that a mid-nineteenth-century Emperor would need to know about.

Because of Zhukovskii's efforts, Alexander became the first Romanov to receive a truly comprehensive education. Baron Feodor Brunnov, soon to become Russia's Ambassador to London, lectured to him about foreign policy, Minister of Finance Count Kankrin discussed state finances, and Konstantin Arsenev delivered lectures on statistics and political economy.[219] Most important, perhaps, Mikhail Speranskii schooled him in law and the nature of autocratic power and insisted that an Emperor could best foster modernization by balancing the conflicting aspirations of various elite groups against each other so that none would gain sufficient power to challenge the Autocrat himself.[220] It was this political principle to which Alexander would adhere most firmly as Emperor, as he balanced statesmen who represented Russia's conservative and progressive elites against each other in an effort to foster change, but keep it within the limits of moderation.

Although Zhukovskii introduced him to some of Russia's greatest minds, Alexander absorbed only a fraction of what they were prepared to offer. He was a dilatory student who, like most Romanovs, preferred the parade ground to the classroom. Merder complained of his inattention, even of his downright laziness, and worried that he lacked the firmness and resolution an autocrat needed in such large measure. "The slightest difficulty or obstacle stops him, and renders him weak and ineffective," he wrote in September 1831. The next day, he added that "there are times when he can spend an hour or more during which not a single thought will enter his head."[221] Even Alexander's passion for military affairs was superficial. He adored parades and loved to give orders at military reviews, but he had little serious interest in military science and little understanding of it. "It seems to me that he loves only the petty details of military affairs," his father once remarked to Merder with some sadness.[222] Nicholas himself drew up a formal plan to guide his son's study of fortifications, strategy, and ballistics, and the Grand Duke studied them because he had no choice. Still, he never developed any genuine interest in these technical aspects of military science.

When his formal education ended in 1837, Alexander Nikolaevich had a good knowledge of French, German, English, Polish, and Russian, despite the faults about which his tutors complained. At that point in life, Grand Dukes traditionally had taken on ceremonial duties in the Russian army, but had done little else. Yet Nicholas I refused to relegate his heir to a minor role such as he himself had played as a Grand Duke, for he was determined to prepare him to govern Russia. To be properly trained, Alexander needed practical experience, and, perhaps most important, he had to see Russia for himself. In the spring of 1837, Nicholas sent him on a seven-month tour, which took him to thirty provinces, including Siberia, in which no Romanov had yet set foot. Alexander got little more than a fleeting glimpse of the Empire he one day would rule because, as Zhukovskii wrote to the Empress, "we are traveling too rapidly, have too many subjects to examine, and our route is too rigidly fixed"; there were also celebrations at every stop along the way that obscured the real condition of the Empire.[223] Still, Alexander Nikolaevich could not have returned to St. Petersburg without a deep awareness of the vastness and diversity of the Russian Empire. Between April and December 1837, he saw the ancient cathedrals and bell towers of Novgorod, Tver, Uglich, and Iaroslavl, the Siberian vastness of Tomsk and Tobolsk, the Volga cities of Kazan and Simbirsk, the sunny southern slopes of the Crimea, the bustling Black Sea port of Odessa, the great domestic *entrepôt* of Nizhnii-Novgorod, the grain fields of the Ukraine that stretched to the horizon and beyond in every direction, and the lands of the Don Cossacks, formerly unruly and rebellious, but by the 1830s among the Emperor's most loyal subjects. No Empire on earth was so far-flung and none held so many different peoples and cultures within its borders. Three of the world's four races lived within it, and nearly all of the world's great religions were practiced by its people. It was a land of great problems, but also one of great potential, and the thought that he would one day reign over it all must have filled Alexander's youthful breast with pride.

The Grand Duke returned to St. Petersburg just four months before his twentieth birthday. Two weeks after it was past, Nicholas sent him to Europe to meet its rulers and take the measure of its statesmen. He also was to consult specialists and take the medicinal waters at Ems in order to cure the chest pains and nagging cough he had developed during the last weeks of his Russian journey. Alexander was away from Russia for more than a year. He visited some forty major cities and every European nation except France, Spain, and Portugal. Everywhere, he met Europe's crowned heads, their ministers and generals. He visited famous landmarks, toured historic buildings, and inspected regiments on parade. He cured his illnesses at the spas in Central Europe, danced the evenings away with England's vivacious young Queen Victoria at Buckingham Palace and Windsor Castle, and became the first Romanov to have an audience with the Pope. He sailed the Rhine in the spring, traveled through the Alps in late summer, and visited the ancient monuments of Rome and the Renaissance wonders of Florence in the winter. It was an exciting and memorable journey, and it filled him with impressions that he never forgot.[224]

The most significant event of Alexander's journey occurred not in Europe's great capitals nor even in the company of great rulers or famous statesmen. Darmstadt was a dormant provincial German city through which he planned to pass as quickly as possible on March 13, 1839, fearing he might be trapped for an evening in one of those rigid, formal, and boring gatherings for which petty German princes had become so notorious. Only with great difficulty did one of his aides convince him that he must pay a formal courtesy call upon Ludwig, Hesse's reigning prince.[225] To the amazement of everyone including himself, the twenty-four hours he spent in Darmstadt totally changed Alexander's life. In the space of a few hours, he fell deeply in love with the Princess Marie of Hesse, Ludwig's youngest daughter. He left Darmstadt the next day as his busy schedule required, but he left his heart behind in the hands of a fifteen-year-old Princess.

While Alexander was growing up, his tutors often remarked about his apparent weakness in the face of adversity. Other contemporaries had much the same impression, although the Marquis de Custine, who saw him at Ems in 1839, recalled that one could also observe "in the lines of his face a power of dissimulation which one trembles to see in so young a man."[226] There was, in fact, a streak of stubborn tenacity in Alexander's character that would not bend before any pressure. It was a quality that surfaced so rarely that even those who knew him best often forgot that it existed. His decision to wed Marie of Hesse was one of those times no power on earth could sway him from the path he had chosen. Nicholas and Aleksandra opposed his choice, for it was well known that Marie's conception had been the product of her mother's not very well concealed liaison with a lover of base origin. Yet her clouded background was of no consequence to Alexander. He threatened to renounce the throne rather than abandon the princess he called "the woman of my dreams" and vowed he would "never marry anyone but her."[227] He left his parents no choice, and they gave way before his determined insistence. In the spring of 1840, he went triumphantly to Darmstadt to claim his bride.[228] In December, Marie embraced Russian Orthodoxy and took the name of Maria Aleksandrovna. On April 16, 1841, Alexander wed her in the Winter Palace chapel. Thus began a love match that endured for more than two decades and produced six sons and two daughters.

Nicholas insisted that Alexander not allow his new-found happiness to interfere with his preparations for ruling Russia. In November 1839, he had appointed him to the State Council, although he did not yet permit him a vote in its decisions. In December 1840, Alexander received the same sort of appointment to the Committee of Ministers, and thus sat on Russia's highest administrative councils.[229] In January 1841, he became the Chancellor of the University of Helsinki, and, during the next two years, Nicholas appointed him to a number of other important policy-making bodies. In late 1842, he began to act as Nicholas's deputy.

Nicholas expected his son to play an important role in the deliberations of those bodies to which he appointed him and involved him in some of the most difficult problems Russia faced. In 1846 and in 1848, he appointed Alexander to secret committees that were discussing serfdom, so that he could gain firsthand experience with the issue that, most statesmen agreed, was Russia's greatest social and economic problem. Nor was the military side of Alexander's training forgotten, as Nicholas assigned him responsibilities that extended far beyond the parade ground.[230] When the Crimean War broke out, Alexander had begun to serve as his father's deputy on a daily basis. For the first time since that day over two centuries before when Mikhail Romanov had ascended the Russian throne, a Romanov sovereign had considered it a major part of his task to train a successor. No longer were the Romanovs insecure autocrats who feared that by training a successor they were creating a potential rival who might one day lead a coup d'état against them. Rather, they had come to realize that the problems Russia faced were so complex that a prince needed long and careful schooling to even hope to attend to them properly.

Because he had served in the upper reaches of Russia's government for nearly fifteen years, Alexander II carried out an extremely smooth transition when he became Russia's Emperor on February 19, 1855. He came to the throne proclaiming his intention to rule in the tradition of "Peter, Catherine, Alexander the Blessed, and Our unforgettable parent." With the help of his father's ministers, he began to govern Russia according to his father's principles. There was a slightly softer tone to his regime, but both father and son believed in the integrity of autocratic power, both idealized military principles, and both devoted all their attention to serving Russia's welfare as they understood it, in this world and in the next. For both, there was a sublime acceptance of death as merely a transition to another stage in their eternal service to Russia. Nicholas had often called upon the "Russian God" for aid and counsel,[231] and Alexander II held the same view of the Autocrat's very personal, yet totally humble, relationship to God.

Deep and abiding though his belief in divine protection was, the events of his first year on the throne tried Alexander's faith sorely. On his deathbed, his father had regretted that Russia's affairs were not "in good order," but they were in far better condition than they would be a year later. Historians often forget that, since Russia's domains stretched halfway around the globe—from Warsaw to Alaska—her war with the Allies in 1854 and 1855 was a worldwide confrontation. At the time of Nicholas's death in February 1855, Russians had driven off an Anglo-French attack against Kamchatka in the Far East, had fought the British and French to a standoff in the Baltic and the Crimea, and had won a series of noteworthy victories against the Turks in the Caucasus and the Transcaucasus.[232] It was during the first year of the new reign that Russia's military effort collapsed as the war turned into a disastrous fiasco in its Crimean theatre. By July 1855, Prince Mikhail Gorchakov concluded that it was hopeless to continue the defense of Sevastopol, Russia's great Crimean naval bastion to which the Allies had laid siege several months earlier.[233] Alexander rejected Gorchakov's advice and continued the struggle, but in September Sevastopol fell to the Allies. The Tsar delayed the final reckoning until December, when the Habsburg Emperor Franz Josef insisted that Russia agree to a peace conference on the Allies' terms immediately or face an Austrian attack. Unable to fight the war on yet another front, Alexander conceded defeat, and a peace conference assembled at Paris to end the conflict. Although the Peace of Paris was moderate and imposed no harsh demands upon Russia, it still made it clear that Russia had been defeated in her first great confrontation with Europe in four decades. It was, without doubt, the end of an era.

Although the Crimean defeat posed no direct threat to Russia's security, it dramatized the utter failure of Nicholas I's domestic and foreign policies, and threatened Russia's continued membership in the European community of Great Powers, where her only claim to status rested upon her military might, as it had done since the time of Peter the Great. Russia either had to modernize along Western lines or risk being pushed back into Asia. Certainly, there were among Europe's statesmen those who would have been delighted to impose the second alternative and remove what they perceived as the continuing threat of Russia's land forces on Europe's eastern frontier.[234]

If Russia were to regain her position as a Great Power in Europe, Alexander would have to resolve a number of very pressing issues. In the mid-nineteenth century, no nation could continue to bear the financial burden of maintaining an army of nearly one and a half million men in peacetime and equipping them with modern weapons. A smaller force, which could be expanded in wartime by a system of reserves such as existed in Prussia, could not be established in a country where the rank and file were drawn from a servile class. As General Dmitrii Miliutin argued when the war ended, it was impossible to train serfs in the use of weapons and tactics and then send them back to their villages as part of a reserve force. Serfs with military training could become the nucleus of increased and greater revolts. Just like the Cossacks in the seventeenth and eighteenth centuries, these men would threaten Russia's entire socioeconomic structure.[235] Other Russians were prepared to argue that serfdom not only prevented the modernization of the army but also was the reason for their nation's economic backwardness.

Yet even these arguments did not at first convince Alexander that he must institute far-reaching social and economic reforms. As his father would have done, he assembled a select committee to discuss the reasons for the Crimean defeat. From that point, an extremely complex interplay of events and political forces set in motion a process that produced the Great Reforms. We shall deal with this body of legislation in a later chapter, but here we should note that it made greater concessions than Alexander originally had intended; he did not set out to become Russia's "Tsar-Liberator."

The Great Reforms Alexander decreed for Russia had side effects neither he nor his advisers had foreseen. By 1855 most educated Russians felt the oppression of Nicholas's regime, but they had little hope that his son would be any different. Wrote one contemporary, "If he will pay attention to public opinion, even to the slightest degree, then ten or even fifteen years of nothing more than that, without any reforms at all, will be more than sufficient."[236] Alexander more than fulfilled such modest expectations. Within a decade, he emancipated millions of serfs and state peasants, created a whole new series of elective bodies to govern Russia's hamlets and districts, replaced trial by secret tribunals with trial by jury, and made Russia's judges independent from all outside influence including his own. It was an immense program of reform legislation, perhaps equaled in modern times only by President Roosevelt's New Deal. One might well expect that the result would have been an era of good feeling between the public and the government and that Alexander would have become a great popular hero. In fact, just the opposite occurred.

Once Alexander freed Russian society from the rigid controls his father had imposed, the expectations of public opinion moved ahead at a far more rapid pace than did his reform program. As a result, even though the Emancipation Acts of 1861 were far more generous than anyone had dared to dream when Alexander ascended the throne, they fell far short of Russians' expectations. All groups in Russia were dissatisfied with the Emancipation Acts, and that disappointment began to drive the nation's youth onto a revolutionary course. Thus it was the more progressive program of Alexander, not the reactionary one of his father, that brought Russia's first real revolutionary movement into being. Young revolutionaries declared open war against the government, its officials, and Alexander himself. Their ultimate weapon was terror and assassination.

By the middle of the nineteenth century, those Summer Gardens that Peter the Great had laid out with such care and whose beautification had so occupied the Empresses Anna and Elizabeth had become one of Petersburgers' favorite promenades, and it was Alexander's custom to join them briefly on some afternoons. Like his father, he enjoyed chance meetings with his subjects from whom he tried to learn more about public opinion in his Empire. On April 4, 1866, he strolled in the Gardens for a short time, spoke briefly with the Duke of Leuchtenburg, and then returned to his carriage. While the policemen on duty at the Gardens' gate were falling over themselves to be of service to their Tsar, a young man stepped from the crowd of onlookers, drew an ancient double-barreled pistol from his tattered coat, and fired one shot at his unsuspecting and amazed Emperor. According to the police reports, a peasant in the crowd jostled the would-be assassin's arm and spoiled his aim. With one shot left in his weapon, he tried to escape, but two policemen chased him and seized his arms before he had gone more than a hundred feet. "Fools, I've done this for you!" he reportedly shouted to the horrified and uncomprehending crowd. Angrily, violently, the police dragged him to Alexander, who asked if he were a Pole. Stubbornly, he shook his head and replied, "Pure Russian." Alexander then asked the young man why he had tried to kill him. "Look at the freedom you gave the peasants!" was his surly reply.[237]

Over the centuries, it had become a tenet almost as certain as the belief that God was in His Heaven that Russia's common folk loved their Tsar and revered him as their "little father." Ever since the Grand Prince of Moscow had risen to rule the Russian land, no commoner had attempted to murder the Tsar. That such a monstrous crime should have been attempted in St. Petersburg, the very symbol of the Romanovs' power and the Empire they had created, appalled most Petersburgers, and they clamored for the authorities to get to the bottom of the attempt. As in the case of the assassination of President Kennedy ninety-seven years later, many were convinced that the assassin must be part of a larger plot, and they demanded that everyone involved be severely punished. Tsarist police officers were usually quite adept at uncovering even obscure and well-hidden plots, as a number of radicals who still languished in the barren wastes of Siberia could readily testify. But there was one man among them who stood out for his cold efficiency and heartless brutality, and public opinion demanded that he be brought in to interrogate the would-be assassin and direct the investigation. Count Mikhail Nikolaevich Muravev, popularly known as the "Hangman of Vilna," a title he had earned during his just-completed assignment as Governor-General of Lithuania, was widely acclaimed as the man for the job. He had just played a major part in crushing those elements of the Polish revolt of 1863 that had spilled into Russia's western provinces and had impressed everyone by his willingness to hang first and ask questions later. When asked which Poles he considered the least dangerous to Russia, he was reputed to have replied, "Those who have been hanged."[238]

Who was the would-be assassin and why had he tried to murder his Emperor? These were questions Muravev needed to answer, but it was several days before he and his assistants resolved even the first one. Their prisoner insisted that he was Aleksei Petrov, a Russian peasant, but they knew from his manner, speech, and general knowledge that, whoever he was, he was not a tiller of the soil. Finally, the keeper of a cheap rooming house reported that one of his lodgers had disappeared, and the police soon confirmed that this was the man they had arrested. When they searched his room, they learned that they held in custody Dmitrii Karakozov, aged twenty-five, who came from a poor noble family living in the Volga province of Saratov. He had been dismissed from the University of Kazan for taking part in student demonstrations. Soon afterward, he had been dismissed from the University of Moscow for not paying his fees. He had "a pale and tired face, hair flowing onto his shoulders, [and] was noticeable for the carelessness of his clothes," one of his professors remembered.[239] He was not distinguished by any particular intellectual or academic achievements. To most who had encountered him in Kazan, Moscow, or St. Petersburg, he must have seemed a nonenity.

Like most Russian student radicals of the 1860s, Karakozov had begun his revolutionary career with a futile effort to educate the masses and spread socialist propaganda among them. Soon he had become deeply depressed by the apparent hopelessness of that task. In frustration, he had concluded that only by killing the Emperor could he do something truly worthwhile to aid the masses' cause. Resolutely, and with little thought for his own fate, he went to St. Petersburg, purchased powder and ball for his old pistol, and tried to shoot down the man he hated with such blind passion. Ironically, his failure damaged the cause he cherished, and many others suffered as a consequence of his reckless act.

Authorities found among Karakozov's belongings the address of Nikolai Ishutin, his cousin and fellow revolutionary, who directed a conspiratorial circle in Moscow that went by the name of Hell. That one piece of information led to the arrest of Ishutin and thirty-one others. Most were sentenced to hard labor in Siberia. Karakozov was condemned to death and hanged at dawn on September 3, 1866. He begged Alexander for mercy. Alexander replied that, as a Christian he could forgive him, but, as Emperor he could not. It was a statement very much in the tradition of Nicholas I who, almost a half-century earlier, had sentenced the Decembrist Kondratii Ryleev to the gallows while he bestowed upon his widow a generous pension to support herself and her fatherless children.[240]

Karakozov's attempt against Alexander shocked public opinion.

Authorities instituted such a brutal policy of repression that no revolutionary group functioned effectively in Russia for several years after the attack. It became impossible even to distribute moderate socialist propaganda without being arrested, so diligent were the police and so anxious were the public to come to their aid. Freed for the moment from the pressure of student revolutionary activism, Alexander and his advisers instituted policies that encouraged Russia's industry, modernized her economy, and restored her diplomatic position in Europe, while they pursued an energetic expansionist policy in Central Asia and the Far East. Under the direction of Prince Aleksandr Gorchakov, Alexander II's foreign policy enjoyed success on all fronts during the 1860s and 1870s. As a result, the first two decades of his reign were for him a time of great personal satisfaction. By 1875, Alexander could take pride in having eradicated the stain of Russia's Crimean defeat at home and abroad.

Alexander's personal life during these years was as turbulent as the changes he imposed upon Russia; the year 1865 was perhaps the most difficult of all. In April his heir, Grand Duke Nikolai Aleksandrovich, died of consumption, and the Emperor felt the loss deeply. The Grand Duke had been all that an Imperial father could wish. Handsome and intelligent, he had charmed all who knew him, and his death was all the more painful because his younger brother Alexander Aleksandrovich seemed less personable and less intelligent. Yet Nikolai's death was not the only emotional crisis Alexander faced that year. Shortly afterward, on one of his courtesy visits to St. Petersburg's elite finishing school for aristocratic young ladies at the Smolnyi Institute, he met Ekaterina Dolgorukova, a young woman of eighteen. Wrote one contemporary, she was "of medium height, with an elegant figure, silky ivory skin, the eyes of a frightened gazelle, a sensuous mouth, and light chestnut tresses."[241] Aging rapidly at fifty, Alexander found her irresistible and saw in her a means to recapture his faded youth and lost happiness.

Hopelessly in love with Ekaterina Dolgorukova, Alexander pursued her discreetly for more than a year and even arranged for her to become one of his wife's ladies-in-waiting. Finally, on July 1, 1866, less than three months after Karakozov had fired his fateful shot outside the Summer Gardens, Alexander and Ekaterina became lovers. He swore to marry her at the first opportunity and proclaimed that "from now on and for always" he considered her as his "wife before God."[242] Thus began a liaison that lasted for the rest of Alexander's life. That his union brought intense grief to the loyal wife with whom he had shared so much happiness in former days seemed of no consequence. He insisted that Ekaterina must continue in her Court post so that he would always have her near him. They met three or four times each week, wrote to each other nearly every day, and had four children during the next fourteen years. Maria Aleksandrovna had to bear the insult of having her husband's mistress and their children always near her. According to some accounts, even as Maria lay dying on May 22, 1880, "she could hear at play in the room above her, her husband's children by his second 'wife.' "[243] Alexander was at Tsarskoe Selo with Ekaterina at the time. As he later confessed to several of his courtiers, the Empress died alone.[244]

The requirements of good taste and decent behavior, not to mention the personal obligation to respect the memory of a departed spouse, decreed that a Russian widower or widow must wait at least a year to remarry, but Alexander hastened to wed his "wife before God" just forty days after the Empress Maria breathed her last. He at first tried to ease the blow of his precipitous action by keeping his second marriage secret from almost everyone, including his heir, the Grand Duke Alexander Aleksandrovich. Only during the remaining months of summer did he gradually disclose to his family and leading advisers that he had wed Ekaterina, who now bore the title of Princess Iurevskaia. General Count Dmitrii Miliutin, who had served Alexander as Minister of War for almost two decades and who was one of his closest advisers on domestic and foreign policy, did not learn of the marriage until late August.[245] Public opinion in St. Petersburg was so shocked at Alexander's behavior that the German Ambassador, General Schweinitz, hearing of the Emperor's death almost a year later, remarked that "God has saved him from losing still more of his dignity and self-respect."[246]

Although others faulted him for his seemingly impetuous behavior, there were reasons for Alexander's haste to marry the woman he loved that had nothing to do with his advancing years or his apparent continued infatuation. Chief among them, as General Miliutin once remarked, Alexander had come to realize that "every day might be his last."[247] "I would have never married before a year of mourning," he wrote to his sister Olga, "if not for the . . . hazardous threats I expose myself to daily which can actually and suddenly end my life."[248] In fact, Alexander's life was in great and continuing peril. The 1870s had seen a resurgence of revolutionary activity in Russia, and, late in the decade, one wing of the movement had decided that its goals could be achieved only through terrorism. On August 26, 1879, a small group of Russian terrorists, who called themselves the Party of the People's Will, met in a forest near Lesnoi to discuss the tactics of their struggle against Alexander. Frustrated in their efforts to spread propaganda among the masses and angry at the Emperor for barring the way to revolution, they decreed that he must die. The "will of the people" demanded it. Thus began a deadly game of cat and mouse, in which the People's Will pursued Alexander relentlessly across the face of Russia, even through the halls of the Winter Palace itself.

One of the terrorists' most dramatic efforts to kill Alexander took place in February 1880, after months of careful preparations. In September 1879, a simple cabinetmaker in search of work had appeared at the Winter Palace and was taken on as a carpenter. The man's passport stated that he was a peasant named Batiushkov from the distant northern province of Olonets. He seemed pleasant, simple, and honest, not overly intelligent, but an able craftsman. The simple country joiner was none other than Stepan Khalturin, one of the leaders of St. Petersburg's nascent workers' movement and a major figure in the terrorist battle organization. Bit by bit, over many weeks, Khalturin smuggled dynamite into the palace and hid it in his bed in the workers' cellar dormitory. Toward the end of January 1880, he planted his patiently collected charge in the cellar, two floors below the palace dining room, with the intention of detonating it while Alexander was at dinner. On February 5, he lit the fuse and calmly left the palace by the workers' entrance. A few moments later, a tremendous explosion shattered the guardroom that stood on the floor between the cellar and the dining room, killing eleven people and injuring fifty-six more. The dining room remained undamaged because Khalturin had used too little explosive, but the psychological impact of the attack was immense. It proclaimed to the world that, even within the walls of his own palace, Alexander was not safe from the revolutionaries' vengeance.[249]

Khalturin's daring assault was the fifth attempt the People's Will had made against Alexander, and they were resolved to try once again. Late in the fall of 1880, they began to organize a new attack that was more complex than any before, because the police security around the Emperor had become almost impenetrable. At the same time, arrests, exiles, and executions continued to thin their sparse ranks, and, for one brief moment, even Andrei Zheliabov, their usually indomitable leader, faltered and suggested they postpone their attack. But Sofia Perovskaia and Anna Iakimova, the terrorists' most ardent advocates of assassination, insisted that the deed must be done without delay. "Our girls are fiercer than our men," remarked Nikolai Kibalchich, their leading chemist and bomb maker. Zheliabov conceded that "the honor of the party demands that the Emperor be killed."[250] Against Alexander's army and secret police, the People's Will marshaled their final force of twenty-seven operatives.

Twenty young men and seven young women, all but six under the age of thirty, only three of them with any knowledge about the use of explosives, and with somewhat less than two hundred rubles among them, prepared to attack the Autocrat of All the Russias. Seven would be dead within six months. Another eleven would not survive the decade. Only six would live to see the revolution come in 1917.[251] With Perovskaia to direct them, a group of five terrorists kept careful watch upon the Winter Palace, noted the routes Alexander followed when he drove to various parts of the city, and began to lay their plans accordingly. The main weapon in their arsenal was the same sort of dynamite charge they had used in past attempts, but now they planned to supplement it with a new and untried weapon. For some months, Kibalchich, a brilliant young scientist and a pioneer in jet propulsion, had been experimenting with the idea of producing nitroglycerine hand grenades, which did not require fuses. In the center of a receptacle filled with jagged bits of metal, he carefully positioned two thin glass vials of nitroglycerine laid crosswise against each other. The vials shattered upon impact, and the grenade exploded. Its principle was deceptively simple, but Kibalchich's grenades were almost suicidally volatile, especially when carried through crowded streets or along icy pavements. The terrorists nevertheless decided to use Kibalchich's new weapon as a second means of attack should their dynamite fail.[252]

The terrorists rented a small basement shop at No. 56 Malaia Sadovaia Street, along the route Alexander often traveled, as a base from which to lay their dynamite mine. To allay suspicion, they opened a cheese shop in their new quarters, and from one of its unused rooms they began to tunnel beneath the street itself. To play the role of cheese sellers, they chose two of their number who were known for their ready wit, but who unfortunately had no experience in business. They soon became a topic of neighborhood gossip as other merchants, servants, and housewives wondered aloud why this pleasant young couple sold cheese to the neighborhood workers at prices far too low to produce a profit. In a city where almost every doorman and janitor was in the pay of the secret police and where each needed to report something out of the ordinary to receive his pay, it was only a matter of time before this gossip reached the ears of the authorities. The possibility of discovery became even greater when the terrorists actually began to dig their tunnel beneath the sidewalk and street, for they risked the sound of their shovels reaching the ears of the police and watchmen who patrolled the street above.

By the latter part of February, the People's Will had nearly completed their preparations. They had no time to lose, for the police were beginning to penetrate the curtain of secrecy with which they had surrounded themselves for eighteen months. Would the police net close before they could mount their final assault against the Tsar? In January, three terrorists had been arrested; a few weeks later, another had fallen into the authorities' clutches. Still another, Natalia Olovennikova, suffered a nervous breakdown and had to be sent away to Moscow. An inspection of the cheese shop by a general from the Imperial Corps of Engineers disguised as a municipal surveyor nearly uncovered the tunnel. Only plain good luck and the glib tongue and artful manner of one of the women threw the inspectors briefly off the scent. But on February 27, Mikhail Trigoni and Zheliabov walked into a police trap. For several days the police did not realize whom they had captured; their ignorance proved a critical factor in the success of the terrorists.

Sofia Perovskaia, the twenty-six-year-old daughter of the man who had been Governor-General of St. Petersburg when Karakozov had fired his fateful pistol shot almost fifteen years before, stepped in to fill the place of her lover Zheliabov after his arrest. She was small and blond, almost childlike in her appearance, but she was a revolutionary to the very depths of her soul and had been so since the age of sixteen. Under her warm encouragement and watchful gaze, her fellow revolutionaries devoted February 28 to preparations for their final assault. The dynamite was properly placed and carefully charged. Kibalchich spent the evening making four nitroglycerine hand grenades to be carried by Ignacy Hryniewicki, Nikolai Rysakov, Timofei Mikhailov, and Ivan Emelianov. Only by working for seventeen hours without rest was Kibalchich able to have his weapons ready.[253]

On the morning of March 1, 1881, the terrorists took up their attack positions. Three were posted at the cheese shop; two of them were to leave just before the attack, while the third, Mikhail Frolenko, was to detonate the mine and probably die beneath the rubble. There were several hours to wait, and one of his fellow terrorists, Vera Figner, later recalled with amazement the calmness with which Frolenko faced almost certain death. "With amazement, I saw him take from a package that he had brought with him a bottle of red wine and a sausage," Figner wrote. " 'What are you doing?' I asked, almost with horror, as I beheld this matter-of-fact procedure on the part of a man who was destined to an almost certain death under the ruin caused by the explosion. 'I must be in full possession of my strength,' calmly replied my comrade, and he imperturbably began to eat."[254]

As the people in the cheese shop awaited Alexander's passage along the street outside their building, Perovskaia took command of the grenade throwers. If, for some reason, Alexander did not follow his usual Sunday route, Perovskaia planned to direct them to other locations through a series of prearranged hand signals. As it turned out, Alexander did not take his usual path. That very morning, Princess Iurevskaia had begged him not to drive along either the Nevskii Prospekt or the Malaia Sadovaia because there had been so many reports about possible terrorist attacks, and he had promised to follow the Catherine Canal Embankment instead. After reviewing a parade, he paid a brief call upon his cousin, the Grand Duchess Ekaterina, and then began his fateful return to the Winter Palace. True to his promise, he drove by way of the Catherine Embankment.

Alexander's changed route had rendered the terrorists' dynamite mine useless. When Sofia Perovskaia had seen him drive to the Grand Duchess's palace, she had signaled her grenadiers to new positions along the Catherine Canal, the most obvious alternate route. They were all in their new positions when the bomb-proof Imperial carriage, a gift from Napoleon III, came racing at full speed along the Inzhenernaia and turned the corner onto the Embankment. Rysakov's grenade damaged the carriage and wounded several onlookers, but Alexander was left unharmed. Then, in the shock and confusion, the Emperor made a fatal mistake. He left his carriage to inspect the damage and to comfort the wounded, unaware that the terrorist Hryniewicki stood leaning against a railing not far away. When his quarry was not two meters away, Hryniewicki hurled his grenade directly between Alexander's feet. A deafening explosion, blood-drenched snow, and the screams of some twenty wounded bystanders filled the air. When the smoke cleared, Alexander lay mortally wounded, both legs smashed and torn by the blast. Not far away, Hryniewicki also lay torn and bleeding, a victim of his own grenade. Alexander died within hours. His assassin followed him in death later that evening. To the very end, he never told the police his name.[255]

At 3:30 on the dark, dreary afternoon of March 1, 1881, the People's Will finally executed the sentence of death they had passed against Alexander almost two years earlier. "The terrible nightmare, which has been oppressing the youth of Russia for the past decade, at last has been lifted," proclaimed Vera Figner, the only one of their Executive Committee to elude the police for several years more. "An overwhelming weight has fallen from our shoulders. Reaction must end in order to make way for the rebirth of Russia."[256] But rebirth did not come, for public opinion, horrified at the terrorists' deed, demanded their punishment. On April 3, five of them, including Zheliabov, Perovskaia, and Kibalchich, died on the gallows. Theirs was a horrible death, as hangings almost always were in nineteenth-century Russia. Death came by slow strangulation, because Russian officials never bothered to construct drop platforms in the scaffold floor beneath their gallows. So unpopular was the hangman's trade that there was only one in all the Empire. This was Frolov, a man who invariably deadened his scruples with large tumblers of raw vodka and became clumsy and befuddled as a result. This time, Frolov was even more besotted than usual. Three of his victims died without incident. For Zheliabov and his friend Mikhailov, death was far more cruel. Twice Mikhailov's noose slipped, and he fell to the platform, only to be hauled up and hanged again by the cursing, drunken Frolov. To prevent the noose from slipping when he hanged Zheliabov, Frolov tied a double knot, which slowed strangulation even more.

It took several minutes for Mikhailov and Zheliabov each to die.[257] With them died the terrorist movement for a quarter-century. Russia embarked upon what is sometimes called the Era of Counterreforms, during which Alexander III held her in a viselike grip that stifled all criticism, or even comment, about government policies. By one of those tragic ironies of history, on the very morning of his death, Alexander II had signed a decree that granted a very limited form of representative government for Russians. Its nullification was one of his son's first acts.

Alexander III was born on February 25, 1845. He was only two years younger than his elder brother Nikolai Aleksandrovich, and the two remained very close throughout their childhood and adolescent years. Grand Duke Nikolai was considerably brighter and had a greater ability to grasp the subjects his tutors taught. Evidently, he transmitted much of what he learned to Alexander and thus served as an important supplement to his education.[258] Beginning in 1853, both boys studied history, geography, Russian, and German with the great academician Iakov Grot, but, as time went on, their studies took different paths. Nikolai Aleksandrovich was to become Russia's Emperor. Alexander was but a junior Grand Duke, and, even as he passed his twentieth birthday, it was not certain just where or how he would serve Russia. By then, he had grown into a giant of a man, "built like a butcher, powerful, and extremely muscular," in a British correspondent's words. "In his youth, he could straighten horseshoes with his bare hands and smash in doors with his shoulders," the correspondent's account continued. "His body was huge and unwieldy, and his movements clumsy, partly the result of his almost morbid shyness. It was as if all the forces of his being had flooded outward to the periphery, for the greater development of bones and muscles, and, as a consequence, had left a lack of passion and intellectualism at the center."[259] His tutors had transmitted to him a rigid sense of morality, a deep awareness of right and wrong, which made it possible for him to perceive the world in uncomplicated terms of good and evil. He once said that he considered himself to be nothing more than "a conscientious regimental commander."[260]

All of the uncertainties about Alexander Aleksandrovich's future disappeared at 12:50 on the morning of April 12, 1865, when Nikolai died of tuberculosis. Within a matter of hours, he was proclaimed heir, even though the entire Imperial family, including the Emperor, was in Nice at the time. Alexander literally stepped into his elder brother's place, even becoming engaged to Princess Dagmar, daughter of King Christian IX and Queen Louisa of Denmark, who had been Nikolai's fiancée. Born into a family that honored peace and was respected throughout Europe, Dagmar was a beautiful young woman who combined sensitivity, modesty, and intelligence with a truly regal presence.[261] She had been devoted to Nikolai and had been with him when he died. It was not love but reasons of state that dictated her subsequent marriage to Alexander in October 1866. Surprisingly, their marriage proved an unusually strong one. Alexander remained devotedly faithful to his Empress Maria Feodorovna, the name Princess Dagmar took when she converted to Orthodoxy. Indeed, he was the only Romanov ruler since Tsar Aleksei Mikhailovich who did not have a mistress or a lover at some point in his life. During the next sixteen years, he and Maria had three sons and two daughters while they lived quietly in their small family circle. Much like his grandfather, and in sharp contrast to his father, Grand Duke Alexander shunned pomp and opulence and chose a life that was notable for its simplicity. Of all the Imperial residences, he preferred Gatchina, where he and Maria Feodorovna lived among a small group of intimate friends, conversed, read, and enjoyed comic threatre and light music. Alexander sometimes played the trombone in a quartet made up of close friends.[262] He had no aspirations to greatness but wanted only to do well the tasks his duty imposed upon him.

Alexander Aleksandrovich's new responsibilities as Russia's heir were reflected almost immediately in the new cadre of tutors who invaded his life just weeks after his brother's death. Although an adult of twenty, he returned to the classroom to prepare himself for the demanding labors that one day would be his. In the fall of 1865, he began to study Russia's past in order to better prepare himself to guide her future. His studies with the great historian Sergei Solovev were particularly significant in shaping his attitudes about his mission as an autocrat and his view of Russia's future. To Solovev, Russia's history represented a vast and intricate mosaic that he sought to portray in his life's work, a twenty-nine-volume history of his motherland. Heavily influenced by Hegel and by the great German historian von Ranke, Solovev saw the state and nation as being inseparably linked. He viewed Russia's history as being the history of her government, and he impressed that view upon Grand Duke Alexander.[263] For a man of Alexander's straightforward views, it was but a small step from Solovev's more sophisticated theories of Russia's national development to the simplistic conclusions that autocracy had played the major role in Russia's past, that the Autocrat personified Russia, and that he himself must play the central part in her present and future. He therefore developed what the historian Florinsky once characterized as "an instinctive elemental attachment to the idea of the unfettered supremacy of the crown, interpreted as the mainstay of the Empire and the very essence of Russia's historical tradition."[264]

If Solovev taught Alexander about Russia's past, others filled his mind with a vision of the future at which the great historian's belief in Russia's political and religious messianism only hinted. During the 1870s, Alexander fell under the spell of Panslav ideas, especially those articulated by the Slavophile Ivan Aksakov. From them Alexander extracted only a crudely formulated Russian chauvinism. He had no sympathy for the nationalistic strivings of such Slavic peoples as the Czechs, the Poles, the Bulgarians, the Serbs, or the Croats. As he noted on a dispatch he received from Russia's Ambassador to Berlin soon after he became Emperor, "We can have no policy except one that is purely

Russian and national."[265] For Alexander Aleksandrovich, Panslavism could never be more than an instrument for furthering Russia's nationalistic and imperialistic aims, and he sought to exploit other Slavic peoples' aspirations for independence from the Ottoman or Habsburg empires in order to further Russian aspirations in the Balkans and Central Europe.

Alexander had even less use for the romantic Slavophile dream of reviving a *zemskii sobor,* such as Tsars Mikhail and Aleksei Mikhailovich had summoned for advice from time to time. Aksakov saw the *zemskii sobor* as an embodiment of an eternal union between Autocrat and people, but to Alexander it smacked of constitutionalism or, at the very least, seemed a threat to his power. "The day may come when flatterers . . . will try to persuade you that it would suffice to grant Russia a so-called constitution on the western model, and all difficulties would disappear," the jurist Konstantin Pobedonostsev warned him in 1876. "This is a lie, and God forbid that a true Russian shall see the day when this lie will become an accomplished fact."[266]

Pobedonostsev, tall, balding, and thin, his cold, slightly myopic stare shielded by thin, wire-rimmed spectacles, became Alexander's favored mentor in the mid-1860s and served as his most trusted friend and adviser throughout his reign. He was a man of rigid morality, uncompromising in his defense of conservative principles, who encouraged his pupil's bigotry and prejudice. On the face of it Pobedonostsev's early background made him an unlikely candidate to become the power behind a man who believed in absolute authority. He had been educated at the Imperial School of Jurisprudence, served in one of Moscow's Senate offices and, by the age of thirty, had become sharply critical of the injustices in Russia's judicial system. "There is no just case which cannot be lost," he wrote bitterly, "nor is there any illegal case which cannot be won, for there are no firm principles according to which the legal can be distinguished from the illegal."[267] He thus became disillusioned with his duties as an administrator of Russia's laws and became a professor of civil law at Moscow University, where he urged the need for a modern court system. In the late 1850s, he championed public jury trials and independent tenure for judges. He became one of Russia's leading jurists and played a major role in drafting the Judicial Reform Act of 1864, which established those very institutions he had championed in his lectures and writings.

Because of his reputation as an enlightened jurist, Alexander II had appointed Pobedonostsev as a tutor to Grand Duke Nikolai Aleksandrovich in 1861. It was a duty Pobedonostsev was reluctant to assume, for it would require him to return to St. Petersburg, a city in which he feared he might lose his integrity. Nevertheless, he obeyed his Emperor's call, began to tutor Nikolai Aleksandrovich in Russian law, and the young Grand Duke asked him to join his suite on a lengthy tour of European Russia in 1863.[268] Two years later, the Grand Duke was dead, but Pobedonostsev's influence over Russia's future rulers was destined to continue. Remembering his elder brother's enthusiasm, Alexander Aleksandrovich invited him to become his own tutor. Alexander discontinued his lessons during his marriage preparations, but resumed them in November 1866. "Dear Konstantin Petrovich," he wrote on November 22. "I want to begin my lessons with you again." He signed his note "your sincerely loving Alexander."[269] From then on, Pobedonostsev would be by his side until his death more than a quarter-century later.

The Pobedonostsev who stood so close to Alexander Aleksandrovich as Grand Duke and later as Emperor Alexander III, was very different from the young man who had agonized over the injustices of his country's courts and cursed the venality of her judges. He had become an unyielding reactionary who regarded the Great Reforms as a threat to the inner fabric of Russian society and a danger to the security of the autocratic system. Pobedonostsev viewed the upsurge of radicalism in the 1870s as a direct consequence of those concessions Alexander II had made in the 1860s, and he impressed that point upon his pupil. It was not a view the Grand Duke needed much urging to accept. Everything in his personal experience had led him to similar, though less clearly articulated, conclusions.

In keeping with Nicholas I's precedent, Alexander II had brought his son into Russia's government soon after he reached his twenty-first birthday. He appointed him to the State Council in the fall of 1866 and to the Committee of Ministers two years later. Grand Duke Alexander thus was closely associated with the formulation of Russian policy from the mid-1860s onward and soon began to oppose his father's Great Reforms. In the highest circles of the administration, he became the leader of a strong conservative political opposition, just as his uncle, Grand Duke Konstantin Nikolaevich, had headed a progressive bloc ever since the mid-1850s. That these factions openly attempted to influence policy at the center of Russia's government was yet another indication of the Romanov dynasty's political maturity. By balancing the conflicting positions of such groups, Alexander II not only attempted to foster change within Russia but to control its pace. One of Alexander III's first acts as Emperor was to destroy that delicate balance his father had maintained with such care for so long.

When Alexander III came to the throne on March 1, 1881, his political principles were firmly established. He lacked polish and had no inclination to compromise in matters of diplomacy and politics. In his evaluations of advisers, foreign diplomats, and even the rulers they served, he was blunt, at times utterly crude. "What a herd of swine!" "What a beast!" were comments he wrote in the margins of reports sent by his ambassadors and ministers. He disliked Catholics, distrusted Protestants, and despised Jews with a passion that was all-pervasive. "He is a rotten, lousy Jew," he once remarked to explain why he had turned down a recommendation that a certain official be promoted to high office.[270] "We must not forget that it was the Jews who crucified our Lord and spilled his precious blood," he wrote at another point.[271] There was a primitive quality about Alexander III's manner and attitudes that cannot be denied, but there also were some virtues in his character. His sense of duty was as pervasive as that of Nicholas I, the Romanov who had raised duty to the level of the sanctioning principle of life itself. Alexander probably was the first truly frugal member of a dynasty that was known for its extravagance. Indeed, Count Sergei Witte, his last Minister of Finance, remarked that the Emperor guarded every kopeck as if it were his own and that he instilled this sense of frugality into the senior officials who served him.[272] Finally, Alexander III was one of the most diligent Romanovs ever to rule Russia. He took his duties seriously, actually read mountains of reports with care, and commented dutifully (though not always politely) in their margins.

The decade of social and political upheaval through which Russia had just passed, and the assassination of his father, convinced Alexander III that he must be firm and unyielding on all social and political questions. He hastened to replace the handful of progressives among his father's ministers with conservatives, with whom he set out to restore the full power of autocracy by attacking every one of the Great Reforms. His domestic program was designed to impose political order and social stability upon Russia, and his foreign policy was directed toward much the same end. With the exception of limited campaigns in Central Asia, his was a reign of peace, for neither he nor his cautious and reserved Foreign Minister Nikolai Giers aspired to achieved grand designs abroad. Stability was an essential prerequisite for attracting the foreign investments that Russia's nascent industrial establishment required, and Alexander was determined to provide it. His regime thus was a time of outward harmony, much as Nicholas I's had been. Within a year after his accession, the revolutionary forces that had appeared so threatening in the late 1870s were in total disarray. Their organizations had been destroyed, their leaders executed, imprisoned, exiled to Siberia, or forced to flee abroad. Order reigned supreme. Even such a catastrophe as the great famine of 1891 could not disturb the tranquility of Alexander III's Russia.

Yet, even though he controlled Russia more firmly than any other Romanov in the nineteenth century, Alexander could not control the caprices of fate. He had always been physically strong and was rarely sick. It seemed unthinkable that such a bull of a man could become ill. But in the spring of 1894 Alexander began to suffer such vague and indefinable malaises as insomnia, loss of appetite, a sense of weakness in the legs. He went to Spala, the Imperial hunting lodge in Poland, thinking that a change of scenery and a brief rest would do him good, but he became worse. A specialist was summoned and diagnosed nephritis, a disease of the kidneys for which there was no cure and little effective treatment. Unable to do much else, he prescribed a trip to Livadia in hopes that the warm and dry Crimean climate might help. No one realized when Alexander boarded the train for the south a few weeks later in mid-September 1894 that he was going to his death. By the end of the month, he actually seemed on his way to recovery. He drove out in his carriage and attended church on several occasions. Yet the improvement was illusory, and he soon became worse. Brief official bulletins, sent to St. Petersburg by the Minister of the Imperial Household, best tell the sad tale of Alexander III's decline into death in the course of one brief fortnight:

> October 5th: The health of the Sovereign Emperor seems worse. A general weakening, and the weakness of the heart increases.

> October 11th: The Sovereign Emperor rested better. Appetite is poor. Strength and heartbeat do not improve. The swelling of the feet increases somewhat.

> October 15th: The Sovereign Emperor ate well. His heart rate has increased a little. The swelling has not increased. He feels better than yesterday.

> October 17th: During the day, the Sovereign Emperor ate little, and felt weaker. The usual cough from which His Majesty has suffered for a long time as the result of a chronic catarrh is worse. A little blood appeared in his urine.

> October 18th: During the day, the Sovereign Emperor continued to have blood in his urine. He had a chill. His temperature is 37.8, his pulse is 90 and weak. Breathing is labored. Appetite is extremely poor. Great weakness. The swelling [in his feet and legs] has increased a great deal.

> October 20th: 9 A.M. Breathing very labored. Heartbeat weakening rapidly. Condition extremely dangerous.

> October 20th: 10 A.M. The Sovereign Emperor managed to take the Last Sacrament. His Majesty was in full possession of all his faculties.

> October 20th: The Sovereign Emperor Alexander III quietly passed away at 2:15 P.M. today.[273]

Alexander III's death ended the last period of calm and stability that Russia would know under the Romanovs. On October 20, 1894, Russia appeared stable, an underdeveloped nation now fully embarked upon the road to rapid industrial development. A brief quarter-century later, the Romanovs would have been swept from the land, the Emperor and his family executed by a Bolshevik firing squad, while Russia writhed in the agonies of civil war. It is one of the ironies of Russia's history under the Romanovs that Alexander III, who believed so firmly in his mission to preserve and strengthen autocracy, failed to prepare his successor in state affairs as Nicholas I and Alexander II had done. Yet both Nicholas I and Alexander II had found willing pupils in their heirs, while Alexander III did not have that same good fortune. Grand Duke Nikolai Aleksandrovich, the future Nicholas II, much preferred to occupy his time with sports, playing with dogs, gathering mushrooms, and shooting. Above all, he enjoyed a carefree life, and everything associated with that received the greater part of his attention. In his diary, there is an account of how he played a delightful game of hide-and-seek with two of his friends. There is another entry that describes the great fun of battles he had at Livadia with Prince George of Greece, in which they pelted each other with chestnuts and pinecones. The first of these entries was made in 1893, when the future Nicholas II was twenty-five years old. The second was dated September 27 and 29, 1894, a scant three weeks before he became Emperor of Russia.[274]

Alexander III had no illusions about his heir and described him with characteristic bluntness on occasion. Concerned about the fact that Nikolai Aleksandrovich was well into his mid-twenties and still had not yet begun to play any serious role in state affairs, Count Witte proposed that he be named to chair the Commitee for Constructing the Trans-Siberian Railway in 1893. According to Witte's account, Alexander III was utterly amazed at his suggestion. "Have you ever tried to discuss anything of any consequence with him?" he asked Witte. "No, Your Majesty, I never have had the pleasure of discussing any such thing with the Heir," Witte replied. "Well, he is still an absolute child," Alexander replied. "His judgments are still truly childish. How could he be the chairman of a committee?"[275] Childish or not, just more than a year later, Nikolai Aleksandrovich ascended the throne as the Emperor Nicholas II. Little did those around him realize that this kind, mild, and not very able man, who presided in 1913, over the three-hundred year anniversary of the Romanovs' accession would lead his country into two disastrous wars and two revolutions, which would make him the last Romanov to rule Russia. Even though Nicholas II brought the Romanov dynasty to ruin, he could not destroy those great achievements with which his nineteenth-century predecessors had adorned Russia. During the century between 1796 and 1894, the Romanovs had turned Peter the Great's capital into a truly Imperial city and had presided over the development of an immensely impressive national culture. We must turn our attention to the achievements and failures of the nineteenth-century Romanovs in order to understand better the reasons why Nicholas II was unable to prevent the fall of his dynasty in 1917.

CHAPTER IX

The New Faces
of St. Petersburg

By the beginning of the nineteenth century, St. Petersburg had become a metropolis thronged with men and women who brought many cultures from many lands, all of them from within the confines of the Romanovs' vast domains. There were Tatars from the Crimea, Germans from the middle Volga and the Baltic provinces, and Finns from the newly conquered Grand Duchy. There were tribesmen from Siberia, the Caucasus, and the vast steppes of Central Asia; there were Armenians, Poles, Lithuanians, Ukrainians, Jews, and Greeks from the newly founded Black Sea port of Odessa. St. Petersburg was the administrative, commercial, and political hub of the Russian Empire, and it was a crucial link in its connection to the West. What happened in Russia usually had its origins in St. Petersburg, and, therefore, Russians were drawn to it by an irresistible force. No one who visited Russia's capital in the nineteenth century could doubt that it was the capital of a vast Empire, for the colossal architectural monuments the Romanovs erected were designed to dramatize and reflect their Imperial grandeur.

Nineteenth-century St. Petersburg preserved the character that the eighteenth-century Romanovs had imparted to it, but Catherine's successors added new dimensions. During the quarter-century after Napoleon's defeat, the city's architecture took on a truly heroic quality reminiscent of the glories of ancient Greece and Rome. Gigantic triumphal arches adorned with huge cast-iron and bronze sculptures, and immense buildings ornamented by ranks of towering columns, proclaimed that the Romanovs had begun to think of Russia as one of the greatest empires in the history of man. In doing so, they diverged sharply from the efforts of Catherine and her predecessors to identify closely with eighteenth-century Europe. Two unique edifices best characterized this transition from the more modest classicism of Catherine's era to the grand Imperial style of the second quarter of the nineteenth century—the Kazan Cathedral and the Bourse.

The Kazan Cathedral was commissioned by Paul I at the very beginning of 1801, and it is symbolic that he chose to dedicate it to the Virgin of Kazan, the holy icon first brought to Moscow by Ivan the Terrible in the sixteenth century to commemorate Muscovy's first great foreign conquest and later moved to St. Petersburg by Peter the Great. Its architect was Andrei Voronikhin, whose mother was a serf girl from the faraway province of Perm and whose father was in all probability Count Aleksandr Stroganov, one of Russia's wealthiest aristocrats and a patron of the arts. Beginning in 1779, just after he turned twenty, Voronikhin came to live with the Stroganovs in St. Petersburg. He began to study architecture under their patronage and showed so much talent that they sent him to Paris to study further. During the 1790s, he designed a number of large buildings for his Stroganov patrons, and it is probable that he won the commission to build the Cathedral of Kazan through the efforts of Count Stroganov himself.[1] From the very first, he set out to build a cathedral that would have ties not with Paris, London, or Amsterdam, but with the glories of Renaissance Italy and the grandeur of the ancient Roman and Greek empires.

Paul was assassinated before Voronikhin even completed drafting his plans, so it was Alexander I who laid the first stone for the cathedral late in 1801. For ten years—through Russia's early struggles with Napoleon, through the trials of Alexander's participation in the Continental System, and through the economic stress of the British blockade—hundreds of stonemasons and thousands of serf artisans labored through St. Petersburg's all too brief summers and long, dark winters. As always, the stone had to be transported over great distances. As always, the cost of a monument to Russia's greatness was no object. In 1811, Voronikhin's unique masterpiece was complete. It was of monumental proportions, its interior ornamented with fifty-six towering Corinthian columns of polished granite, with capitals of cast bronze. Outside, 144 more columns, also of Corthinthian design, fanned outward in an arc, creating a vast semicircular courtyard similar to that of St. Peter's in Rome. Just more than a year after it was completed, Voronikhin's Cathedral began to serve a truly Imperial function when Alexander ordered that Russia's trophies from the struggle against Napoleon be displayed there. Between late 1812 and mid-1814, more than a hundred captured French standards and eagles, seven Persian banners, the baton of Napoleon's great Marshal Davoust, and the keys to those European cities and fortresses that fell to Russian arms during Alexander's march to the West—all were placed on triumphal display. In their midst, the ashes of Field Marshal Prince Kutuzov, the great popular hero who had driven Napoleon from Moscow, reposed in a place of honor. Even before Napoleon's defeat at Waterloo, the Kazan Cathedral had become Russia's first Imperial monument.[2]

Very different, but almost as important in the transition to the heroic style that became so much a part of St. Petersburg's landscape after 1815, was the new Bourse designed by Thomas de Thomon, a foreigner of many talents and interests, who had come to Russia to seek his fortune in 1799, not long before his fortieth birthday. Ever since the time of Peter the Great, the Romanovs and their favorite architects had searched for ways to make the tip of Vasilevskii Island into a dramatic focal point for ships arriving from the West. Many plans had been drawn up, and a few had been attempted with varying degrees of failure. De Thomon's Bourse, dominating its surroundings in much the same style and manner as the Athenian Parthenon, finally achieved the long-sought-after result.

De Thomon surrounded his Bourse with two rows of towering Doric columns. He then framed it with two rostral pillars, their bases ornamented with sitting figures of heroic proportions, the most famous of which was a statue of Neptune by the sculptor Thibault. During those holiday illuminations for which St. Petersburg had become famous, the rostral pillars spouted sheets of flame that seemed to sear the heavens themselves, making the Bourse a sight whose drama was unequaled anywhere in Europe. Even on an ordinary day, and especially during the "white nights" of early summer, it was a beautiful place. Wrote one contemporary, "During a clear night in May or June, a stroll along the Bourse Embankment has a matchless charm. . . . The melancholy accent of a Russian ballad, or the call of a nightingale, are the only sounds to break the silence."[3]

De Thomon's Bourse and Voronikhin's Kazan Cathedral began to change St. Petersburg's appearance in a dramatic fashion. The ornate Baroque of the Elizabethan Age, which Rastrelli had created in his many buildings, and the more subdued classicism of the several architects favored by Catherine the Great, gave way to a style that preserved the clean lines of Catherinian classicism, but substituted Greek for Roman motifs on a truly colossal and heroic scale. In doing so, these two architects laid the groundwork for a great architectural transformation in St. Petersburg that, beginning around 1815, began to reflect the truly Imperial self-image of the Romanovs' Russia.

It is difficult to project oneself back over a space of more than a century and a half to envision the situation in which the Romanovs suddenly, and to their considerable surprise, found themselves in the early years of the nineteenth century. Ever since the time of Peter the Great, they had felt themselves and their subjects inferior to the West. Every technological innovation they imported, every Western specialist they took into their service, every Western custom they adopted reminded them of their comparative backwardness. In order to overcome those feelings, they had proclaimed themselves part of the West and its culture and, by the end of the eighteenth century, had created a reasonably good facsimile of Parisian culture at the highest levels of St. Petersburg's society. As we already have seen, by the end of Catherine's reign great Russian aristocrats often spoke French better than they spoke Russian. On their tables, subtly flavored French sauces and elegantly prepared French entrées replaced the heavy, greasy, sometimes overly spiced traditional dishes upon which their ancestors had dined. By the turn of the century, Russian lords and ladies had become so at ease with French cuisine that their chefs began to create new dishes that have since become famous. At about that time, Count Stroganov's chef produced Beef Stroganov, while others began to create sophisticated versions of such traditional Russian dishes as *kulebiaka,* that unforgettable monument to the culinary art, in which poached fresh salmon is baked in a light pastry crust. Good French wines had long since replaced cloying fruit meads at those aristocratic dinners where the capital's high and mighty wore French fashions and observed French etiquette. No longer was Western culture merely a thin veneer; it had become a way of life, an integral part of their outlook and attitudes. Great aristocrats who conducted themselves "in the Russian manner" were considered boorish and downright crude. Native Russian dress was considered appropriate only for masked balls and other similar occasions.

Yet deep-seated feelings of inferiority remained among Russia's great lords and ladies, and these feelings underlaid the newfound pride Russians expressed in the accomplishments of other Russians. As Nikolai Novikov wrote in the 1770s, "Russians, in their approach to the arts and sciences . . . have as much keenness, understanding, and penetration as the French, but have vastly more firmness, endurance, and industry." Novikov and a number of other educated Russians were willing to admit that their country was not as "civilized" or as enlightened as the societies of Western Europe, but they emphasized how rapidly Russia had progressed. "If we look at the speedy successes which Russians have made in the arts and sciences," Novikov continued, "we shall have to conclude that they will be brought to perfection in a shorter time than in France."[4]

By the second decade of the nineteenth century, Russia no longer had to rationalize her "inferior" position in relation to the West. Russia, the newcomer to Europe, a nation that many Europeans insisted was just beginning to emerge from centuries of backwardness and barbarism, became the savior of Europe, the conqueror of Napoleon. Alexander I and Nicholas I both were enthralled by the new power that lay in their hands. Yet, in their very recognition of it, there also was a certain disbelief. How could Russia, for so long the poor relative in the European community, suddenly have become its most powerful member? At the same time, they needed to reinforce their sense of the awesome power they wielded as autocrats in Russia. As their Empire became more vast, and the problems of administering it more complex, the very existence of their autocratic power seemed more doubtful. Was the Russian Autocrat's command law everywhere in the Russian

Empire? Did his every order command instant obedience no matter where, when, or by whom it was received?

That need for reassurance drove both Alexander and Nicholas into an addiction to the trappings of militarism. What Emperor could doubt his awesome power when fifty, or even eighty, thousand soliders wheeled left or right at his command? Yet, if Romanovs were to drill their armies in the manner so loved by Alexander and Nicholas, it was essential to have an area large enough for up to one hundred thousand troops to maneuver at one time. That area required adequate avenues of approach and departure for tens of thousands of infantry and thousands of cavalry. No city in all of Europe boasted such a gigantic parade ground, but the Romanovs were determined to create one. The nearly mile-long L-shaped area in St. Petersburg—beginning at the Winter Palace Square, extending along the broad Admiralty Boulevard, and ending at the Senate Square, where Falconet's famous statue of Peter the Great reared above the banks of the Neva—answered these requirements perfectly. The total area encompassed 4,305,600 square feet, or just less than 100 acres, and was far larger than any in Paris, Rome, or Berlin.[5] There, the Romanovs could review their armies from the balcony of the Winter Palace itself and, in so doing, connect Russia's military power even more closely to the person of the Emperor. Still, one element more was required. Russia's military might must in some very tangible and meaningful manner be tied to her government and her church, to those secular and ecclesiastical bodies that, at the Emperor's orders, commanded the bodies and souls of all Russian men and women. Therefore, during the first half of the nineteenth century, the Romanovs surrounded this vast parade area with monumental structures that housed the highest administrative echelons of their navy, army, church, and state. These included the central offices of the Senate, the Holy Synod, the Admiralty, the General Staff Headquarters, and St. Isaac's Cathedral, in addition to the Winter Palace.

The first of these great buildings to take shape was the Admiralty. Established by Peter the Great in 1705, its quarters had grown in a haphazard and uncontrolled manner during the next century. Aside from its ornate central section, which Anna's architect Ivan Korobov had designed in the 1730s, the early nineteenth-century Admiralty building was little more than a very long and undistinguished three-storied structure, with row upon monotonous row of windows staring dully out upon more elegant nearby buildings. More than any other edifice in the immediate vicinity of the Winter Palace, the Admiralty stood in need of redesign. A full quarter-mile in length, it was the longest building in St. Petersburg, and it was necessary to make it the focal point for the three great avenues that converged upon it. Its centennial in 1805 seemed an appropriate occasion to begin the work. After considerable debate, and not without some rancor, a special commission chose Andreian Zakharov to design a new facade for the entire structure.

Zakharov's task was immensely complex. Yet he produced a masterpiece of heroic proportions that conformed perfectly to the new self-image of the Romanovs. As both Voronikhin and de Thomon had done, Zakharov used groupings of colossal Greek columns to ornament the facade of his structure. It was a building to commemorate an Empire, and, if its proportions alone did not achieve that end, the various bas-reliefs and sculptures he incorporated into it left no doubt. There at the base of its tower stood four great statues of Achilles, Pyrrhus, Ajax, and Alexander the Great, all of whom served to bind the Russian Empire to the greatness of ancient heroes. From the moment of its completion in 1823, Zakharov's reconstructed Admiralty was, and still is, one of the truly great architectural monuments in St. Petersburg.[6]

Zakharov's Admiralty had not yet been completed when plans were made for another monumental structure to further ornament the periphery of St. Petersburg's vast parade square. Once victory in the Napoleonic Wars had assured Russia's Imperial status, Alexander and a number of his associates began to think of providing St. Petersburg with a monolithic landmark that would dominate its skyline. Alexander decided to reconstruct the smaller St. Isaac's Cathedral that had been built hastily and without proper design nearly a half-century earlier.[7] He assigned the task to August Monferrand, an artist recently arrived from France, who, like so many Europeans who had made their way to Russia in the eighteenth century, had come in search of fame and fortune. Like a number of his more industrious and clever countrymen, Monferrand was destined not to be disappointed, although fame came from a different quarter than he had expected, for he had no training in architecture at all when he first appeared in Russia's capital.

When he arrived in Russia in 1816, Monferrand brought only a genius for producing gemlike miniature drawings of famous buildings, monuments, and statues, and he impressed General Count Augustin Betancourt, chairman of the Imperial Commission for Construction and Hydraulic Works in St. Petersburg, with his minute drawings of Rome's ancient wonders. Anxious to aid a countryman in search of a sinecure, Betancourt urged Monferrand to try his hand at designing plans for St. Isaac's reconstruction. Using his one talent to the fullest, Monferrand produced a beautifully bound little volume of miniature drawings showing how a rebuilt and aggrandized cathedral might appear. There were no blueprints, no detailed drawings, not even specifications of any sort. At best, it was the work of a clever copyist, yet, for an Autocrat used to ordering that buildings be built and that armies be moved, and unaccustomed to worrying about the details of how his orders would be carried out, Monferrand's cleverly done volume was enough. Alexander appointed him chief architect for rebuilding St. Issac's, and left it to men such as Betancourt to determine how Monferrand's sketches would be translated into the reality of stone and mortar.

Alexander's appointment of Monferrand brought protests from a number of St. Petersburg architects who quite rightly complained that the Frenchman had no training in architecture and no knowledge about construction. Especially in raising great buildings upon St. Petersburg's marshy subsoil, inexperience and ignorance could be costly, even fatal, if the structure collapsed during the course of construction. As a result of these protests, it was not until 1824 that a final design for the Cathedral was agreed upon. Its actual construction required another thirty-four years, for even Nicholas I, who succeeded in rebuilding the Winter Palace in a year after it burned down in 1837, could not force the completion of the monumental stonework required for St. Isaac's. The Cathedral was built entirely of granite and marble, its great stone porticoes modeled upon those of the Pantheon in Rome. These were supported by columns of polished Finnish granite, fifty-four feet in height and seven feet thick. Its huge doors were cast of bronze, and its *ikonostas,* carved from richly gilded marble, was 223 feet long. The Cathedral cost twenty-five million rubles to build, a sum that was fully three times as large as the entire budget allocated to the Ministry of Internal Affairs (Russia's largest ministry) in the year of the Cathedral's completion.[8] After St. Peter's in Rome and St. Paul's in London, it was the largest domed structure in the world.

While Zakharov's Admiralty set the style and precedent for a number of other major buildings around Alexander I's vast parade square and Monferrand's St. Isaac's Cathedral added to that vision, neither man became the preeminent architect of the Romanovs' Imperial capital. That distinction belonged to Karl Rossi, who rose from the most improbable beginnings to achieve fame. Just as Rastrelli's architectural creations became the greatest monument to Russia's Elizabethan Age, Rossi's buildings personified the era of Nicholas I.

Born in December 1775 in St. Petersburg, Rossi was the son of an Italian ballerina whose dancing was all the rage in the capital at the time. Scores of young lords flocked to see her perform; a number evidently danced attendance upon her in more private circumstances, and any one of them may have fathered her child. While still in his teens, Rossi studied with the noted Petersburg architect Vincent Brenna, worked with him at Pavlovsk and Gatchina and, in 1796, served as his chief assistant when Brenna was commissioned to build the fortresslike Mikhailovskii Castle for Paul I. Brenna's enthusiasm for his young assistant's talent made it possible for Rossi to spend the first two years of Alexander's reign in Italy, where he studied at the Florentine Academy. Until 1815, he worked in Moscow. Only after much of the reconstruction of the burned city was well under way did he return to St. Petersburg. Almost immediately, he became one of General Betancourt's protégés and received his first Imperial commission in 1818, to build a palace for the Dowager Empress Maria Feodorovna on Elagin Island. The next year, Rossi received a commission to build a palace for Alexander's youngest brother, Grand Duke Mikhail Pavlovich, and his beautiful Württemberg bride Elena Pavlovna. After that, commissions poured in. During the next two decades, he designed St. Petersburg's General Staff Headquarters; the Aleksandra Theatre; all of the buildings along Theatre Street, Mikhailovskaia Street, and around Chernyshev Square; the Mikhailovskii Riding School; the Imperial Senate and Holy Synod buildings, and the 1812 Gallery in the Winter Palace, just to list some of his greatest and best-known works.

Probably no architect since Rastrelli had been so flooded with Imperial commissions. Even today, St. Petersburg remains more the city of Rossi's design than of any other.

Perhaps more than any of his predecessors, Rossi went to extreme efforts to place his architectural jewels in the proper settings. When he built the Mikhailovskii Palace for Grand Duke Mikhail Pavlovich, he redesigned the facades of the buildings on the other three sides of the square it faced, as well as the entire street that led from the square opposite its main entrance. Likewise, when he built the Aleksandra Theatre, he redesigned the facades of the buildings facing the square in front of it, including the Public Library and the pavilion of the Anichkov Palace. Behind his theatre, Rossi built an entire street of buildings to house the theatre's schools and other service and training facilities, and he integrated all of them into the overall plan of the theatre's environment. All his work was characterized by long facades, sometimes separated by great triumphal arches crowned by heroic Greek or Roman figures cast of iron or bronze and dramatized by colossal Doric, Ionic, or Corinthian columns. For Rossi was more than an architect; he was a builder whose artistry took the shape of vast squares, broad avenues, and exquisitely formed palaces. He was the ideal artist to conceive the final integration of all those parts that were needed to complete the great Imperial complex that Zakharov had begun at the Admiralty in 1806.[9]

Rossi began work on this vast project in 1819, when he started to rebuild the General Staff Headquarters that faced the Winter Palace across the great Palace Square. He solved the many complex problems connected with his design by constructing two monumental curved buildings and joining them with a towering arch surmounted by the cast-bronze figure of Victory in a six-horse chariot. The semicircle created by these connected buildings, whose facade equaled the length of six football fields, formed a perfect backdrop for those great military reviews that began on the Palace Square and moved along Admiralty Boulevard. The effect of tens of thousands of troops, with Rossi's majestic buildings and colossal charioteer rising above them, was utterly spectacular, so much so that he repeated many of the design's elements at the other extremity of St. Petersburg's Imperial parade ground, in the vast buildings he raised between 1829 and 1834 to house the Imperial Senate and the Holy Synod. Again, two buildings, this time built in a straight line rather than on a curve, were joined by a great arch and set off by statuesque pillars that dominated their second and third stories. It was a brilliant culmination to a project that had been begun almost three decades earlier and developed with no master plan to harmonize or integrate its various elements.[10]

Rossi's completion of his Senate and Synod buildings marked the culmination of that vast Imperial complex whose construction Alexander I had set into action in 1805 with his commission to Zakharov, although its physical completion had to await the finishing of St. Isaac's Cathedral in 1858. St. Petersburg's major government buildings, streets, and squares had taken shape; construction during the last half-century of the Romanovs' regime would fit into the broad architectural framework that had been established by the middle of the 1840s. By the beginning of Alexander II's reign, St. Petersburg had become an Imperial city such as even Peter the Great could not have envisioned in his most grandiose dreams. It had no counterpart anywhere in the world.

The construction of great buildings to glorify the Imperial aspirations of the Romanov dynasty was only one characteristic of St. Petersburg's development. During the eighteenth century, Russia's new capital had been an aristocratic city, where all of the tasks associated with her administration, navy, and army were performed by nobles who lived and served there. During the nineteenth century, Russia's administration became increasingly the province of professional civil servants who did not share the class outlook and interests of those serfowning nobles who had monopolized the tasks of government a century earlier. In addition to being an aristocratic city, St. Petersburg thus became the domain of a great army of officials whose numbers increased by more than two thousand percent during the nineteenth century.[11] Wealthy nobles, who received immense salaries continued to stand at the top of St. Petersburg's rising bureaucratic pyramid, while its huge base was formed by underpaid, pettifogging scribes, who made up a sort of clerical proletariat, earning pitiful salaries that averaged just more than one percent of what some ministers of state and members of the State Council received.

As the capital's population began to include more people who were not serfowners, and thus could not draft servants from their estates, St. Petersburg experienced a growing demand for servants, hackney drivers, cooks, laundresses, and all sorts of service personnel that upper-class folk required in their daily lives. This brought large numbers of workers into the capital beginning in the early nineteenth century; their numbers increased even more dramatically as St. Petersburg began to emerge as one of Russia's important industrial centers in the 1820s and 1830s, employing thousands of factory hands who suffered the abuses so characteristic of the early stages of the Industrial Revolution. Nineteenth-century St. Petersburg thus developed a number of new faces in addition to its aristocratic and Imperial profiles, and each of these added new and unique elements to the city's life and character.

At the beginning of the nineteenth century, aristocratic life in St. Petersburg still was an extension of the Romanovs' Court and the Court's tastes to other parts of the city where, since the time of Elizabeth, Russia's greatest nobles had vied with each other in building and furnishing elegant palaces and townhouses. By the end of Catherine's reign, a number of Russia's greatest families, such as the Sheremetievs, the Bezborodkos, the Naryshkins, the Golitsyns, and the Iusupovs owned palaces that stood majestically along the banks of the Moika and Fontanka rivers and boasted hundreds of rooms, great art galleries, and even private theatres. The Iusupovs, in fact, had three such palaces within the city limits. The Stroganovs had a magnificent residence, built by Rastrelli in 1754, on the Nevskii Prospekt itself, which was adorned with paintings by such great masters as Van Dyck, Perugino, Tintoretto, and Donatello.[12]

The nineteenth century brought notable changes in this opulent way of life, even though the Romanovs continued to patronize aristocratic culture. The inflation that struck Russia after the Napoleonic Wars and the corresponding crisis of the nobles' serf-based economy caused the cost of living in St. Petersburg to soar. "The building of a house is a much more costly undertaking in St. Petersburg than in any other part of Russia," wrote the German traveler J. G. Kohl in the 1840s. "There are private houses," he added, "the mere ground of which is valued at two hundred thousand rubles, a sum for which, in other parts of the Empire, a man might buy an estate of several square leagues,* with houses, woods, rivers, and lakes, and all the eagles, bears, wolves, oxen, and human creatures that inhabit them."[13] Even a number of truly great and rich Russian aristocrats who maintained private town houses in St. Petersburg owned extremely modest ones. Lady Londonderry visited the capital in 1836 to find the Countess Saltykova living in "a small odd house," while the Countess Razumovskaia's was "small, though *très élégante*."[14] Other nobles who had not the means of the Saltykovs, Iusupovs, or Stroganovs simply became apartment dwellers in response to these economic pressures.

Other factors led Petersburg lords and ladies to abandon private homes for apartments during the nineteenth century. Most obviously, rental lodgings became more plentiful and easier to obtain because the government began to subsidize their construction through low-interest loans to private entrepreneurs. Foreigners in particular tended to become *rentiers,* and names such as Chabot, Olivier, Schmidt, and Ashe appear as the owners of buildings in which prominent Russians lived during the 1820s and 1830s. No social or economic stigma attended living in rented quarters, and people of considerable means did not hesitate to do so. General Count Aleksandr Benkendorf, Chief of the Imperial Gendarmerie that Nicholas I created in 1826, never owned a home in St. Petersburg. Neither did General Count Mikhail Andreevich Miloradovich, St. Petersburg's Governor-General in the early and mid-1820s, nor the architect Vasilii Stasov, nor even Karl Rossi, that great builder of streets, government buildings, and palaces. Count Karl Nesselrode, Russia's Foreign Minister from 1814 until 1856, did not own a home in St. Petersburg until 1844, and virtually all of the great nineteenth-century poets, novelists, composers, and artists who were of noble lineage lived in rented lodgings.[15] Rich and poor often dwelt in the same building, separated by subtle, but rigidly drawn, lines of demarcation. "On the first floor of one building I knew of dwelt two Senators and the families of various other persons of distinction," Kohl wrote. "On the second floor was a school of very high repute, and a host of academicians, teachers, and professors dwelt there with their families. In the back part of the building, not to talk of a multitude of

*One square league was the equivalent of 5,760 acres.

obscure personages, there resided several colonels and majors, a few retired generals, an Armenian priest, and a German pastor."[16]

The settlement of so many aristocrats into apartments brought dramatic, though hardly surprising changes in their patterns of entertainment and hospitality. During the reigns of Elizabeth and Catherine the Great, it had become the style among the city's nobles to entertain others of equal or higher rank at lavish dinners and balls, and the exorbitant cost of doing so left many of them hopelessly in debt. A quarter-century later, costs had risen so precipitously that great entertainments were beyond the means of all but the Romanovs themselves and a bare handful of great lords and ladies. In that sense, the defeat of Napoleon in 1814 marked the end of an age for that group of *nouveaux riches* who had appeared in St. Petersburg during the previous three-quarters of a century, just as the coming of the First World War brought an end to a similar period for a similar group of nineteenth-century Americans.

That those rare celebrations still given in the grand style of the eighteenth century continued to be magnificent is evident from a description left by the Marquis de Custine, a caustic and sharp-tongued French traveler who has left us a lengthy and surprisingly accurate description of life in the Russia of Nicholas I. During the summer of 1839, de Custine attended a fête given by the Grand Duchess Elena Pavlovna at Rossi's newly completed Mikhailovskii Palace and was utterly dazzled by what he saw. "The interior of the grand gallery in which they danced was arranged with marvelous luxury. Fifteen hundred boxes of the rarest plants in flower formed a grove of fragrant verdure. At one of the extremities of the hall, amid thickets of exotic shrubs, a fountain threw up a column of fresh and sparkling water: its spray, illuminated by innumerable wax lights, shone like a dust of diamonds, and refreshed the air, always kept in agitation by the movement of the dance." "It was like a dream," de Custine concluded. "There was not merely luxury in the scene, there was poetry. . . . It seemed like the palace of the fairies: all ideas of limits disappeared, and nothing met the eye but space, light, gold, flowers, reflection, illusion, and the giddy movement of the crowd, which itself seemed multiplied to infinity."[17]

Only a handful of St. Petersburg's aristocrats could offer entertainment on a scale even remotely comparable to the Grand Duchess's. Indeed, when Lady Londonderry, a close friend of Countess Stroganova and a guest of the British Ambassador Lord Durham, spent an entire social season in St. Petersburg, she found few balls and festive dinners at the private residences of the city's great aristocrats. The great majority of her invitations to such lavish entertainments were to the Winter Palace, the Mikhailovskii Palace, and the residences of European ambassadors. From the great aristocrats she received invitations to the theatre, to tea, and to afternoon or evening soirées.[18]

Especially after mid-century, another phenomenon began to intrude upon the style of life and entertainment of the St. Petersburg aristocracy. It had become too expensive for all but a handful to maintain the great staffs and richly stocked kitchens of the size and quality needed for large dinners and balls. Therefore, it became more common practice to have restaurateurs cater celebrations in one's home or even to entertain at public establishments. Such restaurants as St. Georges', Talon's, and Dumet's began to flourish in the 1830s and 1840s, and their number and popularity increased throughout the nineteenth century. The Cubat, A l'ours, Contant, and several others became favorite haunts of the nobility during the last third of the century, while Filippov's became famous among well-bred Petersburgers for its pastries and confections, without which no birthday celebration, afternoon tea, or festive dinner could be complete. Petits fours, pirozhki, or torten from Filippov's became a symbol of prestige in the 1870s, just as having one's own pastry chef had been a mark of distinction a century earlier. Private clubs also became popular among St. Petersburg's wealthy nobles, with the English Club being the most famous and prestigious. Just as their British counterparts gathered at the clubs of St. James and Pall Mall, Russian lords gathered there to discuss sporting events and the great issues of the day, while others read foreign newspapers or lounged in large overstuffed chairs and sofas covered with well-worn leather.

In our portrait of nineteenth-century St. Petersburg, we must remember that its aristocratic life comprised only one of its several faces and, in numerical terms, a rather small one at that. At most, one Petersburger in ten belonged to the nobility; the proportion decreased as the twentieth century approached. Within Russia's vast governmental structures a scrivener army, perched upon high stools at row upon row of copy desks in poorly lit offices, kept the Romanovs' Russia functioning. It was they who copied and recopied instructions, orders, reports, petitions, and all the other types of official papers that the Romanovs' Imperial administration generated in such profusion. Each document that entered or left an office had to be entered in a logbook, further copies often had to be made, and the action taken upon the content of the document had to be recorded. By mid-century, this process produced such an avalanche of documents that senior officials had to devise procedures for destroying some eighty percent of them every five years. In 1850 just the Ministry of Internal Affairs produced thirty-one million separate documents, nearly all of them generated by that burgeoning force of clerks who lived in St. Petersburg and the lesser administrative centers of the Empire.[19]

St. Petersburg's clerical proletariat had become a major element in its population by the 1840s, when the great novelist Nikolai Gogol created in *The Overcoat,* his classic tale of Petersburg life, his famous stereotype of the petty scribe in the person of Akakii Akakievich (whose name derives from the word Russian children use to describe defecation). He was, Gogol wrote, "an official who was singularly undistinguished, rather short, and somewhat pockmarked. He had a rather rusty look about him, and his eyes were somewhat bleary and dim. He had a bald spot in front, his cheeks were uniformly wrinkled on both sides, and the tone of his complexion could best be termed hemorrhoidal, the fault, obviously, of the Petersburg climate."[20] Like so many of his peers, Akakii Akakievich was fascinated not by the greater issues of policy or politics but by the simple process of administration, which moved papers from desk to desk, from office to office, with near-hypnotic regularity. For him, life's central purpose was to keep the flow in motion. He knew not the content, purpose, or destination of the thousands of letters, orders, and files that he saw in any given year. Nor did he care. His part in the seemingly *perpetuum mobile* of the Russian bureaucracy was to prepare exact copies of specific documents in that elegant, copperplate script for which the Romanovs' clerks were famous. That was the focus of his entire life, day and night, on the stool at which he worked and in the miserable corner in which he slept.

Akakii Akakievich represented a type so common, and so much a part of St. Petersburg's life, that his presence lent a universal quality to Gogol's brief tale. Everyone in the capital knew an Akakii Akakievich or, at least, knew of one. In a society obsessed with rank, he personified the failure that dogged the heels of every young official, for he was a middle-aged "perpetual titular counsellor," a man who stood one rank below personal ennoblement, but who never would be able to cross the gap that separated him from it. When he retired, it would be even worse, because the only thing more onerous than the rank of titular councillor for a man past forty was the title of "retired titular counsellor," which proclaimed to the world that an entire career and, hence, an entire lifetime, had ended in failure.

The chasm that separated St. Petersburg's army of Akakii Akakieviches from the aristocratic society that revolved around the Romanovs was immense and virtually unbridgeable. Ever since the time of Peter the Great, the Romanovs had bestowed nobility upon their top civil servants and, in the words of one historian, had tended "to consider the remaining clerks on the same level as military conscripts."[21] In the nineteenth century, they continued to pay this clerical army wages so meager that they could sustain life only in the most marginal sort of way. When dire necessity forced Akakii Akakievich to buy a new overcoat, he was obliged to deny himself such things as candles, tea, tobacco, even heat, for many months in order to save the required sum. Even though sewn from undistinguished materials by a back-alley tailor, his new overcoat cost him eighty rubles, fully one-fifth of his yearly earnings.

Yet even Akakii Akakievich's meager salary was more generous than that of many poor clerks. Fifteen to twenty silver rubles was a very common monthly wage for young men just beginning their careers in St. Petersburg's bureaucracy. For such officials, Akakii Akakievich's mediocre overcoat would have consumed four or five months' wages, and everything else was just as dear. The most modest accommodations, usually without access to kitchen facilities, cost ten or fifteen rubles per month. Because that amounted to one-half, three-quarters, or even all of their pitiful earnings, most young officials shared with several others poor lodgings that were barely suitable for one. Dinners at the most humble sort of eating house, the local *kukhmisterskaia*, cost nearly seven rubles a month in the 1830s, and that reduced price applied only if they were purchased with monthly meal tickets. During the century, even the cost of such poor meals soared, while salaries rose much more slowly. Until the 1860s, they did not rise at all, and petty clerks often shared meal tickets so that each could eat with reasonable regularity.[22]

Poor housing, meager food, and ragged clothing made the St. Petersburg clerical proletariat very similar to the industrial proletariat who lived on the outskirts of the city, although the scribes sought desperately to distinguish their way of life from that of lower-class workers. Poor officials would deny themselves many things, including even wine and vodka, in order to have coffee and sugar, "luxuries" traditionally reserved for the upper classes in Russia, and it was not unusual for such men to spend as much as one-tenth of their income on them.[23] For those Akakii Akakieviches of St. Petersburg who had only a cold, damp corner to call their own, it was that small cup of thick, sweet Turkish coffee, even if drunk only infrequently at a local café, that proclaimed to the world and to themselves that they were not proletarians, but men of "affairs" who spent their days in the service of the Emperor.

For St. Petersburg's poor officials, the glittering life of the great lords and ladies of the Romanov Court was so remote that it almost stood in the realm of fantasy. Yet there were fleeting moments when they could partake of it vicariously—when one of the Romanovs drove past in a carriage, when a high official visited their department, or when they joined the promenade along the Nevskii Prospekt or through the Summer Gardens. Until horse-drawn omnibuses appeared on St. Petersburg's thoroughfares in the middle of the nineteenth century, scribes and high officials also tended to live in the same parts of the city, even in the same buildings, because the distances from one section of the city to another and the difficulty of crossing the Neva during the spring thaw meant that they all had to live near their offices. Most of the city's larger apartment buildings were constructed around a central courtyard, which served not only as a means of letting in air and light, but also as a very precise line of social demarcation. Thus, while a great nobleman and his family might live in an elegant first- or second-floor apartment in the front of a building that stood on the Moika, Fontanka, or Catherine Canal Embankment, a number of poor scribes might share one of the smaller rear apartments on a higher floor.[24] This served to increase that feeling of participation in the life of the high and the mighty that even the lowliest clerk found intoxicating.[25]

Because life in St. Petersburg was so arduous for the rank and file in the Romanovs' clerical army, we might well ask why so many Russians sought to enter its service. The most important reason was that if a young man was not born a peasant, a priest, or a merchant, there were very few career choices open to him. Before the 1860s, there was no private legal profession in Russia, and, because there were very few schools, there was almost no demand for teachers or, even, university professors. It had not yet become possible for a young man to support himself by his pen, as could be done in Europe or the United States, and the practice of medicine offered him limited opportunities at best. Only the nobility made extensive use of physicians in Russia, and they preferred foreign doctors, especially Germans, thinking them better trained and more competent. A young man who did not inherit a large and profitable estate thus had the choice of earning his living in the army or in the civil service. Because an army officer's career required a substantial investment for uniforms and equipment, and because the army placed greater emphasis upon wealth and social connections, those who were totally without means usually chose civil service careers that began in the bureaucracy's lower ranks.

If a young man was to spend his life in the Romanovs' civil service, it benefited him to serve in St. Petersburg. Service there improved his chances of being noticed by some prominent statesman or courtier who might then become his patron. Such a patron was an important prerequisite for a successful career, so much so, in fact, that one cynical senior official advised young men to find one at all costs. "In spite of your talents, try to find shelter under the wing of a successful patron," he wrote. "If you have a patron, you will be considered a genius, competent in everything, and you will advance rapidly. But if you do not have a patron, you will be considered a total fool, fit for nothing, and knowing nothing, and you will never find success in the civil service."[26]

Ambitious young bureaucrats were prepared to suffer years of privation in St. Petersburg for a fleeting chance at success, for that was the only way they could rise into the higher levels of government and society.

Yet the attraction of the capital was something more than simply a beacon for ambitious youths; St. Petersburg exerted a magnetic pull upon the lives of many Russians that even they found hard to explain. "I still do not understand why I came to St. Petersburg," an official from Kazan wrote in 1856. "Among its five hundred thousand inhabitants, I had not one single acquaintance."[27] Mikhail Saltykov-Shchedrin, the bureaucrat-turned-novelist, perhaps best described this mentality in 1872, when he wrote in his *Diary of A Provincial in Petersburg* that "we provincials somehow turn our steps toward Petersburg instinctively. . . . A particular individual will be sitting around and suddenly, as if a light had dawned, he begins to pack his things. 'You're going to Petersburg?'—'To Petersburg!' is the answer. And that is all that needs to be said. It is as if Petersburg, all by itself, with its name, its streets, its fog, rain, and snow could resolve something or shed light on something."[28] Many succumbed to the siren's call of St. Petersburg, but very few were rewarded. Only about one in fifty ever reached that magic rank of State Councillor, which made a man and his descendants noble for all time and brought him a comfortable salary and a decent standard of living.

The more subtle attractions of St. Petersburg, and the excitement of participating vicariously in the comings and goings of the high and the mighty, had no part in the lives of the city's wage laborers, who comprised a full fifty percent of its population by the end of the Crimean War. During the first half of the century, most of these men and women still were serfs who sent their masters substantial payments at each year's end in return for being permitted to work in the capital. Most worked in the service and building trades, although about twelve thousand labored in the city's growing number of factories.[29] These workers generally lived under circumstances that ranged from minimally tolerable to utterly wretched. A commission appointed to investigate their living conditions reported in the early 1840s that it was not unusual to find eighteen to twenty of them crowded into one small apartment. In one case, fifty men, women, and children, including several suffering from such infectious diseases as tuberculosis and syphilis, were discovered living in a single room that measured barely twenty feet square. So urgent was the demand for cheap housing that, by the 1840s, unscrupulous entrepreneurs began to lease entire buildings, convert their interiors into huge barnlike dormitories, and install row upon row of raised plank platforms. Upon these platforms, they marked out sleeping spaces, usually twenty-four inches wide and six feet in length, which they rented by the day. Competition for even these primitive facilities soon became so intense that workers were forced to sleep in shifts, so that two or even three of them might rent the same sleeping space in the course of a single day.[30]

After they paid their dues to their masters and rented some sort of shelter, serf wage laborers had between three and ten rubles left over each month to spend on food and everything else they might need. They lived mainly on cabbage soup, groats, dried peas, and sour black bread, but even that poor diet was so expensive that many could not afford it.[31] All but the poorest dress was beyond their means, and their need for cheap clothing gave rise to a flourishing rag trade in the city's poorer sections. Medical care was a luxury workers rarely, if ever, obtained, and numbers of them died in the street for want of a physician's attention. Entertainment was to be found only at the neighborhood tavern, where they squandered precious kopecks on cheap vodka, which seared the throat as it was drunk and which they usually tempered with swallows of watery beer. Well before the full force of the Industrial Revolution struck Russia during the last three decades of the century, the wage laborers in the Romanovs' capital thus balanced precariously on the brink of abject poverty. Many lost their footing and fell into the abyss, to become part of that destitute and desolate group that lived in the region around the Haymarket, which the great novelist Dostoevskii painted so vividly in *Crime and Punishment*. There, man's inhumanity to man assumed its most demoralizing forms, as fathers drove daughters into prostitution, squandered their earnings on vodka, and lived in squalor so abject as to defy description.

For those workers who survived the never-ending battle against ruin, the suburbs of St. Petersburg, not its center, became the focus of their lives as the nineteenth century progressed. What had been desolate swampland at the beginning of the century began to give way to factories, workshops, and workers' housing by the middle of Nicholas I's reign. A correspondent for the *Northern Bee,* a conservative newspaper published to glorify Nicholas, described this new region at some length in 1839 as he took his readers on an imaginary stroll along the Schlüsselburg Road. "Here one sees silk factories in which a thousand workers labor every day," he exclaimed. "There also is a steam-driven saw-mill and, not far away, a factory which weaves cloth from flax and hemp. A bit further on there is a cotton spinning mill, which employs some two hundred people. Beyond all this, you see the huge stone buildings of the sire, the propagator, of all these factories, the Aleksandrovsk cast-iron foundry, which manufactures among many other things, steam engines for these factories and for steamships."[32] The enraptured correspondent's romanticized account, in fact, described the beginning of St. Petersburg's industrial encirclement, a phenomenon that was to have a marked impact upon the city's character during the last half of the century. By 1900, its population of twelve thousand factory workers grew to ninety-two thousand. Wrote an early twentieth-century commentator, "Factories and industrial plants encircled the city like a ring, gripping the administrative-commercial center in its embrace."[33]

Such a rapid increase in its factory labor force brought new problems to St. Petersburg. Russia's rulers knew only too well the central role the industrial proletariat had played in those waves of revolution that had surged over Western Europe in 1830 and in 1848, and fear that the same thing might happen in St. Petersburg was never far from their minds. Continuing labor unrest in the industrial centers of the West made Nicholas I and Alexander II even more apprehensive about the political security of their capital. Rather than insist that Russia's industrialists provide better housing and working conditions for their workers, they continued their policy of isolating St. Peterburg's proletariat in special suburbs that placed the Neva between them and the center of the city. It was completely possible for a visitor to St. Petersburg in the 1850s and 1860s to travel through the central parts of the city and to see it in all of its Imperial splendor without ever setting eyes upon its squalid industrial slums.

St. Petersburg's workers began to raise political and economic demands in the 1870s, as their already-wretched living and working conditions worsened. The housing shortage had become desperate; there simply were no more places, it seemed, for new waves of workers to find shelter. Even the city's damp and oozing cellars, never used for human habitation even in the cruelest days of serfdom, were pressed into service as greedy landlords rented for exorbitant prices mere corners, which filled with excrement-tainted liquid whenever it rained. Filth and excrement accumulated so rapidly in the courtyards of buildings in the city's poorer sections that, in 1869, one public health physician estimated that more than thirty thousand tons of it were lying unattended throughout the city. Disease flourished to an unprecedented degree. By the 1870s, St. Petersburg had the dubious distinction of suffering the highest mortality rate of any major city in Europe.[34] Cholera, typhus, and, above all, the omnipresent scourge of tuberculosis took a frightful toll among the city's laboring poor.

Wage laborers in the Romanovs' capital suffered extreme moral ills in addition to physical sickness. Most were unmarried men, or men who had left families behind in distant villages. They sought refuge from their poverty and loneliness in liquor to such an extent that, by the late 1860s, the annual number of arrests for drunkenness reached well over thirty thousand. Lonely men demanded not only vodka but also the bodies of women for physical satisfaction, and the daughters of Petersburg's unfortunates soon filled that need. Dostoevskii's memorable prostitute, the gentle and self-sacrificing Sonia Marmeladova who sold her favors in the Haymarket to feed her consumptive mother and starving brothers and sisters, was but one of a veritable army of whores who plied their trade in the city's streets after mid-century. The number of registered prostitutes in the city soared from eighteen hundred to forty-four hundred in the ten years between 1861 and 1870, and reported cases of syphilis rose from just over six thousand to more than fifteen thousand during the same period. By 1870, syphilis was so widespread among Petersburg's workers that, when one physician examined a randomly chosen group at one factory, he found three out of every ten infected with the disease.[35]

But the rapid development of industry and the growth of a wage labor force also indicated that other dramatic changes were taking place within St. Petersburg's boundaries. The city rapidly was becoming a center of industry, even the symbolic hub of capitalism in Russia. As a result, during the second half of the nineteenth century, all of the structures that had become so much a part of capitalist cities in the West began to appear in St. Petersburg: whole streets of shops dealing in ready-made goods of all sorts, private banks and business offices, railroad stations, and all the amenities that a large modern city was expected to offer to the growing number of private travelers who followed the spread of steam transportation across the face of Europe. It was during these years that St. Petersburg came to boast such great and famous hotels as the Astoria, the Hôtel de l'Europe, the Grand Hôtel, and the Hôtel de France.

Other additions to the city's amenities reflected the technological achievements of the nineteenth century. Nicholas I presided over the appearance of gaslights along the Nevskii Prospekt in 1839, and the city's first horse-drawn omnibus line appeared in 1847. The first public railroad station, the Nikolaevskii *vokzal*, was completed in 1851, and the first permanent bridge across the Neva, which until that time had been spanned only by pontoon bridges that were taken up when the river froze, was completed in the same year. Just more than a decade later, in 1862, Petersburgers saw the city's first watertower and waterworks.[36] Once mid-century passed, St. Petersburg evolved more rapidly than ever from an aristocratic city, where its noble dwellers supplied most necessary services from their personal resources, into a modern metropolis of merchants, bureaucrats, shopkeepers, and many others who required that the city provide public services for them.

During the last third of the century, a Soviet historian once remarked, "the demands and tastes of tsarist officials, rich nobles, industrialists, businessmen, and merchants—the 'city fathers' of the time—defined the general character of the buildings which arose in St. Petersburg."[37] These included new public buildings planned and financed by the city's elected municipal government, as well as large structures financed by private entrepreneurs, thus breaking the near-monopoly the Imperial government had held over such construction earlier in the century. Large apartment buildings, built as lucrative investments, began to spring up in profusion along such major thoroughfares as Liteinyi Prospekt, Zagorodnyi Prospekt, and the far end of the Nevskii, as well as on Bolshoi Prospekt, that broad avenue that intersected the whole of Vasilevskii Island. The design of these buildings often clashed with the styles of the majestic structures around them, as untalented architects experimented with extravagant and ill-conceived forms.

All of this was especially unfortunate because St. Petersburg had been spared the taint of mediocre buildings throughout its history. Some of the eighteenth-century Romanovs had been notorious for their bad taste in many things, but the crudity that had led Anna to such famous fiascoes as her "ice palace" wedding and had impelled Elizabeth to appear at public balls with her large breasts and ample hips stuffed into a tight-fitting Preobrazhenskii Guards uniform rarely touched the physical appearance of their capital. Beginning with Peter the Great, the Romanovs had always had the good fortune to be served by talented architects, and they had shared a talent for bringing out the best in them. Thus, it was not the Romanovs but St. Petersburg's emerging bourgeoisie who established a new tradition that was destined to be carried well into the twentieth century, as the Romanovs' successors littered the city landscape with gaudy subway stations, dull and monolithic apartment buildings, and strikingly mediocre monuments to victory in revolution and war.

Of all the changes that had come to the Romanovs' Imperial city during the nineteenth century, the most critical was the growing tension between the institutions of Imperial authority and the city's masses of impoverished wage laborers. A decade and a year after Alexander III's death, these tensions burst into flame, engulfing St. Petersburg in a wave of revolutionary violence. In the fall of 1905, the life of the capital ground to a halt as the Romanovs saw for the first time how crippling a general strike could be in a city grown dependent upon modern goods and services. For a brief moment, it appeared that revolution might triumph in St. Petersburg as it had in Paris in 1789 and on several later occasions. But, unlike Louis XVI in 1789, Charles X in 1830, and Louis Philippe in 1848, the Romanovs won a reprieve from the sentence of revolution in 1905, for the army upon which they had

lavished such pride and attention in the eighteenth and nineteenth centuries defended their Imperial crown. Yet Nicholas II failed to heed
the warnings of 1905 and was unable to realize that he would not be
granted a second reprieve from a revolutionary fate if he refused to
heed the realities of the world in which he lived. Another decade and a
year passed, and revolution again burst forth in St. Petersburg's streets.
In 1917, the Romanovs' Imperial city became the cradle of a new order
when the crowds, who had cheered their Emperors and Empresses for
so long raised their voices in support of such roughly dressed revolutionary heroes as Trotskii and Lenin.

Lenin came to power in a nation that had changed utterly in the
course of a century, a fact reflected with immense clarity in St. Petersburg's changed character. In 1817, the city had just reached the peak
of her Imperial glory, and there was a regularity, a balance, a measured grandeur about the Russian Empire that was reflected in every
aspect of St. Petersburg's life. Aleksandr Pushkin knew the Romanovs'
capital well during the quarter-century after Napoleon's defeat, and he
painted a vivid and memorable portrait of the city during that era in
the introduction to his famous poem, *The Bronze Horseman:*

> *I love thy ruthless winter, lowering*
> *With bitter frost and windless air;*
> *The sledges along Neva scouring;*
> *Girls' cheeks—no rose so bright and fair!*
> *The flash and noise of balls, the chatter;*
> *The bachelor's hour of feasting, too;*
> *The cups that foam and hiss and spatter,*
> *The punch that in the bowl burns blue.*
> *I love the warlike animation*
> *On playing-fields of Mars; to see*
> *The troops of foot and horse in station,*
> *And their superb monotony;*
> *Their ordered, undulating muster;*
> *Flags brazen, tattered on the glorious day;*
> *Those brazen helmets in their lustre*
> *Shot through and riddled in the fray.*[38]

Dire poverty, desperate need, bitter conflict between rich and poor
had no place in Pushkin's poem or in the world he described. St. Petersburg's great conflict in the early nineteenth century was with the el-

ements, most dramatically expressed when the Neva River inundated its streets and wrought havoc with the city that had arisen as a consequence of Peter the Great's implacable opposition to the forces of Nature. Writing of St. Petersburg during the winter of 1917, the poet Aleksandr Blok used very different images to describe very different sorts of conflicts. In "The Twelve," a brief but unforgettable poem, he wrote of a world so different from that described by Pushkin that there seemed no relation between the two:

> *Black night,*
> *White snow.*
> *The wind, the wind!*
> *It stuns you like a blow.*
> *The wind, the wind!*
> *Across the world it gallops to and fro.*
>
> *The wind is weaving*
> *The white snow.*
> *There is ice below.*
> *Stumbling and tumbling,*
> *Folk slip and fall.*
> *God pity all!*
>
> *From house to house*
> *A rope is flung.*
> *On it the sagging sign is hung:*
> *"All Power to the Constituent Assembly!"*
> *A bent old woman,*
> *Tearful, trembly,*
> *Stares at the canvas in despair.*
>
> *Her blear eyes see*
> *How many fine foot-wraps could be*
> *Cut from the linen wasted there,*
> *While the children's feet go bare.*[39]

In less than a hundred years, the power, the grandeur, and the majesty the Romanovs had brought to St. Petersburg after Napoleon's defeat had been irretrievably lost. How and why did that happen? Why were the Romanovs able to build a vast Empire, but unable to respond to the most basic needs of their people? These are questions we now must examine.

CHAPTER X

From Golden Age to Iron Age

T he greatness of Russia's cultural achievement in the nineteenth century can be symbolized most simply by two names: Dostoevskii and Tolstoi. If nineteenth-century Russian culture had produced nothing more than these two colossal figures, it would have been recognized as an era of great artistic achievement. Yet Dostoevskii and Tolstoi merely stood at the peak of a pyramid that overflowed with brilliant novelists, poets, painters, and composers. Without a moment's thought, any Russian schoolchild could produce a list that would include the names of Karamzin, Pushkin, Gogol, Turgenev, Chekhov, Tchaikovsky, Musorgskii, and Repin, while literally dozens of other names could be added without including any whose works were mediocre or second-rate. Between 1801 and 1894, there was such an abundance of talented writers, composers, and painters in Russia that men and women whose work would have won them acclaim at any other time received only passing notice.

Under the first impact of this flood of artistic achievements, Russian culture, and especially Russian letters, reached a golden age during the 1820s and 1830s, which grew out of that aristocratic, Western-oriented, St. Petersburg-centered culture that had evolved during the previous century. But Russia's golden literary age began to fade almost as soon as it blossomed. Compared to the years that had gone before it, the nineteenth century was a difficult time in which to live, and society's growing adoration of technology could not long sustain those exalted emotions of romanticism that, for a short time, characterized Russia's cultural achievement. Writers simply could not wax romantic or sentimental over blast furnaces and locomotives in the manner in which Byron, Schiller, and Pushkin had exalted the passions of love, the glory of freedom, and the heroism of war. The great and beautiful poetry of writers like Pushkin therefore yielded to the more descriptive prose of realism, and this was followed by a similar turn to realism in the other arts.

At about the same time, Russia's culture began to lose its exclusively aristocratic base as the bourgeoisie and even some members of the proletariat gained access to learning. As its audience became increasingly nonaristocratic, the arts and letters of Russia moved away from the Romanovs and their Court. The development of realism, in fact, ushered in an era in which the arts, and especially letters, became antagonistic toward the established order. In the tradition of Novikov and Radishchev, Russian writers began to criticize the Romanovs and to portray a future social and political order far different from that which the Romanovs envisioned. For some critics, the Romanovs had no place in Russia's future at all. After the 1860s, Russia's culture thus was no longer "Romanov," as it had been at the beginning of the century, but more broadly Russian.

Since the Romanovs no longer could motivate this new culture through patronage, they sought to control it through censorship, once they perceived the danger inherent in Western ideas. When Louis XVI and Marie Antoinette died beneath the blade of the guillotine in 1793, Catherine the Great and those aristocrats who aspired to preserve Russia's recently created *ancien régime* society saw that certain ideas of the Enlightenment could lead even to regicide. To insulate Russia from the danger, they were obliged to make what at first was a very awkward distinction between the ideas of the West and the external products of Western culture. While Catherine acted to restrict Russians' access to the writings of the Enlightenment and "all that which their words have spread throughout Europe,"[1] she allowed her grandson Alexander's education under the Swiss Jacobin tutor LaHarpe to continue and permitted certain trustworthy individuals to read and discuss the very works she condemned. At the same time, she insisted that those other aspects of Western culture that the Romanovs and their Court had championed during the eighteenth century must be preserved. Educated Russians still were to dress, act, and speak in the manner of their Western counterparts. They simply were to stop thinking as Westerners did.

By acting in this manner, Catherine set a precedent that would complicate Russians' cultural and intellectual relationship with the West ever afterward. For she established the principle that even the most radical Western ideas were not *totally* forbidden for *all* Russians and that there was a very direct correlation between an individual's attitude toward Western ideas and his loyalty to the Autocrat and to Russia. An individual's status could determine the extent of his access to Western ideas, and, conversely, an individual's attitude toward the West could determine his status in Russia. Catherine's criteria were vague, and never even fully articulated, but it soon became evident that too much commitment to the West was far more risky than too little. During the nineteenth century, this already murky issue became complicated further by a screen of rhetoric about who in Russia was intellectually mature enough to read the writings of Western thinkers and publicists without damage to themselves or Russia. At bottom, however, the real issue was to determine which Russians were sufficiently "loyal" to be able to read and discuss advanced Western European theories but not use them as a basis for criticizing or attacking the established order.

Under Catherine's immediate successor, this question became momentarily irrelevant because the Emperor Paul imposed military discipline upon all strata of Russian society and expected his command principles to define their actions and attitudes. Paul simply dictated his subjects' relationship to the West, and anyone who violated his orders was branded disloyal and punished. The Tsar's prohibitions ranged from the petty to the fundamental. He prohibited French fashions, the use of such words as "society" and "citizen," and the importation of musical scores, because they might contain coded messages. He also forbade Russians to travel abroad, recalled all Russians studying at European universities and, in April 1800, banned the importation of any materials printed outside Russia. So strict was his prohibition that the Empress Maria Feodorovna had to plead at some length for a number of foreign books she had ordered for her personal reading before the ban went into effect.[2]

By the time of Alexander I's sudden elevation to the throne in March 1801, Russians had begun to abandon the rationalism of the Enlightenment and the political activism it had engendered. They turned away from those cosmic philosophical questions that had so occupied the minds of eighteenth-century men and women to more contemplative, inner-directed modes of thought and sought inner fulfillment through emotion rather than reason. What Father George Floróvskii once termed an "awakening of the heart" generated an "irresponsibility of the heart,"[3] which provided most thoughtful Russians with justification for accepting injustices in the world that the Romanovs had created during the course of the eighteenth century. They did so in the comfortable and comforting belief that "social inequality can be tolerated because it is insignificant in comparison to moral equality."[4] By 1801, Russians' commitment to these new sentimentalist truths enabled Alexander and his counselors to bypass the awkward issue of limiting Russians' access to Western thought because the ideas that appealed most to educated men and women carried no threat of political action. Russian letters thus embarked upon the path that brought them to their Golden Age.

In the development of Russian sentimentalism, and its corresponding defense of the Romanovs' state, its social order, and the institution of autocracy, Nikolai Karamzin played an especially important part. A native of the Volga town of Simbirsk, Karamzin grew up very far away from the center of Russia's new Westernized culture. Yet it was indicative of how the new culture was starting to spread outside the large cities that the local doctor taught Karamzin German and the young wife of a neighboring nobleman introduced him to the study of French and proper manners. Evidently she was prepared to teach her precocious eleven-year-old student far sweeter mysteries than those of grammar, syntax, and manners, for Karamzin's father hastily sent him away to Moscow. During the next five years, Karamzin studied there, served in the Guards in St. Petersburg, and returned to his family estate in Simbirsk after his father's sudden death. He might have become just another middling provincial squire if it had not been for the urgings of Ivan Petrovich Turgenev, an absentee Simbirsk nobleman who spent most of his time in Moscow in Novikov's circle of freemasons.

Turgenev recognized in Karamzin a young man of great ability and encouraged him to return to Moscow and begin a literary career.[5] There, Karamzin began to study the writings of the English and German sentimentalists. These intensified his interest in the West, and, to satisfy his curiosity, he left Russia in the spring of 1789 to spend the next fifteen months in Europe. He became one of those rare Russians who saw the French Revolution at first hand.[6]

Unlike such young Russians as Count Pavel Stroganov, who joined Jacobin societies in Paris and reveled in their ferment, Karamzin was not particularly impressed by the Revolution. When he learned that the Bastille had fallen, he hastened away to Switzerland. Not until March 1790 did he visit Paris, and he lived there for two months before he even visited the National Assembly. His first passion for the city had little to do with the Enlightenment or the Revolution. "I am in Paris!" he wrote at the beginning of April. "I run from street to street, from the Tuilleries to the Champs Elysées . . . . as I immerse myself in the noise, the crowds, the theatre, and that magic castle called the Palais Royal." He let the emotions of Paris surge over him for about three months and then moved on to England, where he was far more impressed by the political achievements of the British. "It is not a constitution, but general intelligence, that is the true palladium of the British," he wrote. But he immediately added a note of caution to any in Russia who might think of relying too much upon the institutions of the West. "All civic institutions," he remarked, "ought to conform to the character of a people. What is good in England could be bad in any other country." "Every government whose spirit is permeated by justice," he concluded, "is good and beneficial."[7]

Karamzin left politics and political questions to others for more than a decade after he returned to Russia in the fall of 1790. During those years, he published a tale entitled *Poor Liza*, in which he commented, as Radishchev had two years earlier, upon the vast distance between social classes and the injustices peasants suffered at the hands of Russia's nobles. In Karamzin's tale, the peasant maiden Liza was seduced and abandoned by a young nobleman so intent upon sowing his wild oats that he failed to notice her deep love. Betrayed, she drowned herself in the village pond, but not before she had enjoyed the tearful pleasure of bidding a long and sentimental farewell to her closest friend. Karamzin's tale appears mawkishly overdrawn to today's reader. Yet it was immensely popular with Russians at the time and set the tone for the sentimentalism and romanticism to follow during the next three decades. As one scholar noted not long ago, Karamzin's treatment of social injustice "made the existence of irremediable injustice in a world that was supposed to be good not only tolerable but even pleasurable and uplifting."[8] The very act of shedding tears over Liza's plight served to uplift readers and improve their inner beings. "Ach, I love those themes which touch my heart and compel me to shed tears of tender grief!" Karamzin proclaimed at the beginning of his tale.[9]

Karamzin also defined the model relationship between writers, the Autocrat, and the government in Russia. He thought the major function of every good government was to guarantee freedom and security for its people. Yet it was not political freedom but cultural freedom that he most wanted to defend.[10] Men must be left free to let their spirits soar, immerse themselves in sentiment, and exalt their inner beings. Fearful that any breakdown of authority might threaten such cultural freedom, Karamzin insisted that the ruler and his government must be strong and must use every means to preserve order. He insisted that the writer confine himself to questions of cultural and personal relationships and leave political and social issues to the Autocrat and his counselors. "In Russia, the sovereign is the living law. He favors the good and punishes the bad," he wrote to Alexander, concluding that "a soft heart in a monarch is counted as a virtue only when it is tempered with the sense of duty to use sensible severity."[11]

Even though Karamzin urged writers to confine their interests to cultural questions, he could not remain uninvolved in politics. His monumental *History of the Russian State,* to which he devoted two decades of his life, was inspired by his political interests, as was his *Memoir on Ancient and Modern Russia,* in which he lectured Alexander I about the duties of a ruler and the policies that would best serve Russia's interests. Toward the end of his life, Karamzin became a close adviser to Nicholas I during the troubled weeks just before and after the Decembrist revolt. He helped the young Tsar draft his accession manifesto and advised him about a number of ministerial appointments, including Dmitrii Bludov, who became Minister of Justice and then Minister of Internal Affairs; Dmitrii Dashkov, another future Minister of Justice; and Sergei Uvarov, most famous as Nicholas I's Minister of Public Instruction.[12]

Bludov, Dashkov, and Uvarov were leading members of the Arzamas Society, a literary group founded in 1815 that championed Karamzin's efforts to create an elegant and clear modern Russian style. Among its other members were most of the leading romantic writers of the 1820s and 1830s, including such brilliant poets as Konstantin Batiushkov, Prince Petr Viazemskii, and Aleksandr Pushkin, who had entered Arzamas as a sixteen-year-old student at the Tsarskoe Selo Lyceum.[13] The founder of Arzamas was the poet Vasilii Zhukovskii, who was to become the tutor of the Empress Aleksandra Feodorovna and of the future Alexander II. As a poet, he preached that man must accept reality and conform to it. He believed deeply in Russia's future and cloaked the Romanovs in a heroic, romantic aura, making them the embodiment of Russia's greatest virtues, her moral strength, her national might, and the promise of her greater glory.

During Sergei Uvarov's sixteen-year tenure as Minister of Public Instruction, he established a broad ideological defense of autocracy and the conservative order. Seventeenth- and eighteenth-century Romanovs had given little thought to the need for such a defense, but it became essential as new and more radical Western ideas continued to threaten the institution of autocracy and the integrated conservative outlook that Karamzin first had articulated during the last decade of Alexander's reign.[14] "Russia still is young and virginal," Uvarov said in 1835. "At least for the time being, she ought not to taste the bloody disturbances [being experienced by the West]. We must prolong her youth, and, in the meantime, we must educate her. . . . If I can put off for fifty years that future which these [Western] theories are preparing for Russia, then I shall have fulfilled my duty and can die in peace."[15]

Uvarov himself was a man steeped in Western learning. He was an accomplished diplomat and a talented student of the ancient Near East. As a youth, he had attracted the attention of Napoleon and even the great Goethe. The Emperor Alexander had such confidence in his brilliance that he appointed him President of the Imperial Russian

Academy of Sciences in 1818 when he was not yet thirty-two.[16] As Russia's Minister of Public Instruction, he insisted that it was necessary "to find the principles which form the distinctive character of Russia, and which belong only to Russia . . . to gather into one whole the sacred remnants of Russian nationality and fasten to them the anchor of our salvation." Those principles were summed up in his famous slogan "Orthodoxy, Autocracy, and Nationality." Uvarov considered Orthodoxy to be that assurance of God's love for Russia and the Russians that sustained the nation and its rulers in times of crisis, and he viewed the other two elements in his profane trinity as equally important parts of Russia's past, present, and future greatness. "Autocracy constitutes the main condition of the political existence of Russia," he wrote. "The Russian giant stands on it as on the cornerstone of his greatness. . . . The saving condition that Russia lives and is protected by the spirit of a strong, humane, and enlightened autocracy must permeate popular education and must develop with it. Together with these two national principles there is a third, no less powerful: *Nationality*."[17] Implicit in Uvarov's view was the assumption that, once Russians became fully educated in the precepts of Orthodoxy, Autocracy, and Nationality, they would become just as impervious to radical Western ideas as were, by definition, those censors who read and banned foreign works from being circulated and sold within Russia. Until that happened, of course, he realized that young Russians could not be kept isolated from radical Western ideas but took comfort in the conviction that the handful involved could be placed under police surveillance or, if necessary, even arrested.

The romantic and conservative ideas of Uvarov and Zhukovskii embodied sentiments that appealed to the majority of educated Russians. Indeed, those sentiments had formed an integral part of their lives for several decades, even centuries. But there also were those who responded to that other strain in Western thought that cast romantics in the role of noble opponents of evil tyrants. The hopeless revolt of the Decembrists followed in the footsteps of romantic political dissent in Western Europe, where it usually was connected with the early stages of nationalism.

As we have seen, Nicholas crushed the Decembrists and punished them severely. Yet there was one young poet who shared their passion for freedom, whose writings stirred the soul of every Russian who read them. Whether he would have stood with the Decembrists had he been in St. Petersburg on December 14, 1825, can only be a matter of conjecture, although he once boldly told Nicholas that he would have done so.[18] Certainly, he was frequently in difficulties with the authorities because of his sharp tongue and passionate pen. These characteristics and, most of all, his brilliant poetry made Aleksandr Pushkin, the youngest member of the Arzamas Society, the greatest of Russia's romantic poets and the most resplendent representative of her golden literary age.

Pushkin's biography is a monument to romanticism in the most Byronesque sense of the term. He was a direct descendant of the captive son of an Abyssinian prince, who rose to become a general in the army of Peter the Great. Pushkin lived a romantic life, wrote romantic poetry, and, above all, died a romantic death. His life was more exciting, more adventurous, more turbulent than any he portrayed in his writings. At times, he lived a truly Dionysian existence, gambling wildly and alternating between visiting St. Petersburg's most elegant salons and its most disreputable brothels. He seduced aristocrats' wives and daughters when he could and, when he could not, he bedded whores as a diversion. When he finally married in February 1831, it was to St. Petersburg's most dazzling beauty, the empty-headed and frivolous Natalia Goncharova. "I have known many beautiful women, but none had her classic perfection of face and body," wrote one contemporary. "She was tall and slender, with a delightfully slim waist, a marvelous bosom, a fine head looking like a lily, a wonderfully regular profile. . . . All other women paled next to her."[19] At the age of thirty-seven, Pushkin died fighting to defend his frivolous wife's honor in a duel with the Baron Georges d'Anthès. There is some evidence to suggest that his foe wore armor beneath his coat to protect him from the poet's pistol ball.[20]

It would be impossible even to summarize here the many great works Pushkin wrote during the brief space of about fifteen years, but even a cursory listing can indicate how impressive his achievement was. Even his first poem, which he published at the age of twenty-one under the title of *Russlan and Liudmila,* was so superb that Zhukovskii reportedly sent him his portrait inscribed "to the victorious pupil from the conquered master."[21] After *Russlan and Liudmila,* an avalanche of works poured from Pushkin's pen. He wrote *The Captive of the Caucasus* and *The Fountain of Bakhchissarai* while in exile in southern Russia between 1820 and 1823, at a time when he was almost completely under the influence of Byron. Between 1823 and 1830, he wrote *Eugene Onegin,* one of his greatest creations, and *Boris Godunov,* the first Russian romantic tragedy. Although he wrote less during the last seven years of his life, the works he produced easily qualify among his best, especially *Tsar Saltan* and, most of all, *The Bronze Horseman,* his great poem to Peter the Great and his capital, which we have quoted at some length in our remarks about St. Petersburg's development.

Perhaps Pushkin's most important achievement was his creation of a truly modern Russian literary style. He broke away from the sanctified forms of classicism and replaced them with a language that was as unrestrained and colloquial as it was brilliant. As one critic wrote, Pushkin's poetry not only presented "the best words in the best order" but endowed "the plainest, almost trivial words with poetic meaning."[22] Perhaps even more important, his widely varied writings showed that his new language could be applied not only to poetry but to all forms of literary expression. So rapidly did Russians embroider upon his literary innovations that, by the time of his death, many of them had come to regard him as "a venerable, but obsolete classic, who had outlived his time."[23] Only toward the end of the nineteenth century did Russians begin to recognize the true measure of his genius and pay full tribute to his greatness.

More than any other writer, Pushkin personified the Golden Age of Russian Literature in his poetry. Yet he also personified the spirit of opposition to the Romanov-sponsored cultural and political order. Fresh from the cloistered halls of the Imperial Lyceum, he posed as the champion of liberty and a romantic foe of tryrants, who proclaimed himself "the proud singer of freedom." "Ye tyrants of the world! Tremble!" he wrote in his famous *Ode to Freedom,* which the authorities found in manuscript copies among the papers of so many Decembrists.[24] He cursed Aleksei Arakcheev, Alexander's all-powerful deputy, as a man "full of evil, full of self-importance, mindless, without feeling, without honor,"[25] and, to all who read his early verses, he lamented in *The Village*:

> *O, but if my voice could only move the heart!*
> *Why else this barren passion in my breast should burn*
> *But for this awesome gift of speech bestowed on me by Fate?*
> *When will I see, O friends! the masses free*
> *And slavery struck down by the Sovereign's own hand,*
> *When will that beautiful dawn of freedom so enlightened*
> *At last arise above our land?* [26]

Pushkin's phrases seared the hearts of the young men and women who read them, but the poet proved neither so strong nor so fearless in actual battle with the Emperor. In 1820, when Alexander became angry about his liberal verses, Pushkin sought refuge in the protection of those powerful friends he had known in the Arzamas Society. At the urging of Zhukovskii and Karamzin, Alexander agreed to spare him the pain of Siberian exile and sent him to the south instead. There, the sharp-tongued poet lived comfortably, wrote a great deal, and complained endlessly about his isolation from his friends in St. Petersburg. He became notorious for the duels he fought, the many more that friends prevented him from fighting, and the even greater number of women he seduced. Wives, daughters, and relatives of friends—he considered them all fair game, not to mention native Caucasian and Moldavian women, serving wenches, governesses, and whores of many nationalities. There seemed no way to control his violent temper and raging lust; his only respite would come during fits of creative impulse when he locked himself away for days on end to write some of his most famous poems.[27]

Despite the intercession of Karamzin and Zhukovskii, Pushkin's hopes that Alexander might allow him to return to St. Petersburg never materialized. In desperation, he planned an escape to Europe; then, at the end of November 1825, he learned of Alexander's death, and he looked to the young Emperor Nicholas to free him from his provincial isolation. But the aftermath of the Decembrist revolt dashed Pushkin's hopes almost as soon as they had risen. "You have not been involved in anything—that is true," Zhukovskii wrote to him in mid-

April 1826. "But, in the papers of each of the active figures, [manuscript copies of] your [unpublished] poems have been found." Men had been condemned for less. That so many of the Decembrists obviously had been moved to action by Pushkin's ringing calls to freedom boded ill for him.

For some months, it seemed that Pushkin might well be implicated, but in September Nicholas summoned him to Moscow, "not in the position of a prisoner, and only under the escort of a courier." "Upon his arrival in Moscow," Nicholas ordered, he "must present himself at once to the general of the day at the staff headquarters of his Imperial Majesty." What followed was to become the most exhilarating and most oppressive moment of Pushkin's life. After an hour's interview, Nicholas promised, "From now on, I will be your censor." "Here is the new Pushkin for you," he proclaimed to his courtiers. "Let us forget about the old Pushkin."[28] Freed from exile at last, Pushkin was destined to be enslaved by the Emperor's promise. He was condemned to bear Nicholas's criticisms of his work and listen to recommendations for its improvement. He had to give the impression of considering seriously such ludicrous Imperial "suggestions" as the proposal that he rewrite his play *Boris Godunov* as a novel in the manner of Sir Walter Scott.[29] In this instance, as in others, the purpose of Nicholas's censorship was broadly moral rather than narrowly political. Like his predecessors, he assumed responsibility for Russians' thoughts and deeds and did not conceive of censorship as punitive or oppressive. "The role of the censor was conceived as that of an amiable legal guardian of letters, a foster father of the arts and sciences," a scholar once remarked.[30] Much of educated opinion in Russia shared such a view and found it possible to work creatively within its framework. But for Pushkin, the Emperor's favor soon became a crushing burden that slowed his work; on occasion, it caused him to flee St. Petersburg only to humble himself on his return in contrite and bitterly resented apologies.

Pushkin's untimely death in 1837 coincided with the rise of a young literary critic whose passionate prescriptions dictated the course of Russian letters for the next half-century. Born in 1810, Vissarion Belinskii grew up in Chembar, a small village in his father's native province of Penza, some four hundred miles to the south and east of Moscow. An intellectually and culturally deadening backwater, Chembar left him with no fond childhood memories. For Belinskii, the opportunity to enter Moscow University in 1829 was a priceless chance to escape from the depths of Russia's provinces.

At the university Belinskii joined the circle of Nikolai Stankevich, a young man whose brilliant mind and magnetic personality attracted a number of other intellectuals destined to become famous figures in mid-nineteenth-century Russia. Besides Belinskii, there were the future historian Timofei Granovskii; Mikhail Katkov, later a conservative literary critic and publisher of an important Moscow periodical; Konstantin Aksakov, a famous Slavophile; and Vasilii Botkin, a traveler, writer, and one of the leading Westerners of the 1840s. Perhaps most important of all, Belinskii became a close friend of the leading figure of Stankevich's circle in the 1830s the future anarchist Mikhail Bakunin.[31] These young men rejected the cultural values and political system the Emperor Nicholas imposed upon Russia. As their countrymen had done in the past century, they sought their vision of the future in the West, where they found an immensely rich intellectual smorgasbord, overflowing with new ideas. Between 1826 and 1840, Belinskii later wrote, they "experienced, thought through, and lived through the entire intellectual life of Europe."[32] In doing so, they espoused those very theories from which Uvarov sought to protect Russia, and their belief was fully as passionate as his rejection.

Like his fellows in the Stankevich circle, Belinskii searched for philosophical truth, first in the aesthetics of Schelling, then in the ethics of Fichte, and finally in the logic of Hegel. His encounter with the ideas of these great German thinkers created for him a deep personal crisis that was all the more acute because of his awkward position as a lonely and impoverished commoner among wealthy aristocrats. A deep inner compulsion drove him to preach his new gospels, and he chose literary criticism as his instrument. By the early 1840s, he had begun to argue that man's personality could have meaning only in an open struggle against the oppressions of the external world. He thus challenged Uvarov's slogan of Orthodoxy, Autocracy, and Nationality, by proclaiming that the artist must become the conscience of his time and society. He insisted that every work of literature must be judged according to its social or political message, not merely its artistic merit.[33]

The furious essays Belinskii published during the early and middle 1840s proclaimed that the principles of Uvarov, Zhukovskii, and Nicholas I could not serve as the basis for a Romanov-centered culture that would involve Russian educated society to the extent it had during the eighteenth century. Neither side left any room for compromise in their demands for commitment. One was obliged to accept the system *in toto,* as did Moscow University professor Stepan Shevyrev, when he wrote in 1841 that "there is not a country in all of Europe which can pride itself on possessing such a harmonious political existence as our own."[34] Otherwise, one had to possess the inner fortitude needed to become a stern critic as "furious Vissarion" demanded. "Russia sees her salvation not in mysticism, nor in asceticism, nor in pietism, but in the successes of civilization, in enlightenment, and in humanity," he wrote in 1847. "She needs not sermons (she has heard enough of them already!) nor prayers (she has repeated them too often!), but the awakening in the masses of a sense of their human dignity, lost for so many centuries amidst filth and refuse."[35] It was no longer possible for educated Russians to temporize about the issue of accepting or rejecting the Romanovs' view of their nation's political and cultural destiny. One had to take an uncompromising position or remain utterly silent.

Those who agreed with Belinskii's credo that the true artist must become a critic of the existing order did not share a common vision. Because they hoped to apply the experience of the West to Russia, they became known as Westerners, although they had no definable ideology in common. Among them were such moderates as the historian Granovskii, who believed that Russia should pursue the Western path carefully and gradually. Others, such as the publicists Aleksandr Herzen and Nikolai Ogarev, called for revolution and urged their followers to overthrow the existing order in their homeland if the Emperor refused to heed their demands for a new social and political order. Taken as a whole, their views were a shifting quicksand of devotions to socialism and liberalism, to evolution and revolution, to the glorification of the masses and to a reliance upon an elite, and the men who supported them were notorious for the ease with which they exchanged one view for another. Just before his death in 1848, even Belinskii suddenly shifted his ground to proclaim that "what Russia needed was not socialism but a bourgeoisie."[36] Most of all, the Westerners were not ideologues but critics. Their movement was a thundering of alienated men against the injustices the Romanovs' system heaped upon them as they aspired to become a new conscience for a society that refused them the opportunity to use their talents for the country they loved.

The one thing about which the Westerners agreed, however, was their opposition to the Slavophiles, their major antagonists among those who criticized the Romanovs' society and politics during the 1840s. The most notable among them were Ivan Kireevskii, Aleksei Khomiakov, and Konstantin Aksakov, and they differed from other Russian intellectuals because they rejected the West as a model for Russia's development. Convinced that the rationalism of the West would lead Russia to ruin, they argued that truth could be found only in religious faith. Only Russian Orthodoxy and the communal spirit (*sobornost'*) it fostered, they insisted, preserved true Christian ideals. In their view, the Russian family was patriarchal, while the family in the West was individualistic. In Old Russia, property had been held communally, while in the West there was private ownership. True civilization—Old Russian, pre-Petrine civilization—was based on the land; in the West, civilization was based in the towns and cities. The Slavophiles claimed that Russians, most especially the Romanovs and the nobles who had followed the Western path laid out by Peter the Great, had become alienated from the past of their people and their nation. Only in the peasant commune (*mir*) were Russia's traditional virtues still preserved. It was this *mir,* a unique Russian folk institution, that would lead their nation back to the true path of civilization.[37]

Both Westerners and Slavophiles envisioned Russia's future in terms very different from those espoused by Uvarov and Zhukovskii in defense of the Romanovs' social, political, and cultural regime. Yet there was one defender of the culture of the Romanovs in the 1830s and 1840s who might have established a common ground between its

extreme critics and unyielding defenders had his vision been less distorted by his own psychological torment. Nikolai Gogol, the man whose
literary masterpieces made Russians laugh and weep during the reign
of Nicholas I, was probably the most misunderstood writer of the nineteenth century and perhaps in all of Russia's history. His family were
Ukrainian Cossack squires who owned a small estate and a few serfs.
His parents doted on him, and Gogol grew up surrounded by all the
warmth and affection Belinskii never had known.[38] His were the very
ordinary beginnings commonly found among men who eventually rose
to become middle-ranking bureaucrats in the Romanovs' service.

Prince Dmitrii Mirsky once wrote that "a dark and secretive dispo-
sition, mingled with painful self-consciousness and boundless ambition," characterized Gogol from his youth onward.[39] When he
graduated from the lyceum and was obliged to seek his way in the
world, Gogol responded to that mysterious and magical pull St. Petersburg exerted upon so many Russian provincials. "Fate is driving me off
to Petersburg," he wrote to his uncle. "Perhaps it shall be my lot to live
out my entire life in Petersburg, at least that has long been my dream."
"To live, and to leave no mark of my existence behind, would be terrible for me," he confessed.[40] He wanted to become a great statesman or
at least an important official, but his dreams were dashed almost immediately. Like most young men in search of positions in Russia's capital
during the 1830s and 1840s, Gogol could be nothing more than a petty
clerk, buried deep in the anonymous warrens of St. Petersburg's chanceries, and this empty life crushed him. "Is this what I am supposed to
sell my health and my precious time for?" he asked.[41] Embittered by his
apparent failure, Gogol turned to writing. At first, it was a form of
release. Ultimately, it became a means for wreaking satirical revenge
against the failings of the Romanovs' Russia, while he continued to support the principles that underlay the social, political, and cultural order
they had created.

Gogol's first literary success, *Evenings on a Farm Near Dikanka,* appeared in 1831 and dealt with the life he had known as a child in the
Ukraine. During the next half-decade he published a number of stories
and collections, all of which were well received by enthusiastic readers
in St. Petersburg and the provinces. Perhaps most notable among these

early works was a collection entitled *Arabesques*, in which he examined life in St. Petersburg from the perspective of its lesser folk. Gogol became the first Russian writer to portray the Romanovs' capital in starkly negative terms, as a city where, in the words of one noted scholar, "the smug, the vulgar, the callous, are here to stay," while "the pure of heart are crushed by the unbearable discrepancy between their dreams and 'revolting' reality." [42] "How strangely our fate plays with us!" Gogol himself wrote in one of his tales. "But the strangest of all events take place on the Nevskii Prospekt. O, do not trust this Nevskii Prospekt! I always wrap myself more tightly in my cloak whenever I walk along it, and I try not to take any notice of the things I encounter. Everything's an illusion. Everything's a dream. Everything's not what it seems!" [43] In Gogol's writings, the Nevskii Prospekt and St. Petersburg generally become a place where rank was more important than people, where a Collegial Assessor was obliged to bow to his nose, which had run away and garbed itself in the uniform of a State Councillor and therefore stood three ranks higher than the man from whose face it had come. [44] As he portrayed it, Russia's capital was a city where everything seemed turned upside down, where "the devil himself lights the street lamps only in order to show that everything is not really as it seems." [45]

Gogol did not reject Russia's capital in and of itself, but focused upon those faults that had caused it to fall short of the mark set by the Empire's autocrats. When he dealt with Russia more generally in *The Inspector General*, he continued to critize Russians' failure to measure up to the standards set by their rulers, while he portrayed the Romanovs and their chosen agents, the inspectors general, as representatives of right and justice. *The Inspector General* first was read at one of Zhukovskii's literary evenings late in the winter of 1836. Everyone agreed about its brilliance, but the censors feared to approve it because it seemed to them a satirical and critical account of Russia's provincial administration. Zhukovskii arranged for it to be read at Court, and Nicholas gave his personal permission for it to be performed at the Aleksandra Theatre in mid-April.

The Inspector General also could be seen as a justification for that system of police surveillance the Romanovs had created in an effort to discipline those who strayed from the path of virtue. Obviously, Nicholas took this view, and the best estimates are that that was the meaning Gogol intended for his work. Yet critics saw in the play a brilliant critique of Nicholas's entire system; this so depressed Gogol that he fled from Russia in horror and confusion. He did not see himself as a social or political critic, and the shoe made for him by such men as Belinskii fit poorly. Rather than wear it, he remained in Europe for the next twelve years, except for two brief visits to his homeland.[46]

If critics of Russia's social and political order regarded *The Inspector General* as a negative satire about the Emperor Nicholas's Russia, they misunderstood Gogol's greatest novel, *Dead Souls*, in a like manner. The book recounts the misadventures of Pavel Ivanovich Chichikov, an enterprising swindler who set out to enrich himself at the government's expense by using a quirk in the law that treated dead serfs as being among the living until the next official census. Because Chichikov represented everything that was false, cheap, and dishonest in humanity, there was a universal quality about him that enabled Gogol's tale to transcend even the far-flung boundaries of Russia. Still, he had not conceived of it as social and political criticism of Russia itself, which was how it was hailed by Belinskii and his fellow critics.[47]

The edition of *Dead Souls* Gogol published in 1842 was, in fact, only the first part of a trilogy he envisioned as a Russian *Divine Comedy,* yet he failed to complete the second part of the work.[48] He cast and recast it during the last decade of his life but always remained dissatisfied. About five years before his death, he set aside his work on *Dead Souls* and wrote *Selected Passages from Correspondence with Friends* as an attempt to clarify the misunderstandings that Russia's more radical intellectuals had about his work. "This book is needed, badly needed," he wrote. "Everything will become clear and misunderstandings will be promptly dispelled."[49] He therefore stated very clearly his belief in the social, political, and cultural order the Romanovs had created in Russia and set forth a religious and moral justification for it that bore many similarities to Uvarov's and Nicholas's precepts. Like Uvarov, Gogol saw a superior mercy and virtue in a patriarchal order, in which serfs were subject to their masters, wives to their husbands, and all Russians to their Emperor. "Why is it necessary," he asked, "for one of us to be above everything and, even, above the law? Because the law is like wood, and you will not get very far only by fulfilling the letter of the law. Of course, none of us ought to break the law, or not fulfill its dictates. But you need a superior mercy so as to soften the law, and this only can come to us in the form of absolute monarchy. Without an absolute monarch, a state is an automaton." "A state without an absolute ruler," he concluded, "is like an orchestra without a conductor."[50]

When it appeared in 1847, *Selected Passages* stirred a storm of protest. Belinskii cursed Gogol for preaching "lies and immorality as truth and virtue under the protection of religion and defended by the knout."[51] Again, Gogol was amazed by the reaction to his book. "Oh, Lord, how empty and terrifying your world has grown!" he lamented.[52] Critics persisted in seeing his volume as some sort of bizarre product of his growing obsession with religion, as an outright betrayal of the progressive cause. Yet, perhaps there was something more behind Gogol's surprising tract and, indeed, his entire literary production, than Belinskii and his fellows were prepared to admit. Gogol's criticism was directed against the flaws of mankind and the manner in which they manifested themselves, especially in Russia, but he did not attack the principles that underlay the Romanovs' order. In the final analysis, he perhaps offered his countrymen a means to criticize and improve the existing order without taking the extreme path of outright rejection and revolutionary violence upon which some of them were preparing to embark. Catherine the Great had attempted to enlist literature in her cause during the 1760s. Gogol may well have tried to do so on a vastly more sophisticated level three-quarters of a century later.

Although they disagreed about the meaning of his works, Gogol's past and present critics are agreed that he was the most Russian writer to appear before the middle of the nineteenth century. Unlike such eighteenth-century figures as Fonvizin or Derzhavin, or even such great Golden Age writers as Pushkin, Gogol's language, plots, and style all were exclusively Russian, yet they appealed to a much broader audience than any previous writer's work. While Russian writers generally had focused upon the upper classes, Gogol had broadened his literary portraits to include merchants, minor officials, petty crooks, and provincials of all sorts. Peasants, however, appeared only as fleeting shadows in his tales. Although Belinskii's passionate urgings had driven

Russian literature fully into the realm of realism by the mid-1840s, Russians had yet to see a realistic portrayal in literature or painting of those men and women who comprised some 90 percent of the Empire's population.

It was in 1852, the year of Gogol's death, that Russia's peasants found their first literary portraitist in the person of a wealthy nobleman from the province of Orël. The son of a dashing but poor cavalry officer, and a local heiress who wielded despotic authority over her serfs, Ivan Turgenev grew up in a household dominated by his mother's tyrannical will. He knew what it was to see serfs flogged with the knout, sent off to the army, or forced to marry against their wishes and he had seen peasant families broken up and sold apart. Most of all, he knew the deep, daily agony of serf life, and he knew the manner in which serfs deadened its pain through the opiate of supreme resignation to their fate. They ventured nothing, sought to achieve nothing, and, therefore, stood to lose less than if they permitted personal ambition to rule their lives.

As a student at the universities of Moscow and St. Petersburg, Turgenev met Pushkin and Zhukovskii and was among those who heard Gogol fail in his attempt to become a university lecturer. He studied at the University of Berlin for several years and then, largely at his mother's urging, moved to St. Petersburg in the spring of 1842 to become an official in the Ministry of Internal Affairs, where he served under Nikolai Miliutin, one of the leading architects of the Emancipation of 1861.[53] Yet Miliutin's gradualist approach was not for Turgenev, and he despised his brief stay in the capital's chanceries. He aspired more than ever to become a writer, and during those unhappy months he met Belinskii, who urged him to write a series of short stories about life among Russia's serfs.[54] Turgenev took his advice. The first of his tales appeared in 1847, just a few months before Belinskii's death. Encouraged by its success, he devoted the next several years to writing others and soon began to think of publishing them in a single volume.

The year 1852 saw the publication of two works that had great importance for the cause of freedom and human rights in the Western world. The first of these, Harriet Beecher Stowe's *Uncle Tom's Cabin*, was a diatribe against slavery that reverberated across the length and breadth of America. *Uncle Tom's Cabin* proclaimed that slavery was cruel and utterly evil, that the precepts of Christian morality and the laws of human justice demanded its total abolition. The second of the great abolitionist works to appear in 1852 was Turgenev's, published in St. Petersburg, halfway around the world from Mrs. Stowe's troubled America. A collection of twenty-two sketches of life among Russia's serfs, it bore the innocuous title *Notes of a Huntsman*.

Turgenev's message was more muted, more subtly presented, than was Mrs. Stowe's, for it was neither in accordance with his literary style nor in keeping with the dictates of Tsar Nicholas's censorship for him to proclaim the evils of serfdom in blatant and ringing tones. In any case, most educated Russians were agreed *in theory* by the late 1840s that serfdom was wrong and that it should be abolished.[55] Unlike the situation in the American South, the great difficulty in Russia was not in getting people to admit that bondage should be abolished at some point but in getting them to agree that it should be abolished at that particular time. Turgenev's book played an important part in moving public opinion in that direction, for it reminded educated Russians, and especially serfowners, that serfs were human in every sense. Turgenev showed Russia's aristocracy that serfs were as warmed by love and torn by tragedy as the lords and ladies who bought and sold them. No one could read his poignant descriptions of serf life without feeling that these were noble and virtuous people whom fate and the laws of the Empire had treated cruelly.

For mid-nineteenth-century Russian aristocrats, it was awkward indeed to be confronted by such clear evidence that the chattels they bought, sold, and abused differed from themselves only in their legal status. An official report condemned Turgenev for "ridiculing the landowners, presenting them in a light derogatory to their honor, and, in general, propagating opinions detrimental to the respect due to the nobility from other classes." Nicholas ordered the writer to live in isolation on his country estate for more than a year as punishment for his book.[56] But Turgenev had made his point and made it well; Russians no longer could rationalize serfdom by claiming that peasants were somehow less human than those who owned them. In 1861, less than a decade after *Notes of a Huntsman* appeared and two years before Abraham Lincoln freed America's slaves, serfdom fell in Russia.

Notes of a Huntsman marked the beginning of Turgenev's most brilliant literary decade. More than any other nineteenth-century novelist, he painted the panorama of Russian society and culture in all its doubt, confusion, and conflict on the eve of the Emancipation of 1861. Serfdom was not the only problem he dealt with; one of his other great concerns was the issue of women's emancipation, which had emerged as a major question for Russians when the novels of George Sand first became popular among them in the mid-1840s.[57] Turgenev first described the woman who had freed herself from the shackles of society in *On the Eve* (1859), a short novel in which he painted a brilliant portrait of Elena, a woman of strong will and high ideals, who found the men around her useless, hopelessly pedantic, and utterly uninteresting. Determined to live up to her ideals of freedom, Elena rejected her several Russian suitors and chose instead Insarov, a young Bulgarian freedom fighter.

By Elena's choice of Insarov, Turgenev intimated that Romanov society had not yet produced men worthy of such modern women as she. Nor could it, so long as the conservative precepts of Orthodoxy, Autocracy, and Nationality held sway. Elena herself made that clear in her description of Egor Kurnatovskii, a Chief Secretary in the Senate, whom her parents wished her to marry, and who personified all the Uvarovian virtues. "There is something of iron in him," she wrote to Insarov, "something both empty and dull at the same time. . . . He certainly seems self-assured, hardworking, and capable of self-sacrifice . . . but he is a great despot. How terrible it would be to fall into his hands!"[58]

Almost two decades later, Count Lev Tolstoi developed a more focused, more vibrant portrait of the Kurnatovskii type in the person of Aleksei Karenin, the husband of the heroine in his famous novel *Anna Karenina*. Yet Turgenev's limited portrayal perhaps served a more important function, for it questioned the principles of Orthodoxy, Autocracy, and Nationality at a time when the system they supported had suffered a severe blow in the Crimean War. For all

Russians, the two decades after the Crimean defeat would become a time of searching for new principles. Those who urged Russia's cultural and intellectual development along new paths had many different visions of their country's future. Yet nearly all of them believed it possible to discover the laws that underlay society and governed human behavior, just as man had discovered the scientific laws that governed physical phenomena. Science became their new god as they embarked upon their quest.

Turgenev's most brilliant literary creation, Evgenii Bazarov, the central character in *Fathers and Sons,* published in 1862, personified this uncritical adoration of science that gripped so many young Russians in the mid-nineteenth century. The son of a poor provincial doctor, Bazarov was a university student who believed that science alone held the key to man's future. "A decent chemist is twenty times more useful than any poet," he once proclaimed, summing up his system of values. Bazarov was a nihilist, a term Turgenev coined to describe the new breed of young man "who does not bow before any authority [and] who accepts nothing on faith." Bazarov would argue that there was not a "single convention in our present-day family or civil life that does not demand complete and merciless rejection." Yet his nihilism offered no positive vision of the future. "At the present time, rejection is the most useful thing—therefore, we reject everything," he insisted. When one of Turgenev's "fathers" asked if it were not necessary to build something to replace what he and his kind would destroy, he replied, "That isn't our business. First, it is necessary to clear the way."[59]

Bazarov's nihilism destroyed him, for he died a senseless early death from pyemia as a result of his own carelessness and of the ignorance that pervaded so much of Russia. Despite the elegant palaces, monumental state buildings, and great statues with which the Romanovs adorned Moscow and St. Petersburg and despite the brilliant theatre, ballet, literature, and painting that their patronage had called into being by 1861, ignorance—abysmal, almost universal ignorance—was the greatest blot upon the face of the civilization they had created. "The masses believe that, when the thunder rumbles, it is Elijah the prophet driving his chariot across the heavens," Bazarov once said with disdain.[60] But such primitive superstition was only the tip of a very large iceberg that lay beneath the calm and ordered surface of nineteenth-century Russia. The country's fifty-two million peasants knew only the most primitive agricultural techniques at the time of their emancipation. They knew next to nothing about sanitation, public health, or personal hygiene. They lived in a world peopled by demons, ghosts, elves, and other spectral creatures, whose interventions were used to explain bad luck, good fortune, poverty, prosperity, life, and death. Almost none among them was literate, and therefore they were effectively cut off from the century in which they lived. Newspapers, the only means of mass communication available in the nineteenth century, could have no impact upon them, nor could they be instructed by them. In the entire Russian Empire, not more than 350,000 children out of a total population of 74,000,000 were attending any sort of school at the time of Alexander II's accession.[61]

The dilemma Alexander II and Alexander III confronted in the 1870s and 1880s was that if they fostered education among the newly emancipated masses they would increase many times over the number of Russians involved with radical Western ideas, especially since their predecessors never had bothered to educate them in a defensive, conservative ideology. These newly educated, Western-oriented masses could well pose a serious political threat to the established order. Yet if they failed to educate the masses, then it would become even more difficult for Russia to modernize. Alexander II, Alexander III, and their advisers embarked upon a new political and intellectual path in an attempt to resolve this seemingly insoluble dilemma. They charted their course according to Uvarov's old formula of Orthodoxy, Autocracy, and Nationality, which in the 1870s and 1880s became the basis for an ideological and cultural rejection of the West. Most obviously, this new direction took the form of Russification among non-Russian nationality groups in the Empire. It also involved a more subtle turn toward conservative nationalist themes in Russia's literature, art, and music.

The architect of this new direction in Romanov cultural and intellectual policy in the 1870s and 1880s was Konstantin Pobedonostsev, tutor of Alexander III and Nicholas II, whose greatest talent lay in formulating policy, not in creating an ideological justification for it.

Pobedonostsev erected his policies upon a framework built from the ideas of others. He drew especially upon the precepts of such Slavophiles as Ivan Aksakov and Feodor Tiutchev, as well as such writers as Nikolai Danilevskii and Dostoevskii. On the basis of their writings, he sought to create what he called a "moral union of the people and the government."[62] He insisted that this could be achieved only by destroying the cultural achievements of all non-Russians in the Empire, by repressing all Western incursions that might stimulate Russia's political modernization, and by persecuting Russia's Jews resolutely and without mercy.[63]

Although Pobedonostsev's cultural policy was reactionary, even obscurantist, it did reflect an attempt to heal the breach between Russia's elite and her masses that Peter the Great's policies had opened almost two centuries before. As we have seen, there were in fact two distinct, and mutually exclusive, cultures in Russia by the mid-nineteenth century. One had its roots in Peter the Great's social and cultural reforms, was generally represented by St. Petersburg's splendor, and had evolved into that brilliant elite culture of which the names Pushkin, Gogol, and Turgenev represented but a handful among many outstanding contributors. The other culture had its roots still planted firmly in Old Russia, retained many of its medieval qualities, and combined pagan peasant superstition with a fragile veneer of Christianity.

Pobedonostsev's efforts to recreate a common cultural base such as he imagined had existed in pre-Petrine Russia also meant that he opposed educating all Russians as befitted free citizens in a modern society. He urged that each class be educated "more in keeping with its social status" to fulfill its traditional role and was convinced that higher education would make the lower classes unruly by instilling in them "contempt for parents, [and] dissatisfaction with their own station."[64] He therefore sought to create the basis for a conservative society in which the religious precepts of Orthodoxy, the political and moral power of autocracy, and the messianic aspirations of Russian nationalism would fortify the Romanovs' Empire against further incursions of Western European ideas and culture. His was a sterile and retrograde policy, even within the context of conservatism. As the conservative Konstantin Leontev once remarked, Pobedonostsev was "like a frost that hinders further decay, but he would never get anything to grow."[65]

Pobedonostev's system appeared static and sterile even to his conservative contemporaries, but the minds of the men from whose writings he drew his ideas were far more vibrant. These men were instrumental in creating what might be called Russia's Iron Age of culture, a culture less glittering and less opulent than that of the Golden Age, but more solidly based in Russian experience and accessible to many more people. The art, music, and, most of all, the literature of this new culture were best represented by the paintings of Ilia Repin, the operas of Modest Musorgskii, and, most of all, by the brilliant and ageless novels of Feodor Dostoevskii.

Dostoevskii's life was as tormented and complex as the lives he chronicled in his fiction. Born a commoner in 1821, he saw his father rise to noble rank as a doctor at Moscow's Empress Maria Hospital for the Poor, purchase a small estate to publicize his status, and then die violently at the hands of the serfs he had mistreated so badly. Dostoevskii studied to be a military engineer, but retired a year after he received his commission in order to devote his time to writing. At the age of twenty-eight, he was condemned to death for his part in the revolutionary Petrashevskii circle, which never had formed any concrete plan for revolution in Russia but had spent a great deal of time dreaming about a better, utopian, society. Just before Christmas 1849, he was led out to the Semenovskii Square to be shot, reprieved at the very last possible moment, and sent to Siberia, where he spent four years as a convict laborer and several years more as a private soldier, before Alexander II permitted him to return to St. Petersburg in 1859.[66]

His suffering during the decade he spent in Siberia made Dostoevskii a devout Christian and a passionte conservative who despised all revolutionaries, and he would devote one of his greatest novels, *The Devils*, to a violent attack against them. Yet his personal torment continued even though his political views no longer conflicted with the government. During his years in prison, he had become an epileptic and suffered frequent attacks until his death in 1881. His first marriage, to Maria Isaeva, was a bitter failure, and he sought to erase its pain in a tempestuous love affair with a capricious, cruel, and beautiful woman half his age. Instead of joy, the affair brought him more pain, for his mistress tormented him while she could and then abandoned him for more docile, less complex lovers. In 1867, at the age of forty-six, Dostoevskii finally found happiness in a second marriage to his stenographer, Anna Snitkina. She became his angel of mercy, soothed him, nursed him through his epileptic seizures, and dealt with his many creditors. With her, Dostoevskii found a precious measure of domestic tranquility, but other crises continued to torture him. His incurable addiction to roulette kept him deeply in debt. Even as late as 1877, after all his major novels except *The Brothers Karamazov* had appeared, he did not have one-thousand rubles to buy an amazingly inexpensive summer house in Staraia Russa, a fashionable summer health resort, and Anna had to borrow the sum from her brother. Most of his novels were pledged to publishers, in return for pitifully small advances, long before they were written, and deadlines loomed over Dostoevskii's head every day of his life. He wrote *Crime and Punishment* in two years, *The Idiot* in the same length of time, and *The Devils* in three. Only with *The Brothers Karamazov* did he have a measure of leisure to rewrite and rework what would become his greatest book.[67]

As was the custom in nineteenth-century Russia, *The Brothers Karamazov* first appeared in serialized form in one of the country's famous monthlies. In this case, it was *The Russian Herald,* which had published Dostoevskii's other major novels, as well as works by such famous writers as Turgenev and Count Lev Tolstoi. The installments began in 1879 and ran well into 1880. Long before they were completed, Dostoevskii's fame had soared to a new peak, and his greatness was acclaimed everywhere in Russia. In a letter to his wife, he described the atmosphere that attended a speech he read to the Society of Lovers of Russian Literature in Moscow on June 8, 1880, and it provides some measure of the vast acclaim *The Brothers Karamazov* brought him. "When I came out, the hall resounded with applause and for a long, long time, they would not let me read my speech," he wrote with obvious delight. "At last I began to read: I was interrupted at the end of every page and sometimes at every sentence by a thunder of applause . . . and when I finished—it was not just a roar, but a howl of enthusiasm. . . . They all were embracing and kissing me," he concluded.

"They brought a huge laurel wreath, almost five feet in diameter, and at the end of the meeting over a hundred women rushed onto the platform and crowned me. . . . [Upon the wreath was written] 'From the Russian women about whom you have said so many good things.' "[68] The final irony of his life was that Dostoevskii had little time left in which to enjoy this acclaim he had craved for so long and so obviously relished. The emphysema from which he had suffered for many years finally overwhelmed him and, not long before Christmas, he suffered a pulmonary hemorrhage. He died less than a month later, on January 28, 1881.

Dostoevskii's startling literary creations chronicled a panorama of Russian life and experience that eclipsed all others in their diversity and vastness. He took his readers into the palaces of the rich and the hovels of the poor. He explored St. Petersburg's worst slums, the interiors of the vast government buildings, the deadness of life in prison, the empty existence of political exiles in Siberia, and the pettiness and nastiness of life in Russia's provinces. He analyzed the passions that drove men and women to madness and to saintliness and tried to understand what led them to murder, cheat, and steal. He asked why one man would drive his daughter to sell her body to carters and street sweepers and then squander her pitiful earnings on vodka, while another would curse his son for preferring a monastic cloister to a life of whoring and drinking. He explored why men became inveterate gamblers, why they rejected society when they wished to be a part of it, and why they sought to live within society when they desired to be free from its constraints. He portrayed the lives of great statesmen and petty clerks, rich lords and beggars, grande dames and whores, convicts and their jailers, thieves and their victims, as well as nihilists, soldiers, writers, and the many other human types with which the Empire of the Romanovs was so plentifully endowed. In Dostoevskii's novels, life was harsh, raucous, and cruel. It was never tranquil for long, and his characters rarely were even tempered. His prose never had the neutrality of Turgenev's nor the majestic sweep of Tolstoi's. Dostoevskii's novels throbbed, tore open the flesh of society, and forced readers to gaze upon its exposed nerves and jerking tendons.

But Dostoevskii was not content to portray merely the diversity of the society in which he lived. He sought to extract from his vast tapestry of the human condition profound and relevant conclusions about the purpose of life and the duality that seemed to him to direct man's very nature. This duality was both creative and destructive and could be found in the dilemmas of good and evil, the ever-present split between human and divine law, and the growing alienation of man from his God in the materialistic and technological society of the 1860s and 1870s. More concretely, Dostoevskii saw this duality in the split personality of Russia's culture, which had produced a westernized elite to rule russified masses by means of westernized institutions and laws. These were far more profound manifestations of *raskol* (the Russian term for schism) than that ongoing generational split between the "fathers" and the "sons" about which Turgenev had written earlier in the decade.

Dostoevskii identified this problem of duality in one of his earliest works, *The Double,* published in 1846, long before Turgenev's *Fathers and Sons,* in which he described the miserable existence of the humble clerk Iakov Goliadkin. Crushed by boredom, want, and unrequited love, Goliadkin fantasized a double who took on all the aggressive characteristics that his real *persona* lacked. Goliadkin's visions and fantasies achieved reality in Dostoevskii's tale, as the double became real and the real Goliadkin perished. But Goliadkin was not destroyed merely by outside forces. On the contrary, as one critic wrote, he fell victim to the "creations of his own mind, as do all Dostoevskian heroes who, like Raskolnikov (in *Crime and Punishment*), Ivan Karamazov (in *The Brothers Karamazov*), and the Nihilists of *The Devils,* seek a guiding force in themselves instead of turning toward God."[69]

That was one of the central issues, perhaps *the* central issue, for Dostoevskii. How could man live the sort of life that would enable him to attain salvation, whatever that "salvation" might consist of? At least on one level, that problem was at the heart of each of his four greatest novels. In the first of them, *Crime and Punishment* (1866), he posed the question in nihilistic terms that sought to negate the existence of God and enable man to find salvation within himself. Rodion Raskolnikov, the novel's central figure, was a desperately poor student who conceived of himself as one of an elite, in fact, as one of the elect. This elect, in his view, were "people obviously not made of flesh, but of bronze." By virtue of their great intellect, superior perception, broader vision, and superhuman will, these "extraordinary" men—the men of bronze—stood outside society and the law and thus could justifiably commit acts against society and the law that ordinary men could not. "If his ideas require him to march over corpses and wade through blood, then, in my opinion, he may permit himself to do so in all good conscience," Raskolnikov insisted, in defining such a man's sphere of action.[70]

To prove himself a man of bronze, Raskolnikov rejected society, attempted to live outside it, and brutally murdered an old woman pawnbroker whom he saw as parasitic, worthless, and evil. Yet he could not remain outside society for long; even before he murdered the old pawnbroker, he was drawn back into it when, on the seventh page of the novel, Dostoevskii remarked that Raskolnikov "suddenly felt drawn to people."[71] Indeed, *Crime and Punishment* was far more a study of Raskolnikov's forced return to society than of his rejection of it. In an important sense, *Crime and Punishment* thus became Dostoevskii's first major testing of nihilist ideas—and they failed the test miserably. Certainly they failed Raskolnikov, who found that he could not be a man of bronze and sought repentence, redemption, and resurrection through suffering in Siberia. At last he turned to God to find joy and happiness in his penal servitude. "He did not even know that this new life would not be his for nothing, and that he would have to purchase it dearly at the price of great future struggles," Dostoevskii concluded. "But here begins a new tale," he added, "the tale of the gradual renewal of a man, the tale of his gradual regeneration, and his gradual transition from one world into another."[72] Raskolnikov, at least, found that he could not act outside society and sought to reenter it in the distant wastes of Sibera at tremendous cost to himself and his loved ones.

From Raskolnikov, Dostoevskii turned to portray the perfect man, the true Christian, as he attempted to live within the framework of contemporary society. This was Prince Lev Myshkin, the central character in *The Idiot* (1868–69). Myshkin was openhearted and totally honest. He asked nothing from anyone and gave all he had to anyone and everyone. He was Christ-like in his manner and attitudes. His Christianity, Dostoevskii's Christianity, was pure and simple. Summed up most succinctly, it was, as a peasant woman once told Myshkin, that "God has the same joy every time he sees from heaven that a sinner is praying to him with all his heart as a mother feels when she receives the first smile from her child." That, in Myshkin's view, was "a profound, subtle, and truly religious thought, a thought in which the entire essence of Christianity is at once expressed. That is, the whole idea of God as our true Father, and the whole notion of God's joy in man, is like a father's in his own child—that is the most true and basic idea of Christ!" [73]

It was Myshkin's (and Dostoevskii's) conviction that this idea could be found "more clearly and more readily in the Russian heart." [74] But in the end, Myshkin's Christ-like goodness failed just as miserably in the real world as had Raskolnikov's nihilistic rejection of society. Because of his crime, Raskolnikov became a pariah and was driven to seek redemption. Because of his saintly nature, Myshkin also became a pariah—an idiot in society's view—who was incarcerated in a Swiss asylum. Myshkin's rejection by society thus was even more complete.

If neither nihilism nor Christ-like behavior offered the solution to Dostoevskii's dilemma about how man should live his life and what life's purpose was, what other alternatives were there? Dostoevskii was unable to answer that question when he published the final installments of *The Idiot* in 1869, but he offered a clue in the novel's last few lines. It was almost as if he were speaking directly to that unbroken line of Romanovs who had devoted themselves to creating a European culture in Russia since the time of Peter the Great: "Enough of this being carried away," Dostevskii wrote. "It is time to begin to use our common sense. All of this—this life abroad, this Europe of yours— all of it is mere fantasy, and all of us who have crossed over that boundary are just a fantasy. Remember my words! You'll see for yourself!" [75]

Dostoevskii did not specify just how Russians ought to use their common sense, or what the real, nonfantasy life should be like. Nor did he pursue that question directly in his next great novel, *The Devils* (1871–72). Instead, he returned to the men of bronze and the possibility that such men, whose nihilistic views negated all but themselves, could create a better world. Raskolnikov, of course, had failed. But Raskolnikov's failure had stemmed from his bitter realization that he was not one of the elite, but one of the herd. Therefore, the question remained: What could a *real* man of bronze accomplish if he remained steadfast in his purpose and loyal to himself alone? Dostoevskii examined that issue carefully in *The Devils,* a novel about men of bronze who had become possessed by their exaltation of will and glorification of self. Yet their self-possession ultimately led each of them to ruin and destruction. One committed suicide in order to express his absolute freedom and prove that man can become a god by freely destroying himself. Others lied, cheated, stole, even committed murder.

Each of Dostoevskii's lesser heroes in *The Devils* was destroyed by one particular attribute; for Shatov, it was absolute fraternity; for Shingalëv, absolute equality; for Kirillov, absolute freedom. But what if one man were to embody *all* of these absolutes? To test that hypothesis, Dostoevskii created the novel's central character, a rich and handsome young nobleman by the name of Nikolai Stavrogin. "Everything is contained in the character of Stavrogin," Dostoevskii once wrote. "Stavrogin is EVERYTHING."[76] Stavrogin, a true man of bronze, embodied all the dualities, all the conflicts that Dostoevskii saw in Russian life and in man's nature. He was capable of using people to his own ends and then destroying them without remorse. In some ways, he was the personification of evil in its coldest, most passionless form. As one scholar wrote not long ago, "Stavrogin's evil is reason without faith: cold intellect born in aristocratic boredom, nurtured during a scientific expedition to Iceland, confirmed by study in a German university, and brought by way of St. Petersburg to the Russian people."[77]

Stavrogin thus succeeded completely where Raskolnikov had failed, but his very success proved destructive. In trying to find a solution to the problem of life, Stavrogin set out to experience everything. He was driven by an inner compulsion to taste joy, sin, love, perversion, hate, pain, and tranquility, but once he experienced them, he negated them. "I tested my strength everywhere," he wrote. "But to what was I to apply this strength? That is what I never could see, and still do not see now. . . . Today, as always before, I still find myself capable of wishing to do something good, and I experience pleasure from that fact. But the next moment, I wish to do something evil, and I experience pleasure from that too. But both of these feelings, now as always, are too weak and never will become strong. My desires are far, far too weak. They simply can't direct me." So complete was Stavrogin's negation of everything and everyone that he could not even join the nihilist circle comprised of those lesser men of bronze to whom we referred earlier. "I could not be one of their comrades, because I shared nothing with them," he confessed.[78] Stavrogin soon found he had nothing left to live for; one day they found him in the loft, where he had hanged himself with a carefully soaped silken cord. His last words were written on a scrap of paper that lay nearby: "Blame no one. I did it myself." This time, Dostoevskii offered no message of hope, no alternative path of redemption. Stavrogin's self-destruction was a rational, dispassionate act. "At the autopsy, our doctors absolutely and insistently rejected any verdict of insanity," were the words with which Dostoevskii ended his novel.[79]

The Devils finally proved to Dostoevskii's satisfaction that men of bronze could not create a better world for mankind or, even, for themselves, because the logical result of Raskolnikov's and Stavrogin's theories was moral and physical destruction. But if the path he tested in *Crime and Punishment* and *The Devils* had led to destruction, the extreme alternative that Dostoevskii had explored in *The Idiot* had proven no more promising. Seven years passed before he produced his greatest novel, *The Brothers Karamazov,* which appeared during 1879 and 1880, creating an immense stir among Russia's reading public.

The Brothers Karamazov embodied an immensely complex and subtle statement of Dostoevskii's views about many questions that were troubling Russia and Russians in the 1870s, in addition to his tortured vision of Christianity, which was becoming vitally important to him as his worsening emphysema led him to acknowledge his impending death. The novel also was an effort to perceive where Russia was going. Finally, it was one of the greatest mystery stories ever to appear in world literature, a tale calculated to hold the reader spellbound from the first page until the last. Even a reasonable summary of this vast novel would take us far from our central theme; which must remain the culture that emerged in reaction to the Romanovs' patronage and policies during the nineteenth century. Still, two interrelated problems must concern us briefly. First, how did Dostoevskii attempt to resolve the issue he had raised in his earlier work about how man should live his life and second, what direction did he foresee for Russia? Stated another way, wherein lay the key to Russia's future?

Dostoevskii presented still another version of his men of bronze in *The Brothers Karamazov* in the person of Ivan, the second of the Karamazov brothers. Yet, unlike Raskolnikov and Stavrogin, Ivan's purpose in the novel was not to test a hypothesis but to present a conclusion about the type of man he represented. Ivan was well educated, fully Europeanized, and trained in the natural sciences. He was, Dostoevskii wrote, "one of those modern young men with a brilliant education, and a powerful intellect, who believes in nothing." Ivan, he later added, stood for "Europeanism" in Russia.[80] In a broader sense, he represented the epitome of everything the Romanovs had tried to achieve in terms of westernizing and modernizing their Empire and its people since the time of Peter the Great. But Ivan's "Europeanism" proved devoid of benefit. It destroyed his mind, his most treasured attribute, for he went mad like Prince Myshkin, who also had been Europeanized. Together, Myshkin and Ivan Karamazov represented Dostoevskii's answer to the Romanovs' aspirations to model Russia upon the West by adopting European thought, learning, and science. These borrowings were incompatible with the inner nature of Russia and Russians and could lead only to disaster. Even Uvarov's now sacrosanct trinity of Orthodoxy, Autocracy, and Nationality had emerged within a European intellectual framework, and Dostoevskii, at least obliquely, questioned its viability for Russia. In his brilliant chapter on the legend of the Grand Inquisitor, easily the most famous of any he ever wrote, Dostoevskii had his Inquisitor explain to Christ, who had suddenly and unexpectedly returned to earth, how the Church had corrected his teachings to make them conform more precisely to man's true nature. "We have corrected your work and have based it upon *miracle, mystery, and authority*," he proclaimed with pride. And, as if to fully impress Christ by the greatness of his achievement, he added, "The people have rejoiced that they were again led like a herd, and that that terrible gift [of freedom, given to them by Christ] that had caused them such suffering, had at last been taken from their hearts."[81] Dostoevskii's readers needed only substitute for "miracle, mystery, and authority" the obvious counterpart to be found in "Orthodoxy, Autocracy, and

Nationality" to translate the Grand Inquisitor's message into terms directly relevant to their Russia. Yet, although he made it clear that the Grand Inquisitor would continue on his chosen course, Dostoevskii also hinted that this cause was contrary to the inner nature of Russia and the Russians.

Dostoevskii's alternative to Ivan's "Europeanism" remained somewhat cloudy, but its outlines emerged in the person of Alësha, the youngest Karamazov, who had some of the simple honesty and Christlike qualities of Prince Myshkin. But while Myshkin had been unable to come to grips with the real world and could be true to himself only within the confines of a European psychiatric clinic, Alësha was unable to abandon the real world, even when given an opportunity to do so. He had tried to become a monk and had failed because he felt the compulsion to remain a part of society, even though he found its vice, lust, and baseness painful to behold. With all of its imperfections, he loved life and urged others to do likewise. Dostoevskii saw Alësha as one who stood for "the principles of the [Russian] people,"[82] not as they were, for he considered the eldest brother Dmitrii the personification of Russia at the time, but as a statement of what Russia could become. He made more clear what that meant in the speech he gave in Moscow to honor Pushkin's memory in 1880. "To be a true Russian means to become brother to all men, to become All-Man," he proclaimed. "It means the reconciliation of all European contradictions, the finding of an outlet for the anguish of Europe in the all-human and all-uniting Russian soul." This was Dostoevskii's vision of a future in which Russia would play a dominant cultural (and political) role and would lead Europe to a higher stage of development in which all those endless contradictions so evident in Ivan Karamazov's character would be eliminated by the establishment of "the concert of all nations in the law of Christ."[83] That was Dostoevskii's final answer to the goal he had set himself as a youth, when, in a moment of rashness, he had written to his brother that he would devote himself "to the solution of the mystery of man."[84] There was a rare flash of optimism, a joyful affirmation of hope, in the last lines Dostoevskii penned in *The Brothers Karamazov:* "and forever thus, hand in hand, for all our lives! Hurrah for [Alësha] Karamazov!"[85]

*

We cannot discuss Dostoevskii without devoting equal attention to his contemporary, Lev Tolstoi, the second literary colossus to appear in Russia during the second half of the nineteenth century, who also turned to the masses when his faith in the culture of the elite failed him. Tolstoi's background, life, and ideas were the absolute antithesis of Dostoevskii's. Dostoevskii had been born a commoner; Tolstoi was born into one of Russia's greatest noble families. Dostoevskii spent his childhood in Moscow and saw much of its seamy side, while Tolstoi grew up at his family's vast and beautiful estate, Iasnaia Poliana (Serene Meadow), some one hundred thirty miles south of Moscow. When Tolstoi visited Moscow as a child, it was to stay with rich relatives in opulent surroundings. He never saw that turbulent, churning, frantic world upon whose edge Dostoevskii balanced precariously for much of his early adult life. Tolstoi never knew the slightest twinge of want, while poverty was Dostoevskii's regular companion. Dostoevskii led a life of political conservatism in order to atone for what he considered a misspent radical youth. The young Tolstoi willingly accepted the Romanovs' social and political order only to become its avowed moral foe later in his life. Dostoevskii spent his last years close to the Romanovs and took pleasure in being one of Pobedonostsev's closest friends. Tolstoi devoted the last three decades of his life to opposing the Romanovs' autocracy and stood as Pobedonostsev's arch intellectual rival and moral nemesis. When Dostoevskii died in January 1881, Pobedonostsev arranged a state funeral to honor his remains. When Tolstoi died in 1910, Pobedonostsev had been dead for three years, but the excommunication he had passed against Tolstoi in 1902 still held firm. From beyond the grave, Pobedonostsev thus denied one of Russia's greatest writers the comfort of all Church rites.

Count Lev Nikolaevich Tolstoi was born on August 28, 1828. Fate denied him the comfort of parental love, for his mother died when he was two and his father when he was nine. His favorite aunt became his first guardian, but death took her from him before he turned thirteen, and another aunt took him to live with her in Kazan. In the fall of 1844, just after his sixteenth birthday, Tolstoi entered Kazan University to prepare for a Foreign Service career. The next eight years were chaotic and devoid of any accomplishment except in the dubious realm of "coarse dissoluteness, employed in the service of ambition, vanity, and, above all, lust," as he later recalled.[86]

For a youth who confided to his diary at the age of nineteen that "I would be the unhappiest of mortals if I could not find a purpose in life—a common, useful purpose," Tolstoi took a very long time to find one.[87] He abandoned his diplomatic aspirations at the end of his first term at the university (January 1845) and switched to the study of jurisprudence. Two years later, he abandoned the university altogether to become an enlightened master who bettered the lives of his serfs at Iasnaia Poliana. After a bit more than a year, he moved to Moscow in discouragement. By the beginning of 1849, he had gone on to St. Petersburg, where he vowed to finish his degree and enter Russia's service. Instead, he lost some of his smaller estates at cards. His aspirations changed at least once a month. On May 1, 1849, he wrote to one of his brothers that he planned to enter the Horse Guards as a cadet. By the middle of the month, he had decided instead to reenter St. Petersburg University. At the beginning of June, he abandoned St. Petersburg and fled again to Iasnaia Poliana. That fall, he took a position as a petty clerk in the provincial capital of Tula but was back at Iasnaia Poliana on leave the next summer. Soon, he abandoned his government post altogether and went to Moscow for the winter. Again, he talked about finishing his degree, finding a position in the civil service, and getting married. Instead, he went with his brother to the Caucasus, where he decided to become an artillery cadet in Russia's struggle against the native tribes.[88] After seven years of searching, Tolstoi had chosen a career. It proved to be the wrong one, and one that he soon would abandon.

Even when there seemed to be little purpose or direction in his comings and goings, an inner sense told Tolstoi that his life would not be wasted. "There is within me something which compels me to believe that I was born to be different from other men," he wrote. "Whence comes this feeling? Is it because my abilities are not in harmony? Or, is it that I, in some manner, really do stand on a higher plane than ordinary people?"[89] When he wrote these lines, Tolstoi had nearly completed his first novel, *Childhood*, which the famous poet and editor

Nikolai Nekrasov published in 1852 in the well-known St. Petersburg monthly, *The Contemporary*. Tolstoi's first success in literature heightened his self-esteem, and he began to think seriously of a literary career. Still, he continued to serve in the army until the end of the Crimean War.

The 1850s and 1860s were a time in which Tolstoi won considerable literary fame for a number of novels that were largely autobiographical. Perhaps the most critical year during those two decades was 1862, when he turned his life onto a dramatically different course. After several years of wandering in Russia and Europe, he decided to settle permanently at Iasnaia Poliana, explaining that "it is difficult for me to represent Russia and my sentiment for her without my Iasnaia Poliana."[90] At the end of September, Tolstoi married Sofia Behrs and brought her to live with him on his beloved estate. He was thirty-four; she was a slim, innocent lass just turned eighteen. They would be together until his death forty-eight years later. Sofia bore him thirteen children during the first quarter-century of their marriage and remained faithful to him throughout all his many intellectual wanderings and moral crises. Soon after their marriage, Tolstoi began to formulate his first great epic novel, which he would call *War and Peace*.

Unlike Dostoevskii, whose compulsive gambling and whining relatives kept him impoverished, obliging him to race from novel to novel to pay his debts, the wealthy aristocrat Tolstoi could afford to work at a slower pace. He also approached the task of writing in a very different manner. When Dostoevskii wrote, the words literally burst from him. Because of his temperament as well as his financial need, he was a frenetic, passionate writer, scribbling off whole chapters in a short time, even dictating some of his novels to a stenographer. Tolstoi was calm and careful, in search of perfection and intent upon achieving it. From late 1862 until December 1869, *War and Peace* occupied his attention. He wrote, rewrote, edited, and reedited his work. "For God's sake, stop picking away at it!" wailed his proofreader Petr Bartenev, himself the editor of a famous historical monthly. "I can't help messing it up. But I'm firmly convinced that this messing serves a great use," was Tolstoi's reply.[91] The result was a vast, panoramic novel, more than fifteen hundred pages long, which centered upon Napoleon's invasion of Russia in 1812. It was, the critic and philosopher Nikolai Strakhov wrote, "a complete picture of human life. A complete picture of the Russia of that day. A complete picture of what may be called the history and the struggle of peoples. A complete picture of everything in which people find their happiness and greatness, their grief and humiliation." [92]

War and Peace, an immensely complex novel with a cast of more than five hundred characters, can be read and analyzed on many different levels and understood in as many different ways. Among other things, it was a brilliant portrayal of the life and culture of the elite stratum of the Russian nobility during the reign of Alexander I. On that level, it can be considered a fascinating and vibrant portrait of the aristocratic, European-oriented culture the Romanovs had brought into being in St. Petersburg and Moscow by the beginning of the nineteenth century. The life these nobles lived on their estates, however, was far less central to the novel's plot and its development. *Anna Karenina,* Tolstoi's next epic novel written between 1873 and 1877, portrayed Russia's aristocratic milieu in a somewhat later period. This time, however, he focused much more upon rural Russia, and all of his portraits of the good, satisfying, and virtuous life centered upon the country, not the city. But there were other important differences between the two novels which showed that Tolstoi's concerns were taking a new and critical turn. He was about to reject the values of that aristocratic culture he had portrayed so brilliantly.

The most obvious hint of Tolstoi's changing direction was that the question of morality, relegated to a secondary role in *War and Peace,* occupied a position of prime importance in *Anna Karenina.* He chose a common enough theme in which a woman, married to a man she did not love, had to decide whether to reject or accept the embraces of the man who had captured her heart. Pushkin had posed the same question in the late 1820s in *Eugene Onegin,* his famous "novel in verse," and had resolved it by having the heroine, Tatiana, admit her love for Onegin but remain faithful to her husband. Tolstoi resolved the issue very differently. Anna Karenina abandoned the husband she did not love, went away with Vronskii, the man she adored, and even bore his child, to the shock and scandal of St. Petersburg's high society. Although she sacrificed wealth, position, security, and even the young son she loved, Anna's passion, Tolstoi insisted, was self-centered and purely egotistical. She sacrificed everything *to* it, not *for* it, and it eventually destroyed her. In despair, she threw herself in front of a train and was killed.

To further emphasize the destructive quality of such illicit love as Anna's, Tolstoi counterposed another love story to hers. Lëvin, a noble landowner who loved the land and the country life, fell in love with Princess Kitty, married her, and took her away to share his rural idyll. Together, Kitty and Lëvin brought their children into the world and watched the land yield up its bounty, while society looked on with approval. While Anna's sins brought her a gruesome death, Kitty's virtue was rewarded by a joyful life.

Tolstoi often used Lëvin to speak for his values. Yet Lëvin's eternal rural bliss with his adored Kitty was not to become Tolstoi's fate. By the late 1870s, he had entered into a struggle that would consume the rest of his days as he battled against worldly vanity, man's cruelty to man, and, above all, his own voracious, never-ceasing lust. As one of Tolstoi's most eminent biographers once wrote, he had been searching for God all his life, but "instead of sinning his way to God, like Dostoevskii, he had to reason his way to Him."[93] It was a far more lengthy and painful process as he sought to find the meaning of life in a world that was becoming increasingly complex in technological, social, and moral terms. In frustration he announced that death was the only certainty. Was there any meaning in life that death would not obliterate? If there was not, then what was the point of living at all? And would it not make more sense to accept the inevitable and destroy oneself without waiting for death to come of its own accord?

Tolstoi's search consumed the last thirty years of his life and cost him and his family untold anguish. In the course of it, he denounced his greatest novels and gave away the rights to all of his later writings. His search led him to study the physical and social sciences, the humanities, and the world's religions. It led him to review his past life, seeking out the motives underlying his thoughts, sins, and achievements. Always he seemed to focus upon death: the pain of death, its fearsomeness, its inevitability, its finality. Finally his quest led him to the peasants who seemed to face their end with equanimity. He dressed like them and sought to live like them. He rejected his past, Russia's aristocratic culture, Russia's accomplishments, and Russia's Church. But even when he had thus transformed himself, he still could not conquer his lusts and passions in order to attain that tranquility he so craved. Only in the year before his death did he cease to feel those sexual passions that had impelled him into the arms of so many cooks, laundresses, maids, peasant village women, and prostitutes of all descriptions and nationalities in many cities in Russia and abroad.[94] At the age of eighty-two, he abandoned his home and family to begin a final quest. He died on the journey, at Astapovo, an obscure railroad station far from his home. "Truth . . . I love it much," were his last words, whispered to a world that stood waiting for news that, like all others, Lev Tolstoi also had succumbed to death.[95] His three decades of searching thus ended at 5:45 on the morning of November 7, 1910. His had been a valiant and heroic quest for truth. Yet there also was an element of futility and irony in his long and anguished odyssey. "All his quest for truth and wisdom amounted to no more than a trip around *Iasnaia Poliana*," a critic wrote some years ago. "After having duly admired its proprietors, he ended by idealizing its servants."[96]

Tolstoi, bitter critic of Russia's aristocratic society and culture and the sworn enemy of all earthly authority, and Dostoevskii, the defender of autocracy and the Romanovs' cultural and political order, both turned to the masses as the source of those values they cherished and upon which they hoped to base Russia's future. Both pleaded for healing the vast breach between elite and masses that Peter the Great had opened by his policy of cultural westernization, although each did so for very different reasons. Yet they were not alone in their new direction, for radicals and conservatives generally attempted to base Russia's future development in the masses or, at least, to draw inspiration from them. This turn to the masses went beyond politics and literature into the arenas of painting and music, two other fields of artistic endeavor that had flourished under the Romanovs' aristocratic-centered culture during the first six decades of the nineteenth century. The rich kaleidoscopic tapestry of the masses' daily life and music attracted the attention of many. It became a consuming passion for the aristocratic composer Musorgskii and the peasant painter Repin.

Modest Petrovich Musorgskii, a wealthy nobleman whose father's estates in Pskov province encompassed some twenty-seven thousand acres, grew up surrounded by reminders of Russia's ancient past, studied at the Cadet Corps, and became an officer in the elite Preobrazhenskii Guards. There was little in his appearance as a Guards ensign of seventeen that hinted at the depths to which he soon would plunge in his personal life or the heights to which he would soar in his music. "His manners were polished, aristocratic. He spoke rather through his teeth, and his carefully chosen words were interspersed with French phrases and rather labored," recalled the composer Aleksandr Borodin in describing their first meeting in the fall of 1856. "He showed, in fact, signs of slight pretentiousness; but also, quite unmistakably, of perfect breeding and education. He sat down at the piano and, coquettishly raising his hands, started playing, delicately and gracefully, bits of *Trovatore* and *Traviata,* the circle around him rapturously murmuring the while '*Charmant! Delicieux!*' "[97] As a young man Musorgskii showed talent as a pianist, but he had no formal training in music theory and composition. What musical education he received came after he left school, and it was a scant one at best.

Of all the great writers, painters, and composers nineteenth-century Russia produced, Musorgskii probably lived the most tortured life. While Tolstoi had published *War and Peace* only when he was forty-one and Dostoevskii had not finished *Crime and Punishment* until the age of forty-five, Musorgskii would be dead six days after his forty-second birthday. Born rich, he died desperately poor. He was "very elegant and well-groomed," wrote the critic Vladimir Stasov's daughter in recalling her first meetings with him in the late 1850s. "Everything in him betokened breeding and refinement."[98] Twenty years later, Sergei Rozhdestvenskii, a young professor at St. Petersburg University who saw Musorgskii quite often during the last summer of his life, remarked that "he was always dressed very shabbily and a mutual acquaintance told me later that he often had to buy second-hand clothes for him."[99] Poverty, illness, alcoholism, and madness all joined to destroy Musorgskii, perhaps the greatest of Russia's realist composers, when his creative work had just barely begun. "He is such a physical wreck that he can hardly cease to be the corpse he is at present," wrote the composer Balakirev to a friend in 1879.[100] Evicted from his flat because he had not paid the rent and driven from the civil service because of his chronic alcoholism, Musorgskii was forced to live off friends who tried unsuccessfully to bribe him to finish the two great works he had been working on for almost a decade—*Khovanshchina* and *The Sorochintsy Fair*—in return for their charity.

Musorgskii's only completed operatic masterpiece was *Boris Godunov*, conceived in the heat of two great awakening passions that gripped him in the 1860s. The first of these was his love for Russia, for the Old Russia that had flourished during the centuries before Peter the Great had arisen to change her. His passion was kindled by his "discovery" of Moscow, which he visited for the first time in the summer of 1859. As he roamed the Kremlin, Red Square, the side streets, and the few broad avenues, Musorgskii was enthralled. "Moscow has taken me into another world, the world of antiquity, a dirty world, but one that none the less affects me pleasantly," he wrote to Balakirev. "You know I have been a cosmopolitan," he confessed. "But now—I have undergone a sort of rebirth. I have been brought near to everything Russian."[101] Musorgskii's second passion, conceived at about the same time, was perhaps even more intense. Like his close friend, the painter Ilia Repin, he dedicated himself to realism and, again like Repin, sought his inspiration in Russia's masses. "It is *the people* I want to depict; sleeping or waking, eating or drinking, I have them constantly in my mind's eye—again and again they rise before me, in all their reality, huge, unvarnished, with no tinsel trappings!"[102] While Tolstoi had claimed that man could not even hope to comprehend the meaning of history, Musorgskii seized upon it with a passion. From history he drew the theme of *Boris Godunov*, and from the music of Russia's masses he took many of the motifs that went into it. The same was true of *Khovanshchina*, the opera he never completed, which his friend Nikolai Rimskii-Korsakov edited and orchestrated after his death. This turn away from the aristocratic culture of the Romanovs was further evidence of a movement to create a more broadly based culture in Russia. It was one over which the Romanovs had less influence and of which they were much less a part.

Even more than in music, this movement characterized the work of a group of young artists called the *Peredvizhniki* (Itinerants), who seceded from the Imperial Academy of Fine Arts in 1863 to protest the restraints the authorities sought to impose upon their work. Perhaps the greatest among them, although he was too young to join their protest and entered their ranks more than a decade later, was Musorgskii's close friend Ilia Repin, who was born to a peasant family in Chuguevo, a village of ikon painters in Kharkov province. While Repin was still a small child, his father was drafted into the army, and his mother was left to support her children as a seamstress. As so often happens to a community where the townsfolk have little more than the servants they employ, Repin's mother earned scarcely enough to feed her children. Her eldest son thus grew up in utter poverty, often with no more than a crust of bread for his daily fare. Yet Repin enjoyed a certain amount of good fortune. The local authorities allowed him to attend the district's school for topographers, a rare opportunity for a peasant child, and he learned the rudiments of drawing there. His first real lessons in art, however, came from the village ikon painters. Under their patient guidance, he produced his first paintings, which earned him enough to pay his way to St. Petersburg, where he took the examination to enter the Imperial Academy of Fine Arts.[103]

Repin arrived at the Academy in 1863, the year in which fourteen young artists including the great Ivan Kramskoi, then aged twenty-six, seceded to establish the artel that marked the beginning of the *Peredvizhnik* movement. Poor, provincial, and unsophisticated, Repin at first had no contact with Kramskoi's brilliant young Turks, and he painted canvases on the classical and mythological themes his conservative teachers at the Academy favored. During the late 1860s, he worked especially on *The Resurrection of Jairus's Daughter,* the composition he would enter in the Academy's 1871 competition. At the same time, he worked at home "for myself," as he said, and the realist paintings he produced there were the ones he showed to the dissident artists he had begun to meet through his casual acquaintance with the sharp-eyed critic Vladimir Stasov, whose search for new talent was never ending. By that time, he already had begun to work upon his famous *Volga Barge Haulers.*[104]

Repin won acclaim for his official painting under the Academy's auspices, but it was Stasov who first called public attention to his work. The Academy's 1871 competition also included a separate exhibit of some of the canvases belonging to the *Peredvizhniki,* and in reviewing the *Peredvizhnik* showing, Stasov urged St. Petersburg's gallery-goers to go down the hall to the students' exhibit "where Mr. Repin's marvelous work, *The Resurrection of Jairus's Daughter,* stands out vividly."[105] Repin's early success with this painting was but a faint harbinger of the acclaim that greeted his *Volga Barge Haulers* when he exhibited it two years later. That alone made him the greatest among Russian realist artists.

Repin's *Volga Barge Haulers* portrayed a group of worn and broken men whose lives were rapidly consumed by the backbreaking task of hauling freight barges along Russia's inland waterways. So great was the strain of such labor that, in the United States and Western Europe, it was imposed only upon mules and horses, never upon men. Repin's haulers' arms hung limply at their sides in utter resignation, their faces reflecting the exhaustion, pain, and outright tragedy that consumed their lives. Yet there was one—the only youth in their midst—who stood out among the others by his utterly different pose. Back straight, head erect, eyes gazing beyond his suffering fellows as if looking into the future, his hands were clenched around the harness that bound him to the barge as though he were about to tear it off and fling it aside. "Mr. Repin is a realist," Stasov proclaimed. "He has become totally absorbed in the very depths of the lives, interests, and crushing burdens of the masses."[106] Stasov was notoriously prejudiced in favor of such art, and his comments scarcely were without bias. The true breadth and depth of the emotions *The Barge Haulers* evoked can perhaps best be judged from Dostoevskii's reaction to it. Dostoevskii, who rejected most *Peredvizhnik* art as crude attempts to assault the conscience of Russia's upper classes in order to make them aware of the moral debt they owed to the toiling poor, overflowed with compliments for Repin's work. "The moment I read in the papers about Mr. Repin's haulers, I got frightened," he wrote in an essay directed toward Stasov and critics of similar views. "The theme itself is horrible: somehow we take it for granted that haulers are particularly fit to symbolize the familiar idea of the insolvent debt of the upper classes to the people.

[528]

And I was ready to meet them all in uniforms with well-known labels on their foreheads. And what? Much to my joy, all my fears proved unfounded: haulers, genuine haulers, and nothing more." In seeking to evaluate the content and impact of Repin's painting, Dostoevskii analyzed each of the figures. His attention lingered upon the last hauler, the "drooping little peasant, creeping along separately from the rest, his face not even visible." This figure, Dostoevskii insisted, had a special significance. "This peasant," he wrote, "achieves the purpose —your tendentious, liberal purpose—much more effectively than you suspect! Some spectators will walk away with a sore spot in their hearts, and with love." He concluded with the promise that "this haulers' gang will recur in one's dreams."[107]

Repin had created what has been called "the icon of populism,"[108] and it was an achievement by which Russian realist art would long be measured. The many works that flowed from his brush in the years to come continued to draw from popular and historical themes. *A Refusal of Confession* (1879–85), in which he depicted a condemned political prisoner refusing a priest's offer of confession before his execution, and *The Arrest of a Propagandist* (1880–92) dealt with themes well known to those who were beginning to lead the early revolutionary struggle against the Romanovs' political order. Most of all, Repin captured the meaning of political dissent and the impact it had upon the dissenter and those dearest to him in a canvas entitled *They Did Not Expect Him* (1884), in which he portrayed in the most vivid terms imaginable a political prisoner's return home after years of exile in Siberia. So tragic were the features of the returning exile as he reentered his home and family circle that Pavel Tretiakov, the collector who purchased it, insisted that Repin soften their suffering.[109]

That Pavel Tretiakov should have been the one to purchase Repin's famous canvas was not surprising, since he was one of the leading patrons of the *Peredvizhnik* movement. He spent well over three-quarters of a million rubles on their works during the quarter-century between 1871 and 1897.[110] What was especially unusual about his patronage of art was that he was a merchant. Throughout the nineteenth century, Russian merchants had been viewed as boorish figures, concerned only with petty trade affairs, and uninterested in anything associated with culture or learning. Beginning in the 1850s, however, the sons and grandsons of those Moscow merchants who had attained success and wealth began to seek recognition through philanthropy and patronage of the arts. Pavel Tretiakov and several others began to support the careers of young Russian painters by purchasing their works, and Tretiakov even established a gallery devoted to their paintings that continues to exist in the Soviet Union as one of that nation's greatest museums.[111]

Nothing could have shown more dramatically the shift that had taken place in Russian culture between the Golden Age of Karamzin, Zhukovskii, and Pushkin and the Iron Age of Dostoevskii, Tolstoi, Musorgskii, and Repin than the patronage of the arts by newly risen merchant princes. Pobedonostsev's effort to create a national Russian culture by freezing society into a fixed position had failed, but vibrant, dynamic artists had taken the nationalism he and the Romanovs had fostered and had developed it in a creative and innovative manner. As a result, it was no longer the Romanovs, their Court, and those who sought to emulate its tastes and preferences who served as the chief patrons of art and culture in Russia. Russian art and culture had become national in a far broader and much more fundamental sense.

By the 1880s, the course of Russia's cultural development thus had moved far beyond the Romanovs' control, and their influence was confined generally to the negative realm of censorship. Russia's cultural development became more national in form and content, thereby reintroducing the nation's elite to that heritage they had abandoned under Peter the Great's prodding at the beginning of the eighteenth century. Yet this movement also had disruptive—some would insist, negative—consequences. Much of the clarity, predictability, elegance, and civility that Romanov culture had boasted at the beginning of the nineteenth century had vanished by its end. And those unchallenged precepts that had defined the relationship of social classes, the power of autocracy, the divine nature of absolute authority, even the nature and existence of God—all had been called into question. If Alexander III had managed to bequeath political tranquility to Nicholas II in 1894 because of his energetic application of police repression throughout Russia, he also left his son a nation whose cultural life was in great ferment. At the end of the nineteenth century, Russian culture seethed with excitement, as all types of artists searched for new values and new forms of expression. Their efforts would produce a Silver Age at the dawn of the new century, an age that would outlive the Romanovs and endure well into the 1920s.

CHAPTER XI

The Colossus of the North

When Catherine the Great died in 1796, she bequeathed a great Empire to her son Paul. Russia's domains extended nearly two-thirds of the way around the globe in a vast sweep from the Niemen River on Prussia's eastern frontier, across the rich grainfields of the Ukraine and the great steppes of Eurasia to the Bering Straits, Alaska, and California on the North American continent. It was by far the largest Empire on earth, and one about which Europeans were becoming increasingly fearful. Yet their apprehensions still were based more upon intuitive fears than upon the consequences of any direct confrontation. Such a confrontation had almost occurred several times during the eighteenth century, but Europeans and Russians had veered away from it as if to avoid hearing history's verdict about which was the stronger.

Although scarcely more than a skirmish in comparative terms, the first direct clash between Russia and Europe came within a half-decade of Catherine's death as her son abandoned her more careful ways and embarked upon a more reckless course. Paul had been Emperor for little more than two months when he permitted the Knights of Malta to reestablish their Grand Priory in those regions that Russia had gained by the first two partitions of Poland. It was an amazing step, utterly out of keeping with everything for which the Romanovs stood. Russia's sovereigns always had been champions of Orthodoxy, and sworn enemies of Roman Catholicism, even though they permitted large numbers of Irish and Scots Catholic soldiers of fortune to prosper in their military services. Paul's strange treaty reversed that position. In effect, the most pious and Orthodox Tsar of All the Russias became the patron of a major Roman Catholic military order whose first loyalty obviously could not be to the Russian Autocrat.[1] Yet Paul did not regard this new role as incongruous in the least, for he envisioned himself as a sort of medieval champion destined to restore the *ancien régime* world the French Revolution had so recently toppled. During the first year of his reign, he decreed that France must be humbled "for the safety of all," proclaimed that he "recognized the need to oppose in every way the brutality of the French Republic,"[2] bestowed a pension of 200,000 rubles upon the Comte de Provence who was destined to become Louis XVIII of France some seventeen years later, and offered asylum to Prince Louis-Joseph Condé and his émigré corps of some seven thousand royalists.[3]

Certainly it would be no easy task to employ such thousands of émigrés against revolutionary France in a manner that would destroy the Republic and glorify Russia. Paul saw in the Maltese Order a means for uniting these French royalists and Russian nobles into a great Christian crusade in which an aristocracy of birth, merit, and talent would march beneath Russia's double-headed eagles to crush the revolutionary foe.[4] Such an absurd dream could have been realized only in a world of utter fantasy, and Europe at the end of the eighteenth century was not such a world. Paul's infatuation with the Maltese Order and his dream of himself as a medieval crusader therefore cost Russia very dearly. Events of the late 1790s made the small island of Malta, a pinpoint of land slightly more than one-third the size of the five boroughs of New York City and home of the Maltese Order, into one of the most sought-after domains in the entire Mediterranean. To enforce his claim, Paul had to face not only France but also Russia's frequent eighteenth-century ally, Great Britain. Within three years, he declared war upon them both. A complex series of events forced him to face France first.

Late in the spring of 1797, a young French general by the name of Bonaparte wrote to his superiors that "the island of Malta is of major interest for us" and insisted that it was "worth any price," because it commanded a strategic location in the central Mediterranean.[5] With their approval, he occupied the island's fortress the following year and seized some six million francs from the Maltese Knights to help finance his famous Egyptian campaign.[6] "We now have in the center of the Mediterranean the strongest fortress in Europe," he rejoiced, "and it will cost anyone dear to dislodge us."[7] To dislodge France from this new bastion became Paul's greatest passion, especially after the Maltese Order elected him Grand Master at the end of 1798.

Although Paul was infatuated with the Maltese Order, his original reasons for opposing French ambitions centered further to the East. Ever since the French, again at Napoleon's urging, had seized the Ionian Islands during the summer of 1797,[8] Russia had faced a growing threat of French intervention in the Balkans and the very real possibility that the French fleet might breach the Bosphorus and Dardanelles and confront Russia's Black Sea fleet in its home waters. When Napoleon seized Malta in 1798, Paul ordered Russia's fleet to act in concert with the Turkish and British fleets in the eastern Mediterranean and agreed that a Russo-Turkish fleet under the command of his Admiral Feodor Ushakov should be sent to retake the Ionian Islands. Ushakov completed most of his mission with little difficulty that fall and, in late November, laid siege to the heavily fortified island of Corfu. Four months later, the city and its fortress fell in the greatest victory ever won by the Romanovs' navy against a land objective.[9]

While Corfu still resisted Ushakov's seige, Paul launched an even more dramatic campaign against his French revolutionary foes, and he did so in a region where Russian soldiers had never set foot before. By January 1799, the French had seized all of the Italian peninsula, and the Austrians turned to exploit Paul's anti-French fervor in an effort to regain their former territories. Paul needed little urging to send an army to invade Italy with the Austrians that spring. It was led by the legendary Russian Field Marshal Prince Aleksandr Suvorov.

Within Paul's spit-and-polish military establishment, Suvorov was a sheep of the blackest sort, a maverick of monumental proportions, who preached what Gatchina commanders cursed as rank heresy. Suvorov long had insisted that the way soldiers marched on parade was of little consequence so long as they knew how to fight, and he declared that the tight Prussian uniforms in which Paul had dressed Russia's armies were useless and silly. For more than two years after Catherine's death

Suvorov had lived in disgrace, but there was one point upon which he and his Emperor agreed. Both shared a hatred for France's new regime and a fervent belief that it was Russia's mission to free Europe from its revolutionary threat.[10] Paul therefore called Suvorov out of retirement when Austria sought Russia's aid and placed him in command of the army he had sent to Austria under General Rozenberg.

As a commander, Suvorov devoted himself not to his soldiers' looks but to their needs. He shared their life in the field, often drove them to the limits of endurance, but never asked more of them than he did of himself. Men were devoted to him. For Suvorov, Russian soldiers climbed rugged mountains, swam raging rivers, and charged enemy cannon. Time and again, they proved their devotion in campaigns against the Turks and the Poles in the 1780s and 1790s. They soon repeated all those exploits and more. Now aged sixty-nine, Suvorov proceeded to lead them on one of the most remarkable campaigns the world has ever seen.

Suvorov reached Vienna in mid-March, and by the end of the month he caught up with General Rozenberg's Russian divisions that were already on the march to Italy. Obliged to travel at a snail's pace for the last day of his journey over roads clogged with Rozenberg's baggage-laden columns, Suvorov reached headquarters in a rage. Cursing officers who demanded comfort in the midst of war, he dumped their personal baggage carts, drove out the hordes of whores and camp followers, and tripled the army's rate of march. As always, his tactics were the simplest. "Attack! Cold steel—bayonets and sabers!"[11] Those were his watchwords. He launched his assaults before dawn, in silence, with all possible speed, and without warning. In Suvorov, the ever-victorious armies of revolutionary France began to meet their match.

On April 16, Suvorov hurled his infantry and Cossack brigades across the Adda River, smashed the French General Schérer's forces, and opened the way to Milan. He entered Milan on Russian Easter to shouts of "*Eviva nostro liberatore!*" from throngs of joyous Milanese. In two weeks, he had begun a new advance against Turin, which he took by surprise on May 14 at a cost of only seventy men. His amazing victories were a much-needed tonic to allies who had known defeat at the hands of the French for too long. All the while, however, the supremely conservative and timid Austrian *Hofkriegsrath* continued to siphon off precious troops from Suvorov's command for useless minor siege operations in Lombardy. Desperate for manpower, Suvorov begged to recruit new divisions among the Italians, but the Austrians refused. With the Russians and Austrians who remained under his command, he turned to face the French armies of General Étienne Macdonald as they poured over the Apennines to link up with his main foe, General Jean Moreau.

Covering fifty-three miles in the unheard-of span of thirty-six hours on June 6, Suvorov threw his exhausted men against Macdonald's French infantry and émigré Polish cavalry with dazzling results. Reeling under his furious onslaught, the French fell back. Suvorov's boldness had won the day, and it soon would do so again when he came up against the main French force, now under General Barthélemi Joubert, at the beginning of August. In an immense bloodbath at Novi, Suvorov destroyed two-thirds of the French force, killed Joubert, and captured Generals Grouchy, Perignon, and Colli. He longed to press on, seize Genoa and the Italian Riviera, and strike directly into France by way of the Dauphiné, but his ally's shortsightedness stopped him. Again, the *Hofkriegsrath* refused him troops and supplies. They were about to remove Suvorov from Italy in the belief that lackluster Austrian generals could hold what the Russian genius had won.[12]

Late in August, the *Hofkriegsrath* ordered Suvorov to link up with the Russian army of General Aleksandr Rimskii-Korsakov in Switzerland. The Alps, and Marshal André Masséna's army of eighty thousand crack French troops, barred his way. Spurred on only by their love for their commander, Suvorov's men bayoneted their way through the St. Gotthard Pass and into the Hospenthal to fight one of the most incredible battles in the annals of warfare. In the face of well-positioned French artillery and sharpshooters, Suvorov and his men repaired the destroyed Devil's Bridge and forced a crossing of the Reuss, a roaring torrent that raged through a narrow gorge far beneath their feet. That same day, however, Masséna defeated Rimskii-Korsakov's army at Zurich, and the Austrians were beaten at Linth. Masséna's army now blocked every exit from the mountains, and Suvorov's situation appeared hopeless. Eighty thousand fresh French troops, well fed, well armed, and well positioned, faced some twenty thousand ragged, starving, exhausted Russians.

Suvorov's reaction to Masséna's encirclement was to order a breakout to the north and east. "Mikhail, you'll be in front, face to the enemy!" he told his favorite, Miloradovich, a young field officer who would fight on through some fifty more Napoleonic battles only to die from a Russian pistol ball during the Decembrist revolt. "You are all Russians!" he reminded his men. "Don't let the enemy get on top. Hit him and chase him as you always have done!"[13] That day, Rozenberg's starving infantry and Cossacks drove ten thousand French troops the entire length of the Pragel Pass, slashing and bayoneting them all the way. They left four thousand French casualties and returned with twelve hundred prisoners. Now only the elements barred Suvorov's way, but they proved as ferocious as the French. Only on September 27 did the Russian advance detachments reach Chur on the Rhine. Suvorov had emerged from his incredible ordeal with seventy-five percent of his troops and fourteen hundred French prisoners that his men had captured along the way. At the beginning of October, he at last joined Rimskii-Korsakov's battered army and took them all into winter quarters at Prague.[14]

Two days after the Russians celebrated Christmas in Prague, Paul ordered them back to Russia and abandoned his alliance with Austria. At about the same time, he began to grow disenchanted with the British because Admiral Nelson had prevented his navy from seizing Malta, and he abandoned his alliance with them in September 1800, when British marines occupied Malta for their own purposes. In reply to what he considered an open act of provocation, Paul imposed an embargo upon all British ships and interned more than a thousand seamen who were stranded in Russian ports.[15]

While relations between Paul and his allies were turning sour, several events made closer relations between Russia and France an attractive alternative. On 18 Brumaire (November 9, 1799), General Bonaparte had staged a coup d'état that established the Consulate. To Paul it seemed that France was abandoning her revolutionary precepts and that Bonaparte's rise as First Consul marked a step toward the reestablishment of some sort of monarchy that could stabilize European politics. "In the very near future," he predicted, "a King will be established in France, if not in name then at least in essence." "As far as closer relations with France are concerned," he remarked a few days after he sent the order recalling Suvorov from Austria, "I should be very pleased indeed if she would come over to us, especially if she were to do so as an opponent of Austria."[16] Quite probably to show his good faith, Paul dismissed Prince Condé's corps of French émigrés from Russia's service early in 1800.

Napoleon and his Foreign Minister Talleyrand were quick to respond to Paul's overtures. Bonaparte wrote directly to Feodor Rostopchin, then director of Russia's Foreign Office, that he intended to return six thousand Russian prisoners of war, "without any sort of exchange and with all the honors of war."[17] Realizing that the English were about to seize Malta in any case, he added that he would be pleased indeed to see Malta restored to the Maltese Order under Russia's protection. "Twenty-four hours after Your Imperial Majesty sends someone who has your confidence and knows your desires, and thus has the power to negotiate, the continent and the seas will be at peace," he promised.[18] Paul signed a treaty with Napoleon at the beginning of January 1801 and agreed to commit 120,000 Russian troops to a war against England.[19] Russia had gained absolutely nothing from two years of war against France, and she now stood to gain nothing more from her alliance against England. True, some of Paul's advisers envisioned a fanciful plan for partitioning the Ottoman Empire,[20] but no one with any sense of the real balance of forces in Europe could have taken it seriously. Only Paul gave it his enthusiastic support.

Although dramatic shifts and hasty about-faces characterized Paul's foreign policy, his domestic policy was more sensible and consistent. Count Panin had schooled him well, and Paul's lonely years of solitary study at Gatchina had not been in vain. He had a reasonably clear sense of the difficulties Russia faced and had some serious understanding about how to deal with them. "I fully realize that the Sovereign is a man like anyone else, and that he can be weak and have vices," he once said. Therefore, it was necessary, in his view, to have proper institutions, "such as the Senate, Courts, and such" to serve as the sovereign's deputies. Further, Paul insisted that the Emperor must have the advice of a council, "comprised of men empowered to deal with various areas and types of state affairs." But his recognition of the Autocrat's limitations did not mean that he intended to relinquish any power to such institutions as a State Council, Senate, or law courts. "The [State] Council," he wrote, "is not a place for legislation, but is to be established strictly to help the Sovereign and His ministers."[21] The Autocrat might share other men's frailties, but Paul continued to believe that his office placed him far above them. "Only the person I am speaking to is important, and then, only so long as I am speaking to him," he once told the French Ambassador.[22]

Unlike his predecessors, Paul paid serious attention to improving the conditions under which serfs lived and worked in Russia. In 1797 he forbade field serfs from working for their masters on Sundays and established the principle that they should work no more than three days each week in their masters' fields.[23] Although historians continue to debate whether Paul's three-day rule limited or increased the amount of labor serfs were obliged to render to their masters, the true significance of his decree lay in a more subtle realm. In eighteenth-century Russia, serfdom had been based upon noble masters' usurpation of absolute and arbitrary power over the persons of their bondsmen. They had the right to buy and sell them as they pleased, to rent them out to factory and mine owners, where they labored under the most terrible conditions imaginable, and to take any other liberties they chose. Masters had been known to insist upon having sexual intercourse with serf brides before they gave themselves to their husbands, and it was not unheard of for them to violate their serfs' bodies in other ways. In this world of unlimited power, Paul's decree represented the first effort by any Romanov to place legal limits upon the ability of Russian lords to exploit their serfs, and it served as a symbolic statement that their power was no longer absolute.

Paul aspired to recreate the well-ordered police state Peter the Great had attempted to establish nearly a century before, and which Frederick the Great had refined in Prussia during the middle of the eighteenth century. He therefore insisted that the first obligation of everyone, from the lowest peasant to the greatest lord, was to serve the

Autocrat. Nobles, priests, townsmen, and peasants, each with a clearly established legal identity and a definite function, were to comprise the inhabitants of his state. Certainly, he was not the "nobles' autocrat" as his mother had been. He had no clear preference for any class in Russia and valued each to the extent that it performed its designated function. In contrast to such slave-owning societies as the American antebellum South, where masters feared to educate their human chattels, Paul saw education, in which everyone would be taught "the extent of his duties and obligations," as a powerful instrument for furthering the state's interests.[24] His was to be a state that bestowed privilege only in return for service, and only in proportion to the service rendered. Its underlying premises were very different from those upon which Catherine had encouraged the Russian nobility to build their Golden Age, and the bitter resistance of the nobles to Paul's demands for service was important in bringing about his assassination.

Many of Paul's views about modernizing Russia's government and marshaling her human resources on the eve of the nineteenth century were taken up and implemented by his son, although Alexander I sensibly muted the coercive aspects of his father's principles. Indeed, there were a good many more similarities between Alexander's policies and his father's than between his and his grandmother's, and he dealt with his advisers in much the same manner as his father had. Just more than a year after Alexander's accession, his close friend Count Kochubei complained that "I feel that, as in the time of Paul I, I am in the position of executing orders which I am given." Alexander expected him not to question his policies unless invited to do so. "I am still reduced to saying 'the Emperor wants it thus' [and] 'Such is his supreme will,' " Kochubei confessed with frustration and a touch of bitterness.[25] Much the same could easily have been said by any of Paul's advisers at any time during his reign. Catherine the Great had been able to protect herself from such bitter charges by taking refuge in her feminine temperament. More than once, "a touch of the vapors" or "a slight indisposition" had served as excuses for totally autocratic actions when she thought the proper conduct of state affairs required it.

Alexander's early days on the throne differed from his father's in that his first concern was with domestic policy, not foreign affairs. "If I ever raise arms," he assured his ambassadors to the Courts of Europe, "it will be exclusively in defense against aggression, for the protection of my peoples or of the victims of ambitions that endanger the peace of Europe." "Never," he concluded, "shall I participate in the internal dissensions of foreign states."[26] Alexander therefore turned first to repair the rents that Paul's abrasive policies had torn in the fabric of Russia's society. He ascended Russia's throne proclaiming that he would "govern the people, entrusted to Us by God, according to the laws and in such a manner as would find approval with Our August Grandmother, the Sovereign Empress Catherine the Great, now at rest with God, whose memory We, and all Our homeland, will always cherish."[27]

Although Alexander vowed to rule in the spirit of his grandmother, he devoted much of his attention to implementing the administrative reforms his father had begun to formulate just before his death. Although he and his "Private Committee" failed to draft a "constitution" for Russia, they did create the framework for a modern central bureaucracy. On September 8, 1802, Alexander created eight Ministries to replace those Petrine administrative colleges that still remained at the center of Russia's government. A Committee of Ministers would help the heads of these new agencies to coordinate their work.[28] Although their titles sounded more modern and efficient, Russia's new Ministers still were to serve as the Emperor's personal agents, and the nature of their office remained very traditional. "In any unlimited monarchical state, it is the sovereign alone who possesses the power to make laws," Count Stroganov insisted. "His will in this matter ought to be limited only by the principles of natural justice and universal morality."[29] That principle had guided Peter the Great and every Romanov since his death. It continued to guide Alexander's successors, until the Revolution of 1905.

Despite Alexander's reputation as a child of the French Enlightenment, his understanding about how an autocrat should wield authority remained firmly fixed within the tradition of his seventeenth- and eighteenth-century predecessors, although his view of the society he governed was more modern and progressive. On February 20, 1803, he issued his famous Decree on Free Cultivators, which made it possible for serfs to be freed by their masters under certain conditions.[30] Even though it was a far more moderate measure than those he and his "Private Committee" had discussed at the beginning of his reign, defenders of bondage regarded this decree as a dangerous breach in the defensive wall they had erected around the nobility's most precious institution.

Like his grandmother, who also had dreamed of acting out her fantasies as a philosopher on the throne, Alexander found that Russian conditions imposed a far more effective brake upon his will than he ever had imagined possible. As he reached the end of his second year as Tsar, a gnawing sense of failure began to overwhelm him. In an effort to find those successes that had eluded him at home, he turned to foreign affairs. Soon, he became embroiled so deeply in Europe that he could not avoid sending Russia's armies into battle against Napoleon. As Paul had predicted, Napoleon had become a royal figure. In May 1804, he proclaimed himself France's first Emperor.

As a commander of France's armies, as First Consul, and then as Emperor, Napoleon showed himself to be a dangerous foe. During the first years of Alexander's reign, Europe's rulers continued to search for a sign or weakness or, at least, an indication that they had some reasonable chance of success, before committing themselves to a war with a man whose armies had won victories in all parts of the continent. They considered Alexander's armies an important factor in the success of any coalition against France and watched anxiously for his debut in foreign affairs. The British, especially, were attentive to any gesture he might make, for her statesmen were enthralled by the vision of their great navy acting in concert with Europe's largest army.

Coincidental with Alexander's growing involvement in European affairs, the Imperial Court witnessed a dramatic resurgence of the militarism that had been so pervasive during Paul's brief reign. Alexander had forsaken his infatuation with military parades and uniforms at the beginning of his reign for the chance to prove himself a philosopher on the throne. By 1803 he again had given way to his military passions.[31] Just as he had quietly summoned his "young friends" to advise him about enlightened reforms, so he now recalled General Aleksei Arakcheev from retirement. "Aleksei Andreevich, I need to see you, and ask you to come to St. Petersburg," he wrote to Paul's hated Gatchina drillmaster in the spring of 1803.[32] Little more than two weeks later, Alexander named Arakcheev Inspector-General of the Russian Artillery. If he was to confront Napoleon, the greatest artillerist of modern times, Alexander hoped to be prepared. He ordered Arakcheev to make Russia's artillery into a force that could overwhelm even Napoleon's awesome firepower.

For Alexander, life came to center around army maneuvers more than ever before in the summer and fall of 1803. "I am almost tempted, dear Mama, to date this letter *From General Headquarters,*" the young Empress Elisaveta Alekseevna wrote in the fall of 1803 from Krasnoe Selo, scene of Russia's annual war games. A week later, she confided to her mother that "with his taste for the army, [Alexander] is in his element here, and, when I see him so content and in such a good frame of mind, it makes me the same way very quickly."[33] Booted, spurred, and once again in the company of Arakcheev, Alexander began to see his destiny on foreign battlefields. If he could not now be an enlightened lawgiver in Russia, then he would become the enlightened emancipator of Europe and arbiter of its post-Napoleonic order.

With these new dreams in mind, Alexander drafted his famous Grand Design in 1804 and incorporated it into the instructions he gave that fall to Nikolai Novosiltsev, his friend and special emissary to London. Alexander's document represented the first of several efforts to establish a new political order in Europe. Among other things, he urged Russo-British cooperation in deciding the fate of the Ottoman Empire, the establishment of a German Confederation that would stand independent of both Prussia and Austria, and guarantees to safeguard neutral shipping in time of war. In his Grand Design, Alexander also proposed the principle of collective security based upon the "obligation not to wage war unless all means of mediation had been previously exhausted."[34] It was a remarkable document for its time and contained many of the principles that he would insist upon a decade later at the Congress of Vienna. Some of its precepts would again be presented to the world as new ideas in the twentieth century by America's President Woodrow Wilson in his proposals for a League of Nations.[35]

Negotiations between Russia and England dragged on for a number of months after Novosiltsev reached London. Then, in the late spring of 1805, Napoleon proclaimed himself King of Italy and seized the territory of Genoa and the Ligurian Coast. Infuriated, Britain's Prime Minister William Pitt agreed to pay Russia an annual subsidy of 1,500,000 pounds sterling for every hundred thousand troops Alexander put into the field against Napoleon. Russia and Britain ratified their treaty at the end of July. Less than two weeks later, Austria signed the agreement to round out the system of alliances known as the Third Coalition.[36] The stage was set for Alexander to take the field in his first foreign war.

Alexander and his allies very quickly drafted a grandiose plan for military action against Napoleon and put their armies into the field by the end of summer. On October 15, Napoleon surrounded and captured General Baron Karl von Mack's Austrian army of fifty thousand at Ulm. Six days later, the British Admiral Lord Nelson destroyed the combined French and Spanish fleets at Trafalgar. Nelson had made England undisputed mistress of the seas, but only if Napoleon could be kept from gaining access to the full naval resources of the European continent. If he could seize the shipyards of the Adriatic and the Baltic, he could construct a greater fleet than the one he had lost. Napoleon's first step in that direction was to seize Veinna and Trieste the week after Trafalgar. He then turned to finish with the Russians.

After Napoleon captured General von Mack's army, the burden of the land struggle fell upon Alexander's forces, especially upon General Kutuzov, commander of their advance guard. Kutuzov had learned much from the great Suvorov about the importance of aggressive warfare, but he combined that knowledge with a firm belief in the axiom of Field Marshal Petr Rumiantsev, another great Catherinian general, that "the objective is not the occupation of a geographical position but the destruction of enemy forces."[37] Kutuzov willingly forsook the glory of pitched battles if other means could destroy the enemy. It was a tactic especially suited to those moments when Napoleon's armies held numerical superiority. Therefore, when his advance guard of thirty-five thousand was outnumbered three to one by the army Napoleon had assembled outside Vienna, Kutuzov chose to retreat and abandoned Austria's capital to the French without a battle. His chief concern was to preserve his advance guard and link up successfully with the main body of the Russian army under Count Feodor Buxhoevden at Olmütz. He succeeded in doing so in mid-November, the day after Alexander had arrived at General Headquarters.[38]

At Russia's General Headquarters in the fall of 1805, Alexander provided dramatic evidence of his ignorance of warfare and his inability to judge military talent. His retinue included a number of young men who had made their way by brilliance at Court, and many were bitter rivals. Aside from their personal conflicts, all of these men were wretchedly inexperienced. Unaccustomed to field command, none had ever even been in battle. They all thirsted for glory, recklessly certain that they could overwhelm Napoleon with ease. They referred to Kutuzov as *"Général Lambin"* (General Sluggish) because he seemed so ponderous in his movements,[39] and they were delighted when Alexander named Austria's Chief of Staff, the dashing General Weyrother, as Chief of Operations. Weyrother was known in Austrian circles as a talented military cartographer who swore that he knew "every stream and every undulation in the fields" of Moravia.[40] The more able young Russian generals Bagration and Miloradovich remembered him from Suvorov's Italian campaign, when he had mapped for them a passage through the Alps. Confidently, they had followed his route until it had ended at a sheer mountain face with no way through or around it.[41] Nonetheless, inexperienced Russian officers were impressed by him. Prince Dolgorukii exclaimed that, with the fate of Russia's armies in hands such as Weyrother's, "our success is assured. We need only advance, and the enemy will retreat!"[42] Any knowledgeable historian would find it as difficult to share Dolgorukii's enthusiasm as did experienced generals at the time. Had they been given a choice, they would have cast their lot with "General Sluggish," who knew how to fight almost as well as Weyrother knew how to bow and scrape.

The morning of December 2, 1805 (November 20, according to the Russian calendar), was damp and cold. The temperature hovered near freezing, and heavy mists lay over the fields and forests that surrounded the small Moravian village of Austerlitz. It was the first anniversary of Napoleon's coronation, and he soon hoped to have another great triumph to celebrate. "If the Russians leave the Pratzen Heights, then they will be irrevocably doomed," he remarked to his aides.[43] For Kutuzov, it was a morning filled with gloom and foreboding. Like Napoleon, he understood the strategic significance of the Pratzen Heights on which the Russians were encamped and did not want to lose that advantage simply to gain the fleeting glory of being the first to attack. Yet he was obliged to watch the Russians and their Austrian allies launch their assault from the heights into the valley at precisely 6:30 that morning, just as Weyrother's plan, approved by the Emperor himself, specified. Soon after the attack began, Alexander rode up. Two of Kutuzov's adjutants, Prince Volkonskii and General Berg, reported several conversations in their recollections. "Well, what do you think? Will all go well?" the Emperor asked his commander in chief. Ever the cautious courtier, despite his often disheveled appearance, Kutuzov smiled and replied, "Who could doubt victory under Your Majesty's command?" According to Berg's account, Alexander gave an ominous reply. "No, you command here," he said to Kutuzov. "I am merely an observer." As soon as the Emperor moved out of earshot, Kutuzov evidently muttered in German to Berg, "That's really a good one! I am to command when I did not plan the attack and was against the entire idea from the very beginning!"[44]

Fearful that Napoleon would fall upon the Russians' rear as they advanced from the Pratzen Heights to assault what appeared to be a weak point in the French line, Kutuzov desperately tried to hold back reserves to meet the attack that common sense warned him would come. Alexander "the observer" negated his effort. Not long after their first conversation, the Emperor returned to Kutuzov and saw that Miloradovich's division had not advanced with the others. "Mikhail Andreevich! Why do you not advance?" "I am waiting for all the troops to form up in their columns," was Kutuzov's reply, since he could not reveal his real reason and challenge the wisdom of an attack Alexander had approved personally. "Come now," Alexander continued. "We are not at the Tsaritsyn Meadow, where a parade does not begin until all regiments have assembled." "Sire! It is precisely because we are not at Tsaritsyn Meadow that I am waiting," Kutuzov replied in a last desperate attempt to supply his soverign with a broad hint about his purpose.[45]

Seeing that his Emperor could in no way grasp his meaning, Kutuzov turned to order the full attack he had tried to avoid. Just as he feared, within twenty minutes Napoleon sent Marshal Soult's cavalry to occupy the heights and to attack Miloradovich's division from the rear. A French ball cut Kutuzov's cheek as he sought to rally his troops. For several hours more, the Russians struggled in vain in the cutting wind and driving sleet. By late afternoon, the battle was utterly lost. The tattered Russian army began its march eastward, its numbers reduced by almost thirty thousand casualties. Arakcheev's first efforts to modernize the artillery lay strewn across the field. His army in retreat, Alexander hastened to St. Petersburg, the shame of defeat so bitter that he slipped into the Winter Palace at four o'clock on the morning of December 9 so that no one could witness his return.[46]

Alexander's first effort in war had proved as bitterly disappointing as his first attempt to be an enlightened reformer. Yet, while he had been able to set aside his first failures in domestic affairs, he soon learned that he could not do so as easily in foreign wars. He had to endure eighteen more months of conflict, and several more ignominious defeats, before peace could be made on terms that allowed him to emerge with a semblance of honor. Not until June 13, 1807, did Alexander and Napoleon settle their differences at Tilsit. By then, Napoleon as well as Alexander needed peace to deal with domestic problems. When Alexander brought his Empire into Napoleon's Continental System in 1807, it appeared as if France's Emperor had at last gained control of Europe's resources. He now commanded shipyards on the Adriatic and the Baltic, and England's naval supremacy seemed far less certain.

Russia's domestic affairs had reached a crisis well before Alexander made peace at Tilsit. He had inherited a state whose finances were in a parlous state, and war with France had made them much more desperate.[47] War also had brought other serious problems. War weariness had set in even before Alexander ordered a huge national mobilization in 1806, and it quickly turned to utter exhaustion when he proclaimed the formation of a national militia of more than six hundred thousand men. At a low ebb when the militia was formed, national morale plummeted when Russians learned that their arsenals were so short of muskets that only one-fifth of the men in the new mili-

tia could carry firearms, while the rest would receive medieval pikes.[48]
An epigram circulating in Moscow that year showed how bitter and demoralized Russians had become:

Sin	—has died.
Goodness	—has been driven from the face of the earth.
Candor	—has gone into hiding.
Virtue	—begs for alms.
Charity	—has been placed under arrest.
Sensitivity	—is in the madhouse.
Justice	—has been buried beneath the ruins of the laws.
Credit	—has been bankrupted.
Conscience	—has gone mad and sits on the scales of justice.
Faith	—has been left behind in Jerusalem.
Hope	—with its anchor, lies at the bottom of the sea.
Love	—has fallen ill from the cold.
Honor	—has gone into retirement.
The Law	—dangles from the buttons of the Senators.
And Patience	—will soon be exhausted.[49]

It was an amazing statement of disillusionment with the Emperor whom Russians had greeted with such joyous hopes just a scant half-decade before.

Sentiments such as those expressed by the unknown Moscow epigrammatist grew more intense as nobles who had long been the pillar of the Romanovs' autocracy grew disenchanted with Alexander and his policies. There was much talk among them about stained national honor when Alexander made peace with Napoleon. "We could not maintain our honor by transforming ourselves into an instrument of Napoleon in Europe after we had pledged ourselves to rescue it from his tyranny," one wrote.[50] Even the Empress complained of Alexander's apparent infatuation with Napoleon and worried about the possible consequences. "He has a secret liking for his seducer [Napoleon], which pervades everything," she wrote to her mother at the end of August 1807. "Unfortunately, it is only the Emperor, and a small segment of public opinion that the seducer has conquered," she continued. "The majority have opinions and sentiments that are entirely the opposite." Ominously, she saw danger on the horizon. "The Dowager Empress who, as a *mother*, should have stood forth to defend the interests of her son," she lamented, "has become like a leader of a *Fronde* [a violent political opposition]. All the many dissidents rally around her and praise her to the skies."[51]

Surely, an outpouring of bellicose sentiment was an unusual way to greet a peace treaty that ended an unpopular war. Why should Russians despise a treaty that left their nation's territory intact and demanded no indemnities or other payments? The historian Karamzin spoke the reason for Russians' opposition to Alexander's new alliance in the midst of a lengthy paragraph about national courage and honor. "We should have accepted no peace save on honorable terms," he wrote, insisting that an honorable peace "would not have required us to break our profitable commercial relations with England."[52] Certainly, Alexander did not intend to keep Russia permanently a part of Napoleon's sphere of influence. What made his nobles bitter, however, was that while he awaited the opportunity to strike back, he exacted a very high price from them. Between 1805 and 1807, Russia's peasants had paid for Alexander's war with their bodies and blood. Between 1808 and 1812, the nobility had to surrender their prosperity as the price for his peace. Grain was their chief cash crop; the British blockade of Russia's ports cut grain exports by 75 percent and brought ruin to many.[53]

Alexander was not content to limit his demands for sacrifices from his nobles only to costly economic ones. Once again in quest of that ever-elusive crown of an enlightened sovereign, he took up the reforms he had set aside in 1803. This time, he set out to remove all of the influence peddling and blatant favoritism that had enabled the nobility to gain such an enviable position, for he realized that a government that functioned according to law and not according to the whims of aristocrats was needed to modernize Russia. He placed the impossible task of achieving that goal squarely upon the shoulders of Mikhail Mikhailovich Speranskii, whose name Russians had never heard in the years before Tilsit, but who suddenly emerged at the very pinnacle of Russia's government.

Speranskii, the son of a poor village priest, was born on New Year's Day, 1772, and educated at the Aleksandr Nevskii Seminary in St. Petersburg. He began his studies with an eye to a better position in the Church hierarchy or perhaps even a professorship at the Seminary itself. Certainly, he never dreamed during those days that he would one day sit on the State Council and the Council of Ministers or that he would come to bear the illustrious title of Count. He began his career in government quite by chance, when Prince Kurakin, one of Paul's leading statesmen, asked the authorities at the Seminary to send him one of their best students as a secretary. They chose Speranskii. After Kurakin's retirement, he became the private secretary and most trusted assistant to Alexander's close friend, Count Kochubei. At one point in 1807, Speranskii was sent to report to Alexander when Kochubei was ill. He so impressed the Emperor with his obvious talent that Alexander immediately appointed him his personal secretary. By 1808, Speranskii had become his leading adviser on domestic policy.[54]

Speranskii perceived the total absence of clearly drawn lines of administrative authority and accountability as the major flaw in Alexander's reform efforts. He attempted to remedy that shortcoming in the General Statute on Ministries, which served as the constitutional basis for Russia's central administration from 1811 until the Revolution of 1905.[55] But Speranskii realized that regulations alone could not produce effective administration in Russia's far-flung domains. He therefore argued that officials must be broadly educated, insisting that a modern and progressive curriculum be instituted at the Lyceum that Alexander was in the process of founding at Tsarskoe Selo to prepare young nobles for government service.[56] Equally important, in August 1810, Speranskii urged that officials not be promoted to those ranks that conferred noble status unless they held a university diploma or could pass a special examination.[57] Speranskii's efforts struck directly at the privileged position of the nobility; great nobles clamored for his dismissal. On March 17, 1812, Alexander acceded to their demands.[58]

Alexander's abandonment of Speranskii was the price he had to pay for rallying public opinion behind him on the eve of Napoleon's invasion. Such a confrontation between France and Russia had been several years in the making for reasons that are many and complex. Although Alexander's sister Ekaterina Pavlovna, Russia's greatest lords, and even his mother criticized him for his agreement with Napoleon at Tilsit, Alexander had begun to whittle away at the Continental System almost from the moment he joined it. Russia's increased overland commerce with France could not even begin to compensate for her lost trade with England and, by 1810, American ships had begun, with Alexander's approval, to take advantage of their neutral status to carry cargo between Britain and Russia. It probably was not coincidental that John Quincy Adams became America's first fully accredited diplomatic envoy to Russia at the end of 1809 or that the major portion of his duties in St. Petersburg dealt with the difficulties American ship captains encountered from the French.[59] Despite French protests, Alexander continued· to encourage American vesels to carry cargoes between England and Russia.[60] He was aware of the probable consequences of such anti-French measures and wrote to his sister as early as 1810 that "it appears as though blood must soon flow again."[61]

At that point, Alexander was considering an attack against Napoleon while the bulk of France's armies were occupied in Spain. Yet there was more to his plan than merely the destruction of Napoleon's armies. The day before he warned his sister that "blood must soon flow," he wrote an amazing letter to Prince Czartoryski in which he proposed to restore the Kingdom of Poland in return for Polish support in his attack against Napoleon. Anxious as he was to attack the French, he insisted upon written guarantees of Polish support before he would act.[62] Czartoryski could find little support among Poland's Francophile aristocrats for the cause of the Russians who had ravaged their homeland a scant two decades earlier, and the plan collapsed long before it reached the stage of serious preparation.[63] As a result, the alliance with the French would endure another year before the final confrontation—what Alexander once called "a war to the death" in his letters to Czartoryski—would be at hand.[64] By then, he had decided to await Napoleon's attack on his native soil. "If the Emperor Napoleon makes war upon me, it is possible, even probable, that we shall be defeated," Alexander once told Napoleon's Ambassador General Caulaincourt. But he added the dire warning that "We shall never accept a dictated peace, whatever reverses we may suffer." "I shall not be the first to draw my sword," he told Caulaincourt, "but I shall be the last to sheathe it."[65] Napoleon owed his greatest defeat in large measure to his refusal to heed Alexander's vow when his ambassador dutifully reported it.

Alexander's struggle against Napoleon marked his finest and most dramatic hour. It was a time when all his dreams and fantasies about greatness, heroism, and enlightened princely virtue seemed to come true. Between 1812 and 1815, he became the liberator of Russia, clothed in all the heroic splendor of Aleksandr Nevskii, that saintly prince who had saved the Russian land from a Western invasion some six centuries before. Equally gratifying, he became the conqueror of Napoleon himself. As Alexander rode with his victorious armies along the Champs Elysées and met with his Allies at the Congress of Vienna, no one could doubt the greatness and immense power of the Empire he ruled. Yet the very realization of Russia's vast power disrupted Alexander's relations with his allies during the last decade of his reign. Most of all, it soured Russia's relations with England, a nation with whom she usually had preserved close diplomatic and economic ties since the middle of the eighteenth century. As England came to fear Russia's new power, her statesmen perceived new threats to their nation's well-being wherever Russians and British had any political or economic contact. In Spain, in Italy, in Central Europe, in the Balkans, at Constantinople, in Persia, and in India, the British feared Russian intrigues, plots, and, even, military intervention. None of these threats ever materialized, but diplomats' fears established such an atmosphere of suspicion and distrust in London that England and Russia would be kept apart until the beginning of the twentieth century.[66]

There is no doubt that Alexander relished his new role in European affairs, for he had found there the greatness, glory, and success that had eluded him so persistently within his own domains. He now virtually abandoned his duties in Russia in order to play the part he so craved in Europe. Central to his effort was a system of international conferences, which the Allies at the Congress of Vienna had agreed to summon "for the purpose of consulting upon common interests, and for the consideration of the measures which at each of these periods shall be considered the most salutary for the repose and prosperity of nations and for the maintenance of the peace of Europe."[67] Castlereagh proposed the first of these conferences, which met at Aix-la-Chapelle in the fall of 1818. Its main objectives were to end the allied military occupation of France and to make France a partner in their further discussions. Again, Alexander stood proudly at center stage, not only the champion of France's restoration to the community of European powers but also the defender of the rights of a number of German states.[68] It must have gratified him that the proclamation ending the Allies' occupation of France began with the words: "In the name of the French motherland and the Emperor Alexander," and did not mention the monarchs of Britain, Austria, Prussia, or even France herself.[69]

Before other diplomatic conferences assembled, a wave of revolutionary outbreaks swept across Europe. During the first eight months of 1820, there were revolts in Spain, Naples, Portugal, and Sicily, as well as an unsuccessful attempt to assassinate Britain's entire cabinet and a successful plot to murder Louis XVIII's nephew, the Duc de Berri. Alexander spoke of the need for concerted action against the revolutionary menace, and became so caught up in the excitement of European events that a full year passed before he set foot again in Russia.[70] In his absence, his trusted confidant, General Arakcheev, directed domestic affairs in the Empire. Arakcheev could be brutally efficient in military matters, but he faced serious domestic crises that required his Emperor's personal attention. He used military couriers to keep Alexander involved with his nation's affairs, but it took a month to send a report and receive a reply, and that slowed dangerously the business of Russia's day-to-day government. Many serious problems thus remained unsolved or simply glossed over by palliative measures. Alexander soon would pay a costly price for his neglect.

Early in November 1820, one of Arakcheev's couriers brought Alexander the disturbing news that the elite Semenovskii Guards regiment had "mutinied" against their cruel and perverse commander, Colonel Feodor Schwarz. News of his favorite regiment's disloyalty convinced Alexander that an international conspiracy of radicals was seeking to prevent the Allies from dealing with the revolutionary threat. By the time the Troppau Congress had moved on to Laybach to continue its work in 1821, he had become a firm supporter of Metternich's effort to defend the status quo. He hastened to offer ninety thousand Russian troops to form a reserve for the Austrian army that was marching to suppress new revolts in Italy. Metternich encouraged him, not because Austria needed Russian troops to suppress Italian rebels but, as he later wrote, because Alexander's commitment of troops to the counter-revolutionary cause could be used "to kill Russian liberalism and to demonstrate to Europe that the radicals were opposed by the *two* powers still freest in their actions."[71] Metternich succeeded in his aim. Alexander's hasty reaction to the European revolts of 1820 cost him his treasured image as Europe's liberator. Most sadly, he lost it for no good reason. None of the revolts seriously endangered the security of any Allied government nor had they threatened the stability of Europe.

The Semenovskii "mutiny," which had been so instrumental in driving Alexander into Metternich's web in late 1820, was even less threatening than the revolutionary outbreaks in Europe. Only the most paranoid of minds could have considered it a revolt at all. Beginning in the spring of 1820, Colonel Schwarz had instituted an abusive regime that shocked even the cruel disciplinarians who filled the senior officer ranks of Alexander's army.[72] With grim abandon, he struck soldiers with his fists and, on occasion, was reported to have torn their moustaches out by the roots. In the brief span of five months, he condemned 44 men to an average of 324 blows with birch rods, when anything over 400 was considered equivalent to a death sentence. When he ordered the flogging of several men who wore the Cross of St. George, Russia's highest decoration for bravery, Schwarz's soldiers protested. In response, he imprisoned the entire regiment. Obviously, it was a case of soldiers complaining through proper channels as they had every right to do.

Forced to rely upon the fragmentary reports brought to Troppau by Arakcheev's couriers, Alexander overestimated the seriousness of the situation and sent all of the officers and men to line companies along Russia's frontiers. In doing so, he tarnished irreparably his image in Russia as a liberal prince who believed in fairness and justice.[73] "Some sort of evil genie slandered his good Russian people to the Emperor. He ceased to care for us, and, in loyal subjects, he saw revolutionaries," remembered one young government official. "The Emperor is only concerned with his soldiers," complained another. "He plays with them as if they were toys, never cares for their well-being, and wastes hundreds of millions of rubles on the army." Others saw in Alexander's strange behavior an irresponsible abandonment of his Empire and its concerns in a manner unmatched by any European monarch. "It is shameful," wrote one Russian, "that he personally goes to congresses to which other rulers only send their ministers." "What has his attendance at these congresses gained for us?" asked another.[74]

Part of Russians' disenchantment with Alexander was the product of their hatred for Arakcheev, a man whom many blamed for turning the Tsar away from his loyal subjects' needs. Arakcheev became the object of almost universal fear and hatred throughout Russia during the last decade of Alexander's reign. "Of all Russia, the oppressor,/ Of her governors, the tormentor./ To the Council, he's their mentor,/ To the Tsar, he's friend and brother," wrote Pushkin in a bitter epigram.[75] Others shared his view. "There was no corner his clever spying did not penetrate," wrote one young officer. "No one dared to complain. Let someone make the slightest murmur, and he would disappear forever into the wastes of Siberia."[76]

Clearly, Arakcheev's power exceeded that of any earlier Romanov favorite, even Peter the Great's Menshikov or Catherine's Potemkin. Some historians insist that he even carried blank sheets signed by Alexander upon which he could write out orders to send men to prison or into Siberian exile.[77] But those who saw Arakcheev as all-powerful during Alexander's lengthy absences were wrong to see him as an evil tryant who spent his days plotting personal vengeance against supposed or real enemies. It is true that he was incapable of warmth or kindness in official matters ("you ought occasionally to praise someone, if only by a slip of the tongue," one of his deputies once said)[78] and devoid of that mercy and charity with which Russians expected their Autocrat to temper his absolute decrees. Yet his loyalty was utterly beyond question. Alexander never had to concern himself that Arakcheev might be plotting his overthrow, as Counts Pahlen and Bennigsen had plotted his father's, and that was a matter of no small import to an Emperor who had no surviving children.

Arakcheev presided over Russia at a time of serious domestic difficulties. Perhaps most critical, the cost of participation in the Continental System and the devastation that followed in the wake of Napoleon's invasion and retreat had left the nobility in dire economic straits from which many never recovered. The amount of their indebtedness to the

Government Loan Bank doubled between 1802 and 1820, and then, as the crisis really took hold, it increased ninefold during the next twelve years.[79] Nor was the condition of the treasury much more enviable. Russia's unstable finances had been a cause for serious concern among sober statesmen at the end of Catherine's reign, when the public debt amounted to approximately two hundred million paper rubles. During the next twenty years, Alexander's grandiose foreign policy added another billion rubles to it, even though British subsidies had paid much of the cost of keeping her armies in the field. By 1823, it cost 15 percent of Russia's entire annual revenue just to pay the interest on her public debt.[80]

At the very time when Russia's upper classes were beginning to feel the pain of economic crisis, Alexander imposed upon them a regime of intense political and intellectual control that diverged sharply from his earlier policies. Especially after the assassination of the German dramatist and Russian spy August von Kotzebue by a student from the University of Jena in March 1819, he instituted a rigid system of repression in Russia's universities. His advisers feared that, since Russian universities were modeled upon those of Germany and had preserved close relations with them for three-quarters of a century, there was a real danger of Central European student unrest spreading to Russia.[81] Alexander hastened to agree. Under the direction of his close personal friend, Minister of Spiritual Affairs and Public Instruction Prince Aleksandr Golitsyn, and Golitsyn's special deputy Mikhail Magnitskii, repression began. Eternally vigilant censors drove professors from their posts and restructured curricula to eliminate all subjects that might breed free thinking or encourage criticism of the authorities. Magnitskii himself summed up the principles that underlay these new policies when he wrote, "It is evident that the Prince of Darkness himself has come upon us . . . The word of man—is the means for spreading this diabolical force. The publication of books is its instrument."[82] Magnitskii and his assistants set out to eradicate all sources of this "diabolical force" in Russia. It was a sad conclusion to an educational policy that, less than two decades before, had stressed the Enlightenment and the spirit of free inquiry.

Yet economic crisis and intellectual repression were not the only burdens Alexander imposed upon his subjects during the last years of his reign. He also denied them access to justice on an unprecedented scale. The backlog of cases in Russia's courts mounted, and the avenues for appeals grew endless for those who had access to power and influence. "Often one's life is not long enough to see the end [of a lawsuit]," wrote one Russian. With some bitterness, he concluded that "the poor man who is innocent becomes guilty, while the rich and powerful man who is guilty becomes innocent."[83] Officials in the Ministry of Justice received such miserable salaries that they had no choice but to sell justice and favors in order to feed and clothe themselves.[84] But there was little hope for obtaining better educated and more dedicated officials under Alexander's now oppressive regime. Mikhail Balugianskii, perhaps the first great Russian-born jurist, had set out earlier to establish a renowned juridical faculty at St. Petersburg University, where he was the first rector, but Golitsyn and Magnitskii had destroyed his attempt with a purge so vicious that it cast a pall over Russian jurisprudence for nearly two decades. Not until the 1840s would a course in Russian law be offered at St. Petersburg University. Even more discouraging, Balugianskii was forced to resign his post and the entire university came to a virtual standstill. Only four students graduated in 1824. In 1825 there were only two.[85]

Intellectual repression, economic hardship, and an acute lack of justice in Russia during the last years of Alexander's reign led to increased dissent, as Russia's noble youths became bitterly disillusioned by the discrepancy between conditions they saw and the dreams Alexander had urged upon them as they had marched to free Europe from the yoke of Napoleon. But the most telling statement of Alexander's failure came not from these young men but from Senator Pavel Divov, one of his own appointees, to whom he had entrusted many matters relating to Russia's foreign policy. On the day the news of Alexander's death reached St. Petersburg, Divov penned the following indictment of the monarch who had raised him to great heights in Russia's service:

> St Isaac's Cathedral, in its present half-finished condition, can serve as a true image of the government of Alexander. He tore [the old church] down because he wanted to rebuild a new cathedral from a mass of new materials upon the old foundation, but, at the same

time, he wanted to preserve a worthless part of the old marble building. This cost a huge sum of money, but they had to halt construction when it was discovered how dangerous it was to continue unless the plans were thoroughly revised. It was exactly the same with state affairs under [Alexander]. There was no firm plan, everything was done by trial and error, and everyone groped their way along. Everything that was good and first-rate was destroyed, and replaced by dangerous innovations, part of which were too complex, and part of which were totally impossible to implement. . . . Justice now is paralyzed by all kinds of regulations that have the character of laws but still cause general bitterness because they are saturated with a Jacobin spirit. It is very difficult to explain all of these incongruities. They only can be understood if one realizes that the peculiarities of Alexander's character produced them.[86]

Divov's comments made it clear that a very difficult road lay ahead for Nicholas I when he became Emperor on December 14, 1825. Suppressing the Decembrist revolt was in some ways the easiest of the many painful tasks that lay before the new Tsar.

Unlike Alexander, Nicholas did not hasten to implement farreaching or complex changes when he became Emperor. He was convinced that a new sovereign should at first follow the policies of his predecessor "without the slightest deviation," while he studied the issues and formed a proper judgment about the statesmen who served him. Only when that was accomplished should a new Emperor begin to follow his own course, being "in general, gentle, cautious, and just." "This latter term," he added, was "to encompass both toleration and firmness."[87] During the first half-year of his reign, Nicholas deviated from these precepts only once when, just seven weeks after his accession, he established the Second Section of His Majesty's Own Chancery and charged it with codifying Russia's laws, a task that had defied the best efforts of the Romanovs since the time of Peter the Great.

In contrast to Alexander, who had removed a number of talented and capable men from responsible posts during the last decade of his reign, Nicholas chose some of the best-qualified men in Russia to direct his new Second Section. Balugianskii became its head, but Nicholas placed the real responsibility in the hands of Mikhail Speranskii, now fully restored to favor. Speranskii's talent for bureaucratic organization made the Second Section far more efficient than other government bureaus, and his preference for talent over high birth meant that it was staffed by specialists in jurisprudence, a number of whom he and Balugianskii trained themselves, since there were no law schools in Russia. By 1830 they had completed the entire fifty-five volumes of *The Complete Collection of the Laws of the Russian Empire.* Just more than two years later, they and their staff finished a fifteen-volume *Digest of the Laws of the Russian Empire* as a reference.[88] For the first time in almost two centuries, the Romanovs' Empire possessed a code of laws that reflected its existing political, social, and administrative conditions. Most significant, Speranskii's and Balugianskii's achievement struck at the heart of the bureaucratic arbitrariness that had plagued Russia throughout the Romanov period of her history, for the tyranny officials imposed upon their fellow Russians could now be challenged and their decisions reviewed in the light of a codified body of law.

Although Nicholas professed to believe that Russians' relationships with each other should be governed by the law, he did not see that principle as a limitation upon his government's prerogative to invade his subjects' privacy. Another prominent feature of the system he established thus was increased surveillance over Russians' lives. To carry out this function, he established the Third Section of His Majesty's Own Chancery on June 25, 1826, his thirtieth birthday. It was to be the moral and political guardian of all Russia, to serve as an extension of the Tsar's personal will into every corner of his domain. General Aleksandr Benkendorf, his most trusted adjutant became its director, and under his stewardship the Third Section spread its tentacles far and wide.[89] A mere decade later, at a time when Russia fought no foreign wars and faced no known revolutionary conspiracies, Benkendorf had over sixteen hundred men and women under surveillance, more than a thousand of them for political reasons. The Third Section later extended its surveillance throughout the bureaucracy as the intelligentsia began to denounce the corruption of state officials and as Nicholas and his advisers became more fearful that the revolutions of 1848 might spread to Russia.[90] Mail sent from one city to another was opened regularly, so that police agents might more accurately gauge public opinion and maintain a vigilant watch for the development of conspiracies. By the early 1850s, the chief of the Third Section even detailed an agent to keep Nicholas's second son, Grand Duke Konstantin Nikolaevich, under regular watch. On a number of occasions, this agent clandestinely examined even the secret files Konstantin kept in his private office as Chief of Russia's navy.[91]

This, of course, was done without Nicholas's knowledge. That a Grand Duke was spied upon, even when discovery would have meant utter ruin for those who ordered it, is further evidence that not even so stern an autocrat as Nicholas could control the bureaucratic police apparatus he had unleashed upon Russia in 1826. Since there existed an agency designated as Russia's first guardian against sedition, it followed logically in the minds of the secret police that such sedition must exist. If it did not, then there would be no reason for maintaining such an organization, whose perpetuation obviously involved the livelihoods of many officials.

Once Nicholas had dealt with the Decembrists, created an agency to codify Russia's laws, and taken steps to protect the internal security of his realm through surveillance, he turned to broader questions of domestic reform. In contrast to Alexander, who had assembled his "Private Committee" to plan reforms according to preconceived models, Nicholas ordered a group of senior officials and trusted adjutants to decide what needed to be reformed and how reforms might best be undertaken. This was the famous Committee of December 6, 1826, which included Speranskii, Kochubei, Dmitrii Bludov, Generals Vasilchikov and Dibich, and several other high officials. At no other time during the entire nineteenth century did any Romanov delegate such broad authority for reviewing the social and political situation in Russia and making recommendations for its improvement. Yet the Committee suffered from a flaw that condemned its efforts to failure from the very beginning. Because all of its members considered the Romanov's political system sound, none of them ever contemplated any serious attempt to modernize the manner in which Russia was governed. Their major task, Speranskii reminded them, was "not the full alteration of the existing order or government, but its refinement by means of a few particular changes and additions."[92]

Nicholas based his government upon those very precepts of enlightened conservatism that had proved so vulnerable to revolutionary attack in Europe, and he carried them into the diplomatic arena, where he and his ambassadors were obliged to confront Europe's revolutions much more directly. Again in contrast to his elder brother, who had seen Russia's international security as part of a European system, Nicholas preferred to leave the Europeans to themselves. Much like his Soviet successors, he attempted to construct a *cordon sanitaire* from the Baltic to the Adriatic to insulate Russia from those aspects of Western political life he considered dangerous. To achieve that aim, Nicholas insisted upon acting as his own Foreign Minister from the moment he summoned St. Petersburg's European diplomats to the Winter Palace to hear an account of the Decembrist revolt.

As a diplomat, Nicholas could be utterly charming when it suited his purpose, while revealing himself very little. He could also be extremely blunt, even brutal, as would become very quickly evident in his dealings with the Ottoman Empire. Whereas Alexander had engaged in protracted negotiations with the Sultan about his refusal to evacuate Turkish troops from the Danubian principalities of Wallachia and Moldavia, Nicholas simply gave the Sultan an ultimatum that Turkish troops must evacuate the Danubian principalities within six weeks and that Turkish representatives must conclude those discussions that had been going on without result for a decade. The Sultan conceded without delay, withdrew his troops, and sent his representatives to begin formal negotiations at Akkerman. Nicholas then presented another ultimatum. This time he insisted that the Turks accept his proposals to settle all disputes between Russia and the Ottoman Empire within three months. Again, the Sultan agreed, and in September 1826 signed the Akkerman Convention by which he vowed to observe Turkey's earlier treaty obligations and to grant Russian merchantmen free passage through the Straits.[93] Nicholas's first venture in foreign affairs seemed brilliantly successful; he had issued his orders and the Sultan had obeyed. It must have been an intoxicating experience for a young man still several months short of his thirtieth birthday, who, as recently as nine months before, had been nothing more than the Commander of the Imperial Russian Army Engineers.

But there were other very complex issues involved in Russia's relations with the Sublime Porte in 1826 that were far more responsible for Nicholas's success than his insensitive demands. Most important, the Greeks were in revolt against their Ottoman overlords, and much of Europe supported them. Although he had a strong distaste for the Greeks, Nicholas hastened to join France and England in support of their cause.[94] With all of Europe's Great Powers arrayed against him in the Balkans, the Sultan had little choice but submit to Nicholas's arrogantly stated demands at Akkerman. When the British and French turned away from Russia a year later, Nicholas paid a high price for his blunt diplomacy. At that point, the Sultan disavowed the Akkerman treaty and summoned all faithful Muslims, "rich and poor, great and small" to a Holy War against the Russian infidel.[95] After miscalculating at Akkerman, Nicholas erred again by assuming that the Sultan would not translate his proclamation into armed conflict. To his surprise, the Sultan mobilized his armies, moving large trains of men and supplies northward throughout the early months of 1828 to strengthen his garrisons in the Balkans.

Unable to ignore this growing menace on his southwestern frontier, Nicholas ordered his commander in chief Field Marshal Count Petr Wittgenstein to cross the Pruth River into the Danubian principalities at the end of April. In less than a fortnight, he joined his armies near the Turkish fortress of Braila, anxious to prove himself a commander in battle as well as on the parade ground. It proved a painful and sobering experience, for he had never witnessed the bloody battles of the Napoleonic Wars and did not know how brutal war was. Nor did he learn that hard truth during the early days of the Balkan campaign as Russia's armies seized six Turkish fortresses during the first six weeks of the war. Everywhere, his men sprang to the attack with cheers for Tsar and country. Just as Russia's armies seemed invincible on the parade ground when they marched and wheeled in the tens of thousands, so they seemed invincible in the Balkans in the spring of 1828.

As any military expert who witnessed the inadequacy of Russia's preparations could have predicted, the heady wine of victory began to sour as summer reached its peak, and Nicholas's soldiers fell victim to dysentery and typhus. Rashly overconfident, he ordered his armies to besiege the Turkish fortesses of Varna, Shumla, and Silestria simultaneously, and it was there, with his armies' resources stretched to the breaking point, that he saw men torn apart by cannon shot, split open by sabers, and wasted away by the thousands as dysentery gripped their bowels and fever parched them in the broiling heat of the Balkan summer. Nicolas proved himself brave and calm under fire on a number of occasions during those bitter weeks, but the summer of 1828 showed him that he was not a great general. It was the lesson Alexander had failed to learn after his defeat at Austerlitz, but one Nicholas learned quickly. Never again would he lead troops in the field, and never again would he desert the day-to-day affairs of his Empire in search of glory on the battlefield. When Russia's armies returned to conquer the Turks in 1829, he remained in St. Petersubrg and left the army to General Count Ivan Dibich. In August 1829, Dibich imposed upon the Turks the Treaty of Adrianople, which guranteed Russian freedom to sail the Black Sea, granted practical autonomy to Moldavia and Wallachia, and paved the way for Greece to become independent.[96]

The Treaty of Adrianople made Russia the dominant power in the Near East for the first time in her history. "Russia dominates the world today," Lord Aberdeen commented ruefully to the wife of Nicholas's Ambassador to St. James soon afterward.[97] Yet these victories did not win for Nicholas more than a brief respite from the turmoil of international crises. Soon he faced a far more serious threat within the domains he ruled as King of Poland. On the night of November 29, 1830, revolution erupted in the streets of Warsaw. By all accounts, it should have been crushed·immediately, because the handful of Polish conspirators led by Piotr Wysocki lacked men, organization, and experienced leadership; Wysocki could not find a single senior officer in all of Warsaw to lead his forces. But two factors unexpectedly turned the tide in favor of his tiny band of inexperienced military cadets. Angered by soaring food prices, the Warsaw crowd joined the rebel cause. At the same time, and for reasons that no one has yet explained, Grand Duke Konstantin Pavlovich, Nicholas's Viceroy in Warsaw, refused to order the sixteen thousand crack troops under his command into action against the rebels. Konstantin fled from Warsaw a few hours after the revolt broke out. Ecstatic at their unexpected triumph, Warsaw's citizens seized the city arsenal with its thirty thousand muskets and poured through the streets unchallenged by any of the Grand Duke's troops.

While Konstantin retreated eastward into Russia, the Poles, knowing they could never match the might of Nicholas's armies in a sustained campaign, looked to Europe for aid in their declaration of independence. Their rebellion would be heroic, passionately patriotic, and utterly hopeless. Thousands of fervent patriots donned the red and white colors of a free Poland and raised their voices by the tens of thousands to sing "Poland has not yet perished, so long as we still live." It was the anthem Kósciuszko's rebels had sung as they marched against Catherine's regulars in the 1790s, and it would be sung again and again during Poland's history. As always, the statesmen of the West spoke fervent words in support of Poland's cause and cursed the brutality of the Romanovs' policies. As always, when the time came to transform rhetoric into deeds, the Great Powers did nothing.

Even though the Poles stood alone, Nicholas could not crush them in an instant and had to pay for Konstantin's timidity with a bloody nine-month campaign, which left legions of Russian soldiers dead from wounds and disease. Throughout the summer of 1831, cholera ravaged the Russian army, killing thousands and weakening thousands more. Nor was it confined only to the rank and file. That summer, cholera claimed Grand Duke Konstantin and Nicholas's commander in chief, General Dibich. Field Marshal Prince Ivan Paskevich, the general who had led Russia's armies to victory against Persia in 1827, became the officer to lead Nicholas's troops back across the fields and forests of Eastern Poland to the gates of Warsaw. By the end of August, he had crushed all resistance, and those rebels who survived fled to Prussia, Austria, or France. "Warsaw is at the feet of Your Imperial Majesty," Paskevich reported in another of his famous victory bulletins. "From this day forth," Nicholas replied, "you will be known as the Most Illustrious Prince of Warsaw."[98]

After he had crushed revolution in Poland, Nicholas turned to erect a barrier against it in Europe, for he knew full well that the revolutions of 1830 had driven the final nail into the coffin of that Holy Alliance system in which Alexander had placed such faith. England and France were parliamentary governments, while the three Eastern Powers—Austria, Prussia, and Russia—remained absolute monarchies.

That simple fact assumed overriding importance in the face of Europe's revolutionary upheavals. "There exists in Europe only one issue of any moment," wrote Metternich in the fall of 1830, "and that is Revolution." [99] The nature of their political systems obliged Russia, Prussia, and Austria to confront that issue in a manner very different from that chosen by England and France, and the Polish revolt reminded them even more pointedly how closely their interests were connected. They all had Poles living within their borders as a result of the eighteen-century partitions of Poland, and an outbreak of revolution in the Polish territories of one nation threatened the stability of them all.

This led Nicholas to decide upon a meeting with the Austrian Emperor Franz at Münchengrätz in September 1833. In consultation with their foreign ministers, the two men agreed to act jointly to preserve the Ottoman Empire should it fall before the attacks of the Sultan's rebellious Egyptian vassal Mehemet Ali or some other force and to come to each other's aid if revolution broke out in their Polish provinces. Less than a month later, the Prussian King Frederick William joined them when he signed the Berlin Convention. Nicholas and his two fellow monarchs had committed themselves to defend the status quo in Central and Eastern Europe. [100]

For Nicholas, the conclusion of the Münchengrätz and Berlin agreements marked the culmination of eight years of long diplomatic labors designed to protect Russia from the menace of the West. He had inherited an anomalous situation in Poland, a complex series of conflicts with the Ottoman Empire in the Balkans, a threatening situation in the Transcaucasus, where Persia was about to fall upon Russia's outlying provinces, and a system of relations with Western European states that conflicted with Russia's best interests. By 1833 he had turned this unstable heritage into a conservative, balanced system of alliances. As a result of these diplomatic achievements, from 1831 until 1849 Russia faced no major wars apart from the annual campaigns against the troublesome natives of the Caucasus. The turmoil of the Napoleonic Era and the unsettled times of the Holy Alliance were past. Something resembling a "pax Nicholeana" descended upon Central and Eastern Europe as Nicholas led Russia into a period of economic progress and domestic tranquility.

During the two decades that separated the European revolutions of 1830 and 1848, the crucial question Nicholas faced was how the Romanovs' Russia could meet the challenges posed by the industrializing nations of the West. Even he realized that serfdom was a major obstacle to progress in Russia and publicly said so at a meeting of the State Council in 1842. "There is no doubt that serfdom in the form in which we have it now, is clearly and obviously bad for everyone," he admitted. Yet the solution to this one problem might well create others of greater magnitude. "To attack [serfdom] at this point," he warned, "would be even more destructive," because "a decisive suppression of [serfdom] is impossible without general upheavals."[101]

Nicholas hoped to modernize Russia by "a gradual transformation to another order of things," but two factors interfered.[102] First, he feared that the nobility might rebel if he placed any serious limits upon their power over their serfs. His father's murder and the circumstances of his own accession had shown him the dangers of aristocratic discontent. Yet his success against the Decembrists also had convinced him that he could deal with an aristocratic revolt so long as the army remained loyal. More threatening, in his view, was the specter of a massive peasant war, such as Pugachev had led against Catherine, which might be unleashed if he weakened the nobles' authority over their serfs. In the end, he therefore did very little to resolve the dilemmas serfdom posed for Russia's future development. His most daring effort came in 1842, when he permitted landowners to free their serfs and transfer them into a special category under government authority known as "obligated peasants." Such peasants could rent land from their former lords at a fixed price and no longer be obligated to them in other ways. Few serfowners had any interest in voluntary measures such as Nicholas proposed; by the end of his reign, only about fifty thousand serfs had been freed under his plan.[103]

The cost of Nicholas's failure to resolve these dilemmas did not become evident until the mid-1850s, when Russia's backward social and economic structure became a major factor in her defeat during the Crimean War. It was also then that the major flaw in Nicholas's foreign policy—his failure to reach an understanding with England about Russia's aims in the Near East and the Balkans—took its toll. Yet his failure to resolve the Eastern Question did not mean that he did not recognize its importance. "The Eastern Question occupied the attention of the Emperor [Nicholas] from the very first days of his reign and never ceased to demand his most serious attention," wrote Baron Feodor Brunnov, for many years Nicholas's Ambassador to London.[104] Involving as it did Russia's access to the Straits and the future of Egypt, Greece, and the rest of the Balkans, the Eastern Question stood in the forefront of European affairs during most of Nicholas's reign. It also posed an inevitable tragedy for Europe because Russia and England, the two major powers with the most vital stake in its resolution, regarded each other with such suspicion that they failed to cooperate in the common goal of preserving the Ottoman Empire from collapse. Nicholas never could convince the British that by shoring up the Ottoman Empire he hoped only to guarantee Russia's use of the Black Sea and the Straits as an outlet for her grain. The British continued to fear that he planned to seize the Straits and Constantinople.

The worst British fears seemed confirmed when General Count Aleksei Orlov negotiated the Treaty of Unkiar-Skelessi with the Sultan in mid-1833. In return for his promise to help the Sultan defend his European domains against his rebellious Egyptian vassal Mehemet Ali, Nicholas demanded that Turkey agree "to forbid entry into the Dardanelles of foreign warships," which, he insisted, was nothing more than a formal statement "of a principle which [the Porte] has always held to firmly."[105] When he learned the substance of the treaty, Britain's Foreign Secretary Lord Palmerston warned that his government would "resist to the utmost any attempt on the part of Russia to partition the Turkish Empire." "The integrity and independence of the Ottoman Empire," he added, "are necessary to the maintenance of the tranquility, the liberty, and the balance of power in the rest of Europe."[106] Nicholas was amazed at Palmerston's reaction, but persisted in signing the treaty because he considered it necessary for the protection of Russia's shipping. Nevertheless, he and his ministers tried to allay British fears by explaining their position more fully. "Suppose that the geographical position of England was similar to our own," Ambassador Brunnov told Palmerston. "And [suppose] that your trading fleet was forced to pass through a narrow canal in order to maintain its relations with the rest of the world. And imagine to yourself that Russian warships would be stationed at the entrance of this canal. I leave it to you to imagine what your merchants would say!"[107] Palmerston reacted not with understanding but with anger. Wrote one noted scholar, the Treaty of Unkiar-Skelessi was "a true turning-point in the attitude of English statesmen towards Russia [and] bred in Palmerston a fatal hostility."[108]

In an effort to lessen European political tensions while still protecting Russian merchant shipping, Nicholas made significant concessions; in July 1840, he agreed to relinquish the Treaty of Unkiar-Skelessi in return for a European guarantee of access to the Straits for Russia's merchant ships.[109] By that point, Palmerston had come to take a more dispassionate view of Nicholas's Near Eastern policy, but public and political opinion in England remained sharply anti-Russian. The decisions reached by Lord Ponsonby, Britian's Ambassador to the Porte, were especially colored by a deep-seated hatred for Nicholas and for Russia. "I have always treated as wholly erroneous the belief entertained by some that Russia could act with what people call moderation in these matters or cease for one moment to aim at the subjugation of Turkey," he once wrote.[110] Fully aware that he had failed to explain his Near Eastern policy to the British, Nicholas made a final effort that was more dramatic than any they anticipated.

At ten o'clock on the clear, moonlit night of June 1, 1844, the Dutch channel steamer *Cyclops* docked at Woolwich not far from the spot from which Peter the Great had left England almost a hundred fifty years before. Clad in a pale gray traveling cloak, a tall passenger, known to the captain only as "Count Orlov," hastened down the gangplank. "Count Orlov" was none other than Nicholas traveling incognito to explain his Near Eastern policy to Queen Victoria and her ministers in person.[111] He remained in England for nine days and took advantage of every chance for frank discussions with his British hosts. On one occasion at Windsor Castle, he spoke so loudly and so earnestly to Sir Robert Peel near some open windows that everyone in the courtyard could hear what he said, and Peel had to move him to a more secluded part of the room.[112] But caution lay mainly on the British minister's side, for Nicholas made no secret of his fear that European conflict might follow in the wake of the impending collapse of the Ottoman Empire if England and Russia did not reach an agreement beforehand. He stated his concern most clearly to Lord Aberdeen not long before he left England.

> Turkey is a dying man [he said]. We may endeavor to keep him alive, but we shall not succeed. He will, he must, die. That will be a critical moment. I foresee that I shall have to put my armies into motion and Austria must do the same. . . . In such a case, must not England be on the spot with the whole of her maritime forces? Thus, a Russian army, an Austrian army, a great English fleet, all congregated in those parts. So many powder barrels close to the fire, how shall one prevent the sparks from catching? I do not claim one inch of Turkish soil, but neither will I allow that any other shall have an inch of it. . . . We cannot now stipulate as to what shall be done with Turkey when she is dead. Such stipulations would only hasten her death. I shall therefore do all in my power to maintain the *status quo*. But, nevertheless, we should keep the possible and eventual case of her collapse honestly and reasonably before our eyes. We ought to deliberate reasonably, and endeavor to come to a straightforward and honest understanding on the subject.[113]

Britain's reluctance to reach such a "straightforward and honest understanding" with Nicholas would have terrible consequences. Within ten years of the day he bade a fond farewell to England's Prince Consort on the Woolwich dock, Nicholas put his armies in Southern Russia "into motion," as he had warned Aberdeen he might. Soon the British and the Russians would meet as enemies on the blood-soaked fields of the Crimea.

There were other crises to be weathered before Nicholas's armies faced those of England and France in 1854, however. The year 1848 proved the most difficult time Nicholas had yet lived through. During that year, Russia suffered a famine so great that, in many provinces, peasants harvested less than half of the seed they had sown. There was no surplus grain anywhere and no way to move it quickly even if there had been, because there were only twenty-five miles of railroad in all of Russia. Peasants died by the tens of thousands, and many who lived through the first year died during the next because crops often were so poor that they could not even harvest enough seed for the next season's planting.

A raging cholera epidemic that touched every corner of European

Russia and even some parts of Siberia came on the heels of the famine. No one knew how to halt its spread, and there was no known cure. "It spared no one, but it seized especially many victims from among the poor," wrote one survivor. "After four or five hours, a person would be no more. Terror reigned everywhere."[114] St. Petersburg became a ghost city within a few weeks, as one out of every thirty-six of its half-million inhabitants died, and hordes fled. "About one hundred thousand people have left St. Petersburg during the past two weeks alone," wrote a young schoolgirl in her diary. "In the Merchants' Arcade, many shops have barred their doors. Trade is at a complete standstill."[115] Desperate as the situation seemed in the capital, there were other regions where far fewer people survived. In Novgorod, some one hundred miles away, one out of every nine victims died.[116] Nicholas and his advisers were just as powerless to save Russians from cholera as they were to aid them during the famine. All they could do was to await the approach of winter to drive out the disease.

During 1848 Nicholas saw one out of every seventy Russians die from cholera, and he saw untold thousands more perish from famine. At the same time, he faced the greatest threat from the West he had yet encountered. The revolutions of 1848 threatened the very fabric of his diplomatic system and, for a time, made it seem that he must moderate his role as self-appointed defender of Europe's established order or lead Russia into a major war. That Nicholas found a middle course shows how resilient his foreign policy remained even after two decades.

On the morning of February 21, 1848,* when he was discussing some routine foreign policy matters with Count Nesselrode, Nicholas received word that the July Monarchy had fallen in Paris. It was awesome and awful news. "We all were thunderstruck," the young Grand Duke Konstantin Nikolaevich wrote that evening in his diary. "What will happen now only God knows, but we can see nothing but blood on the horizon. This is what we have come to! A repetition of the terrible

---

*According to the Gregorian calendar used in Western Europe, the first demonstrations occurred at Paris's Place de la Madeleine on February 20. According to Russia's Julian calendar, which was twelve days behind the Gregorian in the nineteenth century, the demonstrations broke out on February 8. Thus it took a bit less than two weeks for the news to travel more than fifteen hundred miles from Paris to St. Petersburg.

events [that followed the French Revolution] at the end of the last century!"[117] Many Russian statesmen feared that a reign of terror would sweep France, and they expected their Emperor to launch an assault against it. But Nicholas was too astute to follow such a perilous course. As in 1830, he was content to "leave the French to fight each other as much as they wish," as he said to Prussia's Frederick William IV.[118] What he feared again was the spread of revolution into Central and Eastern Europe. When revolution struck Berlin and Vienna in mid-March, he and many of St. Petersburg's aristocrats became fearful. "The triumph of revolution in Vienna, where Metternich, patriarch of the conservatives, presided . . . seemed inexplicable," recalled one young army officer. "The turmoil of revolution continued, it seemed, with unrestrained force."[119]

Many Europeans feared that Nicholas would invade the West to crush the revolution, but such an ardent defender of legitimacy as he could not violate the sovereignty of other states in such a blatant fashion. In any case, his first priority was to defend his Russian and Polish domains. He strengthened Russia's security police forces, made censorship truly repressive, and increased the battle-ready troops under Field Marshal Paskevich's command in Poland to 420,000. "The mission of this army," Nicholas explained, "is to defend the integrity of our frontiers, and to thwart any wretches or madmen who dream of restoring Poland in any form other than that which Russian arms so gloriously gained for the Empire. I shall not lay a finger on anyone, but woe unto him who dares to touch us!"[120] Where Europe's monarchs had failed, Nicholas succeeded. Revolution went no further east than Hungary, and, once it had lost its impetus, the monarchs of Central Europe moved to crush it in their domains. By late autumn, Prince von Windischgrätz had triumphed over revolution in Vienna, and General von Wrangel had restored order in Berlin. In March 1849, Field Marshal Radetzky defeated the Italians at Novara and turned aside the revolutionary thrust in Austria's Italian domains. The only revolutionary force in Europe now was in Hungary, where the rebel generals Görgei and Joszef Bem led an army of nearly two hundred thousand against General von Haynau's Austrian regulars; in April 1849, Lajos Kossuth proclaimed Hungary's independence.[121] Desperate to crush this new threat, the young Emperor Franz Josef went to Warsaw to ask for Nicholas's aid against the rebels. Almost immediately, Nicholas ordered Paskevich to cross the Carpathians into the plains of Hungary. With more than 350,000 men under his commnand, Paskevich proceeded to fight a ponderous campaign that contrasted sharply with the rebels' brilliance. Yet the weight of numbers proved overwhelming.[122] Görgei surrendered and Paskevich once again laid a conquered land before his master. "Hungary lies at the feet of Your Imperial Majesty," he reported at the beginning of August.[123]

Nicholas's vast military machine had crushed the Hungarians in less than two months, but the campaign had revealed disquieting flaws in Russia's army. Not only were Paskevich's tactics out of date but his soldiers fought with antiquated weapons. Nicholas found that fact especially disturbing. Flintlock muskets, he knew, were less effective than the more accurate and faster-firing percussion weapons carried by Western infantry. But he also knew that Russia's backward weapons industry could produce only about five percent of the weapons needed to rearm the army in any given year. Since his treasury simply had no funds to order weapons from abroad in large quantities, Nicholas had to be satisfied with token measures to improve the accuracy of his soldiers 1812-vintage muskets.[124] He was just beginning to perceive the terrible dangers that industrial backwardness could pose for a nation in the post-Napoleonic world.

Although Russia's military deficiencies seem obvious in retrospect, neither Europe nor Nicholas really focused upon their broader significance. Even after Paskevich's lackluster showing in Hungary, European diplomats held to their long-standing fears about Russian military power. Indeed, at the end of 1850, Nicholas's power in Europe seemed as awesome as ever, perhaps even more so. "No one," wrote one diplomat, "has been more the master of Europe, except perhaps Napoleon I. No one has inspired so much sympathy, anger, or hatred!"[125] Allies and enemies shared this resentment against Nicholas and Russia. Austria was an embarrassed debtor, having been obliged to beg for Russian aid against the Hungarian rebels. Prussia would not soon forget her humiliation at Olmütz where, in 1850, Nicholas forced her to abandon her dreams of founding a greater Germany. Nicholas had not maintained close relations with France since the revolution of 1830, and he had failed to win the trust of Queen Victoria and her ministers that he had courted so assiduously in 1844. Western statesmen feared his strength as a threat to Europe's stability. In that atmosphere of tension, resentment, suspicion, and misunderstanding, their concern was shifted once again to the "Sick Man" of Europe, the Ottoman Empire.

Nothing proved so inflammatory or so clouded the reason of Christian nations as the dispute over control of the Holy Places in Palestine, which had raged for centuries between the Roman Catholic and Orthodox churches. In the early 1850s, this dispute intensified as it became entangled in the larger web of European politics. To court favor among French Catholics, Louis Napoleon demanded greater control over the shrines in the Holy Land. In reply, Nicholas issued another ultimatum to the Sultan; this time, the Sultan no longer was isolated from Europe's Great Powers. Confident of their support, he declared war on Russia in October 1853. What had begun as a petty dispute had turned into the beginnings of a major war. Nicholas and Russia now faced the might of Western Europe's maritime powers.[126] The long-feared confrontation between Europe and Russia was at hand at a time when no one expected it, and everyone was unprepared.

Nicholas faced the armies of France and England with weakened reserves and inadequate matériel. A third of the French and half of the British troops in the Crimea fought with new percussion rifles, while only one Russian soldier in twenty-five carried one. Flagrant corruption had left even antiquated arms in short supply; Russian arsenals were supposed to contain well over a million small arms, but the Minister of War had to report to an unbelieving Nicholas that they held less than half that number, many in such poor condition that they were unsafe to fire.[127] In combat, the result was catastrophic. A number of Russian troops found their cartridges had been filled with millet by corrupt staff officers who had sold their gunpowder reserves and tried to conceal their crime. Other infantry units received bullet molds that cast balls too large to fit the standard-bore musket. Still others carried weapons with broken triggers, faulty locks, or cracked barrels. Many had no ramrods for their muzzle-loading weapons. In battle, Russian troops were cut down by enemy infantry fire before they could even hope to return it effectively. "Whole regiments melted . . . losing a fourth of their men, while they were coming into musket range," lamented one senior Russian staff officer after watching his infantry advance against the Allies.[128]

Even with these crippling handicaps, Nicholas's soldiers fought so valiantly that the first eighteen months of the Crimean War proved a standoff. When they faced only Turks, they won victories on all fronts, especially in the Caucasus. Outnumbered more than three to one, General Prince Ivan Andronikov drove Ali Pasha's Turks in retreat at Akhaltsike, and, five days later, General Prince Bebutov won an even greater victory over Ahmed Pasha at Başgedikler. Nicholas's brilliant naval strategist Admiral Nakhimov destroyed the Turkish Black Sea fleet at Sinope Harbor on November 20, and the year 1853 closed with every indication that the Russians would repeat their successes of 1829.

Nicholas's campaign against the British and French in 1854 was only somewhat less effective. His armies lost several battles in the Crimea but, in the Baltic they drove back Admiral Sir Charles Napier's attack against the Åland Islands. With a vastly superior force, the French overwhelmed Russian defenders at Bomarsund that August, but only after sustaining murderous losses. In the Far East, Russians drove off an Anglo-French attack at Kamchatka, and, in July, General Bebutov routed Turkey's Army of the Caucasus under Mustafa Zarif Pasha.[129]

Only after Nicholas's death in February 1855 did the Allies' technological superiority begin to tell upon Russia's beleaguered soldiers. The French could fire their new rifled cannon more rapidly and hit targets at ranges that made the Russian gunners shake their heads in wonder. By using newly invented telescopic sights on their modern percussion rifles, British and French sharpshooters could kill Russian officers from distances well out of reach of riflemen in the Sevastopol redoubts. While the Allies shipped ever-increasing quantities of equipment by modern steamships, Russia's planners could not even hope to supply their troops by land. As in 1812, long lines of peasants, driving their primitive two-wheeled creaking carts along roads that became knee deep in thick, sticky mud in spring and fall, were the only means for moving supplies, weapons, and replacements to the front. The Crimean War became a prologue to all the tragedies of the First World War played out on a smaller scale, as men went hungry and fought without ammunition because the General Staff could not supply them. Valor alone could not suffice. During 1855, the French and British generals slowly tightened their grip upon Sevastopol.

During the first months of his reign, a chagrined Alexander II, brought up to believe in the invincibility of Russia's armies, had to confront the magnitude of his nation's defeat. For the first time since Peter the Great had been beaten by the Turks on the Pruth in 1712, Russia's representatives went to a peace conference as supplicants, obliged to bow in defeat to a victorious foreign power. Yet Russia's defeat was not so great that the Allies could impose a ruinous peace upon her. At the Paris Peace Conference, they insisted that the Black Sea be neutralized, that Wallachia and Moldavia be removed from Russia's protection, and that the Bessarabian lands Alexander I had seized in 1812 be returned to Moldavia. The Peace of Paris was a bitter pill for Russia to swallow, but it was far from a disastrous one.[130]

More than any previous Romanov, Alexander II devoted his attention to domestic affairs. His predecessors had sought glory on the field of battle and had won for Russia a permanent place among Europe's Great Powers. But, by the middle of the nineteenth century, the might of rulers and nations had come to be measured by different standards. No longer was it the sovereign with the largest army who necessarily triumphed. The Crimean War had shown that technological superiority, not raw numbers, had become the decisive factor in victory. The conclusion was obvious. If Alexander hoped to preserve the glory his predecessors had won for Russia, he must seek greatness in the less exalted arena of domestic affairs. Russia must modernize if she were still to compete with Europe's Great Powers.

Alexander's awareness of the need for bold measures seemed to be reflected in a speech he made in Moscow on March 30, 1856, just twelve days after his representative signed the Peace of Paris. "The present system of [owning] estates with serfs cannot remain unchanged," he warned. "It is better to begin to abolish serfdom from above than to await that time when it will begin to abolish itself from below."[131] To many, it seemed that he had just tolled the death knell of serfdom in Russia. But Alexander soon proved more cautious than his words to Moscow's assembled nobles had seemed to indicate. Like Nicholas, he feared the intelligentsia and the liberal nobility. He therefore turned to the traditional source of conservative wisdom in Russia's administration. Like his father, he appointed a secret committee of senior statesmen to discuss Russia's future course. This committee was no more effective than any of the ten similar secret committees Nicholas had convened.[132] Yet, during 1857, the basis for real progress on social and economic reform was established in Russia's central government. This came as an indirect result of the secret committee's decision to entrust the task of assembling information about serfdom to the Ministry of Internal Affairs. Led by Nikolai Miliutin, the thirty-nine-year-old director of the Ministry's important Economic Department, a small group of progressive officials entered the reform debate.

Miliutin played a central role in drafting the Emancipation Acts and a number of measures that led men to call the first part of Alexander's reign the Era of the Great Reforms. Born to impoverished noble parents and educated at state expense, he represented a new type of senior government official who had no ties to the serf system and no economic stake in its preservation. "Serfdom serves as the main hindrance—perhaps even the only hindrance—to any development in Russia at the present time," he wrote in 1847. "Only with the emancipation of the serfs," he added, "will the improvement of our rural economy become possible."[133] Miliutin also differed from most senior officials in Russia in that he rose to high office as a consequence of ability, not influential connections. Along with his closest friend, Andrei Zablotskii-Desiatovskii, who headed the Department of Rural Economy in the Ministry of State Domains, and a few other progressive officials, Miliutin controlled the data about the economic and social life in Russia's towns and countryside. These officials had made themselves essential to any senior statesman who wanted to know about the Empire's internal affairs.[134]

Miliutin and his associates knew what an emancipation needed to accomplish; but although they supplied Alexander's secret committee with information, they had no direct input into Russia's legislative process. The situation changed at the beginning of 1859, when Alexander decided to appoint a special commission to draft an emancipation.[135] As its head, he named not a civil official but General Iakov Rostovtsev, a man known for his unswerving loyalty to the Romanovs. Rostovtsev appointed Miliutin, Zablotskii-Desiatovskii, and a number of their close associates to his Editing Commission along with a number of nobles who had distinguished themselves as experts on the complexities of serfdom's economics. For eighteen months, the Editing Commission met several times each week and engaged in often bitter debate. Rostovtsev died in February 1860 before their work was done, but the task of drafting the emancipation that would free Russia's twenty million serfs was completed by Miliutin and the Commission's other progressive members under the unlikely chairmanship of Russia's conservative Minister of Justice, Count Viktor Panin. Panin opposed emancipation, but thought it his duty to set aside his own views and follow his Emperor's orders. "If . . . the sovereign's attitude toward something is different than mine," he once said, "I consider it my duty to abandon my convictions and even to work against them."[136] On February 19, 1861, the Emancipation was published. With seventeen separate enactments and 369 pages, it was one of the most complex pieces of legislation to be produced in Russia before the twentieth century.

The actual juridical process of serfdom's abolition was very complex and took place over several years. Summarized most briefly and without its many qualifications and exceptions, the Emancipation decreed that Russia's former serfs would receive land from their former masters, who would be paid by funds advanced by the government. The former serfs then would repay the government by making annual "redemption payments" over a period of forty-nine years. Despite its many complexities, the Emancipation thus had the great virtue of providing Russia's former bondsmen with land, in sharp contrast to the procedures used in the abolition of American slavery a few years later. Still, the Emancipation was a mixed blessing at best. One of its worst features was that it gave title to all lands in a village to the commune as a whole, not to individuals. This meant that Russia's peasants continued to till scattered plots of land that they plowed, planted, and reaped according to a majority vote of their fellows, as they had since medieval times. Because they did not own the land themselves, they made no effort to improve it, with the result that Russia's grain fields became even less productive. At the same time, there developed among Russia's peasants a land hunger so virulent that it retained its grip upon them even after the Romanovs had been driven from the throne.

So dramatic were the discussions about Emancipation that historians sometimes forget that they were only part of a more extensive debate about even broader social and economic transformation in Russia. Partly in response to this debate and partly because he realized that new institutions must be created to replace the serfowners' authority in Russia's countryside, Alexander instituted a series of other reforms. One of the most complex questions that had to be resolved was how to modernize Russia's ponderous and inefficient administration sufficiently to extend its control over the millions of newly freed serfs. Beginning in 1859, Miliutin and several other experts began to draft legislation that would create for Russia a new institution of local government known as the *zemstvo,* which, they hoped, would involve a broader stratum of the Empire's citizens in its political processes. In the atmosphere of crisis and reconstruction that prevailed, these reformers wanted to draw progressives to the government's cause and to create, as Miliutin once wrote, "a middle-of-the-road party."[137] This would presumably undercut the appeal Russia's embryonic radical movement had for liberal-minded men and women, thus protecting Alexander and his government from violent revolutionary attacks. "The most vital state interests, with which the entire future development of Russia is perhaps connected, urgently demand . . . new rural institutions," Miliutin later remarked.[138]

Although it did not immediately serve the broad function Miliutin and his associates envisioned for it, the *Zemstvo* Statute of January 1, 1864, did in fact establish the basis for a new institution that would emerge as an important political force in the Russian countryside by the end of the century. Because the *zemstva* were to take responsibility for such local matters as public health, education, relief for the poor, and the encouragement of trade, agriculture, and industry, they gradually brought scientists, technicians, and teachers into Russia's countryside, adding an important new element of political awareness to the peasants' lives. Another major breach in the crumbling edifice of Nicholas's system had been repaired with new and different bricks in an effort to reinforce the fortress of the Romanovs' autocracy.[139]

One of the most prominent features of life in the Russian countryside before the Emancipation of 1861 had been the serfowners' control over law and justice. Acting as unpaid judges, they decreed how disputes among serfs should be settled and meted out punishments for many crimes. That they could no longer continue this function once serfdom was abolished made it necessary for the Romanovs to create new courts to replace them. But that was not the only reason Russia's court system needed reform. Under Catherine the Great and her successors, the entire judicial process had become incredibly confused, and its administrators notoriously venal and inept. "Russia resembled a lake, in the depths of which great fish devoured the smaller ones, while, near the surface, everything was calm and it glistened like a mirror," one contemporary lamented.[140] The primary goal of this old judicial order was to protect the interests and prestige of the Romanovs and their leading agents. Of necessity, the new order had to protect the personal and property rights of Russia's newly emerged citizenry. To deal with these problems, the Judicial Reform Statute of November 20, 1864, created an independent judiciary for the first time in Russia's history, along with public jury trials. In doing so, it deprived the Romanovs of absolute control over the dispensation of justice in their Empire, thereby changing the very nature of autocracy in Russia.

One of the most important consequences of Alexander II's Great Reforms was to destroy the *ancien régime* social order upon which the Romanovs had built those vast armies that had defeated Frederick the Great and Napoleon. Once serfdom had been abolished, Russia's army no longer could be based upon servitude and aristocratic privilege alone, because Russians became, *de jure,* citizens, not bondsmen. The Empire required a citizen army, and the task of creating one fell to General Dmitrii Miliutin, Minister of War from 1861 until 1881.[141] Like his younger brother Nikolai, Dmitrii had carved out a brilliant career for himself as an administrator. Choosing the army over the civil service, he became a Major General and member of the Tsar's personal staff at the age of thirty-seven. Toward the end of 1856, he was able to test some of his ideas about modernizing the structure of Russia's army as Chief of Staff to General Prince Aleksandr Bariatinskii's Army of the Caucasus, and his success won him Bariatinskii's confidence.[142] Bariatinskii's support helped secure Miliutin's appointment as Russia's Minister of War in November 1861.

The ministerial portfolio Miliutin took up was bulging with problems, many of them critical, and all of them urgent. Russia's army cost almost a hundred million rubles a year at a time when the national debt had risen to over a billion, or four times the treasury's annual revenue. Major economies in the military budget obviously were needed, but most senior officers found it difficult to see how they could be achieved without drastic reductions in the size of Russia's standing army and a further weakening of the Empire's international prestige.[143] Miliutin knew that the way to reduce military costs and still keep Russia strong was to replace her conscript serf army with an all-class citizen army in which all Russians bore the obligation to serve with the colors. After more than a decade of preparation, he accomplished that aim with the Universal Military Service Statute of 1874.[144] At his urging, Alexander thus rescinded the emancipation from compulsory service that the nobility had wrested from Peter III in 1762.

Although the aristocrats of Alexander's Empire despised the Universal Military Service Statute as a further attack upon their privileges, their lack of action provided very dramatic evidence of how weakened they had become during the previous seven decades. No aristocratic revolt broke out in St. Petersburg in protest nor was there any effort to assassinate Alexander, as there had been when the Emperor Paul had made a far more timid effort to reduce his nobles' privileges. Yet Miliutin was not content only to force Russia's nobles to serve in the ranks as a step toward modernizing Russian society. As Minister of War, he worked diligently to transfer all of the changes wrought by the Great Reforms to the army, traditionally the most conservative institution in the Empire. He made effective citizens out of peasant soldiers by teaching them to read and write, with the result that literacy among soldiers soon rose to be five times greater than it was among peasant men in general.[145] Achievements such as these lend some substance to the contention of one historian who once wrote that "it was in the army, that stronghold of tradition and conservatism, that Russian democracy scored one of its first modest, yet real, successes."[146]

What complicated Miliutin's efforts to streamline Russia's army and reduce military costs was Alexander's insistence that his Empire must pursue a vigorous foreign policy in order to overcome the stigma of her Crimean defeat. The Emperor held firmly to Russia's interests in

Europe; at the same time, he pursued a more aggressive policy in Central Asia and the Far East than had any Romanov before him. Indeed, during his reign it became axiomatic that, when Russia's foreign ventures encountered opposition in the Balkans or elsewhere in Europe, she turned to the East in response. Alexander established regular relations with China and Japan, and in 1876 his diplomats even won grudging Japanese recognition for his claim to Sakhalin, a large island that lay just off the mainland of Russia's Far Eastern territories and just to the north of Japan's own domains. Far more dramatic, Alexander ordered his armies into Central Asia, where his commanders advanced resolutely into Turkestan.

There was something romantic, almost magical, about Russia's Turkestan campaigns in the 1860s and 1870s, for the region was remote, virtually unknown, and obviously exotic. Indeed, we could draw many parallels between nineteenth-century Russians' view of Turkestan and its people and seventeenth-century Europeans' impressions of the Russians. The people of Turkestan were Asiatic. In cities that bore such legendary names as Samarkand and Bukhara, bazaars evoked memories of the spice trade, of great camel caravans moving from the Orient to the West laden with exotic herbs and oils. There was an air of mystery about the region that brought to mind Genghis Khan and Tamerlane, those cruel and barbaric princes whose Asiatic cavalry had swept everything in Russia before them so many centuries before.

But time had turned the tables and had turned them dramatically. For, if they had suffered the disabilities of technological backwardness against the Allies in the Crimea, Alexander's armies enjoyed an overwhelming technological superiority over their Asian foes, just as did the British and the French in Africa at about the same time. During the brief decade after General Mikhail Cherniaev stormed the great Central Asian city of Tashkent in 1865, khanate after khanate fell to Russian arms. Three years later, General Konstantin von Kaufman, Chevniaev's successor as Military Governor of Turkestan, won more and greater victories. Vain, immensely ambitious, and with an insatiable appetite for glory, von Kaufman was determined to win an Asian Empire for his Tsar. During the summer of 1868, he conquered the khanates of Samarkand and Bukhara. Five years later, he took the khanate of Khiva in a swift, well-executed, brutally efficient campaign. Finally, in 1876, he added the khanate of Kokand to Alexander's new possessions. Within a decade, Alexander had increased his Empire by an amount equal to the territories of Austria-Hungary and the newly unified Germany combined.[147]

New policies required new men to formulate and implement them. During his first year on the throne, Alexander replaced Russia's seventy-five-year-old Foreign Minister and Chancellor Count Nesselrode with the much younger Prince Aleksandr Gorchakov, a cousin of Tolstoi, who had been Pushkin's friend and classmate at the Lyceum and was recognized as a diplomat of talent and ingenuity throughout Russia's Foreign Service. Gorchakov had served in Russia's diplomatic corps for some three decades and had represented his Emperor in most of Europe's capitals. In 1854 Nicholas had named him to be Russia's Ambassador to Vienna, one of the most difficult assignments at the time, and he had labored valiantly to keep Austria and the states of Germany from joining France and England against Russia in the Crimean War.

A generation younger than Nesselrode, Gorchakov viewed Russia's diplomatic position in more dynamic terms than those static principles that had dominated her treaty alignments since 1815. He pressured Alexander to fill key diplomatic posts with men who shared his views, and the Emperor usually followed his advice. Only for the critical post of Ambassador to France did they differ, for Alexander insisted upon appointing Count Pavel Kiselev, the man his father had called his "Chief of Staff for Peasant Affairs," whose last diplomatic assignment had come in the early 1830s. Kiselev now was almost seventy, and the only statesman in Russia with sufficient prestige to sign a treaty recognizing Russia's defeat in the Crimea, but his appointment caused Gorchakov difficulties from the outset.

Kiselev had been a senior statesman for more than a quarter-century, and he had grown accustomed to making policy in direct consultation with his Emperor. He found it awkward to work through Gorchakov and compensated for what seemed a lessening of his official rank by making policy in Paris rather than following Gorchakov's detailed instructions. He ardently pressed for an alliance with France at a time when Gorchakov had grown wary of Napoleon III's foreign adventures, especially in Italy. By 1862 these conflicts over policy had become so intense that they forced Kiselev to resign. Still, he had accomplished more than Gorchakov or even Alexander realized at the time. At the Court of Napoleon III, Kiselev's exquisite manners, polished charm, and flawless French made him a favorite. His six years in Paris served to temper Europe's view of Russians as barbaric and brutal and did much to reestablish Russia's status there.[148]

Just after Kiselev's resignation, a new crisis turned Europeans against Russians once again. As in 1830, the reason centered in Poland. On January 22, 1863, Polish patriots launched an attack against their Russian rulers that swept across the length and breadth of the land. To end the rebellion on his terms, Alexander realized that he would have to subjugate Poland much more completely than his father had done. He decided to strike an alliance with the Polish peasantry in order to crush their rebellious noble masters.[149] It seemed a sensible policy. Time and again, Poland's aristocracy had shown its hostility to the Romanovs. At the same time, just like their counterparts in Russia, they had oppressed the peasants on their estates for centuries. Alexander's theory was that if the Russian Emperor granted economic and political concessions to Poland's peasants at the expense of their masters, they would give him their loyalty in his effort to suppress their lords.

To accomplish the subjugation of Poland in this manner, Alexander again turned to Nikolai Miliutin. Like his elder brother, who had become Minister of War just over a year before, Miliutin was convinced that all non-Russian lands must be held firmly within the Empire and that Russia must deal resolutely with the revolt before European public opinion marshaled its full weight on behalf of the Poles.[150] "Only when law and order are firmly established everywhere," he wrote, "will it be possible to begin the treatment of the social ailments engendered long ago in this unfortunate country."[151]

Once order was restored, Miliutin focused his attention upon the economic misery of the Polish peasantry, which, in his words, demanded "a rapid and fundamental resolution."[152] The result, published on February 19, 1864, was an emancipation that was far more generous than that which Russian serfs had received three years earlier. Unlike the Russian serf, the Polish peasant received full title to his land and was not burdened by onerous payments.[153] As in Russia, Miliutin insisted that the emancipation marked only a beginning of a broader reform program.[154] During the next two years, he and his colleagues established secular elementary schools, suppressed the anti-Russian Roman Catholic clergy, and modernized Poland's administration. But this policy was far more fragile than most statesmen realized. When an attack of apoplexy forced Miliutin to retire late in 1866, advocates of intense Russification needed only a few months to gain the upper hand. Well before the end of Alexander II's reign, Poland therefore became an integral part of the Russian Empire. Incensed at Russia's effort to deny them their language, culture, and religion, all Poles, rich and poor, lord and peasant, became virulently anti-Russian. Alexander's wager on the Polish masses had only broadened the base of opposition to Russian rule.

From Alexander's point of view, one of the most troublesome aspects of the Polish revolt had been the outspoken sympathy most Western European governments had expressed on the Poles' behalf. The one exception had been Prussia, whose king and statesmen opposed European efforts to censure Russia. This welcome support paved the way for further cooperation between the two powers. Alexander supported Prussia in the Austro-Prussian War of 1866, and Kaiser Wilhelm assured him that Prussia would support him in repudiating those clauses of the Treaty of Paris that forbade Russia to maintain a fleet in the Black Sea. In June 1870, the Kaiser, Alexander, and their Foreign Ministers Bismarck and Gorchakov, met at Ems, where the Russians assured the Prussians that they would work to neutralize any effort Austria might make to assist France in a war against Prussia. Bismarck thus felt safe in provoking Napoleon III into a declaration of war, and again he assured Alexander of Prussian support in repudiating the Black Sea clauses. On October 19/30, 1870, just three days after Marshal Bazaine capitulated to the Prussians at Metz, Gorchakov sent his famous note to all the governments that had signed the Treaty of Paris. Russia, he announced, no longer would observe any restrictions upon her naval forces in the Black Sea.[155] The Crimean System, born of Russia's defeat in 1856, had reached its end. Alexander had taken the first step to erase the stain of defeat that had so darkened the first years of his reign.

Gorchakov's abrogation of the Black Sea clauses signaled that Alexander was about to pursue a much more active role in Balkan politics, and the support he and the Kaiser had given each other during 1870 paved the way for a reestablishment of that conservative Central European alliance that had flourished during the reign of Nicholas I. But important changes had occurred since the 1830s and 1840s that made this reborn union very different. The alliance of 1873 joined not Russia and Prussia, but Russia and a united and powerful Germany. That single fact changed the entire political complexion of Central Europe. Russia had been the overwhelmingly dominant force in the Central European alliance Nicholas I had forged with Prussia and Austria after the Revolutions of 1830. Germany, her policy directed by her brilliant and ever-resourceful Chancellor Otto von Bismarck, ruled the alliance when it was reestablished in 1873. Indeed, as the historian B. H. Sumner wrote nearly a half-century ago, "Berlin had succeeded Paris as the key capital of Europe" after 1870.[156]

Growing closeness between Russia and Germany was encouraged by other factors in addition to their mutual support during the crises of 1870. Both powers agreed that Russia must be a stern master in Poland, and they had no conflicting interests in the Balkans. Yet Bismarck very wisely did not wish to anchor the security of his newly created Germany in the single harbor of a Russo-German alliance. Ever fearful that Russia and France might achieve a rapprochement and that Austria-Hungary might join them, Bismarck worked for a closer relationship with the Emperor Franz Josef. At the same time, Alexander and his advisers began to perceive that an alliance between Germany, Austria-Hungary, and Russia might lessen conflicts with Austria in the Balkans and neutralize British opposition to Russia's rapid thrust into Central Asia. The basis for such a union was laid during September 1872, when Alexander and Franz Josef met with the Kaiser in Berlin. Soon, they would construct a major diplomatic edifice upon that foundation when they formed the League of the Three Emperors in October 1873.[157]

Alexander, Wilhelm, and Franz Josef had reestablished that conservative alliance with which Nicholas I had bound Central and Eastern Europe together for a quarter-century, but their policy now was affected by two powerful outside ideological forces he had not faced. Of less immediate consequence, Pan-Germanism in Bohemia fostered disagreements between Germany and Austria. More pressing, the doctrines of Pan-Slavism generated intense ideological and political tensions between Russia and Austria. In particular, Russian Pan-Slavism combined extreme chauvinism with a deep messianic passion. One of its first exponents was Nikolai Danilevskii, a natural scientist turned philsopher. In 1869 Danilevskii set forth his views in *Russia and Europe*, a massive treatise of more than five hundred closely printed pages, which his leading biographer has characterized a "a mixture of angry, dated, political Panslavist journalism; primitive, at times brilliant social science; *Realpolitik;* sentimental romanticism and populist-utopian socialism; fanciful theology and philsophy of history; and mad prophecy."[158] Among other things, Danilevskii envisioned the approach of a new cultural and political age in which the Slavic cultural type would triumph over its Latin and German counterparts. As Dostoevskii later said, it would be an age in which "the anguish of Europe" would find an outlet in "the all-human all-uniting Russian soul."[159] Danilevskii and Dostoevskii saw the conflict and its ultimate resolution as a cultural and spiritual issue but, to others, it also was a question of brute force, especially after General Rostislav Fadeev added military and political dimensions to Danilevskii's message. In an essay entitled *Opinion on the Eastern Question* (1870), Fadeev insisted that the coming struggle between East and West was not to be cultural and spiritual, but one that would be decided by a clash of arms between Russians and Germans.[160]

Unlike most ideas that infatuated Russia's impressionable intellectuals during the nineteenth century, Pan-Slavism boasted a solid organizational base among a number of very influential Russians.[161] These men became especially active in the mid-1870s, when the Slavs in the Ottoman provinces of Bosnia, Hercegovina, and Bulgaria rose in revolt against their Moslem overlords and when the independent Balkan Slavic states of Serbia and Montenegro declared war against the Turks so as to fight on behalf of their Slav brothers.[162] Rarely had the Romanovs permitted public opinion to influence their foreign policy, but

Alexander found it awkward to ignore the urgings of such eminent personages as his Turkish Ambassador Count Nikolai Ignatiev and the Metropolitan of Moscow. In any case, Alexander long had been searching for a cause that could help him recapture the glory he had forfeited by Russia's Crimean defeat. Especially after Serbia's army of Russian volunteers went down in defeat to the Turks, he began to take the cause of Bulgaria, Bosnia, and Hercegovina very much to heart. He spoke of the sacrifices of Russia's volunteers in the cause of "our brothers by blood and faith" and warned that if Europe's Powers meeting together in Constantintople in the fall of 1876 could not convince the Turks to meet Russia's "just demands," then he must act independently. "I am certain," he confided to a body of nobles and merchants assembled in the Kremlin Palace, "that all Russia would answer my call."[163] On April 12, 1877, Alexander declared war against the Ottoman Empire.

Although the outcome of the Russo-Turkish War of 1877–78 was never seriously in doubt, Russia's armies advanced clumsily and success came more slowly than expected. Alexander appointed as commander in chief his untalented and timid brother Nikolai Nikolaevich and named the future Alexander III as his deputy. "You can't help being afraid when you think about who holds command," War Minister Miliutin confided to his diary that summer. "The presence of the Sovereign [at army headquarters] not only does not lessen the danger, but actually increases it." "We can only hope," he concluded with a touch of irony, "that the Turks have even more inept commanders than we do."[164]

Speed was the key to Russia's war plan, but the usual problems of transportation and supply crippled the Russian advance from the outset. To make matters worse, Alexander had declared war at a time when his army's weapons were in an awkward stage of transition, and the hodgepodge of weapons his soldiers carried created hopeless ammunition supply problems as desperate ordinance officers struggled to send the proper cartridges to the proper weapons in the thick of battle.[165] These difficulties were compounded by the presence of Alexander and his personal staff at the front during nearly all of the last half of 1877. The Tsar brought with him War Minister Miliutin as well as Foreign Minister Gorchakov and Gorchakov's chief rival, Ambassador Ignatiev. Ignatiev was far more interested in scheming against the man whose post he coveted than he was in the progress of the war. The Gorchakov-Ignatiev feud complicated Russia's foreign policy at a crucial time and rendered Gorchakov ineffective because of his separation from the foreign ambassadors who remained some thirteen hundred miles away in St. Petersburg. Miliutin likewise found it difficult to function efficiently as War Minister when removed from the army's administrative center.

The entire situation bordered upon the absurd. It was as if an American president had gone off to fight a campaign in the Dakota Territory and had insisted that his Secretary of State and Secretary of War accompany him, while the War Office and much of the diplomatic corps remained in Washington, D. C. Worst of all, Alexander seemed utterly incapable of unraveling these problems. Only when he returned to St. Petersburg with his senior statesmen in the late fall did the military situation begin to sort itself out. In late November, the besieging Russian army finally breached the walls of Plevna and then drove southward to seize a number of important Balkan fortresses and towns. On January 8, 1878, they occupied Adrianople; eleven days later, on January 19, the Turks signed an armistice.[166]

Despite the difficulties involved, winning the war proved easier than arranging the peace. In clear violation of the Budapest Convention of January 1877, Ignatiev negotiated a treaty at San Stefano in February 1878 that established a large Bulgarian state and ignored Austria's interests by leaving Bosnia and Hercegovina within the Ottoman Empire. Both Austria and England protested. Alexander evidently concluded that he faced war with both powers if the Treaty of San Stefano was not altered, and he therefore accepted Bismarck's offer to preside as an "honest broker" at a conference of the Great Powers. Yet, when the Congress of Berlin assembled in June 1878, the "honest broker" proved far more concerned with Germany's interests than with Russia's, Austria's, or England's. He therefore pressed Alexander's chief representative, Count Petr Shuvalov, to agree to revisions of the San Stefano Treaty that met Russia's minimal territorial demands but gave far more to Austria-Hungary than she had any right to expect. Russia thus received the territory around the mouth of the Danube and the towns of Kars and Batum in the Caucasus. Austria, whose armies had not fired a shot in anger during the entire war, gained administrative control of Bosnia and Hercegovina. At Austria's insistence, the powers seriously weakened Serbia and vastly reduced the dimensions of Bulgaria.[167]

Alexander had sacrificed, with considerable bitterness, some of the most significant fruits of Russia's victory in exchange for peace with Europe, so necessary as his country embarked upon a vast program of economic modernization and industrialization. When terrorists assassinated him three years later, his son Alexander III inherited an Empire in which this policy had made possible the beginnings of impressive economic development. It would be Alexander III's aim to continue that progress at an even greater rate than his father had envisoned, but he did so within a far more rigidly controlled political framework. As the Autocrat who had launched the Great Reforms in Russia, Alexander II had been reluctant to strike ruthlessly against the political dissent that had arisen during the birth of Russia's new social and economic order. His son labored under no such constraints. Convinced that his father's refusal to crush every stirring of dissent had been directly responsible for his assassination, Alexander III proceeded to institute a regime of rigid political control in Russia.

Alexander III's first step in imposing stability upon Russia was to cast aside the plan Minister of Internal Affairs Count Mikhail Loris-Melikov had prepared for summoning an elective consultative assembly to St. Petersburg, even though Alexander II had approved it on the very morning of his assassination. In protest, Loris-Melikov, War Minister Miliutin, Minister of Finance Abaza, and the State Council's President Grand Duke Konstantin Nikolaevich resigned during the next two months. Alexander calmly replaced them with men who shared his views, so that, by the beginning of 1882, all of the key posts in his new government were firmly in the hands of reactionaries. Count Dmitrii Tolstoi headed the Ministry of Internal Affairs. His close friend Ivan Delianov directed the Ministry of Public Instruction, and the rigidly conservative General Petr Vannovskii reigned as Miliutin's successor in the Ministry of War. They all favored a policy of rapid industrial development, and insisted upon rigid political control. Over them all, firm in his position as Alexander's closest friend and confident, hovered the omnipresent, stark, cold figure of Pobedonostsev, Director General of the Holy Synod.

Alexander set out to restore to the Romanovs' autocracy the power and glory it had known in the early nineteenth century. Convinced that the Great Reforms were the chief cause of the social and political upheavals that Russia had suffered in the 1870s, he and his ministers imposed rigid restrictions upon Russia's periodical press. "It is impossible to make a good beginning at anything until the newspapers are restrained," Pobedonostsev wrote less than two months after his master's accession. Almost without exception, he considered publishers to be "swine or half-wits," insisting that any government that failed to suppress them was utterly irresponsible.[168] At his urging, Alexander instituted a series of censorship regulations in August 1882, that despite their supposedly "provisional" character, continued in effect until the beginning of the twentieth century. These new regulations subjected newspapers and the periodical press to precisely those onerous sorts of censorship that had been abolished with such fanfare in 1865. Only those periodicals that printed an exact reflection of the views held by Alexander and his closest advisers were able to avoid suppression. With the possible exception of the years between 1848 and 1854, Russia's periodical press had never been so rigidly controlled as it was during the reign of Alexander III.

Aside from the "provisional" censorship regulations of August 1882, three particularly important decrees comprised the core of the so-called "counterreforms" that Alexander and his advisers imposed upon Russia. First came the Statute on Land Captains of July 12, 1889, followed by the *Zemstvo* Act of June 12, 1890, and the Municipal Government Statute of June 11, 1892. All three of these decrees became law after the death of the reactionary Minister of Internal Affairs Count Tolstoi, but they often have been regarded as the product of his influence. The first two were drafted by Aleksandr Pazukhin, a bureaucrat working in close league with Pobedonostsev and who had come to Count Tolstoi's attention because of his reactionary critiques of some mildly progressive proposals that had been made for improving Russia's local administration.[169]

Pazukhin was an immensely effective administrator and especially adept at putting the reactionary principles of his masters into the form of draft legislation. When it finally became law in 1889, his Statute on Land Captains imposed stringent state controls upon the freedom of Russia's peasants to conduct their own local affairs by bringing a new type of official into the countryside. Unlike other local officials, land captains were appointed by the Minister of Internal Affairs from names chosen by the provincial nobles and approved by the provincial governor from among the often reactionary hereditary aristocracy. Obviously, such men could be counted upon to support conservative political and social policies and to oppose any effort by the peasantry to gain further control over local affairs. "A sham of self-government [in the peasant villages] was preserved, yet peasant Russia was actually ruled by petty officials drawn from the midst of the landed nobility and controlled by the Minister [of Internal Affairs],"[170] was the way one expert described the new law.

Intense administrative centralization and bureaucratic control were the means Alexander and his advisers used to regain a portion of that uncontrolled autocratic power the Great Reforms had eroded. The second product of Pazukhin's diligent pen, the *Zemstvo* Act of 1890, brought the elective *zemstvo* offices under the firm control of Alexander's personally appointed officials. *Zemstvo* officials had to be confirmed in their posts by Russia's provincial governors, while the Minister of Internal Affairs had the authority to review all *zemstvo* decisions and remove from office any official whose views displeased him. Tolstoi's successor, Ivan Durnovo, used the Municipal Government Statute of 1892 to apply these same principles to elected municipal officials. At the same time, both in town and country, Jews were completely disenfranchised.[171]

Russia's Jews occupied a prominent place in Alexander's thoughts and policies throughout his reign, for he was easily one of the most ardent anti-Semites to sit upon the Russian throne. Given his fervent nationalism and rigid Orthodoxy, it hardly could have been otherwise. To his friends and advisers, he insisted that all Jews were "Christ-killers."

Since much of Russian public opinion shared his loudly voiced sentiments, there were none to protest when at the very beginning of his reign he launched a vicious wave of pogroms against the Jews in southern Russia. During the spring and summer of 1881, the authorities stirred anti-Semitic passions to a fever pitch and then took no action while Jews were robbed, beaten, even murdered, in more than a hundred anti-Jewish riots. Alexander's response to these vicious persecutions was to impose more restrictions upon Russia's Jewry.[172]

Yet Alexander was constrained from pursuing an anti-Semitic policy as freely or as openly as he wished at the beginning of his reign by factors beyond his control. Russia was heavily dependent upon foreign investment capital during the early 1880s, and Western European bankers hastened to exploit that need to force him to moderate his anti-Semitic designs. In discussing efforts to arrange new loans with the Rothschilds, State Secretary Aleksandr Polovtsov confided to his diary that "success with the Rothschilds is possible only in the event that something will be done about the Jewish question [in Russia]. Something in this area could be done by issuing a few Imperial decrees proposing an improvement of Jewish life, decrees which in no way need to get in the way of [anti-Jewish] legislative activity at some future time."[173] The similarities between Polovtsev's remarks and the policies of Nazi Germany during its first half-decade are, of course, striking. Other striking parallels soon became evident as Alexander persisted in his policies against the Jews.

To avoid the unfavorable attention of Western Europeans, Alexander persecuted Jews by means of confidential regulations rather than by public decrees. In 1887, his Minister of Public Instruction Ivan Delianov ordered all school authorities to restrict the number of Jews admitted to their classrooms. With Alexander's support, Minister of Internal Affairs Ivan Durnovo drove some twenty thousand Jewish artisans and tradesmen from Moscow in 1892, and, in January 1893, whole caravans of Jews carrying what few things they could manage to take away moved into those regions in the southwest where they still were permitted to live. Virtually all of them suffered financial ruin as they sold their shops and enterprises at huge losses, since Durnovo had made certain to publicize his expulsion order in the proper places. Finally, Alexander decreed that it was a criminal offense for Jews to bear Christian names. Such persecution at the hands of their Emperor caused a mass exodus of Jews from Russia and drove numbers of those who remained into the resurgent revolutionary movement in the mid-1890s.[174] Some of those who fled went to Western Europe; most chose the United States.

Because he believed that all Romanov subjects should be Russian in language, culture, and outlook, Alexander launched an aggressive campaign against those cultural nationalists who had attempted to revive the art, literature, and music of their people earlier in the century. He intensified the program of Russification that his father had begun in Poland and applied its precepts to the Poles' fellow Slavs, the Ukrainians. He imposed Russification upon the people of Russia's Baltic provinces—present-day Estonia, Lithuania, and Latvia—and did the same with the native populations of Armenia and Georgia in the south. Russian became the language of instruction in the schools, of justice in the courts, and of administration everywhere. At the same time, he authorized campaigns to persecute non-Orthodox religions and to convert native populations to Orthodoxy.[175] The results were all too predictable. By the end of Alexander III's reign, aggressive political separatist movements had taken root among the Estonians, Latvians, Lithuanians, Ukrainians, Armenians, Georgians, and Finns. His ill-advised effort to make all the people in his Empire into Russians had made them violently anti-Russian.

Although Alexander III was relentless in his policies of social and political reaction, he presided over unprecedented growth in Russia's industrial sector. Except for textile production, which continued to employ more workers than all branches of metallurgy until after 1900, most of Russia's economic development was confined to heavy industry because her peasants still were largely self-sufficient and there was no mass market for consumer goods. Railroad mileage increased by almost fifty percent to nearly thirty-one thousand kilometers between 1880 and 1900, and that in turn stimulated the production of coal, iron, and steel.[176] Russian coal production more than quadrupled between 1880 and 1900; the growth figures for iron, steel, and oil were equally impressive.[177] But these gains were achieved only at the cost of immense suffering for Russia's masses as Alexander's aggressively conservative Minister of Finance, Ivan Vyshnegradskii, launched a program to balance the budget, reduce Russia's national debt, stabilize her currency, and put her on the gold standard at a time when world grain prices were in steady decline. "We may not eat enough, but we will export," Vyshnegradskii promised.[178] Under his relentless urging, grain exports increased by almost forty percent before he completed his second year in office. He thus gained for Russia a favorable balance of trade, but he condemned her peasants to utter ruin.

Just as Vyshnegradskii's program seemed certain of success at the close of the 1880s, a yellowish, bitter, coarse bread, baked from such weeds as goosefoot, began to appear in unexpectedly large quantities on peasant tables in Russia's grain belt. It was a fatal sign, for the appearance of "famine bread" when there was no famine was indisputable proof that the peasants had exhausted their grain and cash reserves to meet the government's demands. The slightest crop failure would bring disaster. There was no way to reverse the trend quickly; grain reserves could be replenished only by lowering taxes and waiting for several bountiful harvests to do their work. Then as now, however, rich harvests were the exception in Russia, and it required several years to repair the effects of Vyshnegradskii's policy. In the meantime, the destiny of Russia's millions of peasants lay in the hands of Nature. And Nature proved cruel and fickle during the winter of 1890–91, as hard frosts, but little protective snow, ravaged Russia's central agricultural and Volga River provinces. After the winter frosts, the spring and summer brought intense heat, but no rain, and, by the fall of 1891, Russia was in the grip of the worst crop failure she had experienced since 1848.[179]

Even during normal times, Russian peasants lived a precarious existence. According to a study made by a *zemstvo* doctor about a decade after the famine, abject poverty was still the rule for peasants in Russia's grain belt. Only one household in ten had enough grain to last from harvest until planting season. Syphilis had reached epidemic proportions, and such diseases as malaria, diphtheria, and typhus were commonplace, in large measure because only one household in twenty had a privy. As a rule, the peasants left their excrement in the outer passageway of their cottages, where dogs, chickens, and pigs consumed it. Meat was a rare commodity, but many peasants also had to do without cabbage, cucumbers, and milk. Some of them were so poor that even the vermin abandoned their huts because there was so little food.[180]

Peasants who lived under conditions such as these died in droves during the famine. It was a brutal price to pay for the economic stability that Russia needed to attract foreign investment capital. Amazingly, Russia's peasants remained passive, even when pushed beyond the point of starvation. They died by the tens of thousands, but they remained loyal to Alexander III, their "little father" in St. Petersburg. Even when the famine was at its worst, they did not revolt. A decade of firm repression had achieved all Alexander could have hoped for in terms of political stability in Russia.

If Alexander's domestic program was designed to impose political stability, his foreign policy sought much the same goal. Except for limited military campaigns in Central Asia, his reign was a time of peace, for neither he nor his cautious and reserved Foreign Minister, Nikolai Giers, planned grand foreign designs as their predecessors had. Nonetheless, Alexander changed the direction of Russia's foreign policy in a profound manner, for the latter years of the 1880s brought a serious deterioration in relations with Bismarckian Germany. Conflict over Germany's increased tariff on Russian grain was one important reason for the growing rift between the two powers; others were Germany's renewal of the Triple Alliance with Austria-Hungary and Italy and her refusal to renew the "reinsurance treaty" of 1887 with Russia.[181] Alexander therefore sought new friends in Europe and, despite his apprehensions about France as a hotbed of revolution, began to pay more attention to her as a possible ally against the growing influence of Germany in the affairs of Central Europe. Large French loans in 1889 and 1890 heightened France's appeal,[182] and Alexander began to think that Russia might have something to gain from closer relations with that republican order the Romanovs had shunned since 1870. Alexander and Giers proposed to determine just how worthwhile such a relationship could be, while giving as little in return as possible.

In the world of Great Power politics, a sense of mutual advantage and even economic support are far from a formal alliance, and Alexander postponed making such a commitment to France in the hope that he might yet reestablish better relations with Germany. Yet the steps he and Giers took to demonstrate Russo-French cooperation to Germany soon drove them so close to the French that a full-fledged alliance was the inevitable result. They took their first step in July 1891, when a French squadron anchored at Kronstadt for the purpose of improving relations with Russia. Reported the prestigious and influential *Vossische Zeitung*, "the mighty squadron . . . carries instead of an arsenal of bombs and grenades, an inexhaustible supply of bottles and casks, and intends to open such a cannonade of champagne corks against the walls of the Russian fortress that the hearts of the Russians, already half-open, must infallibly capitulate."[183] Alexander reponded in kind, and even stood bareheaded while a Russian military band played the *Marseillaise* on board one of the French warships.[184] Before the French Admiral Gervais left Kronstadt two weeks later, the Franco-Russian entente had been established. It was not yet a full-scale military alliance, but it was a serious beginning. Russia and France moved a step closer the next year, when General Boisdeffre and the Russian Chief of Staff General Nikolai Obruchev signed a pact that, when approved by their governments, obligated each country to aid the other in the event of attack by Germany. Although Obruchev obviously acted with his Emperor's approval, Alexander postponed confirming the pact until Giers had made one final effort to bring Germany back to Russia's side; when that failed, Russia entered into a full military alliance with France.[185] In doing so, Alexander laid the base for the diplomatic realignments that led to the First World War.

When the alliance was signed at the end of 1893 (January 4, 1894, according to the European calendar), Russia presented a pleasing picture of stability to all who viewed her from abroad. This was in large measure the result of Alexander's policies and personality. Everything about him suggested strength, solidity, and unshakable resolve. He suffered no self-doubts and never questioned that his major purpose was to preserve the Romanovs' autocracy undiluted by concessions to public opinion. To his mind, Russia required a firm hand to guide her along that path of Orthodoxy, Autocracy, and Nationality in which he and his mentor Pobedonostsev so firmly believed. How very illusory this stability was became frighteningly clear once Alexander's hand slipped from Russia's helm. His death on October 24, 1894, ended Romanov Russia's last period of certainty. His son Nicholas II did not possess his singleness of purpose. Nor was Nicholas blessed with Alexander's unshakable belief in the rightness of his judgment. Torn first by war in the Far East, then revolution, then war in Europe, and again by revolution, Russia suffered all those cataclysmic upheavals against which Alexander's policies had shielded her. Less than a quarter-century after he breathed his last, Tsarist Russia would be no more. Along with the Hohenzollerns of Germany and the Habsburgs in Austria-Hungary, the Romanovs slipped from the world's historical stage. Whether their destruction after more than three centuries on the Russian throne was inevitable is a question, of course, that never can be answered with real certitude. It is far more certain that the vacillating regime of the weak and lackluster Nicholas II did a great deal to hasten the dynasty's end. The last Romanov was easily one of the least distinguished in that long line of men and women who ruled Russia between 1613 and 1917.

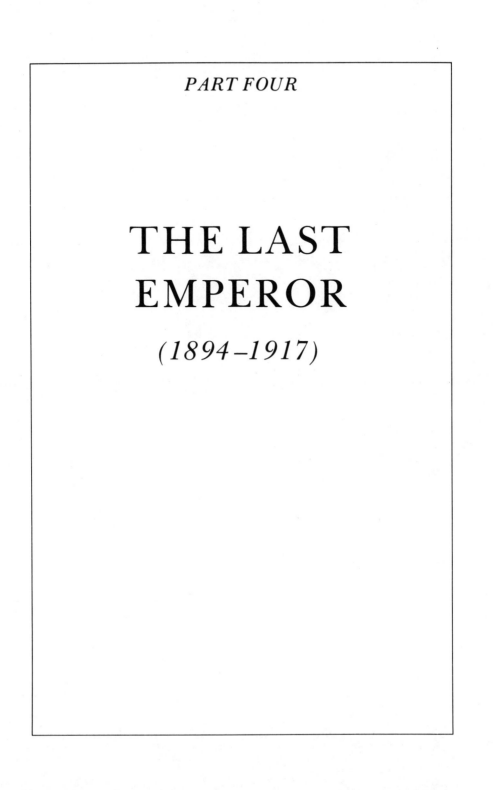

PART FOUR

THE LAST EMPEROR

(1894–1917)

CHAPTER XII

Nicky and Sunny:
The Last Romanovs

Alexander III had begun his reign in the midst of one of the gravest crises ever to face a Romanov. For the first time since the accession of Tsar Mikhail 268 years before, a Romanov had been assassinated, not as part of a palace coup d'état planned to place another member of the family on the throne but as the consequence of a revolutionary plot to destroy the dynasty and abolish autocracy in Russia.

From the moment the scepter became his, however, Alexander III knew who he was, what he should do, and what his policy ought to be. He ruled Russia and the Romanov family with equal firmness. Very quickly, he became notorious for his blunt remarks and fearsome roughness. "Stop playing the Tsar," he telegraphed when his brother Sergei took too much authority. When one of his ministers threatened to resign over a policy dispute, he seized him by the collar, shook him like a rag doll, and bellowed, "Shut up! When I choose to kick you out, you will hear of it in no uncertain terms!"[1]

In sharp contrast to the apprehension and turmoil of 1881, the day of Nicholas II's accession was tranquil and secure. Alexander III died in his bed, and the terrorist movement, which had once seemed so ominous, had long since been crushed. Thanks to his father's stern temper and powerful will, there was no threat to the security of the throne anywhere in the Empire when Nicholas inherited the crown just after a quarter past two on the afternoon of October 20, 1894. Yet his behavior was just the opposite of what his father's had been thirteen years earlier. According to one account, some of his first words after Alexander III breathed his last were, "What is going to happen to me

. . . and to all of Russia?" "I am not prepared to be a Tsar," he lamented. "I never wanted to become one. I know nothing of the business of ruling. I have no idea of even how to talk to the ministers."[2] Nicholas seemed bewildered, even frightened, by the road that lay ahead of him that day. "I saw tears in his blue eyes," his future brother-in-law, Grand Duke Aleksandr Mikhailovich, recalled.[3] This was the carefree, gentle young man with the large soft eyes and the neatly trimmed Vandyke beard, whom everyone in his family called "Nicky." Nicky was a colonel in the Preobrazhenskii Guards and dutifully made token appearances at the Imperial State Council twice a week. Beyond that, very few Russians knew anything about him. "Rarely has a people had a more vague notion about the personality and character of its new sovereign than do Russians at the present moment," reported the German Ambassador to his superiors in Berlin.[4]

Unknown or not, Russians suddenly found Nicholas at the pinnacle of their government. A slender man, only five feet seven inches tall, he felt overshadowed by a number of his relatives. Not the least among them was his massive two-hundred-fifty-pound uncle, the Grand Duke Aleksei Aleksandrovich, Chief of the Russian Admiralty, "admitted to be the best looking man in the Imperial family" and "hopelessly spoiled by women," whom one of his relatives once characterized as being devoted to "fast women and slow ships."[5] Equally formidable was another uncle, General Aide-de-Camp Grand Duke Nikolai Nikolaevich, who, from his great height of six feet five inches, towered a full ten inches above his slight nephew. No Romanov except Peter the Great had grown to greater height, and Nikolai Nikolaevich used it to good advantage whenever he attempted to intimidate Nicholas by pounding the desk with a massive fist and roaring out his demands. From all sides, Nicholas was overwhelmed by demands and counsel from courtiers, who had lived in terror of his bearlike giant of a father, but who now felt free to force themselves upon his mild-mannered son.

During his first days as Emperor, Nicholas thus was urged in as many different directions as there were people to offer advice. But only one among them encouraged him to stand firm against all demands and wheedling. "Show your own mind, and don't let others forget *who you are*," was the advice he received from the Princess Alix Victoria Helena Louise Beatrice of Hesse-Darmstadt, soon to become his wife, the Empress Aleksandra Feodorovna.[6] Nicholas called her "Sunny," as did her parents. She became the greatest, most constant influence upon him. The two of them—Nicky and Sunny—became the last Romanovs to rule Russia. Always in love, never failing in their devotion to each other, they stood hand in hand to preside over the Romanovs' proud three-century anniversary in 1913. Four years later, a revolutionary cataclysm wrested the Imperial scepter from their grasp. Hand in hand, they abdicated and spent long months under ever-worsening conditions of arrest and Siberian exile until they met their deaths in a remote town in the Ural Mountains. They never understood the aspirations of their executioners or their vision of Russia's future.

Perhaps it was chance, or perhaps it was indeed an omen, that Nicholas II, last Autocrat of All the Russias, was born on May 6, 1868, the feast day of Job the Sufferer. From the moment of his birth, unlike every other Romanov ruler born in the nineteenth century, he was Tsarevich, heir to Russia's throne. He spent his childhood at Gatchina in the midst of that sprawling nine-hundred-room palace that the Emperor Paul had enlarged during the late 1780s and early 1790s. There, amidst huge and opulent surroundings, the future Alexander III lived a spartan life and insisted that his children do likewise. As a child, Nicholas ate the simplest foods, bathed in cold water, and even was obliged to go hungry on occasion. Heir of a dynasty that possessed vast lands, rich palaces, such priceless treasures as the Great Hermitage art collection and such royal gems as the 195-carat Orlov diamond and the 40-carat Polar Star ruby, he was obliged to sleep on an army cot, with a hard pallet for a mattress. Nonetheless, Nicholas and his younger brothers and sisters, Georgii, Ksenia, Mikhail, and Olga, led perhaps the least disciplined childhood of any Romanovs. Their mother loved fun and gaiety, and allowed them to grow up quite free of that rigid discipline that had been such a part of their predecessors' lives. When guests were not present at lunch or dinner, it was not unusual for the children to dissolve into peals of laughter as they pelted each other with pellets of rolled-up bread.[7] Such freedom would have been unthinkable for the children of Paul I, Nicholas I, or even Alexander II.

Freedom to romp did not mean freedom from study. An entourage of great Russian scholars tutored Nicholas in history, geography, economics, political economy, and foreign languages. A more apt student than a number of his predecessors had been, he learned French and German fluently. His English was flawless, so much so, in fact, that when he visited England as a young man, people often mistook him for his cousin, the future King George V, to whom he bore an amazing physical resemblance.[8]

Nicholas's father insisted that Pobedonostsev be named chief among his tutors, and this misanthropic statesman trained the son as he had the father. He insisted that "the most precious gift of a statesman is ability to organize" and instilled that view deeply in Nicholas's inner consciousness. Nicholas always kept a diary—neat, concise, and in every way well ordered—and the triviality of its many entries provides a measure of him as a prince. He fell short of a number of Pobedonostsev's other requirements, however, and therein lay the beginnings of tragedy for him and for Russia. "A comprehensive and far-seeing intellect is demanded" in a statesman, Pobedonostsev once wrote. To this quality, he added others: "resolution in action, ability to seize the proper moment, to embrace rapidly the details of all work, without losing sight of its fundamental principles." "Fine observation of men and knowledge of character are indispensable," he continued. A ruler must have a finely developed "knowledge of whom to trust, and experience [to teach him] that the best of men are not free from low instincts and interested motives."[9] Sadly, Nicholas possessed none of these qualities and proved incapable of acquiring them.

If Nicholas needed proof that Pobedonostsev's precepts were the proper ones, his father, whom he held in absolute awe, stood as their living embodiment. Alexander III, the man of iron will and iron body who, in a train wreck in 1888, had held up the collapsing roof of the Imperial dining car to save his wife and children from being crushed beneath it, seemed to his son everything that a Russian Emperor ought to be. There is a story that, when the Austrian Ambassador spoke at a state dinner of mobilizing against Russia in the Balkans, Alexander picked up a silver fork, bent it into a knot, and tossed it to the amazed diplomat with the calm remark that "that is what I am going to do with your two or three army corps." "We have just two allies in this world: our army and our navy," he was fond of telling his advisers when Russia faced a diplomatic crisis.[10] For Nicholas, this giant and stern father was Tsar, Autocrat, and *Bogatyr,* that folk hero who loomed larger than life in the legends of olden times. He dreamed of being like him. Not long after he became Emperor, he swore "to preserve the principles of autocracy as firmly and as steadfastly as did my late and unforgettable father." Men who expected any less (or more) from him, Nicholas insisted in January 1895, were living in a world of "senseless dreams."[11]

While Nicholas saw his father as the embodiment of Pobedonostsev's ideal Romanov Autocrat, there could have been for him no more dramatic affirmation of Pobedonostsev's criticisms of man's nature and his warnings about the dangers of loosening society's bonds than the day of his grandfather's assassination in 1881. An impressionable, shy twelve-year-old boy at the time, Nicholas saw Alexander II's shredded legs and saw him shudder and breathe his last. With a proud but frightened heart, he saw his father and mother, now Emperor and Empress of Russia, speed off in a carriage to begin their reign, "accompanied by a whole regiment of Don Cossacks galloping in attack formation, their red lances shining brightly in the last rays of a crimson March sunset."[12] Before he became Emperor, Alexander III had tried to insulate his family from the affairs of state and had endeavored to create the atmosphere of "a country squire's estate of the 1840s," as one memoirist recalled.[13] All that changed in a moment. If he did not know it before, Nicholas learned on March 1, 1881, what it meant to fear his subjects.

If the day of his grandfather's death left Nicholas with frightening memories, the day of his father's coronation left him with a deep sense of pride. It was the greatest coronation Russians had yet seen. Russia was at peace with Europe, her international prestige restored, and relations with a number of European states cemented by the recent marriages of Alexander II's daughters, sons, nieces, and nephews. Olga Konstantinovna, his niece, had married King George of Greece. His elder daughter Maria Aleksandrovna had married Alfred, Duke of Edinburgh, while his son, Sergei Aleksandrovich, would soon wed Elizabeth of Hesse. This meant that, for the first time, not only Germans but royalty from other countries of Europe were present at a Romanov coronation. Among them were the Archduke Albrecht of Austria and his beautiful wife Maria-Theresa, and Queen Victoria's younger son, the Duke of Edinburgh, handsome in his British Admiral's uniform. All of the Romanov Grand Dukes wore the uniforms of their respective Guard regiments, each with the heavy diamond-studded double eagle around his neck that marked him as a Knight of St. Andrei. It was the most resplendent gathering of European royalty ever seen within the Kremlin's ancient walls. Wrote the Grand Duke Aleksandr Mikhailovich: "The grand duchesses, the princesses of England, Germany, Austria, Denmark, and Greece, and the ladies of the court displayed the biggest accumulation of glittering jewelry ever seen by me or anyone else, before or after May 15, 1883."[14] Grenadier Guards, standing shoulder to shoulder in uniforms from the Great Patriotic War of 1812, lined Alexander's path as he strode to the great Uspenskii Cathedral to crown himself and his wife Emperor and Empress of All the Russias. The opulence, the solemnity, the grandeur of the occasion helped to reassure Russians that the days of doubt and danger were past and that their new Emperor, strong and certain, would lead them to new heights of greatness. At thirty-eight, Alexander looked the picture of robust good health, and everyone expected his reign to be long and prosperous. "Just think, what a great country Russia will have become by the time we will have to escort Nicky to the Cathedral!" the Grand Duke Sergei reportedly mused as he, Nicholas, and some friends sat resting on the banks of the Moscow River a few days later.[15]

Nicholas spent most of the 1880s studying with Pobedonostsev and his other tutors. When he was not in the classroom, he lived a carefree life, unconcerned—indeed unacquainted—with the affairs of state to which his father devoted long hours each day. He built snowhouses and went skating with his sister in the winter, gardened and planted saplings in the spring and summer, and chopped wood in the fall. When he grew a bit older, he went out almost every night during the winter social season, enjoying the great array of entertainments to be found in St. Petersburg during the weeks before Lent. He adored the opera, the theatre, and the ballet. It was then the age of Tchaikovsky,

Rimskii-Korsakov, Balakirev, and Borodin, and their newest compositions, in addition to the standard European operatic and symphonic repertoire, could be heard at the Imperial Mariinskii Theatre, the Italian Opera, and the Imperial Conservatory. Nicholas saw Tchaikovsky's new *Sleeping Beauty* ballet three times in the month after its premiere. He dined, drank, sang, and danced night after night, often the whole night through, as he took in all the pleasures that the vibrant culture of Russia's great capital had to offer. Sometimes, he went to restaurants and private parties with a group of young army officers, whose company he enjoyed and whose life he had begun to share.[16]

Nicholas began to take an interest in army affairs soon after his nineteenth birthday. Like so many Romanovs, he loved the army, its order and its precision. The fixed daily routine of Russia's peacetime army appealed to that sense of order Pobedonostsev had urged upon him for more than a decade. "I am now happier than I can say to have joined the army," he wrote to his "dear, darling Mama" that June.[17] Soon, he received command of a Hussar Life Guards Squadron, and grew to love especially the life of a junior officer, with its freedom from heavy responsibilities. "It appealed to his passive nature," wrote his brother-in-law, the Grand Duke Aleksandr Mikhailovich. "One executed orders and did not have to worry over the vast problems handled by one's superiors."[18]

But these were not the only attractions Nicholas found in army life. For the first time, he was at least partly on his own. From his first days at Krasnoe Selo, site of the army's annual summer maneuvers, he enjoyed the company of his brother officers, the jesting, the drinking, and the camaraderie. "Dinners are very merry," he wrote.[19] To his diary he confided more: "Got a bit soused." "Got stewed." "The officers carried me out." "Wallowed in the grass and drank."[20] It was a happy, rewarding time for a young man who would have loved a life that posed few demands and brought no responsibilities. "He never consented to promote himself to [the rank of] a general," wrote his brother-in-law, because the colonel's rank he held at the time of his father's death "reminded him of his carefree youth."[21]

As one would expect from a young man just past twenty, there was more to Nicholas's carefree youth than drinking, jesting, and lighthearted maneuvers. He was not quite twenty-two when he first met Mathilde Kschessinska, the star graduate of the Imperial Theatre Ballet School. At first, it was she who pursued him. "I fell in love with the Tsarevich on the spot! I can still see his magnificent eyes, his tender, kind expression," she recalled in the memoirs she wrote nearly a half-century, two revolutions, and two world wars later.[22] Kschessinska was small and vivacious, not yet eighteen, with a high, full bosom; deep-set, dark, dancing eyes; and a winning coquettish smile set off by the mass of dark ringlets that framed her face. Eventually, she won not only Nicholas's heart but also those of his cousins, Grand Duke Sergei Mikhailovich, who gave her a summer house at Strelna, and the dashing Grand Duke Andrei Vladimirovich, whom she married in Paris after the revolution that destroyed his family and the prince she had loved first. But those days still were far away in the spring of 1890 when Kschessinska made her debut and lost her heart to Nicholas. Nicholas's diary recorded progress in her campaign to conquer his heart:

> July 17th: I like Kschessinska very much.
>
> July 30th: Gossiped at her window with little Kschessinska.
>
> July 31st: After lunch went, for the last time, to the dear little theatre at Krasnoe Selo. Said goodbye to Kschessinska.
>
> August 1st: Those minutes spent in front of the theatre tantalised my memory.[23]

Nicholas and Kschessinska were not fated to become lovers that summer or even the next, since the little ballerina, who still lived under the watchful eyes of her parents, was sent to Europe with her godfather. A few months after he said goodbye to her at Krasnoe Selo, Nicholas embarked upon a world tour that carried him from St. Petersburg to Egypt's pyramids, to the jungles of India and Ceylon, to the exotic cities of Singapore, Bangkok, Hong Kong, and Tokyo. Everywhere, he was met with pomp and ceremony that obscured the true nature of the world he was seeing for the first time. "My trip is senseless," he told Grand Duke Aleksandr Mikhailovich when they met in Ceylon. "Palaces and generals are the same the world over, and that's all I am permitted to see. I could just as well have stayed at home."[24] He made no secret of how irritating he found his never-ending ceremonial duties. "You must understand that your position brings this with it," his mother wrote to him in India. "You have to *set your personal comfort* aside, be doubly polite and amiable and, above all, never show that you are bored."[25] "You must remember what you represent," she reminded him three months later. "Think how *many eyes* are turned on you."[26]

It was not the eyes of the many but the eyes of just one man that Nicholas had to fear. He reached Japan at the beginning of May and visited a number of the island's most scenic regions. Then, the unthinkable happened. In the small town of Otsu, a minor police official suddenly leaped at Nicholas, swinging a sword at his head. The weapon struck his forehead a glancing blow, which left a gash some two inches in length, cut to the bone. The would-be assassin raised his sword again, but Prince George of Greece acted quickly to deflect the blow with his walking stick.[27] By the narrowest of margins Nicholas escaped death. It was a sobering experience for him, and a frightening one for his family half way around the world in St. Petersburg. "Our cup of sorrow was full, and I assure you Papa and I were at the end of our strength," his mother wrote after hearing the news. "Kiss this good [Prince] Georgie for me and thank him ever so much for knocking over that abominable beast of a Japanese."[28]

After his narrow brush with death, Nicholas sought the safety of Russian soil. He sailed immediately to Vladivostok, Russia's far eastern Pacific bastion, and then made his way back to St. Petersburg across Siberia, a land journey of more than five thousand miles. Nicholas, the last Romanov, thus became the first to travel from one end of his Empire to the other. He left us no clear impressions of this part of his journey, but we know from contemporary accounts that its eastern half must have been rigorous in the extreme. Construction of the Trans-Siberian Railway had only just begun, and the track reached no further east from European Russia than the city of Tomsk, still with fewer than thirty-five thousand inhabitants, in which Siberia's first university had been founded just three years before. The journey from Vladivostok to Tomsk thus had to be made by carriage, on horseback, and by boat.

Nicholas returned to St. Petersburg and his "dear darling Mama" at the end of summer, 1891. "We shall *meet* again *the day after tomorrow* or very nearly so!" she wrote to him on August 1. "I can hardly wait any longer and am all trembling with expectation."[29] Very soon, Nicholas resumed the life he had left behind nearly a year before, still taking no active part in his father's government. Alexander evidently felt that many years lay ahead before age would oblige him to initiate Nicholas into the arts of statecraft. In the meantime, Nicholas continued to pursue Kschessinska. "Since our meeting, I have been in the clouds," he wrote after a few private moments with her in her parents' sitting room early in 1892.[30] Soon, he began to send her gifts—flowers whenever she went to watch the indoor races at the Michael Riding School, and then a gold bracelet with a large sapphire surrounded by diamonds.

As Nicholas's attentions grew more ardent, Kschessinska's career as a ballerina flourished. Although not yet twenty, she had progressed to title roles, always performing under the direction of the brilliant ballet master Petipa. "This young prima ballerina has everything on her side: a charming physique, faultless technique, polished execution, and perfect lightness," proclaimed *Le Monde Artiste* from Paris. When Tchaikovsky saw her dance the role of Aurora in his *Sleeping Beauty*, he came backstage to congratulate her and to promise to write a ballet for her alone.[31] Soon critics began to proclaim her the equal of Russia's greatest.

With her success in the theatre came Kschessinska's final conquest of her Romanov prince. While Nicholas was on a visit to his mother's royal relatives in Copenhagen in the fall of 1892, she left her parents' home and rented "a charming little house," which Nicholas's great-uncle Grand Duke Konstantin Nikolaevich had built for the ballerina Kuznetsova in earlier times. It was a great moment in her life. She now could entertain Nicholas whenever he was free to come to her. Whispered words of passion now could become deeds. "With beating heart I awaited the Tsarevich's return," she confessed.[32] Nicholas did not disappoint her. As a housewarming gift, he gave her a set of eight golden vodka cups inset with precious gems and used to come frequently for supper and long evenings in the "retiring" life they shared together. "I stood by the window, waiting for the regular gallop of his magnificent charger, which rang out from afar on the roadway," she later remembered.[33] To Kschessinska, or, perhaps, *with* her, Nicholas was a paladin, a knight. How different was the Nicholas in her recollections from the Tsar who ended letters to "Sunny," his Empress, with the words, "Your 'poor weak-willed' little hubby."[34] For a brief time in 1893 and early 1894, Nicholas could be for Kschessinska the prince he dreamed of being, the prince she thought him to be. And then, those days were gone. In parting, Nicholas wrote, "whatever happens to my life, my days spent with you will ever remain the happiest memories of my youth."[35]

It was, of course, Princess Alix of Hesse-Darmstadt, not Kschessinska, who would have "Nicky," for it went without saying that he must one day wed the daughter of a ruling house. Born on June 6, 1872, "Sunny" was just four years younger than the prince whose throne she would share. Her mother, the Princess Alice, was a daughter of Queen Victoria and, like all the offspring of England's great queen, she treasured her ties with her homeland even after she wed Grand Duke Louis of Hesse-Darmstadt.[36] At first, Alix was a happy child, "a sweet, merry little person, always laughing," her mother once wrote.[37] But her childhood laughter soon faded. When she was only six, her mother died of diphtheria, and Alix became cool, aloof, and serious. As the Princess Alice would have wished, she grew into a proper English gentlewoman and spent much of her adolescence in England. She was well educated, not merely in the arts generally thought proper for a woman of high breeding but also in history, literature, and languages. By the time she was in her mid-teens, she had a passion for politics and a will of iron.[38]

From the moment of her birth, Alix's life was tied not only to England and Queen Victoria but to the Romanovs and Russia. The Empress Maria Aleksandrovna was her aunt. Soon after her twelfth birthday, in the summer of 1884, an even closer tie was added when her elder sister Elizabeth, known to everyone as "Ella," married Alexander III's younger brother, Grand Duke Sergei Aleksandrovich. Alix went with her sister to St. Petersburg, watched her make her formal entry into the city in Catherine the Great's gilded coach, and stayed with her in the Winter Palace. It was during the days of Ella's wedding that Alix first met Nicholas, then a shy, slender youth of sixteen. According to what she later told Anna Vyrubova, one of her most trusted ladies-in-waiting, Nicholas at that time gave her a brooch, which she first accepted and then, in confusion, returned.[39]

During the five years that separated Alix's first and second visits to St. Petersburg, Ella, now Grand Duchess Elizaveta, seems to have won the hearts of her Romanov relations. Among them, she considered Nicholas and his little sister Ksenia to be her especially "great friends."[40] Meanwhile, Alix grew into a strikingly beautiful young woman. She was tall, with finely chiseled features and large sad eyes, her pale skin set off by masses of red-gold tresses, which she often wore swept up on her head to emphasize her neck and shoulders. Victoria hoped to marry her to her grandson, the Duke of Clarence. Elizaveta was appalled. "I find the idea of [the Duke of Clarence] marrying Alix quite dreadful," she wrote to her brother. "The chief thing is that he does not look overstrong and is too stupid."[41] Even before Alix rejected Clarence's suit in mid-1889, Elizaveta evidently had hopes of marrying her to Nicholas, despite the objections of Queen Victoria, Alexander III, and the Empress Maria Feodorovna. She invited her to spend the entire social season of 1889–90 with her in St. Petersburg and arranged for her path to cross Nicholas's as often as possible.[42] Nicholas had not yet met Kschessinska, and he paid some attention to this tall, flaming-haired beauty, the younger sister his favorite aunt so loved. He took Alix skating, and they went tobogganing on those great "ice hills" Russians built to slide upon in the winter. They met at receptions, and Nicholas even urged his parents to give a special tea dance in Alix's honor.[43]

Just how successful Alix was in winning Nicholas's heart during those winter weeks in St. Petersburg is difficult to judge. Nor is it at all clear that she was even seriously committed to winning it. After all, she and Nicholas were cousins by marriage, shared any number of relatives in common, and thus had a certain family affection between them. For the moment, that sufficed.

Alix returned to Russia in the summer of 1891 to visit her sister at Ilinskoe, the Grand Duke Sergei's great country estate near Moscow. After a year of traveling and contemplation, Nicholas's feelings were somewhat changed. He then was just past twenty-three, had seen the

world, and was at the age when young men of sound Victorian upbringing were supposed to fall in love. Probably his youthful Aunt
Ella's prodding, and the two sisters' physical resemblance, kept Alix
frequently in his thoughts. "O Lord, how I want to go to Ilinskoe," he
wrote in his diary on August 20, just more than a fortnight after he
had returned home from the Far East. "If I do not see her [Alix] now,
I shall have to wait for a whole year, and that will be hard."[44] Still, he
did not want to go badly enough to press the point with his father, and
he remained at Krasnoe Selo and the summer palaces around the capital. Alix continued in his thoughts, however. "My dream is some day to
marry Alix H," he confided to his diary four months later. "I have
loved her for a long while, and still deeper and stronger since 1889."[45]

The key words in Nicholas's "confession" of love were "dream"
and "some day," first of all because his father, mother, and Queen Victoria opposed the idea; second, because Alix, a devout Lutheran, would
have to change her religion; and, finally, because his romance with
Kschessinska enabled him to postpone facing what could be a difficult
and unpleasant confrontation with his father. Clearly, and perhaps not
so unusually, Nicholas enjoyed the process of falling in love, but he was
not inclined to pursue any serious course for the moment. He had confided to Kschessinska that "of all possible fiancées, he liked the Princess
Alice [Alix] best."[46] For the moment, however, he could play the role
of the little ballerina's Prince Charming, who galloped up to her
"charming little house" on his "magnificent charger," in a relationship
that required no commitment and bore no responsibility. When a commitment had to be made, he sought out a woman who, like his mother,
would rule him. Alix had all the will, the fire, and the dedication to
follow difficult courses that Nicholas so obviously lacked. Sadly, her
dedication and her exhortations nearly always pushed him in the
wrong direction.

"I cried like a child and she did too," Nicholas wrote to his "dear
beloved Mama" in describing the moment when Alix accepted his proposal. "But her expression had changed," he added. "Her face was lit
by a quiet content."[47] Understanding this blossoming relationship between Alix and her Nicky is critical to understanding the last days of
Romanov Russia. It is complex in the extreme, and its emotional tang-

les are virtually impossible to unravel. Alix clearly engulfed her husband with a jealous passion and devoured him with a hunger so fierce that it consumed them both. She was deeply, intensely passionate—"a religious *exaltée* with a strong sexual drive," one historian wrote not long ago[48]—and Nicholas loved her deeply, though much less aggressively, in return. Their long-enduring love thus was based for a quarter-century upon a very unequal partnership in which Alix demanded that Nicky submit to her will in all things—their family life, their moments of passion, and their politics. Nicky always couched his submission in words of love and tenderness, but it was near-total submission nonetheless. Alix's demands were expressed in a flurry of love words as well, but it was submission, not equality, that she demanded.

The best documentary record we have of this relationship on a day-to-day basis comes only toward the end of their lives, during the dreadful days of the First World War, but it shows that the pattern Alix established in 1894 had endured and strengthened during the intervening two decades. "I kiss you all over," she wrote, while Nicholas replied, "I love you and long for your caresses!"[49] "Don't laugh at silly old wify, but she has 'trousers' on unseen," she reassured him when he found the pressures at General Headquarters difficult to face and the political crisis in Russia more difficult to cope with.[50] As the war went from bad to worse and as the end of their days on the throne approached, Alix became even more forceful. "Don't hide things from me—I am strong—but listen to me," she insisted in December 1916, less than two months before the revolution drove them from power. "I suffer over you as over a tender, softhearted child—wh[o] needs guiding," she confessed. "Be Peter the Great, John [Ivan] the Terrible, Emperor Paul—crush them all under you," she exhorted him the next day.[51] "Tender thanks for the severe written scolding," Nicholas replied. "God bless you, my darling, my Sunny! Your 'poor weak-willed' little hubby Nicky."[52]

Those terrible days of crisis and defeat were far off and utterly unforeseen when Alix finally granted Nicky her hand in April 1894. Russia was at peace, as she had been for more than a decade. The revolutionary movement, which had sprung into being in the 1870s, had long since been crushed, and what few Russian revolutionaries remained were reduced to trumpeting their cause from the safety of Switzerland. The Russian Social Democratic Labor Party, of which Lenin's Bolsheviks would become one wing, would not be founded for another four years, and the Bolsheviks themselves would not proclaim their independent existence for almost a decade. In 1894 not even the revolutionaries themselves could foresee the rapid resurgence of their cause in Russia; indeed, everything pointed in just the opposite direction. Under Alexander III's strict control and the policies of Finance Minister Sergei Witte, the annual growth rate of Russia's economy stood at 8 percent, the highest anywhere in the world.[53] Russia had just lived through a terrible famine, to be sure, but the government had responded rather effectively to the crisis, and the countryside was on the road to recovery.[54] Clearly, much remained to be accomplished in Russia's agricultural sector, but even there there was some reason for hope, perhaps even cautious optimism.

Most comforting of all for Nicholas, when Alix agreed to marry him, he had no reason to expect that he would be called upon to face a Russian ruler's awesome responsibilities for many years. Those could be left upon his father's powerful shoulders, and he could abandon himself to his infatuation with his fiancée, while she launched her campaign to bind her Nicky to her with the tightest of bonds. Within a few weeks, she had captured his diary, that anchor of precision and neat, daily order, to which he had bound himself since his schoolboy days with Pobedonostsev. There, she wrote reassurances of her love, expressions of deep motherly concern for his well-being, and, perhaps most significant, sympathy for his inexperience, even his inadequacy. From the first moments of their life together, Alix offered her "darling boysy" her everlasting love (and eternal care) as lover, mother, and truest friend. When in mid-July she wrote in his diary that "your Guardian Angel is keeping watch over you,"[55] it was no longer clear whether she referred to the celestial or terrestrial variety of that peculiar species.

It probably would not be an overstatement to say that the summer of 1894 was the happiest of Nicky's life. "Dear darling beloved Mama" seemed to share every bit of her "beloved Nicky's" joy at Alix's acceptance of his proposal, confident that the young princess would not soon replace her in her son's affections. At the same time, Nicky's good friend and cousin "Sandro," Grand Duke Aleksandr Mikhailovich, was about to marry his favorite sister Ksenia, who, his Mama assured him, was "in a seventh heaven of bliss" about it all.[56] Most of all, there was Alix—lovely, regal Alix with the flaming red-gold hair and the soulful blue eyes—for whom he could not be "grateful enough to Providence which has granted me such a treasure for life,"[57] whose consent left Nicky in such a state of ecstasy that, for some time afterward, he confessed, "I couldn't even write [to dearest darling Mama], my hands trembled so."[58] In June, Nicky and Alix went to England to pay their respects to "Granny [Queen Victoria, who] loves me so and doesn't like me missing dinner"[59] and who was so sympathetic to the young couple's blooming love that "she even allowed us *to go out for drives* without a chaperone!"[60]—despite Nicky's confession that whenever he and Alix were alone in the Palace, he could get nothing done "because every moment I simply had to get up and embrace her."[61] In all, it was a near-perfect summer, a time in which "nature, mankind, everything, seem to be good, lovable, and happy."[62] The only cloud on the horizon was very far away to the south, in the mountains of the Caucasus, where Grand Duke Georgii Aleksandrovich, Nicky's younger brother, was languishing in a tuberculosis sanatorium.

Suddenly a cloud greater and blacker than any Nicholas had ever envisioned darkened the sky. On October 20, 1894, nephritis took the life of Alexander III, and Nicholas became Russia's Emperor. His first duty was to bury the man he had loved as a father and revered as a sovereign. As was sadly typical of so much he undertook during the next twenty-three years, Nicholas did the job badly, although things seemed to go well at first. A special train bore Russia's living and dead Emperors from Livadia back to St. Petersburg, after first stopping at Moscow, where Alexander's body lay in state overnight in the Kremlin. The difficulties began in St. Petersburg where Alexander's coffin arrived at ten o'clock on the morning of a dark, cold, wet day. Overwhelmed by grief and, at the same time, consumed by infatuation for his Alix, Nicholas evidently had not made the proper arrangements for the procession to the Peter-Paul Fortress Cathedral. According to one account, "no one knew their proper place. Deputations got lost and stayed away.

Among the groups of clergy, courtiers, high officials and generals
—everywhere, in fact—one heard loud conversations, as people made
observations, exchanged impressions with acquaintances on balconies
and at windows, and laughed loudly at various remarks."[63] Nicholas
followed the hearse, overwhelmed by depression, and looking neither
to the left nor to the right. Alix rode in a separate carriage, heavily
draped in black. Old peasant women in the crowd, those ever-present
harbingers of good and evil, joy and sadness, saw her, crossed themselves one more time, and muttered darkly, "She has entered our land
behind a coffin. She brings misfortune with her."[64] These mutterings,
the lack of planning, the scenes of courtiers squabbling about who
should stand where in the Cathedral, all showed Russians that their
new Tsar was not the iron-willed colossus his father had been. The
same message was proclaimed to the European royalty and statesmen
who had come for the funeral. Nicholas himself realized that such a
shameful display simply could not have occurred during his father's
reign.

Because Nicholas was the first unwed adult male Romanov to ascend Russia's throne since the mid-seventeenth century, it was a matter
of some import that he and Alix be married as soon as possible. So
anxious was he to press on with his wedding that the ceremony of
Alix's conversion to Orthodoxy took place on the very day after
Alexander's death. While the embalmers worked their arts on the
bloated cadaver of the dead Emperor, Alix knelt in the chapel at
Livadia, took the name of Aleksandra Feodorovna, and announced her
acceptance of the True Faith of Nicholas and his fathers.[65] The last
barrier that had stood in the way of her marriage to Nicholas was gone.

On November 14, only a week after Alexander III had been laid to
rest in the Peter-Paul Fortress Cathedral, Nicholas married Aleksandra
Feodorovna in a small ceremony. Dressed in a gown of silver brocade
and wearing the diamond wedding crown of Imperial Grand Duchesses, Alix walked through the long corridors of the Winter Palace to
its chapel where her Nicky awaited her.[66] It is perhaps significant that
he had donned not the uniform of the Preobrazhenskii Guards, of
which he now was the colonel in chief, but that of the Hussar Life
Guards, in which he had found such happiness as a junior officer just a

scant half-decade before. It was the uniform in which he had first met Alix; it also was the uniform in which he had been Kschessinska's Prince Charming. It stood for his carefree youth and for none of his sorrow. Their faces showing the strain of their recent family tragedy but still looking radiant in their love, Nicky and Alix exchanged vows to become man and wife in the presence of family and friends. It was a strange, bittersweet sort of day, so typical of their life together for the next twenty-four years.

"Our marriage seemed to me a mere continuation of the masses for the dead, with this difference that I now wore a white dress instead of a black [one]," Alix later wrote.[67] But happiness took precedence over tragedy for the moment. On their way back to the Anichkov Palace after the ceremony, Nicholas ordered that the soldiers who lined their route be removed so that the masses of Russians who crowded behind them could come close to their new sovereigns. Hordes of Petersburgers crowded around the Imperial sleigh. "This was a daring and beautiful gesture," reported the correspondent of France's *Journal des Débats,* who thought it augured well after the strict regime of Alexander III.[68] It seemed to him that Nicholas intended to become more accessible, and no correspondent from the Third Republic could fail to be impressed by that prospect. George, Duke of York, a future King of England, echoed similar sentiments when he wrote to Queen Victoria that "when they drove from the Winter Palace after the wedding, they got a tremendous reception and ovation from the large crowds in the streets [and] the cheering was most hearty and reminded me of England." Nicholas, he added, "does everything so quietly and naturally . . . [that he] is very popular already.[69]

Nicholas planned his coronation for the spring of 1896. More than any previous Romanov, he wanted the common people, the *narod,* to feel that they were a part of it. The traditional coronation ceremonies would take place within the Kremlin walls in the presence of the usual assortment of statesmen and dignitaries. Afterward, there was to be a mass banquet for the Russian people on a truly gargantuan scale. Tens of thousands of metal mugs were to be manufactured as gifts for the people of Russia from Nicholas and Aleksandra. Each was to bear a raised double-headed Imperial eagle, the date of the coronation, and the initials *Ӂ* and *A* (the Russian monograms for Nicholas II and

Aleksandra), all in gold-colored enamel. There would be dancing, circus performers, tables piled high with food, and twenty booths to dispense thousands upon thousands of gallons of beer to Russia's thirsty peasants. All of this was to be given to the *narod* by their sovereigns.[70] Nicholas ordered proclamations sent throughout his Empire. All of his loyal subjects were invited to a great outdoor celebration, to be held on May 18, the fourth day after his coronation. The people were to assemble at Khodynka Field just outside of Moscow, where the Imperial Army Corps of Engineers held summer maneuvers and practiced constructing entrenchments.[71]

Long before the ice had begun to break up in the Neva outside the Winter Palace in the early months of 1896, the coming coronation had become a lively topic of conversation all over Russia. Muscovites were hard at work, giving their city the face-lift it always received before it greeted a new sovereign. Buildings were repainted, ugly fences and facades concealed behind newly cut evergreens, and banners and bunting made ready to decorate the buildings that lined the Imperial route through the city. People made their plans early. Everywhere, space was at a premium, for the government had bought up most of the rooms in Moscow's hotels for official guests. Small apartments were being rented for the month to out-of-towners for as much as 2,500 rubles, $1,250 at the official rate of exchange in 1894. All the European ambassadors and their staffs had come to Moscow from St. Petersburg, and all were planning lavish balls and entertainments to celebrate the occasion. France's Ambassador had almost a million francs placed at his disposal by his Foreign Minister Gabriel Hanotaux so that he could celebrate the coronation of his country's new ally. It was rumored that the ball he planned to give at the exclusive Hunt Club four nights after the coronation was going to cost nearly a quarter-million rubles. Everyone did his best to wheedle invitations. Even the less prestigious balls still would be worth talking about in years to come. Moscow's Bolshoi Theatre, rebuilt in 1854 to hold four thousand spectators, was going to have a special series of programs. Not only the brilliant stars of the Bolshoi would perform. There also would be some of the most famous ballerinas from the great Imperial Theatre Ballet Company in St. Petersburg. Among them was Kschessinska.[72]

Nicholas and Aleksandra reached the Petrovskii Palace on the outskirts of Moscow on May 6, 1894, Nicholas's twenty-eighth birthday. Three days later, they made their solemn ceremonial entrance into Russia's ancient capital. Watching her Prince Charming from the windows of her room at the Dresden Hotel, which fronted on the Tverskaia just across from the palace of Moscow's Governor-General, stood Kschessinska. Her account of the entrance of her "Niki" into his ancient capital remains one of the best we have:

> The imposing ceremony began at two in the afternoon and finished at about four. Troops lined the whole route. The procession was enormous. Besides detachments from various cavalry regiments of the Guards, there were representatives of the Asian tribes of the Russian Empire in their national dress. There were delegations of Cossacks, members of the high nobility led by the Marshal of the nobles of the Moscow district, all on horseback, followed by the Court orchestra and the Imperial Hunt in their rich uniforms, headed by His Majesty's Master of the Horse and Master of the Hounds. . . .
>
> Finally, the Tsar appeared, riding a white horse whose horseshoes had silver nails. He was followed by the members of the Imperial Family and by the foreign princes who had come to Moscow to attend the Coronation.
>
> Behind the foreign princes came the Empress Maria Feodorovna and the Grand Duchess Olga Aleksandrovna, in a gold carriage with a crown above it, drawn by eight white horses. Two small pages sat on the traces.
>
> In the gold carriage which followed, then Tsarina Aleksandra Feodorovna sat, all alone. Behind her in other carriages came the Grand Duchesses. The weather was magnificent.[73]

For the next four days, European royalty poured into the city: the Queen of Greece; the Kaiser's brother, Prince Henry of Prussia; Queen Victoria's son, the Duke of Connaught; Vittorio Emmanuele, Crown Prince of Italy; Prince Nicholas of Montenegro; Prince Ferdinand of Bulgaria, and many more. In all, the Moscow newspaper *Novoe Vremia* counted one queen, three reigning dukes, two reigning princes, twelve crown princes, and sixteen other princes and princesses who had come from abroad. Among the hundreds of nonroyal dignitaries was a representative from the Emperor of Japan, in whose country Nicholas had received the wound whose scar he still bore. He presented Nicholas and Aleksandra with a magnificent eagle, its plumage made of some two thousand delicate ivory plates, intricately carved to fit together as though they were natural feathers.[74] Finally, on the evening of May 13, Nicholas and Aleksandra moved to the Great Kremlin Palace, that vast two-story building the Russian-German architect Konstantin Thon had built between 1838 and 1849. Covering 500,000 square feet, and 395 feet in length, it had cost some 12 million rubles and had been filled with priceless paintings, sculptures, and artifacts of gold and silver.

The coronation of the Emperor Nicholas II and the Empress Aleksandra Feodorovna, the eighteenth Romanovs to rule Russia, began at nine o'clock on the morning of May 14, 1896. As tradition demanded, the oldest and greatest of the Imperial Guards regiments, the Preobrazhenskiis, stood guard that day. Nicholas observed the coronation ceremonial developed by his ancestors down to the last detail as he and Aleksandra made their way down the ancient Red Staircase and across the square to the great porch of the Uspenskii Cathedral adorned by its huge sacred frescoes. There, Metropolitan Sergei of Moscow, dean of all Russian churchmen, greeted the Tsar. "Most Pious Sovereign!" he began. "You are about to enter this most ancient and holy sanctuary to place upon Your brow the ancient crown of the Tsars and to receive the sacred unction." It was an awesome moment as the Metropolitan continued, "Just as there is no greater power on earth than the Tsar's power, so there is no greater or more difficult burden to bear than the Tsar's duties. Through Your anointing may the invisible might of the Almighty come down upon You and guide Your way as You seek to serve the welfare and happiness of Your faithful subjects."[75]

The Metropolitan's greeting ended, Nicholas and Aleksandra entered the Cathedral to begin a five-hour service during which Nicholas crowned himself and his Empress with the great golden crown of Catherine the Great. Nicholas was anointed by the Metropolitan, said a fervent prayer for Russia's welfare, and took Holy Communion. Then the Kremlin bells pealed, and 101 guns roared in salute to tell all Muscovites that Nicholas was Tsar and Autocrat of All the Russians. For Nicholas, it was the most solemn and inspiring moment of his life. As one historian wrote, "It was as if on that day he had wed Russia."[76] Yet, as so often happened during his life, an omen of disaster darkened even that solemn and joyful moment. As he ascended the altar steps, the chain of the Order of St. Andrei slipped from his shoulders. Only a handful of the great lords who stood closest to him noticed. They all were sworn to secrecy lest superstitious Russians begin to whisper about another evil sign having touched the Romanovs.[77]

On the evening of May 14, more than seven thousand guests assembled for the coronation banquet, among them the descendants of Ivan Susanin, the Russian peasant who, legend had it, had refused to tell the Poles where young Mikhail Romanov was hiding during the dark days of 1612. Susanin has led the Poles deep into a swamp. They had tortured him cruelly as punishment, but young Mikhail had remained safe in hiding. How far Russia had come since those days. And how different it might have been if fate had treated Russia differently. Filled with pride at Russia's greatness, Nicholas and Aleksandra looked down upon the entire assembly from a special dais, where they dined alone as tradition dictated. Afterward, there was a coronation ball made more brilliant by a dazzling array of jewels; Aleksandra in diamonds, her sister the Grand Duchess Elizaveta and Nicholas's sister the Grand Duchess Ksenia in brilliant emeralds, while others were resplendent in sapphires and rubies.[78] Precisely at ten o'clock, Nicholas and Aleksandra stepped onto the balcony of the Great Kremlin Palace, which faced the Moscow River. Aleksandra was presented with a bouquet of roses on a golden tray in which an electric switch had been hidden. The instant she took the flowers and released the switch, hundreds of electric bulbs, the first ever used in an Imperial coronation, illuminated the great Bell Tower of Ivan the Great, and similar illuminations burst forth all over Moscow as if to signal the great technolgical wonders the reign of Nicholas and Aleksandra, and the twentieth century they were about to usher in, would bring to Russia.[79]

While the descendants of Ivan Susanin had been invited to attend the coronation banquet, they were further honored three nights later when the Bolshoi Theatre Company joined with St. Petersburg's Imperial Theatre Ballet in a performance of *A Life for the Tsar*, Glinka's great operatic account of Susanin's patriotic deeds. Pierre d'Alheim, Russian correspondent for *Le Temps* of Paris, sent his newspaper an account of the evening. As at the coronation ball, the theatre was ablaze with color and jewels: officers in "red, blue, green, orange, and multicolored uniforms" and their ladies "covered with diamonds from head to toe." In the top tier of the theatre, there were representatives of the Russian peasantry, invited especially for the occasion, since peasants were not permitted in the theatre on ordinary occasions. This caused d'Alheim to remark that "sometimes autocracy is more courteous than a republic." Suddenly, d'Alheim reported, "there was a loud cheer. Everyone was on their feet. The Emperor and Empress entered their box and bowed to the audience." More shouts. The curtain rose and Glinka's great overture resounded through the theatre. It was a performance worthy of the occasion, yet everyone's eyes kept turning toward their young sovereigns. After the performance, d'Alheim left the theatre to find the streets outside filled with a huge crowd of people, all moving purposefully away from the city's center. It struck him as strange: the Tsar in Moscow and the *narod* leaving? Then he remembered. "Ah, yes! Tomorrow is the people's celebration at Khodynka Field." He joined the crowd and found himself among old women and children, the halt and the blind, the infirm and the robust. He went with them to see what the morrow would bring. Little did he imagine what he would find less than five miles from the Kremlin's walls.[80]

Even before the spring thaws had begun, peasants and workers from all parts of Russia had been moving in the direction of Moscow, intent upon seeing their Tsar and Tsarina and celebrating their coronation. More could do so than ever before because of the railroad construction program that Alexander III and his advisers had begun in the 1880s. Russia now had over forty thousand *versty* (about twenty-six thousand miles) of railroad over which passengers could travel distances that had seemed all but impossible before. Such western Siberian towns as Tomsk and Tobolsk had been many weeks' journey from Moscow in earlier times. Now even a peasant with a third-class ticket on the even cheaper slow train could make the journey in three or four days. It took less than three to make the journey from Kiev in the heart of the Ukraine. One could travel a thousand *versty*, just less than the distance from far away Tobolsk, for less than nine rubles (about $4.40), and the greater the distance one traveled the lower the rate became.[81] The railroad was beginning to bring Russia together as never before. Ironically, it would be these same improved means of travel that would bring workers and peasants from distant parts of Russia to St. Petersburg to help proclaim Nicholas's overthrow a bit more than two decades later.

As third-class passengers in slat-seated railroad cars, as deck passengers on riverboats, in carts, and on foot, the Russian *narod* flowed toward Moscow in the spring of 1896. To Moscow, Russia's ancient capital, Holy Moscow with its forty times forty churches, Moscow the city of the great Tsar, they came from the wilds of Siberia, the grainfields of the Ukraine, the mountains of the Caucasus, and the frozen lands of the far north. As one historian wrote not long ago, "all of Russia was [in Moscow]—that is the Russia of bast shoes, of linen foot-wrappings, or shapeless blouses, blue pantaloons, *tulepy* (greasy sheepskin jackets), heavy capes, kaftans, and worn blackcloth coats."[82] The *narod* had taken Nicholas to their hearts. He was their "little father," and they had come to pay him homage. Before dawn on the morning of May 18, close to a half-million had assembled at Khodynka, ready to cheer their Tsar and Tsarina. For days, they had eaten poorly—a crust of bread, a bowl of watery soup, a raw onion, or a half-cooked potato—as they had made their way to Moscow. Now, they were ready to fill their stomachs with the Tsar's bread, sausage, and pastries, and to slake their neverending thirst for alcohol with free beer to be drunk as toasts to Nicholas and Aleksandra from the commemorative mugs they were to receive.

It was among these people that Pierre d'Alheim found himself as he joined the crowd outside the Bolshoi Theatre that night. He let himself be carried along by the surging throng, impressed by its calmness and deep religious fervor. "From time to time," he reported, "hands would be raised [in prayer] as they came to a chapel or a church, and, for an instant, one caught a glimpse of that white spot on every breast on which they wore emblems of the cross. Women even stopped, crowded together, and offered up brief prayers, bowing low before these sacred places." "I was ecstatic," he continued. "How wonderful it was not to be considered a foreigner in this crowd and to be able to walk in the midst of these people!" D'Alheim moved with the masses through "broad streets, sparsely lit by electric streetlamps, through dark alleys, and then along the chaussée outside the city." Suddenly, they were in the open country in the vicinity of Khodynka Field. The surging stream of people, until that point constricted by buildings and trees along their route, he remembered, "spread out into a wide river, and then became lost in a veritable sea of people into which its noise was absorbed." Here was the Russia of the people, the Russia that Europeans never saw. It was everything that a foreign correspondent in search of the "real" Russia and the "real" Russians could have hoped for, and d'Alheim waxed poetic in his description of the manner in which they passed the predawn hours. There were "old men lying on their stomachs and chatting peacefully. Maidens doing folk dances in a ring. Peasant lads lustily singing humorous ditties and everyone roaring with laughter."

Abruptly, and much to d'Alheim's amazement, the crowd's mood changed just before dawn. "Suddenly, and without any warning, something seemed to seize the crowd," he wrote. "I struggled against it, and tried to turn back. The thought of staying there until morning no longer seemed so pleasant. But a huge crowd was already pressing from behind." Behind that crowd was another, and, behind them, yet another, and another "without end." Suddenly grown fearful, d'Alheim pushed sideways, finally broke free, and took refuge in an all-night restaurant from which he could look out upon the mass of common folk from which he had just escaped. He still was some distance from Khodynka and resigned himself to the obvious realization that he would not reach it that morning. He saw the crowd grow larger and larger, surging toward the stalls they knew had been set up to dispense beer and food in the far distance. D'Alheim continued to watch, fascinated, but at the same time still apprehensive. "Suddenly, there was a terrible, long, drawn-out wail," he recalled. "I caught sight of a small girl, saw her rise above the heads of the crowd, and saw her disappear suddenly. Women and men, somehow being disgorged from the mass, broke away in utter terror." D'Alheim heard them shouting, "There are ditches and trenches in there! People are falling into them! They say that people are simply vanishing!"[83]

That day, d'Alheim got no closer to the disaster than the far edge of the field. As he turned to leave, he came upon a scene so different that he must have thought himself in another world. Indeed, the contrast between his account of the early morning hours and what happened just a few hours later is so great that one would find it difficult to believe the latter part of his report except that other witnesses recorded much the same events. Vladimir Nemirovich-Danchenko, correspondent for the St. Petersburg weekly *Niva* and an associate of Konstantin Stanislavskii in founding the famous Moscow Art Theatre a year later, also had gone to Khodynka later that morning to investigate his cook's hysterical account of "thousands" being crushed to death in the ditches and trenches that crisscrossed the field. Nemirovich-Danchenko and d'Alheim saw the same thing. At the other side of the field, far away from the place where the beer and food stalls had been erected, a chorus of several thousands, conducted by the director of the Moscow Conservatory, sang beautifully. The stands were filled with elegant lords, bejeweled ladies, dashing army officers, and well-dressed merchants, their well-endowed wives especially gussied up for the occasion. Nicholas and Aleksandra appeared on a balcony to respond to the cheers. Toasts were drunk to their health, they received delegations from the Russian people, and everything went with well-orchestrated precision.[84]

After lunch, Nemirovich-Danchenko walked over to the other side of Khodynka Field to that place from which d'Alheim had seen the crowds fleeing from the safety of his restaurant post. The crowd was gone by then, and he walked easily and quickly. What few peasants there were seemed listless, sullen, depressed. Only when he passed beyond the broken stalls that were to have served the Tsar's food and beer did he see the sight that had reduced his cook to hysteria early that morning. Row after row of corpses greeted him; row upon row of trampled, broken, battered bodies that just a few hours before had been men, women, and children happily preparing to greet their Tsar.[85] According to official estimates, 1,389 people lost their lives in the stampede, and another 1,300 suffered injuries.[86] As with all official statistics published about disasters in Imperial Russia, these numbers were very low, and it is generally agreed that the numbers of killed and wounded were several times greater.

Incompetence and tangled bureaucratic lines of authority had been the chief factors in causing the Khodynka tragedy. What had happened, as near as anyone can determine, was that Nicholas's uncle Grand Duke Sergei Aleksandrovich, husband of Aleksandra's sister and Governor-General of Moscow, had gotten into a petty power struggle with the Minister of the Imperial Court, Count Vorontsov-Dashkov. Both men had sent off a flood of contrary and contradictory instructions to the Moscow police, and no one knew which orders to obey. As a result, officials sent far too few police to control the crowd. Nicholas himself was to some extent at fault because he had neglected to oversee the preparations,[87] but it was an even greater tragedy that he failed even to comprehend that fact and tended to excuse the whole catastrophe as one of those sad events that simply could not have been prevented. Muscovites had no such generosity. Wherever the Grand Duke Sergei went during the remaining days of the coronation celebrations and for some time after they had ended, crowds of commoners jeered and shouted their new nickname for him: "Prince Khodynskii."[88]

Nicholas himself was bitterly criticized by Russians and foreigners alike for allowing the coronation celebrations to continue. In fact, Sergei Witte, Nicholas's tough-minded and practical Minister of Finance, urged him to cancel the rest of the festivities, and a number of others shared his opinion.[89] Nonetheless, Nicholas and Aleksandra attended the French Ambassador's ball that very night, although they both appeared deeply distressed. The next day they attended a funeral service for the victims of Khodynka and visited several hospitals to offer their sympathies to those who had been injured. Nicholas donated a thousand rubles (several years' earnings for a peasant and most workers) to the families of each victim and founded a special orphanage for the children whose parents had died in the disaster.[90] These all were noble and generous gestures made by a concerned autocrat saddened by the catastrophe that had struck his people. But their impact was negated by Nicholas's insensitive order to continue with plans for a military review. Just eight days after Khodynka Field had been stained by the blood of innocent workers and peasants, Nicholas stood again on its reviewing stand to receive the salute of 40,592 men, including 67 generals, in a grand finale to the coronation celebrations.[91]

Events did not allow Nicholas and Aleksandra time to dwell upon the Khodynka disaster, although Nicholas, who tended to be introspective about tragedies (he still thought often about his father's death), may well have wished to do so. Just two months later, protocol required that they visit the newly opened All-Russian Exposition of Trade and Industry at Nizhnii Novgorod. The fair was Witte's special creation and was designed to publicize how far Russia had come along the road to modernization and industrial development since the accession of Alexander III. "After touring through the various exhibits, you unconsciously become convinced that Russia is marching forward with rapid strides," the great Moscow industrialist Savva Morozov remarked. "One feels a surge of strength, of energy, and you come to the conclusion without even realizing it that time has been well spent and not wasted."[92] Nicholas and Aleksandra shared Morozov's pride, as well as his hopes for the future. Still, their visit did not pass without incident. Just as they arrived at the central arcade, a violent hailstorm struck, and great balls of ice shattered the glass in many pavilions. Many Russians saw it as another omen. Again, it did not seem a propitious one.[93]

Not long after their visit to Nizhnii Novgorod, Nicholas and Aleksandra visited briefly with the Habsburg Emperor Franz Josef in Vienna, went on to Breslau to meet with the Kaiser Wilhelm, and then traveled on to Copenhagen. In early September, they went to Scotland's Balmoral Castle to visit "Granny [Queen Victoria who] was kinder and more amicable than ever." After traveling south from Scotland in "Granny's own very comfortable railway carriage,"[94] they boarded the Imperial yacht *Polar Star* at Portsmouth Harbor and were escorted across the channel by a squadron of the Royal Navy. In mid-channel, ships of the French fleet steamed out to escort them to Cherbourg. Overwhelmed by the welcoming ceremonies, Nicholas remained on a high emotional peak for the rest of his visit.

Nicholas's description of his stay in France provides a glimpse into the inner workings of the man who stood for Russia in the eyes of millions of men and women throughout the world. It is not a reassuring picture that emerges. While Russia's Autocrat needed to be firm and sober in his judgments, ever-conscious of his nation's and his people's interests, Nicholas was far too busy reveling in the reception he received. He thought long and often of "dear Papa" who, with his Foreign Minister Giers, had been the architect of the Franco-Russian alliance. But his thoughts were not of Alexander's statesmanship, but of his death and how much he was missed. "I nearly cried when the band struck up dear Papa's favorite march 'Sonnez clairons,' the one they played on the *Marengo* during the naval review at Kronstadt," Nicholas wrote. "I was very glad to meet [General] Boisdeffre and [Admiral] Gervais," he added. Both of these men had played an important part in the French visit to St. Petersburg in 1891 and were military planners and diplomats of international stature. Yet Nicholas saw in them another, far less consequential, side. "They are both such kind good men," he continued in his letter to his mother, "and the latter [Gervais] couldn't speak about Papa without tears in his eyes!" These were qualities any loyal bourgeois son would have treasured in an old family friend. They were hardly the characteristics upon which an Autocrat should form his judgments about the men with whom he must deal in the treacherous arena of international politics.

If Nicholas found France's senior officers good, kind, and tender, he was equally impressed by the reception that awaited him in Paris. Clearly, he saw his welcome as a triumph and was beginning to see himself in a totally unearned role as a figure of international significance. He delighted in the formal dinners and receptions, but the insensitive manner in which he treated some of his hosts indicated how little he knew about the political realities of France and provided a preview of how inept he would be in dealing with parliamentary government when it came to Russia a decade later. He and Aleksandra attended a great reception at the Presidential Palace, where "all the members of the higher administration, Ministers of State, Generals, Admirals, Senators, and Deputies were present." There, Nicholas went out of his way to avoid the Deputies, the elected representatives of the French people, and assured his mother that "of course, I talked only to a few better-known ones who had been Ministers." In his view, men of birth, or at least men chosen by a Head of State to serve their nation, were the only company proper for a Russian Autocrat at a reception. Obviously, men chosen by the French *narod* and bourgeoisie were not.

Perhaps best of all, Nicholas loved the military review that concluded his visit to France. He appeared in the uniform of the Cossack Guards, which made him seem taller and more heroic than he was. He felt sad when he and Aleksandra said goodbye to "our dear Boisdeffre and Gervais" at the frontier, especially because they went on to Germany, which Nicholas thought of as "black and dark and boring." He found Germany bearable because the time there was spent not at the Court of the Kaiser, whose overbearing manner made the Tsar feel small and insignificant, but with Aleksandra's family in Darmstadt. "After all," he confessed, "it is very pleasant to take a rest and spend two or three quiet weeks in a small family circle."[95]

"A small family circle." That was what Nicky and his Alix loved best of all, and that is what they labored to create for themselves in Russia. Ill at ease at the Romanov Court and always her mother-in-law's inferior in Court protocol, Aleksandra retreated deeper into that shell she had first erected around herself after her mother's death. She insisted that she and Nicholas abandon the Winter Palace, where all reigning Romanovs had lived since the time of the Empress Anna, and spend their winters at the Alexander Palace at Tsarskoe Selo, where, as one historian wrote not long ago, she attempted "to confine her children and Nicholas himself to a sort of ever-lasting cosy tea-party."[96] It was an unhealthy world that Aleksandra created, peopled by those fawning mediocrities with saccharine and false emotions with whom she felt most at ease. Its mood was perhaps best characterized by her boudoir, the retreat she loved above all others, where the walls were hung with "mauve silk and fragrant with fresh roses and lilacs." There, Aleksandra reclined on a low couch over which hung a large painting of the Virgin Mary "asleep and surrounded by angels"[97] and received that circle of friends unworthy of the Empress of a great Empire. Into this world she sought to entice Nicholas, to draw him away from the company of serious statesmen, diplomats, and generals. It was, in the words of her faithful friend Anna Vyrubova, an "opal-hued" world,[98] the color of the stone thought by superstitious folk to bring ill fortune to all but those born in the month of October.

At Aleksandra's invitation, strange and shady characters came and went to prey upon her guileless faith in quacks, charlatans, and fake holy men. The first and most prominent among this early assortment of psychological and spiritual oddities was the bogus "Dr. Philippe," thrice-convicted of practicing medicine without a license in his native France. "Dr. Philippe" claimed to possess a variety of unusual powers, which included an ability to see into the future, to change the course of events, and to communicate with the world that lay beyond the grave. There is some evidence that he claimed to be in communication with the spirit of Alexander III, whose presence Nicholas still sorely missed and about whose death he still nourished a morbid fixation.

Among his other mysterious powers, "Dr. Philippe" convinced Nicholas and Aleksandra that he could help them produce the male heir whose birth they had awaited so long. His Imperial patrons were so convinced by his predictions that in 1902 they announced Aleksandra's "pregnancy." When, after six months, they finally had to admit that she had never been pregnant in the first place, the embarrassing publicity forced "Dr. Philippe" to leave Russia under a cloud. Nicholas and Aleksandra were sad to see him go and so concerned about his future well-being that Nicholas wrote to Emile Loubet, President of the Third Republic, to recommend his "scholarly" friend to the French Academy. In his turn, "Dr. Philippe" expressed deep concern about the future well-being of his Imperial patrons and made some effort to protect them from harm. Before he left Tsarskoe Selo, he gave Aleksandra a small silver bell he urged her to ring whenever untrustworthy, self-serving, or dangerous advisers approached Nicholas. As one might expect, she rang it on all the wrong occasions. "Dr. Philippe" also promised Aleksandra that "someday you will have another friend like me who will speak to you of God."[99] Aleksandra later took the appearance of the charlatan Rasputin as a fulfillment of that prophecy.

One of the reasons Aleksandra turned to quacks and bogus men of God was her intense and understandable desire for a son and her great sadness that she had not given birth to one after almost a decade of marriage. Every two years, she had borne a daughter—Olga (1895), Tatiana (1897), Maria (1899), and Anastasia (1901). Each time her labor pains commenced, Nicholas and all of Russia anxiously awaited the birth of a son. Each time, Petersburgers had listened for that 300-gun salute that would announce the heir's birth, and each time the firing had ceased after the 101st cannon had discharged its shell, in the traditional salute to the birth of a Grand Duchess. Late in 1903, Aleksandra became pregnant again, and on July 30, 1904, everyone's prayers finally were answered when she gave birth to a son. He seemed a healthy infant, with golden curls and large gray-blue eyes, who weighed a full eight pounds. His delighted parents named him Aleksei, in honor of Tsar Aleksei Mikhailovich, who had been the first son ever born to a reigning Romanov. For a few weeks, all went well. Then, on September 8, Nicholas made a fateful entry in his diary. "Alix and I are very disturbed," he wrote, "at the constant bleeding in little Aleksei. It continued from his navel until evening."[100]

For some time, Nicholas and Aleksandra tried not to admit the sad and frightening truth. Eventually, they had to recognize that their treasured infant son suffered from hemophilia. It was a disease for which there was no known cure and little effective treatment. Because little Aleksei's blood simply could not clot properly, even the smallest bruise could turn into a great, painful, purple swelling. Every minor scrape, the sort that passes unnoticed in most children, was immensely painful. A small wound, or one of the many falls that all small children suffer, could prove fatal. Aleksandra, her friend Anna Vyrubova insisted, "hardly knew a day of happiness after she knew her boy's fate. Her health and spirits declined, and she developed chronic heart trouble. Although the boy's affliction was in no conceivable way her fault," Vyrubova continued, "she dwelt morbidly on the fact that the disease is transmitted through the mother and that it was common in her family."[101] Aleksandra withdrew deeper into her mauve cocoon at Tsarskoe Selo. She sought to draw Nicholas further into her self-imposed isolation as well. Tragically for herself, her son, her husband, and Russia, she enjoyed considerable success in her effort. At the Alexander Palace, surrounded by undistinguished friends of middling talent, narrow views, and staunch middle-class Victorian values, Nicholas became more and more a bourgeois *pater familias*.

But a Romanov Emperor could not simply retreat from St. Petersburg as a good Hessian burgher might do in Darmstadt. The Emperor Nicholas II ruled 130 million people who lived spread out over more than 8.75 million square miles of territory. His Empire had made great economic progress during the past two decades, but that had not been achieved without great cost, the most obvious and tragic payment for which had been the great famine of 1891. It was also a matter of serious concern to thoughtful Russians that, while their country had indeed embarked upon the road to industrialization and economic modernization, a number of pressing problems had been left unattended. Most Russians were illiterate. Only a small percentage of Nicholas's subjects ever saw a doctor in the course of their lives. Almost none among the Empire's vast *narod* ever experienced any of those pleasures that educated men and women ranked in the category of "the finer things of life." Most Russians, in fact, could not be confident of enjoying what were normally classed as life's necessities. They had become so impoverished that economists had begun to express reservations about the continued progress of Russia's industrial development. The great spurt of industrial activity the policies of Alexander III and Sergei Witte had fostered had been confined almost exclusively to the heavy industrial sector. "Upon what basis could light, consumer-oriented industries develop?" these men asked. The sad truth was that, by 1900, Russia still had no widespread demand for consumer goods because most Russians were too poor to buy them. Peasants grew what they hoped would be enough food to get them through the year, made most of the articles they needed in their daily life, and traded for those few odd commodities they could not make themselves.

Conditions such as these had led quickly to the resurgence of a revolutionary movement in Russia once the firm hand of Alexander III had slipped from the helm. These revolutionaries spoke of a new society, in which the people themselves would possess the means of production, a society to which all men and women would contribute according to their ability and from which each would receive according to their needs. It was conceived of as a society founded upon the principles of social justice, in which every man, woman, and child would live free from want and walk with dignity, proud at being useful and valued. To create that society, Russia's socialists insisted that the Romanovs must be swept aside and destroyed by the scourge of revolution. Although the prospect seemed remote in 1900, they would have the opportunity to put their message into practice in 1905, and when they failed on that occasion, they gained another opportunity in 1917.

We shall give more attention to this revolutionary message further on. Here, we should mention that there were other men and women who called for social justice and who begged Nicholas to take the necessary measures before the course called for by the revolutionaries became the only alternative to the Romanovs' regime. Foremost among them was Russia's greatest living novelist, Count Lev Tolstoi, who sent Nicholas a stern warning at the beginning of 1902.

When he wrote his famous letter on January 16, 1902, Tolstoi was seventy-three years of age, a great artist who had enjoyed wealth, success, and fame, only to reject them all in his search for the true meaning of life. He wrote not to Nicholas the Tsar of All the Russias, but to Nicholas the man. To use his own word, Tolstoi wrote to Nicholas as he would have written to a "brother." "I do not want to die," he began, "without having told you what great good you are capable of bringing to yourself and to millions of people, and what great evil you will bring to yourself and to millions if you continue on your present course." It was a stern beginning, and Tolstoi continued in an even more stern vein by setting forth a damning indictment of the Tsar's assistants: "the Tsar does not choose [advisers] from among those thousands of lively, energetic, truly enlightened, honest men who are anxious to take part in civil affairs, but only from those about whom Beaumarchais once said 'be mediocre and servile, and you will achieve everything.' " Tolstoi warned Nicholas not to be lulled into false confidence by the fabled love of the *narod* for their Tsar, for that was an anachronistic dream at best. In fact, Tolstoi insisted that the whole autocratic system of government was outdated. "Autocracy . . . may answer the needs of the people in Central Africa, in a region isolated from the rest of the world, but it no longer answers the needs of the Russian people," he warned. As a result, autocracy was obliged to rely heavily upon the instruments of repression to stay in power, but such measures could hardly serve to govern the *narod* properly. Tolstoi called upon Nicholas to "give the masses the opportunity to express their desires and demands." At the same time, he urged him to make the land the property of all, to abolish private landed property to stave off the threat of a socialist revolution.[102]

At the very least, Tolstoi's advice sounded like a call for parliamentary government. Just as he had risen against Loris-Melikov's call for very limited popular representation in 1881, so Pobedonostsev rose again against those calls Tolstoi and like-minded men issued at the opening of the twentieth century. "The continuation of the regime," Pobedonostsev warned, "depends upon our ability to keep Russia in a frozen state. The slightest warm breath of life would cause the whole thing to rot."[103]

Nicholas saw no reason to heed the pleas and warnings written by Tolstoi and a number of others. The achievements he had seen at Witte's All-Russian Exposition of Trade and Industry at Nizhnii Novgorod and the accomplishments his ministers reported to him each week convinced him that Russia was on the road to great progress that would, in the end, benefit everyone. In the meantime, there were bound to be disruptions, but, like his father, he thought the autocracy was secure behind the wall of its army's bayonets. He could not have been more mistaken in his judgment. Very soon, events in the Far East showed that the wall·was not as secure as Nicholas and his father had thought. Before he had time to adjust his policies to take that fact into account, Nicholas faced that threat of revolution against which Tolstoi and so many others who held progressive views had warned him. Shortly, he was obliged to grant a constitution. Nicholas thought that he had been forced to give Russians too much too soon. In fact, he had given them too little too late.

CHAPTER XIII

The Approach
of Disaster

At eight o'clock on the evening of January 26, 1904, Nicholas and Aleksandra entered the Imperial box at St. Petersburg's great Mariinskii Theatre. As always, the interior of the theatre shone like the architectural gem that it was. The great painted ceiling, the blue walls set off by ornate carvings covered with gold leaf, and the huge crystal chandelier, now ablaze with the light of recently added electric bulbs, all projected a warm and comforting glow, which contrasted sharply with the wet snow and icy wind outside. The performance that night was Dargomyzhskii's *Rusalka,* an opera based on Pushkin's tale of a miller's daughter seduced and betrayed by a young nobleman. It would be a memorable production, and one that Nicholas seemed quite prepared to enjoy. The preceding days had been especially difficult, and he must have been anxious to put thoughts of international crises out of his mind for a few hours. Two days before, the Japanese Ambassador, Shinichiro Kurino, had broken off the negotiations in which Russia and Japan had been attempting to resolve their differences in the Far East, especially in Korea, before their disputes burst into war.[1]

There were those who insisted that a war with Japan would pose few difficulties for Russia, and even thought it desirable. Kaiser Wilhelm, who signed himself "Willy" in the letters he wrote to his young cousin "Nicky," already had begun to address him as "Admiral of the Pacific Ocean";[2] and Minister of Internal Affairs Viacheslav von Plehve had said not long before that "in order to hold back the tide of revolution, we need a short, victorious war."[3] But Witte, now President of the Committee of Ministers, and General Kuropatkin, the Minister of War, warned against it, and Nicholas tended to share Witte's view that war would be "a great disaster for us."[4] A little more than a month earlier, he had told his leading advisers, "War is absolutely impossible [now]. Time—that is Russia's best ally. We grow stronger with each year that passes."[5] Nevertheless, Kurino's departure from St. Petersburg had left Nicholas in an almost fatalistic mood. "War is war, and peace is peace. But this business of not knowing either way is agonizing," he told Kuropatkin.[6] It seemed that it would be a relief just to have the decision made one way or the other. "All day, I was in an excited mood," he confessed, when Minister of Foreign Affairs Count Lamsdorf, Kuropatkin, and several others assembled to discuss the situation with him. He seemed to find a certain consolation in the decision they reached "not to start anything." For the moment, at least, he could turn his attention to *Rusalka,* which he later pronounced "very good" indeed.[7]

Eight o'clock on the evening of that same day found Vice-Admiral Heihachiro Togo, Commander of the Japanese fleet, far away from anything resembling the comfort and civility of Nicholas's surroundings. In every direction, he could see only the cold, dark surface of the sea, as his fleet of ten fast cruisers steamed west by northwest at full speed. At that moment, Togo's fleet was some fifty miles southwest of the southern tip of the Liaotung Peninsula. Unknown to anyone except himself and his superiors in Tokyo, Admiral Togo was going to begin the Russo-Japanese War in just a bit less than four hours from that moment by an attack against Port Arthur, where most of the capital ships of the Imperial Russian Pacific fleet lay at anchor. Among the vessels in the roadstead were seven battleships, led by the flagship *Petropavlovsk* and including the brand-new *Tsarevich,* purchased only a few months before from the French shipyards.[8] Togo's object was to destroy them all. To complete his mission, he needed speed, surprise, and a measure of luck.

While Admiral Togo and his ships' crews steamed resolutely toward Port Arthur, the Russians against whom their guns and torpedos soon would be directed were scandalously unprepared. Not one gun on the battleships was manned or loaded, and only one ship's searchlights were in use. Port Arthur's shore batteries stood immobile, still heavily coated with grease to help them withstand the fierce winter storms. The great ten-inch guns on Electric Hill could not be fired because they had no fluid in their recoil cylinders. Nicholas's Far Eastern Commander in Chief, Admiral Evgenii Alekseev, rumored the illegitimate son of Alexander II, was very well aware of Russia's rapidly worsening relations with Japan; nonetheless, he allowed his great battleships to lie at anchor with all their lights blazing. He had not even taken the elementary textbook precaution of installing torpedo nets around them.[9] That fact later came as no surprise to some. Alekseev's incompetence was notorious.

Alekseev's failure even to take the most basic precautions left his fleet as vulnerable to Japanese attack as the United States' Pacific fleet would be at Pearl Harbor some thirty-seven years and eleven months later. Just as at Pearl Harbor, the Japanese struck without warning. Even more incredible than at Pearl Harbor, they attacked at much closer quarters and still maintained the element of complete surprise. Admiral Togo's cruisers simply steamed into the roadstead, pulled alongside the Russian battleships, fired torpedoes into their hulls, and turned away at top speed. Within minutes, the battleships *Retvizan* and *Tsarevich* and several lesser ships had gaping holes blown in their sides. Not one of Togo's ships was damaged. With them, he then set up a blockade that put the surviving Russian ships out of commission. Even before war was officially declared, the Japanese had seized command of the sea in the Far East, so that they could land troops and supplies on the mainland at will. Without serious opposition from the Russians, they occupied all of Korea and drove northward toward the Yalu River and Manchuria.[10]

Word of Togo's attack reached St. Petersburg about three hours after it began, but it came not from Alekseev's headquarters but from a commercial agent, whose telegram his counterpart in St. Petersburg took to Witte. Witte immediately hurried to the home of an amazed and incredulous Kuropatkin. Kuropatkin, in turn, hastened to confer with Admiral Avelan, Chief of Russia's Admiralty. Five hours after the *Tsarevich* and the *Retvizan* had been torpedoed, Avelan still had received no word from Alekseev.[11] Nor would he for several hours more. From the moment Togo fired the first torpedo of the Russo-Japanese

War, Russia's Far Eastern forces thus felt the weight of timid, slow-witted senior officers and the frustration of impossibly bad communications.

To add to these handicaps, Russia's army and navy suffered under the burden of antiquated training that had not prepared them for the sort of war they must wage against a well-trained enemy, while the problems of supply for a war in the Far East were nearly insurmountable. A victim of its planners' lack of foresight, the Trans-Siberian Railway remained bisected by Lake Baikal, some thirteen thousand square miles of water that lay directly in its path in eastern Siberia. To save the expense of building the especially costly stretch of track around the lake's southern tip, its planners had decided to ferry freight and passengers across it, and that had proven an adequate, though somewhat awkward, stopgap measure so long as there was no great amount of heavy freight to be moved. Well aware of the immense difficulties that this created for supplying troops should war break out in the Far East, Kuropatkin had urged, from the moment he became Minister of War, that the eastern and western banks of the lake be linked by rail with all possible speed, but work went slowly. Forty tunnels had to be blasted through the mountains in order to complete a section of track that was only two hundred fifty *versty* (just less than one hundred seventy miles) in length.[12] At the beginning of 1904, the rail link had not yet been completed, and Kuropatkin estimated that another sixteen months would be needed to finish it even if work were carried on at top speed.[13] Until then, enough ammunition, weapons, food, and clothing had to be laid in before the end of the winter to last the army until after the spring thaw, for during the months when the ice on the lake was breaking up, nothing could be moved across it.

These problems notwithstanding, Nicholas approached war with Japan with confidence. True, the Japanese attack had caught him by surprise, for he had been convinced that they "would not dare" to declare war against Russia.[14] He did not like to think of the bloodshed and suffering war would bring to his people, but the thought that Japan might pose a serious threat to Russia's security seems never to have crossed his mind. In the comments he made in the margins of reports, Nicholas habitually referred to his foes as "little short-tailed monkeys" and made it clear to all around him that he considered the Japanese an inferior race. "The Tsar was supremely confident that, although a few reinforcements might be needed, Japan would be smashed to smithereens," wrote Witte.[15]

Nicholas was also blissfully unconcerned about how the war would be financed. True, his treasury was just beginning to show a surplus after a decade of Witte's careful management, but its balance was precarious. He thought of the money needed to fight Japan as a short-term loan at best. It would be more than recovered, he assured Witte, by the reparations Russia would exact from the Japanese once the war was over.[16] In the meantime, his cousin "Willy" continued to preach about the Yellow Peril and Russia's great mission in the East. Nicholas seemed not to notice that, when the Kaiser had so generously bestowed upon him the title of "Admiral of the Pacific," he had kept for himself the title of "Admiral of the Atlantic." Nor did he seem to realize that every German Chancellor since Bismarck had sought to turn Russia's attention from Europe to Asia whenever possible, a principle of diplomacy that the Kaiser believed in most of all. In strictest confidence, he had told his ministers that "we must try to tie Russia down in East Asia so that she pays less attention to Europe and the Near East."[17]

However much the flattery of the Kaiser and the confident claims of such prowar advisers as Alekseev, von Plehve, and the low-minded adventurer Aleksandr Bezobrazov (who had formed a private company to exploit Russia's advance into Korea) may have stirred Nicholas's confidence, none of them could have touched his emotions as deeply as the spontaneous popular demonstrations that greeted word of the Japanese attack. On January 30, thousands of students gathered in the Palace Square and then went on to join an even larger rally that marched along the Nevskii Prospekt to the Anichkov Palace. Everyone sang "God Save the Tsar" and cheered Russia's army. "Everyone was mixed together," wrote the reporter of the weekly *Niva*. "Generals and tramps marched side-by-side, students with banners, and ladies, their arms filled with shopping. Everyone was united in one general feeling."[18] "The outpouring of feeling exceeded that of any recent war—the Crimean War, the Balkan encounters, the Turkish War," one historian wrote recently.[19] That feeling seemed to be patriotism, but it was a patriotism deeply tinged with a racism that war with the British, the French, or even the Turks had never awakened in the breasts of Russians. Obviously, Russians were incensed that an Asiatic people, in their minds inferior by definition, should have had the audacity to attack the great Russian Empire.

One form of racism soon begat another. The Japanese were far away and far beyond the reach of the average Russian civilian. Yet racial hatred once set loose demanded satisfaction; by the fall of 1904, Russia was in the grip of another wave of pogroms, in which thousands joined in the cry *"Bei zhidov!"* ("Let's smash the Kikes!") in Moscow and in the western and southern regions of the Empire. Many innocent Jews suffered injuries, even death, at the hands of rampaging mobs. Nicholas did nothing to stop the attacks; like his father, he was an inveterate anti-Semite. Unlike Alexander III, however, he was obliged to pay a dear price for his bigotry. As we shall see, mass demonstrations in favor of the war and mass demonstrations against the Jews soon turned into mass protests against autocracy and in favor of a constitutional form of government.

During those days of 1904, Nicholas wanted to "share the dangers and privations of the army," but he allowed his uncle, Grand Duke Aleksei Aleksandrovich, to dissuade him from going to the Far East.[20] Instead, Nicholas settled for reviewing troops and passing out images of St. Seraphim to soldiers about to leave for the front.[21] At the same time, Aleksandra threw herself into the war effort in other ways. "We resigned ourselves to an almost complete cessation of balls and parties," her close friend Anna Vyrubova recalled. "The great salons of the Winter Palace were turned into workrooms, and every day society flocked to sew and knit for our soldiers and sailors fighting such incredible distances away. . . . Every day the Empress came to inspect the work, often sitting down at a table and sewing diligently with the others."[22]

Images of St. Seraphim and mittens knitted by the Empress and her friends did little to offset the army's disabilities in the Far East. Outgeneraled, outmaneuvered, and undersupplied, the Russians stood little chance against those "little short-tailed monkeys," as the press, having seized upon Nicholas's phrase, now called the Japanese. The government might print tens of thousands of postcards with "gaudy representations in blue, and red, and yellow, of a giant Russian guardsman bayoneting a wizened Japanese," as the British correspondent Douglas Story reported,[23] but it could not change the fact that the Japanese continued to defeat the Russians in every major engagement.

"We marched from debacle to debacle for eighteen successive months," the Grand Duke Aleksandr Mikhailovich wrote in his recollections of 1904 and 1905.[24] During the first two months of war, the great battleship *Petropavlovsk* was sunk by a mine (whether Russian or Japanese is not certain), her sister ships the *Tsarevich*, *Pobeda*, and *Retvizan* were seriously damaged, while the *Koreets* and the *Variag* were sunk. The destroyers *Boiarin*, *Vnushitelnyi*, and *Bezstrashnyi* were damaged, the *Strashnyi* sunk, the minelayer *Enisei* blown out of the water by one of her own mines, and the popular hero Admiral Makarov killed in action.[25] Just less than a year after the war began, Port Arthur finally fell to the Japanese after a siege and bombardment that had lasted for 156 days. There was considerable evidence that the Russian commander, General Anatolii Stoessel, had food and ammunition to hold out for much longer than he did, and high officials began to talk about the "shameful surrender of Port Arthur to the enemy."[26] Stoessel was branded a coward and court-martialed, but not before Kaiser Wilhelm had bestowed Germany's highest military order upon him. On the same day, the Kaiser also bestowed the same order upon General Nogi, the Japanese officer who had directed the siege and final assault. Clearly, Wilhelm's hatred of the Yellow Peril did not prevent him from courting favor with the Japanese when they began to look like potentially useful allies against the British in China.[27]

The fall of Port Arthur was only the first of several great defeats Russia suffered in the Far East during 1905. Between February 18 and March 10, Russia and Japan fought the greatest land battle of the war at Mukden. Each side committed more than three hundred thousand troops and more than a thousand pieces of artillery to the struggle. Both lost over more than fifty thousand men killed and wounded in less than a month, and neither won a clear enough victory to force the other to surrender. Nevertheless, Kuropatkin came close to being surrounded by the Japanese, was obliged to withdraw some forty miles to the north, and Mukden became another Russian defeat. Yet Russia's greatest loss was yet to come, and it would be on sea, not on land. Unlike Mukden, its outcome was absolutely clear cut, and no one could doubt its significance.

After a great deal of vacillation, Nicholas decided to send Russia's Baltic fleet under Admiral Zinovii Rozhdestvenskii to the Far East in an effort to reestablish Russia's sea power, even though many of the vessels were unfit for modern warfare and the training of their crews left a good deal to be desired. That the judgment of their officers was little better became dramatically clear off the Dogger Banks in the North Sea, when they mistook several British fishing boats for Japanese torpedo boats. To this day, no one has succeeded in explaining why the Russians had any reason to think that Japanese torpedo boats were anywhere within thousands of miles of the North Sea, but they reached that assumption almost instantly, fired for effect, and provoked a grave incident between Russia and England. To make matters worse, Nicholas, who was so rarely assertive, took an obstinately unyielding position. "I did *not* apologize," he wrote to his mother.[28] His refusal to make amends when amends so obviously were in order led the British to deny Russia's fleet the use of the Suez Canal and all British-held ports in Africa and Asia, which added many weeks and thousands of extra miles to Rozhdestvenskii's voyage.

Still, the Admiral persevered. After steaming halfway around the world in a grueling voyage of many months, he met Togo's fleet on May 14, 1905, in the Tsushima Straits that separated Japan and Korea. He had more ships and more heavy guns than his enemy, but the outcome of the battle was the same as in Togo's earlier attack on Port Arthur. Within the space of a few hours, Rozhdestvenskii lost eight battleships, three cruisers, five minelayers, and four other ships. Four more battleships and a mine layer surrendered. Togo lost a total of three torpedo boats in the course of the entire engagement.[29] Only with the destruction of Rozhdestvenskii's fleet did Nicholas finally perceive the gravity of the situation Russia faced in the Far East. "I fear that we all shall have to drain the bitter cup to the dregs," he wrote soon after he received the news.[30]

Although far from palatable, the dregs proved less bitter than they might have been. Japan's statesmen and military planners realized that more than a year of war had stretched their resources almost to the breaking point and knew that they ran the risk of being overwhelmed by the sheer weight of the Russian forces that slowly but inexorably were being assembled in the Far East against them. Therefore, they accepted President Theodore Roosevelt's invitation to Portsmouth, New Hampshire, and his offer to mediate their differences with Russia. During the summer of 1905, the two sides met, and, by early August, they had worked out an agreement to end the war. Ironically, it was Witte who rescued Nicholas at the bargaining table. He had opposed the war from the very first and had been virtually alone among Nicholas's advisers in predicting Russia's defeat. Nicholas had in fact become so irritated by Witte's criticisms of Russian policies that he had replaced him as Minister of Finance and given him the more ceremonial post of President of the Committee of Ministers just a few months before the war had broken out. Still, Witte answered his Tsar's call and negotiated a peace in the war he had never wanted. His skills as a diplomat enabled Russia to keep all of her Far Eastern possessions except for the Liaotung Peninsula (including Port Arthur), the South Manchurian Railway, and the southern half of Sakhalin Island.[31] Nicholas's Empire remained a Great Power on the Pacific, but there was nothing even Witte could do to shield Nicholas from the stigma of being the first ruler in Europe to suffer defeat at the hands of Asians. For Nicholas, that was perhaps the most bitter pill of all.

While Russia's armies were losing to the Japanese in the Far East, the Empire's factory workers challenged the most fundamental principles of the Romanovs' Russia and forced Nicholas to grant major concessions. It was a new and very frightening threat that Russia's emerging urban proletariat posed to the established order at the beginning of the twentieth century for, unlike those great peasant wars the Romanovs had faced before, the workers' movement was not dispersed over great areas. Also unlike the peasant protests, the men and women who began to demand improvements in the conditions under which they lived and worked in the cities could not be ignored even for a moment, because they were in the very streets of St. Petersburg itself.

By 1905, demand had so outstripped the supply of cheap housing in Russia's capital that workers lived in conditions that were even more crowded and unsanitary than they had been in the 1870s and 1880s. Workers now were obliged to share not only corners of damp and fetid cellars but even the beds in which they slept. Among one group of 1,121 men, women, and children studied in a government survey at the turn of the century, investigators found only 459 beds available.* In some cases, they found as many as five people sharing the use of a single cot. There was, of course, better housing available, but wages still were far too low for the families of industrial workers to be able to afford it. Even an elite metalworker at the great Putilov Works did not earn enough to support a family himself, and that meant that all the abuses of woman and child labor were common coin in Russia's capital.[32] Perhaps worst of all, Nicholas and his ministers buried their heads deeply in the sand at any suggestion of controlling the abuses employers inflicted upon their workers. Even so perceptive a statesman as Witte proclaimed in 1895 that "in Russia, fortunately, there is no working class in the Western sense; therefore there is no labor problem," and confidently insisted that "a patriarchal order of relations between owners and workers prevails in our industry."[33] Less than a decade later, he had to change his view as factory workers began to organize into unions, and strikes became more frequent and widespread. In the first year of Nicholas's reign, there had been sixty-eight strikes in all of Russia. By 1903, the number had risen to five hundred fifty, and almost ninety thousand workers were involved. Perhaps even more dangerous for the established order in Russia, during the first decade of Nicholas's reign, almost a half-million workers had taken part in one strike or another.[34] They were no longer novices in the arena of labor protest.

At the beginning of 1905, the workers in St. Petersburg's Putilov Works went on strike, and about ten thousand others walked off their jobs in sympathy with the strikers' demands. With all of these workers away from their benches, the authorities grew especially nervous as the

* Double beds, such as are common in the United States and Great Britain, were a rarity in Russia and still are. "Beds" thus meant narrow cotlike beds, barely large enough for one person.

festival of the Epiphany approached. On that day—January 6, 1905—Nicholas was to take part in the traditional ceremonial blessing of the Neva's waters, and there were persistent rumors that there would be attempts made to assassinate him or some of his leading ministers. A decade earlier, these might have been considered idle threats, but during the past three years, a number of Russian officials, including Dmitrii Sipiagin (d. 1902) and Viacheslav von Plehve (d. 1904), two of Nicholas's Ministers of Internal Affairs, had been killed by terrorist members of the Combat Detachment of the recently founded Social Revolutionary party.

That morning of January 6, it seemed that St. Petersburg's police had perhaps overemphasized the danger of attacks by revolutionary terrorists. With the capital's high-ranking officials and diplomatic corps looking on from the windows of the great Nicholas Hall in the Winter Palace, the waters were blessed by the Metropolitan Antonii and Nicholas performed his traditional ceremonial role. From across the river, the guns at the Peter-Paul Fortress began to fire in salute. Suddenly, terror gripped the onlookers. "At the third or fourth shot, pieces of broken glass shattered from the window above our heads," wrote Dmitrii Liubimov, who witnessed the scene. "Someone shouted in Russian, 'They are firing live ammunition!' And the shout was repeated in other languages. Small holes could be seen in the upper portions of the windows that left no doubt about what was happening," he concluded.[35] "It seemed like an attack on the lives of the Tsar and the high officials who were present in such large numbers," wrote Grand Duke Konstantin Konstantinovich, who was standing with Nicholas on the embankment when the salutes were fired.[36] Many must have shared his view. Hasty inquiries revealed that a few live rounds had gotten mixed in with the blanks and that no one's life had been in danger because the salutes had been aimed high above the heads of the crowd. Yet the mood had been set. Police officials and the officers who commanded the Petersburg garrison became more nervous than before, especially when the printers joined the Putilov strikers and the newspapers did not appear the next day.[37] The stage was set for more dramatic events.

Although there were no plans to assassinate Nicholas or any of his

leading counselors in early January 1905, there were indeed other
reasons for real concern among those in St. Petersburg who feared any
mass expression of sentiment critical of the regime. By early January, it
was clear that the striking Putilov workers were going to press their
demands more energetically as a result of urgings from a slight, dark-
haired, energetic man known to them all as Father Gapon. Georgii
Gapon was a thirty-four-year-old priest who came from a well-to-do
Ukrainian peasant family. For several years he had been involved with
the Russian trade union movement and was also in the pay of the
Okhrana, Nicholas's secret police. Like a number of others the police
had on their payroll, however, he did not give them his complete loyalty, especially after he discovered that his oratorical skills could bring
large numbers of men and women to his cause.

Although the full extent of Gapon's activities on both fronts remain a subject of some dispute, it nevertheless seems fair to say that his
deep commitment was to the workers' cause, and, for almost a year, he
had been considering a new and dramatic tactic for drawing greater attention to their demands. The Putilov strike provided him with an opportunity to test his idea. On Sunday, January 9, he would lead the St.
Petersburg workers directly to the Tsar and present a petition stating
that "we, the workers of St. Petersburg, our wives, children, and helpless old folk, have come to you to seek justice and protection."[38] They
then would beg Nicholas to come to their aid.

During the days between Epiphany and January 9, Father Gapon
seemed to be everywhere in St. Petersburg's workers' districts as he
exhorted groups of his followers to join his march to the Palace Square.
In the workers' clubs of the Narva Quarter, where the stale air and
stench from hundreds of unwashed bodies made breathing difficult, in
the smoke-filled cafés, teahouses, and taverns where workers sought to
drown their sorrows in watery beer and fiery cheap vodka, and even in
the streets where men and women stood huddled against the biting
wind and fierce cold, Gapon asked the workers the same question.
"Supposing the Tsar will not receive us, and will not read our petition?" Everywhere, the same answer came back with unmistakable resolution. In loud and clear voices the workers proclaimed: "Then we
have no Tsar!"[39] Had he heard the vehemence of their replies,

Nicholas would have been struck by terror. And he might have responded in a different manner when they marched to the Palace Square that Sunday.

The workers who planned to march with Father Gapon knew that they might be fired upon by the police and the soldiers brought in to reinforce them, but they had sworn to lay down their lives in the cause of freedom. "It is better for us to die for our demands than to live as we have lived until now," proclaimed one worker. "Do you swear to die [if necessary]?" he asked those who stood before him. "We swear!" some seven hundred working men and women called back. "But what about those who swear to die [for our cause] today, but get cold feet and don't march with us tomorrow?" he asked again. "Let them be damned!" the crowd roared back.[40] "Suppose the workers do not show up tomorrow?" some of the leading revolutionaries in St. Petersburg asked each other in worried tones.[41] The workers had no such doubts about themselves. Not knowing what lay ahead, they made ready for their march. "If I am killed, then do not weep," wrote one of them in a farewell note to his wife and infant son that night. "Raise Vaniura," he begged, "and tell him that I died a martyr for the freedom and happiness of the people."[42] Only a few hours remained before the march began. "Many turned their attention that evening to the huge blood-red moon that rose above the horizon," one eyewitness remembered. "On this night, Petersburg was the very heart of Russia."[43]

While the workers in their crowded suburbs slept fitfully, paced nervously, wrote notes to loved ones, or prayed to a God in whom many of them no longer believed, the forces St. Petersburg's Governor, General Fullon, had at his command were busy with their own last-minute preparations. Just that afternoon, they had been reinforced by battalions brought in from Pskov and Reval, so that the infantry and cavalry in the capital now numbered some "twelve thousand bayonets and sabres," as one historian later wrote.[44] "Petersburg resembled a city that had been seized by enemy soldiers," he continued. "Bivouacs were laid out in its streets and squares, and campfires burned brightly." Ambulances stood ready to take on the wounded, and great kettles of soup steamed in company mess kitchens that had been set up in the open. At about midnight, orders came down from Guards Commander

Prince Vasilchikov to issue live ammunition and extra rations of vodka. The soldiers were told that the workers were preparing to destroy the Winter Palace and murder the leading state officials and the Imperial family.[45] Before daybreak, General Fullon's "twelve thousand bayonets and sabres" stood waiting for the workers' advance.

The morning of January 9 dawned bright and clear, the temperature about five degrees below freezing. It was one of those rare Petersburg winter days when there was no wind. Gapon's plan was for his marchers to assemble at several points in the distant workers' quarters and, from there, to march along the great avenues that converged on the Winter Palace Square. The workers and their wives and children came dressed in their best, looking sober, serious, and purposeful. "Put on your best dress," they had been told. "Take your children and your wives. No arms, not even penknives."[46] All revolutionary symbols were to be excluded from the demonstration. The theme was to be the workers' peaceful and orderly plea for Nicholas to protect them from the factory owners and to aid them in winning decent conditions in which to live and work. They were to sing religious hymns, not revolutionary songs. They were to carry icons, not revolutionary placards. Portraits of Nicholas and Aleksandra were to rise above their heads, not red banners and revolutionary slogans. They were even urged to be careful about taking red handkerchiefs from their pockets.[47] Nothing was to be done which could give the authorities the least cause for alarm. "Save us, O Lord, your people!" they sang as they marched. "How glorious is our Lord in Zion!"[48] Some thirty thousand strong, they marched to present their petition to Nicholas, the "little father" who, peasants had believed for centuries, was their protector against the strong and cruel masters who ruled their lives.

To stop the workers' march upon the Palace Square, General Fullon had set up barricades across the great avenues that connected the workers' districts with the center of the city. At each of these points, soldiers tried to turn back workers and, at several of them, officers ordered their men to fire into the crowds. The worst slaughter took place on the Winter Palace Square itself, where a company of Preobrazhenskiis, their captain acting on direct orders from Guards Commander Prince Vasilchikov, shot several hundred workers. When the day's bloody work was done, between 150 and 200 men, women, and children lay dead, and another 450 to 800 had been wounded.[49] Among them was Ivan Vasilev, the worker who had left his wife a note that morning begging her to raise their son in the knowledge that his father had died for freedom.

While sabers cut through padded jackets to the flesh beneath and rifle shots rang out in Petersburg's streets, Nicholas remained at Tsarskoe Selo with Aleksandra and their children. When he received the first reports from Fullon and Vasilchikov, he wrote in his diary: "Many were killed and wounded. God, how painful and heartbreaking!"[50] He hastened to receive a carefully chosen delegation of thirty-four workers whom he lectured in the manner of a stern father about the need for order and the evils of revolutionary propaganda. "I believe in the honest feelings of the working people and in their unshakable loyalty to me," he told the workers who stood unwillingly before him. "Therefore, I forgive them their guilt."[51] "The Russian people are deeply and truly devoted to their Sovereign," Aleksandra assured her sister, Princess Victoria of Battenberg later that month.[52] Nicholas and Aleksandra would have been far less smug in their confidence about the workers' loyalty had they seen the letter from Father Gapon, which the Bolshevik writer Maksim Gorkii read at a meeting a few days later. "There is no Tsar!" Gapon proclaimed. "Between him and the people lies the blood of our comrades. Long live then the beginning of the popular struggle for freedom!"[53] Great cheers greeted Gorkii's reading. Workers had died on that terrible day of January 9, 1905. The most momentous casualty of all, however, was the death of the people's belief that Nicholas was their "little father"—that myth, which had been such a vital bulwark for the Romanovs' autocracy for so long.

Bloody Sunday, as that tragic day soon became known, marked the beginning of what the Dowager Empress Maria Feodorovna called the "year of nightmares."[54] Tragedy followed tragedy, crisis piled upon crisis, as Russian workers and revolutionaries struck their first great blows in the cause of freedom. Their first victim was Grand Duke Sergei Aleksandrovich, commander of the Moscow military region and former Military Governor-General of Moscow, who had openly avowed a hatred for revolutionaries. Members of his own family thought him

"obstinate, arrogant, disagreeable," a man who "flaunted his many peculiarities in the face of the entire nation, providing the enemies of the
regime with inexhaustible material for calumnies and libels."[55] He was
both Nicholas's uncle and brother-in-law, the husband of Aleksandra's
elder sister. He was one of those several senior uncles of whom
Nicholas was apprehensive, even fearful.

As Moscow's Governor-General, Sergei Aleksandrovich had
proved himself totally incompetent. He bore a large share of the blame
for the great disaster at Khodynka, and his performance in the eight
years that followed had been scarcely more distinguished. Still,
Nicholas allowed him to remain in office until he himself resigned over
policy disagreements just before the Bloody Sunday killings.

Sergei Aleksandrovich was in the midst of preparing to leave the
position he had occupied for some fourteen years when he fell before
the terrorists' attack. As his carriage passed through one of the Kremlin gates early in the afternoon of February 4, 1905, Ivan Kaliaev, a
member of the Social Revolutionary party's Combat Detachment, threw
a nitroglycerine bomb directly into his lap. The Grand Duke was literally blown to bits. One of the first to reach the scene was his wife, the
gentle and popular Grand Duchess Elizaveta Feodorovna, whose biographer later described the gruesome scene. "Scattered all over the
crimson-stained snow," she wrote, "lay the pieces of scorched cloth, fur
and leather, the stump of a hand, a finger here and a finger there, a
foot severed from the leg and the leg severed from the body, the other
foot still booted lying a few yards away, a ghastly crimson mess where
the torso had been, and, surrounded by the splintered bones of the
skull, the very little that remained of the face when the bomb had done
its work."[56] Some of the Grand Duke's fingers, still adorned with the
rings he habitually wore, were found on the roof of a nearby building.[57] Soon afterward, the Grand Duchess retired from the world that
had dealt so cruelly with her husband and founded the Convent of
Saint Martha and Saint Mary, where she dedicated herself to the care
of Moscow's poor and suffering.[58]

Neither Nicholas nor Aleksandra attended the Grand Duke's funeral because their advisers judged it dangerous for them to set foot
beyond the safety of Tsarskoe Selo. In the brief space of a decade, the

Tsar, who had insisted that the troops be removed from his route so that the people of St. Petersburg could greet him and his bride on the day of their marriage, had come full circle and dared not to go among them even in the presence of armed guards. Wrote Grand Duke Konstantin Konstantinovich in his diary, "These terrible events seem like some kind of dream. In Russia everything is getting worse; if you look back at the autumn, to September and October [1904], you simply can't believe with what quick steps we have advanced to disaster, to unknown misfortunes."[59]

Yet the assassination of Sergei Aleksandrovich signaled only the beginning of a broader wave of popular unrest that had been sparked by the events of Bloody Sunday. As the war in the Far East went from bad to worse and as Nicholas refused to heed pleas that he grant a constitution and summon a national Duma (parliament), agitation and revolutionary terror increased. In mid-June, the crew of the battleship *Potemkin* mutinied in Odessa harbor. A fortnight later, Sergei Aleksandrovich's replacement as Governor-General of Moscow, Count Shuvalov, was killed by another Combat Detachment attack. Throughout the summer and early fall, the members of the Combat Detachment continued their assaults, and the crisis escalated. Strikes increased, and the number of workers involved in protest movements burgeoned.

Not only workers and revolutionaries were involved in these disorders. The base of popular protest broadened throughout the spring and summer of 1905 to include men from such usually conservative professions as medicine, law, and engineering. In May, they and a number of others formed a Union of Unions and demanded a role in making the decisions and policies that would shape Russia's future. Nicholas, they insisted, must grant them those civil and political rights that had accompanied the development of capitalist economic systems in England, France, the United States, even in Germany, Italy, and Austria. Their demands fell upon uncomprehending ears, for neither Nicholas nor Aleksandra clearly understood what was happening in Russia. Nor did they understand how to respond to it. "The lack of what I call 'real' men is great," Aleksandra wrote to her sister at the end of January. "I rack my brains to pieces to find a man and cannot; it is a despairing feeling. One is too weak, another too liberal, the third too

narrow-minded, and so forth."[60] What Nicholas and Aleksandra hoped
to find were not advisers who understood what was going on in Russia
and could make hardheaded and practical judgments but some sort of
magician who could wave a wand and make the problems vanish. One
of the great tragedies of Russia's history during the years between 1905
and 1917 was that, when such a magician could not be found, Nicholas
and Aleksandra settled for men who encouraged them to believe that
the problems *could* be made to vanish or that, at least, *they,* as Russia's
rulers, were in no way at fault for the upheavals that were tearing Russia apart.

By the beginning of September, Nicholas concluded that the worst
of the "year of nightmares" had passed. In mid-August, Witte had
signed the Treaty of Portsmouth to end the Russo-Japanese War, and
less than a fortnight before that, Nicholas had agreed to permit a
Duma, with hopelessly limited powers and elected by a very small electorate, to assemble in St. Petersburg. Certain that this insipidly formulated half-measure would restore order and stability throughout Russia
now that the much-despised war with Japan was past, Nicholas took
Aleksandra, their children, and a few carefully chosen friends on a
two-week Baltic cruise aboard the Imperial yacht *Polar Star*. It was a
happy time for them all. Nicholas and his children climbed the rocks
on shore, hunted for mushrooms, and picked wild berries. Aleksandra
and her new lady-in-waiting, Anna Tanaeva (later Anna Vyrubova),
"spent hours playing four-hand pieces, all our dearly beloved classics,
Bach, Beethoven, and Tschaikovsky," on the piano in the ship's salon.[61]
It was a joyous outing, free from cares about Russia's future. It was the
way a good father expected to spend a holiday with his family and their
friends.

Yet, to the outside observer who looks upon this happy outing
from the distance of three-quarters of a century, a sour, ominous note
mars the portrait of bourgeois family bliss. Nicholas and Aleksandra
chose some of the most mediocre people in their Court to share their
leisure hours, and it would be men and women such as these to whom
they would turn more frequently as the years passed. There was Prince
Aleksei Obolenskii, soon to replace Pobedonostsev as Director-General
of the Holy Synod. "His mind was not a creative one," remembered

one of his fellow Ministers. "It was incapable of cleverness and precision, and, besides, was inclined to paradoxical conclusions and mysticism." Obolenskii evidently loved to speak grandly of "contrasting generalities" and, as Director-General of the Holy Synod, would seek a "quasi-scientific basis" for this strange personal mysticism.[62] Nicholas and Aleksandra also were accompanied by Admiral Aleksei Birilev, a man who liked to express his views forcefully, often emphasizing his points by pounding the table with his fists. Yet for all his bluster, Birilev was a man of little substance or deep conviction. Once he had expressed his views, one of his colleagues remembered, "he never insisted upon his opinion" being accepted. He was satisfied just to have expressed his thoughts in a forceful manner.[63]

During their Baltic cruise, Nicholas and Aleksandra enjoyed most of all the company of Anna Tanaeva, easily one of the most obvious and undisputed nonentities to rise to the surface of the churning cauldron of Court politics in early twentieth-century Russia. Tanaeva was the daughter of the Chief of Nicholas's Personal Chancery. When she became one of Aleksandra's ladies-in-waiting in 1905, she had just turned twenty-one. Her lack of intelligence was amazing and embarrassingly obvious to nearly all who met her. Pierre Gilliard, tutor to the Tsarevich, remembered that she "had the mind of a child." He considered her "lacking in intellect and discrimination" and remarked upon her "limited and puerile understanding."[64] A number of Russian statesmen and foreign diplomats found her to be "an ideal gramophone disc" who could be employed to repeat messages accurately, and without the slightest glimmer of comprehension, to Nicholas or Aleksandra.[65] Tanaeva had visions, was profoundly mystical, and has recently been described as "deeply neurasthenic."[66] Her only virtue was her fierce and unswerving devotion to Nicholas, Aleksandra, and their children, a quality they treasured in the people who served them far above such virtues as candor, intelligence, or talent. "Her boundless affection for the Czarina was a positive danger," wrote Gilliard, "because it was uncritical and divorced from all sense of reality."[67] To Tanaeva, Aleksandra confessed that "God has sent me a friend in you,"[68] and proceeded to marry her "Annia" to naval lieutenant Aleksandr Vyrubov, a half-mad, shell-shocked survivor of the Tsushima Straits debacle who proved unable to consummate their union. Within a year, Vyrubova, as she now was called, obtained a divorce and turned to devote all of her love, passion, and fierce loyalty to her Imperial friends. To Russia's misfortune, as Aleksandra withdrew ever deeper into the seclusion of her private world at Tsarskoe Selo during the next decade, more Vyrubovas, male as well as female, would join her inner circle. As Nicholas followed her further into her retreat, he became surrounded by these nonentities as well.

When Nicholas returned from his Baltic cruise toward the end of September, a crisis larger and more ominous than any he had yet encountered was about to burst upon him. During the past year, Russia's workers had gained their first broad experience in the arena of political action, and they had been aided by a number of revolutionary groups sworn to work for the overthrow of the Romanovs and their autocratic regime. Chief among them were the Mensheviks, Marxists who believed that their party should work with all possible allies and recruit a mass following who could be used as the soldiers of the revolution. Led by Iulii Osipovich Tsederbaum, known in revolutionary circles as Martov, the Mensheviks aspired to replace the autocracy with a bourgeois democratic republic.

The advent of socialism in Russia, they were convinced in 1905, stood very far in the future. Their most bitter rivals were the Bolsheviks, led by Vladimir Ilich Ulianov, better known as Lenin, who insisted that only men and women totally dedicated to the cause of revolution should be accepted as members of the Party and that this small revolutionary cadre should lead the workers to a socialist revolution. Lenin believed that his Bolsheviks should never ally themselves with the liberal forces of the bourgeoisie under any circumstances. Lev Davidovich Bronshtein, soon to become famous under the name of Trotskii, stood between both groups, moving easily from one camp to the other. A more talented orator than either Martov or Lenin, he would play a greater and more active part in the events of 1905 than either of them.

Along with the Bolsheviks and Mensheviks, there was also the Social Revolutionary Party (its members known as SRs), which rejected the more ordered precepts of Marxism and believed that autocracy should be replaced immediately by a socialist order. Led by Viktor Chernov, the SRs had closer ties to Russia's peasant masses than either Bolsheviks or Mensheviks. Their program incorporated elements of earlier Russian populism and terrorism, and it was they who founded the Combat Detachment whose members killed Ministers of Internal Affairs Dmitrii Sipiagin and von Plehve, as well as Grand Duke Sergei Aleksandrovich. During the next two years, they would assassinate another four thousand Russian officials, ranging from village policemen up to and including army generals.[69]

During the first nine months of 1905, agitation by Mensheviks, Bolsheviks, and SRs had done much to acquaint Russia's workers with the tactics of revolutionary struggle, and those months had seen almost sixteen hundred strikes, involving a million men and women.[70] Yet, despite the efforts of the revolutionaries to direct the course of the Russian labor movement, it was the workers themselves, not the young men and women who had hoped to lead them in feats of revolutionary valor, who launched the upheavals that formed the core of the Revolution of 1905. In early October, Lenin was in Switzerland, and Trotskii was in Finland. Neither of them saw the approach of revolution. Then, before either of them realized it, revolution had all of Russia in its grip. Like most mass upheavals, its outbreak had not been planned; it had simply grown spontaneously. For a fortnight, a printers' strike in Moscow had ebbed, surged forward, and ebbed again as other laborers' groups joined it and then returned to work.[71] By October 5, it seemed that the strike was losing force and that the workers' movement had lost its momentum. It proved to be the calm before the storm.

What happened in Russia between October 7 and October 17 was a spontaneous strike movement involving millions of workers that paralyzed the entire Empire. Railroad workers struck the Moscow-Kazan Railway on October 7. Almost as if someone had set up vast strings of dominoes along all of the rail lines that spread out from Moscow like the spokes of a wheel and then had knocked over the one standing in the very center, the strike spread outward in scarcely more time than it took for the trains to travel. It reached Kursk, Nizhnii-Novgorod, Kiev, Riazan, and Voronezh on the 9th, St. Petersburg and Kharkov on the

10th. By October 13, it had reached into the Transcaucasus, Central Asia, and Siberia. Twenty-six thousand miles of track were immobilized, as three-quarters of a million railroad employees struck.[72]

By the time the railway workers' strike had reached Siberia and Central Asia, much of European Russia was in the grip of one of the greatest and most effective general strikes in the history of labor protest anywhere in the world. All of Russia's industry ground to a halt. All of her public services ceased to function. In St. Petersburg, virtually everyone stopped work. Factory workers, servants, postal workers, telegraph operators, janitors, and hackney drivers all walked off their jobs, as did bank clerks, shop clerks, and clerks in government offices. Doctors, lawyers, schoolteachers, university professors, even the entire corps de ballet of the great Imperial Mariinskii Theatre—all joined the strike. There were no newspapers, no streetlights, no tramcars. Food and fuel soon began to grow scarce.[73]

Nicholas's advisers were paralyzed. "The ministers, instead of acting with quick decision, only assemble in council like a lot of frightened hens and cackle about providing united ministerial action," he complained to his mother a few days later.[74] At the same time, the revolutionary groups organized a new body for coordinating the activities of the striking workers and for expressing their joint political and economic demands. On October 13, the St. Petersburg Soviet of Workers' Deputies, patterned upon a body that had been organized by the striking workers at the great Ivanov-Voznesensk textile center some months before, convened for the first time.[75] During the next seven weeks, its numbers increased from about 30 to 562. Trotskii emerged as its leading figure, and it became a testing ground for the platforms and tactics of all revolutionary groups. Perhaps most important of all, it won the confidence and loyalty of Russia's workers.

Fearful that the workers might overthrow the government, Nicholas called in General Dmitrii Trepov and gave him full authority to deal with all outbreaks of violence and disorder in the capital. "Use no blanks, and don't skimp on bullets," was Trepov's first order to the hastily reinforced Petersburg garrison.[76] As Nicholas wrote to his mother a few days later, "Trepov made it quite plain to the populace by his proclamations that any disorder would be ruthlessly put down; and, of course, everybody believed that." But that was by no means the end of the crisis. What Nicholas called "the ominous quiet days" began. "Everybody knew that something was going to happen," he wrote. "The troops were waiting for the signal, but the other side would not begin."[77] Something had to be done to break the impasse, and, if it were to be done without a great deal of bloodshed and violence, Nicholas would have to make concessions to his people's demands for a voice in determining their own and Russia's destiny.

Once again, it was Witte who rose to the occasion to become the man of the hour. "I am sure that the only man who can help you now and be useful is Witte," the sensible Dowager Empress had written to Nicholas earlier. "He certainly is a man of genius, *energetic* and clear-sighted."[78] Nicholas did not fully share his mother's wise opinion; he turned to Witte because he could think of no other alternative. While he was discussing with him the question of what course to follow, he lamented to the Dowager Empress that "I have nobody to rely upon except honest Trepov."[79]

As Nicholas understood Witte, "there were only two ways open: to find an energetic soldier [to lead the army] and crush the rebellion by sheer force. There would be time to breathe then but, as likely as not, one would have to use force again in a few months; and that would mean rivers of blood, and in the end we should be where we had started. . . . The other way out," he continued, "would be to give to the people their civil rights, freedom of speech and press, also to have all laws confirmed by a State Duma—that, of course, would be a constitution."[80] Nicholas much preferred bullets to ballots, but Witte insisted that he himself would have no part in a military dictatorship. Nicholas therefore called in his uncle, Grand Duke Nikolai Nikolaevich, six feet five inches tall, and every inch a soldiers' soldier. He proposed to make Nikolai Nikolaevich military dictator of Russia. According to the oft-repeated tale, the Grand Duke swore to shoot himself on the spot if Nicholas insisted and urged him to follow Witte's advice and grant a constitution.[81] Nicholas agreed. On October 17, 1905, Witte published the famous October Manifesto by which Nicholas granted to all Russians civil rights, agreed to summon a Duma elected by wide (though not universal) suffrage, and agreed that all laws must be approved by the Duma.[82] "God Almighty will be our help," wrote Nicholas. "I feel Him supporting me and putting strength into me, which gives me courage and does not allow me to lose heart."[83] A new era in Russia's history had begun, and Nicholas had just proclaimed himself his country's first constitutional monarch. He found the role an awkward one. In its first months, his new regime brought violence, terror, and bloodshed to Russia.

Russians greeted the October Manifesto in different ways and with a variety of emotions. Moderates accepted the decree at face value and, eventually built a political platform for the so-called Octobrist party upon it. Reactionaries were aghast at what Nicholas and Witte had done. "Fear has driven them out of their minds in St. Petersburg!" fumed Dmitrii Pikhno, the editor of *Kievlianin,* a newspaper so reactionary that it had been the only one in all of Russia to continue its publication during the October general strike. "God alone knows what they are doing! They're actually making the revolution themselves!" Pikhno thought that the Manifesto had destroyed the very foundations upon which Russia had been built. "People have laid down their lives 'For the Faith, Tsar, and Country'—and this is how Russia was created," he exclaimed. "But who is going to lay down his life 'For the State Duma'?" A loyal Russian reactionary could not blame the Tsar for long, however, because there were other scapegoats upon whose heads anger could fall far more easily. To Pikhno's mind, there was a very simple explanation for the Tsar's behavior in the midst of the October crisis, "It's the Jews," he told the young lawyer Vasilii Shulgin. "They [in St. Petersburg] don't realize that in Russia every revolution runs over the carcasses of Jews!"[84]

Reactionaries such as Pikhno immediately organized into Black Hundreds, groups of brutal and bigoted men who vented their fear and rage upon unarmed Jews, the aged poor, and helpless women and children. Their program, as Pikhno indicated in his first outburst against the October Manifesto, was a narrow vision of Orthodoxy, Autocracy, and Nationality, which they used to justify their hatred for all non-Russians in the Empire. Their best-known political organization was the Union of the Russian People, founded at the end of October, in which Nicholas personally accepted badges of honorary membership for himself and the Tsarevich Aleksei.[85] Beatings, even murder, of any who opposed their views were a central part of the Black Hundreds' program.

Men such as Pikhno were correct in one respect. There was a significant proportion of Jews in positions of leadership in the Russian revolutionary movement, but they were not there merely because they bore some perverse sort of hatred for the Christian Orthodox Tsar. Vicious persecution by the Tsar and his agents had left them no other choice.[86] If they did not wish to join the ranks of those tens of thousands of Jews who were fleeing Russia in search of a safer life in Western Europe or the United States, they must work for revolution or resign themselves to seeing their loved ones fall beneath the cudgels of those brutal mobs that continued to sweep through their homes and shops. In St. Petersburg, one of these Jews hastened to speak sentiments shared by all revolutionaries. "A constitution is given, but the autocracy remains," warned the twenty-six-year-old Lev Bronshtein (Trotskii). "Everything is given and nothing is given." Clearly remembering the detachments of Cossack cavalry that the government had used to break the ranks of striking workers with truncheons and whips, he concluded with a ringing condemnation: "The proletariat . . . does not want a *nagaika,* a Cossack whip, wrapped up in a constitution!"[87] Trotskii and other revolutionaries urged workers into the streets to "stand guard over our freedom." After all, he cried, "isn't Trepov's order to spare no bullets hanging by the side of the manifesto about our freedoms?"[88] Together, the revolutionaries urged the workers to collect money to purchase arms to defend their rights and to fight against the agents of autocracy. Browning semiautomatic pistols soon began to make their way into the inside pockets of proletarian jackets.[89]

With weapons in the hands of revolutionary workers and the reactionary lower-middle class—small shopkeepers, minor tradesmen, petty government officials, and other such folk—bloodshed in the streets of St. Petersburg, Moscow, and other cities was inevitable. Left and Right frequently came to blows, and murder became common. Of necessity, the energies of the workers were turned away from the government to parry the very real physical danger they faced. That brief unity the opposition had enjoyed in early and mid-October had been eroded by

Witte's October Manifesto, and they could no longer present a united front against the government or reactionary assaults. If only briefly, Nicholas began to see the wisdom of Witte's program. "More voices are heard protesting that the time has come for the government to take matters firmly in hand," he wrote at the beginning of December. "It is just what Witte has been waiting for—he will now begin to deal with the revolutionary movement energetically."[90] Indeed, Witte did just that. On December 3, troops surrounded the building where the St. Petersburg Soviet of Workers' Deputies was assembled, and arrested some three hundred of its members, including most of its Executive Committee. The Revolution of 1905 in St. Petersburg passed into history. "The Revolution is dead," Trotskii proclaimed. "Long live the Revolution!"[91]

The revolution still had a few gasps of life left elsewhere in the Empire. In Moscow, the Soviet of Workers' Deputies proclaimed a general strike for December 7. When the authorities moved to arrest the strike leaders, an armed uprising broke out. Barricades went up in Presnenskaia, a workers' quarter of the city, and revolutionaries from St. Petersburg, Odessa, and elsewhere joined in the struggle.

Nicholas dispatched the Semenovskii Guards to Moscow to deal with the rebels. Riding on the train that took them there was "Natasha," a young woman revolutionary, and her three-year-old daughter "Lizka." Using "Lizka's" childish charm to divert attention from herself, "Natasha" was carrying a traveling bag full of desperately needed grenades for the rebels barricaded in the Presnenskaia.[92] "Natasha's" brave effort did no good. This time, the Semenovskii Guards were commanded by a man whose thinking ran along the same lines as Trepov's. Colonel Georgii Min simply brought up artillery, bombarded the Presnenskaia for several days until it had been reduced to ruins, and then sent in the Guards to shoot anyone who had not fled. By December 18, the rebellion in Moscow was over. The number killed and wounded totaled over a thousand.[93]

Although Nicholas had thought the killing of the workers on Bloody Sunday was "painful and heartbreaking," he was not overly disturbed by the bloodshed in Moscow. In fact, he was determined to shed a good deal more blood if that was what was needed to restore order. "Terror must be met by terror," he wrote.[94] What especially concerned him, once the Moscow uprising had been suppressed, was the continuing violence in Russia's countryside, where bands of peasants burned manor houses and murdered nobles, landlords, and officials. The solution, Nicholas was convinced, lay in Punitive Expeditions, well-trained detachments of soldiers led by tough, devoted officers, who were sent into the countryside to restore order in a brutal and efficient manner. Punitive Expeditions simply operated as if they were invading foreign territory in which every living soul was an enemy. They executed many villagers at random, burned entire hamlets without mercy, and left people wounded, starving, and homeless. "Don't skimp on bullets, and make no arrests!" were the orders they received.[95] Nicholas was pleased with the results of their work. "Many seditious bands have been dispersed, their homes and property burnt," he wrote with satisfaction to his mother.[96] As he received reports of further burnings and executions, he remarked to one of his aides that "this really tickles me!"[97] No Romanov before Nicholas had ever put down his subjects on such an enormous scale. For the time being he could do so because the army remained loyal. "In December 1905, the Russian proletariat foundered . . . on the bayonets of the peasant army," Trotskii later wrote.[98]

The October Manifesto, which Nicholas had signed at Witte's urging, embodied very clear promises of a parliamentary regime for Russia. Those promises could not be broken, although Nicholas neither liked nor believed in a constitutional regime. As the Revolution of 1905 was crushed, first in St. Petersburg and then in Moscow, Nicholas and his advisers began to face the immense, almost overwhelmingly complex, task of transforming the Russian autocracy into a constitutional government. It was a task that, under the most ideal conditions, would have made the most stalwart statesman shudder. In January 1906, conditions were anything but ideal. A revolution had just been put down in Russia's major cities, but peasants continued to burn barns and manor houses in the countryside. Terrorists still were at work in town and country, and, unlike those members of the People's Will who had pursued Alexander II so clumsily for eighteen months between August 1879 and March 1881, the young men and women in the Social Revolutionary party's Combat Detachment were efficient and dedicated killers. One survey of their attacks against two hundred leading officials

shows that only eight percent of their intended victims escaped unharmed, while they managed to kill seventy percent of their targets
outright.[99] These factors made it difficult for Nicholas and his ministers to establish even a minimum of political stability in the early days
of 1906, and their task was further complicated by the hundreds of
thousands of Russian soldiers in the Far East who were anxiously waiting to return to their homes and families. It had taken many months to
transport them there because of the limited capacity of the Trans-
Siberian Railroad, and it would take even more months to bring them
back because of the strikes among railroad workers. At any moment,
the isolated mutinies among these masses of disgruntled, demoralized
soldiers might turn into a revolt along the entire route of the railroad
and pose a major threat to the fragile peace Witte had established. This
was an especially worrisome problem because Nicholas and his advisers
fully realized the critical role the army had played in enabling the
Romanovs to survive the Revolution of 1905.

If these problems did not make the situation Nicholas and his ministers faced sufficiently difficult, there were others of a more general,
endemic nature to overcome. At a time when the only form of mass
communication was the printed word, most citizens in Nicholas's Empire were illiterate. According to the most recent census (1897), only
one adult Russian in five could read and write, and only one out of
every four school-aged children actually was in school. Among some of
Nicholas's non-Russian subjects (the peoples of Central Asia, for example), the illiteracy rate was virtually one hundred percent.[100] Most
Russians' interests were focused within the very narrow limits of life in
their village or county, and they were not especially anxious to expand
their views beyond those very narrow horizons. Russians had grown
used to having the Empire's vast, and not very competent, bureaucracy
deal with national problems. They simply had no experience with national, or even regional, self-government, and their limited exposure to
such local self-governing councils as the *zemstva* could hardly have
much meaning on the national level. How was the newly enfranchised,
largely illiterate, intensely parochial Russian electorate to be induced to
think in terms of national issues rather than village ones, especially
when there were no political parties in existence to develop constitu-

encies or foster discussions about questions of national significance? And how could debate on questions of national policy take place, given the restraints that censorship had traditionally imposed upon any such discussions?

Not only did all of these problems have to be resolved but they had to be dealt with quickly, something that is never easy for any bureaucracy, especially the one that administered Russia. Between December 1905 and April 1906, when the Duma was to assemble, the apparatus for a constitutional order had to be created, political parties brought into being, rules for the election of deputies set down, and eligible voters registered. Perhaps most critical of all, the Fundamental Laws of the Russian Empire, which stated that the power of the Emperor was "autocratic and unlimited," had to be recast to reflect Russia's transition to a constitutional monarchy. If Nicholas followed the promises he had made in the October Manifesto, he would be obliged to formally renounce one of his most cherished prerogatives, his unlimited power as an Autocrat. "This is the most important issue of all," he warned his ministers. "The question still torments me: do I have the right to change the form of that authority which my ancestors bequeathed to me? I was fully aware of what I was doing when I issued the Manifesto of October 17th," he continued, "and I am firmly resolved to see it through to the end. But I am not convinced that this requires me to renounce the right of supreme power and change the definition of it that has existed for 109 years in the first article of the Fundamental Laws. . . . I am convinced that eighty percent of the people would stand with me in this."[101]

What Nicholas proposed was a clear violation of the spirit, if not the actual letter, of the October Manifesto and the decree of February 20, 1906, that had established the constitutional structure within which Russia's new system of government was to function. "This question will decide the entire future of Russia," Witte warned him. "It was you, Sire, who desired to limit your power [by the October Manifesto]," Count Konstantin Pahlen, a member of the State Council for almost thirty years, remarked. Minister of Justice Mikhail Akimov warned that to insist that the autocratic power remained unlimited "means to throw down the gauntlet." Even the supremely reactionary Petr Durnovo, the

Minister of Internal Affairs who Nicholas thought was "doing splendid work,"[102] admitted that "after the Manifestos of October 17th and February 20th, unlimited monarchy has ceased to exist." Four days later, Nicholas finally heeded his ministers' warnings and agreed that his autocratic power was no longer "unlimited," although he insisted that it was still "autocratic."[103] Nicholas never would really comprehend what that change meant, and his personal view of autocracy continued as before. He distrusted any form of constitutional government; the events of the next two years confirmed him in that view.

The first two Dumas that assembled in 1906 and 1907 proved to be bitter and unworkable experiments in constitutional government. Too many of the deputies were implacably opposed to the government, while Nicholas and his advisers regarded most of them as men of seditious and evil intentions. Most critical of all, neither side understood nor had any experience with compromise, that most vital and fundamental of all political tactics in any parliamentary system. Everyone assumed rigid, unyielding positions. Pavel Miliukov, leader of the powerful Constitutional Democrats, the *Kadety*, called the new Fundamental Laws of April 1906 a "conspiracy against the people,"[104] and his colleague Feodor Rodichev proclaimed that "in Russia there is no justice! In Russia law is made into a joke!" "During this year," he continued, "Russia has lived through sufferings such as she has not seen since the time of Batu Khan."[105]

Obviously, such statements from men who represented respected segments of society—Miliukov was a famous historian and university professor, and Rodichev was a nobleman and a respected lawyer—infuriated Nicholas and his advisers. More important, such sweeping condemnations left the Tsar and his agents no room in which to maneuver in Russia's treacherous new political currents. Their only options were capitulation or opposition, and they obviously chose the latter course. That, in turn, left many Duma members in the same difficult position as the "Establishment." Either they must capitulate before the government's demands or give no ground and oppose the government totally. This forced them into awkward, sometimes unreasonable, positions. They continued to insist upon total political amnesty for everyone who had taken part in the revolutionary events of 1905, for example, a demand that amazed the correspondent from the moderate French journal *Revue des deux Mondes.* "What of the crimes?" he asked. "What of the robberies? What of the killings?"[106]

The first two Dumas were each dissolved after sitting for only a few weeks. Only with the more conservative Third Duma, which first met in November 1907, was the government able to find some ground for joint action. Still, it was a beginning, albeit a modest one. As such, it would establish the framework for Russia's political life until Nicholas's abdication in March 1917.

The man who finally forged Nicholas, his ministers, and the Duma into a workable system of government was Petr Arkadevich Stolypin, Minister of Internal Affairs and Chairman of the Council of Ministers from 1906 until 1911, and one of the most able statesmen ever to serve any Romanov. When he rose to prominence in the days after the First Duma first assembled, he was just forty-four years of age, a big, burly, barrel-chested man who commanded respect from friend and foe alike. Sir George Buchanan, Britain's Ambassador to Russia, wrote that he "combined with rare strength of character a simple, gentle nature" and thought him the "ideal Minister to transact business with." Buchanan called him "a true patriot" and a "great Minister,"[107] a judgment with which his predecessor, Sir Arthur Nicolson, heartily concurred. Nicolson admired Stolypin's "ardent love for his country" and called him "the most notable figure in Europe."[108]

Stolypin understood that the government must work with the Duma and sought to strike an alliance with the Right and the Center, while attacking and weakening the militant Left, whose position he once bluntly summarized by the phrase "hands up!" To that position he replied, "Don't try to scare us."[109] "What you want are great upheavals," he told the militants scornfully. "But what *we* want is a GREAT RUSSIA!"[110] To emphasize that point, he proceeded to propose some of the most dramatic social and economic legislation in Russia's history. His program proved so promising that Lenin lamented in 1908 that "if this should continue for very long periods of time . . . it might force us to renounce any agrarian program at all. . . . It would be empty and stupid democratic phrase-mongering to say that the success of such a policy in Russia is impossible. . . . It *is* possible!"[111]

Nicholas had confidence in Stolypin from the first, and his belief in his minister lasted almost until Stolypin's death in September 1911. "I cannot tell you how much I have come to like and respect this man," the Tsar wrote to his mother some three months after Stolypin had taken office.[112]

Stolypin devoutly believed that "a strong peasant proprietor can serve as an obstacle to the march of revolution" in Russia and that the government had a mission to "rescue the masses from poverty, ignorance, and lawlessness." Because he was convinced that "the land is the guarantee of our strength in the future, that the land *is* Russia," he proposed to stake his government's survival upon "the wise and the strong, not the drunken and weak," among the peasantry.[113] Stolypin's program of agrarian reform comprised several edicts issued between 1906 and 1911, which enabled millions of Russian peasants to gain title to the scattered strips of land they previously had held in common as members of a commune and then enabled them to consolidate those strips into separate, self-contained farms. At the same time, Stolypin convinced Nicholas to make large tracts of Crown lands available for purchase by peasants and to take further measures to encourage the emigration of peasants from crowded areas of European Russia to Siberia. He thus sought to destroy the peasant commune, which for so long had served to dampen Russia's agricultural development by penalizing individual initiative and discouraging private enterprise. In place of the commune, Stolypin hoped to establish a class of more productive small farmers, each with a solid stake in the existing order.[114] The result was a rapid and very dramatic increase in Russia's agricultural production during the next decade, as a new class—the *kulaki,* as "rich" peasants were called—emerged in the Russian countryside. These *kulaki* achieved a level of production on the eve of the First World War that the Soviet state, which soon exterminated them as the bearers of capitalism, would not match until the 1960s.[115]

Despite the apparent success of his programs, Stolypin was not destined to see them through. On the evening of September 1, 1911, during a state visit to Kiev, Nicholas, his daughters Olga and Tatiana, Stolypin, and a number of other ministers attended a festival performance of Rimskii-Korsakov's great *Tale of Tsar Saltan* at the Kiev Opera

House. As was always the case when Nicholas or any of his family appeared in public, extraordinary security precautions were the order of the day, and no one thought seriously that anyone's life could be in danger. Suddenly, during the second intermission, a double agent by the name of Bogrov walked up to Stolypin and shot him at point-blank range.[116] Nicholas was so near that he almost saw it happen. "We had just left the box," he wrote a few days later, "when we heard two sounds as if something had been dropped. I thought an opera glass might have fallen on somebody's head, and ran back into the box to look." From the box, he saw Stolypin standing in the first row of the orchestra. "He slowly turned his face towards us and, with his left hand, made the sign of the cross in the air. Only then did I notice that he was very pale and that his right hand and uniform were bloodstained. He slowly sank into his chair."[117] Four days later, Stolypin died in agony from the chest wounds he had received. Bogrov was mysteriously executed before a full inquiry could be made into all the ramifications of his murderous act, thus giving rise to speculation that he was part of a plot involving high-ranking reactionaries, who hated Stolypin almost as much as the revolutionaries did.[118] Nicholas had lost the last truly able statesman to serve him. Stolypin's successors would range from modestly competent to utterly inept.

The fact that Stolypin could be assassinated with such ease before Nicholas's very eyes, despite the most energetic security measures, provides us with a glimpse into the sort of world in which Nicholas, Aleksandra, and their children lived after the Revolution of 1905 had been crushed. Much of the time, they hid themselves away outside St. Petersburg, that symbol of Romanov grandeur in which they no longer seemed able to share. They almost never stayed at the Winter Palace. Rarely did they appear in public, and only once during the entire nine years that separated Bloody Sunday from the outbreak of the First World War did Nicholas appear unescorted by guards when he walked through Red Square to the Kremlin during the Moscow celebration of the Romanovs' tercentenary in 1913. Nicholas and Aleksandra, who had wanted to be loved by their people, had come to fear them. As their ministers and advisers continued to fall before assassins' attacks, their fear grew more intense until they became virtual prisoners in their own land. Every luxury was theirs for the asking, except the simple freedom to walk or ride where they wished. "You will understand my feelings, my dear Mama, when I tell you I have been unable to go out riding or even outside the gate, and this at one's own home—at Peterhof, usually so peaceful!" Nicholas lamented in 1906.[119]

Usually Nicholas, Aleksandra, and their children left Tsarskoe Selo at the end of March to spend the spring at Livadia in the Crimea. In May, they journeyed north again to Peterhof, and from there they cruised the Baltic, especially the fjords of Finland, on the *Standart* in June and July. In August, they left the Baltic for Spala, and from there they went south to spend September and October at Livadia again. Every year, they wintered at Tsarskoe Selo, from mid-November until March, when they again began their travels. The only variations in this routine occurred between 1905 and 1909, when Nicholas's ministers urged him not to travel anywhere by land in Russia, with the result that the annual visits to Spala and Livadia were cut out.[120] Even on their visit to England in 1909, their advisers feared for them to visit London or Windsor or Balmoral. They went instead to the more easily guarded Isle of Wight for the regatta, where young Prince Edward, later King Edward VIII and Duke of Windsor, remembered with astonishment "the elaborate police guard thrown around his [Nicholas's] every movement."[121] Nicholas and Aleksandra must have thought longingly of those days not so long ago, but seemingly so far away, fifteen years before, when the greatest question of "security" hinged upon whether or not Queen Victoria thought they could properly be allowed to go out without a chaperone.

During the years after the Revolution of 1905, Nicholas and Aleksandra spent more time on the *Standart* than ever before. It was a beautiful yacht, the size of a small cruiser, and the envy of Europe's sovereigns. Kaiser Wilhelm even went so far as to say outright when he visited Peterhof in 1897, that he would be "happy to get it as a present."[122] Aboard the *Standart* Nicholas and Aleksandra lived in staterooms that "were nearly as large as their rooms in the Peterhof villa," amongst furniture covered with "pretty light chintzes."[123] There, Aleksandra seemed to find rare happy moments, while she and Nicholas lived an informal, quiet life among those mediocre friends whose company they loved best. Aleksandra spent her days reclining on a lounge chair on deck (she had begun to spend ever-greater amounts of time in bed because of a "heart condition" that may have been related to her increasingly neurotic behavior), while Nicholas went shooting on the islands that dotted the fjords. "In the mornings we go out in the boats with the children," he wrote to describe their life. "In the afternoon, I usually shoot on one of the islands. In the evening, work for me, because up to now a courier has come every day by torpedo boat." So fearful were Nicholas's advisers that they thought the revolutionaries might even devise a way to attack the Tsar in the midst of the peaceful waters off the Finnish coast. The *Standart* therefore always was surrounded by a squadron of the Imperial Navy. "We have with us here the *Ukraina* and the *Finn,* and the destroyers *Vidnyi, Rezvyi,* the *Gromiashchyi,* also the *Tsarevna,* the *General-Admiral,* and the *Asia,*" Nicholas wrote to his mother. In an effort to make light of their difficulties, he tried to find something cheerful to say about the obviously depressing fact that he had to be guarded from his subjects day and night by battleships. "At night," he continued, "all their searchlights play round the yacht without touching it; a most beautiful sight on the whole."[124]

Once senior police officials decided it was safe for them to travel again by land in Russia, Nicholas and his family resumed their journeys to Livadia, Aleksandra's favorite Imperial residence. As always, a spirit of excitement surrounded their departure from Tsarskoe Selo at the end of March 1909, for they were leaving the gray, cold northern winter behind at last. They traveled in a specially designed railway car, with comfortable sofas and chairs, upholstered in the usual bright chintzes in the sitting room, mauve in Aleksandra's boudoir, and green leather in Nicholas's study. There was a "large and perfectly equipped bathroom" at one end,[125] which contained a tub that was so cleverly designed that the water would not spill over its sides even when the train was in motion.[126] The spring journey from Tsarskoe Selo to Livadia was especially delightful as the still snow-covered fields of the north gave way to warmer regions culminating in the flower-filled Crimean Peninsula.

In the early twentieth century, about half of the Crimea was an

Imperial estate that, in Anna Vyrubova's words, had been "left as far as possible in its natural condition of unbroken forests, wild mountains, and valleys." It was an idyllic, almost subtropical paradise; "the mountains, dark with pines, snow-covered during most of the year, make an impressive background for the profusion of flowering trees, shrubs and vines, making the valleys and plains one continuous garden. . . . Almost every kind of fruit flourished in the valleys," Vyrubova wrote, "and in the spring the wealth of blossoms, pink and white, of apples, cherries, peaches, almonds, made the whole countryside a perfumed garden, while in autumn the masses of golden fruit were a wonder to behold. Flowers bloomed as though they were the very soul of the fair earth. Never have I seen such roses. They spread over every building in great vines as strong as ivy, and they scattered their rich petals over lawns and pathways in a fragrance at times almost overpowering. There was another flower," Vyrubova remembered, "the glycinia, which grew on trailing vines in grapelike clusters, deep mauve in hue, the favorite color of the Empress."[127]

Everything about Livadia and the region that surrounded it was appealing, almost magical, in quality. The local inhabitants were not Russians but Tatars, descendants of those fierce hordes that had swarmed into the Russian land from the east some six centuries before. They now had become sadly backward in the eyes of their Russian masters, who found them interesting for their quaint, anachronistic manners and exotic, colorful costumes. Their presence added another dimension to the picturesque scene that surrounded Nicholas and Aleksandra during those happy southern days. There were "little Tatar villages half buried in the bare sides of the mountains, and the staring white mosques which stood out sharply against the old cypresses in the cemeteries," wrote the Tsarevich Aleksei's tutor Pierre Gilliard some years later. "It seemed fairylike and unreal in its wondrous beauty under this halo of sunshine."[128]

Two years after she and Nicholas resumed their visits to Livadia, Aleksandra had a new palace built of gleaming white limestone. There, she lay in her fragrant, flower-filled world and looked out upon the snowcapped mountains in one direction and the sapphire, sun-swept sea in the other. There, she brought her son Aleksei to regain his strength after those frequent hemophilic hemorrhages that weakened him and made his life a torment throughout his childhood years. There, she could forget that she and Nicholas lived as virtual prisoners in the land they ruled.

In March 1913, Russians began the celebration of the three hundredth anniversary of the Romanovs' accession. Inevitably there ought to have been a great outpouring of patriotic sentiment that could have provided Nicholas and Aleksandra with an ideal means for reestablishing that emotional tie with Russians, and especially Petersburgers, that two decades of their ineptitude and political clumsiness had so seriously weakened. They could not do so, and the fault was largely Aleksandra's. Aleksandra and her constant companion Anna Vyrubova saw "little real enthusiasm, little real loyalty" among Petersburgers, and the Empress was not willing to step forward and make the effort needed to regain their love and respect.[129] More than ever, she suffered from deep feelings of persecution and felt that her subjects found perverse pleasure in misunderstanding her actions. When she was "exhausted," they thought her cold and haughty. When she was concerned about Aleksei's health, they thought her insensitive to their needs. She tried to engage in philanthropic work of various sorts, but knowledge of her goodness never seemed to reach the outside world.[130] She had shrunk so deeply into her cocoon of paranoia and wounded self-pity that she simply could not return to the real world of St. Petersburg and the Winter Palace.

While Aleksandra enjoyed her isolation and was content to blame her lack of rapport with her subjects upon other people and other circumstances, Nicholas's isolation stemmed from his failure to comprehend the new role that had been forced upon him. He would not approach his people after the events of 1905, but insisted that they must earn his "forgiveness" for their revolutionary transgressions. Yet he could not be the stern, forceful but benevolent ruler his father would have been under such circumstances. "I admit I tried to show coldness and reserve towards the Black Sea sailors so that they would feel that the shameful events of 1905 are not easily forgotten," he wrote to his mother in the fall of 1909, although the guilty sailors had long since been punished, and these particular men bore little if any guilt for the mutinies of 1905.[131] Tragically for the Romanovs, Nicholas preserved this primitive political attitude until his very last days on the throne. When, in January 1917, Britain's Ambassador Buchanan urged him to "break down the barrier that separates you from your people and regain their confidence," Nicholas drew himself up and asked haughtily, "Do you mean that *I* am to regain the confidence of my people, or that they are to regain *my* confidence?"[132] It was a statement worthy of a seventeenth-century monarch, not a twentieth-century one.

Although Nicholas and Aleksandra returned to St. Petersburg for the celebrations of their dynasty's great anniversary, they thus took no advantage of the opportunity it offered for reconciliation with their subjects. Ambassador Buchanan's daughter captured some of the disappointment Petersburgers felt. The anniversary, she wrote, "had been eagerly looked forward to and discussed for months beforehand. It had been hoped that these festivities would force the Imperial Family to come out of their seclusion and that the Emperor, when he attended the Duma, would make some public announcement that would relieve the internal situation."[133] Yet Nicholas granted nothing, although it had been customary for centuries for the Tsar to grant amnesties and concessions on important occasions. Nor were any balls given at the Winter Palace to brighten the social season. The entire celebration was permeated by a somberness that amazed Meriel Buchanan, then a young woman in her twenties. When Nicholas, Aleksandra, and their children rode to the great Kazan Cathedral for the memorial Mass, she was astounded to see that his face displayed an "almost stern gravity [that] gave to the celebration no sense of national rejoicing." This was transmitted to the crowds of onlookers, who remained "strangely silent."[134] The ever-loyal Vyrubova perceived the crowds as "undemonstrative masses of people, a typical Petersburg crowd,"[135] a description that contrasted strangely with the actions of those Petersburgers who had greeted Nicholas and Aleksandra on the day of their wedding or of the crowd that had cheered in favor of war with Japan at the beginning of 1904.

During what few celebrations of the Romanovs' three hundredth anniversary there were, Aleksandra preserved an almost total detachment. The Mariinskii Theatre once again performed Glinka's *A Life for the Tsar,* and Aleksandra appeared in the Imperial box for the first time in several years. "Her lovely, tragic face was expressionless, almost austere, as she stood by her husband's side during the playing of the National Anthem, her eyes, enigmatical in their dark gravity, seemed fixed on some secret inward thought that was certainly far removed from the crowded theatre and the people who acclaimed her. Not once did a smile break the immobile somberness of her expression when, the Anthem over, she bent her head in acknowledgment of the cheers that greeted its conclusion," wrote Meriel Buchanan. It proved beyond Aleksandra's emotional strength even to remain in view of her subjects for the evening. "Sitting so close," Miss Buchanan continued in her account, "we could see that the fan of white eagles' feathers the Empress was holding was trembling convulsively, we could see how a dull, unbecoming flush was stealing over her pallor, [and] could almost hear the laboured breathing which made the diamonds which covered the bodice of her gown rise and fall, flashing and trembling with a thousand uneasy sparks of light. Presently, it seemed that this emotion or distress mastered her completely, and with a few whispered words to the Emperor she rose and withdrew to the back of the box, to be no more seen that evening."[136]

High society continued to flourish in St. Petersburg despite the aloofness of the Emperor and Empress. During the winter season, when Nicholas and Aleksandra were cloistered away at Tsarskoe Selo, there was a series of lavish balls and entertainments that the capital's aristocracy continued to enjoy. There was the Bal Blanc, at which young noble damsels wore only white, notable for the "rows of alarming-looking chaperones [who] sat around watching with alert eyes, ready to make none too charitable remarks if one danced more than twice with the same young man." At the Bal Blanc, young ladies danced quadrilles with young lords, the two-step was thought of as "slightly unrefined," and "an order of the Emperor forbade any officer in uniform dancing the one-step."[137] There were "far less conventional and formal and, consequently, a good deal more amusing" balls given for a more mature part of society, and there were dinners, admittedly often "stereotyped and uninteresting, the champagne a little sweet, the flowers badly arranged, the conversation spasmodic and laboured."[138]

Over this world presided the Grand Duchess Maria Pavlovna, a Mecklenberg princess who had wed Nicholas's uncle Grand Duke Vladimir Aleksandrovich, and whose palace became a substitute for the Court that Nicholas and Aleksandra had allowed to fall into such disrepair. Ambassador Buchanan described her as "a *grande dame* in the best sense of the term," a vivacious, intelligent woman who had a gift for bringing out the best in her guests.[139] Maria Pavlovna presided over the great Christmas Bazaar, which officially opened the winter season in the capital, where "the whole of St. Petersburg flocked to buy a few expensive trifles, make a detailed examination of everyone's dresses and hats, and receive a gracious smile from the Grand Duchess."[140] Maria Pavlovna also entertained the so-called "smart set" and boasted such connections with the artistic world as scandalized St. Petersburg's older generation of aristocrats and gave a slightly exotic, mildly dangerous tone to her entertainments.[141]

It was the artistic world, with which the Grand Duchess Maria Pavlovna maintained only the most tenuous ties, that flourished most of all during the years that separated the Revolution of 1905 from that of 1917, for those disordered, chaotic times in which Russians were seeking to plot a course between the political extremes of anarchy and undiminished autocracy produced a new and dramatic burst of culture. This new Silver Age, as it was to be remembered, was a far cry from the elegant Golden Age of Pushkin and from the solid, realistic Iron Age of Dostoevskii and Tolstoi as well. It was marked by shocking scandal, extreme debauchery, frenzied searching, and deep, passionate belief. Among other things, the artists and intellectuals of the Silver Age embarked upon a voyage of unrestrained sexual exploration, which led them to experiments with pederasty, lesbianism, and all varieties of sadomasochism. These were "the children of Russia's terrible years."[142] They awaited the coming of the second revolution in the same manner as religious zealots looked for the Second Coming of Christ.

Suicide, murder, sexual perversion, opium, and alcohol—all were an integral part of life among Russia's avant garde, from the soundless, timeless St. Petersburg "Tower" of the poet Viacheslav Ivanov to the lowest cellars of prostitution and depravity, as depicted in *Among the Dregs,* Maksim Gorkii's portrayal of life in a *trushchoba,* a slum beyond the imagination of almost all Western readers, in which men and women fought and died for a gulp of cheap vodka. This was a world of vast and shocking contrasts, of Valerii Briusov's poem, "The Pale Horse," which took its title from the Book of Revelation 6:8 that proclaimed "behold, a pale horse, and its rider's name was Death," and of Boris Savinkov's novel of the same name, which glorified a deranged cult of assassination. Perhaps most of all, the spirit of the Silver Age was embodied in Andrei Belyi's *Silver Dove,* a strange, awkward novel the young symbolist wrote in 1909, during the space of some five weeks of self-imposed isolation in the tiny village of Bobrovka.

Silver Dove was an amazing allegory of tragedy, whose broader dimensions Belyi himself could not even begin to comprehend in 1909. It centered upon an artist who became "lost in the black pit of Russian ignorance, superstition, hatred, and evil," where the spirit of Russia's artists and poets was "extinguished by the black force of the earth and the forest."[143] There, the carpenter Mitia Kudeiarov, a man with a face that "always looks like half a face; one side of it craftily winking at you, while the other is always spying on something, always afraid of something,"[144] occupied what Belyi called "a still empty place" in Russian life.[145]

Meanwhile, in the nonfictional lives of Nicholas and Aleksandra, that place—evil, destructive, yet holding out a false promise of salvation—had in fact been filled. "We've made the acquaintance of a man of God, Grigorii, from the Tobolsk Guberniia," Nicholas wrote in his diary.[146] The date was November 1, 1905. No single personality would influence the lives of Nicholas, Aleksandra, and their children so directly or so catastrophically. For this was Rasputin, the man "who will speak to you of God," whose coming the fraudulent "Dr. Philippe" had foretold on the eve of his departure from Tsarskoe Selo some two years before.

Variously called a saint, a sinner, and a devil by those who knew him, Grigorii, later to be known as Rasputin (the name was said to have come from the Russian word *rasputnik,* meaning libertine), was born in Siberia, in the village of Pokrovskoe, in 1872. His parents were peasants. He, too, lived the life of a peasant until one day in 1891 when he left his village, wife and children, and set out for Mount Athos in Greece. "Grigorii has turned pilgrim out of laziness," his father is supposed to have remarked at the time.[147] Grigorii insisted that he had seen a vision of the Virgin and that he must follow the path she set for him. Thus, he began his career as a holy wanderer, whose pronouncements excited ecstasy or contempt wherever he went. Aleksandra thought him a saint. When he was away, she liked to imagine that she knelt before him. "My head is bowed, I hear your voice, and feel the touch of your hands," she once wrote.[148] Her daughters wrote him letters too, undoubtedly at their mother's urging, and they contained sentiments that were hardly those that young girls should have been encouraged to write to any adult man. At the age of fourteen, Olga called him her "dear, darling, beloved friend" and signed her letter, "ardently loving you, your Olga," while the eight-year-old Anastasia wrote that she saw him in her dreams.[149] Count Vladimir Kokovtsev, the Minister of Finance who replaced Stolypin as Chairman of the Council of Ministers, told Nicholas that he thought Rasputin was "a typical representative of the sort of Siberian tramp I encountered in the transit prisons soon after I entered the civil service" and warned that these people "always conceal their pasts, besmirched as they are with all sorts of crimes, and are ready, literally, to do anything to attain their goals."[150] Worried by Rasputin's growing influence at Tsarskoe Selo, Kokovtsev spoke to the sensible Dowager Empress about it in 1912. Aware of the danger, but also knowing that she could not avert it, Maria Feodorovna remarked that "my unhappy daughter-in-law does not realize that she is destroying not only herself but the dynasty as well."[151]

Rasputin claimed to be what Russians call a *starets*, a holy man. A true *starets* was a man of God, who had renounced the world to pray for the salvation of the people who still lived in it. "And so, what is a *starets*?" asked Dostoevskii in the fifth chapter of *The Brothers Karamazov*. "A *starets*," he answered, "takes your soul, your will, into his soul and his will. In choosing a *starets*, you renounce any will of your own, and you surrender it to him in complete obedience and with total self-abnegation." Dostoevskii explained further that one surrendered one's soul to a *starets* in the hope that "after a life of complete obedience, one could attain complete freedom, that is, freedom from one's self."[152]

Rasputin, however, was a fake, a fraudulent *starets*, who sought to capture the will, mind, and soul of simple minded believers, high and low, rich and poor, in order to bend them to his will. He preached a doctrine of salvation through sin and emphasized to his flock, especially to the women who flocked to him, that sins of the flesh were especially efficacious for achieving God's forgiveness and, thereby, salvation. "The first word of the Savior was 'Repent,'" he told them. "How can we repent if we have not first sinned?" "Man must sin in order that he have something to repent of," he continued. "If God sends us a temptation, we must yield to it voluntarily and without resistance, so then we may afterwards do penance in utter contrition."[153] Not long after his appearance in St. Petersburg in 1903, Rasputin began to assemble a flock of empty-headed noblewomen who sought his company and, through his rude caresses, his blessings. Bored with their lives, these women found it titillating to be ravished by this smelly, dirty peasant, who ate with his hands, tore at his food with blackened teeth, used the foulest language in their presence, described in coarse detail the sexual acts of the horses on his father's farm in Siberia,[154] and took them quickly and brutally, with the vaguely muttered assurance that "now, Mother. Everything is in order."[155] It was the same sort of bizarre compulsion, the same attraction of repulsive opposites, that Belyi described in *Silver Dove,* when a well-educated young man abandoned a beautiful, sensitive, and wealthy noblewoman for a pockmarked, dirty peasant wench who gave her fat, sweaty, and unattractive body to him with an animal lust so unbridled that he was captured by it and had no will to resist.

In the frenetic world of St. Petersburg after 1905, Rasputin had the personality to attract women who were bored and, at the same time, confused by the upheavals that swirled around them, and he possessed an inner power that many found difficult to turn away from. One of Aleksandra's friends, Lili Dehn, confessed that she was "at once attracted, repelled, disquieted, and reassured" when she first met Rasputin. "At a first glance, he appeared to be a typical peasant from the frozen North," she wrote. "But his eyes held mine, those shining steellike eyes which seemed to read one's inmost thoughts. His face was pale and thin, his hair long, and his beard a lighter chestnut. Rasputin was not tall, but he gave one the impression of being so; he was dressed as a Russian peasant, and wore the [peasant's] high boots, loose shirt, and long black coat."[156] Like Lili Dehn, most people who met Rasputin seemed to remember his eyes. Vyrubova thought he had "the most extraordinary eyes, large, bright, brilliant, and apparently capable of seeing into the very mind and soul of the person with whom he held converse."[157] Lest these descriptions be dismissed as the remarks of two empty-headed and hysterical women (which Vyrubova and Dehn were, in fact), we should recall the account in the diary of Maurice Paléologue, France's Ambassador to Russia, who met Rasputin in February 1915: "The whole expression of the face was concentrated in the eyes—light-blue eyes with a curious sparkle, depth, and fascination. His gaze was at once penetrating and caressing, naïve and cunning, direct and yet remote. When he was excited, it seemed as if his pupils became magnetic."[158]

"Magnetic" eyes, eyes that possessed a "curious sparkle," "shining steellike eyes," eyes that "seemed to read one's inmost thoughts," were the sources of Rasputin's power over his female flock, over Nicholas and Aleksandra, and, eventually, over Russia. It seems that through these eyes he possessed the power to hypnotize, and, with it, he seems to have been able to stem the hemorrhages that threatened the life of the Tsarevich Aleksei. Ever since the day they had discovered that their only son was a victim of hemophilia, Nicholas and Aleksandra had watched him writhe in agony while minor injuries turned into great, painful swellings. Medical experts from St. Petersburg, Moscow, and all of Europe had little to offer in the way of treatment. In desperation, Nicholas and Aleksandra turned to herbalists, such as the Tibetan Dr. Zhimsarian Badmaev, and to outright quacks and itinerant "saints." Dr. Badmaev "prescribed" a number of herbal concoctions for Aleksei on occasion, although there is no evidence that they were of any use.[159]

Modern science, Tibetan herbs, and the ravings of bogus holy men could not cure the Tsarevich's affliction. Nor could they even be counted upon to relieve his sufferings. Nicholas and Aleksandra therefore were more than willing to try the ministrations of Rasputin when the Grand Duchesses Militsa and Anastasia, that notorious pair of Montenegrin princesses who already held the dubious distinction of having discovered "Dr. Philippe" some years before, began to sing his praises. Their urgings were seconded by Aleksandra's inseparable companion, the simpleton Vyrubova, who had revered Rasputin as a saint and a seer ever since he had predicted correctly that her marriage to her shell-shocked, impotent, alcoholic husband would be neither happy nor long lived.[160] Perhaps through his ability to employ some sort of hypnosis, Rasputin managed to take advantage of a then-unknown characteristic of hemophilia (discovered only in the 1960s) that, while emotional stress aggravates hemorrhaging, the induction of emotional tranquility can reduce it sharply and on occasion stem it altogether.[161] On several occasions, Rasputin used his seemingly strange powers to calm Aleksei and to relieve his suffering. To Nicholas and Aleksandra, it was a miracle sent directly by God, and Rasputin's future as a holy man in whom Aleksandra placed absolute confidence was assured. She saw nothing but good in him and would permit no one to speak ill of him in her presence, for he and no one else seemed able to save her son.

Aleksandra's favor toward Rasputin seemed all the more strange and sinister to Russians because no one outside the family's most intimate circle knew that Aleksei suffered from hemophilia. So closely guarded was the nature of his illness that Pierre Gilliard, who tutored the Grand Duchesses Olga, Maria, Tatiana, and Anastasia for eight years between 1905 and 1913 never once heard of it despite the fact that he sometimes lived in the palace, traveled with his pupils to Livadia and Spala, and even sailed with them abroad the *Standart*. Only when he was appointed Aleksei's official tutor in the fall of 1913 did the Tsarevich's personal physician tell Gilliard about his hemophilia in the strictest secrecy.[162] Even with the crises the First World War brought to Russia, the Tsarevich's secret remained closely guarded. As late as December 1915, after he had been at his post for more than a year, the American Ambassador to Russia, George Marye, could not report with certainty the nature of Aleksei's affliction. "We hear all sorts of stories about what is the matter with him," he wrote, "but the best authenticated seems to be that he has some trouble of the circulation."[163]

The total ignorance of the Russian people about Aleksei's disease and, hence, the reason for Aleksandra's initial confidence in Rasputin, created a threatening situation. Sensible Russians found it difficult to retain even a modicum of respect for an Empress who allowed into her presence a crude peasant whose outrageous escapades were known to them all. Even loyal subjects began to worry that something sinister was afoot, and Rasputin's public behavior supported their fears, especially since they almost never saw their Emperor and Empress and could only imagine what was taking place behind the guarded gates of the Alexander Palace at Tsarskoe Selo.

By 1911, it thus had become clear that Rasputin's person was sacrosanct by virtue of the Empress's protection and that, whatever sins he committed in St. Petersburg or elsewhere, he was not to be punished. In response to detailed reports about Rasputin's shocking public behavior, Stolypin attempted to have him sent back to his native Siberian village. He discussed the matter with Nicholas, because he thought that the gossip and rumor about Rasputin and the Imperial family was causing Nicholas and Aleksandra to be held up to ridicule. "I know and believe, Petr Arkadevich, that you are truly loyal to me," Nicholas replied. "Perhaps everything you say is true. But I must ask you never to speak to me again about Rasputin. In any case, I can do nothing at all about it."[164] Aleksandra was so enraged at Stolypin's attempt to exile the rogue whom she now regularly referred to as "our Friend" that she saw his assassination as an act of divine retribution. "Those who have offended God in the person of our Friend may no longer count on divine protection," she explained to the young Grand Duke Dmitrii Pavlovich.[165]

Soon, all sorts of fantastic tales about vast debauches at Tsarskoe Selo, in which Vyrubova, Aleksandra, and all her daughters gave themselves to Rasputin in a wild and unrestrained frenzy of lust, began to circulate from mouth to mouth, and from salon to salon.[166] So much credence was given to these rumors that, in May 1917, the Provisional Government's Supreme Investigating Commission actually ordered Vyrubova to submit to a medical examination after she insisted to them that she could not have had intercourse with Rasputin or Nicholas because she still was a virgin. To the amazement of her interrogators, the examination proved Vyrubova's virginity beyond question.[167]

As the speculations about Rasputin's relationships with the Imperial family spread through Russia between 1911 and 1913, people were consumed by a sense of foreboding and impending doom, which the young writer Dmitrii Merezhkovskii captured when he wrote about the curse of the Romanovs. "In the house of the Romanovs, a mysterious curse descends from generation to generation. Murders and adultery, blood and mud. . . . The block, the rope, and poison—these are the true emblems of Russian autocracy. God's unction on the brows of the Tsars has become the brand of Cain."[168] As the guns of August 1914 boomed out from the Baltic to the Carpathians, many Russians must have thought that the curse had struck with unprecedented fury as their armies suffered defeat after defeat, and as Aleksandra and her treasured Rasputin began to play a far greater and more public role in state affairs.

CHAPTER XIV

Days of War and
Revolution

"The same discouragement prevails everywhere," wrote one Petersburger in assessing the early months of 1914. "No one expects or hopes for anything. Everyone grows indifferent, and gives his thoughts and attention to frivolous subjects, waiting with apathy for the cataclysm which is bound to come."[1] That cataclysm, thoughtful men and women feared, would be a war that pitted England, France, and Russia against Germany and Austria in a conflict that would bring ruin for victor and vanquished alike. "A general European war is mortally dangerous for both Russia and Germany no matter who wins," the reactionary Petr Durnovo warned Nicholas at the beginning of 1914. "There must inevitably break out in the defeated country a social revolution which, by the very nature of things, will spread to the country of the victor."[2]

This fear and pessimism, this sense of fatalistic waiting, evaporated in a wave of hysterical patriotism the moment Nicholas declared war against Germany and Austria. Petersburgers almost seemed relieved that the final step had been taken as they staged demonstrations to show their support of the government. On the Winter Palace Square, where Nicholas's soldiers had shot Petersburg workers in 1905, a huge crowd congregated on August 1 to cheer the war. Again they bore flags, icons, and portraits of Nicholas and Aleksandra. When Nicholas appeared on the Palace balcony, they all knelt as one and sang *"Bozhe Tsaria khrani!"*—"God Save the Tsar!"[3] Three days later, they stormed the German Embassy, a gross structure newly built of red Finnish granite that stood on St. Isaac's Square as a monument to all that was tasteless and crude in Wilhelmian Germany. As enraged crowds turned it into a shambles, the police looked on in that benevolent manner they usually reserved for those moments when they faced pogroms against Jews.[4] Thus, the First War began, as all wars began in Russia, with indiscriminate outbursts of patriotism, best personified, perhaps, by the passion with which reactionaries and extreme liberals in the Duma proclaimed their unity in the common cause of winning victory against the Kaiser. Vladimir Purishkevich, leader of the extreme right-wing party in the Duma, hastened to embrace Pavel Miliukov, leader of the liberal *Kadety*.[5] In return, Miliukov's newspaper, *Rech,* proclaimed to all *Kadety* that "our first duty is to preserve our nation's unity and integrity, and to defend her position as a world power." Miliukov urged them to "put aside our domestic disputes" and insisted that they remember that "our first and only task at this moment is to support our soldiers."[6]

Perhaps without fully realizing it, Miliukov and his supporters had struck the major point for Russian politicians and statesmen to remember. For it was not they who had to face the German artillery shells and machine-gun bullets in Poland and East Prussia. As in all Russian wars, it was the peasants who bore the burden of the fighting and the dying, and it was upon the peasants's devotion and resolve that the issue of victory or defeat hinged. To these peasants, in the words of General Iurii Danilov, "the reasons for the war were never clear," and no one in St. Petersburg ever made much effort to explain it to them.

Peasants were mobilized by the hundreds of thousands all over Russia. In the far north, where the early frosts had just begun; in Siberia; in the Black Earth Region; in the Ukraine, where the rich harvest still stood ripening in the fields; and in the lands of New Russia along the Black Sea, one scene was repeated over and over again. In thousands of villages, the Vanias, Kostias, and Sashas shouldered their rucksacks and bade clumsy, fond farewells to their Tanias, Anniushas, and Matronas, who wept long and sadly waved their kerchiefs, until their loved ones disappeared over the horizon. Had they been asked why they went, they could have given no answer except that the Tsar had called them to defend Russia. Most of them would never see their mothers, wives, or sweethearts again. The men who marched away in the late summer and early fall of 1914 were soon to die in the marshes of Poland, East Prussia, and Galicia in what Aleksandra, in a moment of absurd exaltation, assured Nicholas was a war that "has lifted up spirits, cleansed the many stagnant minds, brought unity in feelings, and is a 'healthy war' in the moral sense."[7]

The scandalous fact, however, was that, although these young men died bravely, many of them died pitifully, without hope, and to little purpose. For the peasant soldiers who marched against the Kaiser's armies in the fall of 1914 often marched without the support of artillery, without ammunition, without even rifles on which to mount the bayonets in which Russian infantrymen had placed such confidence ever since Peter the Great had first brought them into the Russian army. "The only great and serious difficulty for our troops is that we have again an insufficiency of munitions," Nicholas wrote to Aleksandra in mid-November, less than four months after the war began. "In consequence of this," he continued, "our troops have to observe economy and discretion during action, which means that the brunt of the fighting falls upon the infantry. Owing to that, the losses at once become colossal. Some of the Corps of the Line have become divisions; the brigades have shrunk into regiments, and so forth. Reinforcements are coming in well, but half of them have no rifles, as the troops are losing masses. There is nobody to collect them on the battlefields."[8]

By the end of that month, the situation was far, far worse at the front than Nicholas had reported. Indeed, it was far worse than he even realized. Russia entered the war with a million fewer rifles in her arsenals than the number of men who were mobilized, and the same arsenals proved to be almost 600 million rounds of rifle ammunition short. There was only about one machine gun for every six hundred infantry. There was insufficient light artillery, and almost no heavy guns. In 1914, the entire Russian army had only 60 batteries of heavy artillery with which to face the Austrians and the Germans, while the Germans alone had 381 to direct against the Russians. None of Russia's heavy artillery equaled the German weapons in range and caliber. Every German infantry division was supported by exactly twice as many batteries of light artillery as its Russian counterpart, and the Germans had ample shells for their guns, while the Russians did not.[9] So serious was the shortage of ammunition that on the *fourth* day of the war, the general in charge of supplies on Russia's northwestern front wired the following desperate telegram to Minister of War General Vladimir Sukhomlinov:

GENERAL RENNENKAMPF ASKS FOR 108,000 SHRAPNEL SHELLS AND 17,100 ORDINARY, ALSO 56,000,000 RIFLE CARTRIDGES. I CAN SEND AND AM SENDING MY LAST RESERVES: 2,000 ORDINARY SHELLS, 9,000 SHRAPNEL SHELLS, AND 7,000,000 RIFLE CARTRIDGES.[10]

Absurd and unbelievable as it might seem, Nicholas had left his army, the pride of every Russian Emperor since Peter the Great, in such incompetent hands during the decade since the Russo-Japanese War that, in less than a week of fighting, it was running out of ammunition!

All of this was learned by the incredulous French Ambassador on December 18. "I learned yesterday that the Russian artillery is short of ammunition; I learn this morning that the infantry is short of rifles!" Paléologue confided to his diary. "I went at once to General [Mikhail] Belaev, Army Chief of Staff at the Ministry of War, and asked for an explanation. He made a clean breast of everything: 'Our losses in men had been colossal [Belaev confessed], though if it were merely a matter of replacing wastage we could soon do so as we have more than 800,000 men in our depots. But we're short of rifles to arm and train these men. Our original reserve was 5,600,000 rifles; at least we thought so. The Grand Duke Nicholas [Nikolaevich] thought so; I thought so myself. We have been criminally deceived: our magazines are nearly empty. . . . The position is hardly less difficult as regards gun ammunition. The consumption has surpassed all our calculations and anticipations. At the beginning of the war, we had 5,200,000 rounds of 76 mm. shrapnel in our arsenal. Our entire reserve is exhausted. The armies need 45,000 rounds per day. Our maximum output is 13,000; we hope it will reach 20,000 about February 15th.' . . . I thanked him for his candor, made some notes, and withdrew," Paléologue concluded.[11] The shock must have been incredible. Suddenly, France found that the ally upon whom she had counted so heavily to hold the Germans in the east had too few rifles for her infantry and not enough shells to service her artillery. The invincible "Russian steamroller,"[12] about which generals and statesmen had spoken with such pride and assurance in the years before the war, had turned out to be a mirage, the product of wishful thinking that had taken no account of reality.

General Rennenkampf had not demanded vast quantities of shells and cartridges from the desperate general in charge of supplies for the northwestern front without good reason. From the outbreak of the war, he had been locked in a murderous struggle with the German armies in East Prussia, as he and General Aleksandr Samsonov had attacked toward Königsberg from the east and the south. They had enjoyed a brief though illusory moment of success until the Kaiser appointed two new commanders on the Eastern Front in mid-August. Field Marshal Paul von Hindenburg became the army's Commander in Chief, and General Erich von Ludendorff became his Chief of Staff. Together, these two superb military planners decided to face first Samsonov's advance from the south and then to turn against Rennenkampf. It was a daring plan. Samsonov would have to be defeated quickly, and the German forces then would have to turn sharply to meet Rennenkampf's attack against their flank.

The Germans carried out their plan with brilliant and brutal efficiency. By August 30, Hindenburg and Ludendorff had taken over one hundred thousand of Samsonov's soldiers prisoners in an encirclement that became known as the Battle of Tannenberg. Within four days, they had wheeled sharply to face Rennenkampf's drive into the region of the Masurian Lakes. In less than a fortnight, they had captured another forty-five thousand Russians and had driven Rennenkampf's army in headlong retreat. Rennenkampf himself fled so precipitously from the battle that he lost all contact with his own troops for several days.[13] After just a month of war with Germany, the Russians had suffered two major defeats. The one positive result of their amazingly poor performance was that the Germans had been obliged to pull a few divisions out of their thrust toward Paris, and that had weakened their drive just enough to enable the French to halt them at the Marne.

Despite shortages of rifles, artillery, and shells, the Russians did better against Austria, mainly because the Austrian army was less effectively commanded than its German counterpart. Russians and Austrians faced similar problems of supply and transportation, and their weapons were more on a par. Therefore, the great numbers of troops that Nicholas's commanders threw into battle during the first months of the war on the Austrian front had a telling effect, and the Russian armies seized most of Galicia and the Carpathian passes before Christmas. In early March 1915, the great Austrian fortress of Przemysl fell to the Russians after a siege of six months. There, they captured more than 120,000 Austrians and 900 guns. It seemed a great victory indeed, one that helped to offset the embarrassment of Russia's losses in East Prussia.[14] Yet even before the fall of Przemysl, the Russians faced the critical question of where they would get the supplies, weapons, and ammunition to continue their advance in 1915. The sad truth was that the country's industrial establishment could not even hope to produce the quantities of weapons, ammunition, and other matériel needed to supply millions of men spread out along a front more than a thousand miles long. Russia's European Allies could do little to aid her, because their factories at first could barely keep up with the demands of their own armies. Once Allied production got into high gear, the French and English found Russia's Black Sea ports closed to their shipping as a consequence of Turkey's entry into the conflict on the side of Germany and Austria. At the same time, the German navy's U-boat fleet effectively prevented France and England from shipping supplies to Russia through the Baltic.

At the end of April 1915, a combined Austro-German army launched an offensive that drove the Russians in full retreat along the entire Eastern Front. In mid-June, the Austrians captured Lwów. A month later, the Germans breached the Vistula River above Warsaw, and five days afterward the Russians evacuated the city they had held since 1831. By the middle of August, the Russians had lost not only all of the territory they had won from the Austrians between August 1914 and March 1915 but all of Russian Poland and even a portion of those lands Catherine the Great had taken from the Poles in the 1770s. Some of the most fertile grain-growing regions of Eastern Europe had passed into German and Austrian control as a result of these losses. More than 1.5 million Russians had been taken prisoner by the Germans and Austrians, and another 1.5 million had been killed or wounded.[15]

These staggering losses stemmed partly from wretched leadership—the lessons of the Russo-Japanese War had gone unlearned, and senior Russian officers simply had very little understanding about modern warfare. At the height of the Austro-German advance in 1915, the young Grand Duke Andrei Vladimirovich, who later wed Kschessinska, discussed the situation with General F. F. Palitsyn, one of General Alekseev's senior staff officers. Their discussion centered on the defense of Warsaw, which had not yet fallen, and the attitudes expressed by General Palitsyn are sufficiently absurd to justify quoting the conversation at some length.

"What will the High Command do?" the Grand Duke asked Palitsyn.

"I don't know," the General replied.

"But you have some ideas, do you not?"

"Oh, indeed. I have some ideas, some good, very excellent ideas," was the reply.

When he could not extract from Palitsyn any sense of just what his "good, very excellent" ideas were, the Grand Duke, a senior officer on the Russian General Staff, tried another approach with more shocking results.

"Well, then, should we attack?" he asked Palitsyn.

"No, no. That's impossible. We need to conserve our resources," was Palitsyn's response.

"Then we are to make a stand here?"

"Oh, good grief. What are you saying? When we make a stand, it must be where the ground is to our advantage."

"Then you mean we must fall back?" the Grand Duke asked.

"God preserve us! How can we retreat?" Palitsyn asked. "According to all the theories, one loses more in a retreat than in an attack!"

"Then, what shall we do?" asked the amazed Andrei Vladimirovich, appalled at what he had heard and, perhaps, already guessing the hopeless answer his question was about to receive.

"I don't know," General Palitsyn answered again. "But I have some ideas, some good, very excellent ideas."

"I felt my head spinning," the Grand Duke confided to his diary. "It seemed that all those thoughts had gotten twisted into a terrible knot, where neither logic, nor reason, nor force of will could be of any help at all."[16]

It was, in fact, a true Pandora's box that Russia had opened when she went to war with Germany and Austria. The shortages and supply problems of 1914 paled in comparison with those of 1915. When Germany's General Mackensen launched his first assault against the Russian Third Army to open the campaign at Gorlica in May, he brought up more than two hundred heavy guns to open the way for him. The Third Army was stretched along some 130 miles of front, and it was obvious that more men were needed. The most shocking thing of all, however, was that the entire Third Army had a total of exactly 4 guns—two 4.2-inch guns and two 6-inch howitzers—to counter Mackensen's massive barrages.[17] Russian artillery was limited to two or three shells a day, while the Germans fired hundreds.[18] General Nikolai Golovin recalled the awesome effect of the "Mackensen steamroller" in a book he wrote some years later:

> Creeping like some huge beast, the German army would move its advanced units close to the Russian trenches, just near enough to hold the attention of its enemy and to be ready to occupy the trenches immediately after their evacuation. Next . . . the heavy artillery would take up positions in places which were almost or entirely beyond the range of the Russian field artillery, and the heavy guns would start to shower their shells on the Russian trenches, doing it methodically, as was characteristic of the Germans. That hammering would go on until nothing of the trenches remained, and their defenders would be destroyed. Then the beast would cautiously stretch out its paws, the infantry units, which would seize the demolished trenches. In the meantime, the Russian artillery and the Russian rear would be subjected to a fierce fire from the German heavy guns, while the German field artillery and machine guns would protect the advancing infantry from Russian counter attacks.[19]

The effect of such artillery fire was utterly devastating. General Sir Alfred Knox, British military observer with Russia's forces in 1915, described how eighteen hundred raw infantry replacements arrived at the front during one such attack. Not one of these new recruits had a rifle, and had been sent to reserve trenches to wait, in Knox's words, "until casualties in the firing-line should make rifles available" for them. While they were waiting, a German artillery barrage began to rain down, and Knox saw "sixteen hundred of these unarmed drafts churned into gruel by the enemy's guns."[20] It was a shameful waste of men, weapons, and supplies that reached inhuman, if not outright criminal, proportions by September. As a result of it all, General Knox estimated that the total strength of the Russian army facing the Germans and the Austrians at the beginning of the winter of 1915 was "only 650,000 rifles, 2,590 machine guns, and 4,000 three-inch field guns" to defend a front that stretched from the Baltic city of Reval to the Carpathians.[21] If Knox's estimate was reasonably accurate, it meant that the Russian army could field only one armed man, though not always with bullets for his rifle, for every two and a half meters of front. It was a hopelessly inadequate number to offer even a reasonable hope of defense should the Germans and Austrians launch a new offensive.

What was even more shocking than these shortages was the appalling fact that the Russian High Command could not even feed its horses and soldiers, despite the fact that Russia had been a grain-exporting country for more than two centuries. Witte had forced sufficient grain onto the Western European grain markets to finance Russia's great industrial surge in the 1890s and, at the same time, to repair the worst of the ravages of the famine of 1891; Stolypin's agrarian reforms had increased the productivity of the Russian peasant farms by a substantial margin before the outbreak of war. None of this grain could be exported through the Black Sea once Turkey had entered the war against Russia, so much of it now was available for internal consumption. But Russia's military planners and transport personnel simply could not move the grain from the countryside to the front or wherever else it was needed. Instead of twenty pounds of oats each day, horses received only ten; instead of fifteen pounds of hay, they received five. Grand Duke Andrei Vladimirovich protested again and again that his men and their mounts must receive adequate rations if they were to stay in the field. The ministers who came to General Headquarters to discuss the problem told him that "the countryside has already given everything and further pressures for collection from the countryside would bring forth popular revolts." Andrei Vladimirovich and other staff officers insisted that "the war must take precedence over everything else and that troops could not fight without rations." The Ministers remained adamant in insisting that more food could not be sent to the army. "All they wanted was to maintain peace and prevent revolts in the countryside," the Grand Duke concluded.[22]

By the early fall of 1915, it was clear to everyone with any sense that Russia's war effort was on the verge of utter collapse. "Considering the present situation at the front and in the rear of the armies," Minister of War General Aleksei Polivanov reported to the Council of Ministers on August 6, "one can expect an irreparable catastrophe momentarily. The army is no longer retreating—it is simply running away. Its faith in its own forces is completely undermined. The tiniest rumor about the enemy, the appearance of a small German patrol, evokes panic and results in the flight of whole regiments." Russia's statesmen were not surprised by Polivanov's appraisal of the situation, because what he said was quite well known. But they were utterly shocked at the news with which he concluded his report. "There is a far more horrible event which threatens Russia," Polivanov warned his colleagues. "I feel obliged to inform the government that this morning, during my report, His Majesty told me of his decision to remove the Grand Duke [Nikolai Nikolaevich] and to personally assume the supreme command of the army."[23]

When Polivanov made his announcement, the entire Council sat in stunned silence for a moment and then everyone began to talk at once. "One could see to what a degree the majority were shaken by the news they had heard—the latest, stunning blow in the midst of the military misfortunes and internal complications which were being suffered," noted the Council's secretary A. N. Iakhontov.[24] Yet their shock and dismay was not with Nicholas's decision to relieve Grand Duke Nikolai Nikolaevich, for almost all of them agreed that he simply did not have the ability to continue as Commander in Chief of Russia's armies. In their view, the appalling news in Polivanov's report was that Nicholas intended to take over supreme command of the armies. All of them knew he had no talent for strategy and that he was a wretched administrator. All of them knew, too, that Nicholas was weak and usually asserted himself at the wrong time and for the wrong reasons. Most of all, they feared the influence Aleksandra and, through her, Rasputin exercised upon the Emperor. A neurotic Empress suffering from delusions of persecution and a crafty, nearly illiterate peasant would be the two closest advisers of the Commander in Chief of Russia's armies. To use Iakhontov's words, the very thought was indeed "a stunning blow."

"The execution of the Emperor's decision is absolutely impermissible, and one must resist him with all means," was the first reaction to come from Minister of Internal Affairs Prince Nikolai Shcherbatov.[25] After stating very frankly that the representatives of Russia's Allies had "little confidence in the Emperor's firmness of character," Minister of Foreign Affairs Sergei Sazonov concluded that "in general, all this is so terrible that my mind is in chaos. Into what an abyss Russia is being pushed!" Minister of Agriculture Aleksandr Krivoshein thought the the decision "in complete accord with the Emperor's spiritual makeup and with his mystical conception of his Imperial calling" and lamented that "Russia has lived through far more difficult times, but there was never a time when everything was done in order to complicate and confuse an already insoluble situation."[26] Ten of them sent a collective letter to Nicholas to beg him to change his mind, but he remained adamant, despite their utterly unprecedented statement that "the decision you have taken, according to our most thoughtful consideration, threatens Russia, You, and Your dynasty with the direst consequences."[27]

With his ministers predicting disaster from Petrograd,* Nicholas departed for the "Stavka," the headquarters of the Commander in Chief of the Russian armies. "A new, clean page begins," he wrote, "and only God Almighty knows what will be written on it!"[28] Aleksandra sent her Nicky off with passionate assurances of her love, tucked in among strong reminders that "being firm is the only saving," that "God, who is just and near you—will save your country and throne through your firmness." She promised him that "God will give me the strength to help you—because our souls are fighting for the right against the evil." Most of all, Aleksandra sought to comfort the man whom she now called "Russia's Savior" with the reassurance that "our

---

* St. Petersburg, thought by the Russian public to be a German-sounding name, was renamed Petrograd (the Old Slavic equivalent of St. Petersburg) in a wave of anti-German fervor soon after the war broke out in 1914. As we saw in chapter five, the origins of the name actually were Dutch, not German.

Friend's [Rasputin's] prayers arise night and day for you to heaven and God will hear them."²⁹ To remind Nicholas of that comforting fact, she had given him a pocket comb from Rasputin just before he had parted from her at Tsarskoe Selo. "Remember to comb your hair before all difficult tasks and decisions," she reminded him a few days later. "The little comb will bring its help. Don't you feel calm now that you have become 'sure of yourself'—it's not pride or conceit—but sent by God and it will help you in the future and give strength to the others to fulfill your orders."³⁰

Nicholas's activities at Stavka were scarcely those of a great captain intent upon turning near-certain defeat into victory. He moved into the large, comfortable mansion of the local governor and set up a simple routine that hardly seemed in keeping with the activities of the commander of an army in the midst of a great and brutal war. His official day began at ten in the morning, when his Chief of Staff reported on the situation at the various fronts. After that, he received reports from various ministers and senior officers. At about noon, he stopped work for lunch, after which two hours were set aside for rest, walks in the woods, or auto tours of nearby regions. From about 3:30 until 6:00 P.M., there was staff work. Like lunch, the dinner that came just after six was simple—a few *zakuski* (hors d'oeuvres), one or two glasses of vodka, and two, sometimes three, courses, accompanied by a glass or two of port. During the evening, Nicholas and his staff watched movies, listened to music, or enjoyed some similar pleasure.³¹ There were minor discomforts and inconveniences, but nothing of great consequence. "My field bedstead is so hard and stiff," he wrote, but hastened to add that "I must not complain—how many sleep on damp grass and mud!"³² It was a simple life, but certainly not the life of a commander who was in the process of whipping defeated, demoralized troops into fighting trim.

Nicholas obviously did little to advance the cause of victory by his activities at Stavka in 1915, but the most destructive of his decisions concerned Russia's domestic affairs and was communicated in the most offhand manner imaginable. "Think, my Wify," he wrote on August 25, "Will you not come to the assistance of your hubby now that he is absent? What a pity that you have not been fulfilling this duty [as my chief assistant in Petrograd] for a long time or at least during the war! I know of no more pleasant feeling than to be proud of you, as I have been all these past months, when you urged me on with untiring importunity, exhorting me to be firm and to stick to my own opinions."[33] By that time, Aleksandra had already begun to cast herself in the role of Nicholas's deputy. Her utter lack of experience in political affairs did not deter her in the slightest. "Silly old wify . . . has 'trousers' on unseen," were some of the first words of reassurance she wrote to Nicholas only a few hours after he had left Tsarskoe Selo.[34] The next day, in writing about statesmen she thought insufficiently energetic or loyal, she emphasized the trousers again. "I long to show my *immortal* trousers to those poltroons," she remarked.[35] By August 26, just four days after Nicholas had left Petrograd, Aleksandra already had begun to urge ministerial changes upon him. "Samarin [Director-General of the Holy Synod] goes on speaking against me," she complained. "Hope to get you a list of names and trust [we] can find a suitable successor before he can do any more harm."[36] Two days later, Aleksandra insisted that "Shcherbatov is impossible to keep [as Minister of Internal Affairs]." "Better quick to change him," she added in her typically telegraphic style of writing.[37]

Within a week of Nicholas's departure, Aleksandra had taken full control of Russia's domestic affairs with his approval. From then on, she rarely asked his opinion. Instead, she sent advice, suggestions, requests, even orders to him. Often these came not only from her but from Rasputin. "Our Friend begs you not to too much worry over this question of *food supply*—says things will arrange themselves," she wrote in September 1916.[38] A few days later, she sent Nicholas a whole list of assignments, with instructions to "keep my little list before you," so that he would remember just what he should say and do when Aleksandr Protopopov, whom he had just appointed Minister of Internal Affairs at her and Rasputin's urging, came to see him at Stavka. "Forgive my bothering you deary—but am always afraid as you are so terribly hard worked—that you may forget something—& so act as your living notebook," she wrote in explaining the reason she had sent him such a long list of reminders. Most important of all, she wanted Nicholas to remember to tell Protopopov "to listen to our Friend's councils, it will bring him blessings & help his work & Yours."[39] Aleksandra even began to offer military advice. In one of her letters, she explained that losses during bombardments might be reduced if commanders realized that "one must go quickly under their [the Germans' heavy guns] range as they are for great distances and cannot change quickly."[40]

The worst thing about Aleksandra's efforts to play a leading role in Russian affairs during 1915 and 1916 was that she divided the world in which she lived and worked into a large camp of "enemies" and a very small group of "friends," many of whom, she soon became convinced in her paranoid way, were scheming to betray Nicholas, Rasputin, and herself. In her mind, the war effort became centered upon this struggle of the few "good" and "moral" people who supported Nicholas and her circle against the ever-increasing group who opposed them. When she wrote to Nicholas that "you have fought this great fight for your country and your throne—alone and with bravery and decision," she was not referring to any great battle with the Germans or the Austrians but to the fact that Nicholas finally had summoned enough courage to relieve Grand Duke Nikolai Nikolaevich from his post as commander in chief.[41] She had urged that course upon him ever since the Grand Duke had threatened to hang Rasputin if he ever dared set foot in Russian General Headquarters.

Aleksandra's struggle against Nikolai Nikolaevich was still very much on her mind a year later when her paranoia became even more acute. "Its the same story as last year—again against wify," she wrote in November 1916. "They feel that I am your wall and that aggravates them—ah, lovy, dont let them do this, its more serious than you think. It took you long then to realize that last year—& now its the bad party who have got behind [Prime Minister] Trepov. . . . Its difficult writing & asking for oneself, I assure you, but its for y[ou]r and Baby's sake, believe me." "I don't care what bad one says of me," she continued in her semicoherent fashion, "only when one tries to tear devoted, honest people, who care for me—away—its horribly unfair. I am but a woman fighting for her Master & Child, her two dearest ones on earth—& God will help me being your guardian angel."[42] Clearly, Aleksandra had become convinced that her life's great mission was to defend the throne and the autocratic power of her husband and hemophilic son.

In Aleksandra's world, even more than in Nicholas's, the Duma was an object of scorn, even hatred. "Quickly shut [i.e. dissolve] the *Duma*," she urged just a few days after he had left Petrograd.[43] A day later, she reminded him: "The *Duma*, I hope, will at once be closed."[44] When the Duma had reassembled a year later, criticized her meddling, and, especially, damned the influence she allowed Rasputin to have upon state affairs, she renewed her pleas. "Disperse the *Duma* at once," she urged.[45] "They are a 'group,' a poisenous [sic] element in town, whereas dispersed over the country nobody pays any heed to them or respects them," she wrote a few days later.[46] "[Aleksandr] *Guchkov* [one of the leading moderates in the Duma] ought to be got rid of," she insisted at another point. "He hunts after anarchy and [is] against our dynasty, wh[ich] our Friend said God would protect."[47]

Guchkov was only one among many ministers of state against whom Aleksandra railed in her letters to Nicholas, and she usually succeeded in getting them removed from office with considerable dispatch. As the months passed, she became more venomous and gave Nicholas orders much more directly. "[I] should have sent [Prince] *Lvov* [President of the largest Red Cross organization in Russia] to Siberia (one did so for far less grave acts), taken *Samarin*'s *rank* away [he had already been removed as Director-General of the Holy Synod at her urging], [Pavel] *Miliukov* [leader of the *Kadety*, who had just made a bitter attack in the Duma against Rasputin's influence], *Guchkov*, & *Polivanov* [whom she had managed to drive from his post as Minister of War a few months before] also to Siberia. It is war and at such a time interior war is high treason, why don't you look at it like that?" she urged Nicholas. "My soul and brain tell me it w[ou]ld be the saving of Russia," she added.[48] For this sort of scribbled and frantic advice, Nicholas was deeply grateful. As he wrote to her at the very end of 1915, "I do not know how I could have endured . . . if God had not decreed to give you to me as a *wife and friend*!"[49] "It rests with you to keep peace and harmony among the Ministers—thereby you do a great service to me and to our country," he wrote some nine months later. "Oh, my precious Sunny, I am so happy to think that you have found at last a worthy occupation! Now I shall naturally be calm, and at least need not worry over internal affairs."[50]

As a consequence of Aleksandra's meddling and Nicholas's grateful acceptance of her advice in all except the rarest instances, Russia's government was deprived of every reasonably able statesman. By the fall of 1916, Aleksandra's performance of her "worthy occupation" had left her country with a motley assortment of rogues, incompetents, nonentities, and madmen at the head of her government. Basing his judgment upon the wildest assortment of reasons, none of them in any way relevant to state affairs, Rasputin recommended candidates to Aleksandra, who then pressed her choices upon Nicholas. At Rasputin's urging, Aleksei Khvostov became Minister of Internal Affairs in the fall of 1915, not long after he had won favor by adding his lusty bass voice to a gypsy chorus at one of Rasputin's favorite restaurants.[51] Others rose for equally flimsy and meaningless reasons. Perhaps worst of all was Aleksandr Protopopov, a friend of the shadowy herbalist Badmaev and a protégé of Rasputin. After spending two hours with Protopopov at Stavka in September 1916, during which he asked him all the questions from the list Aleksandra and Rasputin had prepared, Nicholas felt confident in reporting to his wife that he found him "inspired by the best intentions," a man with "an excellent knowledge of internal affairs."[52]

Among the many tsarist officials and politicians the Provisional Government's Investigating Commission questioned during the summer of 1917 was President of the Duma Mikhail Rodzianko, a moderate conservative. "Did you consider Protopopov to be a man who suffered from mental illness?" the Commission's President asked Rodzianko. "Unquestionably," Rodzianko replied.[53] Britain's Ambassador Buchanan also characterized Protopopov as "mentally deranged" and went on to say that, after Rasputin's death, Protopopov "would, in his audiences with the Empress, repeat warnings and messages which he had received in his imaginary converse with Rasputin's spirit."[54] "I know for certain," Paléologue reported to his superiors in Paris, "that he once had an infectious disease [syphilis] which has left him with nervous disorders, and that recently the preliminary symptoms of general paralysis have been observed in him."[55] These impediments notwithstanding, on Aleksandra's recommendation Nicholas proceeded to appoint this syphilitic madman Minister of Internal Affairs, the most sensitive and important domestic post in Russia's government.

As Aleksandra followed the inner voice of her conscience and the counsels of Rasputin, ministers came and went with such rapidity that Prince Vladimir Volkonskii remarked that a sign should be put up that read: "Piccadilly—the show changes every Saturday."[56] Miliukov dubbed Aleksandra's rapid cabinet changes as "ministerial leapfrog" and spoke about the "dark forces" behind the throne.[57] Generally every replacement was more subservient and less able than his predecessor had been. It was a ludicrous display, an exercise in absurdity.

In mid-1915, Russia's greatest munitions maker, Aleksei Putilov, told Ambassador Paléologue that "the days of Tsarism are numbered. . . . Revolution is now inevitable. It is only waiting for a favorable opportunity. Such an opportunity will come with some military defeat, a famine in the provinces, a strike in Petrograd, a riot in Moscow, some scandal or tragedy at the palace. . . . From the bourgeois revolution, we shall at once descend to the working class revolution, and soon after to the peasant revolution. And then will begin the most frightful anarchy; interminable anarchy," he said ominously. "We shall see the days of Pugachev again, and perhaps worse!"[58]

By the fall of 1916, those days of chaos were just a few months away. Nicholas and Aleksandra were totally unaware of the impending revolution and saw in every effort to warn them acts of near-treasonous disloyalty. "It is a terrible dilemma," wrote the conservative politician Vasilii Shulgin. "The Tsar offends the nation by what he allows to go on in the palace . . . while the country offends the Tsar by its terrible suspicions. The result is the destruction of those centuries-old ties which have sustained Russia. And what is the cause of all this? The weakness of one man and one woman. . . . Oh, how terrible an autocracy is without an Autocrat!"[59] As if in reply to these prophecies of doom, Aleksandra wrote, "A country, where a man of God helps the sovereign, will never be lost."[60]

Russians' resentment was heightened by their disgust at Rasputin's personal life during 1915 and 1916. He lived in an apartment at No. 64 Gorokhovaia Street, the middle of those three great avenues that radiated outward from the Admiralty. The building was one of those many nondescript apartment houses that had risen in the newer quarters of Petrograd during the quarter-century before the war.

There were several stairways, with several apartments opening onto each landing. Rasputin shared his stairway with a masseuse, a seamstress, and several others who lived in similarly modest circumstances. The sour smell of *shchi,* a type of cabbage soup that was a staple in the diet of common folk, hung in the stairwell. Mingled with it were the smells of rancid butter, hot sheep's cheese, and other similar foods, and one had to make one's way through this stale heavy air to reach Rasputin's apartment at the top of the stairs.[61] Once at the top of the staircase, one entered into a series of rooms with low-arched ceilings and heavy oaken furniture. "The whole contents of the flat, from the cumbersome sideboard to the crowded and abundantly stocked kitchen, bore the stamp of bourgeois well-being and prosperity," Prince Feliks Iusupov recalled. "The lithographs and badly painted pictures on the walls were fully in keeping with the owner's taste."[62] It certainly was not an elegant apartment, nor was it in an elegant part of the city. Its greatest advantage from Rasputin's point of view was that it was very near the railway station from which trains came and went between St. Petersburg and Tsarskoe Selo. Living in a modest part of town also enabled him to preserve his image as a man of the people, something that would have been far more difficult had he lived in a rich apartment along the Moika or the Catherine Canal.

Into this apartment an endless parade of visitors came and went during 1915 and 1916. Among them were the Princess Tatiana Shakhovskaia, the Countesses Maria Golovina and Olga Kreutz, the lady-in-waiting Lidia Nikitina, dozens of women well known in Petrograd society, and many others of less exalted origins. There were shop clerks, cleaning women, whores, and women who thought God spoke to them. They all came seeking favors—one to have her husband transferred away from the front, another to have her husband given a lucrative government contract, yet another to seek counsel about personal problems, and still another to beg a blessing. There was one lady in a low-cut ball gown who wanted Rasputin to have her named *prima donna* at the Imperial Opera. In return for his efforts to grant these pleas, Rasputin received money, wine, sweets, and sexual favors of all sorts. Police agents who kept him under continual surveillance dutifully noted down who spent the night, whose "behavior was very indecorous," and who brought what sorts of bribes. Because Rasputin's closeness to Aleksandra was well known during the days when Nicholas was at Stavka, all of these aspects of his personal life took on added significance and were gossiped about among the police agents and their friends. Human nature being what it is, the tales were elaborated and embroidered upon, and soon all of Petrograd knew some of the fact and much of the fiction.[63]

Far worse than the partially substantiated rumors about his private life were the gross indecencies Rasputin committed in public. These were seen by many people, and what they saw convinced them that the wildest tales about his private life must indeed be true. On one occasion, Rasputin appeared clad in nothing but a shirt at the Villa Rode, a notorious night spot on the outskirts of Petrograd. At the Iar Restaurant, an equally infamous den in Moscow, a number of witnesses agreed that he exposed himself to a number of women and shocked everyone there by his obscene remarks. Ambassador Paléologue got the story from a relative of one of Nicholas's aides-de-camp only a few days later and wrote in his diary that "Rasputin became very excited and with cynical effrontery began to give his audience a description of his amorous feats in Petrograd, naming the women who had accepted his overtures, relating every detail of the scene and pointing out the particular charm and the most spicy or grotesque feature of each occasion. When supper was over . . . Rasputin, dead drunk, began to talk about the Empress, whom he called the 'old girl.' . . . 'I can do anything I like with her' [he said]."[64] Eventually, wrote the British agent Bruce Lockhart, the police dragged him away, "snarling and vowing vengeance."[65]

Rasputin's public behavior heightened Russians' disgust with Nicholas and, especially, Aleksandra, who defended him at every turn. The Empire seemed to have fallen into the hands of a debauchee so dissolute as to defy all polite description. "A scene over which it is best to draw a veil" was the way in which Sir George Buchanan described some of Rasputin's gatherings.[66] "Rasputin's apartments are the scene of the wildest orgies," wrote America's Ambassador George Marye. "They beggar all description and, from the current accounts of them which pass freely from mouth to mouth, the storied infamies of the

Emperor Tiberius on the Isle of Capri are made to seem moderate and tame."[67] "This is the soil on which the long-awaited merging of the intelligentsia with the people has taken place," lamented Vasilii Shulgin. "Grishka [Rasputin] completes the chain. Holding in one hand a hysterical female mystic, and in the other, a hysterical nymphomaniac, he adorns the ballet of Petrograd with his dual countenance—the face of a sorcerer and the face of a satyr."[68] By late 1916, it would have been difficult to find anyone of consequence in Petrograd who did not think that Rasputin should be done away with or that, because they had such total confidence in him, Nicholas and Aleksandra were unfit to rule.

General Vladimir Dzhunkovskii prepared a detailed report on Rasputin's scandalous behavior at Moscow's Iar Restaurant and handed it to Nicholas personally in an attempt to convince him of the very great and immediate danger that lurked on the horizon if Rasputin were not gotten rid of.[69] The moment Aleksandra heard of it, she launched a hysterical and vicious campaign to drive "my enemy" Dzhunkovskii from Russia's service. "Ah, dear, he is not an honest man," she babbled in one of her letters to Nicholas. "He has shown that vile, filthy paper (against our Friend) to [Grand Duke] Dmitrii. . . . Such a sin, & as tho' you had not said to him, that you have had enough of these dirty stories & wish him to be severely punished. . . . Ah, it is so vile—always liars, enemies—I long knew *Dzhunkovskii* hates *Gregory* [Rasputin] & that the 'Preobrazhenskii' clique therefore dislikes me."[70] In response to Aleksandra's continued urging, Nicholas sent Dzhunkovskii into retirement. Not even the Empress's elder sister Ella, regarded by many as a saint for her work among Moscow's poor, could sway her faith. At the beginning of December 1916, Elizaveta Feodorovna left her convent in Moscow to make a rare visit to Tsarskoe Selo to beg Aleksandra to open her eyes to what was happening. "She dismissed me like a dog," the Grand Duchess wept to Iusupov's mother. "Poor Nicky, poor Russia!"[71]

On November 3, 1916, Vladimir Purishkevich arrived at Nicholas's Stavka to dine at his Emperor's invitation. He was one of the leading reactionaries in the Duma, a co-founder of the notorious Union of the Russian People, an ardent patriot who hated Jews and despised all liberals, but a man who possessed an active mind and a deep sense of

honor nonetheless. His arrival was an unusual occasion, because
Nicholas at that time usually received only the flunkies Aleksandra and
Rasputin sent to discuss domestic affairs with him. His staff was delighted to see a man of Purishkevich's stature appear. A number of
Grand Dukes and generals hastened to urge the surprised politician to
tell Nicholas the truth about Russia's impending doom. "Reveal to him
Rasputin's fatal role," they begged. "The Tsar will believe you and your
words may produce a good impression."[72] What Purishkevich said to
Nicholas that evening remains a mystery, but he left Stavka convinced
that the Tsar was surrounded by a staff of "cowards" who valued their
careers more than they valued truth and honor. With these impressions
still sharp in his mind, Purishkevich, who had never before breathed a
word of criticism of his Tsar and his policies, proceeded to deliver a
sensational speech in the Duma on November 19. In his own words, he
ceased to be a "political cadaver" on that day and called upon all ministers to wait upon Nicholas, to "throw themselves at the Tsar's feet, and
to beg him to permit them to reveal all of the horror of the existing
state of affairs," by which he meant Rasputin's influence above all
else.[73]

Yet even as he spoke what were for him such daring phrases,
Purishkevich knew that words were no longer of any account and that
nothing could break Aleksandra's neurotic dependence upon Rasputin
so long as the *starets* lived. Very soon, two even more illustrious allies
joined Purishkevich's cause. The first and most important was Prince
Feliks Iusupov, a younger son of one of the wealthiest and most illustrious families in the Russian Empire. Prince Feliks was a dashing young
officer, married to the strikingly beautiful Grand Duchess Irina Aleksandrovna, whose mother was Nicholas's favorite sister Ksenia. Iusupov
was an enigma, a man of many faces, moods, and interests. The great
ballerina Anna Pavlova, at one time a close friend, once told him that
"you carry God in one eye and the Devil in the other." In view of the
personality quirks that Iusupov exhibited in public and in private, that
description seems especially apt.[74] Among other things, Prince Feliks
loved to dress as a woman and took special pride in telling how, on one
of the occasions he had appeared in drag, he had been ogled by none
other than King Edward VII.[75]

Yet, despite his talent for creating scandal, Prince Iusupov had a firm will and, by early twentieth-century Russian aristocratic standards, a resolute character. Those were the virtues that Purishkevich immediately recognized in him when they first met on November 21, 1916. They talked for a full two hours about the crisis Russia faced. Toward the end of their meeting, according to Purishkevich's diary account, they exchanged some very fateful words.

"What can be done?" Purishkevich asked.

"Eliminate Rasputin," Iusupov replied. Purishkevich remembered that, as the young prince spoke these fateful words, he "smiled enigmatically" and looked him squarely in the eye with an unblinking stare.

"That's easy enough to say," said Purishkevich with a nervous laugh. "But who will carry out such a deed when there are no decisive or resolute men left in Russia. . . ."

"One cannot count upon the government," Iusupov continued. "But it is possible to find such people in Russia nonetheless."

"You think so?" asked Purishkevich. The answer came back almost instantly with icy calmness.

"I am convinced of it, and one of them stands before you at this very moment." [76]

The bargain was struck. Purishkevich and Iusupov agreed to kill Rasputin. Iusupov immediately recruited his best friend, Grand Duke Dmitrii Pavlovich, nephew of Nicholas and Aleksandra, and one of the very few members of the Imperial family in whom they still placed any trust. It was reported that Aleksandra was even thinking of marrying her eldest daughter Olga to him. [77] His "betrayal" of her cause would leave Aleksandra more certain than ever that all of her paranoid fears were real.

For almost a month, the three conspirators laid their plans carefully and with cold calculation. They planned to use the Princess Irina Iusupova, easily one of Petrograd's most beautiful women, as bait to lure Rasputin into their trap. It was well known that Irina was in the Crimea at the time, but Prince Feliks told Rasputin on several occasions that she was planning to come to Petrograd secretly, in advance of her announced return, in order to have a private meeting with him. With his typical flair for the dramatic, as Rasputin began to show interest in a meeting with the Princess Irina, Iusupov prepared a special chamber in which to murder him. On the ground floor of the Iusupov Palace on the Moika, he ordered workmen to refurbish a suite of rooms with costly Persian carpets, antique art objects, and elegant furniture. There was a white bearskin rug in one corner. In the midst of the cozy arrangement of chairs and sofas, Iusupov had his servants place "the table where Rasputin was to take his last cup of tea."[78]

On the night of December 16, 1916, all was ready for the final act of the drama in which Rasputin was to be killed before morning. Iusupov had his servants lay a fire in the great red granite fireplace, and instructed his cook to prepare various sorts of cakes and sweets for the tea to which he had already told Rasputin the Princess Irina had invited him sometime after midnight. There were two sorts of petits fours set out on the table—some with chocolate cream and others filled with Rasputin's favorite rose-flavored cream. While Purishkevich, the Grand Duke Dmitrii, and Iusupov looked on, Dr. Lazovert, a physician in whom Purishkevich placed special confidence and whom he had brought into the conspiracy at the last minute, carefully put potassium cyanide into all the cakes with rose-cream filling. Dr. Lazovert also added cyanide to the glasses set out to serve Madeira and Marsala, the sweet wines Rasputin so loved. Sometime before midnight, all was ready, and Iusupov set out with his car and driver to bring Rasputin to the meeting. When Rasputin arrived, Prince Feliks would tell him that his wife still had guests upstairs, but that they would soon leave. In the meantime, he was to entertain him with poisoned cakes, tea, and wine laced with cyanide. So that Rasputin would believe Iusupov's tale, Purishkevich and the Grand Duke Dmitrii were to play a phonograph record of "Yankee Doodle" in an upstairs room and make sounds of people moving about.[79]

Everything at first went according to plan. Rasputin was waiting, dressed in his best, when Iusupov came for him. His hair was slicked down with oil, his beard carefully trimmed, and he smelled strongly of cheap soap. He wore a silken blouse embroidered with cornflowers, black velvet trousers, and new boots. His blouse was gathered at the waist with a heavy raspberry-colored cord. Iusupov took Rasputin to his palace. Together, they sat in the murder chamber where the

Prince induced Rasputin to drink a glass of poisoned wine and served him several poisoned rose-cream cakes. To his utter amazement, Rasputin continued to eat and drink and asked him to play some gypsy songs on his guitar. The poison seemed to have no effect.

After whispered consultations with the other conspirators at the head of the stairs, Iusupov lost patience. "Vladimir Mitrofanovich," he said to Purishkevich. "You wouldn't have any objections if I just shot him, would you? It would be quicker and simpler." Purishkevich recalled that Iusupov then walked quickly and resolutely to his writing table, took out a Browning pistol, and walked quickly down the stairs. A few moments later, Purishkevich, Grand Duke Dmitrii, and Dr. Lazovert heard a shot, a moan, and the sound of a body falling.[80] Iusupov later wrote that, before he shot Rasputin, he had said, "Grigorii Efimovich, you would do well to look at the crucifix and say a prayer." "Should I fire at his head or his heart?" he asked himself at that moment. He settled the question in an instant. "I aimed at his heart and pressed the trigger," he wrote. "Like a broken marionette," Rasputin fell upon the bearskin rug, shot in the side.[81]

When Rasputin fell before Iusupov's pistol bullet at about 2:00 A.M. on December 17, the conspirators fell to rejoicing that the deed was done. Then, to their amazement and horror, their victim struggled to his feet, threw Iusupov aside, staggered up to the main floor, and reeled through a side door into a sort of courtyard that was formed by the side of the Iuspov Palace and the recessed front of the building next to it. "Shoot, Purishkevich, shoot! He's getting away!" Iusupov shouted. Purishkevich drew his heavy Sauvage pistol from his pocket and released its safety. Twice he fired and missed. He was amazed. He considered himself an expert marksman and had never before thought it possible to miss a man at a mere twenty paces. By then, Rasputin was almost at the gate that opened into the street. Purishkevich stopped, raised his pistol once more, bit into his left wristbone to force utter concentration, and fired. This time the heavy slug struck Rasputin's back. He stopped and began to turn. Purishkevich fired again, this time aiming at Rasputin's head, and his target crumpled into a heap. "I was certain," Purishkevich wrote in his diary, "that this time his song had been sung to the very end and that he would not get up."[82]

Thinking him dead, the conspirators nonetheless tied Rasputin's hands before they dumped his body through a hole in the ice into the river. In their haste, they left one of his boots behind on the ice, thus supplying the police with their first clue in their search for the body.[83] An autopsy found water in Rasputin's lungs, proof that, despite the conspirators' poison and bullets, he had died by drowning. In the streets of Petrograd, men and women quoted with relish the folk saying, "a dog's death for a dog!"[84] Even members of the Imperial family could not restrain their relief. "Prayed for you all darlings," telegraphed the saintly Grand Duchess Elizaveta Feodorovna to Grand Duke Dmitrii as soon as she heard of Rasputin's death. "May God strengthen Feliks after the patriotic deed he fulfilled." To Prince Feliks's mother, she telegraphed, "All my deepest and most tender prayers surround you all because of the patriotic act of your dear son. May God protect you all."[85] The Grand Duchess's sympathy for Rasputin's murderers was symptomatic of the national mood that prevented Nicholas from taking harsh measures against them. Although Aleksandra clamored for him to deal with them severely, he did no more than banish Iusupov to one of his estates and send Grand Duke Dmitrii to the Persian front. Purishkevich remained untouched. His part in the murder had raised his prestige to such heights that Nicholas dared not strike him down.

Even before Rasputin's corpse was found beneath the ice, Ambassador Paléologue had made an ominous entry in his diary. Within a few hours of Rasputin's murder, it was well known within the government and Petrograd's diplomatic community who the leading figures in the plot were. Paléologue thought Purishkevich's role the most significant. "His participation in the murder of Rasputin throws light on the whole attitude of the Extreme Right in the last few months," he wrote. "It means that the champions of autocracy, feeling themselves threatened by the Empress's madness, are determined to defend themselves in spite of the Emperor; and, if necessary, *against* him."[86] A few days later, he added, "the present crisis is a conflict between the Emperor and the natural, official defenders of autocracy"; it was coming to a head with frightening speed as the end of 1916 approached.[87] Everywhere in Russia, prices soared, and profiteering and speculation were rife. On the average, prices rose by more than four hundred percent between 1914 and 1916, while wages barely doubled. By the end of 1916, a pound of black bread cost three times as much as it had in 1914. The price of a pound of beef had increased five and a half times, and the cost of a pound of potatoes had multiplied by eight. For every ruble Petrograders had spent for clothing and shoes in 1914, they now had to spend between four and eight rubles.[88] As the new year dawned, as few as 10 percent of the workers in some Petrograd factories were earning a living wage, while the real wages of civil servants and other white-collar workers had plummeted to less than half of their prewar levels.[89] Rents doubled, even tripled.[90] Fewer and fewer people could afford even basic essentials. All of this meant that, for those tens of thousands of city dwellers who had lived at or near the brink of destitution before the war, ruin became an inevitable consequence of Russia's war effort. The same grim fate awaited many of those whose standard of living might have been characterized as "lower middle class" in 1913. In all, it was a gruesome picture, one that gave good grounds for widespread bitterness and discontent among those growing numbers of people who crowded into cities where public services were beginning to break down on an unprecented scale.

The situation in Russia's cities reached the point of near-collapse when winter arrived with unprecedented force. Bitter frosts lingered for weeks on end. At times the mercury fell to almost fifty degrees below freezing in the central parts of European Russia, and great drifts of snow buried railway cars and supply depots. If Ambassador Paléologue's information was correct, some twelve hundred locomotives were put out of commission, their boiler pipes burst by the frost. Some fifty-seven thousand boxcars could not be moved along the rails of European Russia as a result.[91] Even Protopopov, who in his growing madness had reportedly begun to see Christ standing behind Aleksandra and spent his evening hours in conversation with Rasputin's ghost,[92] could not remain totally unaware of the crisis. Later, he estimated that some sixty thousand boxcars filled with food, firewood, fodder, and other essentials (a figure very close to Paléologue's estimate) lay buried beneath the deep drifts of snow.[93] By the beginning of 1917, Petrograd was in the grip of critical fuel and flour shortages.[94] On some days, it was necessary for poor people to stand in bitter temperatures through the entire night to be close enough to the front of the lines to receive a share of the limited quantities of bread that were available. People's faces began to take on a "sinister expression," to use Paléologue's words.[95] It was no longer a question of *if* there would be a revolution, but only *when* it would break out, unless something very dramatic was done to avert it immediately.

If the changing mood of Petrograd's cold and hungry people was evident to foreigners such as Paléologue, it was also clear to a number of important Russians, including most of the Grand Dukes and conservative Duma politicians, who stood to lose a very great deal if revolution came to Russia. All of them realized that only some truly dramatic concession to public opinion, such as Nicholas's agreement to appoint ministers who had the full confidence of the people's elected representatives and who would be responsible not to the Tsar but to the Duma, could stem Russia's headlong rush toward revolution. During the last weeks of 1916 and the first part of 1917, a number of Nicholas's uncles and cousins, as well as several very conservative great lords, tried desperately to convince him that the sword of Damocles, which hung poised over his head, was indeed about to fall. At the beginning of November, he went to visit his mother in Kiev, where the Grand Dukes Aleksandr Mikhailovich and Pavel Aleksandrovich joined her in an attempt to impress upon him the seriousness of Russia's difficulties. It was a private family conference, and there are no accounts of what was said, but Pierre Gilliard, who had accompanied the Tsarevich Aleksei to Kiev, thought that Nicholas "had never seemed so worried" as after that meeting.[96] Yet in his letters to Aleksandra, Nicholas gave the impression that the meeting in Kiev had been a pleasant one, and his statements do not seem to mark one of his infrequent (and never very successful) efforts to conceal an unpleasant truth from her. "Kiev seems like a wonderful dream; everything passed off so well there," he wrote the day after he returned to his Stavka.[97] Any unpleasant effects from whatever his mother and the Grand Dukes had told him seem to have passed off by the time he returned to Army Headquarters.

If these efforts had failed to make a deep impression on Nicholas, the advice of another cousin, the Romanov historian Grand Duke Nikolai Mikhailovich, proved no more effective. According to the account the Grand Duke related to Vasilii Shulgin a few days later, he had found the Dowager Empress "dreadfully upset" after her meeting with her son. Nikolai Mikhailovich insisted that her distress convinced him to write to Nicholas "with complete frankness" and to tell him "that we are on the path to ruin." He went to Stavka to deliver the letter in person and to warn Nicholas that most men and women in Russia regarded Aleksandra "as the source of all our troubles."[98] Probably nothing could have damaged Nikolai Mikhailovich's effort more than that statement. Just a few weeks earlier, Nicholas had told Grand Duke Aleksandr Mikhailovich that "I believe no one but my wife."[99] He sent the Grand Duke's letter directly to Aleksandra, and it provoked her into a hysterical outburst that effectively ended Nikolai Mikhailovich's role in public affairs. "I read Nikolai's [letter] & am utterly disgusted," she scribbled back in a disjointed letter. "It comes next to high treason. He has always hated & spoken badly of me since 22 years & in the club too (this same conversation I had with him this year).—but during war & at such a time to crawl behind y[ou]r Mama & Sisters & not stick up bravely (agreeing or not) for his Emperor's Wife—is loathsome and treachery." Then, anger and hysteria so overwhelmed her that her letter became all but incoherent. "I don't care personal nastiness, but as y[ou]r chosen wife—they dare not Sweety mine, you must back me up, for your & Baby's sake." She concluded, "*Let* they [sic] scream—we must show we have no fear & are firm. Wify is your staunch One & stands as a rock behind you."[100] Less than two months later, Nicholas sent Grand Duke Nikolai Mikhailovich into exile on one of his estates.

Rasputin was still alive when the Grand Dukes first attempted to talk sense to Nicholas. Once the *starets* was dead, they and others hoped that Nicholas might prove more receptive to their warnings. "Sandro," Grand Duke Aleksandr Mikhailovich, who had been Nicholas's comrade and friend since childhood and was married to the Tsar's favorite sister, made one final attempt to stave off what seemed certain disaster. On February 10, 1917, just thirteen days before revolution erupted in the streets of Petrograd, he went to see Aleksandra at Tsarskoe Selo. We have only the Grand Duke's account of the meeting, but, even if we assume a certain amount of exaggeration, his report clearly indicates that neither Nicholas nor Aleksandra had much comprehension of the immediate dangers they faced. Sandro tried to explain to Aleksandra that Nicholas's only possible course was to appoint a cabinet of ministers who were acceptable to and responsible to the Duma. "All this talk of yours is ridiculous," Aleksandra sneered. "Nicky is an autocrat. How could he share his divine rights with a parliament?" Sandro explained, as he and others had done on numerous occasions, that by his own decree Nicholas had ceased to be an autocrat in October 1905. Aleksandra, he remembered, "answered something incoherent," and he lost his temper. He could not believe that she could be so blind or so stubborn. More than a decade later, he still remembered her last words: "You are exaggerating the danger. Someday, when you are less excited, you will admit that I knew better." To the Grand Duke's amazement, Nicholas "said nothing, and continued to smoke" during the entire discussion.[101]

A number of accounts left by responsible men about their meetings with Nicholas during the last few months of his reign emphasize that he appeared dazed and usually responded only to the stimulus of Aleksandra's hysterical railings against the many "enemies" who surrounded them. By the end of 1916, Ambassador Paléologue had become so concerned about the state of affairs in Russia that he requested an audience with Nicholas during the Christmas holidays. "The moment I entered, I was struck by the Emperor's tired look and his anxious and absorbed expression," he wrote. He then related that Nicholas "answered in a dead, dull voice, which I had never heard before." During their meeting, he was amazed that he could "not succeed in fixing either the Emperor's eyes or attention." As he took the train back to Petrograd, Paléologue concluded that the end was at hand. He wrote: "The Emperor's words, his silences and reticences, his grave, drawn features and furtive, distant gaze, the impenetrability of his thoughts and the thoroughly vague and enigmatical quality of his personality, confirm me in a notion which has been haunting me for months, the notion that Nicholas II feels himself overwhelmed and dominated by events, that he has lost all faith in his mission or his work, that he has, so to speak, abdicated inwardly and now is resigned to disaster."[102]

Former President of the Council of Ministers Count Kokovtsev, whom Aleksandra and Rasputin had driven from office just a few months before war began, saw everything Paléologue had seen, and more. About three weeks after the French Ambassador's visit, the Count also went to Tsarskoe Selo for what was to be his last interview with his Emperor. When he wrote his memoirs some fifteen years later, he still remembered that day—January 19, 1917—with all its pain, shock, and sadness. "The Tsar's appearance so upset me that I could not refrain from asking about his health," he recalled. "I had not seen him for an entire year and he simply was unrecognizable. His cheeks were terribly hollow, his face seemed pinched, and was covered with many tiny wrinkles. His eyes, usually so dark brown and velvety, were completely faded . . . their whites had a definitely yellowish tinge, while the pupils had become a completely washed-out gray and seemed almost lifeless." Kokovtsev remembered that the Tsar "listened to me all the while with a sort of sick smile and kept glancing from side to side in a strange way." The conversation was labored. There seemed little to say, and Kokovtsev saw the smile return again and again. He left convinced that Nicholas was suffering from a nervous breakdown or that, perhaps, he had even become insane.[103]

Similar changes in Nicholas's appearance, personality, and manner were noted by a number who saw him during the last year of his reign, and they were dramatic enough to cause comment and considerable rumor among Petrograd's high social and political circles. Although hardly a reliable witness, the Princess Cantacuzene reported rumors that Nicholas was being drugged at Aleksandra's command by Badmaev, the notorious Tibetan herbalist and medical quack.[104] Aleksandra's fiercely proclaimed loyalty to Nicholas and her paranoid fears of plots against them both hardly make it possible to give much credence to such rumors. Yet there is some circumstantial evidence that Nicholas may perhaps have developed a dependence upon drugs, which hindered his ability to function during the months before the revolution. The constricted pupils that so struck Kokovtsev certainly could have been a symptom of heavy morphine use, as was the constipation from which Nicholas suffered.[105] We know that, as a result of the casual manner in which morphine and other opium derivatives were dispensed in all Russian military hospitals, their use had become so widespread in Russia during 1916 that the Bishop of Viatka felt impelled to speak out against it.[106] We know also that Nicholas and Aleksandra used opium and cocaine quite casually to relieve minor ailments. "I woke up with a shocking cold in the left nostril, so that I am thinking of spraying it with cocaine," Nicholas wrote in November 1915.[107] A few months later, Aleksandra noted that she had told her maid to bring opium for stomach pains that were keeping her awake one night.[108]

To look somewhat further, Rasputin reportedly once told Iusupov that, when Nicholas was upset, he brought him tea, and that "from this tea the blessing of God comes down on him and gives peace to his soul—and everything is well with him and he's happy."[109] According to Purishkevich, Rasputin also told Iusupov that the herbalist Badmaev could provide a variety of herb infusions to induce an especially pleasant state of euphoria. "When your soul is troubled," he reportedly said in recommending Badmaev's preparations, "he'll give you a tiny little cup of liquid made from herbs, you drink it, and, instantly, everything will seem like petty trifles, and you will become genial, so–o ge–enial, and so–o si–lly that you won't worry about anything."[110]

Hallucinogens from Badmaev, morphine from military hospitals, opium from the family medicine chest, cocaine for colds—all of these, singly or in combination, could produce the disorientation, dull gaze, vacant smiles, inability to concentrate, and the apparent unconcern with impending crises that people noted in Nicholas in late 1916 and early 1917. Yet, tempting as it is to do so, the evidence is not solid enough to reach a firm conclusion, and one must remember that Nicholas simply may have become overwhelmed by the pressure of events. One thing is certain, however. Cloistered with Aleksandra at Tsarskoe Selo during the weeks after Rasputin's death, Nicholas had ceased to rule Russia, and he could make no pretense of commanding the army whose loyalty he would need so sorely if revolution broke out. Nicholas and Aleksandra had cut themselves off from all those groups that had formed the very backbone of the Romanov dynasty for more than three centuries.

Like so many of history's momentous events, the beginnings of the Revolution of 1917 were modest, even unimpressive. Thursday, February 23, 1917, later to be remembered as the first day of the Russian

Revolution, dawned cold and clear. It was International Women's Day, a holiday traditionally celebrated by socialists. Petrograd still struggled in the grip of a bitter cold wave that drove temperatures down to forty degrees below freezing at night. Despite the cold, bread lines had begun to form not long after 2:00 A.M. Several days before, the authorities had decided to impose rationing, and it was rumored that each person would be allowed only one pound of bread each day. Such was obviously insufficient to sustain a worker who could buy little else as a consequence of shortages and rampant inflation. People immediately began to buy up whatever bread they could find and to convert it into *sukhariki,* those dried rusks Russians had used as a means for saving bread since time immemorial. *Sukhariki* would last for weeks. Everyone hurried to prepare a supply before rationing was imposed, and the frantic hoarding that ensued caused bakeries to run out long before daylight.[111]

Although International Women's Day was not a major socialist holiday, a number of demonstrations had been planned by the Petrograd workers to celebrate the event. The demonstrations began on a small scale and were confined to the workers' suburbs of the city. But the ranks of those Petrograd working women who had braved the subzero cold to proclaim "Long Live the Working Women!" and similar slogans[112] soon were swelled by striking workers and by those who had just been locked out at the giant Putilov Works. Soon, women who had been turned away empty handed from the bread lines joined them.

Generally, the crowds were in a friendly mood. "It looked like a holiday," in the words of one onlooker.[113] There was no violence, no confrontation with the authorities. People called out for bread, but voiced no political or economic demands.[114] Wrote the Menshevik Nikolai Sukhanov, "Similar disorders had taken place scores of times." He thought that he perceived a certain "irresolution" on the part of the authorities, but was not certain. Neither he nor any other revolutionaries saw anything resembling the beginning of the revolution for which they had all worked and waited for so long.[115] Neither did anyone else in the capital. At the French Embassy that evening, Ambassador Paléologue went ahead with a dinner party for twenty-six guests. He noted a "shade of anxiety" among some of them as the evening began, but saw it slip quickly away in the midst of a lively conversation about who could be expected to be at the Princess Radziwill's long-awaited party that Sunday. Some of his guests got into a spirited discussion about whether Pavlova, Kschessinska, or Karsavina was the best ballerina at the Mariinskii Ballet that season.[116]

While the demonstrations were beginning in Petrograd, Nicholas had arrived at his Stavka from Tsarskoe Selo. "I got your telegram telling me of Olga and Baby [Tsarevich Aleksei] having measles," he wrote to Aleksandra. "I could not believe my eyes—this news was so unexpected." He was very concerned to learn that there was a measles epidemic at the First and Second Cadet Corps in Petrograd as well. "At dinner," he continued, "I saw all the foreign generals—they were very sorry to hear this sad news [about the measles]." He confessed that he greatly missed "my half-hourly game of patience every evening," and vowed to "take up dominoes again in my spare time." On that note, the day of February 23 ended for him.[117]

While Paléologue's guests argued about the merits of the ballerinas at the Mariinskii, while Nicholas worried about his children's measles, and while the women of Petrograd worried about empty bread shops, Minister of Internal Affairs Protopopov ordered Petrograd's newspapers to print reassuring but false reports that large quantities of flour were on hand in the capital.[118] Much to his satisfaction, there were no disorders in Petrograd during the early morning hours of Friday, February 24.[119] Even if they broke out again, senior police officials ordered their men to prevent demonstrators from crossing the Neva bridges from the workers' suburbs into the city's center. Crowds did begin to gather later that morning, and they were much louder and larger than those of the day before. According to the best estimates, there were some 214,000 in the crowds, largely made up of workers from more than 2000 factories and enterprises of various sorts.[120] Petrograd's Commandant General Khabalov noted that cries of "Down with the war!" and even "Down with autocracy!" were mixed with shouts of "Give us bread!"[121]

In contrast to what they had done the day before, the crowds of workers, strikers, and housewives began to converge on the center of Petrograd. When they reached the Neva bridges, the police barred their way as ordered, but the workers found it simple enough to turn aside and cross the river on the ice. The police had orders only to bar the bridges; they made no effort to stop them from pouring across the frozen river itself.[122] At 12:45 P.M., more than three thousand of these workers gathered in the square of the great Kazan Cathedral on Nevskii Prospekt, sang the *"Marseillaise"* and, for the second time that day, shouted "Down with the Tsar!" and "Give us bread!" This time, they bravely unfurled red banners. Two squadrons of Cossacks moved in to disperse them but were not very forceful in doing so. The demonstrators simply moved in another direction and formed up their ranks in still larger numbers. By 3:00 P.M., a larger crowd had gathered at Znamenskaia Square at the far end of the Nevskii, where Prince Trubetskoi's huge statue of Alexander III stood towering and immobile before the railroad station from which trains came and went to Moscow. There were shouts of "Down with the police!" and "Down with the war!" This time, the Cossacks were even less energetic in trying to break up the crowd. One police report noted that the demonstrators applauded the Cossacks, who gallantly bowed in reply.

The crowd's behavior at Znamenskaia Square typified a pattern that emerged during the course of the day in the relations between the demonstrators and the representatives of tsarist authority. Everywhere in the city, crowds shunned conflict with the Cossacks or Guards Cavalry sent against them, and there often were jokes and humorous gestures exchanged between the two sides. It was clear evidence that revolutionary agitators' preachings that workers and soldiers were brothers with common interests had taken a grip upon the minds of the workers during the past several months. As a result, workers generally greeted soldiers with good humor. Against the hated tsarist police, however, they were far more hostile. In several parts of Petrograd, there were clashes between demonstrators and the police that were violent enough to produce casualties. According to official reports, twenty-eight police were injured or wounded, as well as an undetermined number of workers.

At the end of the second day of the revolution that no one had yet recognized, the situation looked more ominous from the authorities' point of view, but only slightly so. Except for scattered battles with the police, the workers had remained reasonably orderly, although there had been some cases of looting in a number of bakeries. That night, General Khabalov made plans to release some reserves of flour to the city's bakers in an effort to shorten bread lines and get more bread into the hands of hungry demonstrators. At the same time, he gave orders for posters to be put up to warn crowds that the army and police would take severe measures to put down any further disorders.[123] No one knew for certain if the measures Khabalov proposed were the best way to deal with the crowds or if they would be sufficient should the workers march again. In an effort to find out, according to Foreign Minister Nikolai Pokrovskii, Protopopov spent "hours in conjuring up the ghost of the *starets* [Rasputin]" that night to ask him what had best be done.[124]

While Khabalov and Protopopov each made his own preparations to deal with the crowds should they reappear the next day, Nicholas was upset to learn that another of his daughters, as well as Anna Vyrubova, had come down with the measles. He felt guilty about not being at Tsarskoe Selo to take some of the burden of nursing the sick children from Aleksandra and promised to return to the palace as soon as possible. In the meantime, he confessed that the "rest" he was getting at Stavka was doing him good. "My brain is resting here—no Ministers, no troublesome questions demanding thought," he wrote that night. Nicholas slept well, got up late the next morning, and hoped to get back to Tsarskoe Selo in a few days to help Aleksandra nurse their children.[125]

Long before Nicholas awakened on the morning of February 25, crowds of strikers, unemployed workers, and housewives, began to congregregate in the outskirts of Petrograd. The most recent estimates are that their numbers had risen to nearly three hundred thousand, and all of them began to converge on the center of the city. By 10:00 A.M., there had been confrontations between workers and police that had produced casualties on both sides, and, throughout the day, more and more workers left their factories to join the demonstrators. The crowds grew larger and voiced their demands with greater force. Not only did they chant "Down with the Tsar!" but made their demand more general as they shouted "Down with tsarism!" That day, three hand grenades were thrown at the police in addition to rocks and chunks of ice. Perhaps the most dramatic event occurred at Znamen-skaia Square, where a revolutionary orator began to address several thousands who had gathered around the statue of Alexander III. Mounted police appeared to break up the demonstration. When their speaker exhorted the crowd to stand fast, their commanding officer, Lieutenant Krylov, raised his pistol and took aim. The crowd fell into shocked silence. At that very moment, a Cossack spurred his horse forward and cut Krylov down with his saber. For the first time since the demonstrations had begun three days before, one representative of tsarist authority had turned against another. It boded ill for the government's cause and gave the workers good reason to rejoice.[126]

While the Cossacks and mounted police were facing ever-growing crowds in Petrograd, Nicholas still was "resting" his brain at Stavka. After a late breakfast, he listened to General Alekseev's staff report for somewhat more than an hour. After lunch, he went to a nearby monastery and sought out the icon of the Holy Virgin. There, as he later wrote to Aleksandra, he "prayed fervently for you, my love, for the dear children, for our country, and also for our Annia [Vyrubova]."[127] Afterward, he took a pleasant walk to complete what evidently had been an enjoyable Saturday afternoon.[128] Only sometime after he returned from his stroll did Nicholas first learn about the disorders in Petrograd. That evening, he sent a stern telegram to General Khabalov:

> I ORDER YOU TO BRING ALL OF THESE DISORDERS IN THE CAPITAL TO A HALT AS OF TOMORROW. THESE CANNOT BE PERMITTED IN THIS DIFFICULT TIME OF WAR WITH GERMANY AND AUSTRIA.
>
> NICHOLAS[129]

In Russian, the text came to just sixteen words, and these were some of the most fateful ones ever sent by a Romanov. For Nicholas's telegram left Khabalov no room for discretion or judgment. As he later told the Supreme Investigating Commission of the Provisional Government, "to be perfectly candid and honest, for me this telegram was like being struck with the head of an axe. How was I to bring the disorders to a halt tomorrow? 'As of tomorrow' was the phrase used. The Emperor ordered them to be stopped and that was it. What was I to do? How was I to bring them to a halt? When they shouted 'Give us bread!' we gave them bread and that was that. But when the banners read 'Down with autocracy!'—the Emperor had given his order. We were going to have to fire [upon the workers to carry it out]."[130] Nicholas, in fact, evidently had in mind the answer to those very questions with which General Khabalov grappled on the evening of February 25. The half-mad Protopopov was the key. As Nicholas wrote to Aleksandra the next day, "Protopopov must give him [Khabalov] clear and definite instructions."[131]

Feeling that he was "absolutely finished," Khabalov walked into the staff meeting he customarily scheduled at ten o'clock every evening during the crisis. When his senior officers were seated, he told them, "Gentlemen! The Emperor has ordered that the disorders must cease as of tomorrow. That's the final word and it must be carried out. Therefore, if the crowd is small, if it is not at all aggressive, and if it is not carrying [red] banners . . . then use your cavalry detachments to disperse it. But if the crowd is in any way threatening, and if it carries banners, then you are to act according to regulations. You are to give three warnings and then—open fire."[132]

Once Khabalov's officers ordered their troops to fire upon Petrograd's workers, the lines of the struggle would be drawn anew. When the first officer gave the new command, Nicholas would have declared war upon his own people at a time when he still expected their support in waging war against the Germans and Austrians. The stakes no longer would be bread, peace, or civic order, but life and death itself. But there was another, equally grave, issue to consider. If the troops refused to fire upon their countrymen, it would mean the end of Nicholas's regime. He had staked his crown and his dynasty's survival upon Khabalov's understanding of a sixteen-word telegram and upon Protopopov's highly questionable ability to "give him clear and definite instructions." Most amazing of all, Nicholas had not even the slightest notion that he had taken such a drastic and irreversible step. Only Aleksandra (who did not yet know that he had sent the telegram to Khabalov) had some inner sense of what an order to fire upon Petrograd's crowds might mean when she wrote to Nicholas on the night of February 25 that "it is essential to have a real cavalry regiment here—one which would immediately restore order—and not mere reserves composed of Petersburg citizens."[133]

What happened on Sunday, February 26, 1917, would determine

whether Nicholas and Aleksandra remained upon the Russian throne. If the soldiers of the Petrograd garrison fired upon the crowds of demonstrators as they had in 1905, Nicholas's regime might still muddle through. If they refused, the crowd would have won the battle for Russia's capital. All through Saturday night and the dark early hours of Sunday morning, the police labored to place machine guns on roofs that commanded clear fields of fire into Petrograd's large squares. At the same time, the Okhrana, the secret police, carried out mass arrests of all known revolutionary agents in the city. Squads, companies, even battalions of soldiers were ordered from their barracks to defend strategic locations.[134] By daybreak the authorities stood ready to confront the workers. The day was to be sunny. Two days before, the cold wave had broken, and the temperature had risen quickly. On Saturday, it had been just eight degrees below freezing. On Sunday, it promised to be even warmer.[135]

As the pale light of the wintry sun began to wash over Petrograd's streets on the morning of February 26, workers appeared dressed in their Sunday best. They seemed cheerful, and there were no demonstrations. It must have been with a great sense of relief that General Khabalov telegraphed to Nicholas that "this morning, February 26, the city is calm."[136] Khabalov had spoken too quickly. Soon, columns of demonstrators began to converge upon Znamenskaia Square where soldiers from the Volynskii Regiment were drawn up to halt their march. As the crowd pressed forward, an officer ordered them to disperse. In reply, the workers struck up conversations with the soldiers who stood before them.[137] A second time the order to disperse rang out. Still, the crowd stood fast. Yet a third time, "according to regulations," the order came. Again, the crowd made no response. The clock in the station tower began to strike twelve, and then the order everyone feared to hear cut through the air: "Fire!" One of the soldiers who had stood on the square that day recalled the drama of the next few moments. "The first volleys were harmless," he remembered, because "the soldiers, by tacit agreement, had fired into the air." An enraged officer walked into the soldiers' ranks and ordered that every man must "fire in turn so that I can see him shoot. Aim for the heart!" he commanded. But that was only the beginning of the bloodshed. "Suddenly, a machine gun aimed at the crowd by the officers started crackling and the workers' blood reddened the snow," wrote the soldier memoirist.[138] Forty demonstrators lay dead, and another forty were wounded. But the soldiers had not fired willingly, and some had not fired at all. Would the bloodshed stiffen their resolve to obey their officers? Or would they turn against the men who had ordered them to fire upon unarmed demonstrators? The answer came that evening.

At some time between four and six o'clock that afternoon, the fourth company of the Pavlovskii Guards joined the revolution for a brief moment. These soldiers had been held in reserve in their barracks. Suddenly, someone rushed in with word that their comrades had shot down some workers in front of the Kazan Cathedral, and a number of the Guards seized rifles and ran out, evidently hoping to convince their comrades to stop killing unarmed demonstrators. Not far from the Church that had been built on the spot where Alexander II had been slain by Hryniewicki's bomb, their path was barred by a detachment of mounted police, and the two groups exchanged fire. Nikolai Sukhanov, the young Menshevik whose day-by-day account of the revolution remains a valuable source for historians, wrote that "the Pavlovskii Regiment [holds] . . . the honour of having performed the first revolutionary act of the military against the armed forces of Tsarism."[139] In 1905 the troops in Petrograd had formed an impenetrable shield around Nicholas's government, and their loyalty had been a crucial factor in enabling him to weather that revolutionary storm. That the autocracy's shield of bayonets had been shattered on February 26, 1917, was indeed, as Sukhanov wrote, "a terrible breach in the stronghold of Tsarism." The revolutionary Rubicon had been crossed when the crowds saw the soldiers fire upon the police. Word spread like wildfire among Petrograd's workers and students that the soldiers were with them. It made no difference that the "Pavlovskii Rebellion" lasted less than two hours and that the soldiers turned themselves over for arrest. The belief that the army was joining their cause strengthened the workers' resolve immensely. Their ranks swelled, and their enthusiasm surged.[140]

Although Nicholas had been reluctant to permit it, the Duma had reassembled in Petrograd on February 14. As the crowds of demonstrators swelled in the city streets, Mikhail Rodzianko, the Duma's President, tried to defend the throne. He telegraphed directly to Nicholas on the evening of February 26 that troops had begun to join the demonstrators. The "immediate appointment of people in whom the nation has trust and who will be empowered to form a government that commands the confidence of all the people," he insisted, was absolutely essential if the throne were not to topple. An hour or so later, he repeated his message and sent copies to Generals Ruzskii, Evert, and Brusilov, who commanded the northern, western, and southwestern fronts. Certain that any further delay would be fatal, he sent another copy of his plea to Nicholas's Chief of Staff General Alekseev and begged him to urge the Emperor to act.[141] If Rodzianko expected Nicholas to agree to a government responsible to the Duma, his hopes were in vain. Count Vladimir Frederiks was present when the second telegram was delivered into Nicholas's hands at Stavka. Nicholas put it aside with the remark, "Again, that fat Rodzianko has written me some sort of nonsense to which I shall not even reply."[142] For the next few hours, Nicholas devoted his full attention to several games of dominoes.[143]

Meanwhile, the soldiers of the Volynskii Regiment had returned to their barracks after the shooting of the demonstrators on Znamenskaia Square. Led by Sergeants Kirpichnikov and Markov, they discussed what they ought to do if their officers ordered them again to shoot down unarmed workers, students, and housewives. "Fathers, mothers, sisters, brothers, even brides are begging for bread," said Kirpichnikov. "Will we strike them down? Have you seen the blood which runs in the streets? I propose that we not march tomorrow. I personally don't want to."[144] The soldiers agreed. The next morning, Monday, February 27, Kirpichnikov told his company's commander that they would not shoot down unarmed demonstrators. When their commander tried to restore discipline, the soldiers shot him. Now there was no turning back. They must fight for the revolution and win, or be hanged as rebels. Within the hour they convinced the Litovskii and Preobrazhenskii Guards to join them.[145] By ten o'clock, they had seized the Liteinyi Arsenal. By noon, the striking workers, students, and rebel soldiers had in their hands some forty thousand rifles, thirty thousand revolvers, and four hundred machine guns. That day, more than sixty-six thousand soldiers went over to the crowd.[146] Frantically, Rodzianko telegraphed again to Nicholas:

> GARRISON TROOPS CAN NO LONGER BE RELIED UPON. RESERVE BATTALIONS OF GUARDS IN REVOLT. THEY ARE KILLING THEIR OFFICERS. SIRE, DO NOT DELAY. IF THE MOVEMENT REACHES THE ARMY, IT WILL MEAN THE RUIN OF RUSSIA. INEVITABLY, THE DYNASTY WILL FALL WITH IT. TOMORROW MAY BE TOO LATE.[147]

Already it was too late. The Petrograd crowd and the Petrograd garrison had seized Russia's capital, and two new centers of power had emerged. One was the Duma, where Rodzianko and other moderate leaders still begged Nicholas to grant concessions in order to save the throne. In the eyes of Petrograd's other new center of power, the revolutionary Petrograd Soviet of Workers' and Soldiers' Deputies, which began to meet on Monday, February 27, Nicholas already had been overthrown. By the afternoon of the 27th, the fifth day of the revolution, Nicholas no longer could have regained control of his capital even by the concessions Rodzianko and his fellow politicians still urged upon him. To reestablish his power in Petrograd, he would have to recapture it by military assault. For Nicholas and Aleksandra, the end was very, very near.

As always, when Nicholas decided to act, his measures were too limited and came too late. On Monday evening, after five days of disorders in his capital, he decided to use force to crush the revolutionary movement. To retake the city in which, according to the best estimates, close to one hundred thousand garrison troops already had gone over to the revolution, Nicholas endowed General Nikolai Ivanov with martial law authority and sent him to Petrograd with a single battalion. He promised to send Ivanov several more regiments as soon as they could be transported from the front. Convinced that he had done all that was needed, Nicholas made preparations to leave the next morning for Tsarskoe Selo. There, he would meet with Ivanov, his loyal troops, and other advisers and lay plans for completing the seizure of his capital if Ivanov had not already succeeded in doing so.[148] Before he went to sleep that night, Nicholas telegraphed to Aleksandra that she should expect him on March 1.[149]

Because he had been with Ivanov and Alekseev until very late, Nicholas was asleep when his train set out for Tsarskoe Selo in the early morning hours of February 28th.[150] By the time he awoke at ten o'clock almost the entire garrison of Petrograd had joined the revolution, and the revolutionary fervor had begun to spread outward from the capital along the rail lines.[151] Nicholas never reached Tsarskoe Selo as Emperor. After hearing a number of contradictory reports, he ordered his train to the ancient city of Pskov, where he consulted with General Ruzskii. Perhaps for the first time, Nicholas was beginning to perceive the full seriousness of the situation he faced, although he did not know that Petrograd was then completely in the hands of the revolution. Nor did he know that even General Ivanov's escort had mutinied and that Ivanov had begun a series of complex train movements that would eventually take him back to Mogilev, far from Petrograd.[152] To his diary that night, Nicholas lamented, "We have detoured via Valdai, Dno, and Pskov, where I am stopping for the night. I have seen Ruzskii. . . . It turns out that Gatchina and Luga also are occupied by insurgents. What a disgrace! Impossible to reach Tsarskoe Selo, but my heart and my thoughts are always there. How distressing that my poor Alix has to face these events alone! May God come to our aid!"[153]

Nicholas's diary perhaps best and most succinctly tells the tale of his last hours as Russia's Emperor. The time for the concessions for which Rodzianko had begged during the last days of February was long since past, even though it was only March 2. No choice remained but abdication. "General Ruzskii came this morning and read to me the transcript of the long conversation he had with Rodzianko over the telephone," Nicholas wrote that night. "According to him, the situation in Petrograd is such that, at this point, a ministry formed by the Duma could accomplish nothing in view of the hostility of the Social Democrats as expressed by the workers' committee [i.e., the Soviet of Workers' and Soldiers' Deputies]." Nicholas concluded that "my abdication is necessary. Ruszkii has sent an account of his conversation [with Rodzianko] to General Headquarters, and Alekseev has told all commanders in chief that it is necessary to take this decision. I have agreed. This evening, [Duma deputies] Guchkov and Shulgin arrived from Petrograd. I talked with them, and they now have returned to the capital carrying the modified manifesto* that I have signed."[154] It was a modest statement to describe a momentous event. In that manifesto, Nicholas declared to Russia and to the world:

> In these days of great struggle against a foreign enemy who has been trying for almost three years to enslave Our Nation, the Lord God has seen fit to send upon Russia a new and terrible ordeal. This new domestic turmoil threatens to have a fatal effect upon the outcome of this hard-fought war. The fate of Russia, the honor of Our heroic army, the well-being of the people, and the entire future of Our Nation require that this war be continued to a victorious end. Our cruel enemy is now drawing upon his last resources and the hour is already near when Our valiant army, together with Our glorious allies, will be able to finally smite the enemy. In these decisive days in the life of Russia, Our Conscience imposes upon Us the duty to draw Our people into a close union and to rally all the forces of Our people for the most rapid attainment of victory. Therefore, and in agreement with the State Duma, We recognize that it is necessary to abdicate from the throne of the Russian State, and to resign the Supreme Power. Not wishing to be separated from Our much-loved Son, We bequeath Our inheritance to Our Brother, Grand Duke Mikhail Aleksandrovich, and We give Our blessing to His accession to the throne of the Russian State. We ask Him to govern in full and indestructible unity with the representatives of the people assembled in legislative bodies and to swear His inviolable oath to them. In the name of Our deeply beloved Nation we summon all true sons of the Motherland to fulfill their sacred obligations to Him who has taken up the duties of Tsar at this very difficult moment of national crisis and to help Him, together with the representatives of the people, to lead the Russian State along the path of victory, prosperity, and glory. May the Lord God help Russia![155]

As he signed his abdication, Nicholas's composure utterly astounded those who stood around him. "He was such a fatalist that I could not believe it," recalled General Dmitrii Dubetskii. "He renounced the Russian throne just as simply as one turns over a cavalry squadron to its new commanding officer."[156] Only to his diary, his

---

*The modification in the abdication manifesto to which Nicholas referred in his diary was his decision to abdicate in favor of his younger brother, rather than his son Aleksei Nikolaevich.

faithful companion since his childhood, did Nicholas betray the depth of his feelings. In one of the diary's scant handful of truly emotional entries, he wrote, "At one o'clock this morning I have left Pskov with a heart that is heavy over what has happened. All around me there is nothing but treason, cowardice, and deceit!"[157] As the morning of March 3 dawned, Nicholas no longer was Emperor of All the Russias. Nor did the Romanovs rule in the Russian land.

CHAPTER XV

The Last Days
of the Romanovs

When Sergei Sazonov, Russia's recently resigned Foreign Minister, heard the details of Nicholas's abdication, he lamented: "Fancy destroying a three-hundred-year-old dynasty and the stupendous work of Peter the Great, Catherine II, and Alexander I! What a tragedy! What a disaster!"[1] No other Romanov had violated Russia's laws of succession as blatantly as Nicholas had when he renounced Tsarevich Aleksei's right to sit upon the throne of his ancestors. In human terms, it was the understandable decision of a father anxious to shield his fragile only son from the awesome and awful burdens of ruling a country torn by war and revolution. In political terms, however, it spelled the end of the Romanov dynasty in Russia. Ironically, it was a decision that Nicholas made alone. For a quarter-century, Aleksandra had dominated his life, had influenced his every thought and act, and had interfered in countless affairs of state. But, on March 2, 1917, separated from her by a hundred miles of railroad and telegraph lines held firmly by revolutionary workers, Nicholas was obliged to make the most monumental decision of his life without her counsel.

It was on the following day at Tsarskoe Selo that Aleksandra learned of Nicholas's abdication and his renunciation of Aleksei's rights to the throne. Lili Dehn, who was with Aleksandra, recalled her reaction to the devastating news. "Her face was distorted with agony, her eyes were full of tears. She tottered rather than walked, and I rushed forward and supported her until she reached the writing table between the windows. She leant heavily against it and, taking my hand in hers, she said brokenly, 'Abdicated!' I could not believe my ears. I waited for

[727]

her next words. They were hardly audible. At last [she said], 'The poor dear. . . . All alone out there . . . and gone through. . . . Oh, my God, what he has gone through! And I was not there to console him.' . . . She paid no attention to me, and kept on repeating, 'My God, how painful. . . . All alone out there.' I put my arms around her and we walked up and down the long room."²

Aleksandra postponed the difficult task of telling Aleksei for five days. On March 8, she asked Pierre Gilliard to tell the Tsarevich because she could not bear to do so. Ever faithful to the family he served and sensitive to the tragedy of what he must say, Gilliard sat down with the twelve-year-old lad he had tutored with such care in the expectation that one day he would become Emperor of All the Russias.

"You know your father does not want to be Tsar any more," Gilliard began.

"What! Why?" exclaimed Aleksei.

"He is very tired and has had a lot of trouble lately," Gilliard explained.

"Oh, yes. Mother told me that they stopped his train when he wanted to come here. But won't Papa be Tsar again afterwards?"

It was then that Gilliard had to tell the Tsarevich that Nicholas had abdicated in favor of the Grand Duke Mikhail, who then had refused the crown unless it was offered to him by a popularly elected constituent assembly.

"But, who's going to be Tsar, then?" Aleksei asked Gilliard in confusion.

"I don't know," his tutor replied. "Perhaps nobody now."³

Not long afterward, the soldiers of the Provisional Government closed the gates in the high iron fence that surrounded the Alexander Palace. Aleksandra, her children, and the handful of loyal courtiers and servants who remained became prisoners of the new government. That night, they could hear the sounds of sporadic gunfire in the park where, on so many happy occasions, they had walked, hunted for mushrooms, and fed the deer that were tame enough to eat from their hands. Their life in a very new and different world had begun.

The next day, March 9, Russia's new rulers permitted Nicholas to rejoin his family after a week of uncertainty. As his auto approached the locked gate of the Alexander Palace, the officer of the day called for the guard to identify its passenger. A rumpled sentry, utterly unlike those perfectly turned-out guardsmen who had stood on duty in earlier times, sauntered forward and peered into the auto's dark interior. "Nicholas Romanov!" he bellowed back to his superior, and the duty officer gave the command for the auto to go through.[4] After a journey of nine days, Nicholas finally had returned to Aleksandra, not as the Emperor of Russia, with a grandiose title that included nearly a hundred words, but simply as Nicholas Romanov.

Once in the palace, Nicholas's composure left him. Anna Vyrubova remembered that "he sobbed like a child on the breast of his wife" during the first hours of their reunion.[5] Yet his tears were brief. As always, Nicholas drew strength from the stiffened resolve Aleksandra seemed to pour into his veins. For years, her will had driven him along the wrong path to the wrong decisions. Now, it strengthened him in the face of the greatest adversity a monarch could face. Nicholas, Aleksandra, and their children had no notion what fate the revolution held in store for them. At best, they might be permitted to live abroad in exile; at worst, they faced the frightening prospect of a humiliating public trial and execution in the tradition of England's Charles I and France's Louis XVI and Marie Antoinette. In large measure, their fate depended upon which course the revolution might follow. In mid-March, no one even dared predict what that might be.

Whatever his hopes, Nicholas's abdication brought neither victory nor peace to Russia. The Provisional Government formed on March 2 to the echo of Aleksandr Kerenskii's ecstatic vow to pass "the sacred cup of power . . . on to the constituent assembly without spilling a single drop,"[6] failed to establish an effective relationship with the Petrograd Soviet of Workers' and Soldiers' Deputies, the true source of power in Russia. The first cabinet of the Provisional Government lasted just two months and three days, until May 5; the second survived until July 24; and the third collapsed on August 6. For most of September, the government was run by Kerenskii, whose star had blazed such a brilliant trail across the sky that spring, and he presided over the formation of yet another cabinet on September 25. Yet Kerenskii's efforts to halt the revolution in mid-course were to no avail. A month later,

Trotskii and Lenin launched a Bolshevik coup that toppled Kerenskii's government and proclaimed the first workers' state in history. The text of the manifesto by which Lenin announced the Bolsheviks' seizure of power on October 25 revealed the vast distance Russia had traveled in a brief six months' span:

TO THE CITIZENS OF RUSSIA!

The Provisional Government is overthrown. Power has passed into the hands of the Military Revolutionary Committee, an organ of the Petrograd Soviet of Workers' and Soldiers' Deputies which stands at the head of the Petrograd proletariat and garrison.

The cause for which the people have struggled: the immediate offer of a democratic peace, the abolition of the landlords' title to the land, the workers' control of production, and the establishment of a Soviet Government—has been victorious.

Long live the Revolution of the Workers, Soldiers, and Peasants! [7]

No longer did Russia's leaders speak of God, Nation, Faith, and Glory, but of The Revolution, The People, and The Peace.

The victory of the Bolsheviks in what is now remembered as the Great October Revolution reflected the steady movement to the Left that Russian public opinion had followed between March and October 1917.[8] The men who had taken the reins of government from Nicholas on March 2 had been sober and successful politicians, still deeply committed to the social and economic order of Imperial Russia. Among them were Pavel Miliukov, historian, university professor, and leader of the liberal Kadet party, who was well known for his belief in constitutional monarchy. There was also Aleksandr Guchkov, leader of the moderately conservative Octobrist party, who came from the ranks of Moscow's merchants and who has been described as "a man of great ability and great ambition, brave and quarrelsome, devoted to liberty but inclined to interpret it in his own way."[9] Both despised Aleksandra and thought Nicholas's abdication essential, but they were sufficiently monarchist to urge the Grand Duke Mikhail to accept the crown and to be dismayed when he rejected their counsels. Miliukov and Guchkov both served under Prince Georgii Lvov, Prime Minister of the Provisional Government, a progressive-minded man who stood as a voice of moderation in the midst of Russia's turmoil. "Nowhere in their country could the Russian people have found better men to lead them out of the darkness of tyranny," wrote the American Consul John Snodgrass. "Lvov and his associates are to Russia what Washington and his associates were to America when it became a nation."[10] In March, the only representative of the Left in the cabinet had been Aleksandr Kerenskii. Kerenskii enjoyed proclaiming himself a brave revolutionary who had volunteered to become "the hostage of democracy" in the camp of the bourgeoisie, but he devoted far more energy to playing upon the aspirations of the masses than to satisfying them.[11]

The moderate politicians soon were replaced by more radical and daring men as the personnel and policies of the Provisional Government moved further to the Left with every cabinet formed in the months after Nicholas's abdication. At the same time, the problems these men faced became more complex, as the Romanovs' political and social structures began to crumble. At the root of Russia's many crises was the war itself, for it had strained her resources beyond the breaking point and had caused the army to collapse as a fighting force on the Eastern Front. By late summer, mass surrenders and desertions had become frequent; by early fall, tens of thousands of peasant soldiers simply began to walk away from their trenches, determined to return to their families and their villages. Only the very heavy demands of war on the Western Front prevented the Kaiser's armies from marching directly on to Petrograd.

The disintegration of Russia's army at the front paralleled an equally serious crisis at home. Sensing the Provisional Government's impotence, hordes of peasants burned down manor houses and murdered their occupants as they hastened to seize those lands they had so long been denied. In the cities, factory workers took control of the factories in which they worked. Along Russia's frontiers, national minorities began to break away from the Empire that had held them in subjugation for so long. If Russia was not to fall into the abyss of utter chaos, a government was needed that could satisfy, or at least appear to satisfy, the aspirations of the masses, while at the same time providing some sort of powerful focus for restoring the national will.[12] Led by Lenin and Trotskii, the Bolsheviks provided those two requisites to a degree that could not be matched by any other political group in Russia at the time. At the end of October, they used their superior party organization and tactical genius to turn the Russian Revolution onto a new and totally untested course. In doing so, they set the lives of their deposed rulers onto a new path as well.

At the beginning of their imprisonment at Tsarskoe Selo, Nicholas, Aleksandra, and their children had suffered few material hardships. They were allowed to live in a wing of the Alexander Palace with those of their inner circle who wished to share their fate, and they did not know the great want and deprivation that so many Russians suffered during those difficult days. It was the psychological strains that were far more difficult for them to bear. No longer Emperor and Empress, they had to adjust overnight to the loss of those courtesies and luxuries they had always taken for granted. Suddenly they were prisoners in what had been their home for many years, with portions of the palace and its grounds forbidden to them, their privacy invaded by revolutionary soldiers whose curiosity impelled them to demand a view of the man and woman who had ruled them so ineptly. That winter, Aleksandra had to do without the fresh flowers special trains had brought to her boudoir from the Crimea every week, even when locomotives could not be found to move grain from the country to the city or to carry food and ammunition to hungry and defenseless soldiers at the front.

Perhaps most painful of all, the "betrayals" Aleksandra had imagined so often became a reality after Nicholas's abdication, as men and women whom they had considered their friends for many years abandoned them utterly. They soon learned that the sailor Derevenko, whom they had thought so devoted to Aleksei, had long been a reluctant servant, bitter at being obliged to spend his days and nights with the Tsarevich for more than a decade. Once freed by the revolution, he gave full vent to his hatred and forced Aleksei to act as his servant for several days before he disappeared from the palace. Still, Aleksandra refused to believe that her "good" Russian people had deserted them. She was convinced that they soon would rise up and demand their rulers' restoration. But the call never came. Aleksandra's vision of the "good" Russian people who loved their Emperor and Empress with unswerving devotion remained the dream it had always been.[13]

Each self-delusion that collapsed was a rude shock. Worst of all, the Romanovs still had no idea what their fate would be. As Minister of Justice in the first cabinet of the Provisional Government, Kerenskii was responsible for their safety; to his credit, he resisted popular demands for revenge. "The Russian Revolution is unstained by bloodshed, and I will not permit it to be disgraced," he told angry deputies from Moscow's Soviet of Workers' and Soldiers' Deputies, as he refused to become "the Marat of the Russian Revolution."[14] With stubborn determination, Kerenskii kept the Romanovs sheltered at Tsarskoe Selo, although he was unable to extend that protection to their devoted companions Anna Vyrubova and Lili Dehn. Late in March, these two women were arrested and taken to Petrograd for interrogation. The authorities released Madame Dehn the next day, but they kept Vyrubova in the Peter-Paul Fortress for five months while they investigated her relationships with Nicholas, Aleksandra, and Rasputin. There had been so many rumors about Rasputin's sexual enslavement of Vyrubova and Aleksandra that the Provisional Government's investigators found it almost impossible to believe that the stories had no basis in fact. Only after a thorough medical examination proved her virginity and after repeated interrogations proved her stupidity did the interrogators order Vyrubova's release, concluding that she could have played no part in intrigues to misdirect state policy.[15]

The spring and summer thus passed with no major threats or crises for Nicholas and Aleksandra. There were periodic disputes with their guards, especially when commanders were changed. For the most part, however, they continued to live like a respectable Victorian middle-class couple, concerned with their children's upbringing and education and anxious to keep themselves occupied with useful tasks. During the first month or so of his imprisonment, Nicholas exercised by shoveling snow every day. Then, when spring finally came, he marshaled his children and companions to plant a kitchen garden in what had once been a large expanse of carefully groomed lawn near the palace. Together, he and his companions cut the sod and carried it away, turned over the earth, and planted the seeds. "We finished our kitchen garden some time ago, and it is now in splendid condition," wrote Gilliard on June 2. "We have every imaginable kind of vegetable and five hundred cabbages," he continued. "To occupy our leisure now that we have finished our work on the garden, we have asked and obtained permission to cut down the dead trees in the park. . . . This will give us a supply of wood for next winter."[16]

That Nicholas, his family, and friends had begun by early summer to lay plans for spending the coming winter at Tsarskoe Selo indicated a bitter failure of the hopes they had entertained during their early weeks of captivity. At first, a number of sane and sober men hoped to send them out of Russia before they fell victim to the hatred of the revolutionary masses. England's Ambassador Sir George Buchanan had several conversations in March and early April with Foreign Minister Miliukov on the subject of providing a refuge for the Romanovs in England, and there seemed to be a good deal of support for the idea in diplomatic and high government circles.[17] The last thing the statesmen of the Provisional Government wanted was to be branded as tsaricides by their counterparts in Europe. Even Kerenskii, the most radical of their number, shared that view, and, when he came to Tsarskoe Selo to question Nicholas and Aleksandra, he made a point of telling them that "the Queen of England asks for news of the ex-Tsarina."[18] It was a painful insult to Aleksandra's self-esteem, but it also assured her and Nicholas that their plight was known to the outside world and that powerful people were concerned about their welfare. "Our captivity at Tsarskoe Selo" wrote Gilliard, "did not seem likely to last long."[19]

At that point, escape seemed relatively simple. "We were only a few hours by railway from the Finnish frontier, and the necessity of passing through Petrograd was the only serious obstacle," Gilliard remembered.[20] But the obstacle of Petrograd proved insurmountable. The Provisional Government still was so weak that it had to defer policy questions to the Petrograd Soviet of Workers' and Soldiers' Deputies.[21] These men and women from the long-suffering lower classes were in no mood to release their prisoners so quickly, and Miliukov and Kerenskii both feared that their indignation would topple the government in an instant if they permitted the Romanovs to take advantage of the asylum offered by the British. Then, when it appeared that there might be a way to send them north to be rescued at the White Sea port of Murmansk, the British government suddenly withdrew its offer, for fear of offending the more radical revolutionary forces in

Russia.[22] The Provisional Government thus had to search for another means to move their captives out of the vicinity of the increasingly volatile Soviet of Workers' and Soldiers' Deputies.

When it became clear that they could not spend the coming winter at Tsarkoe Selo for fear of the Petrograd crowd, Nicholas asked that he and his family be sent to the Crimea, where the weather was warm and the chances for rescue by sea more certain. Kerenskii insisted that it would be impossible to get them through the central provinces of European Russia because angry mobs of peasants, workers, and soldiers, alerted by revolutionary railway workers, would be certain to seize their train. He decided instead to send his prisoners to Tobolsk, a large town in western Siberia.[23] "My choice fell upon Tobolsk," Kerenskii later insisted, "because it was a truly isolated place. It was not on a rail line and, in winter, was almost entirely cut off from the outside world. The home of the governor of Tobolsk was sufficiently comfortable and lent itself to all the arrangements needed for accommodating the Imperial family."[24]

Nicholas, Aleksandra, their children, and the handful of servants and loyal friends who remained with them were told at the end of July that they must pack their belongings and be prepared to leave Tsarskoe Selo within a few days. "We have just learned that they are going to send us not to the Crimea, but to a town in the East, three or four days by train from here," Nicholas wrote in his diary on July 28. "But where, precisely?" he asked. "No one can say. The commandant himself knows nothing about it."[25] Now Prime Minister, Kerenskii kept their destination a closely guarded secret in order to reduce the chances of marauding revolutionary bands waylaying them along their route. "We made all the preparations for their departure in the greatest secrecy," he later explained, "because the least bit of publicity could give rise to all sorts of obstacles and complications. The destination of the Imperial family was not known even to all members of the Provisional Government. Only five or six people in all of Petrograd knew about it."[26] Most important of all, Kerenskii kept the Soviet of Workers' and Soldiers' Deputies in total ignorance about his plans to move his prisoners.

Kerenskii set the departure for August 1. He ordered a special train to carry his prisoners as far as Tiumen and permitted Nicholas one last brief meeting with his younger brother Mikhail. Because he feared that local revolutionaries might attempt to seize the family in revenge for the tortures they had suffered under the tsarist regime, Kerenskii marked the train with signs that identified its occupants as members of the "Japanese Red Cross Mission." To the specially chosen detachment of guards who were to accompany the train to Tobolsk, he gave a stern lecture. "You have been entrusted with guarding the Imperial family here at Tsarskoe Selo, and you will be entrusted with guarding them in Tobolsk, where they are being transferred by órder of the Council of Ministers. Remember: we do not hit people when they are down. Conduct yourselves like gentlemen, not like louts."[27] He then arranged for his prisoners and their baggage to be brought to the train. Just after six o'clock on the morning of August 1, 1917, Nicholas and Aleksandra saw their beloved Tsarskoe Selo fade into the distance. They would never see it again.[28]

Despite the Baroness Buxhoeveden's absurd insistence that "the want of proper arrangements for their departure from Tsarskoe [Selo] had already shown that the former Sovereign was of no importance even to those who were not aggressively hostile,"[29] the fact is that Kerenskii was more than generous in his efforts to ease their journey. Their train had a private sleeping car, a dining car filled with delicacies and fine wines from the Imperial cellars, and several freight cars to carry an immense quantity of baggage. That morning, it had required the efforts of fifty soldiers to load everything the Romanovs and their companions had prepared to take with them, not to mention the belongings of the considerable number of servants they thought necessary. In addition to the several courtiers and ladies who chose to share their new trials, Nicholas and Aleksandra went to Siberia with two valets, six chambermaids, ten footmen, three cooks, four assistant cooks, a clerk, a nurse, a doctor, a barber, a butler, a wine steward, and two pet spaniels.[30] In a land torn by war and revolution, the Romanovs were being treated well indeed, despite Nicholas's complaints that it was "silly and annoying" that they should have to draw the shades whenever their train passed through a station and that the manner in which their schedule was arranged caused "poor Aleksei to stay up until an impossibly late hour" one night.[31]

For almost four days, the train bore them eastward, through Viatka, Perm, across the Urals, and through Ekaterinburg to the river town of Tiumen, where they arrived just before midnight on August 4. There porters labored for the rest of the night to transfer their baggage to the small river steamer *Rus,* which bore them some two hundred miles to the northwest along the Tura and Tobol rivers to Tobolsk. In keeping with Kerenskii's orders, they were given the ship's entire first-class deck, where they strolled and spent long hours looking at the majestic views that lined the river's banks. During the evening of August 5, the *Rus* sailed past the village of Pokrovskoe, and, from her vantage point on the upper deck, Aleksandra could see the home in which Rasputin, to whose memory she still was devoted, once had lived. Finally, on the morning of August 6, just five days after they left Tsarskoe Selo, they reached Tobolsk, their new home, some two thousand miles to the east of Petrograd and its turmoil.[32]

A town of some twenty-one thousand, Tobolsk stood on the bend of the great Irtysh River, opposite the mouth of the Tobol along which the *Rus* had sailed. Formerly an important gateway from European Russia into the lands of the Siberian fur trappers, the town had shrunk to insignificance when the Trans-Siberian Railway had passed some two hundred miles to the south. There, Nicholas, his family, and close friends lived throughout the fall of 1917, the long Siberian winter, and the spring of 1918. They were confined to the governor's house and its fenced-in garden, but their life was far from uncomfortable. Once the governor's house had been painted and repaired, they enjoyed spacious lodgings filled with comfortable furniture and ornamented by the many Persian rugs, paintings, photographs, and icons they had brought from home. Beyond that, the atmosphere was far less hostile than it had been at Tsarskoe Selo. No longer were they in the midst of a bitter and angry populace but among people who still had an affection for their Tsar and Tsarina. Pierre Gilliard, whom the guards allowed to walk about town freely, remembered that, "on the whole, the inhabitants of Tobolsk were still very attached to the Imperial family, and our guards had repeatedly to intervene to prevent them from standing under the windows or removing their hats and crossing themselves as they passed the house."[33]

The fall of 1917 thus passed quickly into winter. Nicholas devoted several hours each day to his favorite pastime of cutting wood, Aleksandra spent hours at her knitting and needlework, and their children still labored at their studies. The routine became comfortably fixed: lunch at one, tea at four, dinner at half-past seven. In between were lessons, exercise, and woodcutting. Games, reading, and energetically performed one-act comedies occupied the evenings, with all of the children taking an active part. Nicholas enjoyed reading out loud, and, when his children were not performing, they got through a great assortment of books ranging from *The Scarlet Pimpernel* and *The Three Musketeers* to a variety of Russian novels by Turgenev, Saltykov-Shchedrin, and Tolstoi. It was, in all, an uneventful winter.[34] Even the Bolshevik victory in the Great October Revolution, which overthrew Kerenskii's weak and vacillating Provisional Government and placed power into the decisive and willing hands of the very men from whom he had hoped to save the Romanovs, had no immediate impact upon their lives.

Though they were far away from the center of events, Nicholas avidly followed the war that winter, and his main concern was that Russia's domestic turmoil not undermine her war effort. From that perspective, he found the news painful and disheartening, as it became clear that Russia could not hope to emerge victorious in her struggle with Germany and Austria. The crowning blow was the Treaty of Brest-Litovsk, which Russia's new masters signed with Austria and Germany on March 3, 1918.* To Nicholas it seemed an utter humiliation for his country and his people. According to at least one account, it caused him to regret the abdication he had made in the hope of strengthening Russia.[35] Still, his ability to lose himself in the trivia of a daily routine had made it possible for Nicholas to come through crises in the past, and he lived through the winter of his Siberian imprisonment in the same manner. Physical exercise tired his body and helped

---

*On February 1, 1918, the Soviet government replaced the Julian calendar with the Gregorian, which had long been in use in the West. Because the old Julian calendar was thirteen days behind the Gregorian in the twentieth century, the Soviet calendar for 1918 simply went from January 31 to February 14. The date of the Brest-Litovsk treaty is according to the new calendar that had just been put into effect. All remaining dates in this chapter will be according to the new calendar.

him to banish sad and depressing thoughts from his mind. In later years, Kerenskii would remember with amazement how the fallen Emperor "threw off authority as formerly he might have thrown off a dress uniform and put on a simpler one. . . . It seemed as if a heavy burden had fallen from his shoulders and that he was greatly relieved."[36]

The strain of the months in Siberia seems to have been far greater for Aleksandra than it was for Nicholas. Perhaps she was beginning to perceive how much her meddling in state affairs and her fanatic faith in Rasputin had contributed to Russia's crises and the Romanovs' ruin. She may have been more sensitive because of her semi-invalid condition, although there is no concrete evidence to indicate just how serious her often referred to "heart problem" really was. For whatever reasons, depression lay heavy upon her as the new year dawned. At the beginning of January 1918, she wrote to Vyrubova, now freed from her Petrograd prison, that "we must have sinned terribly for our Father in Heaven to punish us so frightfully. But I firmly and unfalteringly believe that in the end He will save us. . . . The strange thing about the Russian character," she concluded, "is that it can so suddenly change to evil, cruelty, and unreason, and can as suddenly change back again. This in fact is simply want of character. Russians are in reality big, ignorant children."[37] Aleksandra still had not learned that, in the world of the early twentieth century, the paternalism of seventeenth- and eighteenth-century monarchs was out of place.

When they seized power at the end of October 1917, the Bolsheviks inherited a series of crises that seemed almost hopeless in their complexity. Although Russia's army had fallen into a state of utter collapse, the war ground on. The economy was in a shambles, agricultural and industrial production had fallen to a mere fraction of their prewar levels, and it had become all but impossible to provide Russians with even the most basic goods and services. Aside from these difficulties, Lenin faced the very real dilemma of extending Bolshevik power into areas where national separatist movements, as well as monarchist forces, were beginning to launch counterrevolutionary attacks that would require many months and much bitter fighting to defeat. Within a few months, Tobolsk became the scene of one such Bolshevik power struggle, and Nicholas, Aleksandra, and their children became pawns that rival factions endeavored to seize for their own purposes.

The first act in the drama that would seal the Romanovs' doom began without their knowledge in the city of Ekaterinburg, when the fiercely Bolshevik Regional Soviet of the Urals asked Lenin's permission to transfer Nicholas and his family to their jurisdiction. Before an answer arrived from Moscow,* a detachment of Red Guards from Omsk, Ekaterinburg's rival in the struggle for administrative control of the Ural region, reached Tobolsk on March 2. These Red Guards had been recruited from the ranks of the Trans-Siberian railroad workers, among the toughest and most radical in all of Russia, and they were so well disciplined that Nicholas and Aleksandra at first thought they had come to rescue them. Only Gilliard was more perceptive and realistic; to his diary, he lamented that "our last chance of escape has just been snatched from us."[38]

The purpose of the Omsk detachment was to establish a Bolshevik administration in Tobolsk, where there was growing sympathy for a restoration of the monarchy. For the Red Guards, the Romanovs' presence was a matter of secondary consequence, and they were interested in them only insofar as they might aid or impede their efforts to establish Bolshevik authority in the town.[39] Just a few days later, however, another Bolshevik detachment arrived from Ekaterinburg to challenge the authority of the Omsk guards. There now were three military forces—the guards sent by Kerenskii under Colonel Kobylinskii, the Omsk Red Guards under Commissar Demianov, and the Ekaterinburg Red Guards under Commissar Zaslavskii—to claim custody of the Romanovs. "The atmosphere around us is fairly electrified," Aleksandra wrote to Vyrubova. "We feel that a storm is approaching."[40]

All waited for word from Moscow. Nothing had been heard since February 25, when Colonel Kobylinskii had been ordered to place his prisoners on "soldiers' rations" and to limit their expenses to an

*On March 10 and 11, 1918, Lenin had moved Russia's capital from Petrograd back to Moscow.

average of not more than six hundred rubles per person each month.[41] "We shall have to economize considerably," Nicholas had remarked at the time, sadly agreeing that ten of their servants would have to be let go.[42] Butter and coffee had to be given up, and sugar restricted to a pound and a half each month. Yet local peasants found ways to smuggle extra delicacies to the royal family. Nicholas wrote on March 13: "Recently we have begun to receive butter, coffee, tea biscuits, and jam from various good and kind people who have learned about our restricted provisions funds. How touching!"[43] Charles Gibbes, the English tutor who had taught the Romanov children for several years at Tsarskoe Selo and had rejoined them at Tobolsk, recorded some of the menus served after the order to place the family on "soldiers' rations" had been in effect for about two months:

> *Lunch, April 28/May 11, 1918*
> Russian soup with pearl barley
> Grouse with rice
>
> *Dinner, April 28/May 11, 1918*
> Hot wild duck
> Salad
> Rice pudding
>
> *Lunch, April 29/May 12, 1918*
> Borshch
> Veal rissoles, garnished
>
> *Dinner, April 29/May 12, 1918*
> Leg of veal, garnished
> Macaroni[44]

Not comparable to the fare that once had come from the palace kitchens at Tsarskoe Selo and Livadia, to be sure, but far from what prisoners had been accustomed to receive in tsarist prisons. That the Romanovs lived such an amazingly comfortable life as prisoners angered the newly arrived Red Guards, whose own living conditions were far more spartan.

As various armed detachments vied for authority over them, the Romanovs continued to feel a rising tension. Finally, on April 22, when Vasilii Vasilevich Iakovlev arrived from Moscow, it became clear that interest in the Romanovs' future had been centered in the highest echelons of the Party and the government ever since February when Lenin's Minister of Justice had begun to assemble the documentary evidence needed to put the Tsar and his family on trial. If the Regional Soviet of the Urals hoped to punish the Romanovs in Ekaterinburg, they would have to do so over the very strenuous objections of the central government.

Iakovlev had been sent to Tobolsk by none other than Iakov Sverdlov, then the Bolsheviks' chief organizer, who had played a key role in promoting the Bolshevik cause in the Ural region during the previous year. From his many agents in the Urals, Sverdlov had begun to receive disturbing warnings about plots to free Nicholas and his family and spirit them out of Russia, and he had ordered Iakovlev to transfer the Romanovs to a more secure location. At the same time, Sverdlov also hoped to protect them from the various workers' and soldiers' groups who wished to kill them for personal revenge. If Iakovlev succeeded in moving them to either Omsk or Ufa, it would be easier to keep them out of the vengeful clutches of the Regional Soviet of the Urals. Unfortunately for Nicholas and his family, the Soviet objected so threateningly to Iakovlev's efforts that Sverdlov was obliged to give in and order his reluctant agent to take his charges to Ekaterinburg. Because Aleksei was suffering from a bad bruise that kept him in bed at the time, Iakovlev moved the family in two groups. Nicholas, Aleksandra, and their daughter Maria left Tobolsk on April 26, with the understanding that Aleksei and his sisters Olga, Tatiana, and Anastasia would join them as soon as he could travel.[45]

When Nicholas, Aleksandra, and Maria reached Ekaterinburg on the morning of April 30, they were taken directly to a house owned by a merchant named Ipatiev. It was a large, solid building, and the Ipatiev family had been evicted from it only the previous afternoon when the Regional Soviet learned that they would, in fact, be given custody of Iakovlev's captives. This time, their guards were loyal Bolsheviks, hardened by years of privation and revolutionary struggle. Their commander was Aleksandr Avdeev, a worker who harbored an almost pathological hatred of the Romanovs and devoted considerable effort to making their life uncomfortable. When Nicholas protested the guards' rudeness to Aleksandra on their arrival, Avdeev told him that he would be sentenced to hard labor if he complained again. That, however, was only the beginning.[46]

It was into this confined, brutal atmosphere that Aleksei and his sisters Tatiana, Olga, and Anastasia came three weeks later. By that time, the Ipatiev house had received a new and ominous name from the Ekaterinburg Soviet. They called it "The House of Special Designation," and its prison regime became more severe and degrading as the days passed. The guards insisted upon accompanying the Grand Duchesses to the toilet; there are even some reports that they sketched pictures of Aleksandra engaged in various obscene sexual acts with Rasputin on the toilet walls and insisted that her daughters pay close attention to them.[47] There seemed to be no choice but to bear these humiliations, but Nicholas complained about them bitterly when Egor Berzhin, Commander of the North Ural Siberian Front, arrived in late June to inspect the prisoners. Soon afterward, he was gratified to see that his complaints must have received serious attention. On July 4, Avdeev was replaced by a new officer, Iakov Iurovskii, who at first impressed his prisoners with his apparent honesty and rare efficiency.

Actually, Iurovskii's appearance had nothing to do with Nicholas's complaints to the authorities. Unknown to the inmates of the House of Special Designation, Iurovskii was the chief of the local Cheka, the new Bolshevik secret police organization under the cruelly efficient direction of Feliks Dzerzhinskii that had begun to deal ruthlessly with all real and presumed counterrevolutionaries.[48] Iurovskii's chief concern at first was to prevent his prisoners' escape. The possibility that Nicholas and his family might be rescued had become very real, especially after the violently anti-Bolshevik Czech Legion (a group of Czech prisoners of war whom the Provisional Government had agreed to send to France by way of Siberia and the United States) joined with other "Whites," as the anti-Bolshevik forces were known, in the days after the October Revolution. During the spring and summer of 1918, this White army seized a number of cities and towns along the Trans-Siberian Railway. By early July, their victorious advance was drawing closer and closer to Ekaterinburg, center of Bolshevik power in the Urals, and there seemed a very real possibility that the balance of forces might shift at any moment. "The hour of liberation draws near, and the days of the usurpers are numbered," began one secret message Bolshevik agents discovered before it made its way into Nicholas's hands. Another intercepted letter proclaimed that "the long awaited hour is at hand," and still another was signed by "one of those who is ready to give his life for you—an officer in the Russian army."[49] By the middle of the month, Iurovskii ordered metal gratings installed over the windows in Nicholas's room.[50]

Meanwhile, the Regional Soviet of the Urals met in special session in Ekaterinburg. Well aware that the approaching White armies intended to free Nicholas and his family, they resolved not to be denied their revenge and voted unanimously for Nicholas's execution. Yet, anxious as they were to shed Romanov blood, they did not dare to carry out their sentence without approval from higher authorities. Therefore, they sent Filipp Goloshchëkin, their regional party secretary, to obtain permission from the Bolshevik Central Committee in Moscow. As best we can determine, the Central Committee, especially Lenin and Trotskii, insisted that Nicholas be put on public trial. There also was some talk about submitting the question of the Romanovs' fate to the Fifth All-Russian Congress of Soviets, which had assembled at Moscow's Bolshoi Theatre on July 4 and was still in session. For the moment, however, it was decided that Nicholas and his family should continue as prisoners in the House of Special Designation under the immediate control of the Regional Soviet of the Urals. Thus, when Goloshchëkin returned to Ekaterinburg on July 12, the fate of the Romanovs remained undecided.[51] Assuming that Ekaterinburg remained in Bolshevik hands, the Regional Soviet was not to carry out its plan to execute its prisoners. But what if the White armies continued their advance? Obviously, the Bolsheviks did not intend to permit the Romanovs to fall into friendly hands and become, as Sverdlov later said, "a live banner [for the Whites] to rally around."[52]

The very rapid advance of the Whites on Ekaterinburg in mid-July meant that a decision about the Romanovs' fate had to be made more quickly than the Bolshevik leaders had anticipated. Whether Lenin or Sverdlov actually sent an execution order or merely concurred with the decision of the Regional Soviet is not known, but it is certain that, in mid-July, the local Bolsheviks sent Iurovskii orders to execute all of his prisoners to prevent them from falling into the hands of the advancing monarchists. Precisely how, when, and where the execution was to occur was left to his discretion.[53] Certain of his course and with the help of several close associates, Iurovskii began to lay his plans.

On July 17, only five days after Goloshchëkin's return from Moscow, Iurovskii's colleague Petr Voikov, Ekaterinburg Regional Commissar for Supply, ordered a local chemical warehouse to deliver fifty gallons of sulfuric acid "without delay or excuses" to the deserted Four Brothers Mine, located six miles to the northwest of the city. At the same time, he ordered almost two hundred gallons of gasoline sent to the same location.[54] In consultation with Voikov, Iurovskii had decided that Nicholas, Aleksandra, their children, and attendants all would be shot that night. Because they feared that the crash of rifle fire might attract too much attention from Ekaterinburg's residents, they decided to use handguns for the execution. Hastily, they assembled a variety of weapons: at least one 9 mm. Browning pistol, a Colt .45 caliber pistol, and several 7.62 mm. Nagant revolvers. Voikov and Iurovskii both carried 7.65 mm. Mauser machine pistols.[55]

That night, Nicholas, Aleksandra, and their children went to bed just before midnight as usual. At about 2:00 A.M. (the darkest time of night because the summer daylight time the Bolsheviks had introduced was two hours ahead of standard time), Voikov arrived at the House of Special Designation with word that all was ready. Iurovskii then awakened his prisoners and hurriedly explained that the Whites had advanced more quickly than expected, that the house might come under fire at any moment, and that he had been ordered to move them all to a safer place. They dressed in haste and followed him to a semibasement room, about fifteen feet by seventeen feet in dimensions. There, he asked them to wait while cars were brought up. Nicholas requested chairs for Aleksandra, Aleksei, and himself, and Iurovskii had them brought in with his usual efficiency. Thus they were assembled: Nicholas, Aleksandra, the Tsarevich Aleksei, the Grand Duchesses Tatiana, Olga, Maria, and Anastasia, their family physician Dr. Evgenii Botkin, their footman Aleksei Trupp, the housemaid Anna Demidova, and the cook Ivan Kharitonov. As yet they had no hint of what lay in store for them. During more than a year of imprisonment, they had grown used to delays and strange instructions. Quietly, they waited as they had done so many times before.

But this wait was not to be like the other times when their captors had awakened them for one reason or another. At that very moment, in the hallway outside the room, Iurovskii was checking to make certain that each of his eleven subordinates knew which prisoner he was to shoot, after telling them that he claimed the right to execute Nicholas and Aleksei himself. Voikov glanced at his watch and noted that it was 2:45 A.M. Just then, the truck he had ordered—a four-ton Fiat—arrived, and its driver began to race the engine, as he had been told, to drown the sound of the pistol shots. Satisfied that all was ready, Iurovskii led his men into the room where his unsuspecting prisoners waited, still groggy from being awakened so suddenly. Without hesitating, he strode to where Nicholas sat and announced: "Nicholas Aleksandrovich, by the order of the Regional Soviet of the Urals, you are to be shot, along with all your family."[56] Nicholas leapt to his feet. He barely had time to utter the word *"Chto?"* ("What?") before Iurovskii shot him in the head and turned to fire at Aleksei. Aleksandra and one of her daughters managed to cross themselves before the bullets from their executioners' pistols tore into their bodies. The other Grand Duchesses, who had been standing behind their brother, father, and mother, screamed as they were cut down by a second barrage of pistol fire. As the sound of the shots died away, Aleksei moaned softly. The always efficient Iurovskii promptly stepped over and fired two more shots into his head. All were dead except Anastasia. Only slightly wounded, she cried out, more in fear than in pain. Unwilling to bother with reloading their weapons, the guards seized several rifles that stood nearby and calmly bayoneted her to death. As she collapsed in a motionless heap, it was 3:15 on the morning of July 18, 1918. The Romanov dynasty in Russia had reached its end.[57]

Once the deed was done, Iurovskii, Voikov, and their men hastened to dispose of the bodies, for no one was certain about how long the Whites' advance could be held off. Anxious not to draw attention to their comings and goings, they quietly loaded the bodies onto the back of the Fiat just as dawn was breaking and took them to the Four Brothers Mine. So that no villagers might stumble upon them, Iurov-

skii posted guards around the entire area. Then he and his men proceeded with the grisly task of hacking their victims to pieces.
Determined to destroy all traces of Nicholas and his family, they
poured gasoline over their dismembered corpses and set them ablaze.
When the flames died down, they repeated the process until all of
Voikov's supply of gasoline was consumed. As expected, portions of
larger bones remained after the burning. To destroy them, the men
used the sulfuric acid that Voikov had ordered the day before. After
the acid had finished its work, the remains of the Romanovs were
thrown into the mine shaft. Only the few metal objects they wore, a
handful of corset stays, and the tip of a woman's finger, later thought
by investigators to be Aleksandra's, remained after Iurovskii, Voikov,
and their men left the scene. The only other clue was the charred
earth, which monarchist pathologists later found to be saturated with
melted human fat.[58]

Eight days later, the White army crashed through the Bolshevik
defenses around Ekaterinburg, and a detachment of monarchist
officers raced to Ipatiev's house to free their Emperor and his family.
The building was empty, its interior a shambles. The only living creature they found was a half-starved little English spaniel.[59] It was Aleksei's favorite pet Joy, whom he had named when he lived in another
world. That world—the world of the Romanovs, Autocrats of All the
Russias—was no more. From Moscow, once again restored as Russia's
capital, new rulers launched a new era that would repeat all the trials
and trauma of Peter the Great's time. Peter had labored to bring Russia
into the eighteenth century; Lenin, Trotskii, and Stalin struggled to
bring her firmly into the twentieth. In both cases, the task was accomplished only after untold suffering, great agony, and countless
deaths.

Suffering, agony, and death—these had been as much a part of the
Romanovs' Russia as its riches, splendor, and power. During the course
of three centuries, the successors of the mild and unassuming Tsar
Mikhail had boasted dazzling achievements. They had quadrupled the
size of their domains to more then eight million square miles, built new
cities, brought a new culture into being, and transformed their land
from a medieval semi-Asiatic power into a semimodern European one.

But they had failed in perhaps the most fundamental task of all. Although able to build a great Empire, they had proved incapable of providing for the most basic needs of the people they ruled. Even before the First World War threw their economy and government into chaos, a majority of Russians were illiterate, many were starving, and most lived on the brink of poverty. These conditions were the inevitable results of the manner in which the Romanovs had met the challenge of the West in the century after the French Revolution. Unwilling to see the Old Regime give way in Russia, they had attempted to adopt the economic innovations of Europe's Industrial Revolution but had refused to grant any of the political concessions that had accompanied it in England and France, even in Germany and Austria. The Romanovs thus had denied Russians any effective voice in determining their political destiny even as they had proceeded to establish an economic system in which private initiative flourished and individual decision making was encouraged. This bred among their subjects even greater dissatisfaction with the politics of autocracy, as Russians grew increasingly resentful at having their lives controlled from above by an impersonal and insensitive bureaucracy.

Men and women who felt that their way of life was not worth fighting for proved poor defenders against the Romanovs' foreign and domestic foes. Very few Russians saw any reason to lay down their lives in battle against the armies of Germany and Austria, and even fewer were willing to die to defend the Romanov dynasty from revolutionary attack. Anxious for a stake in their country's future, Russians gave their loyalty to men who promised them basic human dignity and at least a minimal share of what their labor produced. Yet they soon learned that no man and no ideology could solve quickly the crushing problems their nation faced as desperate times drove desperate men to commit desperate acts. "We have seen other tyrants bathing in blood, tyrants more revolting because they come from the people," lamented Kerenskii a decade after he had been driven from his homeland.[60] The last days of the Romanovs thus marked only the beginning of Russia's new struggles: civil war, famine, and purges, all followed by an even greater and more destructive world war than that which had brought down Nicholas and Aleksandra. From that crucible of suffering, agony, and death, Russia emerged more powerful than she had ever been, but the utopia envisioned by the men who had succeeded the Romanovs remained elusive and unrealized.

And so it remains today. "Revolution is the mirror of the coming day," wrote the famous American anarchist Emma Goldman in 1924, the year of Lenin's death. "It is the child that is to be the Man of To-morrow."[61] More than fifty years later, there are many who wonder if the man has realized the promise they perceived in the child, or if, perhaps, Russia simply remains Russia, "a whole world, self-sufficient, independent, and absolute," as the nineteenth-century writer Mikhail Pogodin once explained, a land in which "everything is different."[62]

NOTES AND REFERENCES

KEY TO ABBREVIATIONS IN ARCHIVAL REFERENCES

GPB   Gosudarstvennaia Publichnaia Biblioteka imeni M. E.
Saltykova-Shchedrina. Otdel Rukopisei (Leningrad).
ORGBL   Gosudarstvennaia Biblioteka S.S.S.R. imeni V. I. Lenina.
Otdel Rukopisei (Moscow).
TsGAOR   Tsentral'nyi Gosudarstvennyi Arkhiv Oktiabr'skoi Revoliutsii
(Moscow).
TsGIAL   Tsentral'nyi Gosudarstvennyi Istoricheskii Arkhiv S.S.S.R.
(Leningrad).

KEY TO ABBREVIATIONS IN PUBLISHED REFERENCES

Chteniia   *Chteniia v obshchestve istorii i drevnostei rossiiskikh pri
Imperatorskom Moskovskom universitete* (Moscow, 1845–1916).
IRI   I. E. Grabar, ed., *Istoriia russkogo iskusstva*, 12 vols.
(Moscow, 1953–61).
IV   *Istoricheskii vestnik* (St. Petersburg and Petrograd, 1880–1917).
IZ   *Istoricheskie zapiski* (Moscow, 1937—).
KA   *Krasnyi arkhiv* (Moscow, 1922–41).
OZ   *Otechestvennye zapiski* (St. Petersburg, 1839–1884).
PSZ   *Polnoe sobranie zakonov rossiiskoi imperii*, 2d ed. in 55 vols.
(St. Petersburg, 1830–84).
RS   *Russkaia starina* (St. Petersburg and Petrograd, 1870–1918).
RA   *Russkii arkhiv* (Moscow, 1863–1916).
RBS   *Russkii biograficheskii slovar'*, 25 vols. (St. Petersburg,
Petrograd, and Moscow, 1896–1918).
SEER   *Slavonic and East European Review* (London, 1922–).
SIRIO   *Sbornik Imperatorskago Russkago Istoricheskago Obshchestva*
(St. Petersburg, Moscow, and Iur'ev, 1867–1916).
SR   *Slavic Review* (1941–).
VE   *Vestnik Evropy* (St. Petersburg and Petrograd, 1866–1918).
VI   *Voprosy istorii* (Moscow, 1945–).

ZhMIu   *Zhurnal Ministerstva Iustitsii* (St. Petersburg, 1859–68, 1894–1917).

ZhMNP   *Zhurnal Ministerstva Narodnago Prosveshcheniia* (St. Petersburg and Petrograd, 1834–1917).

ZhMVD   *Zhurnal Ministerstva Vnutrennikh Del* (St. Petersburg, 1829–59).

PROLOGUE

1 B. Vladimirtsov, *Le régime social des Mongols: Le féodalisme nomade* (Paris, 1948), pp. 39–56; D. S. Mirsky, *Russia: A Social History* (London, 1952), pp. 93–97.

2 B. D. Grekov and A. Iakoubovski, *La Horde d'Or et la Russie: La domination Tatare au XIIIe et au XIVe siècle de la mer jaune à la mer noire* (Paris, 1961), pp. 193–95; "The Battle on the River Kalka," *Medieval Russia's Epics, Chronicles, and Tales,* ed. S. A. Zenkovsky (New York, 1954), p. 195.

3 S. M. Solov'ev, *Istoriia Rossii s drevneishikh vremen,* Vol. 2 (Moscow, 1960), pp. 151–55.

4 "The Tale of the Destruction of Riazan," *Medieval Russia's Epics,* p. 201.

5 Grekov and Iakoubovski, *La Horde d'Or,* pp. 201–2.

6 John of Plano Carpini, "History of the Mongols," *The Mongol Mission: Narratives and Letters of the Franciscan Missionaries in Mongolia and China in the Thirteenth and Fourteenth Centuries,* ed. Christopher Dawson (New York, 1955), pp. 29–30.

7 Grekov and Iakoubovski, *La Horde d'Or,* pp. 208–12; Nicholas V. Riasanovsky, *A History of Russia* (New York, 1963), pp. 77–78.

8 A. E. Presniakov, *Obrazovanie velikorusskago gosudarstva* (Petrograd, 1918), pp. 48–64; Grekov and Iakoubovski, *La Horde d'Or,* pp. 208–14.

9 Presniakov, *Obrazovanie,* pp. 136–59; J. L. I. Fennell, *The Emergence of Moscow, 1304–1359* (Berkeley and Los Angeles, 1968), pp. 111–95; Riasanovsky, *History,* pp. 104–16; Princess Zinaida Schakovskoy, *The Fall of Eagles: Precursors of Peter the Great* (New York, 1964), p. 17, n. 1.

10 Fennell, *Emergence of Moscow,* pp. 191–92.

11 P. N. Miliukov, *Ocherki po istorii russkoi kul'tury,* Vol. 3 (St. Petersburg, 1901), pp. 31–32 [all citations are to this edition unless otherwise noted].

12 Solov'ev, *Istoriia Rossii,* Vol. 2, pp. 284–89; L. V. Cherepnin, *Obrazovanie russkago tsentralizovannogo gosudarstva v XIV–XV vekakh* (Moscow, 1960), pp. 596–626.

13 B. D. Grekov, ed., *Ocherki istorii SSSR: Period feodalizma IX–XV vv.,* Vol. 2 (Moscow, 1953), pp. 222–30; Cherepnin, *Obrazovanie,* pp. 629–49.

14 Riasanovsky, *History,* p. 114.

15 Cherepnin, *Obrazovanie,* pp. 855–96; Grekov, *Ocherki: Period feodalizma,* Vol. 2, pp. 287–92.

16 Miliukov, *Ocherki po istorii russkoi kul'tury,* Vol. 2, pp. 21–22.

17 Ibid., pp. 23–24; ibid., Vol. 3, pp. 43–44; Michael Cherniavsky, *Tsar and People: Studies in Russian Myths* (New Haven, 1961), pp. 40–43.

18 Riasanovsky, *History,* pp. 141–42.

19 Quoted in Michael Cherniavsky, "Ivan the Terrible as Renaissance Prince," *Slavic Review, (SR),* Vol. 27, No. 2 (June 1968), p. 200.

20 Ibid., pp. 195–211, especially pp. 195–96.
21 K. Waliszewski, *Ivan the Terrible* (London, 1904), p. 116.
22 R. Iu. Wipper, *Ivan Groznyi* (Moscow, 1922), pp. 34–38; Waliszewski, *Ivan the Terrible*, pp. 120–23.
23 P. A. Sadikov, *Ocherki po istorii oprichniny* (Moscow-Leningrad, 1950), pp. 5–64.
24 A. A. Zimin, *Oprichnina Ivana Groznogo* (Moscow, 1964), p. 479. See also pp. 430–80.
25 Quoted in S. F. Platonov, *Boris Godunov: Tsar of Russia*, trans. L. Rex Pyles (Gulf Breeze, 1973), p. 47.
26 S. F. Platonov, *Boris Godunov* (Petrograd, 1921), p. 142.
27 Ibid., pp. 142–44.
28 Ibid., pp. 144–54; S. F. Platonov, *Smutnoe vremia* (Praga, 1924), pp. 86–119.
29 S. F. Platonov, *Ocherki po istorii smuty v moskovskom gosudarstve XVI–XVII vv. (opyt izucheniia obshchestvennago stroia i soslovnykh otnoshenii v smutnoe vremia)* (St. Petersburg, 1910), pp. 282–460.
30 P. G. Liubomirov, *Ocherk istorii nizhegorodskogo opolcheniia, 1611–1613gg.* (Moscow, 1939), pp. 146–211.

CHAPTER I: *Tsars and Tsarinas*

1 Quoted in P. G. Vasenko, *Boiare Romanovy i votsarenie Mikhaila Feodorovicha* (St. Petersburg, 1913), p. 139. See also pp. 137–38, and P. G. Vasenko, S. F. Platonov, and E. F. Turaeva-Tsereteli, *Nachalo dinastii Romanovykh: istoricheskie ocherki* (St. Petersburg, 1912), pp. 141–42.
2 Vasenko, *Boiare Romanovy*, pp. 142–52; Solov'ev, *Istoriia Rossii*, Vol. 5, pp. 9–16.
3 Quoted in Riasanovsky, *History*, p. 193.
4 Vasenko, *Boiare Romanovy*, pp. 12–56; Platonov, *Smutnoe vremia*, pp. 222–23; A. E. Presniakov, "Moskovskoe gosudarstvo pervoi poloviny XVII veka," *Tri veka*, ed., V. V. Kallash, Vol. 1 (Moscow, 1912), pp. 31–35.
5 Platonov, *Boris Godunov*, pp. 138–40; idem, *Ocherki po istorii smuty*, pp. 230–32.
6 Vasenko, *Boiare Romanovy*, pp. 61–62, 64; Platonov, *Boris Godunov*, pp. 139–40.
7 Vasenko, *Boiare Romanovy*, pp. 57–166.
8 A. A. Kizevetter, "Izbranie na tsarstvo Mikhaila Fedorovicha Romanova," *Istoricheskie otkliti* (Moscow, 1915), pp. 7–23; Platonov, *Smutnoe vremia*, pp. 222–26.
9 Presniakov, "Moskovskoe gosudarstvo pervoi poloviny XVII veka," pp. 40–43.
10 Vasenko, *Boiare Romanovy*, pp. 162–66.
11 M. V. Klochkov, *Zemskie sobory: istoricheskii ocherk* (St. Petersburg, 1914), pp. 49–57; L. V. Cherepnin, *Zemskie sobory russkogo gosudarstva v XVI–XVII vv.* (Moscow, 1978), pp. 216–39.
12 Solov'ev, *Istoriia Rossii*, Vol. 5, pp. 84–97, 112–17.
13 Vasenko, *Boiare Romanovy*, pp. 191–92.

14 M. T. Florinsky, *Russia: A History and an Interpretation*, Vol. 1 (New York, 1967), pp. 250–51; J. L. H. Keep, "The Regime of Philaret (1619–1633)," *Slavonic and East European Review (SEER)*, Vol. 38 (June 1960), pp. 334–60.

15 Aleksandr Barsukov, *Rod Sheremetevykh*, Vol. 3 (St. Petersburg, 1883), pp. 10–17.

16 Quoted in ibid., p. 10. See also Solov'ev, *Istoriia Rossii*, Vol. 5, pp. 125–26.

17 Barsukov, *Rod Sheremetevykh*, Vol. 3, pp. 27–29, 54–61.

18 V. A. Prokof'ev and A. A. Novosel'skii, "Mezhdunarodnoe polozhenie Russkogo gosudarstva v 20–30kh godakh i Smolenskaia voina 1632–1634gg.," *Ocherki istorii SSSR. Period feodalizma: XVII v.*, ed. A. A. Novosel'skii (Moscow, 1955), pp. 468–75; Solov'ev, *Istoriia Rossii*, Vol. 5, pp. 167–80.

19 Solov'ev, *Istoriia Rossii*, Vol. 5, pp. 254–55.

20 George Vernadsky, *The Tsardom of Moscow, 1547–1682*, History of Russia series, Vol. 5 (New Haven and London, 1969), pp. 379–83.

21 N. V. Ustiugov, "Russkaia kul'tura: Prosveshchenie i shkola," *Ocherki istorii SSSR*, ed. Novosel'skii, p. 561; S. F. Platonov, "Tsar Aleksei Mikhailovich (opyt kharakteristiki)," *Tri veka*, ed. Kallash, Vol. 1, p. 86.

22 Solov'ev, *Istoriia Rossii*, Vol. 6, p. 609.

23 Iakov Reitenfel's, "Skazaniia svetleishemu gertsogu Toskanskomu Kos'me Tret'emu o Moskovii," *Chteniia v obshchestve istorii i drevnostei rossiiskikh pri Imperatorskom Moskovskom universitete*, No. 3 (1905), p. 74.

24 Quoted in Ian Grey, *The Romanovs: The Rise and Fall of a Dynasty* (New York, 1970), p. 36.

25 Quoted in Cherniavsky, *Tsar and People*, p. 62.

26 I. E. Zabelin, *Domashnyi byt russkikh tsarits v XVI–XVII stoletiiakh* (Moscow, 1862), pp. 290–92.

27 Cherniavsky, *Tsar and People*, p. 63.

28 S. V. Bakhrushin, "Moskovskoe vosstanie 1648g.," *Nauchnye trudy* (Moscow, 1954), Vol. 2, pp. 61–62.

29 Solov'ev, *Istoriia Rossii*, Vol. 5, p. 481.

30 Samuel H. Baron, ed. and trans., *The Travels of Olearius in Seventeenth-Century Russia* (Stanford, 1967), p. 206.

31 Vernadsky, *Tsardom of Moscow*, Vol. 5, pp. 389–91; Bakhrushin, "Moskovskoe vosstanie," pp. 48–50.

32 Quoted in Bakhrushin, "Moskovskoe vosstanie," p. 50.

33 Baron, ed., *Travels of Olearius*, p. 208.

34 Ibid., p. 211.

35 Cherepnin, *Zemskie sobory*, pp. 275–305.

36 M. N. Tikhomirov, *Klassovaia bor'ba v Rossii XVII v.* (Moscow, 1969), pp. 23–169; B. G. Kurts, *Sostoianie Rossii v 1650–1655gg. po doneseniiam Rodesa* (Moscow, 1914), pp. 20–31, especially n. 1, pp. 23–24.

37 Augustin, Baron de Mayerberg, *Rélation d'un voyage en Moscovie*, Vol. 1 (Paris, 1858), pp. 128–29; V. Ia. Ulanov, "Finansovye reformy tsaria Alekseia Mikhailovicha i 'gil' ' 1662g.," *Tri veka*, ed. Kallash, Vol. 1, p. 187.

38 Mayerberg, *Rélation d'un voyage en Moscovie*, Vol. 2, p. 130.

39 N. V. Ustiugov, "Gosudarstvennyi stroi: finansy," *Ocherki*, p. 434.

40 Quoted in Solov'ev, *Istoriia Rossii*, Vol. 6, p. 194.

41 Ibid., pp. 195–96.

42 Quoted in ibid., p. 195.

43 Ibid., pp. 196–97.
44 Quoted in Paul Avrich, *Russian Rebels, 1600–1800* (New York, 1976), p. 59.
45 Ibid., pp. 17–47. See also I. I. Smirnov, *Vosstanie Bolotnikova, 1606–1607* (Moscow, 1951).
46 Quoted in Avrich, *Russian Rebels,* p. 69.
47 V. I. Lebedev, *Krest'ianskaia voina pod predvoditel'stvom Stepana Razina, 1667–1671gg.* (Moscow, 1955), pp. 46–54.
48 Quotes from Avrich, *Russian Rebels,* pp. 72, 81, 83.
49 Quoted in ibid., p. 87.
50 A. A. Novosel'skii, ed., *Krest'ianskaia voina pod predvoditel'stvom Stepana Razina. Sbornik dokumentov,* Vol. 2 (Moscow, 1957), p. 65.
51 Ibid., p. 78.
52 Ibid., p. 69.
53 A. A. Novosel'skii and N. S. Chaev, "Krest'ianskaia voina pod predvoditel'stvom S. T. Razina," in *Ocherki istorii SSSR,* ed. Novosel'skii, pp. 303–6.
54 Quoted in Avrich, *Russian Rebels,* pp. 109–10.
55 Ibid., pp. 112–13.
56 I. Zabelin, *Domashnyi byt russkikh tsarits v XVI–XVII st.,* pp. 375–86.
57 P. N. Miliukov, *Ocherki po istorii russkoi kul'tury,* Vol. 3 (St. Petersburg, 1901), pp. 97–98.
58 Quoted in Schakovskoy, *Fall of Eagles,* p. 127.
59 Zabelin, *Domashnyi byt,* Vol. 2, p. 302.
60 Schakovskoy, *Fall of Eagles,* p. 127.
61 B. B. Kafengauz, *Peter I i ego vremia* (Moscow, 1948), p. 8.
62 M. M. Bogoslovskii, *Petr Velikii i ego reforma* (Moscow, 1920), p. 3.
63 V. Ia. Ulanov, "XVII vek i reforma Petra Velikago," *Tri veka,* ed. Kallash, Vol. 3, p. 14.
64 Solov'ev, *Istoriia Rossii,* Vol. 7, p. 182.
65 V. Korsakov, "Tsar Feodor Alekseevich," *Russkii biograficheskii slovar'* (*RBS*), Vol. Iab–Fom (New York, 1962), pp. 249–51.
66 Ibid., pp. 250–51; N. Kostomarov, *Russkaia istoriia v zhizneopisaniiakh eia glavneishikh deiatelei,* Vol. 5 (St. Petersburg, 1893), pp. 459–60; V. Berkh, *Tsarstvovanie tsaria Feodora Alekseevicha i istoriia pervago streletskago bunta,* Vol. 1 (St. Petersburg, 1834), pp. 10–16; Solov'ev, *Istoriia Rossii,* Vol. 7, pp. 186–88.
67 Berkh, *Tsarstvovanie Feodora Alekseevicha,* Vol. 1, 18–19; Kostomarov, *Russkaia istoriia,* Vol. 5, pp. 464–65.
68 Solov'ev, *Istoriia Rossii,* Vol. 7, pp. 249–52.
69 Berkh, *Tsarstvovanie Feodora Alekseevicha,* Vol. 1, p. 99.
70 Kostomarov, *Russkaia istoriia,* Vol. 5, p. 465; Korsakov, "Tsar Feodor Alekseevich," p. 263.
71 Solov'ev, *Istoriia Rossii,* Vol. 7, pp. 197–98; Berkh, *Tsarstvovanie Feodora Alekseevicha,* Vol. 1, pp. 83–84; Korsakov, "Tsar Feodor Alekseevich," p. 263.
72 Zabelin, *Domashnyi byt,* Vol. 2, p. 272; Kostomarov, *Russkaia istoriia,* Vol. 5, pp. 466, 471–73; Solov'ev, *Istoriia Rossii,* Vol. 7, pp. 258–60.
73 Zabelin, *Domashnyi byt,* Vol. 2, pp. 271–72; Berkh, *Tsarstvovanie Feodora Alekseevicha,* Vol. 1, pp. 83–85; Schakovskoy, *Fall of Eagles,* pp. 180–81.
74 Solov'ev, *Istoriia Rossii,* Vol. 7, pp. 258–62; Bogoslovskii, *Petr Velikii,* p. 6.
75 M. P. Pogodin, *Semnadtsat' pervykh let v zhizni Imperatora Petra Velikago,*

1672–1689gg. (Moscow, 1875), pp. 28–29; M. M. Bogoslovskii, Vol. 1, *Petr I: Materialy dlía biografii,* Vol. 1 (Moscow, 1940), pp. 38–40.

76 Quoted in C. B. O'Brien, *Russian under Two Tsars, 1682–1689: The Regency of Sophia Alekseevna* (Berkeley and Los Angeles, 1952), p. 18, n. 3.

77 Ibid., pp. 18–22; Kostomarov, *Russkaia istoriia,* Vol. 5, pp. 475–97; Schakovskoy, *Fall of Eagles,* pp. 86–88, 133, 186–89.

78 Quoted in Grey, *The Romanovs,* p. 355.

79 A. A. Brückner, *Istoriia Petra Velikago,* Vol. 1 (St. Petersburg, 1882), pp. 19–27; Bogoslovskii, *Petr I,* Vol. 1, p. 40; L. Jay Oliva, *Russia in the Era of Peter the Great* (Englewood Cliffs, 1969), pp. 30–31.

80 M. D. Rabinovich, "Strel'tsy v pervoi chetverti XVIII v.," *IZ,* Vol. 58 (1956), pp. 273–395; O'Brien, *Russia under Two Tsars,* pp. 21–25.

81 Oliva, *Russia in the Era of Peter the Great,* p. 32.

82 Ian Grey, *Peter the Great: Emperor of All Russia* (Philadelphia and New York, 1960), pp. 41–42.

83 Bogoslovskii, *Petr I,* Vol. 1, pp. 42–43.

84 Solov'ev, *Istoriia Rossii,* Vol. 7, p. 270.

85 Quoted in N. Ustrialov, *Istoriia tsarstvovaniia Petra Velikago* (St. Petersburg, 1858), Vol. 1, appendix 6, p. 334.

86 Solov'ev, *Istoriia Rossii,* Vol. 7, p. 270; Bogoslovskii, *Petr I,* Vol. 1, p. 43.

87 I. A. Zheliabuzhskii, *Zapiski Ivana Afanasievicha Zheliabuzhskago s 1682 po 2 iiulia 1709* (St. Petersburg, 1840), pp. 1–3.

88 Solov'ev, *Istoriia Rossii,* Vol. 7, p. 272.

89 Quoted in Bogoslovskii, *Petr I,* Vol. 1, p. 44.

90 Quoted in Solov'ev, *Istoriia Rossii,* Vol. 7, p. 274.

91 Bogoslovskii, *Petr I,* Vol. 1, pp. 44–45.

92 Brikhner, *Istoriia,* Vol. 1, pp. 34–36; Solov'ev, *Istoriia Rossii,* Vol. 7, pp. 276–77.

93 N. Pavlov-Silvanskii, "Tsar Ioann V Alekseevich," *RBS,* Vol. Ibak–Kliu, pp. 271–72.

94 Schakovskoy, *Fall of Eagles,* pp. 248–50.

95 Quoted in Solov'ev, *Istoriia Rossii,* Vol. 7, p. 409.

CHAPTER II: *In the Eye of the Storm*

1 James H. Billington, *The Icon and the Axe: An Interpretative History of Russian Culture* (London, 1966), p. 119.

2 Ibid.

3 Ibid., pp. 121–26.

4 Baron, ed., *Travels of Olearius,* pp. 62–63.

5 V. O. Kliuchevskii, *Skazaniia inostrantsev o Moskovskom gosudarstve* (Petrograd, 1918), pp. 47–48.

6 Baron, ed., *Travels of Olearius,* pp. 57–58.

7 Ibid., pp. 58–59.

8 Quoted in Geraldine Marie Phipps, "Britons in Seventeenth-Century Russia: A Study in the Origins of Modernization" (Ph.D. diss., University of Pennsylvania, 1971), p. 379.

9 Baron, ed., *Travels of Olearius,* pp. 280–81.

10 "Donesenie Ioganna de Rodesa koroleve Khristine iz Moskvy, 20 oktiabria 1652 goda," Kurts, *Sostianie Rossii*, pp. 126–27.
11 S. F. Platonov, *Moskva i zapad* (Berlin, 1926), p. 58.
12 M. E. Duchesne, trans., *Le Domostroi: ménagier Russe du XVIe siècle* (Paris, 1910), p. 33.
13 Ibid., pp. 47, 53.
14 Platonov, *Moskva i zapad*, pp. 59–68.
15 Zabelin, *Domashnyi byt*, p. 397.
16 Ibid., pp. 421–25.
17 R. Nisbet Bain, *The First Romanovs, 1613–1725: A History of Muscovite Civilization and the Rise of Modern Russia Under Peter the Great and His Forerunners* (London, 1905), p. 27.
18 Iurii Krizhanich, *Politika* (Moscow, 1965), p. 494.
19 Baron, ed., *Travels of Olearius*, p. 143.
20 Bain, *The First Romanovs*, p. 29.
21 Baron, ed., *Travels of Olearius*, p. 144.
22 Quoted in Krizhanich, *Politika*, p. 478.
23 Baron, ed., *Travels of Olearius*, p. 139.
24 Ibid., p. 142.
25 Zabelin, *Domashnyi byt*, pp. 442–44.
26 Kurts, *Sostoianie Rossii*, pp. 126–27; S. K. Bogoiavlenskii, "Moskovskaia nemetskaia sloboda," *Izvestiia Akademiia Nauk SSSR. Seriia istorii i filosofii*, No. 3 (1947), pp. 220–32; Baron, ed., *Travels of Olearius*, pp. 278–82.
27 Pierre Pascal, *Avvakum et les débuts du raskol. La crise réligieuse au XVIIe siècle en Russie* (Paris, 1938), p. 69; Billington, *Icon and the Axe*, p. 120.
28 Quoted in Billington, *Icon and the Axe*, p. 131.
29 N. F. Kapterev, *Patriarch Nikon i Tsar Aleksei Mikhailovich* (Sergiev Posad, 1909), pp. 35–41; Billington, *Icon and the Axe*, pp. 131–32.
30 Billington, *Icon and the Axe*, p. 132.
31 Miliukov, *Ocherki po istorii russkoi kul'tury*, Vol. 2, pp. 42–44.
32 Quoted in Pascal, *Avvakum*, p. 194.
33 Vernadsky, *Tsardom of Moscow*, Vol. 5 (12), pp. 575–83.
34 Quoted in Billington, *Icon and the Axe*, p. 136.
35 Kapterev, *Patriarch Nikon*, pp. 308–93.
36 Pascal, *Avvakum*, pp. 360–402; Solov'ev, *Istoriia Rossii*, Vol. 6, pp. 282–87.
37 Pascal, *Avvakum*, p. 335.
38 Vernadsky, *Tsardom of Moscow*, Vol. 5 (2), pp. 704–6.
39 Pascal, *Avvakum*, pp. 452–63, 498–500, 545.
40 Ibid., pp. 532–33.
41 Billington, *Icon and the Axe*, p. 169. See also pp. 168–70 and Miliukov, *Ocherki po istorii russkoi kul'tury*, Vol. 3, p. 111n.
42 Quoted in Miliukov, *Ocherki po istorii russkoi kul'tury*, Vol. 3, p. 112.
43 Krizhanich, *Politika*, p. 479.
44 Lev Shchepot'ev, *Blizhnii boiarin Artamon Sergeevich Matveev kak kul'turnyi politicheskii deiatel' XVII veka* (St. Petersburg, 1906), pp. 24–27.
45 Platonov, *Moskva i zapad*, pp. 124–25; Vernadsky, *Tsardom of Moscow*, Vol. 5, p. 631; Baroness Sophie Buxhoeveden, *A Cavalier in Muscovy* (London, 1932), pp. 162–65.
46 Billington, *Icon and the Axe*, p. 147.
47 Quoted in ibid.

48 Quoted in N. K. Gudzii, *Istoriia drevnei russkoi literatury,* 6th edn. (Moscow, 1956), p. 474.
49 Miliukov, *Ocherki po istorii russkoi kul'tury,* Vol. 3, pp. 94–95; Billington, *Icon and the Axe,* p. 148.
50 Quoted in N. K. Gudzy, *History of Early Russian Literature,* 2nd edn., trans. Susan Jones (New York, 1949), pp. 507–8.
51 Duchesne, trans., *Le Domostroi,* pp. 52–54, 63–68, 72–74.
52 Quoted in Gudzy, *History,* p. 519. See also pp. 516–20, and V. Varneke, *Istoriia russkogo teatra XVII–XIX vekov* (Moscow-Leningrad, 1939), pp. 21–25.
53 Varneke, *Istoriia,* p. 20.
54 Princess Zinaida Schakovskoy, *La vie quotidienne à Moscou au XVIIe siècle* (Paris, 1963), p. 263.
55 Ibid., pp. 258–60; Schakovskoy, *Fall of Eagles,* pp. 61–63.
56 Reitenfel's, "Skazaniia," p. 93.
57 Schakovskoy, *La vie quotidienne,* pp. 257–58; idem, *Fall of Eagles,* pp. 67–69.
58 Gudzy, *History,* pp. 419–20.
59 Adrien de la Neuville, *Rélation curieuse et nouvelle de la Moscovie* (The Hague, 1699), pp. 14–16.
60 V. O. Kliuchevskii, *Kurs russkoi istorii* (Moscow, 1957), Vol. 3, pp. 352–53.
61 Miliukov, *Ocherki po istorii russkoi kul'tury,* Vol. 3, pp. 134–37; Platonov, *Moskva i zapad,* pp. 125–27; G. V. Plekhanov, *Istoriia russkoi obshchestvennoi mysli* Vol. 2 (Moscow, 1915), pp. 2–13.

CHAPTER III: *The Politics of Muscovy*

1 J. L. I. Fennell, ed. and trans., *The Correspondence between Prince A. M. Kurbsky and Tsar Ivan IV of Russia, 1564–1579* (Cambridge, 1955), p. 67.
2 Quoted in Platonov, *Moskva i zapad,* p. 58.
3 Solov'ev, *Istoriia Rossii,* Vol. 5, pp. 18–20; Cherepnin, *Zemskie sobory,* pp. 172–74.
4 Cherepnin, *Zemskie sobory,* pp. 218–19; Solov'ev, *Istoriia Rossii,* Vol. 5, pp. 21–27; Vernadsky, *Tsardom of Moscow,* Vol. 5, pp. 282–84.
5 E. V. Chistiakova, "Zavershenie bor'by s interventsiei. Organizatsiia novogo pravitel'stva," *Ocherki istorii SSSR. Period feodalizma konets XV v.–nachalo XVII v.* ed. A. N. Nasonov, L. V. Cherepnin, and A. A. Zimin (Moscow, 1955), pp. 601–2.
6 Quoted in Vernadsky, *Tsardom of Moscow,* Vol. 5, p. 287.
7 Quoted in Phipps, "Britons in Seventeenth-Century Russia," p. 104.
8 Ibid., pp. 103–7; Chistiakova, "Zavershenie bor'by s interventsiei," pp. 602–3.
9 Vernadsky, *Tsardom of Moscow,* Vol. 5, p. 290.
10 Solov'ev, *Istoriia Rossii,* Vol. 5, pp. 105–18; Vernadsky, *Tsardom of Moscow,* Vol. 5, pp. 290–91.
11 Quoted in Solov'ev, *Istoriia Rossii,* Vol. 5, p. 17.
12 R. H. Fisher, *The Russian Fur Trade, 1550–1700* (Berkeley and Los Angeles, 1943), pp. 112–14.
13 Iu. V. Got'e, *Zamoskovskii krai v XVII veke* (Moscow, 1937), pp. 157, 164.
14 Jerome Blum, *Lord and Peasant in Russia from the Ninth to the Nineteenth Century* (Princeton, 1961), p. 504.

15 Baron, ed., *Travels of Olearius*, pp. 46, 47.
16 V. G. Geiman and N. V. Ustiugov, "Manufaktura," *Ocherki istorii SSSR*, ed. Novosel'skii, pp. 92–94.
17 Prokof'ev and Novosel'skii, "Mezhdunarodnoe polozhenie Russkogo gosudarstva v 20–30kh godakh i smolenskaia voina 1632–1634gg.," *Ocherki*, pp. 468–470.
18 Quoted in Solov'ev, *Istoriia Rossii*, Vol. 5, p. 165.
19 Ibid., pp. 166–71.
20 Vernadsky, *Tsardom of Moscow*, Vol. 5, pp. 354–57.
21 A. A. Novosel'skii, *Bor'ba moskovskogo gosudarstva s tatarami v pervoi polovine XVII veka* (Moscow-Leningrad, 1948), p. 259.
22 Vernadsky, *Tsardom of Moscow*, Vol. 5, pp. 360.
23 Novosel'skii, *Bor'ba moskovskogo gosudarstva s tatarami*, pp. 286–89.
24 Cherepnin, *Zemskie sobory*, pp. 262–72; A. I. Zaozerskii, "Zemskie sobory," *Ocherki istorii SSSR*, ed. Novosel'skii, pp. 364–65; Vernadsky, *Tsardom of Moscow*, Vol. 5, pp. 366–68.
25 Quoted in Vernadsky, *Tsardom of Moscow*, Vol. 5, p. 440. See also pp. 432–40, and N. Kostomarov, "Malorossiiskii getman Zinovii-Bogdan Khmel'nitskii," in *Russkaia istoriia*, Vol. 2, pp. 236–43.
26 Billington, *Icon and the Axe*, p. 117.
27 Ibid., p. 674, n. 2.
28 Quoted in Vernadsky, *Tsardom of Moscow*, Vol. 5, p. 449.
29 Cherepnin, *Zemskie sobory*, pp. 319–27.
30 Quoted in ibid., pp. 335, 334.
31 Ibid., pp. 327–37.
32 Quoted in Vernadsky, *Tsardom of Moscow*, Vol. 5, p. 469.
33 Ibid., p. 481.
34 Billington, *Icon and the Axe*, p. 119.
35 Quoted in Solov'ev, *Istoriia Rossii*, Vol. 5, p. 627.
36 Quoted in ibid., p. 628.
37 A. N. Mal'tsev, "Pervyi etap russko-pol'skoi voiny za osvobozhdenie Ukrainy i Belorussii (1654–1656)," in *Ocherki istorii SSSR*, ed. Novosel'skii, pp. 483–86.
38 Solov'ev, *Istoriia Rossii*, Vol. 5, pp. 632–33.
39 Quoted in ibid., p. 630.
40 Vernadsky, *Tsardom of Moscow*, Vol. 5, pp. 500–502.
41 Quoted in Solov'ev, *Istoriia Rossii*, Vol. 6, p. 74.
42 Vernadsky, *Tsardom of Moscow*, Vol. 5, p. 539.
43 I. V. Galaktionov, *Iz istorii Russko-Pol'skogo sblizheniia v 50–60kh godakh XVII veka* (Saratov, 1960), pp. 85–98.
44 Quoted in Florinsky, *Russia*, Vol. 1, p. 270.
45 Vernadsky, *Tsardom of Moscow*, Vol. 5, pp. 394–411; Billington, *Icon and the Axe*, p. 119.
46 Novosel'skii, *Bor'ba moskovskogo gosudarstva s tatarami*, pp. 434–42.
47 Ibid., pp. 430–33, Riasanovsky, *History*, p. 167.
48 Novosel'skii, *Bor'ba moskovskogo gosudarstva s tatarami*, pp. 76–77, 150–59; idem, "Russko-turetskie i russko-krymskie otnosheniia v 30–40kh godakh," *Ocherki istorii SSSR*, ed., Novosel'skii, pp. 476–79.
49 Ia. E. Bodarskii, "Mezhdunarodnoe polozhenie Russkogo gosudarstva i russko-turetskaia voina 1676–1681gg.," *Ocherki istorii SSSR*, ed. Novosel'skii, pp. 521–24.

50 Ibid., pp. 525–30.
51 I. B. Grekov and A. N. Mal'tsev, "Mezhdunarodnoe polozhenie Rossii v nachale 80–kh gg., 'Vechnyi mir' 1686 g., i Krymskie pokhody 1687 i 1689gg.," *Ocherki istorii SSSR*, ed. Novosel'skii, pp. 537–41.
52 O'Brien, *Russia under Two Tsars*, pp. 136–38.
53 Ibid., pp. 138–45.

CHAPTER IV: *Eighteenth-Century Emperors and Empresses*

1 Bogoslovskii, *Petr I*, Vol. 1, pp. 18–19.
2 Quoted in Pogodin, *Semnadtsat' pervykh let*, p. 11; Bogoslovskii, *Petr I*, Vol. 1, pp. 20–21.
3 E. F. Shmurlo, "Kriticheskie zametki po istorii Petra Velikago," *Zhurnal Ministerstva Narodnago Prosveshcheniia (ZhMNP)* (August 1900), pp. 229–30; Solov'ev, *Istoriia Rossii*, Vol. 7, pp. 186–92.
4 Bogoslovskii, *Petr I*, Vol. 1, pp. 35–37.
5 Ibid., pp. 49–53.
6 Pogodin, *Semnadtsat' pervykh let*, pp. 103–4.
7 Quoted in Eugene Schuyler, *Peter the Great, Emperor of Russia: A Study of Historical Biography*, Vol. 1 (New York, 1967), p. 106.
8 S. Kniaz'kov, *Ocherki iz istorii Petra Velikago i ego vremeni* (Moscow, 1909), pp. 15–17; Kafengauz, *Petr I*, p. 10.
9 Bogoslovskii, *Petr I*, Vol. 1, pp. 60–61.
10 I. I. Golikov, *Deianiia Petra Velikago, mudrago preobrazovatelia Rossii, sobrannye iz dostovernykh istochnikov*, Vol. 6 (Moscow, 1788–91), p. 72; Knaiz'kov, *Ocherki*, pp. 17–18.
11 *History of the Russian Fleet during the Reign of Peter the Great* (London, 1899), p. xviii; Bogoslovskii, *Petr I*, Vol. 1, pp. 65–66.
12 Patrick Gordon, *Passages from the Diary of General Patrick Gordon* (New York, 1968), pp. 164–66.
13 Bogoslovskii, *Petr I*, Vol. 1, pp. 70–79.
14 Ibid., pp. 81–88; Schuyler, *Peter the Great*, Vol. 1, pp. 173–90.
15 Prince V. I. Kurakin, "Gistoriia o tsare Petre Alekseeviche, 1682–1694," *Arkhiv kniazia F. A. Kurakina*, Vol. 1 (St. Petersburg, 1890), p. 63.
16 Bogoslovskii, *Petr I*. Vol. 1, p. 93.
17 Oliva, *Russia in the Era of Peter the Great*, p. 41.
18 Alexander Gordon, *A History of Peter the Great, Emperor of Russia*, Vol. 2 (London, 1755), pp. 274–75.
19 M. I. Semevskii, *Tsaritsa Katerina Alekseevna, Anna i Villim Mons, 1692–1724. Ocherki iz russkoi istorii* (St. Petersburg, 1884), pp. 21–27.
20 V. O. Kliuchevskii, *Sochineniia*, Vol. 4 (Moscow, 1958), pp. 39–40.
21 Florinsky, *Russia*, Vol. 1, p. 319.
22 Quoted in Solov'ev, *Istoriia Rossii*, Vol. 8, p. 100.
23 Ibid., p. 102; N. B. Golikova, *Politicheskie protsessy pri Petre I* (Moscow, 1957), pp. 8–33.
24 Quoted in Grey, *Peter the Great*, p. 96.
25 Baron de Blomberg, *An Account of Livonia* (London, 1701), p. 295.
26 Florinsky, *Russia*, Vol. 1, p. 321.
27 Bogoslovskii, *Petr I*, Vol. 2, p. 386.

28 Quoted in ibid., pp. 116, 121, 118–19.
29 A. A. Brückner, *Istoriia Petra Velikago*, Vol. 1 (St. Petersburg, 1882), pp. 159–80; Bogoslovskii, *Petr I*. Vol. 2, pp. 128–268; Kliuchevskii, *Sochineniia*, Vol. 4, pp. 21–24; Solov'ev, *Istoriia Rossii*, Vol. 7, pp. 550–54; Grey, *Peter the Great*, pp. 106–13; Schuyler, *Peter the Great*, Vol. 1, pp. 287–98.
30 Grey, *Peter the Great*, p. 113.
31 John Perry, *The State of Russia Under the Present Czar* (London, 1716), pp. 164–65.
32 Bogoslovskii, *Petr I*. Vol. 2, pp. 268–389; Brückner, *Istoriia Petra Velikago*, Vol. 1, pp. 181–87; Schuyler, *Peter the Great*, Vol. 1, pp. 299–309; Grey, *Peter the Great*, pp. 114–24; Kliuchevskii, *Sochineniia*, Vol. 4, pp. 24–26; Solov'ev, *Istoriia Rossii*, Vol. 7, pp. 554–57.
33 *Pis'ma i bumagi Imperatora Petra Velikago*, Vol. 1, pp. 725–27.
34 Gordon, *Diary*, p. 187.
35 *Pis'ma i bumagi Imperatora Petra Velikago*, Vol. 1, No. 238, p. 256.
36 Gordon, *Diary*, pp. 188–92.
37 Pis'mo kniazia Romodanovskago k Petru I, 11 iiunia 1698, Ustrialov, *Istoriia tsarstvovaniia Petra Velikago*, Vol. 3, pp. 474–76.
38 Bogoslovskii, *Petr I*, Vol. 2, pp. 549–56.
39 Johann Georg Korb, *Diary of an Austrian Secretary of Legation at the Court of Czar Peter the Great*, trans. from the original Latin and ed. Count MacDonnell, Vol. 1 (London, 1863), pp. 192–93.
40 Florinsky, *Russia*, Vol. 1, pp. 335–96.
41 Quoted in Philip Longworth, *The Three Empresses: Catherine I, Anne, and Elizabeth of Russia* (London, 1972), p. 5.
42 V. Andreev, "Ekaterina Pervaia," *Osmnadtsatyi vek*, ed. P. Bartenev, Vol. 3 (Moscow, 1869), pp. 1–4; Schuyler, *Peter the Great*, Vol. 1, pp. 435–37; Grey, *Peter the Great*, pp. 197–99; Solov'ev, *Istoriia Rossii*, Vol. 8, pp. 370–72.
43 Pis'mo Petra I k Gosudaryne Ekaterine Alekseevne i Anis'e Kirillovne Tolstoi, 20 marta 1708g., *Pis'ma russkikh gosudarei i drugikh osob tsarskago semeistva*, Vol. 1 (Moscow, 1861), p. 5; V. Andreev, "Ekaterina Pervaia," Vol. 3, pp. 5–9; Schuyler, *Peter the Great*, Vol. 1, pp. 437–41; Grey, *Peter the Great*, pp. 200–202; Longworth, *Three Empresses*, pp. 15–20.
44 Pis'mo Petra I k Gosudaryne Ekaterine Alekseevne, 27 iiunia 1709, *Pis'ma russkikh gosudarei*, Vol. 1, pp. 8–9.
45 Solov'ev *Istoriia Rossii*, Vol. 8, pp. 272–77; Brückner *Istoriia Petra Velikago*, Vol. 2, pp. 456–61; Kniaz'kov, *Ocherki*, 99–104; Grey, *Peter the Great*, pp. 296–305.
46 *Pis'ma i bumagi Imperatora Petra Velikago*, Vol. 9, Bk. 1, No. 3259, p. 231.
47 See, for example, Pis'mo Petra I k Gosudaryne Ekaterine Alekseevne, 2 avgusta 1712, *Pis'ma russkikh gosudarei*, Vol. 1, p. 21.
48 Pis'mo Petra I k Gosudaryne Ekaterine Alekseevne, 23 maia 1716, Vol. 7, p. 45.
49 Golikov, *Deianiia*, Vol. 6, 54–55.
50 Solov'ev, *Istoriia Rossii*, Vol. 9, 105–30; Brückner, Istoriia Petra Velikago, Vol. 2, pp. 329–44; Grey, *Peter the Great*, pp. 348–54.
51 Ustrialov, *Istoriia*, Vol. 6, prilozhenie 46, pp. 346–48.
52 Quoted in Solov'ev, *Istoriia Rossii*, Vol. 9, p. 143.
53 Ustrialov, *Istoriia*, Vol. 6, prilozhenie 48, pp. 349–50.

54 Quoted in Solov'ev, *Istoriia Rossii*, Vol. 9, p 145.
55 Ustrialov, *Istoriia*, Vol. 6, prilozhenie 48, p. 350.
56 Ibid., prilozhenie 52, p. 351.
57 Ibid., prilozhenie 200, p. 586.
58 Ibid., Vol. 6, p. 87.
59 Ibid., prilozhenie 92, p. 389.
60 Quoted in Solov'ev, *Istoriia Rossii*, Vol. 9, p. 168.
61 Ibid., p. 188.
62 Bogoslovskii, *Petr Velikii*, p. 116.
63 Golikov, *Deianiia*, Vol. 9, p. 296.
64 Quoted in Solov'ev, *Istoriia Rossii*, Vol. 9, p. 311.
65 Oliva, *Russia in the Era of Peter the Great*, pp. 75–77.
66 Quoted in Solov'ev, *Istoriia Rossii*, Vol. 9, p. 321.
67 Quoted in Miliukov, *Ocherki po istoriia russkoi kul'tury*, Vol. 3, p. 248.
68 Quoted in Solov'ev, *Istoriia Rossi*, Vol. 9, p. 558.
69 Quoted in ibid.
70 *Polnoe sobranie zakonov rossiiskoi imperii* (PSZ), sobranie 1–oe, No. 4650; P. N. Miliukov, *Gosudarstvennoe khoziaistvo v pervoi chetverti XVIII stoletiia i reforma Petra Velikago* (St. Petersburg, 1892), prilozhenie 4, pp. 141–52; Solov'ev, *Istoriia Rossii*, Vol. 9, p. 570.
71 *PSZ*, sobranie 1–oe, No. 4830.
72 Solov'ev, *Istoriia Rossii*, Vol. 10, pp. 71–74; Florinsky, *Russia*, Vol. 1, pp. 437–38.
73 Solov'ev, *Istoriia Rossii*, Vol. 10, pp. 76–80.
74 C. H. von Manstein, *Contemporary Memoirs of Russia from the Year 1727 to 1744* (New York, 1968), p. 7.
75 Solov'ev, *Istoriia Rossii*, Vol. 10, p. 85.
76 Duke de Liria, "Pis'ma o Rossii v Ispaniiu," *Osmnadtsatyi vek* (Moscow, 1869), Vol. 2, pp. 32–34.
77 Quoted in Manstein, *Memoirs*, p. 8.
78 Solov'ev, *Istoriia Rossii*, Vol. 10, p. 112.
79 "Diplomaticheskie dokumenty, otnosiashchiesia k istorii Rossii v XVIII st.," *Sbornik Imperatorskago Russkago Istoricheskago Obschchestva* (SIRIO), Vol. 3 (1868): 490–91; "Zhurnaly Verkhovnago Tainago Soveta," *SIRIO* Vol. 69: p. 270; *PSZ*, sobranie 1–oe, Nos. 5151, 5152.
80 "Pis'ma Feofana Prokopovicha," *Trudy Kievskoi dukhovnoi akademii*, Vol. 1 (1865), p. 599.
81 Quoted in Solov'ev, *Istoriia Rossii*, Vol. 10, p. 120.
82 Quoted in ibid., p. 141.
83 T. T. Rice, *Elizabeth, Empress of Russia* (London, 1970), pp. 26–27.
84 De Liria, "Pis'ma o Rossii," Vol. 2, p. 36.
85 Ibid., pp. 32, 31.
86 Solov'ev, *Istoriia Rossii*, Vol. 10, pp. 147–48.
87 "Diplomaticheskaia perepiska frantsuzskikh predstavitelei pri russkom dvore, 1681–1772gg," (Dispatches of 23 September 1728 and 23 August 1731), *SIRIO* Vol. 75 (1891), p. 240; *SIRIO* Vol. 81 (1892), p. 235.
88 De Liria, "Pis'ma o Rossii," Vol. 2, p. 181.
89 Manstein, *Memoirs*, p. 22.
90 Quoted by the French Ambassador Magnan in his dispatch of 8 December 1729, "Diplomaticheskaia perepiska," *SIRIO* Vol. 75 (1891), p. 429.

91 Manstein, *Memoirs,* pp. 28–29.
92 D. A. Korsakov, *Votsarenie Imperatritsy Anny Ioannovny* (Kazan, 1880), pp. 3–4.
93 Florinsky, *Russia,* Vol. 1, p. 441.
94 Korsakov, *Votsarenie,* pp. 71, 68–69.
95 Korsakov, *Votsarenie,* prilozhenie 1, pp. 17–18. For an English translation of these "Conditions" and a number of other relevant documents, see Marc Raeff, ed., *Plans for Political Reform in Imperial Russia, 1730–1905* (Englewood Cliffs, N.J., 1966), pp. 41–52.
96 Korsakov, *Votsarenie,* pp. 146–239, and prilozhenie 3, pp. 20–55; P. N. Miliukov, *Iz istorii russkoi intelligentsii* (St. Petersburg, 1903), pp. 26–49; M. M. bogoslovskii, *Konstitutsionnoe dvizhenie 1730g.* (Petrograd, 1918), pp. 12–36.
97 Korsakov, *Votsarenie,* pp. 243–45.
98 Ibid., pp. 265–66.
99 Quoted in ibid., p. 275.
100 Quoted in Solov'ev, *Istoriia,* 10, p. 220.
101 Quoted in Korsakov, *Votsarenie,* p. 276.
102 Manstein, *Memoirs,* p. 35.
103 Kliuchevskii, *Sochineniia,* Vol. 4, p. 294.
104 N. Kostomarov, *Russkaia istoriia v zhizneopisaniiakh eia glavneishikh deiatelei,* pp. 142–144.
105 Quoted in ibid., pp. 144–45.
106 Count Ernst Münnich, *Rossiia i Russkii dvor v pervoi polovine XVIII veka. Zapiski i zamechaniia Gr. Ernsta Minikha* (St. Petersburg, 1891), pp. 168–69.
107 Quoted in Kostomarov, *Russkaia istoriia,* p. 143.
108 Quoted in Mina Curtiss, *A Forgotten Empress: Anna Ivanovna and Her Era, 1730–1740* (New York, 1974), pp. 53, 52. See also p. 119.
109 Manstein, *Memoirs,* p. 45.
110 Münnich, *Rossiia i Russkii dvor,* p. 27.
111 Quoted in Manstein, *Memoirs,* p. 45.
112 Münnich, *Rossiia i Russkii dvor,* p. 165.
113 "Doneseniia i drugiia bumagi angliiskikh poslov, poslannikov, i rezidentov pri russkom dvore s 1728 po 1733 goda," *SIRIO* Vol. 66 (1889), 273–509.
114 Dispatches of Edward Finch to Lord Harrington, 7, 11, and 18 October 1740, in "Donesenie," *SIRIO* Vol. 85 (1893), pp. 231–33, 239–40; Marquis de la Chétardie, *Markiz de-la-Shetardi v Rossii 1740–1742 godov. Perevod rukopisnykh depesh frantsuzskago posol'stva v Peterburge* (St. Petersburg, 1862), pp. 111–34; Münnich, *Rossiia i Russkii dvor,* pp. 84–91.
115 Dispatch of Edward Finch to Lord Harrington, 11 October 1740, in "Donesenie," *SIRIO* Vol. 85 (1893), p. 236.
116 Manstein, *Memoirs,* pp. 275–82; Münnich, *Rossiia i Russkii dvor,* pp. 103–8.
117 Dispatch of Edward Finch to Lord Harrington, 11 November 1740, in "Donesenie," *SIRIO* Vol. 85 (1893), p. 371.
118 Münnich, *Rossiia i Russkii dvor,* pp. 108–9; Dispatch of Edward Finch to Lord Harrington, 11 November 1740, in "Donesenie," *SIRIO* Vol. 85 (1893), pp. 370–81.
119 Manstein, *Memoirs,* p. 296.

120 Dispatch of Edward Finch to Lord Harrington, 2 June 1741, in "Donesenie," *SIRIO* Vol. 91 (1894), p. 110.
121 Manstein, *Memoirs,* pp. 89, 296–97; de la Chétardie, *Markiz de-la-Shetardi v Rossii,* pp. 271–80.
122 Manstein, *Memoirs,* p. 318.
123 Quoted in Aleksandr Veidemeier, *Obzor glavneishikh proisshestvii v Rossii s konchiny Petra Velikago do vstupleniia na prestol Elizavety Petrovny* (St. Petersburg, 1831), Vol. 2, p. 160. See also Kostomarov, *Russkaia istoriia,* Vol. 2, p. 227; Manstein, *Memoirs,* pp. 318–21.
124 Quoted in Kostomarov, *Russkaia istoriia,* Vol. 2, p. 224.
125 De Liria, "Pis'ma o Rossii," Vol. 2, p. 113.
126 *Ibid.,* p. 151.
127 Edward Finch to Lord Harrington, 2 June 1741, in "Donesenie," *SIRIO* Vol. 91 (1894), p. 97.
128 Florinsky, *Russia,* Vol. 1, p. 452.
129 "Her household is short of everything, even such necessities as salt," reported the Saxon Ambassador J. L. Lefort at the beginning of 1730. Dispatch of 2 January, 1730, "Diplomaticheskie dokumenty otnosiashchikhsia k istorii Rossii v XVIII stoletii," *SIRIO* Vol. 5 (1870), pp. 338–39.
130 Rice, *Elizabeth, Empress of Russia,* p. 90.
131 Catherine II, *Mémoires de l'Impératrice Catherine II,* ed. Alexander Herzen (London, 1859), pp. 148–49.
132 Solov'ev, *Istoriia Rossii* Vol. 11, p. 99.
133 Catherine II, *Mémoires de l'Impératrice Catherine II,* pp. 328–29.
134 *Ibid.,* p. 187; J. H. Castera, *Life of Catherine the Great* (London, 1800), Vol. 1, pp. 53–54; Zoe Oldenburg, *Catherine the Great* (New York, 1965), pp. 132–142; Ian Grey, *Catherine the Great* (New York, 1962), pp. 53–54; Daria Olivier, *Elisabeth de Russie* (Paris, 1962), pp. 272–76.
135 Solov'ev, *Istoriia Rossii,* Vol., pp. 162–63.
136 *Ibid.,* pp. 233–39; Manstein, *Memoirs,* pp. 401–2; Rice, *Elizabeth, Empress of Russia,* pp. 79–84; Florinsky, *Russia,* Vol. 1, pp. 453, 470–71.
137 Kostomarov, *Russkaia istoriia,* Vol. 2, p. 247; Solov'ev, *Istoriia Rossii,* Vol. 11, 271–73.
138 P. K. Alefirenko, *Krest'ianskoe dvizhenie i krest'ianskii vopros v Rossii v 30–50kh godakh XVIII veka* (Moscow, 1958), p. 95.
139 *Ibid.,* pp. 137–52.
140 Florinsky, *Russia,* Vol. 1, p. 488.
141 Rice, *Elizabeth, Empress of Russia,* p. 111.
142 Solov'ev, *Istoriia Rossii,* Vol. 12, p. 340.
143 A. Veidemeier, *Tsarstvovanie Elizavety Petrovny* (St. Petersburg, 1834), pp. 107, 112; Rice, *Elizabeth, Empress of Russia,* p. 195.
144 Ia. P. Shakhovskoi, *Zapiski kniazia Iakova Petrovicha Shakhovskago* (St. Petersburg, 1872), pp. 163, 174; Solov'ev, *Istoriia Rossii,* Vol. 12, pp. 635–40.
145 Quoted in M. Semevskii, "Shest' mesiatsev iz russkoi istorii XVIII veka. Ocherk tsarstvovaniia Imperatora Petra III, 1761–1762," *OZ,* Vol. 173, p. 161.
146 Princess Catherine Dashkov, *Memoirs of Princess Dashkov* (London, 1958), p. 45.
147 Semevskii, "Shest' mesiatsev iz russkoi istorii," pp. 161–63.

148 Dashkov, *Memoirs*, pp. 49–50.
149 Semevskii, "Shest' mesiatsev iz russkoi istorii," p. 165.
150 "Ekstrakt iz zhurnala uchebnykh zaniatii velikago kniazia Petra Feodoro-vicha s iiunia 1742 po 1745 gg.," *Chteniia* (1866), Bk. 4, pp. 112–15.
151 Semevskii, "Shest' mesiatsev iz russkoi istorii," p. 168.
152 Catherine II, *Memoirs of Catherine the Great*, trans. Katherine Anthony (New York, 1935), pp. 123–24.
153 Andrei Bolotov, *Zhizn' i prikliucheniia Andreia Bolotova opisannye samim im dlia svoikh potomkov* (Moscow-Leningrad, 1931), Vol. 2, p. 117.
154 Quoted in Catherine II, *Memoirs of Catherine the Great*, p. 137.
155 Semevskii, "Shest' mesiatsev iz russkoi istorii," p. 592.
156 Dashkov, *Memoirs*, p. 67.
157 Florinsky, *Russia*, Vol. 1, p. 497.
158 Ibid., p. 499.
159 V. A. Bilbassov, *Istoriia Ekateriny Vtoroi* (Berlin, 1900), Vol. 1, pp. 426–27; Solov'ev, Istoriia Rossii, Vol. 13, pp. 68–69.
160 Bolotov, *Zhizn' i prikliucheniia*, Vol. 2, p. 105.
161 A. V. Khrapovitskii, *Dnevnik A. V. Khrapovitskago, 1782–1793* (St. Petersburg, 1874), p. 481.
162 Catherine II, *Memoirs of Catherine the Great*, pp. 3–14, 71.
163 Florinsky, *Russia*, Vol. 1, p. 503, 507.
164 Catherine II, *Memoirs of Catherine the Great*, p. 124.
165 Catherine II to Melchior Grimm, 1 October 1778. Quoted in *Memoirs of Catherine the Great*, p. 162.
166 *Perevorot 1762 goda* (Moscow, 1908), pp. 32–39.
167 Bolotov, *Zhizn' i prikliucheniia*, Vol. 2, p. 115.
168 Bilbassov, *Istoriia Ekateriny Vtoroi*, Vol. 2, p. 16.
169 Dashkov, *Memoirs*, pp. 69–71; Bilbassov, *Istoriia Ekateriny Vtoroi*, Vol. 2, pp. 17–19.
170 Bilbassov, *Istoriia Ekateriny Vtoroi*, Vol. 2, pp. 20–27.
171 Ibid., pp. 39–47.
172 Ibid., pp. 48–51; *Perevorot 1762 goda*, pp. 55–63.
173 Bilbassov, *Istoriia Ekateriny Vtoroi*, Vol. 2, pp. 53–58.
174 Ibid., pp. 58–67; *Perevorot 1762 goda*, pp. 65–66.
175 Quoted in Bilbassov, *Istoriia Ekateriny Vtoroi*, Vol. 2, p. 123.
176 *Arkhiv kn. Vorontsovykh*, Vol. 21, p. 430.
177 Bilbassov, *Istoriia Ekateriny Vtoroi*, Vol. 2, pp. 461–69.
178 "Manifesto po povodu vosshestviia na prestol Imperatritsy Ekateriny II," *Osmnadtsatyi vek*, Vol. 4, p. 224.
179 Lettre du Roi au Baron de Breteuil, 10 septembre 1762, "Diplo-maticheskaia perepiska frantsuzskikh predstavitelei pri dvore Impera-tritsy Ekateriny II," *SIRIO* Vol. 140 (1912), p. 57.
180 Bilbassov, *Istoriia Ekateriny Vtoroi*, Vol. 2, pp. 296–341.
181 Ibid., pp. 145–46, 150.
182 Ibid., pp. 150–52.
183 "Sobstvennoruchnye raspisaniia Ekateriny II o nagradakh po sluchaiu vozshestviia eia na prestol i koronatsii," *SIRIO* Vol. 7 (1871), pp. 111–14.
184 Quoted in Florinsky, *Russia*, Vol. 1, p. 505.
185 N. D. Chechulin, ed., *Nakaz Imperatritsy Ekateriny II, dannyi kommissii o sochinenii proekta novago ulozheniia* (St. Petersburg, 1907), pp. 2–4.

186 Pis'mo Ekateriny II k D'Alemberu s predlozheniem priekhat' v Peterburg i zaniat'sia vospitaniem Velikago Kniazia Pavla Petrovicha, 13 noiabria 1762g., *SIRIO* Vol. 7 (1871), p. 179.

187 A. J. Q. Beuchot, ed., *Oeuvres complètes de Voltaire* (Paris, 1832), Vol. 59, pp. 110, 137.

188 Ibid., Vol. 62, p. 311.

189 Kliuchevskii, *Sochineniia*, Vol. 5, p. 75.

190 Chechulin, ed., *Nakaz Imperatritsy Ekateriny II*, pp. cxxix–cxlvii.

191 Quoted in Kliuchevskii, *Sochineniia*, Vol. 5, p. 77.

192 Henry Shirley to the Right Honourable Lord Viscount Weymouth, 28 February 1768, "Diplomaticheskaia perepiska angliiskikh poslannikov pri Russkom dvore," *SIRIO* Vol. 12 (1873), pp. 326–27.

193 Paul Dukes, *Catherine the Great and the Russian Nobility* (Cambridge, 1967), pp. 91–210; Miliukov, *Ocherki po istorii russkoi kul'tury*, Vol. 2, pp. 265–66.

194 Shirley to Viscount Weymouth, 28 February 1768, *SIRIO* Vol. 12 (1873), p. 330.

195 Quoted in Ivanov-Razumnik, *Istoriia russkoi obshchestvennoi mysli: Individualizm i meshchanstvo v russkoi literature i zhizni XIX v.*, Vol. 1 (St. Petersburg, 1908), p. 27.

196 Quoted in W. F. Reddaway, ed., *Documents of Catherine the Great* (Cambridge, 1931), p. 114.

197 Chechulin, ed., *Nakaz Imperatritsy Ekateriny II*, p. 142, article 523.

198 V. O. Kliuchevskii, *A History of Russia*, trans. C. J. Hogarth, Vol. 5 (New York, 1961), p. 45.

199 Chechulin, ed. *Nakaz Imperatritsy Ekateriny II*, p. 3.

200 P. I. Rychkov, *Topografiia Orenburgskaia, to est' obstoiatel'noe opisanie Orenburgskoi gubernii* (St. Petersburg, 1762), pp. 70–93.

201 N. F. Dubrovin, *Pugachev i ego soobshchenniki*, Vol. 1 (St. Petersburg, 1884), pp. 250–53.

202 B. A. Rybakov, ed., *Istoriia SSSR s drevneishikh vremen do nashikh dnei*, Vol. 3 (Moscow, 1967), pp. 466–67; J. T. Alexander, *Autocratic Politics in a National Crisis: The Imperial Russian Government and Pugachev's Revolt, 1773–1775* (Bloomington, 1969), pp. 57–58.

203 Dubrovin, *Pugachev i ego soobshchenniki*, Vol. 1, pp. 67–102.

204 S. A. Golubtsov, ed., *Pugachevshchina*, Vol. 1 (Moscow-Leningrad, 1926), p. 25; Rybakov, ed. *Istoriia SSSR*, Vol. 3, pp. 469–70.

205 Rybakov, ed., *Istoriia SSSR*, Vol. 3, p. 470.

206 "Nastavlenie, dannoe grafu Petru Rumiantsevu, pri naznachenii ego Malorossiiskim general-gubernatorom, s sobstvennoruchnymi pribavkami Ekateriny II, noiabr' 1764 goda," *SIRIO* Vol. 7 (1871), p. 382.

207 Quoted in Grey, *The Romanovs*, p. 201; Florinsky, *Russia*, Vol. 1, p. 590.

208 Quoted in Alexander, *Autocratic Politics*, p. 8.

209 Dubrovin, *Pugachev i ego soobshchenniki*, Vol. 2, pp. 170–73; A. A. Bibikov, *Zapiski o zhizni i sluzhbe Aleksandra Il'icha Bibikova* (Moscow, 1865), *passim*.

210 Pis'mo A. I. Bibikova grafu Z. G. Chernyshevu, 30 dekabria 1773g., in A. S. Pushkin, *Polnoe sobranie sochinenii*, Vol 8 (Moscow, 1965), p. 565.

211 Dubrovin, *Pugachev i ego soobshchenniki*, Vol. 2, pp. 258–397.

212 Rybakov, ed., *Istoriia SSSR*, Vol. 3, pp. 479–81.

213 Bolotov, *Zhizn' i prikliucheniia*, Vol. 3, p. 192.

214 Marie-Daniel Bourrée, Chevalier de Corberon, *Un diplomat français à la*

cour de Catherine II, 1775–1780. Journal intime de Chevalier de Corberon. With an introduction and notes by L.-H. Labande, Vol. 1 (Paris, 1901), p. 93.

215 Quoted in D. M. Lang, *The First Russian Radical: Alexander Radishchev, 1749–1802* (London, 1959), p. 87.

216 *Virginia Gazette*, 16 June 1774.

217 "Sobstvennoruchnoe pis'mo Imperatritsy Ekateriny II grafu P. I. Paninu, 30 oktiabria 1774g.," *SIRIO* Vol. 6 (1871), p. 154.

218 A. Loviagin, "Grigorii Alesksandrovich Potemkin," *RBS*, Vol. 14, pp. 649–50; Bil'bassov, *Istoriia Ekateriny Vtoroi*, Vol. 2, pp. 66, 115, 464, 468.

219 Quotes from Loviagin, "Grigorii Aleksandrovich Potemkin," pp. 651–52.

220 Catherine to Potemkin, 1774, in *Memoirs of Catherine the Great*, p. 324.

221 Khrapovitskii, *Dnevnik*, p. 561.

222 George Soloveytchik, *Potemkin: Soldier, Statesman, Lover and Consort of Catherine of Russia* (New York, 1947), pp. 71–75.

223 Loviagin, "Grigorii Aleksandrovich Potemkin," pp. 653–54.

224 Pis'mo Imperatritsy Ekateriny II k Grimmu, 14 iiulia 1774g., *SIRIO* Vol. 23 (1878), p. 4.

225 Catherine II, *Memoirs of Catherine the Great*, p. 329.

226 Quoted in Grey, *The Romanovs*, p. 209.

227 Charles François Philibert Masson, *Secret Memoirs of the Court of Petersburg* (New York, 1970), p. 84.

228 Count Louis Philippe de Ségur, *Memoirs and Recollections of Count Ségur, Ambassador from France to the Courts of Russia and Prussia, Written by Himself* Vol. III (London, 1825), pp. 91, 108.

229 Soloveytchik, *Potemkin*, p. 286.

230 De Ségur, *Memoirs*, Vol. 3, pp. 148–49.

231 Ibid., pp. 116–18.

232 Quoted in Loviagin, "Grigorii Aleksandrovich Potemkin," p. 657.

233 Khrapovitskii, *Dnenik*, pp. 377–78.

234 Pis'mo Imperatritsy Ekateriny II k Grimmu, 13 oktiabria 1791g., *SIRIO* Vol. 23 (1878), p. 561.

235 Krapovitskii, *Dnevnik*, p. 378.

236 Masson, *Secret Memoirs*, p. 83; Khrapovitskii, *Dnevnik*, p. 503.

237 Masson, *Secret Memoirs*, p. 35; Charles Mazade, ed., *Mémoires du Prince Adam Czartoryski et correspondance avec l'Empereur Alexandre Ier* (Paris, 1887), Vol. 1, p. 124.

238 Khrapovitskii, *Dnevnik*, pp. 297, 312; Masson, *Secret Memoirs*, p. 84; K. Kudriashov, "Platon Aleksandrovich Zubov," *RBS*, Vol. 7, pp. 526–27.

239 Masson, *Secret Memoirs*, p. 84.

240 Mazade, ed., *Mémoires du Prince Adam Czartoryski*, Vol. 1, p. 72.

241 Kudriashov, "Platon Aleksandrovich Zubov," pp. 526–33.

242 A. M. Gribovskii, *Vospominaniia A. M. Gribovskago* (Moscow, 1898), p. 39; Florinsky, *Russia*, Vol. 1, p. 541.

243 Mazade, ed., *Mémoires du Prince Adam Czartoryski*, Vol. 1, pp. 124–25; Masson, *Secret Memoirs*, pp. 34–39.

CHAPTER V: *An Imperial City in the Making*

1   Avrahm Yarmolinsky, ed., *The Poems, Prose and Plays of Alexander Pushkin* (New York, 1936), pp. 95–96.
2   Friedrich Christian Weber, *The Present State of Russia* (New York, 1968), Vol. 1, p. 300.
3   A. V. Predtechenskii, "Osnovanie Peterburga," in *Peterburg petrovskogo vremeni*, ed. A. V. Predtechenskii (Leningrad, 1948), pp. 15–18; P. N. Stolpianskii, *Kak voznik, osnovalsia, i ros Sanktpiterburkh* (Petrograd, 1918), pp. 7–9.
4   Karl Baedeker, *Russia with Tehran, Port Arthur, and Peking: A Handbook for Travellers* (London, Leipzig, and New York, 1914), p. 102. Baedeker's italics.
5   Quoted in Predtechenskii, "Osnovanie Peterburga," p. 24.
6   *Pis'ma i bumagi Imperatora Petra Velikago*, Vol. 3, p. 162.
7   Schuyler, *Peter the Great*, Vol. 2, p. 6.
8   Quoted in ibid.
9   *Pis'ma i bumagi Imperatora Petra Velikago*, Vol. 9, Bk. 1, No. 3259, p. 231.
10 Predtechenskii, "Osnovanie Peterburga," p. 36.
11 I. A. Egorov, *The Architectural Planning of St. Petersburg*, trans. Eric Dluhosch (Athens, Ohio, 1969), pp. 7–9; A. I. Gegello and V. F. Shilkov, "Arkhitektura i planirovka Peterburga do 60-kh godov XVII v.," *Ocherki istorii Leningrada*, ed. M. P. Viatkin, Vol. 1, (Moscow-Leningrad, 1955), pp. 116–17.
12 Weber, *The Present State of Russia*, Vol. 1, pp. 4, 307, 302.
13 I. E. Grabar, "Osnovanie i nachalo zastroiki Peterburga," *Istoriia russkogo iskusstva (IRI)*, ed. I. E. Grabar, Vol. 5, (Moscow, 1960), pp. 71–73; T. T. Rice, "The Conflux of Influences in Eighteenth-century Russian Art and Architecture: A Journey from the Spiritual to the Realistic," *The Eighteenth Century in Russia*, ed. J. E. Garrard (Oxford, 1973), pp. 270–71.
14 V. F. Shilkov, "Arkhitektory-inostrantsy pri Petre I," in *IRI*, Vol. 5, pp. 84–96; Rice, "The Conflux of Influences," pp. 272–74.
15 Egorov, *Architectural Planning of St. Petersburg*, pp. 11–26.
16 Mrs. William Vigor, *Letters from a Lady Who Resided Some Years in Russia* (London, 1777), pp. 3–4.
17 V. F. Shilkov, "Arkhitektory-inostrantsy," pp. 92–94.
18 Weber, *The Present State of Russia*, Vol. 1, pp. 151, 191.
19 P. N. Petrov, *Istoriia Sankt-Peterburga* (St. Petersburg, 1885), p. 57, and appendix, p. 29. See also Arcadius Kahan, "Continuity in Economic Activity and Policy during the Post-Petrine Period in Russia," *The Structure of Russian History: Interpretive Essays*, ed. Michael Cherniavsky (New York, 1970), p. 204.
20 G. E. Kochin, "Naselenie Peterburga do 60-kh godov XVIII v.," *Ocherki istorii Leningrada*, ed. Viatkin, Vol. 1, p. 96; *PSZ*, sobranie 1-oe, No. 2817.
21 *Gorodskie poseleniia v Rossiiskoi Imperii* (St. Petersburg, 1864), Vol. 7, p. xxix.
22 Peter's housing regulations for nobles in 1719 are printed in ibid., pp. 6–7.
23 Kochin, "Naselenie Peterburga do 60-kh godov XVIII v.," p. 103.
24 A. I. Kopanev, "Naselenie Peterburga ot kontsa XVIII v. do 1861g.," *Ocherki istorii Leningrada*, ed. Viatkin, Vol. 1, p. 507.

25 De Ségur, *Memoirs and Recollections,* Vol. 2, p. 181.
26 Kostomarov, *Russkaia istoriia,* Vol. 7, p. 143.
27 B. R. Wipper, "V. V. Rastrelli," *IRI,* Vol. 5, pp. 174–179; D. Arkin, *Rastrelli* (Moscow, 1954), pp. 10–16.
28 Vigor, *Letters from a Lady,* pp. 94–95.
29 Gegello and Shilkov, "Arkhitektura i planirovka Peterburga," p. 138; Egorov, *Architectural Planning of St. Petersburg,* pp. 29–30.
30 S. S. Bronshtein, "Peterburgskaia arkhitetektura 20–30 kh godov XVIII veka," in *IRI,* Vol. 5, pp. 136–37.
31 Egorov, *Architectural Planning of St. Petersburg,* pp. 31–40; Bronshtein, "Peterburgskaia arkitektura," pp. 137–42.
32. N. A. Evsina, *Arkhitekturnaia teoriia v Rossii XVIII v.* (Moscow, 1975), pp. 77–93.
33 Bronshtein, "Peterburgskaia arkhitektura," p. 150.
34 Quoted in P. N. Miliukov, *Ocherki po istorii russkoi kul'tury* (Paris, 1930), Vol. 3, p. 361.
35 Quoted in Miliukov, *Ocherki po istorii russkoi kul'tury,* Vol. 3, p. 206. See also Kliuchevskii, *Sochineniia,* Vol. 5, pp. 164–65.
36 Dispatch of Edward Finch to the Right Honourable Lord Harrington, 2 June, 1741, *SIRIO,* Vol. 91 (1894), pp. 107–8.
37 Miliukov, *Ocherki po istorii russkoi kul'tury,* Vol. 3, pp. 189–90.
38 Rice, "The Conflux of Influences," pp. 279–80.
39 Wipper, "Rastrelli," pp. 199–200; Rice, *Elizabeth, Empress of Russia,* p. 183.
40 Arkin, *Rastrelli,* pp. 36–38.
41 Wipper, "Rastrelli," pp. 191–96; Arkin, *Rastrelli,* pp. 17–26.
42 Quoted in Wipper, "Rastrelli," p. 198.
43 A. N. Petrov, *Pushkin: Dvortsy i parki* (Moscow-Leningrad, 1964), pp. 32–35.
44. Ibid., p. 60.
45 Rice, *Elizabeth, Empress of Russia,* p. 184.
46 Quoted in Wipper, "Rastrelli," p. 202.
47 Rice, *Elizabeth, Empress of Russia,* p. 187; Arkin, *Rastrelli,* p. 46.
48 Arkin, *Rastrelli,* pp. 82–84; Z. Batkowski, *Architekt Rastrelli o swoich praçach* (Lwów, 1939), pp. 64–66.
49 A. N. Petrov, "K voprosu o zodchikh-stroitelaikh Anichkova dvortsa," *Nauchnye soobshcheniia gosudarstvennoi inspektsii po okhrane pamiatnikov Leningrada* (Leningrad, 1959), pp. 22–40; idem, "S. I. Chevakinskii i drugie peterburgskie mastera," *IRI,* Vol. 5, pp. 209–43.
50 Heinrich Storch, *The Picture of Petersburg* (London, 1801), pp. 9–10.
51 De Ségur, *Memoirs and Recollections,* Vol. 2, p. 182.
52 Rice, "The Conflux of Influences," p. 285.
53 Bolotov, *Zhizn' i prikliucheniia,* Vol. 1, pp. 136–37.
54 Storch, *Picture of Petersburg,* pp. 287–90.
55 A. N. Petrov, S. A. Zombe, and T. M. Sitina, "Gradostroitel'stvo," in *IRI,* Vol. 6, pp. 243–46; Egorov, *Architectural Planning of St. Petersburg,* pp. 54–59.
56 I. E. Grabar, S. S. Bronshtein, and G. G. Grimm, "U istokov russkogo klassitsizma," *IRI,* Vol. 6, 68–70; D. A. Kuchariants, *Antonio Rinaldi* (Leningrad, 1976), pp. 9–10; Louis Hautecoeur, *L'Architecture classique à Saint-Pétersbourg à la fin du XVIIIe siècle* (Paris, 1912), pp. 24–25.

57 Kuchariants, *Antonio Rinaldi,* p. 26.
58 Quoted in Egorov, *Architectural Planning of St. Petersburg,* p. 43.
59 Storch, *Picture of Petersburg,* pp. 25–26.
60 I. E. Grabar and G. G. Gun'kin, "V. I. Bazhenov"; M. A. Il'in, "M. F. Kazakov"; A. N. Petrov, "I. E. Starov"; and G. G. Grimm and A. N. Petrov, "Peterburgskie zodchie poslednei chetverty XVIII veka," *IRI,* Vol. 6, pp. 85–235.
61 Quoted in Curtiss, *A Forgotten Empress,* p. 126.
62 Weber, *The Present State of Russia,* Vol. 1, p. 308.
63 Storch, *Picture of Petersburg,* pp. 431–32.
64 Rice, "The Conflux of Influences," p. 283.
65 Stolpianskii, *Kak Voznik, osnovalsia, i ros Sanktpiterburkh,* pp. 264–69.
66 Storch, *Picture of Petersburg,* p. 438.
67 T. T. Rice, *A Concise History of Russian Art* (New York, 1963), pp. 189–90; idem, "Conflux of Influences," p. 189.
68 G. M. Presnov, "Skul'ptura pervoi poloviny XVIII veka," *IRI,* Vol. 5, pp. 460–70.
69 N. N. Kovalenskaia, "F. I. Shubin," ibid., Vol. 6, pp. 329–60.
70 V. N. Petrov, "M. I. Kozlovskii," ibid., pp. 400–435.
71 D. E. Arkin, "E. M. Fal'kone," in ibid., pp. 366–68.
72 Quoted in ibid., p. 371.
73 Quoted in Arthur Wilson, "Diderot in Russia, 1773–1774," *The Eighteenth Century in Russia,* ed. Garrard, pp. 184–85.
74 Yarmolinsky, ed., *The Poems, Prose and Plays of Alexander Pushkin,* pp. 106–7.

CHAPTER VI: *From Debauchery to Philosophy*

1 Marc Raeff, *The Origins of the Russian Intelligentsia: The Eighteenth-Century Nobility* (New York, 1966), pp. 31–32.
2 Quoted in Brückner, *Istoriia Petra Velikago,* Vol. 1, p. 197.
3 James Livingston, "Russia and Western Trade, 1550–1790: A Study in the Origins of Economic Backwardness" (M.A. thesis, Northern Illinois University, 1975), pp. 82–100.
4 Johann Georg Korb, *Diary,* Vol. 1, p. 256.
5 A. N. Pypin, *Istoriia russkoi literatury* (St. Petersburg, 1911), Vol. 3, pp. 187–88; Miliukov, *Ocherki po istorii russkoi kul'tury,* Vol. 2, p. 166.
6 Pypin, *Istoriia,* Vol. 3, pp. 189–95; Miliukov, *Ocherki po istorii russkoi kul'tury,* Vol. 2, pp. 167–68; Florinsky, *Russia,* Vol. 1, pp. 410–1.
7 Plekhanov, *Istoriia,* Vol. 2, pp. 104–6; Pypin, *Istoriia,* Vol. 3, pp. 195–210; E. Vinter, "Feofan Prokopovich i nachalo russkogo Prosveshcheniia," *Rol' i znachenie literatury XVIII veka v istorii russkoi kul'tury,* ed. D. S. Likhachev et al. (Moscow-Leningrad, 1966), pp. 43–46; Florinsky, *Russia,* Vol. 1, p. 416; James Cracraft, "Feofan Prokopovich: A Bibliography of His Works," *Oxford Slavonic Papers,* Vol. 8 (1975), pp. 1–36.
8 Feofan Prokopovich, *Slova i rechi pouchitel'nye, pokhval'nye i pozdravitel'nye Sobraniia, i nekotorye vtorym tisneniem a drugie vnov' napechatannye* (St. Petersburg, 1760), Vol. 357–58. The most recent and best study of Peter's

church reform is James Cracraft, *The Church Reform of Peter the Great* (London, 1971).

9   V. N. Tatishchev, *Istoriia Rossiiskaia* (Moscow-Leningrad, 1962), Vol. 1, p. 87.

10   V. N. Tatishchev, "Razgovor o pol'ze nauk i uchilishch," *Chteniia* (1887), Bk. 1, pp. 137–44.

11   Feofan Prokopovich, "Sermon on the Interment of the Most Illustrious, Most Sovereign Peter the Great, Emperor and Autocrat of All Russia, the Father of His Nation," ed. and trans. Harold B. Segal *The Literature of Eighteenth-Century Russia*, (New York, 1967), Vol. 1, pp. 142–45.

12   Quoted in Plekhanov, *Istoriia*, Vol. 2, p. 102.

13   Miliukov, *Ocherki po istorii russkoi kul'tury*, Vol. 3, p. 187.

14   Schuyler, *Peter the Great*, Vol. 2, pp. 434–35.

15   Miliukov, *Ocherki po istorii russkoi kul'tury*, Vol. 3, pp. 187–88.

16   Quoted in ibid., p. 233.

17   V. V. Kallash and N. E. Efros, eds., *Istoriia russkago teatra* (Moscow, 1914), Vol. 1, p. 70; Miliukov, *Ocherki po istorii russkoi kul'tury*, Vol. 3, p. 187; Jack Weiner, *Mantillas in Muscovy: The Spanish Golden Age Theatre in Tsarist Russia, 1672–1917* (Laurence, Kansas, 1970), pp. 4–15.

18   Vigor, *Letters from a Lady*, pp. 17–19.

19   D. D. Blagoi, *Istoriia russkoi literatury XVIII veka* (Moscow, 1961), pp. 121–30; Hans Rogger, *National Consciousness in Eighteenth-Century Russia* (Cambridge, Mass., 1960), pp. 49–50.

20   Miliukov, *Ocherki po istorii russkoi kul'tury*, Vol. 3, p. 207.

21   Ibid., pp. 234–35; Billington, *Icon and the Axe*, p. 210.

22   Billington, *Icon and the Axe*, p. 190; Vigor, *Letters from a Lady*, pp. 93–95.

23   Raeff, *Origins of the Russian Intelligentsia*, p. 41. See also Marc Raeff, ed., *Peter the Great Changes Russia* (Lexington, Mass., 1972), pp. xv–xix.

24   Pypin, *Istoriia*, Vol. 3, p. 489; quote from B. N. Menshutkin, *Russia's Lomonosov* (Princeton, 1952), p. 186.

25   A. S. Pushkin, *Polnoe sobranie sochinenii*, Vol. 7, pp. 28, 277.

26   Aleksandr Morozov, *Mikhail Vasil'evich Lomonosov, 1711–1765* (Leningrad, 1952), pp. 9–44; Menshutkin, *Russia's Lomonosov*, pp. 7–12.

27   *Calendar of State Papers. Foreign, 1547–1553*, p. 241.

28   T. S. Willan, *The Early History of the Russia Company, 1553–1603* (Manchester, 1956), passim; Menshutkin, *Russia's Lomonosov*, pp. 8–9.

29   Morozov, *Lomonosov*, pp. 31–44; Menshutkin, *Russia's Lomonosov*, pp. 10–11.

30   Morozov, *Lomonosov*, pp. 121–31, 152–54; Plekhanov, *Istoriia*, Vol. 2 pp. 198–99.

31   M. V. Lomonosov, "Ode on the Day of the Ascension to the All-Russian Throne of Her Majesty the Empress Elizabeth Petrovna, the Year 1747," *The Literature of Eighteenth-Century Russia*, and trans. Segal, Vol. 1, p. 197.

32   Morozov, *Lomonosov*, pp. 319–89; Menshutkin, *Russia's Lomonosov*, pp. 48–72.

33   Quoted in Menshutkin, *Russia's Lomonosov*, p. 48.

34   Quoted in Plekhanov, *Istoriia*, Vol. 2, p. 213.

35   Lomonosov, "Ode," p. 201.

36   Morozov, *Lomonosov*, pp. 651–59.

37 D. A. Korsakov, "Artemii Petrovich Volynskii i ego konfidenty," *Russkaia starina (RS,)*, No. 10 (October 1885), pp. 22–24; "Zapiski ob Artemii Volynskom," *Chteniia* (1858), Bk. 2, Sec. 5; Iu. V. Got'e, "Proekt ob popravlenii gosudarstvennykh del Artemiia Petrovicha Volynskago," *Dela i Dni* Vol. 3 (1922), pp. 1–31.

38 Quoted in Rogger, *National Consciousness*, p. 105.

39 Ibid., p. 48.

40 A. P. Sumarokov, "Son—schastlivoe obshchestvo," *N. I. Novikov i ego sovremenniki. Izbrannye sochineniia*, ed. I. V. Malyshev, pp. 354–57.

41 Blagoi, *Istoriia*, p. 228.

42 A. P. Sumarokov, "O blagorodstve," *Novikov i ego sovremenniki*, p. 372.

43 Marc Raeff, "The Enlightenment in Russia and Russian Thought in the Enlightenment," *The Eighteenth Century in Russia*, pp. 30–31; idem., *Origins of the Russian Intelligentsia*, pp. 154–56.

44 Marc Raeff, *Imperial Russia, 1682–1825: The Coming of Age of Modern Russia* (New York, 1972), p. 141.

45 Quoted in *Svodnyi katalog russkoi knigi grazhdanskoi pechati XVIII veka, 1725–1800* (Moscow, 1964), Vol. 2, p. 489.

46 Miliukov, *Ocherki po istorii russkoi kul'tury*, Vol. 3, p. 336.

47 Quoted in Emile Haumant, *La Culture Française en Russie (1700–1900)*, (Paris, 1913), p. 87.

48 Quoted in Ibid., p. 86.

49 Marquis de Corberon, *Un diplomat français à la cour de Catherine II, 1775–1780* (Paris, 1901), Vol. 2, p. 324.

50 Haumant, *La Culture Française en Russie*, pp. 86–87.

51 Ibid., pp. 87–88.

52 Quoted in Miliukov, *Ocherki po istorii russkoi kul'tury*, Vol. 3, pp. 340–41.

53 Kazimirz Waliszewski, *The Romance of an Empress: Catherine II of Russia* (New York, 1894), p. 234.

54 Ibid., p. 344.

55 Quoted in Ibid., p. 346. See also pp. 332, 345.

56 Quoted in Blagoi, *Istoriia*, p. 481.

57 G. R. Derzhavin, "Zapiski, 1743–1812," *Sochineniia G. R. Derzhavina* (St. Petersburg, 1871), Vol. 6, pp. 542–46; Richard Wortman, *The Development of a Russian Legal Consciousness* (Chicago, 1976), p. 100; Blagoi, *Istoriia*, pp. 483–84.

58 G. R. Derzhavin, "Ode to the Wise Princess Felitsa of the Kirghiz-Kazakh Horde, Written by a Certain Murza, Long a Resident of Moscow, But Now Living in St. Petersburg Because of His Affairs, 1782," *The Literature of Eighteenth-Century Russia*, ed. and trans. Segal, Vol. 2, pp. 270, 276, 278.

59 Quoted in Wortman, *Development of Russian Legal Consciousness*, pp. 100–101.

60 G. R. Derzhavin, "To Rulers and Judges," *The Literature of Eighteenth-Century Russia*, ed. and trans. Segal, Vol. 2, p. 261.

61 D. I. Fonvizin, "Poslanie k slugam moim Shumilovu, Van'ke i Petrushke," *Izbrannye proizvedeniia russkikh myslitelei vtoroi poloviny XVIII veka* (Moscow, 1952), Vol. 2, p. 221.

62 D. I. Fonvizin, *The Brigadier* in *The Literature of Eighteenth-Century Russia*, ed. and trans. Segal, Vol. 2, pp. 349, 368.

63 Quoted in Marc Slonim, *The Epic of Russian Literature: From Its Origins Through Tolstoi* (New York, 1964), p. 40.

64 For a complete listing of these numerous translations, see *Svodnyi katalog russkoi knigi grazhdanskoi pechati XVIII veka, 1725–1800,* Volumes 1–4.

65 A. Bolotov, *Zhizn' i prikliucheniia,* Vol. 1, pp. 446–47.

66 Ibid., p. 44.

67 Fonvizin, *The Brigadier,* p. 349.

68 A. S. Pushkin, "Zametki po russkoi istorii XVIII veka," *Polnoe sobranie sochinenii,* Vol. 8, p. 127.

69 A. G. Dement'ev et al., eds., *Russkaia periodicheskaia pechat'* (*1702–1894*). *Spravochnik* (Moscow, 1959), pp. 14–49.

70 P. N. Berkov, "Satiricheskaia zhurnalistika 1769–1774gg.," *Ocherki po istorii russkoi zhurnalistiki i kritiki* (Leningrad, 1950), Vol. 1, pp. 46–49; G. Gareth Jones, "Novikov's Naturalized *Spectator,*" *The Eighteenth Century in Russia,* pp. 152–53.

71 G. P. Makogonenko, *Nikolai Novikov i russkoe prosveshchenie XVIII veka* (Moscow-Leningrad, 1952), pp. 63–66, 83–91.

72 Miliukov, *Ocherki po istorii russkoi kul'tury,* Vol. 3, pp. 297–303; Berkov, "Satiricheskaia zhurnalistika 1769–1774," pp. 50–73; Jones, "Novikov's Naturalized *Spectator,*" pp. 156–65.

73 N. I. Novikov, "Avtor k samomu sebe," in *Novikov i ego sovremenniki,* p. 92.

74 N. I. Novikov, "Otryvok puteshestviia v*** I*** T***," in ibid., p. 100.

75 N. K. Piksanov, "I. V. Lopukhin," in *Masonstvo v ego proshlom i nastoiashchem,* ed. S. P. Mel'gunov and N. P. Sidorov (Moscow, 1915), Vol. 1, pp. 227–50; In-Ho L. Ryu, "Moscow Freemasons and the Rosicrucian Order: A Study in Organization and Control," *The Eighteenth Century in Russia,* pp. 203–23; I. V. Lopukhin, "Zapiski nekotorykh obstoiatel'stv zhizni i sluzhby deistvitel'nago tainago sovetnika, Senatora I. V. Lopukhina, sochineniia im samin," *Russkii arkhiv* (*RA*) Vol. 22, (1884), Bk. 1, pp. 1–154; JoAnn Schrampfer [Ruckman], "A Russian Freemason: I. V. Lopukhin" (M. A. thesis, University of Chicago, 1963), pp. 5–18.

76 Raeff, *Origins of the Russian Intelligentsia,* p. 164.

77 G. P. Makogonenko, *Radishchev i ego vremia* (Moscow, 1956), pp. 23–52; Lang, *Alexander Radishchev,* pp. 39–41.

78 A. N. Radishchev, "Zhitie Fedora Vasil'evicha Ushakova," *A. N. Radishchev: Izbrannye filosofskie i obshchestvenno-politicheskie proizvedeniia,* ed. I. Ia. Shchipanov (Moscow, 1952), pp. 232–38; Makogonenko, *Radishchev i ego vremia,* pp. 43–54.

79 Quoted in A. Startsev, *Radishchev v gody "Puteshestviia"* (Moscow, 1960), p. 21.

80 There have been numerous editions of Radishchev's *Journey,* and extensive commentary about it, in Russian. See, among others, Makogonenko, *Radishchev i ego vremia,* pp. 417–514; V. P. Semennikov, *Radishchev: Ocherki i issledovaniia* (Moscow-Petrograd, 1923); and A. Startsev, *Radishchev v gody "Puteshestviia."* A good English translation, together with useful notes and an introductory commentary, is R. P. Thaler, ed., and Leo Wiener, trans., *A Journey from St. Petersburg to Moscow* (Cambridge, Mass., 1958).

81 Khrapovitskii, *Dnevnik,* p. 340.

82 "Zamechaniia Ekateriny II na knigi A. N. Radishcheva," *Protsess A. N. Radishcheva,* ed. D. A. Babkin (Moscow-Leningrad, 1952), pp. 157–64.

83 "Smertnyi prigovor A. N. Radishchevu, 24 iiulia 1790g.," ibid., p. 244.

84 Pis'mo Ekateriny II k D'Alemberu, 13 noiabria 1762g., *SIRIO* Vol. 7 (1871), p. 179.

85 Quoted in Grand Duke Nikolai Mikhailovich, *Le Comte Paul Stroganov* (Paris, 1905), Vol. 1, p. xxxviii.

86 Quoted in Haumant, *La Culture Française en Russie*, p. 172.

87 De Ségur, *Memoirs and Recollections*, Vol. 3, p. 420.

88 Quoted in Haumant, *La Culture Française en Russie*, p. 176. See also A. M. Skabichevskii, *Ocherki istorii russkoi tsenzury, 1700–1863gg.* (St. Petersburg, 1892), p. 64.

89 Haumant, *La Culture Française en Russie*, p. 189.

90 L. vicomte de Puibusque, *Lettres sur la guerre de Russie en 1812; sur la ville de Saint-Pétersbourg, les moeurs et les usages des habitans de la Russie et de la Pologne* (Paris, 1817), pp. 270–71.

CHAPTER VII: *Imperial Aspirations*

1 Baron, ed., *Travels of Olearius*, p. 163.

2 Quoted in Livingston, "Russia and Western Trade, 1550–1790," pp. 78, 79.

3 Quoted in M. N. Pokrovskii, *Russkaia istoriia s drevneishikh vremen* (Moscow, 1933), Vol. 2, p. 177.

4 Willan, *Early History of the Russian Company*, pp. 55–56; Violet Barbour, *Capitalism in Amsterdam in the Seventeenth Century* (Ann Arbor, 1963), p. 119; Joseph T. Fuhrmann, *The Origins of Capitalism in Russia: Industry and Progress in the Sixteenth and Seventeenth Centuries* (Chicago, 1972), pp. 78, 248–50.

5 Quoted in Pokrovskii, *Russkaia istoriia*, Vol. 2, p. 201.

6 Quoted in Miliukov, *Gosudarstvennoe khoziaistvo Rossii*, p. 528.

7 Novosel'skii, *Bor'ba moskovskogo gosudarstva s tatarami*, pp. 435–42.

8 Schuyler, *Peter the Great*, Vol. 1, p. 244.

9 Bogoslovskii, *Petr I*, Vol. 1, pp. 210–18.

10 Quoted in Schuyler, *Peter the Great*, Vol. 1, p. 245.

11 Bogoslovskii, *Petr I*, Vol. 1, pp. 227–70.

12 Ibid., pp. 271–301.

13 *Pis'ma i bumagi Imperatora Petra Velikago*, Vol. 1, No. 99.

14 E. V. Tarle, *Severnaia voina i shvedskoe nashestvie na Rossii* (Moscow, 1958), pp. 49–50.

15 Prince M. M. Shcherbatov, ed., *Journal de Pierre le Grand depuis l'année 1698 jusqu'à l'année 1714 inclusivement* (Stockholm, 1774), pp. 38–40.

16 Riasanovsky, *History of Russia*, p. 246; Plekhanov, *Istoriia*, Vol. 2, pp. 226–31; N. B. Golikova, "K istorii Astrakhanskogo vosstaniia 1705–1706gg.," *Rossiia v period reform Petra I* ed. N. I. Pavlenko (Moscow, 1973), pp. 249–88.

17 Plekhanov, *Istoriia*, Vol. 2, pp. 231–33; Solov'ev, *Istoriia Rossii*, Vol. 8, pp. 183–93; Reinhard Wittram, *Peter I: Czar und Kaiser* (Göttingen, 1964), Vol. 1, pp. 278–80.

18 Wittram, *Peter I*, Vol. 1, pp. 288–94; Solov'ev, *Istoriia Rossii*, Vol. 8, pp. 198–205.

19 Brückner, *Istoriia Petra Velikago*, Vol. 4, pp. 447–56.

20 *Pis'ma i bumagi Imperatora Petra Velikago*, Vol. 8 (1), pp. 169–71.

21 Shcherbatov, ed., *Journal de Pierre le Grand*, p. 230.

22 Solov'ev, *Istoriia Rossii*, Vol. 8, p. 206.

23 Wittram, *Peter I*, Vol. 1, pp. 311–20.
24 Quoted in F. Martens, *Sobranie traktatov i konventsii, zakliuchennykh Rossieiu s inostrannymi derzhavami* (St. Petersburg, 1892–94), Vol. 13, p. lxxiv.
25 Quoted in Brückner, *Istoriia Petra Velikago*, Vol. 4, p. 461.
26 *PSZ*, sobranie 1-oe, Nos. 2321, 2328.
27 N. A. Voskresenskii, ed., *Zakonodatel'nye akty Petra I* (Moscow-Leningrad, 1945), Vol. 1, p. 199.
28 Brückner, *Istoriia Petra Velikago*, Vol. 4, p. 487.
29 Solov'ev, *Istoriia Rossii*, Vol. 8, pp. 386—87.
30 Ibid., Vol. 9, p. 273.
31 Quoted in Martens, *Sobranie traktatov*, Vol. 9, p. 49.
32 Quoted in ibid., Vol. 13, pp. 21, 22.
33 Quoted in B. H. Sumner, *Peter the Great and the Emergence of Russia* (London, 1950), p. 126.
34 Voskresenskii, ed., *Zakonodatel'nye akty*, Vol. 1, p. 220; Miliukov, *Gosudarstvennoe khoziaistvo*, pp. 565–89.
35 Miliukov, *Gosudarstvennoe khoziaistvo*, pp. 543–53.
36 Quoted in Blum, *Lord and Peasant in Russia* p. 464.
37 Arcadius Kahan, "Continuing Economic Activity and Policy During the Post-Petrine Period in Russia," *The Structure of Russian History: Interpretive Essays* pp. 194–95; P. I. Liashchenko, *Istoriia narodnogo khoziaistva SSSR*, Vol. 1 (Moscow, 1956), pp. 346–89.
38 R. O. Crummey, "The Reconstruction of the Boiar Aristocracy, 1613–1645," *Forschungen zur osteuropäischen Geschichte* Vol. 18 (1973), pp. 187–200; idem, "The Origins of the Noble Official: The Boiar Elite, 1613–1689," *Russian Officialdom from the Seventeenth to the Twentieth Century*, ed. W. M. Pintner and D. K. Rowney (forthcoming), Chapter 3.
39 Martens, *Sobranie traktatov*, Vol. 1, pp. 48–49; Vol. 9, pp. 63–65.
40 Ibid., Vol. 13, pp. 42–43; O. Halecki, *A History of Poland* (New York, 1943), p. 185.
41 Solov'ev, *Istoriia Rossii*, Vol. 10, pp. 346–60; Münnich, *Zapiski*, pp. 37–47; Manstein, *Memoirs*, pp. 69–83; Martens, *Sobranie traktatov*, Vol. 13, pp. 42–43.
42 Florinsky, *Russia*, Vol. 1, pp. 463–64; Solov'ev, *Istoriia Rossii*, Vol. 10, pp. 377–95.
43 Martens, *Sobranie traktatov*, Vol. 1, pp. 70–71; Solov'ev, *Istoriia Rossii*, Vol. 10, pp. 400–462; Florinsky, *Russia*, Vol. 1, pp. 464–65.
44 K. Waliszewski, *La Dernière des Romanovs: Elisabeth Ier, Impératrice de Russie* (Paris, 1902), pp. 110–23; Solov'ev, *Istoriia Rossii*, Vol. 10, pp. 294–96, 686–89; Dispatch of C. Wich to the Right Honourable Lord Carteret, 7 June 1742, in "Diplomaticheskaia perepiska angliiskikh poslov i poslannikov pri russkom dvore," *SIRIO* Vol. 91 (1894), p. 490.
45 Quoted in Martens, *Sobranie traktatov*, Vol. 13, p. 67.
46 Quoted in ibid., p. 68.
47 Quoted in ibid., Vol. 9, pp. 136–37.
48 Ibid., pp. 191–200.
49 Solov'ev, *Istoriia Rossii*, Vol. 12, pp. 444–461.
50 Ibid., pp. 402–12, 463–69.
51 *Perevorot 1762 goda*, p. 27.
52 Quoted in Martens, *Sobranie traktatov*, Vol. 5, p. 368.

53 V. I. Lebedev, ed., *Reformy Petra I: Sbornik dokumentov* (Moscow, 1937), pp. 73–74; Solov'ev, *Istoriia Rossii*, Vol. 7, pp. 462–64; Vol. 10, pp. 223–25; Raeff, ed., *Plans for Political Reform in Imperial Russia*, pp. 48–50.
54 Blum, *Lord and Peasant in Russia*, p. 368.
55 Kostomarov, *Russkaia istoriia*, Vol. 7, pp. 175–77.
56 *PSZ*, sobranie 1–oe, No. 7142.
57 Manstein, *Memoirs*, p. 262.
58 Solov'ev, *Istoriia Rossii*, Vol. 10, pp. 470–71.
59 Raeff, *Origins of the Russian Intelligentsia*, p. 74.
60 *PSZ*, sobranie 1–oe, No. 11,444; M. I. Semevskii, "Shest' mesiatsev iz russkoi istorii," pp. 761–64.
61 Quoted in Semevskii, "Shest' mesiatsev iz russkoi istorii," p. 775.
62 See, for example, Alexei Rzhevskii's poem written to honor the occasion, entitled "Oda vsepresvetleishemu, derzhavneishemu, velikomu i miloserdomu gosudariu, istinnomu ottsu poddannykh imperatoru Petru Fedorovichu, samoderzhtsu vserossiiskomu. Prinositsia v znak blagodarnosti za bezprimernoe i miloserdoe pozhalovan'e vol'nostiu rossiiskikh dvorian." Quoted in ibid., pp. 772–74.
63 Florinsky, *Russia*, Vol. 1, pp. 484–86.
64 Arcadius Kahan, "The Costs of 'Westernization' in Russia: The Gentry and the Economy in the Eighteenth Century," *The Structure of Russian History*, pp. 231–36.
65 Quoted in Florinsky, *Russia*, Vol. 1, p. 514.
66 Quoted in Solov'ev, *Istoriia Rossii*, Vol. 13, p. 161.
67 Quoted in A. Brückner, *Istoriia Ekateriny Vtoroi* (St. Petersburg, 1885), Vol. 3, p. 269.
68 Quoted in Martens, *Sobranie traktatov*, Vol. 2, p. 2.
69 Quoted in Solov'ev, *Istoriia Rossii*, Vol. 13, p. 182.
70 Quoted in Martens, *Sobranie traktatov*, Vol. 10, p. 215.
71 Quoted in ibid., pp. 215–16.
72 Quoted in ibid., Vol. 13, pp. 119–20.
73 David L. Ransel, *The Politics of Catherinian Russia: The Panin Party* (New Haven and London, 1975), p. 128.
74 Quoted in Florinsky, *Russia*, Vol. 1, p. 517.
75 Quoted in Martens, *Sobranie traktatov*, Vol. 7, pp. 9–10.
76 Ransel, *Politics of Catherinian Russia*, pp. 128–29.
77 Solov'ev, *Istoriia Rossii*, Vol. 13, pp. 356–58.
78 Quoted in Herbert H. Kaplan, *The First Partition of Poland* (New York and London, 1962), p. 36. See also p. 43.
79 "Spisok s zapiski Ekateriny II k N. Paninu o novom korole pol'skom i o svoem zdorove," *SIRIO* Vol. 7 (1871), p. 373.
80 Florinsky, *Russia*, Vol. 1, p. 517.
81 Brückner, *Istoriia Ekateriny Vtoroi*, Vol. 3, pp. 306–13; Kaplan, *First Partition*, pp. 46–105; Gladys Scott Thomson, *Catherine the Great and the Expansion of Russia* (New York, 1965), pp. 92–100.
82 Albert Sorel, *The Eastern Question in the Eighteenth Century* (London, 1898), pp. 24–26.
83 Kaplan, *First Partition*, pp. 104–5.
84 Quoted in Solov'ev, *Istoriia Rossii*, Vol. 14, p. 280.
85 Florinsky, *Russia*, Vol. 1, p. 521; Brückner, *Istoriia Ekateriny Vtoroi*, Vol. 3, pp. 332–35.

86 Martens, *Sobranie traktatov,* Vol. 2, pp. 9–10; Vol. 7, pp. 65–66.
87 Ibid., Vol. 2, pp. 13–29; Vol. 7, pp. 65–81; Kaplan, *First Partition,* pp. 147–88; Riasanovsky, *History of Russia,* pp. 297–98.
88 Brückner, *Istoriia Ekateriny Vtoroi,* Vol. 3, pp. 352–53.
89 Quoted in Solov'ev, *Istoriia Rossii,* Vol. 14, p. 549.
90 *SIRIO* Vol. 13 (1873), p. 260.
91 Brückner, *Istoriia Ekateriny Vtoroi,* Vol. 3, pp. 354–57; Solov'ev, *Istoriia Rossii,* Vol. 15, pp. 7–30, 76–88; Riasanovsky, *History of Russia,* pp. 293–94.
92 Brückner, *Istoriia Ekateriny Vtoroi,* Vol. 3, pp. 358–59.
93 Ibid., p. 375–77.
94 Pis'mo Imperatritsy Ekateriny II k Melkioru Grimmu, 27 maia 1780, *SIRIO,* Vol. 23 (1878), pp. 180–81.
95 Quoted in Brückner, *Istoriia Ekateriny Vtoroi,* Vol. 3, pp. 379, 381.
96 Quoted in ibid., p. 381.
97 Martens, *Sobranie traktatov,* Vol. 2, pp. 96–116.
98 Brückner, *Istoriia Ekateriny Vtoroi,* Vol. 3, pp. 400–405.
99 De Ségur, *Memoirs and Recollections,* Vol. 3, pp. 109, 116–18, 148–49.
100 Quoted in ibid., pp. 19–20.
101 Quoted in Brückner, *Istoriia Ekateriny Vtoroi,* Vol. 3, p. 418.
102 Martens, *Sobranie traktatov,* Vol. 2, p. 187.
103 Brückner, *Istoriia Ekateriny Vtoroi,* Vol. 3, pp. 426–67, 476–86.
104 Martens, *Sobranie traktatov,* Vol. 2, pp. 193–94.
105 Quoted in R. H. Lord, *The Second Partition of Poland: A Study in Diplomatic History* (Cambridge, Mass., 1915), p. 92.
106 O. Balzer, "Reformy społeczne i polityczne konstytucyi 3. maja," *Przgłąd Polski* (1891), pp. 222–60, 416–96.
107 Lord, *Second Partition,* pp. 199–200.
108 Pis'mo Imperatritsy Ekateriny II k Melkioru Grimmu, 10 maia 1791, *SIRIO,* Vol. 23 (1878), pp. 534–35.
109 Lord, *Second Partition,* p. 249.
110 Quotes from ibid., p. 275.
111 Władysław Smoleński, *Konfederacya Targowicka* (Krakow, 1903), pp. 45–47, 177–79.
112 Quoted in Lord, *Second Partition,* p. 291.
113 W. F. Reddaway, ed., *The Cambridge History of Poland from Augustus II to Pilsudski (1697–1935)* (Cambridge, 1941), Vol. 2, pp. 152–53.
114 Ibid., pp. 160–73; R. H. Lord "The Third Partition of Poland," *SEER,* Vol. 3, No. 9 (March 1925), pp. 482–83.
115 Quoted in Lord, "Third Partition," p. 488.
116 Pis'mo Imperatritsy Ekateriny II k Melkioru Grimmu, 3 sentiabria 1794, *SIRIO,* Vol. 23 (1878), p. 610.
117 Quoted in Martens, *Sobranie traktatov,* Vol. 2, p. 613.
118 Ibid., p. 229.
119 Florinsky, *Russia,* Vol. 1, p. 544.
120 Arcadius Kahan, "The Costs of 'Westernization,' " p. 233.
121 P. A. Shtorkh, "Materialy dlia istorii gosudarstvennykh denezhnykh znakov v Rossii s 1653 po 1840 god.," *ZhMNP,* Vol. 137 (1868), pp. 822–23.
122 Edmond Genet to the Comte de Montmorin, quoted in Lang, *Alexander Radishchev,* p. 127.
123 *PSZ,* sobranie 1–oe, No. 14,392.

124 Ibid., No. 16,187.
125 Quoted in Kahan, "The Costs of 'Westernization,' " p. 224.
126 Bilbassov, *Istoriia Ekateriny Vtoroi*, Vol. 2, pp. 461–73; S. V. Voznesenskii, *Ekonomika Rossii XIX–XX vv. v tsifrakh* (Leningrad, 1924), p. 47.
127 Kahan, "Costs of 'Westernization,' " p. 233.
128 Blum, *Lord and Peasant in Russia*, p. 438.
129 V. I. Semevskii, *Krest'iane v tsarstvovanie imperatritsy Ekateriny II* (St. Petersburg, 1888), Vol. 1, pp. 155–56; V. Gitermann, *Geschichte Russlands* (Zurich, 1947), Vol. 2, pp. 489–91.

CHAPTER VIII: *The Imperial Dynasty*

1 Catherine II, *Mémoires de l'Impératrice Catherine II*, p. 215.
2 Ibid., pp. 216–17.
3 Bilbassov, *Istoriia Ekateriny Vtoroi*, Vol. 1, p. 274; Catherine II, *Mémoires de l'Impératrice Catherine II*, p. 223.
4 Bilbassov, *Istoriia Ekateriny Vtoroi*, Vol. 1, p. 274.
5 N. K. Shilder, *Imperator Pavel Pervyi: Istoriko-biograficheskii ocherk* (St. Petersburg, 1901), p. 5.
6 Dmitrii Kobeko, *Tsesarevich Pavel Petrovich, 1754–1796* (St. Petersburg, 1883), pp. 5–6; Shilder, *Pavel Pervyi*, p. 7; V. Chizh, "Imperator Pavel I," *Voprosy filosofii i psikhologii* Vol. 18, No. 3 (May–June 1907), pp. 223, 225.
7 E. S. Shumigorskii, *Imperator Pavel I: Zhizn' i tsarstvovanie* (St. Petersburg, 1907), pp. 10–11; S. A. Poroshin, *Zapiski* (St. Petersburg, 1881), entries for 1 December 1764 and 7 January, 28 March, 19 April, and 14 September, 1765; Ransel, *Politics of Catherinian Russia*, pp. 10–33, 206.
8 N. I. Panin, "Vsepoddanneishee pred'iavlenie slabago poniatiia i mneniia o vospitanii ego imperatorskago vysochestva gosudaria velikago kniazia Pavla Petrovicha," in Shilder, *Pavel Pervyi*, p. 509.
9 Ibid., pp. 509–11; Kobeko, *Tsesarevich Pavel Petrovich*, pp. 52–57; Shilder, *Pavel Pervyi*, pp. 56–62; Ransel, *Politics of Catherinian Russia*, p. 215.
10 Quoted in Ransel, *Politics of Catherinian Russia*, pp. 223, 225.
11 Ia. L. Barskov, "Pis'ma Imperatritsy Ekateriny II k grafu P. V. Zavadovskomu," *Russkii istoricheskii zhurnal*, No. 5 (1918), pp. 225–26; D. I. Fonvizin, *Sobranie sochinenii* (Moscow, 1959), Vol. 2, pp. 187–93; Ransel, *Politics of Catherinian Russia*, pp. 220–21, 227.
12 Shilder, *Pavel Pervyi*, pp. 87–88.
13 Quoted in ibid., p. 91.
14 De Corberon, *Un diplomat français à la cour de Catherine II*, Vol. 2, p. 19.
15 Ibid., Vol. 1, p. 245.
16 Shumigorskii, *Imperator Pavel I*, p. 36.
17 Quoted in Kobeko, *Tsesarevich Pavel Petrovich*, p. 119.
18 Shilder, *Pavel Pervyi*, p. 96.
19 Shumigorskii, *Imperator Pavel I*, p. 35.
20 Pis'mo Imperatritsy Ekateriny II k frau B'elke, 28 aprelia 1776g., *SIRIO*, Vol. 27 (1880), p. 79.
21 Kobeko, *Tsesarevich Pavel Petrovich*, p. 122.
22 Pis'mo Imperatritsy Ekateriny II k Melkioru Grimmu, 29 iiunia 1776g., *SIRIO*, Vol. 23 (1878), pp. 49–50.

23   E. S. Shumigorskii, *Imperatritsa Mariia Feodorovna, 1759–1828. Eia biografiia* (St. Petersburg, 1892), Vol. 1, pp. 51–55.
24   Quoted in ibid., pp. 79–80.
25   K. Waliszewski, *Paul the First of Russia, the Son of Catherine the Great* (London, 1913), p. 17.
26   Quoted in Shilder, *Pavel Pervyi*, p. 115.
27   Quoted in Kobeko, *Tsesarevich Pavel Petrovich*, p. 138.
28   Quoted in Shilder, *Pavel Pervyi*, pp. 126–28.
29   Quoted in Shumigorskii, *Imperatritsa Mariia Feodorovna*, Vol. 1, p. 131.
30   Quoted in ibid., p. 148.
31   Ibid., pp. 149–50.
32   Quoted in Waliszewski, *Paul the First*, p. 54.
33   Quoted in Shilder, *Pavel Pervyi*, p. 161.
34   Quoted in Shumigorskii, *Imperator Pavel I*, p. 49.
35   Quoted in Shilder, *Pavel Pervyi*, p. 162.
36   "Kharakteristika tsesarevicha Pavla Petrovicha, velikoi kniagini Marii Feodorovny, i lits ikh svity, napisannaia v 1782 godu imperatorom Iosifom II dlia svoego brata, velikago gertsoga toskanskago Leopol'dam," *Pavel Pervyi*, p. 549.
37   Quoted in Shumigorskii, *Imperatritsa Mariia Feodorovna*, Vol. 1, p. 258.
38   Quoted in Shilder, *Pavel Pervyi*, p. 192.
39   Quoted in Waliszewski, *Paul the First*, p. 55.
40   Shumigorskii, *Imperatritsa Mariia Feodorovna*, Vol. 1, pp. 317–18; Kobeko, *Tsesarevich Pavel Petrovich*, pp. 275–82.
41   Quoted in Shumigorskii, *Imperatritsa Mariia Feodorovna*, Vol. 1, p. 333.
42   Quoted in ibid., p. 334.
43   E. S. Shumigorskii, *Ekaterina Ivanovna Nelidova, 1758–1839. Ocherk iz istorii imperatora Pavla* (St. Petersburg, 1898), pp. 30–64. See also Princess Liza Troubetskaia, ed., *Correspondance de Sa Majesté l'Impératrice Marie Féodorovna avec Mademoiselle de Nélidoff, sa démoiselle d'honneur, 1797–1801* (Paris, 1896), pp. 1–160.
44   Pis'mo F. V. Rostopchina k grafu S. R. Vorontsovu, 28 maia 1794 goda," in *Arkhiv kniazia Vorontsova*, Vol. 8, p. 93.
45   Quoted in Shilder, *Pavel Pervyi*, p. 161.
46   Charles Masson, *Secret Memoirs*, pp. 107–9.
47   Quoted in Shilder, *Pavel Pervyi*, p. 343.
48   Ibid.
49   Paul and Maria Feodorovna had drafted this manifesto as early as 1788 in preparation for this moment. See "Akt, Vysochaishe utverzhdennyi v den' sviashchennoi koronatsii Ego Imperatorskago Velichestva i polozhennyi dlia khraneniia na prestole Uspenskago sobora," in Shilder, *Pavel Pervyi*, pp. 561–63.
50   A. E. Presniakov, *Apogei samoderzhaviia: Nikolai I* (Leningrad, 1925), p. 7.
51   "Nagrady, pozhalovannye v den' koronovaniia imperatora Pavla I, 5–go aprelia 1797 goda (po spisku, sostavlennomu kniazem Lobanovym-Rostovskim)," *Pavel Pervyi*, pp. 565–72.
52   "Zapiski N. A. Sablukova," *Tsareubiistvo 11 marta 1801 goda: Zapiski uchastnikov i sovremennikov* (St. Petersburg, 1908), p. 28.
53   Florinsky, *Russia*, Vol. 1, p. 627.
54   Waliszewski, *Paul the First*, p. 412.

55 "Aufzeichnung der Fürstin Darja Christophorowna Liewen geb. Baronesse Benkendorff," *Die Ermordung Pauls und die Thronbesteigung Nikolaus I. Neue Materialen*, ed. Theodor Schiemann, (Berlin, 1902), p. 39.

56 Quoted in Waliszewski, *Paul the First*, p. 416.

57 Ibid., pp. 416–17.

58 James J. Kenney, Jr., "Lord Whitworth and the Conspiracy Against Tsar Paul I: The New Evidence of the Kent Archive," *Slavic Review* (*SR*) Vol. 36, No. 2 (June 1977), pp. 205–11; Waliszewski, *Paul the First*, pp. 412–13.

59 Shilder, *Pavel Pervyi*, pp. 469–72, 481–82.

60 Th. Schiemann and A. Brückner, *Smert' Pavla Pervago* (Moscow, 1909), pp. 117–18; "Die Ermordung Pauls I. Aufzeichnungen von A. N. Weljaminow-Sernow," *Die Ermordung Pauls und die Thronbesteigung Nikolaus I. Neue Materialen*, ed. Schiemann, pp. 21–22; "Zapiski N. A. Sablukova" and "Zapiski Avgusta Kotsebu," *Tsareubiistvo*, pp. 64–65, 372–74.

61 Waliszewski, *Paul the First*, p. 434.

62 Quoted in "Zapiski Sablukova," p. 86.

63 Schiemann and Brückner, *Smert' Pavla Pervago*, pp. 131–33; "Izvlechenie iz memuarov grafa Bennigsena," *Tsareubiistvo*, pp. 144–48.

64 "Izvlechenie iz memuarov grafa Bennigsena," pp. 148–149; "Zapiski Sablukova," pp. 88–89; Waliszewski, *Paul the First*, pp. 455–58.

65 Quoted in Allen McConnell, *Tsar Alexander I: Paternalistic Reformer* (New York, 1970), p. 19.

66 Quoted in Shilder, *Pavel Pervyi*, p. 493.

67 Quoted in ibid.

68 Richard Pipes, ed. and trans., *Karamzin's Memoir on Ancient and Modern Russia: A Translation and an Analysis* (Cambridge, Mass., 1959), p. 135.

69 F. F. Vigel', *Zapiski* (Moscow, 1928), Vol. 1, p. 125.

70 "Stikhotvorenie A. S. Shishkova po sluchaiu vosshestviia na prestol imperatora Aleksandra I," N. K. Shilder, *Imperator Aleksandr Pervyi: Ego zhizn' i tsarstvovanie* (St. Petersburg, 1897), Vol. 2, p. 405.

71 "Iz donesenii Viatsoli. Riga, 17–go marta 1801 goda," and "Iz donesenii Lokatelli. St. Petersburg, 15–go marta 1801 goda," in Shilder, *Aleksandr Pervyi*, Vol. 2, pp. 309–10.

72 Quoted in Shilder, *Pavel Pervyi*, p. 496.

73 "Detskie pis'ma velikago kniazia Aleksandra Pavlovicha imperatritse Ekaterine II," in Shilder, *Aleksandr Pervyi*, Vol. 1, appendix 4, p. 261.

74 F.-C. LaHarpe, *Mémoires de Frédéric-César LaHarpe* (Paris-Geneva, 1864), p. 75.

75 Florinsky, *Russia*. Vol. 2, p. 630.

76 Mazade, ed., *Mémoires du Prince Adam Czartoryski*, Vol. 1, pp. 108–9.

77 Quoted in Velikii Kniaz' Nikolai Mikhailovich, *Imperatritsa Elisaveta Alekseevna supruga Imperatora Aleksandra I* (St. Petersburg, 1908), Vol. 1, pp. 26–27.

78 Pis'mo imperatritsy Ekateriny II k Melkioru Grimmu, 7 aprelia 1793g., *SIRIO*, Vol. 23 (1878), p. 583.

79 Nikolai Mikhailovich, *Imperatritsa Elisaveta Alekseevna*, Vol. 1, pp. 20, 24.

80 Published in ibid., p. 21.

81 Pis'mo imperatritsy Ekateriny II k Melkioru Grimmu, 14 maia 1793g., *SIRIO*, Vol. 23 (1878), p. 583.

82 Quoted in Shilder, *Aleksandr Pervyi*, Vol. 1, p. 86.

83 Mazade, ed., *Mémoires du Prince Adam Czartoryski*, Vol. 1, p. 72.
84 Pis'mo velikoi kniagini Elisavety Alekseevny k materi, Markgrafine Badenskoi, 19 fevralia 1794g., *Imperatritsa Elisaveta Alekseevna*, Vol. 1, p. 138.
85 E. M. Almedingen, *The Emperor Alexander I* (New York, 1964), p. 33.
86 Pis'mo velikago kniazia Aleksandra Pavlovicha k kniaziu Viktoru Pavlovichu Kochubeiu, ot 1–go maia 1796 goda, in Shilder, *Aleksandr Pervyi*, Vol. 1, Appendix 11, p. 277.
87 Shilder, *Aleksandr Pervyi*, Vol. 2, pp. 12–18.
88 Quoted in ibid., pp. 65–66.
89 Quoted in ibid., p. 69.
90 Velikii Kniaz' Nikolai Mikhailovich, *Imperator Aleksandr I. Opyt istoricheskago izsledovaniia* (Petrograd, 1914), p. 6.
91 Quoted in McConnell, *Tsar Alexander I*, p. 20.
92 Count P. A. Stroganov, "Résultat d'une conférence avec l'Empéreur le 24 juin 1801," *Graf P. A. Stroganov 1774–1817: Istoricheskoe izsledovanie epokhi Imperatora Aleksandra I*, ed., Nikolai Mikhailovich (St. Petersburg, 1903), Vol. 2, p. 61.
93 Count P. A. Stroganov, "De l'état de notre constitution," ibid., p. 41.
94 Count P. A. Stroganov, "Essai sur le système à suivre dans la réformation de l'administration de l'Empire," *Le Comte Paul Stroganov*, Vol. 2, Appendix 8, p. 9.
95 Almedingen, *Emperor Alexander I*, p. 84.
96 Pis'mo imperatritsy Elisavety Alekseevny k materi, Markgrafine Badenskoi, in Nikolai Mikhailovich, *Imperatritsa Elisaveta Alekseevna*, Vol. 2, p. 133.
97 Quoted in Florinsky, *Russia*, Vol. 2, p. 632.
98 Shilder, *Aleksandr Pervyi*, Vol. 2, pp. 117–71.
99 Quoted in Martens, *Sobranie traktatov*, Vol. 13, p. 296.
100 Quoted in ibid., p. 298.
101 Ibid., p. 300.
102 Pis'mo Imperatora Aleksandra I–go velikoi kniagine Ekaterine Pavlovne, 17 maia [iiunia?] 1807g., Tilsit, *Perepiska Imperatora Aleksandra I s sestroi velikoi kniaginei Ekaterinoi Pavlovnoi*, ed. Velikii Kniaz' Nikolai Mikhailovich (St. Petersburg, 1910), p. 15.
103 Pis'mo Imperatora Aleksandra I–go velikoi kniagine Ekaterine Pavlovne, 26 maia [iiunia?], 1807g., Weimar, in ibid., p. 17.
104 Pipes, ed. and trans., *Karamzin's Memoir on Ancient and Modern Russia*, pp. 63–75, 139–205.
105 Nikolai Mikhailovich, ed., *Perepiska Aleksandra I s velikoi kniaginei Ekaterinoi Pavlovnoi*, pp. 57, 64, 71, and passim.
106 Quoted in Shilder, *Aleksandr Pervyi*, Vol. 3, p. 42.
107 Quoted in ibid., Vol. 3, p. 83.
108 M. Iu. Lermontov, *Sochineniia* (Moscow, 1970), Vol. 1, p. 263.
109 Quoted in Nikolai Mikhailovich, *Imperator Aleksandr I*, p. 125.
110 Quoted in Florinsky, *Russia*, Vol. 2, p. 675.
111 Quoted in Shilder, *Aleksandr Pervyi*, Vol. 3, p. 89.
112 L. N. Tolstoi, *Sobranie sochinenii* (Moscow, 1962), Vol. 6, pp. 106–13.
113 Quoted in Eugene Tarle, *Napoleon's Invasion of Russia, 1812* (London, 1942), p. 145.
114 Quoted in ibid.

115   Quoted in Armand de Caulaincourt, *With Napoleon in Russia. The Memoirs of General de Caulaincourt, Duke of Vicenza* (New York, 1935), p. 135.
116   Quoted from Shilder, *Aleksandr Pervyi*, Vol. 3, p. 110. See also Tarle, *Napoleon's Invasion*, pp. 151–56.
117   Quoted in Tarle, *Napoleon's Invasion*, p. 165.
118   Caulaincourt, *With Napoleon in Russia*, pp. 111–15. See also Tarle, *Napoleon's Invasion*, pp. 164–66.
119   Quoted in Tarle, *Napoleon's Invasion*, p. 171.
120   Pis'mo Imperatora Aleksandra I–go velikoi kniagine Ekaterine Pavlovne, 7 sentiabria 1812g., *Perepiska Aleksandra I s velikoi kniaginei Ekaterinoi Pavlovnoi*, p. 84.
121   Tarle, *Napoleon's Invasion*, p. 184.
122   Quoted in ibid., p. 231.
123   Quoted in ibid., p. 278.
124   Florinsky, *Russia*, Vol. 2, p. 680.
125   Shilder, *Aleksandr Pervyi*, Vol. 3, p. 174.
126   Quoted in A. N. Pypin, *Obshchestvennoe dvizhenie v Rossii pri Aleksandre I* (St. Petersburg, 1885), p. 40.
127   Alexander Mikhailofsky-Danilefsky, *History of the Campaign in France in the Year 1814* (London, 1839), pp. 365–70; Almedingen, *Alexander I*, p. 150.
128   Quoted in Shilder, *Aleksandr Pervyi*, Vol. 3, p. 387, n. 297.
129   McConnell, *Tsar Alexander I*, pp. 125–26.
130   Pis'mo Imperatora Aleksandra I–go velikoi kniagine Ekaterine Pavlovne, 8 noiabria 1812g., *Perepiska Aleksandra I s velikoi kniaginei Ekaterinoi Pavlovnoi*, p. 103.
131   Pis'mo Imperatora Aleksandra I–go k kniaziu A. N. Golitsynu, 15 fevralia 1813g., Nikdai Mikhailovich, *Imperator Aleksandr I*, Appendix 4, p. 403.
132   "Zapiska Imperatora Aleksandra I k R. A. Koshelevu, 25 ianvaria 1813g., Nikdai Mikhailovich, *Imperator Aleksandr I*, Appendix 6, pp. 454–55.
133   Florinsky, *Russia*, Vol. 2, pp. 640–41.
134   See Pis'ma baronessy Kriudener k Imperatoru Aleksandru I, in Nikdai Mikhailovich, *Imperator Aleksandr I*, Appendix 8, pp. 527–49.
135   Quoted in N. K. Shilder, *Imperator Nikolai Pervyi: Ego zhizn' i tsarstvovanie* (St. Petersburg 1903), Vol. 1, p. 349.
136   Quoted in C. K. Webster, ed., *British Diplomacy, 1813–1815* (London, 1921), p. 383.
137   Quoted in Harold Nicolson, *The Congress of Vienna: A Study in Allied Unity, 1812–1822* (New York, 1946), p. 250.
138   Ibid., p. 249.
139   S. S. Tatishchev, *Vneshniaia politika imperatora Nikolaia I* (St. Petersburg, 1887), p. 4; McConnell, *Tsar Alexander I*, p. 58.
140   Quoted in Nicolson, *Congress of Vienna*, p. 249.
141   Pis'mo Imperatora Aleksandra I k kniaziu A. N. Golitsynu, 8–15 fevralia 1821g., Nikdai Mikhailovich, *Imperator Aleksandr I*, Appendix 4, pp. 416–20.
142   Pis'mo Imperatora Aleksandra I k kniaziu A. N. Golitsynu, 10 marta 1821g., in ibid., pp. 430–31.
143   W. Bruce Lincoln, *Nicholas I: Emperor and Autocrat of All the Russias* (Bloomington and London, 1978), pp. 17–31.
144   Pis'mo Konstantina Pavlovicha k Nikolaiu Pavlovichu, 2 dekabria 1825g.,

Schiemann, ed., *Die Ermordung Pauls und die Thronbesteigung Nikolaus I*, p. 94.

145 Shilder, *Nikolai Pervyi*, Vol. 1, pp. 216, 227; A. E. Presniakov, *14 dekabria 1825 goda* (Moscow-Leningrad, 1926), pp. 66–78.

146 W. Bruce Lincoln, "A Re-Examination of Some Historical Stereotypes: An Analysis of the Career Patterns and Backgrounds of the Decembrists," *Jahrbücher für Geschichte Osteuropas*, Vol. 24, No. 3 (1976), pp. 357–68.

147 M. V. Nechkina, *Dvizhenie dekabristov* (Moscow, 1955), Vol. 1, pp. 304–426; V. I. Semevskii, *Politicheskie i obshchestvennye idei dekabristov* (St. Petersburg, 1909), pp. 286–499; Anatole Mazour, *The First Russian Revolution: The Decembrist Movement, Its Origins, Development, and Significance* (Berkeley, 1937), pp. 46–65; Marc Raeff, ed., *The Decembrist Movement* (Englewood Cliffs, 1966), pp. 1–29.

148 Quoted in A. D. Borovkov, "A. D. Borovkov i ego avtobiograficheskie zapiski," *RS*, Vol. 96, No. 11 (November, 1898), p. 333.

149 Presniakov, *14 dekabria 1825 goda*, pp. 101–2; Shilder, *Nikolai Pervyi*, Vol. 1, p. 281; Th. Schiemann, *Geschichte Russlands unter Kaiser Nikolaus I* (Berlin, 1908), Vol. 2, p. 44.

150 "Zapiski Nikolaia I o vstuplenii ego na prestol'," *Mezhdutsarstvie 1825 goda i vosstanie dekabristov v perepiske i memuarakh chlenov tsarskoi sem'i*, ed. B. E. Syroechkovskii (Moscow-Leningrad, 1926), p. 22.

151 Ibid., pp. 22–23; Presniakov, *14 dekabria 1825 goda*, p. 116.

152 "Zapiski Nikolaia I o vstuplenii ego na prestol'," p. 27.

153 Shilder, *Nikolai Pervyi*, Vol. 1, p. 290; Baron M. A. Korf, *The Accession of Nicholas I* (London, 1857), p. 255.

154 Quoted in Korf, *The Accession*, p. 258.

155 Pis'mo Nikolaia I k Konstantinu Pavlovichu, 14–16 dekabria 1825 goda, in Schiemann, ed., *Die Ermordung Pauls und die Thronbesteigung Nikolaus I*, p. 103.

156 Marquis Astolphe de Custine, *La Russie en 1839* (Paris, 1843), Vol. 1, pp. 317–19.

157 Queen Victoria to Leopold, King of the Belgians, 11 June 1844 (NS), *The Letters of Queen Victoria: A Selection of Her Majesty's Correspondence between the Years 1837–1861*, ed. A. C. Benson and Viscount Escher (London, 1907), pp. 16–17.

158 Pis'mo Imperatritsy Ekateriny II k Melkioru Grimmu, 5 iiulia 1796g., *SIRO*, Vol. 23 (1878), p. 681.

159 Baron M. A. Korf, "Materialy i cherty k biografii Imperatora Nikolaia I i k istorii ego tsarstvovaniia. Rozhdenie i pervyia dvadtsat' let zhizni (1796–1817gg.)," *Materialy i cherty k biografii Imperatora Nikolaia I i k istorii ego tsarstvovaniia*, ed. N. F. Dubrovin (St. Petersburg, 1896), p. 17.

160 Ibid., pp. 22–23.

161 Quoted in ibid., p. 26. See also Shilder, *Nikolai Pervyi*, Vol. 1, p. 11.

162 Quoted in Korf, "Materialy," p. 30.

163 Quoted in Paul LaCroix, *Histoire de la vie et du règne de Nicolas Ier* (Paris, 1864), Vol. 1, p. 39.

164 Korf, "Materialy," p. 36.

165 Constantin de Grunwald, *Tsar Nicholas I*, trans. from the French Brigit Patmore (London, 1954), p. 23.

166 Quoted in Shilder, *Nikolai Pervyi*, Vol. 1, p. 454. Italics mine.

167 Quoted in I. D. Iakushkin, *Zapiski, stat'i, i pis'ma dekabrista I. D. Iakushkina* (Moscow, 1951), pp. 82–83.

168 These quotations are taken from "Zaveshchanie Nikolaia I synu," *Krasnyi arkhiv (KA)*, Vol. 3, (1923), pp. 291–93.

169 Grunwald, *Nicholas I*, p. 29.

170 "Imperatritsa Aleksandra Feodorovna v svoikh vospominaniiakh," *RS*, Vol. 88, No. 10 (October 1896), p. 21; I. N. Bozherianov, *Zhizneopisanie imperatritsy Aleksandry Feodorovny, suprugi Imperatora Nikolaia I* (St. Petersburg, 1898), Vol. 1, pp. 51–53.

171 "Imperatritsa Aleksandra Feodorovna v svoikh vospominaniiakh," p. 25.

172 "Zapiski Nikolaia I o vstuplenii ego na prestol'," p. 14.

173 Quoted in Grunwald, *Nicholas I*, p. 154.

174 Lincoln, *Nicholas I*, pp. 78–82.

175 Queen Victoria to Leopold, King of the Belgians, 4 June 1844 (NS), *Letters of Queen Victoria*, Vol. 2, p. 14.

176 A. Kh. Benkendorf, "Imperator Nikolai v 1828–1829 i v 1830–1831gg.," *RS*, Vol. 87, No. 7 (July 1896), pp. 6–7; "Perepiska Imperatora Nikolaia Pavlovicha s velikim kniazem tsesarevichem Konstantinom Pavlovichem, 1825–1829, 1830–1831gg.," *SIRO*, Vols. 131–132 (1910–11), passim.

177 S. V. Bakhrushin, "Velikaia kniaginia Elena Pavlovna," in *Osvobozhdenie krest'ian: deiateli reformy* (Moscow, 1911), pp. 116–17.

178 LaCroix, *Histoire de la vie*, Vol. 7, p. 5.

179 Pis'mo velikago kniazia Aleksandra Pavlovicha k kniaziu Viktoru Kochubeiu, ot 1–go maia 1796 goda, *Aleksandr Pervyi*, Vol. 1, Appendix 11, p. 277.

180 Bakhrushin, "Velikaia kniaginia Elena Pavlovna," p. 131.

181 LaCroix, *Histoire de la vie*, Vol. 7, p. 4.

182 Th. Schiemann, "Imperator Nikolai Pervyi (iz zapisok i vospominanii sovremennikov)," *RA*, No. 2 (February 1902), pp. 464–65; Grunwald, *Nicholas I*, pp. 139–40.

183 Quoted in Th. Schiemann, *Geschichte Russlands*, Vol. 3, pp. 317–18.

184 Quoted in Bozherianov, *Zhizneopisanie*, Vol. 1, p. 37.

185 M. Mundt, *Ein deutscher Arzt am Hofe Kaiser Nikolaus I von Russland* (Munich-Leipzig, 1917), p. 437.

186 Schiemann, *Geschichte Russlands*, Vol. 3, p. 318; see also Vol. 2, pp. 366–80, 318.

187 Baroness M. P. Frederiks, "Iz vospominanii baronessy M. P. Frederiksa," *Istoricheskii vestnik (IV)*, Vol. 71, No. 1 (January 1898), pp. 58–60.

188 A. E. Tsimmerman, 'Vospominaniia Generala A. E. Tsimmermana,' ORGBL, fond 325, kartonka 1, papka 1/142.

189 Quoted in A. S. Nifontov, *Rossiia v 1848 godu* (Moscow, 1949), p. 19.

190 The Austrian Ambassador Colloredo to Metternich, 31 August 1846 (NS), quoted in Grunwald, *Tsar Nicholas I*, pp. 228–29.

191 Ibid., p. 229, n. 1.

192 Memoirs of Captain Haffner, quoted in ibid., p. 216.

193 See, for example, A. F. Tiutcheva (Aksakova), *Pri dvore dvukh imperatorov. Vospominaniia-Dnevnik* (Moscow, 1928), Vol. 1, p. 168.

194 De Custine, *La Russie en 1839*, Vol. 1, p. 316.

195 'Otnoshenie Deistvitel'nago Tainago Sovetnika Dmitriia Buturlina 17–go

marta 1849g., k Ministru Narodnago Prosveshcheniia Grafu Uvarovu,' (konfidential'no), TsGIAL, fond 772, opis' 1, delo No. 2242/1–2; A. V. Nikitenko, *Zapisk i dnevnik*, Vol. 1 (Moscow, 1956), p. 338.

196 "Zaveshchanie Nikolaia I synu," *KA*, Vol. 3 (1923), p. 292; quoted in Presniakov, *Apogei samoderzhaviia*, p. 13.

197 Nicholas I to Prince Ivan Paskevich, 30 March 1848, in Prince A. Shcherbatov, *General-Fel'dmarshal kniaz' Paskevich. Ego zhizn' i deiatel'nost'* (St. Petersburg, 1892), Vol. 6, p. 214.

198 Aleksandr Kaminskii, "Vsepoddanneishaia zapiska Kaminskago, 1850 goda," *RS*, Vol. 122, No. 6 (June 1905), p. 629.

199 General Castelbajac to M. Thouvenel, 16 September 1853 and 11 February 1854, in L. Thouvenel, *Nicolas Ier et Napoleon III. Les préliminaires de la guerre de Crimée* (Paris, 1891), pp. 218, 334.

200 Tiutcheva, *Pri dvore dvukh imperatorov*, Vol. 1, entry for 4 October, 1853, p. 124.

201 General Castelbajac to M. Thouvenel, 11 February 1854, in *Nicolas Ier et Napoleon III*, p. 333.

202 Tiutcheva, *Pri dvore dvukh imperatorov*, Vol. 1, entry for 24 November 1854, pp. 167–68.

203 Baroness M. P. Frederiks, "Iz vospominanii," *IV*, Vol. 71, No. 2 (February 1898), p. 477. Her italics.

204 Tiutcheva, *Pri dvore dvukh imperatorov*, Vol. 1, entry for 19 February 1855, p. 184.

205 Ibid., p. 180.

206 Quoted in M. Polievktov, *Nikolai I: Biografiia i obzor tsarstvovaniia* (Moscow, 1918), p. 376.

207 Quoted in Grunwald, *Tsar Nicholas I*, p. 286.

208 Aleksandr Ivanovich Gertsen, *Polnoe sobranie sochinenii i pisem*, ed. M. K. Lemke (Petrograd, 1919), Vol. 13, p. 616.

209 K. D. Kavelin to T. N. Granovskii, 4 March 1855, in Sh. M. Levin, "K. D. Kavelin o smerti Nikolaia I," *Literaturnoe nasledstvo*, Vol. 67 (Moscow, 1959), p. 610.

210 A. V. Nikitenko, *Zapiski i dnevnik*, Vol. 1, p. 553.

211 Tiutcheva, *Pri dvore dvukh imperatorov*, Vol. 1, entry for 19 February 1855, pp. 179, 185.

212 Quoted in N. S. Shtakel'berg, "Zagadka smerti Nikolaia I," *Russkoe proshloe*, Vol. 1, (1923), p. 60.

213 Quoted in Bozherianov, *Zhizneopisanie*, Vol. 1, p. 96.

214 K. K. Merder, *Zapiski K. K. Merdera, vospitatelia tsesarevicha Aleksandra Nikolaevicha, 1824–1834gg.* (St. Petersburg, 1885), pp. 1–2.

215 Quoted in S. S. Tatishchev, *Imperator Aleksandr II: Ego zhizn' i tsarstvovanie* (St. Petersburg, 1911), Vol. 1, pp. 11–12.

216 Quoted in S. S. Tatishchev, "Aleksandr II, Imperator Vserossiiskii," *RBS*, Vol. 1, p. 390.

217 Pis'mo V. A. Zhukovskago imperatritse Aleksandre Feodorovne, 2–go oktiabria 1826g., in Tatishchev, *Imperator Aleksandr II*, Vol. 1, p. 16.

218 Dnevnik K. K. Merdera, in ibid., Vol. 1, p. 46.

219 M. V. Ptukha, *Ocherki po istorii statistiki v SSSR* (Moscow, 1959), Vol. 2, pp. 299, 362; Tatishchev, *Imperator Aleksandr II*, Vol. 1, pp. 84–85.

220 M. M. Speranskii, "O zakonakh. Besedy grafa M. M. Speranskago s Ego

Ímperatorskom Vysochestvom Gosudarem Naslednikom Tsesarevichem Velikim Kniazem Aleksandrom Nikolaevichem s 12 oktiabria 1835 po 10 aprelia 1836 goda," *SIRIO,* Vol. 30 (1880), pp. 363–65.

221 *Zapiski Merdera,* p. 112.

222 Quoted in Tatishchev, *Imperator Aleksandr II,* Vol. 1, pp. 48.

223 Pis'mo V. A. Zhukovskago imperatritse Aleksandre Feodorovne, 6–go maia 1837g., in ibid., Vol. 1, pp. 68–69.

224 Tatishchev, "Aleksandr II, Imperator Vserossiiskii," pp. 431–39.

225 Pis'mo V. A. Zhukovskago imperatritse Aleksandre Feodorovne, 14–go marta 1839g., *Imperator Aleksandr II,* Vol. 1, p. 96.

226 Marquis Astolphe de Custine, *Russia* (Cincinnati, 1856), p. 3.

227 Quoted in W. E. Mosse, *Alexander II and the Modernization of Russia* (New York, 1962), p. 30.

228 LaCroix, *Histoire de la vie,* Vol. 8, pp. 361–65.

229 Ibid., pp. 320–22.

230 Tatishchev, *Imperator Aleksandr II,* Vol. 1, pp. 108–14.

231 Riasanovsky, *Nicholas I and Official Nationality in Russia,* p. 85.

232 Lincoln, *Nicholas I,* pp. 345–47.

233 E. V. Tarle, *Sochineniia v dvenadtsati tomakh* (Moscow, 1959), Vol. 9, pp. 441–43.

234 M. Poggenophl au Directeur de la Chancellerie de St. Pétersbourg, 20 mars 1854, in Count K. V. Nesselrode, *Letters et papiers du Chancellier Comte de Nesselrode, 1760–1850* (Paris, 1912), Vol. 11, pp. 30–31.

235 P. A. Zaionchkovskii, "D. A. Miliutin: biograficheskii ocherk," *Dnevnik D. A. Miliutina, 1873–1875gg.* ed. P. A. Zaionchkovskii (Moscow, 1947), Vol. 1, p. 17.

236 Pis'mo K. D. Kavelina k T. N. Granovskomu, 4 marta 1855 goda, Sh. M. Levin, "K. D. Kavelin o smerti Nikolaia I," *Literaturnoe nasledstvo,* Vol. 67 (1959), p. 610.

237 Quoted from Franco Venturi, *Roots of Revolution: A History of the Populist and Socialist Movements in Nineteenth-Century Russia* (New York, 1966), p. 347. See also Adam Ulam, *In the Name of the People: Prophets and Conspirators in Prerevolutionary Russia* (New York, 1977), pp. 2–5.

238 Quoted in Ulam, *In the Name of the People,* p. 8.

239 Quoted in Venturi, *Roots of Revolution,* p. 344.

240 Ibid., pp. 344–49; K. F. Ryleev, *Polnoe sobranie sochineniia* (Moscow, 1934), pp. 501, 518.

241 Quoted in Alexandre Tarsaidzé, *Katia, Wife Before God* (New York, 1970), p. 90.

242 Quoted in ibid., p. 98.

243 Mosse, *Alexander II,* p. 143.

244 P. A. Zaionchkovskii, ed., *Dnevrik D. A. Miliutina, 1876–1877* (Moscow, 1951), Vol. 3, p. 251; A. A. Polovtsov, *Dnevnik gosudarstvennogo sekretaria A. A. Polovtsova, 1883–1886gg.* (Moscow, 1966), Vol. 1, p. 189.

245 D. A. Miliutin, *Dnevnik,* Vol. 3, pp. 269, 275, 278.

246 Quoted in Mosse, *Alexander II,* p. 147.

247 D. A. Miliutin, *Dnevnik,* Vol. 3, p. 269.

248 Quoted in Tarsaïdzé, *Katia,* p. 217.

249 S. S. Volk, *Narodnaia volia* (Moscow-Leningrad, 1966), pp. 102–3; David Footman, *Red Prelude* (New Haven, 1945), pp. 130–37; W. Bruce Lincoln,

"Murder Near the Cathedral," *History Today,* Vol. 25, No. 3 (March 1975), pp. 177–78.
250 Quoted in Footman, *Red Prelude,* p. 167.
251 Ibid., pp. 244–57.
252 M. F. Frolenko, *Sobranie sochineniia* (Moscow, 1932), Vol. 2, p. 63.
253 Vera Figner, *Memoirs of a Revolutionist* (New York, 1927), pp. 97–102; Footman, *Red Prelude,* pp. 109–93.
254 Figner, *Memoirs,* p. 102.
255 Venturi, *Roots of Revolution,* pp. 712–13; Footman, *Red Prelude,* pp. 194–200.
256 Vera Figner, *Zapechatlennyi trud* (Moscow, 1964), Vol. 1, p. 268.
257 Footman, *Red Prelude,* pp. 242–43.
258 Konstantin Korol'kov, *Zhizn' i tsarstvovanie Imperatora Aleksandra III (1881–1894gg)* (Kiev, 1901), pp. 17–19.
259 Dillon, "Aleksandr III," *Golos minuvshago,* Nos. 5–6 (May–June 1917), p. 85.
260 Quoted in W. Bruce Lincoln, "Alexander III of Russia," *History Today,* Vol. 26, No. 10 (October 1976), p. 645.
261 Nicolas Notovitch, *L'Empereur Alexandre III et son entourage* (Paris, 1893), pp. 71–73.
262 Florinsky, *Russia,* Vol. 2, p. 1087; Notovitch, *Alexandre III,* pp. 69–79.
263 Anatole G. Mazour, *Modern Russian Historiography* (New York and Princeton, 1958), pp. 98–106.
264 Florinsky, *Russia,* Vol. 2, p. 1087.
265 Quoted in ibid., p. 1088.
266 Quoted in ibid., p. 1089.
267 K. P. Pobedonostsev, "Graf V. N. Panin," *Golosa iz Rossii,* No. 7 (1859; reprint ed., Moscow, 1974–75), pp. 137–38.
268 Robert F. Byrnes, *Pobedonostsev: His Life and Thought* (Bloomington, 1968), pp. 25–26; Korol'kov, *Zhizn' Aleksandra III,* p. 16.
269 Pis'mo Tsesarevicha Aleksandra Aleksandrovicha k Konstantinu Petrovichu Pobedonostsevu, 22 noiabria 1866gg., in *K. P. Pobedonostsev i ego korrespondenty* (Moscow-Petrograd, 1923), Vol. 1 (2), p. 1103.
270 Dillon, "Aleksandr III," pp. 87, 92.
271 Quoted in Florinsky, *Russia,* Vol. 2, p. 1119.
272 S. Iu. Witte, *Vospominaniia* (Moscow, 1960), Vol. 1, p. 408.
273 *Pamiati Imperatora Aleksandra III* (Moscow, 1894), pp. 4–6.
274 Florinsky, *Russia,* Vol. 2, pp. 1141–42.
275 Witte, *Vospominaniia,* Vol. 1, pp. 434–35.

CHAPTER IX: *The New Faces of St. Petersburg*

1 S. Bezsonov, *Krepostnye arkhitektory* (Moscow, 1938), pp. 39–54; V. Panov, *Arkhitektor A. N. Voronikhin* (Moscow, 1937), pp. 25–30; M. A. Il'in, "A. N. Voronikhin," in *IRI,* Vol. 8 (1), pp. 62–64.
2 I. E. Grabar, ed., *Istoriia arkhitektury: Peterburgskaia arkhitektura v XVIII i XIX veke* (Moscow, 1911), Vol. 3, pp. 485–88; Pavel Svin'in, *Dostopamiatnosti Sanktpeterburga i ego okrestnostei* (St. Petersburg, 1816), Vol. 1, pp. 52–57.

3   Svin'in, *Dostopamiatnosti Sanktpeterburga*, Vol. 2, p. 111. See also pp. 98–109; I. E. Grabar, "T. Tomon," in *IRI*, Vol. 8, pp. 106–122.

4   Quoted in Rogger, *National Consciousness*, pp. 74–75.

5   Egorov, *Architectural Planning of St. Petersburg*, pp. 193–95.

6   Svin'in, *Dostopamiatnosti Sanktpeterburga*, Vol. 5, pp. 105–121; M. A. Il'in, "A. D. Zakharov," *IRI*, Vol. 8 (1), pp. 86–104; G. Grimm, *Arkhitektor Andreian Zakharov* (Moscow, 1940), pp. 7–62.

7   Egorov, *Architectural Planning of St. Petersburg*, pp. 121–22, 156–57.

8   Baedeker, *Russia*, pp. 109–10; L. V. Tengoborskii, 'Kratkoe izlozhenie nashego finansovago polozheniia,' (mai, 1856g.), TsGIAL, fond 958, opis' 1, delo No. 742/3.

9   G. G. Grimm, M. A. Il'in, and Iu. A. Egorov, "K. I. Rossi," *IRI*, Vol. 8 (1), pp. 128–64; Grabar, *Istoriia arkhitektury*, Vol. 3, pp. 527–60.

10 Egorov, *Architectural Planning of St. Petersburg*, pp. 131–82.

11 P. A. Zaionchkovskii, *Pravitel'stvennyi apparat samoderzhavnoi Rossii v XIX v.* (Moscow, 1978), pp. 66–72.

12 Baedeker, *Russia*, pp. 103, 124.

13 J. G. Kohl, *Russia: St. Petersburg, Moscow, Kharkoff, Riga, Odessa, the German Provinces on the Baltic, the Steppes, the Crimea, and the Interior of the Empire* (London, 1844), p. 7.

14 Lady Londonderry, *The Russian Journal of Lady Londonderry, 1836–1837*, ed. W. A. L. Seaman and J. R. Sewell (London, 1973), pp. 121, 113.

15 B. V. Tomashevskii, ed., *Pushkinskii Peterburg* (Leningrad, 1949), pp. 379–408; Edward Jerrmann, *Pictures from St. Petersburg* (New York, 1852), pp. 36–37.

16 Kohl, *Russia*, p. 6.

17 Marquis de Custine, *Russia*, pp. 115–16.

18 Lady Londonderry, *Russian Journal*, pp. 96–128.

19 A. G. Rashin, *Naselenie Rossii za sto let (1811–1913): statisticheskii ocherk* (Moscow, 1956), p. 124; L. A. Perovskii, 'O prichinakh umnozheniia deloproizvodstva vo vnutrennem upravlenii,' (mart, 1851g.), TsGIAL, fond 1287, opis' 36, delo No. 137/41.

20 N. V. Gogol', *Sobranie sochinenii* (Moscow, 1959), Vol. 3, p. 128.

21 S. Frederick Starr, *Decentralization and Self-Government in Russia, 1830–1870* (Princeton, 1972), p. 22.

22 F. G. Terner, *Vospominaniia F. G. Ternera* (St. Petersburg, 1910), Vol. 1, p. 68; A. A. Kharitonov, "Iz vospominanii A. A. Kharitonova," *RS*, Vol. 81, No. 1 (January 1894), pp. 116–17; I. V. Roskovshenko, "Peterburg v 1831–1832gg.," *RS*, Vol. 101, No. 3 (February 1900), p. 487.

23 P. I. Nebolsin, "Biudzhety Peterburgskikh chinovnikov," *Ekonomicheskii ukazatel'*, No. 11 (16 March 1857), pp. 241–50.

24 See, for example, Pis'mo N. A. Miliutina k D. A. Miliutinu, 29 ianvaria 1837g., ORGBL, fond 169, karton 69, papka No. 5/35–36.

25 Roskovshenko, "Peterburg v 1831–1832gg.", pp. 477–80.

26 S. I. Zarudnyi, "Pis'mo opytnago chinovnika sorokovykh godov mladshemu sobratu, postupaiushchemu na sluzhbu," *RS*, Vol. 100 (1899), p. 543.

27 A. I. Artem'ev, 'Dnevnik, l ianvaria–31 iiulia 1856g.,' GPB, fond 37, delo No. 158/8. Entry for 11 January, 1856.

28 M. E. Saltykov-Shchedrin, *Sobranie sochinenii* (Moscow, 1970), Vol. 10, p. 271.

29 E. Karnovich, *Sanktpeterburg v statisticheskom otnoshenii* (St. Petersburg, 1860), pp. 43–46; A. I. Kopanev, *Naselenie Peterburga v pervoi polovine XIX veka* (Moscow, 1957), p. 58.

30 Reginald Zelnik, *Labor and Society in Tsarist Russia: The Factory Workers of St. Petersburg, 1855–1870* (Stanford, 1971), p. 52; 'O polozhenii chernorabozhikh v S.-Peterburge,' TsGIAL, fond 869, opis' 1, delo No. 350/1–16.

31 Zelnik, *Labor and Society,* p. 56.

32 Quoted in M. P. Viatkin, "Ekonomicheskaia zhizn' Peterburga v period razlozheniia i krizisa krepostnichestva," *Ocherki istorii Leningrada,* Vol. 1, p. 462.

33 Stolpianskii, *Kak voznik, osnovalsia, i ros Sanktpiterburkh,* pp. 357–58.

34 Zelnik, *Labor and Society,* pp. 241–44.

35 Ibid., pp. 234–36; 250–51; 414, n. 45.

36 S. P. Luppov and N. N. Petrov, "Gorodskoe upravlenie i gorodskoe khoziaistvo Peterburga ot kontsa XVIII v. do 1861g.," *Ocherki istorii Leningrada,* Vol. 1, pp. 623–24; I. A. Bartenev, "Arkhitektura Peterburga," in ibid., Vol. 2, pp. 797–800.

37 Bartenev, "Arkhitektura Peterburga," p. 809. See also pp. 796–808.

38 Aleksandr Pushkin, *The Bronze Horseman,* in *The Poems, Prose and Plays of Alexander Pushkin,* p. 97.

39 Aleksandr Blok, *The Twelve,* trans. Babette Deutsch and Avrahm Yarmolinsky (New York, 1931).

CHAPTER X: *From Golden Age to Iron Age*

1 Letter of Catherine the Great to Melchior Grimm, 23 June 1790. Quoted in Haumant, *La Culture Française en Russie,* p. 176.

2 Pypin, *Obshchestvennoe dvizhenie v Rossii pri Aleksandre I,* pp. 72–74; A. A. Kornilov, *Kurs istorii Rossii XIX v.* (Moscow, 1918), Vol. 1, pp. 60–61; V. I. Semevskii, "Vvedenie," in A. A. Brückner ed., *Smert' Pavla I* (St. Petersburg, 1907), pp. xxxiii–xxxiv; *PSZ,* Vol. sobranie 1–oe, No. 19,387; Florinsky, *Russia,* Vol. 1, pp. 626–27.

3 Prot. Georgii Florovskii, *Puti russkago bogosloviia* (Paris, 1937), p. 128.

4 Iu D. Levin, "Angliiskaia poeziia i literatura russkogo sentimentalizma, *Ot klassitsizma k romantizmu,* ed. M. D. Alekseev (Leningrad, 1970), p. 233.

5 Blagoi, *Istoriia,* pp. 626–27; Pypin, *Istoriia,* Vol. 4, pp. 209–11; Richard Pipes, "The Background and Growth of Karamzin's Political Ideas Down to 1810," in *Karamzin's Memoir on Ancient and Modern Russia,* pp. 21–24; Henry M. Nebel, Jr., *N. M. Karamzin: A Russian Sentimentalist* (The Hague-Paris, 1967), pp. 24–26.

6 Pipes, "Karamzin's Political Ideas," pp. 27–29.

7 N. M. Karamzin, "Pis'ma russkogo puteshestvennika," *Izbrannye sochineniia* (Moscow-Leningrad, 1964), Vol. 1, pp. 370, 593.

8 Wortman, *Development of a Russian Legal Consciousness,* p. 129.

9 N. M. Karamzin, "Bednaia Liza," *Izbrannye sochineniia,* Vol. 1, p. 607.

10 Wortman, *Development of a Russian Legal Consciousness,* p. 130; Pipes, "Karamzin's Political Ideas," pp. 37, 39–40.

11 Pipes, ed. and trans., *Karamzin's Memoir on Ancient and Modern Russia,* pp. 197–98.

12 Ibid., pp. 103–205; Wortman, *Development of a Russian Legal Consciousness*, pp. 129–30; Lincoln, *Nicholas I*, pp. 86–87.

13 P. N. Sakulin, "Literaturnye techeniia v Aleksandrovskuiu epokhu," *Istoriia russkoi literatury XIX veka*, ed. D. N. Ovsianiko-Kulikovskii (Moscow, 1908), Vol. 1, pp. 95–97; A. N. Shebunin, "Brat'ia Turgenevykh v dvorianskoe obshchestvo aleksandrovskoi epokhi," in *Dekabrist N. I. Turgenev: Pis'ma k bratu S. I. Turgenevu* (Moscow-Leningrad, 1936), pp. 31–37; Barry Hollingsworth, "Arzamas: Portrait of a Literary Society," *SEER*, Vol. 44, No. 103 (July 1966), pp. 310–26.

14 Pipes, "Karamzin's Political Ideas," pp. 5–6.

15 Quoted in Nikitenko, *Dnevnik*, Vol. 1, p. 174.

16 Riasanovsky, *Nicholas I and Official Nationality in Russia*, pp. 71–72; Cynthia H. Wittaker, "The Ideology of Sergei Uvarov: An Interpretive Essay," *Russian Review*, Vol. 37, No. 2 (April 1978), pp. 158–76.

17 Quoted in Riasanovsky, *Nicholas I and Official Nationality in Russia*, pp. 74–75.

18 Ernest J. Simmons, *Pushkin* (New York, 1964), p. 253.

19 Quoted in Slonim, *Epic of Russian Literature*, p. 105.

20 Simmons, *Pushkin*, p. iv.

21 Quoted in ibid., p. 101.

22 Slonim, *Epic of Russian Literature*, pp. 81–82.

23 Prince D. S. Mirsky, *A History of Russian Literature* (New York, 1927), p. 126.

24 A. S. Pushkin, "Vol'nost'. Oda," *Polnoe sobranie sochinenii* (Moscow, 1962), Vol. 1, p. 321.

25 A. S. Pushkin, "Na Arakcheeva," ibid., Vol. 1, p. 406.

26 A. S. Pushkin, "Derevnia," ibid., Vol. 1, pp. 360–61.

27 A. N. Pypin, *Kharakteristiki literaturnykh mnenii ot dvadtsatykh do piatidesiatykh godov* (St. Petersburg, 1909), pp. 59–67; V. V. Gippius et al., "Pushkin," *Istoriia russkoi literatury*, ed. D. D. Blagoi and B. P. Gorodetskii (Moscow-Leningrad, 1953), Vol. 6, pp. 187–93.

28 The preceding quotations are taken from Simmons, *Pushkin*, pp. 246, 248, and 253.

29 Slonim, *Epic of Russian Literature*, p. 102.

30 Sidney Monas, *The Third Section: Police and Society in Russia under Nicholas I* (Cambridge, Mass., 1961), p. 145.

31 Ivanov-Razumnik, "Obshchestvennye i umstvennye techeniia tridtsatykh godov," *Istoriia*, ed. Ovsianiko-Kulikovskii, Vol. 1, pp. 260–267; G. V. Plekhanov, "Vissarion Grigor'evich Belinskii," ibid., Vol. 2, pp. 227–34; P. N. Miliukov, "Liubov' u idealistov tridtsatykh godov," *Iz istorii russkoi intelligentsii*, pp. 81–94; A. N. Pypin, *Belinskii: Ego zhizn' i perepiska* (St. Petersburg, 1908), pp. 6–76.

32 Quoted in Ivanov-Razumnik, "Obshchestvennye i umstvennye techeniia," p. 247.

33 Herbert E. Bowman, *Vissarion Belinsky, 1810–1848: A Study in the Origins of Social Criticism in Russia* (Cambridge, Mass., 1954), pp. 127–30.

34 S. P. Shevyrev, "Vzgliad russkago na sovremennoe obrazovanie Evropy," *Moskvitianin*, No. 1 (1841), pp. 292–93.

35 V. G. Belinskii, *Sobranie sochinenii V. G. Belinskago*, ed. Ivanov-Razumnik (Petrograd, 1919), Vol. 3, p. 822.

36 Richard Pipes, *Russia under the Old Regime* (New York, 1974), p. 269. Some of the best and most recent studies of the Westerners include the following: Martin Malia, *Alexander Herzen and the Birth of Russian Socialism* (Cambridge, Mass., 1961); Edward Brown, *Stankevich and His Moscow Circle, 1830–1840* (Stanford, 1961); Bowman, *Vissarion Belinsky,* and a vast number of specialized studies in Russian that can be found in the bibliographies to these works.

37 A great deal has been written about the Slavophiles, and their most important works have long since been published. The best summaries of their views can be found in Ch. Vetrinskii, "Umstvennoe i obshchestvennoe dvizhenie sorokovykh godov," *Istoriia,* ed. Ovsianiko-Kulikovskii, Vol. 2, pp. 67–130; Ivanov-Razumnik, *Istoriia russkoi obshchestvennoi mysli,* Vol. 1, pp. 290–331; N. Riasanovsky, *Russia and the West in the Teachings of the Slavophiles* (Cambridge, Mass., 1952); Malia, *Alexander Herzen* passim, but especially pp. 279–312; and P. K. Christoff, *An Introduction to Nineteenth-Century Slavophilism,* 2 vols. (The Hague, 1961, 1972).

38 L. N. Stepanov, "Gogol'," *Istoriia russkoi literatury,* ed. B. P. Gorodetskii (Moscow-Leningrad, 1955), Vol. 7, pp. 132–34; Victor Erlich, *Gogol* (New Haven and London, 1969), pp. 7–14.

39 Mirsky, *History of Russian Literature,* p. 184.

40 Pis'mo N. V. Gogolia k P. P. Kosiarovskomu, 3–go sentiabria 1827g., published in Gogol', *Sobranie sochinenii,* Vol. 6, p. 273.

41 Quoted in Erlich, *Gogol,* p. 17.

42 Ibid., p. 79.

43 N. V. Gogol', "Nevskii Prospekt," in *Sobranie sochinenii,* Vol. 3, p. 42.

44 N. V. Gogol', "Nos," in ibid., pp. 44–70, especially pp. 50–51.

45 Gogol', "Nevskii Prospekt," p. 43.

46 Vladimir Nabokov, *Nikolai Gogol* (New York, 1961), pp. 54–60; Erlich, *Gogol,* pp. 108–11.

47 V. G. Belinskii, "Pokhozhdeniia Chichikova ili Mertvye Dushi," *Sobranie sochinenii Belinskago,* Vol. 2, Cols. 401–16.

48 Billington, *Icon and the Axe,* pp. 338–39.

49 Quoted in Erlich, *Gogol,* pp. 184–85.

50 N. V. Gogol', *Polnoe sobranie sochinenii N. V. Gogolia* (Moscow, 1913), Vol. 8, p. 42.

51 V. G. Belinskii, "Pis'mo k Gogoliu," *Sobranie sochinenii Belinskago,* Vol. 3, Col. 821.

52 Quoted in Erlich, *Gogol,* p. 194.

53 W. Bruce Lincoln, *Nikolai Miliutin: An Enlightened Russian Bureaucrat of the Nineteenth Century* (Newtonville, Mass., 1977), pp. 32–34.

54 Pis'mo V. G. Belinskago k V. P. Botkinu, 3 aprelia 1843g., in *Belinskii: Pis'ma,* ed. E. A. Liatskii (St. Petersburg, 1914), Vol. 2, p. 360. See also L. M. Lotman et al., "Proza shestidesiatykh godov," *Istoriia russkoi literatury,* ed. M. K. Dobrynin (Moscow-Leningrad, 1956), Vol. 8(1), pp. 316–319; A. E. Gruzinskii, "Ivan Sergeevich Turgenev," *Istoriia,* ed. Ovsianiko-Kulikovskii, Vol. 3, pp. 278–80.

55 Terence Emmons, *The Russian Landed Gentry and the Peasant Emancipation of 1861* (Cambridge, 1968), p. 30.

56 Quoted in Slonim, *Epic of Russian Literature,* p. 253.

57 Malia, *Alexander Herzen,* pp. 265–74.

58 I. S. Turgenev, *Nakanune,* in *Sobranie sochinenii* (Moscow, 1961), Vol. 3, p. 79.
59 I. S. Turgenev, *Ottsy i deti,* ibid., Vol. 3, pp. 139, 142, 159, 162.
60 Ibid., p. 159.
61 Florinsky, *Russia,* Vol. 2, pp. 784, 806.
62 Quoted in ibid., p. 1089.
63 Byrnes, *Pobedonostsev,* pp. 290–91, 332–57; Edward C. Thaden, *Conservative Nationalism in Nineteenth-Century Russia* (Seattle, 1964), pp. 187–200.
64 Quoted in Florinsky, *Russia,* Vol. 2, pp. 1114–15.
65 Quoted in Thaden, *Conservative Nationalism,* p. 202.
66 G. M. Fridlender, "Dostoevskii," *Istoriia russkoi literatury,* ed. B. I. Bursov (Moscow-Leningrad, 1956), Vol. 9 (2), pp. 7–14, 30–34.
67 Ibid., pp. 34–39; Byrnes, *Pobedonostsev,* pp. 93–108; Slonim, *Epic of Russian Literature,* pp. 272–78. See also E. J. Simmons, *Dostoevski: The Making of a Novelist* (Oxford, 1940); David Magarshack, *Dostoevsky* (New York, 1962); and E. H. Carr, *Dostoevsky* (London, 1949), for three very useful English-language studies of Dostoevskii's life and work.
68 Quoted in Magarshack, *Dostoevsky,* pp. 380–81.
69 Slonim, *Epic of Russian Literature,* p. 281.
70 F. M. Dostoevskii, *Prestuplenie i nakazanie,* in *Polnoe sobranie sochinenii v tridtsati tomakh* (Leningrad, 1973), Vol. 6, pp. 211, 200.
71 Ibid., p. 11.
72 Ibid., p. 422.
73 F. M. Dostoevskii, *Idiot,* in *Polnoe sobranie sochinenii,* Vol. 8, pp. 183–84.
74 Ibid., p. 184.
75 Ibid., p. 510.
76 Quoted in Billington, *Icon and the Axe,* p. 419.
77 Ibid., p. 421. Billington's discussion of Dostoevskii's work is easily one of the most provocative available, and perhaps the most outstanding brief essay in English.
78 F. M. Dostoevskii, *Besy,* in *Polnoe sobranie sochinenii,* Vol. 10, p. 514.
79 Ibid., p. 515–516.
80 F. M. Dostoevskii, *Brat'ia Karamazovy,* in *Polnoe sobranie sochinenii,* Vol. 15, pp. 126, 128.
81 Ibid., Vol. 14, p. 234.
82 Ibid., Vol. 15, p. 125.
83 Quoted in Slonim, *Epic of Russian Literature,* pp. 296–97.
84 Quoted in Magarshack, *Dostoevsky,* p. 388.
85 Dostoevskii, *Polnoe sobranie sochinenii,* Vol. 15, p. 197.
86 Quoted in E. J. Simmons, *Leo Tolstoy* (Boston, 1946), p. 49.
87 Quoted in ibid., p. 59.
88 B. I. Bursov and L. D. Opul'skaia, "Lev Tolstoi," *Istoriia russkoi literatury,* ed. Bursov, Vol. 9 (2), pp. 436–50; V. Shklovskii, *Lev Tolstoi* (Moscow, 1967), pp. 18–135.
89 L. N. Tolstoi, *Dnevniki, 1847–1894gg.,* in *Sobranie sochinenii v dvadtsati tomakh* (Moscow, 1965), Vol. 19, p. 88.
90 Quoted in Slonim, *Epic of Russian Literature,* p. 311.
91 Quoted in Simmons, *Tolstoy,* p. 273.
92 Quoted in ibid., p. 274.
93 Ibid., p. 315.
94 Ibid., p. 443.

95   Quoted in Shklovskii, *Lev Tolstoi*, p. 628.
96   Slonim, *Epic of Russian Literature*, p. 312.
97   Quoted in M. D. Calvocoressi, *Modest Mussorgsky: His Life and Works* (Fair Lawn, N. J., 1956), pp. 18–19.
98   Quoted in ibid., pp. 35–36.
99   Quoted in M. D. Calvocoressi and Gerald Abraham, *Masters of Russian Music* (New York, 1936), p. 241.
100 Quoted in Calvocoressi, *Mussorgsky*, p. 195.
101 Quoted in Calvocoressi and Abraham, *Masters*, p. 185.
102 Quoted in Billington, *Icon and the Axe*, p. 407.
103 E. Gomberg-Verzhbinskaia, *Peredvizhniki* (Leningrad, 1970), pp. 80–81; I. E. Grabar, "Chuguevskie uchitelia Repina," *Khudozhestvennoe nasledstvo*, ed. I. E. Grabar and I. S. Zil'bershtein (Moscow-Leningrad, 1948), Vol. 1, pp. 16–17.
104 D. V. Sarab'ianov, "I. E. Repin," *IRI*, Vol. 9 (1), pp. 447–49.
105 Quoted in Gomberg-Verzhbinskaia, *Peredvizhniki*, p. 84.
106 Quoted in Sarab'ianov, "I. E. Repin," pp. 462–63.
107 F. M. Dostoevsky, *The Diary of a Writer*, trans. and ann. Boris Brasol (New York, 1954), p. 81.
108 Billington, *Icon and the Axe*, p. 406.
109 Elizabeth Valkenier, *Russian Realist Art: The Peredvizhniki and Their Tradition* (Ann Arbor, 1977), p. 67.
110 Ibid., p. 65.
111 Ibid., pp. 63–65; JoAnn (Schrampfer) Ruckman, "The Business Elite of Moscow: A Social Inquiry" (Ph.D. diss., Northern Illinois University, 1975), pp. 161–237, 322–64.

CHAPTER XI: *The Colossus of the North*

1   Norman E. Saul, *Russia and the Mediterranean, 1797–1807* (Chicago, 1970), pp. 37–38.
2   Quoted in Martens, *Sobranie traktatov*, Vol. 13, p. 249.
3   K. E. Dzhedzhula, *Rossiia i velikaia frantsuzskaia burzhuaznaia revoliutsiia kontsa XVIII veka* (Kiev, 1972), p. 423; R. S. Lanin, "Vneshniaia politika Pavla I v 1796–1798gg.," *Uchenye zapiski Leningradskogo Gosudarstvennogo Universiteta* [seriia istoricheskikh nauk] Vol. 10 (1941), pp. 22–25.
4   M. V. Klochkov, *Ocherki pravitel'stvennoi deiatel'nosti vremeni Pavla I* (Petrograd, 1916), pp. 133–34.
5   Dispatch of General Bonaparte to the Executive Directory, 26 May 1797, *Letters and Documents of Napoleon*, ed. and trans. John Eldred Howard (New York, 1961), Vol. 1, p. 191.
6   Saul, *Russia and the Mediterranean*, p. 42.
7   Dispatch of General Bonaparte to the Executive Directory, 17 June 1797, *Letters and Documents of Napoleon*, Vol. 1, p. 244.
8   Dispatch of General Bonaparte to the Executive Directory, 26 May 1797, in ibid., p. 191.
9   Saul, *Russia and the Mediterranean*, p. 91.
10 See, for example, G. P. Meshcheriakov, ed., *A. V. Suvorov: Sbornik dokumentov* (Moscow, 1952), Vol. 3, p. 557.
11 Ibid., Vol. 4, p. 12.

12 Philip Longworth, *The Art of Victory: The Life and Achievements of Field-Marshal Suvorov, 1729–1800* (New York, 1966), pp. 236–69.
13 Quoted in ibid., p. 282.
14 Ibid., pp. 270–90.
15 A. M. Stanislavskaia, *Russko-Angliiskie otnosheniia i problemy Sredizemnomor'ia, 1798–1807gg.* (Moscow, 1962), pp. 144–54; Saul, *Russia and the Mediterranean*, pp. 129–31.
16 Quoted in S. B. Okun', *Ocherki istorii SSSR: konets XVIII–pervaia chetverty XIX veka* (Leningrad, 1956), pp. 105, 106.
17 Quoted in Martens, *Sobranie traktatov*, Vol. 13, p. 250.
18 Quoted in ibid., p. 251.
19 Okun', *Ocherki*, p. 107.
20 Florinsky, *Russia*, Vol. 1, p. 621.
21 Quoted in Klochkov, *Ocherki*, pp. 113–14.
22 Quoted in ibid., p. 124.
23 For a thorough and important discussion of this law, see Klochkov, *Ocherki*, pp. 528–29.
24 Quoted in ibid., p. 124. For an outstanding discussion of the development of police states in seventeenth- and eighteenth-century Europe and Russia, see Marc Raeff, "The Well-Ordered Police State and the Development of Modernity in Seventeenth- and Eighteenth-Century Europe: An Attempt at a Comparative Approach," *The American Historical Review*, Vol. 80, No. 5 (December 1975), pp. 1221–43.
25 Quoted in Patricia Kennedy Grimsted, *The Foreign Ministers of Alexander I: Political Attitudes and the Conduct of Russian Diplomacy, 1801–1825* (Berkeley and Los Angeles, 1969), p. 89.
26 Quoted in Florinsky, *Russia*, Vol. 2, p. 651.
27 Quoted in Shilder, *Aleksandr Pervyi*, Vol. 2, p. 6.
28 A. N. Filippov, "Istoricheskii ocherk obrazovaniia ministerstv v Rossii," *Zhurnal Ministertva Iustitsii* (*ZhMIu*), No. 9 (September 1902), pp. 39–73.
29 Count P. A. Stroganov, "Essai sur un règlement organique de toutes les branches du gouvernement de Russie," in Nikolai Mikhailovich, *Graf P. A. Stroganov*, Vol. 1, p. 253.
30 Kornilov, *Kurs*, Vol. 1, pp. 120–21.
31 Alan Palmer, *Alexander I: Tsar of War and Peace* (London, 1974), p. 77.
32 Quoted in Michael Jenkins, *Arakcheev, Grand Vizier of the Russian Empire* (New York, 1969), p. 94.
33 Pis'ma Imperatritsy Elisavety Alekseevny k materi, Markgrafine Badenskoi, l i 8 sentiabria 1803g., in Nikolai Mikhailovich, *Imperatritsa Elisaveta Alekseevna*, Vol. 2, pp. 105, 109.
34 Quoted in Palmer, *Alexander I*, p. 84.
35 Ibid., pp. 82–84; Marian Kukiel, *Czartoryski and European Unity, 1770–1861* (Princeton, 1955), pp. 42–51; and Grimsted, *Foreign Ministers*, pp. 127–31.
36 Palmer, *Alexander I*, pp. 84–87; Kukiel, *Czartoryski*, pp. 57–60; Grimsted, *Foreign Ministers*, pp. 131–41.
37 Quoted in Palmer, *Alexander I*, p. 96.
38 N. S. Kiniapina, *Vneshniaia politika Rossii pervoi poloviny XIX veka* (Moscow, 1963), pp. 28–30; Shilder, *Aleksandr Pervyi*, Vol. 2, pp. 131–32; Palmer, *Alexander I*, pp. 96–98.

39 Quoted in Shilder, *Aleksandr Pervyi*, Vol. 2, p. 283.

40 Palmer, *Alexander I*, p. 99.

41 Ibid.

42 Quoted in Shilder, *Aleksandr Pervyi*, Vol. 2, p. 136.

43 Ibid., p. 140.

44 Quoted in ibid., pp. 139–40.

45 Quoted in ibid., p. 140.

46 Ibid., pp. 140, 285, 144–45; Pis'mo Imperatritsy Elisavety Alekseevny k materi, Markgrafine Badenskoi, 11/23 dekabria 1805g., in Nikolai Mikhailovich, *Imperatritsa Elisaveta Alekseevna*, Vol. 2, pp. 176–78.

47 P. A. Shtorkh, "Materialy," *ZhMNP*, Vol. 137 (1868), p. 822.

48 Shilder, *Aleksandr Pervyi*, Vol. 2, pp. 287, 155.

49 Th. Schiemann, *Aleksandr Pervyi* (Moscow, 1908), p. 37.

50 Pipes, ed. and trans., *Karamzin's Memoir on Ancient and Modern Russia*, p. 145.

51 Pis'mo Imperatritsy Elisavety Alekseevny k materi, Markgrafine Badenskoi, 29 avgusta 1807g., in Nikolai Mikhailovich, *Imperatritsa Elisaveta Alekseevna*, Vol. 2, pp. 255–56.

52 Pipes, ed. and trans., *Karamzin's Memoir on Ancient and Modern Russia*, p. 145.

53 I. M. Kulisher, *Ocherk istorii russkoi torgovli* (St. Petersburg, 1923), pp. 273–76.

54 Marc Raeff, *Michael Speransky: Statesman of Imperial Russia* (The Hague, 1957), p. 55.

55 *PSZ*, sobranie 1-oe, No. 24,686.

56 D. F. Kobeko, *Imperatorskii Tsarskosel'skii litsei* (St. Petersburg, 1911), pp. 6–7.

57 *PSZ*, sobranie I-oe, No. 23,771; H.-J. Torke, "Das Russische Beamtentum in der ersten Hälfte des 19. Jahrhunderts," *Forschungen zur osteuropäischen Geschichte*, Vol. 13 (1967), pp. 58–70.

58 Raeff, *Speransky*, pp. 63–65.

59 See John Quincy Adams, *Memoirs of John Quincy Adams*, Charles Francis Adams, ed. (Philadelphia, 1874), Vol. 2, especially pp. 191–245.

60 Hugh Seton-Watson, *The Russian Empire, 1801–1917* (Oxford, 1967), p. 123; Albert Vandal, *Napoléon et Alexandre Ier* (Paris, 1907), Vol. 2, pp. 530–31.

61 Pis'mo Aleksandra I–go velikoi kniagine Ekaterine Pavlovne, 26 dekabria 1810, in Nikolai Mikhailovich, ed, *Perepiska Aleksandra I s velikoi kniaginei Ekaterinoi Pavlovnoi*, p. 35.

62 Lettres de l'Empereur Alexandre Ier au prince Adam Czartoryski, 25 décembre 1810 et 31 janvier 1811, *Mémoires du Prince Adam Czartoryski et correspondance avec l'Empereur Alexandre Ier*, ed. Mazade, Vol. 2, pp. 248–54, 277.

63 Kukiel, *Czartoryski*, pp. 94–99.

64 Lettre de l'Empereur Alexandre Ier au prince Adam Czartoryski, 25 décembre 1810, *Mémoires du Prince Czartoryski*, Vol. 2, p. 252.

65 Quoted in Caulaincourt, *With Napoleon in Russia*, pp. 5–6.

66 For a summary of the British perception of these threats, see C. K. Webster, *The Foreign Policy of Castlereagh, 1815–1822: Britain and the European Alliance* (London, 1958), pp. 88–96.

67 Article 6 of the Quadruple Alliance Treaty of 20 November, 1815. Quoted in C. K. Webster, *The Congress of Vienna, 1814–1815* (New York, 1966), p. 163.

68 Kiniapina, *Vneshniaia politika Rossii pervoi poloviny XIX veka*, pp. 100–101; Shilder, *Aleksandr Pervyi*, Vol. 4, pp. 116–22.

69 Quoted in Shilder, *Aleksandr Pervyi*, Vol. 4, p. 463.

70 Palmer, *Alexander I*, p. 370.

71 Quoted in Henry Kissinger, *A World Restored: Metternich, Castlereagh, and the Problems of Peace, 1812–1822* (Boston, 1957), p. 280. See also pp. 279–81.

72 Semevskii, *Politicheskie i obshchestvennye idei dekabristov*, p. 163.

73 Ibid., pp. 135–47.

74 Quoted in ibid., pp. 79–80.

75 A. S. Pushkin, "Na Arakcheeva," *Polnoe sobranie sochinenii* (Moscow, 1962), Vol. 1, p. 406.

76 Quoted in Semevskii, *Politicheskie i obshchestvennye idei*, p. 84.

77 Ibid., pp. 84–85.

78 Quoted in Jenkins, *Arakcheev*, p. 71.

79 Blum, *Lord and Peasant in Russia*, pp. 379–83.

80 Florinsky, *Russia*, Vol. 2, p. 709; Shtorkh, "Materialy," pp. 822–23.

81 McConnell, *Tsar Alexander I*, pp. 156–57.

82 Quoted in I. N. Borozdin, "Universitety v Rossii v pervoi polovine XIX veke," *Istoriia Rossii v XIX veke* (St. Petersburg, 1907), Vol. 2, p. 361.

83 Quoted in Semevskii, *Politicheskie i obshchestvennye idei*, p. 88.

84 Ibid., p. 90. This situation continued through the next quarter-century. See Tengoborskii, 'Kratkoe izlozhenie nashego finansovago polozheniia' (mai, 1856g.), TsGIAL, fond 958, opis' 1, delo No. 742/5.

85 G. M. Kosachevskaia, *Mikhail Andreevich Balug'ianskii i Peterburgskii universitet pervoi chetverti XIX veka* (Leningrad, 1971), pp. 76–90, 135–51.

86 Quoted in Schiemann, *Aleksandr Pervyi*, p. 38.

87 Nicholas I, "Zaveshchanie Nikolaia I synu," *KA*, Vol. 3 (1923), p. 293.

88 Raeff, *Speransky*, pp. 322–32; G. Tel'berg, "Uchastie Imperatora Nikolaia I v kodifikatsionnoi rabote ego tsarstvovaniia," *ZhMIu*, Vol. 22, No. 1 (January 1916), pp. 233–44.

89 Monas, *Police and Society in Russia under Nicholas I*, pp. 62–65.

90 V. Bogucharskii, "Tret'e otdelenie sobstvennoi ego imperatorskago velichestva kantseliarii o sebe samom," *Vestnik Evropy (VE)*, Vol. 52, No. 3 (March 1917), p. 99.

91 A. V. Golovnin, 'Prodolzhenie zapisok A. V. Golovnina s dekabria 1870g. po fevral' 1871g.,' TsGIAL, fond 851, opis' 1, delo No. 9/7–8.

92 "Zhurnaly komiteta uchrezhdennago Vysochaishim reskriptom 6 dekabria 1826 goda," *SIRIO*, Vol. 74 (1891), p. 264.

93 Quoted in Tatishchev, *Vneshniaia politika*, pp. 145–53; S. Zhigarev, *Russkaia politika v vostochnom voprose: Istoriko-iuridicheskie ocherki* (Moscow, 1896), p. 330.

94 Count Zichy to Prince Metternich, 24 April 1828 (NS), in Prince Clemens von Metternich, *Memoirs of Prince Metternich* (New York, 1879–82), Vol. 4, p. 489.

95 Quoted in Tatishchev, *Vneshniaia politika*, p. 179. See also Lincoln, *Nicholas I*, pp. 115–22.

96 I. P. Dubetskii, "Zapiski I. P. Dubetskago," *RS*, Vol. 83, No. 4 (April 1895), pp. 113–44; Pis'ma Imperatora Nikolaia I –go k velikomu kniaziu Konstantinu Pavlovichu, 16 maia, 9 i 30 iiunia 1828g., *SIRIO*, Vol. 131 (1910), pp. 230–47; Lincoln, *Nicholas I*, pp. 122–29.

97 Princess Daria Lieven to General A. Kh. Benkendorf, 10 (22) October 1829, in *Letters of Dorothea, Princess Lieven, during Her Residence in London, 1812–1834*, ed. L. G. Robinson (London, 1902), p. 199.

98 Quotes from LaCroix, *Historie de la vie*, Vol. 5, p. 518, and Shilder, *Nikolai Pervyi*, Vol. 2, p. 375. See also R. F. Leslie, *Polish Politics and the Revolution of November, 1830* (London, 1956), pp. 51–263.

99 Metternich to Count Apponyi, 14 May 1832, in *Memoirs of Prince Metternich*, Vol. 5, p. 189.

100 Martens, *Sobranie traktatov*, Vol. 4, pp. 445–62; Lincoln, *Nicholas I*, pp. 143–47.

101 *Gosudarstvennyi Sovet, 1801–1901gg.* (St. Petersburg, 1902), p. 64.

102 Ibid.

103 Florinsky, *Russia*, Vol. 2, p. 778.

104 Baron F. I. Brunnov, "Obzor politiki russkago dvora v nyneshnee tsarstvovanie," quoted in Tatishchev, *Vneshniaia politika*, p. 307.

105 Quoted in S. M. Gorianinow, *Le Bosphore et les Dardanelles* (Paris, 1910), p. 40.

106 Quoted in Harold Temperley, *England and the Near East: The Crimea* (London and New York, 1936), p. 73.

107 Quoted in Martens, *Sobranie traktatov*, Vol. 12, p. 116.

108 Temperley, *England and the Near East*, pp. 73–74.

109 Martens, *Sobranie traktatov*, Vol. 12, pp. 130–41.

110 Quoted in Temperley, *England and the Near East*, pp. 75–76.

111 *Times* (London), 3 June 1844, p. 6.

112 V. Puryear, *England, Russia, and the Straits Question, 1844–1856* (Berkeley, 1931), p. 44.

113 Quoted in Baron C. F. von Stockmar, *Memoirs of Baron Stockmar*, trans. G. A. M. and ed. F. Max Müller (London, 1872), Vol. 2, pp. 107–8.

114 Nikitenko, *Dnevnik*, Vol. 1, p. 312.

115 V. P. Bykova, *Zapiski staroi smolianki* (St. Petersburg, 1898), p. 180.

116 Nikitenko, *Dnevnik*, Vol. 1, p. 312; "Obozrenie khoda i deistvii kholernoi epidemii v Rossii v techenie 1848 goda," *Zhurnal Ministerstva Vnutrennikh Del* (*ZhMVD*), Vol. 27, No. 9 (September 1849), pp. 319–28.

117 Grand Duke Konstantin Nikolaevich, 'Dnevnik za 1848g.,' TsGAOR, fond 722, opis' 1, delo No. 89/29–30. Entry for 21 February 1848.

118 Nicholas I to Frederick William IV, 24 February 1848, *KA*, Vols. 89–90 (1938), p. 170.

119 Tsimmerman, 'Vospominaniia Generala A. E. Tsimmermana,' ORGBL, fond 325, kartonka 1, papka 2/8.

120 Nicholas I to Frederick William IV, 3(15) July 1848, quoted in Martens, *Sobranie traktatov*, Vol. 8, p. 274.

121 Lincoln, *Nicholas I*, pp. 268–70; Nifontov, *Rossiia v 1848 godu*, pp. 269–70; E. Andics, *Das Bündnis Habsburg-Romanow. Vorgeschichte der zaristichen intervention in Ungarn im Jahre 1849* (Budapest, 1963), pp. 106–36; W. L. Langer, *Political and Social Upheaval, 1832–1852* (New York-London, 1969), pp. 469–70.

122 J. S. Curtiss, *The Russian Army under Nicholas I, 1825–1855* (Durham, 1965), pp. 297–302.

123 Quoted in Graf Otto von Bray-Steinberg, "Imperator Nikolai i ego spodvizhniki," *RS*, Vol. 109, No. 1 (January 1890), p. 121.

124 Lincoln, *Nicholas I*, pp. 315–16; L. Gorev, *Voina 1853–1856gg. i oborona Sevastopolia* (Moscow, 1955), pp. 14–15.

125 Quoted in Grunwald, *Nicholas I*, p. 255.

126 Lincoln, *Nicholas I*, pp. 330–39.

127 Gorev, *Voina 1853–1856gg.*, pp. 15–16.

128 Quoted in Curtiss, *The Russian Army*, p. 127. See also pp. 125–128.

129 Lincoln, *Nicholas I*, pp. 345–48.

130 Seton-Watson, *The Russian Empire*, pp. 328–30.

131 Quoted in Tatishchev, *Imperator Aleksandr II*, Vol. 1, p. 278.

132 P. I. Liashchenko, *Poslednyi sekretnyi komitet po krest'ianskomu delu. 3 ianvaria 1857g.–16 fevralia 1858g. (po materialam arkhiva Gosudarstvennago Soveta)*, (St. Petersburg, 1911), passim.

133 N. A. Miliutin, 'Mysli o sposobakh unichtozheniia krepostnago sostoianiia v Rossii,' (6 fevralia 1847g.), TsGIAL, fond 869, opis' 1, delo No. 449/55.

134 Lincoln, *Nikolai Miliutin*, pp. 3–47.

135 Emmons, *The Russian Landed Gentry and the Peasant Emancipation*, pp. 52–61; Daniel Field, *The End of Serfdom: Nobility and Bureaucracy in Russia, 1855–1861* (Cambridge, Mass., 1976), pp. 79–82; P. A. Zaionchkovskii, *Otmena krepostnogo prava v Rossii* (Moscow, 1968), pp. 63–124.

136 Quoted in Field, *End of Serfdom*, p. 326.

137 Lettre de N. A. Milutine à D. A. Milutine, 11/23 décembre 1861, published in Anatole Leroy-Beaulieu, *Un Homme d'état Russe (Nicolas Milutine) d'après sa corréspondance inédite. Étude sur la Russie et la Pologne pendant le règne d'Alexandre II (1855–1872)*, (Paris, 1884), p. 118.

138 N. A. Miliutin, 'Zapiska po voprosu o preobrazovanii zemskikh uchrezhdeniiakh,' (22 maia 1862 g.), TsGIAL, fond 869, opis' 1, delo No. 397/28.

139 Starr, *Decentralization and Self-Government in Russia*, passim.

140 I. I. Mikhailov, "Kazanskaia starina (iz vospominanii Iv. Iv. Mikhailova)," *RS*, Vol. 100, No. 10 (October 1899), p. 102.

141 On Miliutin's early life and career, see briefly, W. Bruce Lincoln, "General Dmitrii Miliutin and the Russian Army," *History Today*, Vol. 26, No. 1 (January 1976), pp. 40–43.

142 Zaionchkovskii, "D. A. Miliutin: biograficheskii ocherk," pp. 17–19. 17–19.

143 I. Bliokh, *Finansy v Rossii XIX stoletiia* (St. Petersburg, 1882), Vol. 2, pp. 15–16, 21–28, 37–61; *Istoriia Ministerstva Finansov, 1802–1902* (St. Petersburg, 1902), Vol. 1, p. 634.

144 See especially, P. A. Zaionchkovskii, *Voennye reformy, 1860–1870 godov v Rossii* (Moscow, 1952), pp. 85–99; P. Bobrovskii, "Vzgliad na grammotnost' i uchebnye komandy (ili polkovye shkoly) v nashei armii," *Voennyi sbornik*, Vol. 76, No. 12 (December 1870), 281–84; Forrestt A. Miller, *Dmitrii Miliutin and the Reform Era in Russia* (Nashville, 1968), pp. 88–90.

145 Miller, *Dmitrii Miliutin*, pp. 88–90.

146 Florinsky, *Russia*, Vol. 2, p. 909.

147 N. S. Kiniapina, *Vneshniaia politika Rossii vtoroi poloviny XIX veka* (Moscow, 1974), pp. 223–49; Seymour Becker, *Russia's Protectorates in Central Asia: Bukhara and Khiva, 1865–1924* (Cambridge, Mass., 1968), pp. 14–92.

148 A. P. Zablotskii-Desiatovskii, *Graf P. D. Kiselev i ego vremia* (St. Petersburg, 1882), Vol. 3, pp. 1–330.

149 I. I. Kostiushko, *Krest'ianskaia reforma 1864 g. v Tsarstve Pol'skom* (Moscow, 1962), p. 79; R. F. Leslie, *Reform and Insurrection in Poland, 1856–1865* (London, 1963).

150 Kostiushko, *Krest'ianskaia reforma*, p. 79.

151 "Vypiska iz zapiski Mikiutina ot 21 dekabria 1863g.," *Izsledovaniia v Tsarstve Pol'skom, po vysochaishemu poveleniiu, proizvedenie pod rukovodstvom Senatora, Stats-Sekretaria Miliutina*, ed. N. A. Miliutin (St. Petersburg, 1863), Vol. 1, pp. 4–5. Pages in this work are not numbered consecutively. Each report is paginated separately.

152 Ibid.

153 "Zhurnal Komiteta Vysochaishe uchrezhdennago dlia razsmotreniia proektov ob ustroistve krest'ian v Tsarstve Pol'skom," *Izsledovaniia*, Vol. 1, pp. 9–27.

154 Pis'mo N. A. Miliutina k Ia. A. Solov'evu, 23 marta/4 aprelia 1864g., *RS*, Vol. 54 (1887), p. 183.

155 Prince Heinrich Reuss to Prince Otto von Bismarck, 9 September 1870, and Bismarck to Reuss, 16 September 1870, in K. Rheindorf, *Die Schwarze Meer Frage, 1856–1871* (Berlin, 1925), pp. 149–51; Goriainow, *Le Bosphore et les Dardanelles*, pp. 154–67; W. E. Mosse, *The Rise and Fall of the Crimean System, 1855–1871: The Story of a Peace Settlement* (London, 1963), pp. 159–62; Florinsky, *Russia*, Vol. 2, pp. 966–67.

156 B. H. Sumner, *Russia and the Balkans, 1870–1880* (London, 1962), p. 81.

157 A. F. Pribaum, *The Secret Treaties of Austria-Hungary, 1879–1914* (Cambridge, Mass., 1921), Vol. 2, pp. 184–86; Kiniapina, *Vneshniaia politika Rossi vtoroi poloviny XIX veka*, p. 135.

158 Robert E. MacMaster, *Danilevsky: A Russian Totalitarian Philosopher* (Cambridge, Mass., 1967), p. 119.

159 Quoted on Slonim, *Epic of Russian Literature*, p. 297.

160 Thaden, *Conservative Nationalism*, pp. 150–51.

161 M. B. Petrovich, *The Emergence of Russian Panslavism, 1856–1870* (New York, 1956), pp. 145–50.

162 Mihailo D. Stojanović, *The Great Powers and the Balkans, 1875–1878* (Cambridge, 1939), pp. 12–27, 55–57, 78–94.

163 Quoted in Tatishchev, *Imperator Aleksandr II*, Vol. 2, p. 310.

164 Zaionchkovskii, ed., *Dnevnik D. A. Miliutina, 1876–1877*, Vol. 2, p. 195.

165 Zaionchkovskii, *Voennye reformy*, pp. 176–79.

166 Tatishchev, *Imperator Aleksandr II*, Vol. 2, pp. 342–87.

167 Sumner, *Russia and the Balkans*, pp. 425–553, and especially p. 499. See also A. J. P. Taylor, *The Struggle for the Mastery of Europe, 1848–1918* (Oxford, 1954), pp. 247–50; W. N. Medlicott, *The Congress of Berlin and After: A Diplomatic History of the Near Eastern Settlement, 1878–1880* (London, 1938), pp. 36–136; Seton-Watson, *The Russian Empire*, pp. 457–59.

168 Quoted in P. A. Zaionchkovskii, *Krizis samoderzhaviia na rubezhe 1870–1880kh godov* (Moscow, 1964), p. 411.

169 P. A. Zaionchkovskii, *Rossiiskoe samoderzhavie v kontse XIX stoletiia (politicheskaia reaktsiia 80kh–nachala 90kh godov)* (Moscow, 1970), p. 366; Florinsky, *Russia*, Vol. 2, p. 1093.

170 Florinsky, *Russia*, Vol. 2, p. 1095. For a discussion of the legislative pro-

cess that produced this statute, see Zaionchkovskii, *Rossiiskoe samoderzhavie,* pp. 366–401.

171 L. G. Zakharova, *Zemskaia kontrreforma 1890g.* (Moscow, 1968), p. 91–150; Zaionchkovskii, *Rossiiskoe samoderzhavie,* pp. 401–28.

172 Zaionchkovskii, *Krizis samoderzhaviia,* pp. 413–19; Florinsky, *Russia,* Vol. 2, p. 1120.

173 A. A. Polovtsov, *Dnevnik gosudarstvennogo sekretaria A. A. Polovtsova, 1883–1892,* ed. P. A. Zaionchkovskii (Moscow, 1966), Vol. 1, p. 131. Entry for 17 October 1883.

174 Zaionchkovskii, *Rossiiskoe samoderzhavie,* pp. 131–38; Florinsky, *Russia,* Vol. 2, pp. 1120–21.

175 Zaionchkovskii, *Rossiiskoe samoderzhavie,* pp. 117–30.

176 P. A. Khromov, *Ekonomicheskoe razvitie Rossii v XIX i XX vekakh* (Moscow, 1950), pp. 460–62.

177 Ibid., pp. 454–60.

178 Quoted in Richard G. Robbins, Jr., *Famine in Russia, 1891–1892* (New York and London, 1975), p. 6.

179 Ibid., pp. 1–12, 188–89.

180 John Maynard, *The Russian Peasant and Other Studies* (London, 1942), Vol. 1, pp. 48–52.

181 Kiniapina, *Vneshniaia politika Rossii vtoroi poloviny XIX veka,* pp. 190–213.

182 Seton-Watson, *The Russian Empire,* p. 573.

183 Quoted in William L. Langer, *The Franco-Russian Alliance, 1890–1894* (New York, 1967), p. 186.

184 Ibid., pp. 184–185.

185 Ibid., pp. 254–65, 350–91; Baron Boris E. Nolde, *L'Alliance Franco-Russe* (Paris, 1936), pp. 616–92.

CHAPTER XII: *Nicky and Sunny: The Last Romanovs*

1 Quoted in Alexander, Grand Duke of Russia, *Once a Grand Duke* (New York, 1932), p. 174.

2 Quoted in ibid., pp. 168–69.

3 Ibid., p. 168.

4 Quoted in S. S. Ol'denburg, *Tsarstvovanie Imperatora Nikolaia II* (Belgrad, 1939), Vol. 1, p. 38.

5 Alexander, *Once a Grand Duke,* pp. 138–39.

6 Quoted in Edward Crankshaw, *The Shadow of the Winter Palace: Russia's Drift to Revolution, 1825–1917* (New York, 1976), p. 306.

7 A. Mosolov, *Pri dvore Imperatora* (Riga, n.d.), pp. 6–7; *Nikolai II: Materialy dlia kharakteristiki lichnosti i tsarstvovaniia* (Moscow, 1917), pp. 40–42.

8 Robert K. Massie, *Nicholas and Alexandra* (New York, 1978), pp. 24–25.

9 Konstantin Pobedonostsev, *Reflections of a Russian Statesman* (Ann Arbor, 1965), p. 265.

10 Quoted in Alexander, *Once a Grand Duke,* pp. 66–67.

11 Quoted in S. G. Sviatikov, *Obshchestvennoe dvizhenie v Rossii 1700–1895* (Rostov-on-the-Don, 1905), Vol. 2, p. 197.

12 Alexander, *Once a Grand Duke,* p. 61.

13 The memoirs of V. P. Obninskii, as excerpted in *Nikolai II: Materialy,* p. 41.
14 Alexander, *Once a Grand Duke,* p. 73.
15 Quoted in ibid., p. 77.
16 Massie, *Nicholas and Alexandra,* p. 18.
17 Nicholas to the Empress Maria Feodorovna, 25 June 1887, *The Letters of Tsar Nicholas and Empress Marie,* ed. Edward J. Bing (London, 1937), p. 33.
18 Alexander, *Once a Grand Duke,* p. 166.
19 Nicholas to the Empress Maria Feodorovna, 25 June 1887, in *Letters of Nicholas and Marie,* p. 34.
20 Quoted in Massie, *Nicholas and Alexandra,* p. 19.
21 Alexander, *Once a Grand Duke,* p. 166.
22 The Princess Romanovsky-Krassinsky, *Dancing in Petersburg: The Memoirs of Kschessinska* (New York, 1961), p. 29.
23 Quoted in ibid., p. 34.
24 Quoted in Alexander, *Once a Grand Duke,* p. 167.
25 The Empress Maria Feodorovna to Nicholas, 16 January 1891, in *Letters of Nicholas and Marie,* p. 47.
26 The Empress Maria Feodorovna to Nicholas, 23 April 1891, in ibid., p. 58.
27 V. N. Lamsdorf, *Dnevnik, 1891–1892* (Moscow-Leningrad, 1934), pp. 112–25. Diary entries for 29 April–5 May 1891.
28 The Empress Maria Feodorovna to Nicholas, 6 May 1891, *Letters of Nicholas and Marie,* pp. 59–60.
29 The Empress Maria Feodorovna to Nicholas, 1 August 1891, ibid., p. 67.
30 Quoted in Romanovsky-Krassinsky, *Memoirs of Kschessinska,* p. 37.
31 Ibid., p. 46–47.
32 Ibid., p. 43.
33 Ibid., p. 44.
34 Nicholas to the Empress Aleksandra Feodorovna, especially the letters of 14, 15, and 16 December 1916, in A. L. Hynes, trans., *The Letters of the Tsar to the Tsaritsa, 1914–1917* (Hattiesburg, 1970), pp. 307–10.
35 Quoted in Romanovsky-Krassinsky, *Memoirs of Kschessinska,* p. 51.
36 Baroness Sophie Buxhoeveden, *The Life and Tragedy of Alexandra Feodorovna, Empress of Russia* (London, 1928), pp. 2–9.
37 Quoted in Massie, *Nicholas and Alexandra,* p. 27.
38 Ibid., pp. 28–30; Buxhoeveden, *Alexandra Feodorovna,* pp. 9–15.
39 Anna Viroubova, *Memories of the Russian Court* (New York, 1923), p. 19.
40 Quoted in E. M. Almedingen, *An Unbroken Unity: A Memoir of Grand-Duchess Serge of Russia, 1864–1918* (London, 1964), p. 31.
41 Quoted in ibid., pp. 33–34.
42 Ibid., p. 37.
43 Buxhoeveden, *Alexandra Feodorovna,* pp. 23–26.
44 Quoted in Sir Bernard Pares, *The Fall of the Russian Monarchy: A Study of the Evidence* (New York, 1961), p. 33.
45 Quoted in ibid.
46 Romanovsky-Krassinsky, *Memoirs of Kschessinska,* p. 39.
47 Nicholas to the Empress Maria Feodorovna, 10 April 1894, *Letters of Nicholas and Marie,* p. 76.
48 Crankshaw, *Shadow of the Winter Palace,* p. 308.
49 Aleksandra Feodorovna to Nicholas, 4 April 1915, *Letters of the Tsaritsa to the Tsar, 1914–1916,* ed. Sir Bernard Pares (Hattiesburg, 1970), p. 115;

Nicholas to Aleksandra Feodorovna, 17 June 1916, *Letters of the Tsar to the Tsaritsa,* p. 212.

50 Aleksandra Feodorovna to Nicholas, 22 August 1915, *Letters of the Tsaritsa to the Tsar,* p. 114.

51 Aleksandra Feodorovna to Nicholas, 13 and 14 December 1916, ibid., pp. 454–55.

52 Nicholas to Aleksandra Feodorovna, 14 December 1916, *Letters of the Tsar to the Tsaritsa,* pp. 307–8.

53 John P. McKay, *Pioneers for Profit: Foreign Entrepreneurship and Russian Industrialization, 1885–1914* (Chicago, 1970), p. 4.

54 Robbins, *Famine in Russia,* pp. 170–76.

55 Quoted in Pares, *Fall of the Russian Monarchy,* p. 36.

56 The Empress Maria Feodorovna to Nicholas, 27 June 1894, *Letters of Nicholas and Marie,* p. 87.

57 Nicholas to the Empress Maria Feodorovna, 3 September 1895, ibid., p. 102.

58 Nicholas to the Empress Maria Feodorovna, 10 April 1894, ibid., p. 76.

59 Nicholas to the Empress Maria Feodorovna, 27 June 1894, ibid., p. 85.

60 Nicholas to the Empress Maria Feodorovna, 14 June 1894, ibid., p. 82.

61 Nicholas to the Empress Maria Feodorovna, 27 June 1894, ibid., p. 84.

62 Nicholas to the Empress Maria Feodorovna, 10 April 1894, ibid., p. 76.

63 *Nikolai II: Materialy,* p. 54.

64 Quoted in Pierre Gilliard, *Le Tragique destin de Nicolas II et de sa famille* (Paris, 1938), p. 35.

65 Massie, *Nicholas and Alexandra,* pp. 41–42.

66 Ibid., p. 44.

67 Quoted in René Fülöp-Miller, *Rasputin: The Holy Devil* (New York, 1928), p. 80.

68 Quoted in Ol'denburg, *Tsarstvovanie Nikolaia II,* Vol. 1, p. 47.

69 Quoted in Harold Nicolson, *King George the Fifth: His Life and Reign* (New York, 1953), p. 57.

70 Harrison E. Salisbury, *Black Night, White Snow: Russia's Revolutions, 1905–1917* (New York, 1978), pp. 51–53.

71 Alexander, *Once a Grand Duke,* p. 171.

72 Salisbury, *Black Night, White Snow,* pp. 51–53.

73 Romanovsky-Krassinsky, *Memoirs of Kschessinska,* pp. 58–59.

74 Ol'denburg, *Tsarstvovanie Nikolaia II,* Vol. 1, p. 59; B. A. Rybakov, *Treasures in the Kremlin* (London, Prague, and Moscow, 1962), p. 127.

75 Quoted in Ol'denburg, *Tsarstvovanie Nikolaia II,* Vol. 1, p. 59.

76 Ibid., p. 60; *Zhivopisnoe obozrenie,* No. 21 (19 maia 1896), pp. 27–43.

77 Massie, *Nicholas and Alexandra,* p. 52.

78 Ibid., p. 53–54.

79 *Zhivopisnoe obozrenie,* No. 22 (26 maia 1896), pp. 55–59; Romanovsky-Krassinsky, *Memoirs of Kschessinska,* p. 59.

80 *Nikolai II: Materialy,* p. 106.

81 Baedeker, *Russia,* p. xxii.

82 Salisbury, *Black Night, White Snow,* p. 53.

83 *Nikolai II: Materialy,* pp. 107–8.

84 Ibid., pp. 111–13; Witte, *Vospominaniia,* Vol. 2, pp. 67–68. For a summary of Nemirovich-Danchenko's account, see Salisbury, *Black Night, White Snow,* pp. 54–56.

85 Salisbury, *Black Night, White Snow*, p. 56.
86 N. P. Eroshkin, "Administrativno-politseiskii apparat," *Istoriia Moskvy*, ed. A. M. Pankratova (Moscow, 1955), Vol. 5, pp. 665–66.
87 Alexander, *Once a Grand Duke*, p. 170.
88 *Nikolai II: Materialy*, p. 59.
89 Witte, *Vospominaniia*, Vol. 2, pp. 68–70; Alexander Iswolsky, *Memoirs* (London, 1920), pp. 258–60.
90 Ol'denburg, *Tsarstvovanie Nikolaia II*, Vol. 1, p. 61.
91 Salisbury, *Black Night, White Snow*, pp. 57–58.
92 Quoted in Ol'denburg, *Tsarstvovanie Nikolaia II*, Vol. 1, p. 63.
93 Ibid., p. 64.
94 Nicholas to the Empress Maria Feodorovna, 2 Obtober 1896, *Letters of Nicholas and Marie*, p. 120.
95 This description of Nicholas's impressions of his visit to France is drawn from his letter to the Empress Maria Feodorovna of 2 October 1896, ibid., pp. 120–25.
96 Crankshaw, *Shadow of the Winter Palace*, p. 308.
97 Viroubova, *Memories*, p. 54.
98 Ibid., p. 60.
99 Quoted in Pares, *Fall of the Russian Monarchy*, p. 131. For information on "Dr. Philippe," see *Nikolai II: Materialy*, pp. 60–62; Salisbury, *Black Night, White Snow*, pp. 205, 657 n. 7; and Alexander, *Once a Grand Duke*, pp. 181–82.
100 Quoted in Salisbury, *Black Night, White Snow*, p. 108.
101 Viroubova, *Memories*, pp. 10–11.
102 L. N. Tolstoi, "Pis'mo Nikolaiu II," *Sobranie sochinenii* (Moscow 1965), Vol. 18, pp. 289–97.
103 Quoted in Alexander, *Once a Grand Duke*, p. 177.

CHAPTER XIII: *The Approach of Disaster*

1 Nicholas's diary for Monday, 26 January 1904. Quoted in Salisbury, *Black Night, White Snow*, p. 89; Andrew Malozemoff, *Russian Far Eastern Policy, 1881–1904, with Special Emphasis on the Causes of The Russo-Japanese War* (Berkeley and Los Angeles, 1958), pp. 248–49.
2 Quoted in Salisbury, *Black Night, White Snow*, p. 95.
3 Quoted in Witte, *Vospominaniia*, Vol. 2, p. 291.
4 Quoted in David Walder, *The Short Victorious War: The Russo-Japanese Conflcit, 1904–1905* (London, 1973), p. 53.
5 Quoted in A. N. Kuropatkin, "Dnevnik A. N. Kuropatkina," *KA*, Vol. 2 (1922), p. 95.
6 Ibid., p. 106.
7 Nicholas's diary for 26 January 1904. Quoted in Salisbury, *Black Night, White Snow*, p. 89.
8 Walder, *Short Victorious War*, pp. 58–59.
9 Ibid., p. 58.
10 Ibid., pp. 60–65.
11 Kuropatkin, "Dnevnik" pp. 109–10.
12 Baedeker, *Russia*, p. 533.
13 Kuropatkin, "Dnevnik," p. 105.

14 Quoted in Alexander, *Once a Grand Duke*, p. 214.
15 Witte, *Vospominaniia*, Vol. 2, p. 292.
16 Ibid.
17 Quoted in Massie, *Nicholas and Alexandra*, p. 84.
18 Quoted in Salisbury, *Black Night, White Snow*, p. 91.
19 Ibid.
20 Nicholas to the Dowager Empress Maria Feodorovna, 23 September 1904, *Letters of Nicholas and Marie*, p. 177.
21 Massie, *Nicholas and Alexandra*, p. 88.
22 Viroubova, *Memories*, p. 9.
23 Douglas Story, *The Campaign with Kuropatkin* (London, 1904), p. 299.
24 Alexander, *Once a Grand Duke*, p. 219.
25 Walder, *Short Victorious War*, pp. 69–71.
26 Witte, *Vospominaniia*, Vol. 2, p. 374.
27 Walder, *Short Victorious War*, pp. 230–44; Seton-Watson, *The Russian Empire*, pp. 592–95.
28 Nicholas to the Dowager Empress Maria Feodorovna, 13 October 1904, *Letters of Nicholas and Marie*, p. 178.
29 Alexander, *Once a Grand Duke*, pp. 221–23; Seton-Watson, *The Russian Empire*, pp. 595–97; Walder, *Short Victorious War*, pp. 267–88.
30 Nicholas to the Dowager Empress Maria Feodorovna, 18 May 1905, *Letters of Nicholas and Marie*, p. 179.
31 Seton-Watson, *The Russian Empire*, p. 597.
32 Walter Sablinsky, *The Road to Bloody Sunday: Father Gapon and the St. Petersburg Massacre of 1905* (Princeton, 1976), pp. 12–14.
33 Quoted in ibid., pp. 3, 19.
34 Ibid., p. 29; V. I. Nevskii, *Rabochee dvizhenie v ianvarskie dni 1905 goda* (Moscow, 1930), pp. 8–9.
35 D. N. Liubimov, "Gapon i 9 ianvaria," *Voprosy Istorii (VI)*, Vol. 40, No. 8 (August 1965), p. 123.
36 Quoted in Sablinsky, *Road to Bloody Sunday*, p. 198.
37 Ibid., pp. 198–99; A. V. Bogdanovich, *Tri poslednykh samoderzhtsa: Dnevnik A. V. Bogdanovicha* (Moscow-Leningrad, 1924), pp. 328–30; V. I. Gurko, *Features and Figures of the Past: Government and Opinion in the Reign of Nicholas II* (Stanford, 1939), pp. 344–45.
38 Quoted in Liubimov, "Gapon i 9 ianvaria," p. 126.
39 L. Gurevich, "Narodnoe dvizhenie v Peterburge 9–go ianvaria 1906 goda," *Byloe*, Vol. 1, No. 1 (January 1906), p. 210; Liubimov, "Gapon i 9 ianvaria," p. 126.
40 Quoted in Nevskii, *Rabochee dvizhenie v ianvarskie dni*, p. 92.
41 Quoted in Sablinsky, *Road to Bloody Sunday*, p. 228.
42 Quoted in ibid., p. 222.
43 Gurevich, "Narodnoe dvizhenie," p. 213.
44 S. N. Semanov, *Krovavoe voskresen'e* (Leningrad, 1965), p. 72.
45 Ibid., pp. 72–73.
46 Quoted in Sablinsky, *Road to Bloody Sunday*, p. 214.
47 Ibid., p. 215.
48 Semanov, *Krovavoe voskresen'e*, p. 86; Liubimov, "Gapon i 9 ianvaria," *VI*, Vol. 40, No. 9 (September 1965), p. 114.
49 Nevskii, *Rabochee dvizhenie v ianvarskie dni*, pp. 124–27; Liubimov, "Gapon i 9 ianvaria," No. 9 (September 1965) pp. 114–21.

50　Quoted in Sablinsky, *Road to Bloody Sunday*, p. 278.
51　Quoted in ibid., p. 281.
52　Aleksandra Feodorovna to Princess Victoria of Battenberg, 27 January 1905, in Buxhoeveden, *Alexandra Feodorovna*, p. 109.
53　Quoted in Sablinsky, *Road to Bloody Sunday*, p. 269.
54　Bing, *Letters of Nicholas and Marie*, p. 206.
55　Alexander, *Once a Grand Duke*, p. 139.
56　Almedingen, *An Unbroken Unity*, p. 52.
57　Prince Felix Yousoupoff, *Avant l'éxil, 1887–1919* (Paris, 1952), p. 122.
58　Ibid., pp. 123–25; Almedingen, *An Unbroken Unity*, pp. 59–79.
59　Quoted in Salisbury, *Black Night, White Snow*, p. 136.
60　Aleksandra Feodorovna to Princess Victoria of Battenberg, 27 January 1905, in Buxhoeveden, *Alexandra Feodorovna*, pp. 108–9.
61　Viroubova, *Memories*, p. 18.
62　Gurko, *Features and Figures*, p. 209.
63　Ibid., p. 410.
64　Pierre Gilliard, *Thirteen Years at the Russian Court* (New York, 1970), p. 83.
65　Quoted in Pares, *Fall of the Russian Monarchy*, p. 129.
66　Salisbury, *Black Night, White Snow*, p. 151.
67　Gilliard, *Thirteen Years*, p. 83.
68　Viroubova, *Memories*, p. 23.
69　Florinsky, *Russia*, Vol. 2, p. 1195.
70　V. I. Nevskii, *Sovety i vooruzhennoe vosstanie v 1905 godu* (Moscow, 1932), p. 197.
71　Ibid., pp. 193–220.
72　Ibid., pp. 220–22; Bertram D. Wolfe, *Three Who Made a Revolution: A Biographical History* (New York, 1948), p. 320.
73　Wolfe, *Three Who Made a Revolution*, pp. 320–21.
74　Nicholas to the Dowager Empress Maria Feodorovna, 19 October 1905, *Letters of Nicholas and Marie*, p. 187.
75　Nevskii, *Sovety i vooruzhennoe vosstanie*, pp. 14–26.
76　"Prikaz Peterburgskogo General-Gubernatora, D. F. Trepova o besposhchadnom podavlenii revoliutsionnogo dvizheniia," *Vserossiiskaia politicheskaia stachka v oktiabria 1905*, ed. L. M. Ivanov (Moscow-Leningrad, 1955), Vol. 1, p. 354.
77　Nicholas to the Dowager Empress Maria Feodorovna, 19 October 1905, *Letters of Nicholas and Marie*, p. 187.
78　The Dowager Empress Maria Feodorovna to Nicholas, 16 October 1905, ibid., p. 184.
79　Nicholas to the Dowager Empress Maria Feodorovna, 19 October 1905, ibid., p. 188.
80　Ibid., pp. 187–88.
81　Witte, *Vospominaniia*, Vol. 3, pp. 14–38; Pares, *Fall of the Russian Monarchy*, pp. 85–86.
82　Gurko, *Features and Figures*, p. 399.
83　Nicholas to the Dowager Empress Maria Feodorovna, 19 October 1905, *Letters of Nicholas and Marie*, p. 189.
84　V. V. Shul'gin, *Dni* (Belgrad, 1925), pp. 6–7.
85　Ol'denburg, *Tsarstvovanie Nikolaia II*, Vol. 1, p. 331.
86　Leopold Haimson, *The Russian Marxists and the Origins of Bolshevism* (Cambridge, Mass., 1955), pp. 60–62.

87 Quoted in Wolfe, *Three Who Made a Revolution*, p. 323.
88 Leon Trotsky, *1905* (New York, 1971), p. 117.
89 Salisbury, *Black Night, White Snow*, p. 164.
90 Nicholas to the Dowager Empress Maria Feodorovna, 1 December 1905, *Letters of Nicholas and Marie*, p. 197.
91 Quoted in Florinsky, *Russia*, Vol. 2, p. 1183.
92 Elizaveta Drabkina, *Chernye sukhari* (Moscow, 1963), pp. 31–32.
93 Ol'denburg, *Tsarstvovanie Nikolaia II*, Vol. 1, pp. 334–35.
94 Nicholas to the Dowager Empress Maria Feodorovna, 29 December 1905, *Letters of Nicholas and Marie*, p. 207.
95 Quoted in *Nikolai II: Materialy*, p. 23.
96 Nicholas to the Dowager Empress Maria Feodorovna, 29 December 1905, *Letters of Nicholas and Marie*, p. 207.
97 Quoted in *Nikolai II: Materialy*, p. 23.
98 Trotsky, *1905*, p. 296.
99 Oliver H. Radkey, *The Agrarian Foes of Bolshevism: Promise and Default of the Russian Socialist Revolutionaries, February to October 1917* (New York, 1958), p. 69.
100 Seton-Watson, *The Russian Empire*, p. 477.
101 Quoted in Ol'denburg, *Tsarstvovanie Nikolaia II*, Vol. 1, p. 343.
102 Nicholas to the Dowager Empress Maria Feodorovna, 12 January 1906, *Letters of Nicholas and Marie*, p. 212.
103 Quotes from Ol'denburg, *Tsarstvovanie Nikolaia II*, Vol. 1, p. 344.
104 Quoted in Florinsky, *Russia*, Vol. 2, p. 1189.
105 Quoted in Ol'denburg, *Tsarstvovanie Nikolaia II*, Vol. 1, p. 355.
106 Quoted in ibid.
107 Sir George Buchanan, *My Mission to Russia and Other Diplomatic Memories* (Boston, 1923), Vol. 1, p. 160.
108 Harold Nicolson, *Sir Arthur Nicolson, Bart., First Lord Carnock* (London, 1930), p. 225.
109 Quoted in P. N. Miliukov, *Vospominaniia, 1859–1917* (New York, 1955), Vol. 1, p. 425.
110 "Rech' P. A. Stolypina, 10 maia 1907 goda," in M. P. Bok, *Vospominaniia o moem ottse P. A. Stolypine* (New York, 1953), p. 248.
111 Quoted in Wolfe, *Three Who Made a Revolution*, p. 361.
112 Nicholas to the Dowager Empress Maria Feodorovna, 11 October 1906, *Letters of Nicholas and Marie*, p. 220.
113 "Rech' P. A. Stolypina, 5–go dekabria 1908g.," *Vospominaniia*, pp. 290–92.
114 See especially S. M. Dubrovskii, *Stolypinskaia zemel'naia reforma* (Moscow, 1963), pp. 65–230; Geroid T. Robinson, *Rural Russia Under the Old Regime* (New York, 1932), pp. 208–343.
115 Crankshaw, *Shadow of the Winter Palace*, p. 369.
116 Graf V. N. Kokovtsev, *Iz moego proshlago. Vospominaniia 1903–1919gg.* (Paris, 1933), Vol. 1, pp. 475–77.
117 Nicholas to the Dowager Empress Maria Feodorovna, 10 September 1911, *Letters of Nicholas and Marie*, pp. 265–66.
118 Salisbury, *Black Night, White Snow*, p. 212.
119 Buxhoeveden, *Alexandra Feodorovna*, p. 120; Massie, *Nicholas and Alexandra*, p. 156.
120 Nicholas to the Dowager Empress Maria Feodorovna, 30 August 1906, *Letters of Nicholas and Marie*, p. 217.

121 Edward, Duke of Windsor, *A King's Story* (New York, 1947), p. 69.
122 Nicholas to the Dowager Empress Maria Feodorovna, 1 August 1897, *Letters of Nicholas and Marie*, p. 130.
123 Buxhoeveden, *Alexandra Feodorovna*, p. 119.
124 Nicholas to the Dowager Empress Maria Feodorovna, 13 September 1906, *Letters of Nicholas and Marie*, p. 218.
125 Viroubova, *Memories*, p. 97.
126 Massie, *Nicholas and Alexandra*, p. 156.
127 Viroubova, *Memories*, pp. 37–38.
128 Gilliard, *Thirteen Years*, p. 91.
129 Viroubova, *Memories*, p. 99.
130 This impression permeates the memoirs of that "ideal gramophone disc" Anna Vyrubova and, to a lesser extent, the account of Aleksandra's biographer, the Baroness Buxhoeveden.
131 Nicholas to the Dowager Empress Maria Feodorovna, 12 September 1909, *Letters of Nicholas and Marie*, p. 248.
132 Quoted in George Buchanan, *Mission to Russia*, Vol. 2, p. 46.
133 Meriel Buchanan, *The Dissolution of an Empire* (London, 1932), pp. 34–35.
134 Ibid., p. 35.
135 Viroubova, *Memories*, p. 98.
136 Meriel Buchanan, *Dissolution of an Empire*, p. 36.
137 Ibid., pp. 14–15.
138 Ibid., p. 19.
139 George Buchanan, *Mission to Russia*, Vol. 1, p. 176.
140 Meriel Buchanan, *Dissolution of an Empire*, p. 14.
141 Ibid., p. 47.
142 Quoted in Salisbury, *Black Night, White Snow*, p. 198.
143 Andrei Belyi, *The Silver Dove*, trans. George Reavey, with a preface by Harrison E. Salisbury (New York, 1974), p. ix.
144 Andrei Belyi, *Serebrianyi golub'* (Munich, 1967), p. 42.
145 Quoted in Belyi, *Silver Dove*, p. x.
146 Quoted in Salisbury, *Black Night, White Snow*, p. 176.
147 Quoted in Colin Wilson, *Rasputin and the Fall of the Romanovs* (New York, 1964), p. 33.
148 Quoted in Kokovtsev, *Iz moego proshlago*, Vol. 2, p. 42.
149 "Pis'ma velikikh knaizhen Ol'gi i Anastasii k Rasputinu, 1909g.," *Za kulisami tsarizma (arkhiv Tibetskogo vracha Badmaeva)*, ed. V. P. Semennikov (Leningrad, 1925), pp. 9–10.
150 Kokovtsev, *Iz moego proshlago*, Vol. 2, p. 40.
151 Quoted in ibid., p. 35.
152 F. M. Dostoevskii, *Brat'ia Karamazovykh*, in *Polnoe sobranie sochinenii* (Leningrad, 1976), Vol. 14, p. 26.
153 Quoted in Fülöp-Miller, *Rasputin*, p. 215.
154 Ibid., p. 271; Salisbury, *Black Night, White Snow*, p. 206.
155 Quoted in Salisbury, *Black Night, White Snow*, p. 302.
156 Lili Dehn, *The Real Tsaritsa* (Boston, 1922), pp. 100–101.
157 Viroubova, *Memories*, p. 153.
158 Maurice Paléologue, *An Ambassador's Memoirs*, trans. F. A. Holt (New York, n.d.), Vol. 1, p. 292.
159 Semennikov, ed., *Za kulisami tsarizma*, p. 17.

160 Viroubova, *Memories*, pp. 152–54; Pares, *Fall of the Russian Monarchy*, pp. 133–38.
161 Massie, *Nicholas and Alexandra*, p. 190.
162 Gilliard, *Thirteen Years*, pp. 17–37.
163 George Thomas Marye, *Nearing the End in Imperial Russia* (Philadelphia, 1929), p. 394.
164 Quoted in V. I. Gurko, *Tsar i Tsaritsa* (Paris, 1927), p. 90.
165 Quoted in Salisbury, *Black Night, White Snow*, p. 169.
166 Massie, *Nicholas and Alexandra*, p. 218.
167 V. M. Rudnev, "The Truth Concerning the Russian Imperial Family: Statement by Vladimir Michailovitch Roudneff, appointed by Minister of Justice Kerensky Special High Commissioner for Revision and Investigation of the actions of Ministers and other High Personages of the Imperial Government," in Viroubova, *Memories*, pp. 395–96.
168 Quoted in Paléologue, *Ambassador's Memoirs*, Vol. 1, p. 260.

CHAPTER XIV: *Days of War and Revolution*

1 Count Paul Vassili (Princess Catherine Radziwill), *Behind the Veil at the Russian Court* (New York, 1914), p. 390.
2 Quoted in Salisbury, *Black Night, White Snow*, p. 240.
3 Paléologue, *Ambassador's Memoirs*, Vol. 1, p. 52.
4 Iu. N. Danilov, *Rossiia v mirovoi voine, 1914–1915gg.* (Berlin, 1925), pp. 111–12.
5 Ibid., 110–11.
6 Miliukov, *Vospominaniia*, Vol. 2, p. 190.
7 Aleksandra to Nicholas, 24 September 1914, *Letters of the Tsaritsa to the Tsar*, p. 9.
8 Nicholas to Aleksandra, 19 November 1914, *Letters of the Tsar to the Tsaritsa*, p. 14.
9 Nicholas N. Golovine, *The Russian Army in the World War* (New Haven, 1931), pp. 32, 126–27, 131; Danilov, *Rossiia v mirovoi voine*, pp. 256–58.
10 Published in Golovine, *The Russian Army* p. 143.
11 Paléologue, *Ambassador's Memoirs*, Vol. 1, p. 222.
12 Quoted in Florinsky, *Russia*, Vol. 2, p. 1320.
13 Ibid., p. 1323.
14 Ibid., p. 1326.
15 Golovine, *The Russian Army*, pp. 90–91, 222; Seton-Watson, *The Russian Empire*, pp. 709–10.
16 Grand Duke Andrei Vladimirovich, *Dnevnik za 1915g.* (Moscow-Leningrad, 1925), pp. 49–50.
17 Golovine, *The Russian Army*, p. 220.
18 Andrei Vladimirovich, *Dnevnik*, p. 42.
19 Golovine, *The Russian Army*, pp. 220–21.
20 Major General Sir Alfred Knox, *With the Russian Army, 1914–1917* (London, 1921), Vol. 1, p. 319.
21 Ibid., p. 348.
22 Andrei Vladimirovich, *Dnevnik*, p. 31.

23   Michael Cherniavsky, ed., *Prologue to Revolution: Notes of A. N. Iakhontov on the Secret Meetings of the Council of Ministers, 1915* (Englewood Cliffs, 1967), p. 76.
24   Ibid., pp. 76–77.
25   Ibid., p. 78.
26   Ibid., p. 80.
27   Ibid., p. 166.
28   Nicholas to Aleksandra, 25 August 1915, *Letters of the Tsar to the Tsaritsa*, p. 71.
29   Aleksandra to Nicholas, 22 August 1915, *Letters of the Tsaritsa to the Tsar*, p. 114.
30   Aleksandra to Nicholas, 23 August 1915, ibid., p. 117.
31   A. Bubnov, *V Tsarskoi stavke* (New York, 1955), pp. 180–81.
32   Nicholas to Aleksandra, 7 September 1915, *Letters of the Tsar to the Tsaritsa*, p. 84.
33   Nicholas to Aleksandra, 25 August 1915, ibid., pp. 71–72.
34   Aleksandra to Nicholas, 22 August 1915, *Letters of the Tsaritsa to the Tsar*, p. 114.
35   Aleksandra to Nicholas, 23 August 1915, ibid., p. 119.
36   Aleksandra to Nicholas, 26 August 1915, ibid., p. 123.
37   Aleksandra to Nicholas, 28 August 1915, ibid., p. 127.
38   Aleksandra to Nicholas, 22 September 1916, ibid., p. 408.
39   Aleksandra to Nicholas, 27 September 1916, ibid., p. 417.
40   Aleksandra to Nicholas, 2 September 1915, ibid., p. 135.
41   Aleksandra to Nicholas, 22 August 1915, ibid., p. 114.
42   Aleksandra to Nicholas, 12 November 1916, ibid., p. 441.
43   Aleksandra to Nicholas, 30 August 1915, ibid., p. 131.
44   Aleksandra to Nicholas, 31 August 1915, ibid., p. 132.
45   Aleksandra to Nicholas, 14 December 1916, ibid., p. 456.
46   Aleksandra to Nicholas, 16 December 1916, ibid., p. 459.
47   Aleksandra to Nicholas, 30 August 1915, ibid., p. 130.
48   Aleksandra to Nicholas, 14 December 1916, ibid., p. 456.
49   Nicholas to Aleksandra, 13 December 1915, *Letters of the Tsar to the Tsaritsa*, p. 122.
50   Nicholas to Aleksandra, 23 September 1916, ibid., p. 269.
51   Massie, *Nicholas and Alexandra*, p. 325.
52   Nicholas to Aleksandra, 29 September 1916, *Letters of the Tsar to the Tsaritsa*, p. 275.
53   P. E. Shchegolev, ed., *Padenie tsarskogo rezhima* (Moscow-Leningrad, 1927), Vol. 7, p. 145.
54   George Buchanan, *Mission to Russia*, Vol. 2, p. 51.
55   Paléologue, *Ambassador's Memoirs*, Vol. 3, p. 46.
56   Shchegolev, ed., *Padenie tsarskogo rezhima*, Vol. 6, p. 138.
57   Miliukov, *Vospominaniia*, Vol. 2, p. 276.
58   Quoted in Paléologue, *Ambassador's Memoirs*, Vol. 1, pp. 349–50.
59   Shul'gin, *Dni*, pp. 100–101.
60   Aleksandra to Nicholas, 5 December 1916, *Letters of the Tsaritsa to the Tsar*, p. 444.
61   Fülöp-Miller, *Rasputin*, pp. 181–82.
62   Prince Felix Yousoupoff, *Rasputin* (New York, 1928), pp. 90–91.

63 Fülöp-Miller, *Rasputin*, pp. 182–200; Massie, *Nicholas and Alexandra*, pp. 319–22.
64 Paléologue, *Ambassador's Memoirs*, Vol. 1, p. 331.
65 Bruce Lockhart, *British Agent* (New York, 1933), pp. 125–26.
66 George Buchanan, *Mission to Russia*, Vol. 1, p. 241.
67 Marye, *Nearing the End in Imperial Russia*, pp. 444, 446.
68 Shul'gin, *Dni*, p. 115.
69 Shchegolev, ed., *Padenie tsarskogo rezhima*, Vol. 5, pp. 103–6.
70 Aleksandra to Nicholas, 22 June 1915, *Letters of the Tsaritsa to the Tsar*, pp. 105–6.
71 Yousoupoff, *Avant l'éxil*, p. 199.
72 Quoted in V. M. Purishkevich, *Dnevnik chlena gosudarstvennoi dumy Vladimira Mitrofanovicha Purishkevicha* (Riga, 1934), p. 7.
73 Ibid., insert facing p. 7.
74 Yousoupoff, *Avant l'éxil*, p. 154.
75 Ibid., p. 86.
76 Purishkevich, *Dnevnik*, pp. 11–12.
77 Salisbury, *Black Night, White Snow*, p. 293.
78 Yousoupoff, *Avant l'éxil*, p. 236.
79 Purishkevich, *Dnevnik*, pp. 64–66.
80 Ibid., pp. 74–75.
81 Yousoupoff, *Avant l'éxil*, p. 245.
82 Purishkevich, *Dnevnik*, p. 81.
83 "Ubiistvo Rasputina. Ofitsial'noe doznanie," *Byloe*, No. 1 (July 1917), p. 65.
84 Paléologue, *Ambassador's Memoirs*, Vol. 3, p. 135.
85 "Ubiistvo Rasputina," pp. 81–82.
86 Paléologue, *Ambassador's Memoirs*, Vol. 3, p. 133.
87 Ibid., p. 137.
88 B. M. Kochakov, "Petrograd v gody pervoi mirovoi voiny i Fevral'skoi burzhuazno-demokraticheskoi revoliutsii," *Ocherki istorii Leningrada* ed. B. M. Kochakov (Moscow-Leningrad, 1956), Vol. 3, pp. 950–51.
89 Marc Ferro, *The Russian Revolution of February 1917*, trans. J. L. Richards (Englewood Cliffs, 1972), pp. 20–22.
90 Pares, *Fall of the Russian Monarchy*, p. 332.
91 Paléologue, *Ambassador's Memoirs*, Vol. 3, p. 213.
92 Ibid., pp. 119, 215.
93 Shchegolev, ed., *Padenie tsarskogo rezhima*, Vol. 4, p. 21.
94 V. S. Diakin, *Russkaia burzhuaziia i tsarizm v gody pervoi mirovoi voiny* (Leningrad, 1967), pp. 312–14.
95 Paléologue, *Ambassador's Memoirs*, Vol. 3, p. 213.
96 Gilliard, *Thirteen Years*, p. 178.
97 Nicholas to Aleksandra, 30 October 1916, *Letters of the Tsar to the Tsaritsa*, p. 287.
98 Shul'gin, *Dni*, pp. 117–18.
99 Quoted in Alexander, *Once a Grand Duke*, p. 275.
100 Aleksandra to Nicholas, 4 November 1916, *Letters of the Tsaritsa to the Tsar*, pp. 433–34.
101 Alexander, *Once a Grand Duke*, pp. 283–84.
102 Paléologue, *Ambassador's Memoirs*, Vol. 3, pp. 151–52.

103 Kokovtsev, *Iz moego proshlago*, Vol. 2, pp. 402–4.
104 Princess Cantacuzene, *Revolutionary Days: Recollections of Romanovs and Bolsheviki, 1914–1917* (Boston, 1919), pp. 97, 188–89.
105 For example, see references to this in Aleksandra to Nicholas, 21 June and 7 October 1915, in *Letters of the Tsaritsa to the Tsar*, pp. 105, 191.
106 Paléologue, *Ambassador's Memoirs*, Vol. 3, p. 212.
107 Nicholas to Aleksandra, 13 November 1915, *Letters of the Tsar to the Tsaritsa*, p. 265.
108 Aleksandra to Nicholas, 14 January 1916, *Letters of the Tsaritsa to the Tsar*, p. 265.
109 Yousoupoff, *Rasputin*, p. 110.
110 Quoted in Purishkevich, *Dnevnik*, p. 77.
111 Shchegolev, ed., *Padenie tsarskogo rezhima*, Vol. 1, pp. 184–85.
112 L. S. Gaponenko, ed., *Revoliutsionnoe dvizhenie v Rossii posle sverzheniia samoderzhaviia* (Moscow, 1957), p. 8.
113 Quoted in Ferro, *Russian Revolution*, p. 36.
114 Shchegolev, ed., *Padenie tsarskogo rezhima*, Vol. 1, p. 183.
115 N. N. Sukhanov, *The Russian Revolution, 1917*, ed., abr., and trans. Joel Carmichael (Oxford, 1955), p. 5.
116 Paléologue, *Ambassador's Memoirs*, Vol. 3, p. 214; Louis de Robien, *The Diary of a Diplomat in Russia, 1917–1919*, trans. Camilla Sykes (London, 1969), p. 7.
117 Nicholas to Aleksandra, 23 February 1917, *Letters of the Tsar to the Tsaritsa*, pp. 313–14.
118 Shchegolev, ed., *Padenie tsarskogo rezhima*, Vol. 4, p. 96.
119 Ibid.
120 I. I. Mints, *Istoriia velikogo oktiabria* (Moscow, 1967), Vol. 1, p. 500.
121 Shchegolev, ed., *Padenie tsarskogo rezhima*, Vol. 4, p. 183.
122 William Henry Chamberlin, *The Russian Revolution, 1917–1921* (New York, 1965), Vol. 1, p. 75.
123 Mints, *Istoriia velikogo oktiabria*, Vol. 1, pp. 502–6; Chamberlin, *Russian Revolution*, Vol. 1, pp. 76–77; Shchegolev, ed., *Padenie tsarskogo rezhima*, Vol. 1, p. 185.
124 Quoted in Paléologue, *Ambassador's Memoirs*, Vol. 3, p. 215.
125 Nicholas to Aleksandra, 24 February 1917, *Letters of the Tsar to the Tsaritsa*, p. 315; Nicholas II, *Journal intime de Nicolas II (juillet 1914–juillet 1918)* (Paris, 1934), p. 91.
126 Mints, *Istoriia velikogo oktiabria*, Vol. 1, pp. 511–19.
127 Nicholas to Aleksandra, 26 February 1917, *Letters of the Tsar to the Tsaritsa*, p. 316.
128 Nicholas to Aleksandra, 25 February 1917, ibid., p. 315.
129 Shchegolev, ed., *Padenie tsarskogo rezhima*, Vol. 1, p. 190.
130 Ibid.
131 Nicholas to Aleksandra, 26 February 1917, *Letters of the Tsar to the Tsaritsa*, pp. 316–17.
132 Shchegolev, ed., *Padenie tsarskogo rezhima*, Vol. 1, p. 191.
133 Quoted in Mints, *Istoriia velikogo oktiabria*, Vol. 1, p. 520.
134 Ibid., pp. 521–22.
135 Aleksandra to Nicholas, 25 February 1917, quoted in ibid., p. 519.
136 Quoted in ibid., p. 523.

137 Ibid., pp. 522–27.
138 Quoted in Ferro, *Russian Revolution*, p. 39.
139 Sukhanov, *Russian Revolution*, p. 29.
140 Shchegolev, ed., *Padenie tsarskogo rezhima*, Vol. 1, pp. 194–96; Mints, *Istoriia velikogo oktiabria*, Vol. 1, pp. 526–27; Salisbury, *Black Night, White Snow*, pp. 349–50.
141 Mints, *Istoriia velikogo oktiabria*, Vol. 1, p. 528.
142 Shchegolev, ed., *Padenie tsarskogo rezhima*, Vol. 5, p. 38.
143 Nicholas II, *Journal intime*, p. 92.
144 Quoted in Mints, *Istoriia velikogo oktiabria*, Vol. 1, p. 534.
145 Ferro, *Russian Revolution*, pp. 42–43.
146 I. P. Leiberov, "Petrogradskii proletariat v Fevral'skoi revoliutsii 1917g.," *Istoriia rabochikh Leningrada*, ed. V. S. Diakin (Leningrad, 1972), Vol. 1, pp. 528–29.
147 Quoted in Diakin, *Russkaia burzhuaziia i tsarizm*, p. 326.
148 Ferro, *Russian Revolution*, pp. 67–70.
149 *Letters of the Tsar to the Tsaritsa*, p. 318.
150 Nicholas II, *Journal intime*, p. 92.
151 Leiberov, "Petrogradskii proletariat v Fevral'skoi revoliutsii 1917g.," Vol. 1, p. 529.
152 Shchegolev, ed., *Padenie tsarskogo rezhima*, Vol. 5, pp. 321–27.
153 Nicholas II, *Journal intime*, pp. 92–93.
154 Ibid., p. 93.
155 Published in Ol'denburg, *Tsarstvovanie Nikolaia II*, Vol. 2, pp. 257–58.
156 Shchegolev, ed., *Padenie tsarskogo rezhima*, Vol. 6, p. 393.
157 Nicholas II, *Journal intime*, p. 93.

CHAPTER XV: The Last Days of the Romanovs

1 Quoted by Paléologue, *Ambassador's Memoirs*, Vol. 3, p. 266.
2 Dehn, *The Real Tsaritsa*, p. 165.
3 Gilliard, *Thirteen Years*, p. 215.
4 Buxhoeveden, *Alexandra Feodorovna*, p. 271.
5 Viroubova, *Memories*, p. 212.
6 These were Kerenskii's words to Grand Duke Mikhail Aleksandrovich as reported to Paléologue by an eyewitness. Paléologue, *Ambassador's Memoirs*, Vol. 3, pp. 241–42.
7 From the Russian text published in Alexander Rabinowitch, *The Bolsheviks Come to Power: The Revolution of 1917 in Petrograd* (New York, 1976), p. 275.
8 The best description of this movement to the Left, and the process by which the Bolsheviks seized power in October, is to be found in Rabinowitch, *Bolsheviks Come to Power*, passim.
9 Seton-Watson, *The Russian Empire*, p. 618.
10 Quoted in Rabinowitch, *Bolsheviks Come to Power*, p. xxii.
11 Quoted in Florinsky, *Russia*, Vol. 2, p. 1388.
12 Perhaps the most useful study to date of the urban and rural masses, their aspirations, and actions in 1917 is J. L. H. Keep, *The Russian Revolution: A Study in Mass Mobilization* (New York, 1976).

13 Buxhoeveden, *Alexandra Feodorovna*, pp. 271–77; Gilliard, *Thirteen Years*, pp. 216–26; Dehn, *The Real Tsaritsa*, pp. 196–212; Viroubova, *Memories*, pp. 213–28.

14 Alexander Kerensky, *The Catastrophe* (New York and London, 1927), p. 259.

15 Viroubova, *Memories*, pp. 229–68; 395–96; Shchegolev, ed., *Padenie tsarskogo rezhima*, Vol. 2, p. 215; Vol. 3, p. 247.

16 Gilliard, *Thirteen Years*, p. 231.

17 Alexandre Kerenski, *La vérité sur le massacre des Romanov* (Paris, 1936), pp. 160–61; George Buchanan, *Mission to Russia*, Vol. 2, pp. 90–106.

18 Quoted in Gilliard, *Thirteen Years*, p. 222.

19 Ibid., p. 217.

20 Ibid.

21 S. P. Mel'gunov, *Sud'ba Imperatora Nikolaia II posle otrecheniia* (Paris, 1951), pp. 41–59.

22 Ibid., pp. 162–71.

23 Ibid., pp. 172–79.

24 Alexandre Kerenski, *La Revolution Russe, 1917* (Paris, 1928), p. 268.

25 Nicholas II, *Journal intime*, p. 136.

26 Quoted in Mel'gunov, *Sud'ba Imperatora Nikolaia II*, pp. 192–93.

27 Quoted in ibid., p. 197.

28 Nicholas II, *Journal intime*, p. 138.

29 Buxhoeveden, *Alexandra Feodorovna*, p. 310.

30 Massie, *Nicholas and Alexandra*, p. 449.

31 Nicholas II, *Journal intime*, p. 139.

32 Ibid., pp. 139–40; V. M. Verchinin, "Journal officiel," in Kerenskii, *La vérité*, pp. 186–89.

33 Gilliard, *Thirteen Years*, p. 242.

34 Ibid., pp. 239–265; "Tobol'skii dnevnik odnoi iz priblizhennykh k Tsarskoi Sem'e," *Arkhiv Russkoi Revoliutsii*, ed. G. V. Gessen (Berlin, 1926), Vol. 17, pp. 301–303; Nicholas II, *Journal intime*, pp. 155–90.

35 Gilliard, *Thirteen Years*, pp. 243–44, 257.

36 Kerensky, *The Catastrophe*, pp. 268–69.

37 Aleksandra Feodorovna to Anna Vyrubova, 9 January 1918, in Viroubova, *Memories*, p. 318.

38 Gilliard, *Thirteen Years*, pp. 257–58.

39 Mel'gunov, *Sud'ba Imperatora Nikolaia II*, pp. 244–46.

40 Aleksandra Feodorovna to Anna Vyrubova, 21 March/4 April 1918, in Viroubova, *Memories*, p. 341.

41 Gilliard, *Thirteen Years*, p. 254.

42 Nicholas II, *Journal intime*, p. 179.

43 Nicholas II, "Dnevnik Nikolaia Romanova," *KA*, Vol. 27 (1928), p. 118.

44 J. C. Trewin, *Tutor to the Tsarevich* (London, 1975), p. 101.

45 Mel'gunov, *Sud'ba Imperatora Nikolaia II*, pp. 276–96.

46 Massie, *Nicholas and Alexandra*, p. 482.

47 Ibid., p. 484; Mel'gunov, *Sud'ba Imperatora Nikolaia II*, pp. 370–74; Trewin, *Tutor to the Tsarevich*, pp. 106–7.

48 Mel'gunov, *Sud'ba Imperatora Nikolaia II*, pp. 378–79.

49 P. M. Bykov, "Poslednie dni poslednego tsaria," *Arkhiv Russkoi Revoliutsii*, Vol. 17, p. 313.

50 Nicholas II, *Journal intime*, p. 214.

51 Mel'gunov, *Sud'ba Imperatora Nikolaia II*, p. 400.
52 Quoted in Salisbury, *Black Night, White Snow*, pp. 591–92.
53 Mel'gurov, *Sud'ba Imperatora Nikolaia II*, pp. 401–2; Bykov, "Poslednie dni," pp. 512–13.
54 John F. O'Connor, ed. and trans., *The Sokolov Investigation of the Alleged Murder of the Russian Imperial Family* (New York, 1971), pp. 173–75.
55 Ibid., pp. 134–41; Mel'gunov, *Sud'ba Imperatora Nikolaia II*, p. 382.
56 Quoted in Mel'gunov, *Sud'ba Imperatora Nikolaia II*, p. 383. See also Bykov, "Poslednie dni," p. 314.
57 E. E. Alfer'ev, ed., *Pis'ma tsarskoi sem'i iz zatocheniia* (Jordanville, N.Y., 1974), pp. 395–402; Mel'gunov, *Sud'ba Imperatora Nikolaia II*, pp. 382–83.
58 Alfer'ev, ed., *Pis'ma tsarskoi sem'i*, pp. 404–10; O'Connor, *Sokolov Investigation*, pp. 190–91.
59 Trewin, *Tutor to the Tsarevich*, p. 113.
60 Kerensky, *The Catastrophe*, p. 265.
61 Emma Goldman, *My Further Disillusionment in Russia* (Garden City, N.Y., 1924), p. 178.
62 M. P. Pogodin, *Istoriko-politicheskie pis'ma i zapiski v prodolzhenii krymskoi voiny, 1853–1856* (Moscow, 1874), pp. 3, 254.

WORKS CITED

Adams, John Quincy. *Memoirs of John Quincy Adams*, ed. Charles Francis Adams. Vol. 2. Philadelphia, 1874.

Alefirenko, P. K. *Krest'ianskoe dvizhenie i krest'ianskii vopros v Rossii v 30–50kh godakh XVIII veka.* Moscow, 1958.

Aleksandra Feodorovna (I). "Imperatritsa Aleksandra Feodorovna v svoikh vospominaniiakh." *RS*, Vol. 88, No. 10 (October 1896), pp. 5–60.

Aleksandra Feodorovna (II). *Letters of the Tsaritsa to the Tsar, 1914–1916*, ed. Sir Bernard Pares. Hattiesburg, 1970.

Alekseev, M. D., ed. *Ot klassitsizma k romantizmu.* Leningrad, 1970.

Alexander, J. T. *Autocratic Politics in a National Crisis: The Imperial Russian Government and Pugachev's Revolt, 1773–1775.* Bloomington, Ind., 1969.

Alexander [Mikhailovich], Grand Duke. *Once a Grand Duke.* New York, 1932.

Alfer'ev, E. E., ed. *Pis'ma tsarskoi sem'i iz zatocheniia.* Jordanville, N.Y., 1974.

Almedingen, E. M. *The Emperor Alexander I.* New York, 1964.

———. *An Unbroken Unity: A Memoir of Grand-Duchess Serge of Russia, 1864–1918.* London, 1964.

Andics, E. *Das Bündnis Habsburg-Romanow. Vorgeschichte der zaristichen Intervention in Ungarn im Jahre 1849.* Budapest, 1963.

Andreev, V., "Ekaterina Pervaia." *Osmnadtsatyi vek*, ed. P. Bartenev, Vol. 3 (1869), pp. 1–26.

Andrei Vladimirovich, Grand Duke. *Dnevnik za 1915g.* Moscow-Leningrad, 1925.

Arkin, D. E. "E. M. Fal'kone," *IRI*, Vol. 6 (1953–61), pp. 366–83.

———. *Rastrelli.* Moscow, 1954.

Artem'ev, A. I. 'Dnevniki, 1855–1858gg.' GPB, fond 37, dela Nos. 155–161.

Avrich, Paul. *Russian Rebels, 1600–1800.* New York, 1976.

Babkin, D. A. *Protsess A. N. Radishcheva.* Moscow-Leningrad, 1952.

Baedeker, Karl. *Russia, with Teheran, Port Arthur, and Peking: A Handbook for Travellers.* Leipzig and London, 1914.

Bain, R. Nisbet. *The First Romanovs, 1613–1725: A History of Muscovite Civilization and the Rise of Modern Russia Under Peter the Great and His Forerunners.* London, 1905.

Bakhrushin, S. V. *Nauchnye trudy.* Vol. 3. Moscow, 1954.

———. "Velikaia kniaginia Elena Pavlovna," *Osvobozhdenie krest'ian: deiateli reformy*, pp. 155–72. Moscow, 1911.

Balzer, O. "Reformy spoleczne i politiczne konstytucyi 3. maja." *Przgląd Polski* (1891), pp. 222–60, 461–96.

Barbour, Violet. *Capitalism in Amsterdam in the Seventeenth Century.* Ann Arbor, 1963.

Barsukov, Aleksandr. *Rod Sheremetevykh.* Vol. 3. St. Petersburg, 1883.

Bartenev, I. A. "Arkhitektura Peterburga." *Ocherki istorii Leningrada,* ed. M. P. Viatkin, Vol. 2, pp. 793–809.

Bartenev, P., ed. *Arkhiv kniazia Vorontsova.* 40 vols. Moscow, 1870–95.

———, ed. *Osnmadtsatyi vek.* 4 vols. Moscow, 1869.

Batkowski, Z. *Architekt Rastrelli o swoich pracach.* Lwów, 1939.

Becker, Seymour. *Russia's Protectorates in Central Asia: Bukhara and Khiva, 1865–1924.* Cambridge, Mass., 1968.

Belinskii, V. G. *Sobranie sochinenii V. G. Belinskago,* ed. Ivanov-Razumnik. 3 vols. Petrograd, 1919.

Belyi, Andrei. *Serebrianyi golub'.* Munich, 1967.

———. *The Silver Dove,* trans. George Reavey, with a preface by Harrison E. Salisbury. New York, 1974.

Benkendorf, A. Kh. "Graf A. Kh. Benkendorf o Rossii v 1827–1830gg." *KA,* Vol. 37 (1929); Vol. 38 (1930).

———. "Imperator Nikolai v 1828–1829 i v 1830–1831gg. (iz zapisok Grafa A. Kh. Benkendorfa)." *RS,* Vol. 87, No. 6 (June 1896); Vol. 87, No. 7 (July 1896); Vol. 88, No. 10 (October 1896).

Benson, A. C., and Viscount Escher, eds. *The Letters of Queen Victoria: A Selection of Her Majesty's Correspondence between the Years 1837–1861.* 3 vols. London, 1907.

Berkh, V. *Tsarstvovanie tsaria Feodora Alekseevicha i istoriia pervago streletskago bunta.* 2 vols. St. Petersburg, 1834.

Berkov, P. N. "Satiricheskaia zhurnalistika 1769–1774gg." *Ocherki po istorii russkoi zhurnalistiki i kritiki,* ed. V. E. Evgen'ev-Maksimov, et al. Vol. 1, pp. 45–81.

Beuchot, A. J. Q. ed. *Oeuvres complètes de Voltaire.* Vol. 59. Paris, 1832.

Bezsonov, S. *Krepostnye arkhitektory.* Moscow, 1938.

Bibikov, A. A. *Zapiski o zhizni i sluzhbe Aleksandra Il'icha Bibikova.* Moscow, 1865.

Bilbassov, V. A. *Istoriia Ekateriny Vtoroi.* 2 vols. Berlin, 1900.

Billington, James, H. *The Icon and the Axe: An Interpretative History of Russian Culture.* London, 1966.

Bing, Edward J., ed. *The Letters of Tsar Nicholas and Empress Marie.* London, 1937.

Blagoi, D. D. *Istoriia russkoi literatury XVIII veka.* Moscow, 1961.

———, and B. P. Gorodetskii, eds. *Istoriia russkoi literatury.* Vol. 6. Moscow-Leningrad, 1953.

Bliokh, I. *Finansy v Rossii XIX stoletiia.* 2 vols. St. Petersburg, 1882.

Blok, Aleksandr. *The Twelve,* trans. Babette Deutsch and Avrahm Yarmolinsky. New York, 1931.

Blomberg, Baron de. *An Account of Livonia.* London, 1701.

Blum, Jerome. *Lord and Peasant in Russia from the Ninth to the Nineteenth Century.* Princeton, 1961.

Bobrovskii, P. "Vzgliad na grammotnost' i uchebnye komandy (ili polkovye shkoly) v nashei armii." *Voennyi sbornik,* Vol. 76, No. 12 (December 1870).

Bodarskii, Ia. E. "Mezhdunarodnoe polozhenie Russkago gosudarstva i russko-turetskaia voina 1676–1681gg." *Ocherki istorii SSSR, Period feodalizma: XVII v.*, ed. A. A. Novosel'skii, pp. 518–31.

Bogdanovich, A. V. *Tri poslednykh samoderzhtsa: Dnevnik A. V. Bogdanovicha.* Moscow-Leningrad, 1924.

Bogoiavlenskii, S. K. "Moskovskaia nemetskaia sloboda." *Izvestiia Akademiia Nauk SSSR. Seriia istorii i filosofii*, No. 3 (1947), pp. 220–32.

Bogoslovskii, M. M. *Konstitutsionnoe dvizhenie 1730g.* Petrograd, 1918.

———. *Petr I: Materialy dlia biografii.* 5 vols. Moscow, 1940–48.

———. *Petr Velikii i ego reforma.* Moscow, 1920.

Bogucharskii, V. "Tret'e otdelenie sobstvennoi ego imperatorskago velichestva kantseliarii o sebe samom." *VE*, Vol. 52, No. 3 (March 1917), pp. 85–125.

Bok, M. P. *Vospominaniia o moem ottse P. A. Stolypine.* New York, 1953.

Bolotov, Andrei. *Zhizn' i prikliucheniia Andreia Bolotova opisannye samim im dlia svoikh potomkov.* 3 vols. Moscow-Leningrad, 1931.

Borovkov, A. D. "A. D. Borovkov i ego avtobiograficheskie zapiski." *RS*, Vol. 96, No. 11 (November 1898), pp. 331–63; No. 12 (December 1898), pp. 591–616.

Borozdin, I. N. "Universitety v Rossii v pervoi polovine XIX veke." *Istoriia Rossii v XIX veka.* Vol. 2 (1907), pp. 349–78.

Bowman, Herbert E. *Vissarion Belinsky, 1810–1848: A Study in the Origins of Social Criticism in Russia.* Cambridge, Mass., 1954.

Bozherianov, I. N. *Zhizneopisanie imperatritsy Aleksandry Feodorovny, suprugi Imperatora Nikolaia I.* 2 vols. St. Petersburg, 1898.

Bray-Steinberg, Graf Otto von. "Imperator Nikolai i ego spodvizhniki." *RS*, Vol. 109, No. 1 (January 1890), pp. 115–39.

Bronshtein, S. S. "Peterburgskaia arkhitektura 20–30-kh godov XVIII veka." *IRI*, Vol. 5 (1953–61), pp. 122–50.

Brown, Edward. *Stankevich and His Moscow Circle, 1830–1840.* Stanford, 1961.

Brückner, A. A. *Istoriia Ekateriny Vtoroi.* 5 vols. St. Petersburg, 1882–86.

———. *Istoriia Petra Velikago.* 6 vols. St. Petersburg, 1882.

———. *Smert' Pavla I.* St. Petersburg, 1907.

Bubnov, A. *V Tsarskoi stavke.* New York, 1955.

Buchanan, Sir George. *My Mission to Russia and Other Diplomatic Memories.* 2 vols. Boston, 1923.

Buchanan, Meriel. *The Dissolution of an Empire.* London, 1932.

Bursov, B. I., ed. *Istoriia russkoi literatury.* Vol. 9 (2). Moscow-Leningrad, 1956.

———, and L. D. Opul'skaia, eds. "Lev Tolstoi." *Istoriia russkoi literatury.* Vol. 9 (2) (1956), pp. 435–620.

Buxhoeveden, Baroness Sophie. *A Cavalier in Muscovy.* London, 1932.

———. *The Life and Tragedy of Alexandra Feodorovna, Empress of Russia.* London, 1928.

Bykov, P. M. "Poslednie dni poslednego tsaria." *Arkhiv Russkoi Revoliutsii*, ed. G. V. Gessen. Vol. 17 (1926), pp. 305–6.

Bykova, V. P. *Zapiski staroi smolianki.* St. Petersburg, 1898.

Byrnes, Robert F. *Pobedonostsev: His Life and Thought.* Bloomington, 1968.

Calvocoressi, M. D. *Modest Mussorgsky: His Life and Works.* Fair Lawn, N.J., 1956.

———, and Gerald Abraham, *Masters of Russian Music.* New York, 1936.

Cantacuzene, Princess. *Revolutionary Days: Recollections of Romanovs and Bolsheviki, 1914–1917.* Boston, 1919.

Carr, E. H. *Dostoevsky.* London, 1949.

WORKS CITED

Castera, J. H. *Life of Catherine the Great.* 2 vols. London, 1800.
Catherine II. "Bumagi Imperatritsy Ekateriny II," *SIRIO,* Vol. 27 (1880).
———. *Mémoires de l'Impératrice Catherine II,* ed. Alexander Herzen. London, 1859.
———. *Memoirs of Catherine the Great,* trans. Katherine Anthony. New York, 1935.
———. *Nakaz Imperatritsy Ekateriny II, dannyi kommissii o sochinenii proekta novago ulozheniia,* ed. N. D. Chechulin. St. Petersburg, 1907.
———. "Pis'ma Imperatritsy Ekateriny II baronu Mel'kioru Grimmu, 1774–1796," *SIRIO,* Vol. 23 (1878).
———. "Sobstvennoruchnye raspisaniia Ekateriny II o nagradakh po sluchaiu vozshestviia eia na prestol i koronatsii." *SIRIO,* Vol. 7 (1871), pp. 111–14.
Caulaincourt, Armand de. *With Napoleon in Russia. The Memoirs of General de Caulaincourt, Duke of Vicenza.* New York, 1935.
Chamberlin, William Henry. *The Russian Revolution, 1917–1921.* 2 vols. New York, 1965.
Cherepnin, L. V. *Obrazovanie russkago tsentralizovannogo gosudarstva v XIV–XV vekakh.* Moscow, 1960.
———. *Zemskie sobory russkogo gosudarstva v XVI–XVII vv.* Moscow, 1978.
Cherniavsky, Michael. "Ivan the Terrible as Renaissance Prince," *SR,* Vol. 27, No. 2 (June 1968), pp. 195–211.
———. *Tsar and People: Studies in Russian Myths.* New Haven, 1961.
———, ed. *Prologue to Revolution: Notes of A. N. Iakhontov on the Secret Meetings of the Council of Ministers, 1915.* Englewood Cliffs, 1967.
———, ed. *The Structure of Russian History: Interpretive Essays.* New York, 1970.
Chétardie, Marquis de la. *Markiz de-la-Shetardi v Rossii 1740–1742 godov. Perevod rukopisnykh depesh frantsuzskago posol'stva v Peterburge.* St. Petersburg, 1862.
Chistiakova, E. V. "Zavershenie bor'by s interventsiei. Organizatsiia novogo pravitel'stva." *Ocherki istorii SSSR,* ed. A. N. Nasonov, et al., pp. 593–603.
Chizh, V. "Imperator Pavel I." *Voprosy filosofii i psikhologii.* Vol. 18, No. 3 (May–June 1907), pp. 221–90; No. 4 (Sept.–Oct. 1907), pp. 391–468; No. 5 (Nov.–Dec. 1907), pp. 585–678.
Christoff, P. K. *An Introduction to Nineteenth-Century Slavophilism.* 2 vols. The Hague, 1961, 1972.
Corbéron, Marie-Daniel Bourrée, Chevalier de. *Un diplomat français à la cour de Catherine II, 1775–1780. Journal intime de Chevalier de Corbéron.* 2 vols. Paris, 1901.
Cracraft, James. *The Church Reform of Peter the Great.* London, 1971.
———. "Feofan Prokopovich: A Bibliography of His Works," *Oxford Slavonic Papers,* Vol. 8 (1975), pp. 1–36.
Crankshaw, Edward. *The Shadow of the Winter Palace: Russia's Drift to Revolution, 1825–1917.* New York, 1976.
Crummey, R. O. "The Origins of the Noble Official: The Boiar Elite, 1613–1689." *Russian Officialdom from the Seventeenth to the Twentieth Century,* ed. W. M. Pintner and D. K. Rowney. Forthcoming, University of North Carolina Press, Fall 1980/Spring 1981.
———. "The Reconstruction of the Boiar Aristocracy, 1613–1645," *Forschungen zur osteuropäischen Geschichte,* Vol. 18 (1973), pp. 187–220.
Curtiss, J. S. *The Russian Army under Nicholas I, 1825–1855.* Durham, 1965.
Curtiss, Mina. *A Forgotten Empress: Anna Ivanovna and Her Era, 1730–1740.* New York, 1974.

Custine, Astolphe Louis Lénor, Marquis de. *La Russie en 1839.* 4 vols. Paris, 1843.

———. *Russia.* Cincinnati, 1856.

Czartoryski, Prince Adam. *Mémoires du Prince Adam Czartoryski et correspondance avec l'Empereur Alexandre Ier,* ed. Charles Mazade. 2 vols. Paris, 1887.

Danilov, Iu. N. *Rossiia v mirovoi voine, 1914–1915 gg.* Berlin, 1924.

Dashkov, Princess Catherine. *Memoirs of Princess Dashkov.* London, 1958.

Davydov, N. V., and N. N. Polianskii, eds. *Sudebnaia reforma.* Vol. 1. Moscow, 1915.

Dawson, Christopher, ed. *The Mongol Mission: Narratives and Letters of the Franciscan Missionaries in Mongolia and China in the Thirteenth and Fourteenth Centuries.* New York, 1955.

Dehn, Lili. *The Real Tsaritsa.* Boston, 1922.

Deiateli revoliutsionnogo dvizheniia v Rossii. Bio-bibliograficheskii slovar'. 4 vols. Moscow, 1927–34.

Dement'ev, A. G., et al., eds. *Russkaia periodicheskaia pechat' (1702–1894). Spravochnik.* Moscow, 1959.

Derzhavin, G. R. "Ode to the Wise Princess Felitsa of the Kirghiz-Kazakh Horde, Written by a Certain Murza, Long a Resident of Moscow, But Now Living in St. Petersburg Because of His Affairs, 1782." *The Literature of Eighteenth-Century Russia,* ed. and trans. Harold B. Segal. Vol. 2, pp. 270–79.

———. "To Rulers and Judges." *Literature of Eighteenth-Century Russia,* ed. and trans. Segal. Vol. 2, p. 261.

———. "Zapiski, 1743–1812." *Sochineniia G. R. Derzhavina.* Vol. 6. St. Petersburg, 1871.

Diakin, V. S. *Russkaia burzhuaziia i tsarizm v gody pervoi mirovoi voiny.* Leningrad, 1967.

———, ed. *Istoriia rabochikh Leningrada.* 2 vols. Leningrad, 1972.

Dillon. "Aleksandr III." *Golos minuvshago,* No. 5–6 (May–June 1917), pp. 85–95.

"Diplomaticheskaia perepiska angliiskikh poslov i poslannikov pri Russkom dvore, 1694–1776 gg." *SIRIO,* Vol. 12 (1874); Vol. 19 (1876); Vol. 39 (1884); Vol. 51 (1886); Vol. 61 (1888); Vol. 66 (1889); Vol. 71 (1891); Vol. 80 (1892); Vol. 85 (1893); Vol. 91 (1894); Vol. 99 (1897); Vol. 102 (1898); Vol. 110 (1901); Vol. 148 (1916).

"Diplomaticheskaia perepiska frantsuzskikh predstavitelei pri Russkom dvore, 1681–1772 gg." *SIRIO,* Vol. 34 (1881); Vol. 40 (1884); Vol. 49 (1885); Vol. 52 (1886); Vol. 57 (1887); Vol. 64 (1888); Vol. 75 (1891); Vol. 81 (1892); Vol. 86 (1893); Vol. 92 (1894); Vol. 96 (1896); Vol. 100 (1897); Vol. 105 (1899); Vol. 140 (1912); Vol. 141 (1913); Vol. 142 (1913).

"Diplomaticheskaia perepiska prusskago korolia Fridrikha II s grafa Sol'msa, poslannikom pri Russkom dvore." *SIRIO,* Vol. 37 (1893); Vol. 72 (1891).

"Diplomaticheskaia perepiska prusskikh poslannikov pri Russkom dvore, 1763–1766 gg." *SIRIO,* Vol. 22 (1878).

"Diplomaticheskie dokumenty, otnosiashchiesia k istorii Rossii v XVIII st." *SIRIO,* Vol. 3 (1868).

Dobrynin, M. K., ed. *Istoriia russkoi literatury.* Vol. 8 (1). Moscow-Leningrad, 1956.

"Donesenie i drugiia bumagi angliiskikh poslov, poslannikov, i rezidentov pri russkom dvore s 1728 po 1733 goda." *SIRIO,* Vol. 66 (1889), pp. 273–509.

Dostoevskii, F. M. *The Diary of a Writer,* trans. and ann. Boris Brasol. New York, 1954.

———. *Polnoe sobranie sochinenii v tridtsati tomakh.* Leningrad, 1972–.

Drabkina, Elizaveta. *Chernye sukhari.* Moscow, 1963.

Druzhinin, N. M. *Gosudarstvennye krest'iane i reforma P. D. Kiseleva.* 2 vols. Moscow-Leningrad, 1946, 1958.

Dubrovin, N. F. ed. *Materialy i cherty k biografii Imperatora Nikolaia I i k istorii ego tsarstvovaniia.* St. Petersburg, 1896.

———, ed. "Protokoly, zhurnaly, i ukazy Verkhovnago Tainago Soveta s l iiulia po konets dekabria 1727g." *SIRIO* (1889).

———. *Pugachev i ego soobshchenniki.* 3 vols. St. Petersburg, 1884.

Dubrovskii, S. M. *Stolypinskaia zemel'naia reforma.* Moscow, 1963.

Duchesne, M. E., trans. *Le Domostroi: ménagier Russe du XVIe siècle.* Paris, 1910.

Dukes, Paul. *Catherine the Great and the Russian Nobility.* Cambridge, 1967.

Dzhanshiev, G. *Epokha velikikh reform.* St. Petersburg, 1905.

———. *S. I. Zarudnyi i sudebnaia reforma.* Moscow, 1889.

Dzhedzhula, K. E. *Rossiia i velikaia frantsuzskaia burzhuaznaia revoliutsiia kontsa XVIII veka.* Kiev, 1972.

Dzhevelegov, A. K. "Graf V. N. Panin." *Velikaia Reforma,* Vol. 5, pp. 147–55.

———, S. P. Mel'gunov, and V. I. Picheta, eds. *Velikaia Reforma: Russkoe obshchestvo i krest'ianskii vopros v proshlom i nastoiashchem.* 6 vols. Moscow, 1911.

Edward, Duke of Windsor. *A King's Story.* New York, 1947.

Egorov, I. A. *The Architectural Planning of St. Petersburg,* trans. Eric Dluhosch. Athens, Ohio, 1969.

"Ekstrakt iz zhurnala uchebnykh zaniatii velikago kniazia Petra Feodorovicha s iiunia 1742 po 1745 gg." *Chteniia,* Bk. 4 (1866), pp. 112–16.

Emmons, Terence. *The Russian Landed Gentry and the Peasant Emancipation of 1861.* Cambridge, 1968.

Erlich, Victor. *Gogol.* New Haven and London, 1969.

Eroshkin, N. P. "Administrativno-politseiskii apparat." *Istoriia Moskvy,* ed. A. M. Pankratova. Vol. 5, pp. 663–75.

Evgen'ev-Maksimov, V. E., et al., eds. *Ocherki po istorii russkoi zhurnalistiki i kritiki.* Vol. 1. Leningrad, 1950.

Evsina, N. A. *Arkhitekturnaia teoriia v Rossii XVIII v.* Moscow, 1975.

Fennell, J. L. I. *The Emergence of Moscow, 1304–1359.* Berkeley and Los Angeles, 1968.

———, ed. and trans. *The Correspondence between Prince A. M. Kurbsky and Tsar Ivan IV of Russia, 1564–1579.* Cambridge, 1955.

Ferro, Marc. *The Russian Revolution of February 1917,* trans. J. L. Richards. Englewood Cliffs, 1972.

Field, Daniel. *The End of Serfdom: Nobility and Bureaucracy in Russia, 1855–1861.* Cambridge, Mass., 1976.

Figner, Vera. *Memoirs of a Revolutionist.* New York, 1927.

———. *Zapechatlennyi trud.* 2 vols. Moscow, 1964.

Filippov, A. N. "Istoricheskii ocherk obrazovaniia ministerstv v Rossii." *ZhMIu,* No. 9 (September 1902), pp. 39–73.

Fisher, R. H. *The Russian Fur Trade, 1550–1700.* Berkeley and Los Angeles, 1943.

Florinsky, M. T. *Russia: A History and an Interpretation.* 2 vols. New York, 1967.

Florovskii, Prot. Georgii. *Puti russkago bogosloviia.* Paris, 1937.

Fonvizin, D. I. "The Brigadier." *Literature of Eighteenth-Century Russia.* Vol. 2, pp. 318–73.

———. "Poslanie k slugam moim Shumilovu, Van'ke i Petrushke." *Izbrannye proizvedeniia russkikh myslitetei vtoroi poloviny XVIII veka,* ed. I. Ia. Shchipanov. Vol. 2, pp. 219–22.

———. *Sobranie sochinenii.* Vol. 2. Moscow, 1959.

Footman, David. *Red Prelude.* New Haven, 1945.

Frederiks, Baroness M. P. "Iz vospominanii baronessy M. P. Frederiksa." IV, Vol. 71, No. 1 (January 1898), pp. 52–88; Vol. 71, No. 2 (February 1989), pp. 454–84.

Fridlender, G. M. "Dostoevskii," *Istoriia russkoi literatury,* ed. B. I. Bursov, pp. 7–120.

Frolenko, M. F. *Sobranie sochinenii.* Vol. 2. Moscow, 1932.

Fuhrmann, Joseph T. *The Origins of Capitalism in Russia: Industry and Progress in the Sixteenth and Seventeenth Centuries.* Chicago, 1972.

Fülöp-Miller, René. *Rasputin: The Holy Devil.* New York, 1928.

Galaktionov, I. V. *Iz istorii Russko-Pol'skogo sblizheniia v 50–60kh godakh XVII veka.* Saratov, 1960.

Gaponenko, L. S., ed. *Revoliutsionnoe dvizhenie v Rossii posle sverzheniia samoderzhaviia.* Moscow, 1957.

Garrard, J. E., ed. *The Eighteenth Century in Russia.* Oxford, 1973.

Gegello, A. I., and V. F. Shilkov. "Arkhitektura i planirovka Peterburga do 60-kh godov XVIII v.," *Ocherki istorii Leningrada,* ed. M. P. Viatkin, Vol. 1. Moscow-Leningrad, 1955, pp. 115–57.

Geiman, V. G., and N. V. Ustiugov. "Manufaktura." *Ocherki istorii SSSR,* ed. A. A. Novosel'skii, pp. 87–113.

Gertsen, Aleksandr Ivanovich. *Polnoe sobraine sochinenii i pisem,* ed. M. K. Lemke. 22 vols. Petrograd, 1918–22.

Gessen, G. V., ed. *Arkhiv Russkoi Revoliutsii.* 22 vols. Berlin, 1921–37.

Gilliard, Pierre. *Thirteen Years at the Russian Court.* New York, 1970.

———. *Le tragique destin de Nicolas II et de sa famille.* Paris, 1938.

Gippius. V. V., et al. "Pushkin," *Istoriia russkoi literatury,* ed. Blagoi and Gorodetskii, Moscow-Leningrad, 1953, pp. 161–330.

Gitermann, V. *Geschichte Russlands.* 3 vols. Zurich, 1944–49.

Gogol', N. V. *Polnoe sobranie sochinenii N. V. Gogolia.* Vol. 8. Moscow, 1913.

———. *Sobranie sochinenii.* 6 vols. Moscow, 1959.

Goldman, Emma. *My Further Disillusionment in Russia.* Garden City, 1924.

Golikov, I. I. *Deianiia Petra Velikago, mudrago preobrazovatelia Rossii, sobrannye iz dostovernykh istochnikov.* 15 vols. Moscow, 1788–91.

Golikova, N. B. "K istorii Astrakhanskogo vosstaniia 1705–1706gg." *Rossiia v period reform Petra I,* ed. N. I. Pavlenko. Moscow, 1973, pp. 249–88.

———. *Politicheskie protsessy pri Petre I.* Moscow, 1957.

Golovine, Nicholas N. *The Russian Army in the World War.* New Haven, 1931.

Golovnin, A. V. 'Zapiski Aleksandra Vasil'evicha Golovnina s maia 1866 do ianvaria 1867gg.,' TsGIAL, fond 851, opis' 1, delo No. 6.

———. 'Zapiski Aleksandra Vasil'evicha Golovnina s marta 1867 goda,' TsGIAL, fond 851, opis' 1, delo No. 7.

———. 'Prodolzhenie zapisok, 1868–1870gg.,' TsGIAL, fond 851, opis' 1, delo No. 8.

———. 'Prodolzhenie zapisok Aleksandra Vasil'evicha Golovnina s dekabria 1870g. po fevral' 1871g.,' TsGIAL, fond 851, opis' 1, delo No. 9.

Golubtsov, S. A., ed. *Pugachevshchina*. 3 vols. Moscow-Leningrad, 1926–31.

Gomberg-Verzhbinskaia, E. *Peredvizhniki*. Leningrad, 1970.

Gordon, Alexander. *A History of Peter the Great, Emperor of Russia*. 2 vols. London, 1755.

Gordon, Patrick. *Passages from the Diary of General Patrick Gordon*. New York, 1968.

Gorev, L. *Voina 1853–1856gg. i oborona Sevastopolia*. Moscow, 1955.

Gorianinow, S. M. *Le Bosphore et les Dardanelles*. Paris, 1910.

Gorodetskii, V. P., ed. *Istoriia russkoi literatury*. Vol. 7. Moscow-Leningrad, 1955.

Gorodskie poseleniia v Rossiiskoi Imperii. Vol. 7. St. Petersburg, 1864.

Gosudarstvennyi Sovet, 1801–1901gg. St. Petersburg, 1902.

Got'e, Iu. V. "Proekt ob popravlenii gosudarstvennykh del Artemiia Petrovicha Volynskago." *Dela i dni*, Vol. 3 (1922), pp. 1–31.

———. *Zamoskovskii krai v XVII veke*. Moscow, 1937.

Grabar, I. E. "Chuguevskie uchitelia Repina," *Khudozhestvennoe nasledstvo*, ed. I. E. Grabar and I. S. Zil'bershtein. Moscow-Leningrad, 1948. Vol. 1, pp. 17–32.

———. "Osnovanie i nachalo zastroiki Peterburga." *IRI*, Vol. 5 (1953–61), pp. 65–83.

———. "T. Tomon." *IRI*, Vol. 8 (1) (1953–61), pp. 106–22.

———, ed. *Istoriia arkhitektury: Peterburgskaia arkhitektura v XVIII i XIX veke*. Vol. 3. Moscow, 1911.

———, ed. *Istoriia russkogo iskusstva*. 12 vols. Moscow, 1953–61.

———, S. S. Bronshtein, and G. G. Grimm. "U istokov russkogo klassitsizma." *IRI*, Vol. 6 (1953–61), pp. 41–84.

———, and G. G. Gun'kin. "V. I. Bazhenov." *IRI*, Vol. 6 (1953–61), pp. 85–129.

Grekov, B. D., ed. *Ocherki istorii SSSR: Period feodalizma IX–XV vv*. Moscow, 1953.

———, and A. Iakoubovski. *La Horde d'Or et la Russie: La domination Tatare au XIIIe et au XIVe siècle de la mer jaune à la mer noire*. Paris, 1961.

Grekov, I. B., and A. N. Mal'tsev. "Mezhdunarodnoe polozhenie Rossii v nachale 80–kh gg., 'Vechnyi mir' 1686g., i Krymskie pokhody 1687 i 1689gg.," in *Ocherki istorii SSSR*, ed. A. A. Novosel'skii, pp. 531–41.

Grey, Ian. *Catherine the Great*. New York, 1965.

———. *Peter the Great: Emperor of All Russia*. Philadelphia and New York, 1960.

———. *The Romanovs: The Rise and Fall of a Dynasty*. New York, 1970.

Gribovskii, A. M. *Vospominaniia A. M. Gribovskago*. Moscow, 1898.

Grimm, G. G. *Arkhitektor Andreian Zakharov*. Moscow, 1940.

———, M. A. Il'in, and Iu. A. Egorov. "K. I. Rossi." *IRI*, Vol. 8 (1) (1953–61), pp. 128–64.

———, and A. N. Petrov. "Peterburgskie zodchie poslednei chetverty XVIII veka." *IRI*, Vol. 6 (1953–61), pp. 186–235.

Grimm, Baron Melchior. "Pis'ma barona Mel'kiora Grimma k imperatritse Ekaterine II." *SIRIO*, Vol. 32 (1891).

Grimsted, Patricia Kennedy. *The Foreign Ministers of Alexander I: Political Attitudes and the Conduct of Russian Diplomacy, 1801–1825*. Berkeley and Los Angeles, 1969.

Grunwald, Constantin de. *Tsar Nicholas I*, trans. from the French Brigit Patmore. London, 1954.

Gruzinskii, A. E. "Ivan Sergeevich Turgenev." *Istoriia russkoi literatury XIX veka*, ed. D. N. Ovsianiko-Kulikovskii. Vol. 3, pp. 278–331.

Gudzii, N. K. *Istoriia drevnei russkoi literatury*. 6th edn. Moscow, 1956.

Gudzy, N. K. *History of Early Russian Literature*, trans. Susan Jones. New York, 1949.

Gurevich, L. "Narodnoe dvizhenie v Peterburge 9–go ianvaria 1906 goda." *Byloe*, Vol. 1, No. 1 (January 1906), pp. 200–229.

Gurko, V. I. *Features and Figures of the Past: Government and Opinion in the Reign of Nicholas II*. Stanford, 1939.

———. *Tsar i Tsaritsa*. Paris, 1927.

Haimson, Leopold. *The Russian Marxists and the Origins of Bolshevism*. Cambridge, Mass., 1955.

Halecki, O. *A History of Poland*. New York, 1943.

Haumant, Emile. *La Culture Française en Russie (1700–1900)*. Paris, 1913.

Hautecoeur, Louis. *L'Architecture classique à Saint-Pétersbourg à la fin du XVIIIᵉ siècle*. Paris, 1912.

Herman, E., ed. "Diplomaticheskie dokumenty, otnosiashchiesia k istorii Rossii v XVIII stoletii. Soobshcheno iz del saksonskago gosudarstvennago arkhiv v Drezdene." *SIRIO* (1868).

History of the Russian Fleet during the Reign of Peter the Great. London, 1899.

Hollingsworth, Barry. "Arzamas: Portrait of a Literary Society." *SEER*, Vol. 44, No. 103 (July 1966), pp. 310–26.

Iakushkin, I. D. *Zapiski, stat'i, i pis'ma dekabrista I. D. Iakushkina*. Moscow, 1951.

Il'in, M. A. "A. D. Zakharov." *IRI*, Vol. 8 (1) (1953–61), pp. 86–104.

———. "A. N. Voronikhin." *IRI*, Vol. 8 (1) (1953–61), pp. 62–85.

———. "M. F. Kazakov." *IRI*, Vol. 6 (1953–61), pp. 130–65.

Istoriia Ministerstva Finansov, 1802–1902. 2 vols. St. Petersburg, 1902.

Istoriia Rossii v XIX veke. 9 vols. St. Petersburg, 1907.

Iswolsky, Alexander. *Memoirs*. London, 1920.

———. *Recollections of a Foreign Minister*. Garden City, 1921.

———. *Au service de la Russie: Correspondance diplomatique*. 2 vols. Paris, 1937–39.

Ivanov, L. M. *Vserossiiskaia politicheskaia stachka v oktiabria 1905*. Pt. 1. Moscow-Leningrad, 1955.

Ivanov-Razumnik. *Istoriia russkoi obshchestvennoi mysli: Individualizm i meshchanstvo v russkoi literature i zhizni XIX v*. 2 vols. St. Petersburg, 1908.

———. "Obshchestvennye i umstvennye techeniia tridtsatykh godov." *Istoriia russkoi literatury XIX veka*, ed. D. N. Ovsianiko-Kulikovskii. Vol. 1, pp. 247–76.

Jenkens, Michael. *Arakcheev, Grand Vizier of the Russian Empire*. New York, 1969.

Jerrmann, Edward. *Pictures from St. Petersburg*. New York, 1852.

Jones, G. Gareth. "Novikov's Naturalized *Spectator*," *The Eighteenth Century in Russia*, ed. J. E. Garrard, pp. 149–65.

Kafengauz, B. B. *Petr I i ego vremia*. Moscow, 1948.

Kahan, Arcadius. "Continuity in Economic Activity and Policy during the Post-Petrine Period in Russia," *The Structure of Russian History*, ed. Michael Cherniavsky. New York, 1970, pp. 191–211.

———. "The Costs of 'Westernization' in Russia: The Gentry and the Economy in the Eighteenth Century." *The Structure of Russian History*, ed. Michael Cherniavsky, pp. 224–50.

Kaiser, F. B. *Die russische Justizreform von 1864: Zur Geschichte der russischen Justiz von Katharina II bis 1917*. Leiden, 1972.

Kallash, V. V., ed. *Tri veka.* 6 vols. Moscow, 1912.

Kallash, V. V., and N. E. Efros, eds. *Istoriia russkago teatra.* Moscow, 1914.

Kaminskii, Aleksandr. "Vsepoddanneishaia zapiska A. Kaminskago, 1850 goda." *RS,* Vol. 122, No. 6 (June 1905), pp. 629–57.

Kaplan, Herbert H. *The First Partition of Poland.* New York and London, 1962.

Kapterev, N. F. *Patriarkh Nikon i Tsar Aleksei Mikhailovich.* Sergiev Posad, 1909.

Karamzin, N. M. *Izbrannye sochineniia.* 2 vols. Moscow-Leningrad, 1964.

Karnovich, E. *Sanktpeterburg v statisticheskom otnoshenii.* St. Petersburg, 1860.

Keep, J. L. H. "The Regime of Philaret (1619–1633)." *SEER,* Vol. 38 (June 1960), pp. 334–60.

———. *The Russian Revolution: A Study in Mass Mobilization.* New York, 1976.

Kennan, George F. *The Marquis de Custine and his "Russia in 1839."* Princeton, 1971.

Kenney, James J., Jr. "Lord Whitworth and the Conspiracy Against Tsar Paul I: The New Evidence of the Kent Archive." *SR,* Vol. 36, No. 2 (June 1977), pp. 205–11.

Kerensky, Alexander. *The Catastrophe.* New York and London, 1927.

———. *La Revolution Russe, 1917.* Paris, 1928.

———. *La vérité sur le massacre des Romanov.* Paris, 1936.

Kharitonov, A. A. "Iz vospomonanii A. A. Kharytonova." *RS,* Vol. 81, No. 1 (January 1894), pp. 101–32.

Khrapovitskii, A. V. *Dnevnik A. V. Khrapovitskago, 1782–1793.* St. Petersburg, 1874.

Khromov, P. A. *Ekonomicheskoe razvitie Rossii v XIX i XX vekakh.* Moscow, 1950.

Khudriashov, K. "Platon Aleksandrovich Zubov." *RBS,* Vol. 7 (1896–1918), pp. 526–46.

Kiniapina, N. S. *Vneshniaia politika Rossii pervoi poloviny XIX veka.* Moscow, 1963.

———. *Vneshniaia politika Rossii vtoroi poloviny XIX veka.* Moscow, 1974.

Kissinger, Henry. *A World Restored: Metternich, Castlereagh, and the Problems of Peace, 1812–1822.* Boston, 1957.

Kizevetter, A. A. *Istoricheskie ocherki.* Moscow, 1912.

———. *Istoricheskie otkliki.* Moscow, 1915.

———. "Tabel' o rangakh." *Entsiklopedicheskii slovar' Brokgauza-Eifrona,* Vol. 32 (a), pp. 439–41.

Kliuchevskii, V. O. *A History of Russia,* trans. C. J. Hogarth. 5 vols. New York, 1961.

———. *Skazaniia inostrantsev o Moskovskom gosudarstve.* Petrograd, 1918.

———. *Sochineniia.* Vols. 1–5. (*Kurs russkoi istorii.*) Moscow, 1958.

Klochkov, M. V. *Ocherki pravitel'stvennoi deiatel'nosti vremeni Pavla I.* Petrograd, 1916.

———. *Zemskie sobory: istoricheskii ocherk.* St. Petersburg, 1914.

Kniaz'kov, S. *Ocherki iz istorii Petra Velikago i ego vremeni.* Moscow, 1909.

Knox, Sir Alfred. *With the Russian Army, 1914–1917.* 2 vols. London, 1921.

Kobeko, D. F. *Imperatorskii Tsarskosel'skii litsei.* St. Petersburg, 1911.

———. *Tsesarevich Pavel Petrovich, 1754–1796.* St. Petersburg, 1883.

Kochakov, B. M., ed. *Ocherki istorii Leningrada.* Vol. 3. Moscow-Leningrad, 1956.

———. "Petrograd v gody pervoi mirovoi voiny i Fevral'skoi burzhuazno-demokraticheskoi revoliutsii." *Ocherki istorii Leningrada,* ed. B. M. Kochakov. Vol. 3. Moscow-Leningrad, 1956, pp. 932–1002.

Kochin, G. E. "Naselenie Peterburga do 60-kh godov XVIII v.," *Ocherki istorii Leningrada*, ed. M. P. Viatkin. Vol. 1, pp. 94–114.

Kohl, J. G. *Russia: St. Petersburg, Moscow, Kharkoff, Riga, Odessa, the German Provinces on the Baltic, the Steppes, the Crimea, and the Interior of the Empire.* London, 1844.

Kokovtsev, Graf V. N. *Iz moego proshlago. Vospominaniia 1903–1919gg.* 2 vols. Paris, 1933.

Konstantin Nikolaevich, Grand Duke. 'Dnevniki v. k. Konstantina Nikolaevicha, 1836–1889gg.,' TsGAOR, fond 722, opis' 1, dela Nos. 74–124.

Kopanev, A. I. "Naselenie Peterburga ot kontsa XVIII v. do 1861g.," *Ocherki istorii Leningrada*, ed. M. P. Viatkin. Vol. 1, pp. 506–49.

———. *Naselenie Peterburga v pervoi polovine XIX veka.* Moscow, 1957.

Korb, Johann Georg. *Diary of an Austrian Secretary of Legation at the Court of Czar Peter the Great*, trans. from the original Latin and ed. Count MacDonnell. 2 vols. London, 1863.

Korf, Baron M. A. *The Accession of Nicholas I.* London, 1857.

———. 'Dnevnik barona M. A. Korfa, 1838–1852gg.,' TsGAOR, fond 728, opis' 1, dela Nos. 1817/i–xiv.

———. "Materialy i cherty k biografii Imperatora Nikolaia I i k istorii ego tsarstvovaniia. Rozhdenie i pervyia dvadtsat' let zhizni (1796–1817gg.)," *Materialy i cherty k biografii Imperatora Nikolaia I i k istorii ego tsarstvovaniia*, ed. N. F. Dubrovin. St. Petersburg, 1896.

Kornilov, A. A. *Kurs istorii Rossii XIX v.* 3 vols. Moscow, 1918.

Korol'kov, Konstantin. *Zhizn' i tsarstvovanie Imperatora Aleksandra III (1881–1894gg.).* Kiev, 1901.

Korsakov, D. A. "Artemii Petrovich Volynskii i ego konfidenty." *RS*, Vol. 47, No. 10 (October 1885), pp. 17–54.

———. *Votsarenie Imperatritsy Anny Ioannovny.* Kazan, 1880.

Korsakov, V. "Tsar Feodor Alekseevich." *RBS*, Vol. Iab–Fom, pp. 249–64.

Kosachevskaia, G. M. *Mikhail Andreevich Balug'ianskii i Peterburgskii universitet pervoi chetverti XIX veka.* Leningrad, 1971.

Kostiushko, I. I. *Krest'ianskaia reforma 1864 g. v Tsarstve Pol'skom.* Moscow, 1962.

Kostomarov, N. *Russkaia istoriia v zhizneopisaniiakh eia glavneishikh deiatelei.* 7 Pts. in 3 Vols. St. Petersburg, 1874–93.

Kovalenskaia, N. N. "F. I. Shubin." *IRI*, Vol. 6 (1953–61), pp. 329–60.

Krizhanich, Iurii. *Politika.* Moscow, 1965.

Kuchariants, D. A. *Antonio Rinaldi.* Leningrad, 1976.

Kukiel, Marian. *Czartoryski and European Unity, 1770–1861.* Princeton, 1955.

Kulisher, I. M. *Ocherk istorii russkoi torgovli.* Petersburg, 1923.

Kurakin, Prince V. I. "Gistoriia o tsare Petre Alekseeviche, 1682–1694." *Arkhiv Kniazia F. A. Kurakina.* St. Petersburg, 1890. Vol. 1, pp. 39–74.

Kuropatkin, A. N. "Dnevnik A. N. Kuropatkina." *KA*, Vol. 2 (1920).

Kurts, B. G. *Sostoianie Rossii v 1650–1655g. po doneseniiam Rodesa.* Moscow, 1914.

LaCroix, Paul. *Histoire de la vie et du règne de Nicolas Ier.* 8 vols. Paris, 1864–69.

LaHarpe, F.-C. *Mémoires de Frédéric-César LaHarpe.* Paris-Geneva, 1864.

Lamsdorf, V. N. *Dnevnik, 1891–1892.* Moscow-Leningrad, 1934.

Lang, D. M. *The First Russian Radical: Alexander Radishchev, 1749–1802.* London, 1959.

Langer, William L. *The Franco-Russian Alliance, 1890–1894.* New York, 1967.

————. *Political and Social Upheaval, 1832–1852.* New York-London, 1969.

Lanin, R. S. "Vneshniaia politika Pavla I v 1796–1798gg." *Uchenye zapiski Leningradskogo Gosudarstvennogo Universiteta* (seriia istoricheskikh nauk). Vol. 10 (1941).

Lebedev, V. I. *Krest'ianskaia voina pod predvoditel'stvom Stepana Razina, 1667–1671gg.* Moscow, 1955.

————, ed. *Reformy Petra I: Sbornik dokumentov.* Moscow, 1937.

Leiberov, I. P. "Petrogradskii proletariat v Fevral'skoi revoliutsii, 1917g.," *Istoriia rabochikh Leningrada,* ed. V. S. Diakin. Vol. 1. Leningrad, 1972, pp. 512–25.

Lemke, M. *Ocherki po istorii russkoi tsenzury i zhurnalistiki XIX stoletiia.* St. Petersburg, 1904.

Lermontov, M. Iu. *Sochineniia.* 2 vols. Moscow, 1970.

Leroy-Beaulieu, Anatole. *Un Homme d'état Russe (Nicolas Milutine) d'après sa correspondance inédite. Étude sur la Russie et la Pologne pendant le règne d'Alexandre II (1885–1872).* Paris, 1884.

Leslie, R. F. *Polish Politics and the Revolution of November, 1830.* London, 1956.

————. *Reform and Insurrection in Poland, 1856–1865.* London, 1963.

Levin, Iu. D. "Angliiskaia poeziia i literatura russkogo sentimentalizma," *Ot klassitsizma k romantizmu,* ed. M. D. Alekseev. Leningrad, 1970, pp. 195–297.

Levin, Sh. M. "K. D. Kavelin o smerti Nikolaia I," *Literaturnoe nasledstvo.* Moscow, 1959. Vol. 67, pp. 596–612.

Liashchenko, P. I. *Istoriia narodnogo khoziaistva SSSR.* 2 vols. Moscow, 1956.

————. *Poslednyi sekretnyi komitet po krest'ianskomu delu, 3 ianvaria 1857g.–16 fevralia 1858g. (po materialam arkhiva Gosudarstvennago Soveta).* St. Petersburg, 1911.

Liatskii, E. A., ed. *Belinskii: Pis'ma.* 3 vols. St. Petersburg, 1914.

Lieven, Princess Daria. *Letters of Dorothea, Princess Lieven, during her Residence in London, 1812–1834,* ed. L. G. Robinson. London, 1902.

Likhachev, D. S., et al., eds. *Rol' i znachenie literatury XVIII veka v istorii russkoi kul'tury.* Moscow-Leningrad, 1966.

Lincoln, W. Bruce. "Alexander III of Russia." *History Today,* Vol. 26, No. 10 (October 1976), pp. 644–53.

————. "The Circle of Grand Duchess Elena Pavlovna, 1847–1861." *SEER,* Vol. 48, No. 112 (July 1970), pp. 373–87.

————. "The Daily Life of St. Petersburg Officials in the Mid-Nineteenth Century." *Oxford Slavonic Papers,* Vol. 8 (1975), pp. 82–100.

————. "General Dmitrii Miliutin and the Russian Army." *History Today,* Vol. 26, No. 1 (January 1976), pp. 40–48.

————. "Murder Near the Cathedral." *History Today,* Vol. 25, No. 3 (March 1975), pp. 175–84.

————. *Nicholas I: Emperor and Autocrat of All the Russias.* London and Bloomington, 1978.

————. *Nikolai Miliutin: An Enlightened Russian Bureaucrat of the Nineteenth Century.* Newtonville, Mass., 1977.

————. *Petr Petrovich Semenov-Tian-Shanskii: The Life of a Russian Geographer.* Newtonville, Mass., 1980.

————. "A Profile of the Russian Bureaucracy on the Eve of the Great Reforms." *Jahrbücher für Geschichte Osteuropas,* Vol. 27, No. 2 (1979), pp. 181–96.

————. "A Re-Examination of Some Historical Stereotypes: An Analysis of the Career Patterns and Backgrounds of the Decembrists." *Jahrbücher für Geschichte Osteuropas,* Vol. 24, No. 3 (1976), pp. 357–68.

————. "Reform and Reaction in Russia: A. V. Golovnin's Critique of the 1860s." *Cahiers du monde russe et soviétique,* Vol. 16, No. 2 (April–June 1975), pp. 167–79.

————. "Western Culture Comes to Russia." *History Today,* Vol. 20, No. 10 (October 1970), pp. 677–86.

Liria, Duke de. "Pis'ma o Rossii v Ispaniiu." *Osmnadtsatyi vek* (1869). Vol. 2, pp. 5–198; Vol. 3, pp. 27–132.

Liubimov, D. N. "Gapon i 9 ianvaria." *VI,* Vol. 40, No. 8 (August 1965), pp. 123–31; No. 9 (September 1965), pp. 114–12.

Liubomirov, P. G. *Ocherk istorii nizhegorodskogo opolcheniia, 1611–1613 gg.* Moscow, 1939.

Livingston, James. "Russia and Western Trade, 1550–1970: A Study in the Origins of Economic Backwardness." M.A. thesis, Northern Illinois University, 1975.

Lockhart, Bruce. *British Agent.* New York, 1933.

Lomonosov, M. V. "Ode on the Day of the Ascension to the All-Russian Throne of Her Majesty the Empress Elizabeth Petrovna, the Year 1747," *Literature of Eighteenth-Century Russia,* ed. and trans. Harold B. Segal. Vol. 1, pp. 193–201.

Londonderry, Lady. *The Russian Journal of Lady Londonderry, 1836–1837,* ed. W. A. L. Seaman and J. R. Sewell. London, 1973.

Longinov, M. *Novikov i moskovskie martinisty.* Moscow, 1867.

Longworth, Philip. *The Art of Victory: The Life and Achievements of Field-Marshal Suvorov, 1729–1800.* New York, 1966.

————. *The Three Empresses: Catherine I, Anne, and Elizabeth of Russia.* London, 1972.

Lopukhin, I. V. "Zapiski nekotorykh obstoiatel'stv zhizni i sluzhby deistvitel'nago tainago sovetnika Senatora I. V. Lopukhina, sochineniia im samin." *RA,* Vol. 22 (1884). Bk. 1, pp. 1–154.

Lord, R. H. *The Second Partition of Poland: A Study in Diplomatic History.* Cambridge, Mass., 1915.

————. "The Third Partition of Poland." *SEER,* Vol. 3, No. 9 (March 1925).

Lotman, L. M., et al. "Proza shestidesiatykh godov." *Istoriia russkoi literatury,* ed. M. K. Dobrynin. Vol. 8 (1), pp. 277–315.

Loviagin, A. "Grigorii Aleksandrovich Potemkin." *RBS,* Vol. 14 (1896–1918), pp. 649–70.

Luppov, S. P., and N. N. Petrov. "Gorodskoe upravlenie i gorodskoe khoziaistvo Peterburga ot kontsa XVIII v. do 1861g." *Ocherki istorii Leningrada,* ed. M. P. Viatkin. Vol. 1, pp. 601–29.

McConnell, Allen. *Tsar Alexander I: Paternalistic Reformer.* New York, 1970.

McKay, John P. *Pioneers for Profit: Foreign Entrepreneurship and Russian Industrialization, 1885–1914.* Chicago, 1970.

MacMaster, Robert E. *Danilevsky: A Russian Totalitarian Philosopher.* Cambridge, Mass., 1967.

Magarshack, David. *Dostoevsky.* New York, 1962.

Makogonenko, G. P. *Nikolai Novikov i russkoe prosveshchenie XVIII veka.* Moscow-Leningrad, 1952.

————. *Radishchev i ego vremia.* Moscow, 1956.

Malia, Martin. *Alexander Herzen and the Birth of Russian Socialism.* Cambridge, Mass., 1961.

Malozemoff, Andrew. *Russian Far Eastern Policy, 1881–1904, with Special Emphasis on the Causes of the Russo-Japanese War.* Berkeley and Los Angeles, 1958.

Mal'tsev, A. N. "Pervyi etap russko-pol'skoi voiny za osvobozhdenie Ukrainy i Belorussii (1654–1656)." *Ocherki istorii SSSR,* ed. A. A. Novosel'skii, pp. 480–96.

Malyshev, I. V., ed. *N. I. Novikov i ego sovremenniki. Izbrannye sochineniia.* Moscow, 1961.

"Manifesta po povodu vosshestviia na prestol Imperatritsy Ekateriny II," *Osmnadtsatyi vek.* Vol. 4. Moscow, 1869, pp. 216–24.

Manstein, C. H. von. *Contemporary Memoirs of Russia from the Year 1727 to 1744.* New York, 1968.

Mariia Feodorovna. *Correspondance de Sa Majesté l'Impératrice Marie Féodorowna avec Mademoiselle de Nélidoff, sa demoiselle d'honneur, 1797–1801,* ed. Princess Liza Troubetskaia. Paris, 1896.

Martens, F. *Sobranie traktatov i konventsii, zakliuchennykh Rossieiu s inostrannymi derzhavami.* 15 vols. St. Petersburg, 1874–1908.

Marye, George Thomas. *Nearing the End in Imperial Russia.* Philadelphia, 1929.

Massie, Robert K. *Nicholas and Alexandra.* New York, 1978.

Masson, Charles François Philibert. *Secret Memoirs of the Court of Petersburg.* New York, 1970.

Mayerburg, Baron Augustin de. *Rélation d'un voyage en Moscovie.* 2 vols. Paris, 1858.

Maynard, John. *The Russian Peasant and Other Studies.* London, 1942.

Mazour, Anatole. *The First Russian Revolution: The Decembrist Movement, Its Origins, Development, and Significance.* Berkeley, 1937.

———. *Modern Russian Historiography.* New York and Princeton, 1958.

Medlicott, W. N. *The Congress of Berlin and After: A Diplomatic History of the Near Eastern Settlement, 1878–1880.* London, 1938.

Meehan-Waters, Brenda. "Catherine the Great and the Problem of Female Rule." *Russian Review,* Vol. 34, No. 3 (July 1975), pp. 293–307.

Mel'gunov, S. P. *Sud'ba Imperatora Nikolaia II posle otrecheniia.* Paris, 1951.

———, and N. P. Sidorov, eds. *Masonstvo v ego proshlom i nastoiashchem.* 2 vols. Moscow, 1915.

Menshutkin, Boris N. *Russia's Lomonosov.* Princeton, 1952.

Merder, K. K. *Zapiski K. K. Merdera, vospitatelia tsesarevicha Aleksandra Nikolaevicha, 1824–1834gg.* St. Petersburg, 1885.

Meshcheriakov, G. P., ed. *A. V. Suvorov: Sbornik dokumentov.* 4 vols. Moscow, 1952.

Metternich, Prince Clemens von. *Memoirs of Prince Metternich.* 5 vols. New York, 1879–82.

Mikhailofsky-Danilefsky, Alexander. *History of the Campaign in France in the Year 1814.* London, 1839.

Mikhailov, I. I. "*Kazanskaia starina (iz vospominaii Iv. Iv. Mikhailova).*" RS, Vol. 100, No. 10 (October 1899).

Miliukov, P. N. *Iz istorii russkoi intelligentsii.* St. Petersburg, 1903.

———. *Gosudarstvennoe khoziaistvo v pervoi chetverti XVIII stoletiia i reforma Petra Velikago.* St. Petersburg, 1892.

———. *Ocherki po istorii russkoi kul'tury.* 3 vols. St. Petersburg, 1901.

———. *Ocherki po istorii russkoi kul'tury.* 3 vols. Paris, 1937.

————. *Vospominaniia, 1859–1917.* 2 vols. New York, 1955.

Miliutin, D. A. *Dnevnik D. A. Miliutina,* ed. P. A. Zaionchkovskii. 4 vols. Moscow, 1947–53.

————.'Moi starcheskie vospominaniia za 1816–1873gg.' ORGBL, fond 169, kartonki 12–16.

Miliutin, N. A. 'Mysli o sposobakh unichtozheniia krepostnago sostoianiia v Rossii,' 6 fevralia 1847g., TsGIAL, fond 869, opis' 1, delo No. 449.

————. 'Pis'ma N. A. Miliutina k D. A. Miliutinu, 1837g.,' ORGBL, fond 169, karton 69, papka No. 5.

————. 'Zapiska po voprosu o prebrazovanii zemskikh uchrezhdeniiakh,' 22 maia 1862g., TsGIAL, fond 869, opis' 1, delo No. 397.

————, ed. *Izsledovaniia v Tsarstve Pol'skom, po vysochaishemu poveleniiu, proizvedenie pod rukovodstvom Senatora, Stats-Sekretaria Miliutina.* 6 vols. St. Petersburg, 1863–66.

Miller, Forrestt A. *Dmitrii Miliutin and the Reform Era in Russia.* Nashville, 1968.

Mints, I. I. *Istoriia velikogo oktiabria.* 3 vols. Moscow, 1967–73.

Mirsky, Prince D. S. *A History of Russian Literature.* New York, 1927.

————. *Russia: A Social History.* London, 1952.

Monas, Sidney. *The Third Section: Police and Society in Russia under Nicholas I.* Cambridge, Mass., 1961.

Morozov, Aleksandr. *Mikhail Vasil'evich Lomonosov, 1711–1765.* Leningrad, 1952.

Mosolov, A. *Pri dvore Imperatora.* Riga, n.d.

Mosse, W. E. *Alexander II and the Modernization of Russia.* New York, 1962.

————. *The Rise and Fall of the Crimean System, 1855–1871: The Story of a Peace Settlement.* London, 1963.

Mundt, M. *Ein deutscher Arzt am Hofe Kaiser Nikolaus I von Russland.* Munich-Leipzig, 1917.

Münnich, Count Ernst. *Rossiia i russkii dvor v pervoi polovine XVIII veka. Zapiski i zamechaniia Gr. Ernsta Minikha.* St. Petersburg, 1891.

Nabokov, Vladimir. *Nikolai Gogol.* New York, 1961.

Nabokov, V. "Raboty po sostavleniiu sudebnykh ustavov." *Sudebnaia reforma,* ed. N. V. Davydov and N. N. Polianskii. Vol. 1. Moscow, 1915, pp. 303–53.

Napoleon I. *Letters and Documents of Napoleon,* ed. and trans. John Eldred Howard. Vol. 1. New York, 1961.

Nasonov, A. N., L. V. Cherepnin, and A. A. Zimin, eds. *Ocherki istorii SSSR. Period feodalizma konets XV v.–nachalo XVIII v.* Moscow, 1955.

Nebel, Henry M., Jr. *N. M. Karamzin: A Russian Sentimentalist.* The Hague-Paris, 1967.

Nebolsin, P. I. "Biudzhety Peterburgskikh chinovnikov." *Ekonomicheskii ukazatel',* No. 11 (16 March 1857), pp. 241–50.

Nechkina, M. V. *Dvizhenie dekabristov.* 2 vols. Moscow, 1955.

Nesselrode, Count K. V. *Lettres et papiers du Chancellier Comte de Nesselrode, 1760–1850.* 11 vols. Paris, 1905–12.

Neuville, Adrian de la. *Rélation curieuse et nouvelle de la Moscovie.* La Haye, 1699.

Nevskii, V. I. *Rabochee dvizhenie v ianvarskie dni 1905 goda.* Moscow, 1930.

————. *Sovety i vooruzhennoe vosstanie v 1905 godu.* Moscow, 1932.

Nicholas I. "Perepiska Imperatora Nikolaia Pavlovicha s velikim kniazem tsesarevichem Konstantinom Pavlovichem, 1825–1829, 1830–1831gg." *SIRIO,* Vols. 131–132 (1910–11).

————. "Zaveshchanie Nikolaia I synu." *KA,* Vol. 3 (1923), pp. 291–93.

Nicholas II. "Dnevnik Nikolaia Romanova." *KA,* Vol. 20. (1927); Vol. 21 (1927); Vol. 22 (1927); Vol. 27 (1918).

———. *Journal intime de Nicolas II à juillet 1914.* Paris, 1925.

———. *Journal intime de Nicolas II (juillet 1914–juillet 1918).* Paris, 1934.

———. *Letters of the Tsar to the Tsaritsa, 1914–1917,* trans. A. L. Hynes. Hattiesburg, 1970.

———. *The Willy-Nicky Correspondence.* New York, 1918.

Nicolson, Harold. *The Congress of Vienna: A Study in Allied Unity, 1812–1822.* New York, 1946.

———. *King George the Fifth: His Life and Reign.* New York, 1953.

———. *Sir Arthur Nicolson, Bart., First Lord Carnock.* London, 1930.

Nifontov, A. S. *Rossïia v 1848 godu.* Moscow, 1949.

Nikitenko, A. V. *Dnevnik.* 3 vols. Moscow, 1956.

———. *Zapiski i dnevnik, 1826–1877.* 2 vols. St. Petersburg, 1893.

Nikolai II: Materialy dlia kharakteristiki lichnosti i tsarstvovaniia. Moscow, 1917.

Nikolai Mikhailovich, Grand Duke. *Graf P. A. Stroganov, 1774–1817: Istoricheskoe izsledovania epokhi Imperatora Aleksandra I.* 2 vols. St. Petersburg, 1903.

———. *Le Comte Paul Stroganov.* 3 vols. Paris, 1905.

———. *Imperator Aleksandr I. Opyt istoricheskago izsledovaniia.* 2 vols. Petrograd, 1914.

———. *Imperatritsa Elisaveta Alekseevna supruga Imperatora Aleksandra I.* 2 vols. St. Petersburg, 1908.

———, ed. *Perepiska Imperatora Aleksandra I s sestroi velikoi kniaginei Ekaterinoi Pavlovnoi.* St. Petersburg, 1910.

Nolde, Boris E. *L'Alliance Franco-Russe.* Paris, 1936.

Notovitch, Nicolas. *L'Empereur Alexandre III et son entourage.* Paris, 1893.

Novikov, N. I. "Avtor k samomu sebe." *N. I. Novikov i ego sovremenniki,* ed. I. V. Malyshev. Moscow, 1961, pp. 91–94.

———. "Otryvok puteshestviia V*** I*** T***." *N. I. Novikov i ego sovremenniki,* ed. I. V. Malyshev. Moscow, 1961, pp. 100–103.

Novosel'skii, A. A. *Bor'ba moskovskogo gosudarstva s tatarami v pervoi polovine XVII veka.* Moscow-Leningrad, 1948.

———. "Russko-turetskie I russko-krymskie otnosheniia v 30–40kh godakh." *Ocherki istorii SSSR,* ed. A. A. Novosel'skii, pp. 476–80.

———. ed. *Krest'ianskaia voina pod predvoditel'stvom Stepana Razina. Sbornik dokumentov.* 2 vols. Moscow, 1957.

———. ed. *Ocherki istorii SSR. Period feodalizma: XVII v.* Moscow, 1955.

———, and N. S. Chaev. "Krest'ianskaia voina pod predvoditel'stvom S. T. Razina," *Ocherki istorii SSSR,* ed. A. A. Novosel'skii, pp. 277–311.

Obolenskii, Prince D. A. "Moi vospominaniia o velikoi kniagine Elene Pavlovne." *RS,* Vol. 137, No. 3 (March 1909), pp. 504–28; Vol. 138, No. 4 (April 1909), pp. 37–62.

"Obozrenie khoda i deistvii kholernoi epidemii v Rossii v techenie 1848 goda." *ZhMVD,* Vol. 27, No. 9 (September 1849), pp. 319–28.

O'Brien C. B., *Russia under Two Tsars, 1682–1689: The Regency of Sophia Alekseevna.* Berkeley and Los Angeles, 1952.

O'Connor, John F., ed. and trans., *The Sokolov Investigation of the Alleged Murder of the Russian Imperial Family.* New York, 1971.

Ocherki istorii Leningrada, ed. M. P. Viatkin, et al. 3 vols. Leningrad, 1955–1956.

Okun', S. B. *Ocherki istorii SSSR: konets XVIII–pervaia chetverty XIX veka*. Leningrad, 1956.

Ol'denburg, S. S. *Tsarstvovanie Imperatora Nikolaia II*. 2 vols. Belgrad, 1939.

Oldenburg, Zoe. *Catherine the Great*. New York, 1965.

Olearius, Adam. *The Travels of Olearius in Seventeenth-Century Russia*, ed. and trans. Samuel H. Baron. Stanford, 1967.

Oliva, L. Jay. *Russia in the Era of Peter the Great*. Englewood Cliffs, 1969.

Olivier, Daria. *Elisabeth de Russie*. Paris, 1962.

'O polozhenii chernorabochikh v S.-Peterburge,' TsGIAL, fond 869, opis' 1, delo No. 350.

Oreus, I. *Opisanie vengerskoi voiny 1849g*. St. Petersburg, 1880.

Orlov, Vl. *Russkie prosvetiteli 1790–1800kh godov*. Leningrad, 1950.

'Otnoshenie Deistvitel'nago Tainago Sovetnika Dmitriia Buturlina 17–go marta 1849g., k Ministru Narodnago Prosveshcheniia Grafu Uvarovu,' (Konfidential'no), TsGIAL, fond 772, opis' 1, delo No. 2242.

Ovsianiko-Kulikovskii, D. N., ed. *Istoriia russkoi literatury XIX veka*. 5 vols. Moscow, 1908.

Paléologue, Maurice. *An Ambassador's Memoirs*, trans. F. A. Holt. 3 vols. New York, n.d.

Palmer, Alan. *Alexander I: Tsar of War and Peace*. London, 1974.

Pamiati Imperatora Aleksandra III. Moscow, 1894.

Panin, V. N., ed. "Bumagi grafa Petra Ivanovicha Panina o pugachevskom bunte." *SIRIO*, Vol.6 (1871), pp. 74–218.

Pankratova, A. M. ed. *Istoriia Moskvy*. Vol. 5. Moscow, 1955.

Panov, V. *Arkhitektor A. N. Voronikhin*. Moscow, 1937.

Pares, Sir Bernard. *The Fall of the Russian Monarchy: A Study of the Evidence*. New York, 1961.

Pascal, Pierre. *Avvakum et les débuts du raskol. La crise religieuse au XVIIe siècle en Russie*. Paris, 1938.

Paul I. "Zapiska Imperatora Pavla I ob ustroistve raznykh chastei gosudarstvennago upravleniia." *SIRIO*, Vol. 90 (1894), pp. 1–4.

Pavlenko, N. I., ed. *Rossiia v period reform Petra I*. Moscow, 1973.

Pavlov-Silvanskii, N. "Tsar Ioann V Alekseevich." *RBS*, Vol. Ibak–Kliu, pp. 271–72.

Perevorot 1762 goda. Moscow, 1908.

Perovskii, L. A. 'O prichinakh umnozheniia deloproizvodstva vo vnutrennem upravlenii,' mart, 1851g., TsGIAL, fond 1287, opis' 36, delo No. 137.

Perry, John. *The State of Russia Under the Present Czar*. London, 1716.

Peter I. *Journal de Pierre le Grand dépuis l'année 1698 jusqu'à l'année 1714 inclusivement*, ed. Prince M. M. Shcherbatov. Stockholm, 1774.

———. *Pis'ma i bumagi Imperatora Petra Velikago*. 12 vols. Petrograd, 1916–.

Petrov, A. N. "I. E. Starov." *IRI*, Vol. 6, (1953–61), pp. 166–85.

———. "K voprosu o zodchikh-stroiteliakh Anichkova dvortsa," *Nauchnye soobshcheniia gosudarstvennoi inspektsii po okhrane pamiatnikov Leningrada*. Leningrad, 1959, pp. 22–40.

———. *Pushkin: Dvortsy i parki*. Moscow-Leningrad, 1964.

———. "S. I. Chevakinskii i drugie peterburgskie mastera." *IRI*, Vol. 5 (1953–61), pp. 209–43.

———, S. A. Zombe, and T. M. Sitina. "Gradostroitel'stvo." *IRI*, Vol. 6 (1953–61), pp. 236–77.

Petrov, P. N. *Istoriia Sanktpeterburga.* St. Petersburg, 1885.

Petrov, V. N. "M. I. Kozlovskii." *IRI,* Vol. 6, (1953–61), pp. 400–35.

Petrovich, M. B. *The Emergence of Russian Panslavism, 1856–1870.* New York, 1956.

Phipps, Geraldine Marie. "Britons in Seventeenth-Century Russia: A Study in the Origins of Modernization." Ph.D. diss., University of Pennsylvania, 1971.

Piksanov, N. K. "I. V. Lopukhin." *Masonstvo v ego proshlom i nastoiashchem,* ed. S. P. Mel'gunov and N. P. Sidorov. Vol. 1. Moscow, 1915, pp. 227–50.

Pipes, Richard, ed. and trans. *Karamzin's Memoir on Ancient and Modern Russia: A Translation and an Analysis.* Cambridge, Mass., 1959.

———. *Russia Under the Old Regime.* New York, 1974.

Pis'ma russkikh gosudarei i drugikh osob tsarskago semeistva. 5 vols. Moscow, 1861–62.

Platonov, S. F. *Boris Godunov.* Petrograd, 1921.

———. *Boris Godunov: Tsar of Russia,* trans. L. Rex Pyles. Gulf Breeze, 1973.

———. *Moskva i zapad.* Berlin, 1926.

———. *Ocherki po istorii smuty v moskovskom gosudarstve XVI–XVII vv. (opyt izucheniia obshchestvennago stroia i soslovnykh otnoshenii v smutnoe vremia).* St. Petersburg, 1910.

———. *Smutnoe vremia.* Prague, 1924.

———. "Tsar Aleksei Mikhailovich (opyt kharakteristiki)." *Tri veka,* ed. V. V. Kallash. Vol. 1, pp. 85–114.

Plekhanov, G. V. *Istoriia russkoi obshchestvennoi mysli.* 3 vols. Moscow, 1915.

———. "Vissarion Grigor'evich Belinskii." *Istoriia russkoi literatury XIX veka,* ed. D. N. Ovsianiko-Kulikovskii. Vol. 2, pp. 227–68.

Pobedonostsev, K. P. "Graf V. N. Panin." *Golosa iz Rossii,* no. 7 (1859). Reprint., Moscow, 1974–75, pp. 3–142.

———. *K. P. Pobedonostsev i ego korrespondenty.* Vol. 1(2). Moscow-Petrograd, 1923.

———. *Reflections of a Russian Statesman.* Ann Arbor, 1965.

Pogodin, M. P. *Istoriko-politicheskie pis'ma i zapiski v prodolzhenii krymskoi voiny, 1853–1856gg.* Moscow, 1874.

———. *Semnadtsat' pervykh let v zhizni Imperatora Petra Velikago, 1672–1689 gg.* Moscow, 1875.

Pokrovskii, M. N. *Russkaia istoriia s drevneishkikh vremen.* 4 vols. Moscow, 1933.

Polievktov, M. *Nikolai I: Biografiia i obzor tsarstvovaniia.* Moscow, 1918.

Polnoe sobranie zakonov rossiiskoi imperii. 2d ed. 55 vols. St. Petersburg, 1830–84.

Polovtsov, A. A. *Dnevnik gosudarstvennogo sekretaria A. A. Polovtsova, 1883–1892.* 2 vols. Moscow, 1966.

Poroshin, S. A. *Zapiski S. A. Poroshina.* St. Petersburg, 1881.

Predtechenskii, A. V. "Osnovanie Peterburga," *Peterburg petrovskogo vremeni,* ed. A. V. Predtechenskii, pp. 3–48.

———. ed. *Peterburg petrovskogo vremeni.* Leningrad, 1948.

Presniakov, A. E. *Apogei samoderzhaviia: Nikolai I.* Leningrad, 1925.

———. *14 dekabria 1825 goda.* Moscow-Leningrad, 1926.

———. "Moskovskoe gosudarstvo pervoi poloviny XVII veka," *Tri veka,* ed. V. V. Kallash. Vol. 1, pp. 4–84.

———. *Obrazovanie velikorusskago gosudarstva.* Petrograd, 1918.

Presnov, G. M. "Skul'ptura pervoi poloviny XVIII geka." *IRI*, Vol. 5, pp. 460–70.

Pribaum, A. F. *The Secret Treaties of Austria-Hungary, 1879–1914.* Vol. 2. Cambridge, Mass., 1921.

Prokof'ev, V. A., and A. A. Novosel'skii. "Mezhdunarodnoe polozhenie russkogo gosudarstva v 20–30kh godakh i Smolenskaia voina 1632–1634gg.," *Ocherki istorii SSSR*, ed. A. A. Novosel'skii, pp. 462–75.

Prokopovich, Feofan. "Pis'ma Feofana Prokopovicha." *Trudy Kievskoi Dukhovnoi Akademii*, Vol. 1 (1865), pp. 141–59.

———. "Sermon on the Interment of the Most Illustrious, Most Sovereign Peter the Great, Emperor and Autocrat of All Russia, the Father of His Nation," *The Literature of Eighteenth-Century Russia*. ed. Harold B. Segal. Vol. 1. New York, 1967, pp. 141–48.

———. *Slova i rechi pouchitel'nye, pokhval'nye i pozdravitel'nye sobraniia, i nekotorye vtorym tisneniem a drugie vnov' napechatannye.* St. Petersburg, 1760.

Protasov, A. Ia. "Dnevnik A. Ia. Protasova." *Drevniaia i novaia Rossiia*, Vol. 17, No. 8 (August 1880), pp. 761–75.

Ptukha, M. V. *Ocherki po istorii statistiki v SSSR.* 2 vols. Moscow, 1959.

Puibusque, L. vicomte de. *Lettres sur la guerre de Russie en 1812; sur la ville de Saint-Pétersbourg, les moeurs et les usages des habitans de la Russie et de la Pologne.* Paris, 1817.

Purishkevich, V. M. *Dnevnik chlena gosudarstvennoi dumy Vladimira Mitrofanovicha Purishkevicha.* Riga, 1924.

Puryear, V. *England, Russia, and the Straits Question, 1844–1856.* Berkeley, 1931.

Pushkin, A. S. *Polnoe sobranie sochinenii.* 10 vols. Moscow, 1962–66.

———. *The Poems, Prose and Plays of Alexander Pushkin*, ed. Avrahm Yarmolinsky. New York, 1936.

Pypin, A. N. *Belinskii: Ego zhizn' i perepiska.* St. Petersburg, 1908.

———. *Istoriia russkoi literatury.* 4 vols. St. Petersburg, 1911–13.

———. *Kharakteristiki literaturnykh mnenii ot dvadtsatykh do piatidesiatykh godov.* St. Petersburg, 1909.

———. *Obshchestvennoe dvizhenie v Rossii pri Aleksandre I.* St. Petersburg, 1885.

Rabinowitch, Alexander. *The Bolsheviks Come to Power: The Revolution of 1917 in Petrograd.* New York, 1976.

Rabinovich, M. D. "Strel'tsy v pervoi chetverti XVIII v." *IZ* 58 (1956): 273–305.

Radishchev, A. N. *A Journey from St. Petersburg to Moscow.* Edited by R. P. Thaler and translated by Leo Wiener. Cambridge, Mass., 1958.

———. *Izbrannye filosofskie i obshchestvenno-politicheskie proizvedeniia.* Moscow, 1952.

———. "Zhitie Fedora Vasil'evicha Ushakova," *A. N. Radishchev: Izbrannye . . . proizvedeniia*, ed. I. Ia. Shchipanov, pp. 232–38.

Radkey, Oliver H. *The Agrarian Foes of Bolshevism: Promise and Default of the Russian Socialist Revolutionaries, February to October 1917.* New York, 1958.

Raeff, Marc. "The Enlightenment in Russia and Russian Thought in the Enlightenment," *The Eighteenth Century in Russia*, ed. J. E. Garrard, pp. 25–47.

———. *Imperial Russia, 1682–1825: The Coming of Age of Modern Russia.* New York, 1972.

———. *Michael Speransky: Statesman of Imperial Russia.* The Hague, 1957.

———. *The Origins of the Russian Intelligentsia: The Eighteenth-Century Nobility.* New York, 1966.

———. "The Well-Ordered Police State and the Development of Modernity in Seventeenth- and Eighteenth-Century Europe: An Attempt at a Comparative Approach." *The American Historical Review*, Vol. 80, No. 5 (December, 1975), pp. 1221–43.

———, ed. *The Decembrist Movement.* Englewood Cliffs, 1966.

———, ed. *Peter the Great Changes Russia.* Lexington, Mass., 1972.

———, ed. *Plans for Political Reform in Imperial Russia, 1730–1905.* Englewood Cliffs, 1966.

Ransel, David L. *The Politics of Catherinian Russia: The Panin Party.* New Haven and London, 1975.

Rashin, A. G. *Naselenie Rossii za sto let (1811–1913): statisticheskii ocherk.* Moscow, 1956.

Reddaway, W. F., ed. *The Cambridge History of Poland from Augustus II to Pilsudski (1697–1935).* 2 vols. Cambridge, 1941.

———, ed. *Documents of Catherine the Great.* Cambridge, 1931.

Reitenfel's, Iakov. "Skazaniia svetleishemu gertsogu Toskanskomu Kos'me Tret'emu o Moskovii," *Chteniia*, No. 3 (1905), pp. 1–128.

Rheindorf, K. *Die Schwarze Meer Frage, 1856–1871.* Berlin, 1925.

Riasanovsky, N. V. *A History of Russia.* New York, 1963.

———. *Nicholas I and Official Nationality in Russia, 1825–1855.* Berkeley and Los Angeles, 1959.

———. *Russia and the West in the Teachings of the Slavophiles.* Cambridge, Mass., 1952.

Rice, Tamara Talbot. *A Concise History of Russian Art.* New York, 1963.

———. "The Conflux of Influences in Eighteenth-Century Russian Art and Architecture: A Journey from the Spiritual to the Realistic," *The Eighteenth Century in Russia*, ed. J. E. Garrard, pp. 268–99.

———. *Elizabeth, Empress of Russia.* London, 1970.

Robbins, Richard G., Jr. *Famine in Russia, 1891–1892.* New York and London, 1975.

Robien, Louis de. *The Diary of a Diplomat in Russia, 1917–1919,* trans. Camilla Sykes. London, 1969.

Robinson, Geroid T. *Rural Russia under the Old Regime.* New York, 1932.

Rogger, Hans. *National Consciousness in Eighteenth-Century Russia.* Cambridge, Mass., 1960.

Romanovsky-Krassinsky, Princess. *Dancing in Petersburg: The Memoirs of Kschessinska.* New York, 1961.

Roskovshenko, I. V. "Peterburg v 1831–1832gg." *RS*, Vol. 101, No. 3 (February 1900), pp. 477–90.

Ruckman, JoAnn. "The Business Elite of Moscow: A Social Inquiry." Ph.D. diss., Northern Illinois University, 1975.

(———), JoAnn Schrampfer. "A Russian Freemason: I. V. Lopukhin." M.A. thesis, University of Chicago, 1963.

Rybakov, B. A. *Treasures in the Kremlin.* London, Prague, and Moscow, 1962.

———, ed. *Istoriia SSSR s drevneishikh vremen do nashikh dni.* 6 vols. Moscow, 1966–69.

Rychkov, P. I. *Topografiia Orenburgskaia, to est' obstoiatel'noe opisanie Orenburgskoi gubernii.* St. Petersburg, 1762.

Ryleev, K. F. *Polnoe sobranie sochineniia.* Moscow, 1934.

Ryu, In-Ho L. "Moscow Freemasons and the Rosicrucian Order: A Study in

Organization and Control," *The Eighteenth Century in Russia*, ed. J. E. Garrard, pp. 198–232.

Sablinsky, Walter. *The Road to Bloody Sunday: Father Gapon and the St. Petersburg Massacre of 1905*. Princeton, 1976.

Sablukhov, N. A. "Zapiski N. A. Sablukhova," *Tsareubiistvo 11 marta 1901 goda: Zapiski uchastnikov i sovremennikov*. St. Petersburg, 1908.

Sadikov, P. A. *Ocherki po istorii oprichniny*. Moscow-Leningrad, 1950.

Sakulin, P. N. "Literaturnye techeniia v Aleksandrovskuiu epokhu," *Istoriia russkoi literatury XIX veka*, ed. D. N. Ovsianiko-Kulikovskii. Vol. 1, pp. 58–112.

Salisbury, Harrison E. *Black Night, White Snow: Russia's Revolutions, 1905–1917*. New York, 1978.

Saltykov-Shchedrin, M. E. *Sobranie sochinenii*. 10 vols. 1967–70.

Sarabi'anov, D. V. "I. E. Repin." *IRI*, Vol. 9 (1), pp. 445–563.

Saul, Norman E. *Russia and the Mediterranean, 1797–1807*. Chicago, 1970.

Schakovskoy, Princess Zinaida. *The Fall of Eagles: Precursors of Peter the Great*. New York, 1964.

———. *La vie quotidienne à Moscou au XVIIe siècle*. Paris, 1963.

Schiemann, Th. *Aleksandr Pervyi*. Moscow, 1908.

———. *Geschichte Russlands unter Kaiser Nikolaus I*. 4 vols. Berlin, 1907–13.

———. "Imperator Nikolai Pervyi (iz zapisok i vospominanii sovremennikov)." *RA*, No. 2 (February 1902), pp. 459–75.

———. ed. *Die Ermordung Pauls und die Thronbesteigung Nikolaus I. Neue Materialen*. Berlin, 1902.

———, and A. Brückner. *Smert' Pavla Pervago*. Moscow, 1909.

Schuyler, Eugene. *Peter the Great, Emperor of Russia: A Study of Historical Biography*. 2 vols. New York, 1967.

Segal, Harold B., ed. and trans. *The Literature of Eighteenth-Century Russia*. 2 vols. New York, 1967.

Ségur, Count Louis Philippe de. *Memoirs and Recollections of Count Ségur, Ambassador from France to the Courts of Russia and Prussia, Written by Himself*. 3 vols. London, 1825.

Semanov, S. N. *Krovavoe voskresen'e*. Leningrad, 1965.

Semennikov, V. P. *Radishchev: Ocherki i issledovaniia*. Moscow-Petrograd, 1923.

———, ed. *Za kulisami tsarizma (arkhiv Tibetskogo vracha Badmaeva)*. Leningrad, 1925.

Semevskii, M. I. "Shest' mesiatsev iz russkoi istorii XVIII veka. Ocherk tsarstvovaniia Imperatora Petra II, 1761–1762." *OZ*, Vol. 173 (1839–84).

———. *Tsaritsa Katerina Alekseevna, Anna i Villim Mons, 1692–1724. Ocherki iz russkoi istorii*. St. Petersburg, 1884.

Semevskii, V. I. *Krest'iane v tsarstvovanie imperatritsy Ekateriny II*. 2 vols. St. Petersburg, 1888.

———. *Politicheskie i obshchestvennye idei dekabristov*. St. Petersburg, 1909.

"Sergei Ivanovich Zarudnyi." *RBS*, Vol. 7 (1896–1918), pp. 241–47.

Seton-Watson, Hugh. *The Russian Empire, 1801–1917*. Oxford, 1967.

Shakhovskoi, Ia. P. *Zapiski kniazia Iakova Petrovicha Shakhovskago*. St. Petersburg, 1872.

Shchegolev, P. E., ed. *Padenie tsarskogo rezhima*. 7 vols. Moscow-Leningrad, 1924–27.

Shchepot'ev, Lev. *Blizhnii boiarin Artamon Sergeevich Matveev kak kul'turnyi politicheskii deiatel' XVII veka*. St. Petersburg, 1906.

Shcherbatov, Prince A. *General-Fel'dmarshal kniaz' Paskevich. Ego zhizn' i deiatel'nost'*. 7 vols. St. Petersburg, 1892.

Shchipanov, I. Ia., ed. *A. N. Radishchev: Izbrannye filosofskie i obshchestvenno-politicheskie proizvedeniia*. Moscow, 1952.

———, ed. *Izbrannye proizvedeniia russkikh myslitelei vtoroi poloviny XVIII veka*. Vol. 2, Moscow, 1952.

Shebunin, A. N., ed. *Dekabrist N. I. Turgenev: Pis'ma k bratu S. I. Turgenevu*. Moscow-Leningrad, 1936.

Shevyrev, S. P. "Vzgliad russkago na sovremennoe obrazovanie Evropy." *Moskvitianin*, No. 1 (1841), pp. 219–96.

Shilder, N. K. "Aleksandr I, Imperator Vserossiiskii." *RBS*, pp. 141–384.

———. *Imperator Aleksandr Pervyi: Ego zhizn' i tsarstvovanie*. 2 vols. St. Petersburg, 1897.

———. *Imperator Nikolai Pervyi: Ego zhizn' i tsarstvovanie*. 2 vols. St. Petersburg, 1903.

———. *Imperator Pavel Pervyi: Istoriko-biograficheskii ocherk*. St. Petersburg, 1901.

Shilkov, V. F. "Arkhitektory-inostrantsy pri Petre I." *IRI*, Vol. 5 (1953–61), pp. 84–86.

Shklovskii, V. *Lev Tolstoi*. Moscow, 1967.

Shmurlo, E. F. "Kriticheskie zametki po istorii Petra Velikago." *ZhMNP*, Vol. 329 (May–June 1900), pp. 54–96; Vol. 330 (July–August 1900), pp. 193–234; Vol. 331 (September–October 1900), pp. 335–66.

Shtakel'berg, N. S. "Zagadka smerti Nikolaia I." *Russkoe proshloe*, Vol. 1 (1923), pp. 58–73.

Shtorkh, P. A. "Materialy dlia istorii gosudarstvennykh denezhnykh znakov v Rossii s 1653 po 1840 god." *ZhMNP*, Vol. 137 (1868), pp. 772–847.

Shubin-Pozdeev, D. "K kharakteristike lichnosti i sluzhebnoi deiatel'nosti S. I. Zarudnago." *RS*, Vol. 57, No. 2 (February 1888), pp. 477–84.

Shul'gin, V. V. *Dni*. Belgrad, 1925.

Shumigorskii, E. S. *Ekaterina Ivanovna Nelidova, 1758–1839. Ocherk iz istorii imperatora Pavla*. St. Petersburg, 1898.

———. *Imperator Pavel I: Zhizn' i tsarstvovanie*. St. Petersburg, 1907.

———. *Imperatritsa Mariia Feodorovna, 1759–1828. Eia biografiia*. St. Petersburg, 1892.

Simmons, E. J. *Dostoevskii: The Making of a Novelist*. Oxford, 1940.

———. *Leo Tolstoy*. Boston, 1946.

———. *Pushkin*. New York, 1964.

Sivkov, K. "S. N. Glinka." *RBS*, Vol. 5 (1896–1918), pp. 290–97.

Skabichevskii, A. M. *Ocherki istorii russkoi tsenzury, 1700–1863gg*. St. Petersburg, 1892.

Slonim, Marc. *The Epic of Russian Literature: From Its Origins through Tolstoi*. New York, 1964.

Smirnov, I. I. *Vosstanie Bolotnikova, 1606–1607*. Moscow, 1951.

Smoleński, Władysław. *Konfederacya Targowicka*. Krakow, 1903.

Sokolov, N. *Ubiistvo tsarskoi sem'i*. Berlin, 1925.

Solov'ev, S. M. *Istoriia Rossii s drevneishikh vremen*. Vols. 4–15. Moscow, 1960–66.

Soloveytchik, George. *Potemkin: Soldier, Statesman, Lover and Consort of Catherine of Russia*. New York, 1947.

Sorel, Albert. *The Eastern Question in the Eighteenth Century.* London, 1898.

Speranskii, M. M. "O zakonakh. Besedy grafa M. M. Speranskago s Ego Imperatorskim Vysochestvom Gosudarem Naslednikom Tsesarevichem Velikim Kniazem Aleksandrom Nikolaevichem s 12 oktiabria 1835 po 10 aprelia 1836 goda." *SIRO,* Vol. 30 (1880).

Stanislavskaia, A. M. *Russko-Angliiskie otnosheniia i problemy Sredizemnomor'ia, 1798–1807gg.* Moscow, 1962.

Starr, S. Frederick. *Decentralization and Self-Government in Russia, 1830–1870.* Princeton, 1972.

Startsev, A. *Radishchev v gody "Puteshestviia."* Moscow, 1960.

Stepanov, L. N. "Gogol'," *Istoriia russkoi literatury,* ed. V. P. Gorodetskii. Vol. 7, pp. 263–380.

Stockmar, Baron C. F. von. *Memoirs of Baron Stockmar,* trans. from the German G. A. M. and ed. F. Max Müller. 2 vols. London, 1872.

Stojanović, Mihailo D. *The Great Powers and the Balkans, 1875–1878.* Cambridge, 1939.

Stolpianskii, P. N. *Kak voznik, osnovalsia, i ros Sanktpiterburkh.* Petrograd, 1918.

Storch, Heinrich. *The Picture of Petersburg.* London, 1801.

Story, Douglas. *The Campaign with Kuropatkin.* London, 1904.

Sudebnye ustavy 20 noiabria 1864g. za piat'desiat' let. Vol. 1. Petrograd, 1914.

Sukhanov, N. N. *The Russian Revolution, 1917,* ed., abr., and trans. Joel Carmichael. Oxford, 1955.

Sumarokov, A. P. "O blagorudstve," *N. I. Novikov i ego sovremenniki,* ed. I. V. Malyshev. Moscow, 1961, pp. 370–72.

———. "Son—schastlivoe obshchestvo," *N. I. Novikov i ego sovremenniki,* ed. I. V. Malyshev. Moscow, 1961, pp. 354–57.

Sumner, B. H. *Peter the Great and the Emergence of Russia.* London, 1950.

———. *Russia and the Balkans, 1870–1880.* London, 1962.

Sviatikov, S. G. *Obshchestvennoe dvizhenie v Rossii, 1700–1895.* 2 vols. Rostov-on-the-Don, 1905.

Svin'in, Pavel. *Dostopamiatnosti Sanktpeterburga i ego okrestnostei.* 5 vols. St. Petersburg, 1816–23.

Svodnyi katalog russkoi knigi grazhdanskoi pechati XVIII veka, 1725–1800. 6 vols. Moscow, 1963–75.

Syroechkovskii, B. E., ed. *Mezhdutsarstvie 1825 goda i vosstanie dekabristov v perepiske i memuarakh chlenov tsarskoi sem'i.* Moscow-Leningrad, 1926.

Tarle, Eugene. *Napoleon's Invasion of Russia.* London, 1942.

———. *Severnaia voina i shvedskoe nashestvie na Rossii.* Moscow, 1958.

———. *Sochineniia v dvenadtsatyi tomakh.* Vols. 8 and 9. Moscow, 1959.

Tarsaidzé, Alexandre. *Katia, Wife Before God.* New York, 1970.

Tatishchev, S. S. "Aleksandr II, Imperator Vserossiiskii." *RBS,* Vol. 1 (1896–1918), pp. 385–892.

———. *Imperator Aleksandr II: Ego zhizn' i tsarstvovanie.* 2 vols. St. Petersburg, 1911.

———. *Vneshniaia politika imperatora Nikolaia I.* St. Petersburg, 1887.

———. "Votsarenie Imperatora Nikolaia." *Russkii vestnik,* Vol. 224, Nos. 3–4 (1893), pp. 89–113.

Tatishchev, V. N. *Istoriia Rossiiskaia.* 7 vols. Moscow-Leningrad, 1962–68.

———. "Razgovor o pol'ze nauk i uchilishch." *Chteniia* (1887), Bk. 1, pp. 137–44.

Taylor, A. J. P. *The Struggle for the Mastery of Europe, 1848–1918.* Oxford, 1954.

Tel'berg, G. "Uchastie Imperatora Nikolaia I v kodifikatsionnoi rabote ego tsarstvovaniia." *ZhMIu,* Vol. 22, No. 1 (January 1916), pp. 233–44.

Temperley, Harold. *England and the Near East: The Crimea.* London and New York, 1936.

Tengoborskii, L. V. 'Kratkoe izlozhenie nashego finansovago polozheniia' mai, 1856g., TsGIAL, fond 958, opis' 1, delo No. 742.

Terner, F. G. *Vospominaniia F. G. Ternera.* 2 vols. St. Petersburg, 1910.

Thaden, Edward C. *Conservative Nationalism in Nineteenth-Century Russia.* Seattle, 1964.

Thomson, Gladys Scott. *Catherine the Great and the Expansion of Russia.* New York, 1965.

Thouvenel, L. *Nicolas Ier et Napoléon III. Les préliminaires de la guerre de Crimée.* Paris, 1891.

Tikhomirov, M. N. *Klassovaia bor'ba v Rossii XVII v.* Moscow, 1969.

Tiutcheva (Aksakova), A. F. *Pri dvore dvukh imperatorov. Vospominaniia-Dnevnik.* 2 vols. Moscow, 1928.

Tolstoi, L. N. *Sobranie sochinenii.* 20 vols. Moscow, 1960–65.

Tomashevskii, B. V., ed. *Pushkinskii Peterburg.* Leningrad, 1949.

Torke, H.-J. "Das Russische Beamtentum in der ersten Hälfte des 19. Jahrhunderts." *Forschungen zur osteuropäischen Geschichte,* Vol. 13 (1967).

Trewin, J. C. *Tutor to the Tsarevich.* London, 1975.

Troitskii, S. M. *Russkii absoliutizm i dvorianstvo v XVIII v: Formirovanie biurokratii.* Moscow, 1974.

Trotsky, Leon. *The History of the Russian Revolution,* trans. Max Eastman. Ann Arbor, 1960.

———. *1905.* New York, 1971.

Tsimmerman, A. E. 'Vospominaniia Generala A. E. Tsimmermana,' ORGBL, fond 325, kartonka 1, papki 1–2, kartonka 2, papka 1.

Turgenev, I. S. *Sobranie sochinenii.* 10 vols. Moscow, 1961–62.

Ulam, Adam. *In the Name of the People: Prophets and Conspirators in Prerevolutionary Russia.* New York, 1977.

Ulanov, V. Ia. "XVII vek i reforma Petra Velikago," *Tri veka,* ed. V. V. Kallash. Vol. 3, pp. 1–14.

———. "Finansovye reformy tsaria Alekseia Mikhailovicha i gil' 1662g." *Tri veka,* ed. V. V. Kallash. Vol. 1, pp. 178–205.

Uroff, Benjamin P. "Grigorii Karpovich Kotoshikhin, 'On Russia in the Reign of Alexis Mikhailovich': An Annotated Translation." Ph.D. diss., Columbia University, 1970.

Ustiugov, N. V. "Gosudarstvennyi stroi: finansy," *Ocherki istorii SSSR,* ed. A. A. Novosel'skii, pp. 411–38.

———. "Russkaia kul'tura: Prosveshchenie i shkola," *Ocherki istorii SSSR,* ed. A. A. Novosel'skii, pp. 554–67.

Ustrialov, N. *Istoriia tsarstvovaniia Petra Velikago.* 6 vols. St. Petersburg, 1858–63.

Valkenier, Elizabeth. *Russian Realist Art: The Peredvizhniki and Their Tradition.* Ann Arbor, 1977.

Valuev, P. A. "Duma russkago vo vtoroi polovine 1855g." *RS,* Vol. 70, No. 5 (May 1891).

Vandal, Albert. *Napoléon et Alexandre Ier.* 3 vols. Paris, 1907.

Varneke, V. *Istoriia russkogo teatra XVII–XIX vekov.* Moscow-Leningrad, 1939.

Vasenko, P. G. *Boiare Romanovy i votsarenie Mikhaila Feodorovicha*. St. Petersburg, 1913.

———, S. F. Platonov, and E. F. Turaeva-Tsereteli. *Nachalo dinastii Romanovykh: istoricheskie ocherki*. St. Petersburg, 1912.

Vassilii, Count Paul. [Princess Catherine Radziwill.] *Behind the Veil at the Russian Court*. New York, 1914.

Veidemeier, Aleksandr. *Obzor glavneishikh proisshestvii v Rossii s konchiny Petra Velikago do vstupleniia na prestol Elizavety Petrovny*. 3 vols. St. Petersburg, 1830–32.

———. *Tsarstvovanie Elizavety Petrovny*. St. Petersburg, 1834.

Venturi, Franco. *Roots of Revolution: A History of the Populist and Socialist Movements in Nineteenth-Century Russia*. New York, 1966.

Vernadsky, George. *The Tsardom of Moscow, 1547–1682*. New Haven and London, 1969.

Vetrinskii, Ch. "Umstvennoe i obshchestvennoe dvizhenie sorokovykh godov," *Istoriia russkoi literatury XIX veka*, ed. D. N. Ovsianiko-Kulikovskii. Vol. 2, pp. 67–130.

Viatkin, M. P. "Ekonomicheskaia zhizn' Peterburga v period razlozheniia i krizisa krepostnichestva," *Ocherki istorii Leningrada*, ed. M. P. Viatkin. Vol. 1, pp. 447–505.

Vigel', F. F. *Zapiski*. 2 vols. Moscow, 1928.

Vigor, Mrs. William. *Letters from a Lady Who Resided Some Years in Russia*. London, 1777.

Vintner, E. "Feofan Prokopovich i nachalo russkogo prosveshcheniia," *Rol' i znachenie literatury*, ed. D. S. Likhachev, et al., pp. 43–46.

Virginia Gazette, 16 June 1774.

Viroubova, Anna. *Memories of the Russian Court*. New York, 1923.

Vladimirtsov, B. *Le régime social des Mongols: Le féodalisme nomade*. Paris, 1948.

Volk, S. S. *Narodnaia Volia*. Moscow-Leningrad, 1966.

Voskresenskii, N. A., ed. *Zakonodatel'nye akty Petra I*. Moscow-Leningrad, 1945.

Voznesenskii, S. V. *Ekonomika Rossii XIX–XX vv. v tsifrakh*. Leningrad, 1924.

Walder, David. *The Short Victorious War: The Russo-Japanese Conflict, 1904–1905*. London, 1973.

Waliszewski, Kazimirz. *La Dernière des Romanovs: Elisabeth Ier, Impératrice de Russie*. Paris, 1902.

———. *Ivan the Terrible*. London, 1904.

———. *Paul the First of Russia, the Son of Catherine the Great*. London, 1913.

———. *The Romance of an Empress: Catherine II of Russia*. New York, 1894.

Weber, Friedrich Christian. *The Present State of Russia*. 2 vols. New York, 1968.

Webster, C. K. *The Congress of Vienna, 1814–1815*. New York, 1966.

———. *The Foreign Policy of Castlereagh, 1815–1822: Britain and the European Alliance*. London, 1958.

———, ed. *British Diplomacy, 1813–1815*. London, 1921.

Weiner, Jack. *Mantillas in Muscovy: The Spanish Golden Age Theatre in Tsarist Russia, 1672–1917*. Lawrence, Kans., 1970.

Wilhelm II. *The Willy-Nicky Correspondence*. New York, 1918.

Willan, T. S. *The Early History of the Russia Company, 1553–1603*. Manchester, 1956.

Wilson, Arthur. "Diderot in Russia, 1773–1774," *The Eighteenth Century in Russia*, ed. J. E. Garrard, pp. 166–97.

Wilson, Colin. *Rasputin and the Fall of the Romanovs.* New York, 1964.

Wipper, B. R. "V. V. Rastrelli." *IRI,* Vol. 5, pp. 174–208.

Wipper, R. Iu. *Ivan Groznyi.* Moscow, 1922.

Wittaker, Cynthia H. "The Ideology of Sergei Uvarov: An Interpretative Essay." *Russian Review,* Vol. 37, No. 2 (April 1978), pp. 158–76.

Witte, S. Iu. *Vospominaniia.* 3 vols. Moscow, 1960.

Wittram, Reinhard. *Peter I: Czar und Kaiser.* 2 vols. Göttingen, 1964.

Wolfe, Bertram D. *Three Who Made a Revolution: A Biographical History.* New York, 1948.

Wortman, Richard. *The Development of a Russian Legal Consciousness.* Chicago, 1976.

Yousoupoff, Prince Felix. *Avant l'exil, 1887–1919.* Paris, 1952.

———. *Rasputin.* New York, 1928.

Zabelin, I. E. *Domashnyi byt russkikh tsarits v XVI–XVII stoletiiakh.* Moscow, 1862.

Zablotskii-Desiatovskii, A. P. *Graf P. D. Kiselev i ego vremia.* 4 vols. St. Petersburg, 1882.

Zaionchkovskii, P. A. "D. A. Miliutin: biograficheskii ocherk," in *Dnevnik D. A. Miliutina, 1873–1875gg,* ed. P. A. Zaionchkovskii. Vol. 1. Moscow, 1947, pp. 5–72.

———. *Krizis samoderzhaviia na rubezhe 1870–1880kh godov.* Moscow, 1964.

———. *Otmena krepostnogo prava v Rossii.* Moscow, 1968.

———. *Pravitel'stvennyi apparat samoderzhavnoi Rossii v XIX v.* Moscow, 1978.

———. *Provedenie v zhizn' krest'ianskoi reformy 1861g.* Moscow, 1958.

———. *Rossiiskoe samoderzhavie v kontse XIX stoletiia (politicheskaia reaktsiia 80kh–nachala 90kh godov).* Moscow, 1970.

———. *Voennye reformy, 1860–1870 godov v Rossii.* Moscow, 1952.

Zakharova, L. G. *Zemskaia kontrreforma 1890g.* Moscow, 1968.

Zaozerskii, A. I. "Zemskie sobory," *Ocherki istorii SSSR,* ed. A. A. Novosel'skii, pp. 360–366.

Zarudnyi, S. I. "Pis'mo opytnago chinovnika sorokovykh godov mladshemu sobratu, postupaiushchemu na sluzhbu." *RS,* Vol. 100 (1889), pp. 543–46.

Zelnik, Reginald. *Labor and Society in Tsarist Russia: The Factory Workers of St. Petersburg, 1855–1870.* Stanford, 1971.

Zenkovsky, S. A., ed. *Medieval Russia's Epics, Chronicles, and Tales.* New York, 1954.

Zheliabuzhskii, I. A. *Zapiski Ivana Afanasievicha Zheliabuzhskago s 1682 po 2 iiulia 1709.* St. Petersburg, 1840.

Zhigarev, S. *Russkaia politika v vostochnom voprose: Istoriko-iuridicheskie ocherki.* Moscow, 1896.

Zhivopisnoe obozrenie, Nos. 21 and 22 (19 i 26 maia 1896).

Zhukovskii, V. A. "Pis'ma V. A. Zhukovskago k F. P. Litke." *RA,* Bk. 2 (1887).

"Zhurnaly komiteta uchrezhdennago Vysochaishim reskriptom 6 dekabria 1826 goda." *SIRO,* Vol. 74 (1891).

"Zhurnaly Verkhovnago Tainago Soveta." *SIRIO,* Vol. 69 (1890).

Zimin, A. A. *Oprichnina Ivana Groznogo.* Moscow, 1964.

INDEX

Names of Romanov rulers are set in **boldface** type.